MW01420414

ENCYCLOPEDIA OF BUSINESS CHARTS

ENCYCLOPEDIA OF BUSINESS CHARTS

Robert D. Carlsen and Donald L. Vest

PRENTICE-HALL, INC. ENGLEWOOD CLIFFS, N.J.

Prentice-Hall International, Inc., *London*
Prentice-Hall of Australia, Pty. Ltd., *Sydney*
Prentice-Hall of Canada, Ltd., *Toronto*
Prentice-Hall of India Private Ltd., *New Delhi*
Prentice-Hall of Japan, Inc., *Tokyo*
Prentice-Hall of Southeast Asia Pte. Ltd., *Singapore*
Whitehall Books, Ltd., *Wellington, New Zealand*

Fourth Printing . . . . . June, 1980

© 1977, *by*

PRENTICE-HALL, INC.

Englewood Cliffs, N.J.

All rights reserved. No part of this book may be reproduced in any form or by any means, without permission in writing from the publisher.

Library of Congress Cataloging in Publication Data

Carlsen, Robert D.

Encyclopedia of business charts.

1. Business—Graphic methods. I. Vest, Donald L., joint author. II. Title.
HA31.C27 1977   658.4'5   76-54251
ISBN 0-13-275321-9

Printed in the United States of America

PREFACE

This is an encyclopedia of business charts. It is designed as an invaluable reference book for employees and managers of small, medium, and large business and industrial firms, educators, public service employees . . . all those who find themselves called upon to prepare charts for reports, meetings, briefings, customers, or the monitoring of their own activities.

The encyclopedia is unique in that it is not limited to a single subject but rather offers a selection of business charts and chart styles that can be used to cover virtually all normal operational activities. Chart example categories include:

    Schedules
    Budgets
    Technical Performance
    Financial Ratios
    Selling
    Proposals and Quotations
    Reliability
    Quality Control
    Accuracy
    Facilities
    Equipment
    Manpower
    Maintenance
    Overhaul and Repair
    Problems and Actions
. . . and many more!

Also included is a section on "Chartsmanship" with clear, illustrated guidelines for preparing effective business charts.

The main body of the encyclopedia (Sections 1.0 through 58.0) contains hundreds of chart examples, all organized by category and arranged in alphabetical order. Within each category a broad selection of styles are presented so that the user can easily find and choose the graphic method best suited to his purpose.

People who work in, or manage, various aspects of private or public enterprises have needs and preferences that vary widely when it comes to charts. Some prefer or need simple, "uncluttered" charts that quickly indicate trends. Others prefer or need charts that itemize detailed information in great abundance. The primary benefit to the user of this encyclopedia is that examples are presented that fulfill all of these needs and preferences. One style is not recommended as preferable to another, but rather the best examples possible are shown covering a broad spectrum of styles, from *simple trend style charts* to *complex detailed charts*.

The user benefits, too, in that he does not have to spend an excessive amount of time developing or inventing a graphic method for displaying important information. Instead, he can go directly to the proper section of the encyclopedia where examples are presented in ascending order from the simplest to the most fact-packed style for presenting information. He can quickly "shop" within that category for the specific style that suits his own particular needs, for the examples are presented with a minimum of comment or narrative description. He can choose a graphic approach, a tabular approach, or a combination graphic/tabular approach. His selection can be a simple, uncluttered, trend-indicating format, or one that is packed with detail . . . the choice is up to the user.

Once the selection has been made, that format can easily be communicated to others in the organization because a clear, visual example exists within the covers of this unique reference book.

In the "Chartsmanship" part of the encyclopedia (Sections 59.0 through 77.0), guidelines for preparing effective business charts are given. Basic types of business charts are first described: line charts, surface charts, column charts, bar charts, symbol charts, and circle charts. Then, every aspect of chart preparation is described and illustrated: format and nomenclature, titles, grids, line weight and shading, amount scales, time scales, goals and limits, time-now dating, notes, keys and authentication, emphasizing key points, and data layout.

The *Encyclopedia of Business Charts* is comprehensive and complete. It is a *must* reference book for every type of business, public service, and educational activity, designed to take its place on the bookshelf in these applications alongside the dictionary and thesaurus.

Robert D. Carlsen
Donald L. Vest

TABLE OF CONTENTS

Preface — v

PART I — BUSINESS CHART EXAMPLES

1.0 Accuracy

	Text	Figure
1.1 Accuracy — Version 1	3	4
1.2 Accuracy — Version 2	3	5
1.3 Accuracy — Version 3	3	6
1.4 Accuracy — Version 4	3	7

2.0 Average Collection Period of Receivables

	Text	Figure
2.1 Average Collection Period of Receivables — Version 1	9	11
2.2 Average Collection Period of Receivables — Version 2	9	12
2.3 Average Collection Period of Receivables — Version 3	9	13
2.4 Average Collection Period of Receivables — Version 4	9	14
2.5 Average Collection Period of Receivables — Version 5	9	15
2.6 Average Collection Period of Receivables — Version 6	9	16
2.7 Average Collection Period of Receivables — Version 7	10	17
2.8 Average Collection Period of Receivables — Version 8	10	18

3.0 Budgets — Detail

	Text	Figure
3.1 Budget — Detail — Version 1	19	21
3.2 Budget — Detail — Version 2	19	22
3.3 Budget — Detail — Version 3	19	23
3.4 Budget — Detail — Version 4	19	24
3.5 Budget — Detail — Version 5	19	25
3.6 Budget — Detail — Version 6	19	26
3.7 Budget — Detail — Version 7	19	27

	Text	Figure
3.8 Budget — Detail — Version 8	19	28
3.9 Budget — Detail — Version 9	20	29
3.10 Budget — Detail — Version 10	20	30
3.11 Budget — Detail — Version 11	20	31
3.12 Budget — Detail — Version 12	20	32
3.13 Budget — Detail — Version 13	20	33
3.14 Budget — Detail — Version 14	20	34
3.15 Budget — Detail — Version 15	20	35
3.16 Budget — Detail — Version 16	20	36
3.17 Budget — Detail — Version 17	20	37

4.0 Budgets — Expenditures and Commitments

	Text	Figure
4.1 Budget — Expenditures and Commitments — Version 1	39	41
4.2 Budget — Expenditures and Commitments — Version 2	39	42
4.3 Budget — Expenditures and Commitments — Version 3	39	43
4.4 Budget — Expenditures and Commitments — Version 4	39	44
4.5 Budget — Expenditures and Commitments — Version 5	39	45
4.6 Budget — Expenditures and Commitments — Version 6	39	46
4.7 Budget — Expenditures and Commitments — Version 7	40	47

5.0 Budgets — Expenditures and Funding

	Text	Figure
5.1 Budget — Expenditures and Funding — Version 1	49	51
5.2 Budget — Expenditures and Funding — Version 2	49	52
5.3 Budget — Expenditures and Funding — Version 3	49	53
5.4 Budget — Expenditures and Funding — Version 4	49	54
5.5 Budget — Expenditures and Funding — Version 5	49	55
5.6 Budget — Expenditures and Funding — Version 6	49	56
5.7 Budget — Expenditures and Funding — Version 7	49	57
5.8 Budget — Expenditures and Funding — Version 8	50	58

6.0 Budget — Expenditures, Funding, and Commitments

	Text	Figure
6.1 Budget — Expenditures, Funding, and Commitments — Version 1	59	60
6.2 Budget — Expenditures, Funding, and Commitments — Version 2	59	61
6.3 Budget — Expenditures, Funding, and Commitments — Version 3	59	62
6.4 Budget — Expenditures, Funding, and Commitments — Version 4	59	63
6.4 Budget — Expenditures, Funding, and Commitments — Version 5	59	64
6.6 Budget — Expenditures, Funding, and Commitments — Version 6	59	65

7.0 Budgets — Summaries

	Text	Figure
7.1 Budget — Summary — Version 1	67	71
7.2 Budget — Summary — Version 2	67	72
7.3 Budget — Summary — Version 3	67	73

Table of Contents

ix

	Text	Figure
7.4 Budget — Summary — Version 4	67	*74*
7.5 Budget — Summary — Version 5	67	*75*
7.6 Budget — Summary — Version 6	67	*76*
7.7 Budget — Summary — Version 7	68	*77*
7.8 Budget — Summary — Version 8	68	*78*
7.9 Budget — Summary — Version 9	68	*79*
7.10 Budget — Summary — Version 10	68	*80*
7.11 Budget — Summary — Version 11	68	*81*
7.12 Budget — Summary — Version 12	68	*82*
7.13 Budget — Summary — Version 13	68	*83*
7.14 Budget — Summary — Version 14	68	*84*
7.15 Budget — Summary — Version 15	68	*85*
7.16 Budget — Summary — Version 16	68	*86*
7.17 Budget — Summary — Version 17	68	*87*
7.18 Budget — Summary — Version 18	68	*88*
7.19 Budget — Summary — Version 19	69	*89*
7.20 Budget — Summary — Version 20	69	*90*
7.21 Budget — Summary — Version 21	69	*91*
7.22 Budget — Summary — Version 22	69	*92*
7.23 Budget — Summary — Version 23	69	*93*
7.24 Budget — Summary — Version 24	69	*94*
7.25 Budget — Summary — Version 25	69	*95*
7.26 Budget — Summary — Version 26	69	*96*
7.27 Budget — Summary — Version 27	69	*97*
7.28 Budget — Summary — Version 28	70	*98*
7.29 Budget — Summary — Version 29	70	*99*

8.0 Cash Flow

	Text	Figure
8.1 Cash Flow — Version 1	101	*102*
8.2 Cash Flow — Version 2	101	*103*
8.3 Cash Flow — Version 3	101	*104*
8.4 Cash Flow — Version 4	101	*105*
8.5 Cash Flow — Version 5	101	*106*

9.0 Cost Comparisons

	Text	Figure
9.1 Cost Comparisons — Version 1	107	*108*
9.2 Cost Comparisons — Version 2	107	*109*
9.3 Cost Comparisons — Version 3	107	*110*
9.4 Cost Comparisons — Version 4	107	*111*
9.5 Cost Comparisons — Version 5	107	*112*
9.6 Cost Comparisons — Version 6	107	*113*
9.7 Cost Comparisons — Version 7	107	*114*

10.0 Costs as a Percent of Sales

	Text	Figure
10.1 Costs as a Percent of Sales — Version 1	115	*117*
10.2 Costs as a Percent of Sales — Version 2	115	*118*
10.3 Costs as a Percent of Sales — Version 3	115	*119*
10.4 Costs as a Percent of Sales — Version 4	115	*120*
10.5 Costs as a Percent of Sales — Version 5	115	*121*
10.6 Costs as a Percent of Sales — Version 6	115	*122*
10.7 Costs as a Percent of Sales — Version 7	116	*123*
10.8 Costs as a Percent of Sales — Version 8	116	*124*
10.9 Costs as a Percent of Sales — Version 9	116	*125*
10.10 Costs as a Percent of Sales — Version 10	116	*126*
10.11 Costs as a Percent of Sales — Version 11	116	*127*

11.0 Current Assets to Current Liabilities

	Text	Figure
11.1 Current Assets to Current Liabilities — Version 1	129	*130*
11.2 Current Assets to Current Liabilities — Version 2	129	*131*
11.3 Current Assets to Current Liabilities — Version 3	129	*132*

	Text	Figure
11.4 Current Assets to Current Liabilities — Version 4	129	*133*
11.5 Current Assets to Current Liabilities — Version 5	129	*134*
11.6 Current Assets to Current Liabilities — Version 6	129	*135*
11.7 Current Assets to Current Liabilities — Version 7	129	*136*

12.0 Current Liabilities to Tangible Net Worth

	Text	Figure
12.1 Current Liabilities to Tangible Net Worth — Version 1	137	*138*
12.2 Current Liabilities to Tangible Net Worth — Version 2	137	*139*
12.3 Current Liabilities to Tangible Net Worth — Version 3	137	*140*
12.4 Current Liabilities to Tangible Net Worth — Version 4	137	*141*
12.5 Current Liabilities to Tangible Net Worth — Version 5	137	*142*
12.6 Current Liabilities to Tangible Net Worth — Version 6	137	*143*

13.0 Distribution of Income

	Text	Figure
13.1 Distribution of Income — Version 1	145	*146*
13.2 Distribution of Income — Version 2	145	*147*
13.3 Distribution of Income — Version 3	145	*148*
13.4 Distribution of Income — Version 4	145	*149*

14.0 Earnings

	Text	Figure
14.1 Earnings — Version 1	151	*154*
14.2 Earnings — Version 2	151	*155*
14.3 Earnings — Version 3	151	*156*
14.4 Earnings — Version 4	151	*157*
14.5 Earnings — Version 5	151	*158*
14.6 Earnings — Version 6	151	*159*
14.7 Earnings — Version 7	151	*160*
14.8 Earnings — Version 8	151	*161*
14.9 Earnings — Version 9	151	*162*
14.10 Earnings — Version 10	152	*163*
14.11 Earnings — Version 11	152	*164*
14.12 Earnings — Version 12	152	*165*
14.13 Earnings — Version 13	152	*166*
14.14 Earnings — Version 14	152	*167*
14.15 Earnings — Version 15	152	*168*
14.16 Earnings — Version 16	152	*169*
14.17 Earnings — Version 17	152	*170*
14.18 Earnings — Version 18	152	*171*
14.19 Earnings — Version 19	152	*172*
14.20 Earnings — Version 20	153	*173*
14.21 Earnings — Version 21	153	*174*

15.0 Earnings and Sales

	Text	Figure
15.1 Earnings and Sales — Version 1	175	*177*
15.2 Earnings and Sales — Version 2	175	*178*
15.3 Earnings and Sales — Version 3	175	*179*
15.4 Earnings and Sales — Version 4	175	*180*
15.5 Earnings and Sales — Version 5	175	*181*
15.6 Earnings and Sales — Version 6	175	*182*
15.7 Earnings and Sales — Version 7	175	*183*
15.8 Earnings and Sales — Version 8	175	*184*
15.9 Earnings and Sales — Version 9	176	*185*
15.10 Earnings and Sales — Version 10	176	*186*

Table of Contents

16.0 Earnings as a Percent of Sales

	Text	Figure
16.1 Earnings as a Percent of Sales — Version 1	187	189
16.2 Earnings as a Percent of Sales — Version 2	187	190
16.3 Earnings as a Percent of Sales — Version 3	187	191
16.4 Earnings as a Percent of Sales — Version 4	187	192
16.5 Earnings as a Percent of Sales — Version 5	187	193
16.6 Earnings as a Percent of Sales — Version 6	187	194
16.7 Earnings as a Percent of Sales — Version 7	187	195
16.8 Earnings as a Percent of Sales — Version 8	188	196
16.9 Earnings as a Percent of Sales — Version 9	188	197
16.10 Earnings as a Percent of Sales — Version 10	188	198
16.11 Earnings as a Percent of Sales — Version 11	188	199
16.12 Earnings as a Percent of Sales — Version 12	188	200

17.0 Earnings, Sales, and Costs

	Text	Figure
17.1 Earnings, Sales, and Costs — Version 1	201	203
17.2 Earnings, Sales, and Costs — Version 2	201	204
17.3 Earnings, Sales, and Costs — Version 3	201	205
17.4 Earnings, Sales, and Costs — Version 4	201	206
17.5 Earnings, Sales, and Costs — Version 5	201	207
17.6 Earnings, Sales, and Costs — Version 6	201	208
17.7 Earnings, Sales, and Costs — Version 7	201	209
17.8 Earnings, Sales, and Costs — Version 8	202	210
17.9 Earnings, Sales, and Costs — Version 9	202	211
17.10 Earnings, Sales, and Costs — Version 10	202	212

18.0 Equipment Capacity Versus Workload

	Text	Figure
18.1 Equipment Capacity Versus Workload — Version 1	213	214
18.2 Equipment Capacity Versus Workload — Version 2	213	215
18.3 Equipment Capacity Versus Workload — Version 3	213	216
18.4 Equipment Capacity Versus Workload — Version 4	213	217
18.5 Equipment Capacity Versus Workload — Version 5	213	218
18.6 Equipment Capacity Versus Workload — Version 6	213	219
18.7 Equipment Capacity Versus Workload — Version 7	213	220

19.0 Facilities

	Text	Figure
19.1 Facilities — Version 1	221	222
19.2 Facilities — Version 2	221	223
19.3 Facilities — Version 3	221	224
19.4 Facilities — Version 4	221	225
19.5 Facilities — Version 5	221	226
19.6 Facilities — Version 6	221	227
19.7 Facilities — Version 7	221	228
19.8 Facilities — Version 8	221	229

20.0 Facility Capacity Versus Workload

	Text	Figure
20.1 Facility Capacity Versus Workload — Version 1	231	233
20.2 Facility Capacity Versus Workload — Version 2	231	234
20.3 Facility Capacity Versus Workload — Version 3	231	235
20.4 Facility Capacity Versus Workload — Version 4	231	236

xii   Table of Contents

	Text	Figure
20.5 Facility Capacity Versus Workload — Version 5	231	237
20.6 Facility Capacity Versus Workload — Version 6	231	238
20.7 Facility Capacity Versus Workload — Version 7	232	239
20.8 Facility Capacity Versus Workload — Version 8	232	240
20.9 Facility Capacity Versus Workload — Version 9	232	241
20.10 Facility Capacity Versus Workload — Version 10	232	242

21.0 Financial Summaries

	Text	Figure
21.1 Financial Summary — Version 1	243	244
21.2 Financial Summary — Version 2	243	245
21.3 Financial Summary — Version 3	243	246
21.4 Financial Summary — Version 4	243	247
21.5 Financial Summary — Version 5	243	248

22.0 Fixed Assets to Tangible Net Worth

	Text	Figure
22.1 Fixed Assets to Tangible Net Worth — Version 1	249	250
22.2 Fixed Assets to Tangible Net Worth — Version 2	249	251
22.3 Fixed Assets to Tangible Net Worth — Version 3	249	252
22.4 Fixed Assets to Tangible Net Worth — Version 4	249	253
22.5 Fixed Assets to Tangible Net Worth — Version 5	249	254
22.6 Fixed Assets to Tangible Net Worth — Version 6	249	255

23.0 Gross Assets

	Text	Figure
23.1 Gross Assets — Version 1	257	258
23.2 Gross Assets — Version 2	257	259
23.3 Gross Assets — Version 3	257	260
23.4 Gross Assets — Version 4	257	261
23.5 Gross Assets — Version 5	257	262
23.6 Gross Assets — Version 6	257	263
23.7 Gross Assets — Version 7	257	264
23.8 Gross Assets — Version 8	257	265

24.0 Gross Assets Turnover

	Text	Figure
24.1 Gross Assets Turnover — Version 1	267	268
24.2 Gross Assets Turnover — Version 2	267	269
24.3 Gross Assets Turnover — Version 3	267	270
24.4 Gross Assets Turnover — Version 4	267	271
24.5 Gross Assets Turnover — Version 5	267	272
24.6 Gross Assets Turnover — Version 6	267	273

25.0 Inventory

	Text	Figure
25.1 Inventory — Version 1	275	277
25.2 Inventory — Version 2	275	278
25.3 Inventory — Version 3	275	279
25.4 Inventory — Version 4	275	280
25.5 Inventory — Version 5	275	281
25.6 Inventory — Version 6	275	282
25.7 Inventory — Version 7	275	283
25.8 Inventory — Version 8	275	284
25.9 Inventory — Version 9	275	285
25.10 Inventory — Version 10	276	286

Table of Contents

xiii

26.0 Maintenance

	Text	Figure
26.1 Maintenance — Version 1	287	288
26.2 Maintenance — Version 2	287	289
26.3 Maintenance — Version 3	287	290
26.4 Maintenance — Version 4	287	291
26.5 Maintenance — Version 5	287	292
26.6 Maintenance — Version 6	287	293
26.7 Maintenance — Version 7	287	294

27.0 Manpower and Facilities

	Text	Figure
27.1 Manpower and Facilities — Version 1	295	296
27.2 Manpower and Facilities — Version 2	295	297
27.3 Manpower and Facilities — Version 3	295	298
27.4 Manpower and Facilities — Version 4	295	299
27.5 Manpower and Facilities — Version 5	295	300
27.6 Manpower and Facilities — Version 6	295	301

28.0 Manpower by Assignment

	Text	Figure
28.1 Manpower by Assignment — Version 1	303	305
28.2 Manpower by Assignment — Version 2	303	306
28.3 Manpower by Assignment — Version 3	303	307
28.4 Manpower by Assignment — Version 4	303	308
28.5 Manpower by Assignment — Version 5	303	309
28.6 Manpower by Assignment — Version 6	303	310
28.7 Manpower by Assignment — Version 7	303	311
28.8 Manpower by Assignment — Version 8	303	312
28.9 Manpower by Assignment — Version 9	304	313
28.10 Manpower by Assignment — Version 10	304	314
28.11 Manpower by Assignment — Version 11	304	315
28.12 Manpower by Assignment — Version 12	304	316
28.13 Manpower by Assignment — Version 13	304	317
28.14 Manpower by Assignment — Version 14	304	318
28.15 Manpower by Assignment — Version 15	304	319
28.16 Manpower by Assignment — Version 16	304	320
28.17 Manpower by Assignment — Version 17	304	321
28.18 Manpower by Assignment — Version 18	304	322
28.19 Manpower by Assignment — Version 19	304	323

29.0 Manpower by Experience

	Text	Figure
29.1 Manpower by Experience — Version 1	325	326
29.2 Manpower by Experience — Version 2	325	327

30.0 Manpower Summaries

	Text	Figure
30.1 Manpower Summary — Version 1	329	331
30.2 Manpower Summary — Version 2	329	332
30.3 Manpower Summary — Version 3	329	333
30.4 Manpower Summary — Version 4	329	334
30.5 Manpower Summary — Version 5	329	335
30.6 Manpower Summary — Version 6	329	336
30.7 Manpower Summary — Version 7	329	337
30.8 Manpower Summary — Version 8	329	338
30.9 Manpower Summary — Version 9	330	339
30.10 Manpower Summary — Version 10	330	340
30.11 Manpower Summary — Version 11	330	341
30.12 Manpower Summary — Version 12	330	342
30.13 Manpower Summary — Version 13	330	343
30.14 Manpower Summary — Version 14	330	344
30.15 Manpower Summary — Version 15	330	345

31.0 Manpower Turnover

	Text	Figure
31.1 Manpower Turnover — Version 1	347	348
31.2 Manpower Turnover — Version 2	347	349
31.3 Manpower Turnover — Version 3	347	350

32.0 Manpower Versus Workload

	Text	Figure
32.1 Manpower Versus Workload — Version 1	351	353
32.2 Manpower Versus Workload — Version 2	351	354
32.3 Manpower Versus Workload — Version 3	351	355
32.4 Manpower Versus Workload — Version 4	351	356
32.5 Manpower Versus Workload — Version 5	351	357
32.6 Manpower Versus Workload — Version 6	351	358
32.7 Manpower Versus Workload — Version 7	351	359

33.0 Net Profits to Tangible Net Worth

	Text	Figure
33.1 Net Profits to Tangible Net Worth — Version 1	361	362
33.2 Net Profits to Tangible Net Worth — Version 2	361	363
33.3 Net Profits to Tangible Net Worth — Version 3	361	364
33.4 Net Profits to Tangible Net Worth — Version 4	361	365
33.5 Net Profits to Tangible Net Worth — Version 5	361	366
33.6 Net Profits to Tangible Net Worth — Version 6	361	367

34.0 Net Sales to Inventory

	Text	Figure
34.1 Net Sales to Inventory — Version 1	369	370
34.2 Net Sales to Inventory — Version 2	369	371
34.3 Net Sales to Inventory — Version 3	369	372
34.4 Net Sales to Inventory — Version 4	369	373
34.5 Net Sales to Inventory — Version 5	369	374

35.0 Overhaul and Repair

	Text	Figure
35.1 Overhaul and Repair — Version 1	375	377
35.2 Overhaul and Repair — Version 2	375	378
35.3 Overhaul and Repair — Version 3	375	379
35.4 Overhaul and Repair — Version 4	375	380
35.5 Overhaul and Repair — Version 5	375	381
35.6 Overhaul and Repair — Version 6	375	382
35.7 Overhaul and Repair — Version 7	375	383
35.8 Overhaul and Repair — Version 8	375	384
35.9 Overhaul and Repair — Version 9	376	385
35.10 Overhaul and Repair — Version 10	376	386
35.11 Overhaul and Repair — Version 11	376	387
35.12 Overhaul and Repair — Version 12	376	388
35.13 Overhaul and Repair — Version 13	376	389
35.14 Overhaul and Repair — Version 14	376	390
35.15 Overhaul and Repair — Version 15	376	391

36.0 Overtime

	Text	Figure
36.1 Overtime — Version 1	393	394
36.2 Overtime — Version 2	393	395
36.3 Overtime — Version 3	393	396
36.4 Overtime — Version 4	393	397
36.5 Overtime — Version 5	393	398
36.6 Overtime — Version 6	393	399
36.7 Overtime — Version 7	393	400

37.0 Percent Return on Gross Assets

	Text	Figure
37.1 Percent Return on Gross Assets — Version 1	401	403
37.2 Percent Return on Gross Assets — Version 2	401	404
37.3 Percent Return on Gross Assets — Version 3	401	405
37.4 Percent Return on Gross Assets — Version 4	401	406

Table of Contents

	Text	Figure
37.5 Percent Return on Gross Assets — Version 5	401	407
37.6 Percent Return on Gross Assets — Version 6	401	408
37.7 Percent Return on Gross Assets — Version 7	401	409
37.8 Percent Return on Gross Assets — Version 8	401	410
37.9 Percent Return on Gross Assets — Version 9	402	411
37.10 Percent Return on Gross Assets — Version 10	402	412
37.11 Percent Return on Gross Assets — Version 11	402	413
37.12 Percent Return on Gross Assets — Version 12	402	414

38.0 Problems and Actions

	Text	Figure
38.1 Problems and Actions — Version 1	415	417
38.2 Problems and Actions — Version 2	415	418
38.3 Problems and Actions — Version 3	415	419
38.4 Problems and Actions — Version 4	415	420
38.5 Problems and Actions — Version 5	415	421
38.6 Problems and Actions — Version 6	415	422
38.7 Problems and Actions — Version 7	415	423
38.8 Problems and Actions — Version 8	416	424

39.0 Product Usage

	Text	Figure
39.1 Product Usage — Version 1	425	426
39.2 Product Usage — Version 2	425	427
39.3 Product Usage — Version 3	425	428
39.4 Product Usage — Version 4	425	429
39.5 Product Usage — Version 5	425	430
39.6 Product Usage — Version 6	425	431

40.0 Proposals/Quotations

	Text	Figure
40.1 Proposals/Quotations — Version 1	433	435
40.2 Proposals/Quotations — Version 2	433	436
40.3 Proposals/Quotations — Version 3	433	437
40.4 Proposals/Quotations — Version 4	433	438
40.5 Proposals/Quotations — Version 5	433	439
40.6 Proposals/Quotations — Version 6	433	440
40.7 Proposals/Quotations — Version 7	433	441
40.8 Proposals/Quotations — Version 8	434	442
40.9 Proposals/Quotations — Version 9	434	443
40.10 Proposals/Quotations — Version 10	434	444
40.11 Proposals/Quotations — Version 11	434	445
40.12 Proposals/Quotations — Version 12	434	446
40.13 Proposals/Quotations — Version 13	434	447
40.14 Proposals/Quotations — Version 14	434	448

41.0 Quality

	Text	Figure
41.1 Quality — Version 1	449	451
41.2 Quality — Version 2	449	452
41.3 Quality — Version 3	449	453
41.4 Quality — Version 4	449	454
41.5 Quality — Version 5	449	455
41.6 Quality — Version 6	449	456
41.7 Quality — Version 7	449	457
41.8 Quality — Version 8	449	458
41.9 Quality — Version 9	450	459
41.10 Quality — Version 10	450	460
41.11 Quality — Version 11	450	461
41.12 Quality — Version 12	450	462
41.13 Quality — Version 13	450	463
41.14 Quality — Version 14	450	464
41.15 Quality — Version 15	450	465

42.0 Receivables

	Text	Figure
42.1 Receivables — Version 1	467	468
42.2 Receivables — Version 2	467	469
42.3 Receivables — Version 3	467	470
42.4 Receivables — Version 4	467	471
42.5 Receivables — Version 5	467	472
42.6 Receivables — Version 6	467	473
42.7 Receivables — Version 7	467	474
42.8 Receivables — Version 8	467	475

43.0 Reliability

	Text	Figure
43.1 Reliability — Version 1	477	480
43.2 Reliability — Version 2	477	481
43.3 Reliability — Version 3	477	482
43.4 Reliability — Version 4	477	483
43.5 Reliability — Version 5	477	484
43.6 Reliability — Version 6	477	485
43.7 Reliability — Version 7	477	486
43.8 Reliability — Version 8	477	487
43.9 Reliability — Version 9	477	488
43.10 Reliability — Version 10	478	489
43.11 Reliability — Version 11	478	490
43.12 Reliability — Version 12	478	491
43.13 Reliability — Version 13	478	492
43.14 Reliability — Version 14	478	493
43.15 Reliability — Version 15	478	494
43.16 Reliability — Version 16	478	495
43.17 Reliability — Version 17	478	496
43.18 Reliability — Version 18	478	497
43.19 Reliability — Version 19	478	498
43.20 Reliability — Version 20	478	499
43.21 Reliability — Version 21	478	500
43.22 Reliability — Version 22	479	501
43.23 Reliability — Version 23	479	502
43.24 Reliability — Version 24	479	503
43.25 Reliability — Version 25	479	504
43.26 Reliability — Version 26	479	505
43.27 Reliability — Version 27	479	506
43.28 Reliability — Version 28	479	507

44.0 Revenue Versus Costs

	Text	Figure
44.1 Revenue Versus Costs — Version 1	509	511
44.2 Revenue Versus Costs — Version 2	509	512
44.3 Revenue Versus Costs — Version 3	509	513
44.4 Revenue Versus Costs — Version 4	509	514
44.5 Revenue Versus Costs — Version 5	509	515
44.6 Revenue Versus Costs — Version 6	509	516
44.7 Revenue Versus Costs — Version 7	509	517
44.8 Revenue Versus Costs — Version 8	509	518
44.9 Revenue Versus Costs — Version 9	509	519
44.10 Revenue Versus Costs — Version 10	510	520
44.11 Revenue Versus Costs — Version 11	510	521

45.0 Sales

	Text	Figure
45.1 Sales — Version 1	523	526
45.2 Sales — Version 2	523	527
45.3 Sales — Version 3	523	528
45.4 Sales — Version 4	523	529
45.5 Sales — Version 5	523	530
45.6 Sales — Version 6	523	531
45.7 Sales — Version 7	523	532
45.8 Sales — Version 8	523	533
45.9 Sales — Version 9	523	534
45.10 Sales — Version 10	524	535
45.11 Sales — Version 11	524	536
45.12 Sales — Version 12	524	537

Table of Contents

xvii

	Text	Figure
45.13 Sales — Version 13	524	538
45.14 Sales — Version 14	524	539
45.15 Sales — Version 15	524	540
45.16 Sales — Version 16	524	541
45.17 Sales — Version 17	524	542
45.18 Sales — Version 18	524	543
45.19 Sales — Version 19	524	544
45.20 Sales — Version 20	524	545
45.21 Sales — Version 21	524	546
45.22 Sales — Version 22	525	547
45.23 Sales — Version 23	525	548
45.24 Sales — Version 24	525	549
45.25 Sales — Version 25	525	550
45.26 Sales — Version 26	525	551
45.27 Sales — Version 27	525	552
45.28 Sales — Version 28	525	553
45.29 Sales — Version 29	525	554

46.0 Sales Backlog

	Text	Figure
46.1 Sales Backlog — Version 1	555	557
46.2 Sales Backlog — Version 2	555	558
46.3 Sales Backlog — Version 3	555	559
46.4 Sales Backlog — Version 4	555	560
46.5 Sales Backlog — Version 5	555	561
46.6 Sales Backlog — Version 6	555	562
46.7 Sales Backlog — Version 7	555	563
46.8 Sales Backlog — Version 8	556	564
46.9 Sales Backlog — Version 9	556	565
46.10 Sales Backlog — Version 10	556	566

47.0 Sales Effort

	Text	Figure
47.1 Sales Effort — Version 1	567	568
47.2 Sales Effort — Version 2	567	569
47.3 Sales Effort — Version 3	567	570
47.4 Sales Effort — Version 4	567	571
47.5 Sales Effort — Version 5	567	572
47.6 Sales Effort — Version 6	567	573
47.7 Sales Effort — Version 7	567	574

48.0 Sales per Employee

	Text	Figure
48.1 Sales per Employee — Version 1	575	577
48.2 Sales per Employee — Version 2	575	578
48.3 Sales per Employee — Version 3	575	579
48.4 Sales per Employee — Version 4	575	580
48.5 Sales per Employee — Version 5	575	581
48.6 Sales per Employee — Version 6	575	582
48.7 Sales per Employee — Version 7	575	583
48.8 Sales per Employee — Version 8	575	584
48.9 Sales per Employee — Version 9	575	585
48.10 Sales per Employee — Version 10	576	586
48.11 Sales per Employee — Version 11	576	587
48.12 Sales per Employee — Version 12	576	588

49.0 Schedule, Cost, and Technical Performance

	Text	Figure
49.1 Schedule, Cost, and Technical Performance — Version 1	589	591
49.2 Schedule, Cost, and Technical Performance — Version 2	589	592
49.3 Schedule, Cost, and Technical Performance — Version 3	589	593
49.4 Schedule, Cost, and Technical Performance — Version 4	589	594
49.5 Schedule, Cost, and Technical Performance — Version 5	589	595

xviii   Table of Contents

	Text	Figure
49.6 Schedule, Cost, and Technical Performance — Version 6	589	*596*
49.7 Schedule, Cost, and Technical Performance — Version 7	590	*597*
49.8 Schedule, Cost, and Technical Performance — Version 8	590	*598*
49.9 Schedule, Cost, and Technical Performance — Version 9	590	*599*

50.0 Schedule and Costs

	Text	Figure
50.1 Schedule and Costs — Version 1	601	*603*
50.2 Schedule and Costs — Version 2	601	*604*
50.3 Schedule and Costs — Version 3	601	*605*
50.4 Schedule and Costs — Version 4	601	*606*
50.5 Schedule and Costs — Version 5	601	*607*
50.6 Schedule and Costs — Version 6	601	*608*
50.7 Schedule and Costs — Version 7	601	*609*
50.8 Schedule and Costs — Version 8	602	*610*
50.9 Schedule and Costs — Version 9	602	*611*
50.10 Schedule and Costs — Version 10	602	*612*
50.11 Schedule and Costs — Version 11	602	*613*
50.12 Schedule and Costs — Version 12	602	*614*
50.13 Schedule and Costs — Version 13	602	*615*

51.0 Schedules — End Item — Multiple Products

	Text	Figure
51.1 Schedule — End Item — Multiple Products — Version 1	617	*619*
51.2 Schedule — End Item — Multiple Products — Version 2	617	*620*
51.3 Schedule — End Item — Multiple Products — Version 3	617	*621*
51.4 Schedule — End Item — Multiple Products — Version 4	617	*622*
51.5 Schedule — End Item — Multiple Products — Version 5	617	*623*
51.6 Schedule — End Item — Multiple Products — Version 6	617	*624*
51.7 Schedule — End Item — Multiple Products — Version 7	617	*625*
51.8 Schedule — End Item — Multiple Products — Version 8	618	*626*
51.9 Schedule — End Item — Multiple Products — Version 9	618	*627*
51.10 Schedule — End Item — Multiple Products — Version 10	618	*628*
51.11 Schedule — End Item — Multiple Products — Version 11	618	*629*
51.12 Schedule — End Item — Multiple Products — Version 12	618	*630*
51.13 Schedule — End Item — Multiple Products — Version 13	618	*631*

52.0 Schedules — End Item — Single Product Type

	Text	Figure
52.1 Schedule — End Item — Single Product Type — Version 1	633	*637*
52.2 Schedule — End Item — Single Product Type — Version 2	633	*638*
52.3 Schedule — End Item — Single Product Type — Version 3	633	*639*
52.4 Schedule — End Item — Single Product Type — Version 4	633	*640*
52.5 Schedule — End Item — Single Product Type — Version 5	633	*641*

Table of Contents   xix

	Text	Figure		Text	Figure
52.6 Schedule — End Item — Single Product Type — Version 6	633	*642*	52.23 Schedule — End Item — Single Product Type — Version 23	635	*659*
52.7 Schedule — End Item — Single Product Type — Version 7	634	*643*	52.24 Schedule — End Item — Single Product Type — Version 24	635	*660*
52.8 Schedule — End Item — Single Product Type — Version 8	634	*644*	52.25 Schedule — End Item — Single Product Type — Version 25	635	*661*
52.9 Schedule — End Item — Single Product Type — Version 9	634	*645*	52.26 Schedule — End Item — Single Product Type — Version 26	635	*662*
52.10 Schedule — End Item — Single Product Type — Version 10	634	*646*	52.27 Schedule — End Item — Single Product Type — Version 27	635	*663*
52.11 Schedule — End Item — Single Product Type — Version 11	634	*647*	52.28 Schedule — End Item — Single Product Type — Version 28	635	*664*
52.12 Schedule — End Item — Single Product Type — Version 12	634	*648*	52.29 Schedule — End Item — Single Product Type — Version 29	636	*665*
52.13 Schedule — End Item — Single Product Type — Version 13	634	*649*	52.30 Schedule — End Item — Single Product Type — Version 30	636	*666*
52.14 Schedule — End Item — Single Product Type — Version 14	634	*650*	52.31 Schedule — End Item — Single Product Type — Version 31	636	*667*
52.15 Schedule — End Item — Single Product Type — Version 15	634	*651*	52.32 Schedule — End Item — Single Product Type — Version 32	636	*668*
52.16 Schedule — End Item — Single Product Type — Version 16	634	*652*			
52.17 Schedule — End Item — Single Product Type — Version 17	634	*653*	**53.0 Schedules — First or Single Article**		
52.18 Schedule — End Item — Single Product Type — Version 18	635	*654*	53.1 Schedule — First or Single Article — Version 1	669	*674*
52.19 Schedule — End Item — Single Product Type — Version 19	635	*655*	53.2 Schedule — First or Single Article — Version 2	669	*675*
52.20 Schedule — End Item — Single Product Type — Version 20	635	*656*	53.3 Schedule — First or Single Article — Version 3	669	*676*
52.21 Schedule — End Item — Single Product Type — Version 21	635	*657*	53.4 Schedule — First or Single Article — Version 4	669	*677*
52.22 Schedule — End Item — Single Product Type — Version 22	635	*658*	53.5 Schedule — First or Single Article — Version 5	669	*678*

	Text	Figure
53.6 Schedule — First or Single Article — Version 6	670	*679*
53.7 Schedule — First or Single Article — Version 7	670	*680*
53.8 Schedule — First or Single Article — Version 8	670	*681*
53.9 Schedule — First or Single Article — Version 9	670	*682*
53.10 Schedule — First or Single Article — Version 10	670	*683*
53.11 Schedule — First or Single Article — Version 11	670	*684*
53.12 Schedule — First or Single Article — Version 12	670	*685*
53.13 Schedule — First or Single Article — Version 13	670	*686*
53.14 Schedule — First or Single Article — Version 14	670	*687*
53.15 Schedule — First or Single Article — Version 15	671	*688*
53.16 Schedule — First or Single Article — Version 16	671	*689*
53.17 Schedule — First or Single Article — Version 17	671	*690*
53.18 Schedule — First or Single Article — Version 18	671	*691*
53.19 Schedule — First or Single Article — Version 19	671	*692*
53.20 Schedule — First or Single Article — Version 20	671	*693*
53.21 Schedule — First or Single Article — Version 21	671	*694*
53.22 Schedule — First or Single Article — Version 22	671	*695*

	Text	Figure
53.23 Schedule — First or Single Article — Version 23	672	*696*
53.24 Schedule — First or Single Article — Version 24	672	*697*
53.25 Schedule — First or Single Article — Version 25	672	*698*
53.26 Schedule — First or Single Article — Version 26	672	*699*
53.27 Schedule — First or Single Article — Version 27	672	*700*
53.28 Schedule — First or Single Article — Version 28	672	*701*
53.29 Schedule — First or Single Article — Version 29	672	*702*
53.30 Schedule — First or Single Article — Version 30	673	*703*
53.31 Schedule — First or Single Article — Version 31	673	*704*
53.32 Schedule — First or Single Article — Version 32	673	*705*
53.33 Schedule — First or Single Article — Version 33	673	*706*
53.34 Schedule — First or Single Article — Version 34	673	*707*
53.35 Schedule — First or Single Article — Version 35	673	*708*
53.36 Schedule — First or Single Article — Version 36	673	*709*

54.0 Schedules — In-Process

	Text	Figure
54.1 Schedule — In-Process — Version 1	711	*716*
54.2 Schedule — In-Process — Version 2	711	*717*
54.3 Schedule — In-Process — Version 3	711	*718*

Table of Contents

	Text	Figure
54.4 Schedule — In-Process — Version 4	711	719
54.5 Schedule — In-Process — Version 5	712	720
54.6 Schedule — In-Process — Version 6	712	721
54.7 Schedule — In-Process — Version 7	712	722
54.8 Schedule — In-Process — Version 8	712	723
54.9 Schedule — In-Process — Version 9	712	724
54.10 Schedule — In-Process — Version 10	712	725
54.11 Schedule — In-Process — Version 11	712	726
54.12 Schedule — In-Process — Version 12	712	727
54.13 Schedule — In-Process — Version 13	712	728
54.14 Schedule — In-Process — Version 14	713	729
54.15 Schedule — In-Process — Version 15	713	730
54.16 Schedule — In-Process — Version 16	713	731
54.17 Schedule — In-Process — Version 17	713	732
54.18 Schedule — In-Process — Version 18	714	733
54.19 Schedule — In-Process — Version 19	714	734
54.20 Schedule — In-Process — Version 20	714	735
54.21 Schedule — In-Process — Version 21	714	736
54.22 Schedule — In-Process — Version 22	714	737
54.23 Schedule — In-Process — Version 23	714	738
54.24 Schedule — In-Process — Version 24	714	739
54.25 Schedule — In-Process — Version 25	714	740
54.26 Schedule — In-Process — Version 26	714	741
54.27 Schedule — In-Process — Version 27	714	742

55.0 Tangible Net Worth Turnover

	Text	Figure
55.1 Tangible Net Worth Turnover — Version 1	743	744
55.2 Tangible Net Worth Turnover — Version 2	743	745
55.3 Tangible Net Worth Turnover — Version 3	743	746
55.4 Tangible Net Worth Turnover — Version 4	743	747
55.5 Tangible Net Worth Turnover — Version 5	743	748
55.6 Tangible Net Worth Turnover — Version 6	743	749

56.0 Technical Performance Summaries

	Text	Figure
56.1 Technical Performance Summary — Version 1	751	752
56.2 Technical Performance Summary — Version 2	751	753
56.3 Technical Performance Summary — Version 3	751	754
56.4 Technical Performance Summary — Version 4	751	755
56.5 Technical Performance Summary — Version 5	751	756
56.6 Technical Performance Summary — Version 6	751	757
56.7 Technical Performance Summary — Version 7	751	758

57.0 Unit Cost/Time

	Text	Figure
57.1 Unit Cost/Time — Version 1	759	761
57.2 Unit Cost/Time — Version 2	759	762
57.3 Unit Cost/Time — Version 3	759	763
57.4 Unit Cost/Time — Version 4	759	764
57.5 Unit Cost/Time — Version 5	759	765
57.6 Unit Cost/Time — Version 6	759	766
57.7 Unit Cost/Time — Version 7	759	767
57.8 Unit Cost/Time — Version 8	760	768
57.9 Unit Cost/Time — Version 9	760	769
57.10 Unit Cost/Time — Version 10	760	770
57.11 Unit Cost/Time — Version 11	760	771
57.12 Unit Cost/Time — Version 12	760	772
57.13 Unit Cost/Time — Version 13	760	773
57.14 Unit Cost/Time — Version 14	760	774
57.15 Unit Cost/Time — Version 15	760	775

58.0 Working Capital Turnover

	Text	Figure
58.1 Working Capital Turnover — Version 1	777	779
58.2 Working Capital Turnover — Version 2	777	780
58.3 Working Capital Turnover — Version 3	777	781
58.4 Working Capital Turnover — Version 4	777	782

Table of Contents

	Text	Figure
58.5 Working Capital Turnover — Version 5	777	783
58.6 Working Capital Turnover — Version 6	777	784
58.7 Working Capital Turnover — Version 7	777	785
58.8 Working Capital Turnover — Version 8	778	786

PART II—CHARTSMANSHIP

59.0 Basic Types of Business Charts

	Text	Figure
59.1 Basic Chart Types — Two-Scale	789	790
59.2 Basic Chart Types — One-Scale	789	791

60.0 Line Chart Variations

	Text	Figure
60.1 Line Chart Variations — Single Sets of Scales	793	794
60.2 Line Chart Variations — Repeated and Multiple Scales	793	795
60.3 Examples of Uses of Line Charts	793	796
60.4 Examples of Line Charts Used to Display Frequency Distributions	793	797
60.5 Examples of Line Charts Used for Ration Analysis	793	798

61.0 Surface Chart Variations

	Text	Figure
61.1 Surface Chart Variations — Simple	799	800
61.2 Surface Chart Variations — Band and Variance Styles	799	801
61.3 Examples of Uses of Surface Charts	799	802

62.0 Column Chart Variations

	Text	Figure
62.1 Column Chart Variations — Basic	803	804
62.2 Column Chart Variations — Floating and Area	803	805
62.3 Examples of Uses of Column Charts	803	806

63.0 Bar Chart Variations

	Text	Figure
63.1 Bar Chart Variations — Basic	807	808
63.2 Bar Chart Variations — Step Style	807	809
63.3 Examples of Uses of Bar Charts	807	810

64.0 Symbol Chart Variations

	Text	Figure
64.1 Symbol Chart Variations — Basic	811	812
64.2 Milestone Symbol Chart	811	813

65.0 Circle Chart Variations

	Text	Figure
65.1 Circle Chart Variations — Basic	815	816
65.2 Examples of Uses of Circle Charts	815	817

66.0 Format and Nomenclature

	Text	Figure
66.1 Basic Chart Format	819	820
66.2 Chart Nomenclature	819	821

67.0 Shape, Position, and Size

	Text	Figure
67.1 Chart Shape	823	824
67.2 Chart Position on Page	823	825

Table of Contents

xxiii

	Text	Figure
67.3 Chart Proportions Related to Pages	823	826
67.4 Film Projection Proportions	823	827

68.0 Titles

	Text	Figure
68.1 Chart Title Location	829	830
68.2 Chart Title Types	829	831

69.0 Grids

	Text	Figure
69.1 Grid Rulings	833	834
69.2 Use of Tick Marks	833	835
69.3 Column Chart Grids	833	836
69.4 Grid Patterns for Bar and Symbol Charts	833	837

70.0 Line Weight and Shading

	Text	Figure
70.1 Line Weight	839	840
70.2 Curve Line Weight	839	841
70.3 Preferred Line and Shading Patterns	839	842
70.4 Effective Shading	839	843

71.0 Amount Scales

	Text	Figure
71.1 Amount Scale Selection	845	847
71.2 Amount Data Anomalies	845	848
71.3 The Zero Base	845	849
71.4 Compression of the Amount Scale	845	850
71.5 Amount Scale Intervals	845	851
71.6 Reading Curve or Column Values	845	852
71.7 Location of Amount Scale Designations	845	853
71.8 Line Chart Amount Designations	845	854
71.9 Column Chart Amount Designations	846	855
71.10 Location of Amount Scale Caption	846	856

72.0 Time Scales

	Text	Figure
72.1 Time Scale Location	857	858
72.2 Time Scale Range	857	859
72.3 Time Scale Anomalies	857	860
72.4 Time Scale Designations	857	861
72.5 Data Carried Over from Previous Time Period	857	862

73.0 Goals and Limit

	Text	Figure
73.1 Goals and Limits — Basic Concepts	863	864
73.2 Goals as Related to One- and Two-Scale Charts	863	865
73.3 Other Examples of Goals and Limits	863	866

74.0 Time-Now Dating

	Text	Figure
74.1 Time-Now Dating — Arrows and Lines	867	868
74.2 Time-Now Dating — Shading, Bars, and Call-Outs	867	869

75.0 Notes, Keys, and Authentication

	Text	Figure
75.1 Location for Notes	871	872
75.2 Labels Versus Keys	871	873
75.3 Data Authentication	871	874

76.0 Emphasizing Key Points

	Text	Figure
76.1 Special Horizontal and Vertical Rulings	875	876
76.2 Special Uses of Shading	875	877
76.3 Highlighting Problems and Exceptions	875	878

77.0 Data Layout

	Text	Figure
77.1 Trend Versus Detail Charts	879	881
77.2 Cumulative and Rate Charts	879	882
77.3 Plotting Points	879	884
77.4 Surface Versus Column Charts	879	885
77.5 Planning Surface Charts	880	886

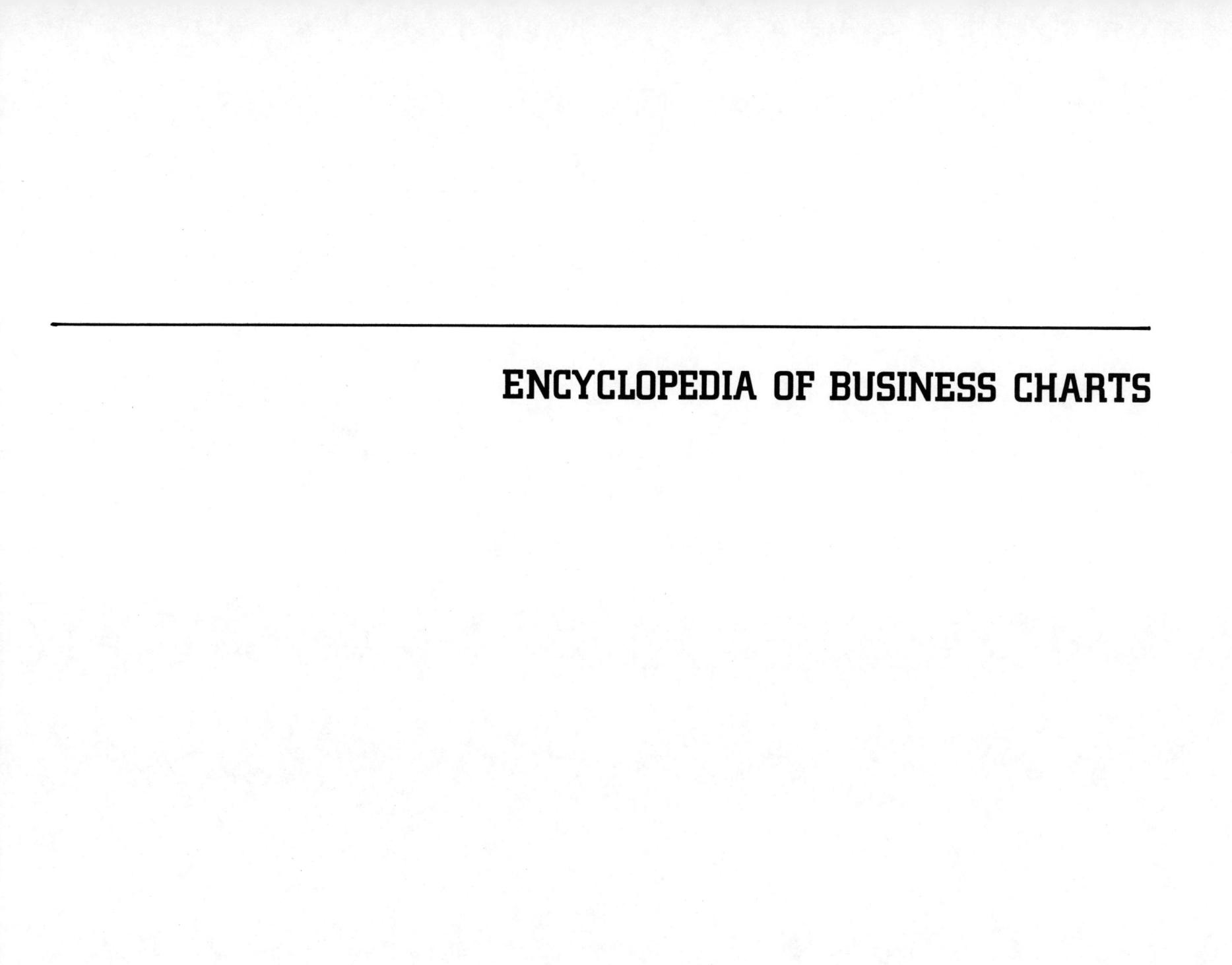

ENCYCLOPEDIA OF BUSINESS CHARTS

I

BUSINESS CHART EXAMPLES

Introduction

The types of graphics used in operating a business fall into three main categories: diagrams, maps, and charts. Diagrams, such as organization diagrams, flow diagrams, and networks, are usually intended to graphically portray <u>how</u> an activity should be, or is being, accomplished, and <u>who</u> is responsible for that accomplishment. Maps such as route maps, location maps, and density maps, illustrate <u>where</u> an activity is, or should be, taking place, and <u>what</u> exists there.

The emphasis in this part of the encyclopedia is on the <u>chart</u> form of business graphics. Charts such as line charts, column charts, and surface charts, are normally constructed to show the businessman <u>how much</u> and <u>when</u>. Charts have the ability to graphically display the past, present, and anticipated future of an activity. They can be plotted so as to indicate the current direction that is being followed in relationship to what should be followed. They can indicate problems and potential problems, hopefully in time for constructive corrective action to be taken.

The emphasis, too, is on <u>tracking</u> charts. In this capacity, they are used to monitor an activity's schedule, its costs, its general financial position, and its technical performance, such as accuracy, reliability, and quality. In all of these applications, the tracking chart must have at least two elements of data. One is the plan, or goal, of the activity. The second element is the actual performance plotted against that plan. Business charts are also used for analytical and information purposes. All three categories of charts . . . tracking, analytical, information . . . are included in this encyclopedia. They each have special and useful purposes in the operation of an enterprise.

Chart categories are presented in alphabetical order (Accuracy, Average Collection Period of Receivables, Budgets, etc.). The index can be used to locate subjects that are known by two or more terms of identical or similar meaning. Within each category charts are arranged in an ascending order of complexity, from the simple to the detailed. Further, the tracking type charts are presented first, each section usually ending with tabular versions of tracking charts followed by one-time status report styles of charts.

Many of the graphic conventions used in the chart examples that follow (the use of time-now lines, for instance) are explained and described, together with alternate conventions, in the "Chartsmanship" part (Part II) of this encyclopedia.

1.0 ACCURACY

Charts that show the technical performance of a product in terms of accuracy are displayed in this section. Also see Section 56.0, *Technical Performance Summaries*.

1.1 Accuracy—Version 1: Accuracy is tracked in terms of errors per month as a percent of total product usage in Version 1 of an accuracy chart, Figure 1.1. Actual performance, in this example, is tracked against a goal.

1.2 Accuracy—Version 2: In Version 2 of an accuracy tracking chart, Figure 1.2, test performance is shown in terms of distance from a target. Performance within 5 feet of the target is acceptable. The acceptable area is shaded on this chart example.

1.3 Accuracy—Version 3: Graphics are used in a one-time status report version of an accuracy chart, Figure 1.3. In this example, 90.2% of the units performed within the specified 5-foot distance from the target while 9.8% of the units performed beyond the specified limit.

1.4 Accuracy—Version 4: A target circle chart style is used as a one-time status report in Version 4 of an accuracy chart, Figure 1.4. In this example the center of the circle represents the goal, and the outer tolerance limit of 3 miles is shown with a dashed line. Target "hits" are recorded, and the percentages of hits within versus out-of-tolerance are given in note form.

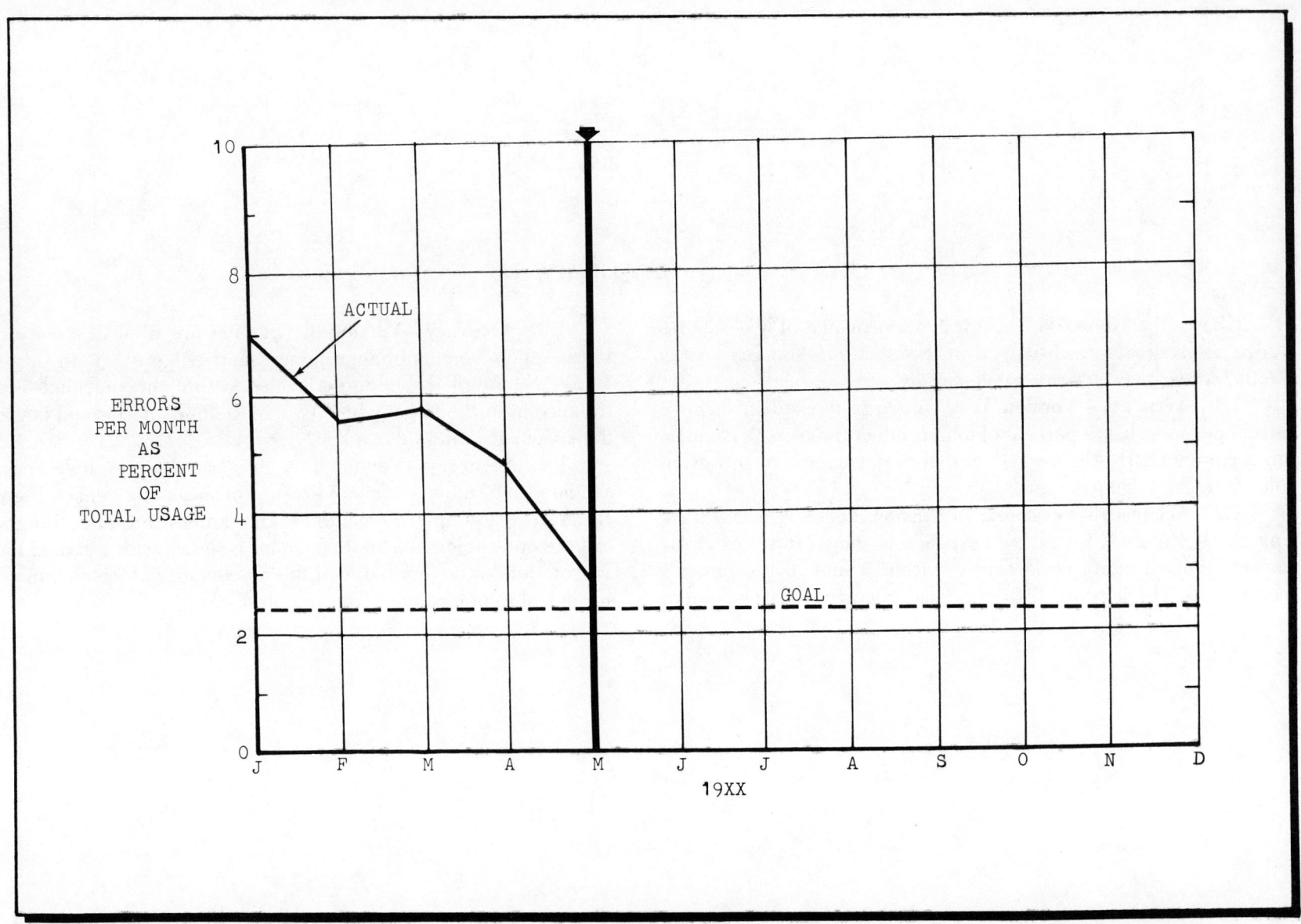

Figure 1.1   Accuracy—Version 1

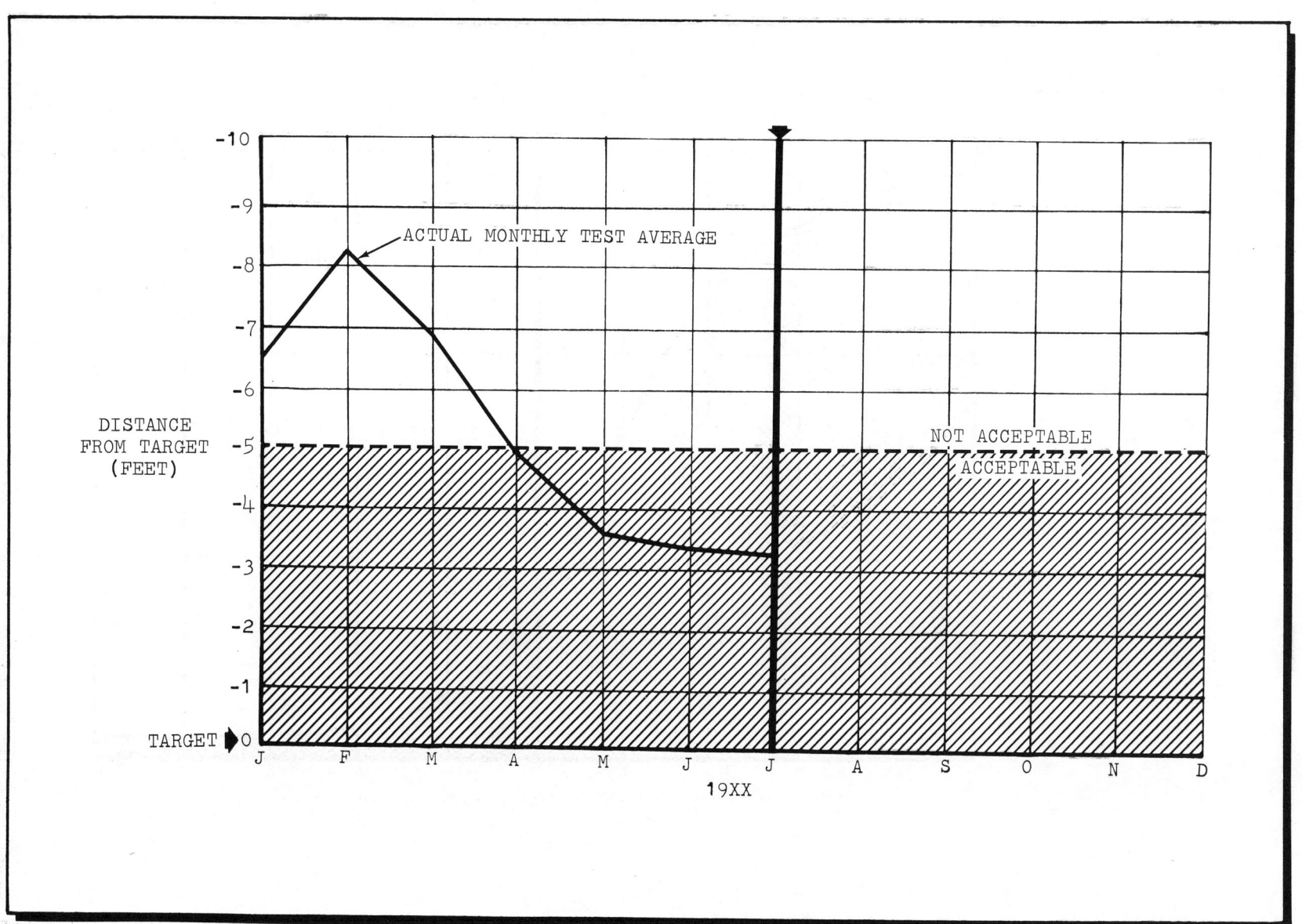

Figure 1.2 Accuracy—Version 2

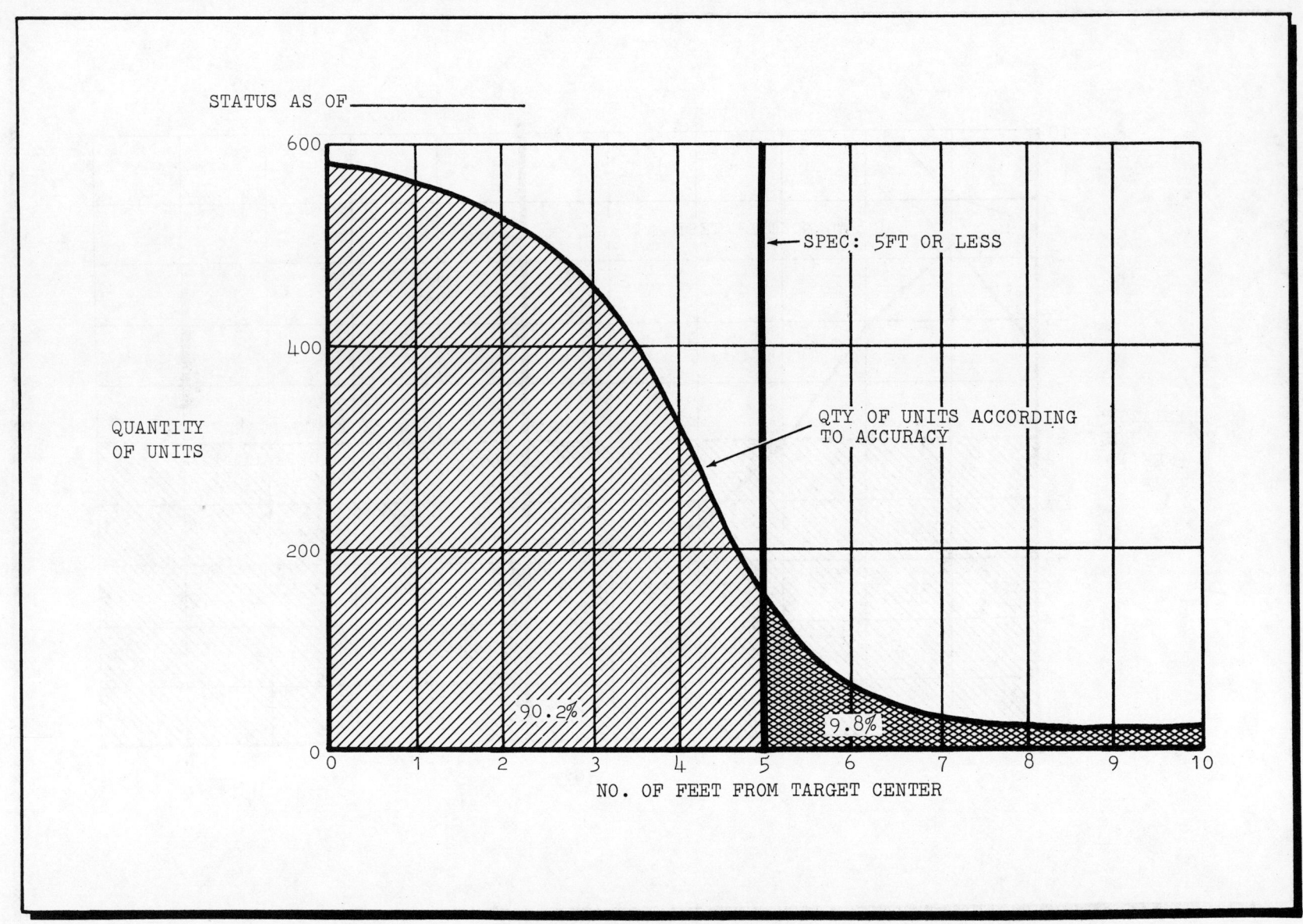

Figure 1.3 Accuracy—Version 3

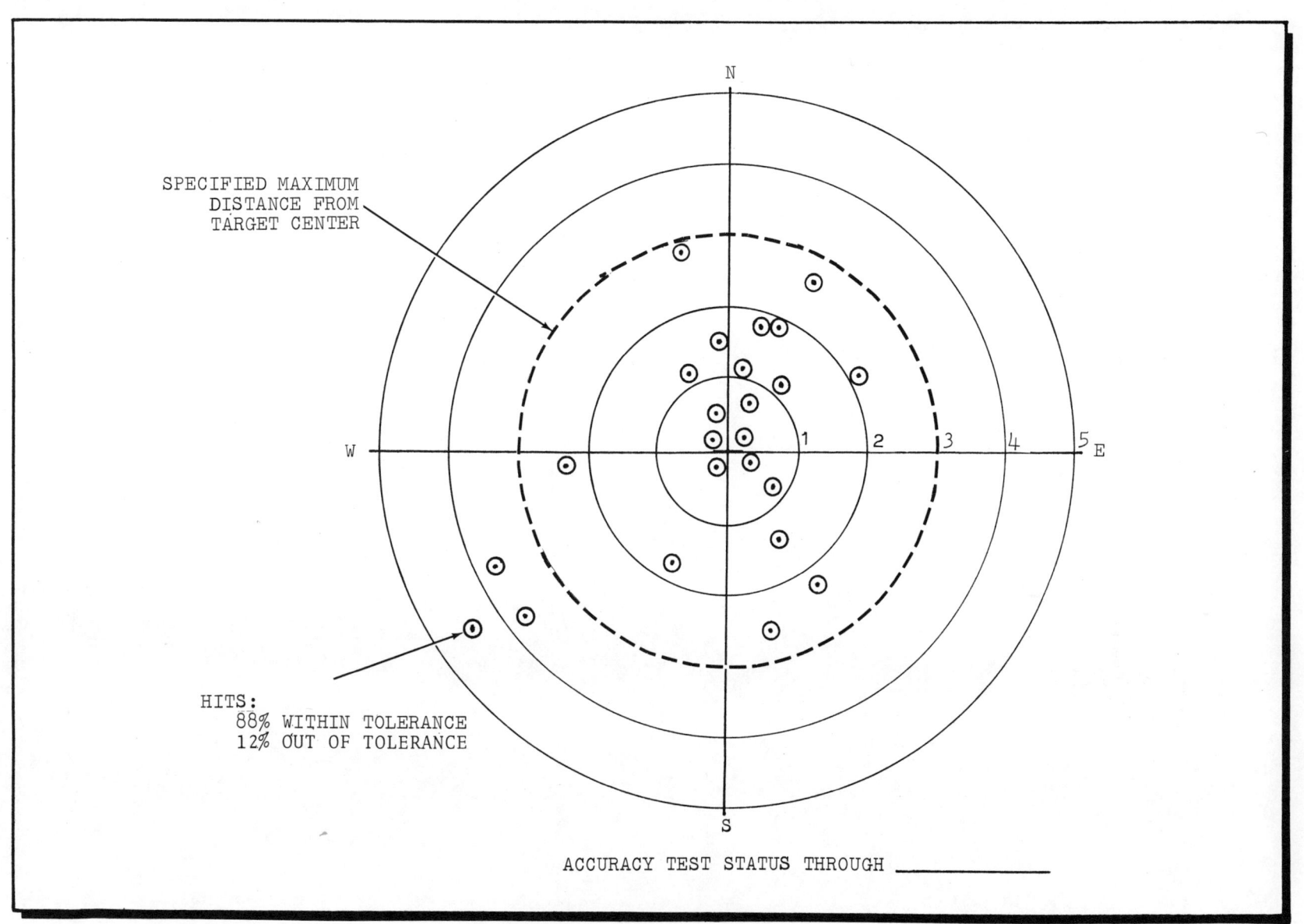

Figure 1.4 Accuracy—Version 4

2.0 AVERAGE COLLECTION PERIOD OF RECEIVABLES

Charts that display the average period of time (usually days) normally required to convert accounts and notes receivable into cash are shown in this section. Average collection periods that are excessively high may indicate a danger of having too many uncollectable receivables. Collection periods that are too low may indicate that too few credit risks are being taken when the cultivation of new business may well depend upon a certain amount of risk taking. Also see Section 42.0, *Receivables*.

2.1 Average Collection Period of Receivables—Version 1: A line chart style is used for Version 1 of a tracking chart for displaying the average collection period of receivables, Figure 2.1. In this example, the amount scale is in days. The goal is shown with a dashed line, and actuals to date are shown with a solid line. An arrowhead on the amount scale highlights that it does not start from a zero base.

2.2 Average Collection Period of Receivables—Version 2: Version 2 of an average collection period of receivables chart, Figure 2.2, is similar to Version 1 except in this example the amount scale starts with zero and shading has been added to enhance the readability of the actuals. The problem with using shading is the extra effort required for its application.

2.3 Average Collection Period of Receivables—Version 3: Column and line chart styles are combined in Version 3 of a tracking chart used for displaying the average collection period of receivables, Figure 2.3. A dashed line shows the plan, and solid columns are used to display actuals to date.

2.4 Average Collection Period of Receivables—Version 4: Dual amount scales are used on Version 4 of an average collection period of receivables tracking chart, Figure 2.4. Dashed and solid lines are used to display the collection period and are in register with the left-hand amount scale. Ball-and-line and dotted lines are used to display the dollar value of the receivables and are in register with the right-hand amount scale.

2.5 Average Collection Period for Receivables—Version 5: Examination of performance over a long time span is possible with the format utilized in Version 5 of a chart used for displaying the average collection period of receivables, Figure 2.5. In this example, actuals for four previous years are shown. The plan and actuals for the current year are displayed in the center grid, and the right-hand grid shows the plan for the coming year.

2.6 Average Collection Period for Receivables—Version 6: Six lines of statistics are combined with graphics in Version 6 of a tracking chart for displaying the average collection period for receivables, Figure 2.6. Average daily sales are first given. These figures are derived from dividing the annualized monthly sales by 365. Forecasted and actual receivables are then shown, followed by the collection period in terms of days. The planned and actual collection period statistics are also plotted on the graphic portion of the chart.

2.7 Average Collection Period of Receivables—Version 7: A non-graphic format is used for Version 7 of a tracking chart for displaying the average collection period for receivables, Figure 2.7. In this version, statistics for planned and actual net sales, receivables, and the collection period are given.

2.8 Average Collection Period of Receivables—Version 8: Version 8 of an average collection period of receivables chart, Figure 2.8, is useful as a one-time status report. Statistics for net sales, receivables, and the average collection period are given in terms of plans, actuals, and variances from plans.

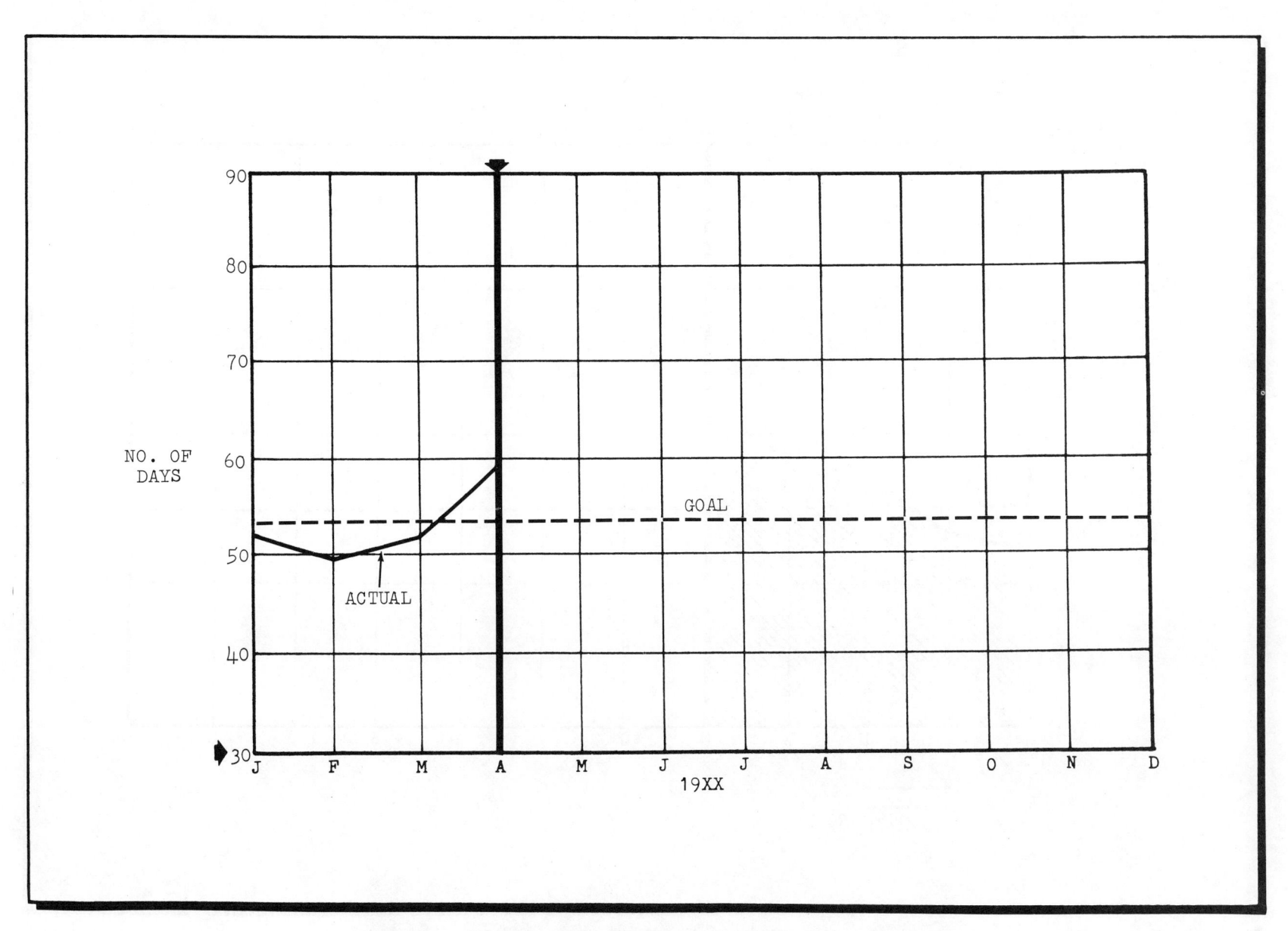

Figure 2.1 Average Collection Period of Receivables—Version 1

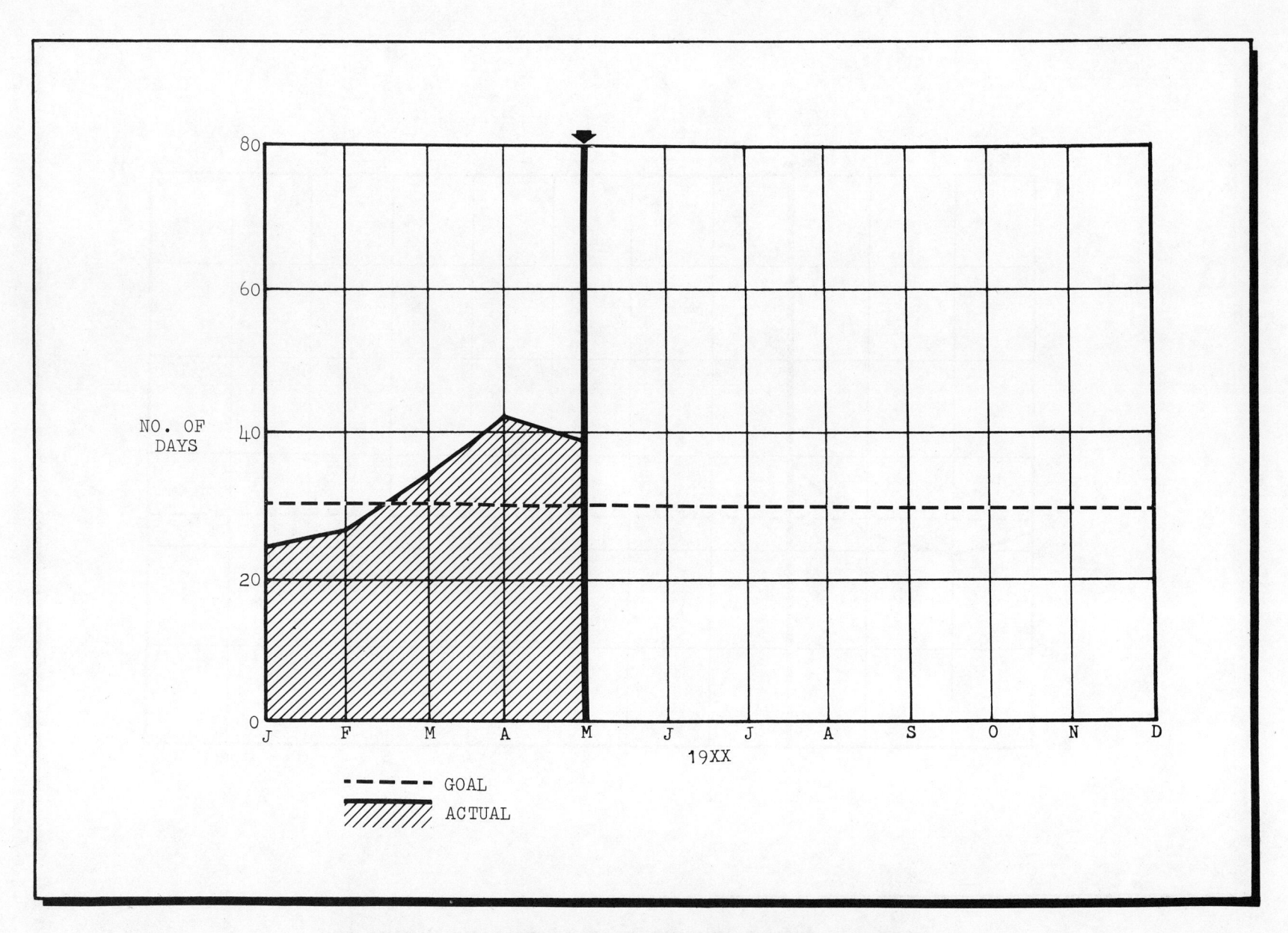

Figure 2.2   Average Collection Period of Receivables—Version 2

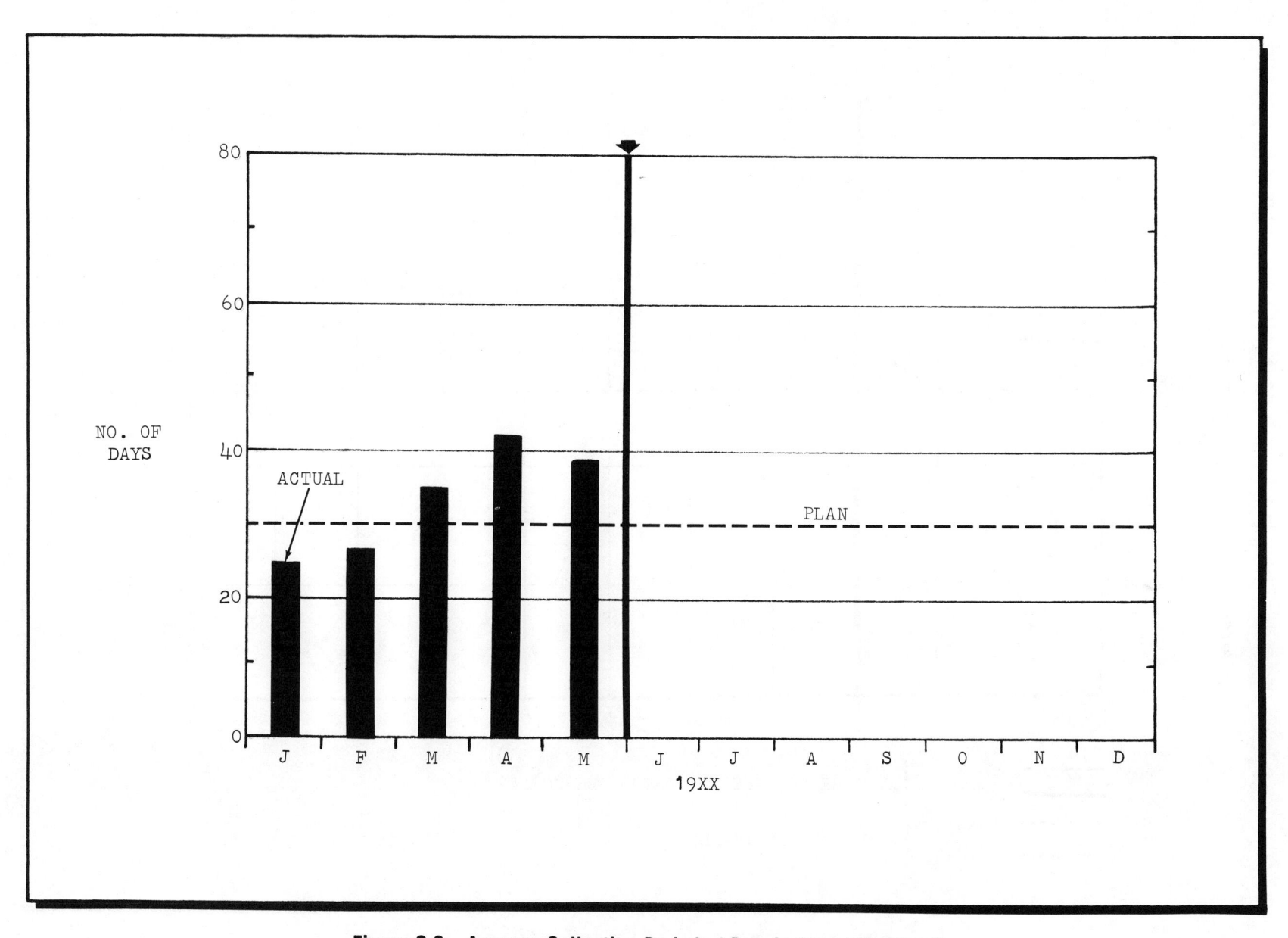

Figure 2.3 Average Collection Period of Receivables—Version 3

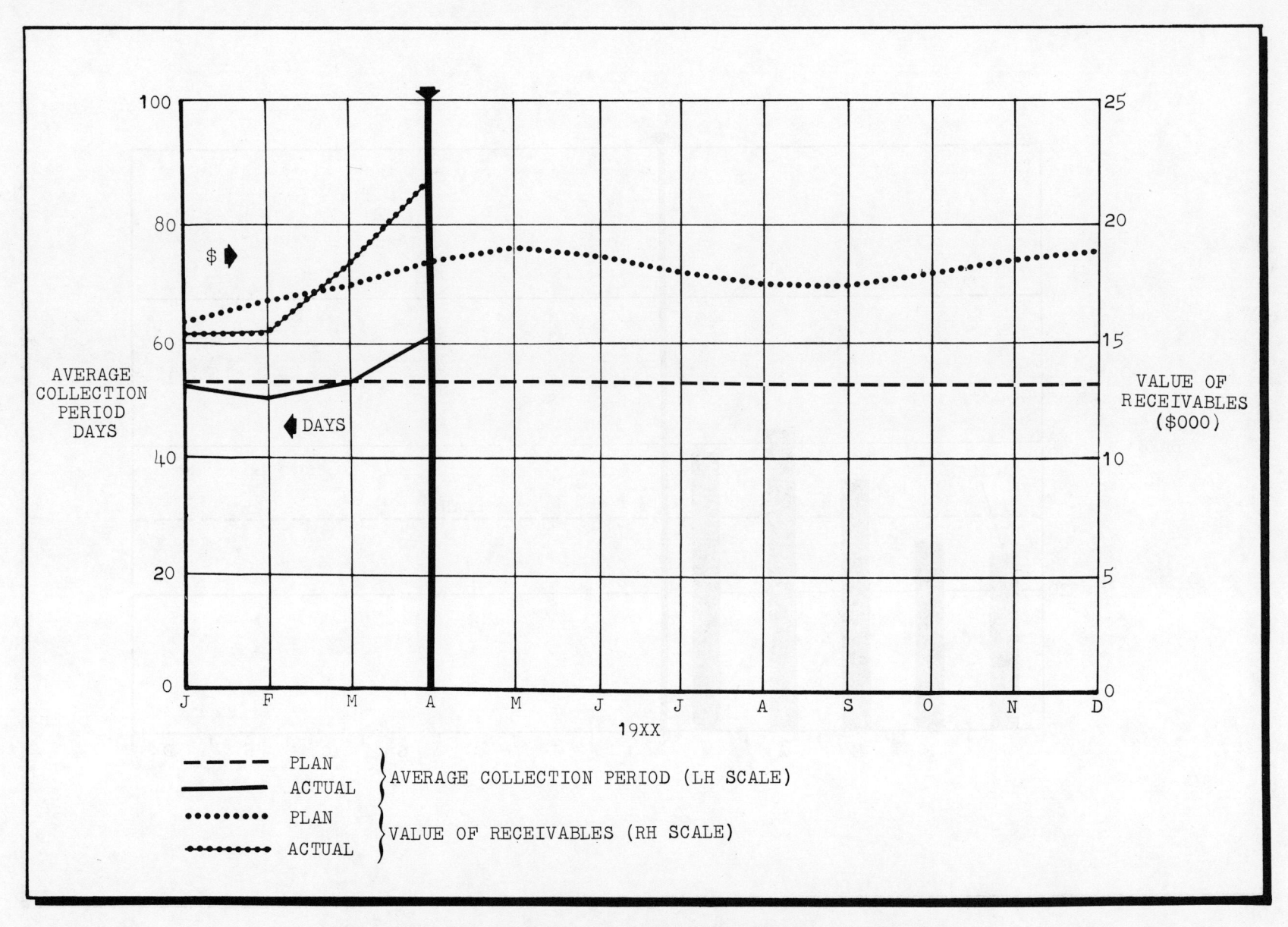

Figure 2.4 Average Collection Period of Receivables—Version 4

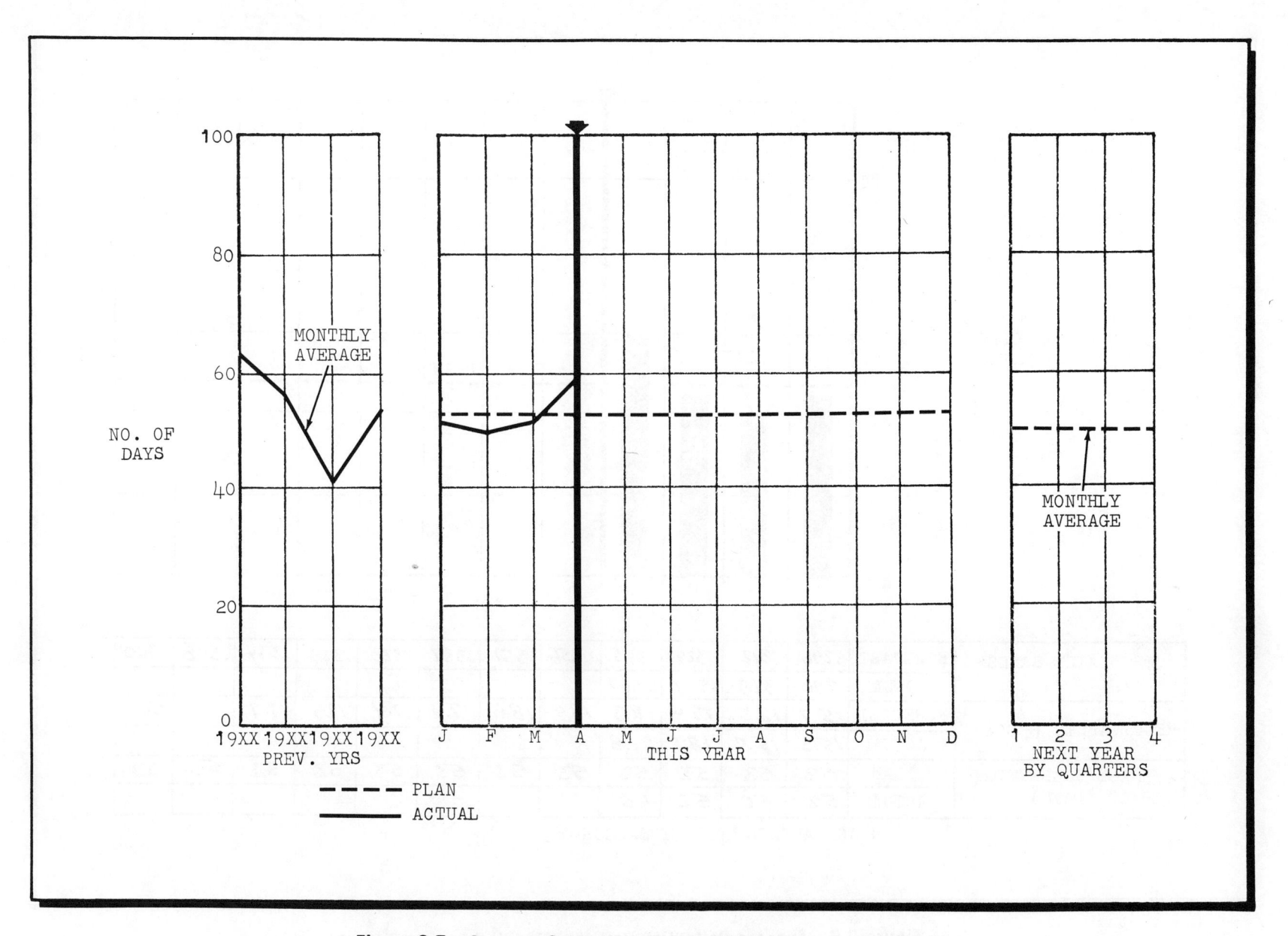

Figure 2.5 Average Collection Period of Receivables—Version 5

AVER. DAILY SALES* ($000)	FORECAST	.296	.312	.329	.345	.356	.351	.337	.329	.329	.334	.348	.350
	ACTUAL	.296	.329	.351	.362								
RECEIVABLES ($000)	FORECAST	15.7	16.5	17.4	18.3	18.9	18.6	17.9	17.4	17.4	17.7	18.4	18.6
	ACTUAL	15.3	15.5	18.1	21.8								
AVERAGE COLLECTION PERIOD (DAYS)	PLAN	53	53	53	53	53	53	53	53	53	53	53	53
	ACTUAL	52	50	52	60								

* ANNUALIZED MONTHLY SALES ÷ 365

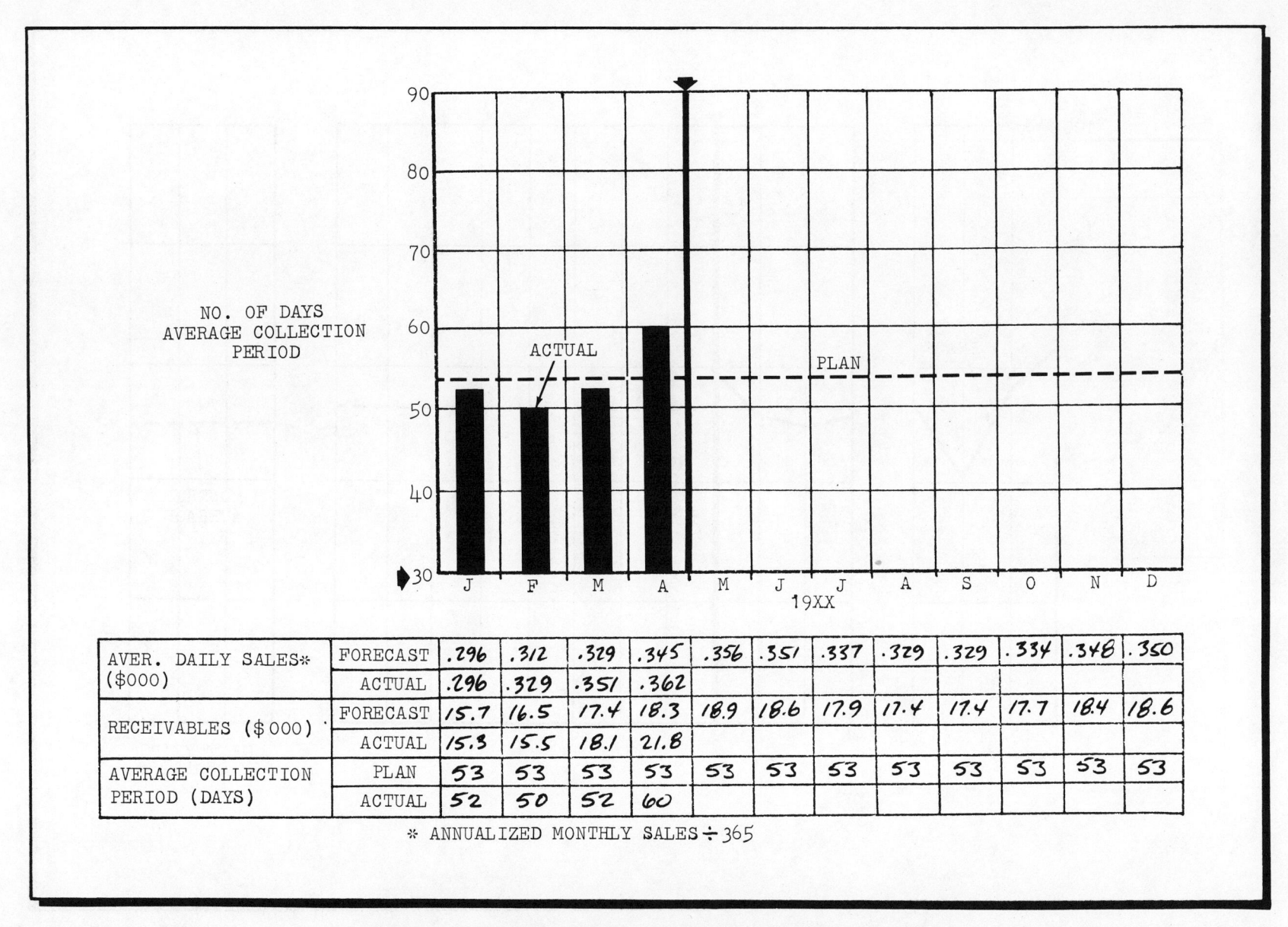

Figure 2.6 Average Collection Period of Receivables—Version 6

ITEM			J	F	M	A	19XX M	J	J	A	S	O	N	D
NET SALES ($000)	PER MO.	FORECAST	9.0	10.0	11.0	12.0	12.0	10.0	8.0	8.0	10.0	12.0	14.0	14.0
		ACTUAL	9.0	11.0	12.0	12.0								
	YTD	FORECAST	9.0	19.0	30.0	42.0	54.0	64.0	72.0	80.0	90.0	102.0	116.0	130.0
		ACTUAL	9.0	20.0	32.0	44.0								
	ANNUALIZED	FORECAST	108.0	114.0	120.0	126.0	130.0	128.0	123.0	120.0	120.0	122.0	127.0	130.0
		ACTUAL	108.0	120.0	128.0	132.0								
	AVER. DAILY SALES*	FORECAST	.296	.312	.329	.345	.356	.351	.337	.329	.329	.334	.348	.350
		ACTUAL	.296	.329	.351	.362								
TOTAL RECEIVABLES ($000)		FORECAST	15.7	16.5	17.4	18.3	18.9	18.6	17.9	17.4	17.4	17.7	18.4	18.6
		ACTUAL	15.3	15.5	18.1	21.8								
AVERAGE COLLECTION PERIOD (DAYS)		GOAL	53	53	53	53	53	53	53	53	53	53	53	53
		ACTUAL	52	50	52	60								
		VARIANCE	-1	-3	-4	+7								

*ANNUALIZED SALES ÷ 365 = AVERAGE DAILY SALES

Figure 2.7 Average Collection Period of Receivables—Version 7

STATUS AS OF _____

ITEM		PLAN	ACTUAL	VARIANCE
NET SALES ($000)	PER MONTH	12.0	12.0	0
	YEAR-TO-DATE	42.0	44.0	+2
	ANNUALIZED	126.0	132	+6
	AVERAGE DAILY SALES*	.345	.362	+.017
RECEIVABLES ($000)		18.3	21.8	+3.5
AVERAGE COLLECTION PERIOD (DAYS)		53	60	+7

* ANNUALIZED SALES ÷ 365 = AVERAGE DAILY SALES

Figure 2.8 Average Collection Period of Receivables—Version 8

3.0 BUDGETS—DETAIL

Budget charts dealing with budgeted and actual expenditures broken down and compared in terms of labor, material, and other similar cost elements are shown in this section. This includes comparisons between elements, units, or departments. Also see Budget Sections 4.0 through 7.0.

3.1 Budget—Detail—Version 1: A combination graph and statistical table showing a breakdown of labor, material, and total costs is displayed in Figure 3.1. All of the statistics in this example are given in cumulative form. The graphic portion of the chart displays only the total costs, giving the current variance between budgeted and actual expenditures, as well as an estimated cost at completion.

3.2 Budget—Detail—Version 2: The graphic portion of a combined graph and statistical table shown in Figure 3.2 displays the total budgeted and actual expenditures divided into the two components, labor and material. Activity is plotted on the graph in terms of total costs and material costs, the labor being the difference between those two elements.

3.3 Budget—Detail—Version 3: A rate per month budget chart is shown in Version 3, Figure 3.3. The budgeted and actual expenditures columns on the chart are segmented into two components, labor and material. The disadvantage of this style chart is that if there is a variance between the budgeted and actual figures at the bottom of the columns ("material" for January, February, and March, in this example), the top portion of the columns (labor) is offset and cannot be easily compared.

3.4 Budget—Detail—Version 4: In the combined graphic and statistical table chart shown in Figure 3.4, labor is divided into two components, direct and indirect. In this example, also, only the total costs are plotted on the graph. If, as shown in the example, there is a current over-budget condition, the chart reader must look at the statistical portion of the chart to determine what element of the budget plan is causing this condition. In the example, it can be seen that the actual cost of material is the problem.

3.5 Budget—Detail—Version 5: Labor, overtime, supplies and materials, and travel and per diem are the elements that make up the total costs in the example chart shown in Figure 3.5. As with Version 4, only the totals are shown on the graphic portion of the chart, and the chart reader must examine the statistical table in order to determine the source of the over-budget condition.

3.6 Budget—Detail—Version 6: Version 6 of a budget chart, Figure 3.6, is identical to Version 5 except that the elements that make up the total cost, in this example, are departments.

3.7 Budget—Detail—Version 7: A method for comparing two separate elements, such as departments or divisions or programs, is shown in Version 7 of a budget tracking chart, Figure 3.7.

3.8 Budget—Detail—Version 8: A trio of deviation style charts are used in Version 8 of a budget chart, Figure 3.8. The performance of three different elements (in this case, departments) is compared.

3.9 Budget—Detail—Version 9: Eight separate cost elements related to a single cost "package" are shown in Version 9 of a budget tracking chart, Figure 3.9. In this example, the budget data relative to the separate processing steps that make up a total assembly are shown.

3.10 Budget—Detail—Version 10: A series of deviation-from-budget style charts are used in Version 10, Figure 3.10. In this example, the performance of various departments is compared.

3.11 Budget—Detail—Version 11: A statistical table showing budgeted and actual expenditures in five different departments is displayed in the example in Figure 3.11. The most significant variance in this example has been circled to attract the chart reader's attention.

3.12 Budget—Detail—Version 12: Version 12 of a budget tracking statistical table, Figure 3.12, is identical to Version 11 except that in this example a remarks section has been provided.

3.13 Budget—Detail—Version 13: A comparison of a fewer number of units, departments, or items permits a broader coverage of statistical cost elements, as shown in the statistical table in Figure 3.13. In this example, six sets of statistics are displayed for each unit. Also in this example, an estimate to complete (revised forecast) has been made for only that unit (Unit 2) that shows a current over-budget condition.

3.14 Budget—Detail—Version 14: A format for displaying statistical data on a weekly basis is shown in Version 14 of a budget chart, Figure 3.14. The various cost elements are listed in the left-hand column. Each chart covers a one-month segment. The cumulative status regarding budgeted and actual expenditures to the end of the previous month is first shown. Then weekly rate figures together with cumulative figures are shown for each week of the month being tracked. On the right-hand side of the table the cumulative budgeted and *estimated* position for the end of that month is shown, including an estimate as to the variance.

3.15 Budget—Detail—Version 15: A "box score" style table is shown as Version 15, Figure 3.15. This table shows status for only one point in time. It has the disadvantage of needing to be completely redone for each new reporting date. It has the advantage of clearly showing variances from budget.

3.16 Budget—Detail—Version 16: Another version of a "Box score" is shown in Figure 3.16. This example is similar to Version 15 except that a column has been added to show the estimated overrun or underrun at completion. This example also provides a column for showing the name of the persons responsible for the functions being monitored.

3.17 Budget—Detail—Version 17: Another form of a box score is shown in Figure 3.17. In this table, three sets of figures are shown in relationship to each item: the costs for the current month, cumulative costs to date, and the estimated costs at completion. A check mark is used on this particular example to highlight the most significant anticipated overrun condition. The bottom line of the table shows each variance as a percentage of the budget.

$-THOUSANDS
(CUMULATIVE)

EST. COST AT COMPLETION 47.0

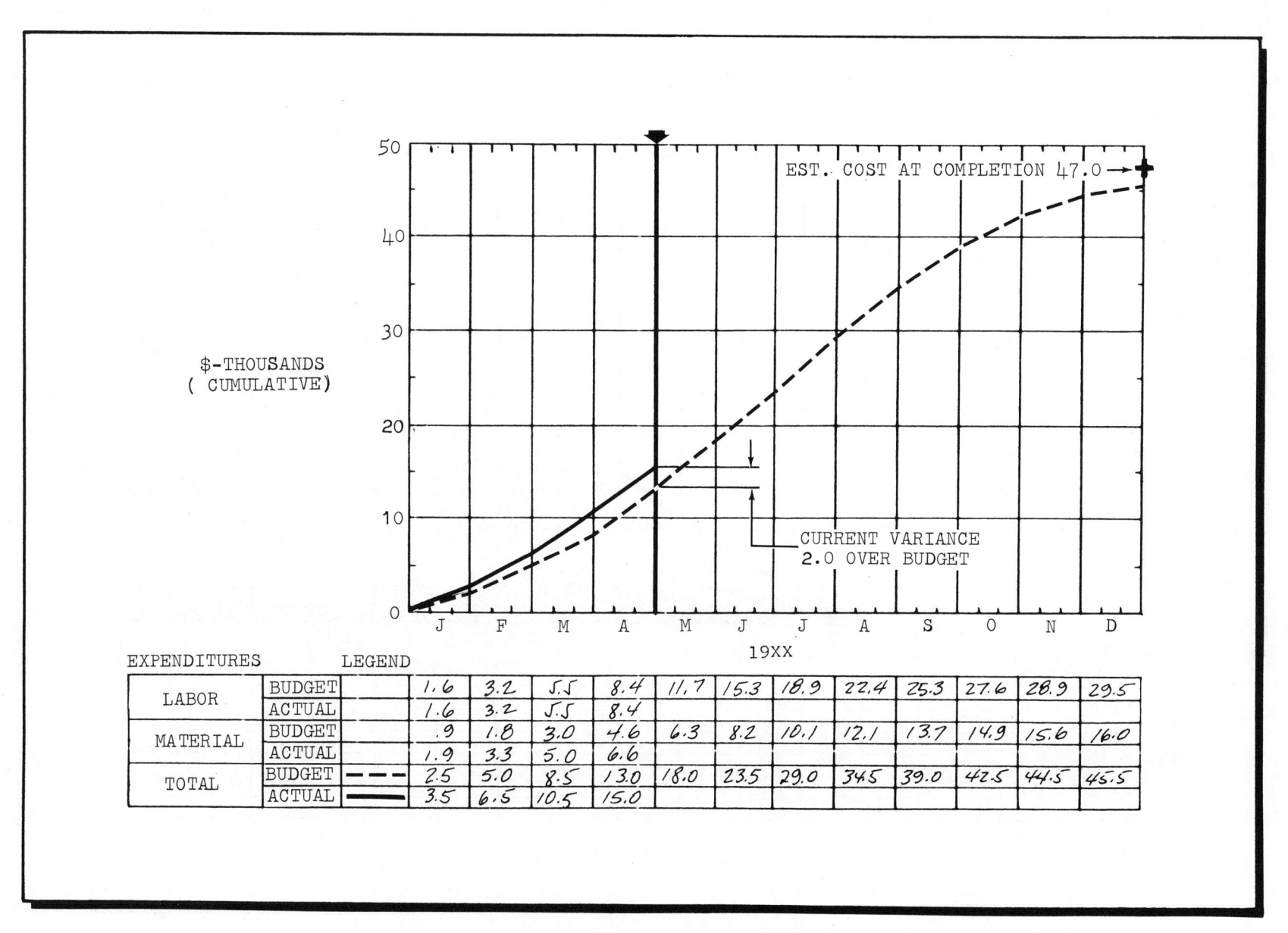

CURRENT VARIANCE
2.0 OVER BUDGET

19XX

EXPENDITURES	LEGEND		J	F	M	A	M	J	J	A	S	O	N	D
LABOR	BUDGET		1.6	3.2	5.5	8.4	11.7	15.3	18.9	22.4	25.3	27.6	28.9	29.5
	ACTUAL		1.6	3.2	5.5	8.4								
MATERIAL	BUDGET		.9	1.8	3.0	4.6	6.3	8.2	10.1	12.1	13.7	14.9	15.6	16.0
	ACTUAL		1.9	3.3	5.0	6.6								
TOTAL	BUDGET	-----	2.5	5.0	8.5	13.0	18.0	23.5	29.0	34.5	39.0	42.5	44.5	45.5
	ACTUAL	———	3.5	6.5	10.5	15.0								

Figure 3.1   Budget—Detail—Version 1

$-THOUSANDS
(CUMULATIVE)

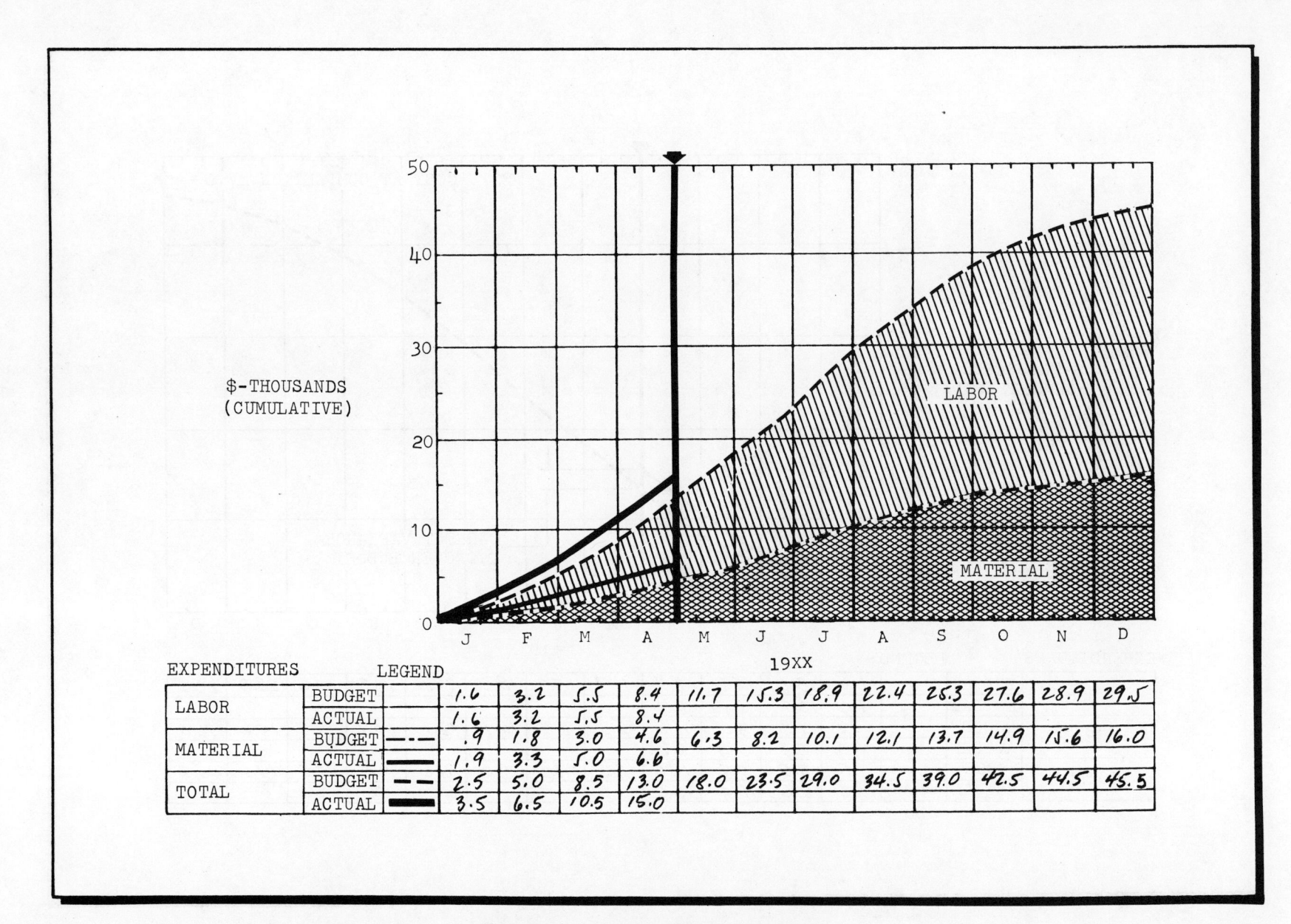

EXPENDITURES		LEGEND	J	F	M	A	M	J	J	A	S	O	N	D
LABOR	BUDGET		1.6	3.2	5.5	8.4	11.7	15.3	18.9	22.4	25.3	27.6	28.9	29.5
	ACTUAL		1.6	3.2	5.5	8.4								
MATERIAL	BUDGET	—·—	.9	1.8	3.0	4.6	6.3	8.2	10.1	12.1	13.7	14.9	15.6	16.0
	ACTUAL	——	1.9	3.3	5.0	6.6								
TOTAL	BUDGET	— —	2.5	5.0	8.5	13.0	18.0	23.5	29.0	34.5	39.0	42.5	44.5	45.5
	ACTUAL	▬▬	3.5	6.5	10.5	15.0								

Figure 3.2   Budget—Detail—Version 2

$-THOUSANDS
(RATE PER MONTH)

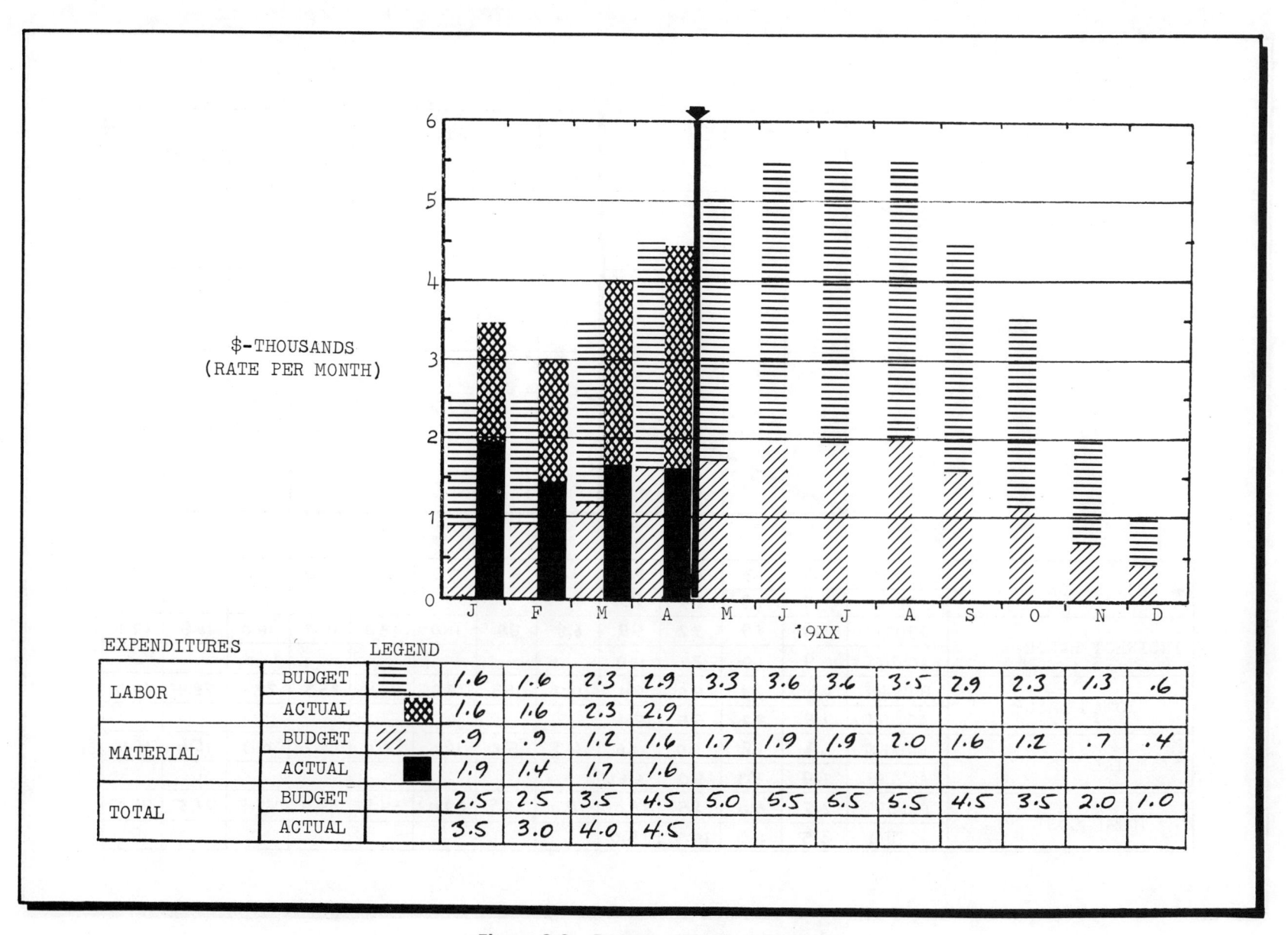

EXPENDITURES		LEGEND												
LABOR	BUDGET	≡	1.6	1.6	2.3	2.9	3.3	3.6	3.6	3.5	2.9	2.3	1.3	.6
	ACTUAL	▩	1.6	1.6	2.3	2.9								
MATERIAL	BUDGET	▨	.9	.9	1.2	1.6	1.7	1.9	1.9	2.0	1.6	1.2	.7	.4
	ACTUAL	■	1.9	1.4	1.7	1.6								
TOTAL	BUDGET		2.5	2.5	3.5	4.5	5.0	5.5	5.5	5.5	4.5	3.5	2.0	1.0
	ACTUAL		3.5	3.0	4.0	4.5								

Figure 3.3   Budget—Detail—Version 3

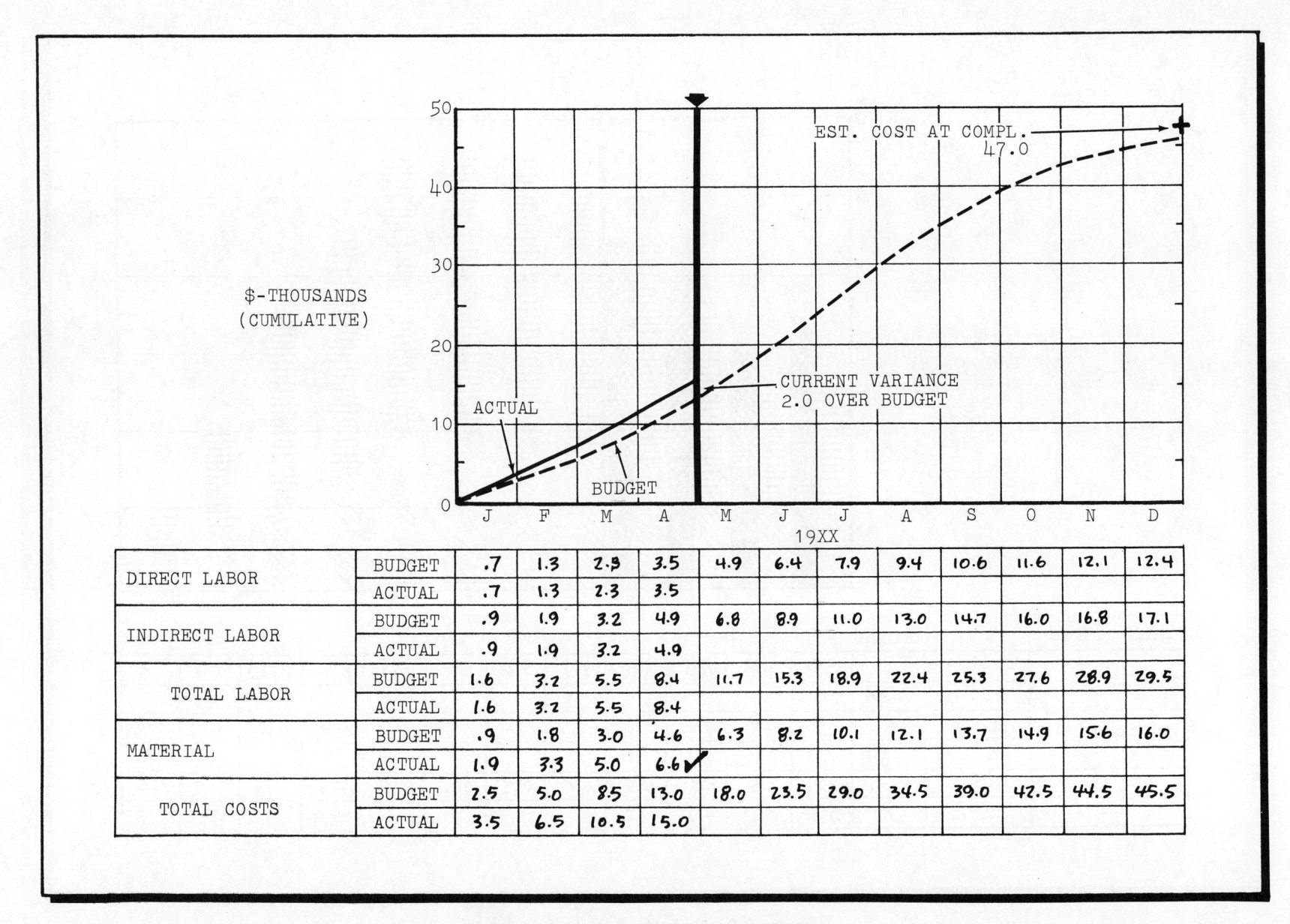

		J	F	M	A	M	J	J	A	S	O	N	D
DIRECT LABOR	BUDGET	.7	1.3	2.3	3.5	4.9	6.4	7.9	9.4	10.6	11.6	12.1	12.4
	ACTUAL	.7	1.3	2.3	3.5								
INDIRECT LABOR	BUDGET	.9	1.9	3.2	4.9	6.8	8.9	11.0	13.0	14.7	16.0	16.8	17.1
	ACTUAL	.9	1.9	3.2	4.9								
TOTAL LABOR	BUDGET	1.6	3.2	5.5	8.4	11.7	15.3	18.9	22.4	25.3	27.6	28.9	29.5
	ACTUAL	1.6	3.2	5.5	8.4								
MATERIAL	BUDGET	.9	1.8	3.0	4.6	6.3	8.2	10.1	12.1	13.7	14.9	15.6	16.0
	ACTUAL	1.9	3.3	5.0	6.6								
TOTAL COSTS	BUDGET	2.5	5.0	8.5	13.0	18.0	23.5	29.0	34.5	39.0	42.5	44.5	45.5
	ACTUAL	3.5	6.5	10.5	15.0								

Figure 3.4   Budget—Detail—Version 4

$-THOUSANDS
(CUMULATIVE)

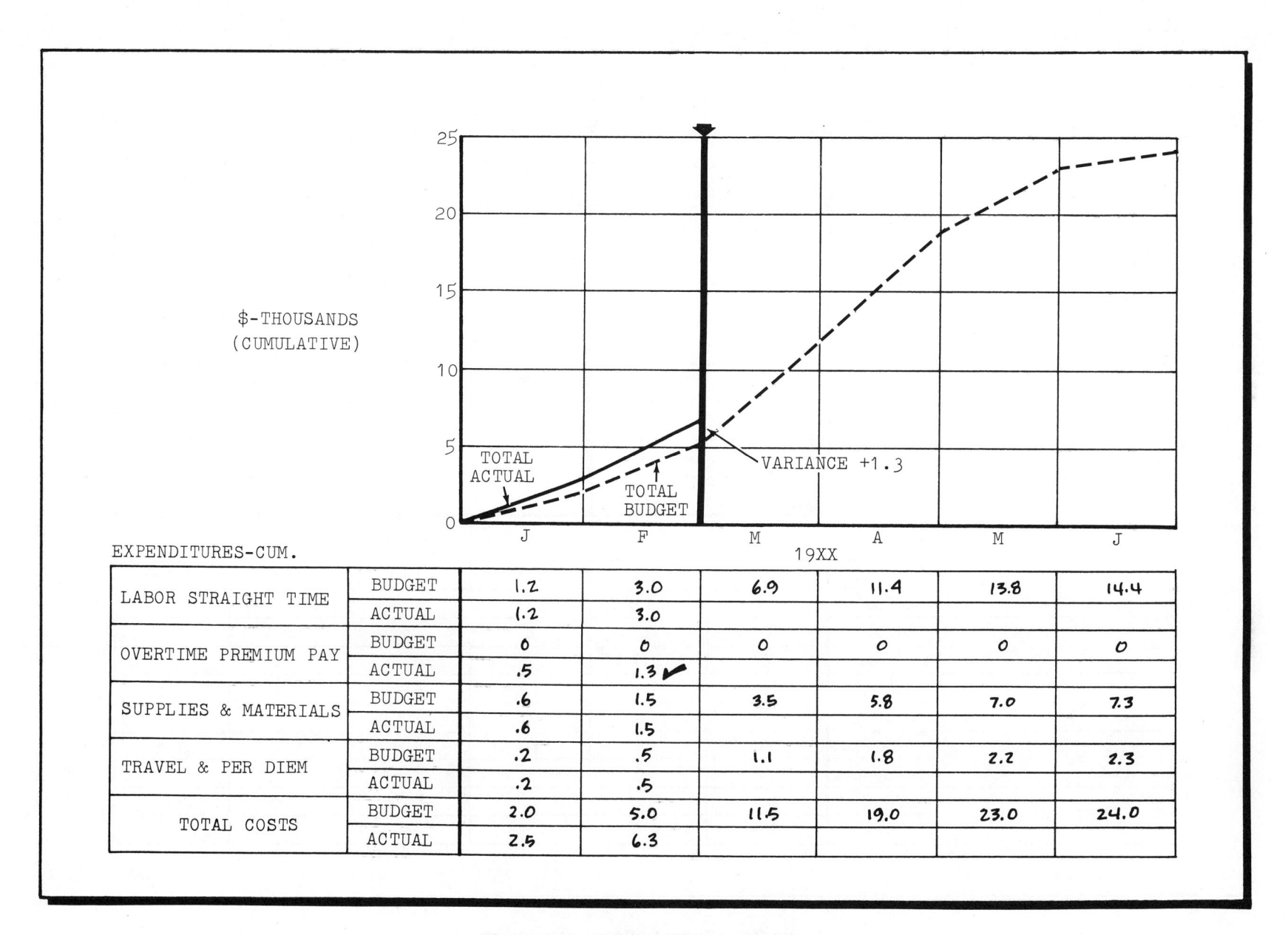

TOTAL ACTUAL
TOTAL BUDGET
VARIANCE +1.3

J F M A M J
19XX

EXPENDITURES-CUM.

		J	F	M	A	M	J
LABOR STRAIGHT TIME	BUDGET	1.2	3.0	6.9	11.4	13.8	14.4
	ACTUAL	1.2	3.0				
OVERTIME PREMIUM PAY	BUDGET	0	0	0	0	0	0
	ACTUAL	.5	1.3				
SUPPLIES & MATERIALS	BUDGET	.6	1.5	3.5	5.8	7.0	7.3
	ACTUAL	.6	1.5				
TRAVEL & PER DIEM	BUDGET	.2	.5	1.1	1.8	2.2	2.3
	ACTUAL	.2	.5				
TOTAL COSTS	BUDGET	2.0	5.0	11.5	19.0	23.0	24.0
	ACTUAL	2.5	6.3				

Figure 3.5 Budget—Detail—Version 5

$-THOUSANDS
(CUMULATIVE)

ACTUAL

BUDGET

VARIANCE +1.3

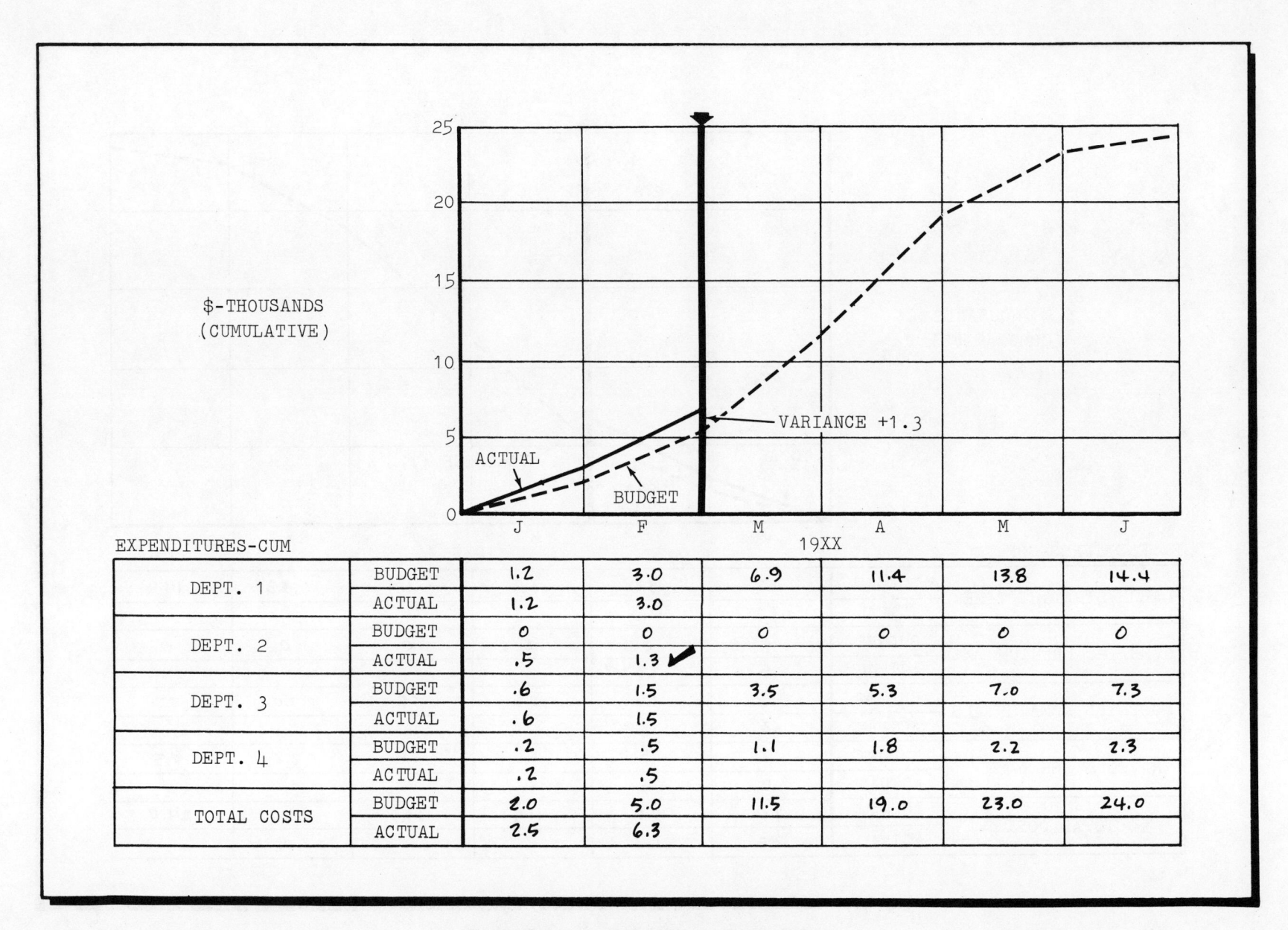

J F M A M J
19XX

EXPENDITURES-CUM							
DEPT. 1	BUDGET	1.2	3.0	6.9	11.4	13.8	14.4
	ACTUAL	1.2	3.0				
DEPT. 2	BUDGET	0	0	0	0	0	0
	ACTUAL	.5	1.3				
DEPT. 3	BUDGET	.6	1.5	3.5	5.3	7.0	7.3
	ACTUAL	.6	1.5				
DEPT. 4	BUDGET	.2	.5	1.1	1.8	2.2	2.3
	ACTUAL	.2	.5				
TOTAL COSTS	BUDGET	2.0	5.0	11.5	19.0	23.0	24.0
	ACTUAL	2.5	6.3				

Figure 3.6   Budget—Detail—Version 6

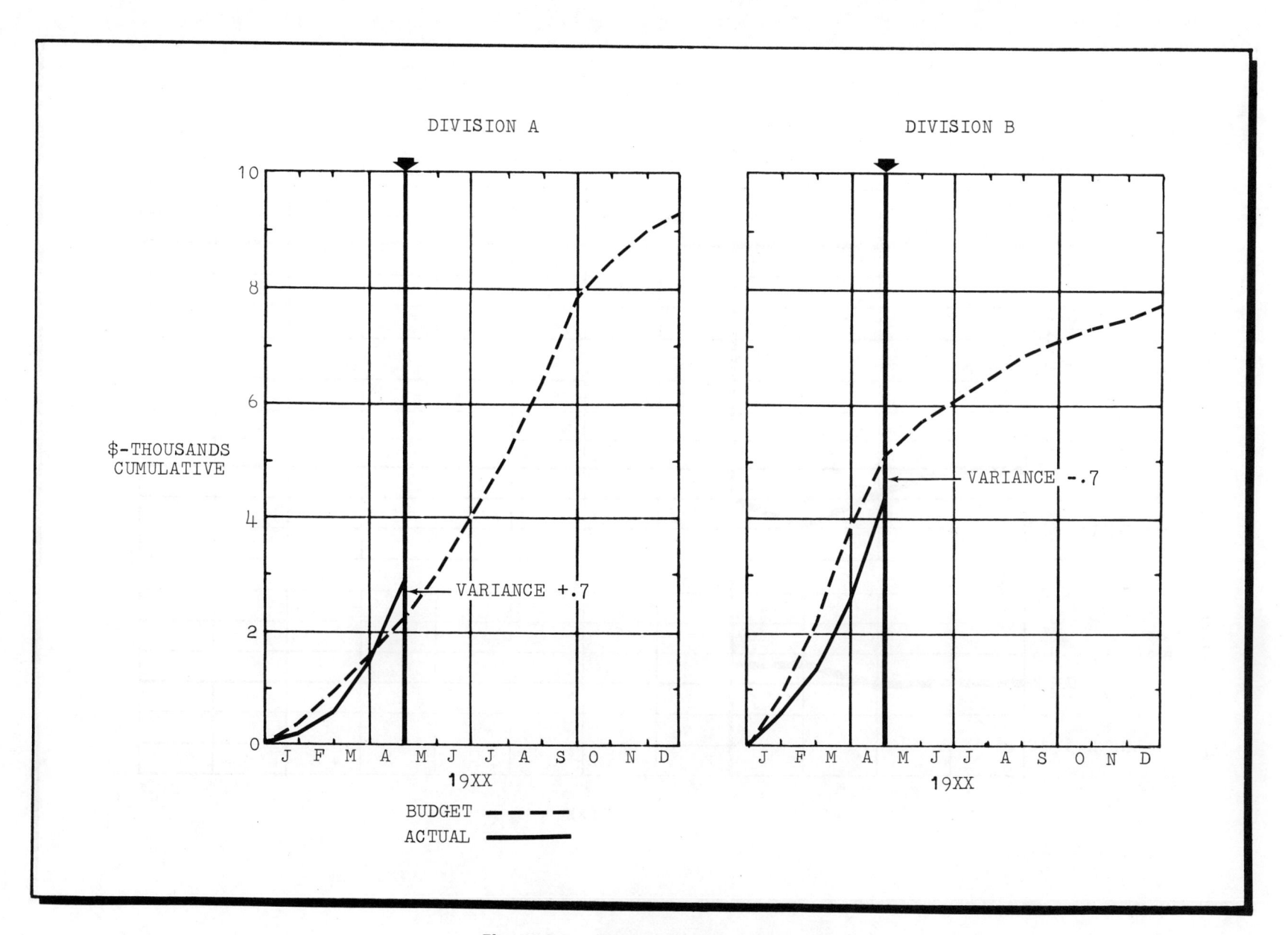

Figure 3.7 Budget—Detail—Version 7

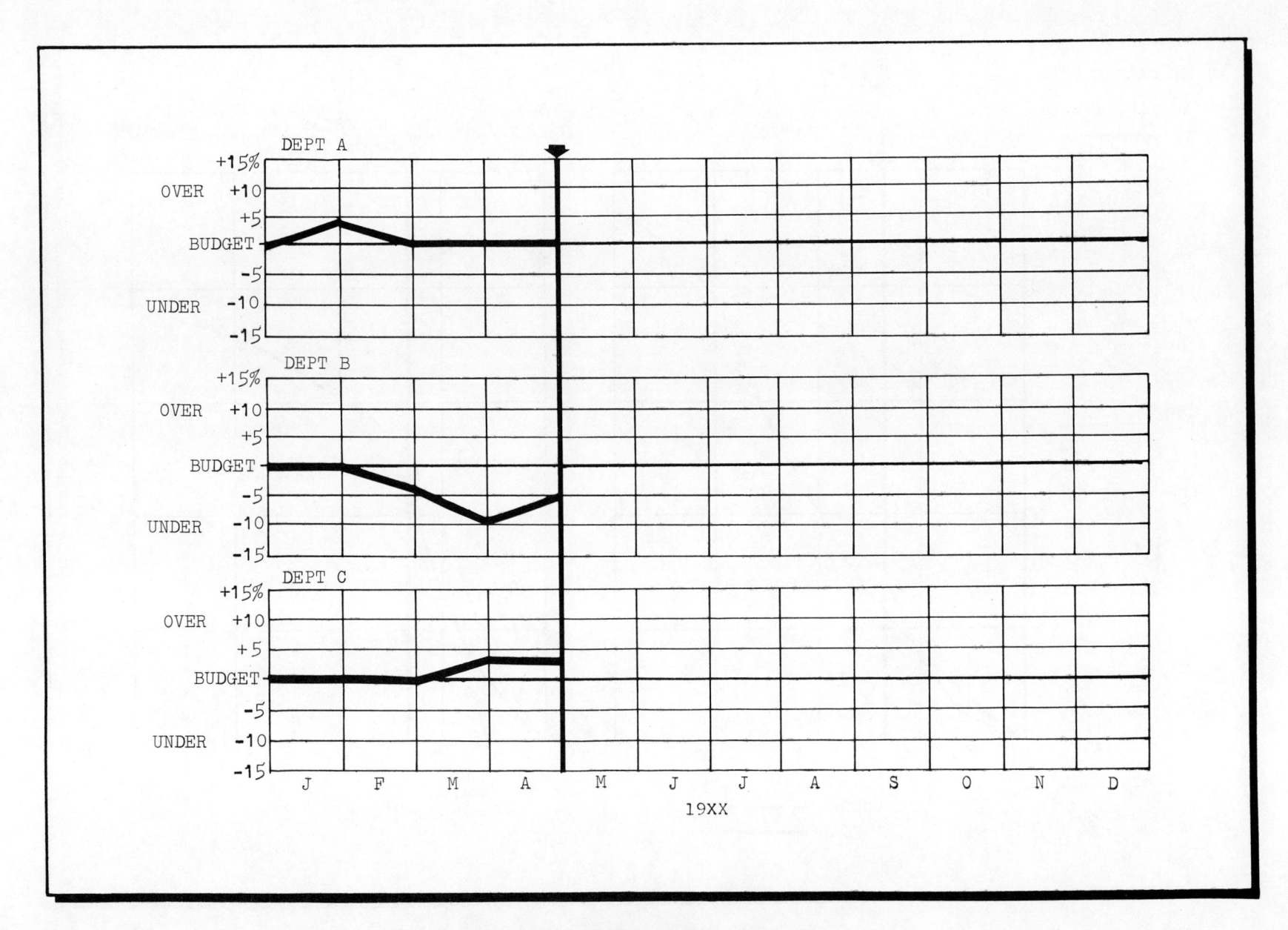

Figure 3.8 Budget—Detail—Version 8

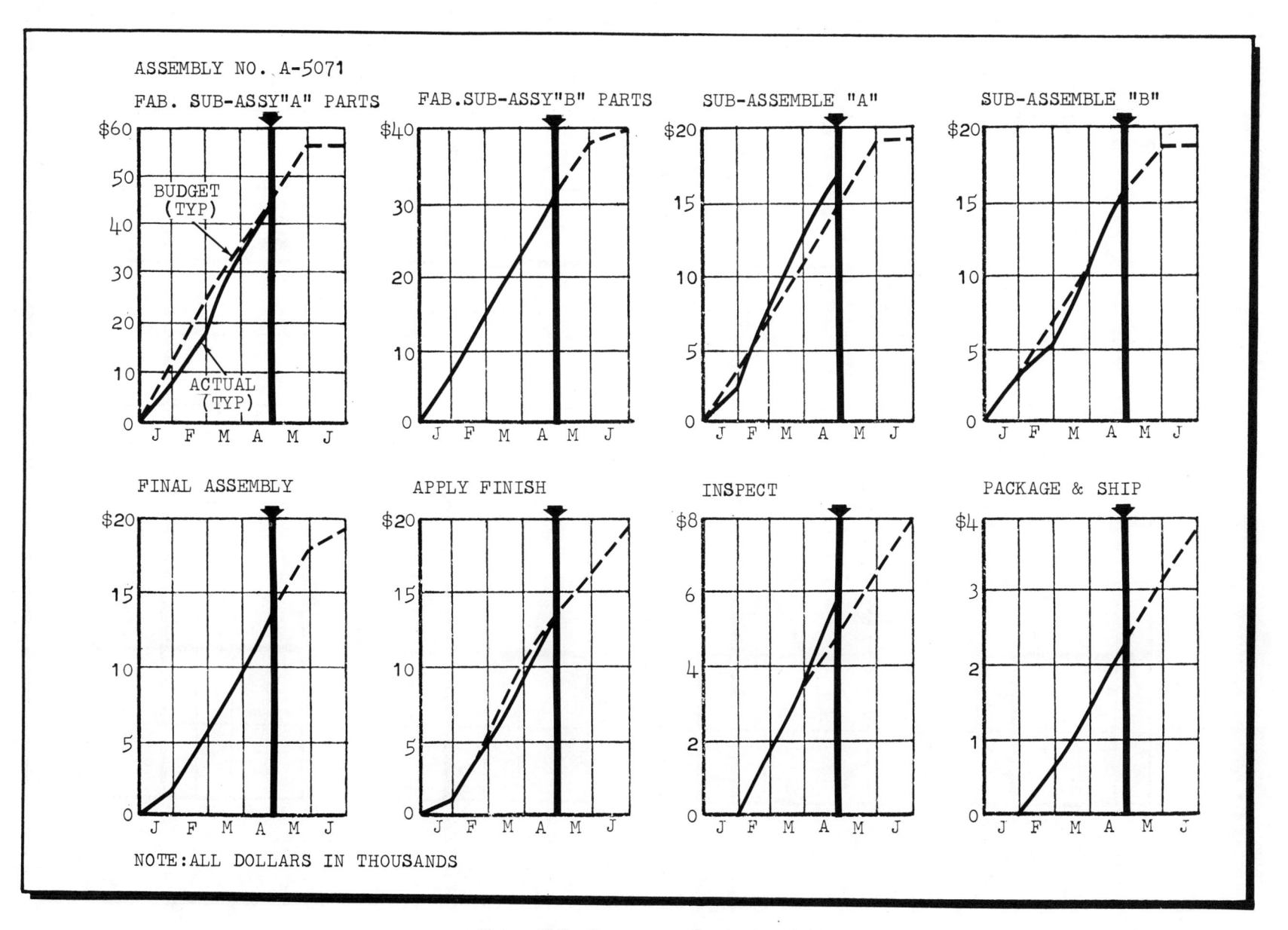

Figure 3.9 Budget—Detail—Version 9

NOTE: ALL DOLLARS IN THOUSANDS

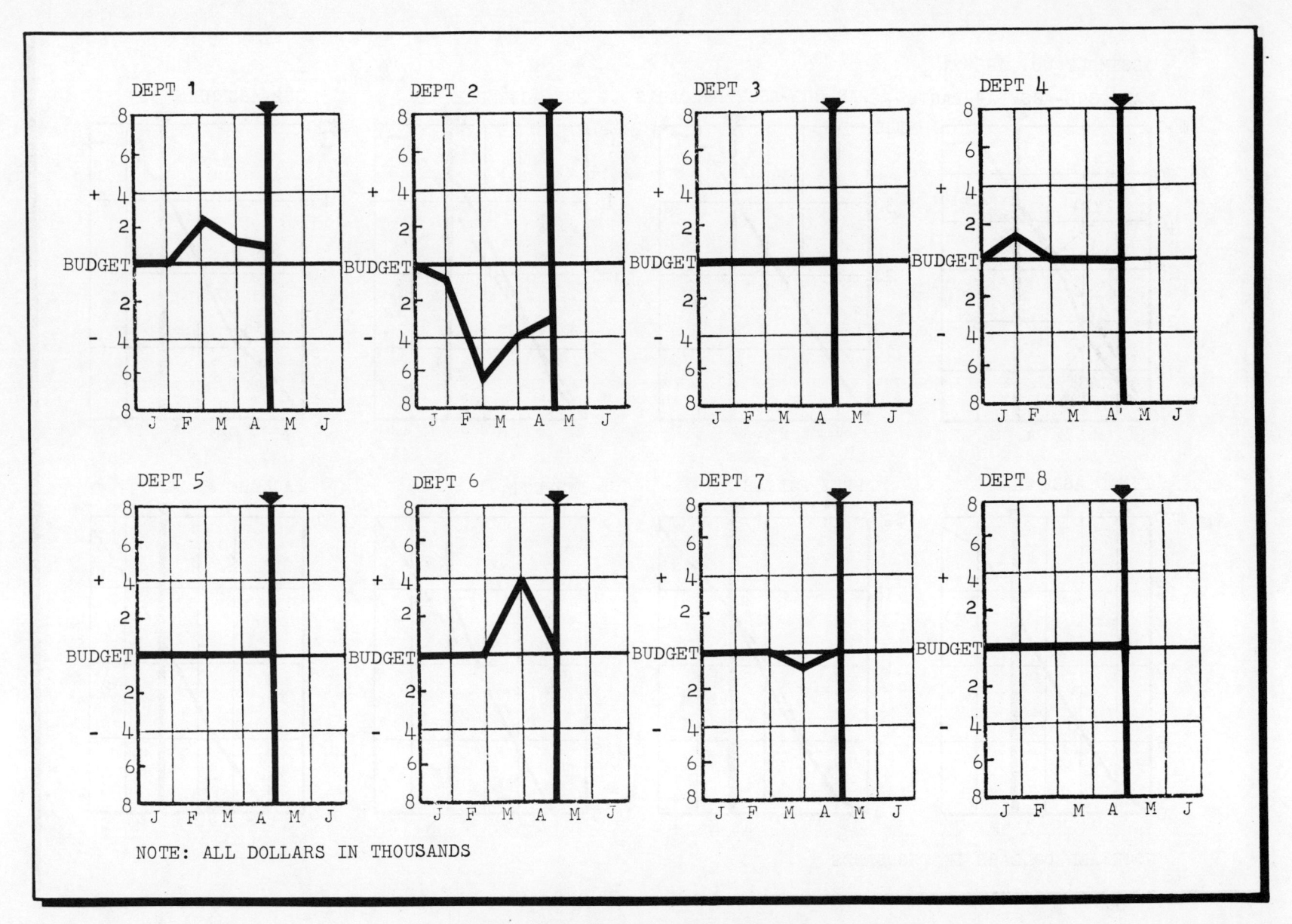

Figure 3.10 Budget—Detail—Version 10

CUM STATUS

		J	F	M	A	M	J	J	A	S	O	N	D
DEPT 1	BUDGET	.4	1.0	1.6	2.3	3.1	4.0	5.1	6.5	7.7	8.4	9.0	9.3
	ACTUAL	.1	.6	1.5	3.0								
	VARIANCE	-.3	-.4	-.1	+.7								
DEPT 2	BUDGET	.4	1.3	2.7	4.2	5.3	6.2	6.9	7.6	8.2	8.8	9.3	9.8
	ACTUAL	.6	1.5	2.9	4.2								
	VARIANCE	+.2	+.2	+.2	0								
DEPT 3	BUDGET	.2	.4	.6	1.2	1.9	2.7	3.3	3.9	4.4	4.9	5.2	5.5
	ACTUAL	.2	.4	.6	1.2								
	VARIANCE	0	0	0	0								
DEPT 4	BUDGET	.6	1.3	1.8	2.4	3.0	3.6	4.2	4.8	5.4	6.0	6.6	7.2
	ACTUAL	.5	1.1	1.5	2.0								
	VARIANCE	-.1	-.2	-.3	-.4								
DEPT 5	BUDGET	.3	.5	.9	1.2	1.8	2.9	3.8	4.9	5.9	6.9	7.8	8.8
	ACTUAL	.3	.6	.9	1.2								
	VARIANCE	0	+.1	0	0								

19XX

NOTE: ALL DOLLARS IN THOUSANDS

Figure 3.11   Budget—Detail—Version 11

	CUM STATUS	J	F	M	A	M	J	J	A	S	O	N	D	REMARKS
DEPT 1	BUDGET	.4	1.0	1.6	2.3	3.1	4.0	5.1	6.5	7.7	8.4	9.0	9.3	VENDOR X HAS INCREASED PRICE OF RAW MATERIALS. SECOND SOURCE BEING SOUGHT
	ACTUAL	.1	.6	1.5	3.0									
	VARIANCE	-.3	-.4	-.1	+.7									
DEPT 2	BUDGET	.4	1.3	2.7	4.2	5.3	6.2	6.9	7.6	8.2	8.8	9.3	9.8	
	ACTUAL	.6	1.5	2.9	4.2									
	VARIANCE	+.2	+.2	+.2	0									
DEPT 3	BUDGET	.2	.4	.6	1.2	1.9	2.7	3.3	3.9	4.4	4.9	5.2	5.5	
	ACTUAL	.2	.4	.6	1.2									
	VARIANCE	0	0	0	0									
DEPT 4	BUDGET	.6	1.3	1.8	2.4	3.0	3.6	4.2	4.8	5.4	6.0	6.6	7.2	
	ACTUAL	.5	1.1	1.5	2.0									
	VARIANCE	-.1	-.2	-.3	-.4									
DEPT 5	BUDGET	.3	.5	.9	1.2	1.8	2.9	3.8	4.9	5.9	6.9	7.8	8.8	
	ACTUAL	.3	.6	.9	1.2									
	VARIANCE	0	+.1	0	0									

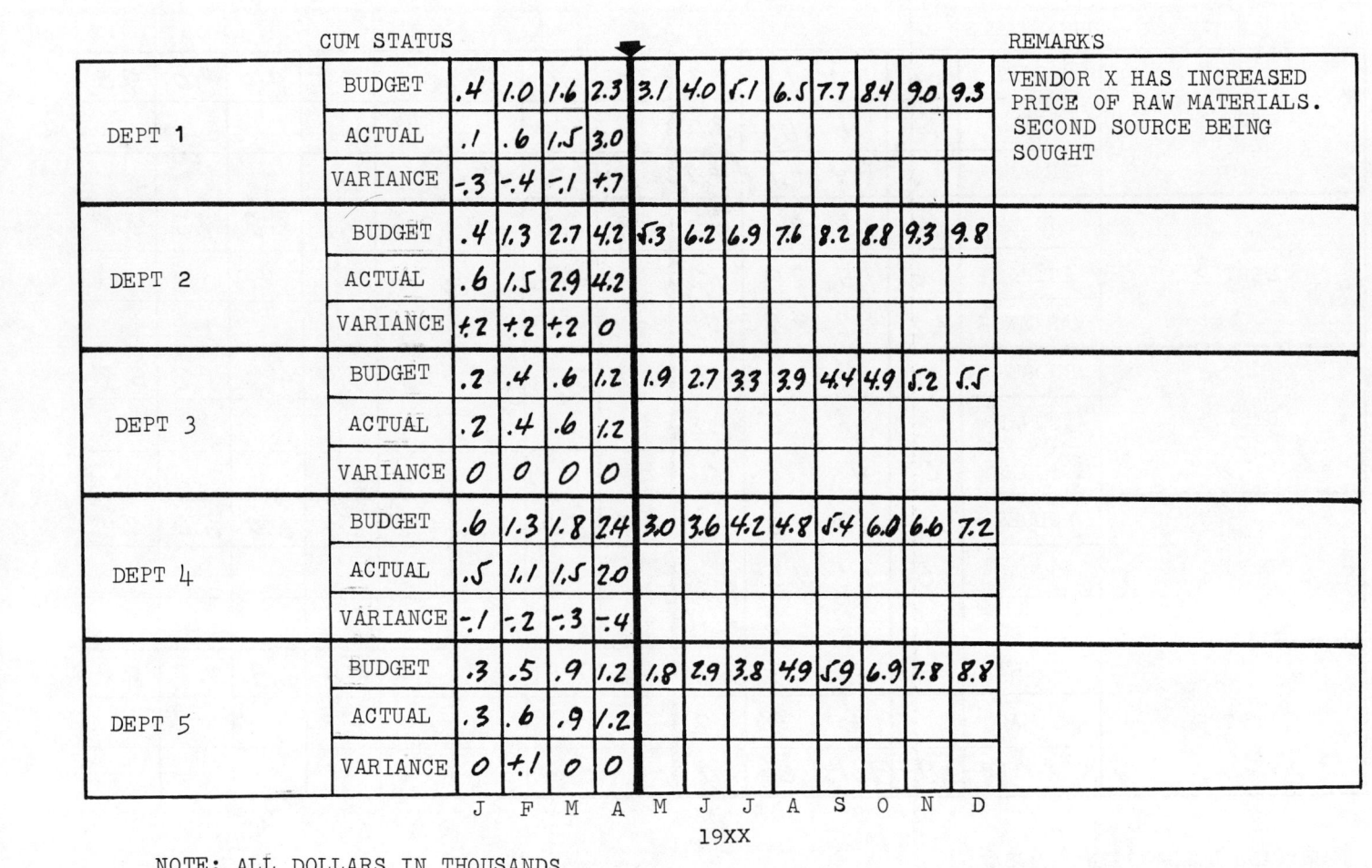

19XX

NOTE: ALL DOLLARS IN THOUSANDS

Figure 3.12   Budget—Detail—Version 12

						▼																
UNIT 1	BUDGET RATE	1.0	1.0	1.0	1.0	1.0	1.0	1.0	1.0	1.0	1.0	1.0	1.0	1.0	1.0	1.0	1.0	1.0	1.0	1.0	1.0	1.0
	ACTUAL RATE	1.0	1.0	1.0	1.0	1.0	1.0	1.0	1.0	1.0												
	BUDGET CUM	1.0	2.0	3.0	4.0	5.0	6.0	7.0	8.0	9.0	10.0	11.0	12.0	13.0	14.0	15.0	16.0	17.0	18.0	19.0	20.0	21.0	22.0
	ACTUAL CUM	1.0	2.0	3.0	4.0	5.0	6.0	7.0	8.0	9.0												
	CUM VARIANCE																					
	EST TO COMPL																					
UNIT 2	BUDGET RATE	1.1	1.2	1.3	1.4	1.4	1.4	1.4	1.4	1.4	1.4	1.5	1.5	1.5	1.5	1.5	1.5	1.6	1.6	1.6	1.6	1.6	1.6
	ACTUAL RATE	1.0	1.0	1.6	1.5	1.6	1.7	1.6	1.4	1.4												
	BUDGET CUM	1.1	2.3	3.6	5.0	6.4	7.8	9.2	10.6	12.0	13.4	14.9	16.4	17.9	19.4	20.9	22.4	24.0	25.6	27.2	28.8	30.4	32.0
	ACTUAL CUM	1.0	2.0	3.6	5.1	6.7	8.4	10.0	11.4	12.8												
	CUM VARIANCE	-.1	-.3		+.1	+.3	+.6	+.8	+.8	+.8												
	EST TO COMPL										14.2	15.6	17.0	18.4	19.8	21.2	22.6	24.0					
UNIT 3	BUDGET RATE	.3	.3	.3	.3	.4	.5	.5	.5	.5	.5	.5	.5	.5	.5	.5	.5	.5	.5	.5	.5	.5	.5
	ACTUAL RATE	.3	.3	.3	.3	.4	.5	.5	.5	.5												
	BUDGET CUM	.3	.6	.9	1.2	1.6	2.1	2.6	3.1	3.6	4.1	4.6	5.1	5.6	6.1	6.6	7.1	7.6	8.1	8.6	9.1	9.6	10.1
	ACTUAL CUM	.3	.6	.9	1.2	1.6	2.1	2.6	3.1	3.6												
	CUM VARIANCE																					
	EST TO COMPL																					
		3	10	17	24	3	10	17	24	31	7	14	21	28	5	12	19	26	2	9	16	23	30
		FEB				MAR					APR				MAY				JUN				

NOTE: ALL DOLLARS IN THOUSANDS

Figure 3.13 Budget—Detail—Version 13

CONTRACT ITEM	CUM STATUS END OF JULY		AUGUST ACTUAL (WEEKLY/CUM)					CUM TOTAL THROUGH AUGUST		EST VAR AT END OF AUGUST
	BUDGET	ACTUAL	2	9	16	23	30	BUDGET	EST	
INERTIAL NAVIGATION SYSTEM A	$286.7	$300.0	2.7/302.7	3.4/306.1	2.9/309.0			$298.6	$314.0	+$15.4
INERTIAL NAVIGATION SYSTEM B	54.0	54.0	1.3/55.3	1.7/57.0	1.5/58.5			61.5	61.5	0
PLATFORM	107.5	104.0	.9/104.9	1.2/106.1	1.2/107.3			109.7	109.5	−.2
CONTROL UNIT	23.6	25.0	1.0/26.0	1.0/27.0	1.0/28.0			28.0	30.0	+2.0
COMPUTER	210.3	210.3	3.4/213.7	4.0/217.7	2.9/220.6			225.0	226.5	+1.5
LINE TEST SET	48.0	48.0	0/48.0	0/48.0	0/48.0			48.0	48.0	0
PLATFORM TEST BENCH	27.3	27.3	0/27.3	0/27.3	0/27.3			27.3	27.3	0
ELECTRONIC TEST BENCH	72.0	71.0	2.0/73.0	2.1/75.1	2.2/77.3			80.0	80.0	0
LINE ANALYZER	56.0	56.0	0/56.0	0/56.0	0/56.0			56.0	56.0	0

NOTE: ALL DOLLARS IN THOUSANDS

Figure 3.14 Budget—Detail—Version 14

STATUS THROUGH __JUNE__

LOT NUMBER	CUSTOMER	BUDGET CUM	ACTUAL CUM	VARIANCE CUM
6579	SLDKFJGMKS	$187.3	$187.3	0
6580	SLDKWODKSM	44.6	44.5	-.1
6581	SLDKFJGMCJ	384.0	388.0	+4.0
6582	WOEKFJVMS	27.6	27.6	0
6583	SLDKFJGS	CANCELLED		
6584	SLDKFJSDF	281.0	281.0	0
6585	WLDKFJEODK	197.3	226.0	+28.7
6586	OWIERUTJS	63.0	60.0	-3.0
6587	WOEKFKJSHD	38.0	38.0	0
	TOTALS:	$1,222.8	$1,252.4	$+29.6

NOTE: ALL DOLLARS IN THOUSANDS

Figure 3.15 Budget—Detail—Version 15

STATUS THROUGH __JUNE__

FUNCTION	RESPONSIBLE MANAGER	BUDGET THROUGH __JUNE__	EXPENDED THROUGH __JUNE__	CURRENT VARIANCE	ESTIMATED OVERRUN(+) UNDERRUN(−) AT COMPLETION
ENGINEERING	SMITH	$10,700	$12,000	$ +1,300	$ +3,000
MANUFACTURING	JONES	13,650	13,650	0	0
QUALITY ASSURANCE	BROWN	3,145	2,980	−165	−500
TEST	JOHNSON	4,300	4,150	−150	0
PROGRAM OFFICE	GREEN	3,800	3,800	0	0
	TOTALS	$35,595	$36,580	$ +985	$ +2500

Figure 3.16   Budget—Detail—Version 16

STATUS THROUGH **FEB**

ITEM	COSTS THIS MONTH			CUM COSTS TO DATE			EST COSTS AT COMPLETION		
	BUDGET	ACTUAL	VAR	BUDGET	ACTUAL	VAR	BUDGET	ACTUAL	VAR
A ~~PHILSKSLA~~	$26.5	$26.4	$ -.1	$286.3	$285.0	$ -1.3	$350.0	$347.0	$ -3.0
B ~~CHPADKSLA~~	15.6	26.5	+10.9	140.5	175.0	+34.5	245.7	325.7	+80.0 ✓
C ~~MLSKLLVH~~	3.4	3.5	+.1	27.6	27.6	0	40.3	40.3	0
D ~~ALBHDJYHG~~	8.5	8.0	-.5	98.2	97.0	-1.2	150.0	148.0	-2.0
E ~~ABSKDYHG~~	2.0	2.0	0	15.7	15.7	0	32.0	32.0	0
F ~~QVRKTPRY~~	1.2	1.2	0	14.0	14.0	0	28.0	28.0	0
TOTALS	$57.2	$67.6	$10.4	$582.3	$614.3	$32.0	$846.0	$921.0	$+75.0
VAR. AS % OF BUDGET			18.1%			5.5%			8.9%

NOTE: ALL DOLLARS IN THOUSANDS

Figure 3.17   Budget—Detail—Version 17

4.0 BUDGETS—EXPENDITURES AND COMMITMENTS

Certain types of activities, such as purchasing parts or materials, involve tracking not only the actual expenditure of funds, but the making of commitments to expend funds, as well. This section displays methods of showing these two factors. Also see Budget Sections 3.0, and 5.0 through 7.0.

4.1 Budget—Expenditures and Commitments—Version 1: A simple combination line curve chart and column chart is used to display expenditure and commitment budget status in Figure 4.1. Budgeted and actual expenditures are shown in line curve form with the current cumulative variance and the current estimated cost at completion shown in note form at the bottom of the chart. The column chart, representing the total budget, is shaded to that point indicating current expenditures plus current outstanding commitments.

4.2 Budget—Expenditures and Commitments—Version 2: A graph and statistical table are combined in Version 2 of an expenditures and commitments budget tracking chart, Figure 4.2. In this example it can be seen that, as of the reporting date (end of February), actual commitments exceed planned commitments by $200. This is an indication that the expenditures, too, will exceed the budget in subsequent reporting periods. The note section shows that the current estimated cost at completion does, in fact, exceed the budget by $200.

4.3 Budget—Expenditures and Commitments—Version 3: Version 3 of an expenditures and commitments budget chart, Figure 4.3, is identical to Version 2 except that in the statistical table, lines have been added to show variances.

4.4 Budget—Expenditures and Commitments—Version 4: Ten lines of statistical data are combined with graphics in Version 4 of an expenditures and commitments budget chart, Figure 4.4. Both commitments and expenditures are shown in terms of planned and budgeted activity, actual performance, and variance, all in terms of rate per month and cumulative statistics. Only the cumulative statistics are shown in graphic form in this example.

4.5 Budget—Expenditures and Commitments—Version 5: If an activity was to be cancelled before it was completed, the cancellation liability of the activity might not be expenditures alone, but expenditures plus either all, or at least a portion, of the outstanding commitments. In Version 5 of an expenditures and commitments budget chart, Figure 4.5, budgeted, actual, and variance figures for both expenditures and expenditures plus outstanding commitments are shown.

4.6 Budget—Expenditures and Commitments—Version 6: A combination of commitment and expenditure factors is shown in Version 6, Figure 4.6. The first element of data concerns planned and actual commitments, which is followed by budgeted and actual expenditures. The third set of statistics involves commitment liability. In this example, this represents that portion of outstanding commitments that would have to be paid in the event the activity or project was cancelled. The final set of statistics, called "exposure" in this example, represents the expenditures plus commitment liability, thus showing the total liability for each time segment of the project. Variances are shown in note form, as is the current estimated cost at completion.

4.7 Budget—Expenditures and Commitments—Version 7: Figure 4.7 shows a tabular display of statistics relative to expenditures and commitments. Both rate per month and cumulative statistics are given. The last set of statistics (expenditure rate and expenditure cum. plus outstanding commitments liability) shows total liability in the event the activity is stopped or cancelled. In this particular example, also, a check mark is used to indicate the probable source of the current over-budget condition.

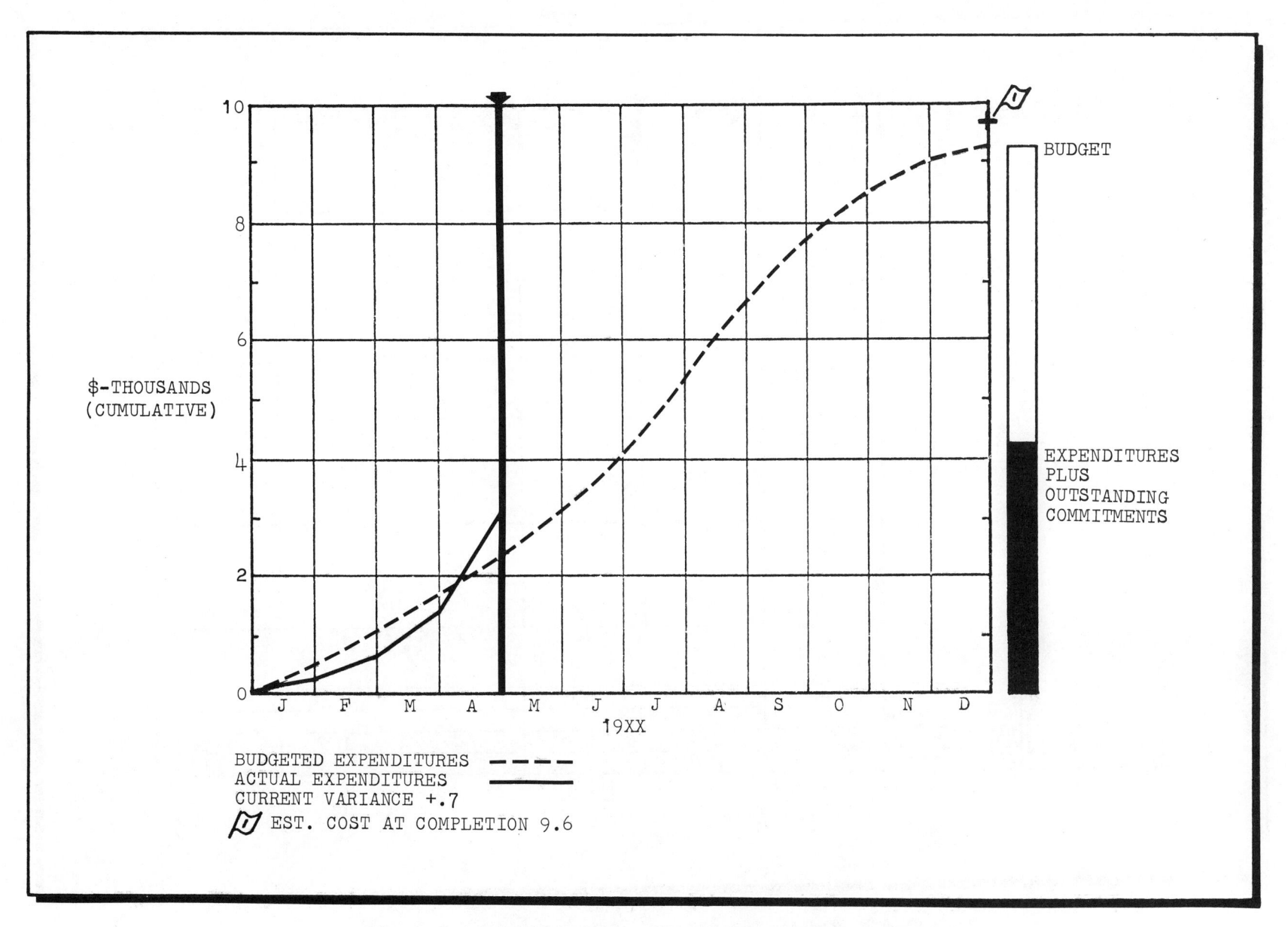

Figure 4.1   Budget—Expenditures and Commitments—Version 1

CUMULATIVE							
COMMITMENTS	PLAN ●●●●●●	1.0	2.3	4.1	5.9	6.5	
	ACTUAL ●●●●●●	1.0	2.5				
EXPENDITURES	BUDGET – – –		1.0	2.3	4.1	5.9	6.5
	ACTUAL ———		1.0				

EST. COST AT COMPLETION: 6.7

VARIANCE +.2

$-THOUSANDS CUMULATIVE

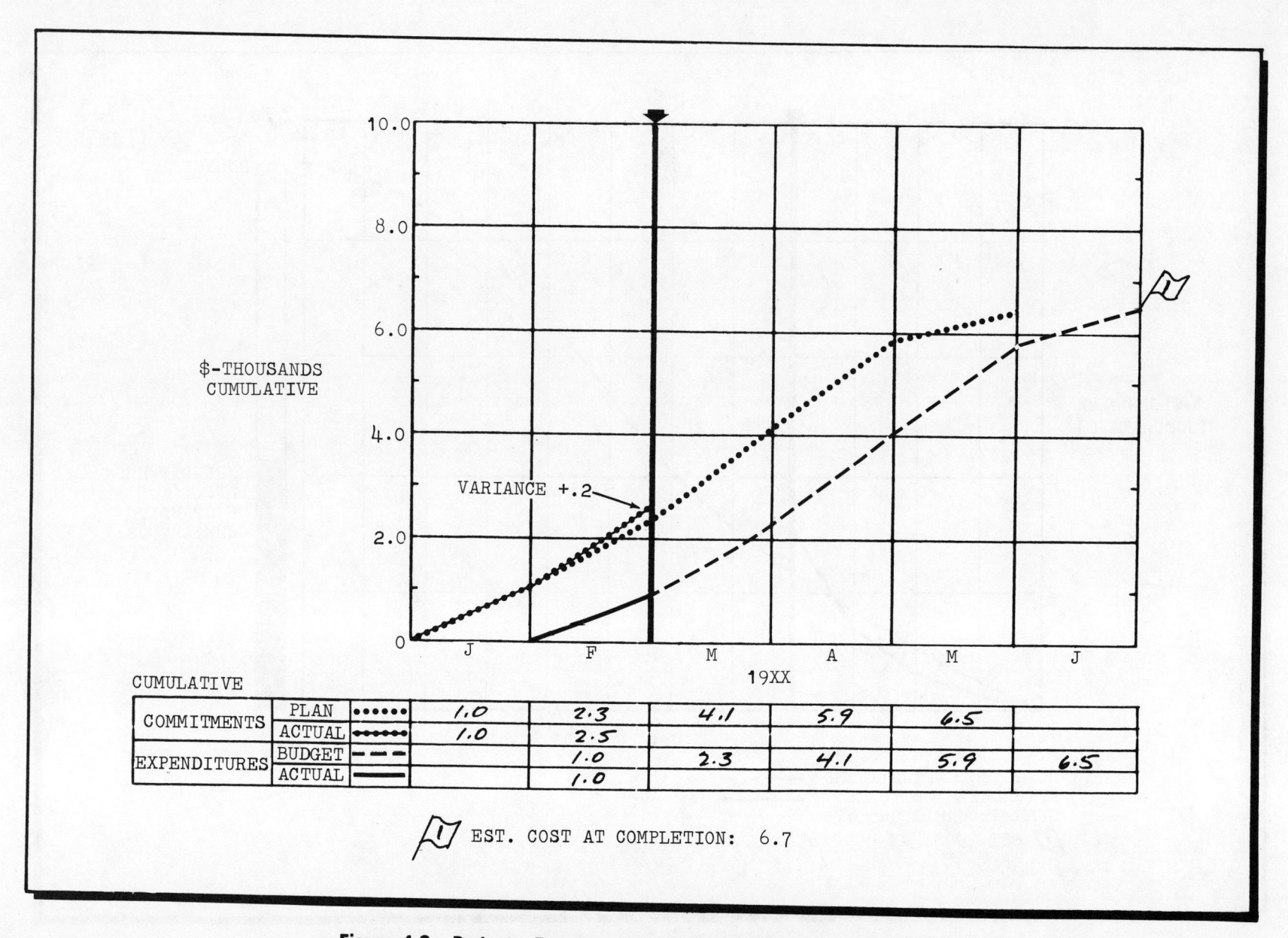

Figure 4.2   Budget—Expenditures and Commitments—Version 2

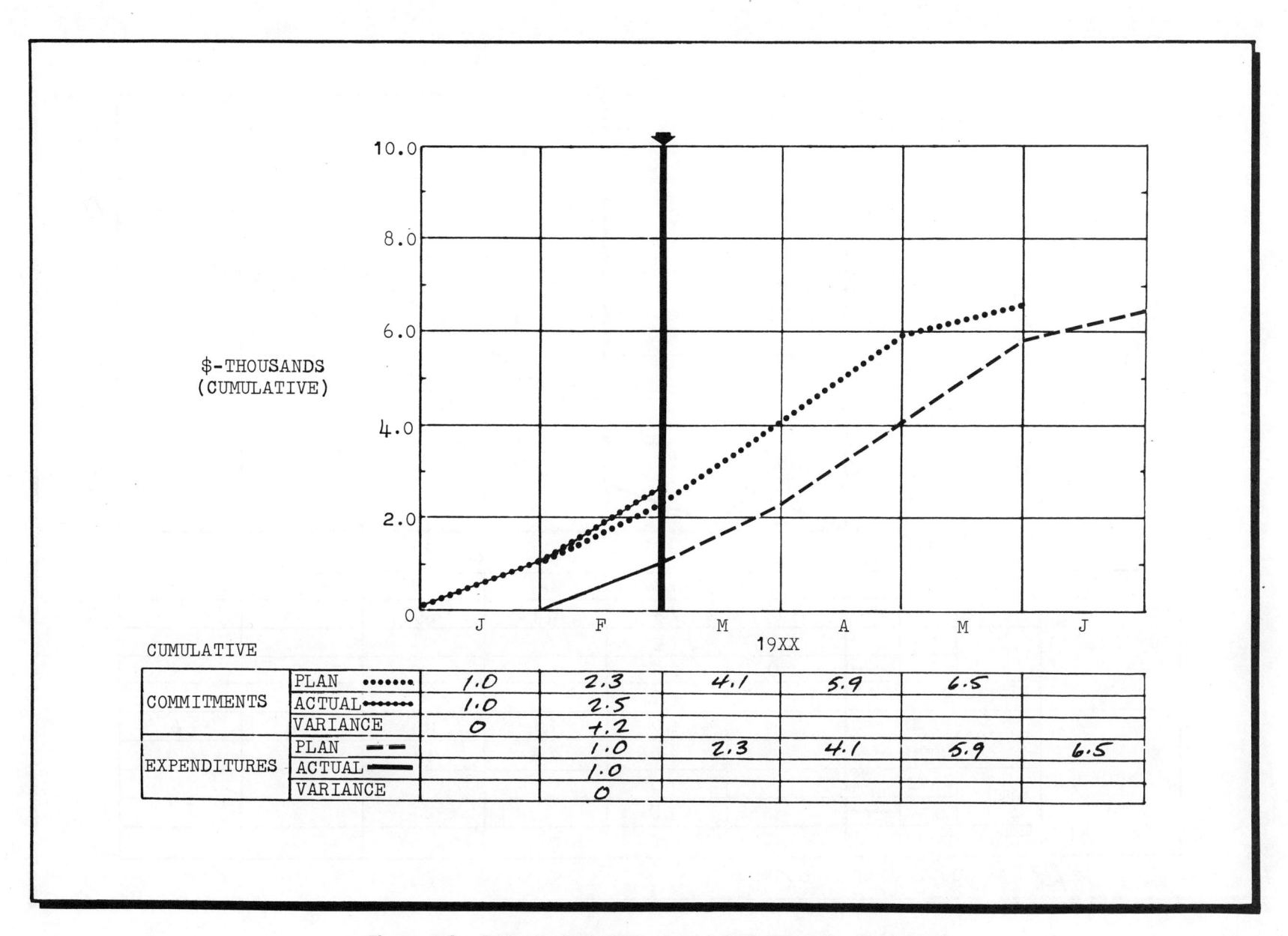

	CUMULATIVE						
COMMITMENTS	PLAN	1.0	2.3	4.1	5.9	6.5	
	ACTUAL •••••••	1.0	2.5				
	VARIANCE	0	+.2				
EXPENDITURES	PLAN – –		1.0	2.3	4.1	5.9	6.5
	ACTUAL ▬▬▬		1.0				
	VARIANCE		0				

Figure 4.3 Budget—Expenditures and Commitments—Version 3

COMMITMENTS	PLAN			1.0	1.3	1.8	1.8	.6
		• • • • •		1.0	2.3	4.1	5.9	6.5
	ACTUAL			1.0	1.5			
		••••••		1.0	2.5			
	VARIANCE				+.2			
EXPENDITURES	BUDGET	RATE			1.0	1.3	1.8	1.8	.6
		CUM	— —		1.0	2.3	4.1	5.9	6.5
	ACTUAL	RATE			1.0				
		CUM	——		1.0				
	VARIANCE				0				

⚑ EST COST AT COMPLETION: 6.7

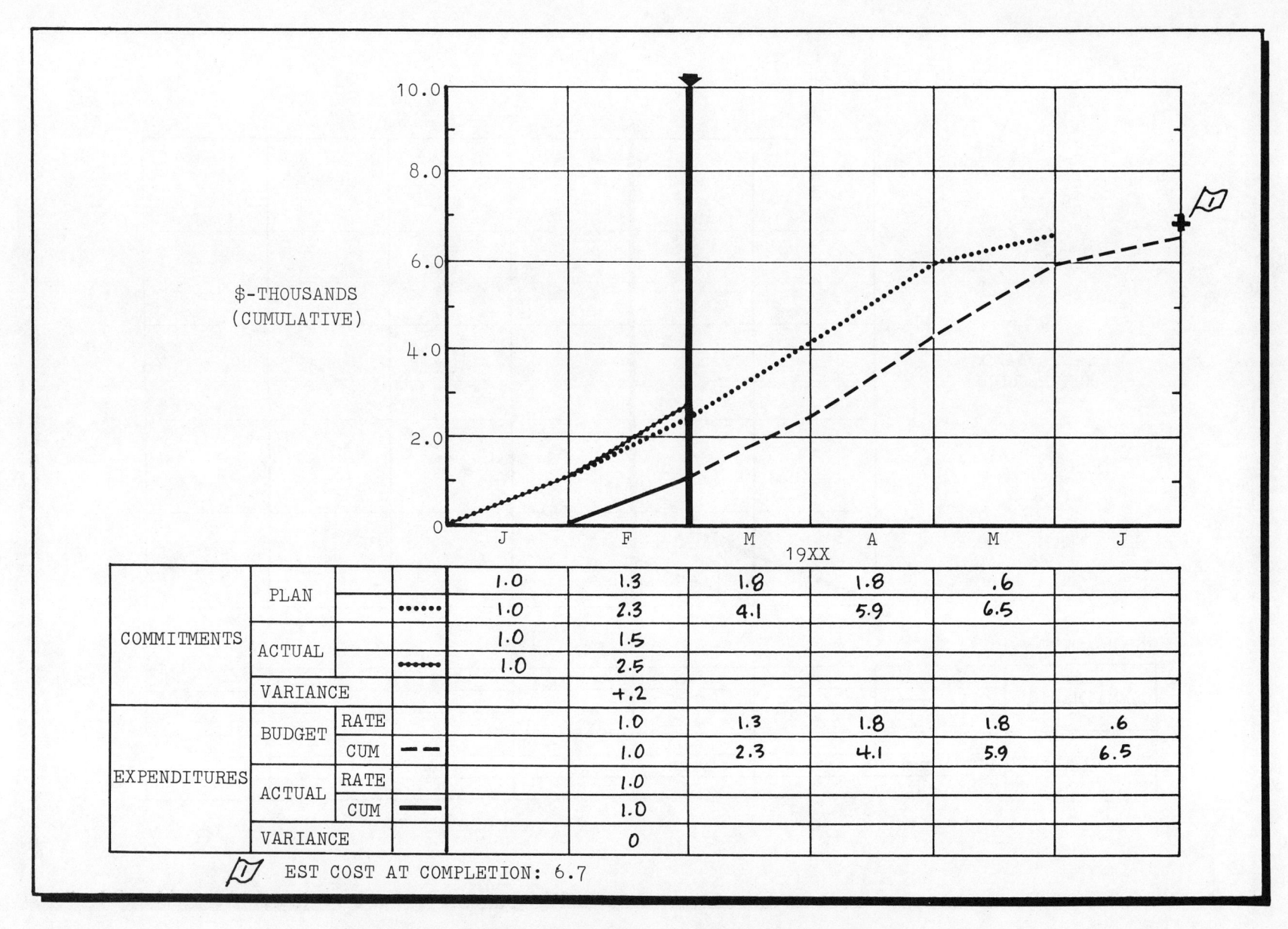

Figure 4.4 Budget—Expenditures and Commitments—Version 4

EXPENDITURES	BUDGET - - -			1.0	2.3	4.1	5.9	6.5
	ACTUAL ▬▬▬			1.0				
	VARIANCE			0				
EXPENDITURES PLUS OUTSTANDING COMMITMENTS	BUDGET ······	1.0	2.3	4.1	5.9	6.5	6.5
	ACTUAL ●●●●●●	1.0	2.5				
	VARIANCE		+.2				

⚑ EST. COST AT COMPLETION: 6.7

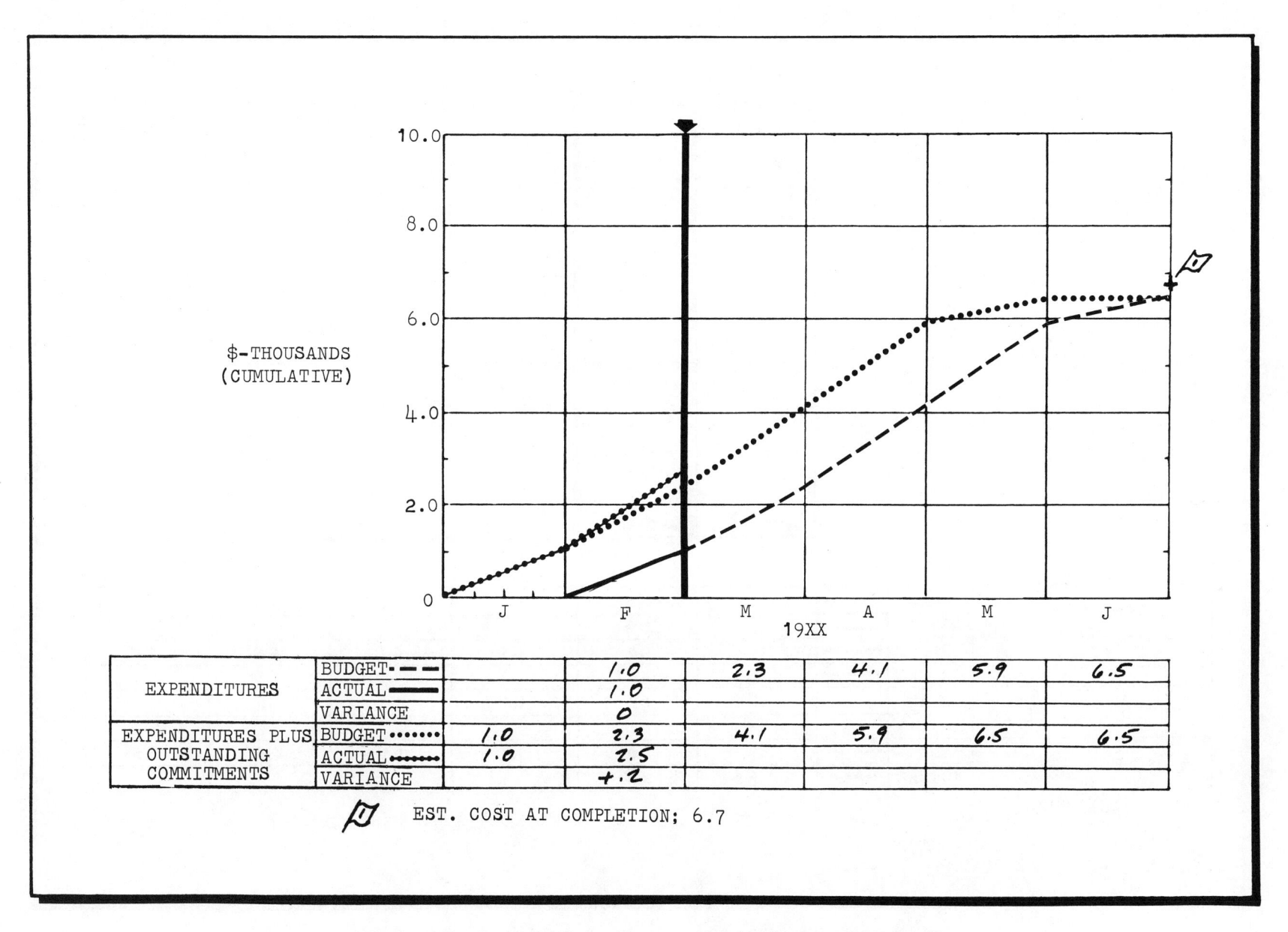

Figure 4.5 Budget—Expenditures and Commitments—Version 5

COMMITMENTS	PLAN ········	1.0	2.3	4.1	5.9	6.5	
	ACTUAL ●●●●●●●	1.0	2.5				
EXPENDITURES	BUDGET ─ ─ ─		1.0	2.3	4.1	5.9	6.5
	ACTUAL ▬▬▬		1.0				
COMMITMENT LIABILITY	PLAN	.8	1.0	1.4	1.4	.5	
	ACTUAL	.8	1.2				
EXPOSURE	PLAN ··········	.8	2.0	3.7	5.5	6.4	6.5
	ACTUAL ··········	.8	2.2				

VARIANCES:
    COMMITMENTS +.2
    EXPENDITURES 0
    EXPOSURE +.2

⚑ EST. COST AT COMPLETION: 6.7

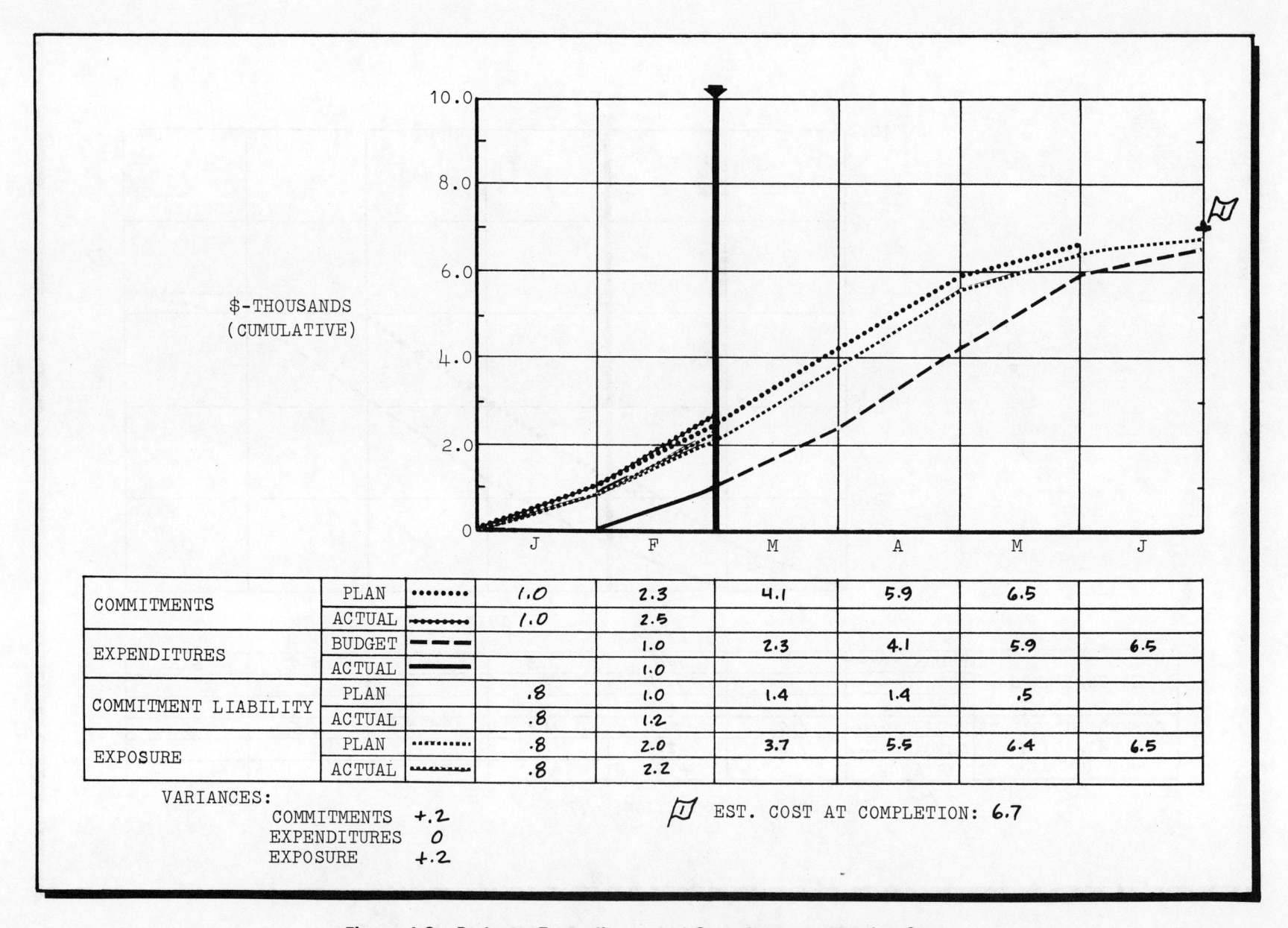

Figure 4.6 Budget—Expenditures and Commitments—Version 6

			J	F	M	A	M	J
EXPENDITURES	BUDGET	RATE		1.0	1.3	1.8	1.8	.6
		CUM		1.0	2.3	4.1	5.9	6.5
	ACTUAL	RATE		1.0				
		CUM		1.0				
	VARIANCE	CUM		0				
COMMITMENTS	PLAN	RATE	1.0	1.3	1.8	1.8	.6	
		CUM	1.0	2.3	4.1	5.9	6.5	
	ACTUAL	RATE	1.0	1.5				
		CUM	1.0	2.5				
	VARIANCE	CUM		+.2 ✓				
OUTSTANDING COMMITMENTS LIABILITY	PLAN		.8	1.0	1.4	1.4	.5	
	ACTUAL		.8	1.2				
EXPENDITURE RATE & EXPENDITURE CUM. PLUS OUTSTANDING COMMITMENTS LIABILITY	BUDGET	RATE	.8	2.0	2.7	3.2	2.3	.6
		CUM	.8	2.0	3.7	5.2	6.4	6.5
	ACTUAL	RATE	.8	2.2				
		CUM	.8	2.2				
	VARIANCE	CUM	0	+.2				

NOTE: ALL DOLLARS IN THOUSANDS

19XX

Figure 4.7 Budget—Expenditures and Commitments—Version 7

5.0 BUDGETS—EXPENDITURES AND FUNDING

This section contains budget charts that display budgeted and actual expenditures in relationship to the anticipated and actual receipt of funds. Also see Budget Sections 3.0, 4.0, 6.0, and 7.0.

5.1 Budget—Expenditures and Funding—Version 1: The budget tracking chart shown in Figure 5.1 displays data relative to the budget, actual expenditures, and estimated costs to complete. In addition, a column on the right-hand side of the line chart displays total funding segmented as to planned profit, the budget, and funds already received at the time of the report (end of April, in this example). It can be seen that the current estimate to complete, in this example, cuts into the activity's planned profit.

5.2 Budget—Expenditures and Funding—Version 2: An alternate method of showing funding is displayed as Version 2 of an expenditures and funding chart, Figure 5.2. In this example funds, which are received periodically throughout the life of this particular activity, are shown in step line form. Budgeted and actual expenditures are shown in line curve form. In this example it can be seen that, as of the reporting date of this chart (end of April), expenditures have exceeded on-hand funds by $5000.

5.3 Budget—Expenditures and Funding—Version 3: A chart that combines graphics and statistics is shown in Figure 5.3. The graphic portion of the chart is identical to Version 2, except that a "flag" has been added noting the current anticipated cost at completion. The statistical portion of the chart carries the funding plan and actual funds received, and the budgeted and actual expenditures. In addition, expenditures made in excess of on-hand funds are shown in the fifth line of the table as "vulnerability."

5.4 Budget—Expenditures and Funding—Version 4: Version 4 of an expenditures and funding budget chart, Figure 5.4, is identical to Version 3 except that an additional line of statistics has been added, "variance from budget."

5.5 Budget—Expenditures and Funding—Version 5: Both rate per month and cumulative statistics are shown in the tabular portion of the expenditures and funding chart, Version 5, Figure 5.5. The graphic portion of the chart is used to display the cumulative data.

5.6 Budget—Expenditures and Funding—Version 6: A combination step line chart and paired column chart, as applied to an expenditures and funding budget tracking chart, is shown in Figure 5.6. Funding, both actual and anticipated, is shown in step line form. Columns are used to display budgeted and actual expenditures.

5.7 Budget—Expenditures and Funding—Version 7: A statistical table version of an expenditures and funding tracking chart is shown in Figure 5.7. In this example, the bottom line of the table shows the "vulnerability" of the activity, expenditures

$5000 in excess of funds received. A variation of this table would add a cumulative variance line which would show the project activity to be $15,000 overrun as of the reporting date in this example.

5.8 Budget—Expenditures and Funding—Version 8: A one-time report style is shown in Figure 5.8. Separate subjects (engineering, manufacturing, etc.) are shown across the top of the table, and the measurement factors are shown in the left-hand column. The anticipated variance for the total activity is at the bottom of the table, in this case showing anticipated final costs exceeding funds by a total of $900.

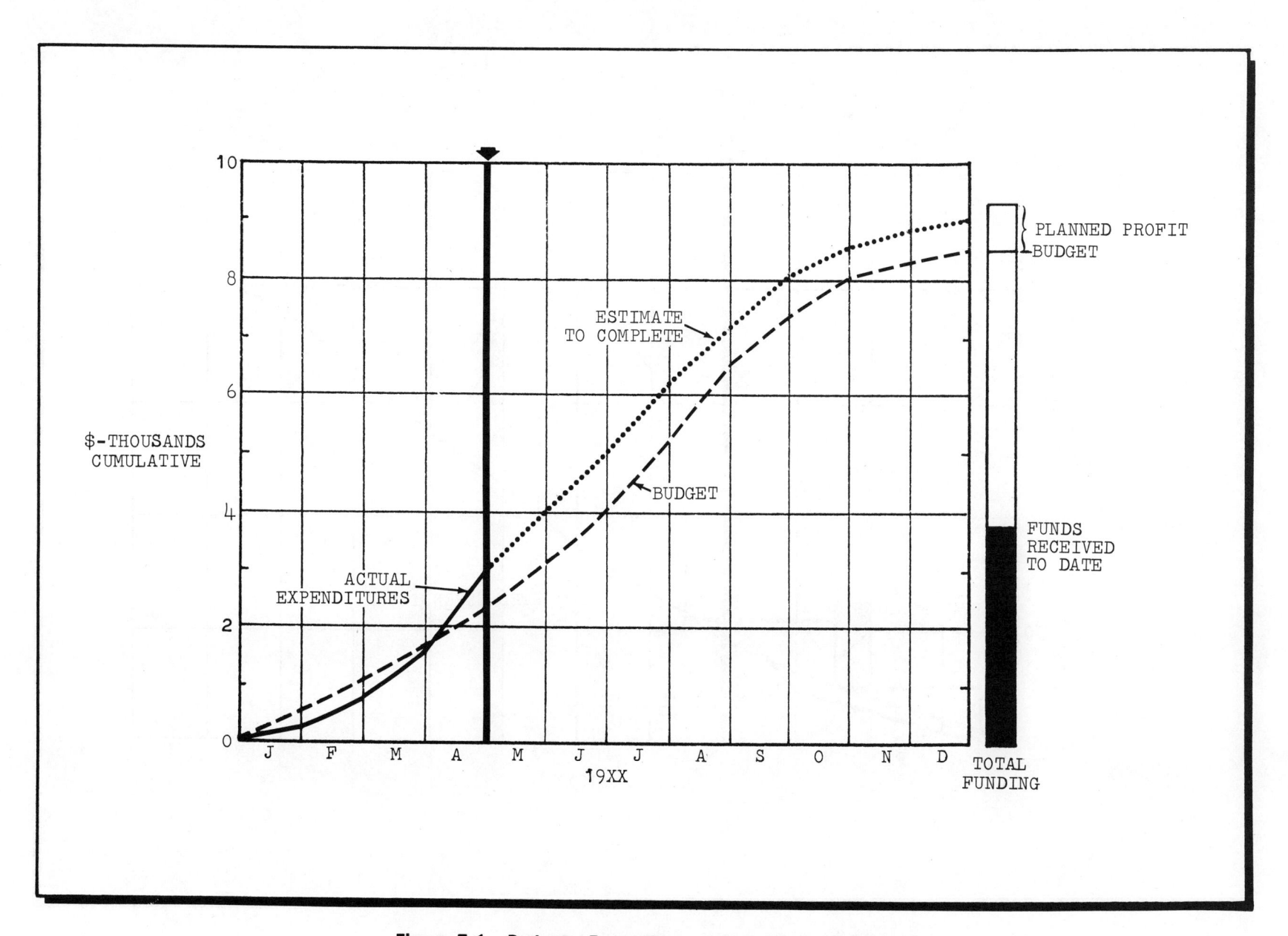

Figure 5.1   Budget—Expenditures and Funding—Version 1

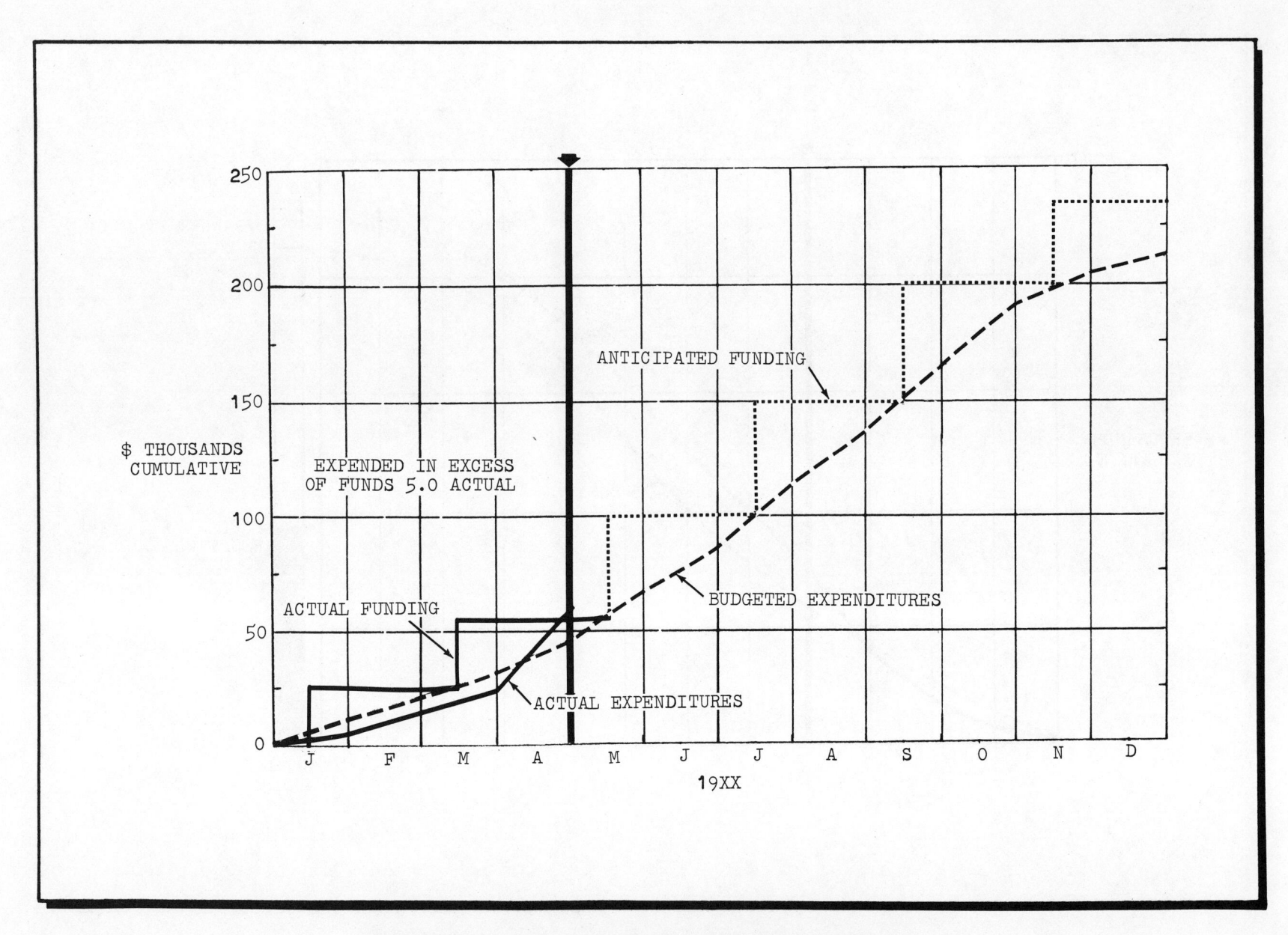

Figure 5.2   Budget—Expenditures and Funding—Version 2

CUMULATIVE													
FUNDING	PLAN	25	25	55	55	100	100	150	150	200	200	235	235
	ACTUAL ⎯⎯	25	25	55	55								
EXPENDITURES	BUDGET ⎯ ⎯ ⎯	10	20	30	45	63	85	110	135	162	190	204	210
	ACTUAL ⎯⎯⎯	5	13	32	6								
VULNERABILITY*					5								

* EXPENDITURES IN EXCESS OF FUNDS

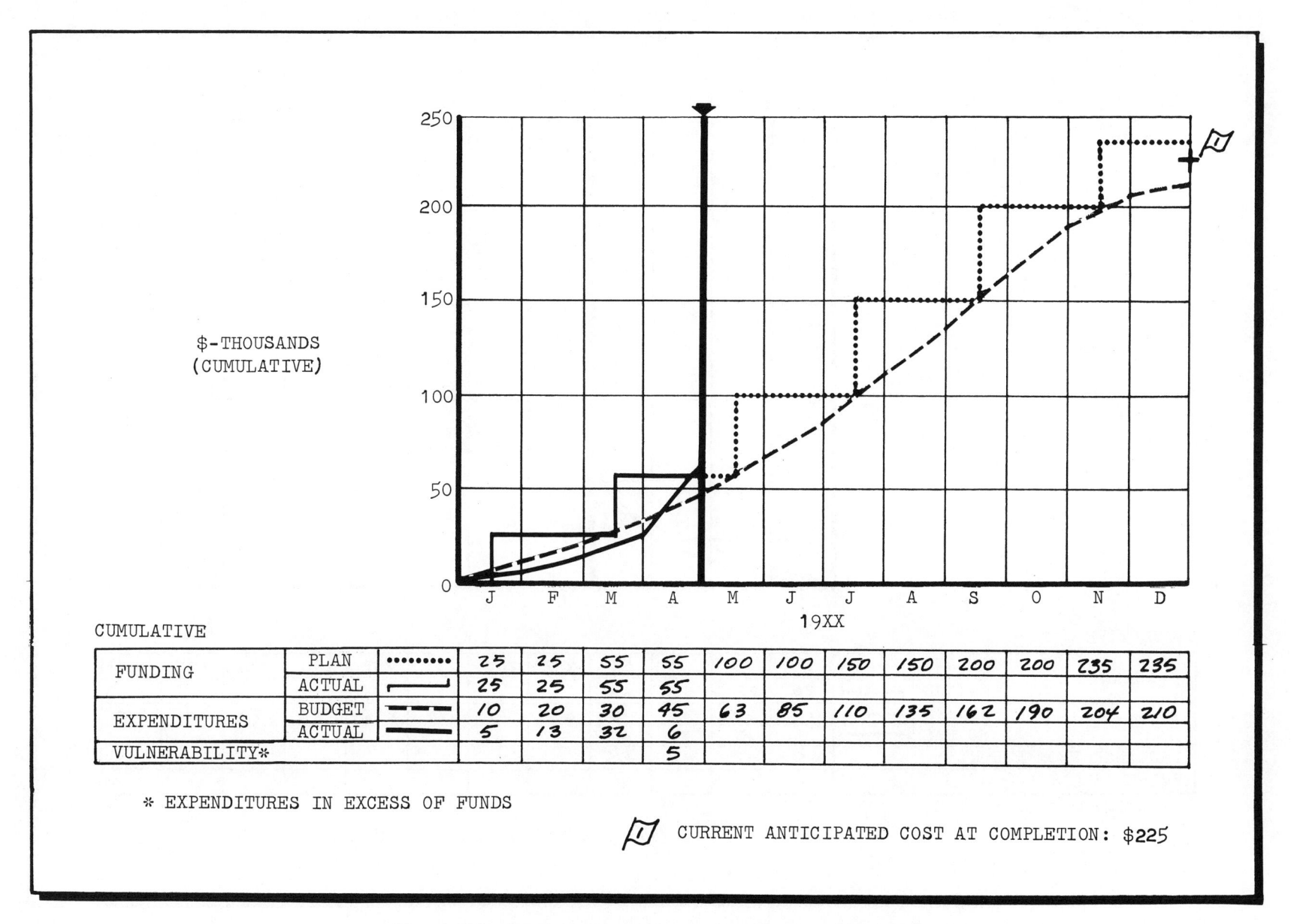

🚩 CURRENT ANTICIPATED COST AT COMPLETION: $225

Figure 5.3   Budget—Expenditures and Funding—Version 3

$-THOUSANDS
(CUMULATIVE)

CUMULATIVE														
FUNDING	PLAN	··········	25	25	55	55	100	100	150	150	200	200	235	235
	ACTUAL		25	25	55	55								
EXPENDITURES	BUDGET	– – –	10	20	30	45	63	85	110	135	162	190	204	210
	ACTUAL	——	5	13	22	60								
VARIANCE FROM BUDGET			-5	-7	-8	+15								
VULNERABILITY*						5								

* EXPENDITURES IN EXCESS OF FUNDS

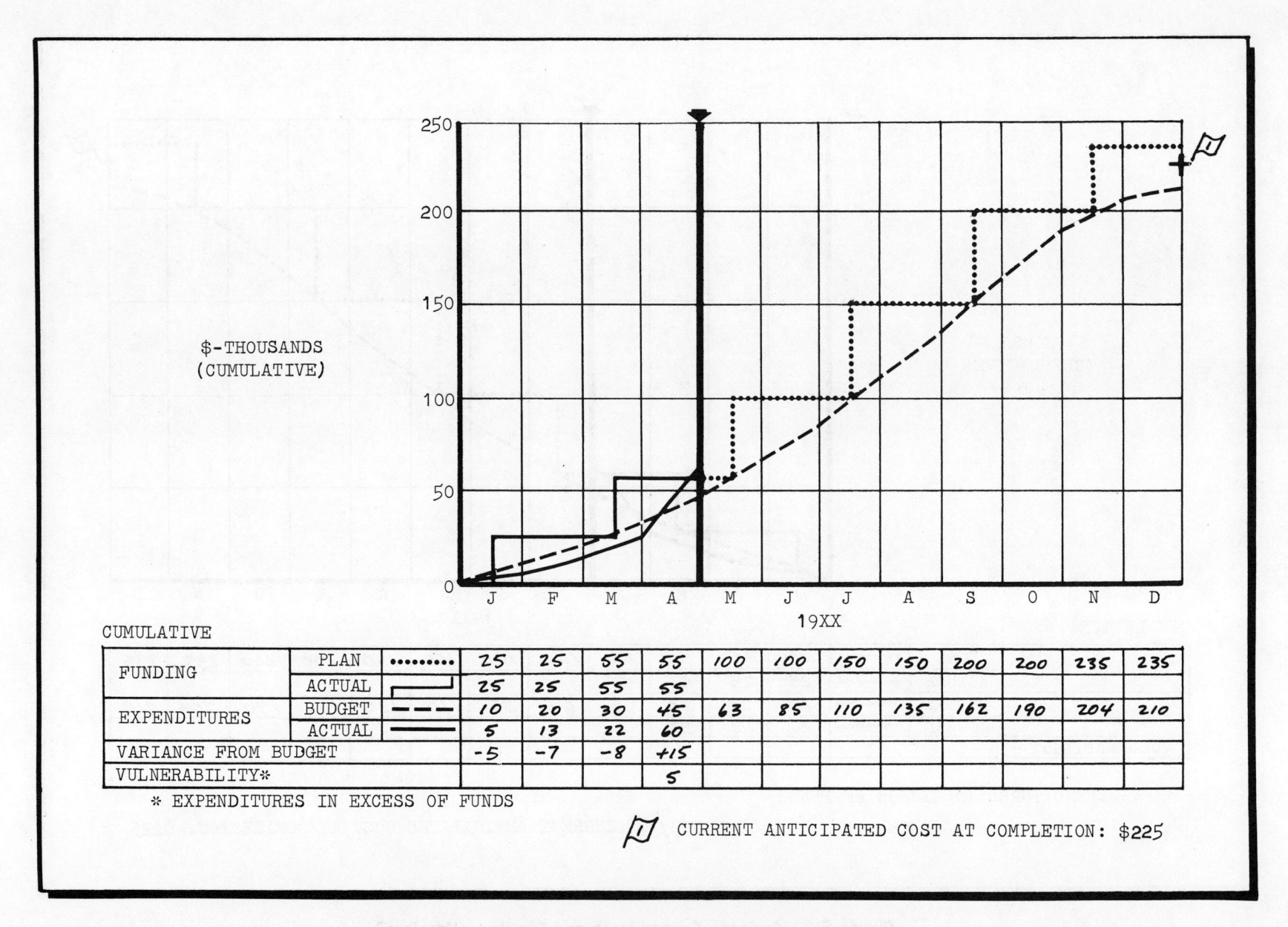

🚩 CURRENT ANTICIPATED COST AT COMPLETION: $225

Figure 5.4 Budget—Expenditures and Funding—Version 4

			J	F	M	A	M	J	J	A	S	O	N	D
FUNDING	PLAN	RATE	25	0	30	0	45	0	50	0	50	0	35	0
		CUM ⋯⋯	25	25	55	55	100	100	150	150	200	200	235	235
	ACTUAL	RATE	25	0	30	0								
		CUM ⌐	25	25	55	55								
EXPENDITURES	BUDGET	RATE	10	10	10	15	18	22	25	25	27	28	14	6
		CUM - - -	10	20	30	45	63	85	110	135	162	190	204	210
	ACTUAL	RATE	5	8	9	38								
		CUM ――	5	13	22	60								
VULNERABILITY*		CUM				5								

* EXPENDITURES IN EXCESS OF FUNDS

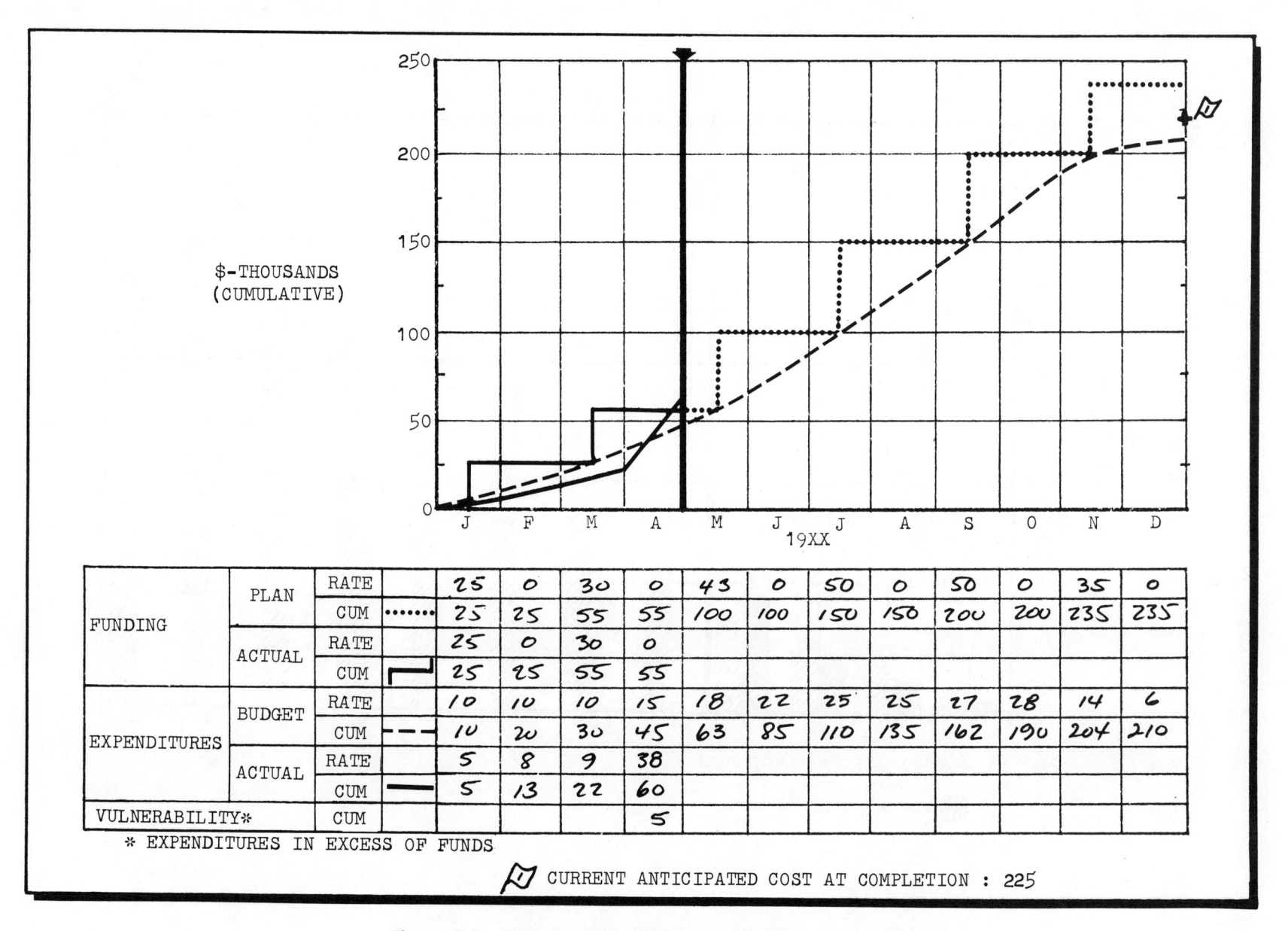

⚑ CURRENT ANTICIPATED COST AT COMPLETION : 225

Figure 5.5   Budget—Expenditures and Funding—Version 5

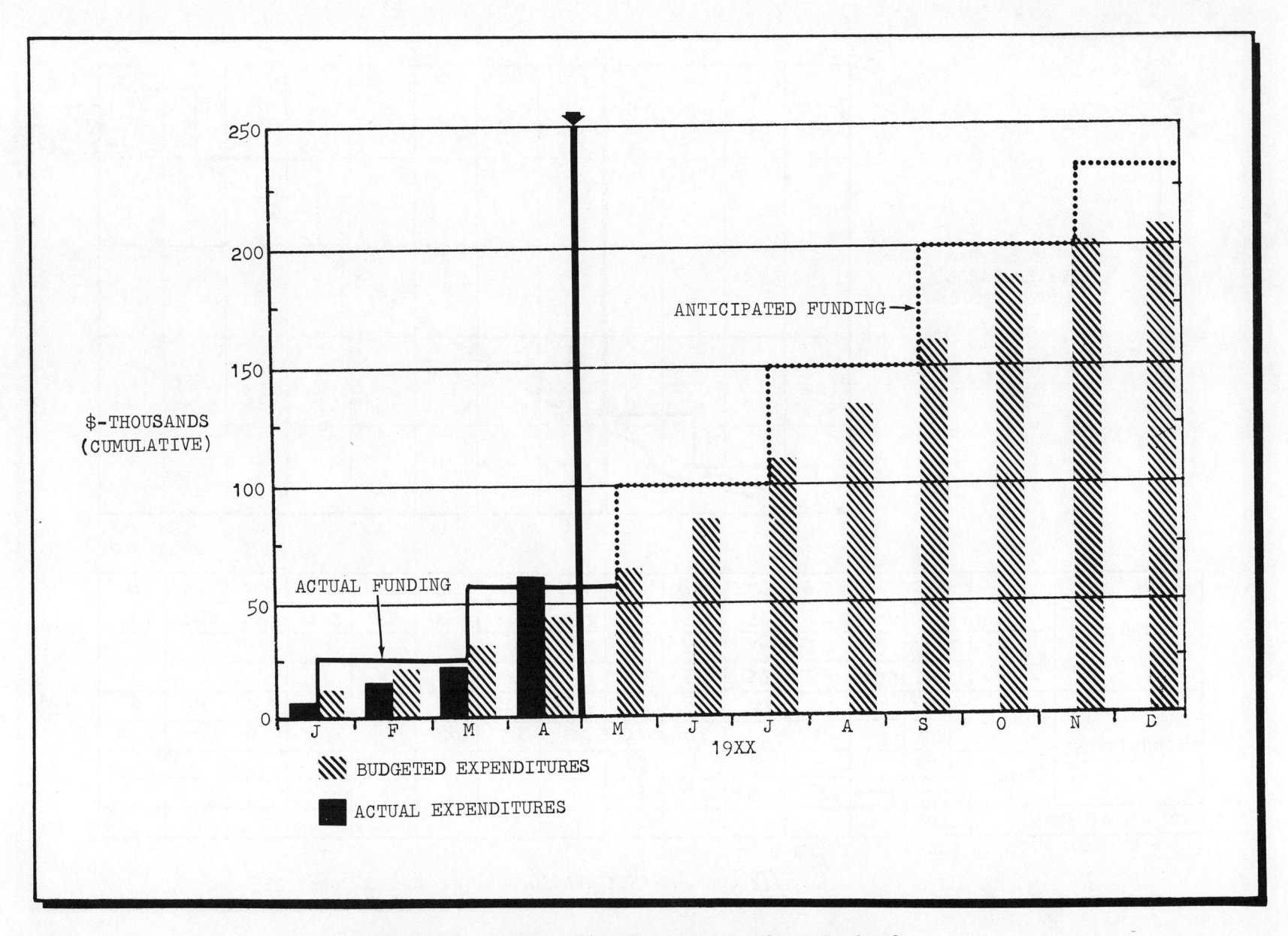

Figure 5.6   Budget—Expenditures and Funding—Version 6

			J	F	M	A	M	J	J	A	S	O	N	D
FUNDING	PLAN	RATE	25	0	30	0	45	0	50	0	50	0	35	0
		CUM	25	25	55	55	100	100	150	150	200	200	235	235
	ACTUAL	RATE	25	0	30	0								
		CUM	25	25	55	55								
EXPENDITURES	BUDGET	RATE	10	10	10	15	18	22	25	25	27	28	14	6
		CUM	10	20	30	45	63	85	110	135	162	190	204	210
	ACTUAL	RATE	5	8	9	38								
		CUM	5	13	22	60								
VULNERABILITY*						5								

19XX

*EXPENDITURES IN EXCESS OF FUNDS
NOTE: ALL DOLLARS IN THOUSANDS

Figure 5.7 Budget—Expenditures and Funding—Version 7

STATUS AS OF _____

FACTOR	TOTALS	DETAIL				
		ENGR'G	MFG	QUAL. ASSUR.	TEST	PROG. OFFICE
EXPENDITURES TO <u>JUNE 30</u>	$144.4	$17.4	$105.9	$5.0	$13.5	$2.6
EST. REMAINING EXPENDITURES	94.6	17.4	56.6	5.0	13.0	2.6
EST. FINAL COST	239.0	34.8	162.5	10.0	26.5	5.2
CONTRACT BUDGET	230.0	34.8	158.5	10.0	21.5	5.2
ENGINEERING CHANGES- EXISTING	4.2					
ENGINEERING CHANGES- ANTICIPATED	3.9					
TOTAL ANTICIPATED CONTRACT FUNDS	238.1					
COSTS EXCEEDING FUNDS	$.9					
FUNDS EXCEEDING COSTS						

NOTE: ALL DOLLARS IN THOUSANDS

Figure 5.8 Budget—Expenditures and Funding—Version 8

6.0 BUDGETS—EXPENDITURES, FUNDING, AND COMMITMENTS

Budget charts which display three related factors, expenditures, funding, and commitments, are shown in this section. Also see Budget Sections 3.0 through 5.0, and 7.0.

6.1 Budget—Expenditures, Funding, and Commitments—Version 1: In Version 1 of an expenditures, funding, and commitments budget chart, Figure 6.1, planned and actual funding is shown in step line form. Line curves are used to display budgeted and actual expenditures, and expenditures plus outstanding commitments. The current estimated cost at completion is shown, in this example, in note form at the bottom of the chart.

6.2 Budget—Expenditures, Funding, and Commitments—Version 2: Version 2 of an expenditures, funding, and commitments budget tracking chart is shown in Figure 6.2. It differs from Version 1 in two respects. First, variance statistics have been added to the tabular portion of the chart. Second, commitments are summed with expenditures in terms of *liability* rather than in terms of total commitments, commitment liabilities representing only a portion of total commitments.

6.3 Budget—Expenditures, Funding, and Commitments—Version 3: The most complex form of an expenditures, funding, and commitments budget tracking chart is shown as Version 3, Figure 6.3. In this example the planned and actual funding is shown in step line form, and expenditures, exposure, and expenditures and outstanding commitments are all shown in line curve form. The current estimated cost at completion is given in the note section of the chart.

6.4 Budget—Expenditures, Funding, and Commitments—Version 4: A tabular form of an expenditures, funding, and commitments budget tracking chart is shown in Figure 6.4. In this version, both rate per month and cumulative statistics are given for all of the main elements. A check mark has been used to draw the chart reader's attention to the primary anomaly in this statistical table.

6.5 Budget—Expenditures, Funding, and Commitments—Version 5: A "box score" type of status report is shown in Figure 6.5. As with all similar type status reports, it has the disadvantage of needing to be redone for each reporting period. Also, as with other such charts, a check mark has been used to draw attention to the most significant anomaly presented in this example.

6.6 Budget—Expenditures, Funding, and Commitments—Version 6: A tabular method for displaying the significant budget factors relative to a total activity or project is displayed as Version 6, Figure 6.6. This shows total funding, the allocation of that funding, all of the current expenditures, the forecast to complete, and the estimated position, both percentage-wise and cost-wise, at the end of the project or activity. As a one-time status report, this table has the disadvantage of needing to be redone for each new reporting period.

$-THOUSANDS
CUMULATIVE

FUNDING	PLAN	••••••	5.7	5.7	14.5	14.5	19.7	19.7
	ACTUAL	━━━━━	5.7	5.7				
EXPENDITURE PLUS OUTSTANDING COMMITMENTS	PLAN	oooooo	2.0	5.2	9.4	14.5	17.1	17.9
	ACTUAL	●●●●●●	2.0	5.4				
EXPENDITURES	BUDGET	-----	1.0	3.9	7.6	12.7	16.5	17.9
	ACTUAL	———	1.0	3.9				

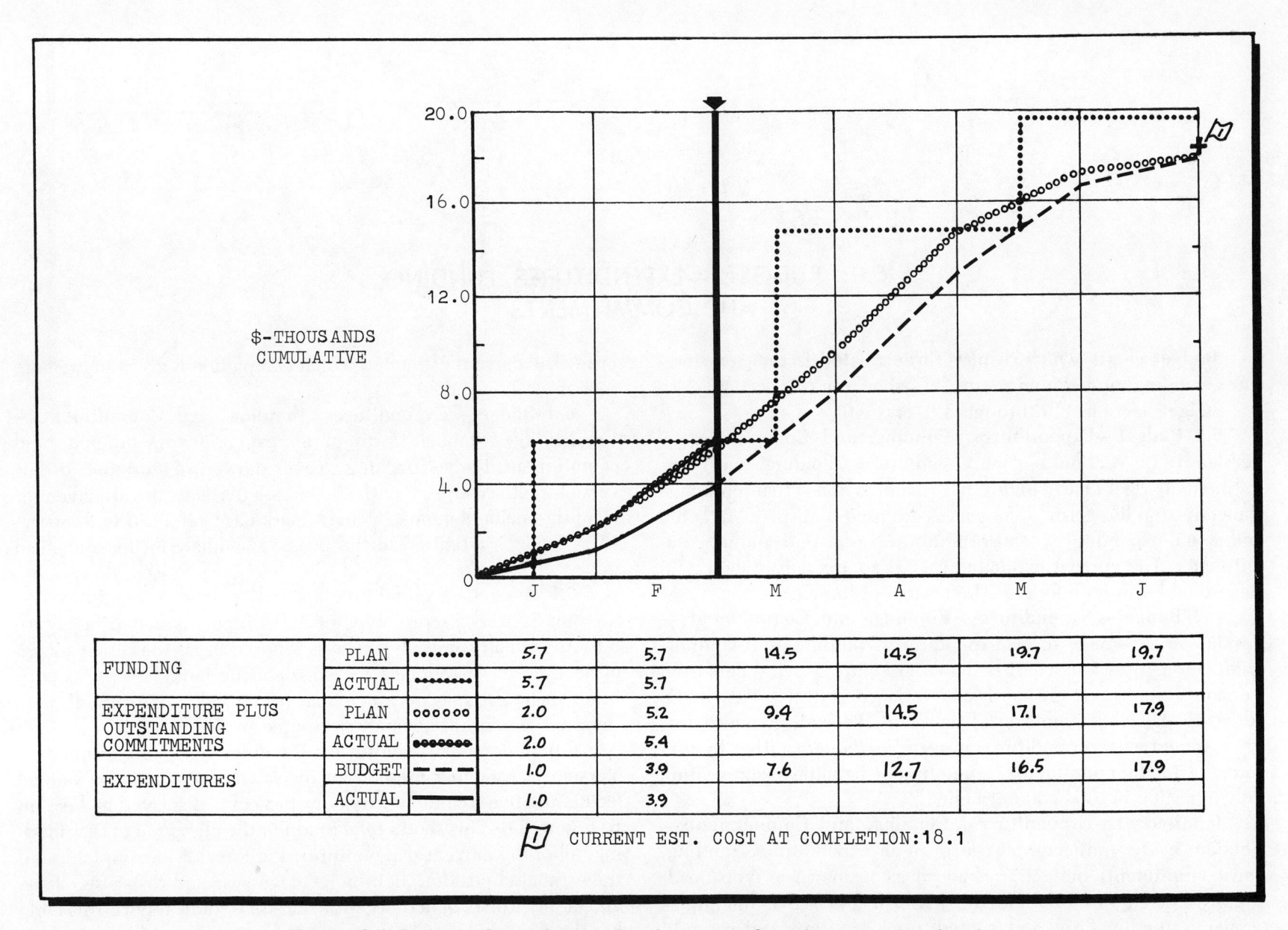

⚑ CURRENT EST. COST AT COMPLETION: 18.1

Figure 6.1 Budget—Expenditures, Funding, and Commitments— Version 1

$-THOUSANDS
(CUMULATIVE)

FUNDING	PLAN	•••••••	5.7	5.7	14.5	14.5	19.7	19.7
	ACTUAL	••••••	5.7	5.7				
	VARIANCE		0	0				
EXPENDITURES PLUS COMMITMENT LIABILITY	PLAN	—·—	1.8	4.9	9.0	14.1	17.0	17.9
	ACTUAL	—+—	1.8	5.1				
	VARIANCE		0	+.2				
EXPENDITURES	BUDGET	— — —	1.0	3.9	7.6	12.7	16.5	17.9
	ACTUAL	———	1.0	3.9				
	VARIANCE		0	0				

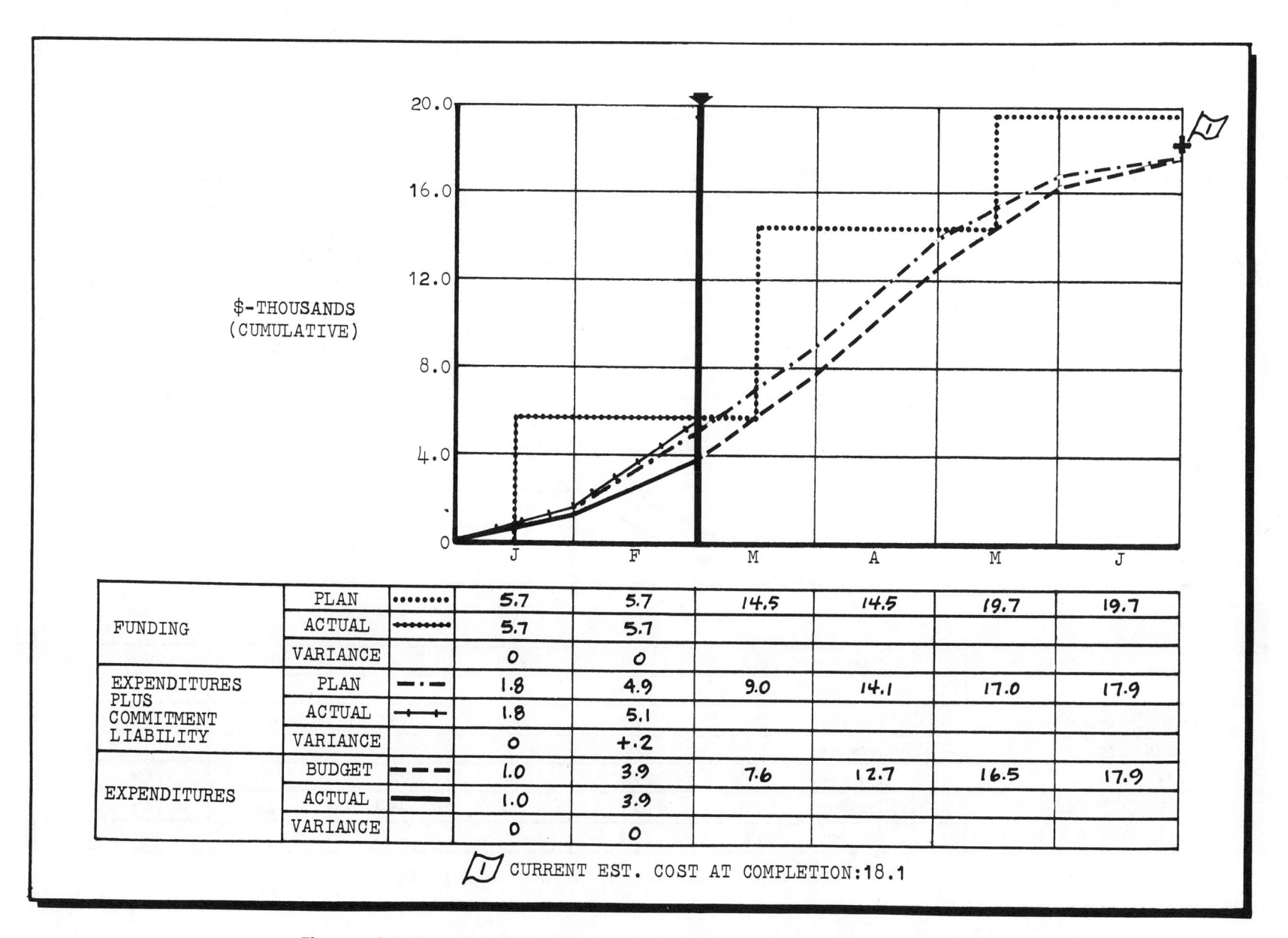

⌐1 CURRENT EST. COST AT COMPLETION: 18.1

Figure 6.2 Budget—Expenditures, Funding and Commitments—Version 2

FUNDING	PLAN	·······	5.7	5.7	14.5	14.5	19.7	19.7
	ACTUAL	●●●●●●●	5.7	5.7				
EXPENDITURES PLUS OUTSTANDING COMMITMENTS	BUDGET	ooooooo	2.0	5.2	9.4	14.5	17.1	17.9
	ACTUAL	⊙⊙⊙⊙⊙⊙⊙	2.0	5.4				
EXPOSURE		—·—·—	1.8	4.9	9.0	14.1	17.0	17.9
EXPENDITURES (LABOR & MAT'L)	BUDGET	— — —	1.0	3.9	7.6	12.7	16.5	17.9
	ACTUAL	———	1.0	3.9				

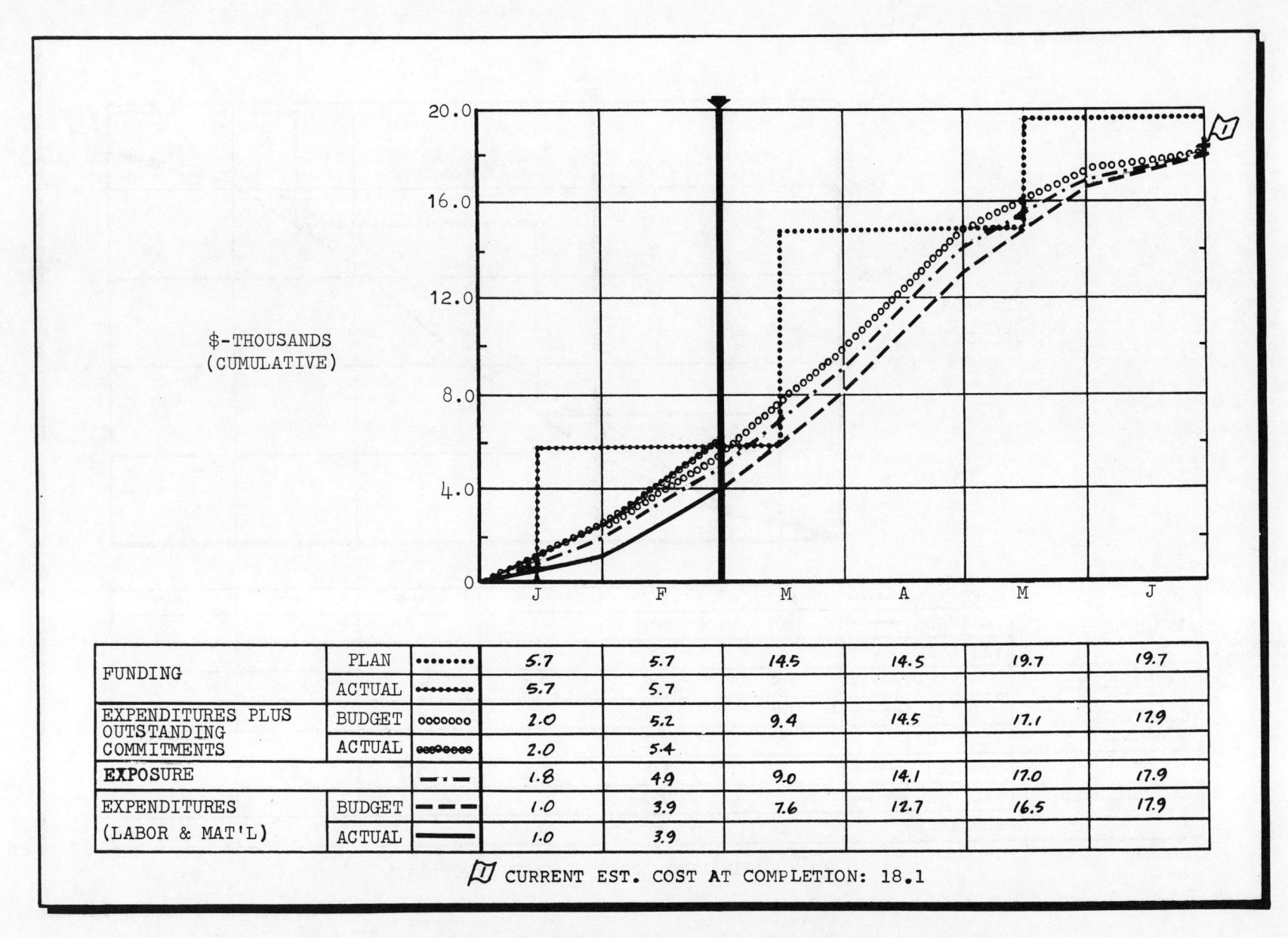

⚑ CURRENT EST. COST AT COMPLETION: 18.1

Figure 6.3 Budget—Expenditures, Funding, and Commitments— Version 3

FUNDING	PLAN	RATE	5.7	0	8.8	0	5.2	0
		CUM	5.7	5.7	14.5	14.5	19.7	19.7
	ACTUAL	RATE	5.7	0				
		CUM	5.7	5.7				
	VARIANCE	CUM	0	0				
EXPENDITURES (LABOR & MATERIAL)	BUDGET	RATE	1.0	2.9	3.7	5.1	3.8	1.4
		CUM	1.0	3.9	7.6	12.7	16.5	17.9
	ACTUAL	RATE	1.0	2.9				
		CUM	1.0	3.9				
	VARIANCE	CUM	0	0				
OUTSTANDING COMMITMENTS	PLAN		1.0	1.3	1.8	1.8	.6	0
	ACTUAL		1.0	1.5				
EXPENDITURE RATE & EXPENDITURE CUM PLUS OUTSTANDING COMMITMENTS	BUDGET	RATE	2.0	4.2	5.5	6.9	4.4	1.4
		CUM	2.0	5.2	9.4	14.5	17.1	17.9
	ACTUAL	RATE	2.0	4.4				
		CUM	2.0	5.4				
	VARIANCE	CUM	0	+.2				

NOTE: ALL DOLLARS IN THOUSANDS

J F M A M J

19XX

Figure 6.4 Budget—Expenditures, Funding, and Commitments— Version 4

STATUS THROUGH __FEB__

ITEM	STATUS THIS MONTH			CUM STATUS TO DATE			EST POSITION AT COMPLETION		
	BUDGET	ACTUAL	VAR	BUDGET	ACTUAL	VAR	BUDGET	ACTUAL	VAR
FUNDING	0	0	0	5.7	5.7	0	19.7	19.7	0
EXPENDITURES PLUS OUTSTANDING COMMITMENTS	4.2	4.4	+.2 ✓	5.2	5.4	+.2	17.9	18.1	+.2
LABOR	1.9	1.9	0	2.9	2.9	0	11.4	11.4	0
MATERIAL	1.0	1.0	0	1.0	1.0	0	6.5	6.7	+.2
TOTAL EXPENDITURES (LABOR + MAT'L)	2.9	2.9	0	3.9	3.9	0	17.9	18.1	+.2

NOTE: ALL DOLLARS IN THOUSANDS

Figure 6.5 Budget—Expenditures, Funding, and Commitments—Version 5

STATUS AS OF __MAY 1__

TOTAL FUNDING			$200,000
LESS FEE @ 10%			
FUNDS AVAIL. FOR ALLOCATION	$180,000		
FUNDS ALLOCATED		$180,000	
CURRENT EXPENDITURES:			
DIRECT LABOR	36,000		
APPLIED OVERHEAD @ 120%	43,200		
MATERIALS COMMITTED	7,400		
PURCHASED PARTS COMMITTED	3,000		
SUBCONTRACTING	3,800		
TRAVEL	600		
SUB-TOTAL	94,000		
G & A @ 10%	9,400		
TOTAL CURRENT EXPENDITURES		$103,400	
FUNDS REMAINING FROM ALLOCATION	76,600		
FORECAST TO COMPLETE		58,500	
FORECAST COST AT COMPLETION			161,900
COST VARIANCE (OVERRUN)			38,100
PERCENT VARIANCE (OVERRUN)			19.1%

Figure 6.6 Budget—Expenditures, Funding, and Commitments—Version 6

7.0 BUDGETS—SUMMARIES

This section contains examples of charts that show budgeted and actual expenditure activity. The section is limited to charts that display this information only in terms of *total* budgeted and actual costs, such as would be summarized in terms of total material costs, or total labor costs, or total department costs, or total program or project costs. Also see Budget Sections 3.0 through 6.0.

7.1 Budget—Summary—Version 1: The basic ingredients of a budget chart are shown in Figure 7.1. The budget for an activity is first plotted. As time passes, the actual expenditures are plotted in relationship to the budget, and the cumulative variance between the two sets of statistics is shown. It is common practice to periodically make new forecasts or "estimates to complete." Sometimes this is done quarterly, and in still other instances it is done only when there is an over-budget condition, such as shown in the example. Also in this example, the expected cost position at the end of the project is indicated.

7.2 Budget—Summary—Version 2: The same information that was shown in Version 1 is shown in Version 2 of the budget chart displayed in Figure 7.2. This particular example also shows the use of a target, a target being a cost goal different from the budget, or from the estimated cost at completion. Also in this example, the current cumulative variance ($700 over budget) is shown as a note rather than on the main body of the chart.

7.3 Budget—Summary—Version 3: In Figure 7.3, a "budget column" has been added to supplement a line curve budget chart. The column is shaded to show funds expended as of the reporting date. In this example, the detailed monthly forecast (estimate to complete) that was in Versions 1 and 2 has been omitted except for a year-end point: current estimated cost at completion. It can be seen, in this example, that the current estimate cuts into the profit planned for this particular activity.

7.4 Budget—Summary—Version 4: A statistical table has been added to a cumulative line curve chart, Version 4, Figure 7.4. The single line statistical entry in this example shows the cumulative variance between budgeted and actual expenditures for each reporting period.

7.5 Budget—Summary—Version 5: In situations where expenditures activity must be tracked, but the nature of the subject is such that the exact dollar value of the budget must be concealed, a chart such as shown in Figure 7.5 might be used. In this example, the budget is tracked in relationship to a target from which negative and positive deviation values are shown. Since the zero base line has been omitted, the exact amount of the target is not revealed.

7.6 Budget—Summary—Version 6: Two lines of statistical data are used in conjunction with a cumulative line curve chart shown in Figure 7.6. The two lines of statistics, in this example, are the cumulative budgeted and actual expenditures. The estimate to complete is shown only in graphic form.

7.7 Budget—Summary—Version 7: Three lines of statistical data are shown in Version 7 of a budget chart, Figure 7.7. In addition to the cumulative budgeted and actual expenditure statistics shown in Version 6, the cumulative variance statistics are shown in this example.

7.8 Budget—Summary—Version 8: In Version 8 of a budget chart, Figure 7.8, shading has been added to make the cumulative actual expenditure curve more visible to the chart reader. As with Version 7, this example also presents three lines of statistical data, the third line in this example, though, being the cumulative estimate to complete statistics rather than cumulative variance statistics.

7.9 Budget—Summary—Version 9: A rate per month style of budget chart is shown in Figure 7.9. This example is shown in line curve form.

7.10 Budget—Summary—Version 10: Four lines of statistics are shown in conjunction with a cumulative line curve budget chart in Figure 7.10. In this case, the budgeted and actual expenditures are shown, statistically, in terms of both rate per month and cumulatively. Only the cumulative figures are plotted on the graph.

7.11 Budget—Summary—Version 11: Four sets of statistical data are shown in relationship to the cumulative line curve budget chart in Figure 7.11. In this example, all four sets of statistics are relative to cumulative data: budgeted and actual expenditures, the variance between these two sets of numbers, and the current estimate to complete.

7.12 Budget—Summary—Version 12: Five lines of statistical data are shown with the line curve budget chart in Figure 7.12.

This example is identical to Version 10 except that cumulative variance statistics have been added.

7.13 Budget—Summary—Version 13: Version 13 of a budget chart, Figure 7.13, combines six lines of statistical data with a cumulative line curve chart. In this version, all cumulative statistics that are shown in the table are also plotted on the graph. In addition, the table also displays the budgeted and actual rate per month statistics.

7.14 Budget—Summary—Version 14: Version 14 of a budget chart, Figure 7.14, is identical to Version 13, except that, in this example, the estimates to complete statistics are shown both in terms of rate per month and cumulative.

7.15 Budget—Summary—Version 15: A full complement of statistics is shown in Version 15 of a budget chart, Figure 7.15. The table includes cumulative and rate per month statistics. The cumulative figures are also plotted on the graphic portion of the chart.

7.16 Budget—Summary—Version 16: Version 16 of a budget chart, Figure 7.16, is identical to Version 15 except that shading has been added to highlight the over-budget condition. A variation of this chart would be to shade only that portion of the over-budget condition up to the time-now line.

7.17 Budget—Summary—Version 17: A cumulative step line chart is shown as Version 17 of a budget chart, Figure 7.17. The disadvantage of this type of chart is that the vertical lines often coincide making the graphic portion of the chart difficult to read. Shading has been added, in this example, to make the cumulative actual expenditure portion of the chart easier to read.

7.18 Budget—Summary—Version 18: A step line chart and a column chart have been combined in the budget chart example shown in Figure 7.18. Budgeted expenditures, in this example, are shown in step line form. Actual expenditures are shown in column

Budgets—Summaries

chart form. This particular technique helps to overcome the problem of coinciding vertical lines associated with step line charts that use multiple lines. Also, in this particular example, the columns have been segmented to show different elements of the actual expenditures (in-house versus subcontracted).

7.19 Budget—Summary—Version 19: A rate per month version of a budget chart is shown in paired column chart form in Figure 7.19. In this example, three columns are used, one to show budgeted expenditures, the second to show actual expenditures, and the third to show the estimate to complete. The columns, in this example, are overlayed in such a manner that when actual expenditure columns are added to the chart, they do not obliterate those columns representing budgeted and estimated performance.

7.20 Budget—Summary—Version 20: An example of a budget chart where a statistical table has been added on the right-hand side of the graph is shown as Version 20, Figure 7.20. The disadvantage of this style chart as compared to previously shown combined statistic/graphic charts is that there is a need to have two date lines, one horizontal and the other vertical.

7.21 Budget—Summary—Version 21: One of the most complex versions of a budget tracking chart is shown in Figure 7.21. In this example, three separate elements have been combined: a cumulative line curve chart, a columnar rate per month chart, and a statistical table. The table carries a full complement of statistics, all of which are shown, with the exception of the variances, on one or the other of the two graphs.

7.22 Budget—Summary—Version 22: Version 22 of a budget chart, Figure 7.22, combines a cumulative chart and a rate per month chart, and provides space on the right-hand side of both graphs for a written analysis. Since, in an analysis, comments from a previous reporting period may be useful if they are carried over, an additional column has been, provided to highlight, with an arrow, the items that are new for the latest reporting period. This example also shows a multi-year grid where the current year, by months, is shown in relationship to the previous year and the coming year.

7.23 Budget—Summary—Version 23: The budget performance of a number of separate projects, or departments, can be summarized on the percentage type chart shown in Figure 7.23. Actuals, in this example, are displayed against a minimum performance goal.

7.24 Budget—Summary—Version 24: A deviation style chart is shown in Figure 7.24. The budget plan is the center line, and actuals, in terms of over- and under-budget, are tracked against it. This example also shows limit lines for management action. When performance exceeds these limits, it is management's responsibility to step in and take corrective action.

7.25 Budget—Summary—Version 25: Another version of a deviation chart is shown in Figure 7.25. This is a chart similar to Version 24, except the grid, in this case, is laid out to show performance in prior years.

7.26 Budget—Summary—Version 26: The techniques of a step line chart and a column chart are combined in the deviation budget chart shown as Version 26, Figure 7.26. In this example, as with previous examples of deviation charts, the budget plan is represented by the center line of the chart. Actual performance, in terms of over- or under-budget activity, is shown in column form. An estimate to complete is shown in step line form. It shows, in this example, that the project is expected to be completed under budget.

7.27 Budget—Summary—Version 27: A deviation chart combined with a statistical table is shown in Version 27, Figure 7.27. The statistics, in this example, show budgeted and actual expenditures. The deviation chart, however, reflects only the variances from budget. An additional element of this chart is that the existing over-budget condition is shaded to emphasize that point to the chart reader.

7.28 Budget—Summary—Version 28: A statistical table version of a budget tracking chart is shown in Figure 7.28. In this example cumulative figures are shown. It is useful, in a table of this sort, to use some method to indicate that portion of the table where the chart reader's attention should be focused. In this example an arrow has been used.

7.29 Budget—Summary—Version 29: A full complement of statistics is shown in the table, Figure 7.29. Both rate per month and cumulative sets of statistics are shown. As with Version 28, the anomaly to which the chart readers should focus their attention is highlighted, in this case with a circle.

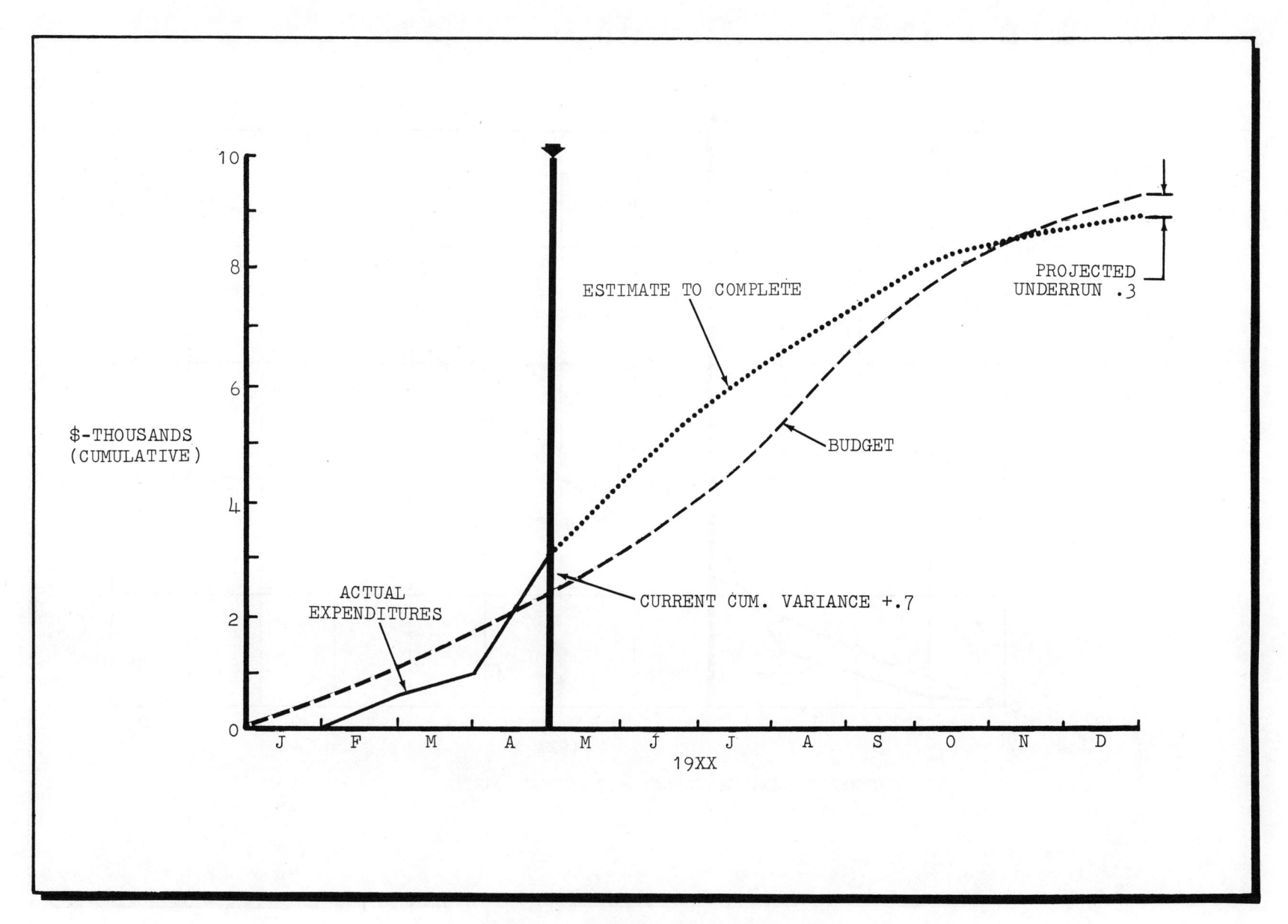

Figure 7.1 Budget—Summary—Version 1

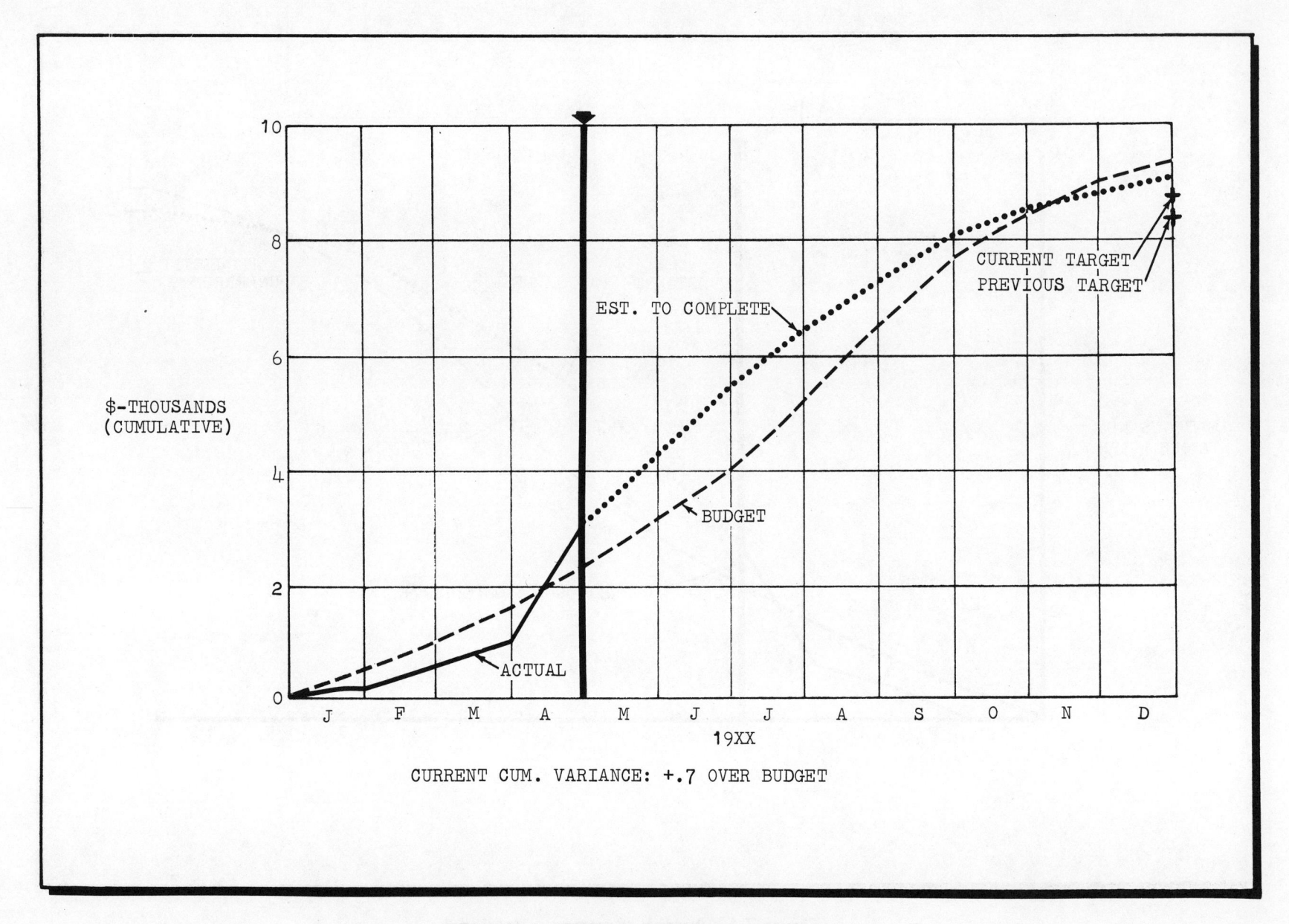

Figure 7.2   Budget—Summary—Version 2

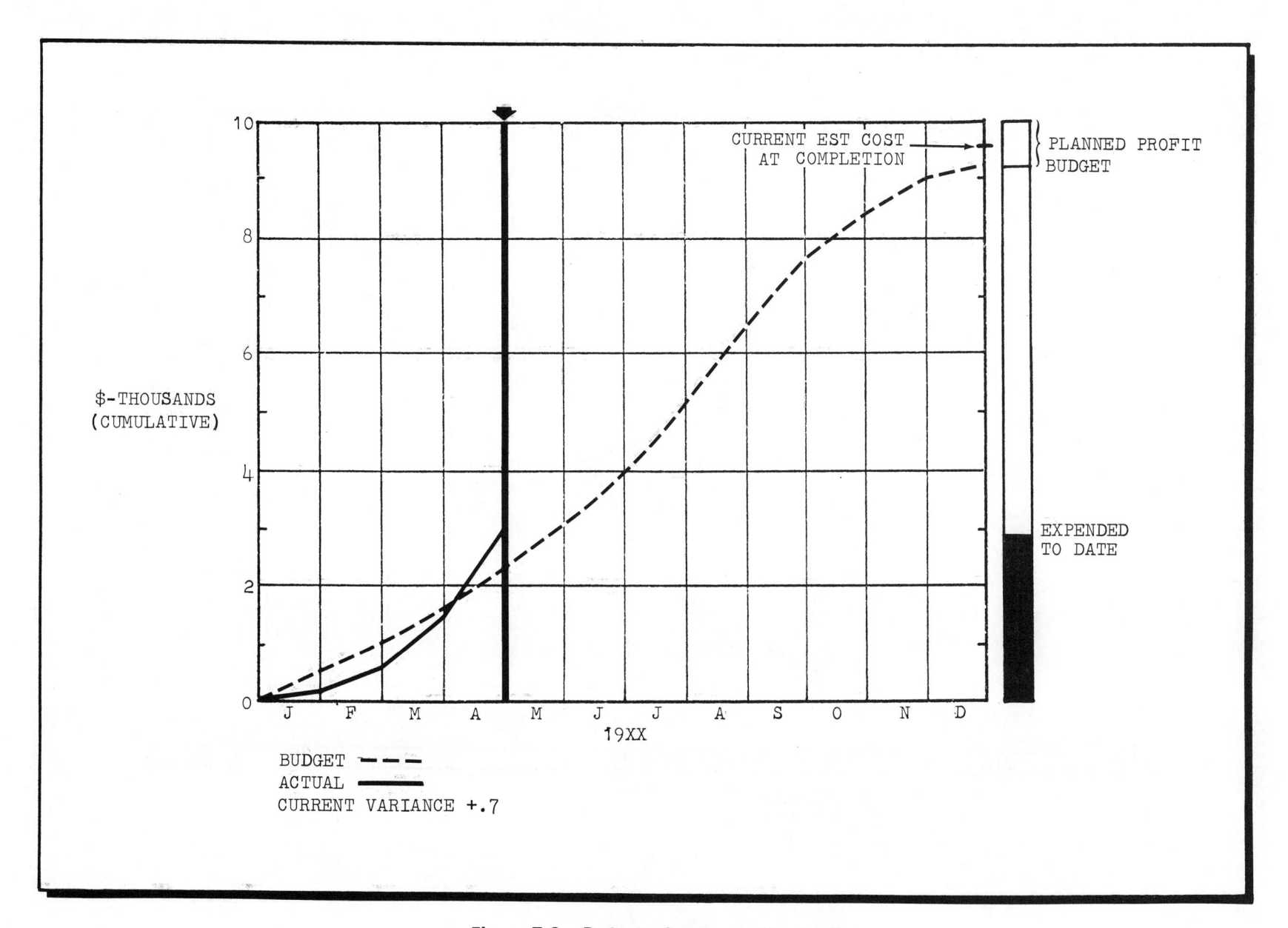

Figure 7.3 Budget—Summary—Version 3

73

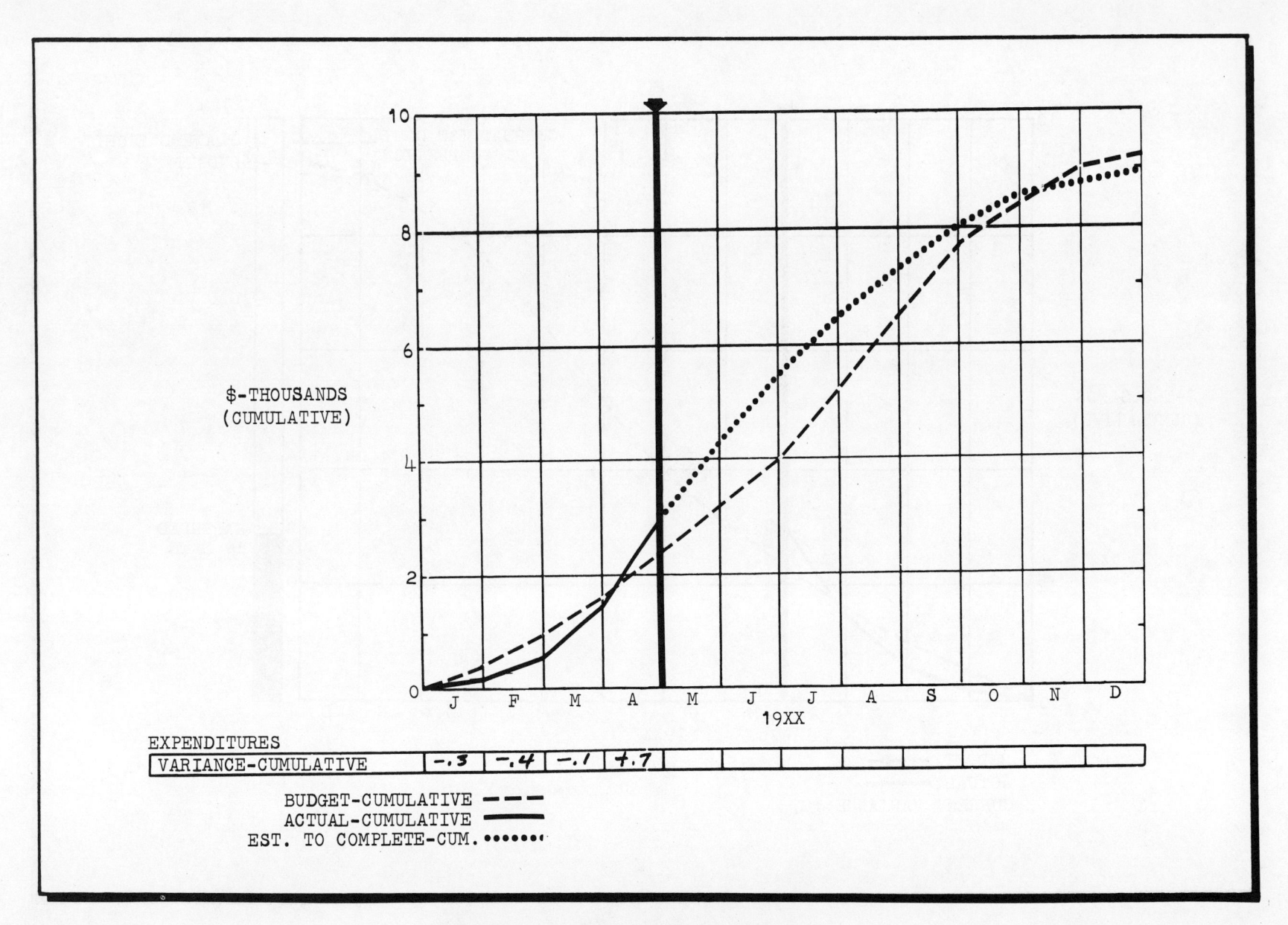

Figure 7.4 Budget—Summary—Version 4

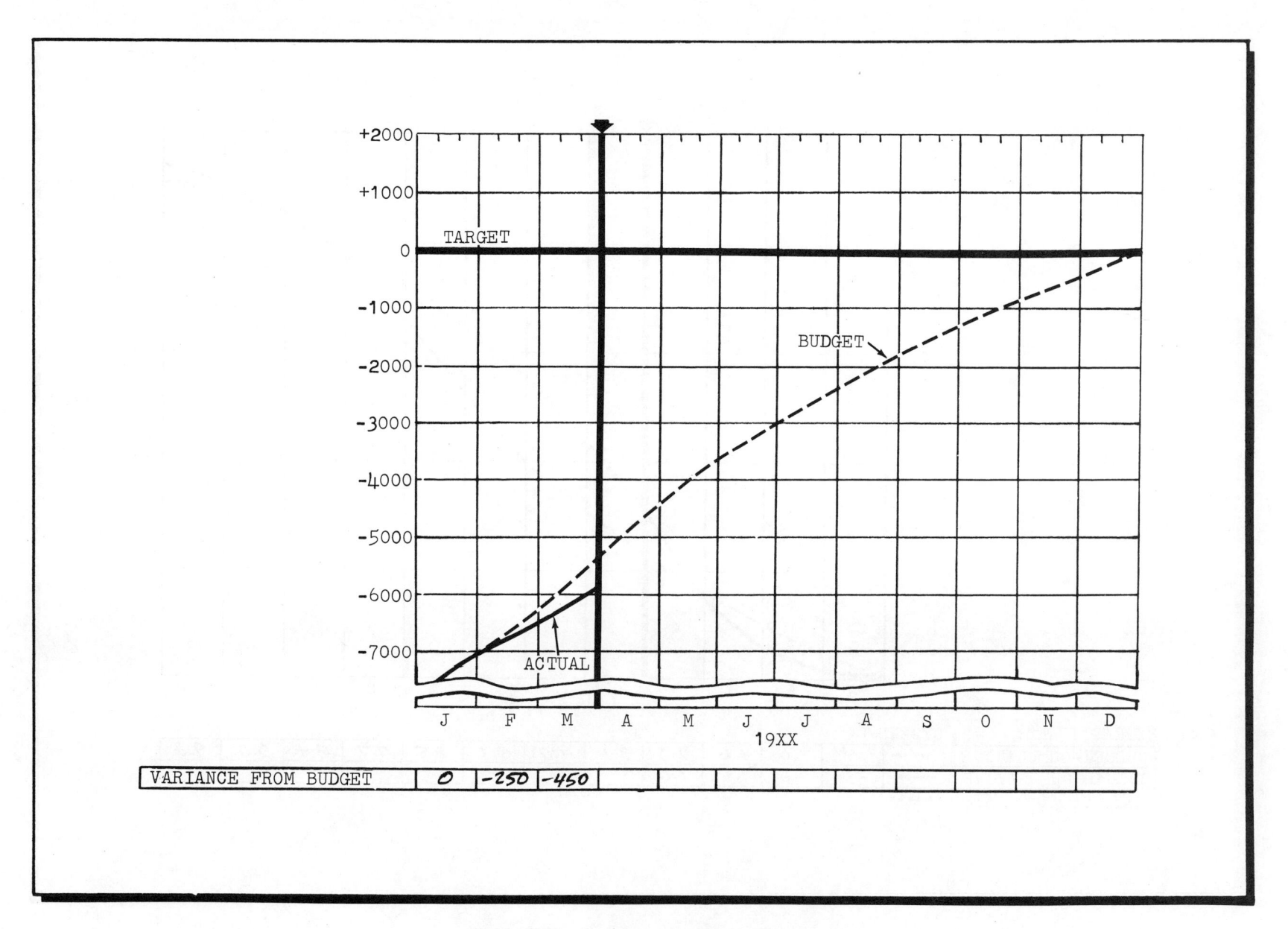

Figure 7.5 Budget—Summary—Version 5

$-THOUSANDS
(CUMULATIVE)

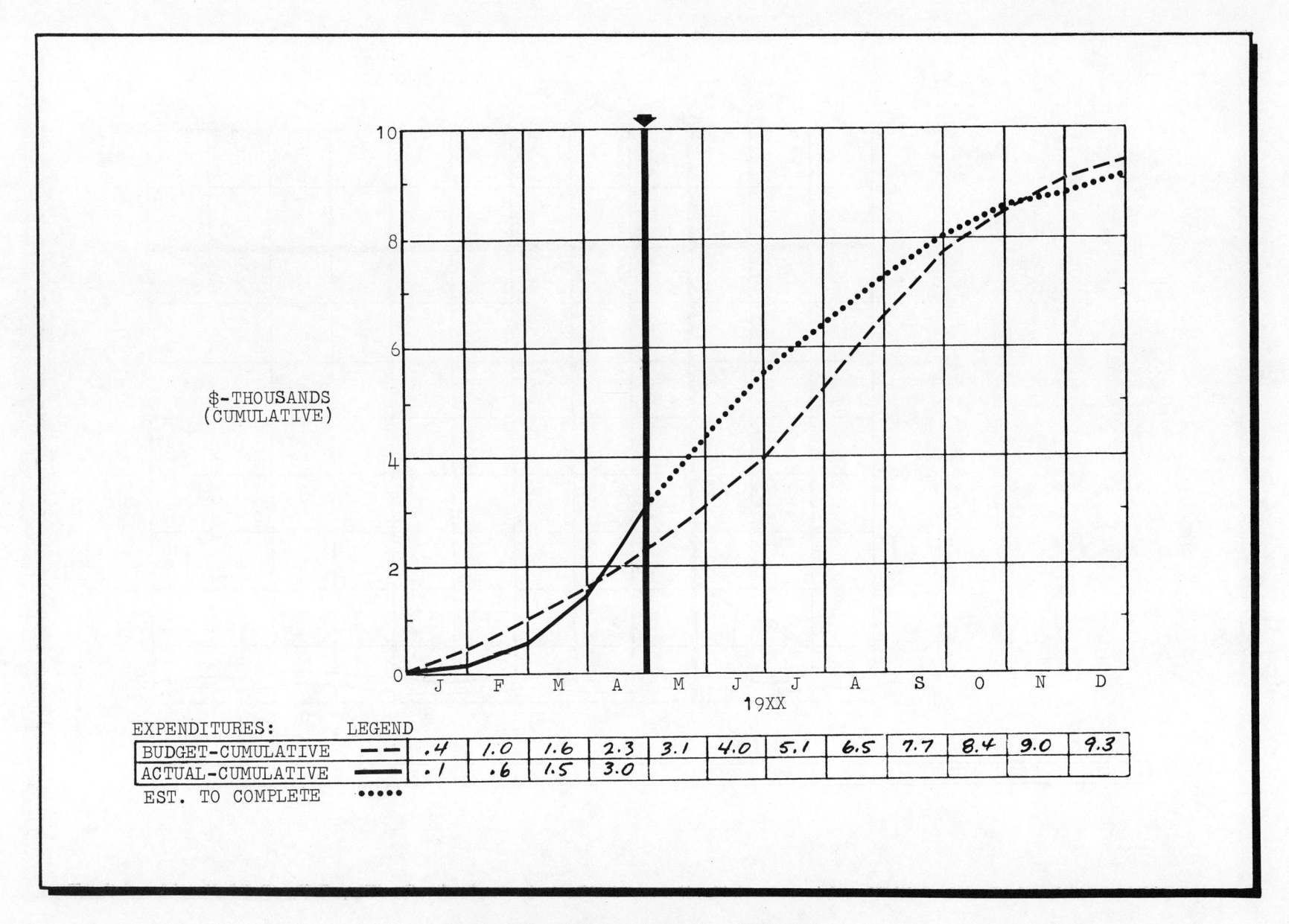

EXPENDITURES:	LEGEND											
BUDGET-CUMULATIVE	— —	.4	1.0	1.6	2.3	3.1	4.0	5.1	6.5	7.7	8.4	9.0	9.3
ACTUAL-CUMULATIVE	——	.1	.6	1.5	3.0								
EST. TO COMPLETE	•••••												

Figure 7.6 Budget—Summary—Version 6

$-THOUSANDS
(CUMULATIVE)

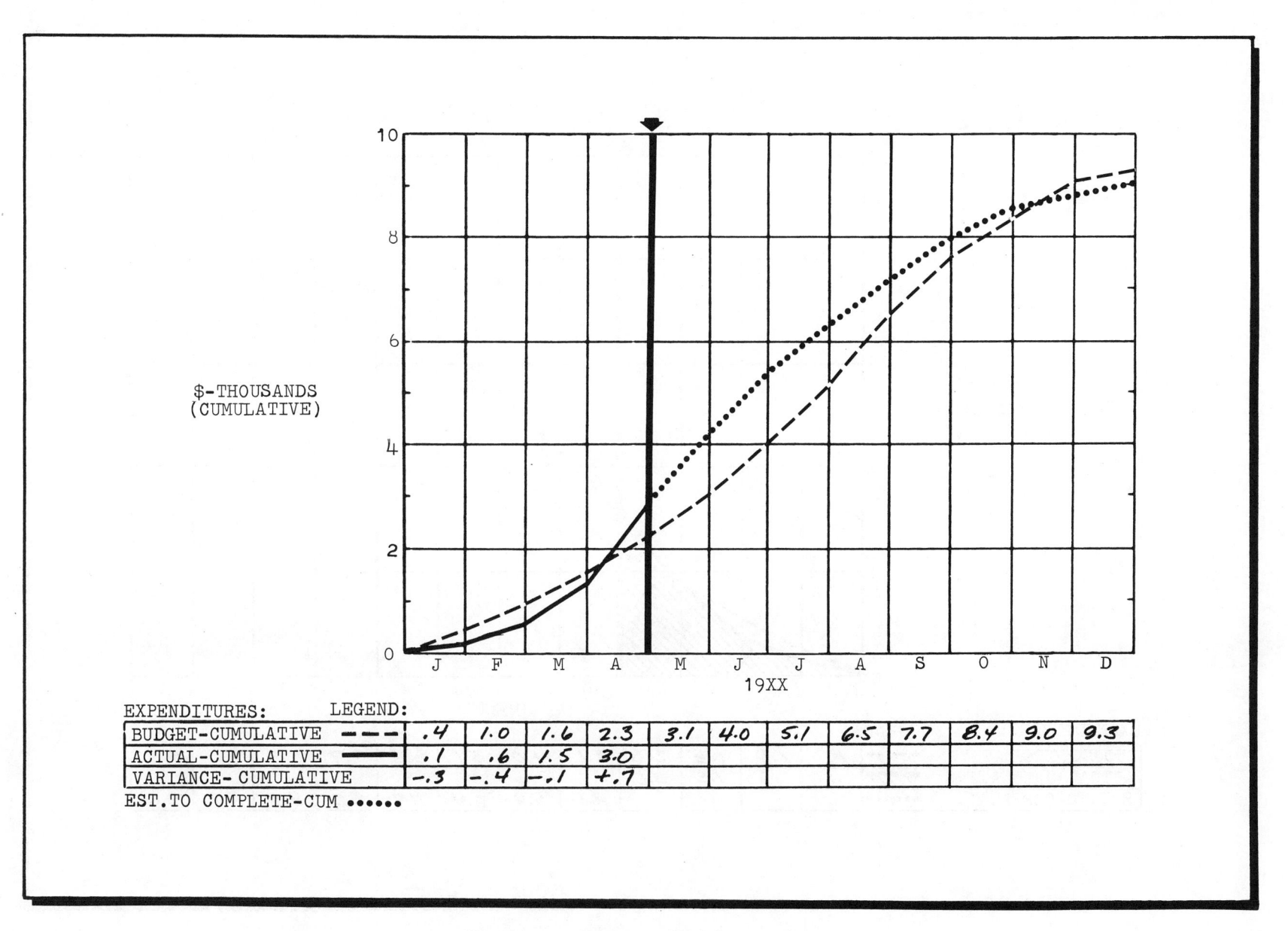

EXPENDITURES:	LEGEND:											
BUDGET-CUMULATIVE	– – –	.4	1.0	1.6	2.3	3.1	4.0	5.1	6.5	7.7	8.4	9.0	9.3
ACTUAL-CUMULATIVE	——	.1	.6	1.5	3.0								
VARIANCE- CUMULATIVE		-.3	-.4	-.1	+.7								
EST.TO COMPLETE-CUM	•••••												

Figure 7.7 Budget—Summary—Version 7

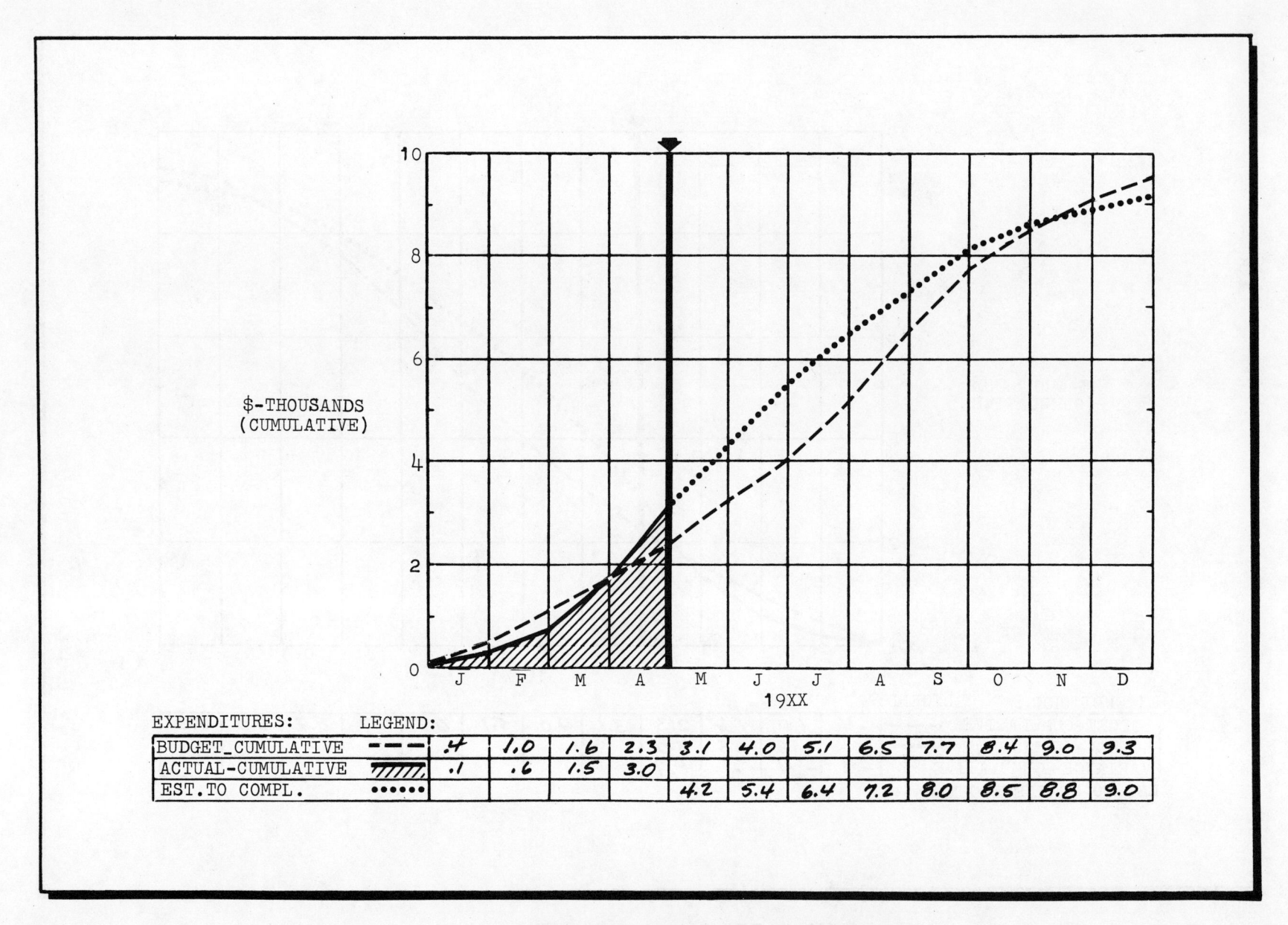

EXPENDITURES:	LEGEND:											
BUDGET-CUMULATIVE	– – –	.4	1.0	1.6	2.3	3.1	4.0	5.1	6.5	7.7	8.4	9.0	9.3
ACTUAL-CUMULATIVE	/////	.1	.6	1.5	3.0							
EST. TO COMPL.	••••••					4.2	5.4	6.4	7.2	8.0	8.5	8.8	9.0

Figure 7.8   Budget—Summary—Version 8

EXPENDITURES: LEGEND:

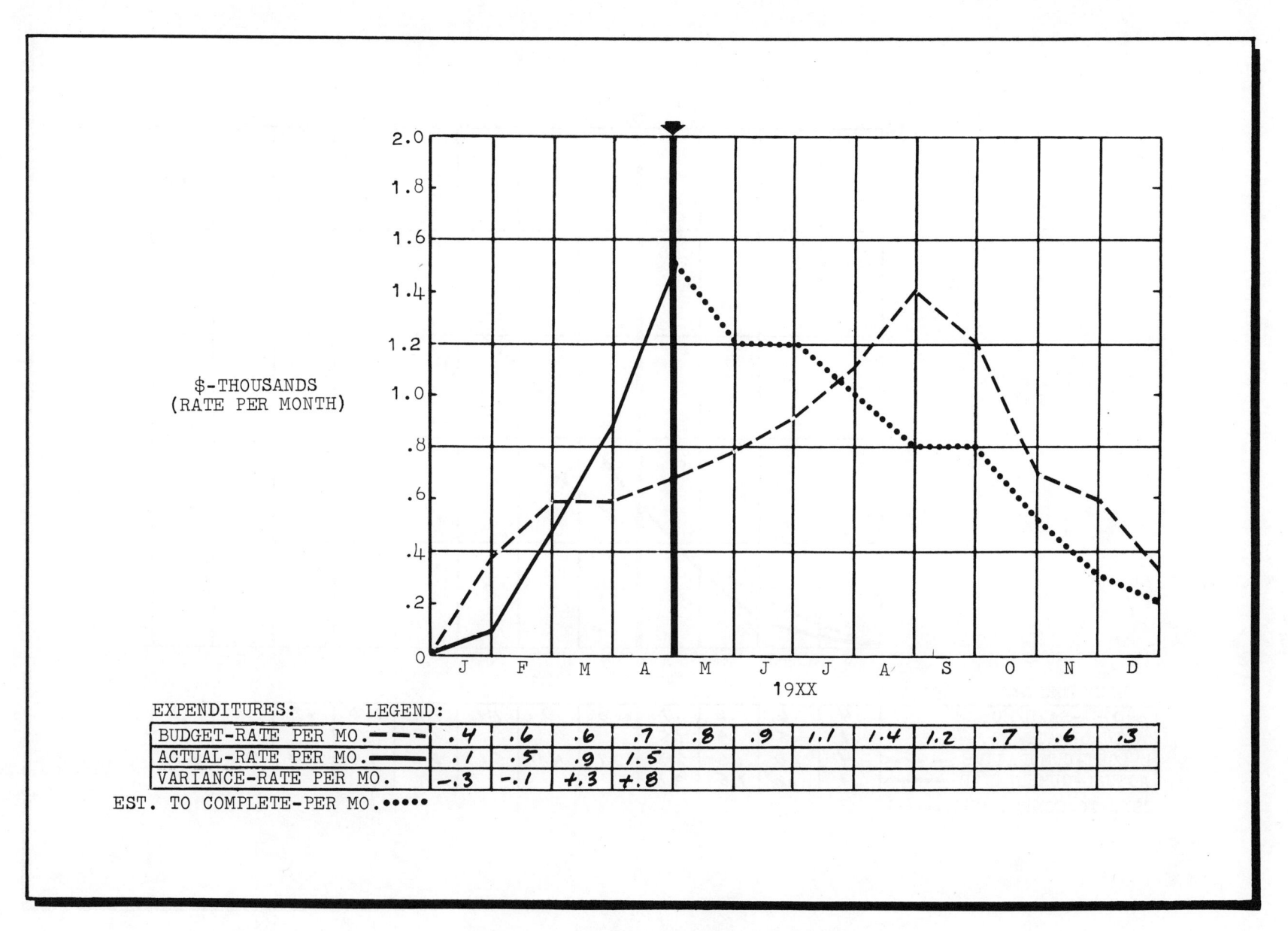

	J	F	M	A	M	J	J	A	S	O	N	D
BUDGET-RATE PER MO. -----	.4	.6	.6	.7	.8	.9	1.1	1.4	1.2	.7	.6	.3
ACTUAL-RATE PER MO. ————	.1	.5	.9	1.5								
VARIANCE-RATE PER MO.	-.3	-.1	+.3	+.8								

EST. TO COMPLETE-PER MO. •••••

Figure 7.9 Budget—Summary—Version 9

$-THOUSANDS
(CUMULATIVE)

EXPENDITURES:	LEGEND:												
BUDGET-RATE/MO.		.4	.6	.6	.7	.8	.9	1.1	1.4	1.2	.7	.6	.3
ACTUAL-RATE/MO.		.1	.5	.9	1.5								
BUDGET-CUMULATIVE	– – –	.4	1.0	1.6	2.3	3.1	4.0	5.1	6.5	7.7	8.4	9.0	9.3
ACTUAL-CUMULATIVE	——	.1	.6	1.5	3.0								
EST. TO COMPL.-CUM.	••••••												

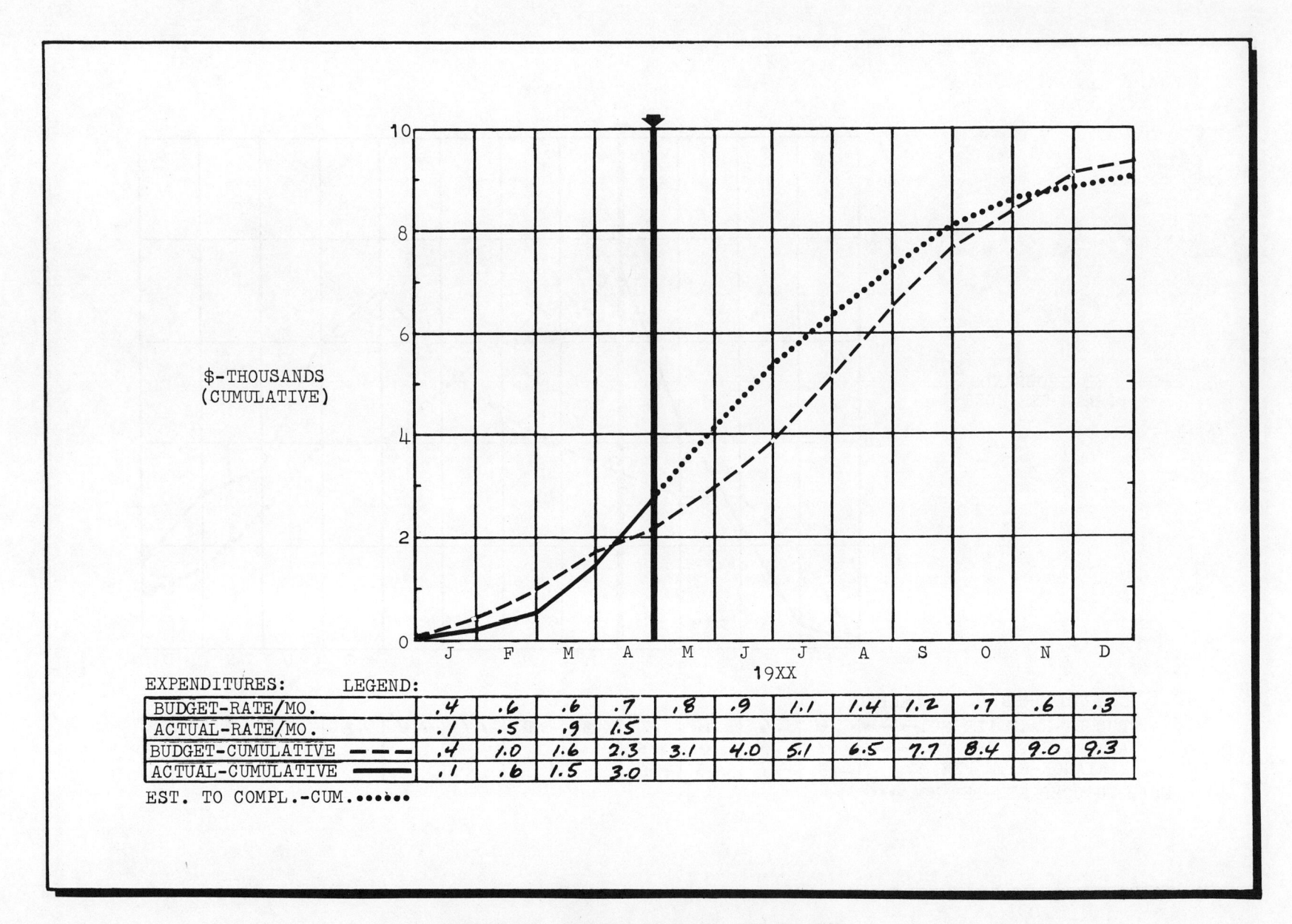

Figure 7.10 Budget—Summary—Version 10

80

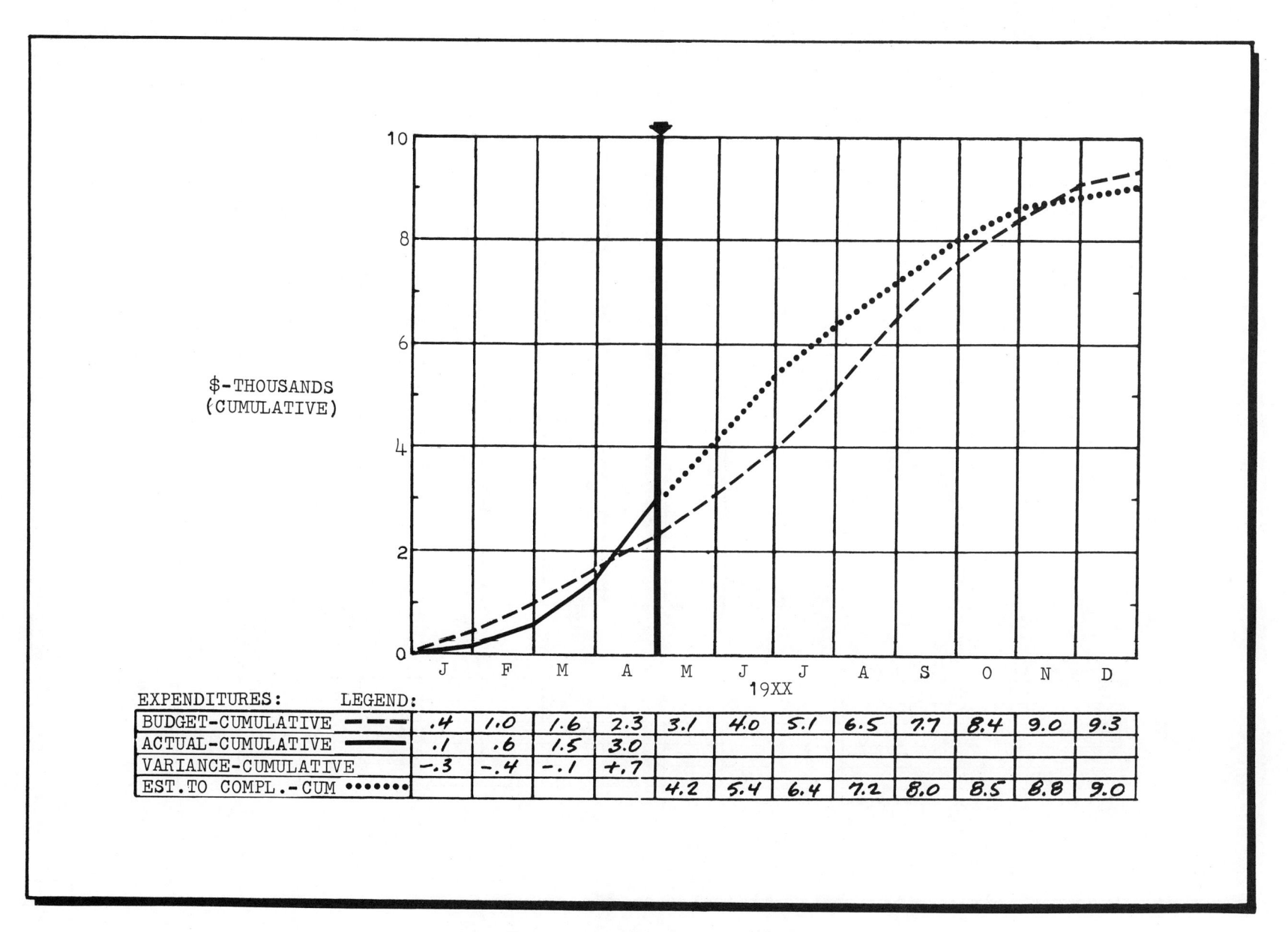

EXPENDITURES:	LEGEND:											
BUDGET-CUMULATIVE	– – –	.4	1.0	1.6	2.3	3.1	4.0	5.1	6.5	7.7	8.4	9.0	9.3
ACTUAL-CUMULATIVE	———	.1	.6	1.5	3.0								
VARIANCE-CUMULATIVE		-.3	-.4	-.1	+.7								
EST. TO COMPL.-CUM	•••••••					4.2	5.4	6.4	7.2	8.0	8.5	8.8	9.0

Figure 7.11 Budget—Summary—Version 11

EXPENDITURES:	LEGEND:	J	F	M	A	M	J	J	A	S	O	N	D
BUDGET-RATE/MO.		.4	.6	.6	.7	.8	.9	1.1	1.4	1.2	.7	.6	.3
ACTUAL-RATE/MO.		.1	.5	.9	1.5								
BUDGET-CUMULATIVE	– – –	.4	1.0	1.6	2.3	3.1	4.0	5.1	6.5	7.7	8.4	9.0	9.3
ACTUAL-CUMULATIVE	———	.1	.6	1.5	3.0								
VARIANCE-CUMLATIVE		-.3	-.4	-.1	+.7								

EST TO COMPL.-CUM. ● ● ● ● ● ● ●

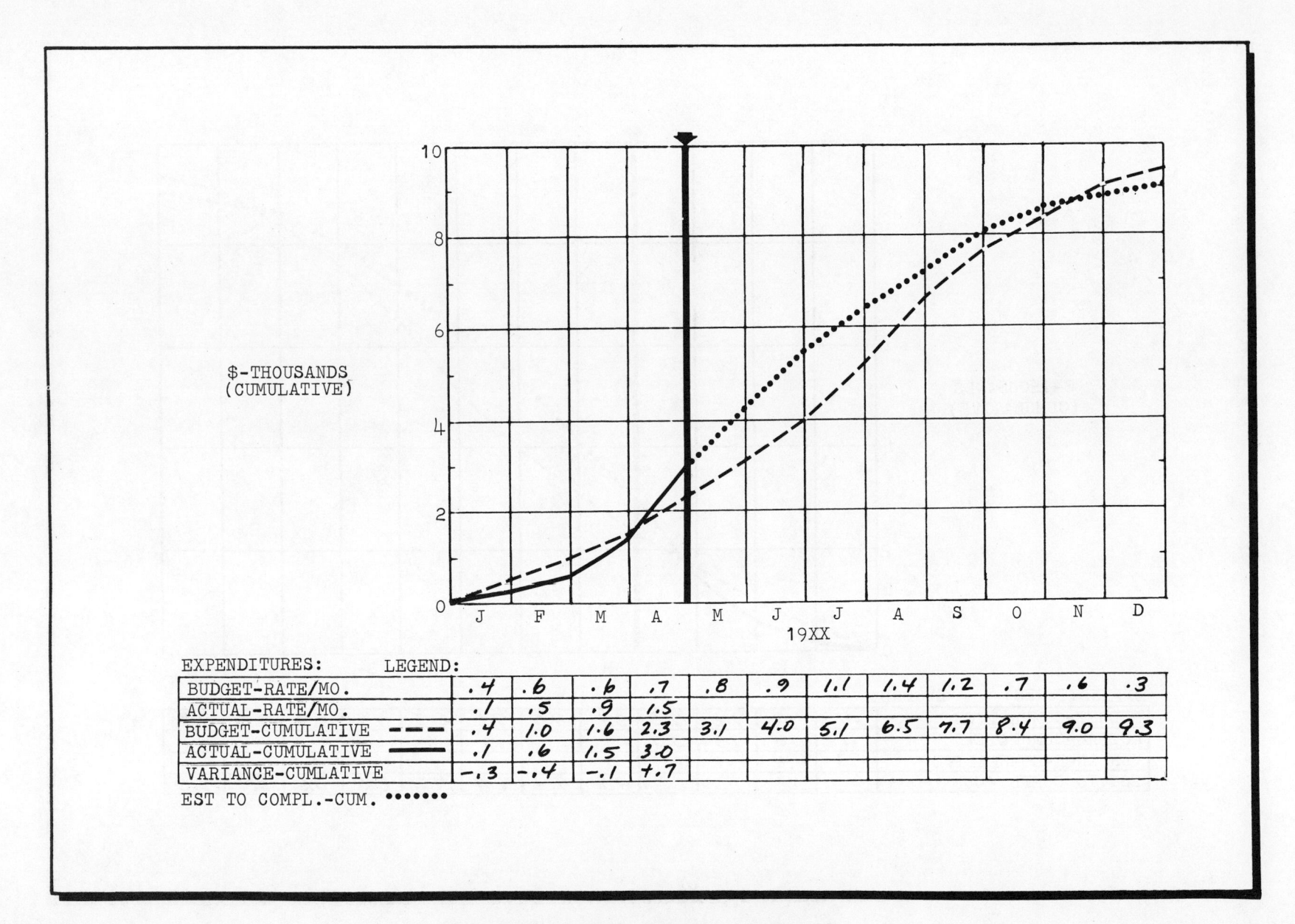

Figure 7.12   Budget—Summary—Version 12

$-THOUSANDS
(CUMULATIVE)

EXPENDITURES:	LEGEND											
BUDGET-RATE/MO.		.4	.6	.6	.7	.8	.9	1.1	1.4	1.2	.7	.6	.3
ACTUAL-RATE/MO.		.1	.5	.9	1.5								
BUDGET-CUMULATIVE	— —	.4	1.0	1.6	2.3	3.1	4.0	5.1	6.5	7.7	8.4	9.0	9.3
ACTUAL-CUMULATIVE	——	.1	.6	1.5	3.0								
VARIANCE/CUMULATIVE		-.3	-.4	-.1	+.7								
EST.TO COMPL.-CUM.	•••••					4.2	5.4	6.4	7.2	8.0	8.5	8.8	9.0

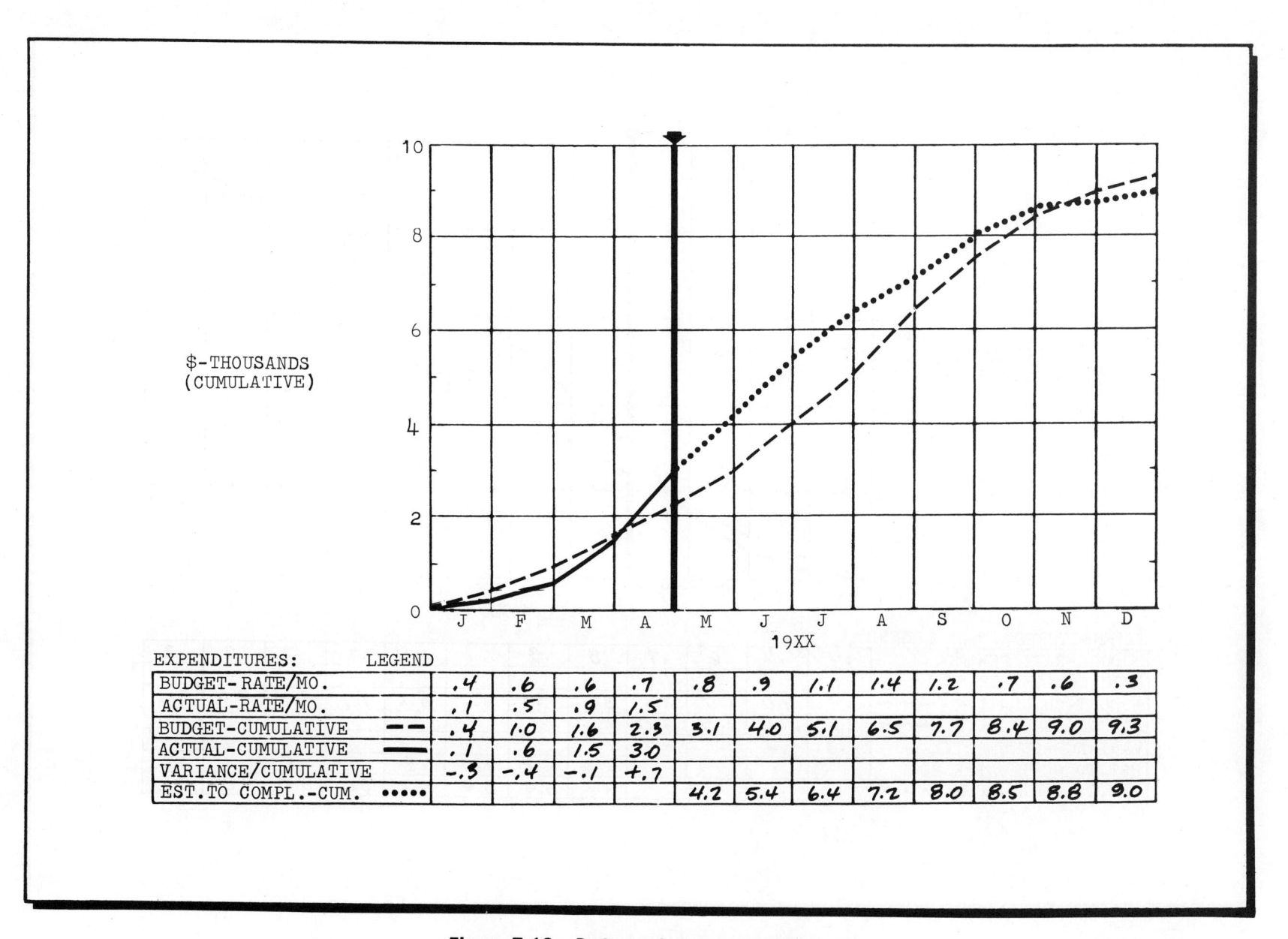

Figure 7.13   Budget—Summary—Version 13

EXPENDITURES	LEGEND											
BUDGET-RATE PER MO.		.4	.6	.6	.7	.8	.9	1.1	1.4	1.2	.7	.6	.3
ACTUAL-RATE PER MO.		.1	.5	.9	1.5								
BUDGET-CUMULATIVE	- - -	.4	1.0	1.6	2.3	3.1	4.0	5.1	6.5	7.7	8.4	9.0	9.3
ACTUAL-CUMULATIVE	——	.1	.6	1.5	3.0								
VARIANCE-CUMULATIVE		-.3	-.4	-.1	+.7								
EST.TO COMPL.-PER MO.						1.2	1.2	1.0	.8	.8	.5	.3	.2
EST.TO COMPL.-CUM.	••••••					4.2	5.4	6.4	7.2	8.0	8.5	8.8	9.0

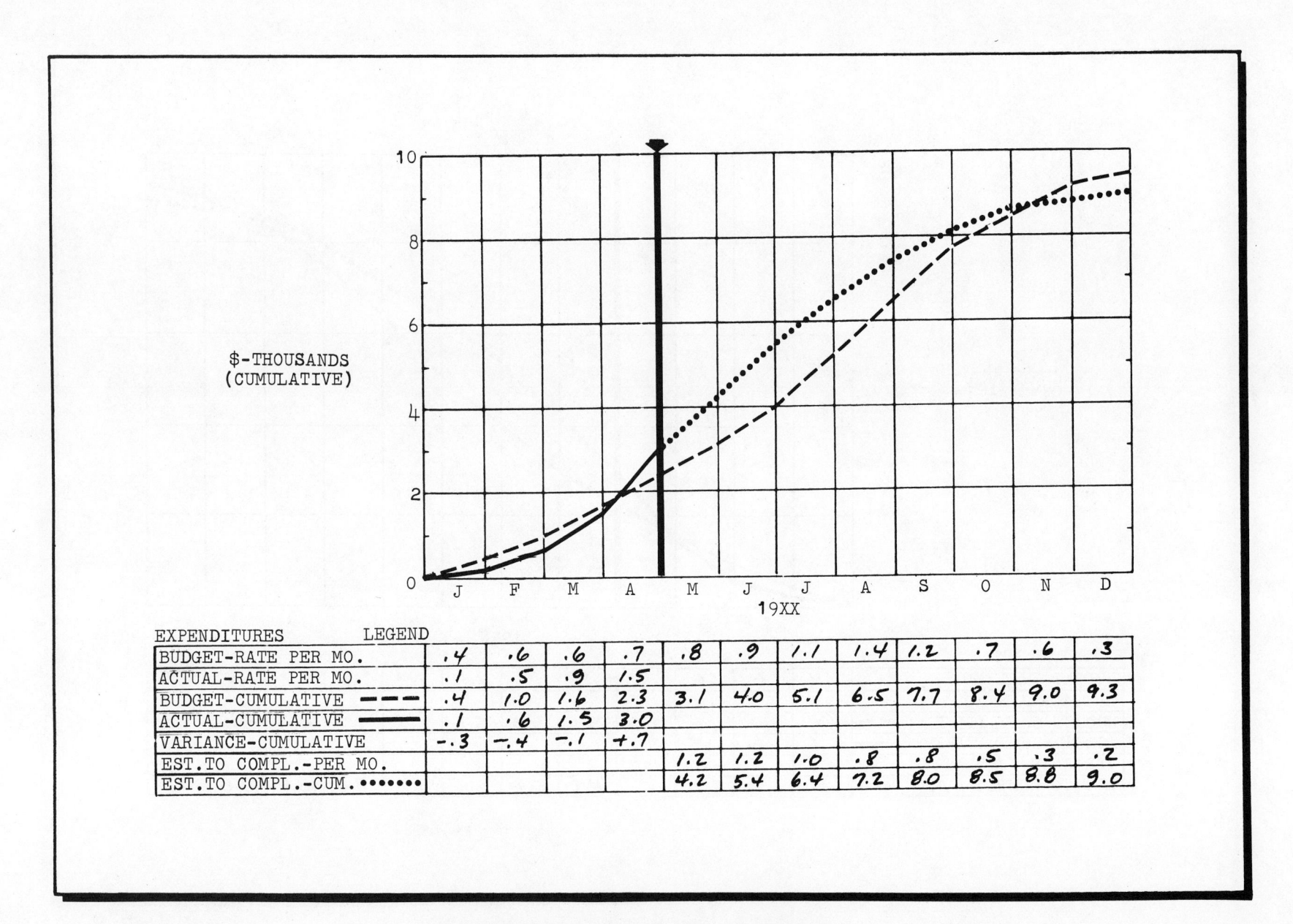

Figure 7.14   Budget—Summary—Version 14

$-THOUSANDS
(CUMULATIVE)

EXPENDITURES	LEGEND	J	F	M	A	M	J	J	A	S	O	N	D
BUDGET-RATE PER MO.		.4	.6	.6	.7	.8	.9	1.1	1.4	1.2	.7	.6	.3
ACTUAL-RATE PER MO.		.1	.5	.9	1.5								
VARIANCE-RATE PER MO.		-.3	-.1	+.3	+.8								
EST. TO COMPL-RATE PER MO.						1.2	1.2	1.0	.8	.8	.5	.3	.2
BUDGET-CUMULATIVE	-----	.4	1.0	1.6	2.3	3.1	4.0	5.1	6.5	7.7	8.4	9.0	9.3
ACTUAL-CUMULATIVE	———	.1	.6	1.5	3.0								
VARIANCE-CUMULATIVE		-.3	-.4	-.1	+.7								
EST. TO COMPL-CUMULATIVE	········					4.2	5.4	6.4	7.2	8.0	8.5	8.8	9.0

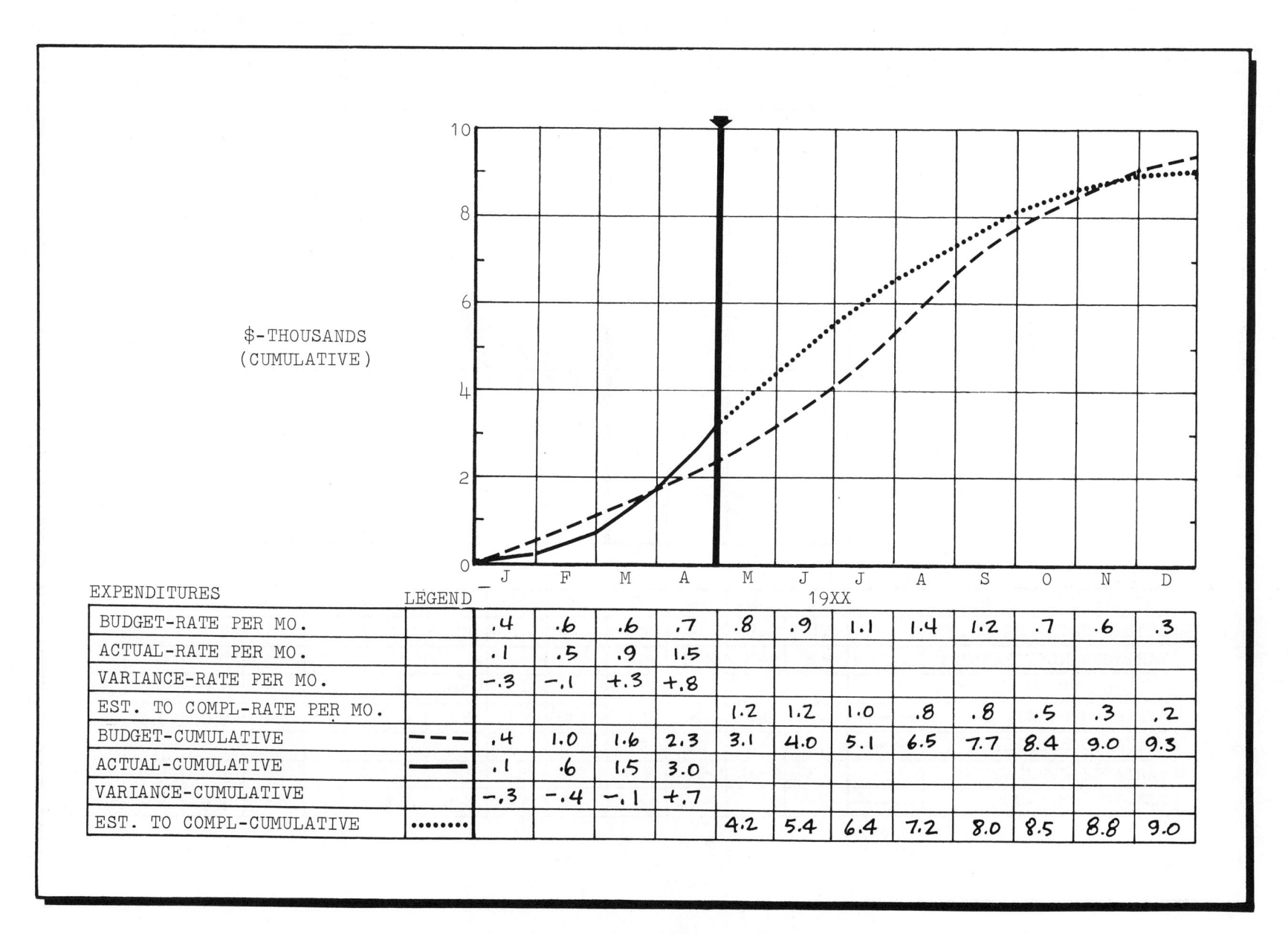

Figure 7.15   Budget—Summary—Version 15

EXPENDITURES:	LEGEND:	J	F	M	A	M	J	J	A	S	O	N	D
BUDGET-RATE PER MO.		.4	.6	.6	.7	.8	.9	1.1	1.4	1.2	.7	.6	.3
ACTUAL-RATE PER MO.		.1	.5	.9	1.5								
VARIANCE-RATE PER MO.		−.3	−.1	+.3	+.8								
EST. TO COMPL-RATE / MO.						1.2	1.2	1.0	.8	.8	.5	.3	.2
BUDGET-CUMULATIVE	– – –	.4	1.0	1.6	2.3	3.1	4.0	5.1	6.5	7.7	8.4	9.0	9.3
ACTUAL-CUMULATIVE	——	.1	.6	1.5	3.0								
VARIANCE-CUMULATIVE		−.3	−.4	−.1	+.7								
EST. TO COMPL-CUM	....					4.2	5.4	6.4	7.2	8.0	8.5	8.8	9.0
OVER BUDGET	/////												

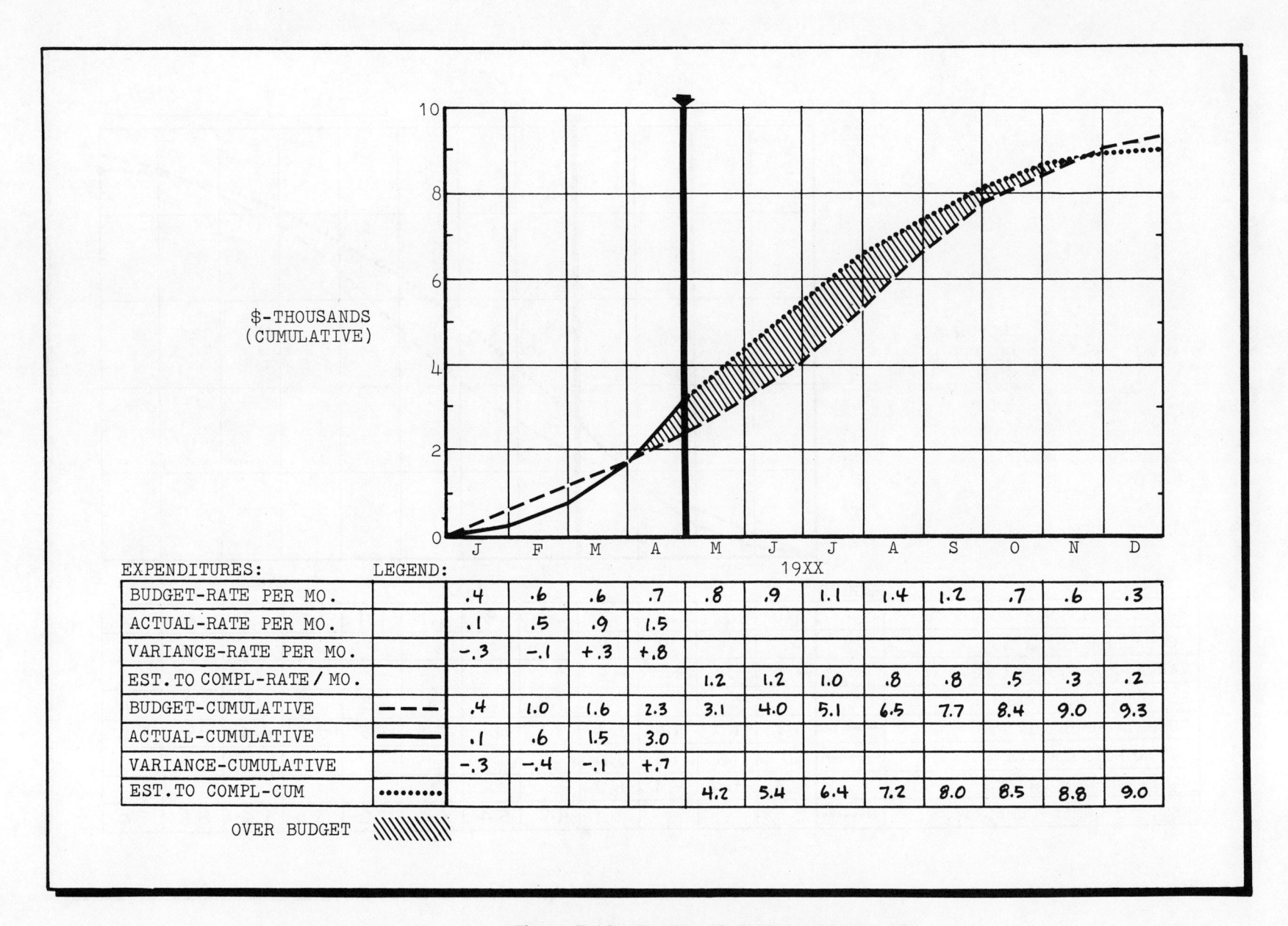

Figure 7.16   Budget—Summary—Version 16

EXPENDITURES:	LEGEND:	J	F	M	A	M	J	J	A	S	O	N	D
BUDGET-RATE PER MO		.4	.6	.6	.7	.8	.9	1.1	1.4	1.2	.7	.6	.3
ACTUAL-RATE PER MO.		.1	.5	.9	1.5								
VARIANCE-RATE PER MO.		-.3	-.1	+.3	+.8								
EST. TO COMPL-RATE PER MO.						1.2	1.2	1.0	.8	.8	.5	.3	.2
BUDGET-CUMULATIVE	– – –	.4	1.0	1.6	2.3	3.1	4.0	5.1	6.5	7.7	8.4	9.0	9.3
ACTUAL-CUMULATIVE	▥▥▥	.1	.6	1.5	3.0								
VARIANCE-CUMULATIVE		-.3	-.4	-.1	+.7								
EST. TO COMPL-CUMULATIVE	········					4.2	5.4	6.4	7.2	8.0	8.5	8.8	9.0

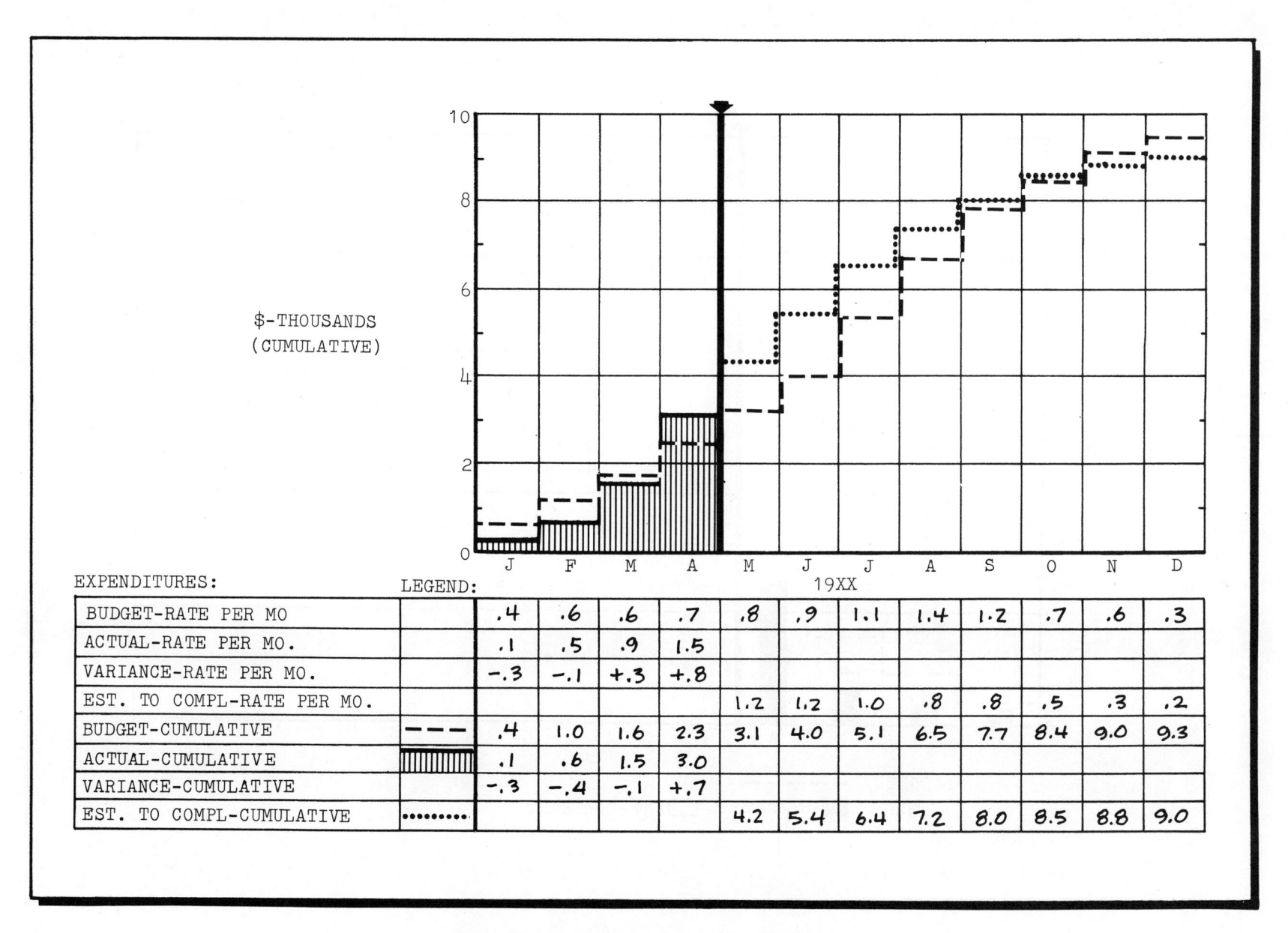

Figure 7.17   Budget—Summary—Version 17

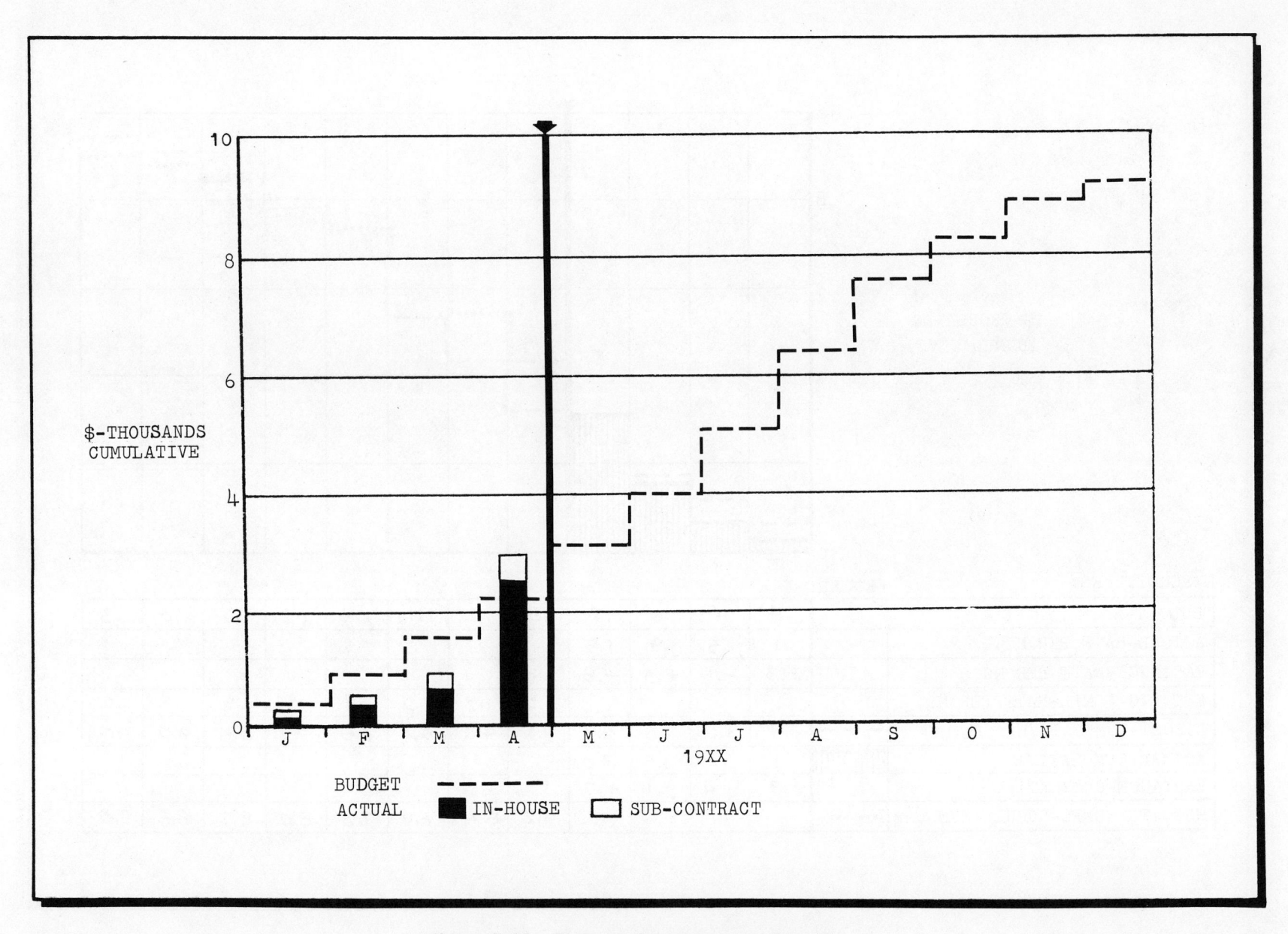

Figure 7.18   Budget—Summary—Version 18

$-THOUSANDS
(RATE PER MONTH)

EXPENDITURES:	LEGEND:	J	F	M	A	M	J	J	A	S	O	N	D
BUDGET-RATE PER MO.	▨	.4	.6	.6	.7	.8	.9	1.1	1.4	1.2	.7	.6	.3
ACTUAL-RATE PER MO.	■	.1	.5	.9	1.5	1.1							
VARIANCE-RATE PER MO.		-.3	-.1	+.3	+.8	+.3							
EST. TO COMPL-RATE PER MO.	▩						1.2	1.2	1.0	.8	.8	.5	.3	.2
BUDGET-CUMULATIVE		.4	1.0	1.6	2.3	3.1	4.0	5.1	6.5	7.7	8.4	9.0	9.3
ACTUAL-CUMULATIVE		.1	.6	1.5	3.0	4.1							
VARIANCE-CUMULATIVE		-.3	-.4	-.1	+.7	+1.0							
EST. TO COMPL-CUMULATIVE							4.2	5.4	6.4	7.2	8.0	8.5	8.8	9.0

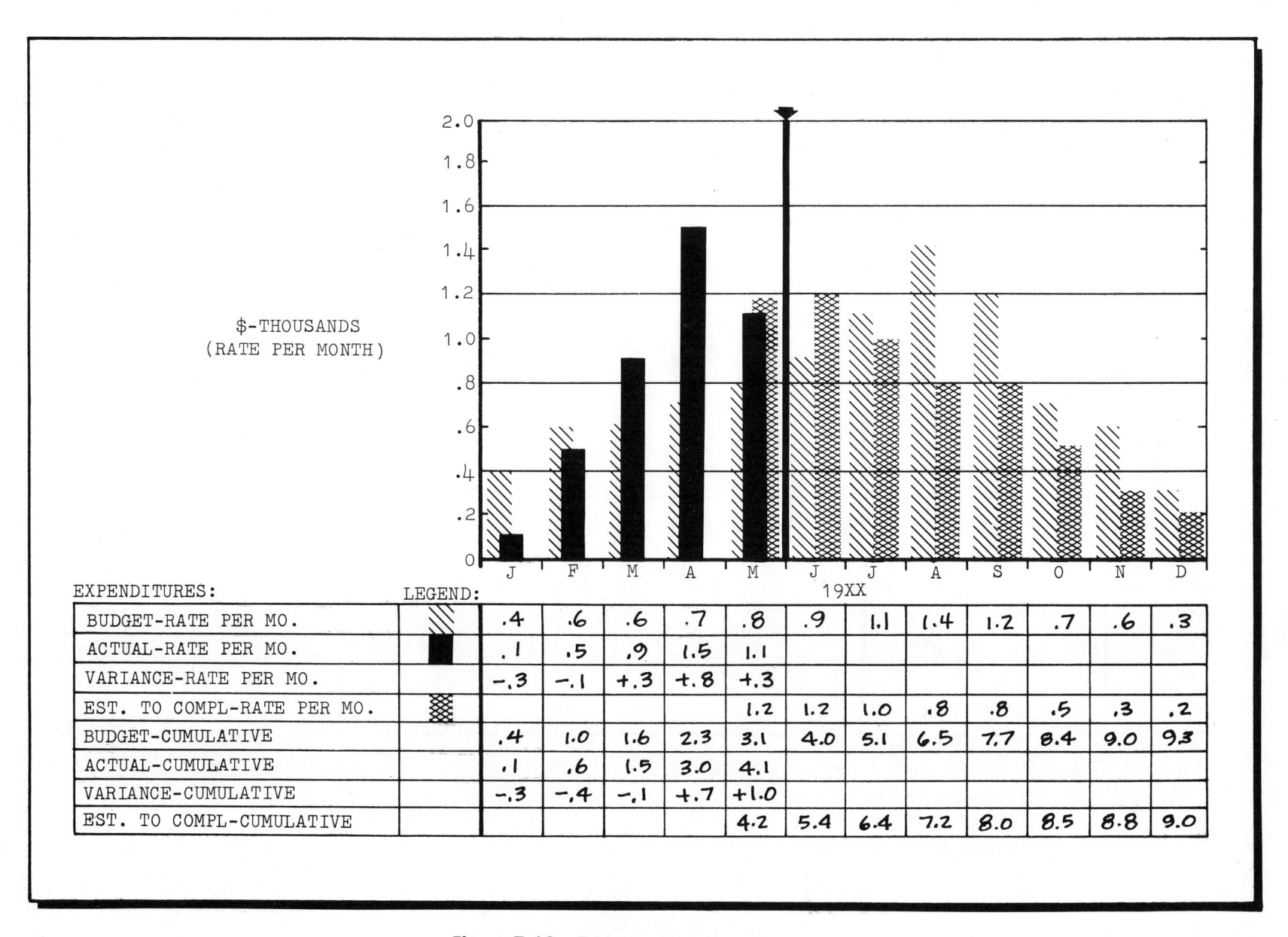

Figure 7.19   Budget—Summary—Version 19

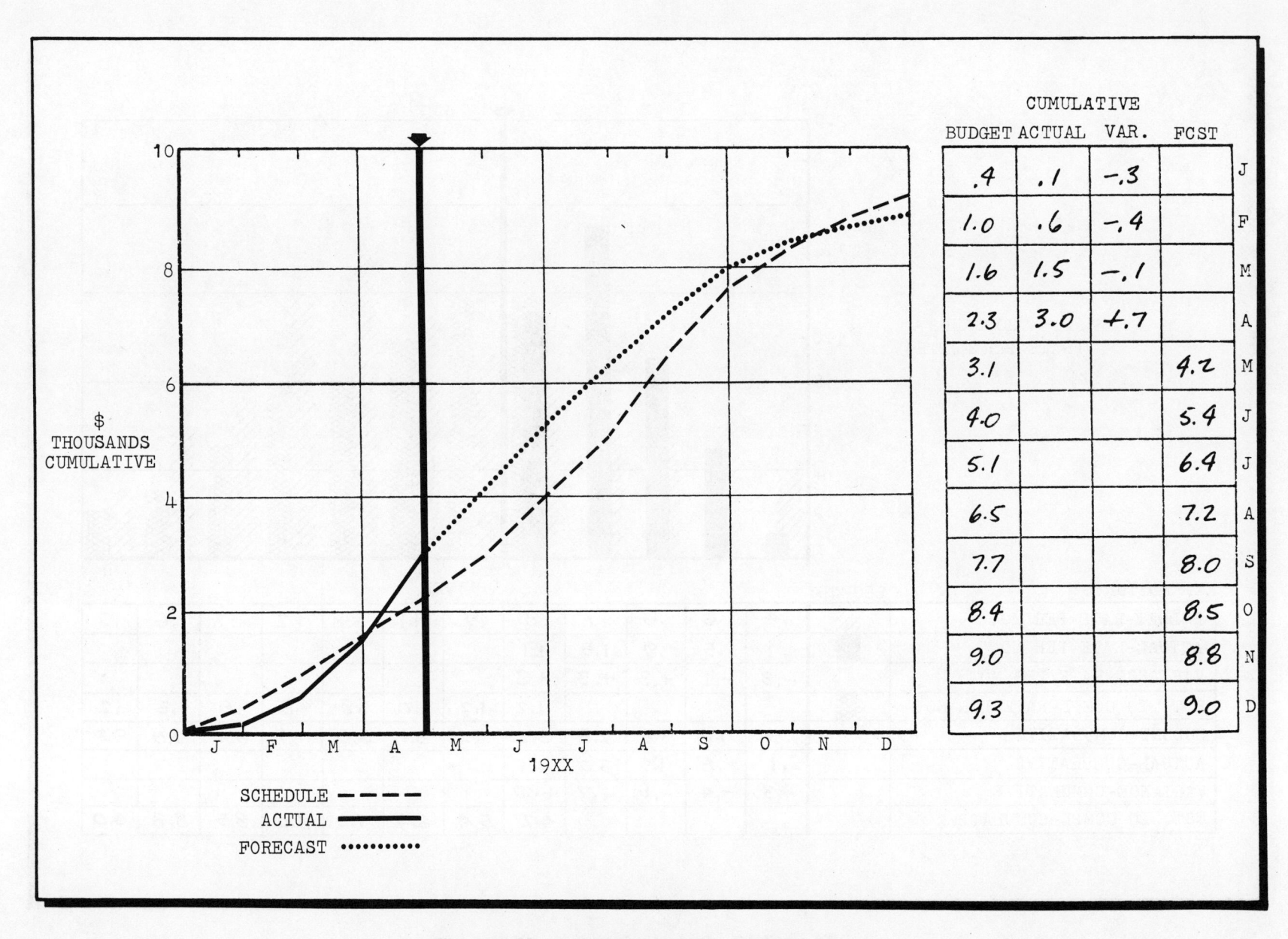

CUMULATIVE				
BUDGET	ACTUAL	VAR.	FCST	
.4	.1	-.3		J
1.0	.6	-.4		F
1.6	1.5	-.1		M
2.3	3.0	+.7		A
3.1			4.2	M
4.0			5.4	J
5.1			6.4	J
6.5			7.2	A
7.7			8.0	S
8.4			8.5	O
9.0			8.8	N
9.3			9.0	D

SCHEDULE -- -- --
ACTUAL ———
FORECAST ....

Figure 7.20   Budget—Summary—Version 20

$-THOUSANDS
(CUMULATIVE)

$-THOUSANDS
(RATE PER MONTH)

19XX

EXPENDITURES:	LEGEND:	J	F	M	A	M	J	J	A	S	O	N	D
BUDGET-RATE PER MO.	-----	.4	.6	.6	.7	.8	.9	1.1	1.4	1.2	.7	.6	.3
ACTUAL-RATE PER MO.	■	.1	.5	.9	1.5								
VARIANCE-RATE PER MO.		-.3	-.1	+.3	+.8								
EST. TO COMPL-RATE PER MO.	·······					1.2	1.2	1.0	.8	.8	.5	.3	.2
BUDGET-CUMULATIVE	-----	.4	1.0	1.6	2.3	3.1	4.0	5.1	6.5	7.7	8.4	9.0	9.3
ACTUAL-CUMULATIVE	——	.1	.6	1.5	3.0								
VARIANCE-CUMULATIVE		-.3	-.4	-.1	+.7								
EST. TO COMPL-CUMULATIVE	·······					4.2	5.4	6.4	7.2	8.0	8.5	8.9	9.0

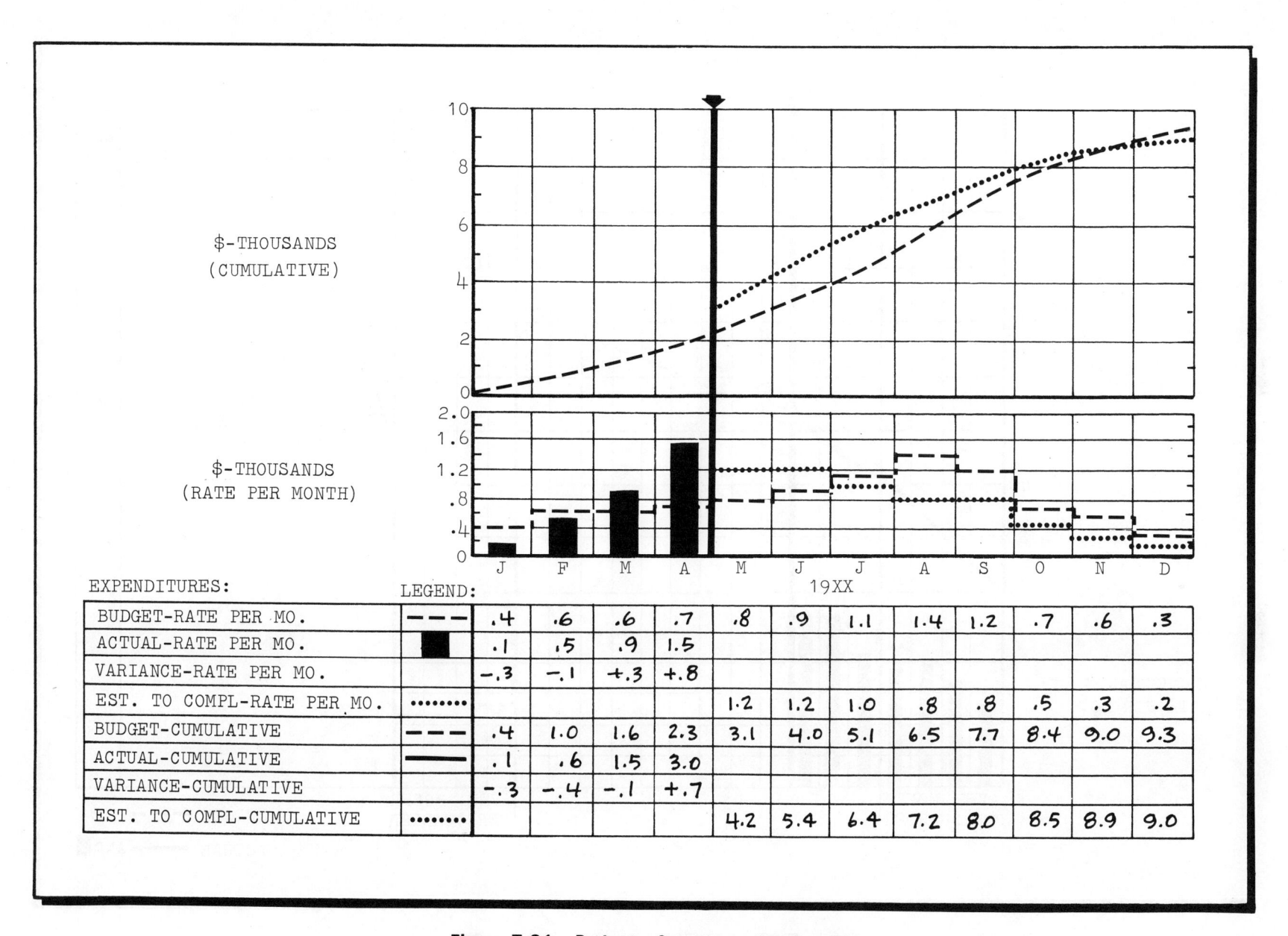

Figure 7.21   Budget—Summary—Version 21

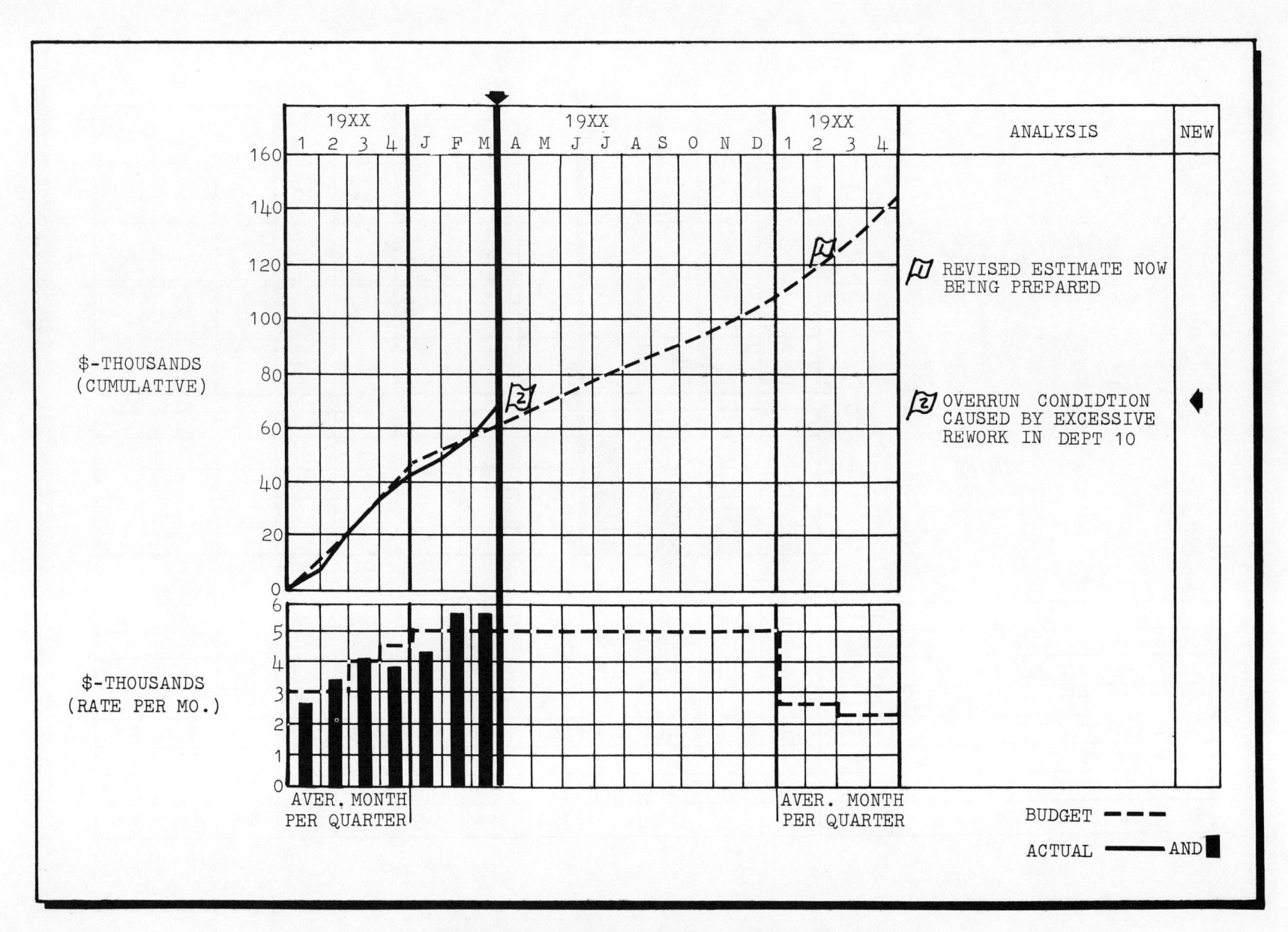

Figure 7.22 Budget—Summary—Version 22

92

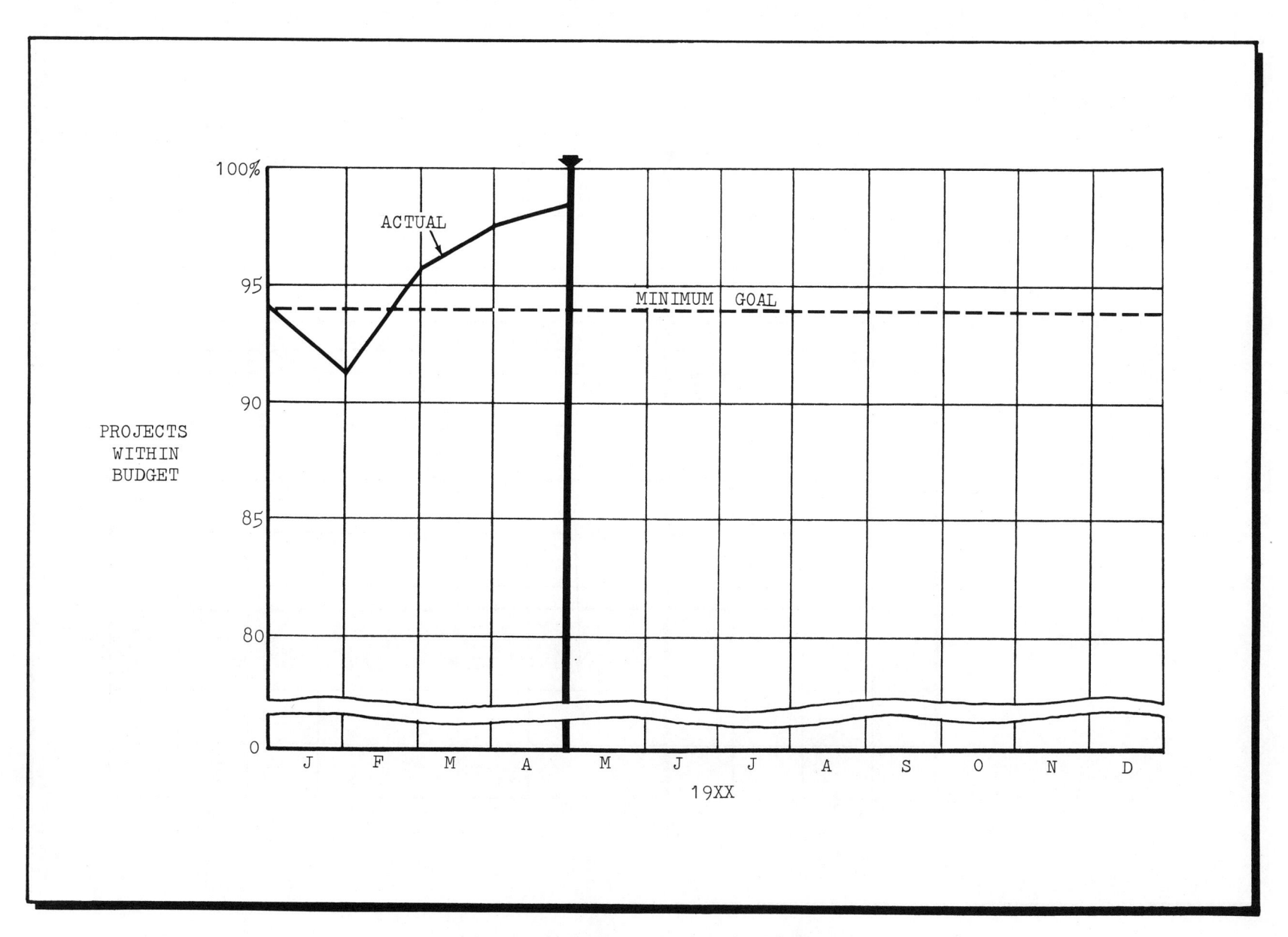

Figure 7.23   Budget—Summary—Version 23

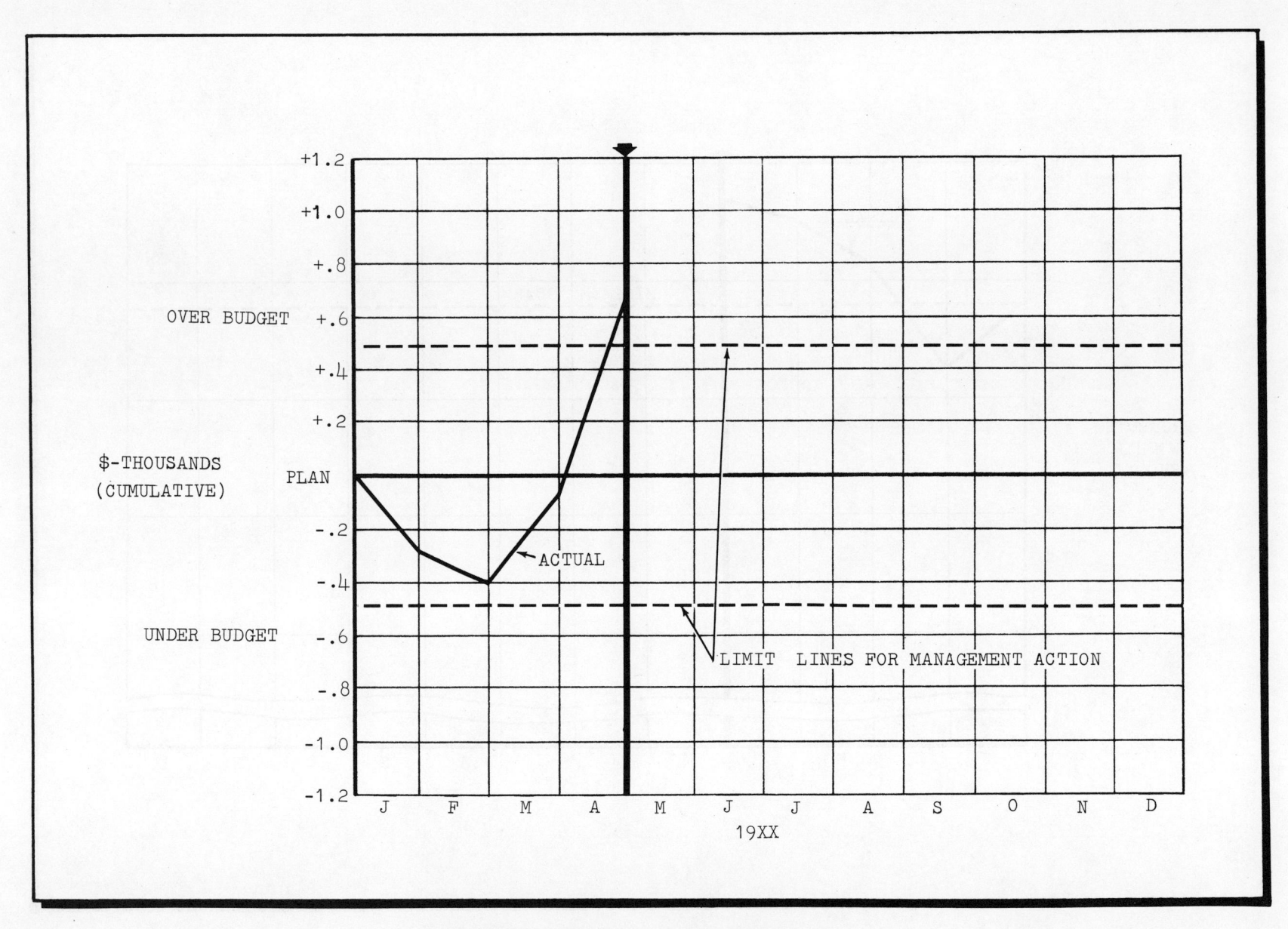

Figure 7.24 Budget—Summary—Version 24

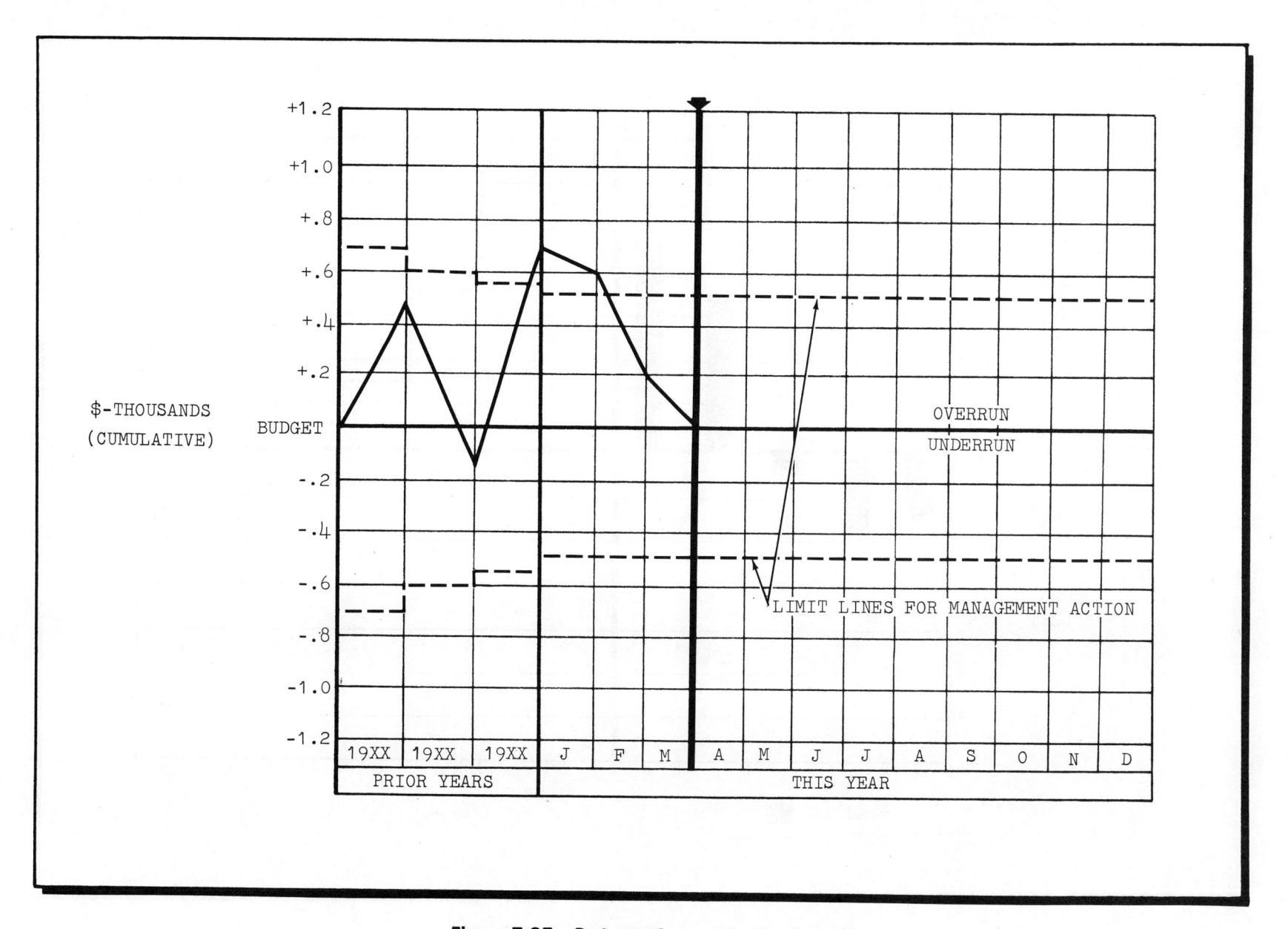

Figure 7.25 Budget—Summary—Version 25

95

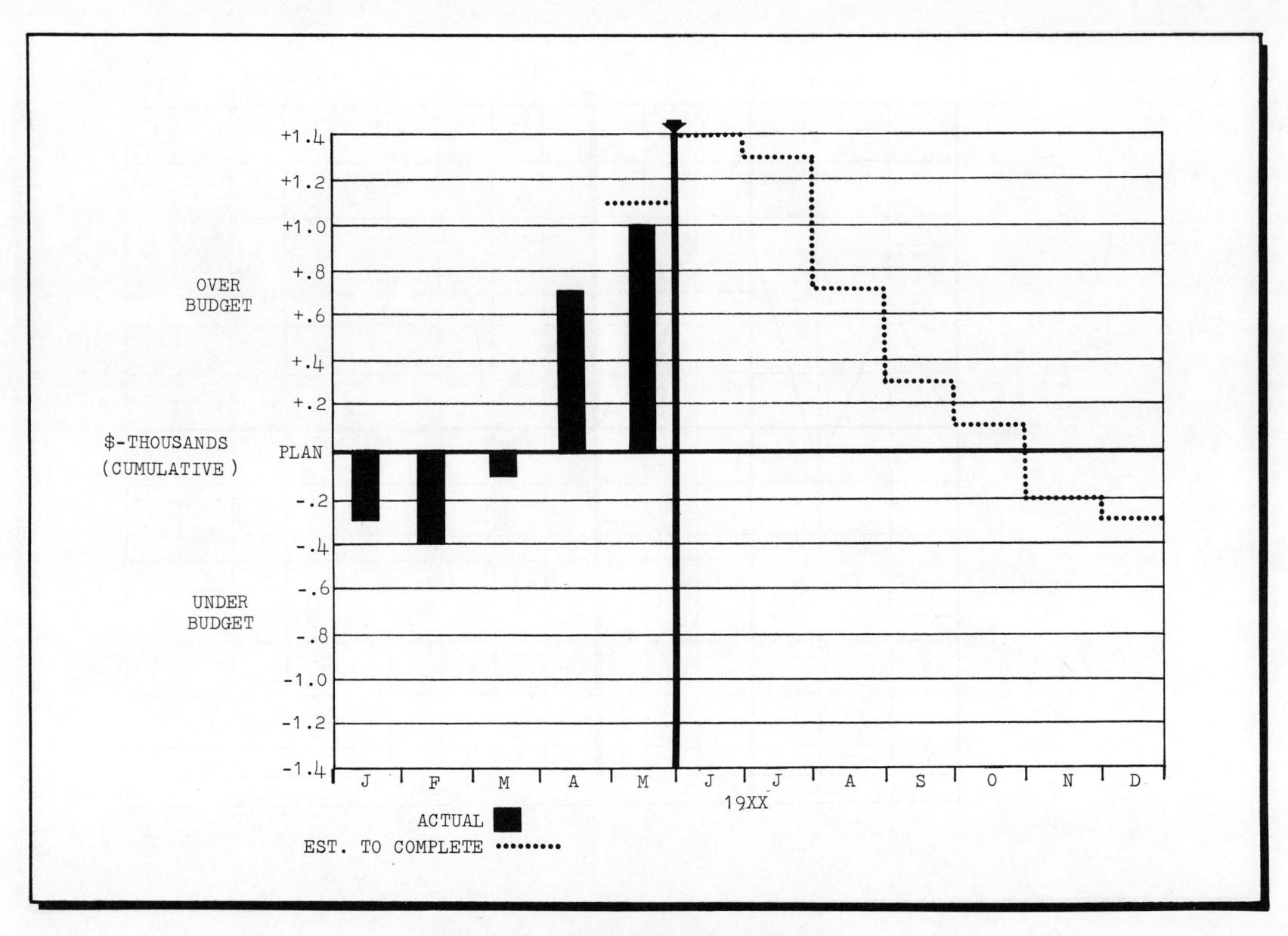

Figure 7.26   Budget—Summary—Version 26

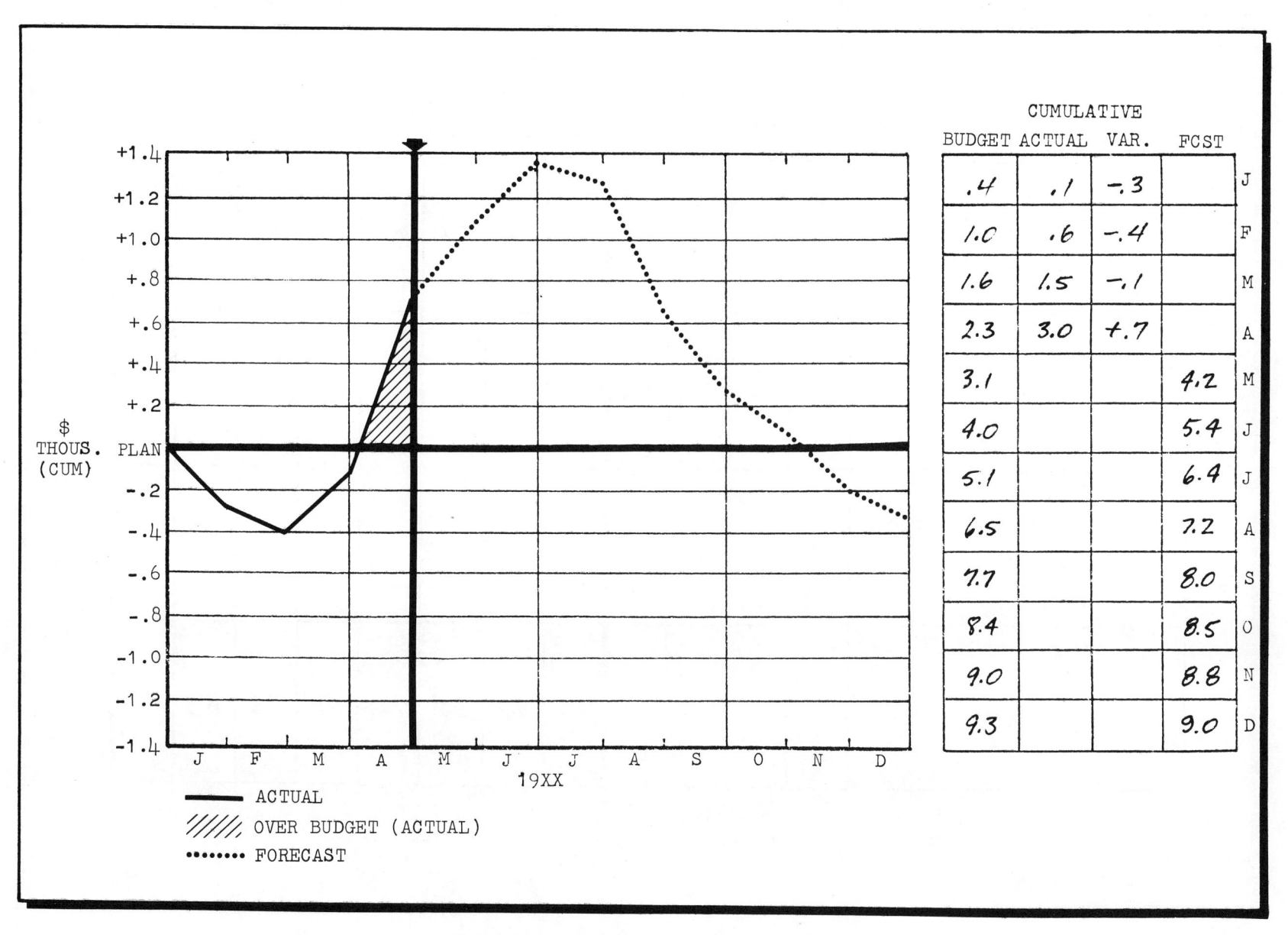

CUMULATIVE				
BUDGET	ACTUAL	VAR.	FCST	
.4	.1	-.3		J
1.0	.6	-.4		F
1.6	1.5	-.1		M
2.3	3.0	+.7		A
3.1			4.2	M
4.0			5.4	J
5.1			6.4	J
6.5			7.2	A
7.7			8.0	S
8.4			8.5	O
9.0			8.8	N
9.3			9.0	D

——— ACTUAL
////// OVER BUDGET (ACTUAL)
••••••• FORECAST

Figure 7.27   Budget—Summary—Version 27

EXPENDITURES-CUMULATIVE

	J	F	M	A	M	J	J	A	S	O	N	D
BUDGET	.4	1.0	1.6	2.3	3.1	4.0	5.1	6.5	7.7	8.4	9.0	9.3
ACTUAL	.1	.6	1.5	3.0								
VARIANCE	-.3	-.4	-.1	+.7								
ESTIMATE TO COMPLETE					4.2	5.4	6.4	7.2	8.0	8.5	8.8	9.0

19XX

Figure 7.28   Budget—Summary—Version 28

EXPENDITURES

	J	F	M	A	M	J	J	A	S	O	N	D
BUDGET-RATE PER MO.	.4	.6	.6	.7	.8	.9	1.1	1.4	1.2	.7	.6	.3
ACTUAL-RATE PER MO.	.1	.5	.9	1.5								
VARIANCE-RATE PER MO.	-.3	-.1	+.3	+.8								
EST. TO COMPL.-RATE PER MO.					1.2	1.2	1.0	.8	.8	.5	.3	.2
BUDGET-CUMULATIVE	.4	1.0	1.6	2.3	3.1	4.0	5.1	6.5	7.7	8.4	9.0	9.3
ACTUAL-CUMULATIVE	.1	.6	1.5	3.0								
VARIANCE-CUMULATIVE	-.3	-.4	-.1	(+.7)								
EST. TO COMPL.-CUMULATIVE					4.2	5.4	6.4	7.2	8.0	8.5	8.8	9.0

19XX

Figure 7.29 Budget—Summary—Version 29

8.0 CASH FLOW

Cash flow is the sum of net income after all expenses and deductions, except depreciation, amortization, and stock dividends, have been made. Examples of cash flow charts are shown in this section.

8.1 Cash Flow—Version 1: Cash flow is normally examined on a quarterly or annual basis. Version 1, Figure 8.1, compares the current year's cash flow against the previous year on a quarterly basis. The columns which display actuals for the current year are segmented to show dividends, depreciation, and retained earnings.

8.2 Cash Flow—Version 2: Cash flow is shown on a per share basis in Version 2 of a cash flow tracking chart, Figure 8.2. The columns that represent the current year's quarterly actuals, and the dashed step lines that show the previous year's actuals, are divided so as to show the proportions of net income and depreciation to the total.

8.3 Cash Flow—Version 3: A surface chart version of a cash flow chart is shown in Figure 8.3. This example, which is not a tracking chart, compares cash flow per common share over a ten-year time span.

8.4 Cash Flow—Version 4: Version 4 of a cash flow chart, Figure 8.4, is identical to Version 3 except that a column chart style is used in this example. The columns are subdivided to show the proportions of depreciation and net income to the total cash flow per share.

8.5 Cash Flow—Version 5: A column chart style with the columns segmented as to dividends, depreciation, and retained earnings is shown as Version 5 of a cash flow chart, Figure 8.5. As with Versions 3 and 4, this is a non-tracking style of chart.

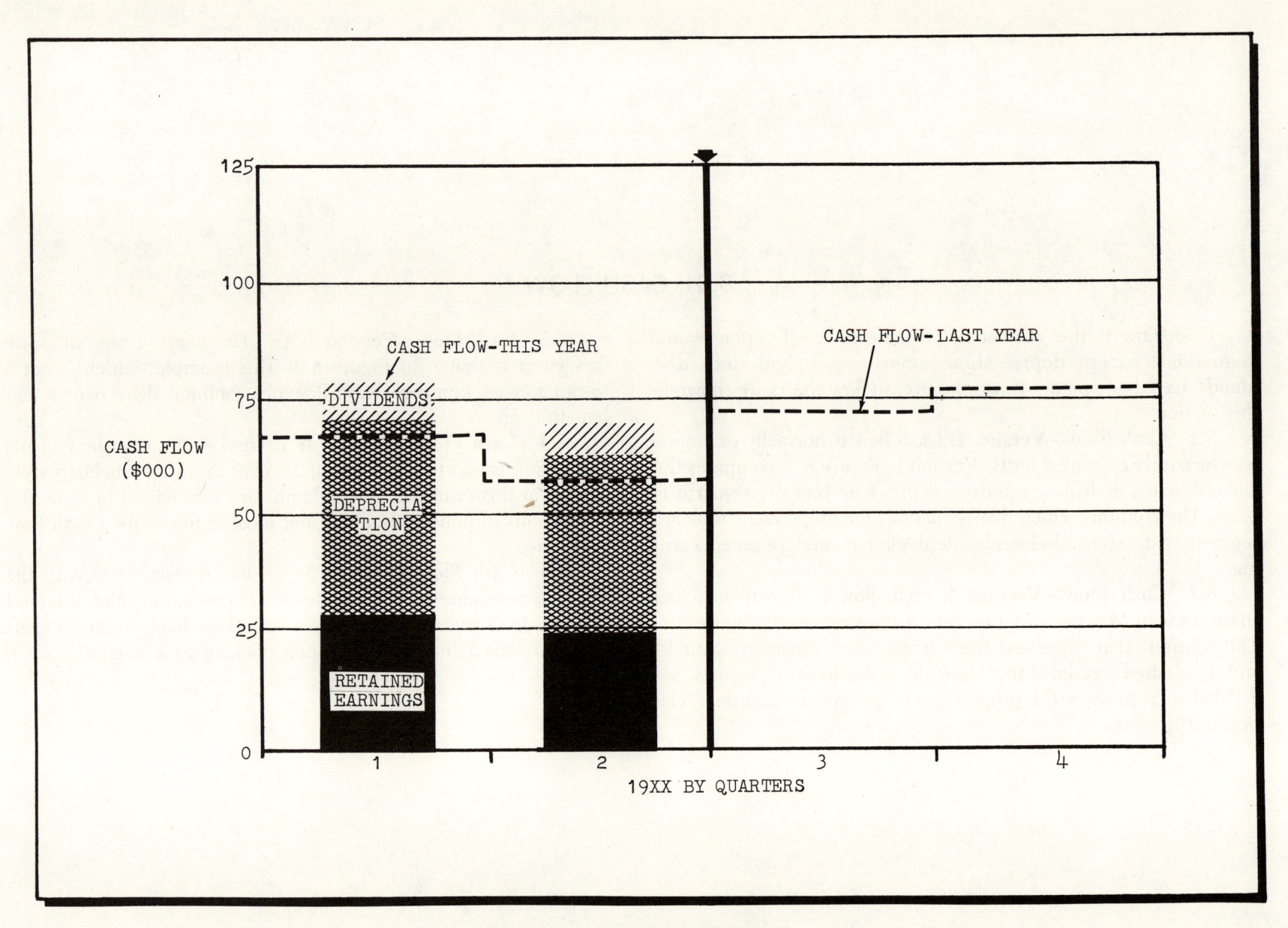

Figure 8.1   Cash Flow—Version 1

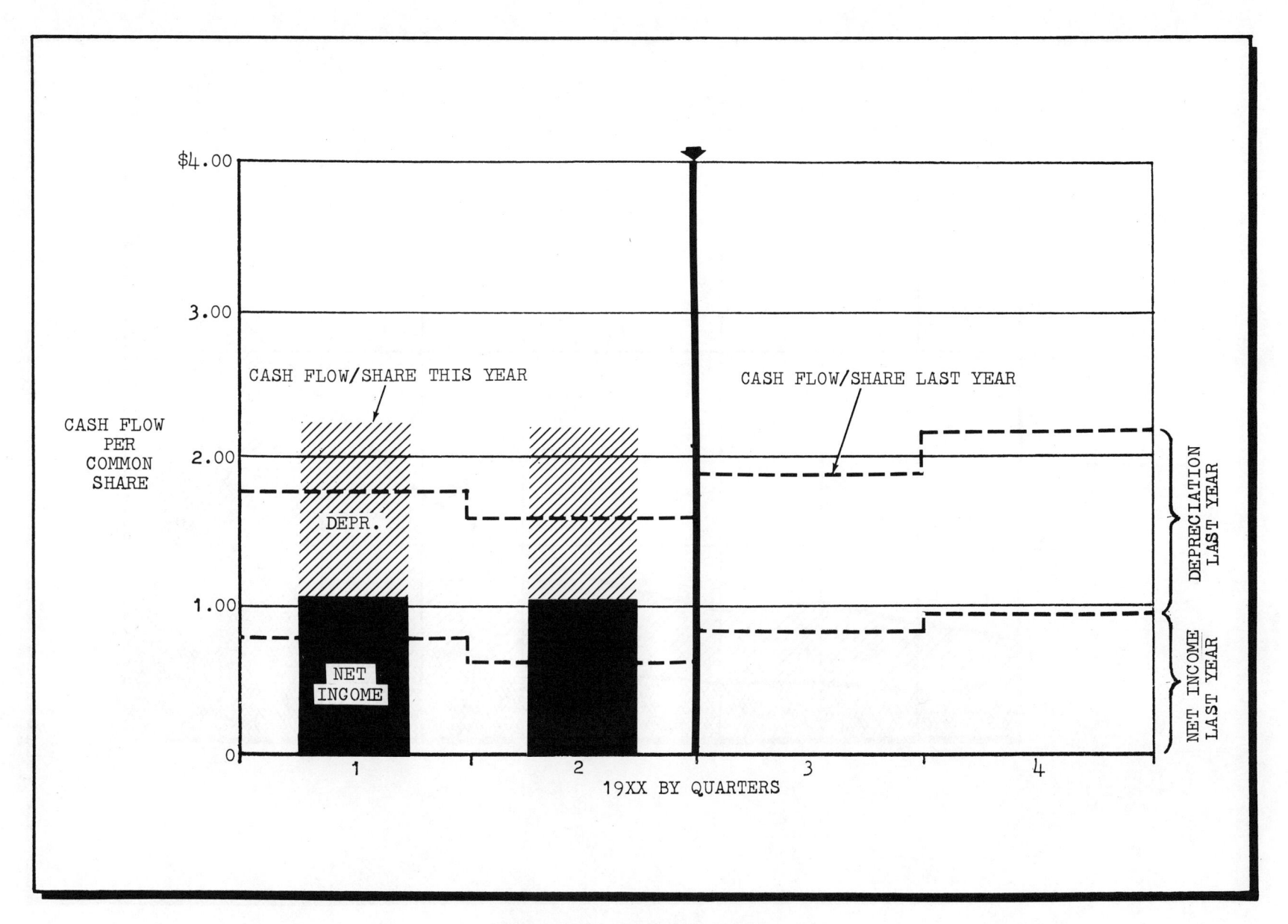

Figure 8.2 Cash Flow—Version 2

103

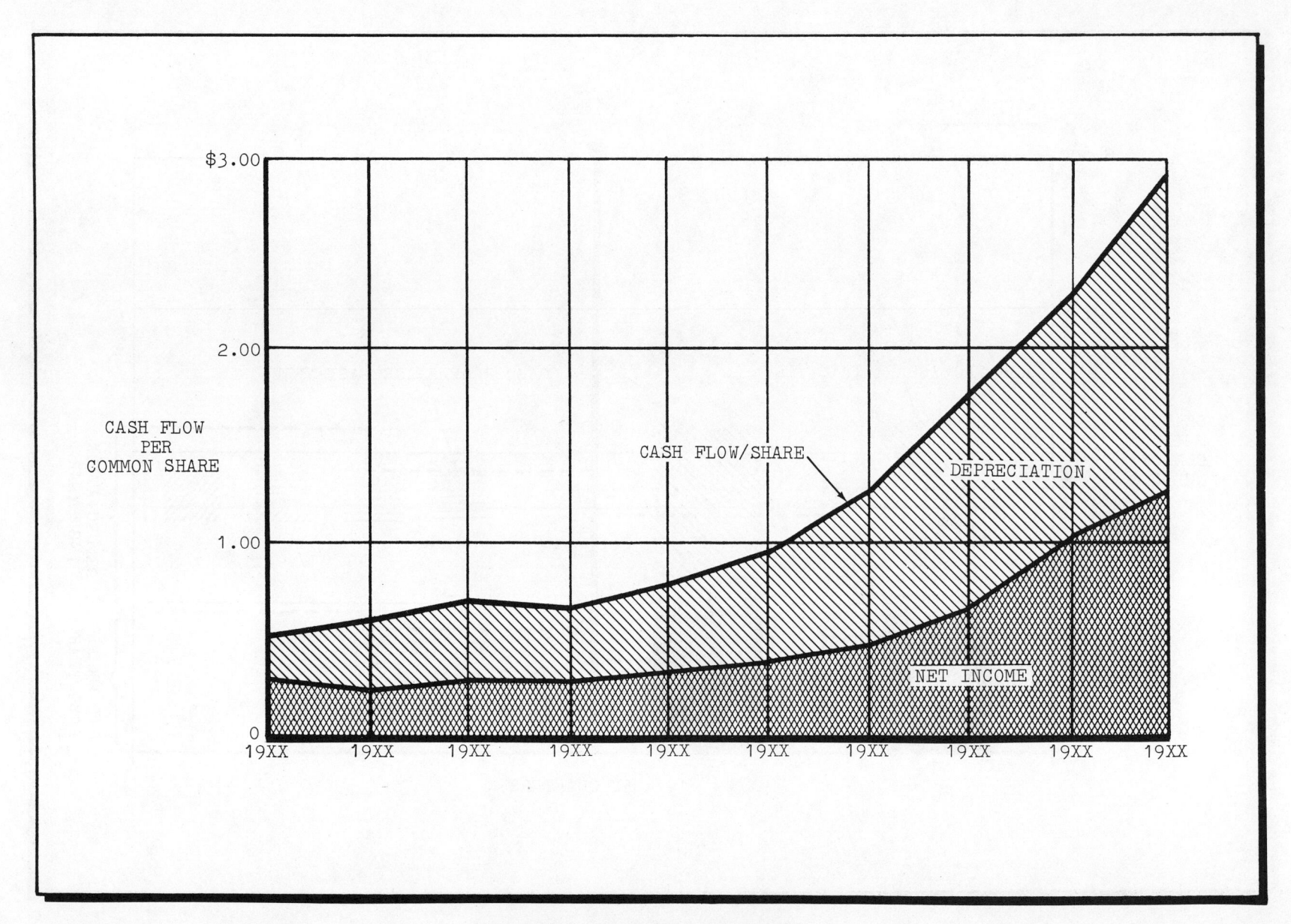

Figure 8.3 Cash Flow—Version 3

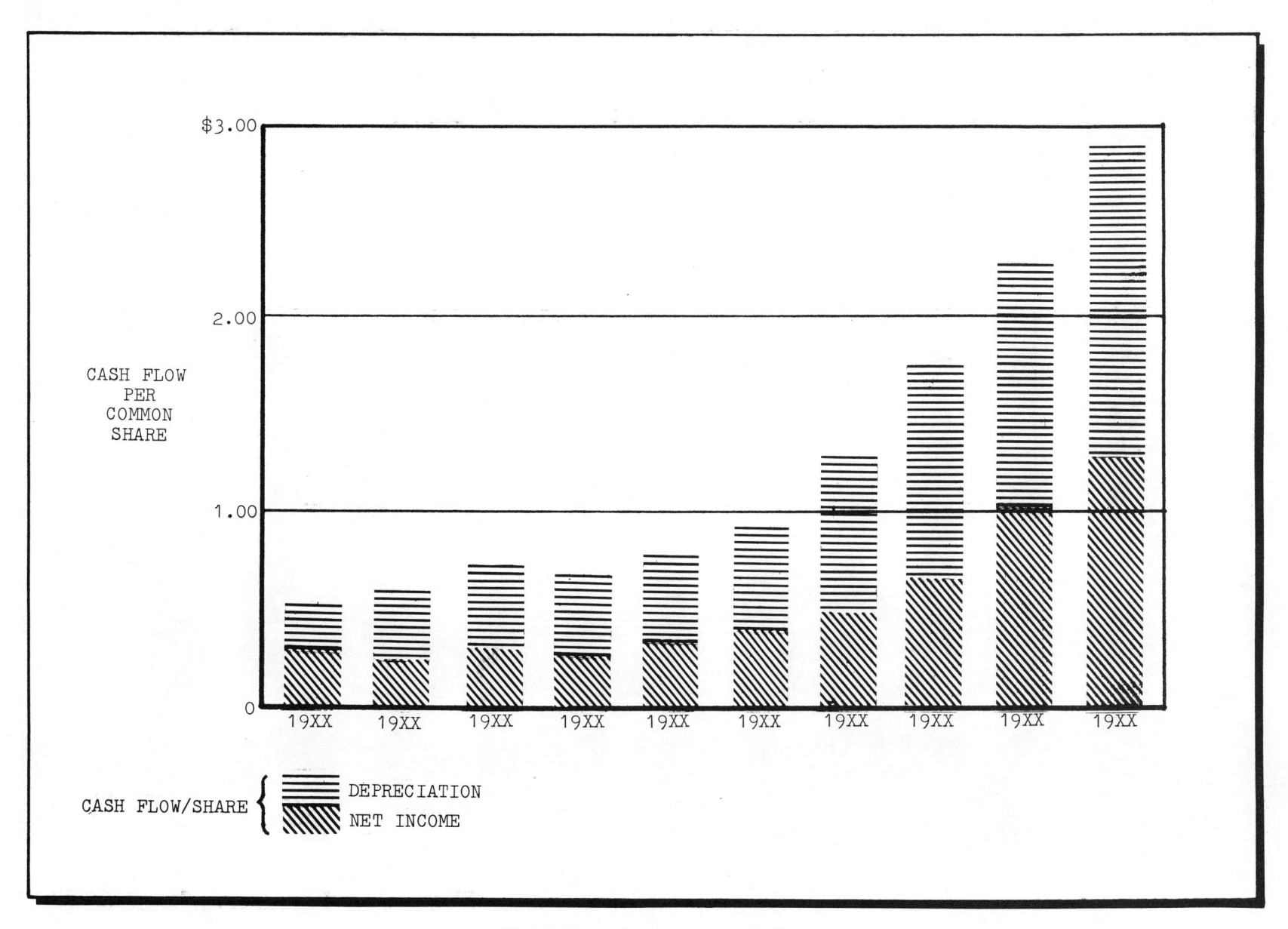

Figure 8.4   Cash Flow—Version 4

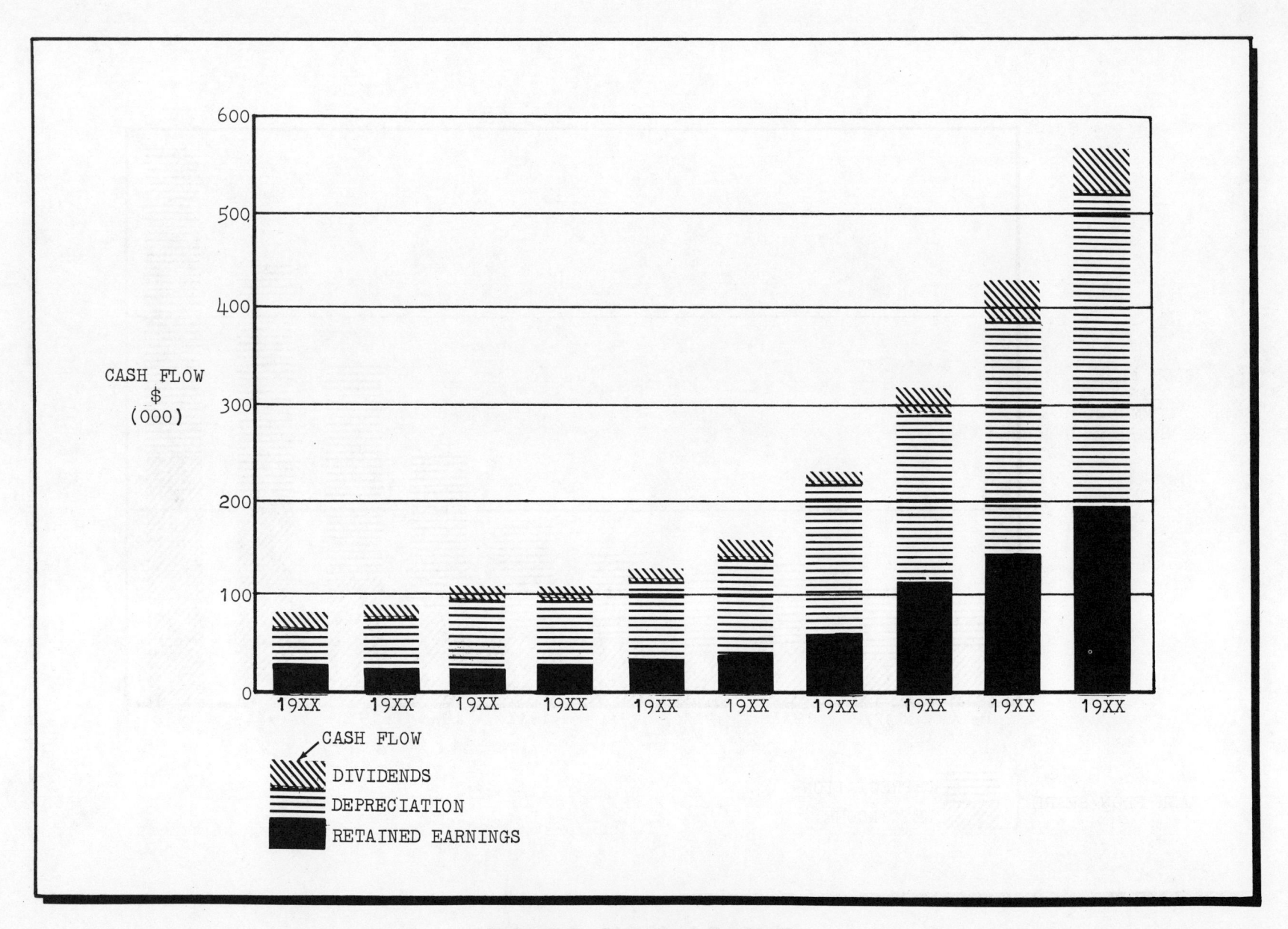

Figure 8.5   Cash Flow—Version 5

9.0 COST COMPARISONS

Charts that compare costs with related factors such as employment or performance during a previous time period are shown in this section. Charts showing costs in terms of actual expenditures versus planned expenditures will be found in the "Budget" sections of this encyclopedia. Also see Section 10.0, *Costs as a Percent of Sales* and Section 57.0, *Unit Cost/Time*.

9.1 Cost Comparisons—Version 1: In Version 1 of a cost comparison chart, Figure 9.1, the current year's delivery costs are compared to that of the previous year. In this example, costs are on a cumulative basis with the previous year's costs shown with a dashed line, and the current year's costs to date shown with a solid line.

9.2 Cost Comparisons—Version 2: A column chart style is used in Version 2 of a cost comparison chart, Figure 9.2. In this example, advertising costs for the current year (solid columns) are compared with the corresponding costs of the previous year (hatched columns) on a month-by-month basis.

9.3 Cost Comparisons—Version 3: Version 3 of a cost comparison chart, Figure 9.3, displays the monthly telephone costs in relationship to the number of employees. The left-hand amount scale is in terms of dollars, and the right-hand scale is in terms of the number of employees. This particular example shows a significant increase in telephone costs despite the fact that employment has remained relatively stable.

9.4 Cost Comparisons—Version 4: Rework and scrap costs for the current year are compared to those of the previous year in Version 4 of a cost comparison chart, Figure 9.4. In this particular example, a segment of time has been cross-hatched to indicate when a new material handling program was introduced resulting in a significant drop in monthly costs.

9.5 Cost Comparisons—Version 5: Details of a cost improvement program are shown in Version 5 of a cost comparison chart, Figure 9.5. Planned cost improvements are shown in dashed step line form with numbers keyed to the right-hand side where each planned upward step in cost savings is explained. Actual costs savings to date are shown with a solid line.

9.6 Cost Comparisons—Version 6: The grid on Version 6 of a cost comparison chart, Figure 9.6, has been constructed to show costs as well as savings relative to a cost improvement program. The initial costs may be, for instance, an investment in new equipment. When the investment has been recovered, savings are both anticipated (dashed line) and actually being achieved (solid line).

9.7 Cost Comparisons—Version 7: Version 7 of a cost comparison chart, Figure 9.7, is a non-tracking style of column chart. The current year's average weekly payroll cost is compared to costs for the same factor for the previous nine years.

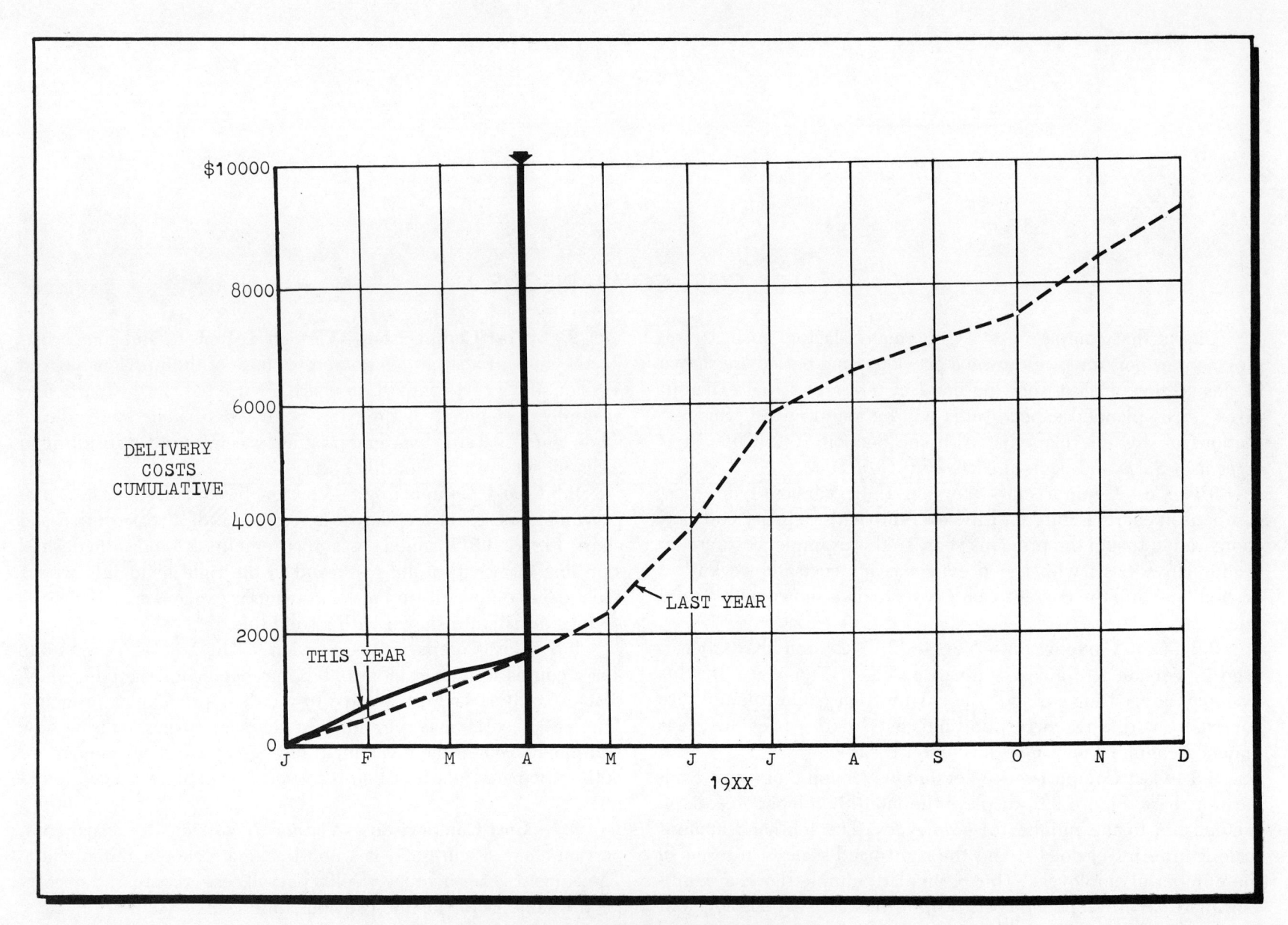

Figure 9.1 Cost Comparisons—Version 1

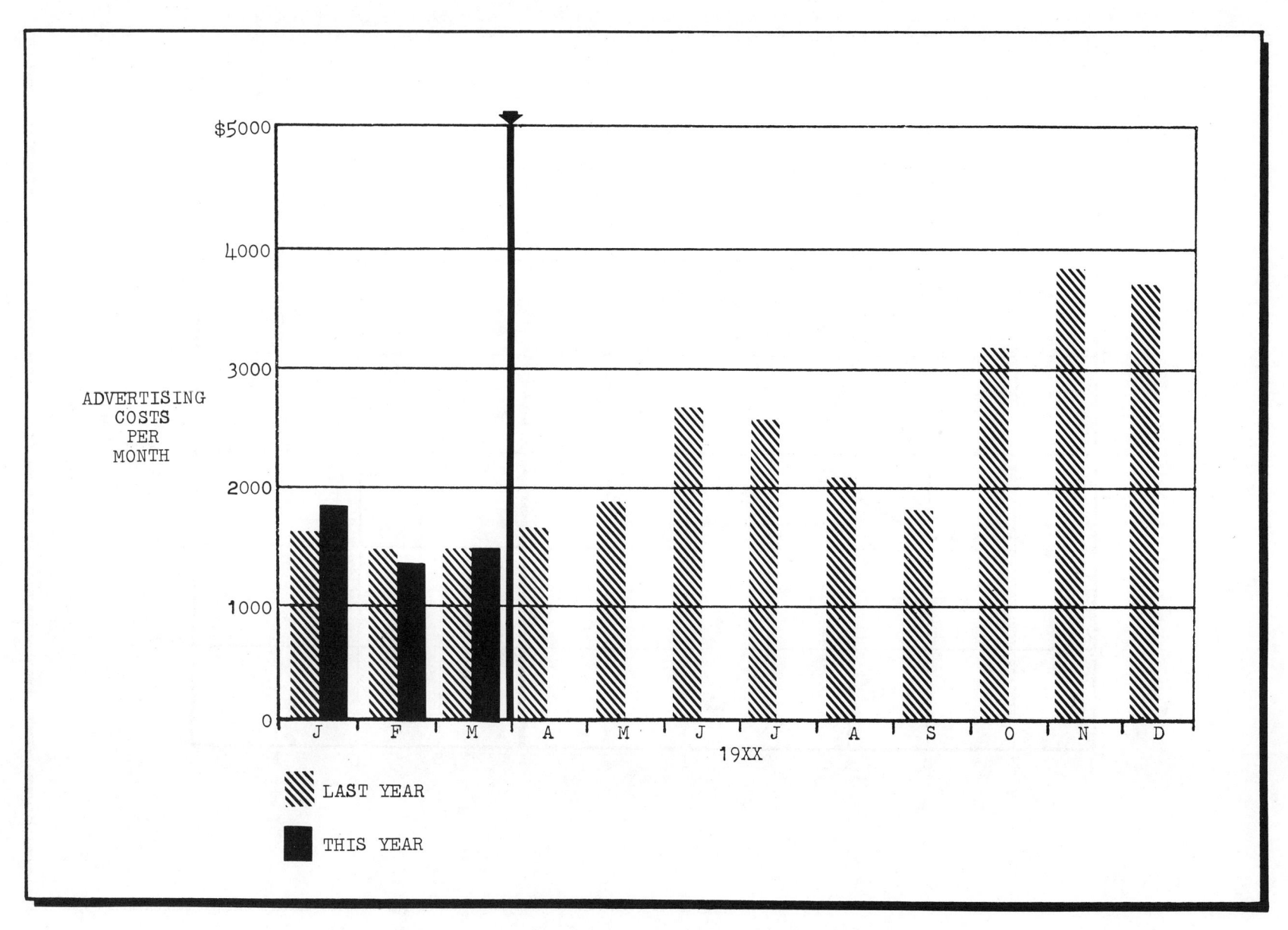

Figure 9.2 Cost Comparisons—Version 2

109

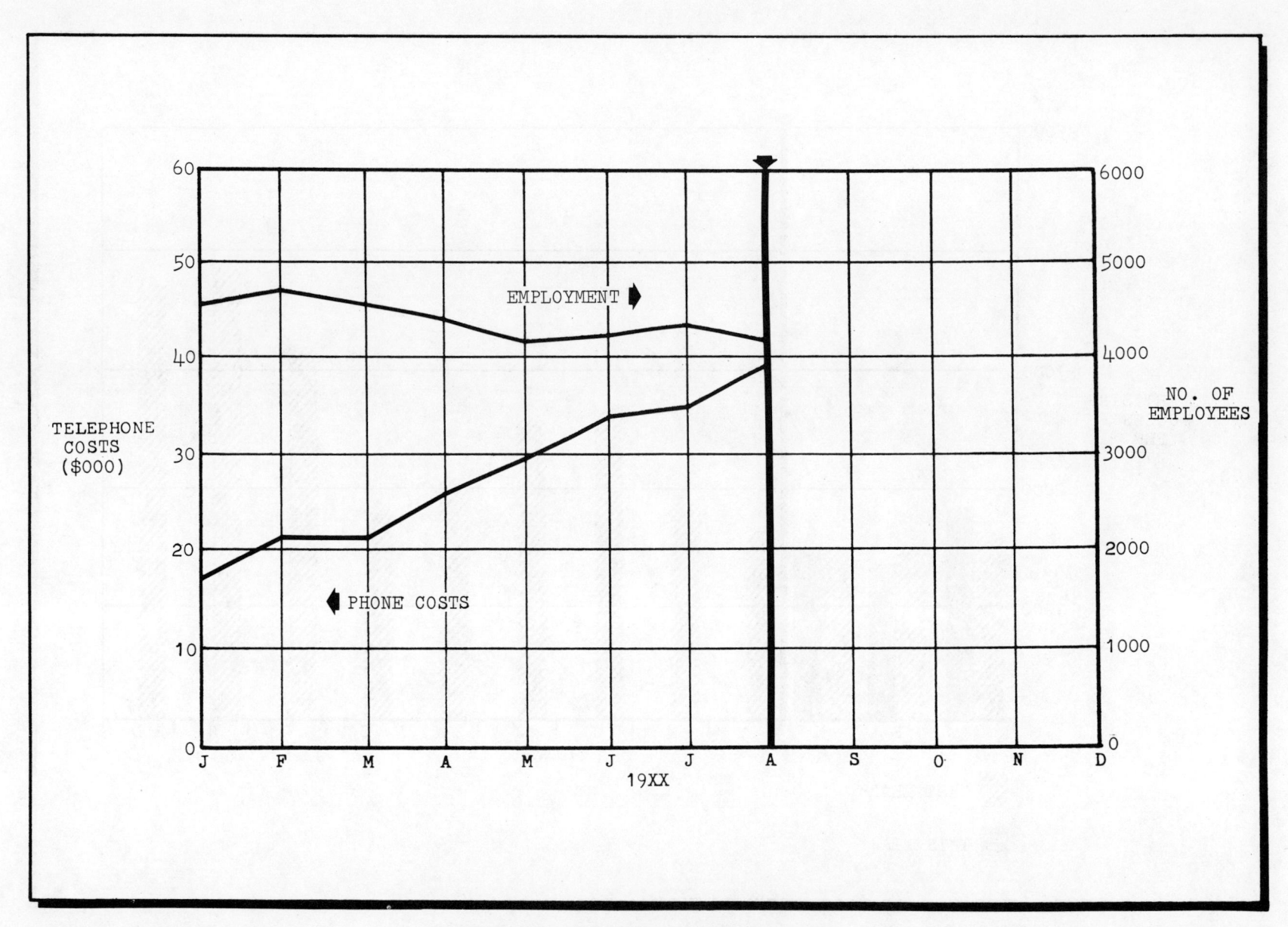

Figure 9.3 Cost Comparisons—Version 3

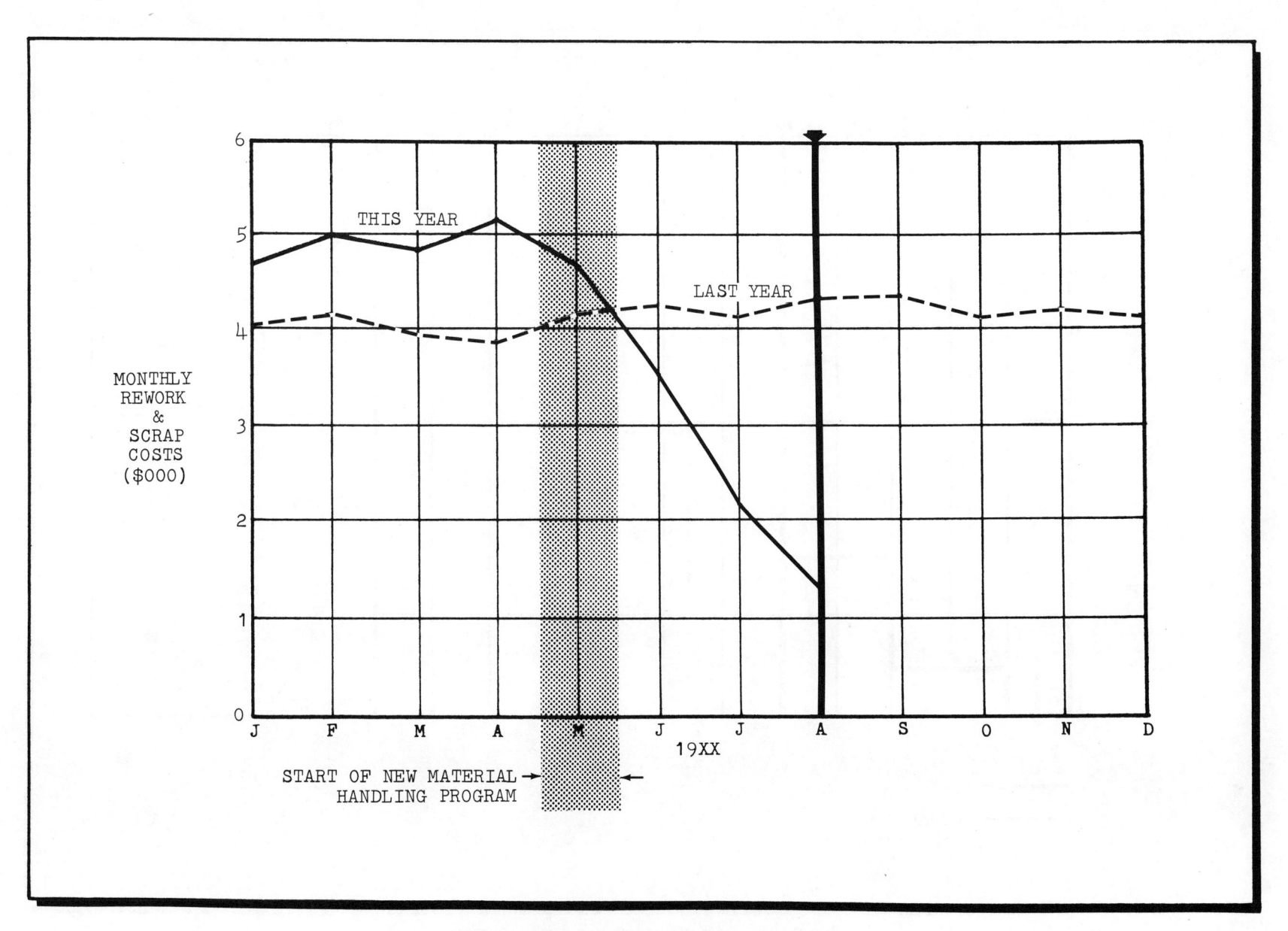

Figure 9.4   Cost Comparisons—Version 4

111

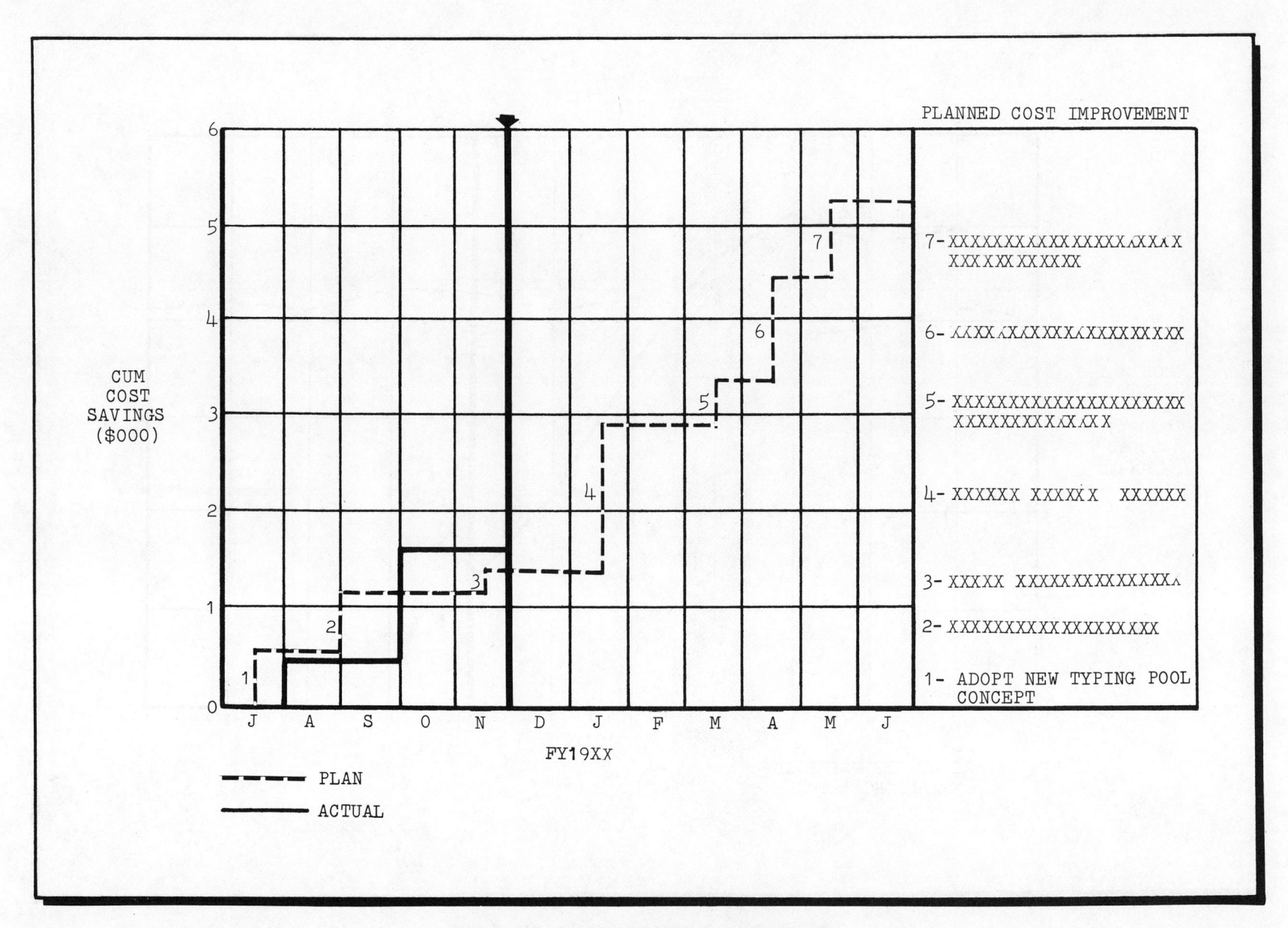

Figure 9.5   Cost Comparisons—Version 5

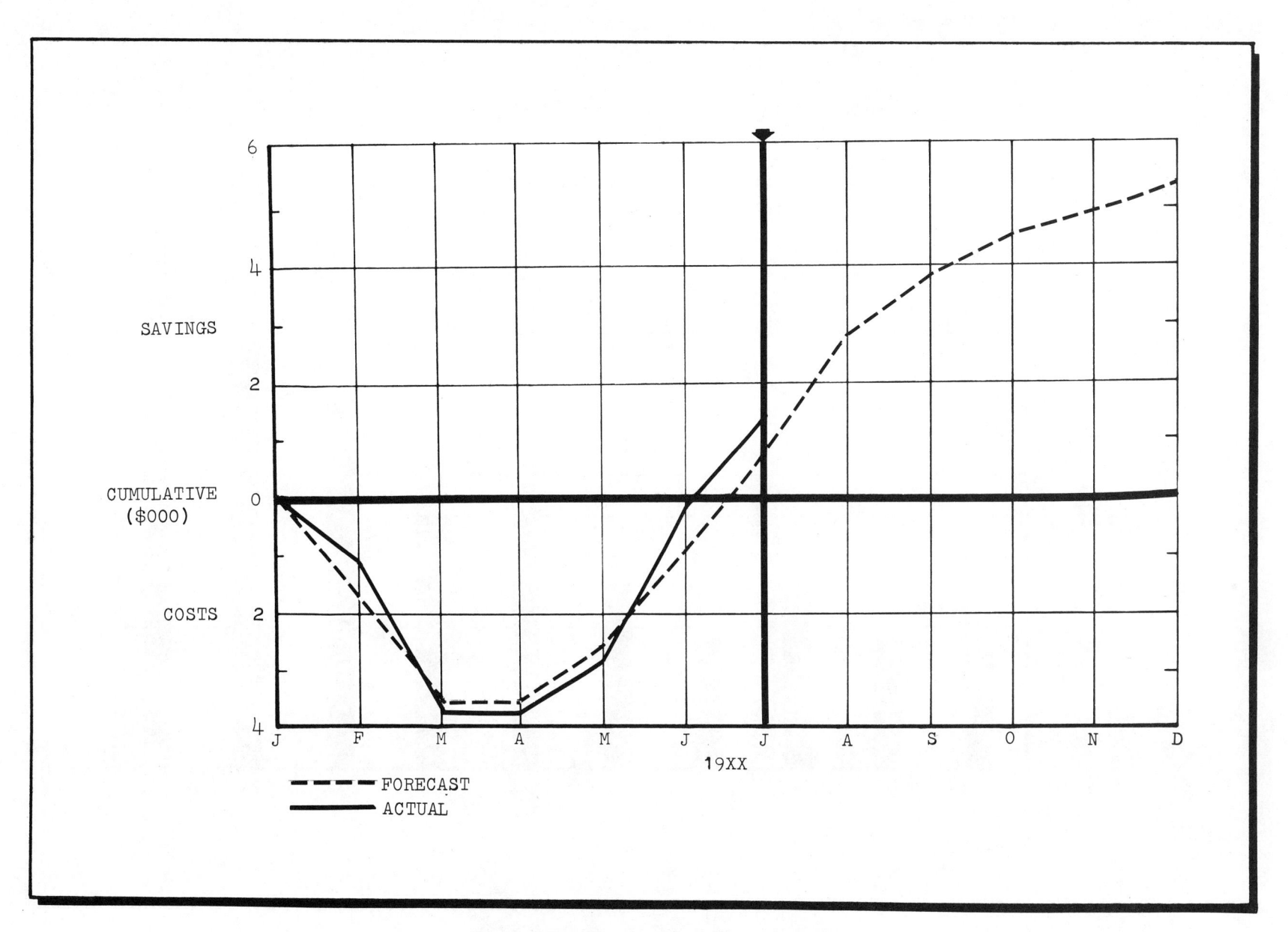

Figure 9.6   Cost Comparisons—Version 6

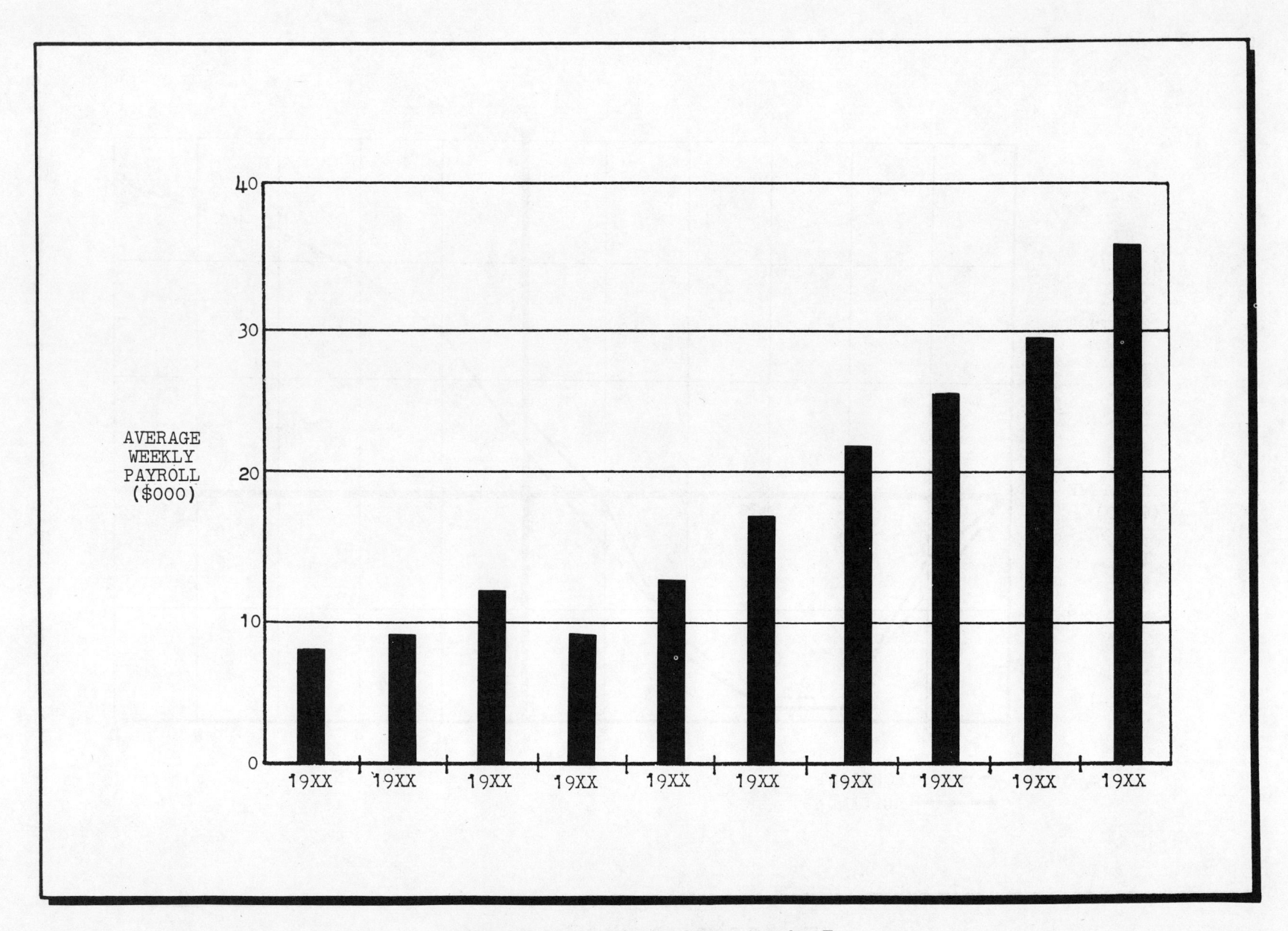

Figure 9.7 Cost Comparisons—Version 7

10.0 COSTS AS A PERCENT OF SALES

The ratio of costs to sales is an essential measurement in most businesses. This section shows methods for displaying various categories of costs and expenses as a percent of sales. Also see Section 44.0, *Revenue Versus Costs*.

10.1 Costs as a Percent of Sales—Version 1: A simple version of a costs as a percent of sales tracking chart is shown in Figure 10.1. In this example a goal of 76% has been established and is shown with a dashed line. Actuals to date (solid line) are plotted against this goal. An arrowhead has been used on the amount scale to emphasize that it does not start from a zero base. If the plotting were in terms of monthly operating costs to sales instead of monthly cost of goods to sales, the percentage would be called the Operating Ratio.

10.2 Costs as a Percent of Sales—Version 2: A column chart style has been combined with a line chart style in Version 2 of a costs as a percent of sales tracking chart, Figure 10.2. A dashed line is used in this example to show an industry average for selling expenses to sales. Such averages vary from one industry to the next, and the average for a given industry can usually be obtained from banks or trade associations. The actual ratio to date in Version 2 is shown with solid columns.

10.3 Costs as a Percent of Sales—Version 3: The ratio of manufacturing costs to sales is shown on Version 3 of a costs as a percent of sales tracking chart, Figure 10.3. In this example, actual performance to date (solid line with shading) is compared against two factors: the goal for the current year and the previous year's actual monthly ratios. A variation of this chart would be to use year-to-date averages instead of monthly figures.

10.4 Costs as a Percent of Sales—Version 4: Two amount scales are used in Version 4 of a costs as a percent of sales tracking chart, Figure 10.4. The left-hand scale is in terms of the dollar cost of goods, and is related to the columns. The right-hand scale is in terms of the percent of cost of goods to sales and is related to the line chart. An arrowhead on the right-hand column points out that the scale does not begin with zero.

10.5 Costs as a Percent of Sales—Version 5: A pair of grids is used in Version 5 of a costs as a percent of sales tracking chart, Figure 10.5. The upper grid shows forecasted and actual sales per month. The lower grid displays the ratio of the cost of goods to sales, with actuals plotted against a goal. In both grids, a broken line is used to indicate that the amount scales do not have zero bases.

10.6 Costs as a Percent of Sales—Version 6: Forecasted and actual sales dollars, selling expenses, and the ratio of selling expenses to sales are shown by quarters on side-by-side grids in Version 6, Figure 10.6. Each grid in this example has its own amount scale, the left-hand scale being the only one in this set that does not start from a zero base.

10.7 Costs as a Percent of Sales—Version 7: The ratio of costs to sales is shown in three categories in Version 7 of a costs as a percent of sales tracking chart, Figure 10.7. Plotting in this example is by quarters.

10.8 Costs as a Percent of Sales—Version 8: A statistical table has been combined with graphics in Version 8 of a costs as a percent of sales tracking chart, Figure 10.8. In this example, the graphic portion of the chart shows the monthly actuals (solid columns) plotted in relationship to the budget (dashed line). The statistical portion of the chart gives the corresponding dollar values including the variances between the budgeted and actual figures.

10.9 Costs as a Percent of Sales—Version 9: Version 9 of a costs as a percent of sales tracking chart, Figure 10.9, is identical to Version 8 except that additional statistics have been added to the tabular section of the chart.

10.10 Costs as a Percent of Sales—Version 10: A statistical table version of a costs as a percent of sales tracking chart is shown as Version 10, Figure 10.10. In this example, forecasted and actual sales dollars are given as well as the budgeted and actual manufacturing costs, the latter in both dollars and the ratio to sales.

10.11 Costs as a Percent of Sales—Version 11: Version 11 of a costs as a percent of sales chart, Figure 10.11, is in the form of a one-time status report. This style of chart displays the planned and actual status for a single point in time without showing past or anticipated performance.

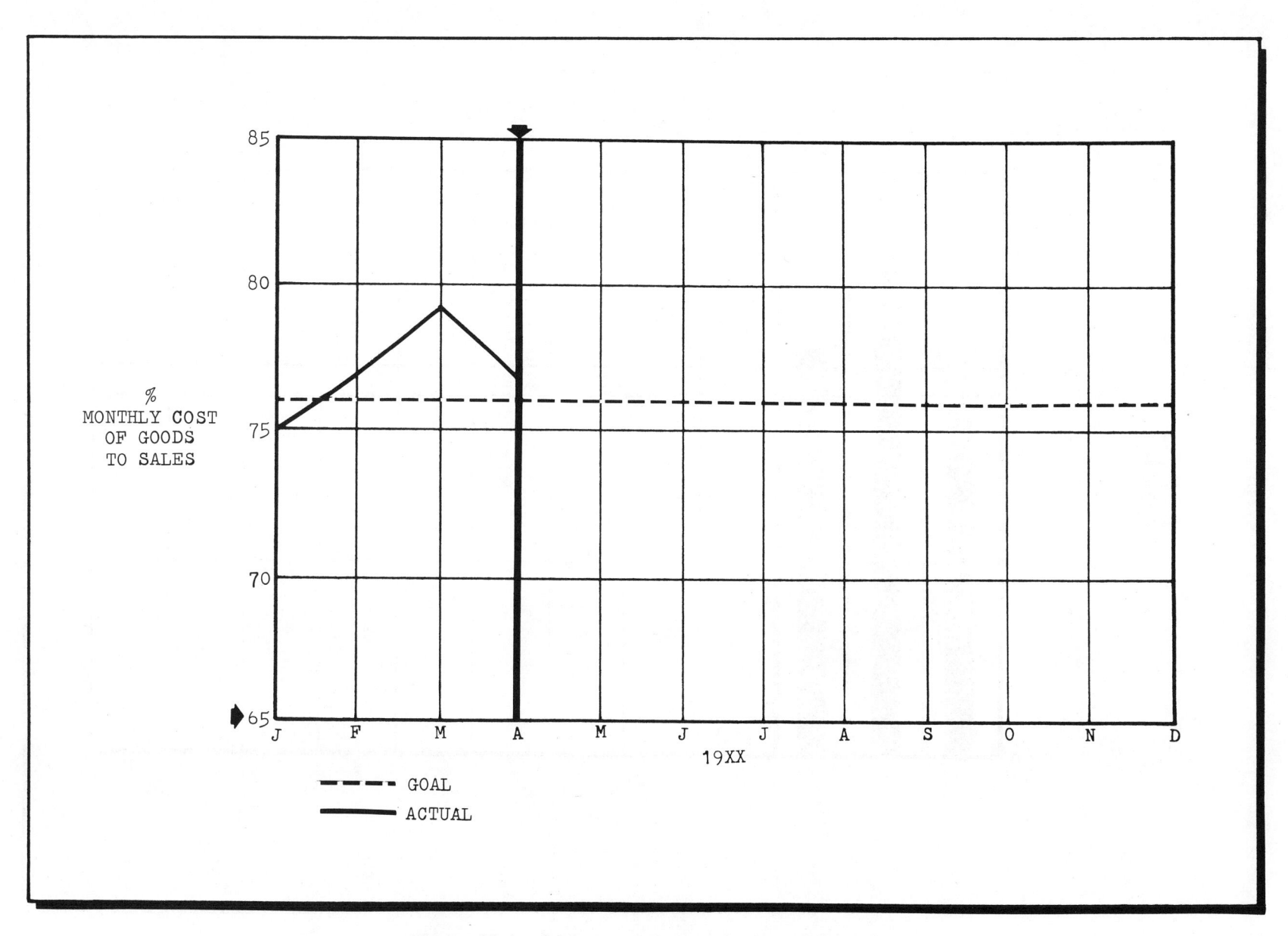

Figure 10.1 Costs as a Percent of Sales—Version 1

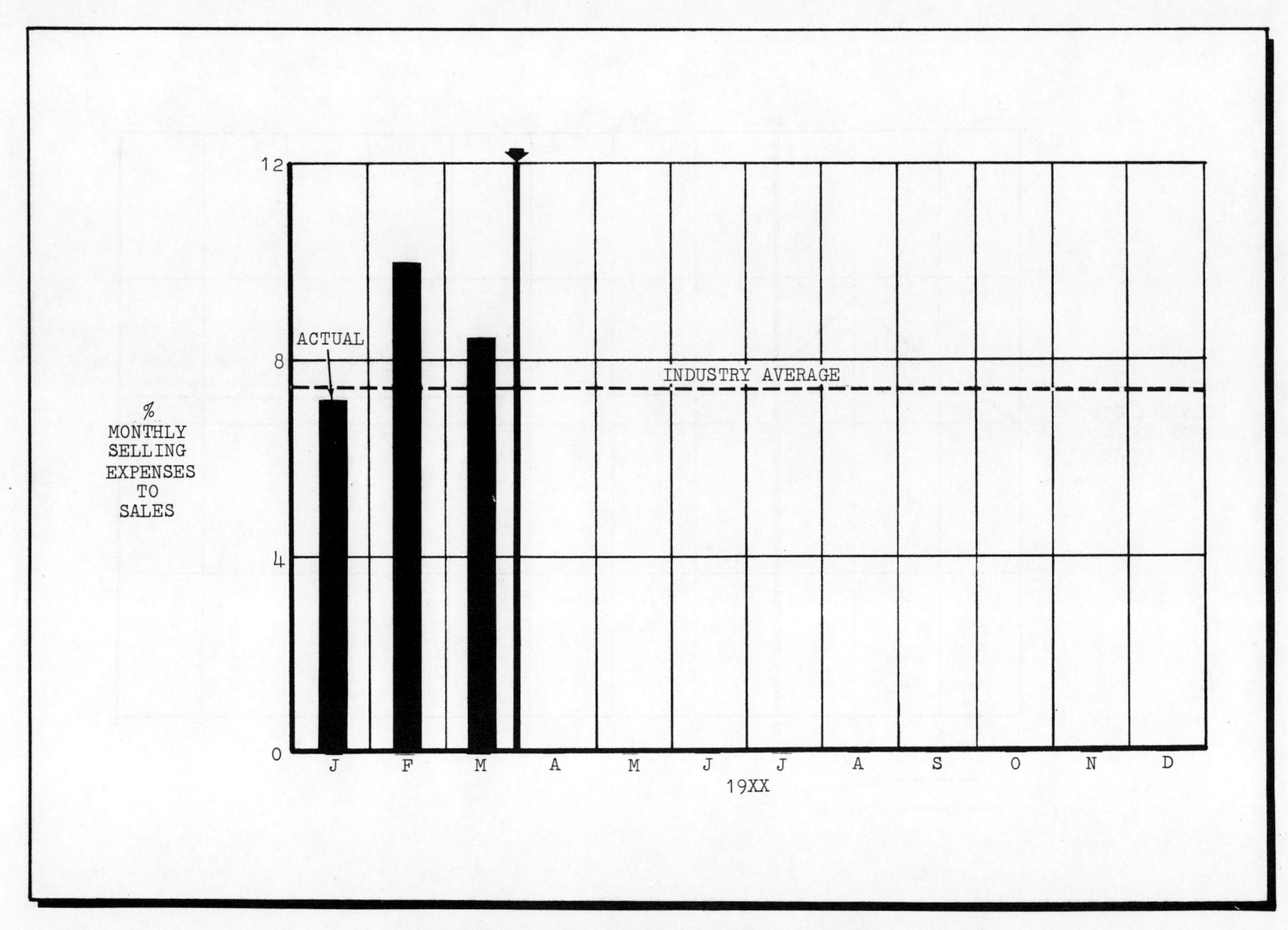

Figure 10.2 Costs as a Percent of Sales—Version 2

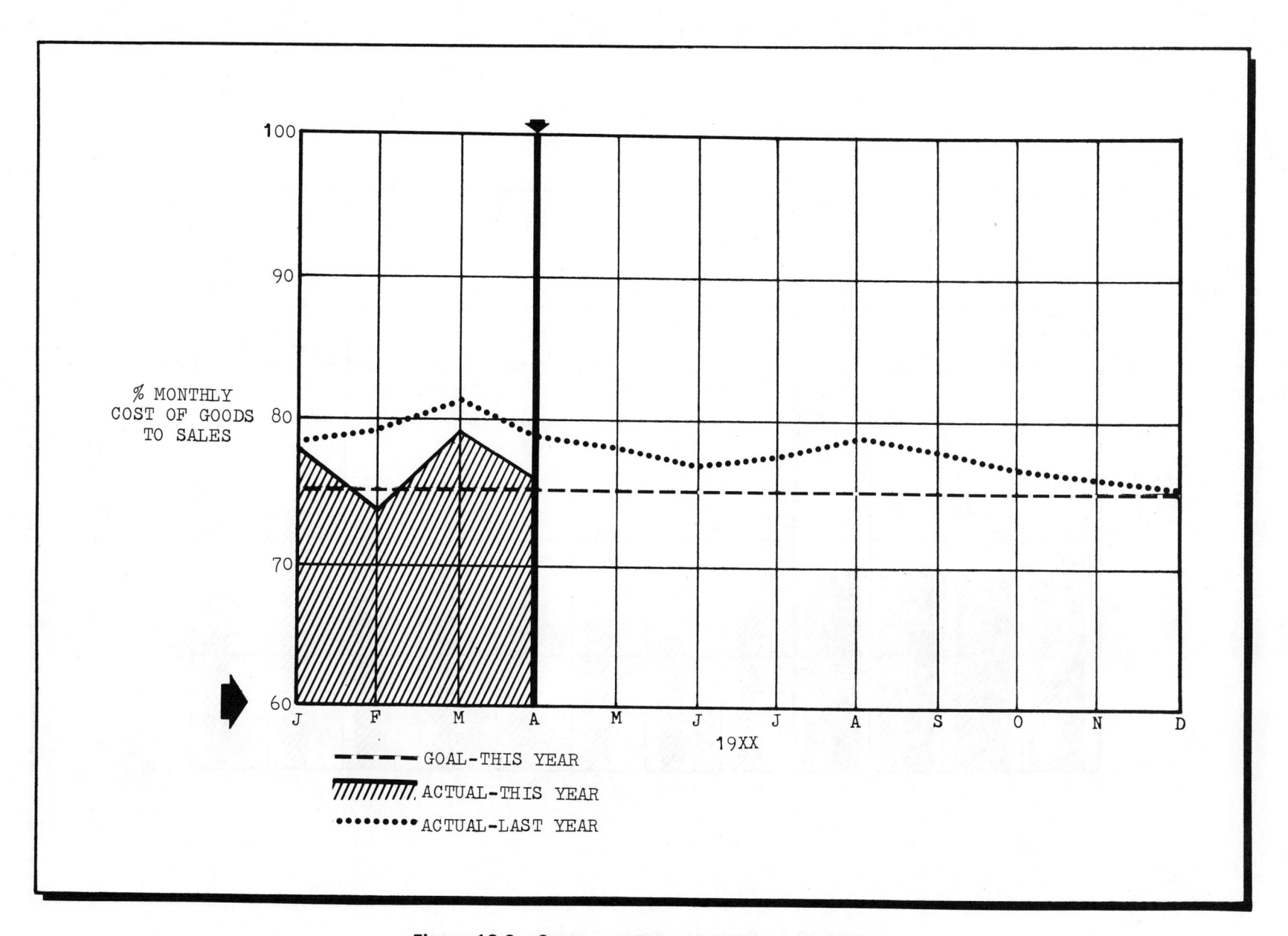

Figure 10.3   Costs as a Percent of Sales—Version 3

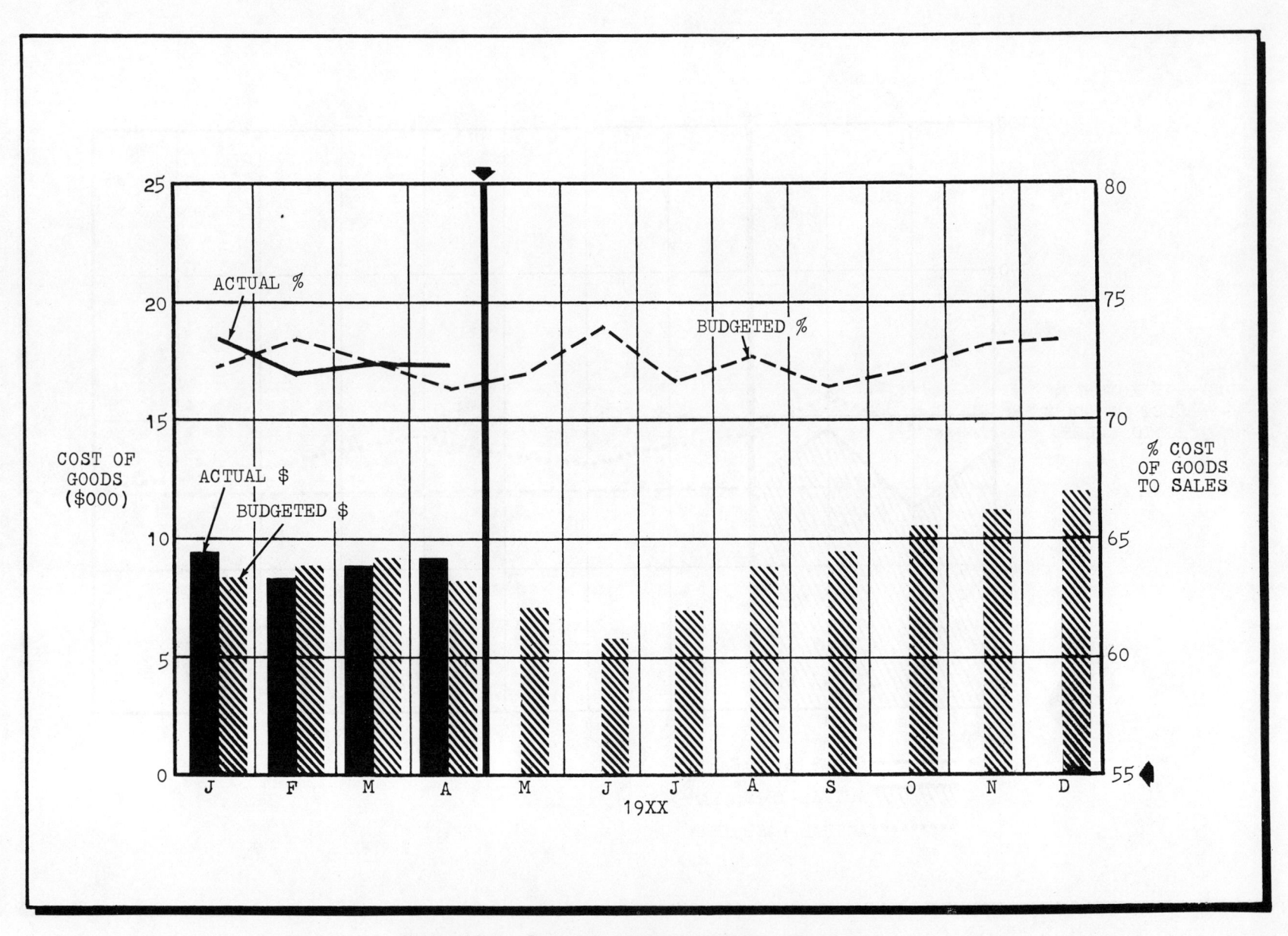

Figure 10.4 Costs as a Percent of Sales—Version 4

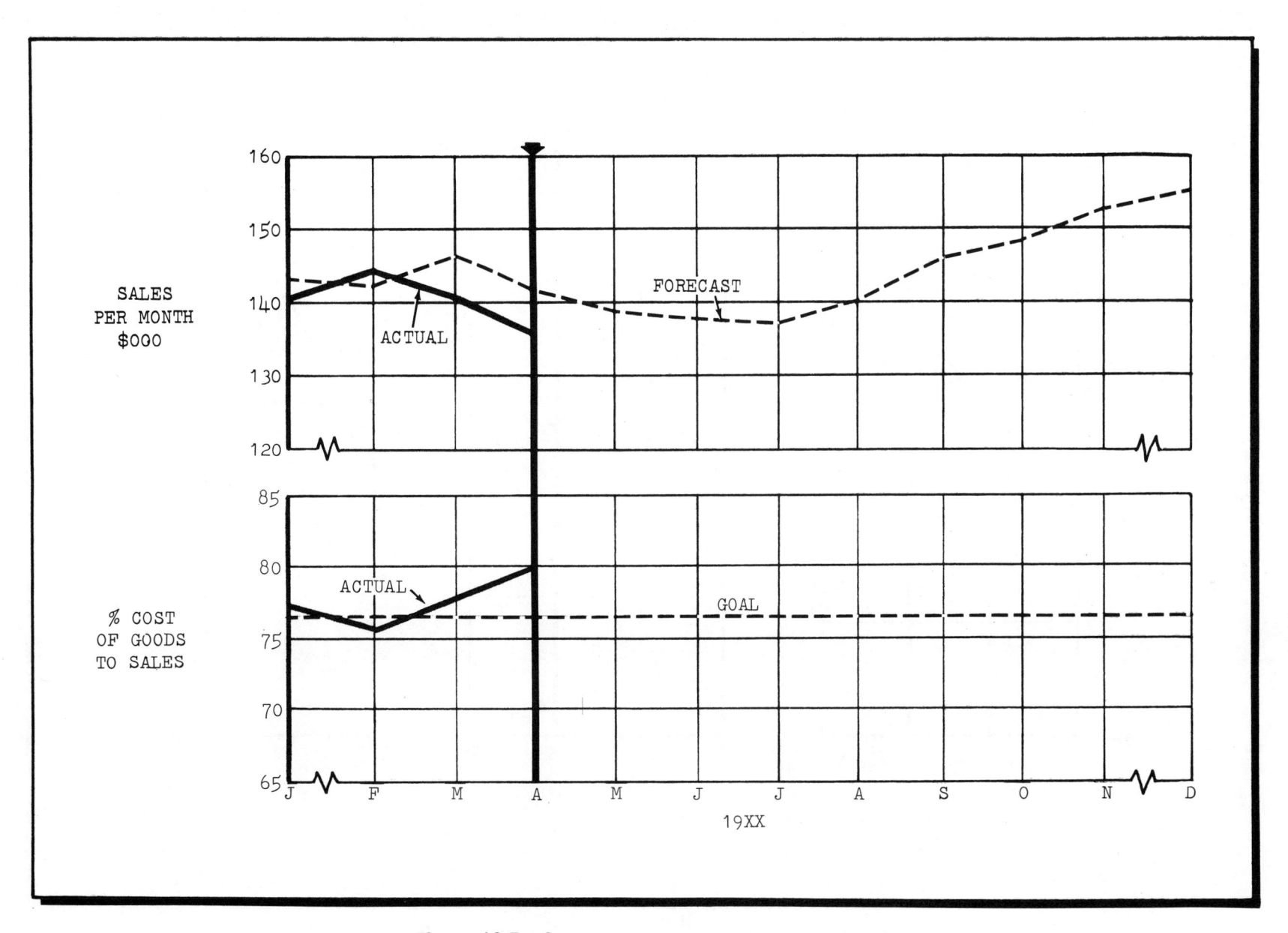

Figure 10.5 Costs as a Percent of Sales—Version 5

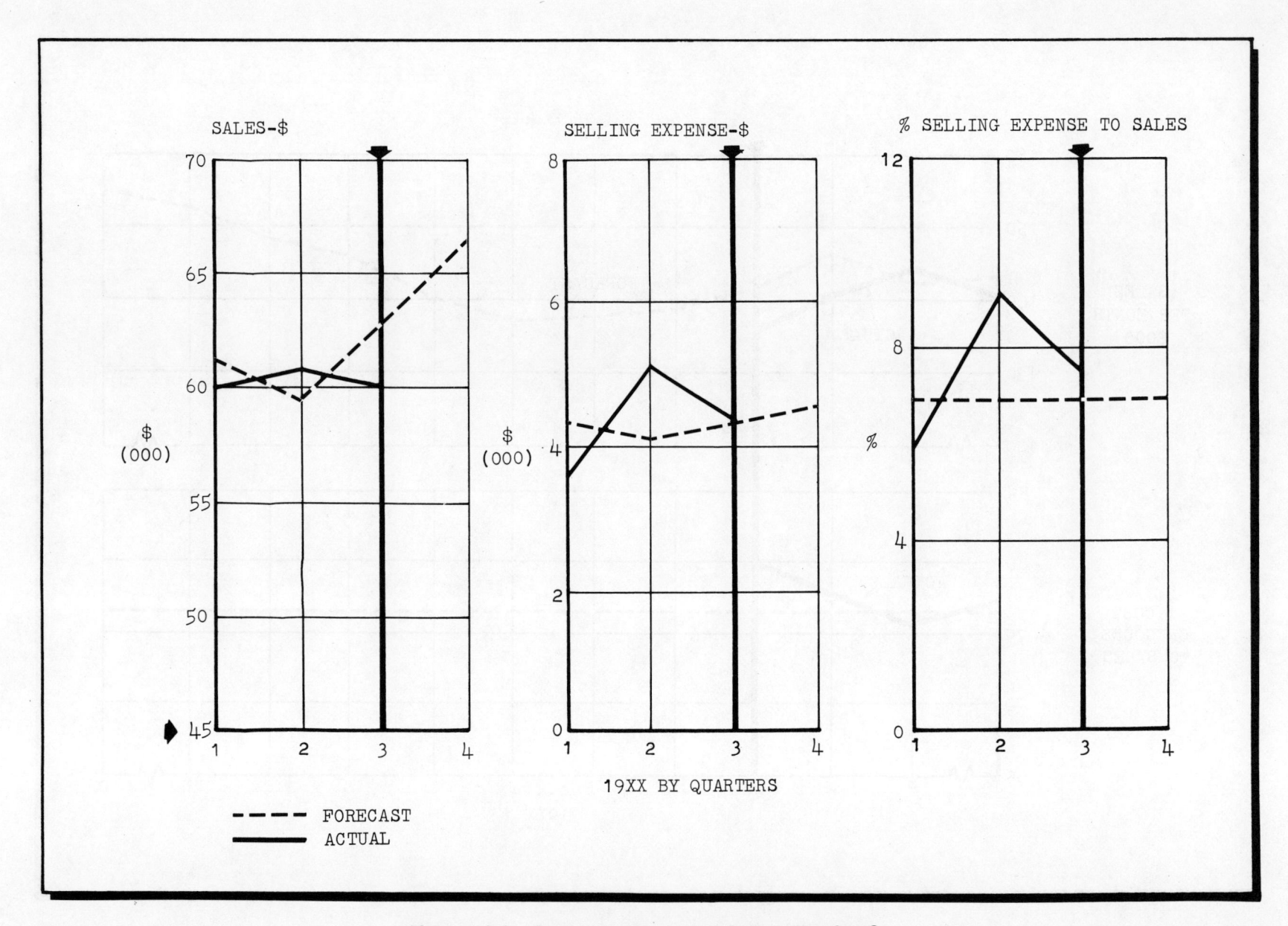

Figure 10.6 Costs as a Percent of Sales—Version 6

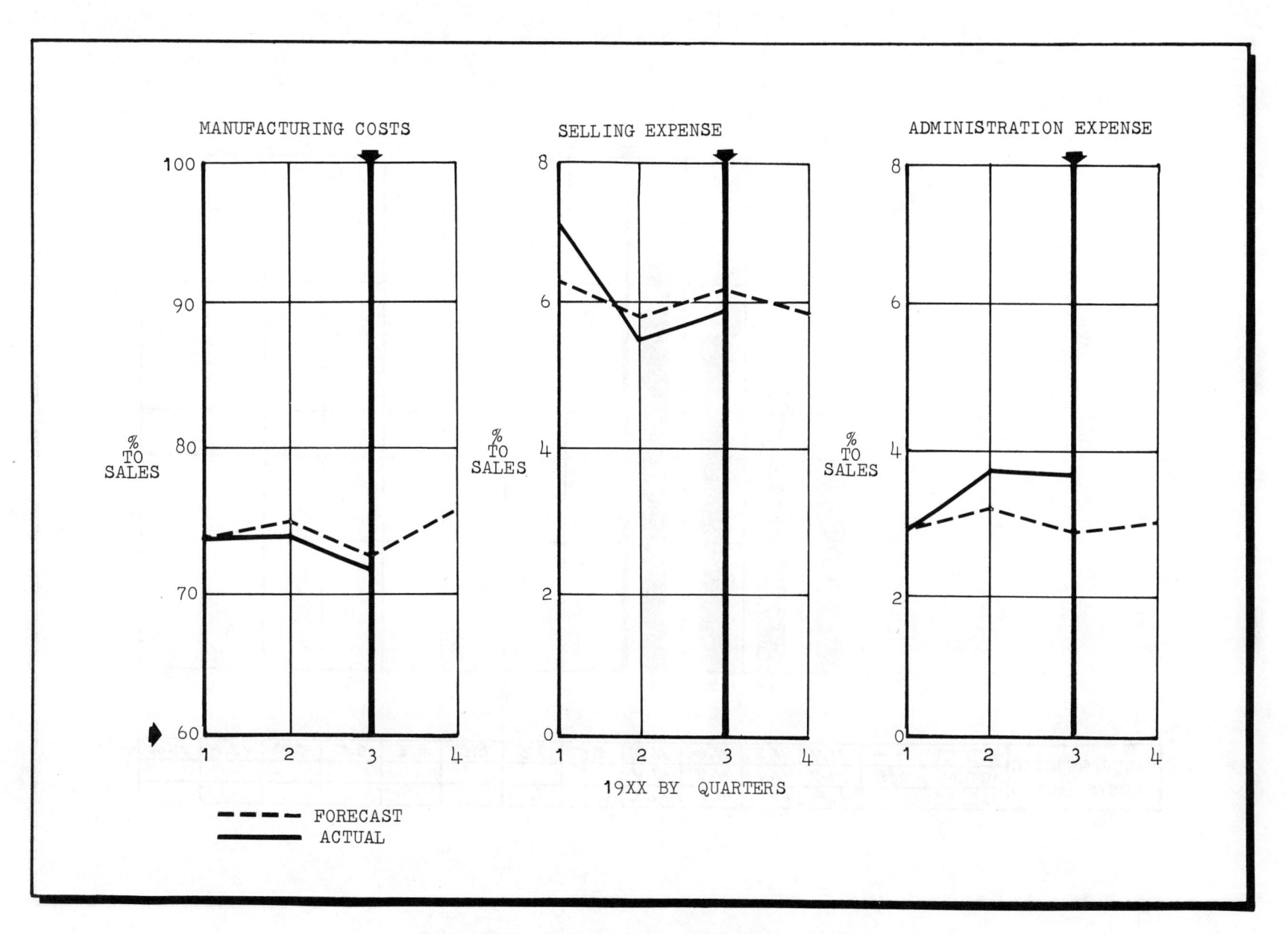

Figure 10.7 Costs as a Percent of Sales—Version 7

% MONTHLY
MANUFACTURING
COSTS TO SALES

MANUFACTURING COSTS ($000)	BUDGET ——	11.9	11.2	11.6	11.2	9.5	9.3	8.5	8.2	9.5	10.9	12.6	14.6
	ACTUAL ■	12.7	11.4	11.7	12.4								
	VARIANCE	+.8	+.2	+.1	+1.2								

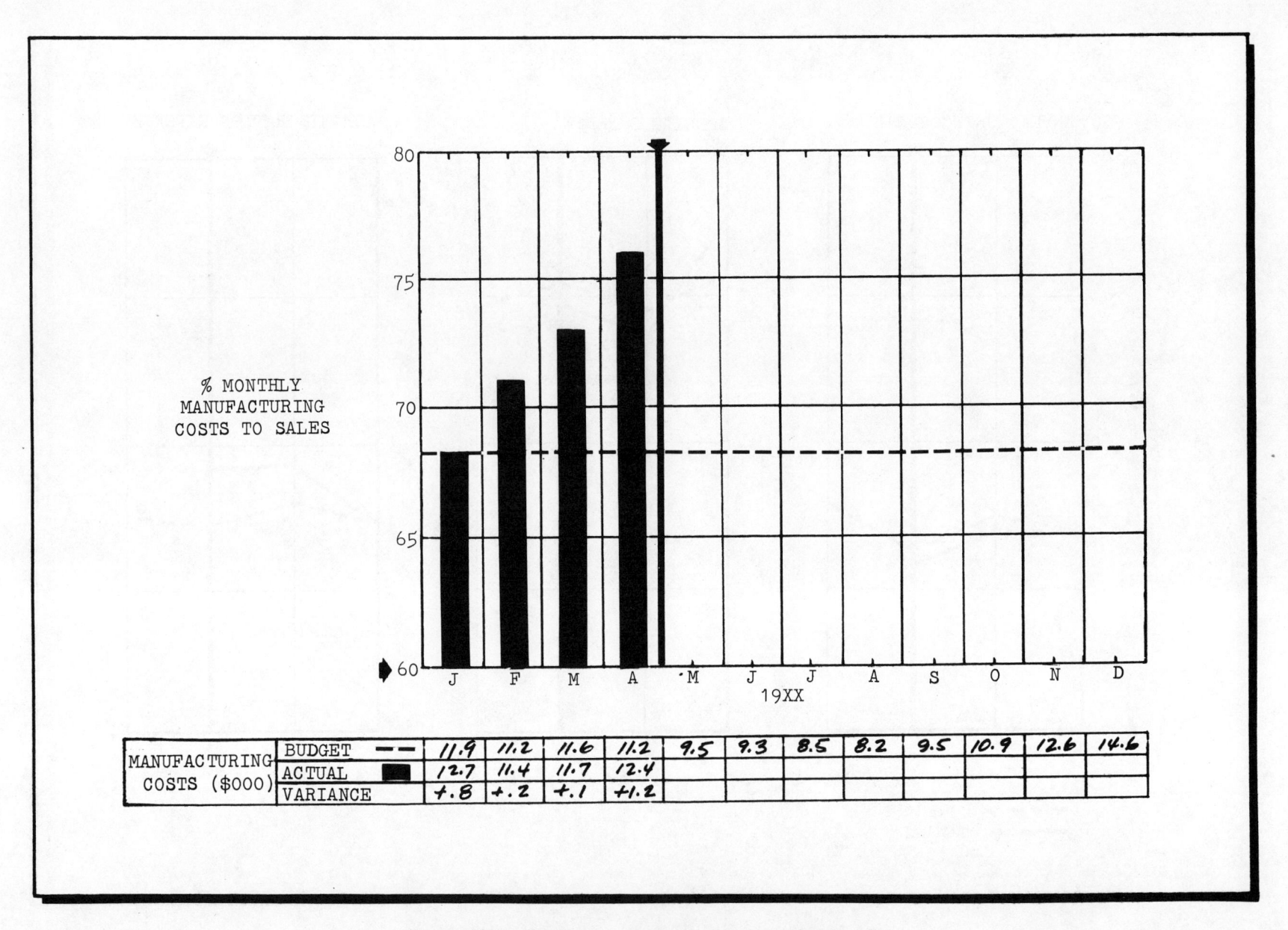

Figure 10.8 Costs as a Percent of Sales—Version 8

% MONTHLY
MANUFACTURING
COST TO SALES

ACTUAL

BUDGETED

19XX

SALES PER MO.	$000	FORECAST	17.5	16.5	17.0	16.5	14.0	13.7	12.5	12.0	13.9	16.0	18.5	21.5
		ACTUAL	18.7	16.0	16.0	16.1								
MANUFAC-TURING COSTS	$000	BUDGET	11.9	11.2	11.6	11.2	9.5	9.3	8.5	8.2	9.5	10.9	12.6	14.6
		ACTUAL	12.7	11.4	11.7	12.4								
	% TO SALES	BUDGET	68	68	68	68	68	68	68	68	68	68	68	68
		ACTUAL	68	71	73	77								

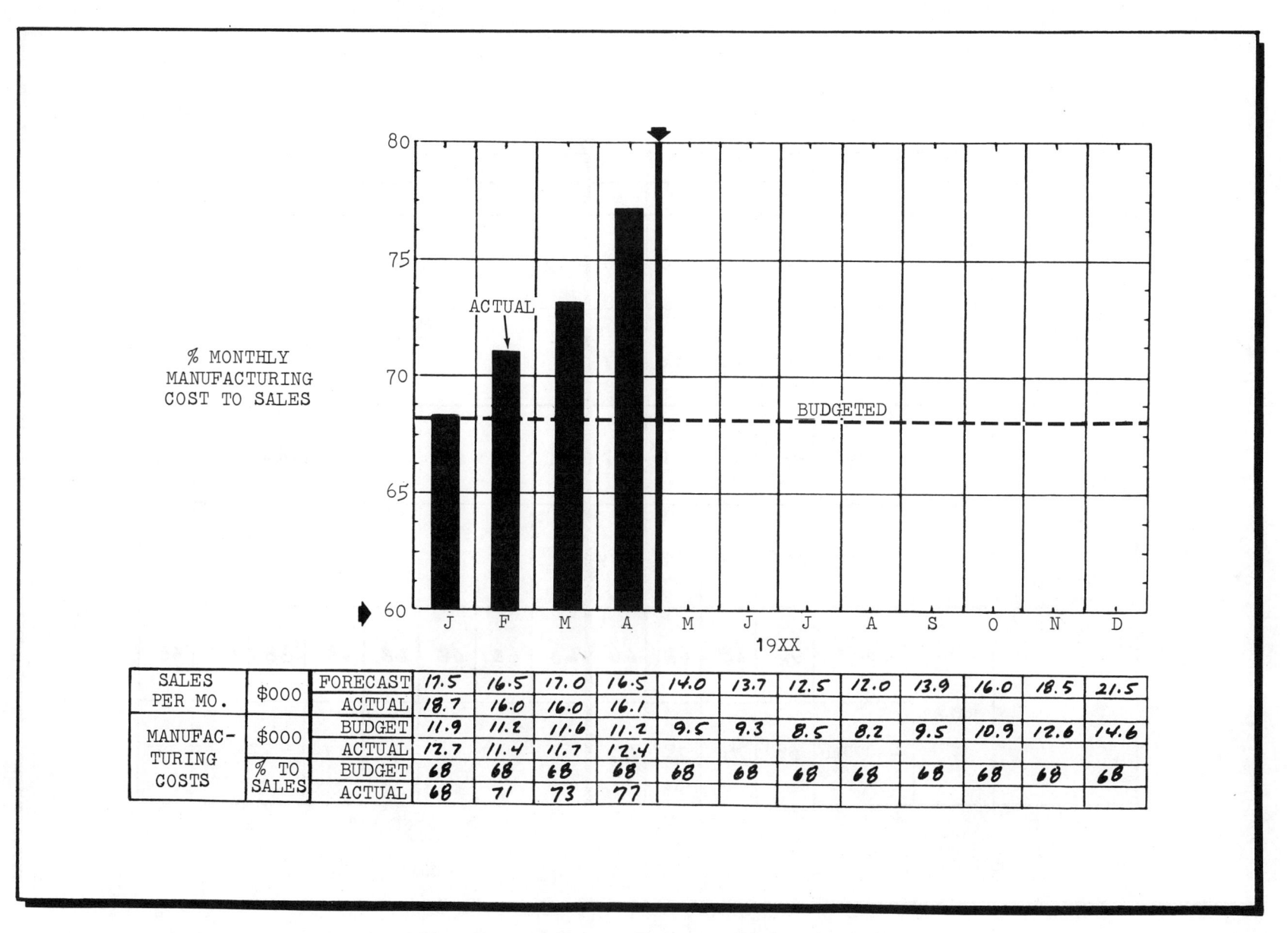

Figure 10.9 Costs as a Percent of Sales—Version 9

CATEGORY			19XX											
			J	F	M	A	M	J	J	A	S	O	N	D
SALES PER MONTH	$ 000	FORECAST	17.5	16.5	17.0	16.5	14.0	13.7	12.5	12.0	13.9	16.0	18.5	21.5
		ACTUAL	18.7	16.0	16.0	16.1								
MANUFAC- TURING COSTS	$ 000	BUDGET	11.9	11.2	11.6	11.2	9.5	9.3	8.5	8.2	9.5	10.9	12.6	14.6
		ACTUAL	12.7	11.4	11.7	12.4								
	% TO SALES	BUDGET	68	68	68	68	68	68	68	68	68	68	68	68
		ACTUAL	68	71	73	77								

Figure 10.10   Costs as a Percent of Sales—Version 10

STATUS AS OF _____

ITEM	PLAN	ACTUAL	VARIANCE
SALES ($000)	16.5	16.1	-.4
MANUFACTURING COSTS ($000)	11.2	12.4	+1.2
% MANUFACTURING COSTS TO SALES	68%	77%	+9%

Figure 10.11 Costs as a Percent of Sales—Version 11

11.0 CURRENT ASSETS TO CURRENT LIABILITIES

Charts that display the multiple of current assets to current liabilities, sometimes called the current ratio, are displayed in this section. The multiple is found by dividing the current assets (cash, accounts receivable, inventories, and other assets that will normally become cash) by current liabilities (notes and accounts payable, taxes, and other payables).

11.1 Current Assets to Current Liabilities—Version 1: A simple method for displaying the multiple of current assets to current liabilities is shown in Version 1, Current Assets to Current Liabilities, Figure 11.1. The actuals for the year to date are displayed against the year's forecast.

11.2 Current Assets to Current Liabilities—Version 2: The actual monthly multiple of current assets to current liabilities is displayed in relationship to an "industry average" in Version 2, Figure 11.2. Industry average statistics are usually available from banks or trade associations.

11.3 Current Assets to Current Liabilities—Version 3: Version 3 of a current assets to current liabilities chart, Figure 11.3, is identical to Version 2, except a line representing the actual year-to-date average has been added to Version 3.

11.4 Current Assets to Current Liabilities—Version 4: A column chart style is used in Version 4 of a current assets to current liabilities chart, Figure 11.4. In this example hatched columns represent the forecasted multiple, and solid columns show the actuals up to the reporting date (end of May).

11.5 Current Assets to Current Liabilities—Version 5: A multi-year version of a current assets to current liabilities chart is shown in Figure 11.5. The current year's forecasted and actual performance is shown in relationship to four previous years and the forecast for the coming year.

11.6 Current Assets to Current Liabilities—Version 6: A table of statistics has been added to a graphic chart in Version 6 of a current assets to current liabilities chart, Figure 11.6. The table displays the forecasted and actual multiples of current assets to current liabilities by the month. The graphic portion of the chart displays the forecast in step line form, and actuals in solid column form.

11.7 Current Assets to Current Liabilities—Version 7: An example of a one-time status report is shown as Version 7 of a current assets to current liabilities chart, Figure 11.7. In this example, detailed statistics for current assets and current liabilities are given together with the forecasted and actual ratio.

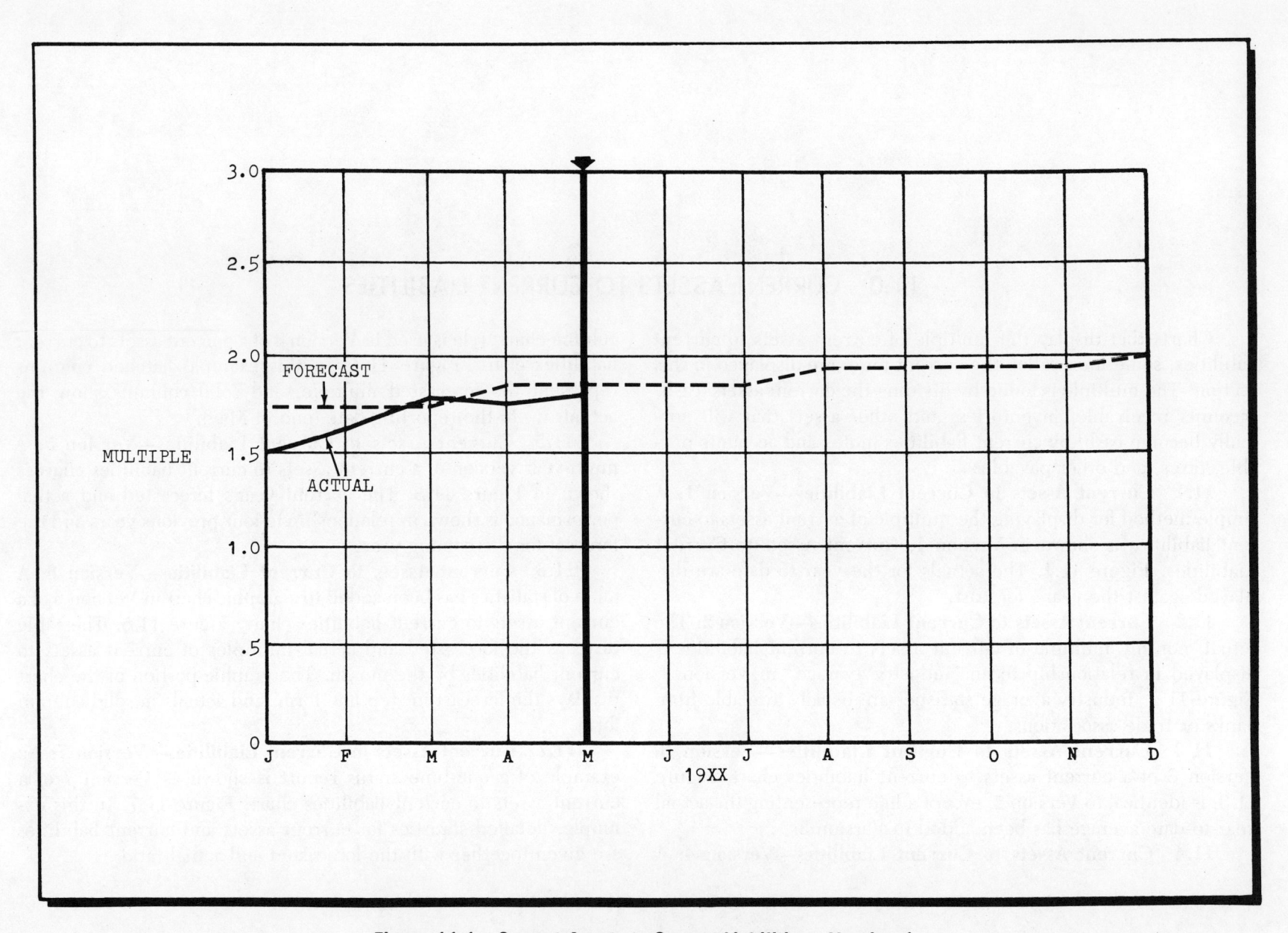

Figure 11.1   Current Assets to Current Liabilities—Version 1

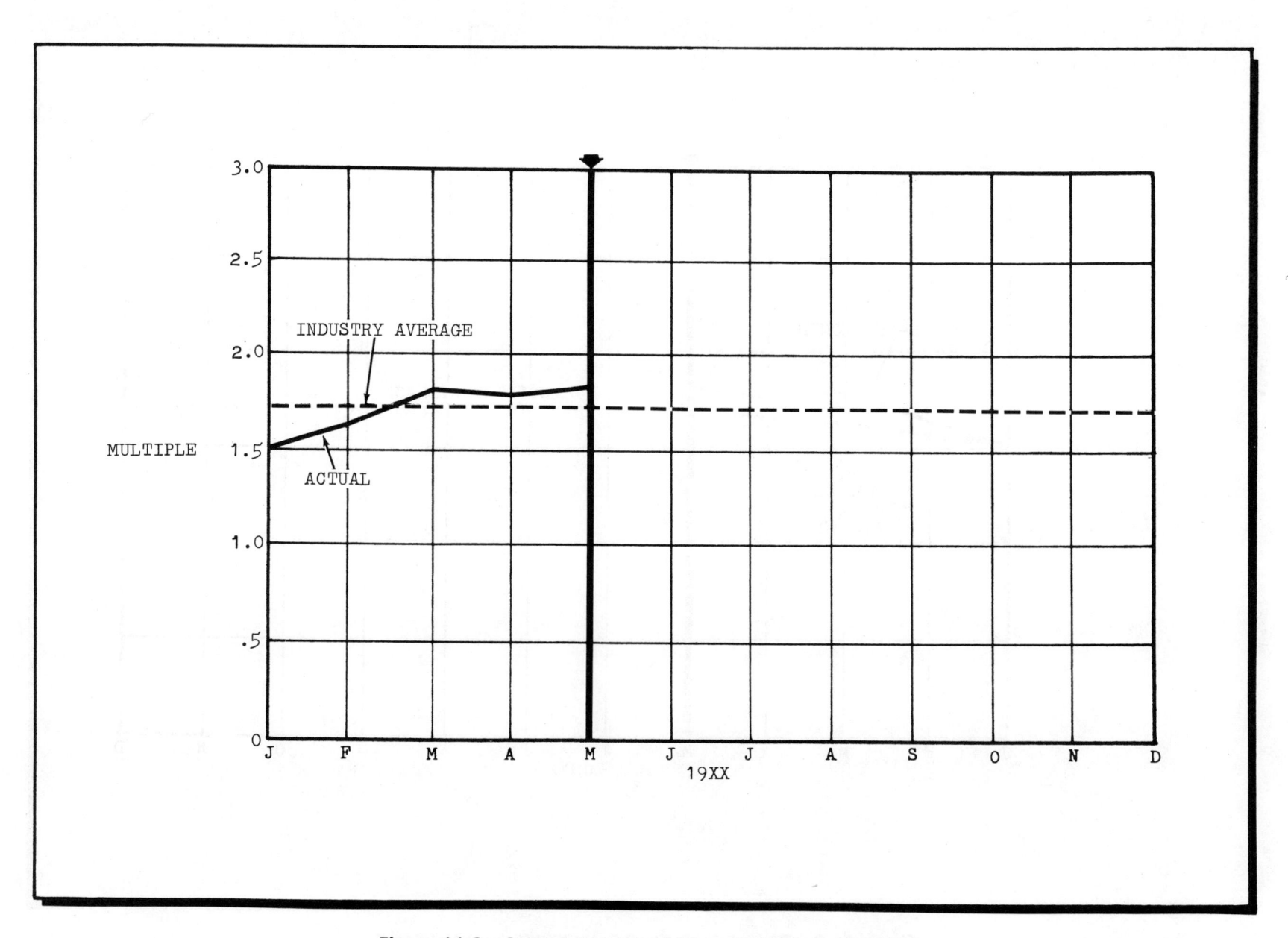

Figure 11.2 Current Assets to Current Liabilities—Version 2

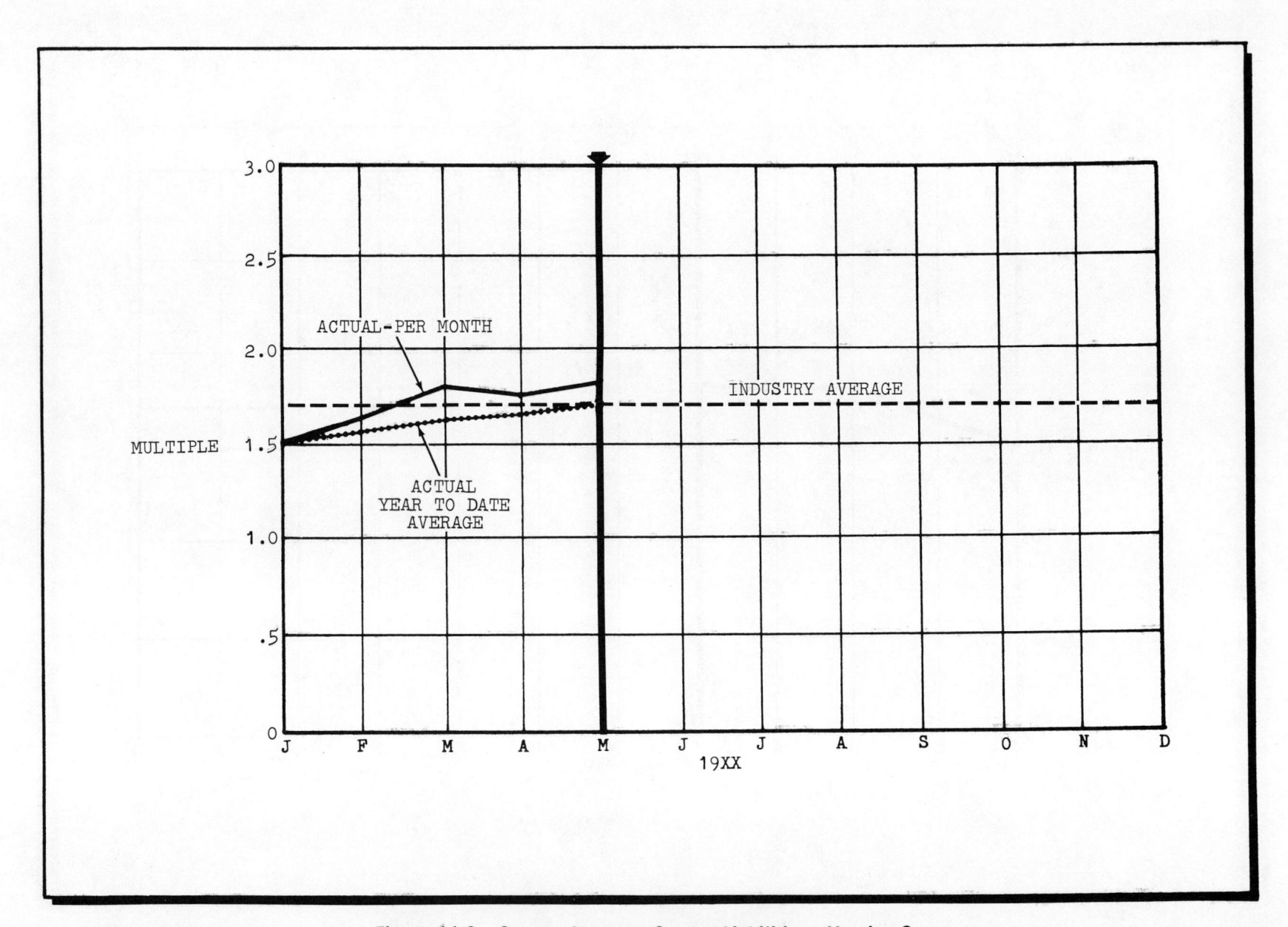

Figure 11.3   Current Assets to Current Liabilities—Version 3

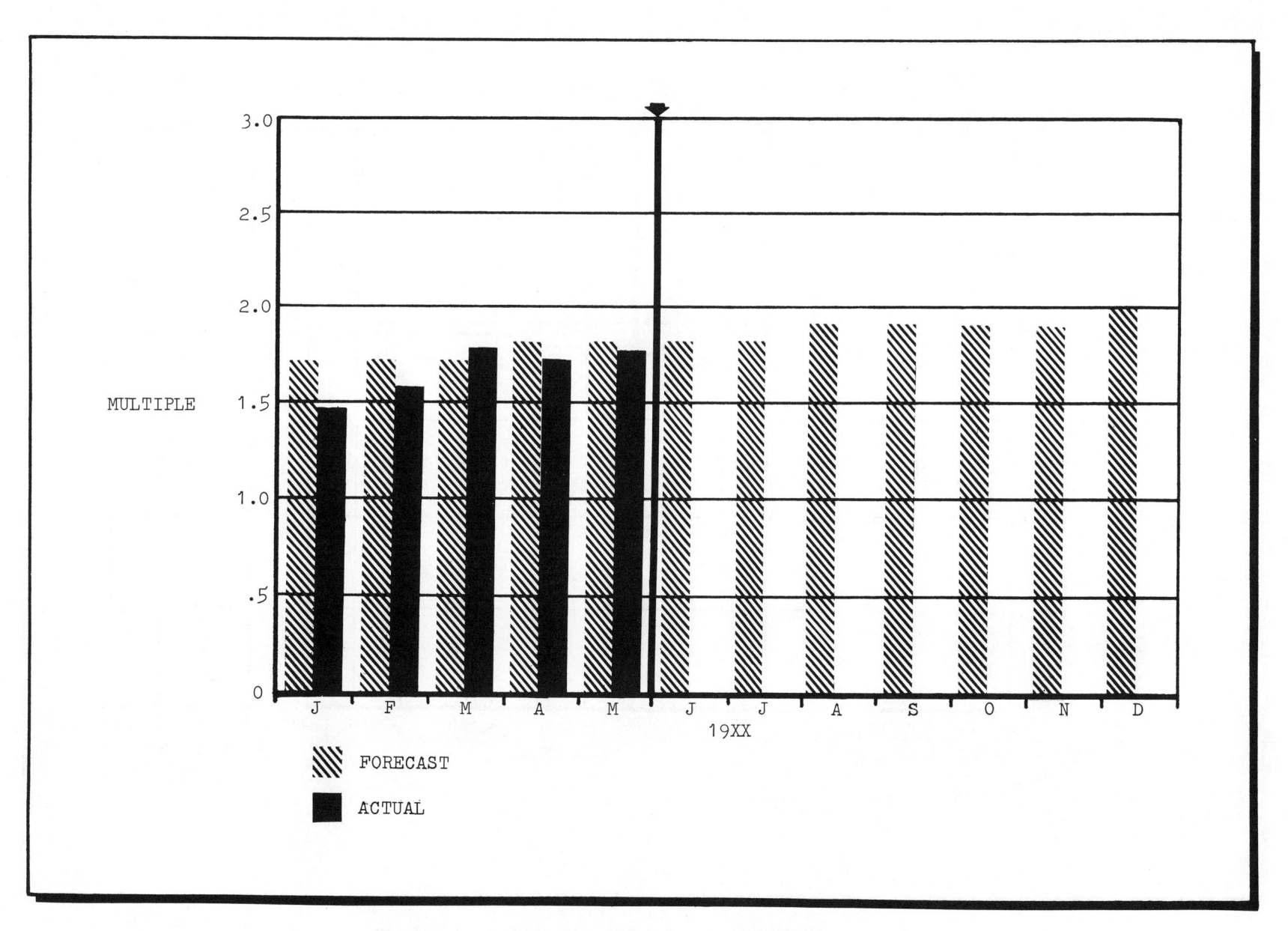

Figure 11.4 Current Assets to Current Liabilities—Version 4

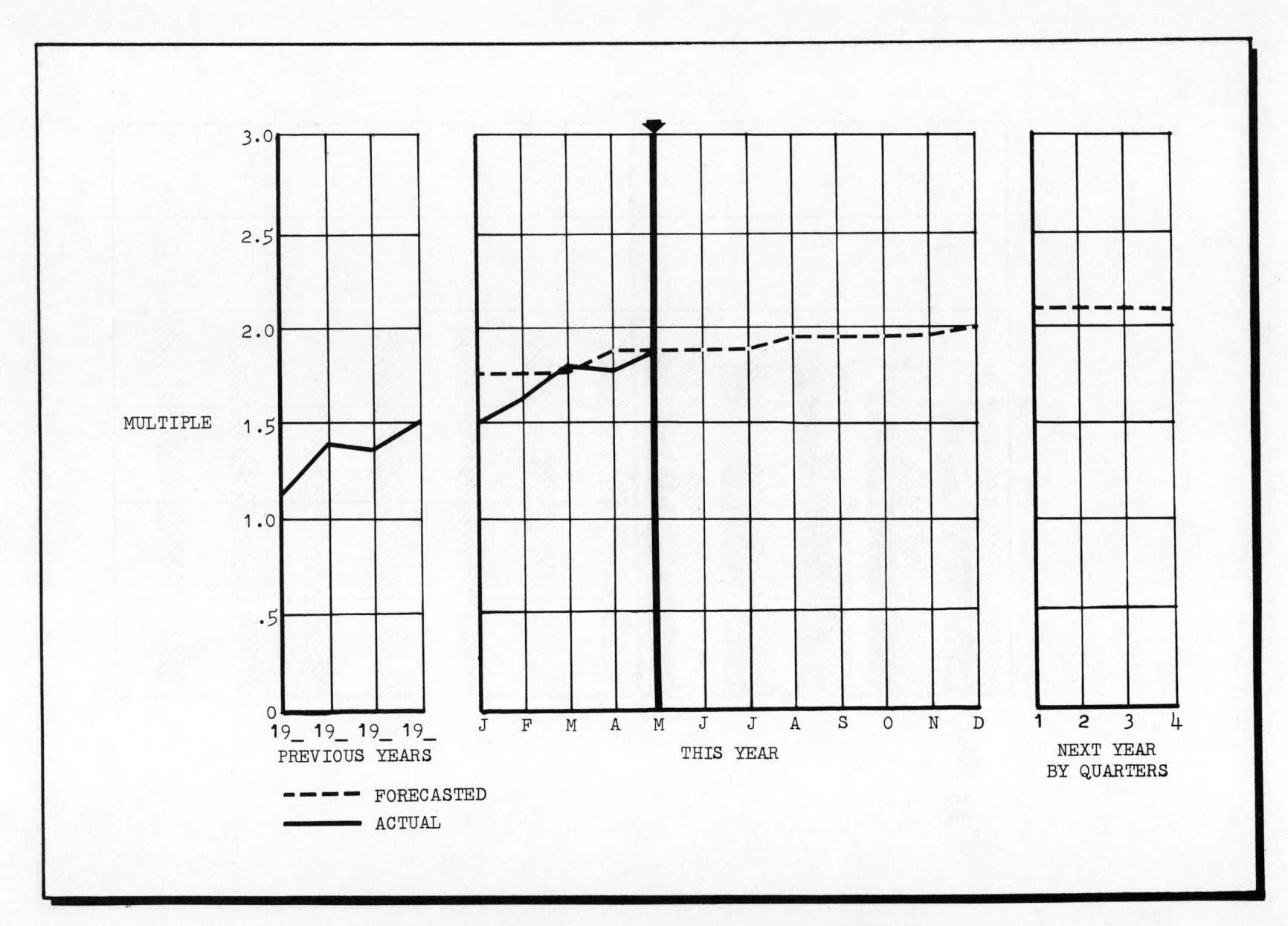

Figure 11.5 Current Assets to Current Liabilities—Version 5

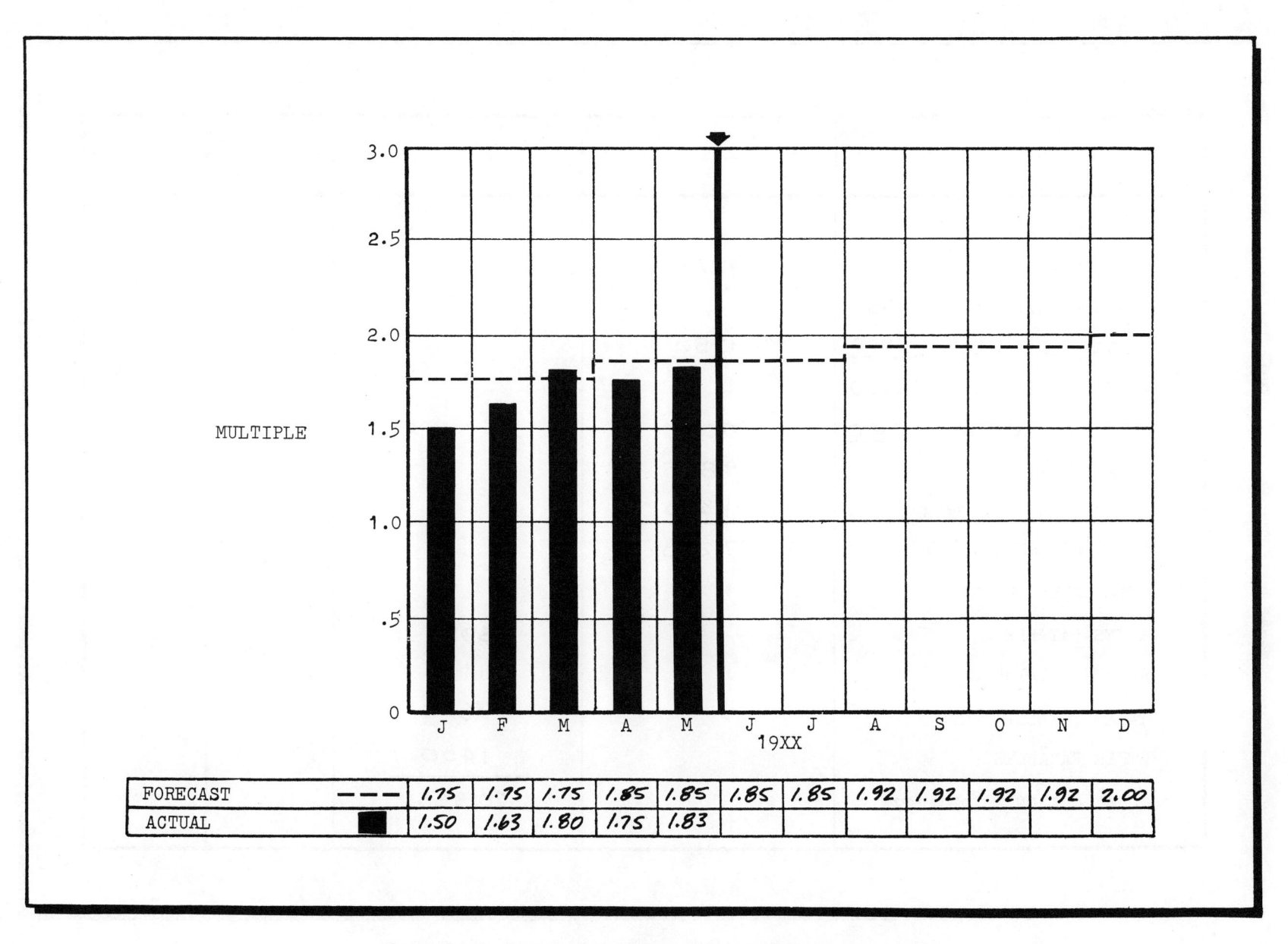

FORECAST — — —	1.75	1.75	1.75	1.85	1.85	1.85	1.85	1.92	1.92	1.92	1.92	2.00
ACTUAL ■	1.50	1.63	1.80	1.75	1.83							

Figure 11.6 Current Assets to Current Liabilities—Version 6

STATUS AS OF JUNE 1

ITEM	ASSETS	LIABILITIES	RATIO	
			FORECAST	ACTUAL
CURRENT ASSETS:				
CASH ON HAND	$4260			
NOTES RECEIVABLE 4680				
LESS DISCOUNTED 2900	1780			
ACCNTS RECEIVABLE 22150				
LESS BAD DEBT RES 2100	20050		1.85	1.83
INVENTORIES	9855			
PREPAYMENT OF EXPENSES	1300			
TOTAL CURRENT ASSETS	37 245			
CURRENT LIABILITIES				
NOTES PAYABLE		$3970		
ACCOUNTS PAYABLE		11165		
TAXES PAYABLE		3800		
OTHER PAYABLES		1400		
TOTAL CURRENT LIABILITIES		20,335		

Figure 11.7   Current Assets to Current Liabilities—Version 7

12.0 CURRENT LIABILITIES TO TANGIBLE NET WORTH

The ratio of current liabilities to tangible net worth compares what is owed to what is owned. This section displays examples of charts that show this ratio. Current liabilities consist of accounts and notes payable, taxes payable, and other payables. Tangible net worth consists of the total worth of a business less intangible assets such as goodwill, trademarks, and organization expenses.

12.1 Current Liabilities to Tangible Net Worth—Version 1: A simple method for displaying the ratio of current liabilities to tangible net worth is shown as Version 1, Figure 12.1. In this example an upper limit of 62% is shown with a dashed line. When actuals (solid line) go above that limit, it is an indication that special management action is required to reduce the ratio.

12.2 Current Liabilities to Tangible Net Worth—Version 2: In Version 2 of a current liabilities to tangible net worth tracking chart, Figure 12.2, a dashed line is used to define an "upper limit" for the ratio, and solid columns show the actual ratio for each month. In this example the actual ratio of current liabilities to tangible net worth for the month of March has exceeded the upper limit, indicating the need for special management action to reduce the ratio.

12.3 Current Liabilities to Tangible Net Worth—Version 3: Version 3 of a current liabilities to tangible net worth tracking chart, Figure 12.3, permits an examination of the current year's performance in relationship to that of previous years. In this example, the upper limit is shown with a dashed line for the current year and for the coming year. Actual performance to date is shown with a solid line.

12.4 Current Liabilities to Tangible Net Worth—Version 4: A statistical table has been combined with graphics in Version 4 of a current liabilities to tangible net worth tracking chart, Figure 12.4. Statistics for current liabilities, tangible net worth, and the ratio are given in the tabular portion of the chart. On the graphic portion solid columns are used to show the actual ratio in relationship to the upper limit (62% in this example).

12.5 Current Liabilities to Tangible Net Worth—Version 5: Version 5, Figure 12.5, displays a tabular form of a current liabilities to tangible net worth tracking chart. Detailed statistics for current liabilities and tangible net worth are given as well as the ratio in terms of actual performance, the upper limit, and the variance, each month, between actual performance and the upper limit. A circle has been used in the example to emphasize the over-the-limit condition for March.

12.6 Current Liabilities to Tangible Net Worth—Version 6: A one-time status report style is used as Version 6 of a current liabilities to tangible net worth chart, Figure 12.6. The statistics for current liabilities, tangible net worth, and the ratio are given in terms of what has been planned, the actuals for the reporting date, and the variances.

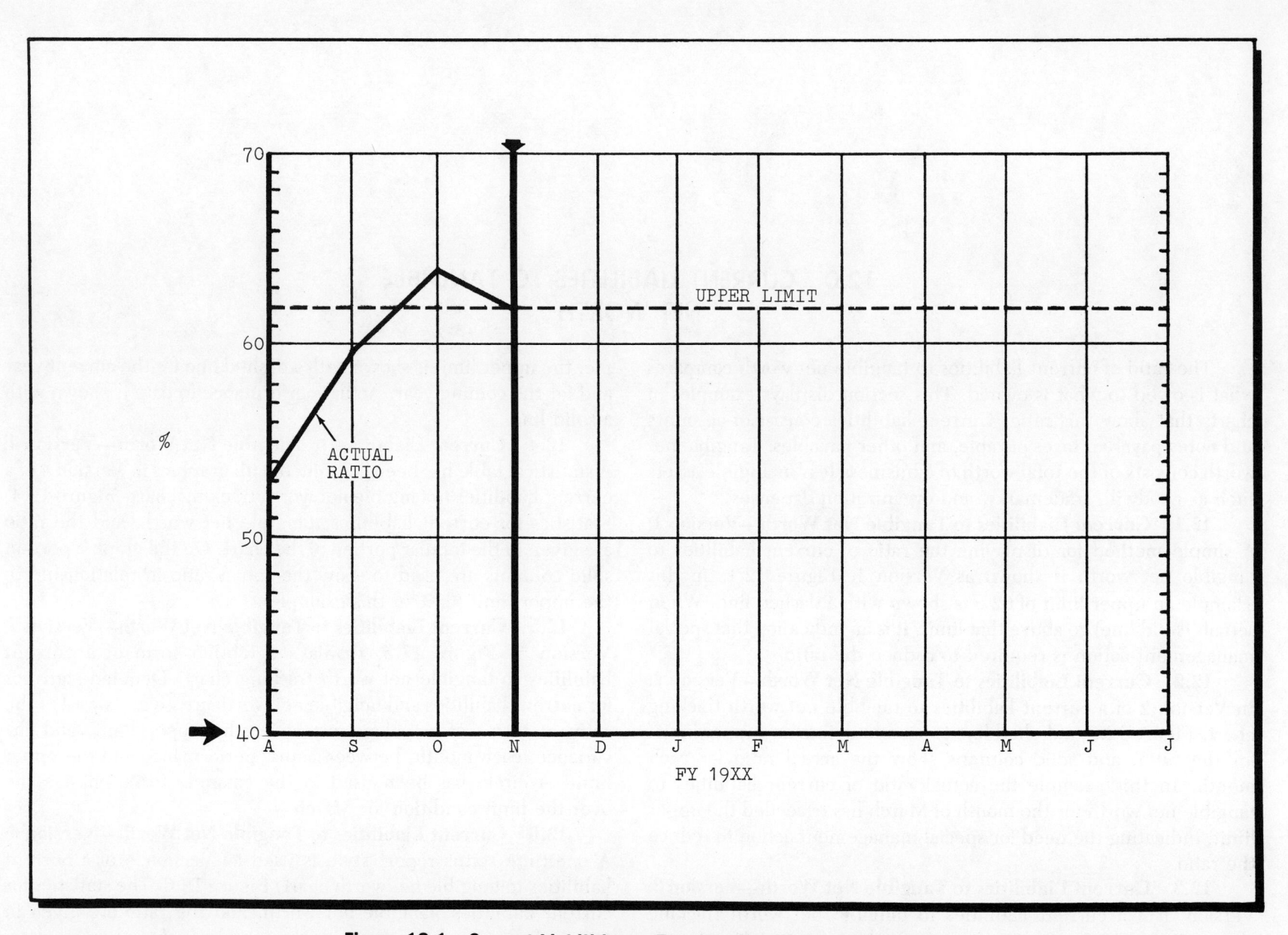

Figure 12.1 Current Liabilities to Tangible Net Worth—Version 1

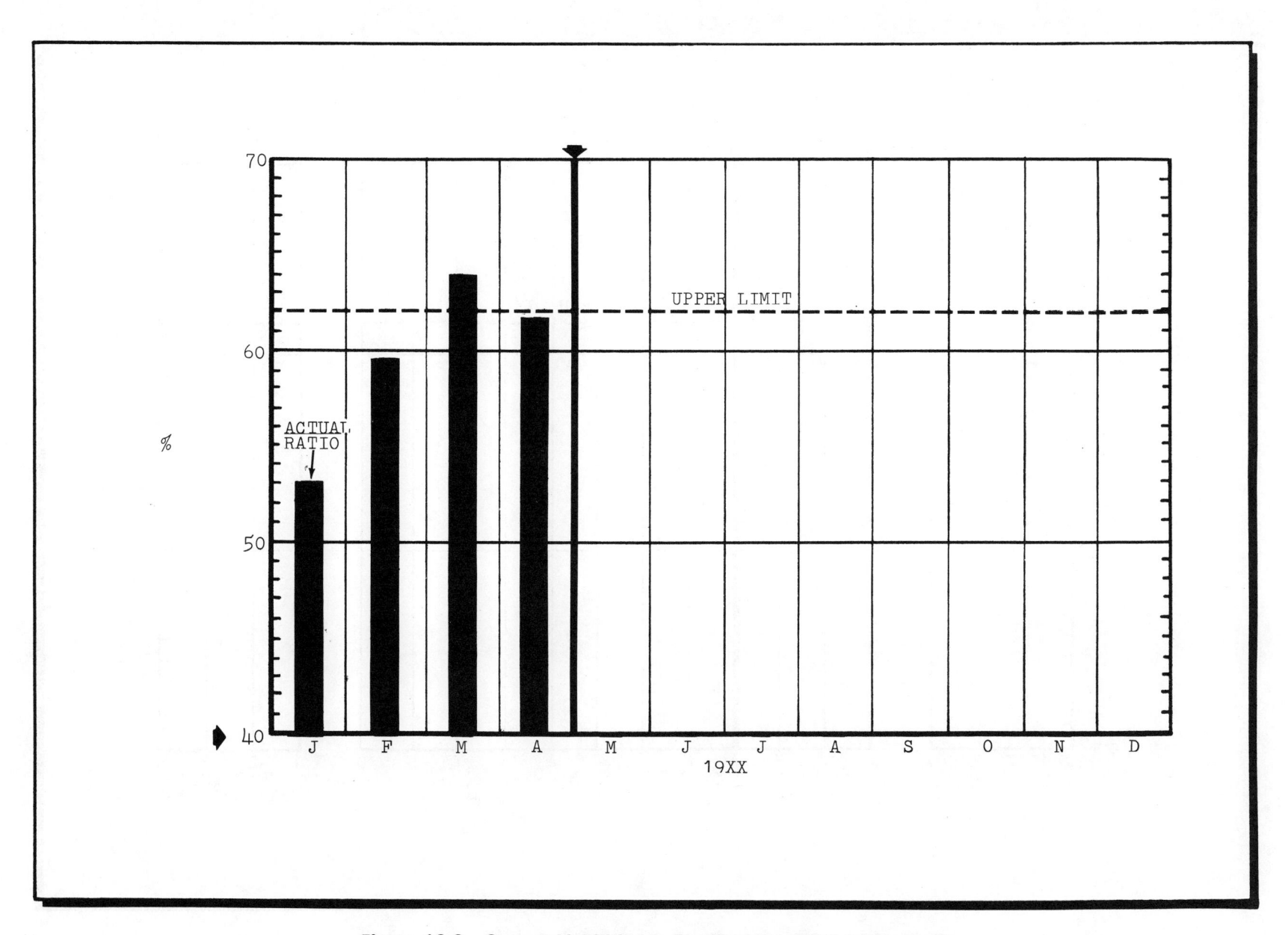

Figure 12.2 Current Liabilities to Tangible Net Worth—Version 2

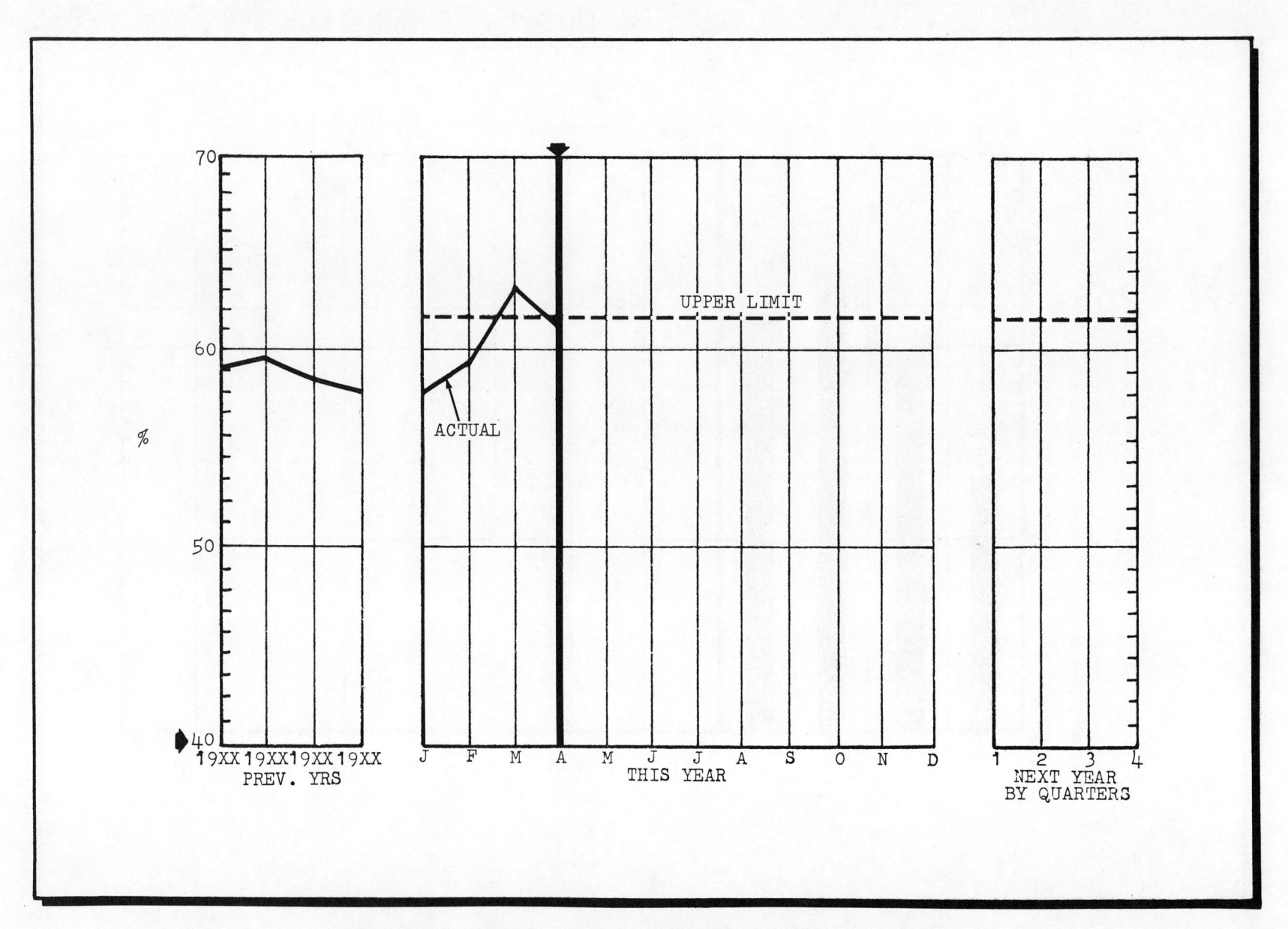

Figure 12.3   Current Liabilities to Tangible Net Worth—Version 3

CURRENT LIABILITIES(CL) $000	15.8	18.4	22.0	20.3								
TANGIBLE NET WORTH(TNW) $000	29.9	30.9	34.4	32.9								
RATIO-CL TO TNW %	53.0	59.5	64.0	61.7								

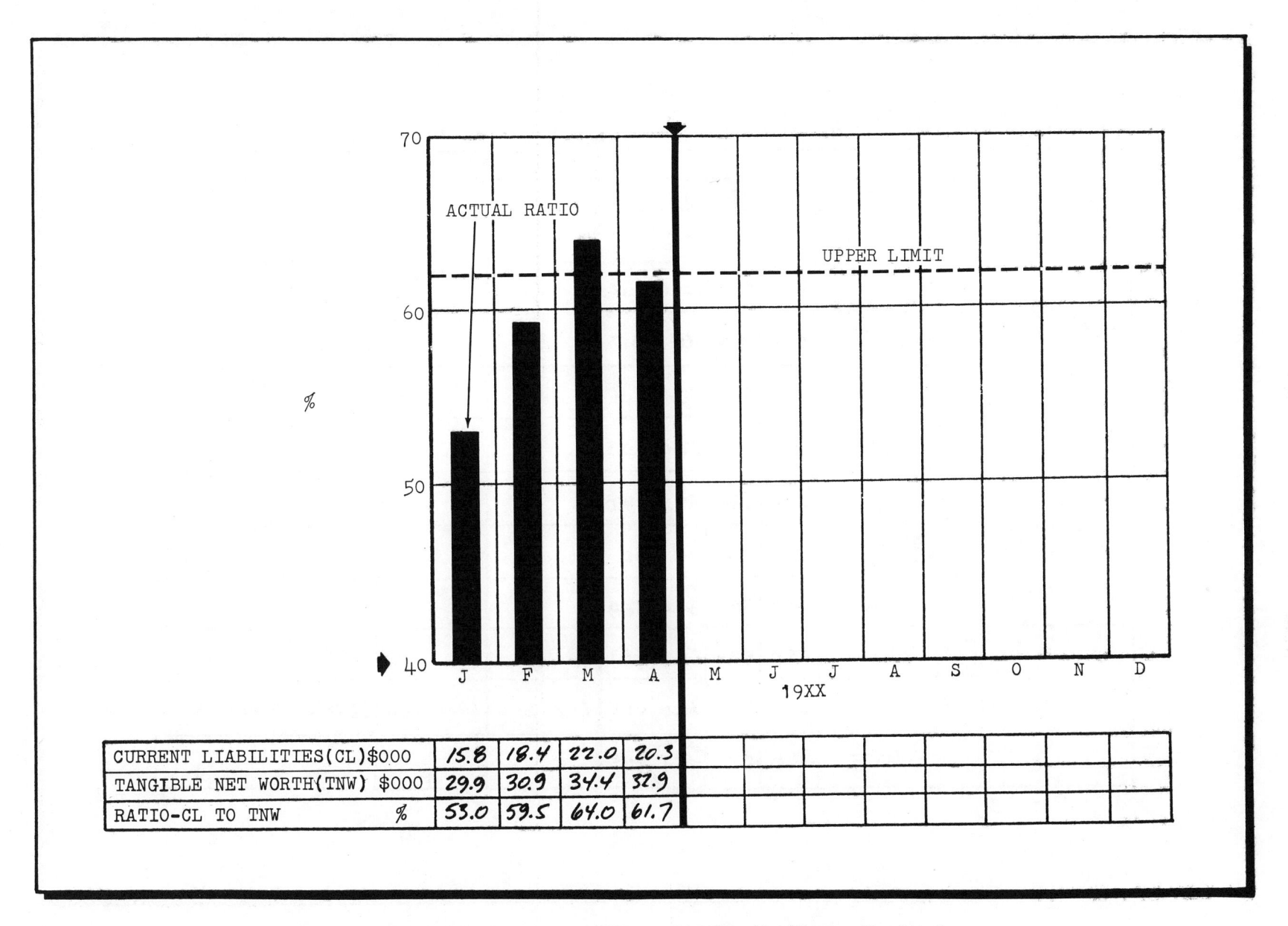

Figure 12.4 Current Liabilities to Tangible Net Worth—Version 4

ITEM		19XX											
		J	F	M	A	M	J	J	A	S	O	N	D
CURRENT LIABILITIES (CL) $ 000	NOTES PAYABLE	3.1	3.6	4.3	4.0								
	ACCOUNTS PAYABLE	8.7	10.2	12.1	11.2								
	TAXES PAYABLE	2.9	3.3	4.0	3.7								
	OTHER PAYABLES	1.1	1.3	1.6	1.4								
	TOTAL	15.8	18.4	22.0	20.3								
TANGIBLE NET WORTH (TNW) $ 000	TOTAL NET WORTH	31.0	32.0	35.5	34.0								
	MINUS INTAG. ASSETS	1.1	1.1	1.1	1.1								
	TOTAL	29.9	30.9	34.4	32.9								
RATIO CL TO TNW %	ACTUALS	53.0	59.5	64.0	61.7								
	UPPER LIMIT	62.0	62.0	62.0	62.0	62.0	62.0	62.0	62.0	62.0	62.0	62.0	62.0
	VARIANCE	-9.0	-2.5	+2.0	-.3								

Figure 12.5 Current Liabilities to Tangible Net Worth—Version 5

STATUS AS OF __APRIL__

	PLAN	ACTUAL	VARIANCE
CURRENT LIABILITIES (CL) $000	20.0	20.3	+.3
TANGIBLE NET WORTH (TNW) $000	32.3	32.9	+.6
RATIO-CL TO TNW %	62.0	61.7	-.3

Figure 12.6 Current Liabilities to Tangible Net Worth—Version 6

13.0 DISTRIBUTION OF INCOME

Charts that display the distribution of income after all costs and expenses except taxes have been deducted are shown in this section. Also see Section 8.0, *Cash Flow*.

13.1 Distribution of Income—Version 1: Distribution of income is usually examined on a quarterly or annual basis. Version 1 of a distribution of income tracking chart, Figure 13.1, compares the current year's actuals against performance during the previous year by quarters. The previous year's performance is shown with dashed step lines. The current year's actuals are shown with segmented columns.

13.2 Distribution of Income—Version 2: A segmented column chart format is used for Version 2 of a distribution of income chart, Figure 13.2. This is a non-tracking style of chart, comparing the distribution of income over a ten-year period.

13.3 Distribution of Income—Version 3: The same data shown in Version 2 of a distribution of income chart are used in Version 3, Figure 13.3. In this example, a surface chart style is used.

13.4 Distribution of Income—Version 4: Segmented circle charts ("pie" charts) are used to compare the current year with the previous year as to the distribution of income, Figure 13.4. As with Versions 2 and 3, this style is non-tracking in nature.

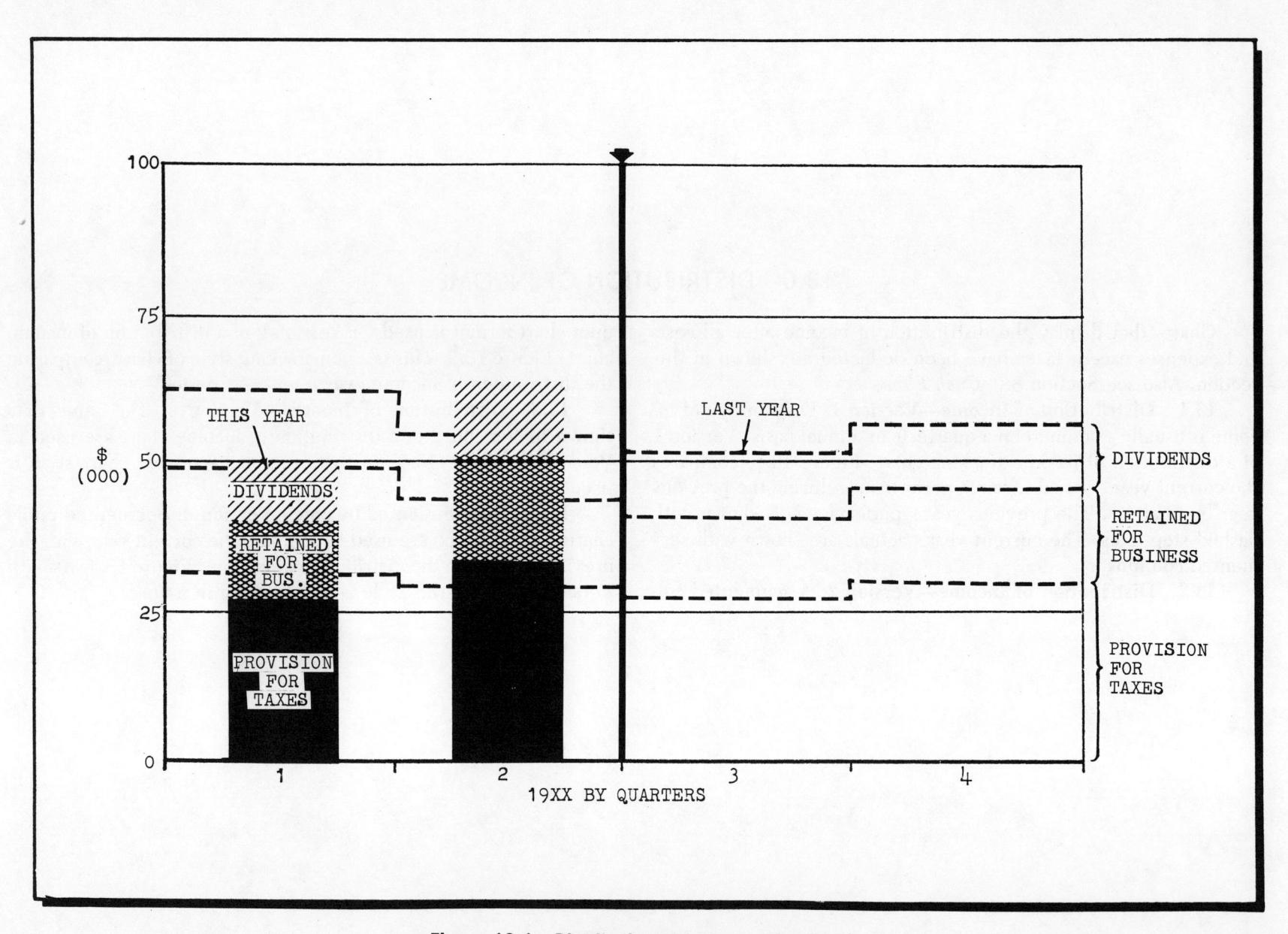

Figure 13.1 Distribution of Income—Version 1

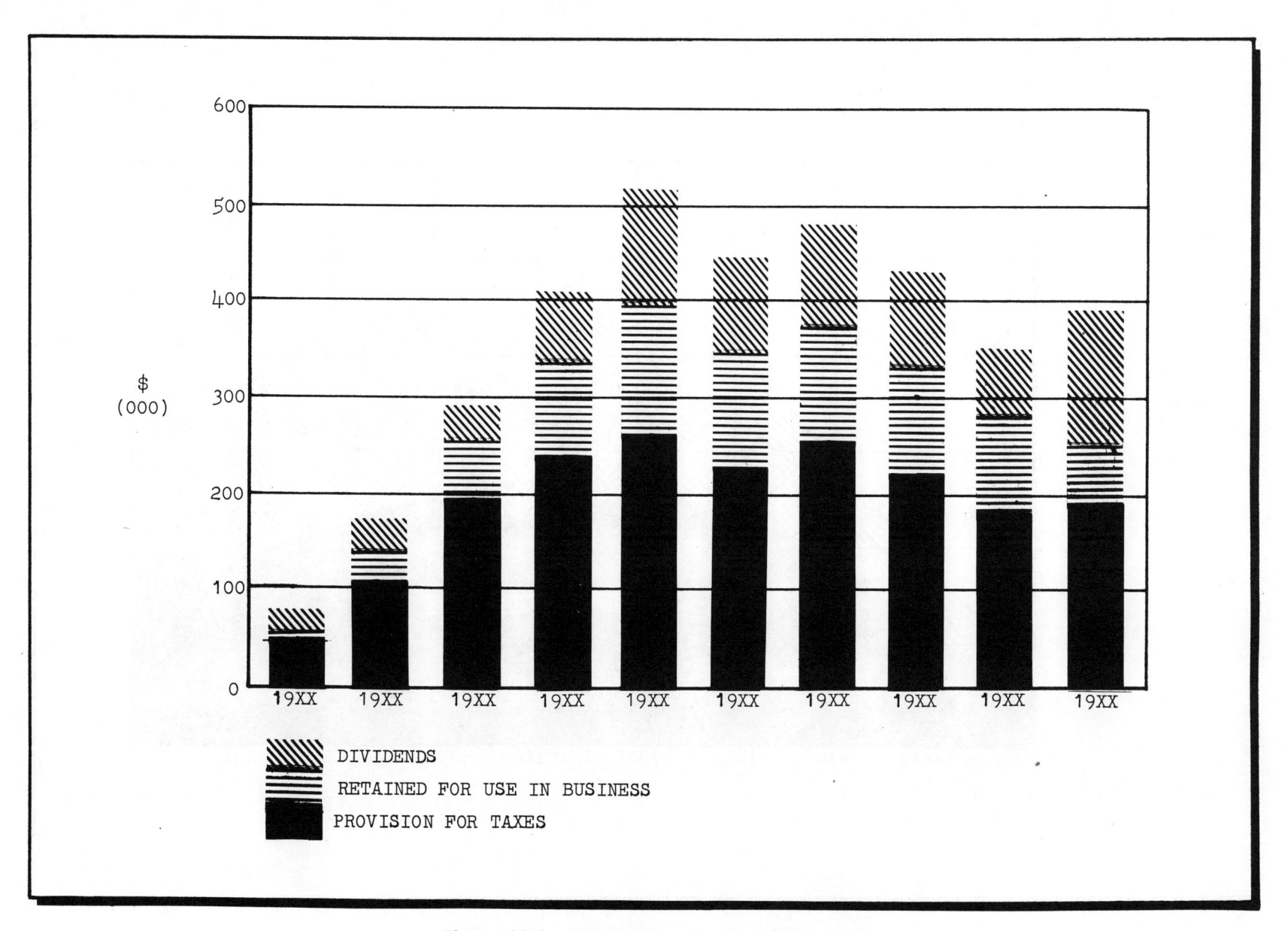

Figure 13.2 Distribution of Income—Version 2

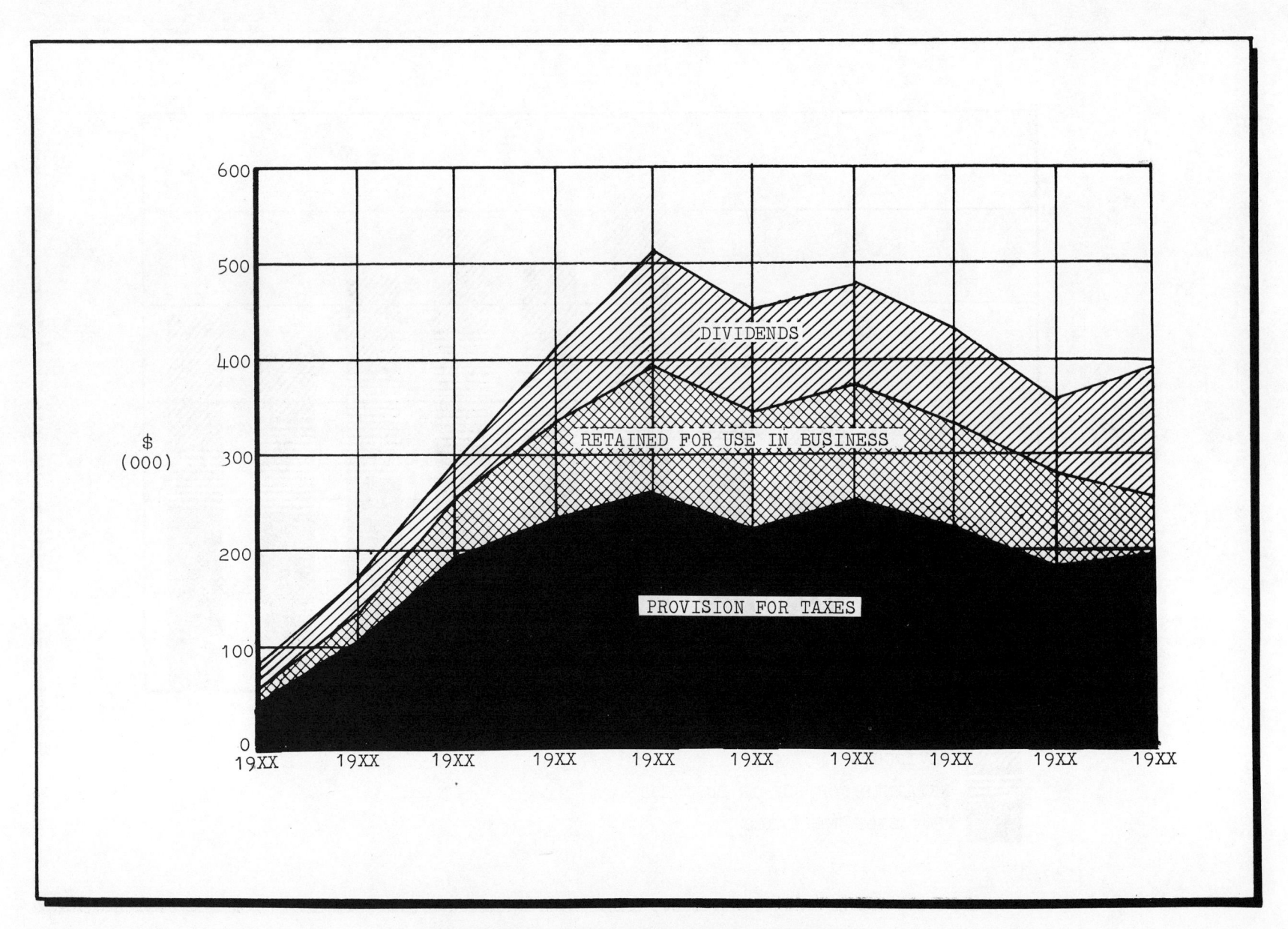

Figure 13.3 Distribution of Income—Version 3

LAST YEAR

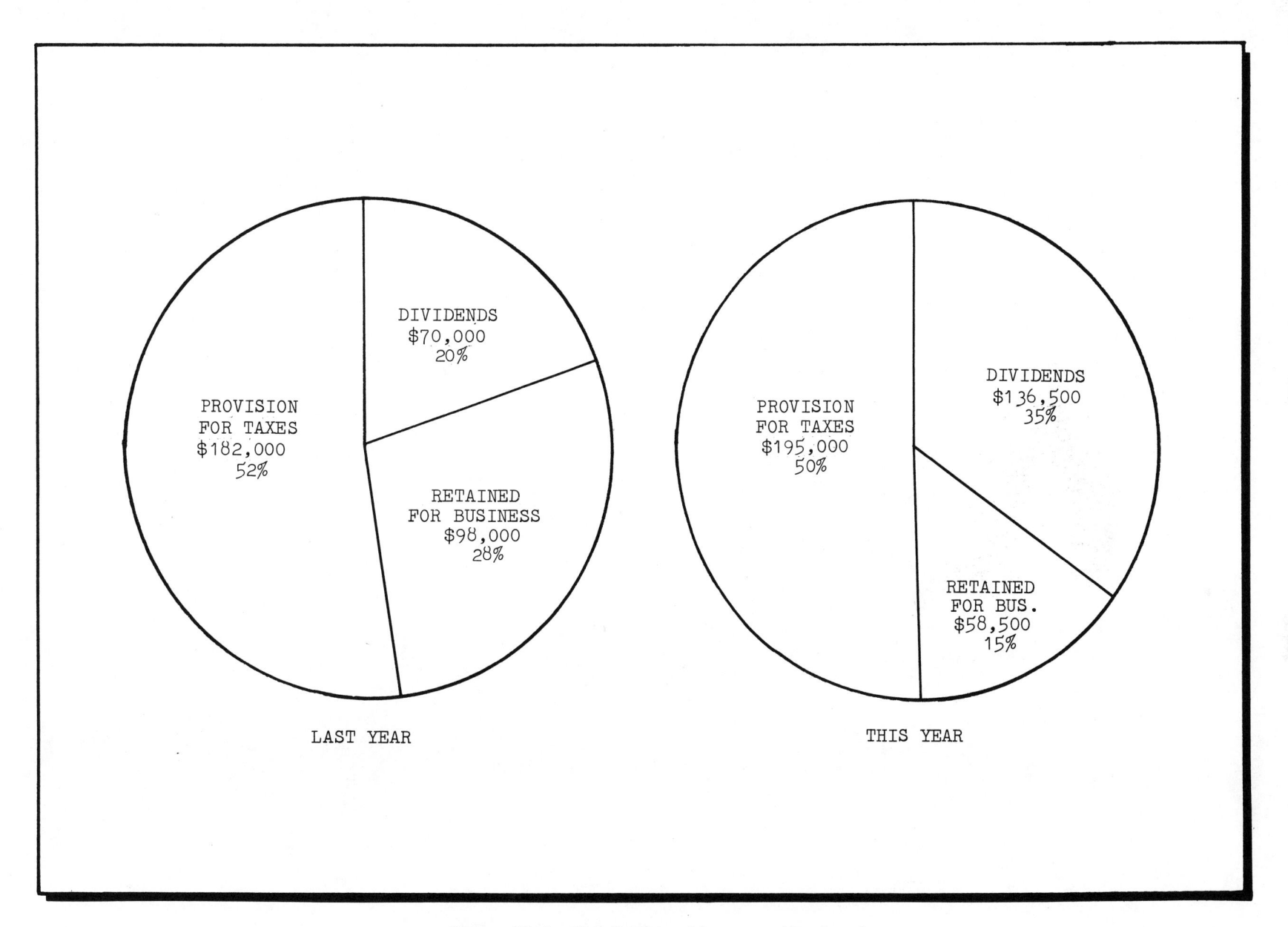

- DIVIDENDS
  $70,000
  20%
- PROVISION FOR TAXES
  $182,000
  52%
- RETAINED FOR BUSINESS
  $98,000
  28%

THIS YEAR

- DIVIDENDS
  $136,500
  35%
- PROVISION FOR TAXES
  $195,000
  50%
- RETAINED FOR BUS.
  $58,500
  15%

Figure 13.4 Distribution of Income—Version 4

14.0 EARNINGS

This section displays examples of charts that can be used for showing performance as it relates to earnings (profits). In actual application, these charts would normally be identified more specifically; i.e., operating earnings, pre-tax profit, operating margin, net profit, net earnings, etc. Also see Sections 15.0, *Earnings and Sales,* 16.0, *Earnings as a Percent of Sales,* and 17.0, *Earnings, Sales, and Costs.*

14.1 Earnings—Version 1: A simple version of an earnings tracking chart is shown as Version 1, Figure 14.1. The grid, in this example, has been constructed to provide for showing losses as well as profits. Planned earnings, on a rate per month basis, are shown with a dashed line. Actual earnings to the reporting date are shown with a solid line.

14.2 Earnings—Version 2: Version 2 of an earnings tracking chart, Figure 14.2, is identical to Version 1, except actual earnings (in this example) are shown using solid columns instead of a line. A variation of this example would be to hatch, or color-code, the loss columns differently from the profit columns.

14.3 Earnings—Version 3: Earnings are shown in the example earnings tracking chart, Version 3, Figure 14.3, on a cumulative basis. The plan is shown with a dashed line, and actual earnings up to the reporting date are shown with a solid line.

14.4 Earnings—Version 4: An earnings tracking chart that shows the plan, or forecast, in step line form and actuals with solid columns is shown as Version 4 of an earnings tracking chart, Figure 14.4.

14.5 Earnings—Version 5: In Version 5, an earnings tracking chart, Figure 14.5, the monthly plan and actual profit figures have been annualized on a year-to-date basis. This approach makes it easier for the chart reader to relate month-by-month activity with the year-end objective.

14.6 Earnings—Version 6: Planned and actual earnings on an annualized year-to-date basis are shown as Version 6 of an earnings tracking chart, Figure 14.6. The plan, in this example, is shown in step line form. The actual earnings are shown using solid columns.

14.7 Earnings—Version 7: Earnings in terms of percent deviation from plan are shown in Version 7 of an earnings tracking chart, Figure 14.7. This example uses cumulative figures as the basis. The same style chart could also be used for rate per month or annualized figures.

14.8 Earnings—Version 8: In some situations it is useful to look at the current year's planned and actual earnings in relationship to past performance. The earnings tracking chart shown as Version 8, Figure 14.8, shows the current year's planned and actual cumulative earnings in relationship to the previous year's actual cumulative earnings.

14.9 Earnings—Version 9: Earnings on a rate per month

basis are shown as Version 9 of an earnings tracking chart, Figure 14.9. The plan is shown in step line form with a dashed line, and the current year's actual performance to date is shown using solid columns. The previous year's actual earnings are shown using a solid line.

14.10 Earnings—Version 10: The tracking of earnings is done on the basis of quarters in Version 10 of an earnings tracking chart, Figure 14.10. Paired columns are used to show the current year's forecasted and actual earnings. The previous year's actual earnings are shown with a solid step line.

14.11 Earnings—Version 11: A method for showing earnings performance covering a span of several years is shown in Version 11 of an earnings tracking chart, Figure 14.11. The actual earnings for four previous years are shown in line curve style, with a solid line, on the left-hand side of the chart. The current year's planned earnings and actual earnings to date are annualized on a year-to-date basis so they can be more easily compared with performance in previous years. The coming year's forecasted earnings are shown by quarters, also annualized.

14.12 Earnings—Version 12: A percent deviation from plan style chart is used to show earning performance on both a rate per month and an annualized basis in Version 12 of an earnings tracking chart, Figure 14.12. The deviation from plan for monthly earnings is shown with a solid line. A dashed line is used to show these deviations on an annualized basis.

14.13 Earnings—Version 13: A pair of charts is utilized to display earnings status in Version 13 of an earnings tracking chart, Figure 14.13. The top grid shows forecasted and actual earnings on a cumulative basis. The bottom chart shows rate per month status in terms of percent deviation from plan.

14.14 Earnings—Version 14: Three separate elements are combined on the earnings tracking chart shown as Version 14, Figure 14.14. Planned and actual earnings on a cumulative basis are shown in the upper left-hand grid. Below that earnings are shown in terms of rate per month. The right-hand side of the chart provides space for a narrative analysis.

14.15 Earnings—Version 15: A statistical table has been combined with a graphic chart in Version 15 of an earnings tracking chart, Figure 14.15. Forecasted and actual earnings, and the variance between these two factors, are shown in the statistical table portion of the chart in cumulative form. The forecasted and actual cumulative earnings are also plotted on the graphic portion of the chart.

14.16 Earnings—Version 16: A statistical table with nine lines of data has been combined with a graphic chart in Version 16 of an earnings tracking chart, Figure 14.16. Forecasted and actual earnings, and the variance between these two factors, are given in terms of rate per month, cumulative, and annualized statistics in the table. The annualized figures are also plotted on the graphic portion of the chart.

14.17 Earnings—Version 17: A statistical table that can be used for tracking earnings status is shown in Figure 14.17. Forecasted and actual earnings, variances in terms of dollars, and deviations from plans in terms of percentages are given on the basis of rate per month, cumulative, and annualized statistics.

14.18 Earnings—Version 18: A one-time status report in the form of a statistical table is shown in Figure 14.18. In this example, the dollar and percentage performance of several different divisions of an enterprise are compared in terms of the previous year's earnings, the current year's forecasted and actual earnings to the date of the report, and the anticipated, or forecasted, earnings for the coming year. The most significant anomaly in this example has been underlined to attract the chart reader's attention.

14.19 Earnings—Version 19: Another version of a one-time status report is shown in Figure 14.19. Forecasted and actual earnings, as well as variances and percentage deviations from plans, are

Earnings

153

given for the month just concluded at the time of the status report, and also in terms of annualized earnings for that month, cumulative earnings to date, and the anticipated year-end earnings.

14.20 Earnings—Version 20: An information style chart covering a ten-year time span is shown as Version 20 of an earnings chart, Figure 14.20. This example is not a tracking chart and is useful primarily in examining trends.

14.21 Earnings—Version 21: In Figure 14.21, a segmented circle chart ("pie" chart) is used to show the performance of separate divisions of an enterprise and their related contribution to overall earnings. Status is shown for one point in time. As with Version 20 this is not a tracking chart.

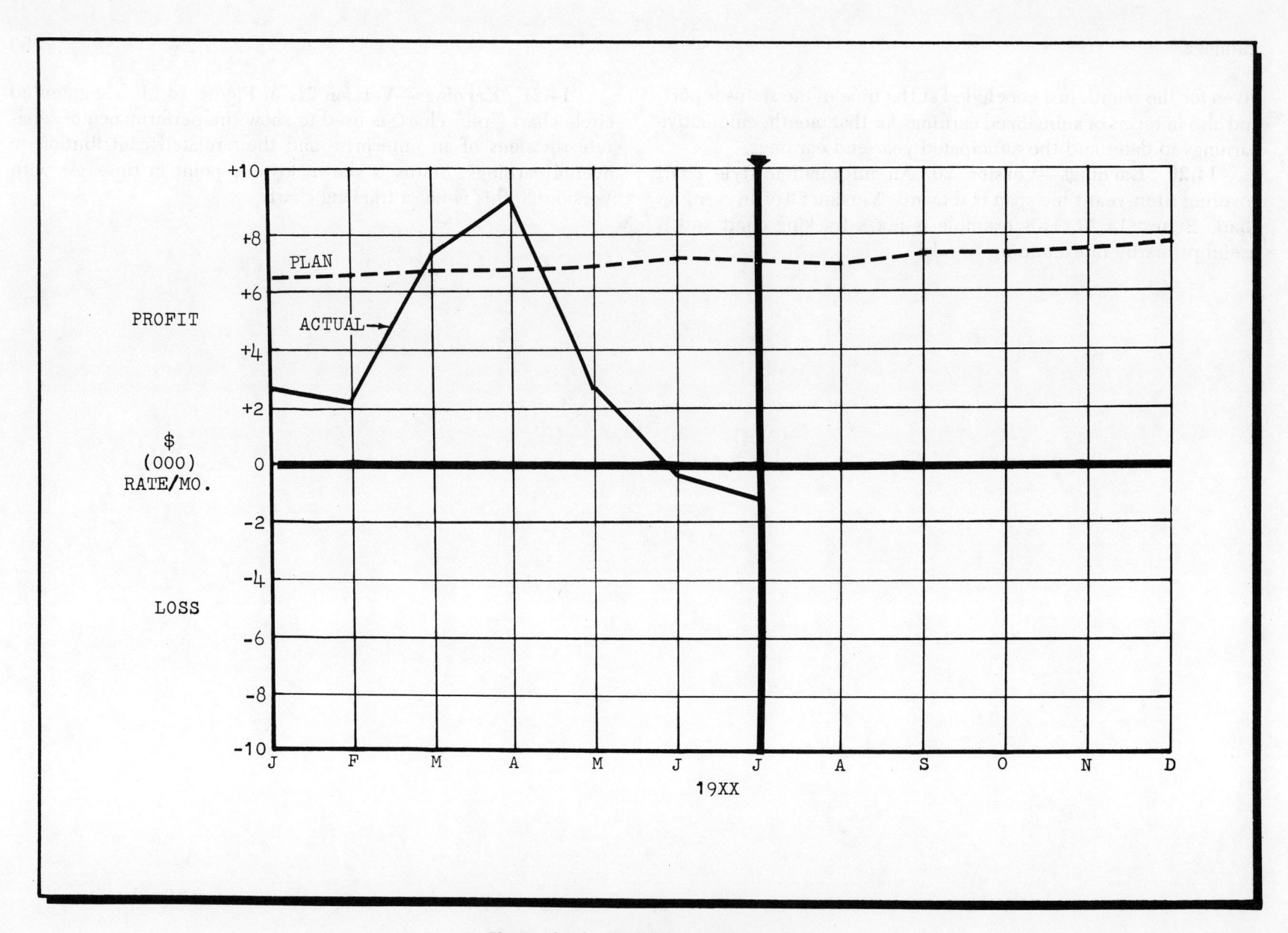

Figure 14.1   Earnings—Version 1

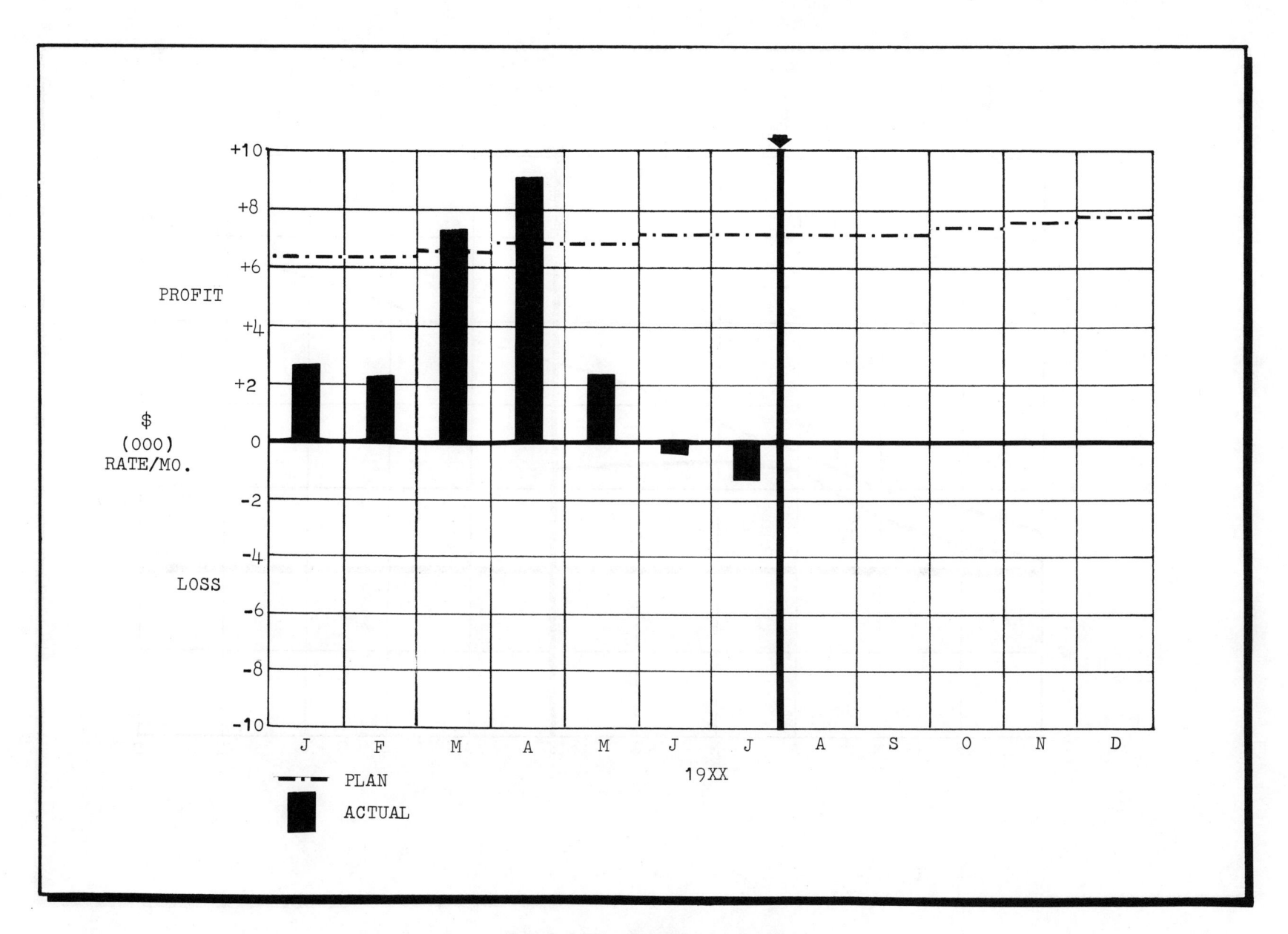

Figure 14.2   Earnings—Version 2

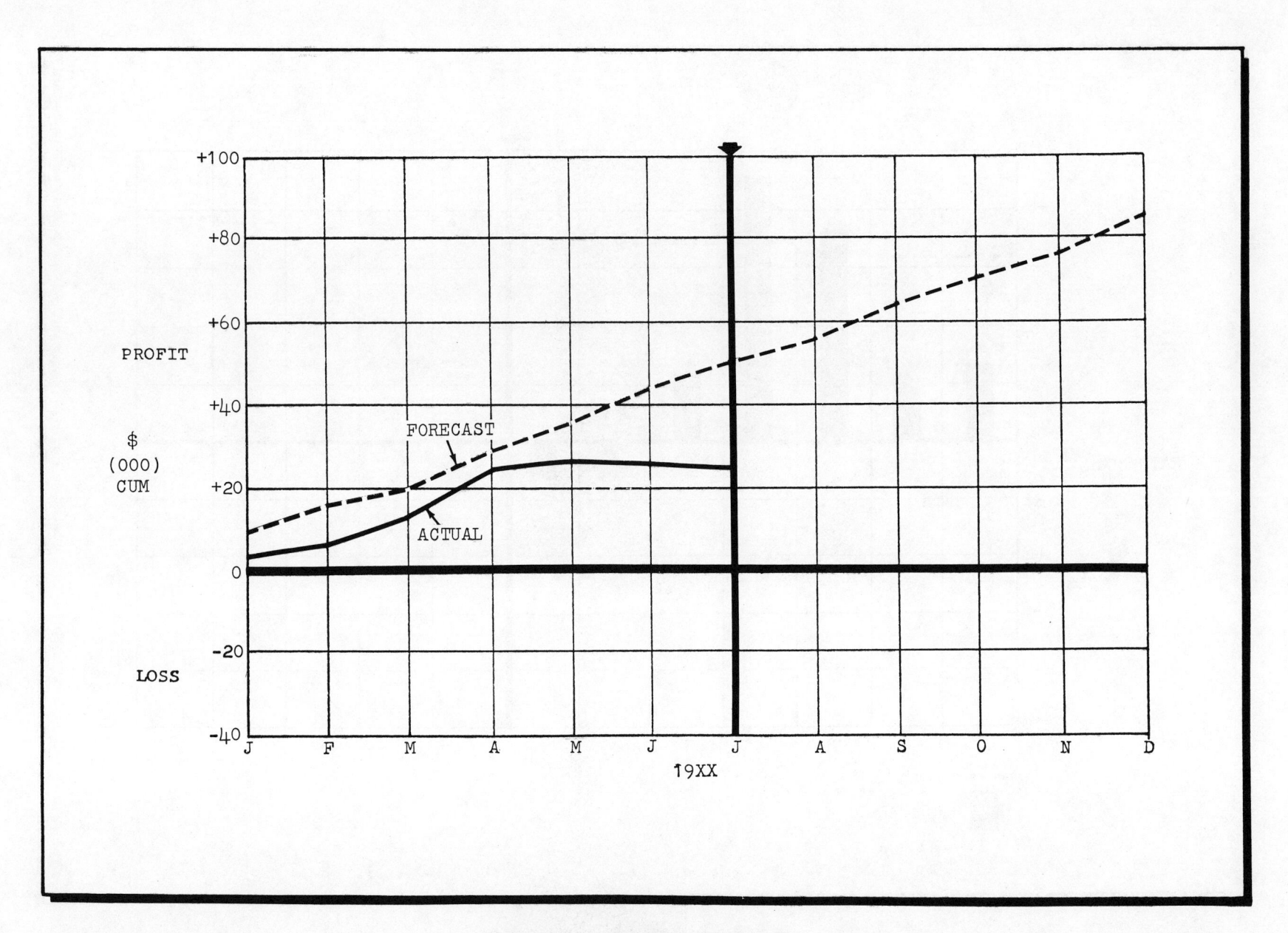

Figure 14.3 Earnings—Version 3

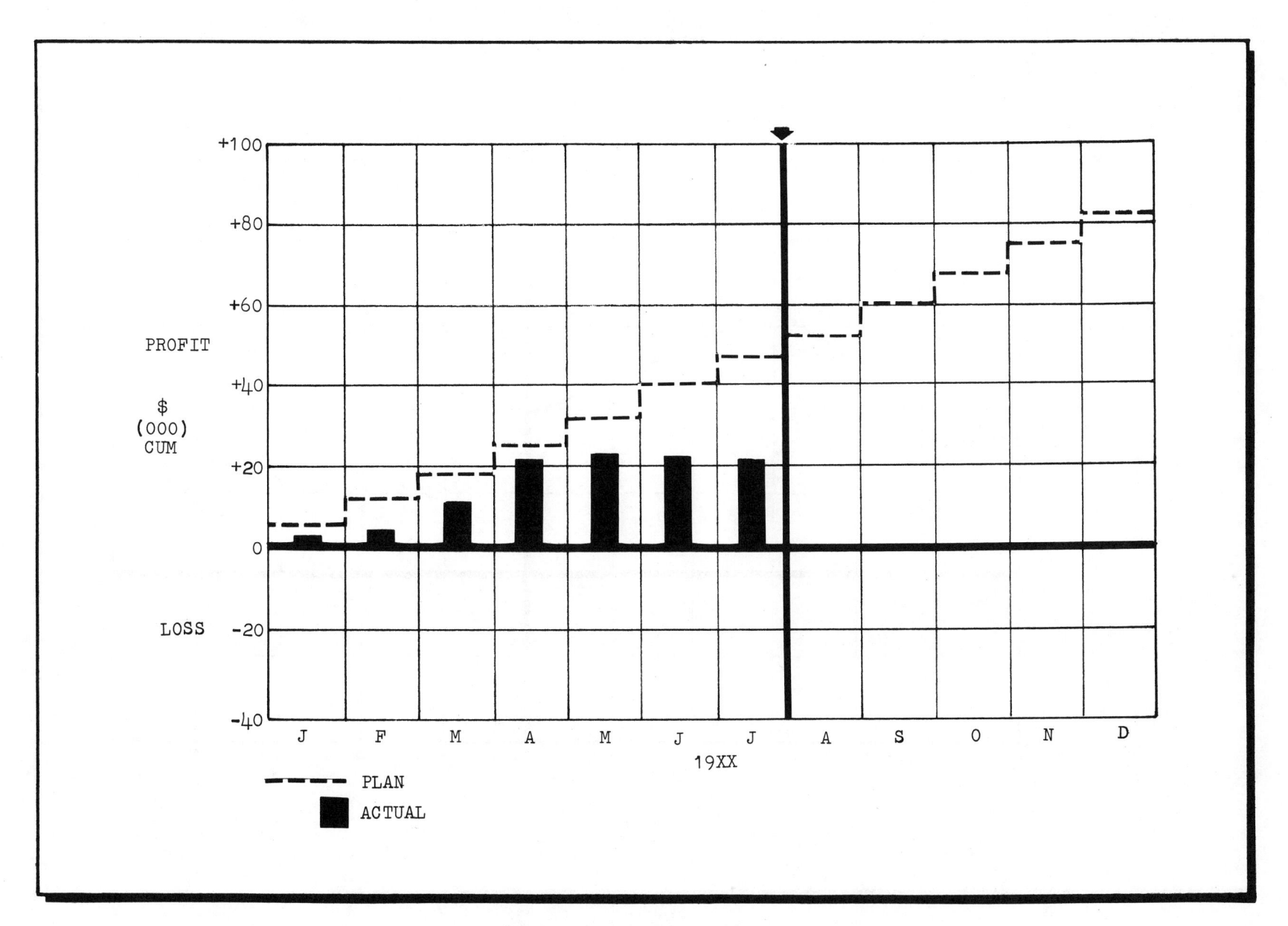

Figure 14.4   Earnings—Version 4

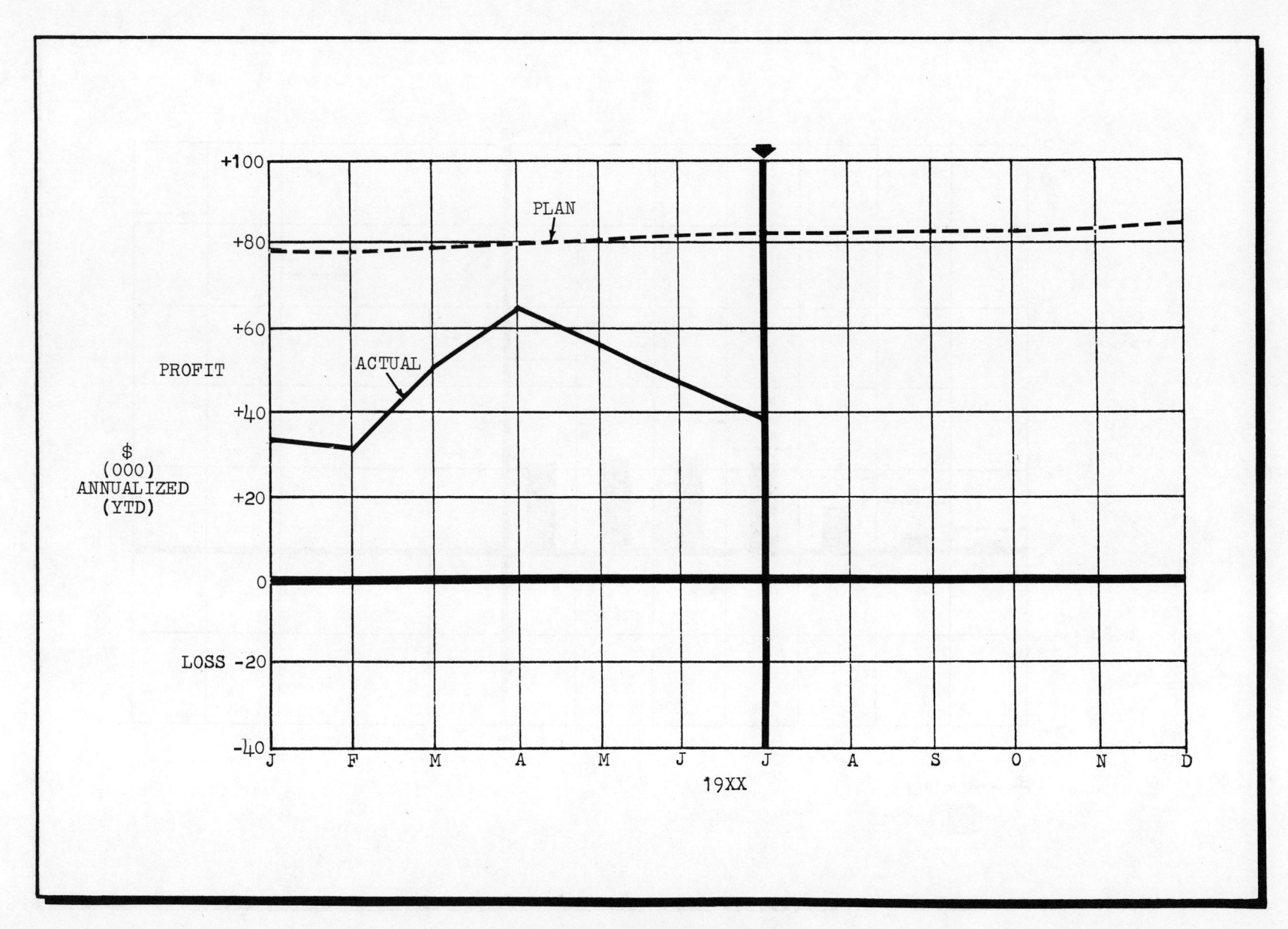

Figure 14.5 Earnings—Version 5

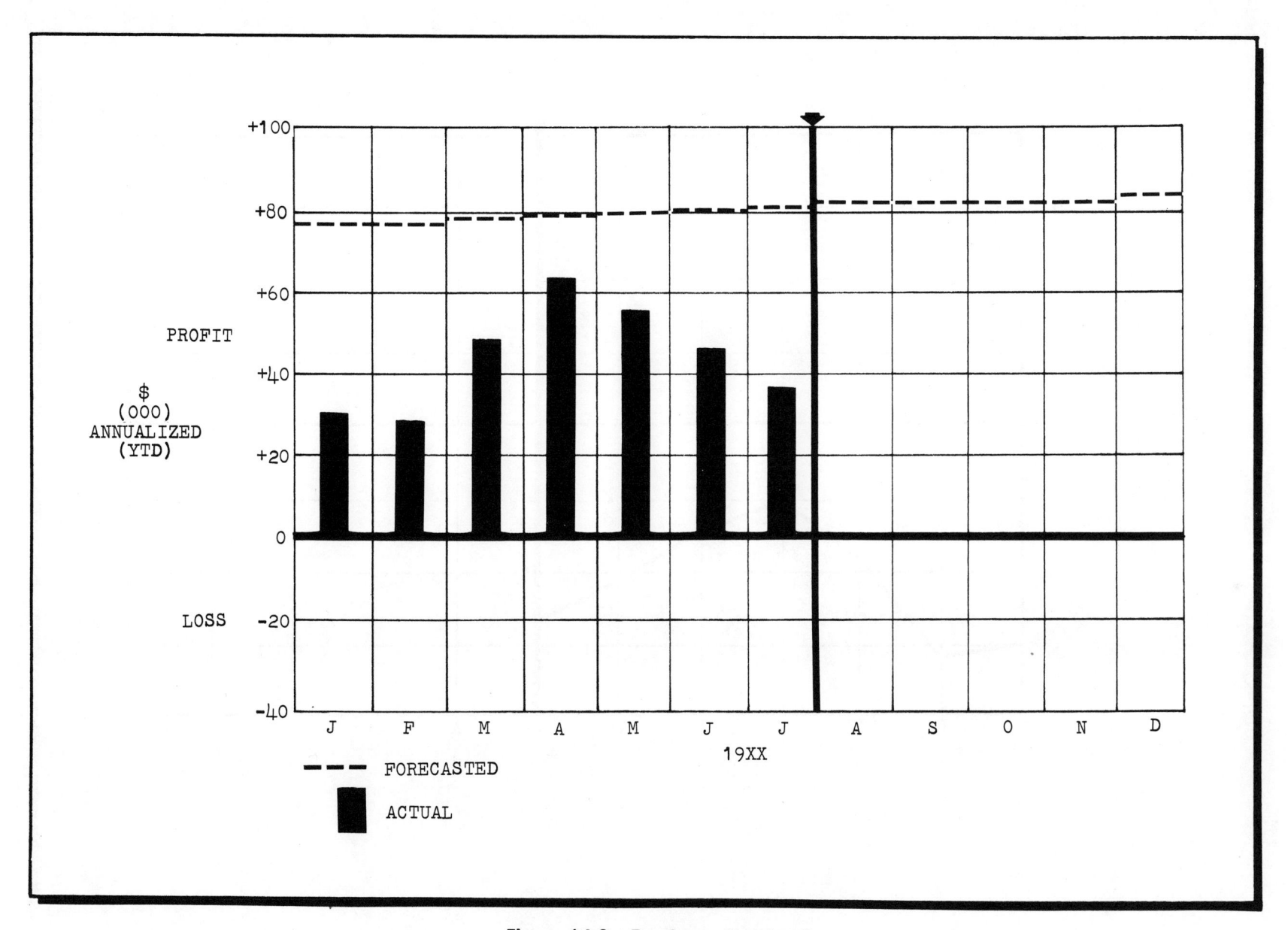

Figure 14.6   Earnings—Version 6

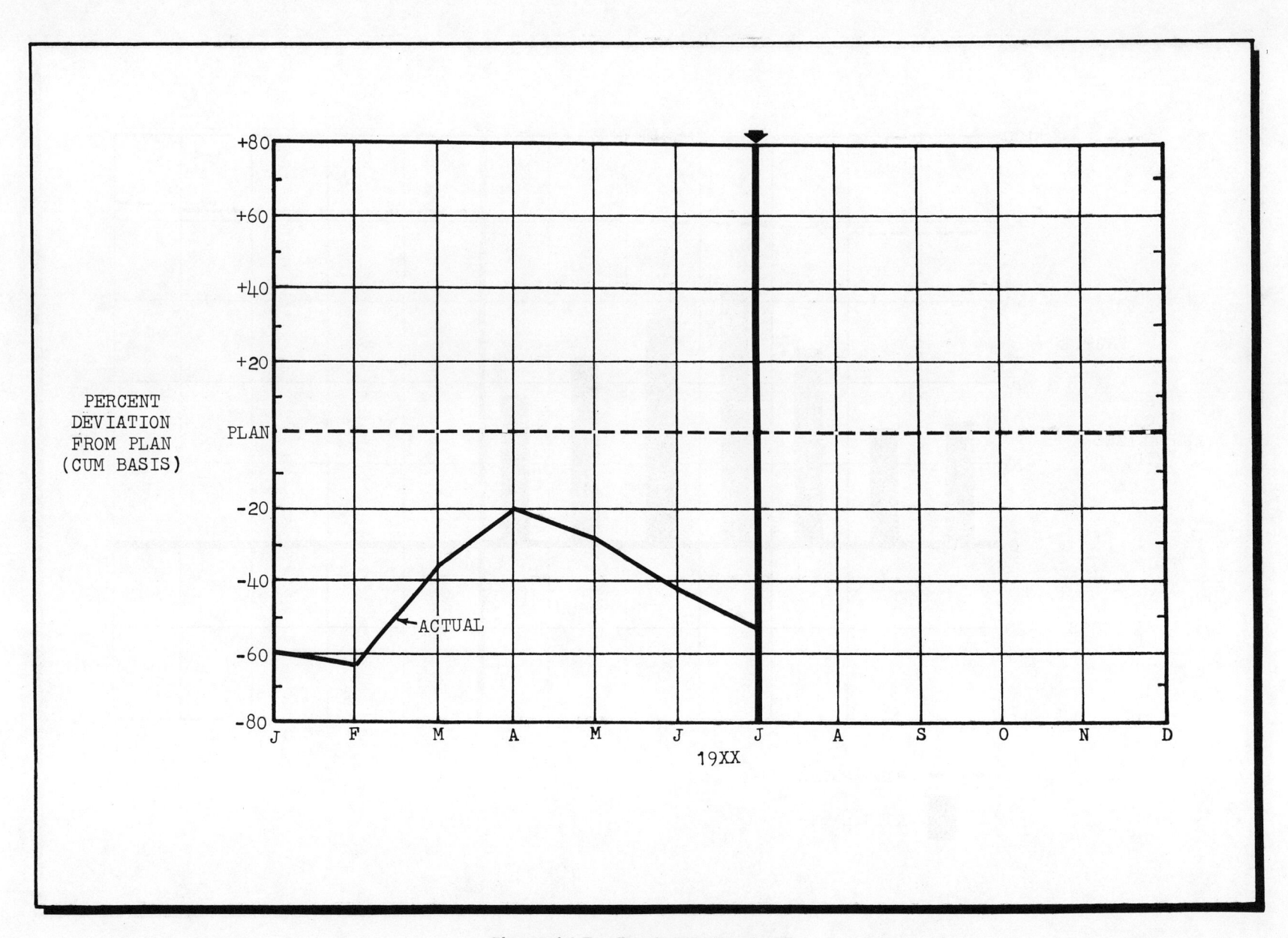

Figure 14.7 Earnings—Version 7

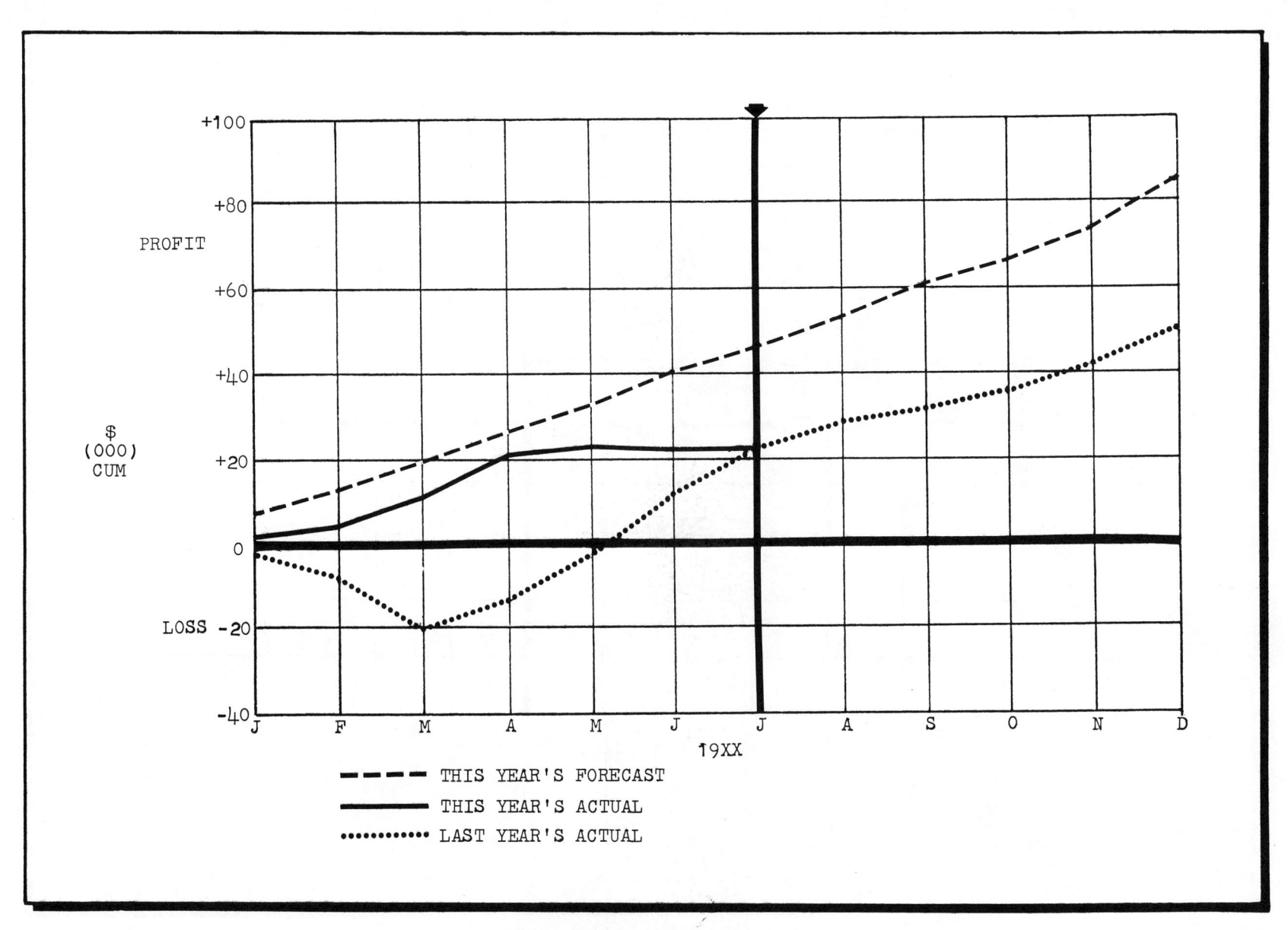

Figure 14.8 Earnings—Version 8

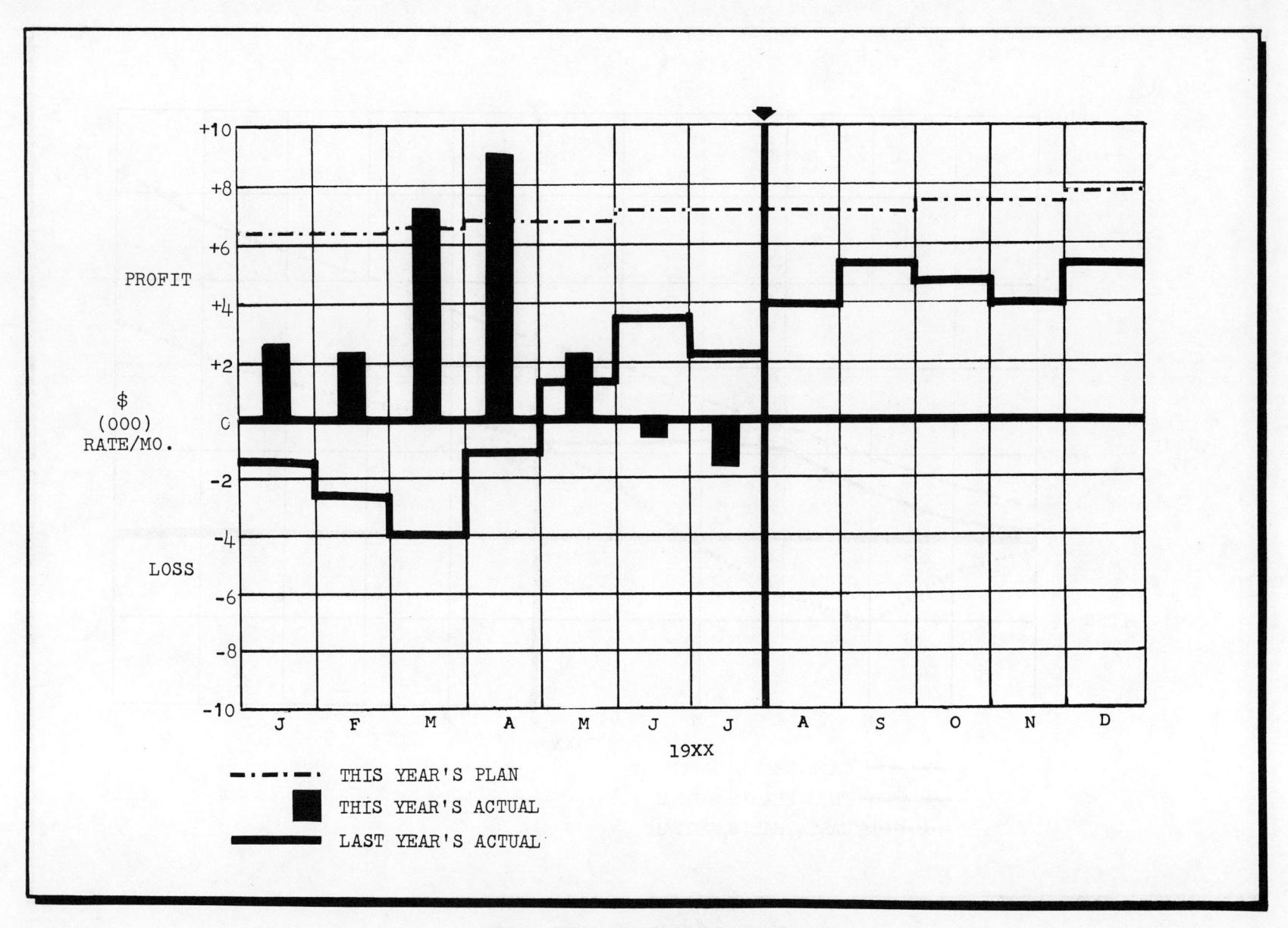

Figure 14.9   Earnings—Version 9

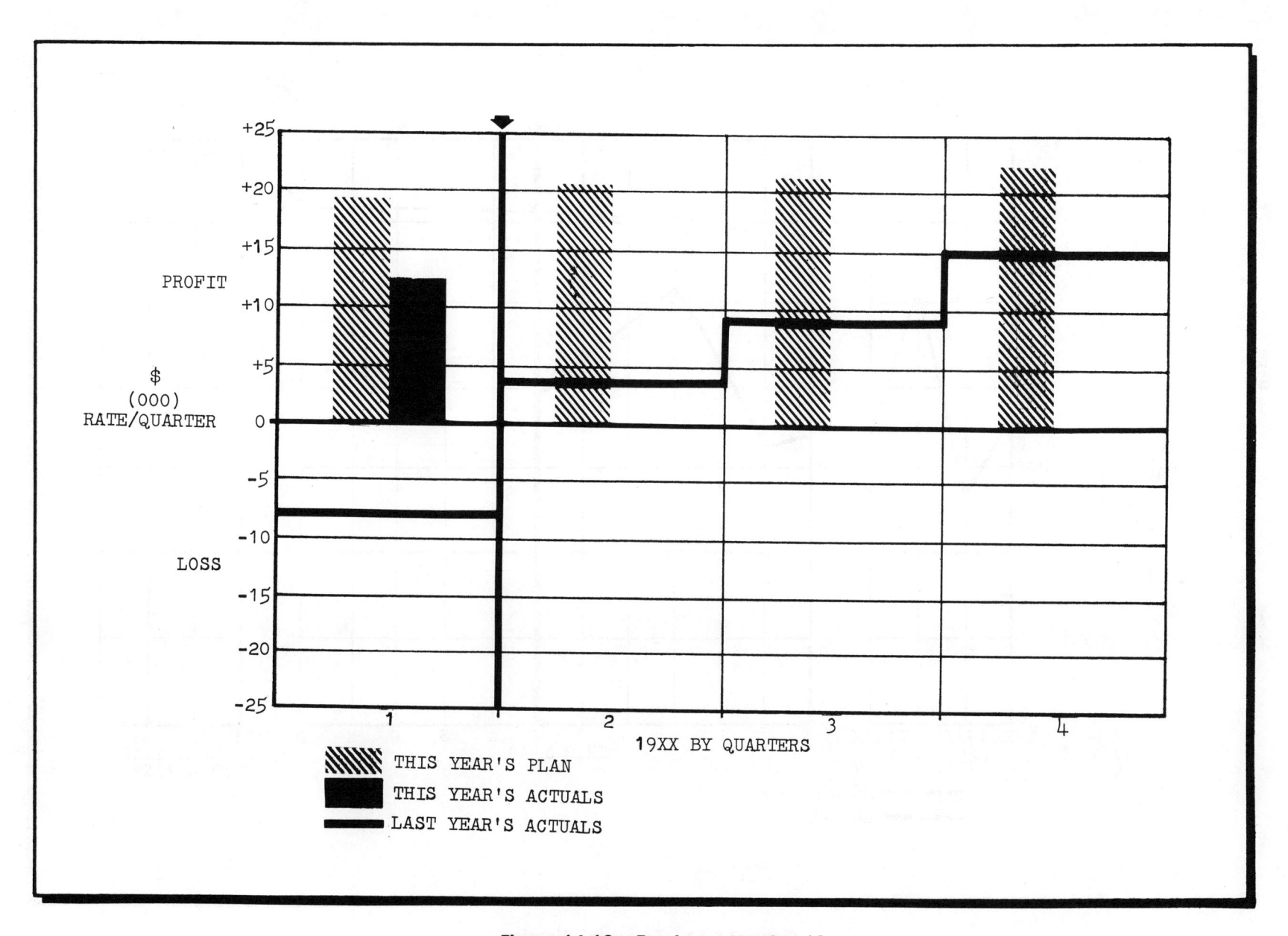

Figure 14.10   Earnings—Version 10

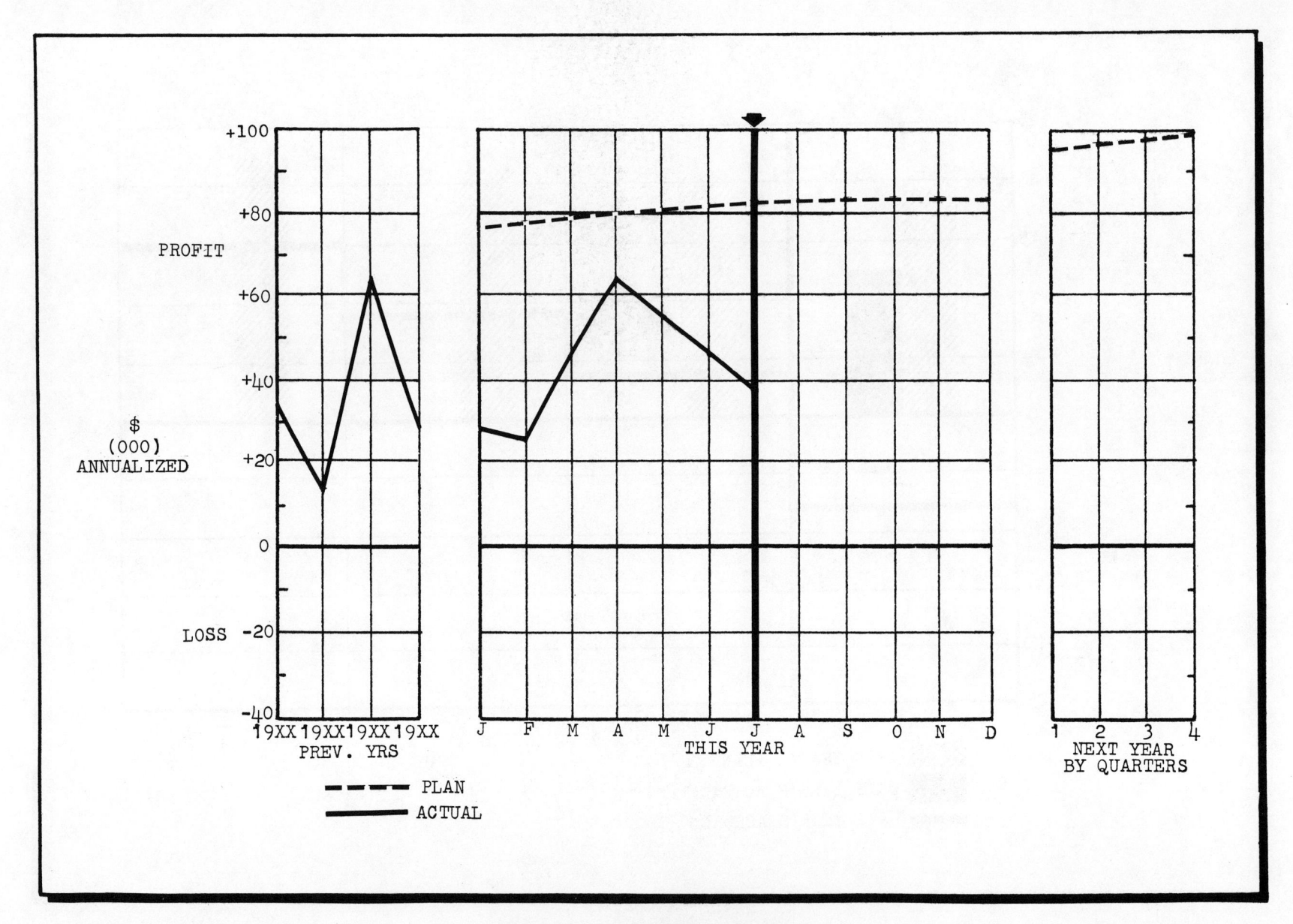

Figure 14.11 Earnings—Version 11

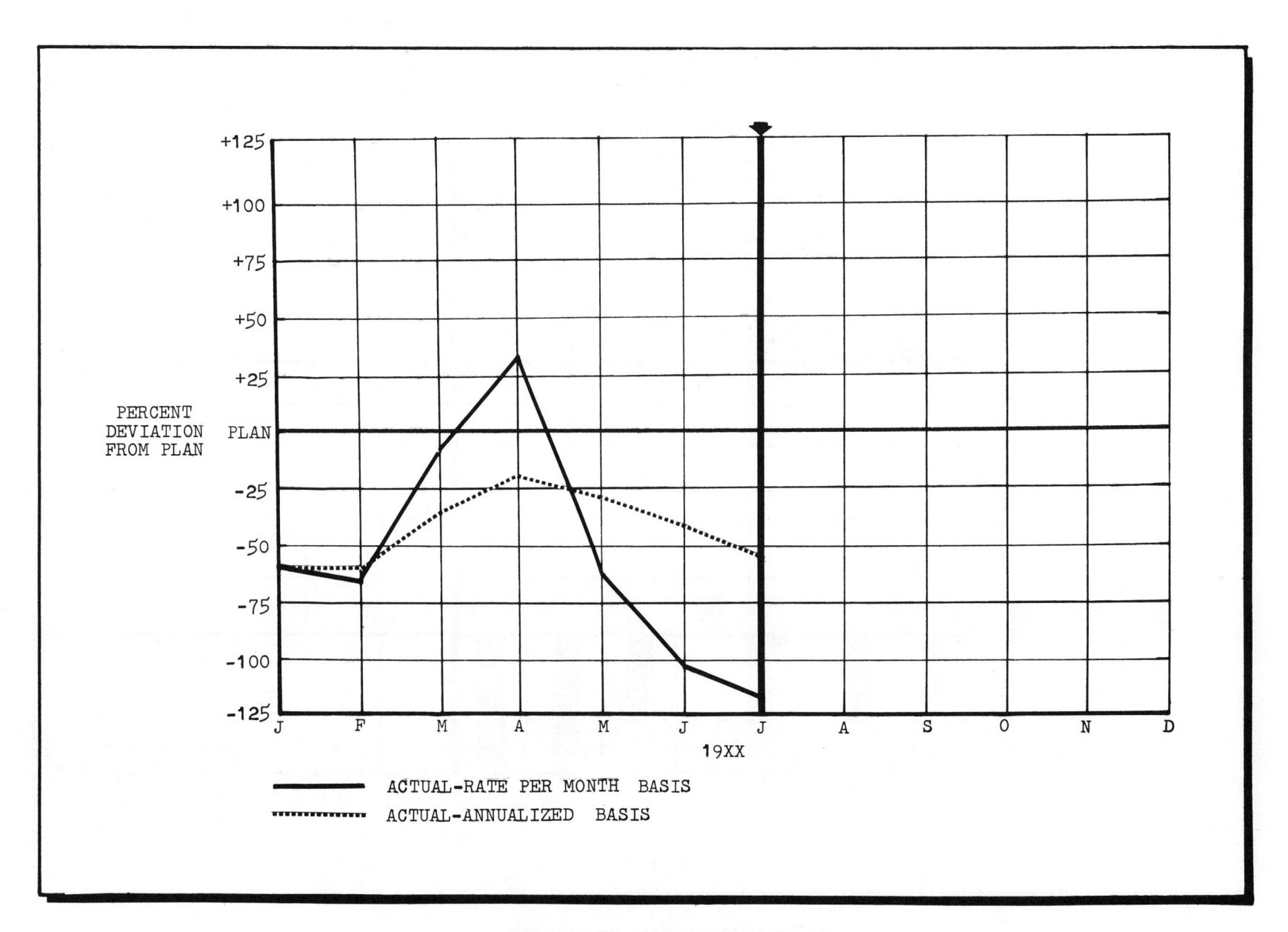

Figure 14.12 Earnings—Version 12

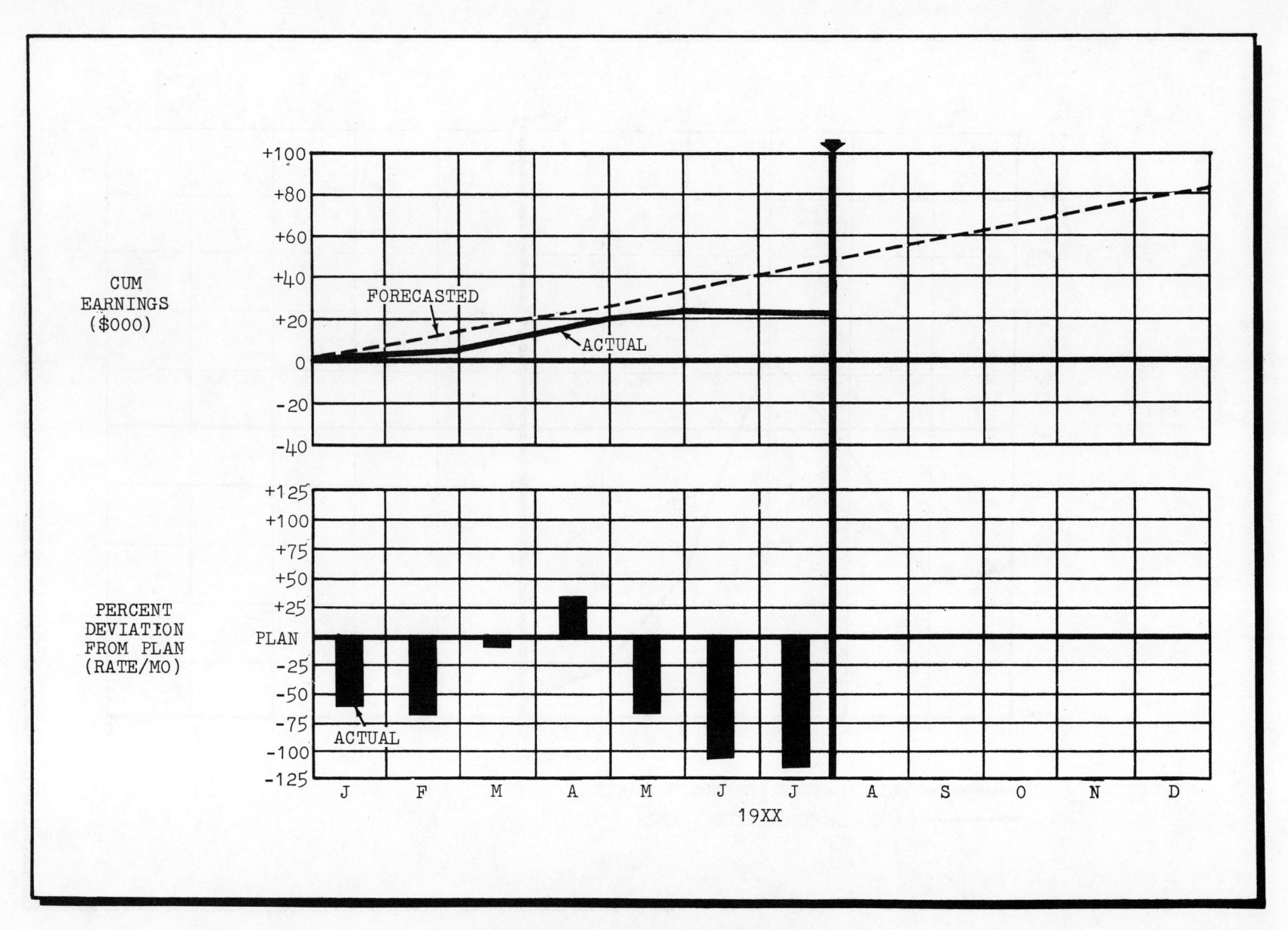

Figure 14.13 Earnings—Version 13

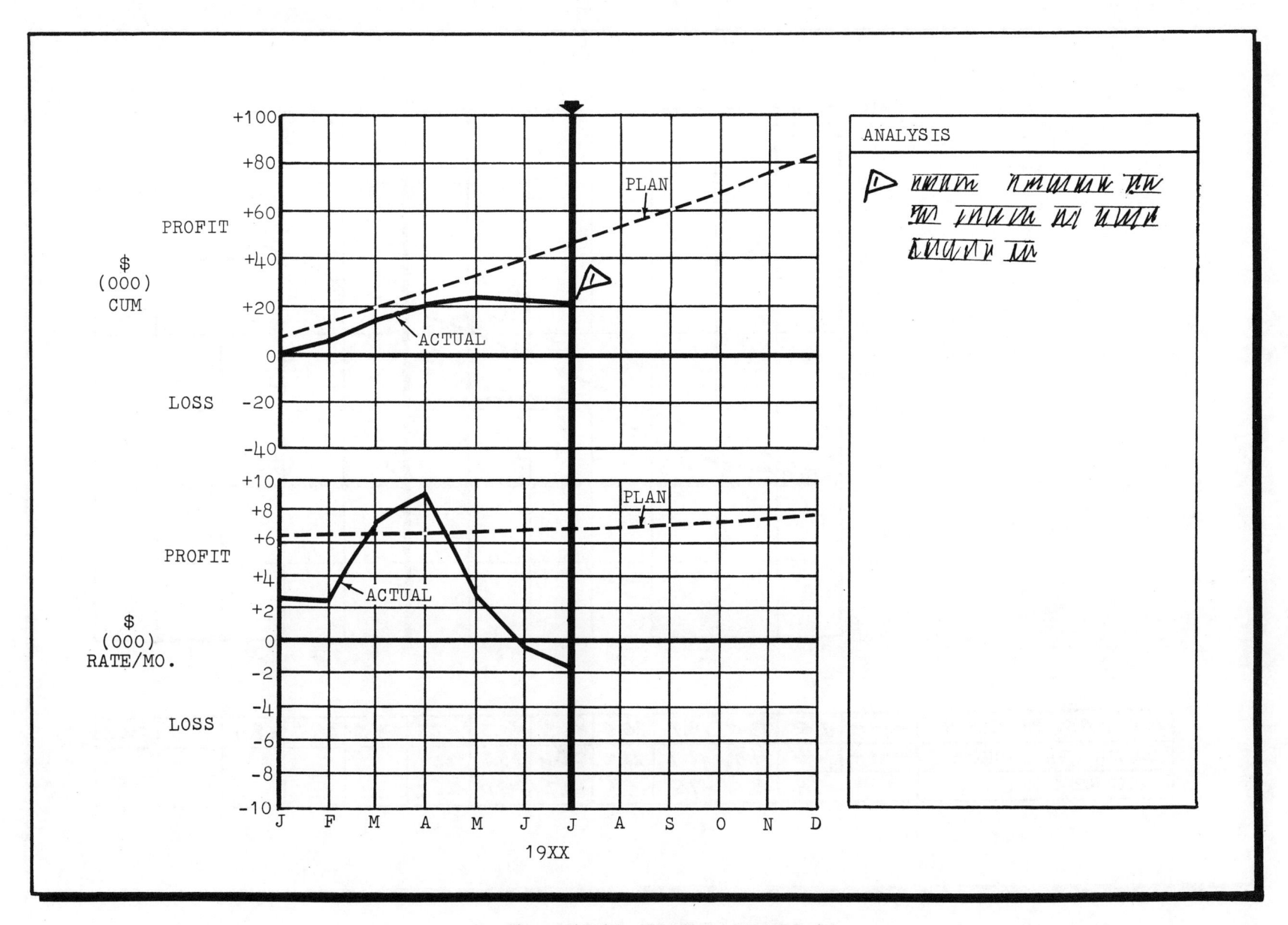

Figure 14.14 Earnings—Version 14

		J	F	M	A	M	J	J	A	S	O	N	D
FORECASTED PROFIT-CUM	-----	6.5	13.0	19.7	26.5	33.3	40.3	47.3	54.3	61.5	68.9	76.4	84.2
ACTUAL PROFIT-CUM	———	2.6	4.9	12.2	21.2	23.6	23.3	22.1					
VARIANCE-CUM		-3.9	-8.1	-7.5	-5.3	-9.7	-17.0	-25.2					

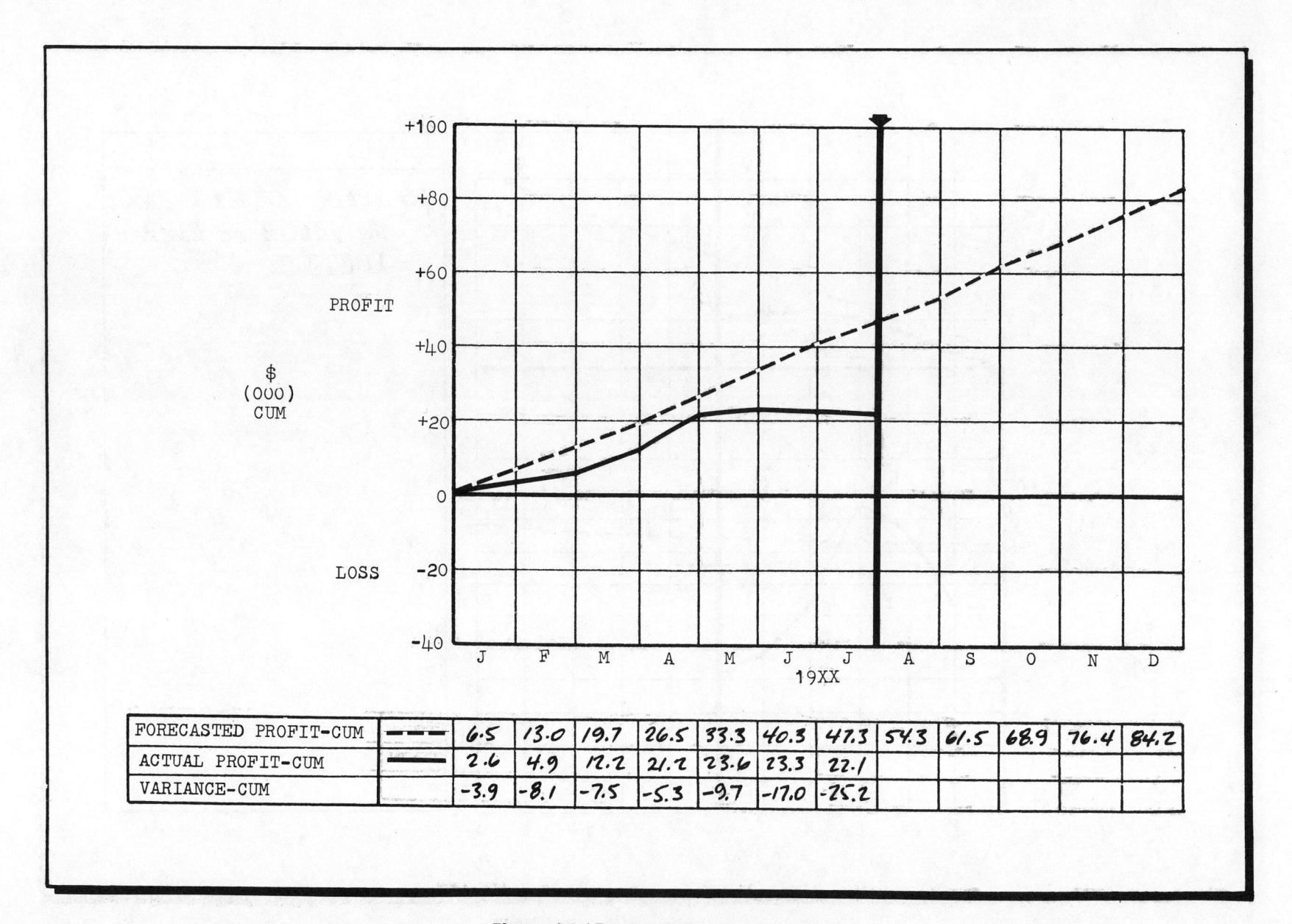

Figure 14.15 Earnings—Version 15

		J	F	M	A	M	J	J	A	S	O	N	D
RATE PER MO	FORECAST	6.5	6.5	6.7	6.8	6.8	7.0	7.0	7.0	7.2	7.4	7.5	7.8
	ACTUAL	2.6	2.3	7.3	9.0	2.4	-.3	-1.2					
	VARIANCE	-3.9	-4.2	+.6	+2.2	-4.4	-7.3	-8.2					
CUMULATIVE	FORECAST	6.5	13.0	19.7	26.5	33.3	40.3	47.3	54.3	61.5	68.9	76.4	84.2
	ACTUAL	2.6	4.9	12.2	21.2	23.6	23.3	22.1					
	VARIANCE	-3.9	-8.1	-7.5	-5.3	-9.7	-17.0	-25.2					
ANNUALIZED (YTD)	FORECAST	78.0	78.0	78.8	79.5	79.9	80.6	81.1	81.5	82.0	82.7	83.3	84.2
	ACTUAL	31.2	29.4	48.8	63.6	56.6	46.6	37.9					
	VARIANCE	-46.8	-48.6	-30.0	-15.9	-23.3	-34.0	-43.2					

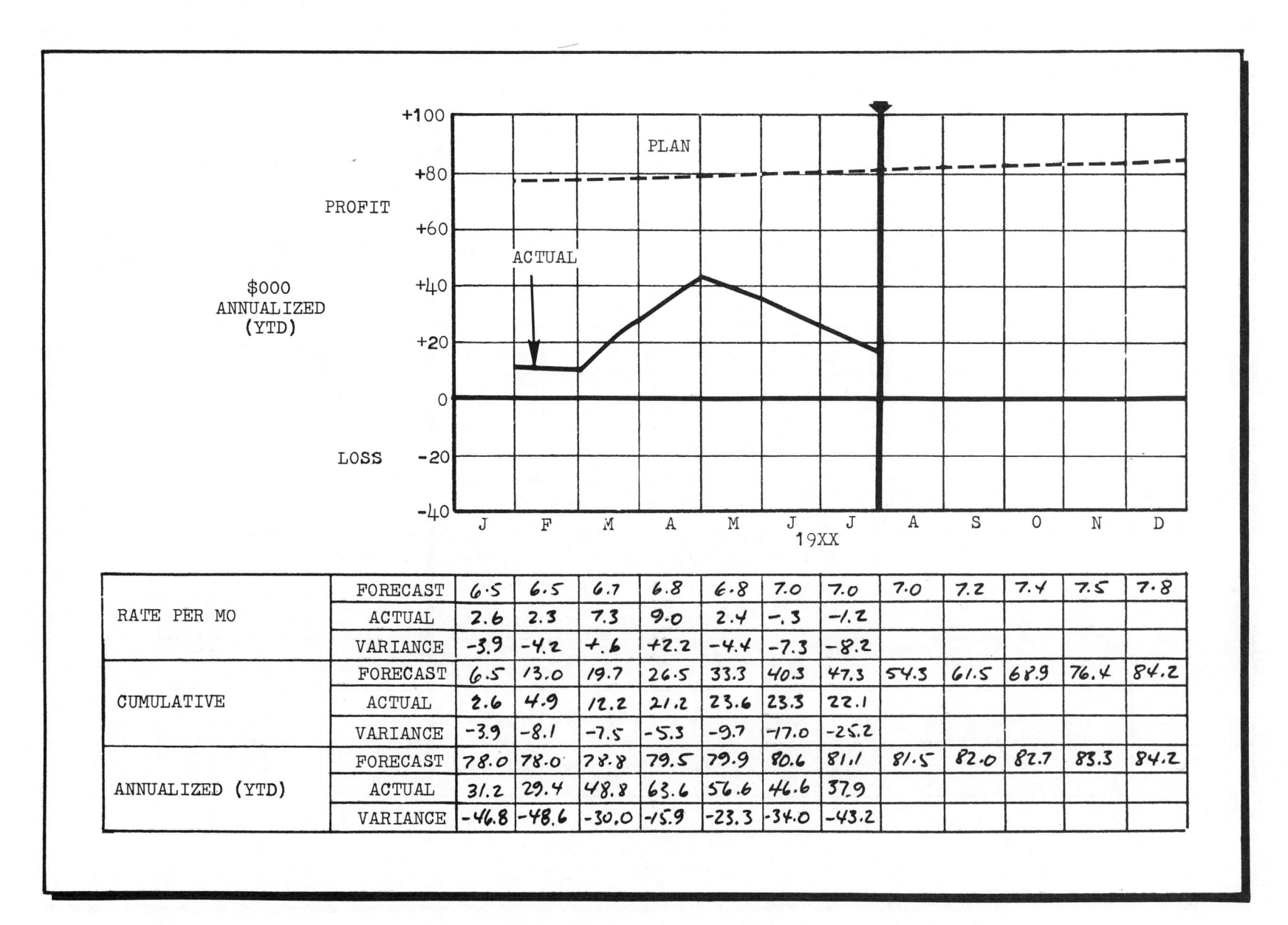

Figure 14.16   Earnings—Version 16

FACTOR		19XX											
		J	F	M	A	M	J	J	A	S	O	N	D
FORECAST ($000)	RATE PER MO.	6.5	6.5	6.7	6.8	6.8	7.0	7.0	7.0	7.2	7.4	7.5	7.8
	CUMULATIVE	6.5	13.0	19.7	26.5	33.3	40.3	47.3	54.3	61.5	68.9	76.4	84.2
	ANNUALIZED-YTD	78.0	78.0	78.8	79.5	79.9	80.6	81.1	81.5	82.0	82.7	83.3	84.2
ACTUAL ($000)	RATE PER MO.	2.6	2.3	7.3	9.0	2.4	-.3	-1.2					
	CUMULATIVE	2.6	4.9	12.2	21.2	23.6	23.3	22.1					
	ANNUALIZED-YTD	31.2	29.4	48.8	63.6	56.6	46.6	37.9					
VARIANCE ($000)	RATE PER MO.	-3.9	-4.2	+.6	+2.2	-4.4	-7.3	-8.2					
	CUMULATIVE	-3.9	-8.1	-7.5	-5.3	-9.7	-17.0	-25.2					
	ANNUALIZED-YTD	-46.8	-48.6	-30.0	-15.9	-23.3	-34.0	-43.2					
DEVIATION FROM PLAN (PERCENT)	RATE	-60	-65	-9	+32	-65	-104	-117					
	CUM. & ANNUAL'Z'D	-60	-62	-38	-20	-29	-42	-53					

Figure 14.17 Earnings—Version 17

STATUS AS OF __MARCH 31__

UNIT	LAST YEAR $000/%	THIS YEAR ANNUALIZED $000/%		NEXT YEAR $000/%
		FORECAST	ACTUAL	
DIVISION A	7.3/10%	17.6/21%	19.5/26%	26.9/27%
DIVISION B	25.4/35%	13.5/16%	12.7/17%	9.0/9%
DIVISION C	18.2/25%	21.9/26%	18.0/24%	23.9/24%
DIVISION D	5.7/8%	15.2/18%	15.8/21%	27.8/28%
DIVISION E	16.0/22%	16.0/19%	<u>9.0/12%</u>	12.0/12%
TOTALS	72.6/100%	84.2/100%	75.0/100%	99.6/100%

Figure 14.18 Earnings—Version 18

STATUS AS OF __AUGUST 1__

	FORECAST ($000)	ACTUAL ($000)	VARIANCE ($000)	DEVIATION FROM PLAN (%)
EARNINGS FOR PAST MONTH	7.0	-1.2	-8.2	-117
ANNUALIZED EARNINGS FOR PAST MONTH	81.1	37.9	-43.2	-53
CUM EARNINGS TO DATE	47.3	22.1	-25.2	-53
ANTICIPATED YEAR-END EARNINGS	84.2	75.0	-9.2	-11

Figure 14.19 Earnings—Version 19

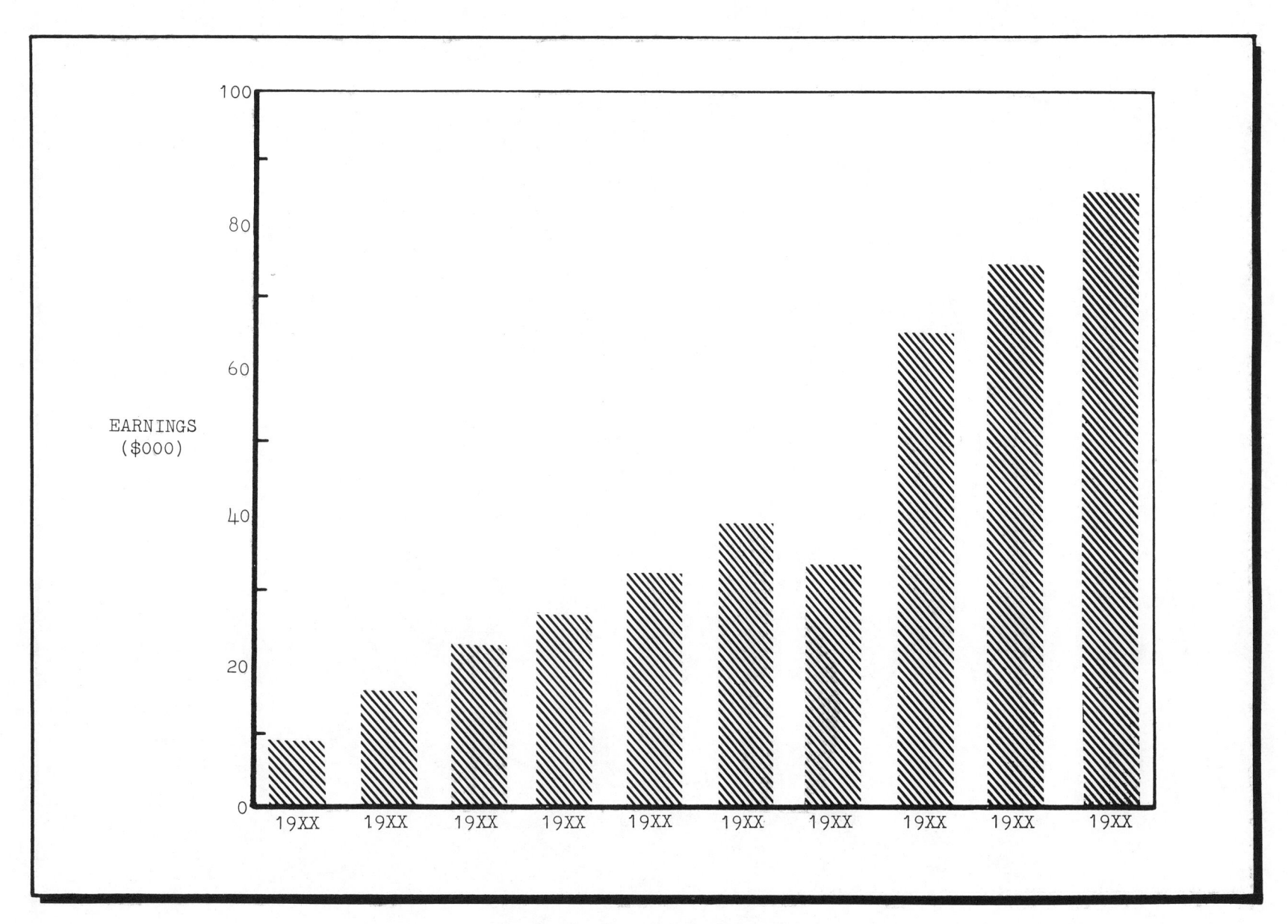

Figure 14.20   Earnings—Version 20

DIV. A
$5,900
7%

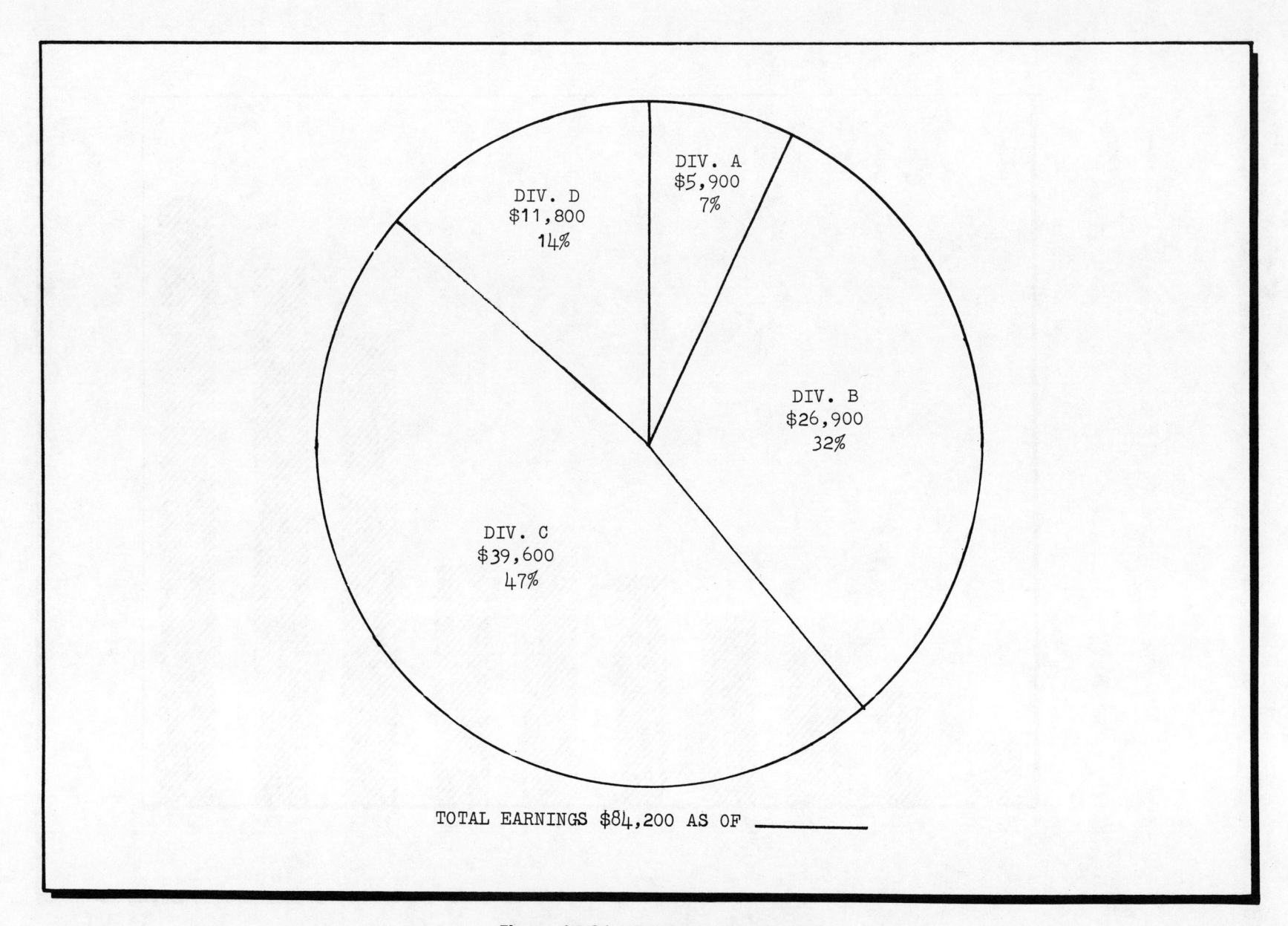

DIV. D
$11,800
14%

DIV. B
$26,900
32%

DIV. C
$39,600
47%

TOTAL EARNINGS $84,200 AS OF _____

Figure 14.21   Earnings—Version 21

15.0 EARNINGS AND SALES

The two factors of earnings (profits) and sales (revenues) are shown, combined, in the charts in this section. Also see Section 14.0, *Earnings*, Section 16.0, *Earnings as a Percent of Sales*, and Section 17.0, *Earnings, Sales, and Costs*.

15.1 Earnings and Sales—Version 1: The data related to both earnings and sales have been plotted in Version 1 of an earnings and sales tracking chart, Figure 15.1. In this example, sales and earnings are both shown in terms of forecasted and actual performance. The grid has been constructed to accommodate the showing of losses as well as profits.

15.2 Earnings and Sales—Version 2: Two scales have been used in Version 2 of an earnings and sales tracking chart, Figure 15.2, so as to make the earnings portion of the chart easier to read than in Version 1. The left-hand scale is used for reading the forecasted and actual sales plottings. The right-hand scale is expanded and is used for reading the profit/loss plottings.

15.3 Earnings and Sales—Version 3: Version 3 of an earnings and sales tracking chart, Figure 15.3, utilizes two grids. The left-hand grid displays the sales data. The right-hand grid displays profit and loss data. Both factors are shown in terms of forecasted and actual performance.

15.4 Earnings and Sales—Version 4: Earnings and sales are shown in Version 4, Figure 15.4, in terms of rates per month. Both the sales and the profit forecasts are shown in step line form. Actual sales are shown with a solid column, and actual profits and losses are shown with hatched columns.

15.5 Earnings and Sales—Version 5: A semi-logarithmic grid has been used in Version 5 of an earnings and sales tracking chart, Figure 15.5. This approach has the advantage of exaggerating the profit and loss columns so that they are more easily read. It has the disadvantage of distorting the relationship between the profit/loss factor and the sales factor.

15.6 Earnings and Sales—Version 6: Sales and earnings which are annualized on a year-to-date basis are shown in Figure 15.6. Both sales and earnings forecasts are in step line form. Actual sales and actual profits and losses are shown in column form.

15.7 Earnings and Sales—Version 7: A multi-year version of an earnings and sales tracking chart is shown as Version 7, Figure 15.7. In this example, annualized sales and profit/loss figures are shown for the previous four years, the current year, and the coming year.

15.8 Earnings and Sales—Version 8: A statistical table has been combined with two graphic charts in Version 8 of an earnings and sales tracking chart, Figure 15.8. The table gives cumulative sales and cumulative profit and loss statistics in terms of forecasted and actual performance and the variance therefrom. The cumulative forecasted and actual sales statistics are plotted on the top graph, and the profit and loss figures are plotted on the lower graph.

15.9 Earnings and Sales—Version 9: A statistical table type of earnings and sales tracking chart is shown as Version 9, Figure 15.9. Forecasted and actual sales and profit/loss are given in terms of rate per month, cumulative, and annualized statistics. The cumulative variances are also given.

15.10 Earnings and Sales—Version 10: A one-time status report version of an earnings and sales chart is shown as Version 10, Figure 15.10. Status for the just-completed month, the year to date, and the estimated year-end position are shown in this example. Detailed sales are summarized, and the bottom line provides the profit or loss information.

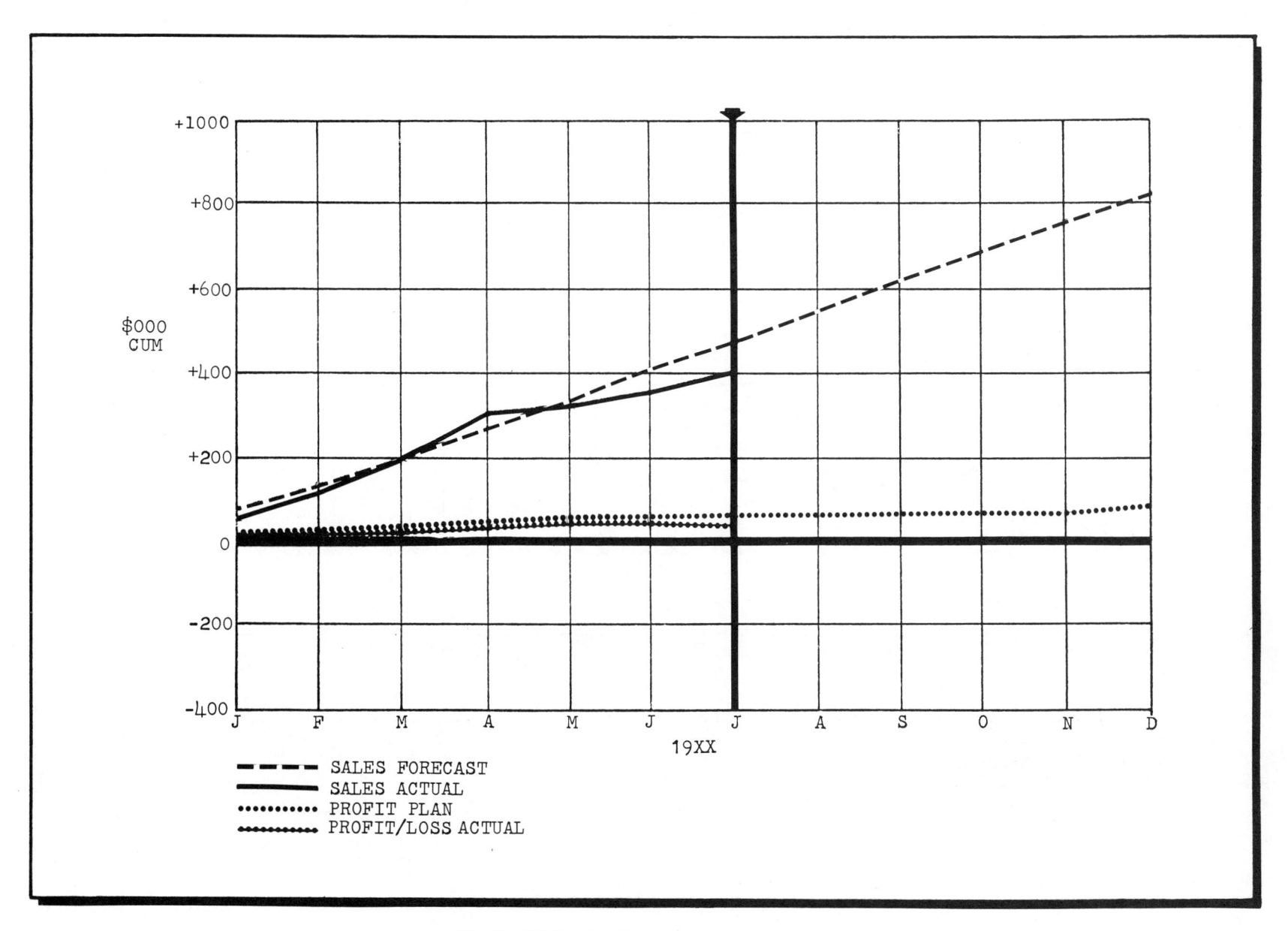

Figure 15.1 Earnings and Sales—Version 1

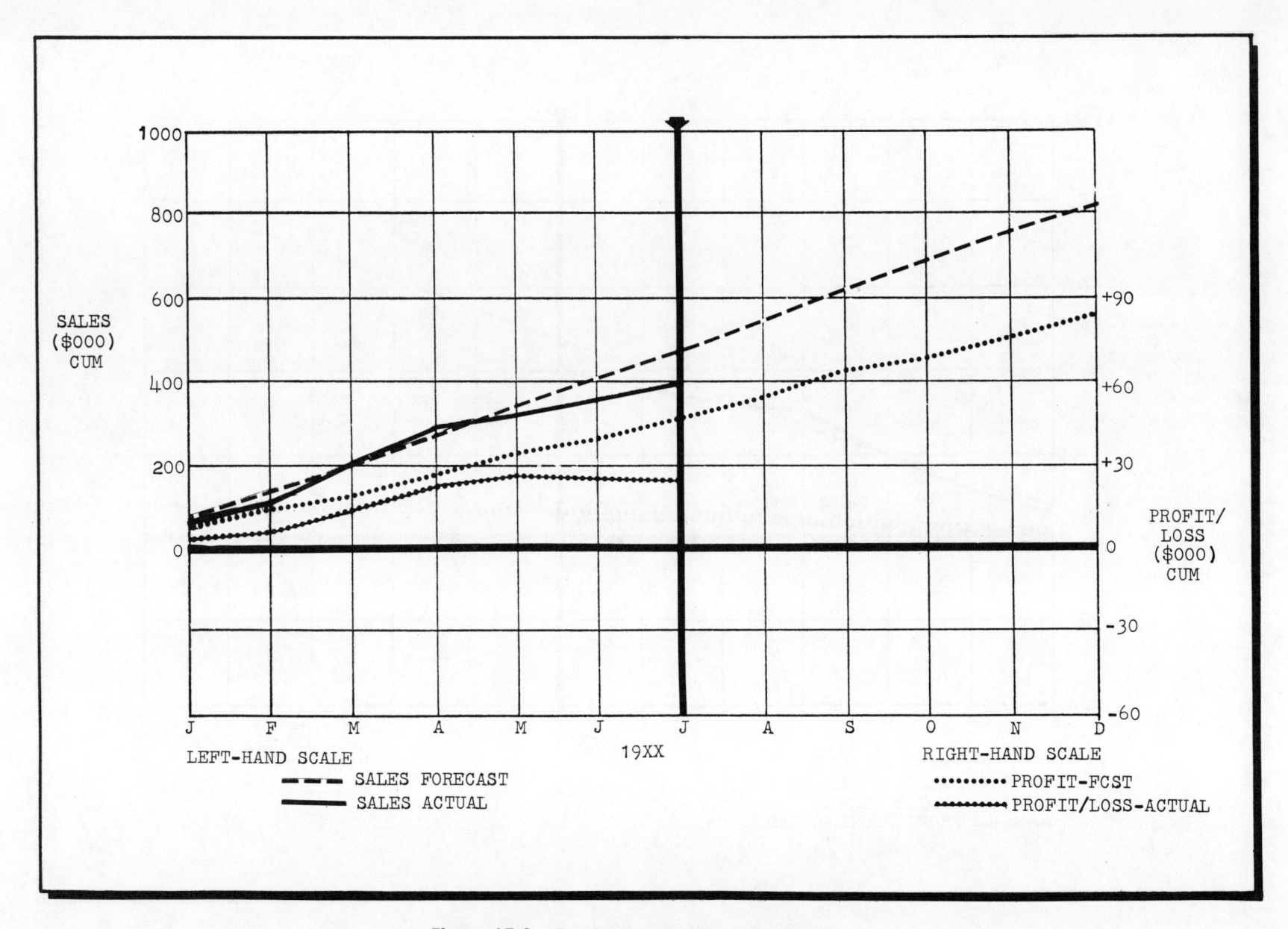

Figure 15.2 Earnings and Sales—Version 2

178

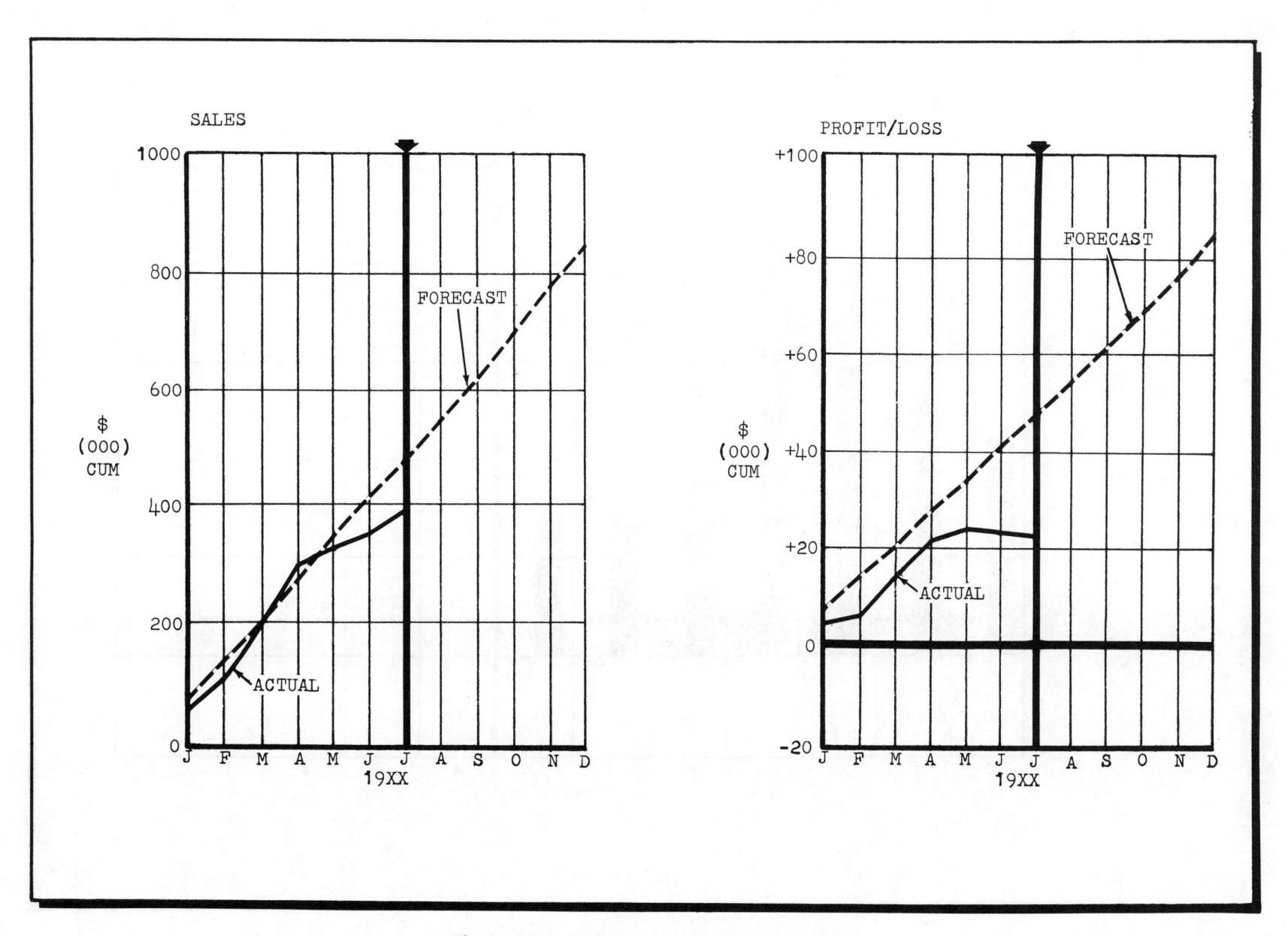

Figure 15.3 Earnings and Sales—Version 3

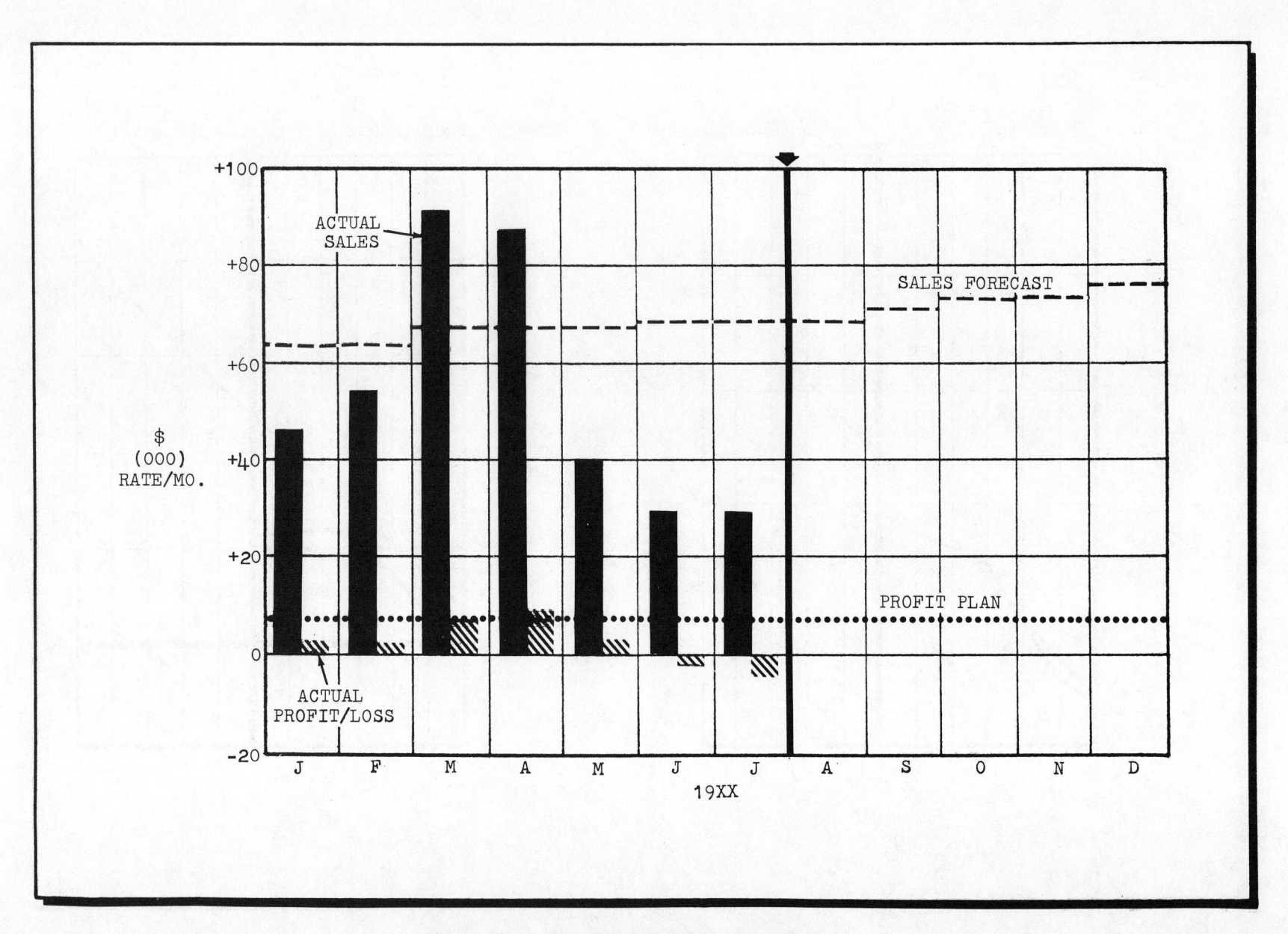

Figure 15.4 Earnings and Sales—Version 4

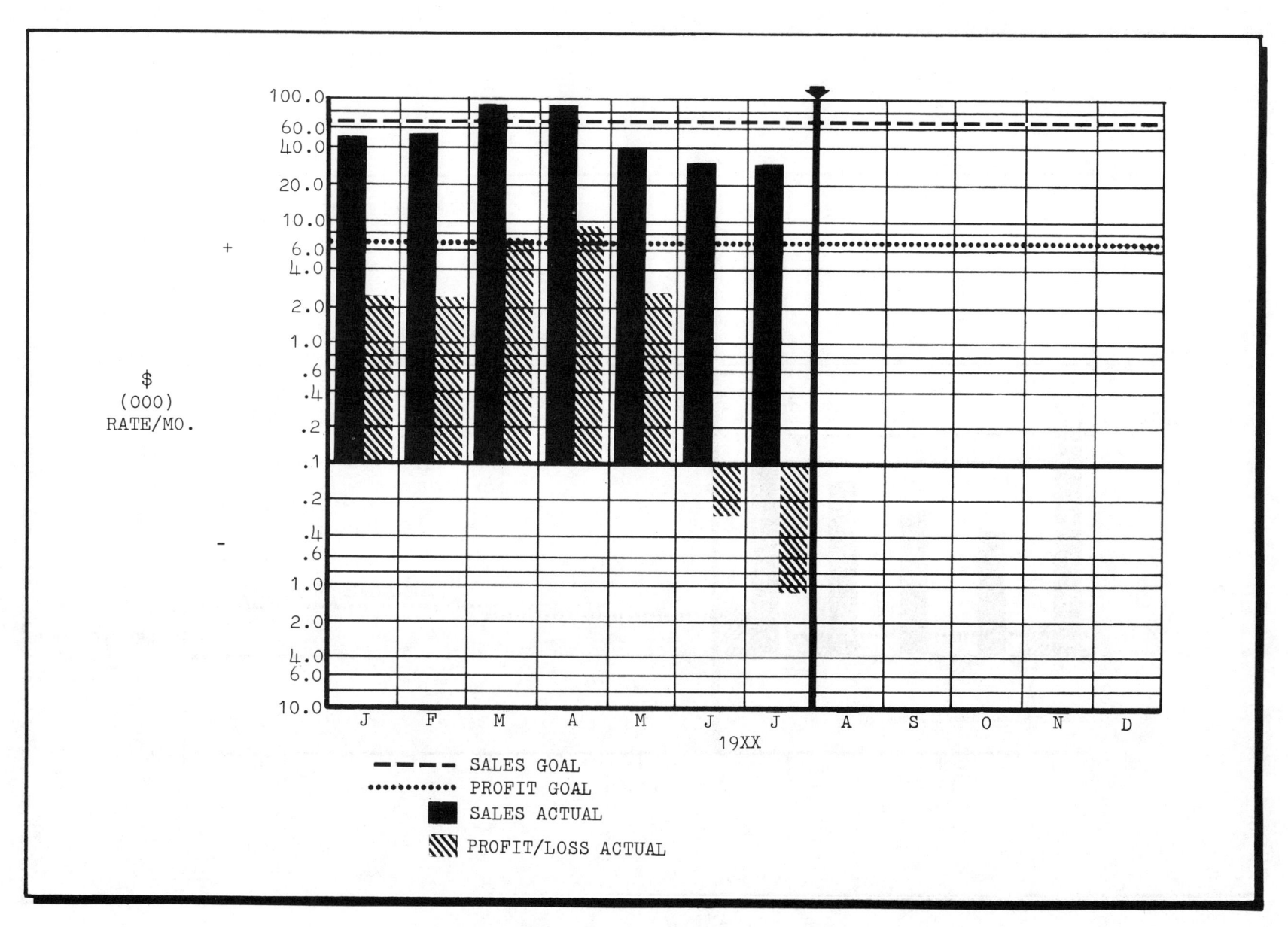

Figure 15.5   Earnings and Sales—Version 5

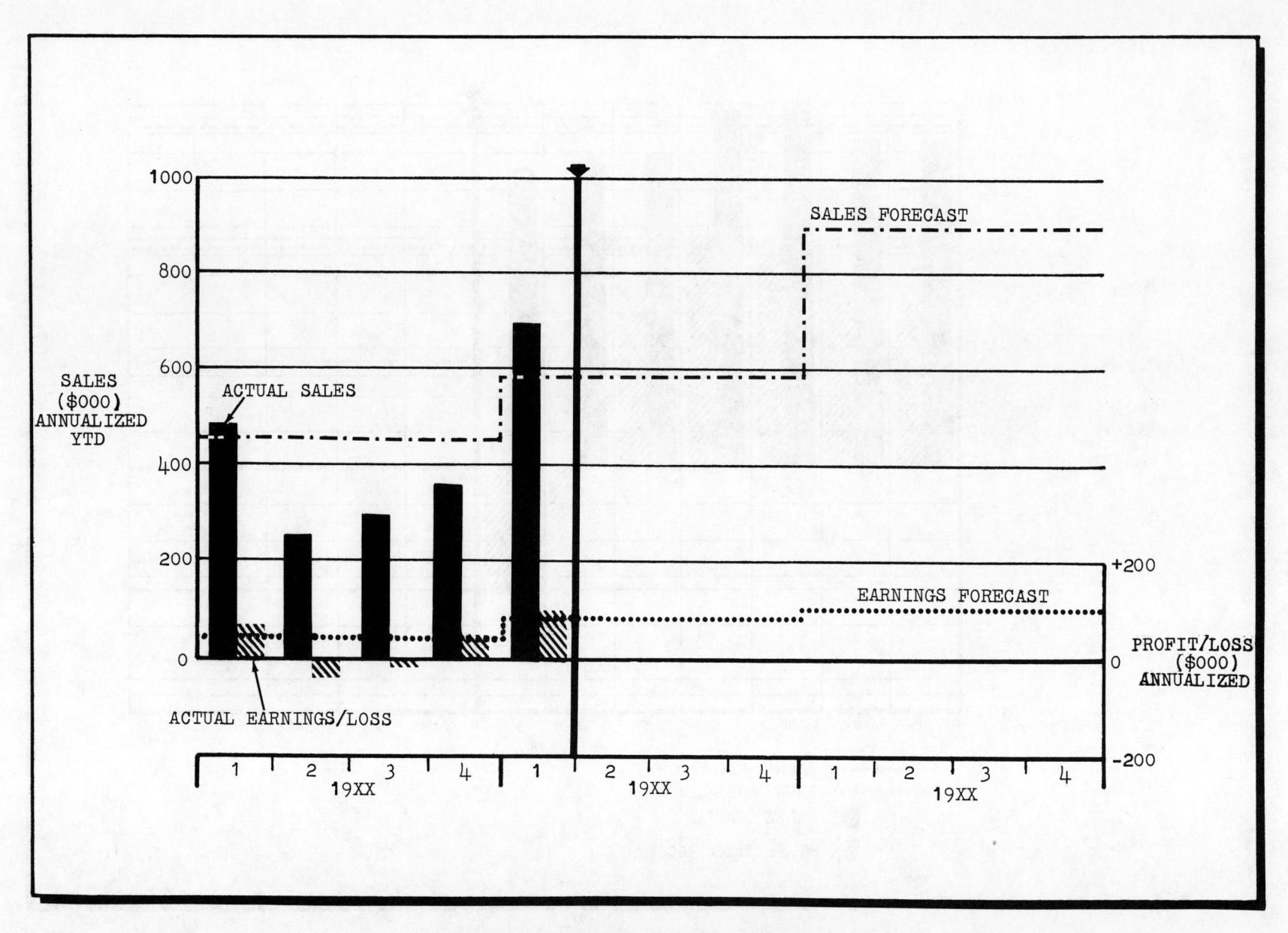

Figure 15.6 Earnings and Sales—Version 6

182

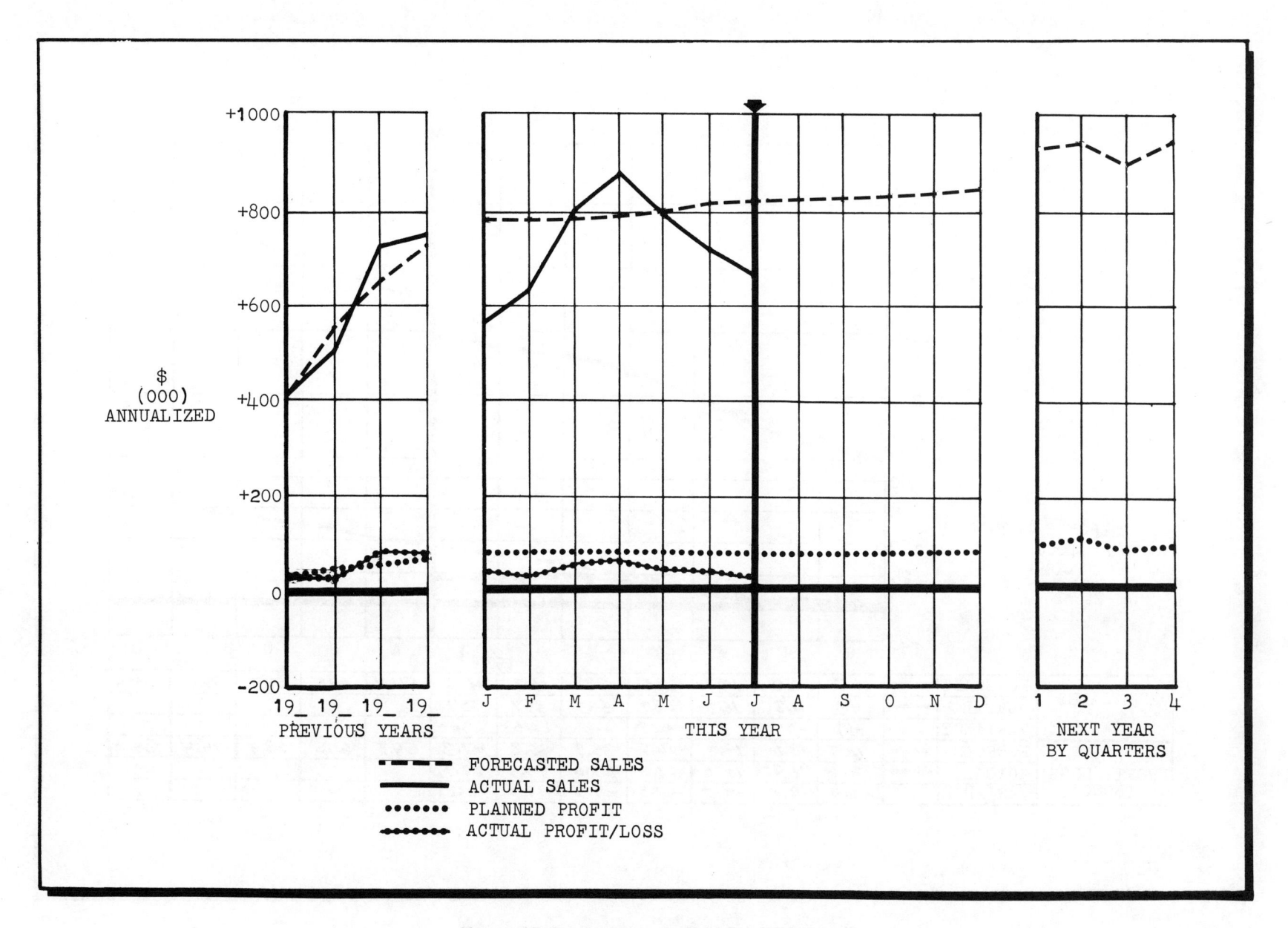

Figure 15.7   Earnings and Sales—Version 7

		J	F	M	A	M	J	J	A	S	O	N	D
CUM SALES ($000)	FORECAST -- --	65	130	197	265	333	403	473	543	615	689	764	842
	ACTUAL ———	48	103	197	287	327	357	387					
	VARIANCE	-17	-27	0	+22	-6	-46	-86					
CUM PROFIT/LOSS ($000)	FORECAST -- --	6.5	13.0	19.7	26.5	33.3	40.3	47.3	54.3	61.5	68.9	76.4	842
	ACTUAL ———	2.6	4.9	12.2	21.2	23.6	23.3	22.1					
	VARIANCE	-3.9	-8.1	-7.5	-5.3	-9.7	-17.0	-25.2					

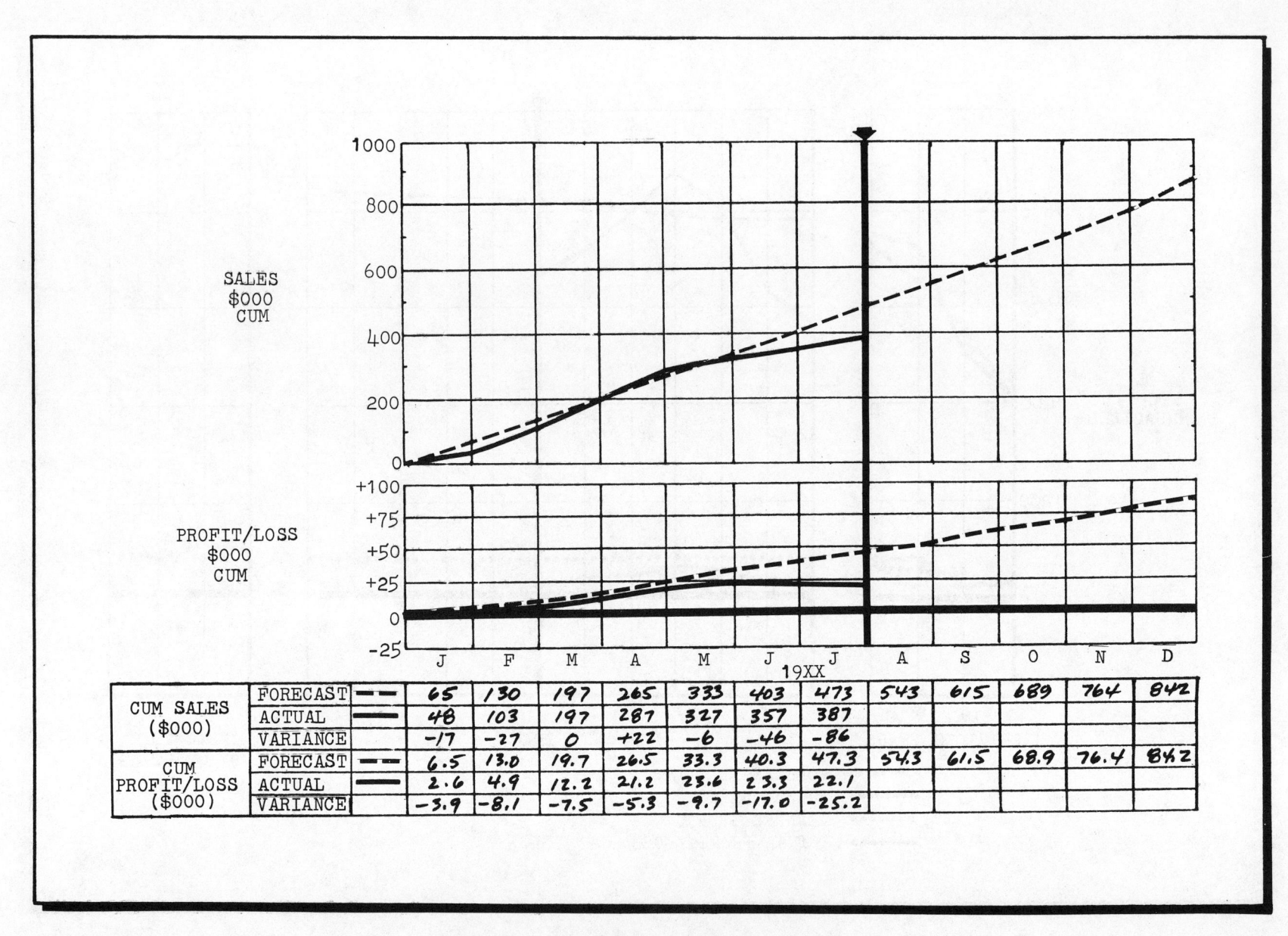

Figure 15.8 Earnings and Sales—Version 8

FACTOR			19XX											
			J	F	M	A	M	J	J	A	S	O	N	D
SALES ($000)	FORECAST	RATE/MO	65	65	67	68	68	70	70	70	72	74	75	78
		CUM	65	130	197	265	333	403	473	543	615	689	764	842
		ANNUAL'D	780	780	788	795	799	806	811	815	820	827	833	842
	ACTUAL	RATE/MO	48	55	94	90	40	30	30					
		CUM	48	103	197	287	327	357	387					
		ANNUAL'D	576	618	788	861	785	714	633					
	VARIANCE	CUM	-17	-27	0	+22	-6	-46	-86					
PROFIT/ LOSS ($000)	FORECAST	RATE/MO	6.5	6.5	6.7	6.8	6.8	7.0	7.0	7.0	7.2	7.4	7.5	7.8
		CUM	6.5	13.0	19.7	26.5	33.3	40.3	47.3	54.3	61.5	68.9	76.4	84.2
		ANNUAL'D	78.0	78.0	78.8	79.5	79.9	80.6	81.1	81.5	82.0	82.7	83.3	84.2
	ACTUAL	RATE/MO	2.6	2.3	7.3	9.0	2.4	-.3	-1.2					
		CUM	2.6	4.9	12.2	21.2	23.6	23.3	22.1					
		ANNUAL'D	31.2	29.4	48.8	63.6	56.6	46.6	37.9					
	VARIANCE	CUM	-3.9	-8.1	-7.5	-5.3	-9.7	-17.0	-25.2					

Figure 15.9 Earnings and Sales—Version 9

STATUS THROUGH __JUNE__

	STATUS THIS MONTH			YEAR TO DATE STATUS			EST. YEAR-END STATUS		
	FCAST	ACT	VAR	FCAST	ACT	VAR	FCAST	ACT	VAR
SALES ($000)									
ITEM A	6	6	0	36	36	0	72	72	0
ITEM B	3	3	0	20	22	+2	40	44	+4
ITEM C	4	4	0	27	27	0	53	53	0
ITEM D	2	2	0	9	10	+1	19	20	+1
ITEM E	7	10	+3	41	50	+9	82	95	+13
TOTAL SALES	22	25	+3	133	145	+12	266	284	+18
PROFIT/LOSS ($000)	2.2	2.4	+.2	13.3	15.0	+1.7	26.6	28.4	+1.8

Figure 15.10   Earnings and Sales—Version 10

16.0 EARNINGS AS A PERCENT OF SALES

Examples of charts that display the ratio of earnings (or income) to revenue (or sales) are displayed in this section. Also see Section 14.0, *Earnings*, Section 15.0, *Earnings and Sales*, and Section 17.0, *Earnings, Sales, and Costs*.

16.1 Earnings as a Percent of Sales—Version 1: An example of a simple method for displaying earnings as a percent of sales is shown in Version 1, Figure 16.1. The goal, 9% in this example, is plotted on the grid with a dashed line. The actual monthly earnings percentage is plotted with a solid line.

16.2 Earnings as a Percent of Sales—Version 2: A column chart style is used in Version 2 of an earnings as a percent of sales tracking chart, Figure 16.2. The hatched columns indicate the plan, or forecast, and the solid columns indicate actual earnings to date. Both the plan and actuals are plotted in terms of the rate per month in this example.

16.3 Earnings as a Percent of Sales—Version 3: The current year is compared against the previous year in Version 3 of an earnings as a percent of sales tracking chart, Figure 16.3. Columns are used, in this example, to show the previous year's performance. A dashed step line is used to show the current forecast of earnings.

16.4 Earnings as a Percent of Sales—Version 4: The grid in Version 4 of an earnings as a percent of sales tracking chart, Figure 16.4, is constructed to show six years of activity. On the left-hand side, the actual earnings to sales percentages for four previous years are shown. The center grid displays the forecasted and actual performance for the current year. The right-hand grid shows the forecast, by quarters, for the coming year.

16.5 Earnings as a Percent of Sales—Version 5: In Version 5 of an earnings as a percent of sales tracking chart, Figure 16.5, sales for each month are shown as a percentage, total sales equaling 100%. Columns, representing costs and broken down by cost category, display the application of the sales dollars. Columns that fall below the 100% line indicate a profit (right-hand scale) for the month. Columns that go above the 100% line indicate a loss for that particular month. Numbers on the tops of the columns indicate the gross sales in terms of dollars.

16.6 Earnings as a Percent of Sales—Version 6: Statistics have been combined with a graphic display in Version 6 of an earnings as a percent of sales tracking chart, Figure 16.6. In this example, statistics are given in terms of rate per month for the forecast, the actual earnings to sales percentages, and the variances between these latter two factors. Except for the variance figures, the data that are given in the table are also plotted on the graph.

16.7 Earnings as a Percent of Sales—Version 7: Six lines of statistics are given in Version 7 of an earnings as a percent of sales tracking chart, Figure 16.7. The earnings to sales percentages, in terms of rate per month and year-to-date averages, are given in the table. The year-to-date average statistics are also plotted on the graphic portion of the chart.

16.8 Earnings as a Percent of Sales—Version 8: Sales, earnings, and earnings as a percent of sales are given on a rate-per-month basis in the table in Version 8 of an earnings as a percent of sales tracking chart, Figure 16.8. The earnings to sales percentage statistics, forecasted and actual, are also plotted on the graphic portion of the chart.

16.9 Earnings as a Percent of Sales—Version 9: A statistical table version of an earnings as a percent of sales tracking chart is shown as Version 9, Figure 16.9. Forecasted, actual, and variance statistics on both a rate-per-month and year-to-date basis are given for sales, earnings, and earnings as a percent of sales.

16.10 Earnings as a Percent of Sales—Version 10: A one-time status report type of statistical table is shown as Version 10 of an earnings as a percent of sales chart, Figure 16.10. Sales, profit, and the percentage of profit to sales are given. The bottom of the table shows the totals.

16.11 Earnings as a Percent of Sales—Version 11: A non-tracking type of chart is used in Version 11 of an earnings as a percent of sales chart, Figure 16.11. This example shows earnings performance over a ten-year period plotted against an industry average.

16.12 Earnings as a Percent of Sales—Version 12: A segmented circle chart ("pie" chart) is shown as Version 12 of an earnings as a percent of sales chart, Figure 16.12. This, as with Version 11, is a non-tracking type of chart.

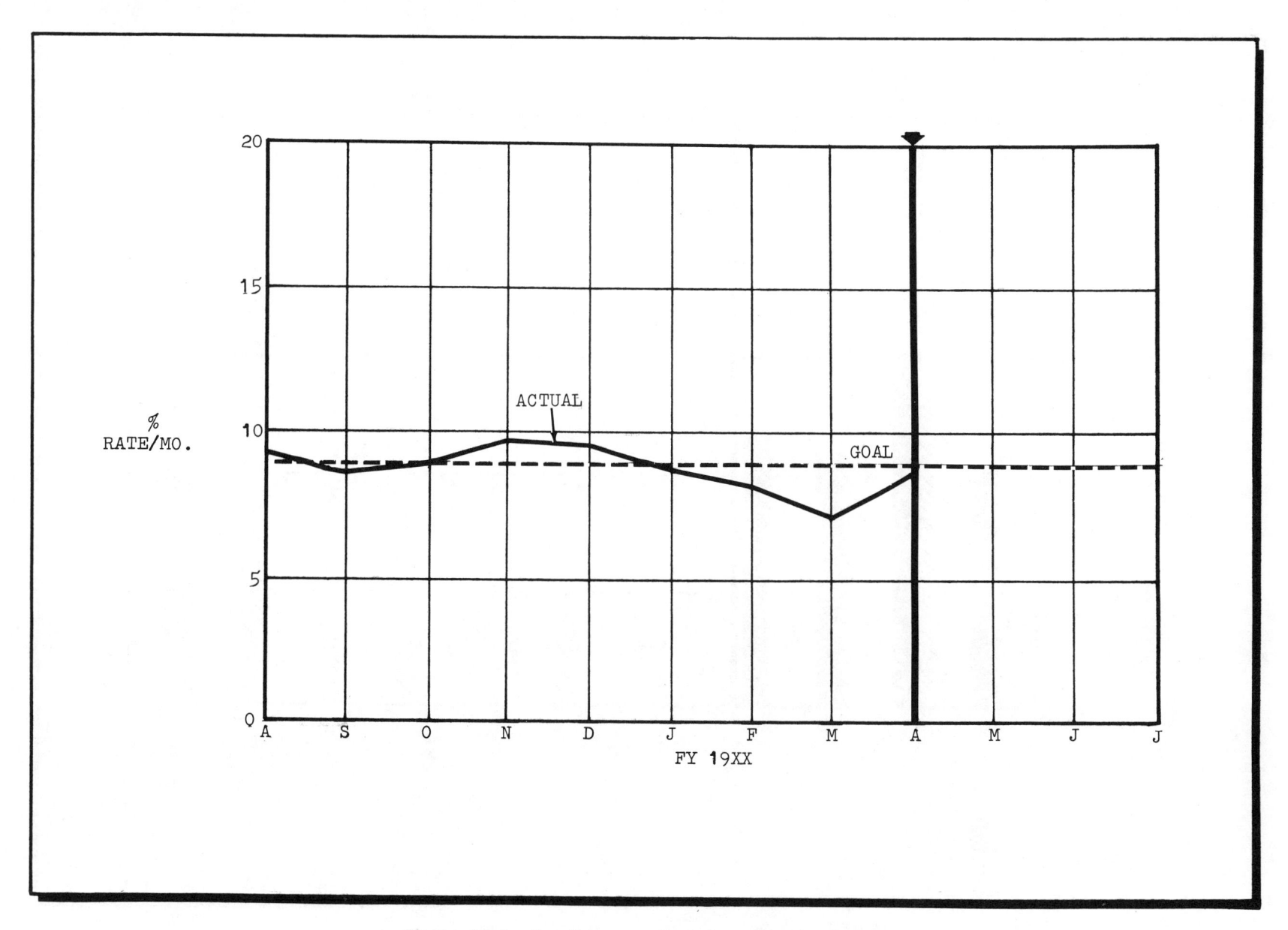

Figure 16.1   Earnings as a Percent of Sales—Version 1

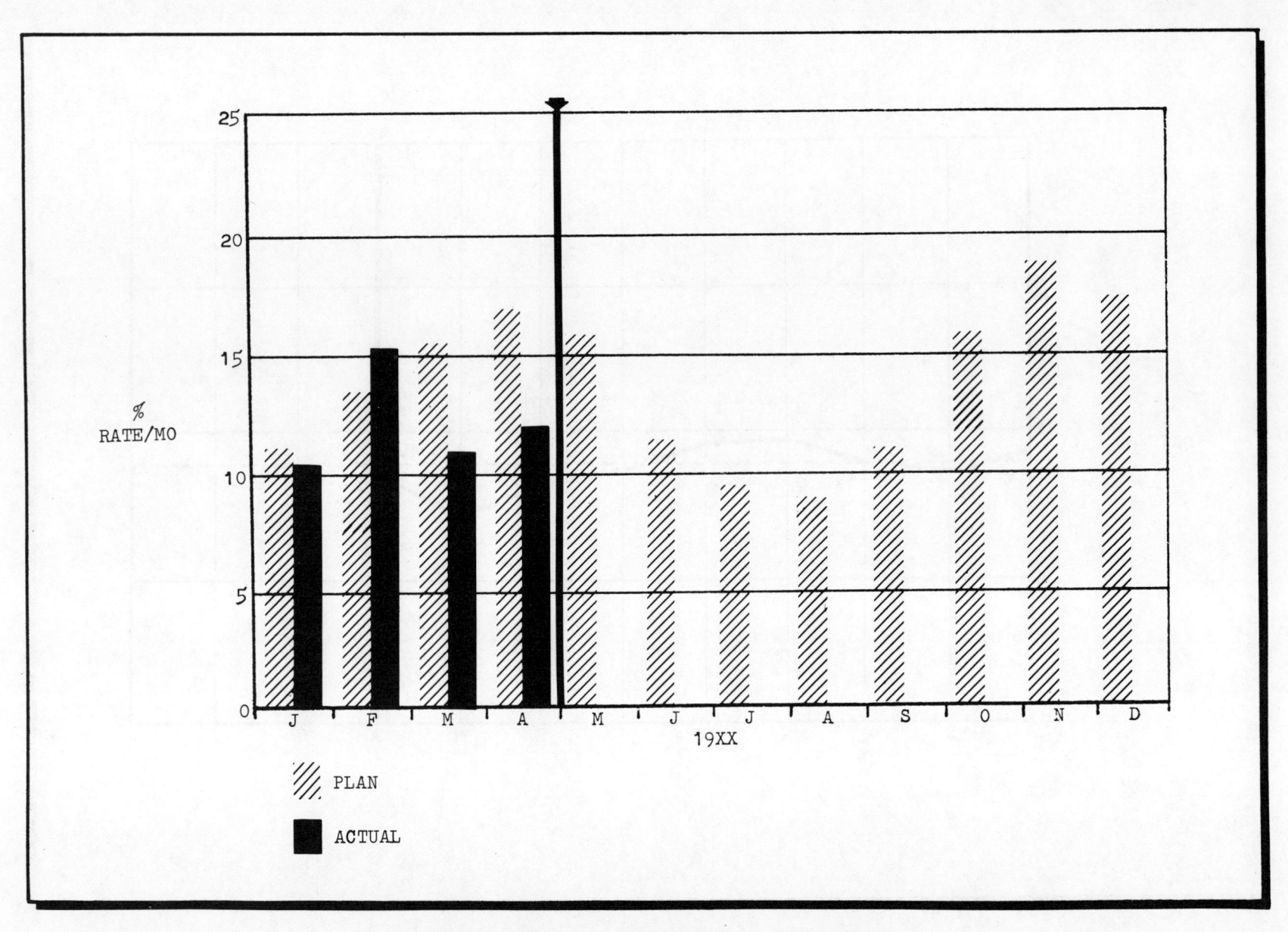

Figure 16.2   Earnings as a Percent of Sales—Version 2

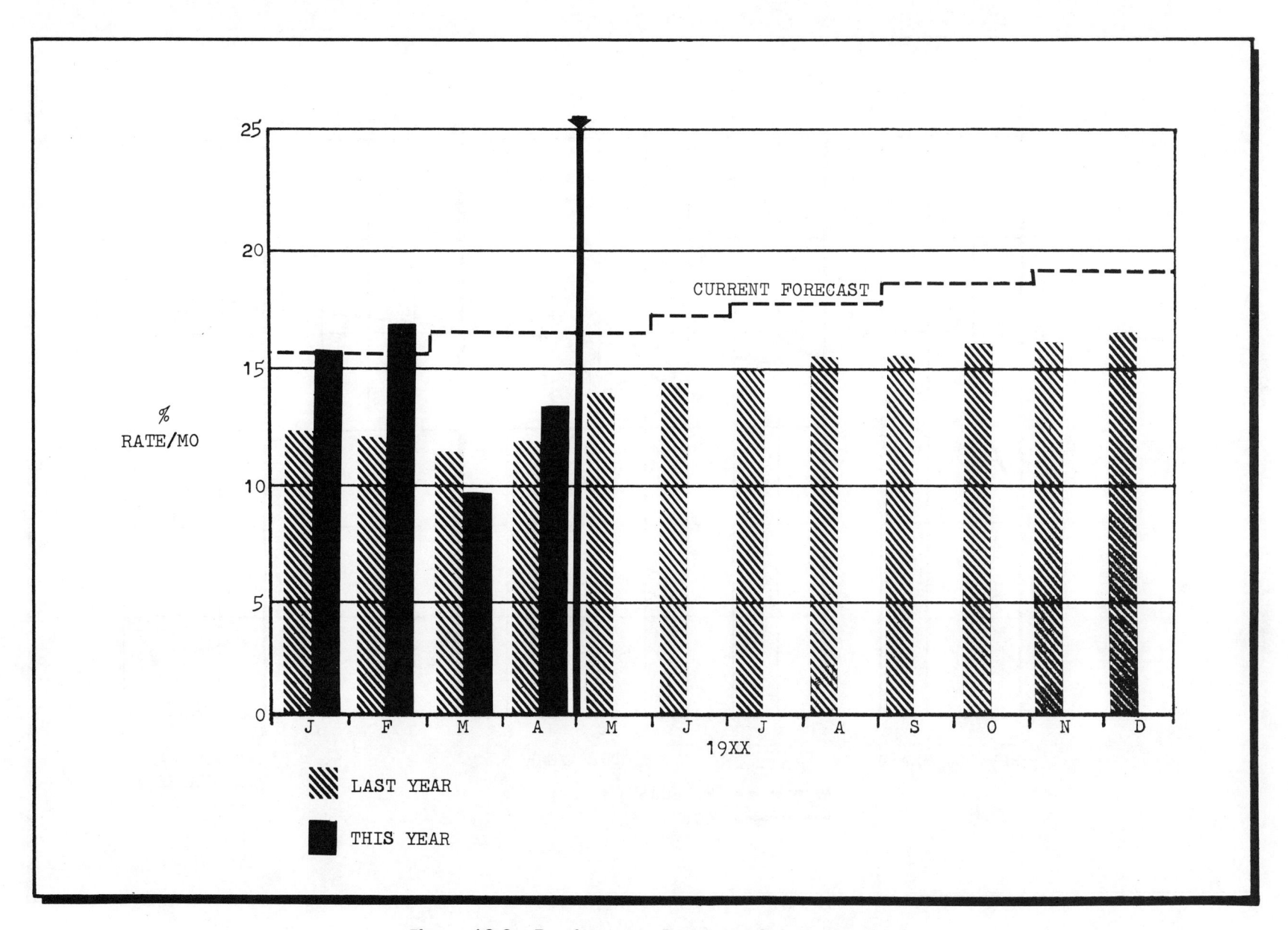

Figure 16.3 Earnings as a Percent of Sales—Version 3

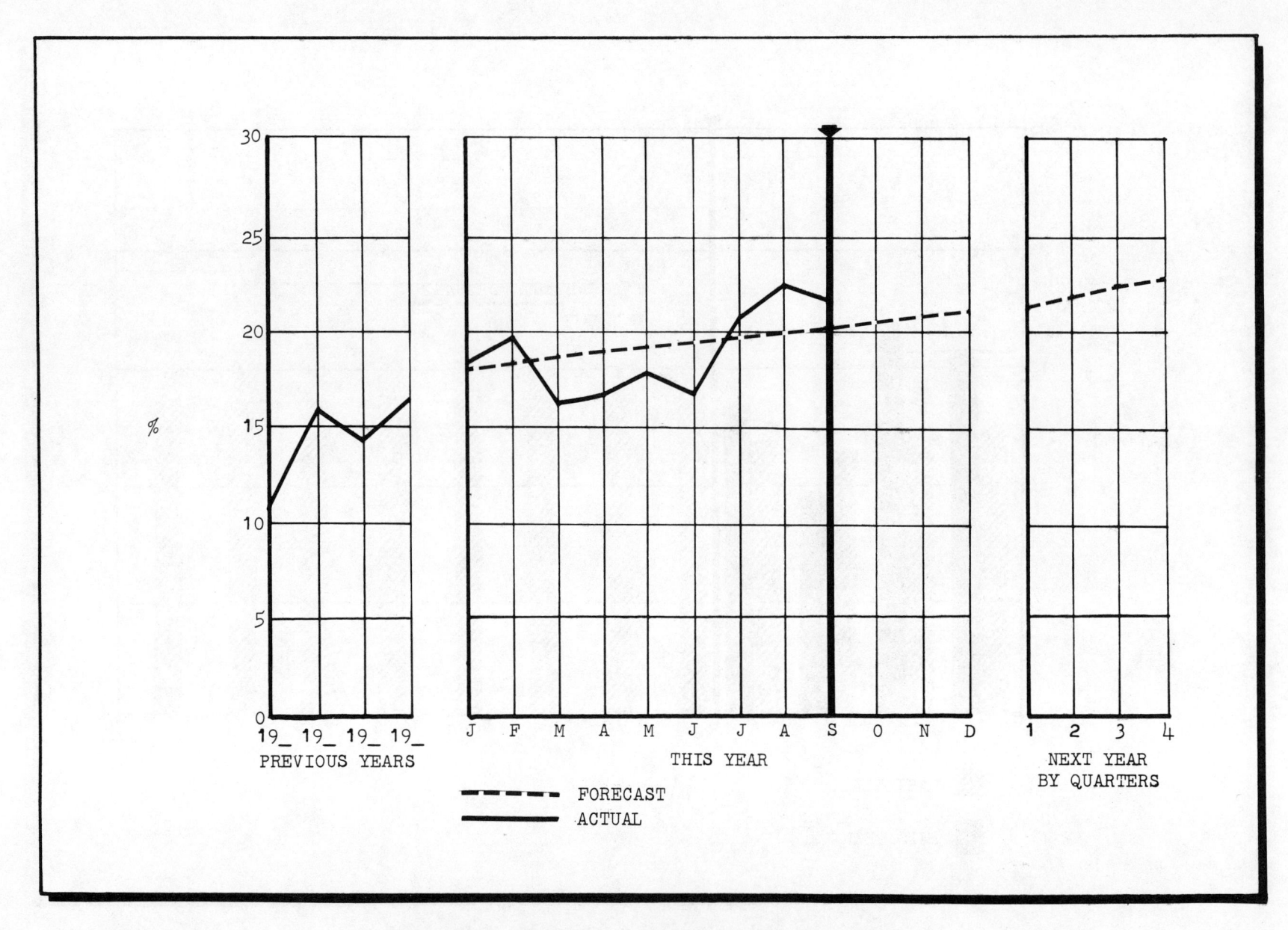

Figure 16.4   Earnings as a Percent of Sales—Version 4

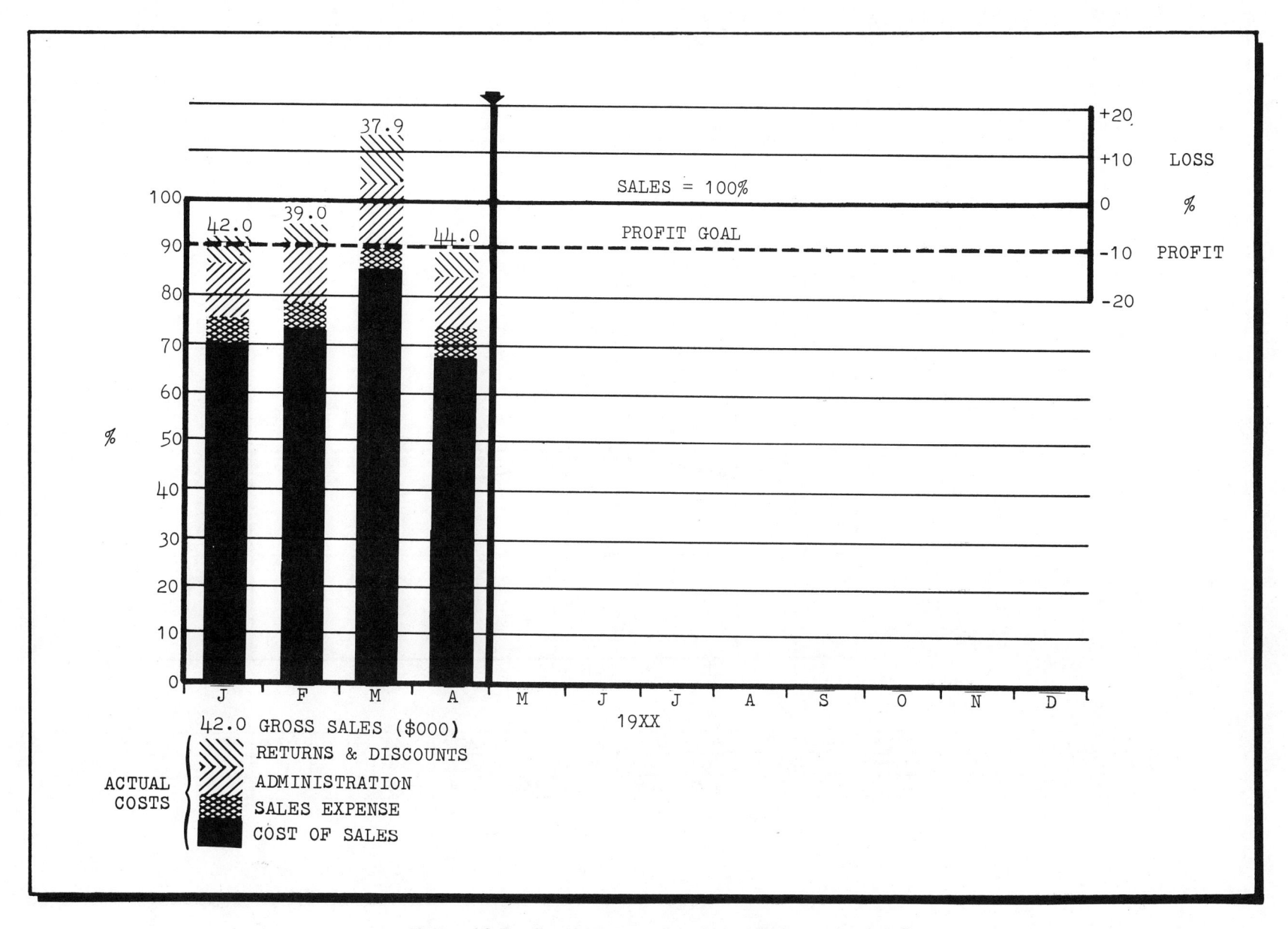

Figure 16.5 Earnings as a Percent of Sales—Version 5

RATE/MO.													
FORECASTED	-----	10.0	10.0	10.0	10.0	10.0	10.0	10.0	10.0	10.0	10.0	10.0	10.0
ACTUAL	———	9.4	8.8	9.0	9.6	9.5	8.6	8.2	7.1				
VARIANCE		-.6	-1.2	-1.0	-.4	-.5	-1.4	-1.8	-2.9				

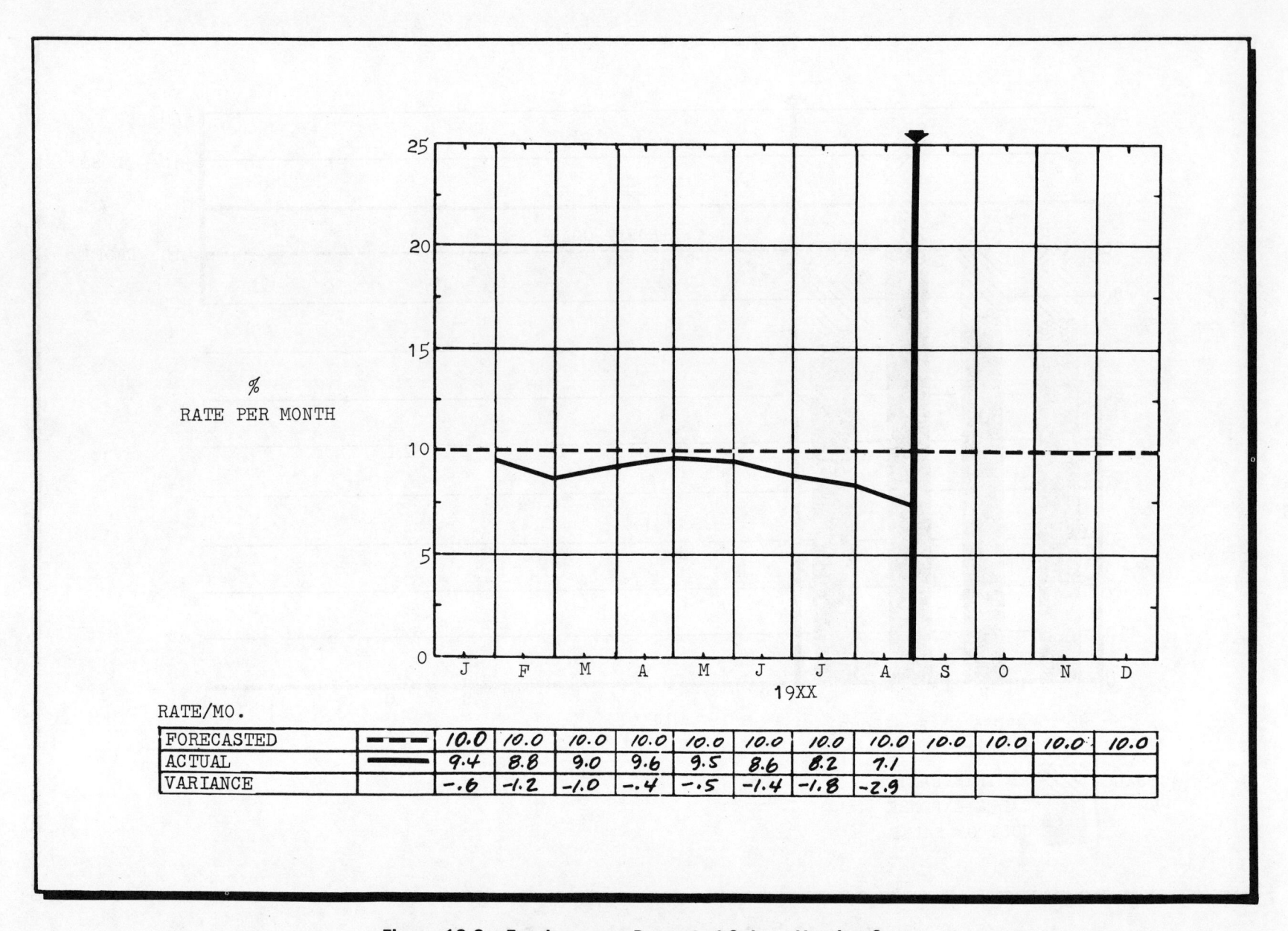

Figure 16.6   Earnings as a Percent of Sales—Version 6

%
YEAR-TO-DATE AVERAGE

		J	F	M	A	M	J	J	A	S	O	N	D
RATE PER MO.	FORECASTED	10.0	10.0	10.0	10.0	10.0	10.0	10.0	10.0	10.0	10.0	10.0	10.0
	ACTUAL	9.4	8.8	9.0	9.6	9.5	8.6	8.2	7.1				
	VARIANCE	-.6	-1.2	-1.0	-.4	-.5	-1.4	-1.8	-2.9				
YEAR-TO-DATE AVERAGE	FORECASTED --	10.0	10.0	10.0	10.0	10.0	10.0	10.0	10.0	10.0	10.0	10.0	10.0
	ACTUAL ——	9.4	9.1	9.1	9.2	9.2	9.1	9.0	9.0				
	VARIANCE	-.6	-.9	-.9	-.8	-.8	-.9	-1.0	-1.0				

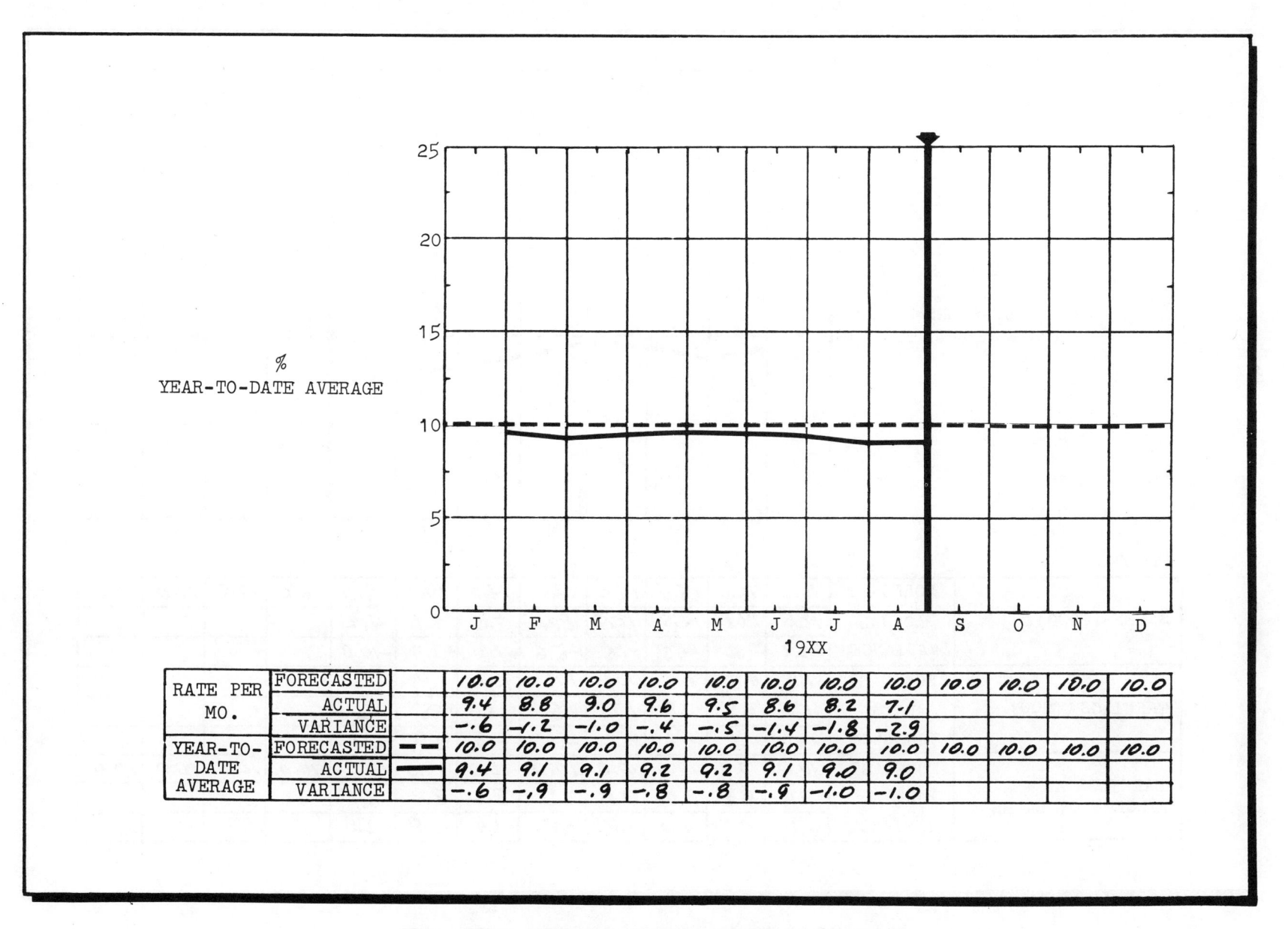

Figure 16.7   Earnings as a Percent of Sales—Version 7

EARNINGS
AS A %
OF SALES
(RATE PER MONTH)

FORECAST

ACTUAL

J F M A M J J A S O N D
19XX

RATE/MO.														
SALES ($000)	FORECAST	15.0	15.0	15.0	14.0	14.0	14.0	14.0	15.0	16.0	17.0	17.0	17.0
	ACTUAL	12.8	14.8	14.5	12.5	8.4	7.0	6.1	4.2				
	VARIANCE	-2.2	-.2	-.5	-1.5	-5.6	-7.0	-7.9	-10.8				
EARNINGS ($000)	FORECAST	1.5	1.5	1.5	1.4	1.4	1.4	1.4	1.5	1.6	1.7	1.7	1.7
	ACTUAL	1.2	1.3	1.3	1.2	.8	.6	.5	.3				
	VARIANCE	-.3	-.2	-.2	-.2	-.6	-.8	-.9	-.12				
EARNINGS AS A PERCENT OF SALES	FORECAST	10.0	10.0	10.0	10.0	10.0	10.0	10.0	10.0	10.0	10.0	10.0	10.0
	ACTUAL	9.4	8.8	9.0	9.6	9.5	8.6	8.2	7.1				
	VARIANCE	-.6	-1.2	-1.0	-.4	-.5	-1.4	-1.8	-2.9				

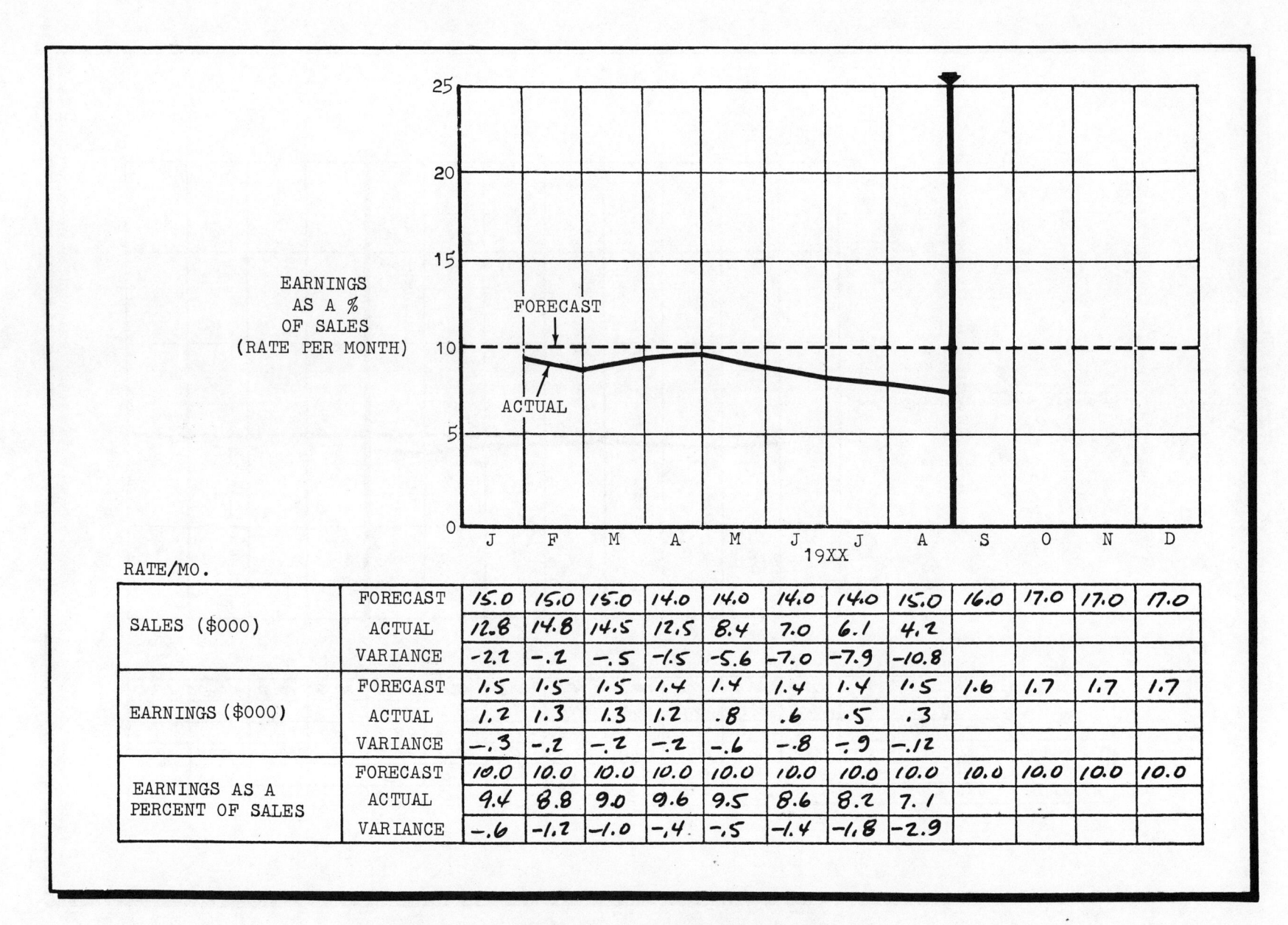

Figure 16.8 Earnings as a Percent of Sales—Version 8

FACTOR			19XX											
			J	F	M	A	M	J	J	A	S	O	N	D
SALES ($000)	RATE/MO	FORECAST	15.0	15.0	15.0	14.0	14.0	14.0	14.0	15.0	16.0	17.0	17.0	17.0
		ACTUAL	12.8	14.8	14.5	12.5	8.4	7.0	6.1	4.2				
		VARIANCE	-2.2	-.2	-.5	-1.5	-5.6	-7.0	-7.9	-10.8				
	YTD	FORECAST	15.0	30.0	45.0	59.0	73.0	87.0	101.0	116.0	132.0	149.0	166.0	183.0
		ACTUAL	12.8	27.6	42.1	54.6	63.0	70.0	76.1	80.3				
		VARIANCE	-2.2	-2.4	-2.9	-4.4	-10.0	-17.0	-24.9	-35.7				
EARNINGS ($000)	RATE/MO	FORECAST	1.5	1.5	1.5	1.4	1.4	1.4	1.4	1.5	1.6	1.7	1.7	1.7
		ACTUAL	1.2	1.3	1.3	1.2	.8	.6	.5	.3				
		VARIANCE	-.3	-.2	-.2	-.2	-.6	-.8	-.9	-1.2				
	YTD	FORECAST	1.5	3.0	4.5	5.9	7.3	8.7	10.1	11.6	13.2	14.9	16.6	18.3
		ACTUAL	1.2	2.5	3.8	5.0	5.8	6.4	6.9	7.2				
		VARIANCE	-.3	-.5	-.7	-.9	-1.5	-2.3	-3.2	-4.4				
EARNINGS AS A PERCENT OF SALES	RATE/MO	FORECAST	10.0	10.0	10.0	10.0	10.0	10.0	10.0	10.0	10.0	10.0	10.0	10.0
		ACTUAL	9.4	8.8	9.0	9.6	9.5	8.6	8.2	7.1				
		VARIANCE	-.6	-1.2	-1.0	-.4	-.5	-1.4	-1.8	-2.9				
	YTD	FORECAST	10.0	10.0	10.0	10.0	10.0	10.0	10.0	10.0	10.0	10.0	10.0	10.0
		ACTUAL	9.4	9.1	9.1	9.2	9.2	9.1	9.0	9.0				
		VARIANCE	-.6	-.9	-.9	-.8	-.8	-.9	-1.0	-1.0				

Figure 16.9 Earnings as a Percent of Sales—Version 9

STATUS THROUGH __JUNE__

PROJECT	SALES	PROFIT	% TO SALES
A	$28,879	$2,839	9.5%
B	4,025	394	9.8%
C	14,768	2,112	14.3%
D	1,650	185	11.2%
E	8,926	0	0
F	20,147	685	3.4%
G	11,008	1024	9.3%
TOTALS	$90,403	$7239	8.0%

Figure 16.10 Earnings as a Percent of Sales—Version 10

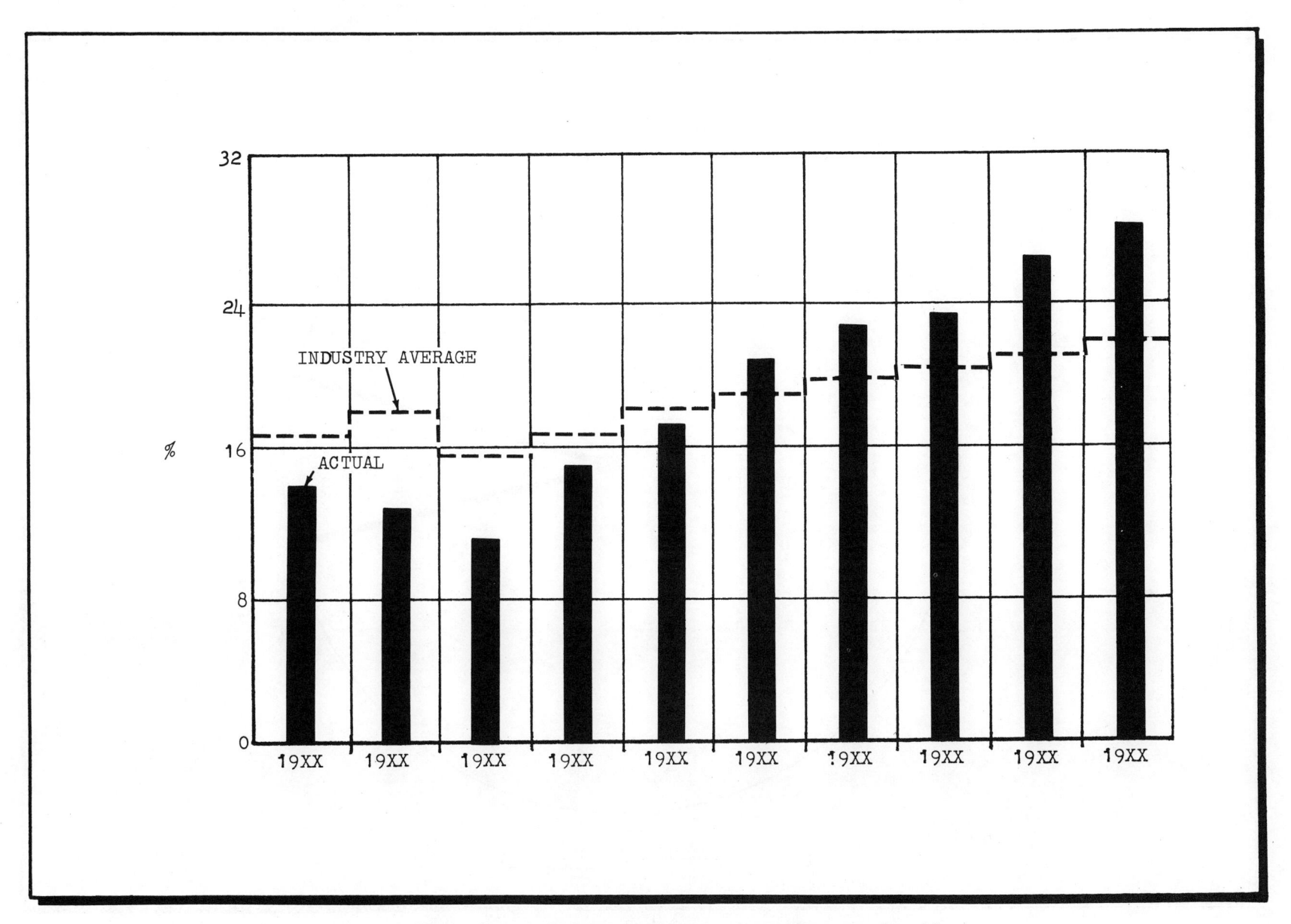

Figure 16.11 Earnings as a Percent of Sales—Version 11

199

SALES
EXPENSE
9.6%

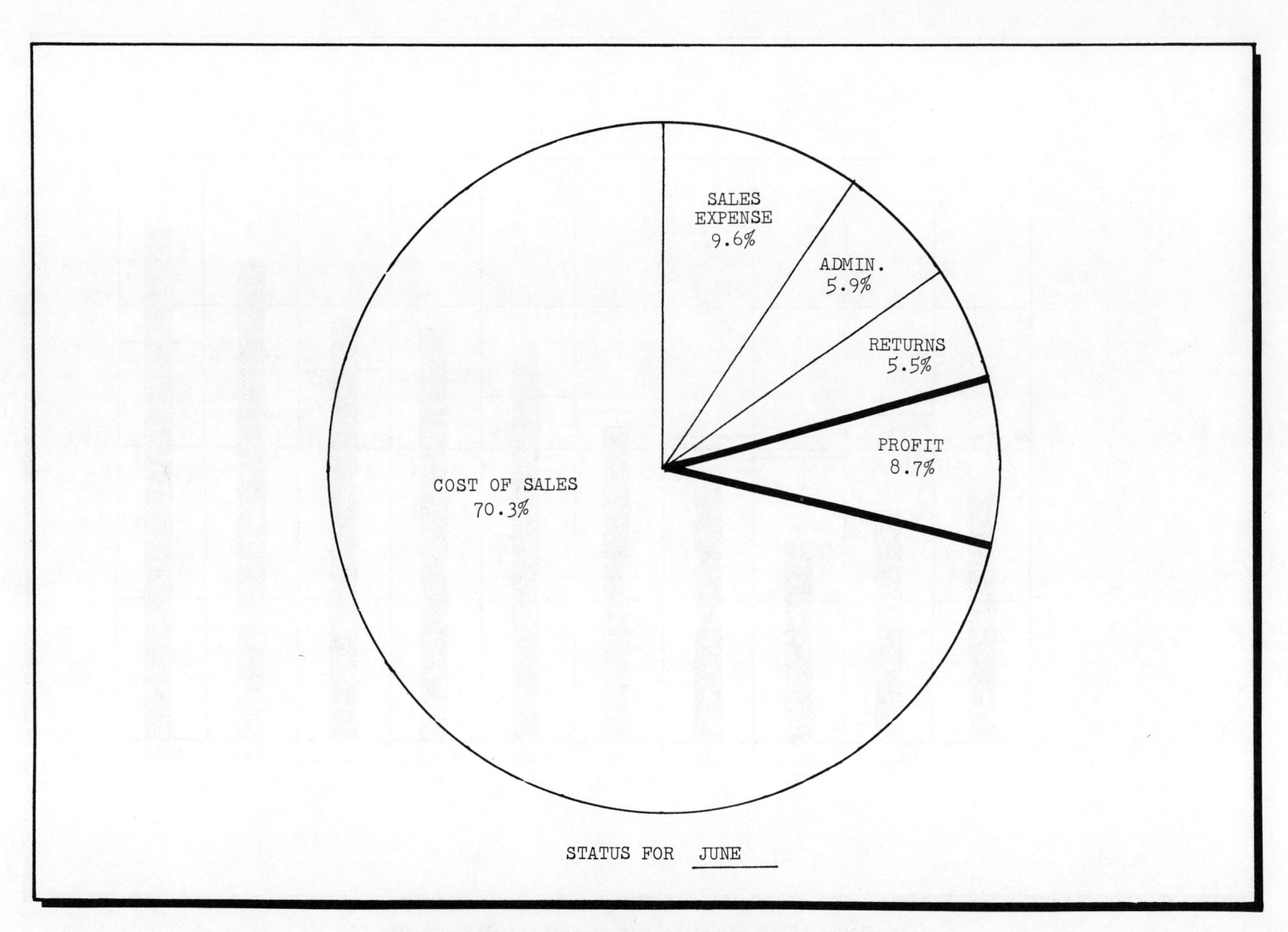

ADMIN.
5.9%

RETURNS
5.5%

PROFIT
8.7%

COST OF SALES
70.3%

STATUS FOR   JUNE

Figure 16.12   Earnings as a Percent of Sales—Version 12

17.0 EARNINGS, SALES, AND COSTS

This section contains chart examples that combine, on one chart, three factors: earnings, sales, and costs. Also see Section 14.0, *Earnings*, Section 15.0, *Earnings and Sales*, Section 16.0, *Earnings as a Percent of Sales*, and Section 44.0, *Revenue Versus Costs*.

17.1 Earnings, Sales, and Costs—Version 1: The basic elements of an earnings, sales, and costs chart are shown as Version 1, Figure 17.1. In this example, actual sales and costs are plotted on a rate-per-month basis. The net variance between these two factors is shaded to show profit and loss. In this example tracking is against forecasted sales, only.

17.2 Earnings, Sales, and Costs—Version 2: A cumulative (year to date) style chart is used as Version 2 of an earnings, sales, and costs chart, Figure 17.2. Forecasted sales are shown with a dashed line. Actual sales and costs are plotted against this forecast, and the net variance between these two actual performance factors is shaded to highlight profit or loss.

17.3 Earnings, Sales, and Costs—Version 3: Sales, costs, and the profit and loss are shown on an annualized year-to-date basis in Version 3 of an earnings, sales, and costs chart, Figure 17.3. As with Versions 1 and 2, tracking in this example is in terms of forecasted sales, only. Since there is no zero base in this example, an arrow has been used to highlight that fact.

17.4 Earnings, Sales, and Costs—Version 4: Grouped columns are used in Version 4 of an earnings, sales, and costs chart, Figure 17.4. In this example, the sales forecast is plotted with a dashed step line. Actual sales, actual costs, and the resulting profit or loss are shown with columns.

17.5 Earnings, Sales, and Costs—Version 5: In Version 5 of an earnings, sales, and costs chart, Figure 17.5, the cost data are plotted downward, using the actual sales as a base line. The bottom of the cost data, then, indicates a profit when it falls above the zero base line, and a loss when it falls below that line.

17.6 Earnings, Sales, and Costs—Version 6: A display of earnings, sales, and costs data on a multi-year basis is shown in Version 6, Figure 17.6. Actual sales and costs for the previous four years and the current year to date are shown. The net variance between these two factors is hatched to show the profit or loss. The current year, plotted with data annualized on a rate-per-month basis, is shown in relationship to the sales forecast. The coming year's forecast is shown annualized by quarters.

17.7 Earnings, Sales, and Costs—Version 7: Three separate grids are used to show earnings, sales, and costs in Version 7, Figure 17.7. All charts are on a cumulative (year to date) basis. The left-hand grid displays forecasted and actual sales. The center grid shows forecasted and actual costs. The right-hand grid, constructed to show both profit and loss, displays forecasted and actual earnings.

17.8 Earnings, Sales, and Costs—Version 8: Statistics have been combined with a graphic chart in Version 8 of an earnings, sales, and costs chart, Figure 17.8. In this example, the graphic portion of the chart shows the actual sales and costs plotted in relationship to the sales forecast. The net variance between the sales and costs lines has been shaded to highlight the profit or loss. The table contains all of the supportive statistics for the graph, plus the statistics for the variance between the actual and forecasted sales.

17.9 Earnings, Sales, and Costs—Version 9: A statistical table version of an earnings, sales, and costs tracking chart is shown in Figure 17.9. In this example, forecasted and actual sales, costs, and earnings are shown in terms of rate per month, cumulative, and annualized statistics.

17.10 Earnings, Sales, and Costs—Version 10: A one-time status report style of earnings, sales, and costs chart is shown as Version 10, Figure 17.10. Sales, costs, and profit are shown in three categories: status for the month, the year-to-day status, and the estimated year-end status.

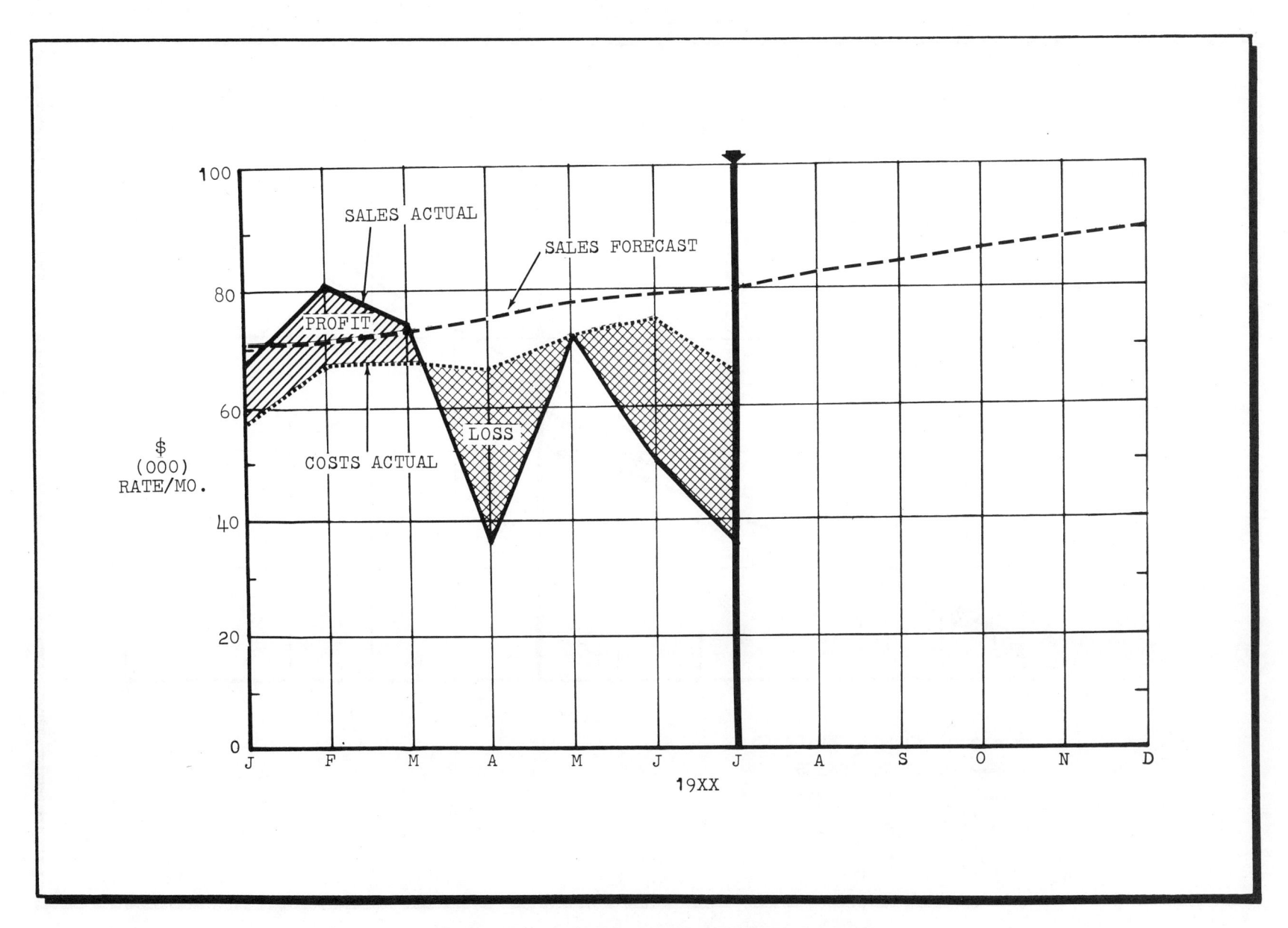

Figure 17.1   Earnings, Sales, and Costs—Version 1

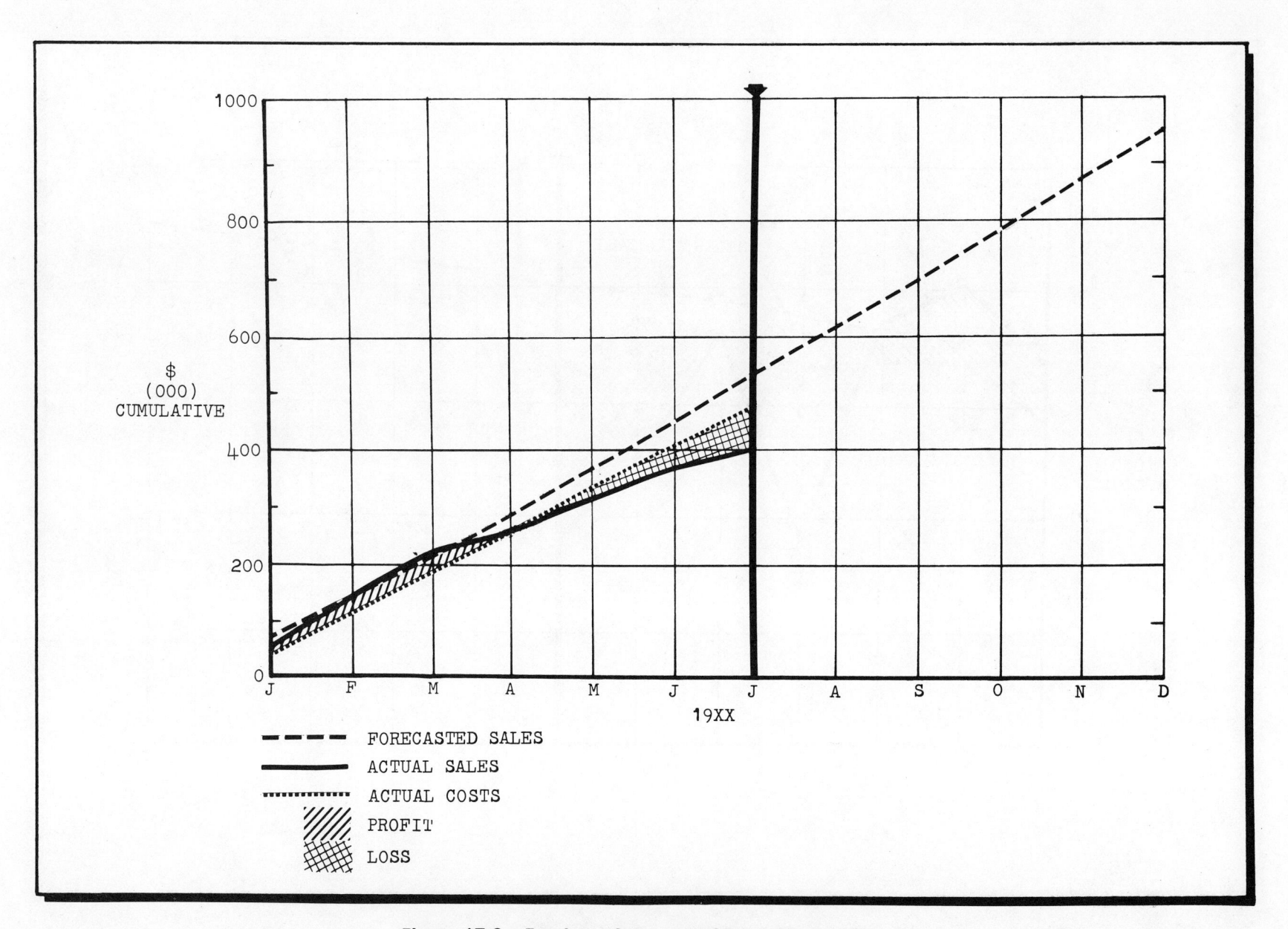

Figure 17.2 Earnings, Sales, and Costs—Version 2

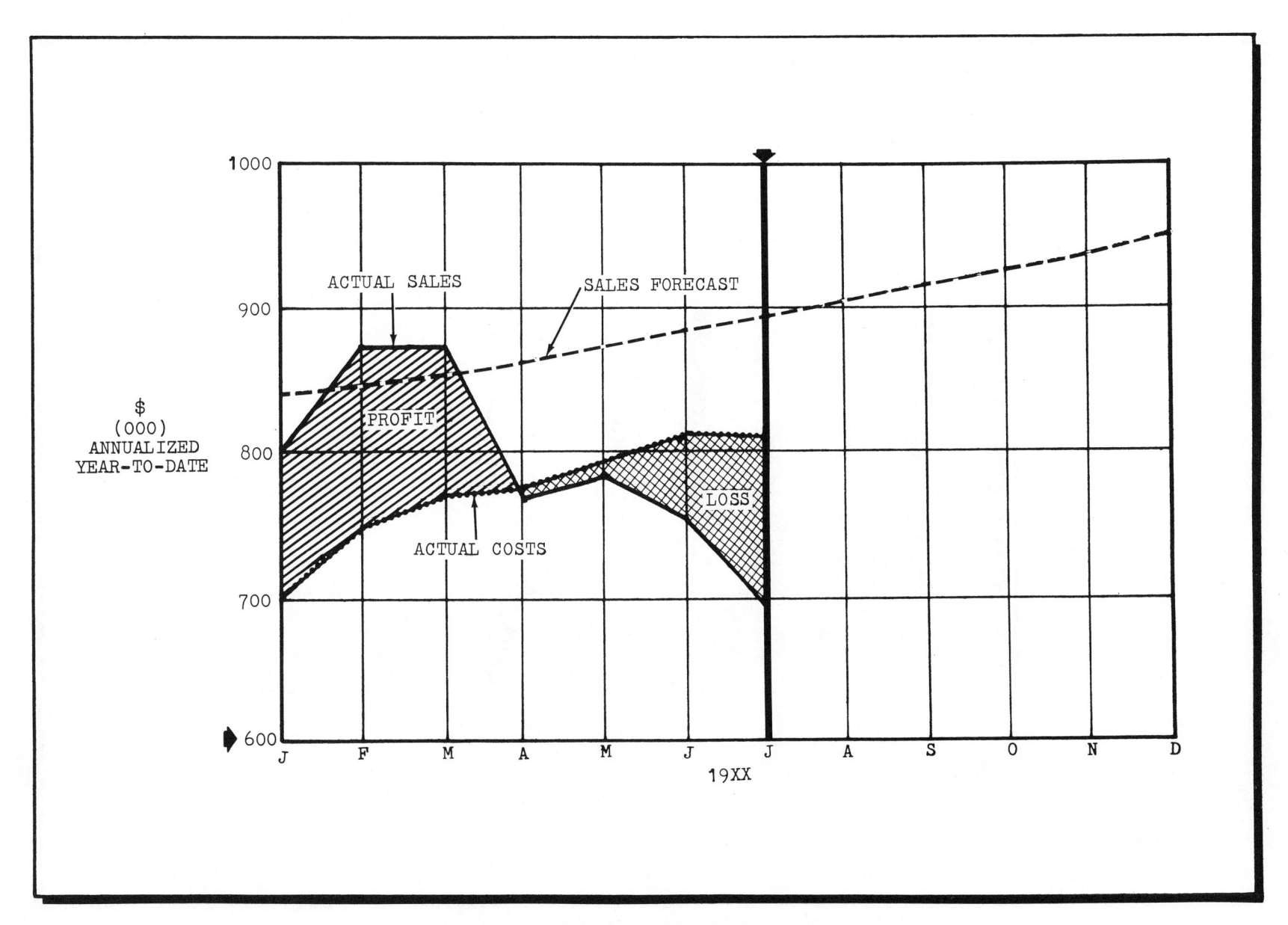

Figure 17.3　Earnings, Sales, and Costs—Version 3

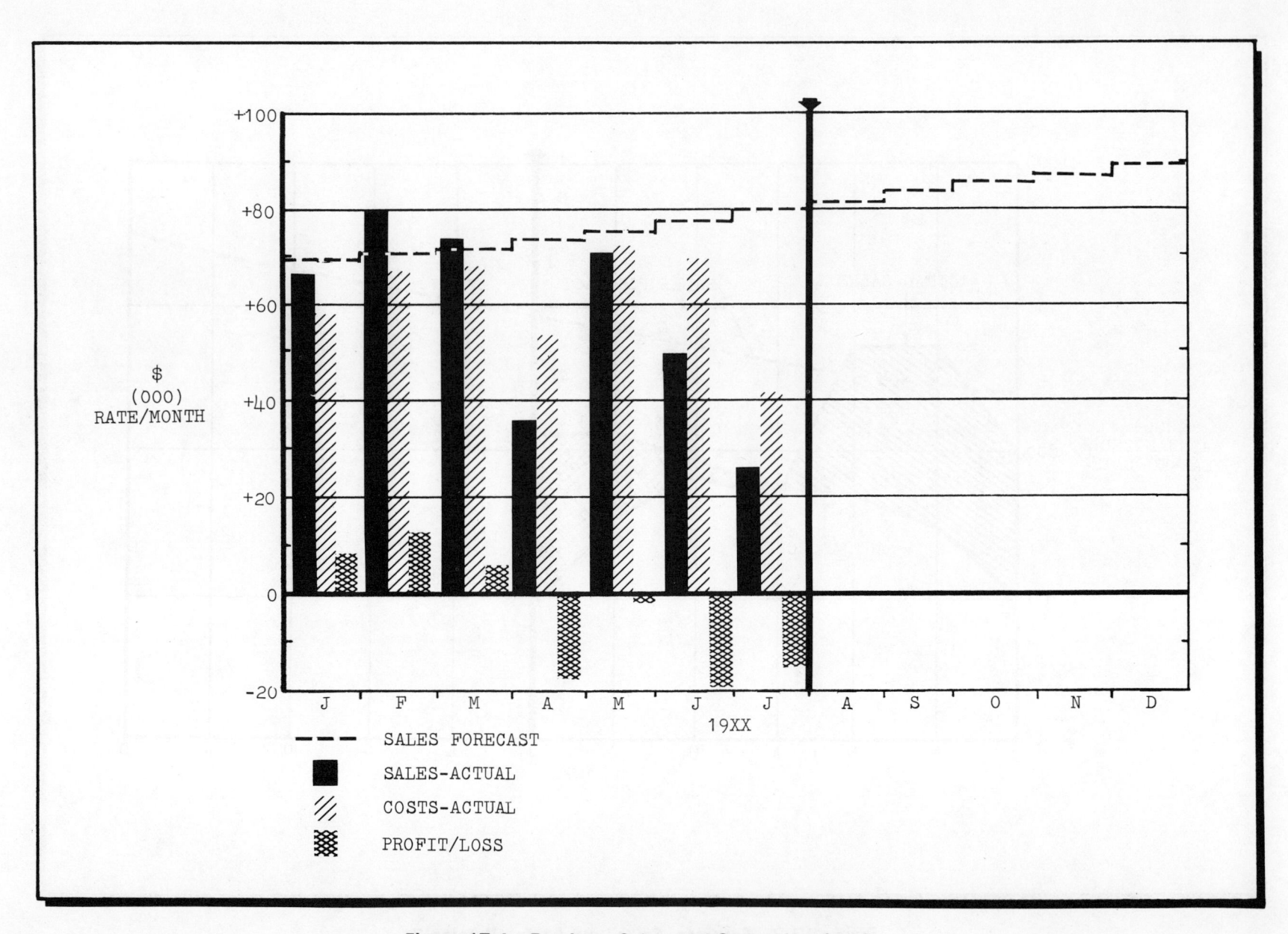

Figure 17.4 Earnings, Sales, and Costs—Version 4

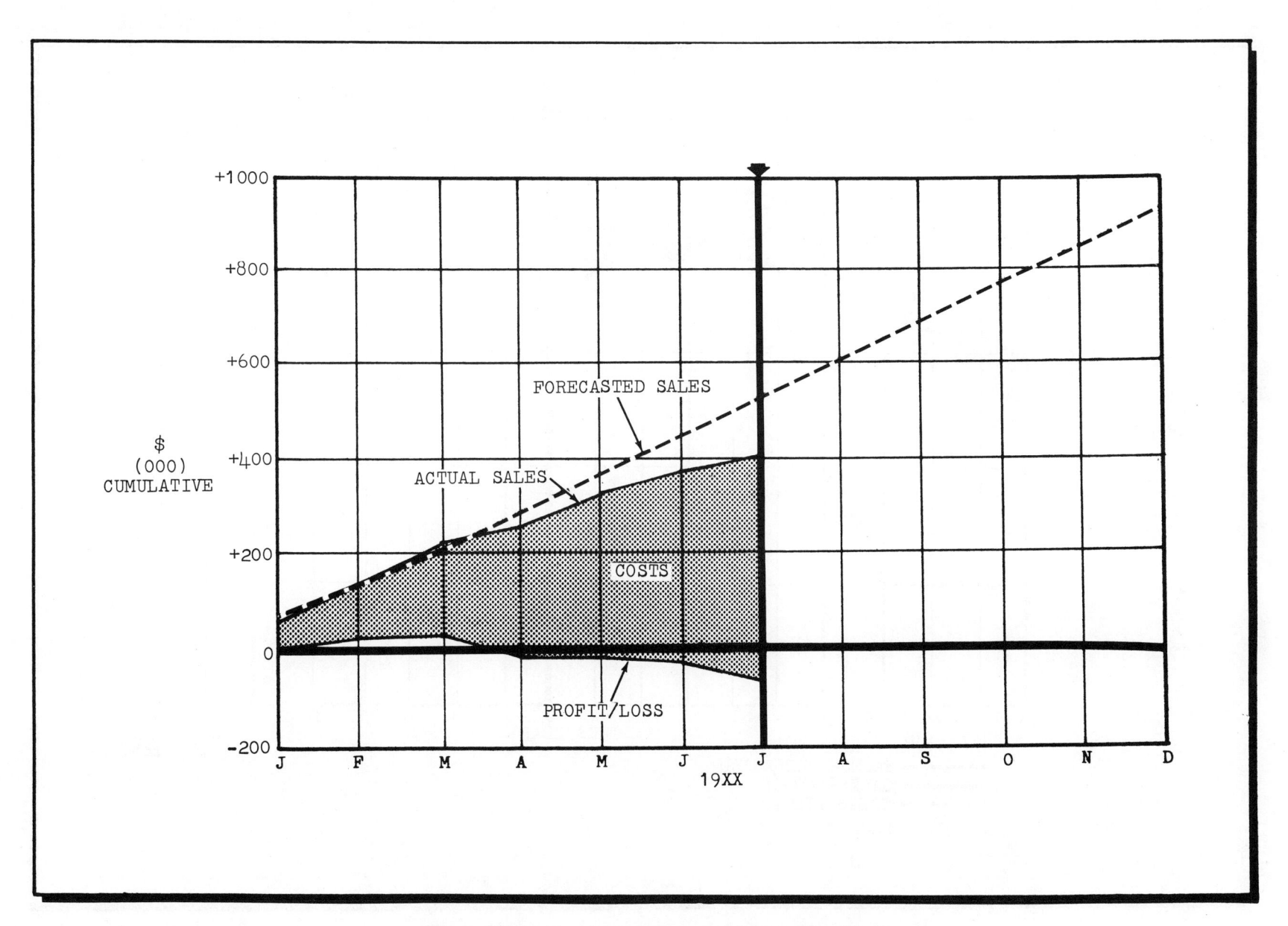

Figure 17.5 Earnings, Sales, and Costs—Version 5

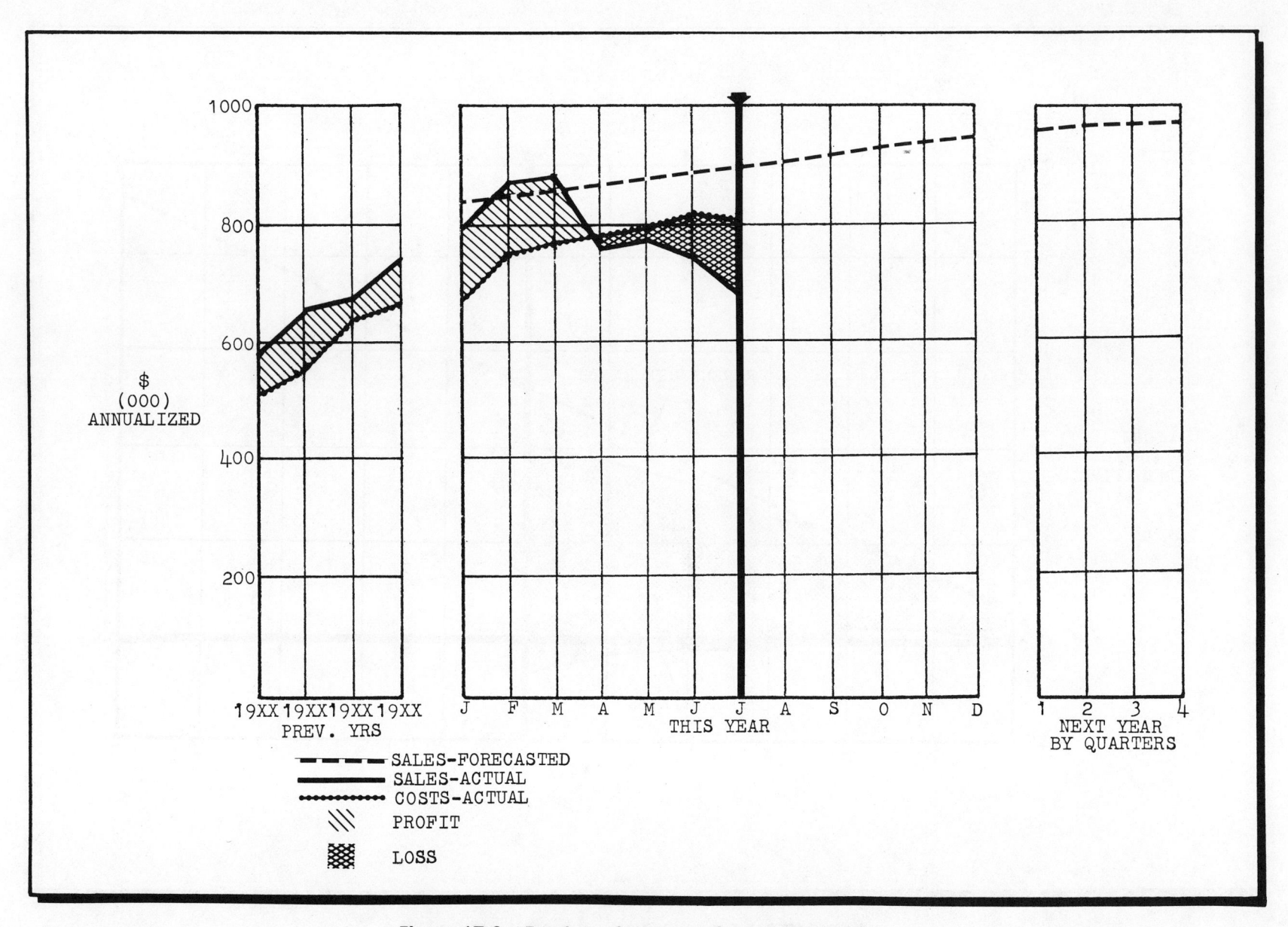

Figure 17.6 Earnings, Sales, and Costs—Version 6

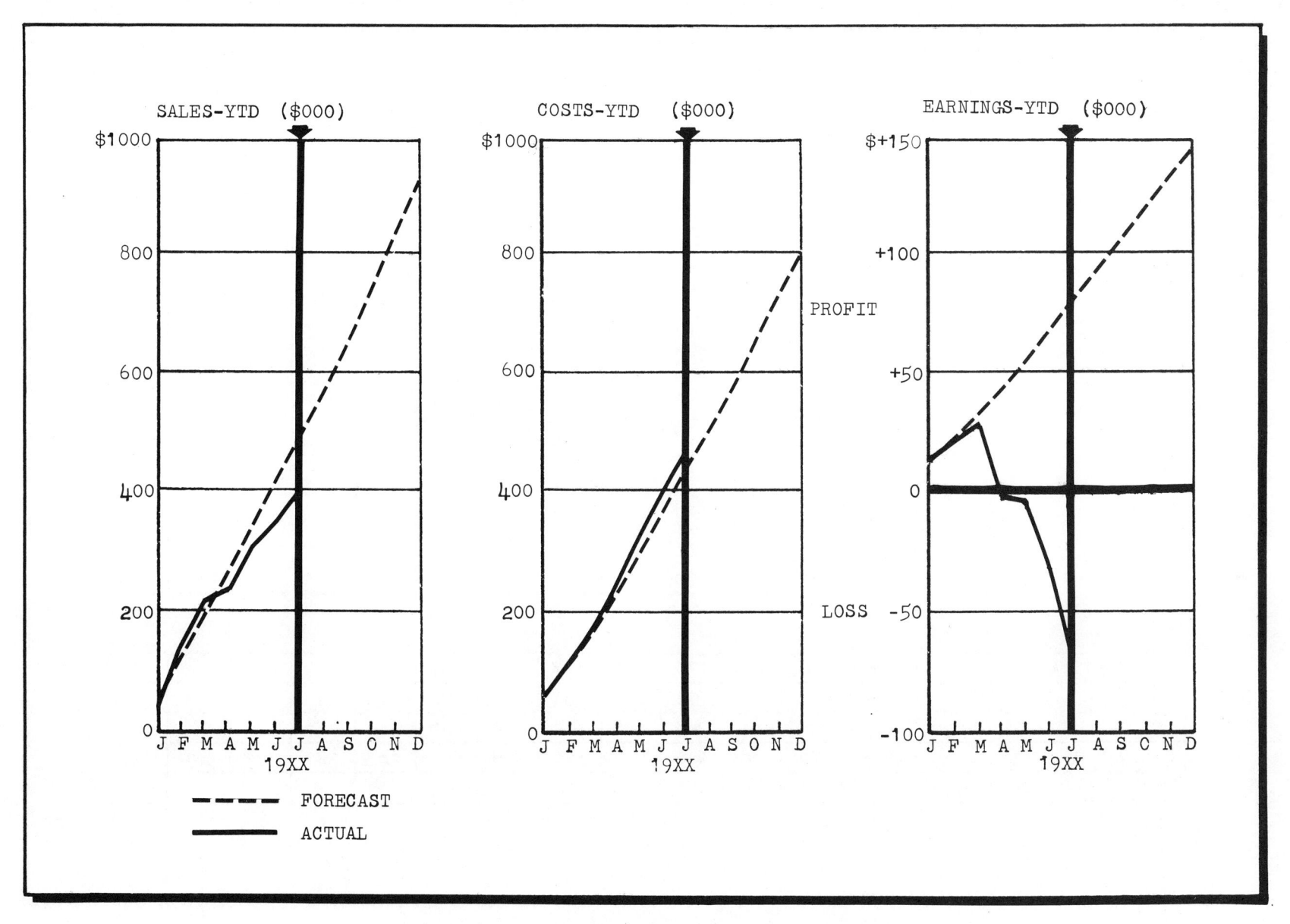

Figure 17.7   Earnings, Sales, and Costs—Version 7

$
(000)
CUMULATIVE

		J	F	M	A	M	J	J	A	S	O	N	D
SALES-ACT. CUM	———	66	146	220	256	327	377	403					
COSTS-ACT. CUM	••••••	58	125	193	259	331	406	472					
PROFIT/LOSS-ACT. CUM	‖‖‖ / ▨	8	21	27	-3	-4	-29	-69					
SALES-F'CST CUM	— — —	70	141	213	287	363	441	521	603	687	773	861	951
VARIANCE-ACT & F'CST SALES		-4	+5	+7	-31	-36	-64	-64					

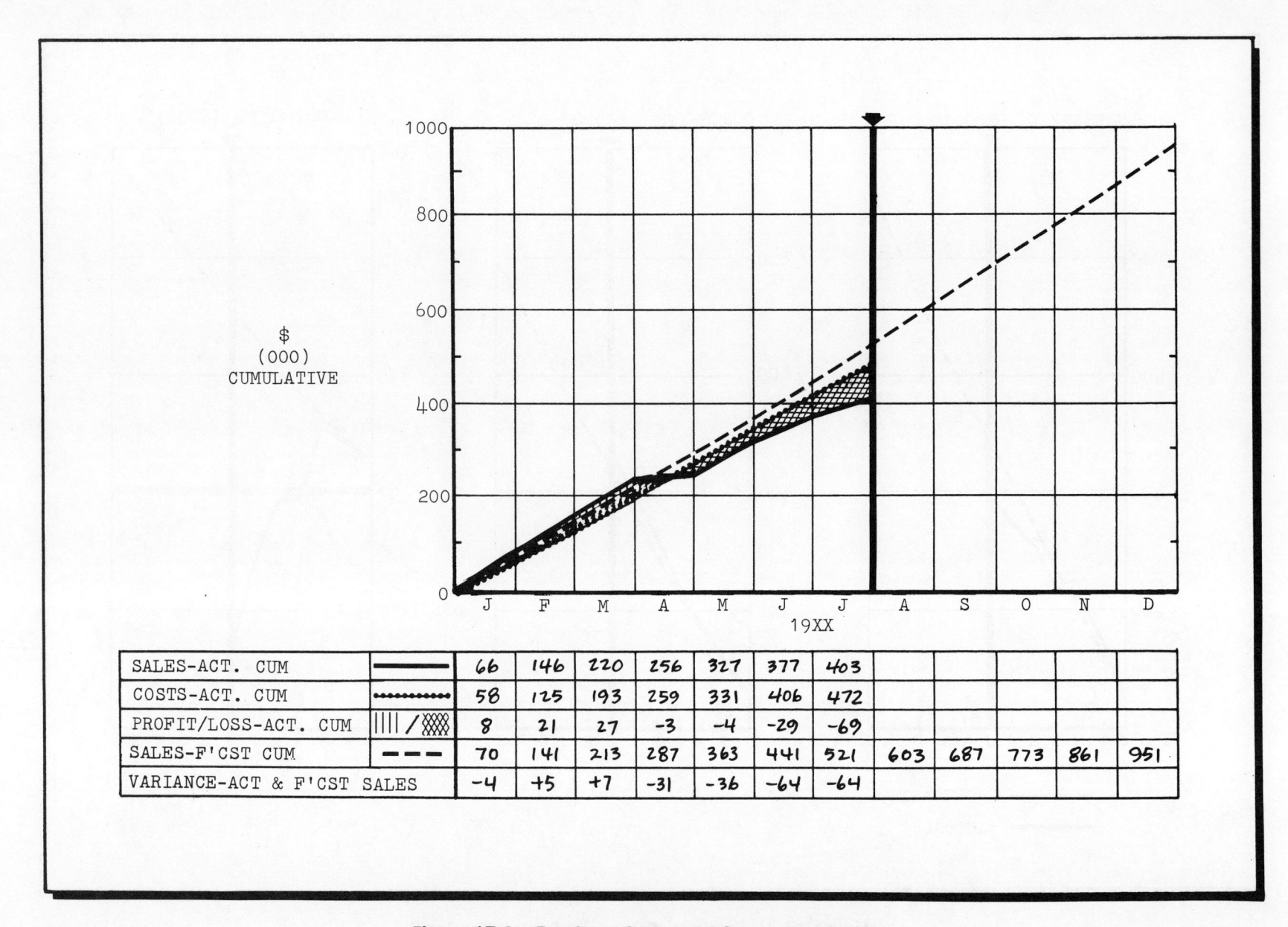

Figure 17.8 Earnings, Sales, and Costs—Version 8

FACTOR			19XX											
			J	F	M	A	M	J	J	A	S	O	N	D
SALES ($000)	FCST	RATE/MO	70	71	72	74	76	78	80	82	84	86	88	90
		CUM	70	141	213	287	363	441	521	603	687	773	861	951
		ANNUAL'D YTD	840	846	852	861	871	882	893	905	916	928	939	951
	ACT	RATE/MO	66	80	74	36	71	50	26					
		CUM	66	146	220	256	327	377	403					
		ANNUAL'D YTD	792	876	880	768	785	754	691					
COSTS ($000)	FCST	RATE/MO	60	60	61	63	65	66	68	70	71	73	75	77
		CUM	60	120	181	244	309	375	443	513	584	657	732	809
		ANNUAL'D YTD	720	720	724	732	742	750	759	770	779	788	799	809
	ACT	RATE/MO	58	67	68	66	72	75	66					
		CUM	58	125	193	259	331	406	472					
		ANNUAL'D YTD	696	750	772	777	794	812	809					
EARNINGS ($000)	FCST	RATE/MO	10	11	11	11	11	12	12	12	13	13	13	13
		CUM	10	21	32	43	54	66	78	90	103	116	129	142
		ANNUAL'D YTD	120	126	128	129	130	132	134	135	137	139	141	142
	ACT	RATE/MO	8	13	6	-30	-1	-25	-40					
		CUM	8	21	27	-3	-4	-29	-69					
		ANNUAL'D YTD	96	126	108	-9	-9	-58	-118					

Figure 17.9   Earnings, Sales, and Costs—Version 9

STATUS THROUGH __FEB__

FACTOR	STATUS THIS MONTH			YTD STATUS			EST YEAR-END STATUS		
	FCST	ACT	VAR	FCST	ACT	VAR	FCST	ACT	VAR
SALES ($000)	71	80	+9	141	146	+5	951	951	0
COSTS ($000)	60	67	+7	120	125	+5	809	809	0
PROFIT ($000)	11	13	+2	21	21	0	142	142	0

Figure 17.10 Earnings, Sales, and Costs—Version 10

18.0 EQUIPMENT CAPACITY VERSUS WORKLOAD

Charts that show the relationship between existing and planned equipment capacity and workload are shown in this section. Also see Section 20.0, *Facility Capacity Versus Workload*.

18.1 Equipment Capacity Versus Workload—Version 1: Version 1 of an equipment capacity versus workload tracking chart, Figure 18.1, compares the actual and forecasted number of systems processed per month with the capacity of the system test consoles. The consoles are rates with a yield of eight units per month, each, on a two-shift, six-day work week basis, giving a total capacity for 26 consoles or 208 systems per month. The acquisition of four additional test consoles in August will increase the equipment capacity to 240 systems per month.

18.2 Equipment Capacity Versus Workload—Version 2: Equipment capacity is examined in terms of its actual yield in Version 2 of an equipment capacity versus workload tracking chart, Figure 18.2. The amount scale can be in terms of a single piece of equipment (as shown), or multiples of the same equipment all producing the same production unit. The scheduled workload in this example is shown with a dotted line. The actual yield (solid line) can also be compared with the yield from the previous year (dashed line).

18.3 Equipment Capacity Versus Workload—Version 3: The planned and actual quantities of units produced per month are compared against a machine shop with a tooling and machine tool rating of 3300 units per month in Version 3 of an equipment capacity versus workload tracking chart, Figure 18.3. In this example the shop rating is on the basis of one shift, so one possible solution to the current excessive workload could be to open up a second shift.

18.4 Equipment Capacity Versus Workload—Version 4: Version 4 of an equipment capacity versus workload chart, Figure 18.4, looks at actual workload in relationship to the yield of existing equipment on a three-shift basis. In this example, the current workload can be handled on a one-shift basis. In two months, either a second shift will have to be added or additional equipment acquired.

18.5 Equipment Capacity Versus Workload—Version 5: A family of related test equipment is compared in Version 5 of an equipment capacity versus workload tracking chart, Figure 18.5. The purpose is to attempt to spot potential bottlenecks in the flow as with the module tester on the flow.

18.6 Equipment Capacity Versus Workload—Version 6: A tabular version of an equipment capacity versus workload tracking chart is shown as Version 6, Figure 18.6. A column on the right-hand side of the table shows, with a check mark, the equipment with the most critical capacity versus workload problem.

18.7 Equipment Capacity Versus Workload—Version 7: A table that can be used to analyze equipment requirements based on their capacities versus varying workloads is shown as Version 7 of an equipment capacity versus workload chart, Figure 18.7. Equipment costs and equipment costs per unit are summarized at the bottom of the table.

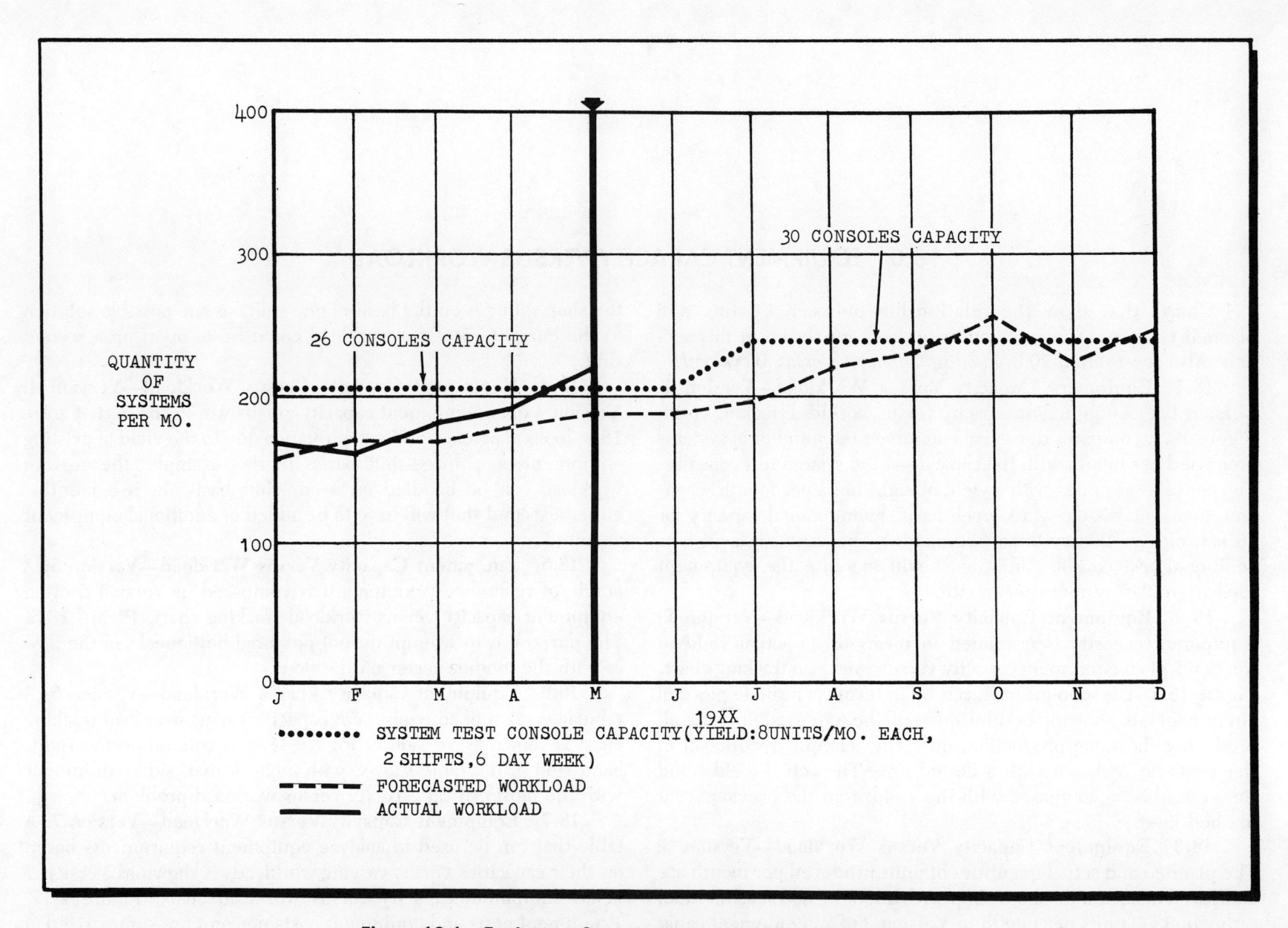

Figure 18.1 Equipment Capacity Versus Workload—Version 1

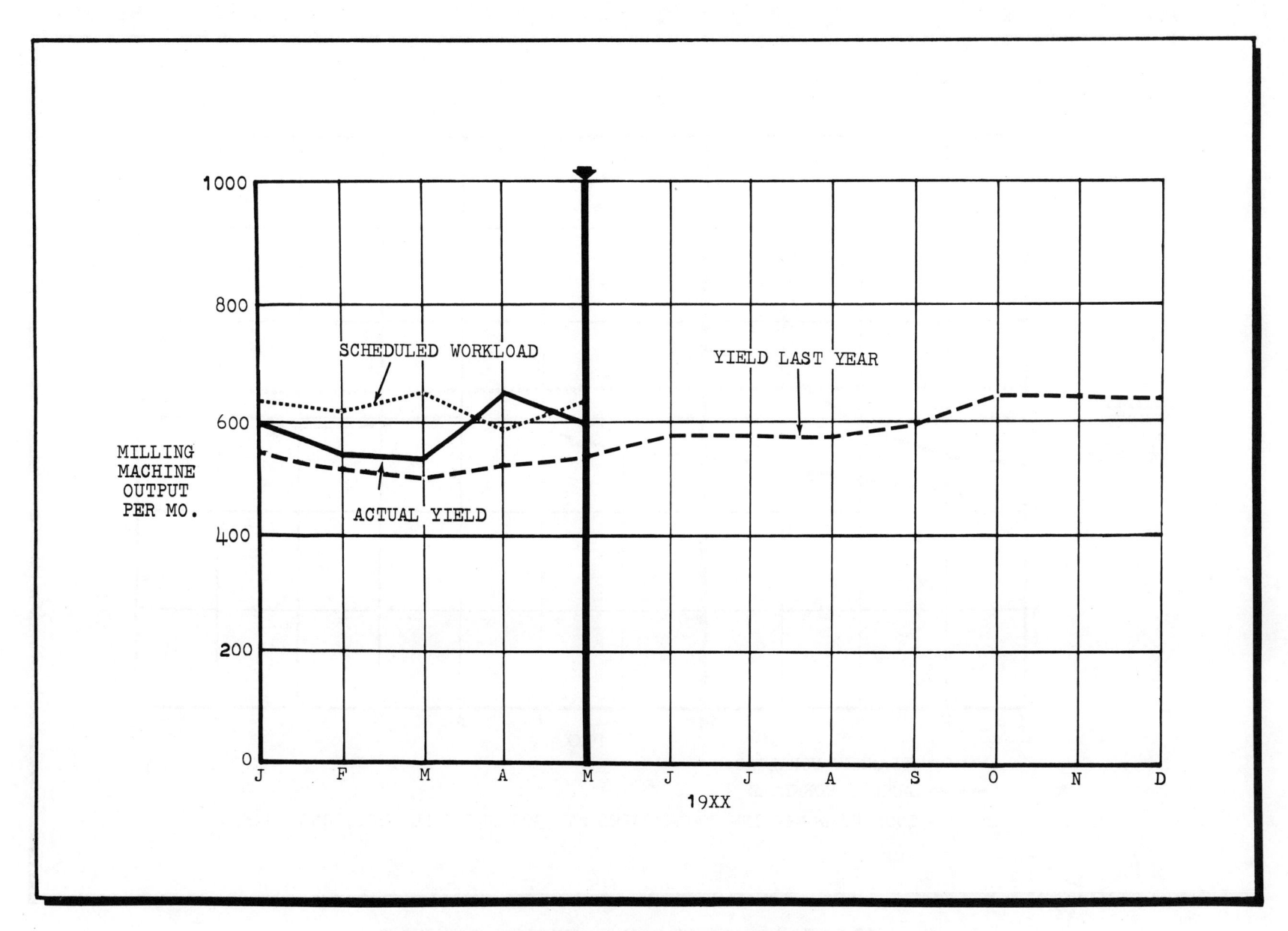

Figure 18.2 Equipment Capacity Versus Workload—Version 2

215

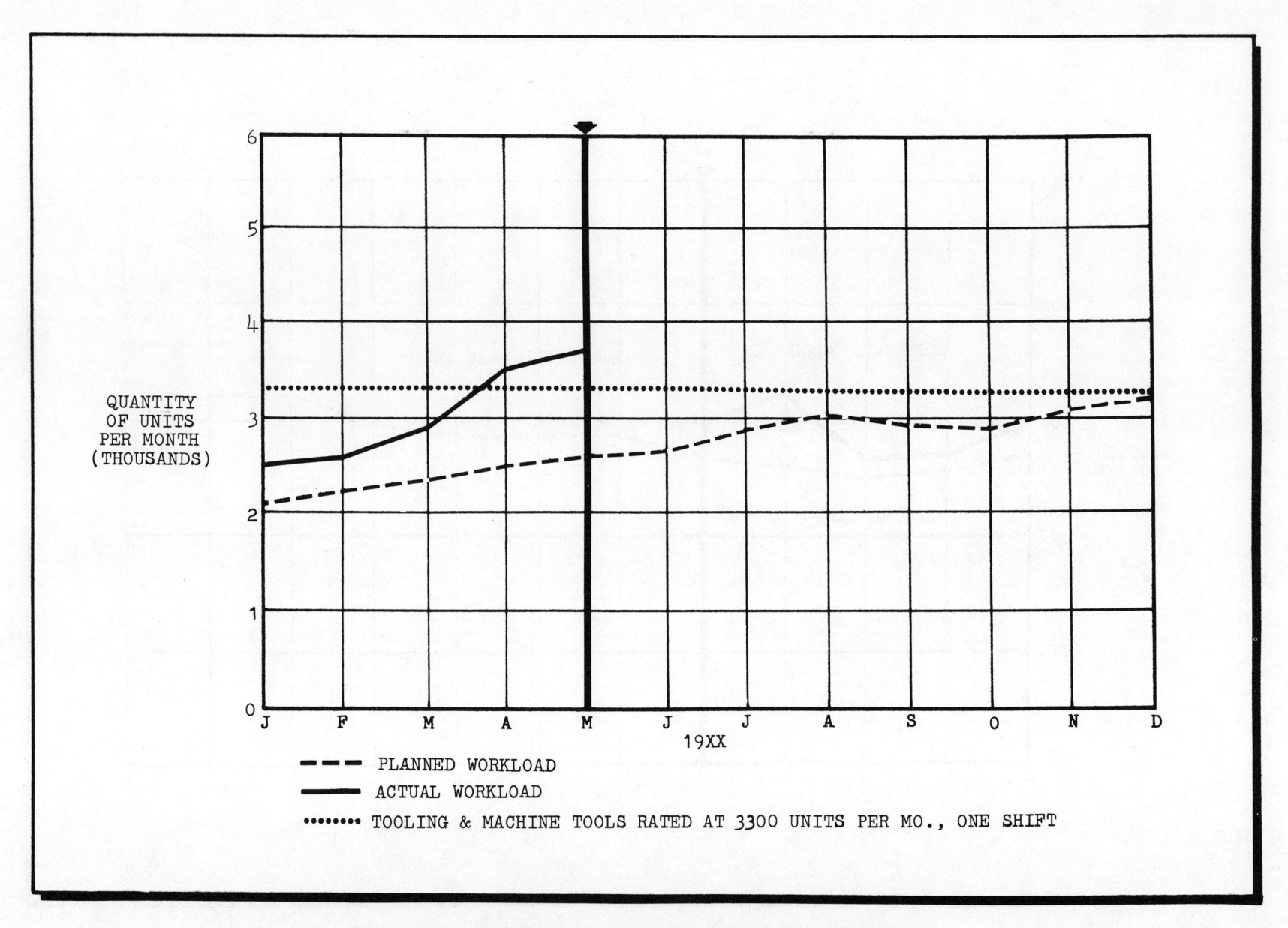

Figure 18.3 Equipment Capacity Versus Workload—Version 3

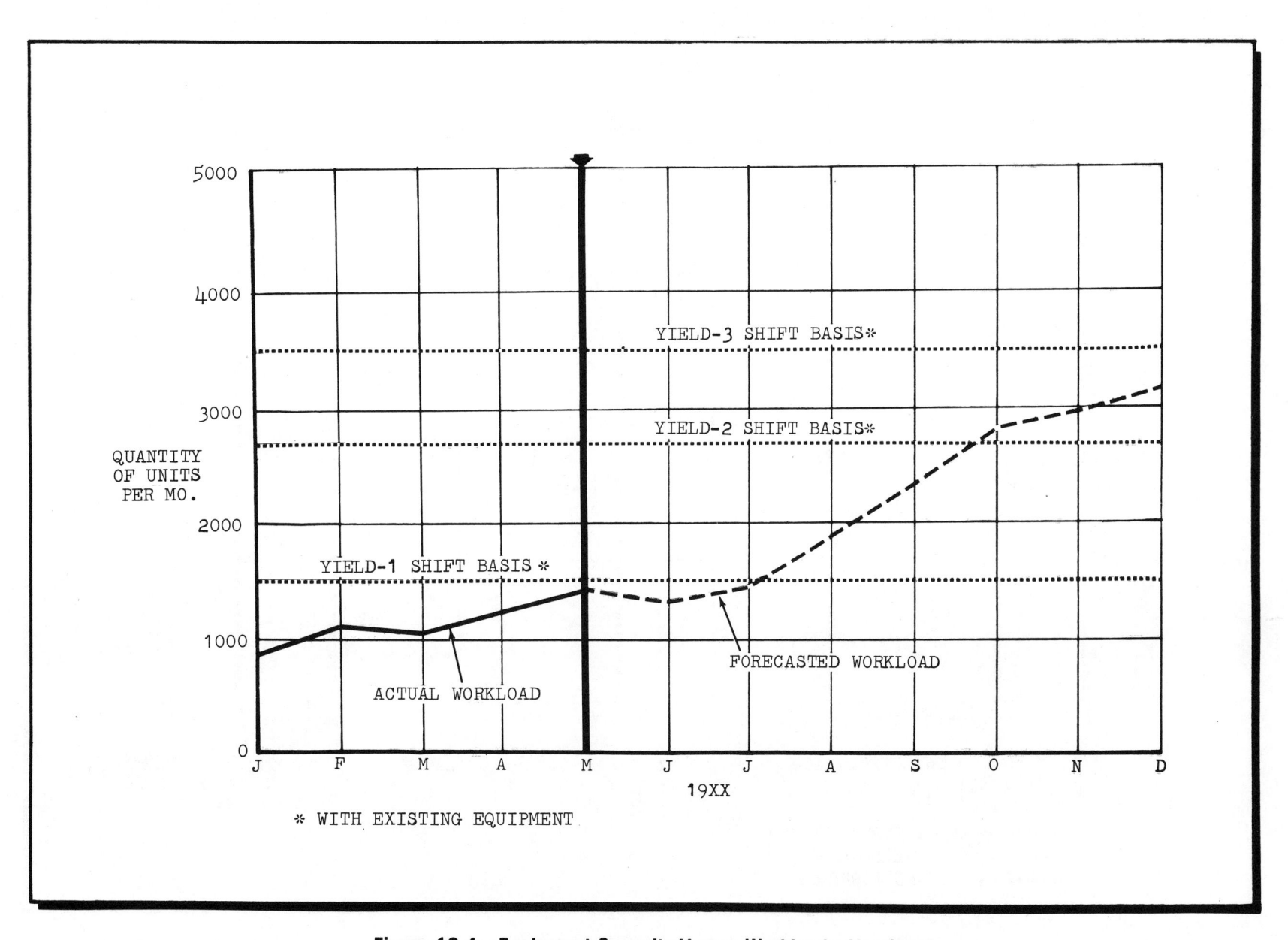

Figure 18.4 Equipment Capacity Versus Workload—Version 4

217

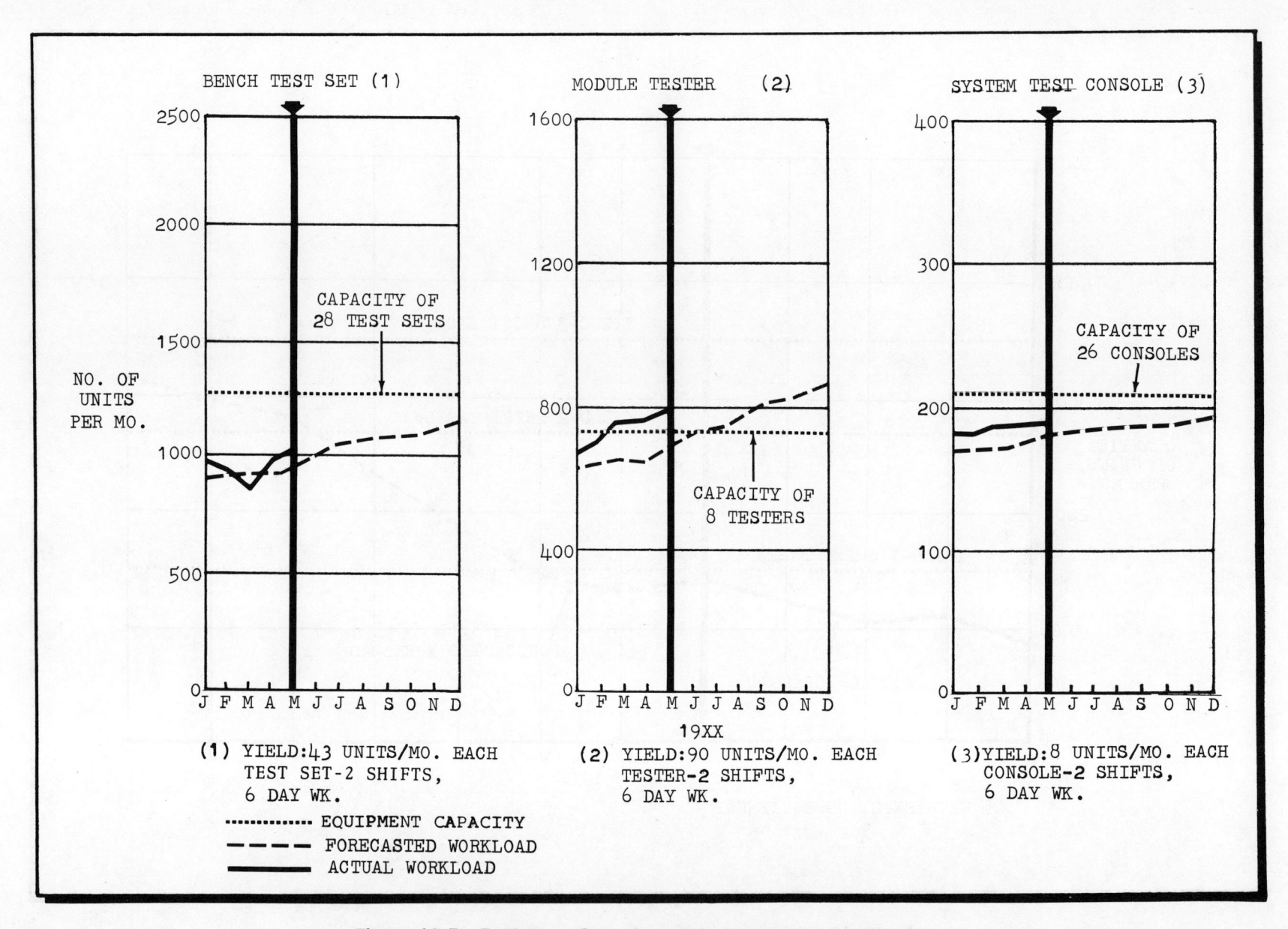

Figure 18.5 Equipment Capacity Versus Workload—Version 5

EQUIPT	CAPAC-ITY	FCST/ACTUAL	(1)	\multicolumn{12}{c	}{19XX}	CRIT-ICAL (✓)
				J	F	M	A	M	J	J	A	S	O	N	D	
VIBRATION	26 UNITS/ MONTH	FCST	W	21	22	22	23	24	25	26	27	28	26	22	20	
			V	+5	+4	+4	+3	+2	+1	0	-1	-2	0	+4	+6	
		ACTUAL	W	20	23	22	24									
			V	+6	+3	+4	+2									
SHOCK	13 UNITS/ MONTH	FCST	W	10	9	9	12	12	12	10	11	10	10	9	9	
			V	+3	+4	+4	+1	+1	+1	+3	+2	+3	+3	+4	+4	
		ACTUAL	W	10	10	8	12									
			V	+3	+3	+5	+1									
LOADS	40 UNITS/ MONTH	FCST	W	40	39	39	40	40	40	40	39	39	39	40	40	
			V	0	+1	+1	0	0	0	0	+1	+1	+1	0	0	
		ACTUAL	W	40	40	40	47									✓
			V	0	0	0	-7									
HUMIDITY	15 UNITS/ MONTH	FCST	W	10	11	10	9	9	8	9	8	8	9	9	8	
			V	+5	+4	+5	+6	+6	+7	+6	+7	+7	+6	+6	+7	
		ACTUAL	W	10	10	11	10									
			V	+5	+5	+4	+5									

(1) W = WORKLOAD
V = VARIANCE BETWEEN CAPACITY & WORKLOAD
+ = EXCESS CAPACITY
− = EXCESS WORKLOAD

Figure 18.6 Equipment Capacity Versus Workload—Version 6

STATUS AS OF _____

EQUIPMENT	COST ($000)	YIELD PER MO.	EQUIP. QUANTITY REQUIRED TO SUPPORT UNITS PER MO. WORKLOAD OF:									
			10	20	30	40	50	60	70	80	90	100
SYSTEM TEST CONS.	15	8	2	3	4	5	7	8	9	10	12	13
MODULE TESTER	6	27	1	1	2	2	2	3	3	3	4	4
BENCH TEST SET	4	43	1	1	1	1	2	2	2	2	3	3
ELECT SYST. TESTER	10	18	1	2	2	3	3	4	4	5	5	6
PNEUMATIC SYST. TEST	9	23	1	1	2	2	3	3	4	4	4	5
LAB CHECKOUT UNIT	5	50	1	1	1	1	1	2	2	2	2	2
EQUIPMENT COSTS ($000)			49	89	119	144	187	223	243	272	312	346
EQUIPMENT COST PER UNIT ($000)			4.90	4.45	3.97	3.60	3.74	3.72	3.47	3.40	3.47	3.46

Figure 18.7 Equipment Capacity Versus Workload—Version 7

19.0 FACILITIES

Charts that display information relative to the size, use, and location of facilities are shown in this section. Also see Sections 20.0, *Facility Capacity Versus Workload* and 27.0, *Manpower and Facilities*.

19.1 Facilities—Version 1: Changes in facilities usually occur less often than other factors that are monitored in business. The example chart shown in Figure 19.1 covers a seven-year time period. It shows the facility square footage for the previous five years and predicts requirements for the coming two years.

19.2 Facilities—Version 2: Version 2 of a facilities chart, Figure 19.2, tracks facility costs per square foot over a long time span. A solid line shows actuals to date, and a dashed line projects square footage costs for the next three years. An arrowhead is used on the amount scale to call attention to the fact that it does not start from a zero base.

19.3 Facilities—Version 3: The total square footage shown in Version 3 of a facilities chart, Figure 19.3, is segmented to show its use. The footnote section of this example carries additional information regarding capabilities.

19.4 Facilities—Version 4: A bar chart style is used for Version 4 of a facilities chart, Figure 19.4. In the form of a one-time status report, square footage is shown by department as to what exists, what is under construction, and what is planned. A dashed line shows the square footage by department for the previous year.

19.5 Facilities—Version 5: A statistical table is used as Version 5 of a facilities chart, Figure 19.5. As a one-time status report, gross and net square footage figures are given for what exists, what is under construction, what is planned, and the total.

19.6 Facilities—Version 6: A facilities plot plan is the basis for Version 6 of a facilities chart, Figure 19.6. Square footage figures are given for each of the structures and are summarized for the current and previous years in bar form at the bottom of the chart.

19.7 Facilities—Version 7: A map is used for Version 7 of a facilities chart, Figure 19.7. Square footage figures are given by location and are summarized at the bottom of the chart.

19.8 Facilities—Version 8: A one-time status report in the form of a segmented circle is used as Version 8 of a facilities chart, Figure 19.8. Square footage and percentage figures are given for each segment. The total square footage is summarized at the bottom of the chart.

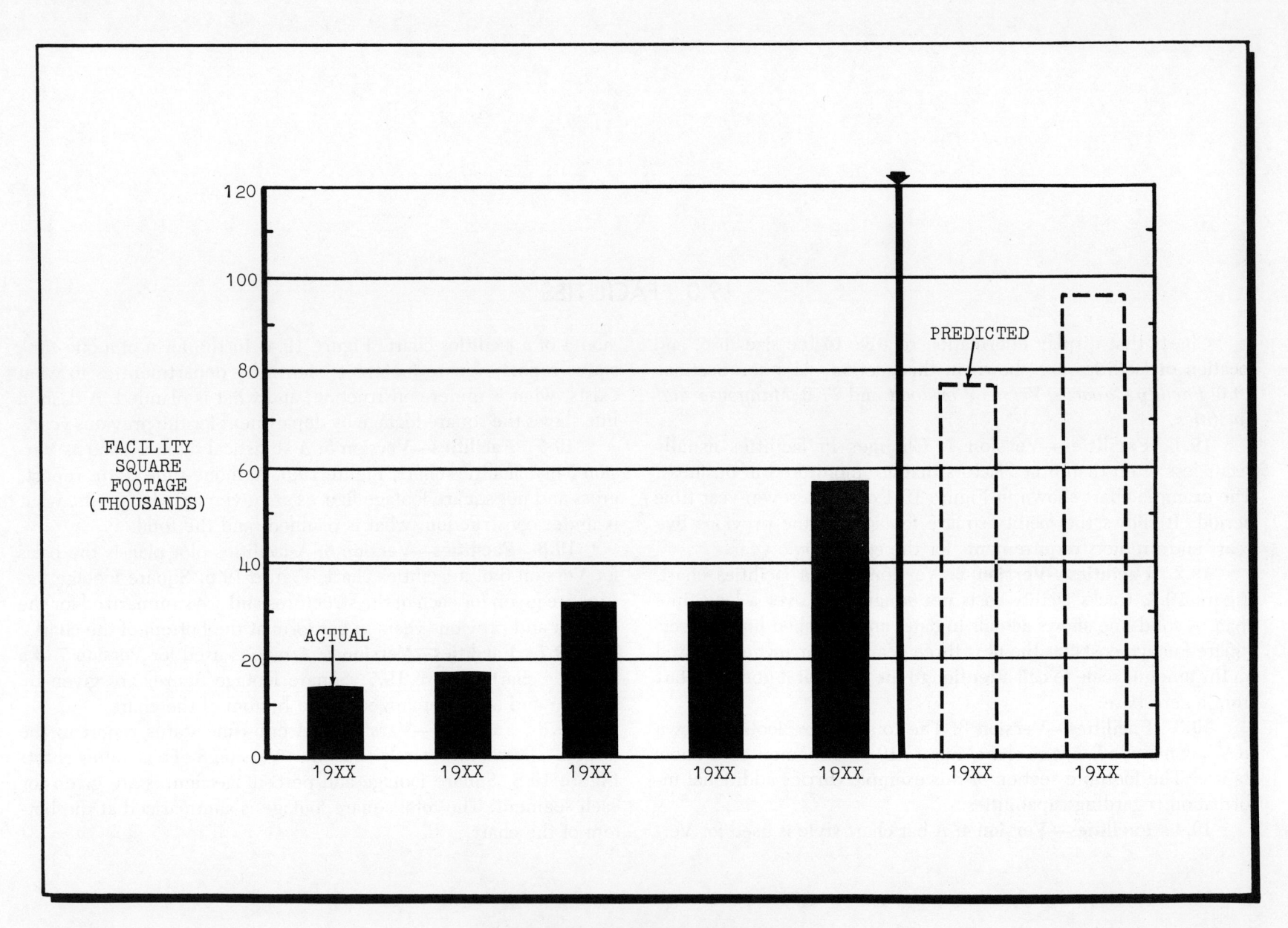

Figure 19.1   Facilities—Version 1

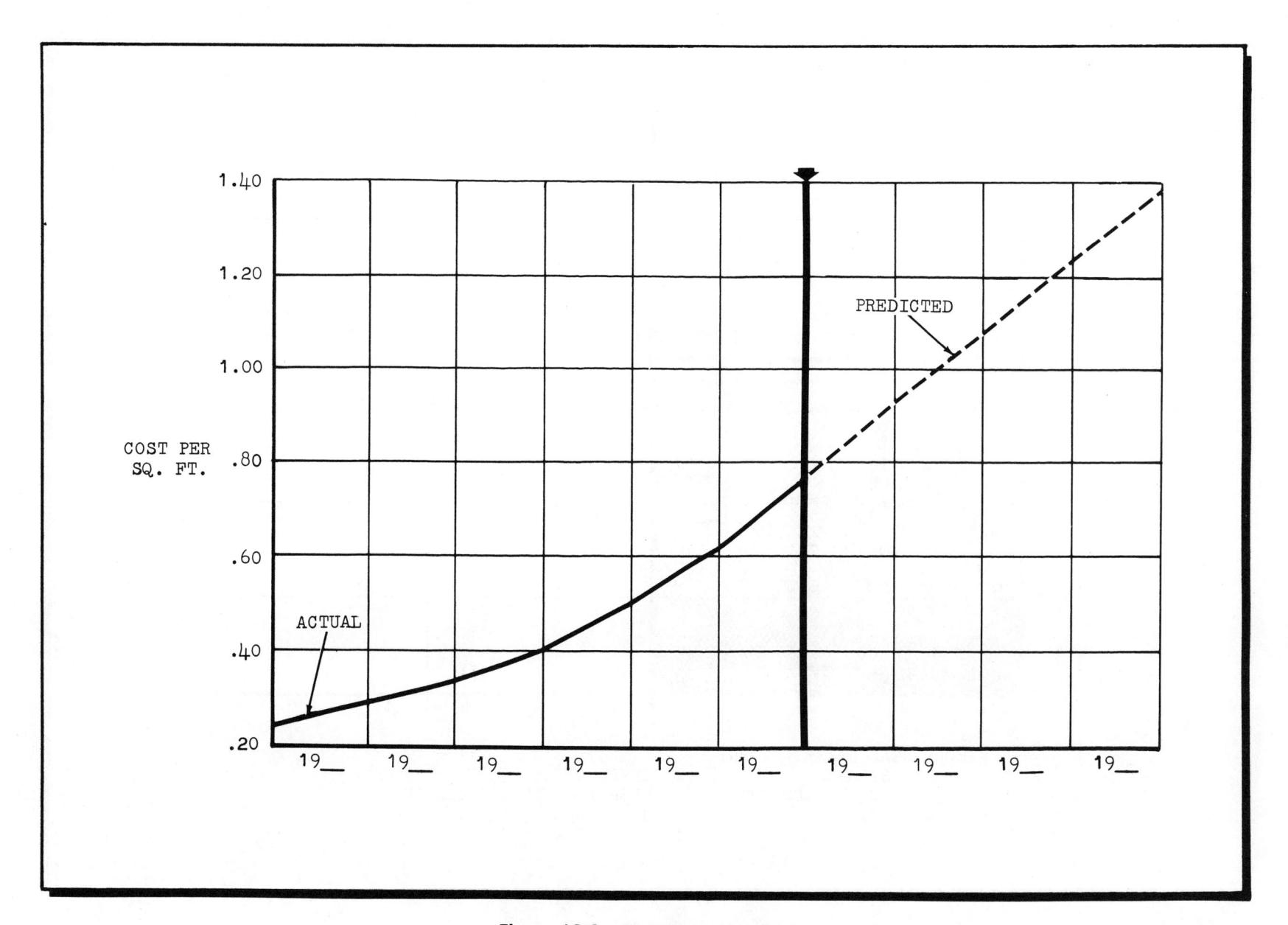

Figure 19.2 Facilities—Version 2

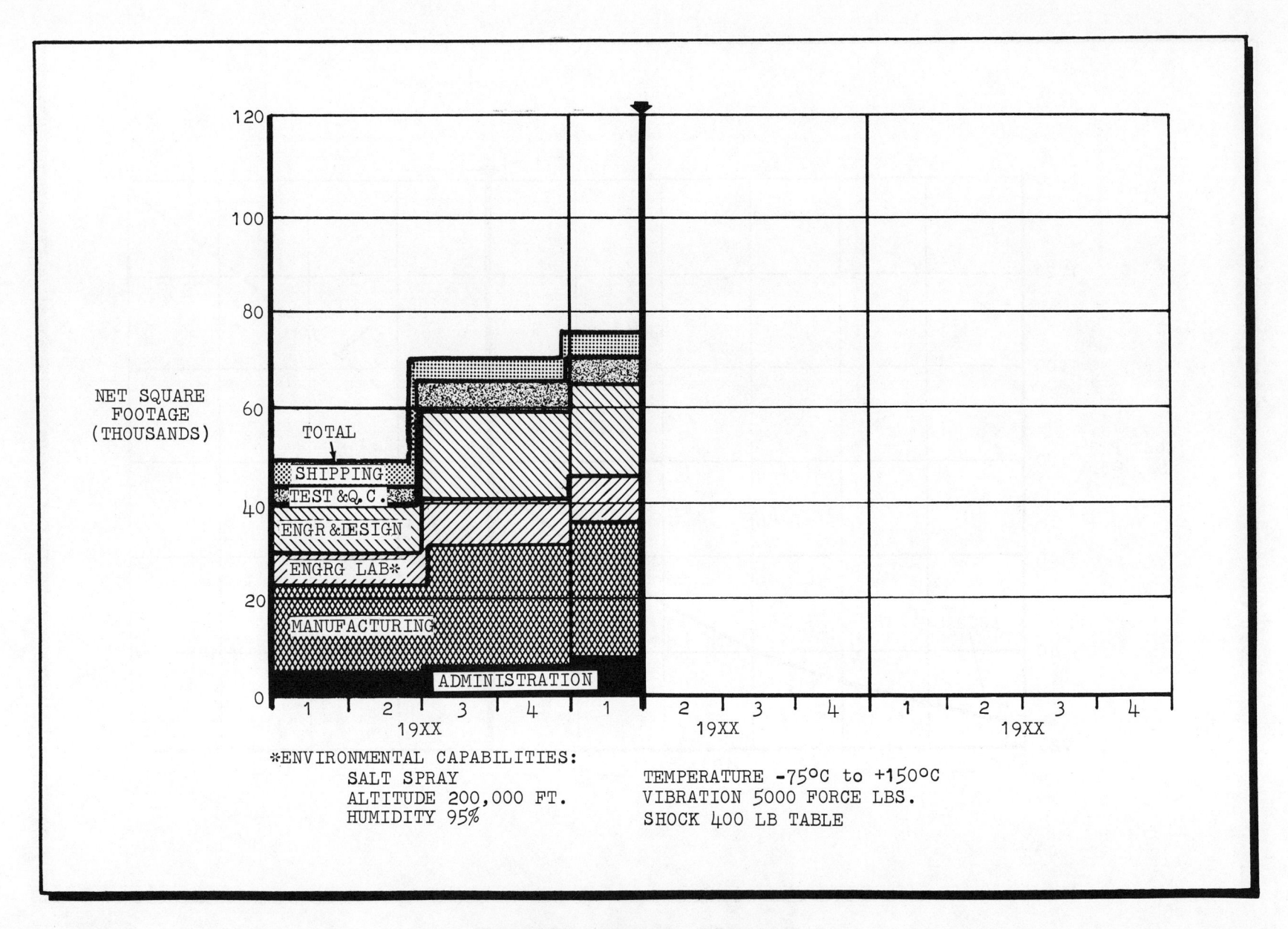

Figure 19.3 Facilities—Version 3

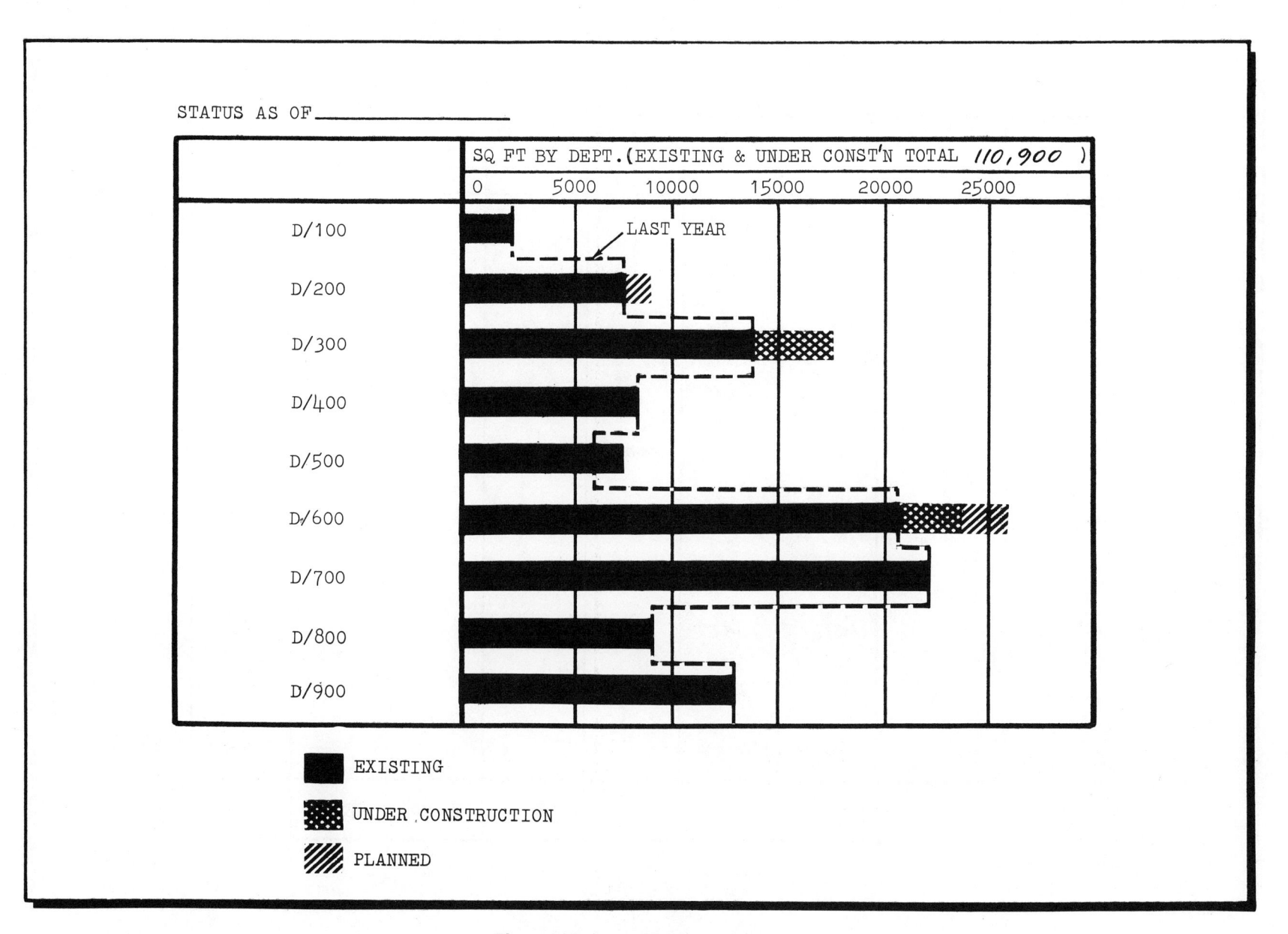

Figure 19.4 Facilities—Version 4

STATUS AS OF

DEPARTMENT	FACILITY SQUARE FOOTAGE							
	EXISTING		UNDER CONSTRUCT.		PLANNED		TOTAL	
	GROSS	NET	GROSS	NET	GROSS	NET	GROSS	NET
ADMINISTRATION	3312	3015					3312	3015
FINANCE	2208	1921					2208	1921
SALES	3036	2763					3036	2763
ENGINEERING	7176	6243			2000	1850	9176	8093
TOOL SHOP	6072	5526	1000	910			7072	6436
MACHINE SHOP	3864	3362					3864	3362
MAINTENANCE	2263	2059					2263	2059
ASSEMBLY	18161	16527	3000	2780			21161	19307
QUALITY CONTROL	2484	2161					2484	2161
WAREHOUSE	6624	6028					6624	6028
TOTALS	55,200	49,605	4000	3690	2000	1850	61,200	55,145

Figure 19.5 Facilities—Version 5

STATUS AS OF _____

RENO LOS ANGELES BAKERSFIELD

- 2500 (planned)
- 2500 (on hand)
- 4000 (under construction)
- 4000 (on hand)
- 4000 (planned)
- 15,600
- 22,000
- 12,000
- 5000

FACILITIES:
- ——————— ON HAND
- – – – – – UNDER CONSTRUCTION
- ············ PLANNED
- [XXX] SQUARE FOOTAGE

TOTAL SQUARE FOOTAGE

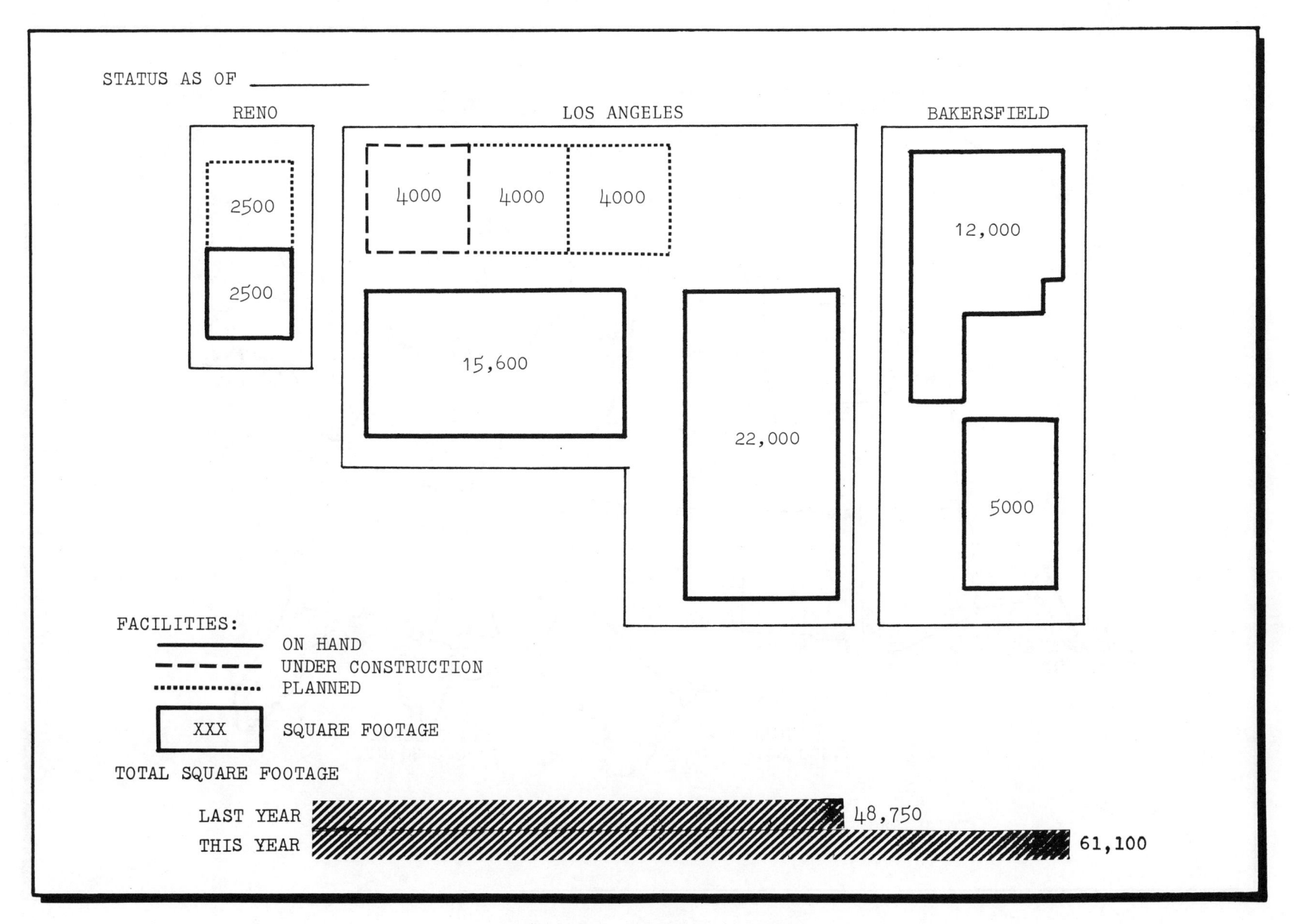

LAST YEAR 48,750
THIS YEAR 61,100

Figure 19.6 Facilities—Version 6

PORTLAND
12,750 SQ.FT.

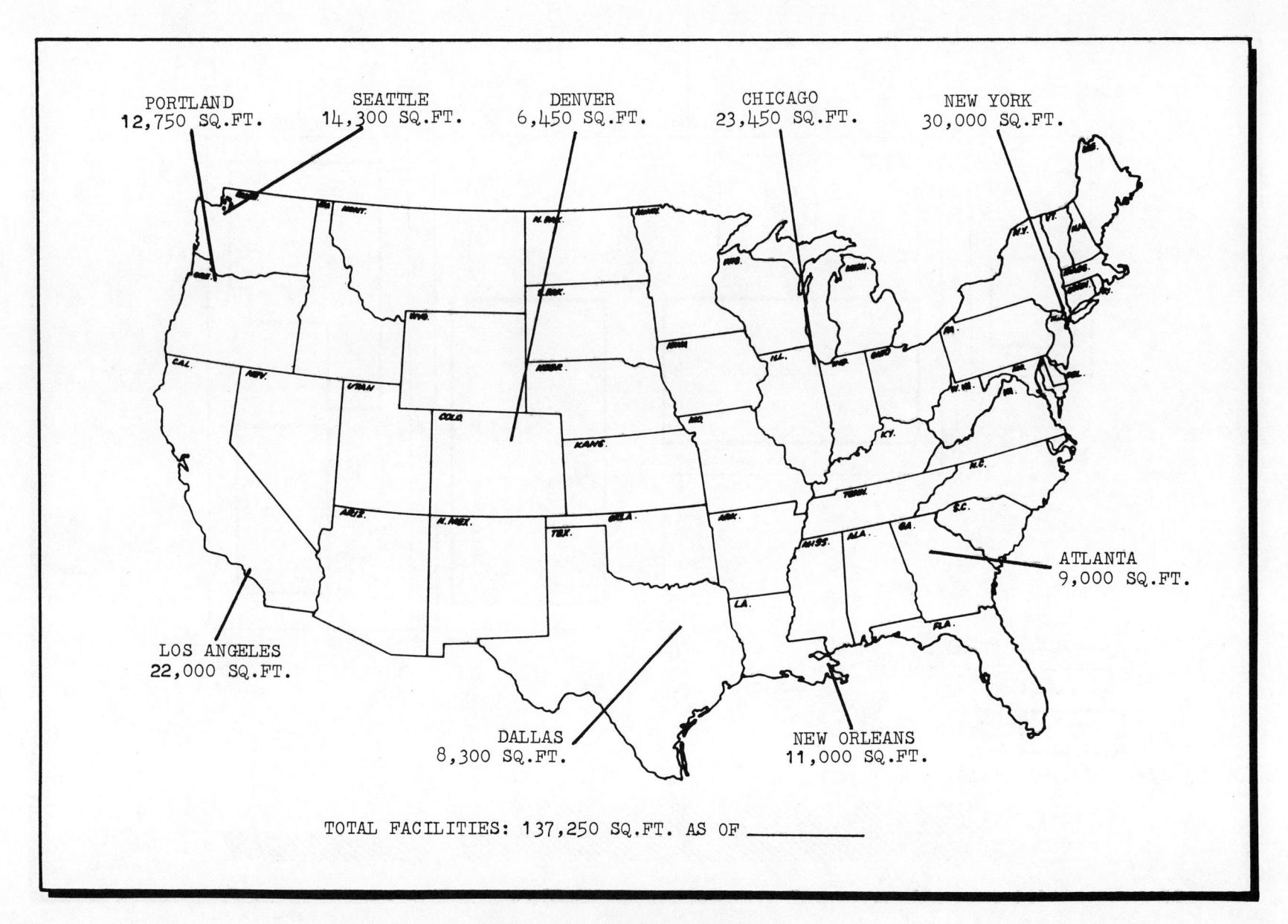

SEATTLE
14,300 SQ.FT.

DENVER
6,450 SQ.FT.

CHICAGO
23,450 SQ.FT.

NEW YORK
30,000 SQ.FT.

ATLANTA
9,000 SQ.FT.

LOS ANGELES
22,000 SQ.FT.

DALLAS
8,300 SQ.FT.

NEW ORLEANS
11,000 SQ.FT.

TOTAL FACILITIES: 137,250 SQ.FT. AS OF _____

Figure 19.7 Facilities—Version 7

STATUS AS OF _____

FACILITIES
GOVERNMENT
FURNISHED

13,585 SQ.FT.
24.5%

FACILITIES OWNED
10,150 SQ.FT.
18.3%

FACILITIES LEASED
31,703 SQ.FT.
57.2%

TOTAL SQUARE FOOTAGE   55,438

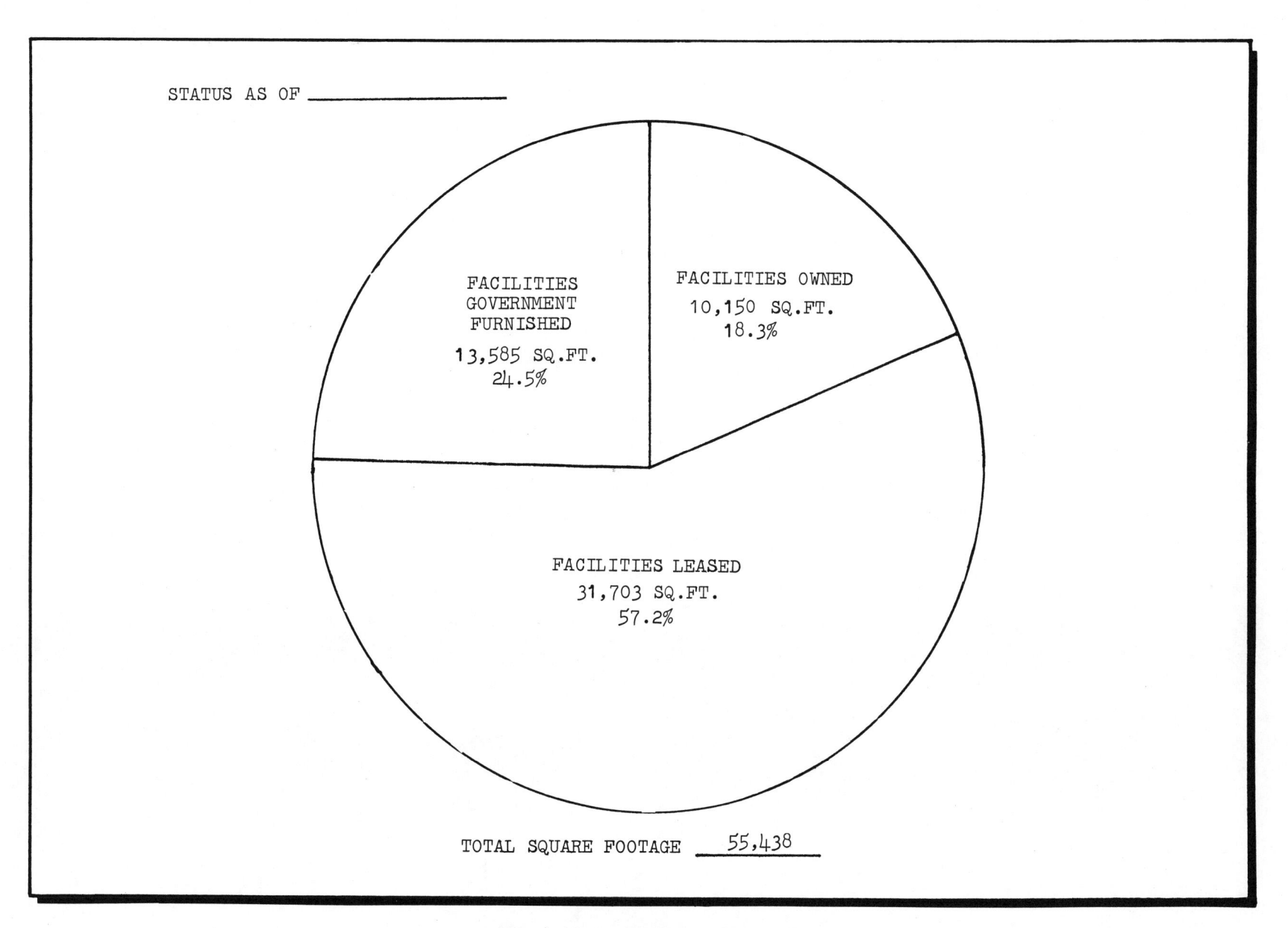

Figure 19.8 Facilities—Version 8

20.0 FACILITY CAPACITY VERSUS WORKLOAD

Charts that relate workload requirements to the existing and planned capacity of facilities are shown in this section. Also see Sections 18.0, *Equipment Capacity Versus Workload*, 19.0, *Facilities*, and 27.0, *Manpower and Facilities*.

20.1 Facility Capacity Versus Workload—Version 1: Workload is compared to capacity in Version 1, Figure 20.1, in terms of the production per month as a percent of capacity. The previous year's actuals are shown as a gauge of the current year's performance. The bottom of the chart grid is broken to indicate that the amount scale does not start from zero base.

20.2 Facility Capacity Versus Workload—Version 2: In Version 2 of a facility capacity versus workload tracking chart, Figure 20.2, the actual production per month as a percent of capacity is compared to an annual forecast. For comparison purposes, a plotting representing the actual production *costs* as a percent of sales is also given.

20.3 Facility Capacity Versus Workload—Version 3: Forecasted and actual production per month as a percent of capacity is shown over a six-year period in Version 3 of a facility capacity versus workload tracking chart, Figure 20.3. The actual monthly average is given in the left-hand grid for the previous four years. Forecasted and actual percentages are given for the current year, and the forecasted monthly average is shown by quarters for the coming year. An arrowhead on the amount scale emphasizes that it does not start from zero.

20.4 Facility Capacity Versus Workload— Version 4: Version 4, Figure 20.4, is an example of a tracking chart used to display the capacity of a facility in terms of being able to produce a certain quantity of items, a certain dollar volume, or a certain number of transactions during a specific time period. In this example, the planned and actual number of transactions per month are compared with the facility's capacity.

20.5 Facility Capacity Versus Workload—Version 5: Dual amount scales are used in Version 5 of a facility capacity versus workload tracking chart, Figure 20.5. Both scales can be used to read the comparative values of forecasted units, actual units, and available square footage.

20.6 Facility Capacity Versus Workload—Version 6: The actual and projected workloads, converted to square footage requirements, are compared with existing and proposed facility square footage in Version 6 of a facility capacity versus workload tracking chart, Figure 20.6. The workload square footage requirement is found by converting sales to employees at the rate of $1140 sales per month per employee, then converting the number of employees to square footage requirements using 85 square feet per employee with 80% on the first shift as the factors.

20.7 Facility Capacity Versus Workload—Version 7: Version 7 of a facility capacity versus workload tracking chart, Figure 20.7, is similar to Version 6, except, in this example, shading has been added to emphasize the existing and planned facility capacity portion of the chart.

20.8 Facility Capacity Versus Workload—Version 8: Paired, segmented columns are used in Version 8 of a facility capacity versus workload tracking chart, Figure 20.8. The segmented columns show the planned workload square footage requirement. The segments break down the total to show the portions of direct and indirect labor, with the direct portion further broken down by product line. Solid columns show the total actuals per quarter. The planned and actual workloads are compared against the amount of square footage in existing facilities (solid line), facilities under construction (dotted line), and planned facilities (dashed line).

20.9 Facility Capacity Versus Workload—Version 9: Version 9 of a facility capacity versus workload tracking chart, Figure 20.9, is similar to versions 6 and 7, except, in this example, a table of statistics has been added.

20.10 Facility Capacity Versus Workload—Version 10: A complex tabular version of a facility capacity versus workload tracking chart is shown as Version 10, Figure 20.10. The table contains the sales forecast statistics, and shows the conversion of these basic numbers to square footage requirements.

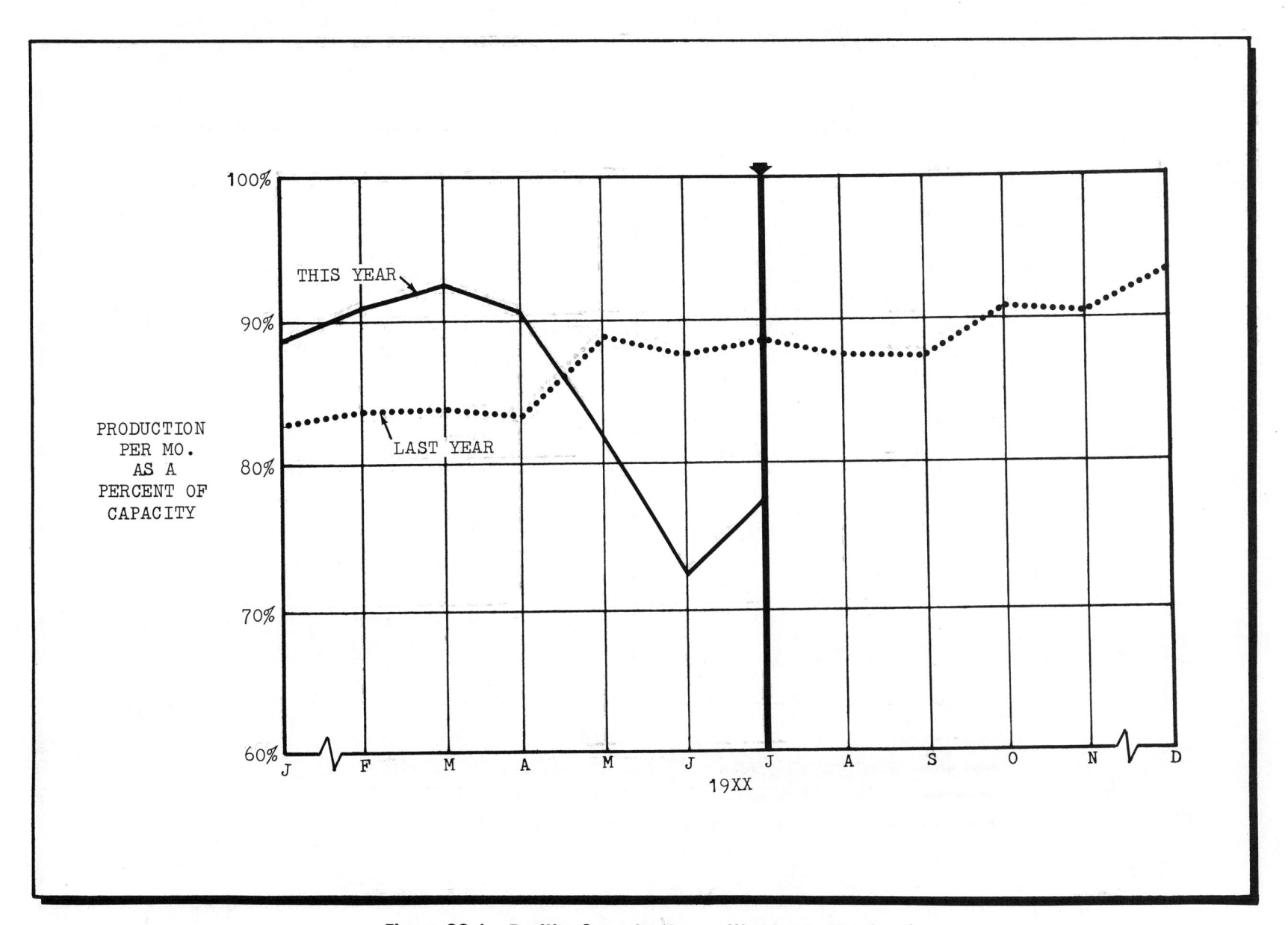

Figure 20.1 Facility Capacity Versus Workload—Version 1

233

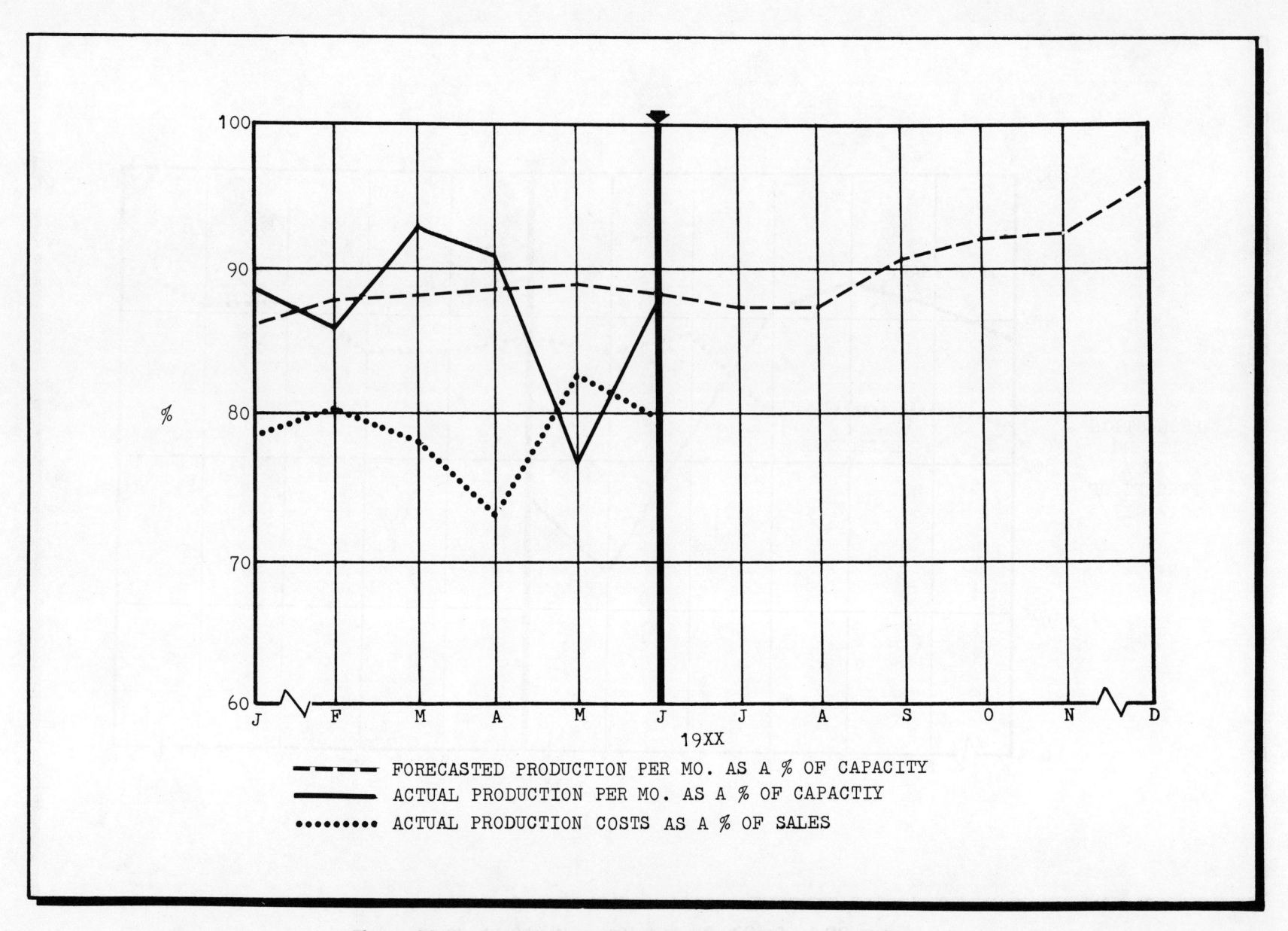

Figure 20.2 Facility Capacity Versus Workload—Version 2

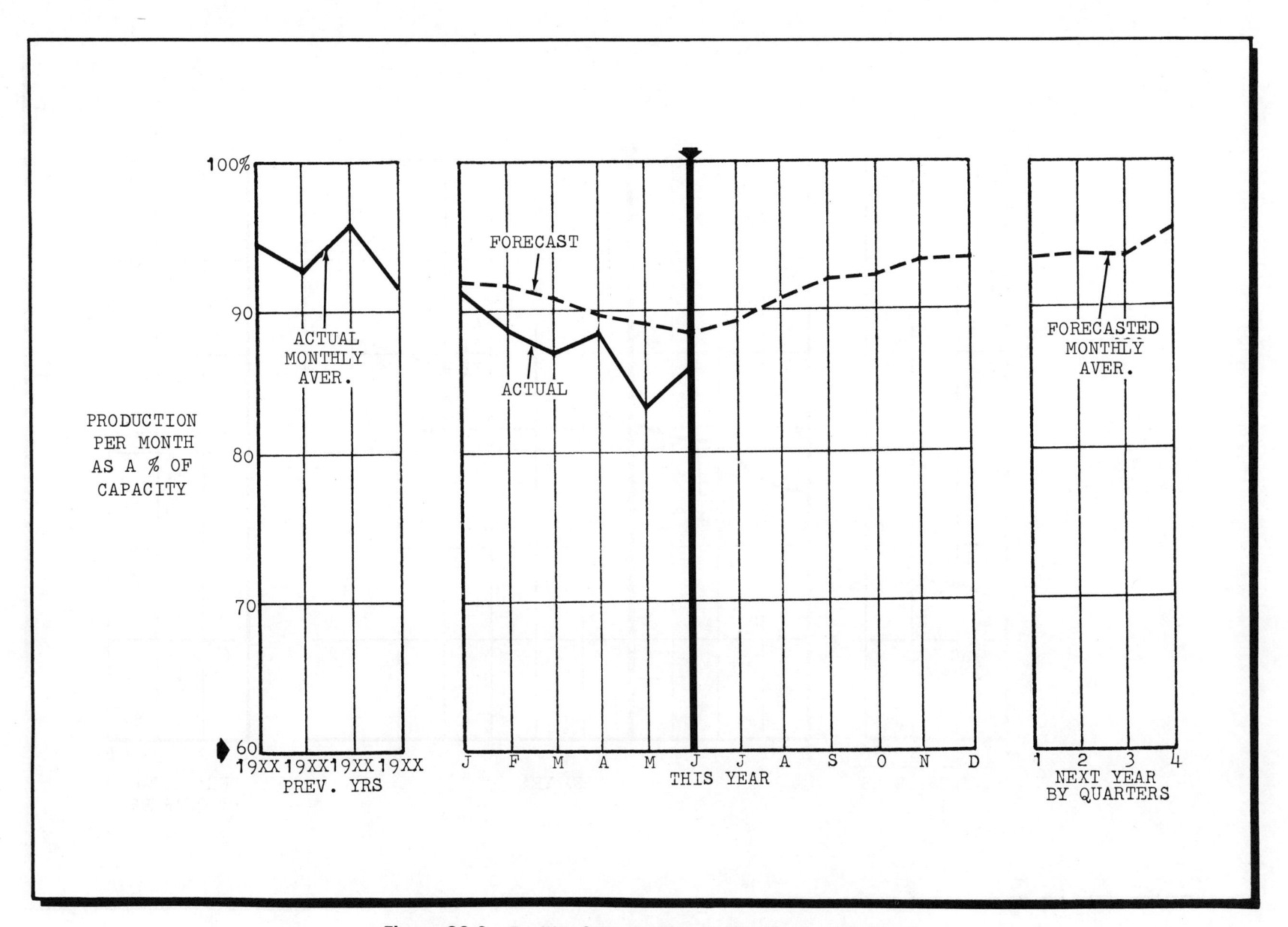

Figure 20.3 Facility Capacity Versus Workload—Version 3

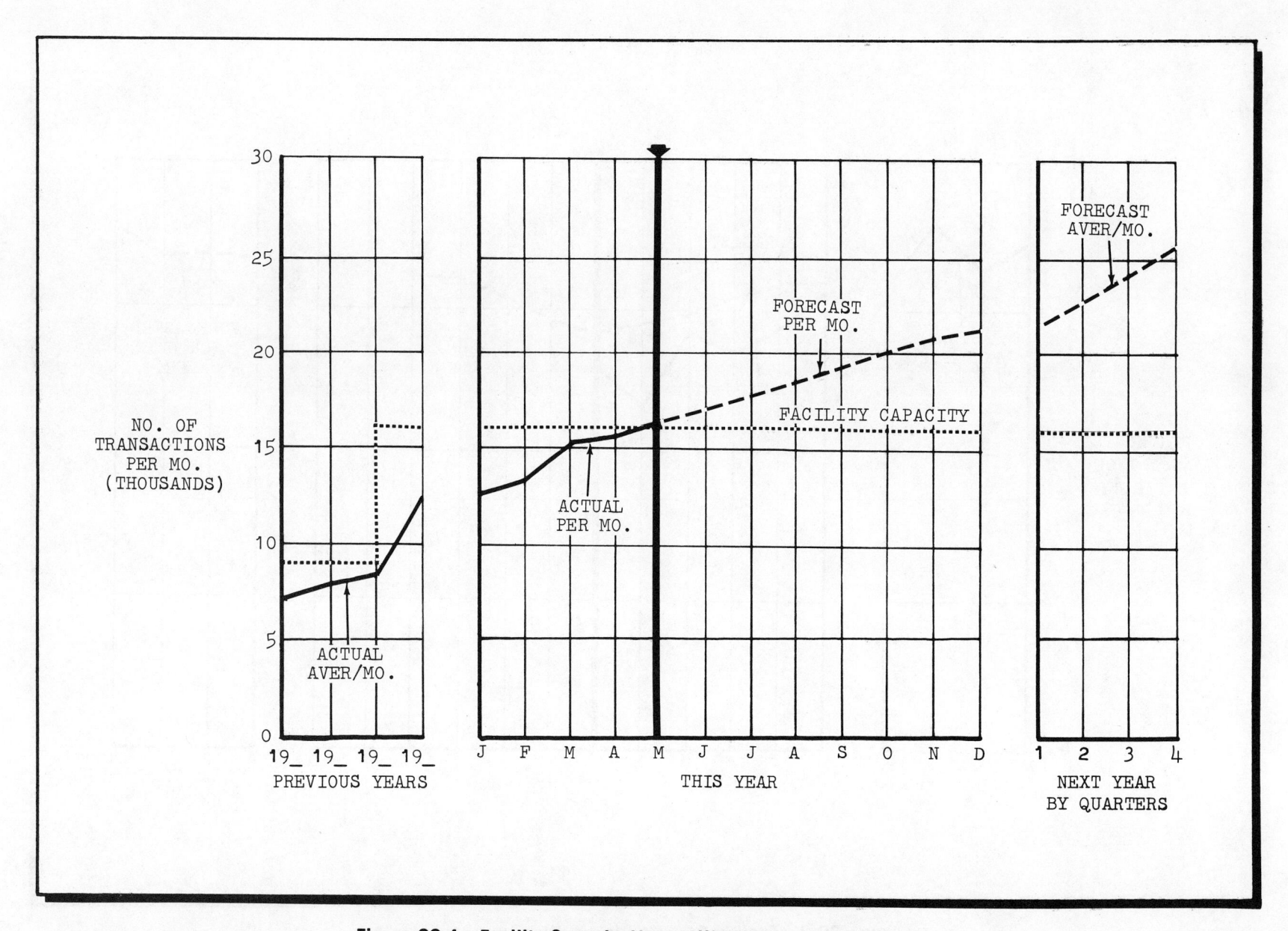

Figure 20.4   Facility Capacity Versus Workload—Version 4

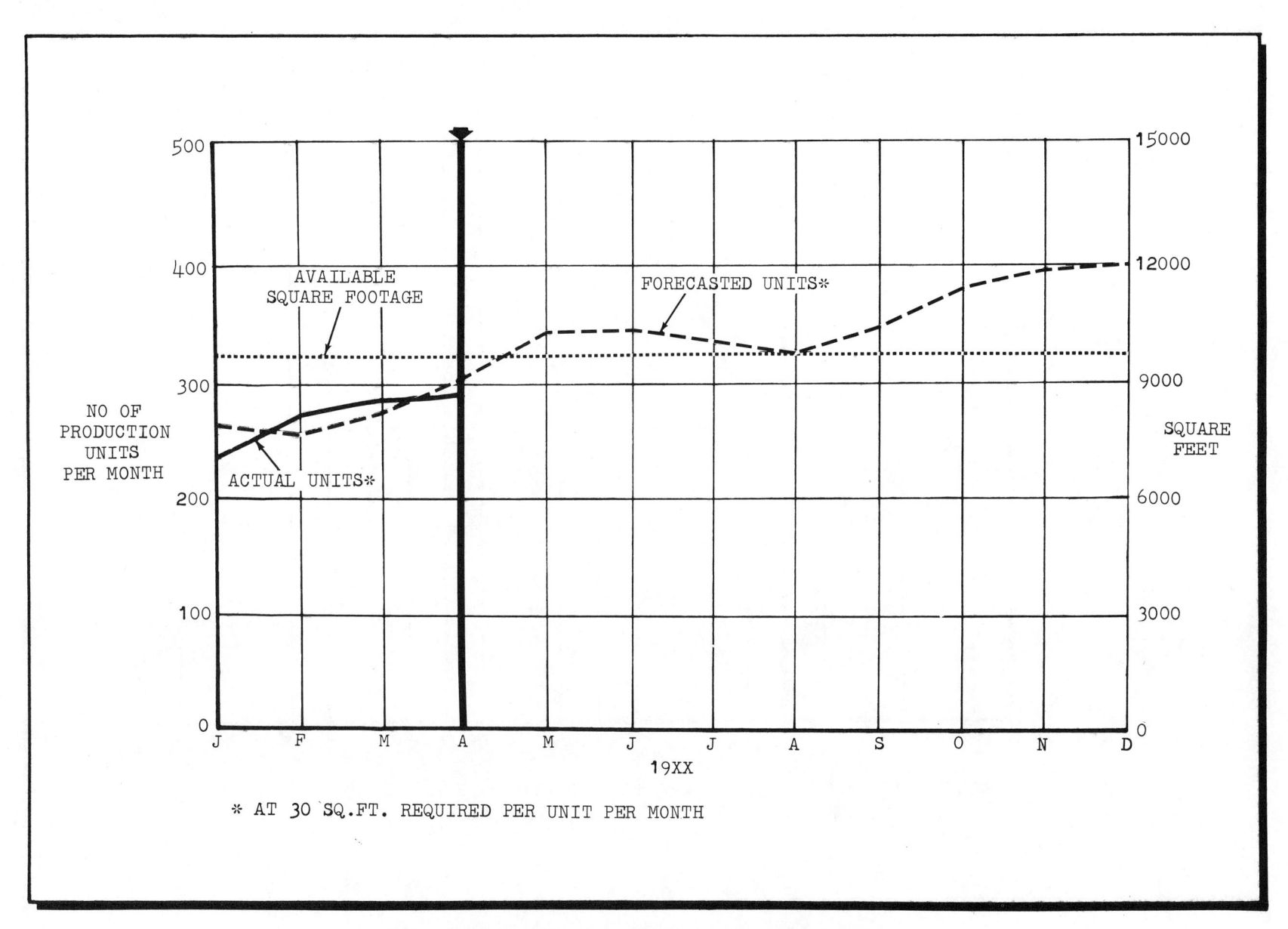

Figure 20.5 Facility Capacity Versus Workload—Version 5

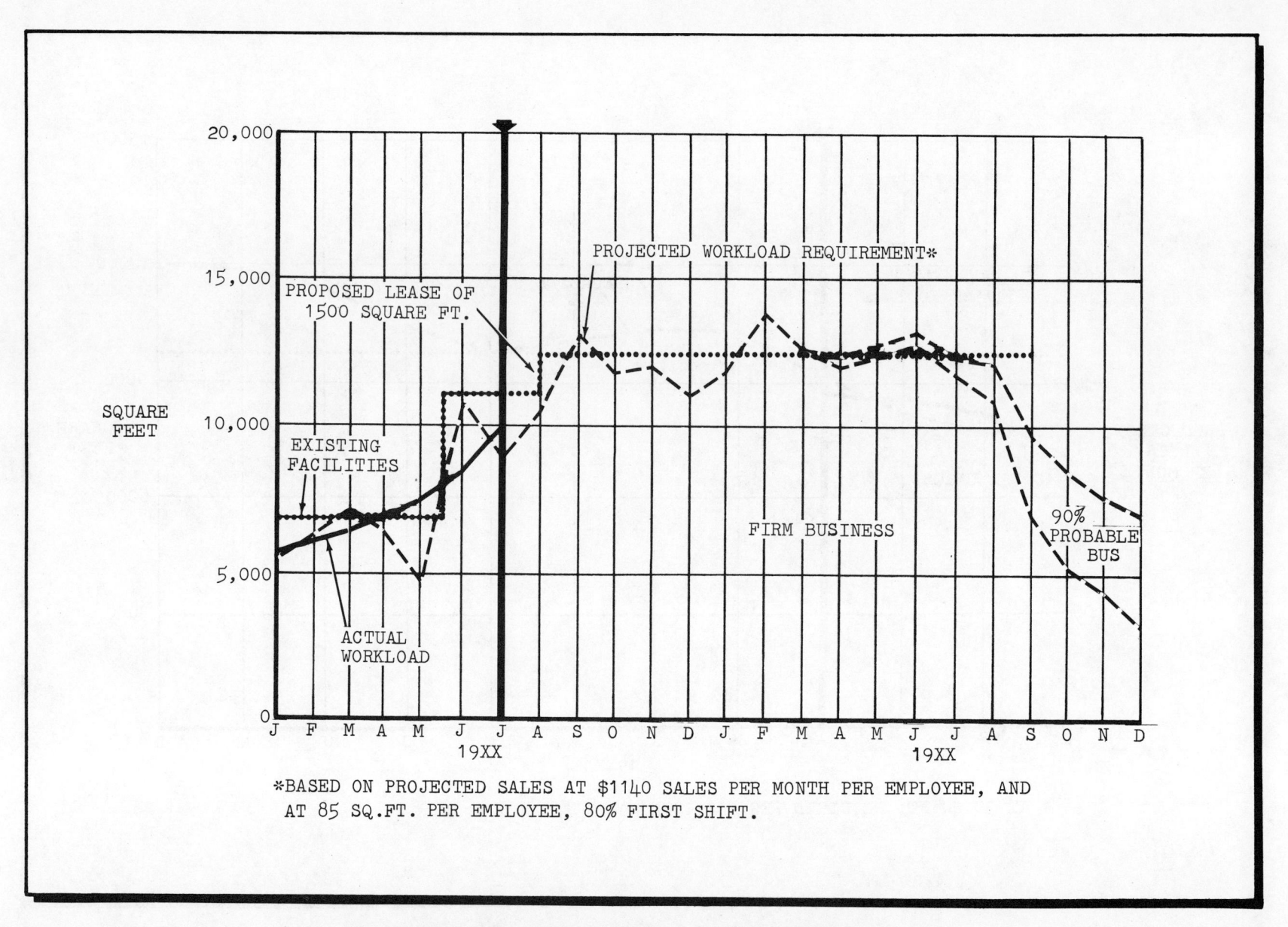

Figure 20.6 Facility Capacity Versus Workload—Version 6

238

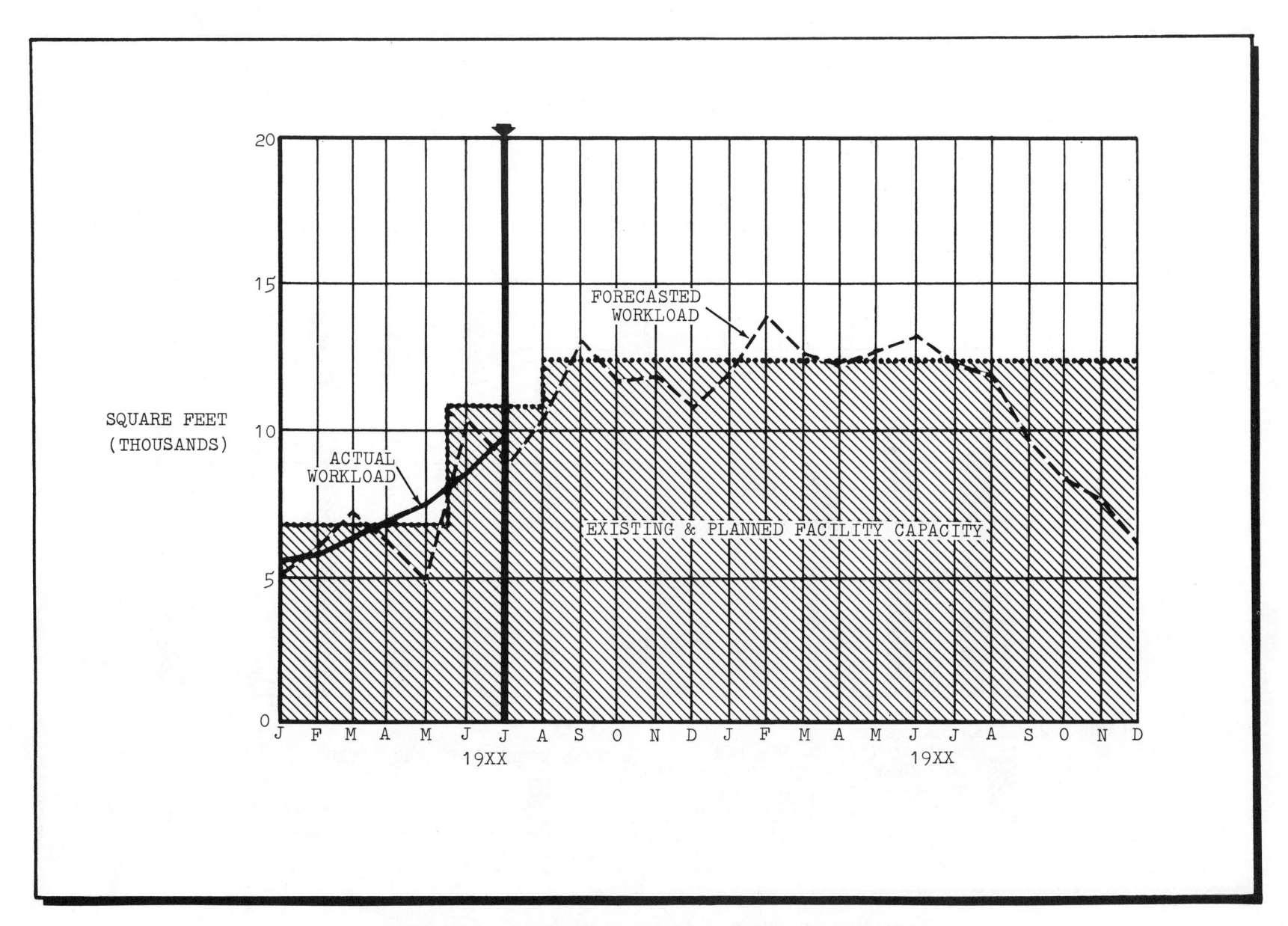

Figure 20.7   Facility Capacity Versus Workload—Version 7

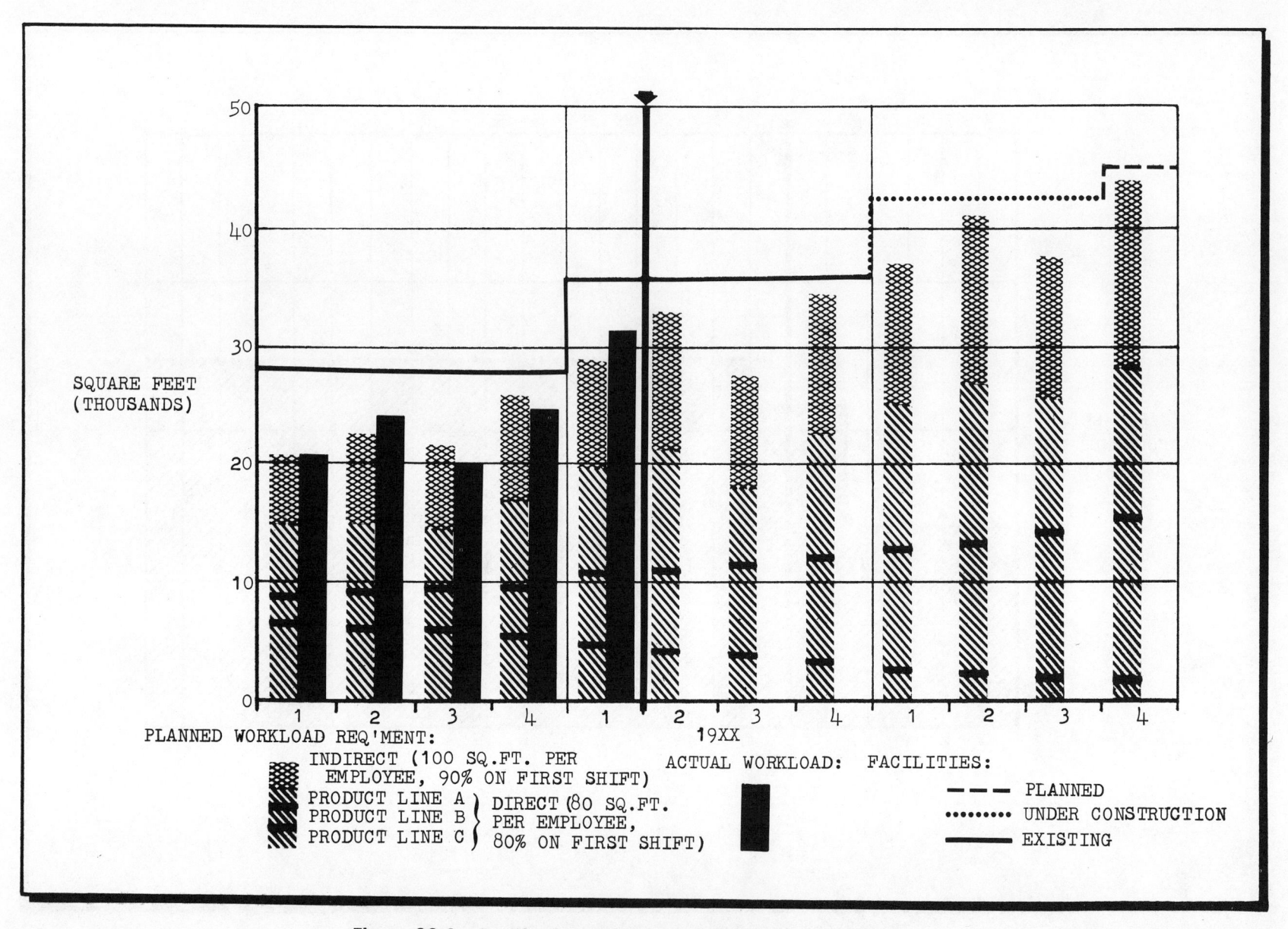

Figure 20.8 Facility Capacity Versus Workload—Version 8

240

SQUARE FEET (THOUSANDS)

LEASE 1500 SQ.FT.

FIRM PLUS 90% PROBABLE BUSINESS

J F M A M J J A S O N D J F M A M J J A S O N D
19XX — 19XX

PER MONTH:

		J	F	M	A	M	J	J	A	S	O	N	D	J	F	M	A	M	J	J	A	S	O	N	D
SALES ($000)	ACTUALS	89	105	121	101	79	176	146																	
	FORECAST								177	219	199	201	185	201	235	211	207	216	222	208	206	161	139	127	104
EMPLOYEE FACTOR(1)	ACTUALS	80	85	92	100	111	125	141																	
	FORECAST	78	92	106	89	69	154	128	155	192	175	176	162	172	206	185	181	189	195	183	181	141	122	112	91
SQ.FT. FACTOR-WORKLOAD (000) (2)	ACTUALS ————	5.4	5.8	6.3	6.8	7.5	8.5	9.6																	
	FORECAST – – – –	5.3	6.3	7.2	6.1	4.7	10.5	8.7	10.5	13.1	11.9	12.0	11.0	12.0	14.0	12.6	12.3	12.8	13.3	12.4	12.3	9.6	8.3	7.7	6.2
FACILITIES SQ. FOOTAGE (000)	EXISTING •••••••	6.8	6.8	6.8	6.8	6.8	11.0	11.0	11.0																
	PLANNED •••••••									12.5	12.5	12.5	12.5	12.5	12.5	12.5	12.5	12.5	12.5	12.5	12.5	12.5	12.5	12.5	12.5

(1) FORECAST AT $1140 MONTHLY SALES PER EMPLOYEE
(2) FORECAST AT 85 SQ.FT. PER EMPLOYEE AT 80% ON FIRST SHIFT

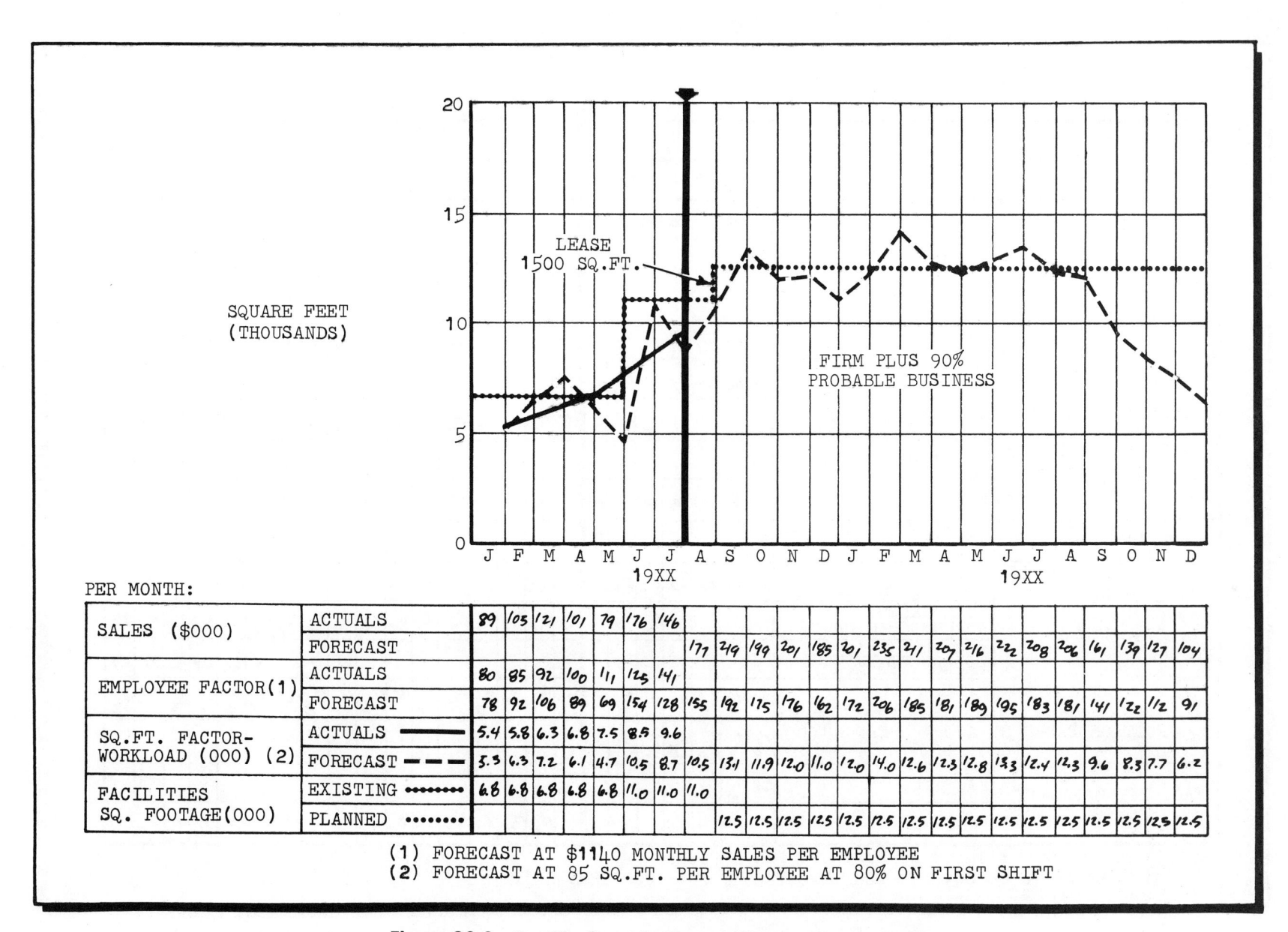

Figure 20.9 Facility Capacity Versus Workload—Version 9

ACTIVITY PER MONTH		19XX												19XX											
		J	F	M	A	M	J	J	A	S	O	N	D	J	F	M	A	M	J	J	A	S	O	N	D
SALES ($000)	ACTUAL	89	105	121	101	79	176	146																	
	FIRM								177	219	199	201	185	201	235	211	202	210	249	198	188	121	87	76	55
	90% PROBABLE																5	6	3	10	18	40	52	51	49
	TOTAL	89	105	121	101	79	176	146	177	219	199	201	185	201	235	211	207	216	222	208	206	161	139	127	104
EMPLOYEE FACTOR (1) FORECAST BASED ON:	ACTUAL SALES	78	82	106	89	69	154	128																	
	FIRM SALES								155	192	178	176	162	176	206	185	177	184	192	174	165	106	76	67	48
	90% PROB. SALES																4	5	3	9	16	35	46	45	43
	TOTAL	78	82	106	89	69	154	128	155	192	178	176	162	176	206	185	181	189	195	183	181	141	122	112	91
HEADCOUNT	ACTUAL	80	85	92	100	111	125	141																	
SQ. FOOTAGE FACTOR (2) (000) WORKLOAD FORECAST BASED ON:	ACTUAL SALES EMPLOY. FACTOR	5.3	6.3	7.2	6.1	4.7	10.5	8.7																	
	FIRM SALES EMPLOY. FACTOR								10.5	13.1	11.9	12.0	11.0	12.0	14.0	12.6	12.0	12.5	13.1	11.8	11.2	7.2	5.2	4.6	3.3
	90% PROB. SALES EMPLOY. FACTOR																.3	.3	.2	.6	1.1	2.4	3.1	3.1	2.9
	TOTAL SALES EMPLOY. FACTOR	5.3	6.3	7.2	6.1	4.7	10.5	8.7	10.5	13.1	11.9	12.0	11.0	12.0	14.0	12.6	12.3	12.8	13.3	12.4	12.3	9.6	8.3	9.7	6.2
SQ. FOOTAGE BASED ON ACTUAL HEADCOUNT (000)		5.4	5.8	6.3	6.8	7.5	8.5	9.6																	
FACILITY CAPACITY SQ. FOOTAGE (000)	EXISTING	6.8	6.8	6.8	6.8	6.8	11.0	11.0	11.0																
	PLANNED									12.5	12.5	12.5	12.5	12.5	12.5	12.5	12.5	12.5	12.5	12.5	12.5	12.5	12.5	12.5	12.5

(1) FORECAST @ $1140 MONTHLY SALES PER EMPLOYEE
(2) FORECAST @ 85 SQ. FT. PER EMPLOYEE AT 80% ON FIRST SHIFT

Figure 20.10 Facility Capacity Versus Workload—Version 10

21.0 FINANCIAL SUMMARIES

Methods for displaying financial summary information are shown in this section. Charts or tables of this type are, by nature, usually complex because of the need to show a greater number of facts.

21.1 Financial Summary—Version 1: A method for tracking profit, taxes, general and administrative expenses, selling expenses, and the cost of goods in terms of their percent of sales is shown in Figure 21.1. The plan, or goal, for each factor is shown in step line form. Actuals to date are shown with segmented columns. The broken line at the bottom of the chart emphasizes that the amount scale does not begin with zero.

21.2 Financial Summary—Version 2: A status report style of financial summary chart is shown as Version 2, Figure 21.2. In tabular form, the basic income statement actual performance statistics are given for the current month. Actual and forecasted figures are given on a year-to-date basis, and the year-to-date forecast through the following month is also given.

21.3 Financial Summary—Version 3: Essential ratios are used in the one-time status report style of a financial summary, Figure 21.3. In this example, the current ratios are compared to those of the previous year.

21.4 Financial Summary—Version 4: Version 4 of a financial summary, Figure 21.4, is similar to Version 3 except that in this example the current actuals are compared against a plan. Variance figures are also given in this version.

21.5 Financial Summary—Version 5: Version 5 of a financial summary chart, Figure 21.5, compares key elements of the income statement over a ten-year period. Sales dollars are given in statistical form at the bottom of the graph. This example is not suitable for tracking purposes.

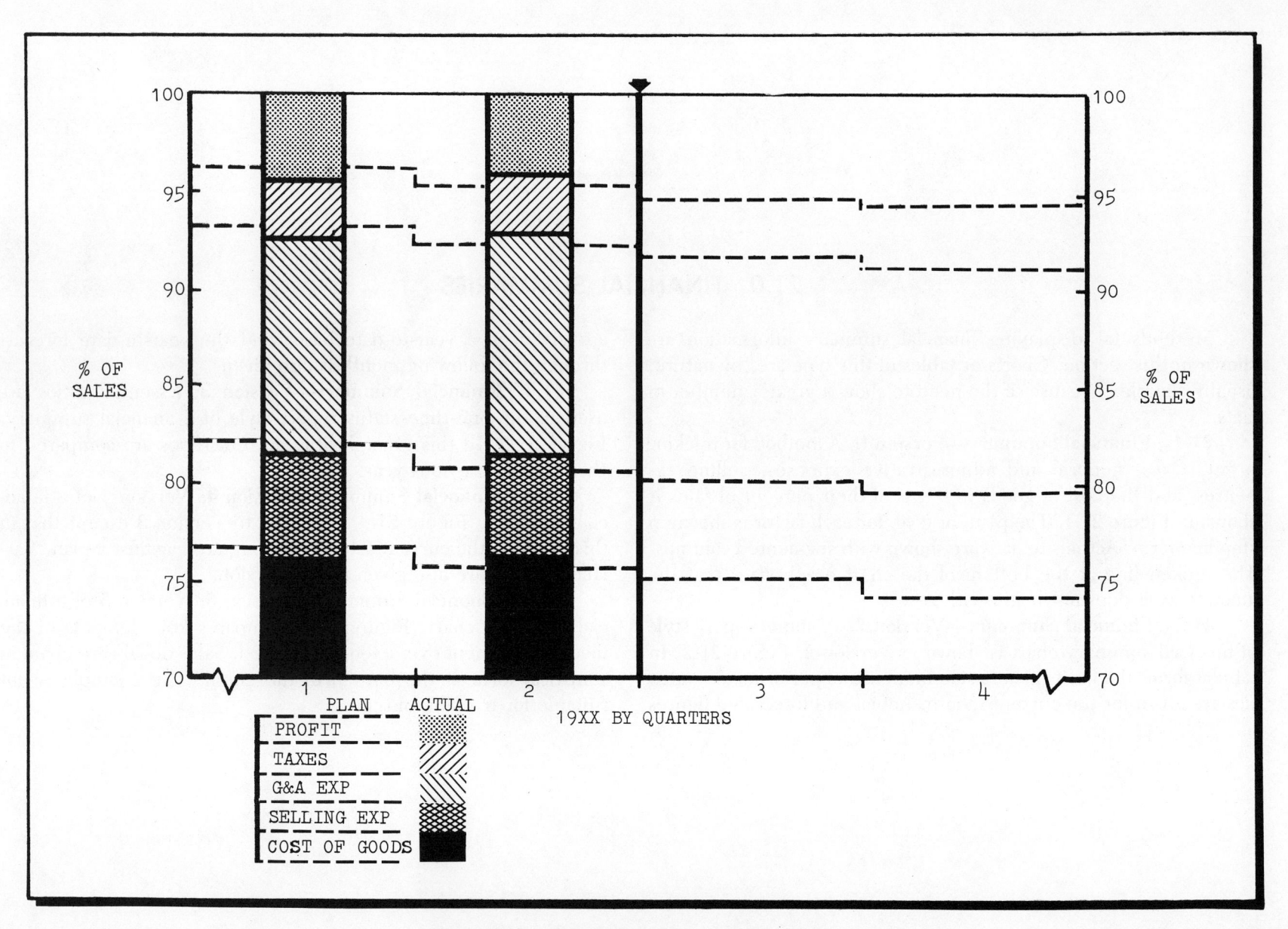

Figure 21.1   Financial Summary—Version 1

STATUS AS OF __JUNE__

ITEM		THIS MONTH	YEAR TO DATE		NEXT MO.-YTD
		ACTUAL	ACTUAL	FORECAST	FORECAST
NET SALES	$	17,156	96,580	110,034	129,134
COST OF GOODS SOLD	$	13,090	74,173	81,645	95,688
	% OF SALES	76.3	76.8	74.2	74.1
SELLING EXPENSE	$	995	5,505	6,162	7,232
	% OF SALES	5.8	5.7	5.6	5.6
GEN'L & ADMIN. EXPENSE	$	1,990	11,107	12,434	14,463
	% OF SALES	11.6	11.5	11.3	11.2
TAXABLE INCOME	$	1,081	5,795	9,793	11,751
	% OF SALES	6.3	6.0	8.9	9.1
ALLOW FOR TAXES	$	335	1,796	3,040	3,640
	% OF SALES	2.0	1.9	2.8	2.8
EST. NET PROFIT	$	746	3,999	6,753	8,111
	% OF SALES	4.3	4.1	6.1	6.3

Figure 21.2   Financial Summary—Version 2

STATUS AS OF DEC 31, 19xx

RATIO:	LAST YEAR	THIS YEAR
PERCENT RETURN ON GROSS ASSETS	19.6%	13.0%
CURRENT ASSETS TO CURRENT LIABILITIES	2.01 TIMES	1.83 TIMES
NET PROFIT (AFTER TAXES) AS A PERCENT OF SALES	5.6%	3.6%
GROSS ASSETS TURNOVER	3.5 TIMES	3.6 TIMES
TANGIBLE NET WORTH TURNOVER	5.57 TIMES	6.00 TIMES
WORKING CAPITAL TURNOVER	9.97 TIMES	11.4 TIMES
AVERAGE COLLECTION PERIOD OF RECEIVABLES	50.6 DAYS	50.9 DAYS
CURRENT LIABILITIES TO TANGIBLE NET WORTH	55.2%	61.8%
NET PROFIT TO TANGIBLE NET WORTH	30.9%	21.0%
FIXED ASSETS TO TANGIBLE NET WORTH	44.2%	48.6%
COSTS AS A PERCENT OF SALES	91.1%	93.6%
NET SALES TO INVENTORY	19.1 TIMES	19.6 TIMES
SALES PER EMPLOYEE	$24,452	$21,462

Figure 21.3 Financial Summary—Version 3

STATUS AS OF **DEC 31, 19xx**

RATIO	PLAN	ACTUAL	VARIANCE
PERCENT RETURN ON GROSS ASSETS	19.6%	13.0%	-6.6%
CURRENT ASSETS TO CURRENT LIABILITY	2.01 TIMES	1.83 TIMES	-.18 TIMES
NET PROFIT (AFTER TAXES) AS A PERCENT OF SALES	5.6%	3.6%	-2.0%
GROSS ASSETS TURNOVER	3.5 TIMES	3.6 TIMES	+.1 TIMES
TANGIBLE NET WORTH TURNOVER	5.57 TIMES	6.00 TIMES	+.43 TIMES
WORKING CAPITAL TURNOVER	9.97 TIMES	11.4 TIMES	+1.43 TIMES
AVERAGE COLLECTION PERIOD OF RECEIVABLES	50.6 DAYS	50.9 DAYS	+.3 DAYS
CURRENT LIABILITIES TO TANGIBLE NET WORTH	55.2%	61.8%	+6.6%
NET PROFIT TO TANGIBLE NET WORTH	30.9%	21.0%	-9.9%
FIXED ASSETS TO TANGIBLE NET WORTH	44.2%	48.6%	+4.4%
COSTS AS A PERCENT OF SALES	91.1%	93.6%	+2.5%
NET SALES TO INVENTORY	19.1 TIMES	19.6 TIMES	+.5 TIMES
SALES PER EMPLOYEE	$24,452	$21,462	-$2990

Figure 21.4 Financial Summary—Version 4

| SALES $000 | 61 | 78 | 102 | 135 | 195 | 180 | 205 | 240 | 300 | 365 |

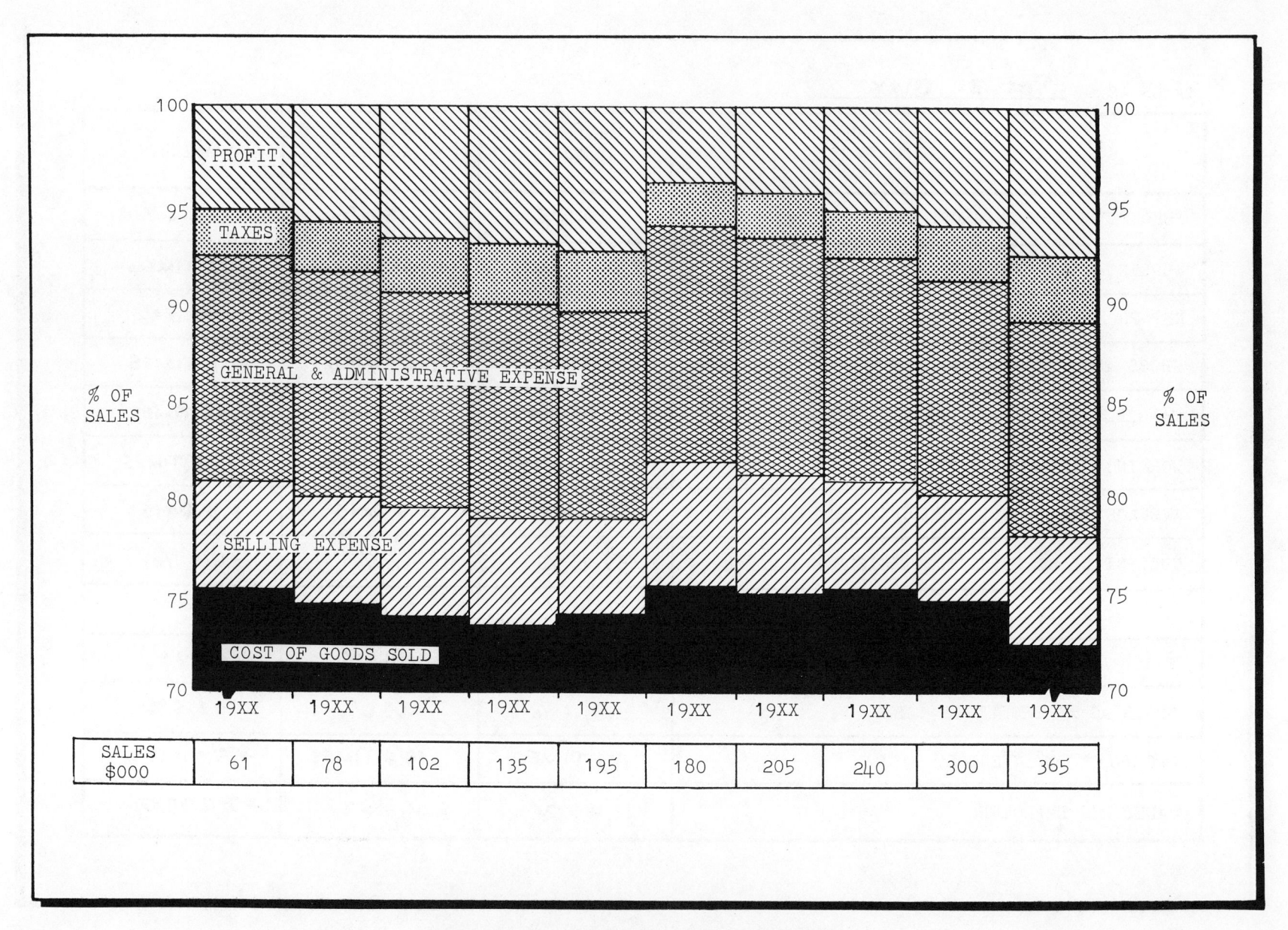

Figure 21.5   Financial Summary—Version 5

22.0 FIXED ASSETS TO TANGIBLE NET WORTH

Methods for displaying the ratio of fixed assets to tangible net worth are shown in this section. Fixed assets include the value of land, buildings, equipment, tools, fixtures, and furniture, less any allowances that have been made for depreciation. Tangible net worth consists of the total net worth of the enterprise less any amount that has been classified as intangible (goodwill, trademarks, organization expenses, etc.).

22.1 Fixed Assets to Tangible Net Worth—Version 1: A simple method for displaying the ratio of fixed assets to tangible net worth is shown as Version 1, Figure 22.1. A goal of 50% is shown as a dashed line in this example. Actual performance, plotted up to the reporting date, is shown with a solid line. An arrow has been used to highlight that the amount scale on this example does not start with zero.

22.2 Fixed Assets to Tangible Net Worth—Version 2: A column chart, by quarters, is shown as Version 2 of a fixed assets to tangible net worth tracking chart, Figure 22.2. The predicted monthly ratios of fixed assets to tangible net worth are shown using hatched columns in this example. The actual ratios to date are shown with solid columns.

22.3 Fixed Assets to Tangible Net Worth—Version 3: A multi-year version of a fixed assets to tangible net worth chart is shown in Figure 22.3. The goal, which could be an industry average, is shown in this example using a dashed line. The actual ratio is plotted using a solid line and is shaded for emphasis.

22.4 Fixed Assets to Tangible Net Worth—Version 4: A statistical table has been combined with graphics in Version 4 of a fixed assets to tangible net worth tracking chart, Figure 22.4. The graphic portion of the chart shows the actual monthly ratio in relationship to a goal of 50%. The tabular portion of the chart gives the supporting statistics.

22.5 Fixed Assets to Tangible Net Worth—Version 5: A statistical table that has been constructed to serve as a tracking chart is shown as Version 5 of a fixed assets to tangible net worth chart, Figure 22.5. In this example, the basic statistics for fixed assets (FA) and tangible net worth (TNW) are given, together with the ratio of FA to TNW in terms of the goal, the actual performance, and the variance therefrom.

22.6 Fixed Assets to Tangible Net Worth—Version 6: Figure 22.6 displays a one-time status report style for showing the ratio of fixed assets to tangible net worth. One of the problems with this style of report is that it has to be totally redone for each new reporting date.

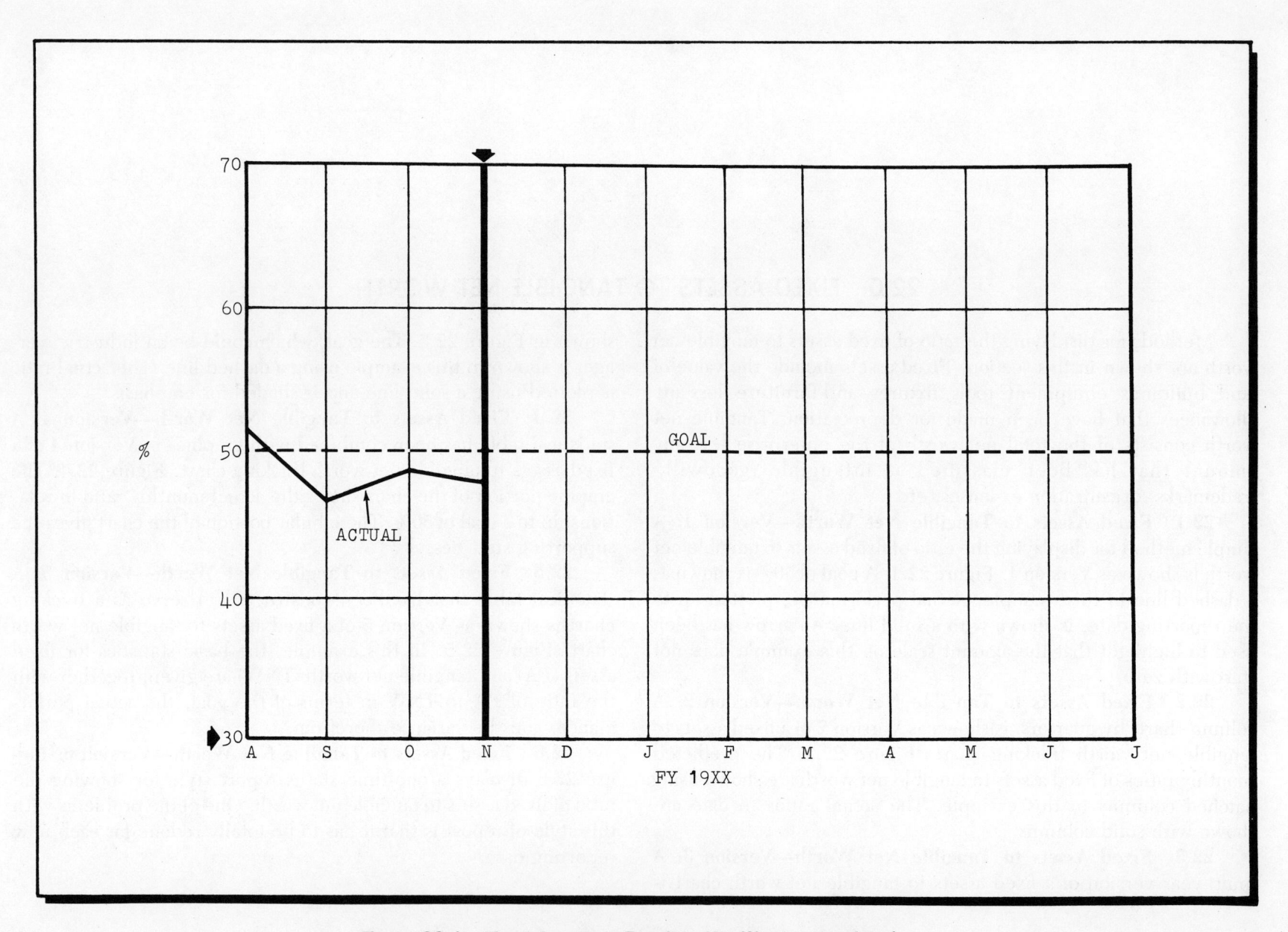

Figure 22.1 Fixed Assets to Tangible Net Worth—Version 1

250

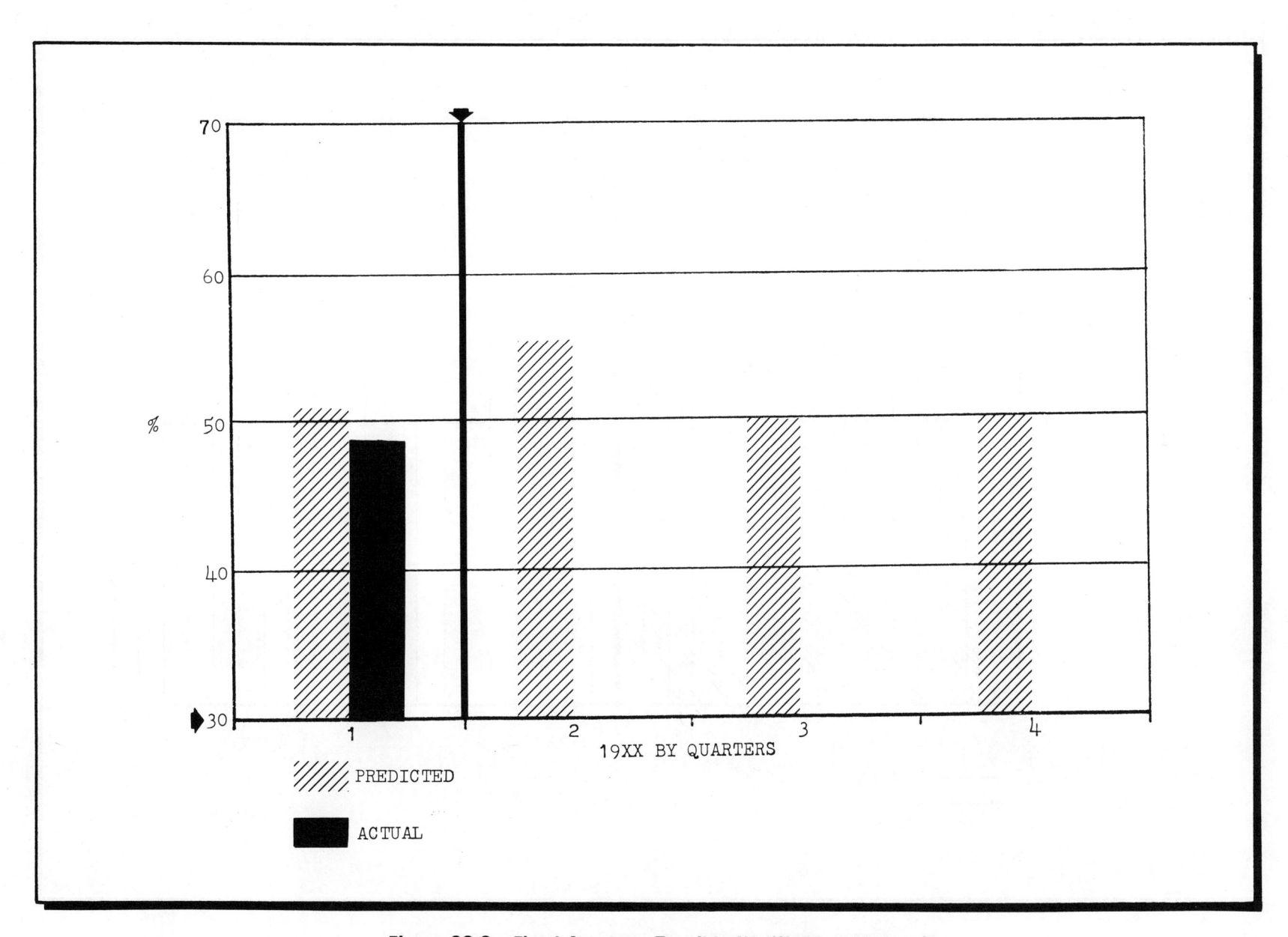

Figure 22.2   Fixed Assets to Tangible Net Worth—Version 2

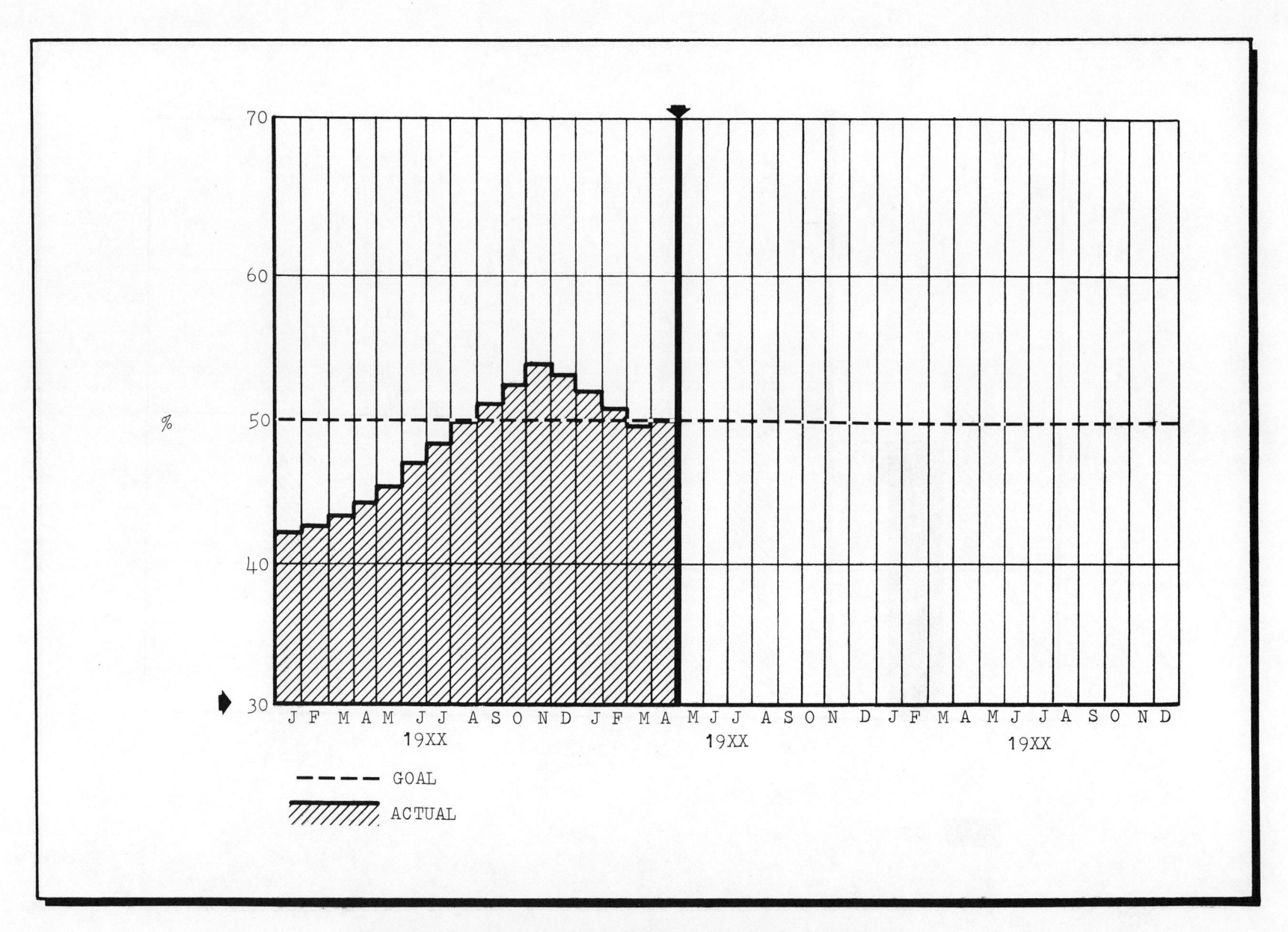

Figure 22.3 Fixed Assets to Tangible Net Worth—Version 3

		J	F	M									
FIXED ASSETS(FA)	$000	16.0	16.0	16.0									
TANGIBLE NET WORTH(TNW)	$000	30.9	34.4	32.9									
RATIO-FA TO TNW	%	51.8	46.5	48.6									

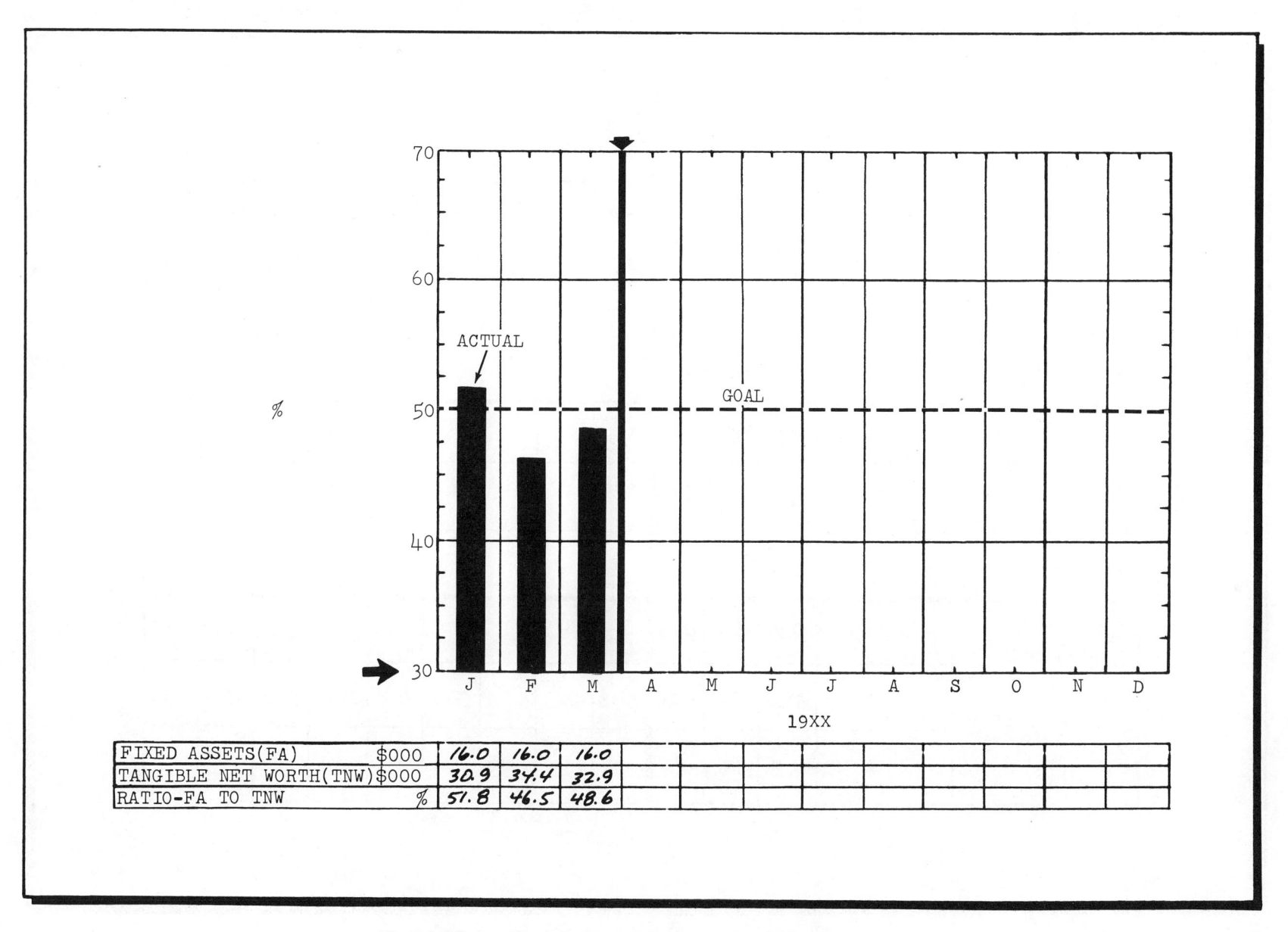

Figure 22.4 Fixed Assets to Tangible Net Worth—Version 4

ITEM	19XX											
	J	F	M	A	M	J	J	A	S	O	N	D
PLANT, EQUIP, ETC ($000)	20.1	20.1	20.1									
LESS DEPREC. ALLOW ($000)	4.1	4.1	4.1									
FIXED ASSETS ($000)	16.0	16.0	16.0									
NET WORTH ($000)	32.0	35.5	34.0									
LESS INTANG. ASSETS ($000)	1.1	1.1	1.1									
TANGIBLE NET WORTH ($000)	30.9	34.4	32.9									
PERCENT FIXED ASSETS TO TANGIBLE NET WORTH — ACTUAL	51.8	46.5	48.6									
PERCENT FIXED ASSETS TO TANGIBLE NET WORTH — GOAL	50.0	50.0	50.0	50.0	50.0	50.0	50.0	50.0	50.0	50.0	50.0	50.0
PERCENT FIXED ASSETS TO TANGIBLE NET WORTH — VARIANCE	+1.8	-3.5	-1.4									

Figure 22.5 Fixed Assets to Tangible Net Worth—Version 5

STATUS AS OF _____

ITEM	PLAN	ACTUAL	VARIANCE
FIXED ASSETS (FA) $000	16.0	16.0	0
TANGIBLE NET WORTH (TNW) $000	32.0	32.9	+.9
RATIO-FA TO TNW	50.0%	48.6%	-1.4%

Figure 22.6 Fixed Assets to Tangible Net Worth—Version 6

23.0 GROSS ASSETS

Gross assets represent the total of all that is owned by an enterprise. This section contains examples of ways to display the value of gross assets. Also see Sections 24.0, *Gross Assets Turnover* and 37.0, *Percent Return on Gross Assets*.

23.1 Gross Assets—Version 1: Version 1 of a gross assets tracking chart, Figure 23.1, displays the actual value of gross assets (solid line) against a forecast (dashed line). The bottom of the grid is broken to indicate that the amount scale (in thousands of dollars) does not start from a zero base.

23.2 Gross Assets—Version 2: A combination line chart style and surface chart style is used in Version 2 of a gross assets tracking chart, Figure 23.2. The actual value of gross assets for the current year (solid line with shading) is compared against two factors: the forecast for the year and the value of assets during the previous year.

23.3 Gross Assets—Version 3: A format that displays gross assets on a multi-year basis is used in Version 3 of a gross assets tracking chart, Figure 23.3. In this example, the actual value of assets for each of four previous years is shown on the left-hand grid. The center grid displays the current year's forecast and performance to date. The forecast for the coming year (right-hand grid) is given by quarters.

23.4 Gross Assets—Versión 4: A column chart style has been combined with a step line chart style in Version 4 of a gross assets tracking chart, Figure 23.4. In this example, the forecast and the actuals are both broken down into the two main components of gross assets, working capital and permanent investment.

23.5 Gross Assets—Version 5: Three grids are used in Version 5 of a gross assets tracking chart, Figure 23.5. The two right-hand grids display forecasted and actual values of working capital and permanent investment, by quarters. The left-hand grid summarizes these as gross assets. The bottom lines of all three grids are broken to indicate that the amount scales do not start from zero.

23.6 Gross Assets—Version 6: The graphic portion of Version 6 of a gross assets tracking chart, Figure 23.6, displays the forecasted and actual value of gross assets. The table portion of the chart gives the statistical backup, including the forecasted and actual dollar value of the permanent investment and working capital. An arrowhead is used on the amount scale to highlight the fact that the scale does not begin with a zero base.

23.7 Gross Assets—Version 7: A gross assets tracking chart in the form of a statistical table is shown as Version 7, Figure 23.7. In this example, forecasted and actual statistics are given for working capital, permanent investment, and gross assets.

23.8 Gross Assets—Version 8: A non-tracking version of a gross assets chart is shown as Version 8, Figure 23.8. In this example, the current year's gross asset value is compared with that of nine previous years. A variation of this chart would be to segment the columns according to working capital and permanent investment.

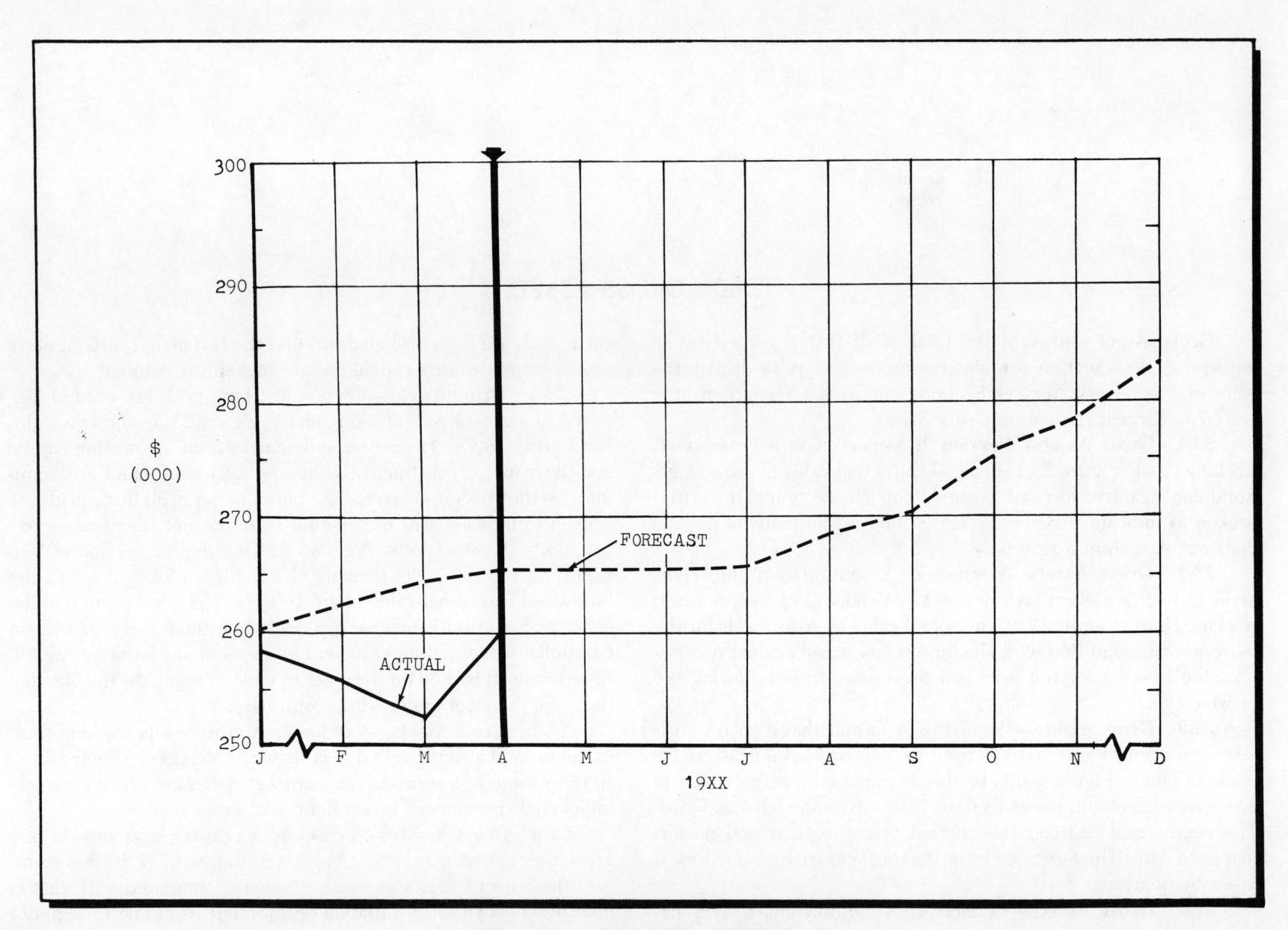

Figure 23.1   Gross Assets—Version 1

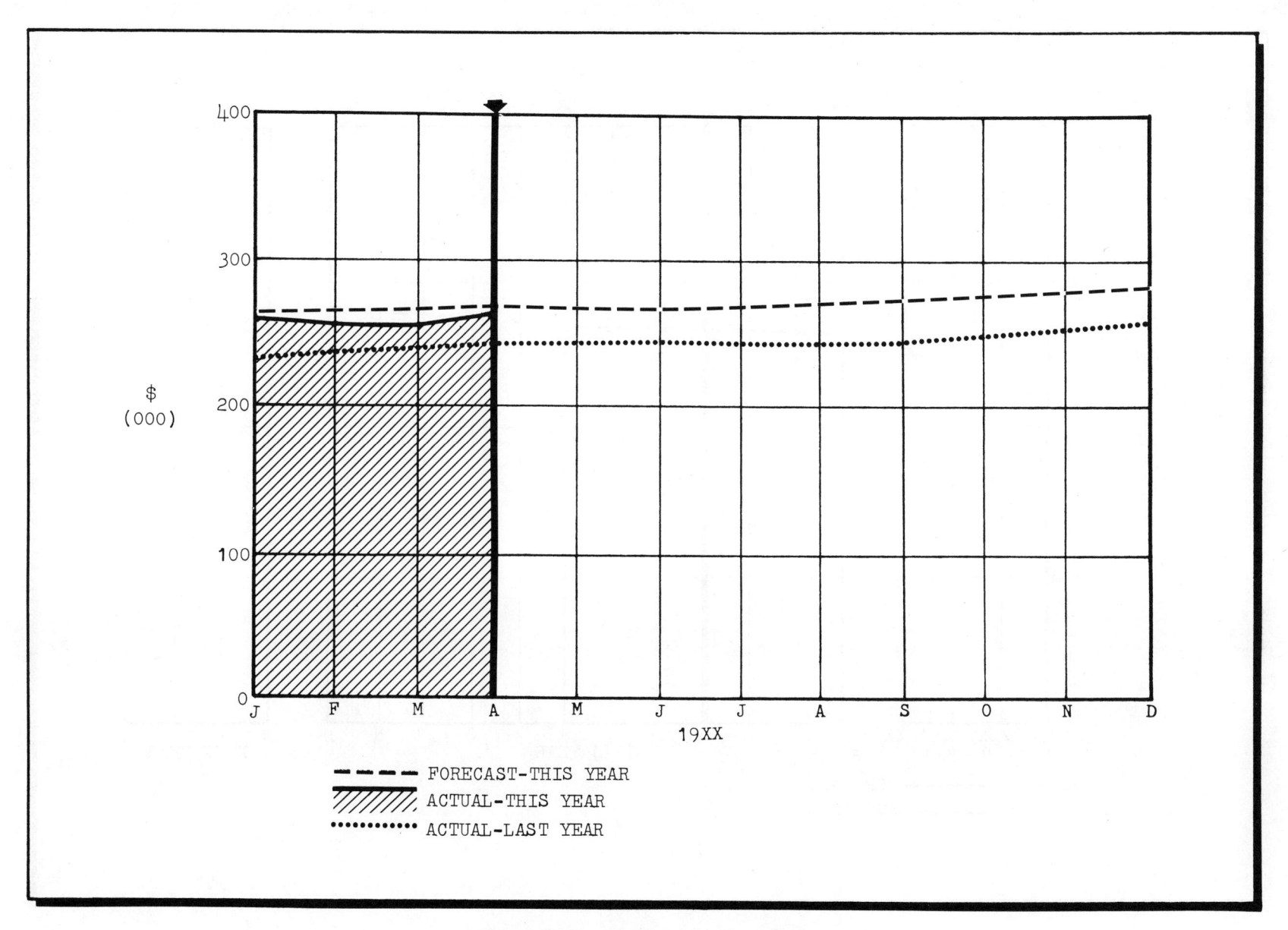

Figure 23.2 Gross Assets—Version 2

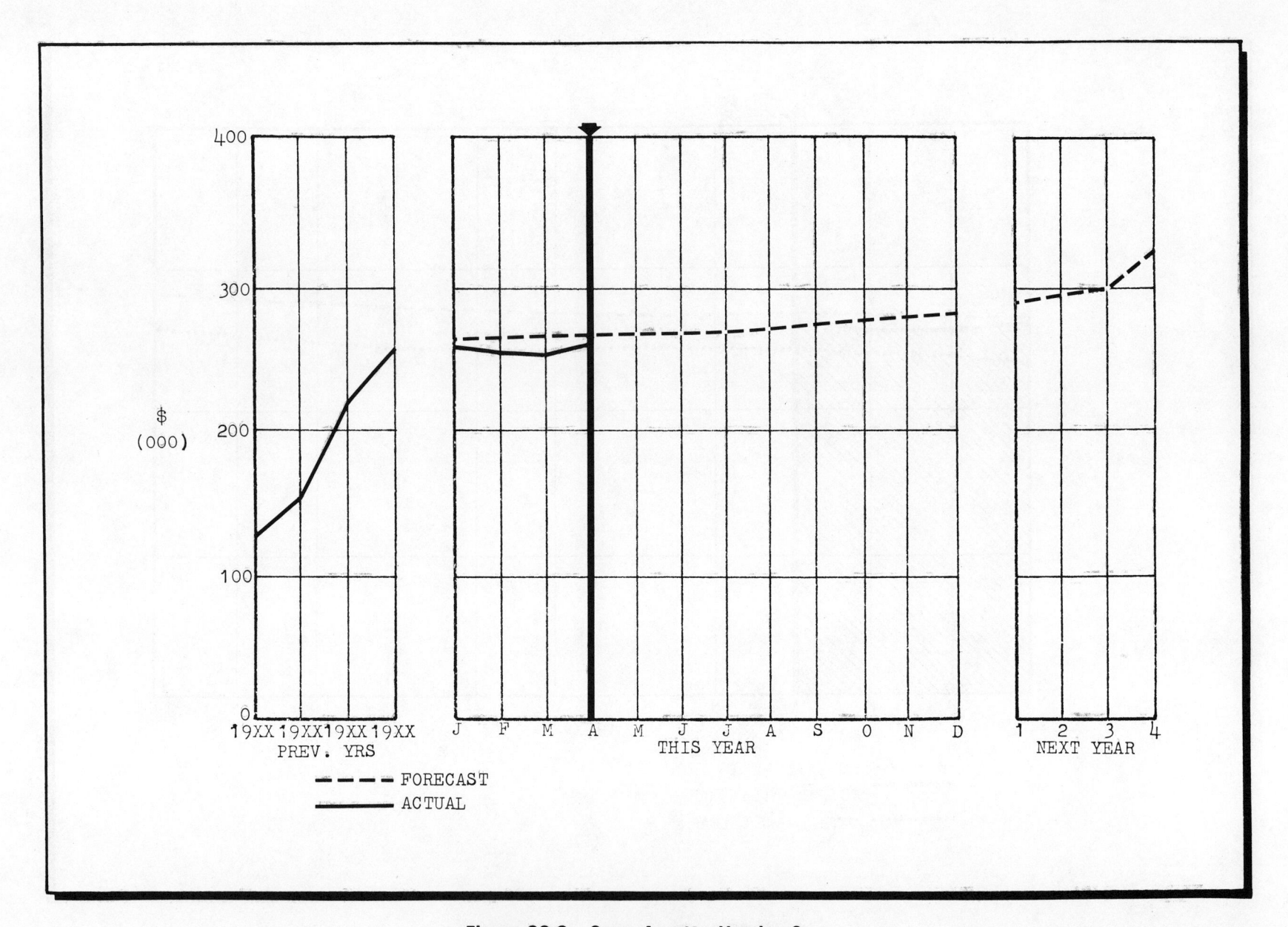

Figure 23.3　Gross Assets—Version 3

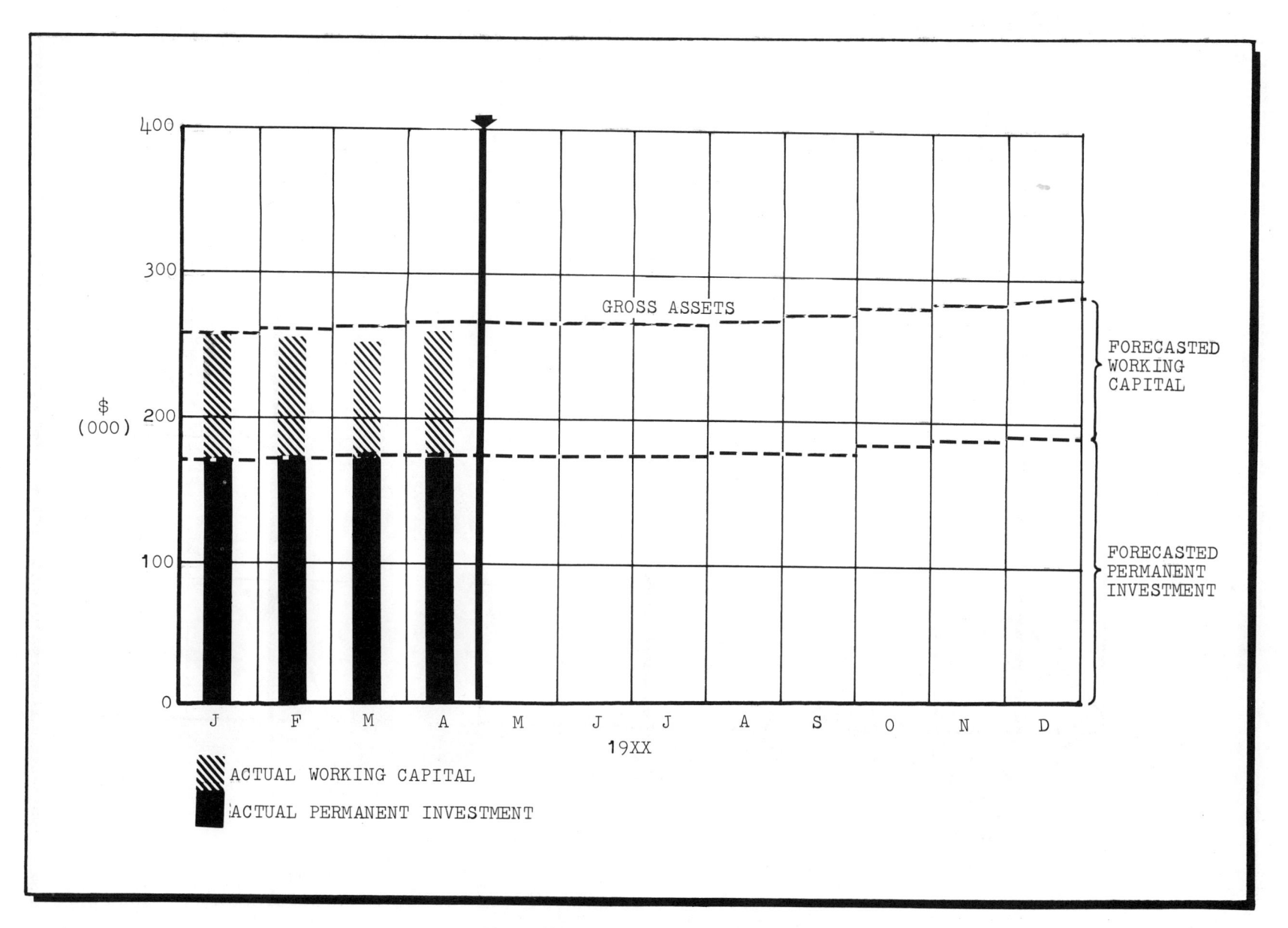

Figure 23.4 Gross Assets—Version 4

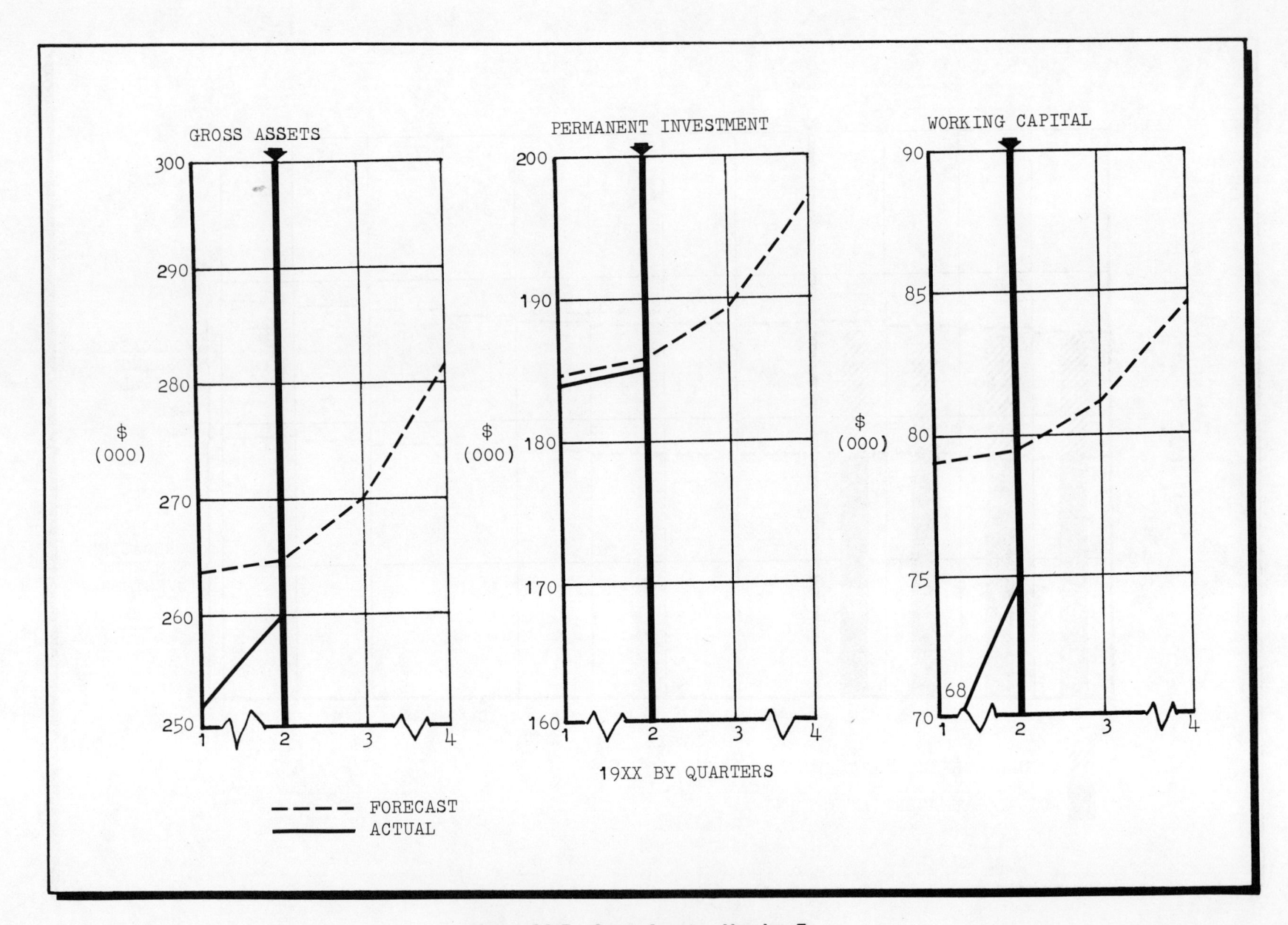

Figure 23.5 Gross Assets—Version 5

GROSS ASSETS
($000)

FORECAST

ACTUAL

		J	F	M	A	M	J	J	A	S	O	N	D
WORKING CAPITAL	FORECAST	78.0	78.6	79.2	79.5	79.5	79.5	79.5	80.4	81.0	82.5	83.4	84.6
	ACTUAL	76.5	73.4	68.0	76.0								
PERMANENT INVESTMENT	FORECAST	182.0	183.4	184.8	185.5	185.5	185.5	185.5	187.6	189.0	192.5	194.6	197.4
	ACTUAL	182.0	182.0	184.0	184.0								
GROSS ASSETS	FORECAST	260.0	262.0	264.0	265.0	265.0	265.0	265.0	268.0	270.0	275.0	278.0	282.0
	ACTUAL	258.5	255.4	252.0	260.0								

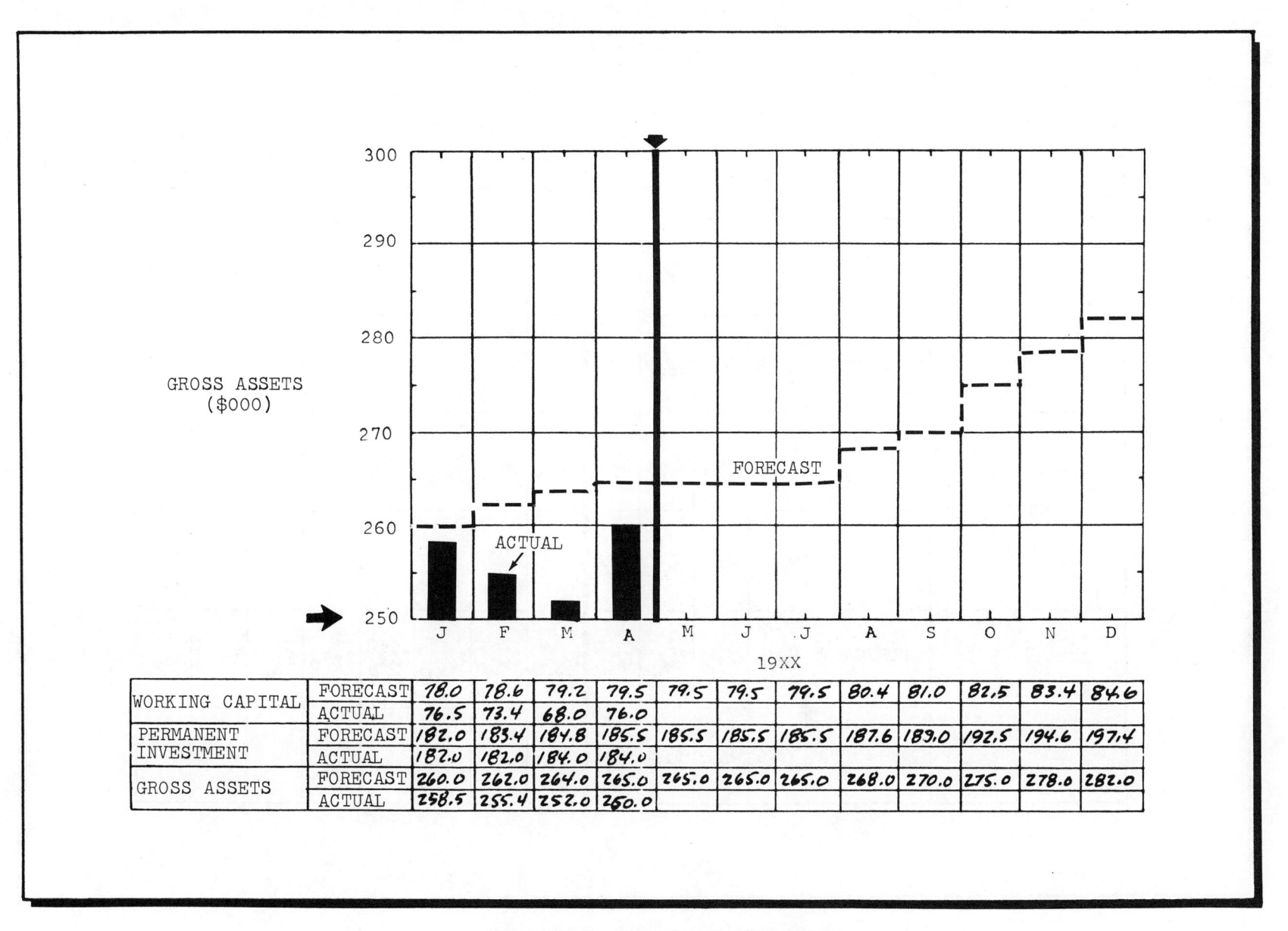

Figure 23.6   Gross Assets—Version 6

ITEM ($000)		19XX											
		J	F	M	A	M	J	J	A	S	O	N	D
WORKING CAPITAL (WC)	FORECAST	78.0	78.6	79.2	79.5	79.5	79.5	79.5	80.4	81.0	82.5	83.4	84.6
	ACTUAL	76.5	73.4	68.0	76.0								
PERMANENT INVESTMENT (PI)	FORECAST	182.0	183.4	184.8	185.5	185.5	185.5	185.5	187.6	189.0	192.5	194.6	197.4
	ACTUAL	182.0	182.0	184.0	184.0								
GROSS ASSETS (WC+PI)	FORECAST	260.0	262.0	264.0	265.0	265.0	265.0	265.0	268.0	270.0	275.0	278.0	282.0
	ACTUAL	258.5	255.4	252.0	260.0								

Figure 23.7   Gross Assets—Version 7

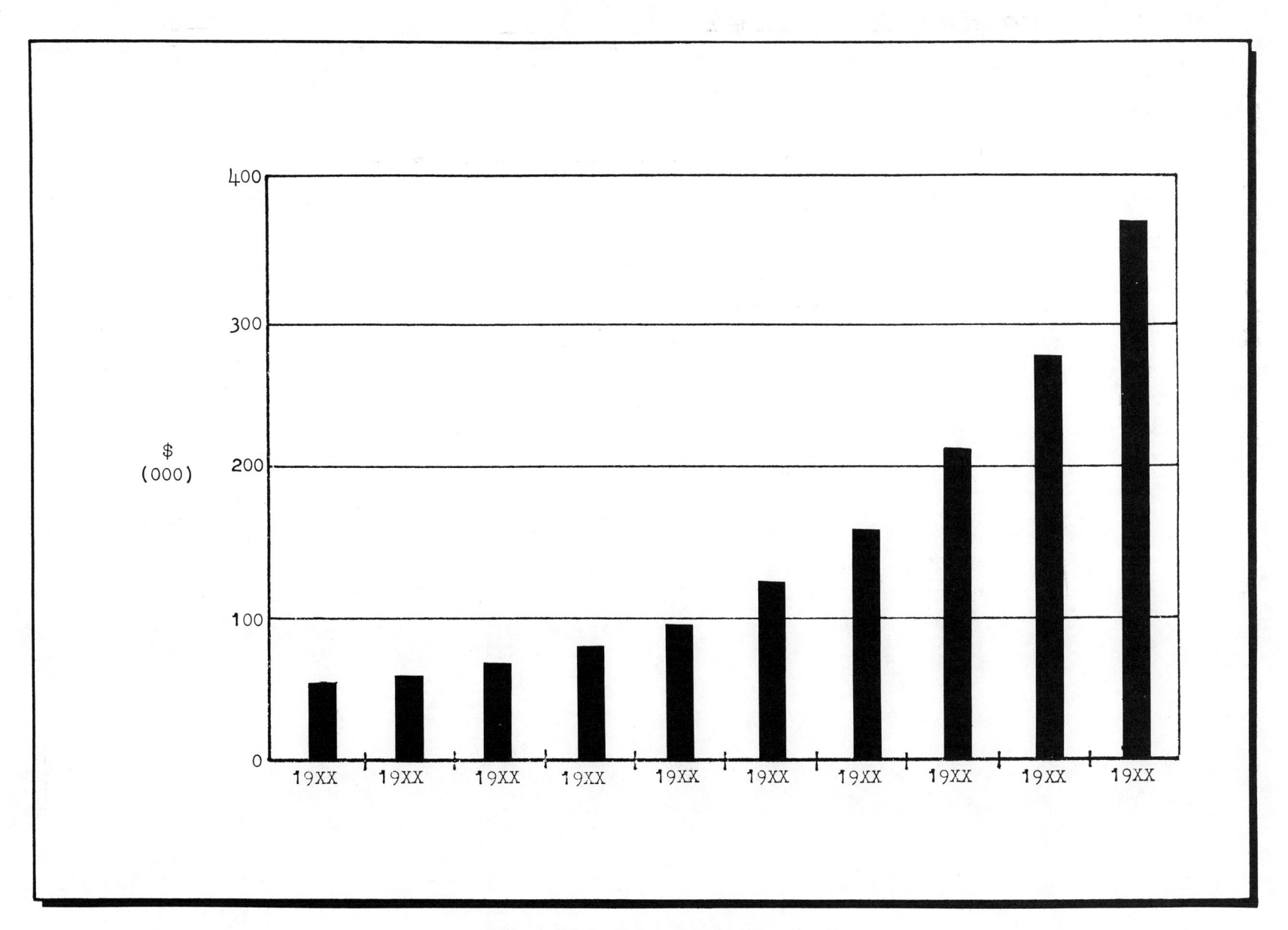

Figure 23.8   Gross Assets—Version 8

24.0 GROSS ASSETS TURNOVER

Charts that display the turnover of gross assets are shown in this section. Gross assets turnover is determined by dividing sales by gross assets. Also see Sections 23.0, *Gross Assets* and 37.0, *Percent Return on Gross Assets*.

24.1 Gross Assets Turnover—Version 1: A simple version of a gross assets turnover tracking chart is shown as Version 1, Figure 24.1. In this example, the forecasted and actual gross assets turns per year are displayed on a year-to-date average basis.

24.2 Gross Assets Turnover—Version 2: Version 2 of a gross assets turnover tracking chart, Figure 24.2, utilizes a dashed step line to show the forecast and solid columns to show actuals to date. Gross assets turns per year in this example have been calculated on the basis of monthly annualized sales divided by the month-end value of gross assets. On this basis the plotting will have a tendency to be somewhat erratic if sales vacillate significantly for seasonal or other reasons.

24.3 Gross Assets Turnover—Version 3: A multi-year format such as shown in Version 3, Figure 24.3, provides the opportunity of evaluating the current year's turnover of gross assets not only against the forecast, but against performance in previous years as well. In this example, solid lines are used to show actual turnover and dashed lines are used to show the current and following years' forecast.

24.4 Gross Assets Turnover—Version 4: A chart with two amount scales is used for Version 4 of a gross assets turnover tracking chart, Figure 24.4. In this example, the turnover is compared with the monthly earnings as a percent of sales.

24.5 Gross Assets Turnover—Version 5: A statistical table has been combined with graphics in Version 5 of a gross assets turnover tracking chart, Figure 24.5. Forecasted and actual monthly and year-to-date average figures appear in the table. The year-to-date average figures are also plotted on the graph, the stepped dashed line representing the forecast and solid columns showing actuals.

24.6 Gross Assets Turnover—Version 6: A detailed tabular form of a gross assets turnover tracking chart is shown as Version 6, Figure 24.6. The bottom of the table presents the gross assets turnover figures on both a monthly and year-to-date average basis. The top of the table gives the detailed sales and gross assets data from which the turnover rates are derived.

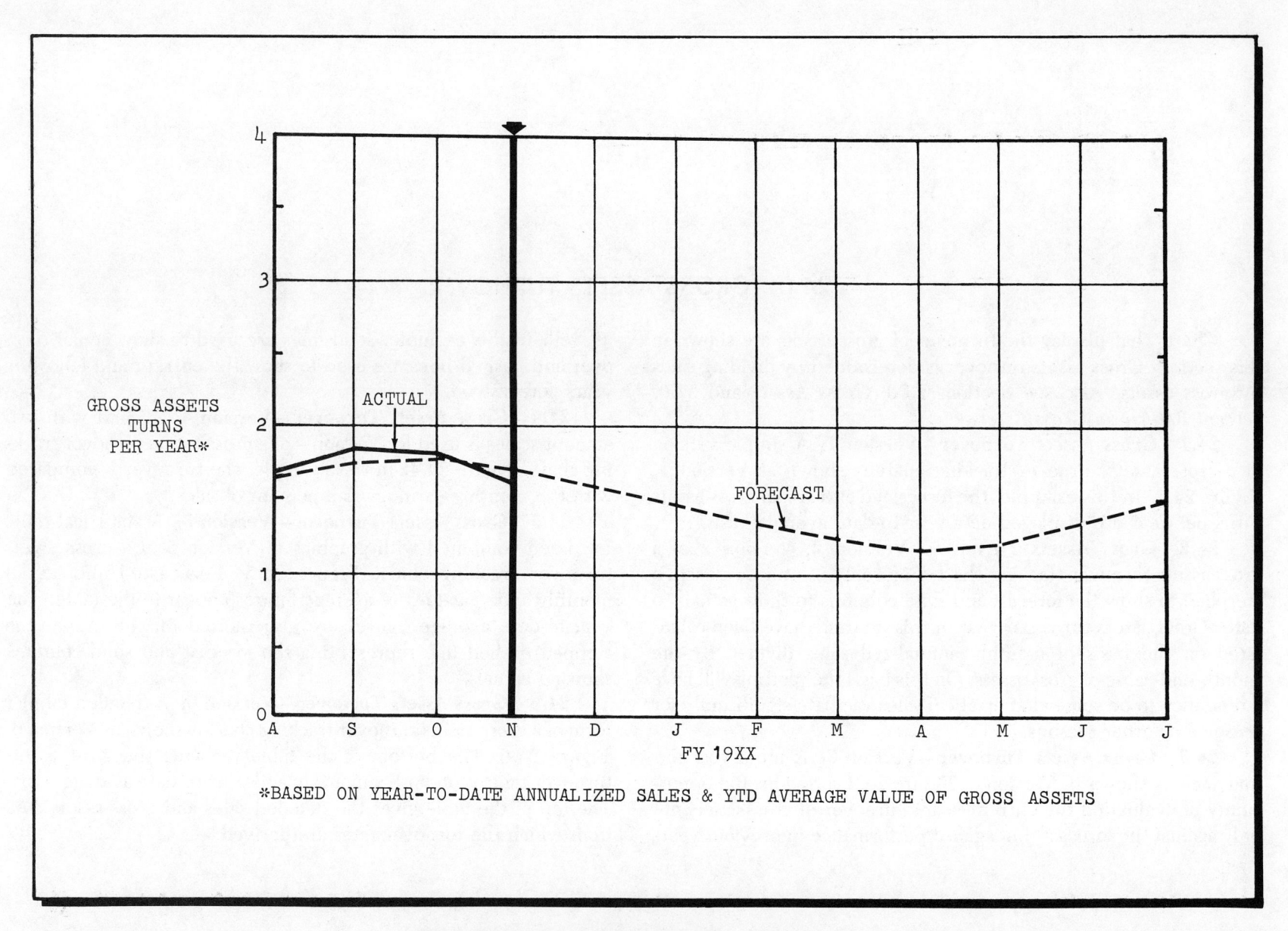

Figure 24.1 Gross Assets Turnover—Version 1

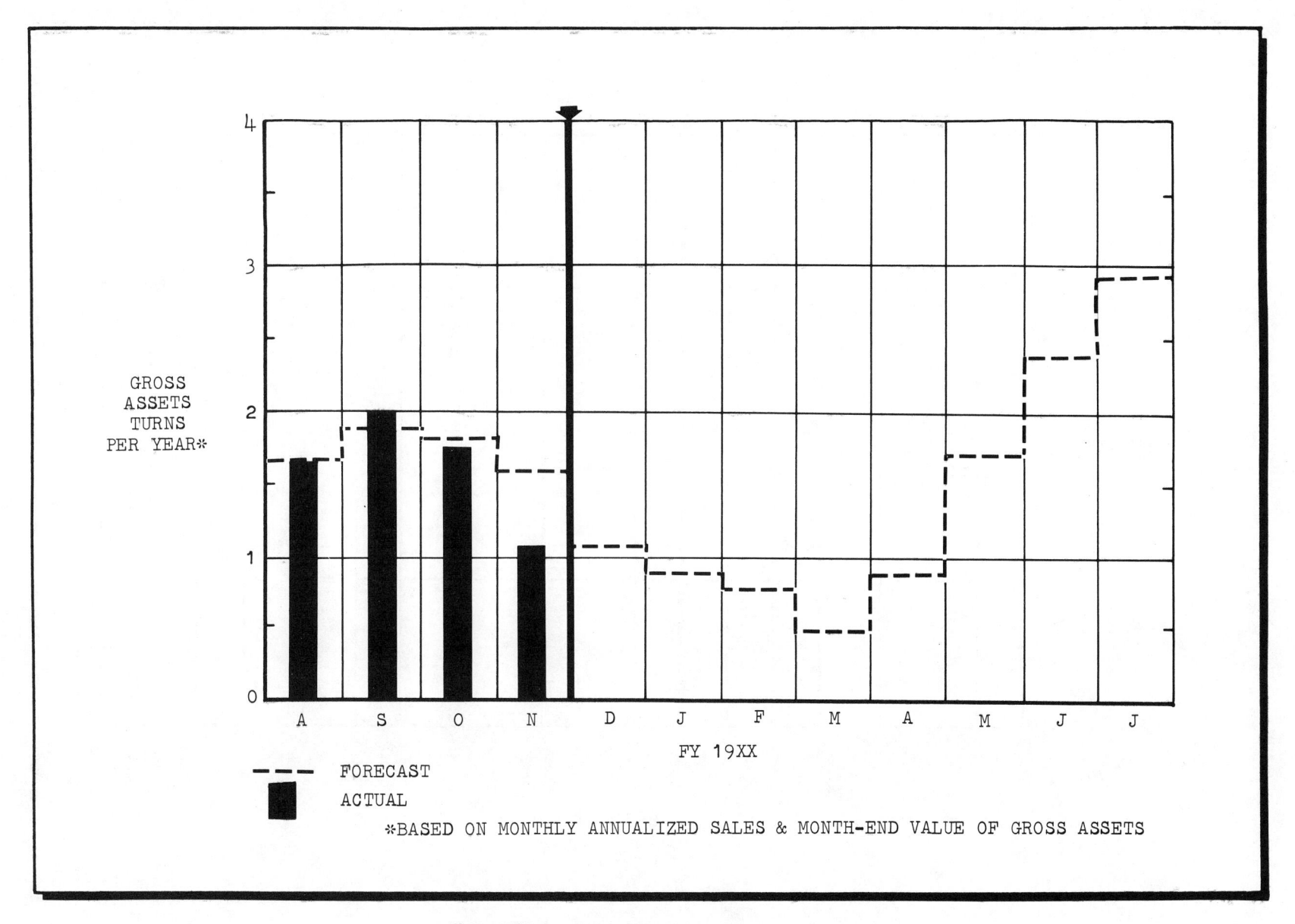

Figure 24.2 Gross Assets Turnover—Version 2

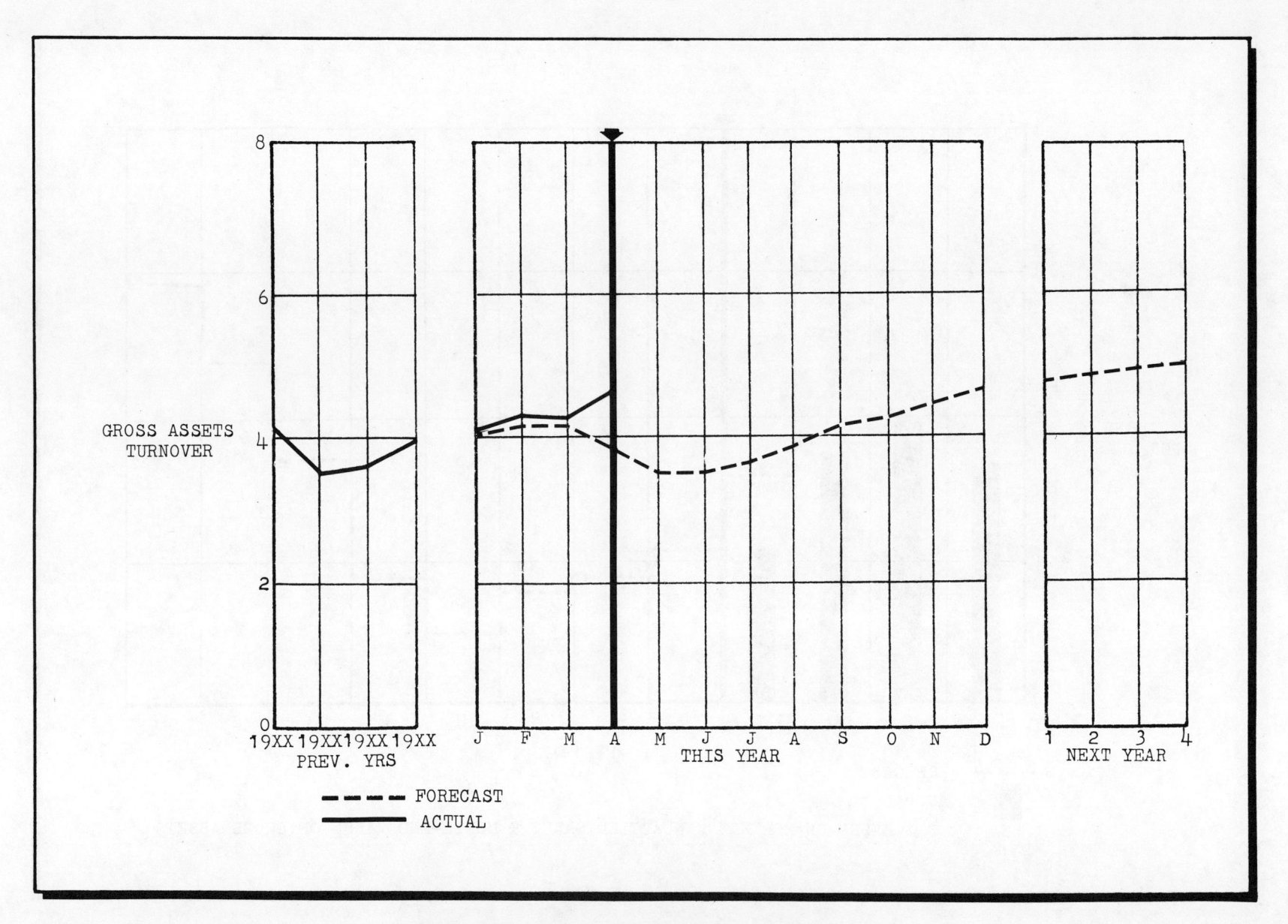

Figure 24.3 Gross Assets Turnover—Version 3

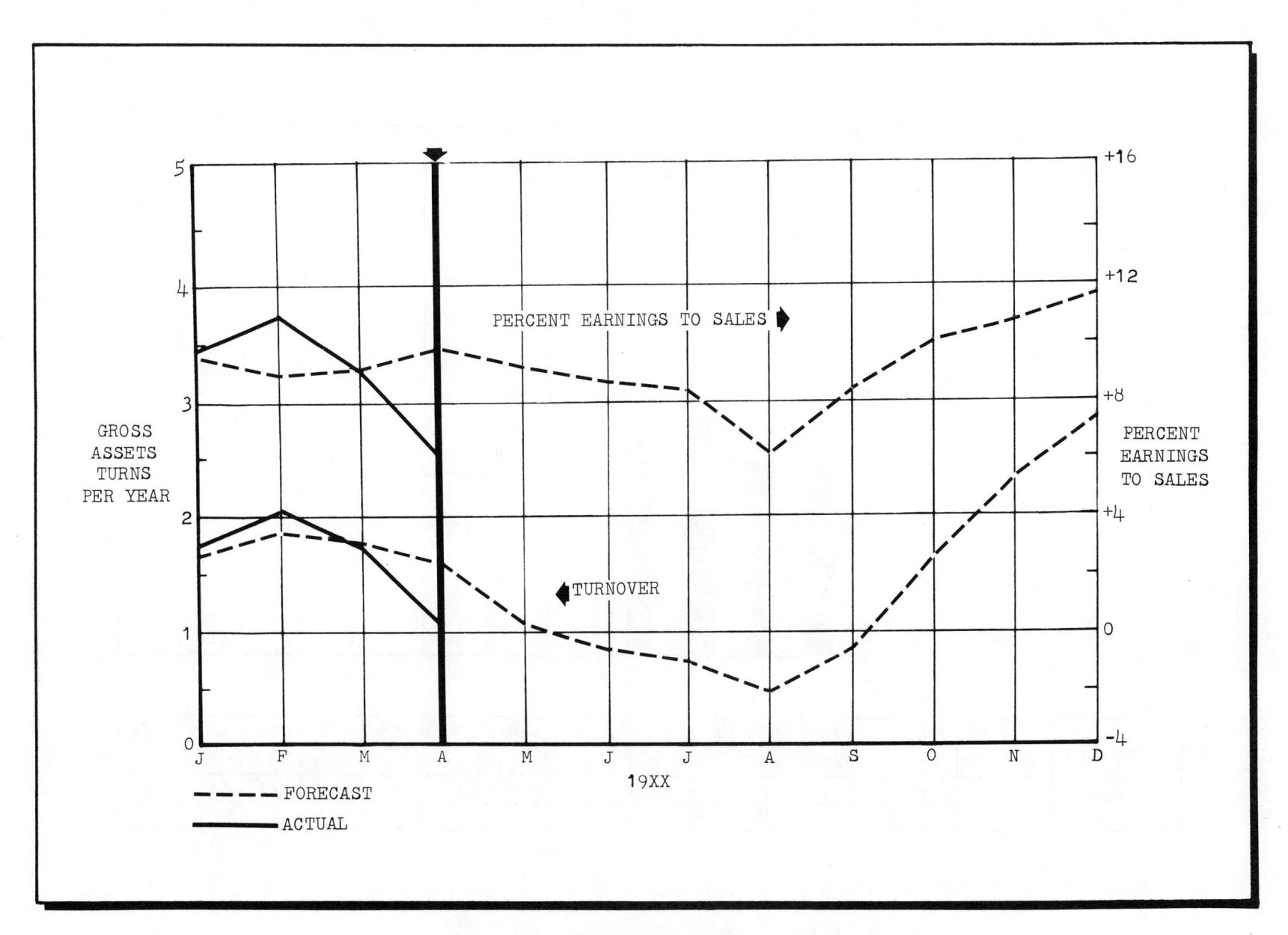

Figure 24.4 Gross Assets Turnover—Version 4

GROSS ASSETS
TURNS PER YEAR

			J	F	M	A	M	J	J	A	S	O	N	D
GROSS ASSETS TURNOVER	MONTHLY	F		1.65	1.87	1.80	1.58	1.07	.88	.74	.46	.87	1.66	2.33	2.90
		A		1.68	2.00	1.74	1.08								
	YTD AVERAGE	F	----	1.65	1.76	1.77	1.73	1.60	1.48	1.37	1.24	1.19	1.25	1.36	1.50
		A	■	1.68	1.84	1.81	1.63								

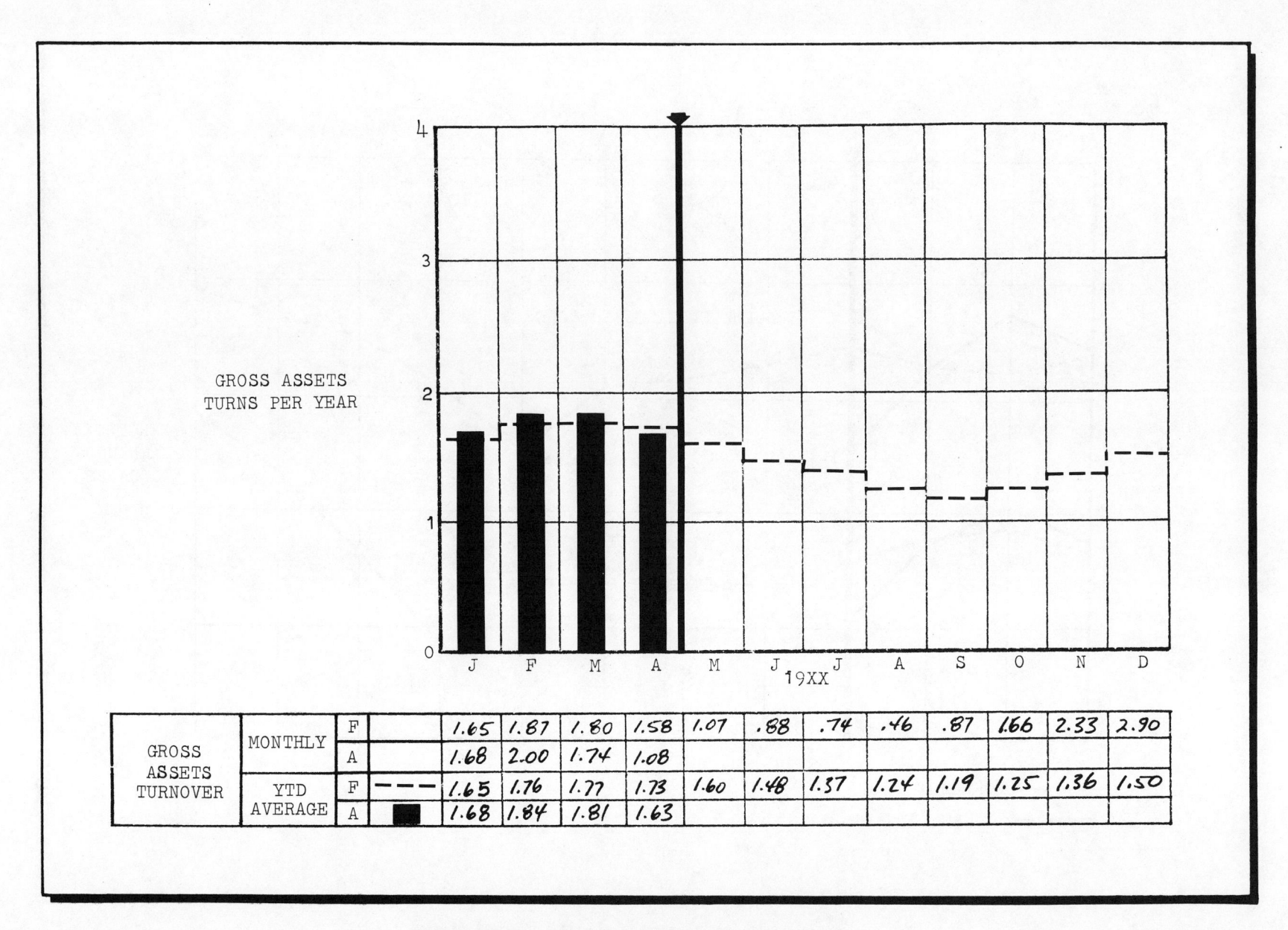

Figure 24.5   Gross Assets Turnover—Version 5

			J	F	M	A	M	J	J	A	S	O	N	D
							19XX							
SALES ($000)	MONTHLY	F	12.8	14.8	14.5	12.5	8.4	7.0	6.1	4.2	8.0	15.3	22.0	27.8
		A	13.0	16.0	14.0	8.0								
	MONTHLY ANNUAL'D	F	153.6	177.6	174.0	150.0	100.8	84.0	73.2	50.4	96.0	183.6	264.0	333.6
		A	156.0	192.0	168.0	96.0								
	YEAR-TO-DATE (CUM)	F	12.8	27.6	42.1	54.6	63.0	70.0	76.1	80.3	88.3	103.6	125.6	153.4
		A	13.0	29.0	43.0	51.0								
	YTD ANNUAL'D	F	153.6	165.6	168.4	163.8	151.2	140.0	130.1	120.5	117.4	124.3	136.9	153.4
		A	156.0	174.0	172.0	153.0								
GROSS ASSETS ($000)	MONTH-END	F	92.9	95.0	96.8	94.8	94.0	95.7	97.8	108.9	110.1	110.7	113.3	114.9
		A	93.0	96.0	96.5	89.0								
	YTD AVER	F	92.9	94.0	94.9	94.9	94.7	94.9	95.3	97.0	98.4	99.7	100.9	102.1
		A	93.0	94.5	95.2	93.6								
GROSS ASSETS TURNOVER	MONTHLY	F	1.65	1.87	1.80	1.58	1.07	.88	.74	.46	.87	1.66	2.33	2.90
		A	1.68	2.00	1.74	1.08								
	YTD AVER	F	1.65	1.76	1.77	1.73	1.60	1.48	1.37	1.24	1.19	1.25	1.36	1.50
		A	1.68	1.84	1.81	1.63								

F=FORECAST
A=ACTUAL

Figure 24.6   Gross Assets Turnover—Version 6

25.0 INVENTORY

Charts that examine inventory in relationship to plans or standards are shown in this section. Inventory above a plan or standard indicates an excess investment resulting in an adverse effect on Return on Investment. Inventory below a plan or standard would indicate shortages that could have an adverse effect on production or customer service. Also see Section 34.0, *Net Sales to Inventory*.

25.1 Inventory—Version 1: Version 1 of an inventory chart, Figure 25.1, compares the actual inventory against the planned inventory. The left-hand amount scale is in terms of the number of weeks supply.

25.2 Inventory—Version 2: Version 2 of an inventory tracking chart, Figure 25.2., utilizes a deviation chart format. Actuals are plotted according to the number of weeks the inventory supply is above or below the plan. The amount scale could also be in terms of the dollar value of the inventory or the percent deviation from plan.

25.3 Inventory—Version 3: A deviation column chart style is used in Version 3 of an inventory tracking chart, Figure 25.3. As with Version 2, the amount scale is in terms of the number of weeks the inventory supply is above or below the plan.

25.4 Inventory—Version 4: The actual number of weeks of inventory supply on hand is tracked against a standard that varies from week to week in Version 4 of an inventory tracking chart, Figure 25.4. Shading those portions that are over and under the standard enhances the chart's readability.

25.5 Inventory—Version 5: The amount scale in Version 5 of an inventory tracking chart, Figure 25.5, is in terms of the dollar value of the inventory investment. The plan is shown with a dashed line, and actuals with a solid line.

25.6 Inventory—Version 6: Paired columns are used in Version 6 of an inventory tracking chart, Figure 25.6. The plan for the year, in this example, is shown with hatched columns. Actuals to date (end of March) are shown with solid columns.

25.7 Inventory—Version 7: Double amount scales are used in Version 7 of an inventory tracking chart, Figure 25.7. The dashed and solid lines relate to the left-hand scale, showing inventory in terms of the number of weeks supply on hand. The ball and line and dotted lines display inventory in terms of dollar investment and are in register with the right-hand amount scale.

25.8 Inventory—Version 8: Segmented columns are used to show the composition of the actual inventory in Version 8 of an inventory tracking chart, Figure 25.8. In this example, the plan is shown with a dashed step line. A variation would be to also segment the plan as to the inventory components.

25.9 Inventory—Version 9: Three separate grids are used in Version 9 of an inventory tracking chart, Figure 25.9. Shown are the plans and actual inventories (in terms of dollar value) of raw material, work in process, and finished goods.

25.10 Inventory—Version 10: A statistical table has been combined with graphics in Version 10 of an inventory tracking chart, Figure 25.10. The graphic portion of the chart displays planned and actual inventory in terms of dollar value. The table shows the inventory activity for each month.

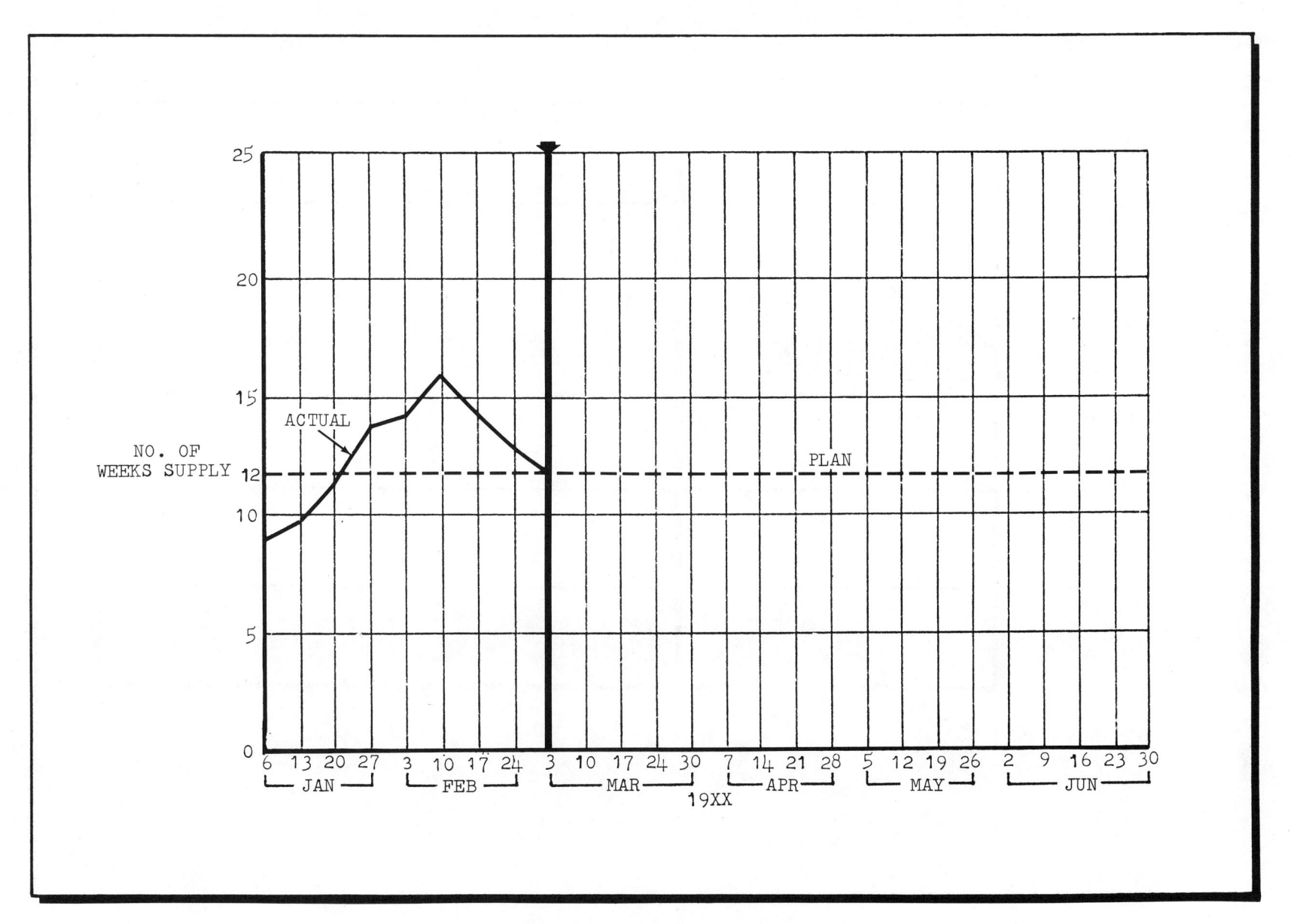

Figure 25.1   Inventory—Version 1

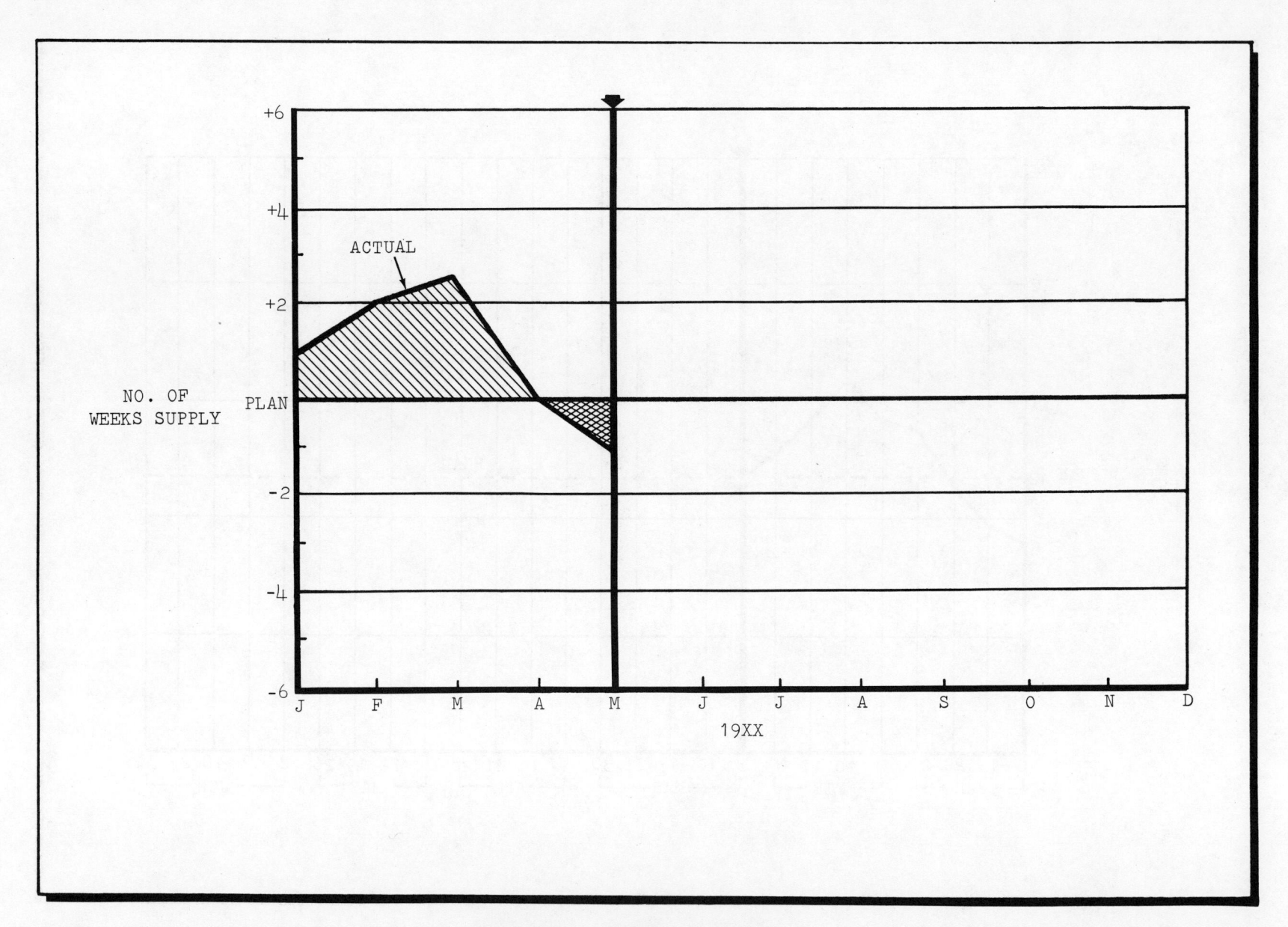

Figure 25.2   Inventory—Version 2

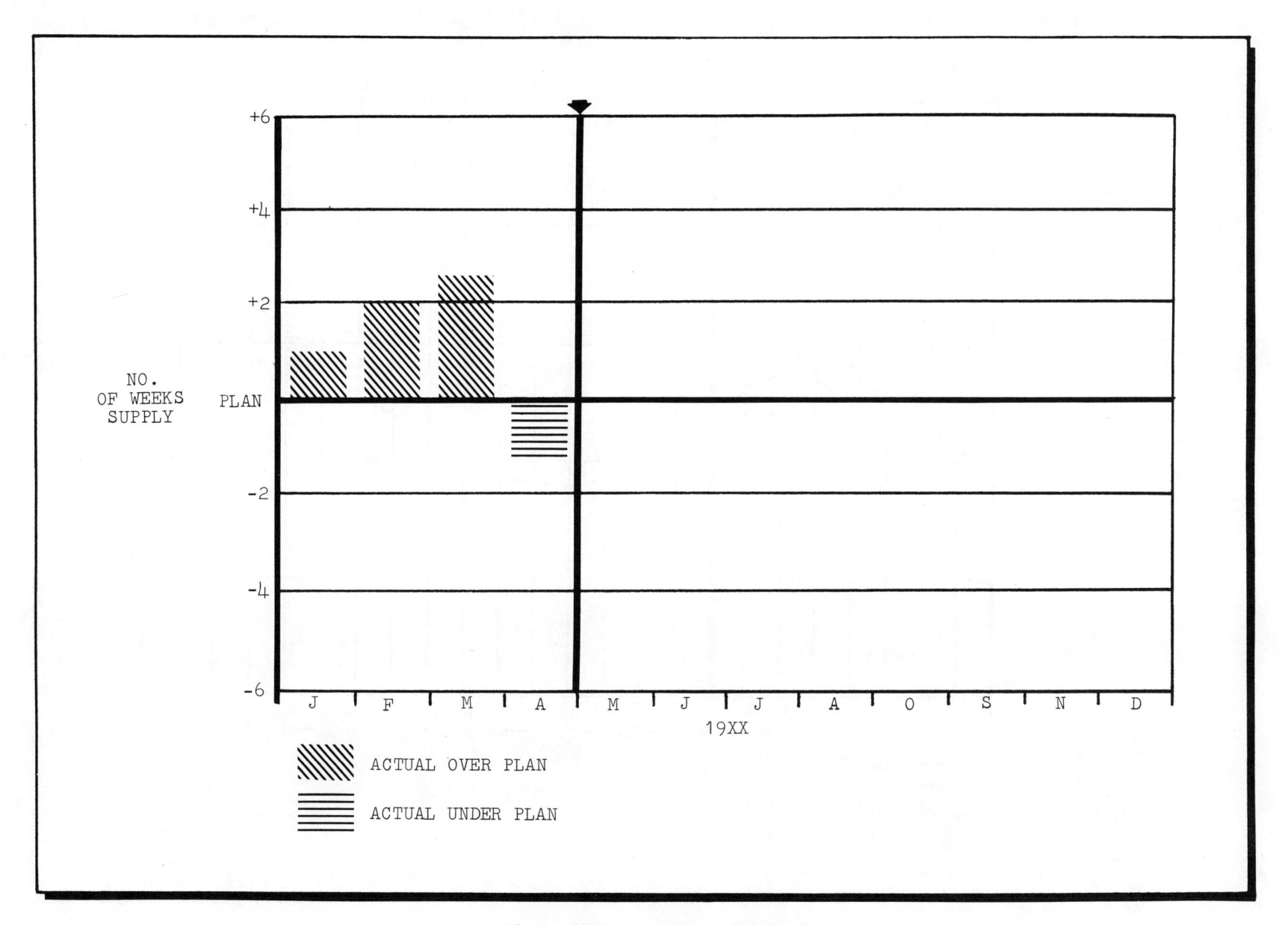

Figure 25.3   Inventory—Version 3

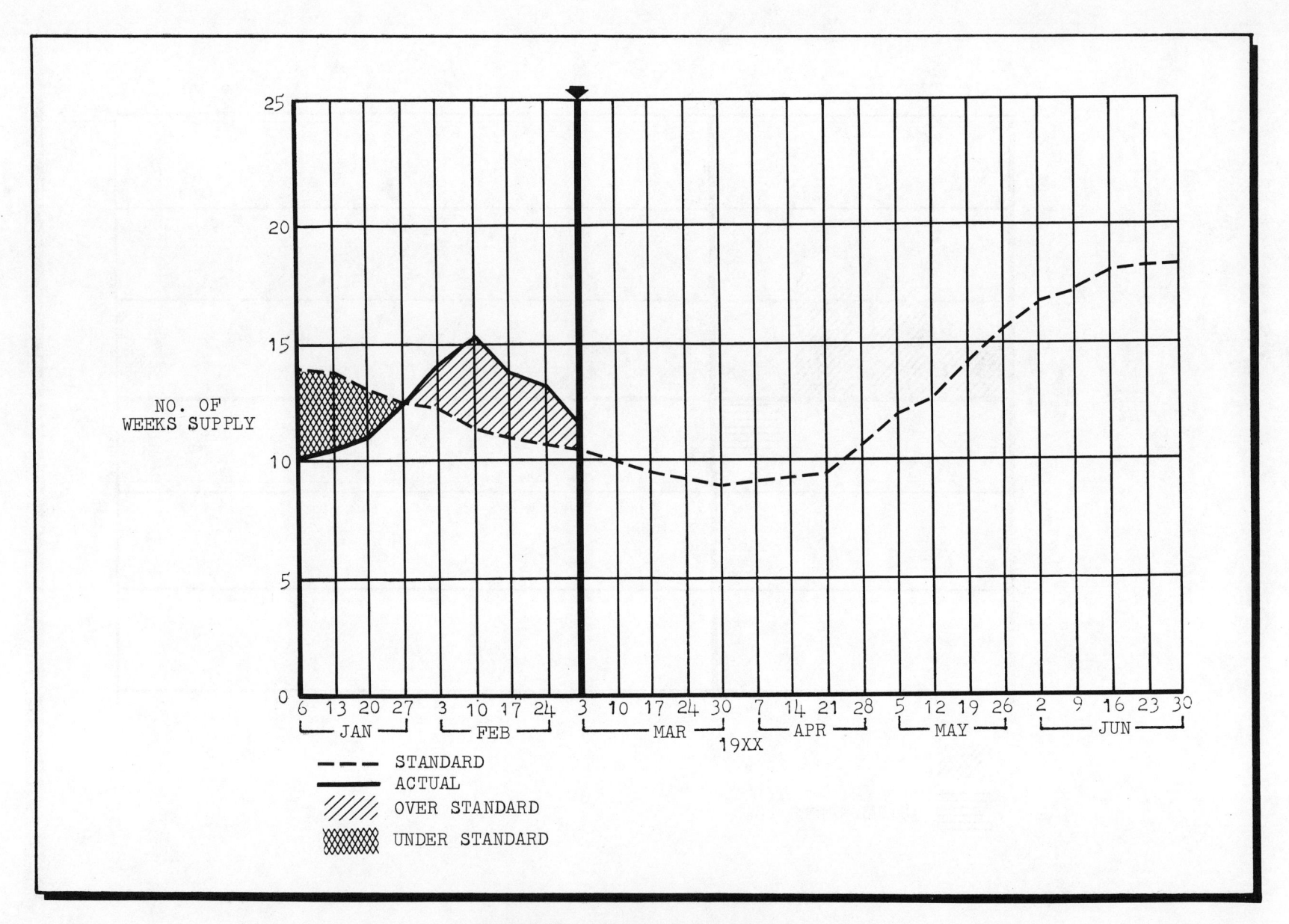

Figure 25.4   Inventory—Version 4

280

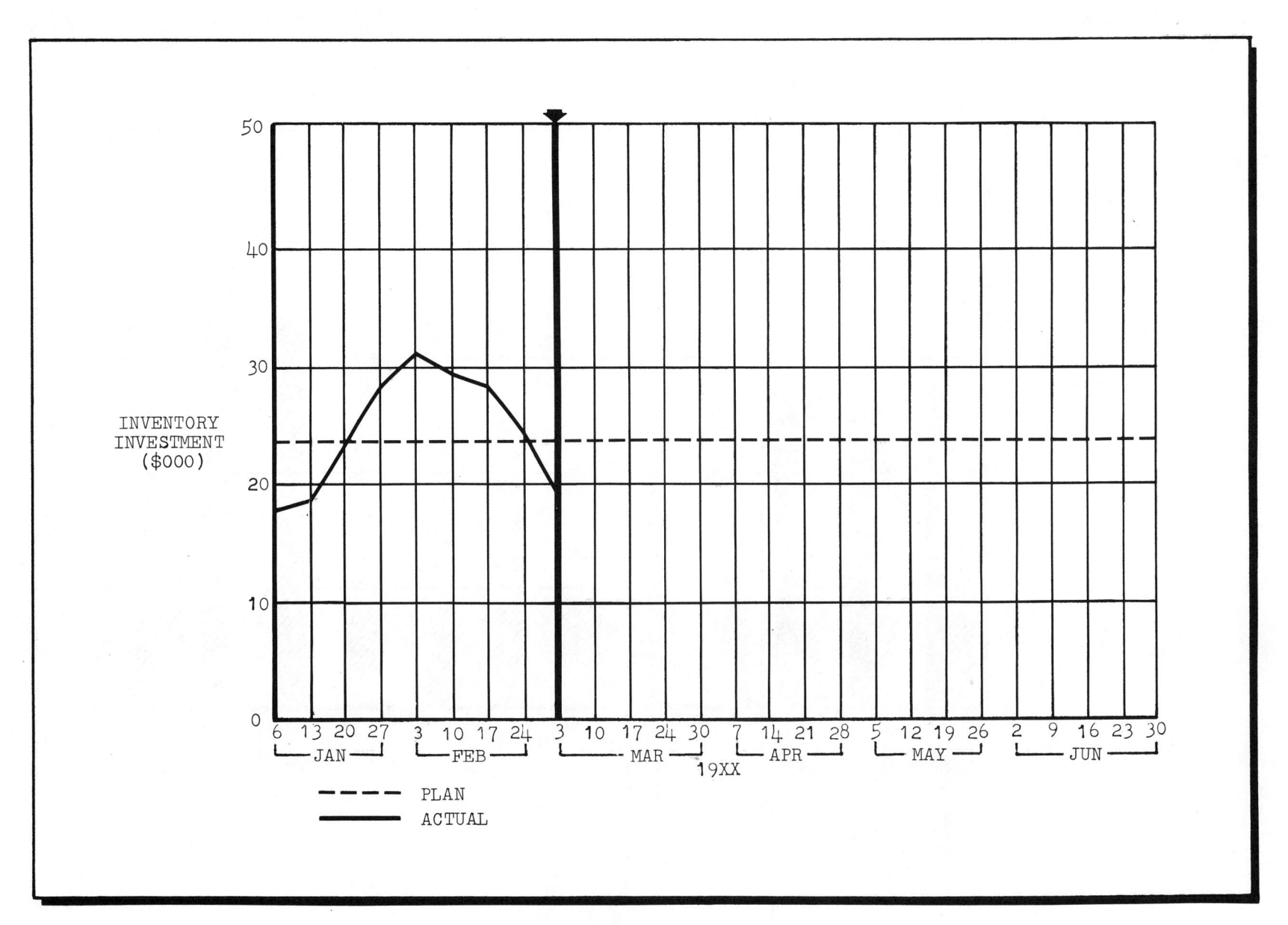

Figure 25.5 Inventory—Version 5

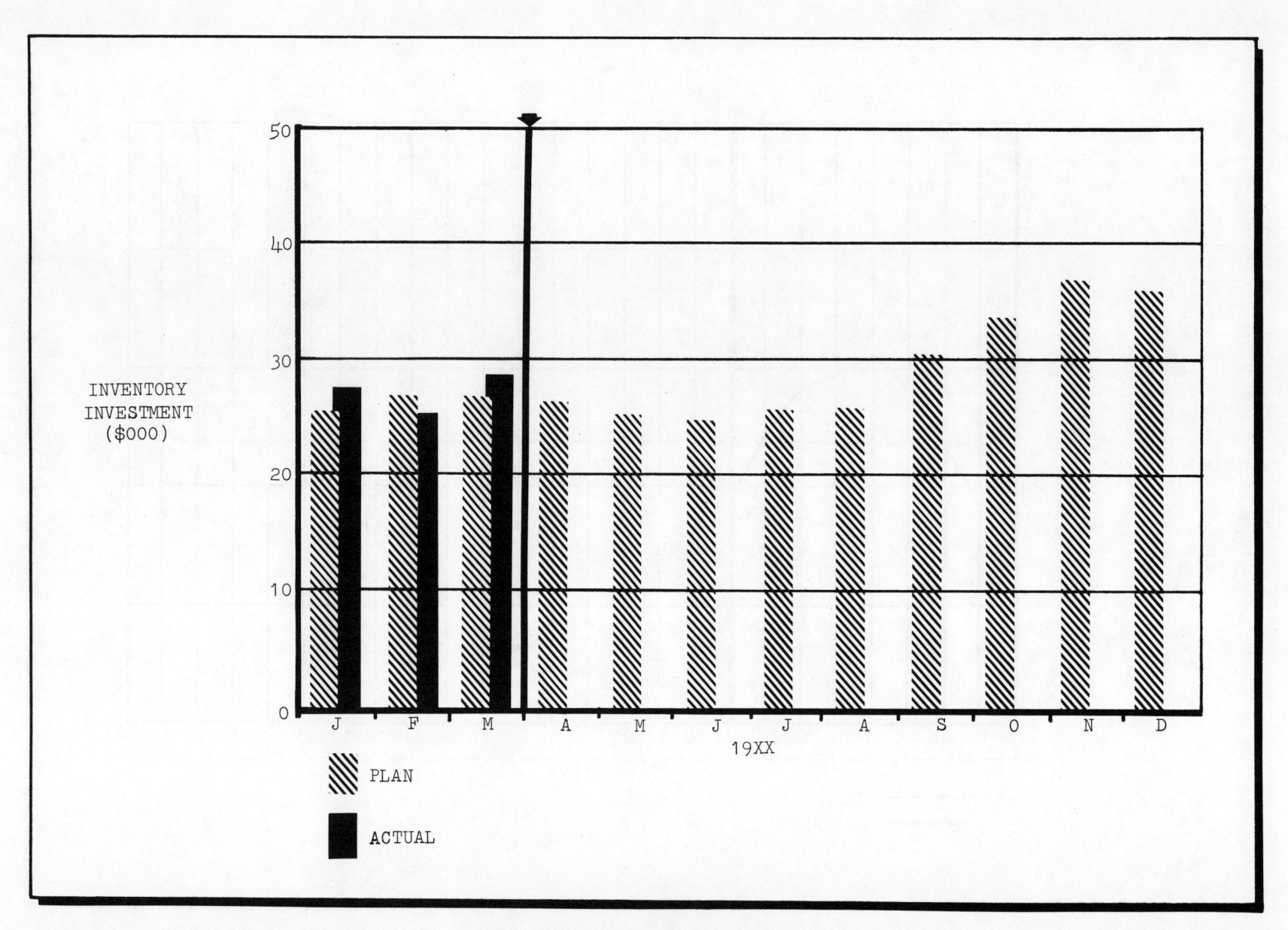

Figure 25.6   Inventory—Version 6

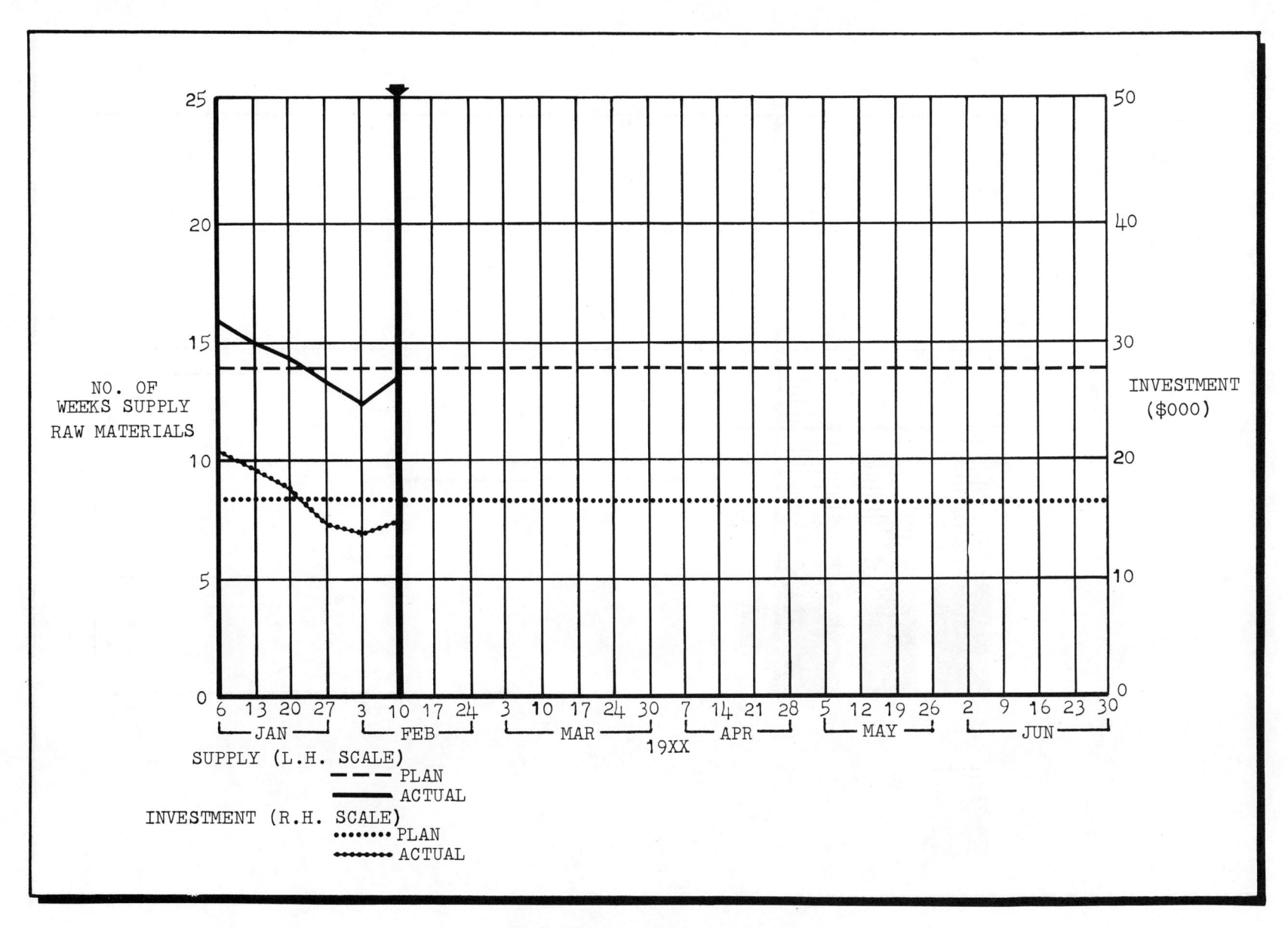

Figure 25.7   Inventory—Version 7

283

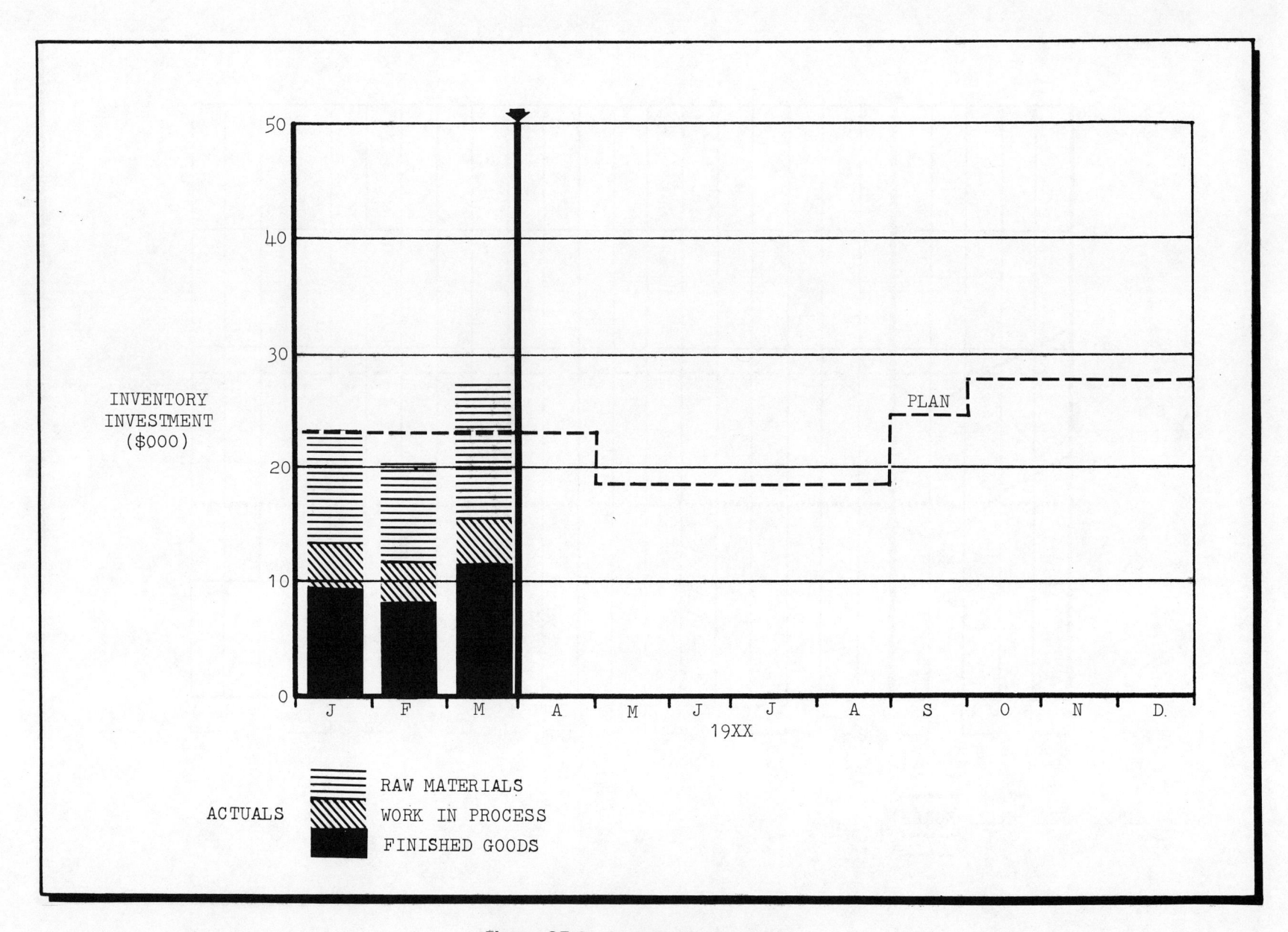

Figure 25.8 Inventory—Version 8

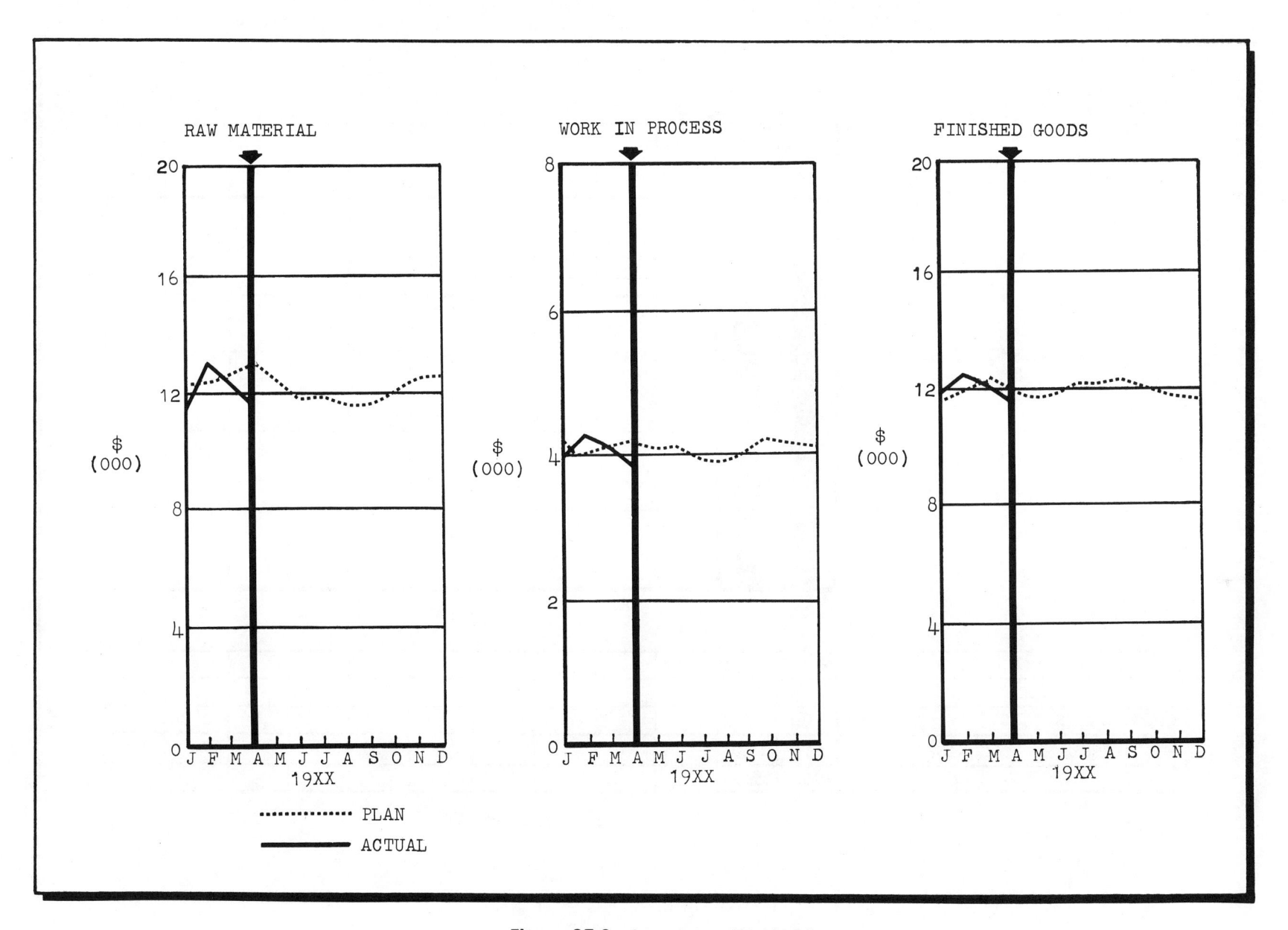

Figure 25.9 Inventory—Version 9

MONTH END
INVENTORY
($000)

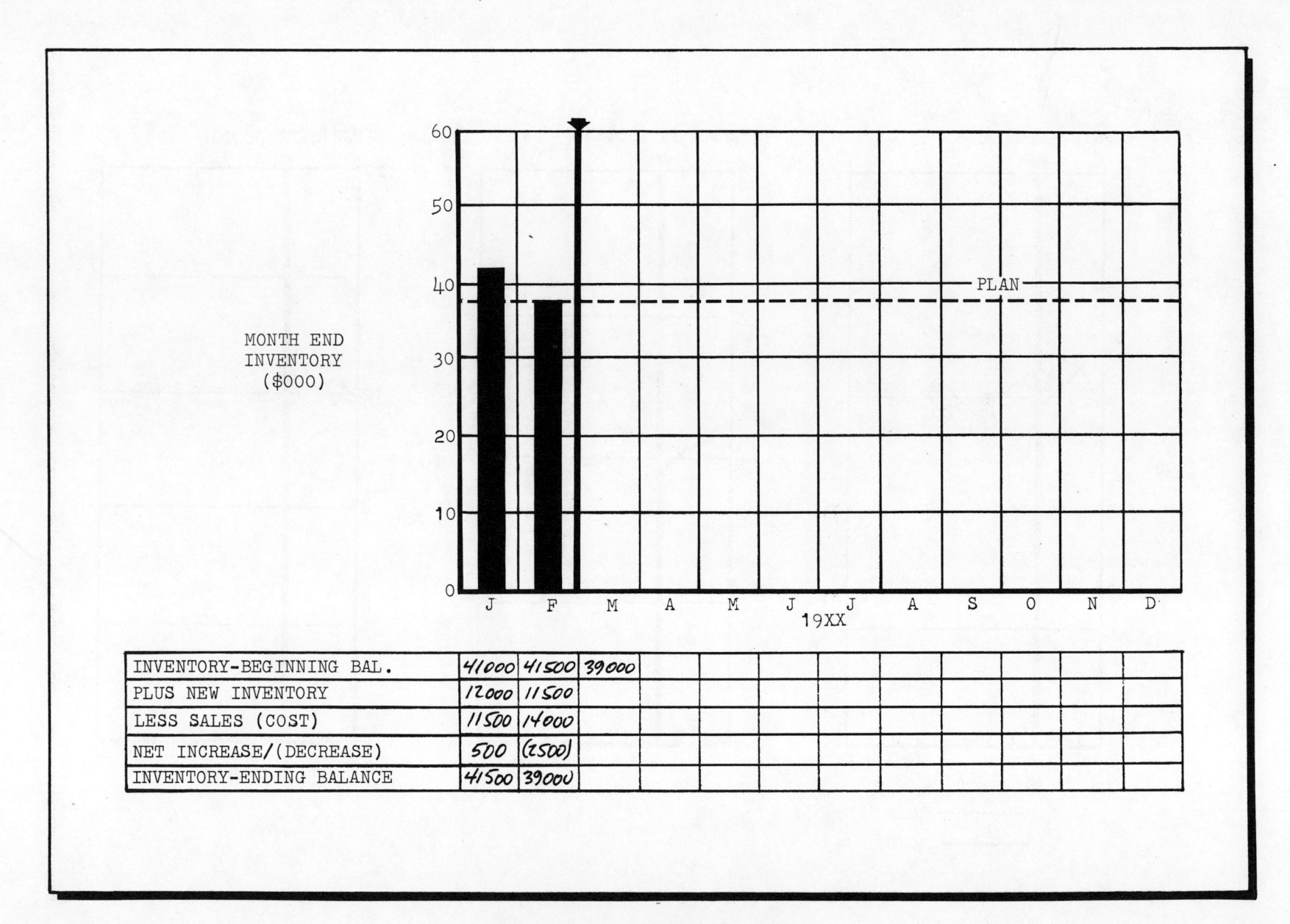

	J	F	M	A	M	J	J	A	S	O	N	D
INVENTORY-BEGINNING BAL.	41000	41500	39000									
PLUS NEW INVENTORY	12000	11500										
LESS SALES (COST)	11500	14000										
NET INCREASE/(DECREASE)	500	(2500)										
INVENTORY-ENDING BALANCE	41500	39000										

Figure 25.10   Inventory—Version 10

26.0 MAINTENANCE

Charts that display the status of product and equipment maintenance activities are shown in this section. Also see Sections 35.0, *Overhaul and Repair* and 43.0, *Reliability*.

26.1 Maintenance—Version 1: The actual maintenance efforts on two separate models of equipment are compared against a forecast in Version 1 of a maintenance tracking chart, Figure 26.1. The maintenance effort in this example is in terms of hours per month.

26.2 Maintenance—Version 2: The total hours of actual maintenance effort per month are compared against a predicted workload level in Version 2 of a maintenance tracking chart, Figure 26.2. The total is segmented and shaded to show the portions of the effort that consist of scheduled and non-scheduled maintenance.

26.3 Maintenance—Version 3: Version 3 of a maintenance tracking chart, Figure 26.3, compares scheduled maintenance costs with equipment down time costs so the effect of maintenance can be evaluated on a continuing basis. Two scales are used in this example, the left-hand scale for maintenance costs, and the right-hand scale for the cost of equipment down time.

26.4 Maintenance—Version 4: Maintenance hours are compared with equipment or product usage hours in Version 4 of a maintenance tracking chart, Figure 26.4. The tabular portion of the chart shows the hours per month for each factor and the percent of direct maintenance hours to usage hours. The graphic portion of the chart displays the percentage in column chart form and compares the monthly total against the average for the previous year.

26.5 Maintenance—Version 5: Maintenance effort is tracked on the basis of minutes of effort per equipment usage hour in Version 5 of a maintenance tracking chart, Figure 26.5. Actuals are shown on the graphic portion of the chart in relationship to actuals for the previous year.

26.6 Maintenance—Version 6: A breakdown of maintenance activity is given in tabular form in Version 6 of a maintenance tracking chart, Figure 26.6. In this example, tracking is in terms of the quantity of complaints and a breakdown of how the complaints were handled.

26.7 Maintenance—Version 7: A one-time status report version of a maintenance chart is shown as Version 7, Figure 26.7. Both graphics and statistics are employed in this example to show field maintenance activity for the reporting period.

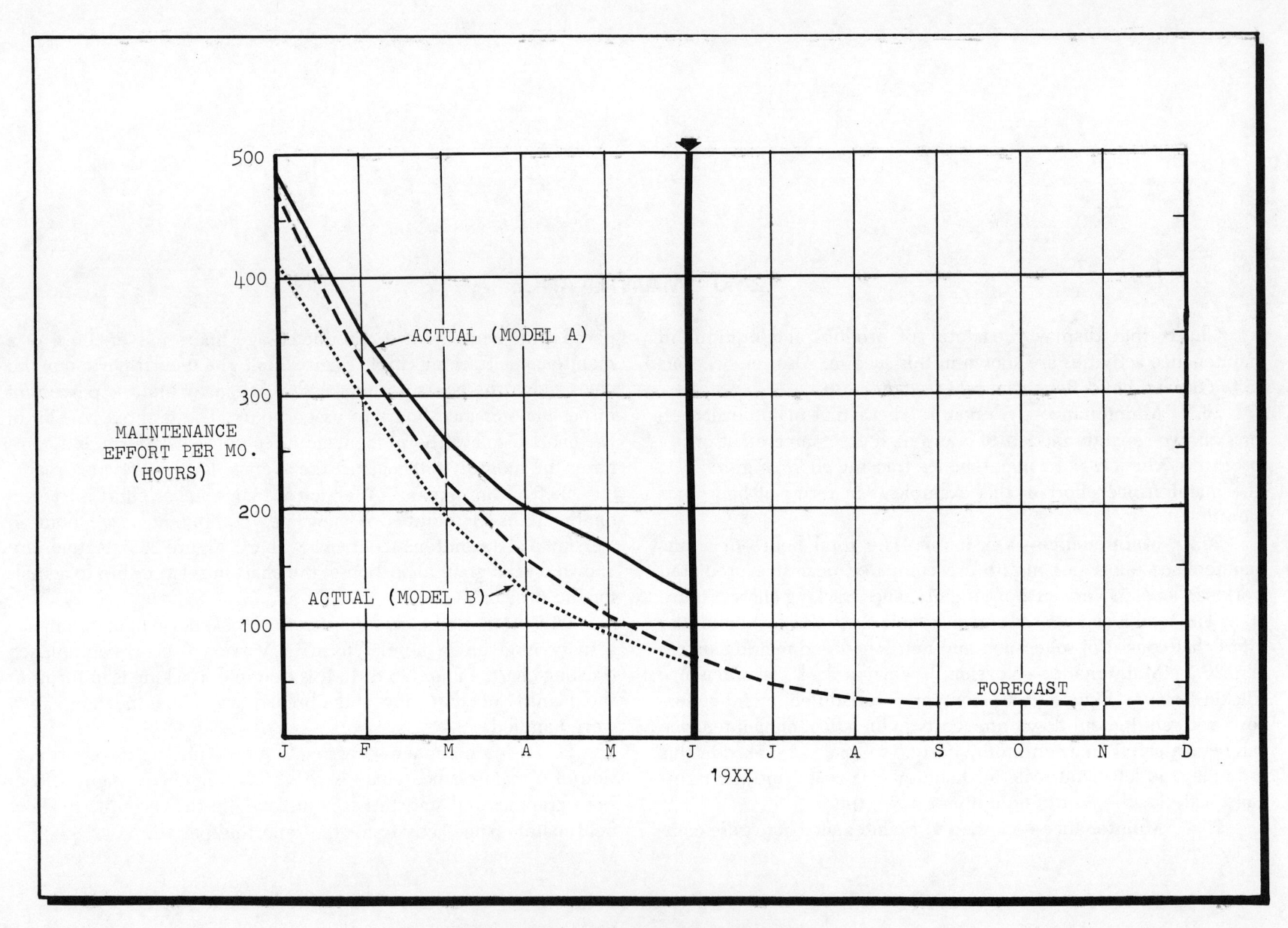

Figure 26.1   Maintenance—Version 1

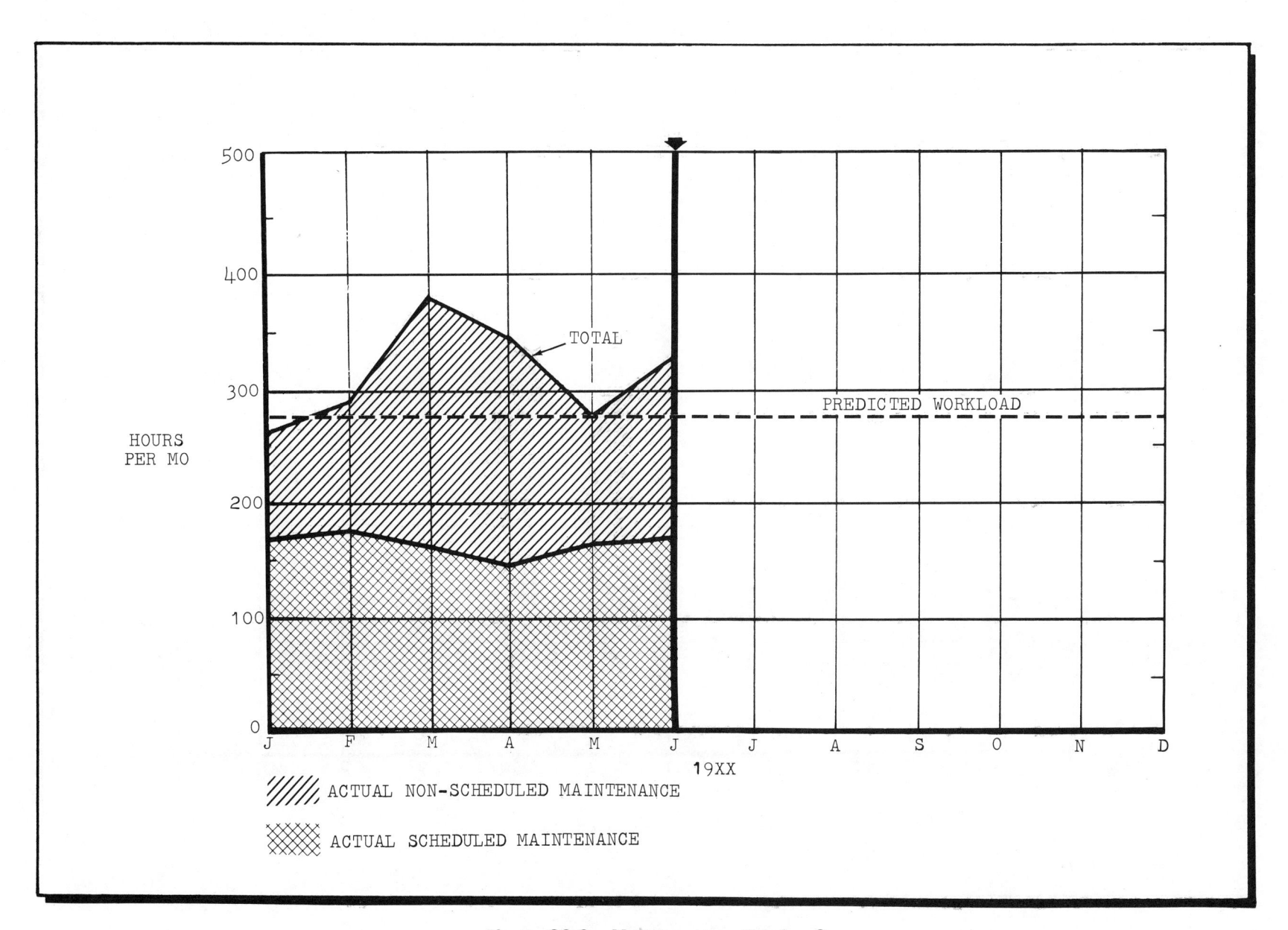

Figure 26.2 Maintenance—Version 2

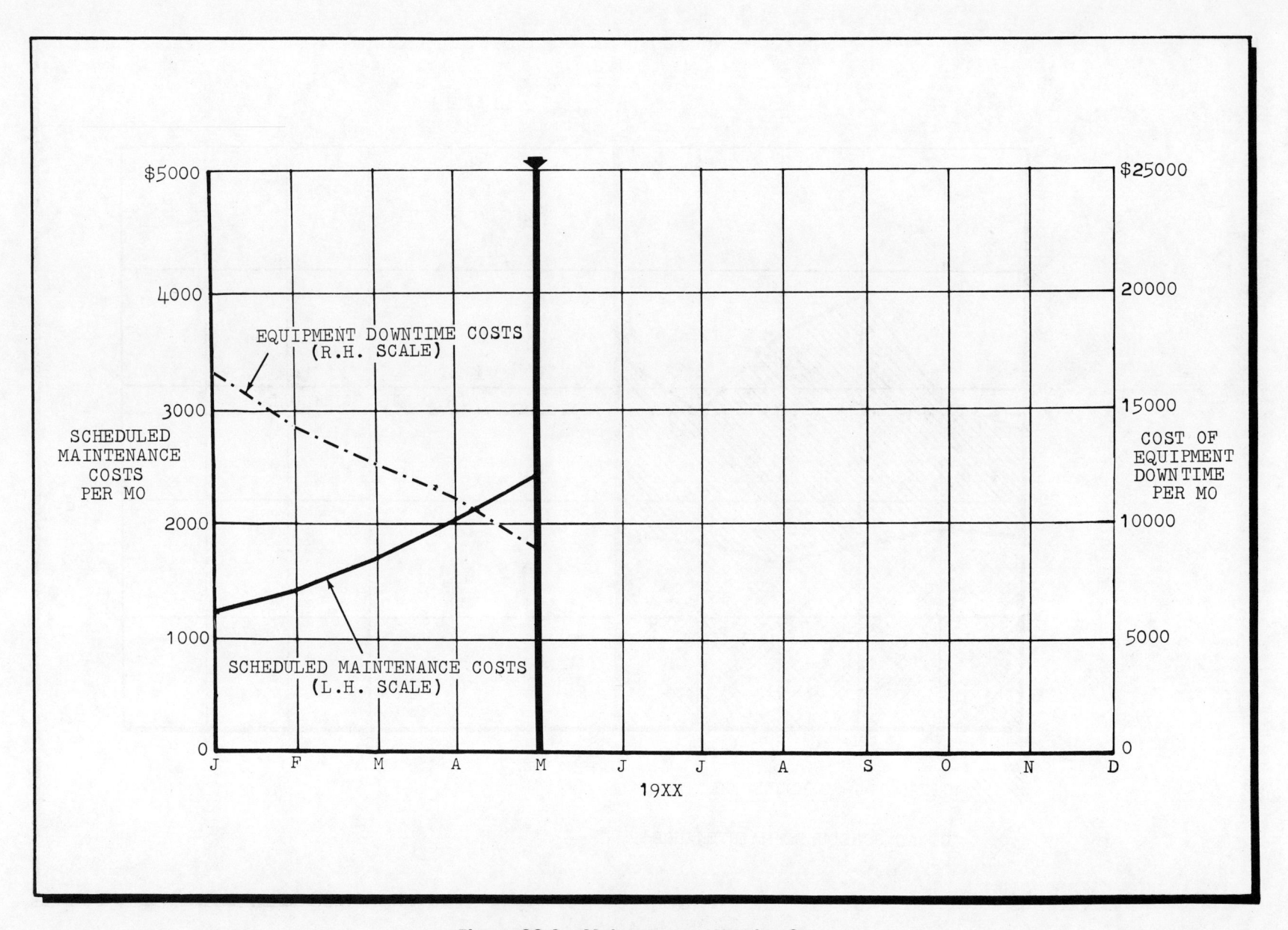

Figure 26.3   Maintenance—Version 3

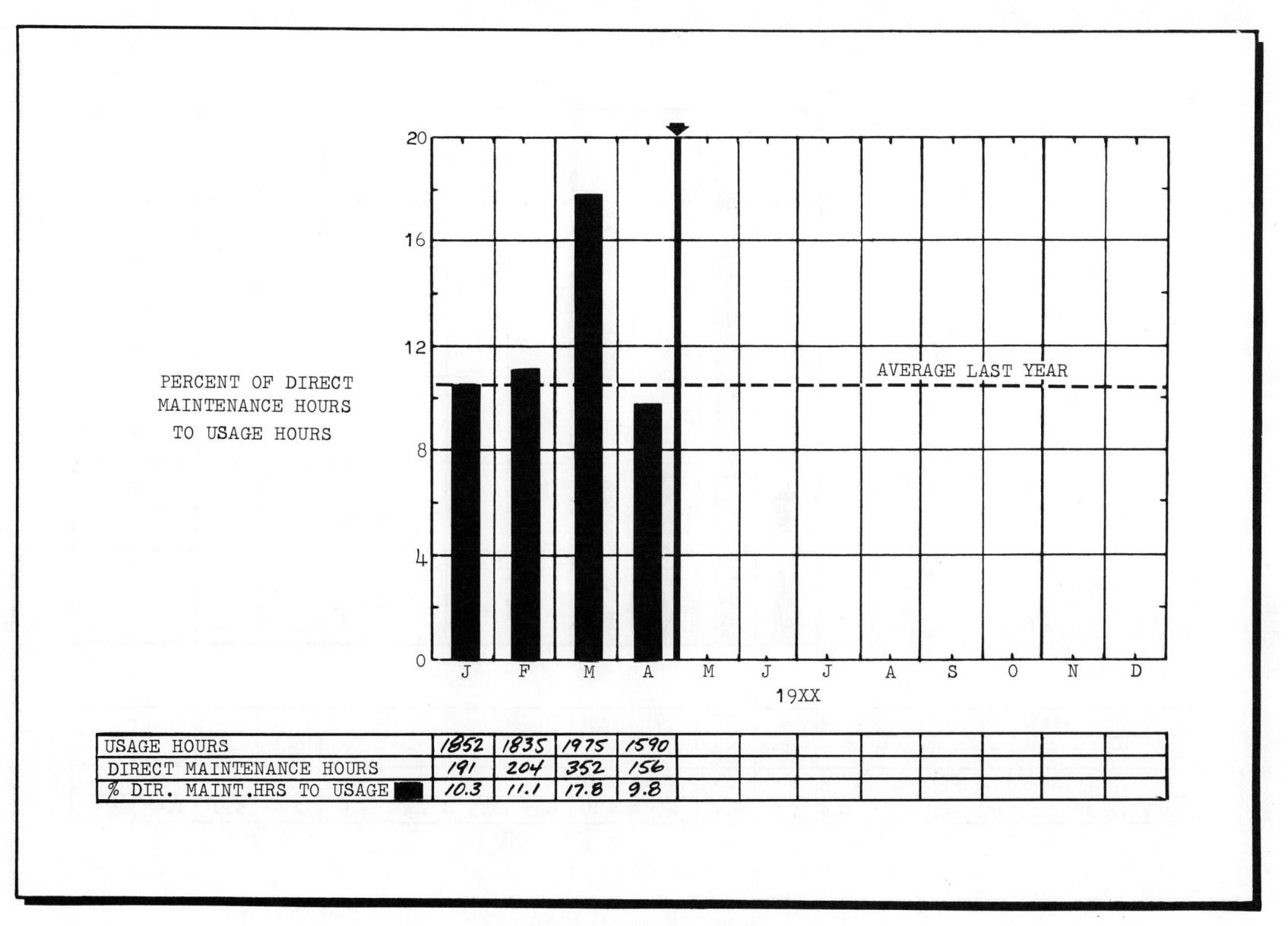

PERCENT OF DIRECT
MAINTENANCE HOURS
TO USAGE HOURS

AVERAGE LAST YEAR

19XX

USAGE HOURS	1852	1835	1975	1590								
DIRECT MAINTENANCE HOURS	191	204	352	156								
% DIR. MAINT. HRS TO USAGE	10.3	11.1	17.8	9.8								

Figure 26.4   Maintenance—Version 4

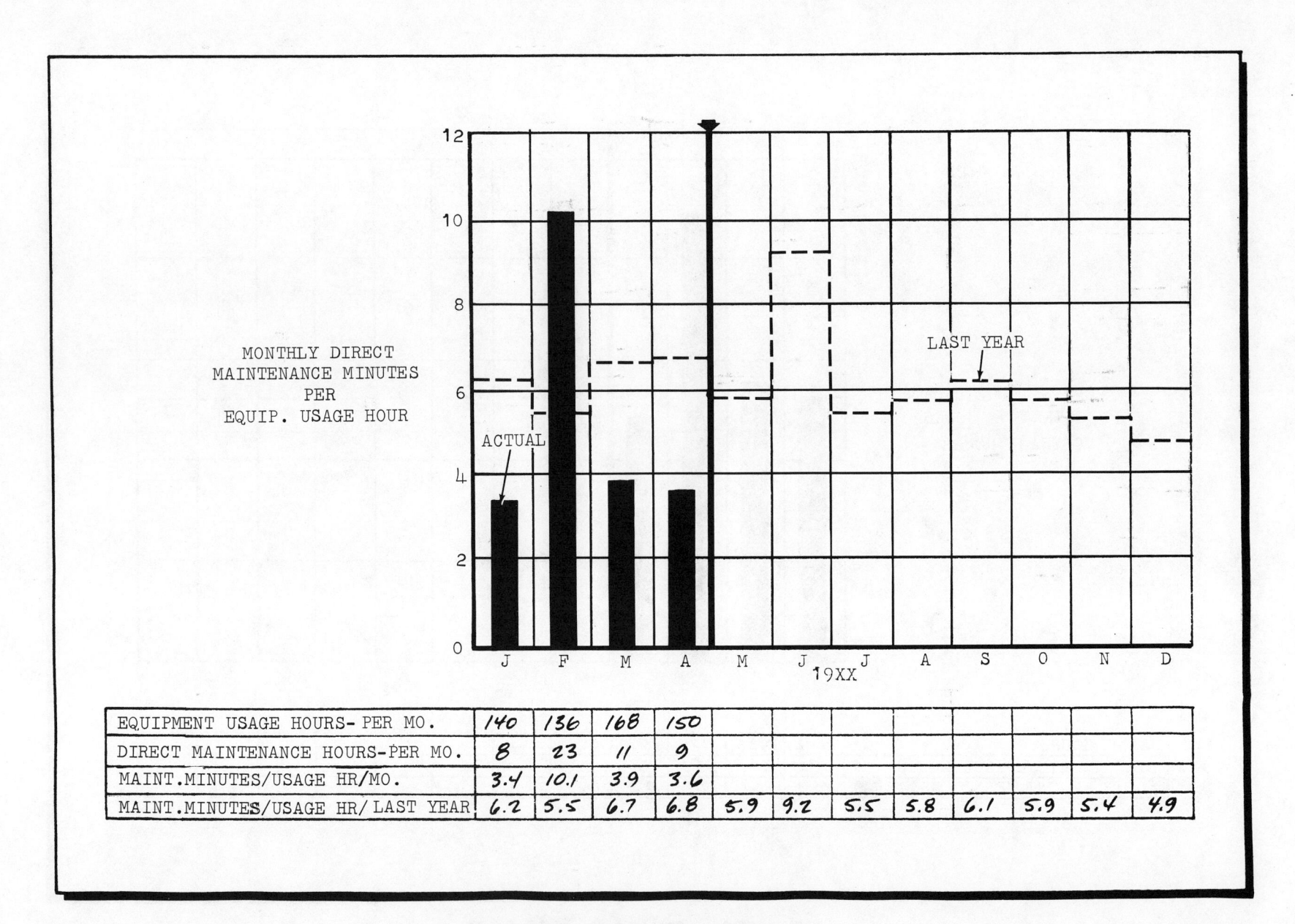

MONTHLY DIRECT
MAINTENANCE MINUTES
PER
EQUIP. USAGE HOUR

ACTUAL

LAST YEAR

19XX

	J	F	M	A	M	J	J	A	S	O	N	D
EQUIPMENT USAGE HOURS- PER MO.	140	136	168	150								
DIRECT MAINTENANCE HOURS- PER MO.	8	23	11	9								
MAINT. MINUTES/USAGE HR/MO.	3.4	10.1	3.9	3.6								
MAINT. MINUTES/USAGE HR/ LAST YEAR	6.2	5.5	6.7	6.8	5.9	9.2	5.5	5.8	6.1	5.9	5.4	4.9

Figure 26.5 Maintenance—Version 5

MAINTENANCE ACTIVITY			19XX					
			JAN	FEB	MAR	APR	MAY	JUN
PRODUCT PERFORMANCE	USAGE HOURS	PER MO.	5178	4860				
		CUM	5178	10038				
	% GOOD	PER MO.	87	85				
		CUM AVER	87	86				
	% BAD	PER MO.	13	15				
		CUM AVER	13	14				
FIELD MAINTENANCE (PER MO.)	TOTAL COMPLAINTS		673	729				
	CLEARED BY	OPERATOR INSTR.	209	197				
		ON-SITE ADJUSTMENT	404	452				
		RETURN TO FACTORY	60	80				
FACTORY REPAIR (PER MO.)	UNIT AT FAULT	SUBSYSTEM A	1	3				
		SUBSYSTEM B	12	16				
		SUBSYSTEM C	41	59				
		SUBSYSTEM D	6	2				

Figure 26.6   Maintenance—Version 6

STATUS AS OF _____

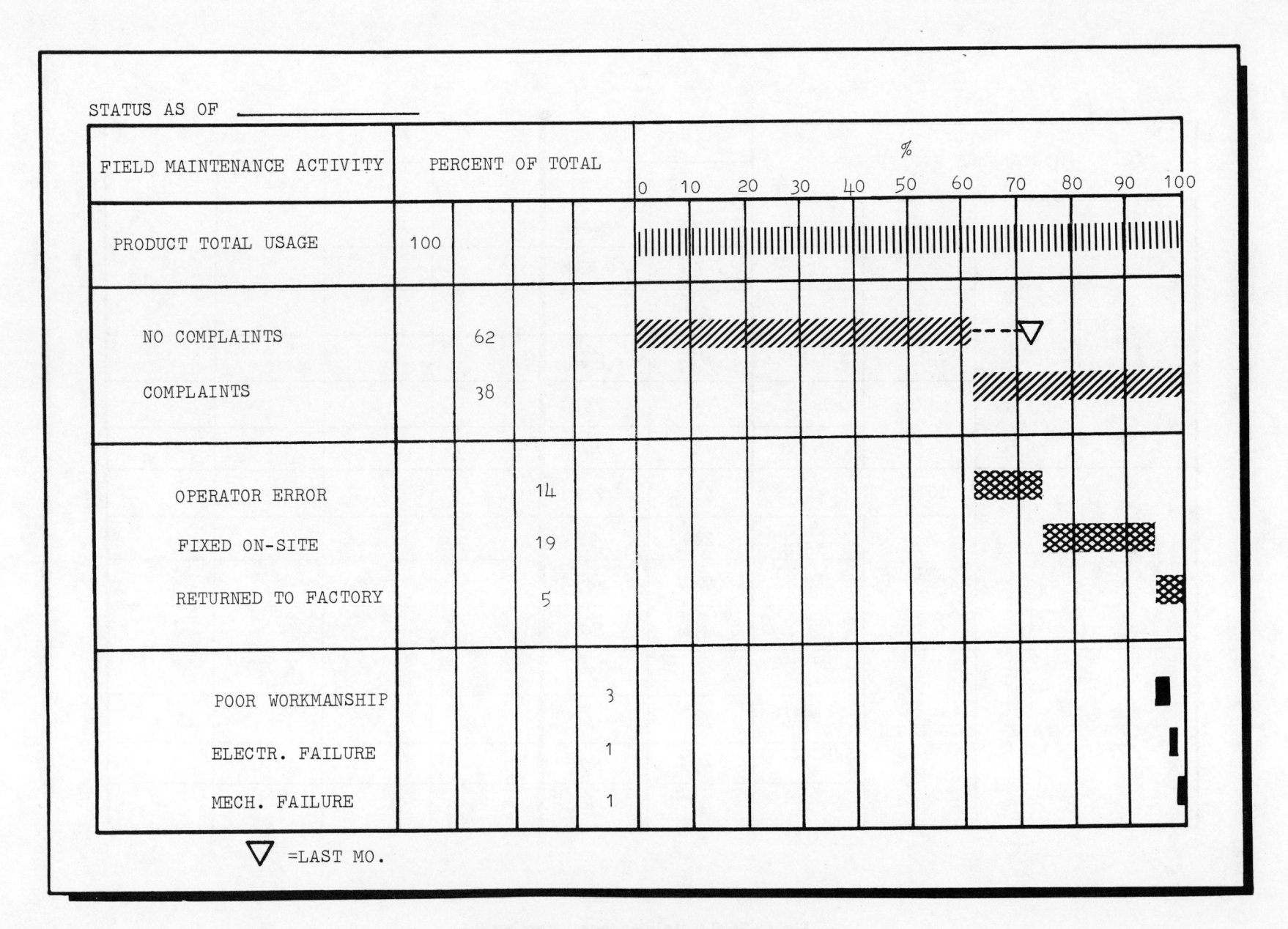

FIELD MAINTENANCE ACTIVITY	PERCENT OF TOTAL			% 0 10 20 30 40 50 60 70 80 90 100
PRODUCT TOTAL USAGE	100			||||||||||||||||||||||||||||||||||||||||||||||||||||||||
NO COMPLAINTS		62		▨▨▨▨▨▨▨▨▨----▽
COMPLAINTS		38		▨▨▨▨▨
OPERATOR ERROR			14	▩▩
FIXED ON-SITE			19	▩▩▩
RETURNED TO FACTORY			5	▩
POOR WORKMANSHIP				3 ■
ELECTR. FAILURE				1 ■
MECH. FAILURE				1 ■

▽ = LAST MO.

Figure 26.7   Maintenance—Version 7

27.0 MANPOWER AND FACILITIES

Charts that show manpower in relationship to existing and planned facilities are shown in this section. Also see manpower sections 28.0 through 32.0, and Section 20.0, *Facility Capacity Versus Workload*.

27.1 Manpower and Facilities—Version 1: Dual scales are used on Version 1 of a manpower and facilities tracking chart, Figure 27.1. The left-hand scale is in terms of floor space square footage and relates to the dashed and solid lines on the graph. The right-hand scale is in terms of the number of employees and is in register with the left-hand scale at the rate of 100 square feet per employee.

27.2 Manpower and Facilities—Version 2: Version 2 of a manpower and facilities tracking chart, Figure 27.2, is similar to Version 1 except in this example paired columns and a step line have been used to display the data. The step line shows planned and actual floor space. The paired columns show the actual and planned number of employees.

27.3 Manpower and Facilities—Version 3: The hatched and cross-hatched portions of Version 3 of a manpower and facilities tracking chart, Figure 27.3, show facilities square footage divided as to use. The line curves, in register with the right-hand amount scale, show the actual and forecasted number of employees in need of each of the areas.

27.4 Manpower and Facilities—Version 4: An analytical version of a manpower and facilities chart, showing status as of one point in time, is shown in Figure 27.4. The vertical scale in this example is in terms of floor space square footage. The horizontal scale is in terms of the number of employees. Plottings are made according to the number of square footage utilized per employee for each of six separate departments.

27.5 Manpower and Facilities—Version 5: An area plot plan is used for a one-time status report version of a manpower and facilities chart, Figure 27.5. Facilities are shown in terms of what is on hand, what is under construction, and what is planned. Manpower is given in terms of what exists, and what the coming capacities will be, broken down by shifts.

27.6 Manpower and Facilities—Version 6: Facility square footage and employment are displayed on a format that covers ten years in Version 6 of a manpower and facilities chart, Figure 27.6. Facilities are shown with hatched columns and are in register with the left-hand amount scale. Columns representing employment are across-hatched and are in register with the right-hand amount scale.

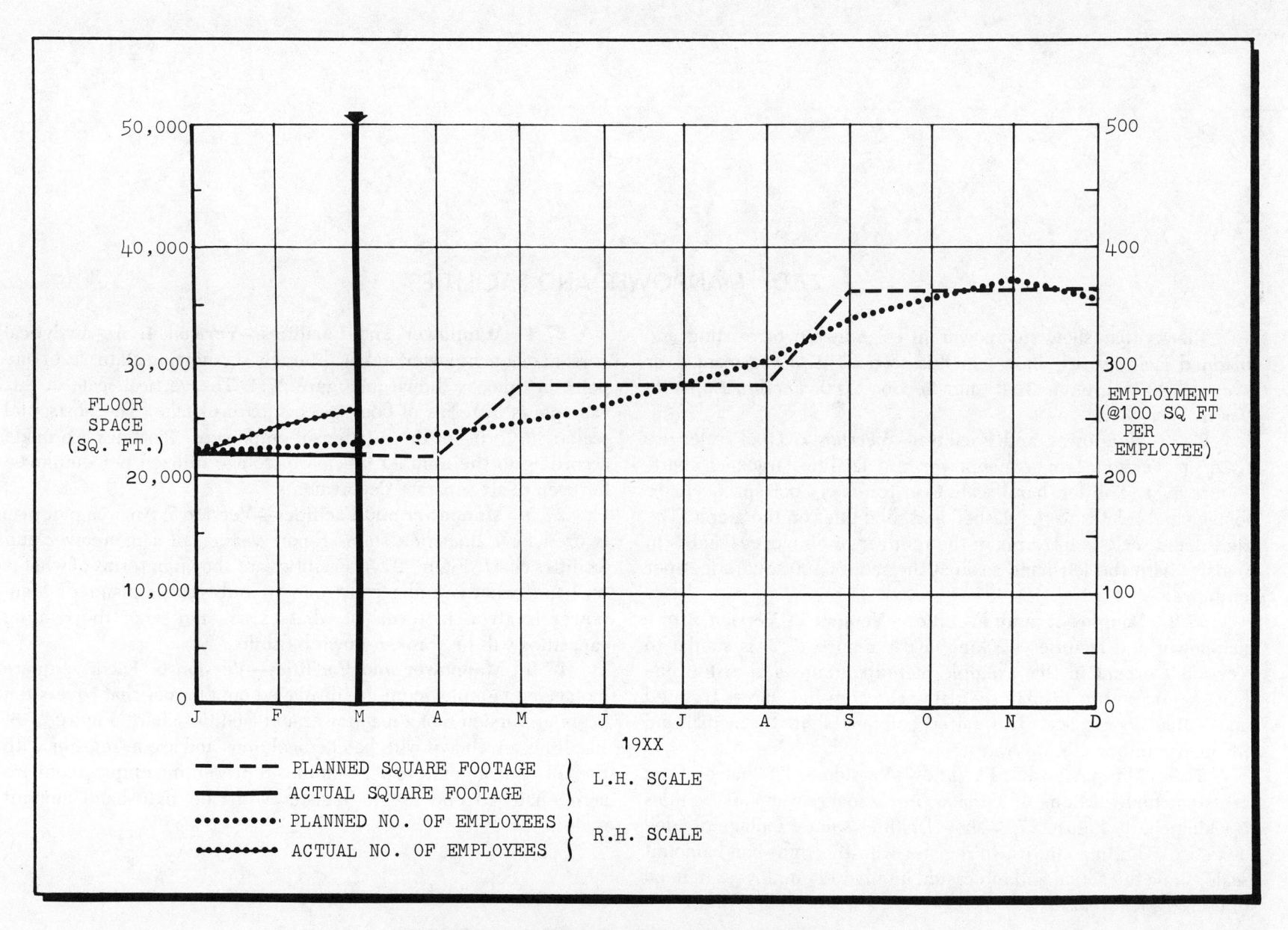

Figure 27.1 Manpower and Facilities—Version 1

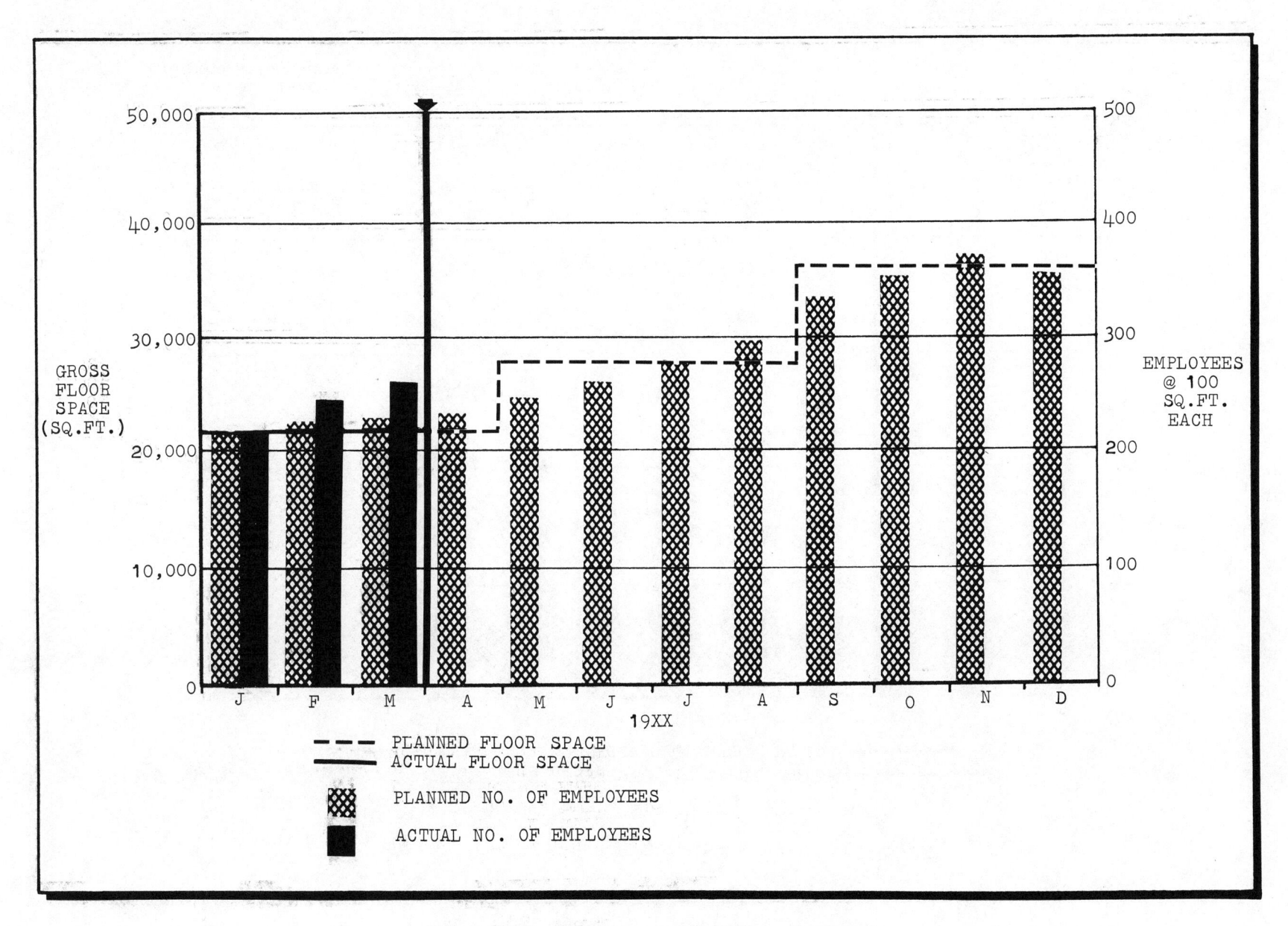

Figure 27.2 Manpower and Facilities—Version 2

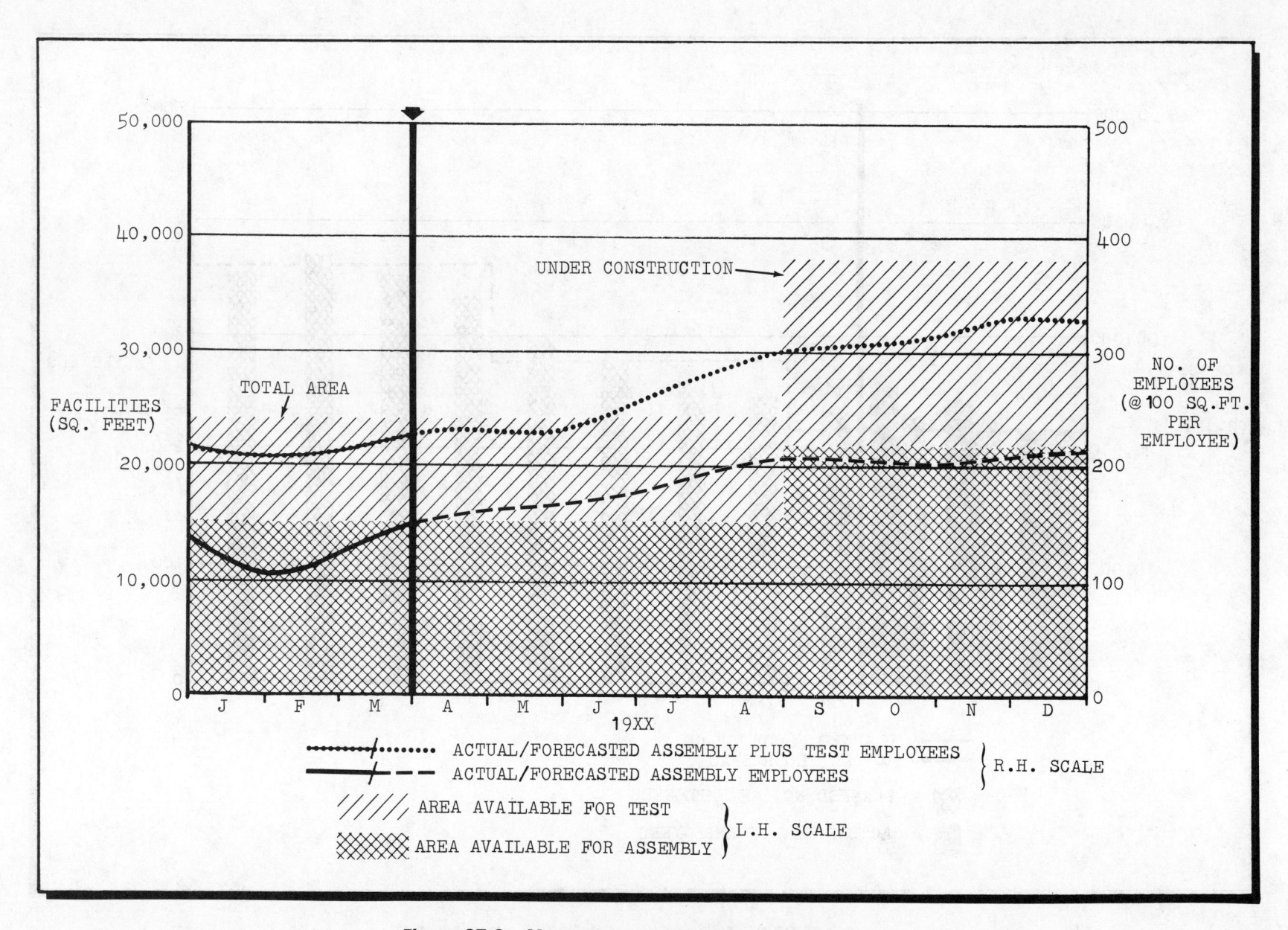

Figure 27.3 Manpower and Facilities—Version 3

STATUS AS OF _____

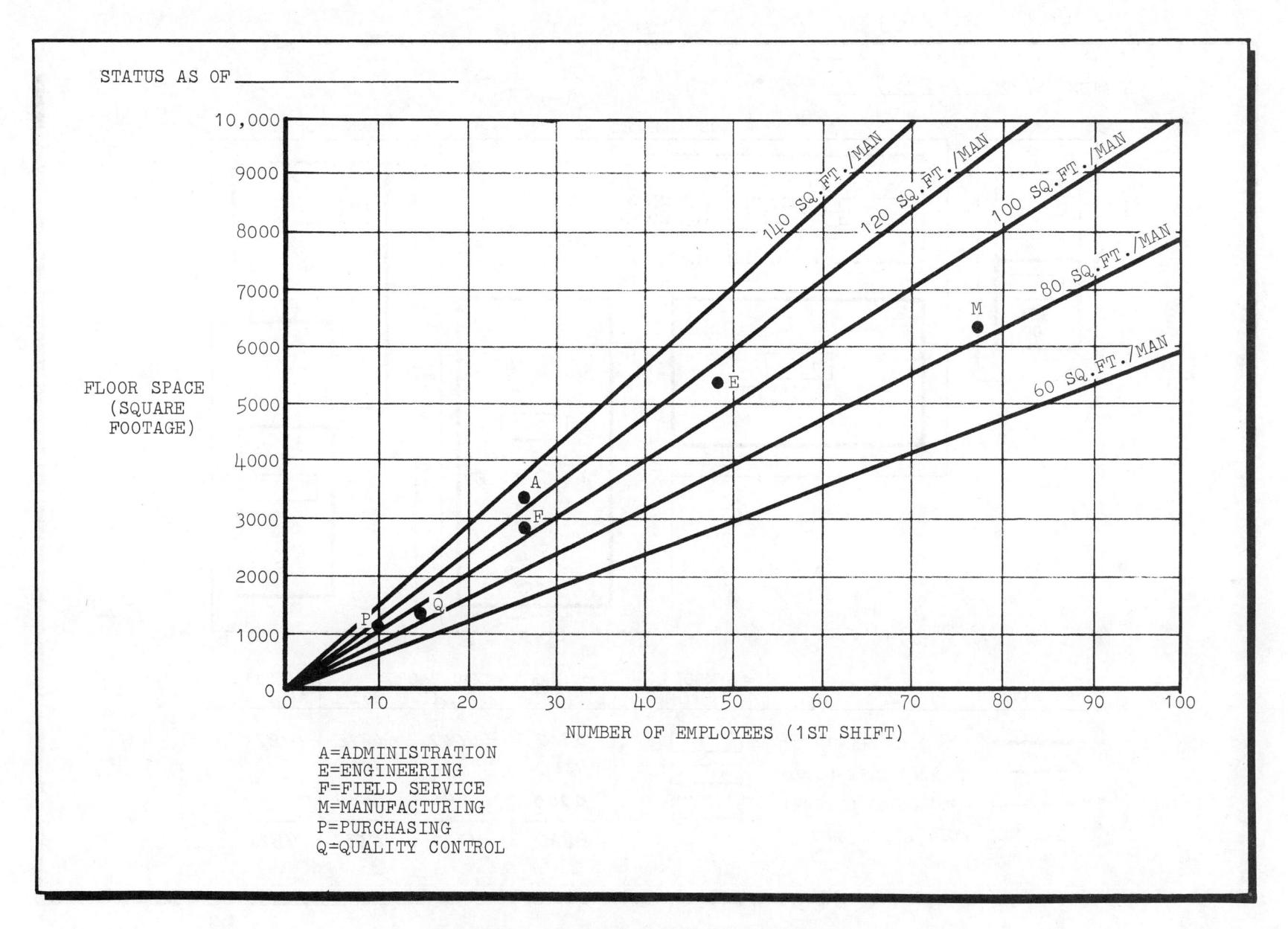

Figure 27.4 Manpower and Facilities—Version 4

STATUS AS OF _____

| | | RENO | | LOS ANGELES | | | | BAKERSFIELD | |

(Figure showing facility diagrams with the following labels:)

RENO:
- (8/28) 250 [under construction]
- 250, 92% OCC

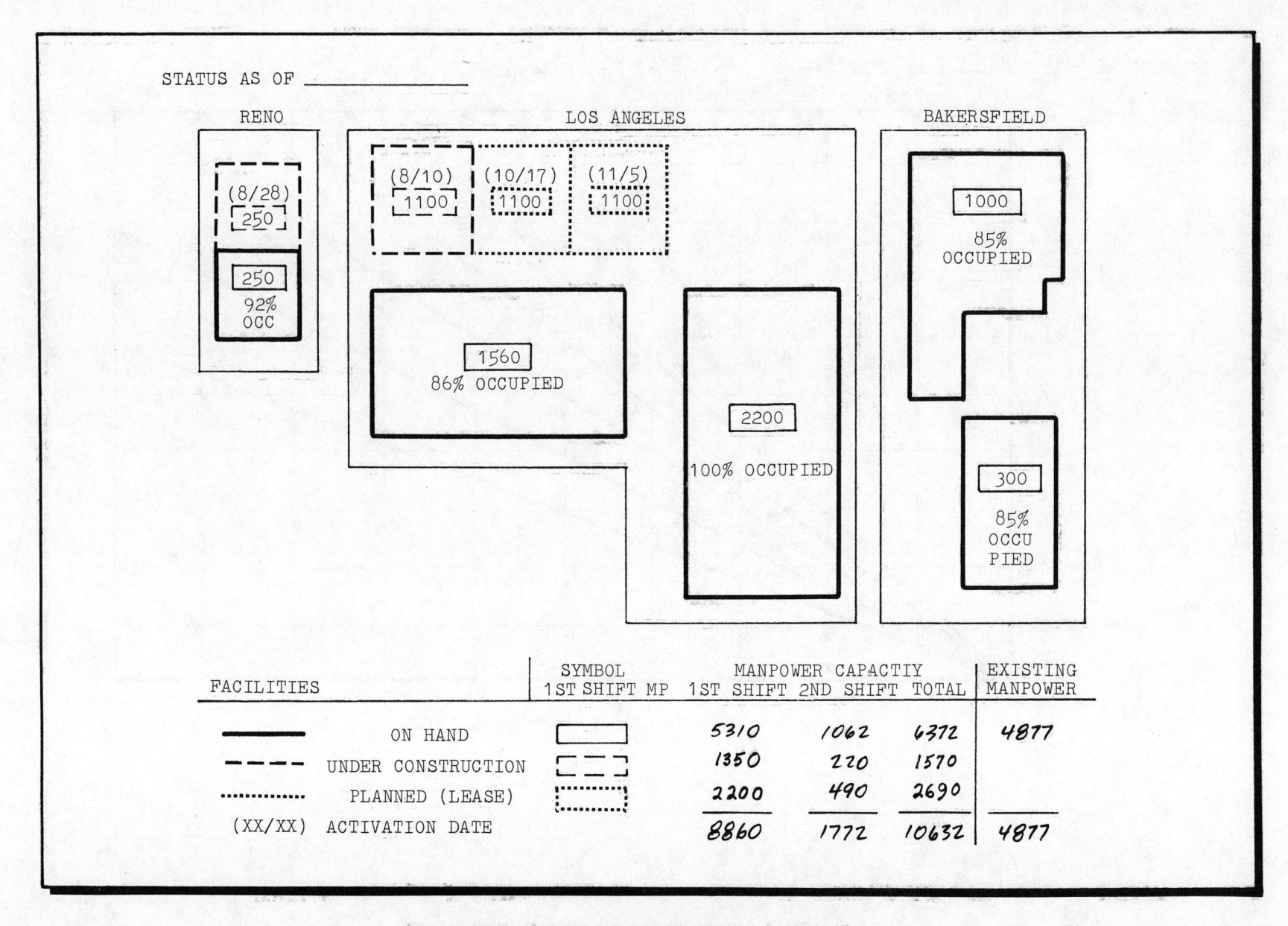

LOS ANGELES:
- (8/10) 1100 [under construction]
- (10/17) 1100 [planned lease]
- (11/5) 1100 [planned lease]
- 1560, 86% OCCUPIED
- 2200, 100% OCCUPIED

BAKERSFIELD:
- 1000, 85% OCCUPIED
- 300, 85% OCCUPIED

FACILITIES		SYMBOL 1ST SHIFT MP	MANPOWER CAPACTIY			EXISTING MANPOWER
			1ST SHIFT	2ND SHIFT	TOTAL	
————	ON HAND	▭	5310	1062	6372	4877
– – – –	UNDER CONSTRUCTION	▭	1350	220	1570	
··········	PLANNED (LEASE)	▭	2200	490	2690	
(XX/XX)	ACTIVATION DATE		8860	1772	10632	4877

Figure 27.5 Manpower and Facilities—Version 5

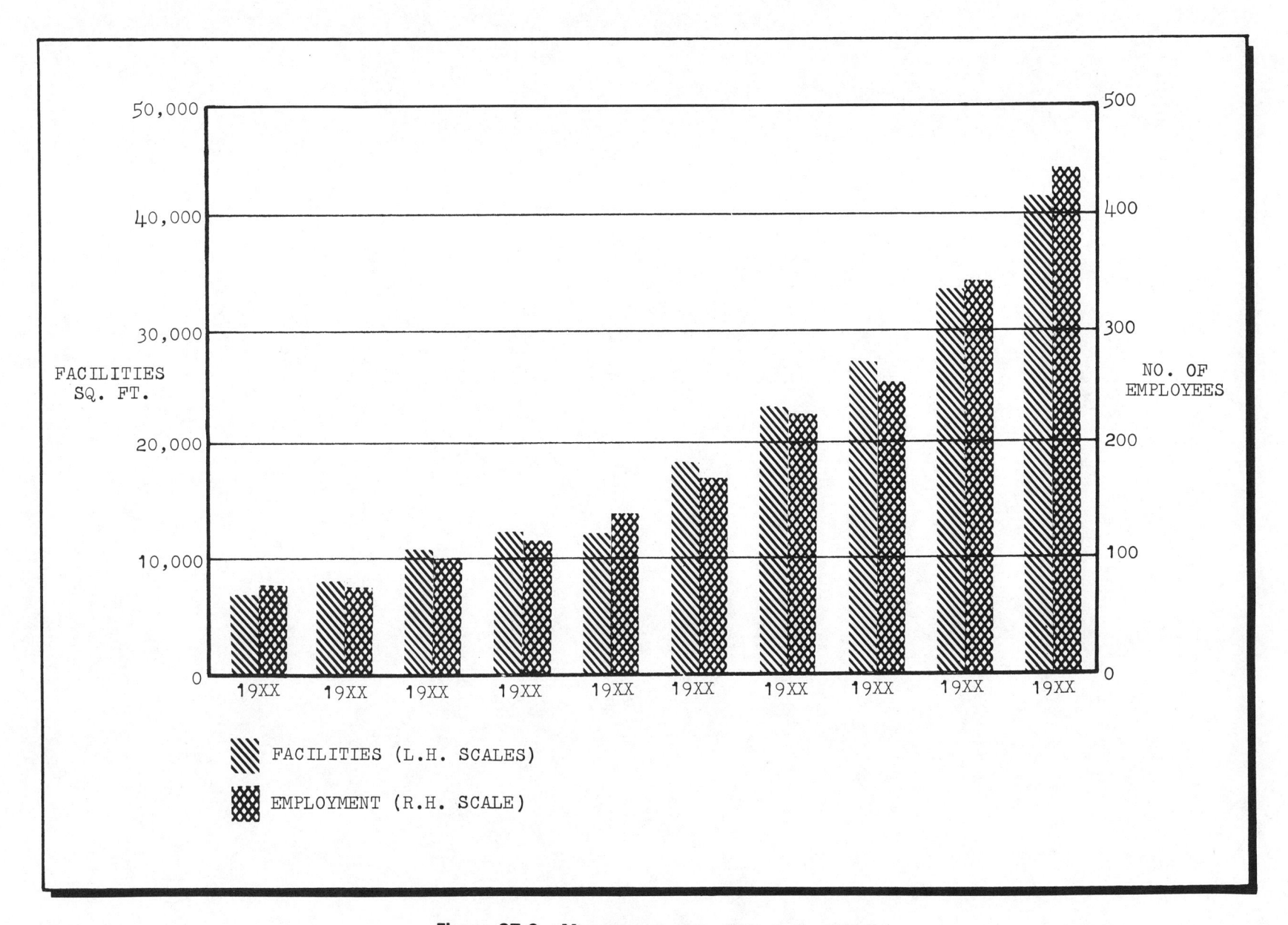

Figure 27.6 Manpower and Facilities—Version 6

28.0 MANPOWER BY ASSIGNMENT

Charts that show manpower broken down by assignment (i.e., organizational unit, project, product line, function, etc.) are displayed in this section. Also see manpower sections 27.0, and 29.0 through 32.0.

28.1 Manpower by Assignment—Version 1: Version 1 of a manpower by assignment tracking chart, Figure 28.1, displays budgeted direct manpower, actuals to date, and the current revised forecast. It also shows in the note section of the chart the current month's breakdown of the quantity of direct charging people, by department.

28.2 Manpower by Assignment—Version 2: The graphic showing the total number of employees is segmented to display the portions assigned to each of several facilities in Version 2 of a manpower by assignment tracking chart, Figure 28.2. In this example, which covers a five-year time span, historical performance (actuals versus plans) is not shown.

28.3 Manpower by Assignment—Version 3: A display of direct labor in relationship to product line assignments (could be "projects") is shown as Version 3 of a manpower by assignment tracking chart, Figure 28.3. Actuals on this example are shown with solid lines. The forecast is shown with dashed lines.

28.4 Manpower by Assignment—Version 4: A step line chart style is used for Version 4 of a manpower by assignment tracking chart, Figure 28.4. A solid line is used to show total actuals to date. Circled numbers represent the monthly quantity for each segment of the total. Numbers to the right of the time-now line represent planned manpower. Numbers to the left of the time-now line represent actual manpower.

28.5 Manpower by Assignment—Version 5: Dashed step lines are used in Version 5 of a manpower by assignment chart, Figure 28.5, to show forecasted direct labor requirements by product line. Actual head count to date is shown for each month with segmented columns.

28.6 Manpower by Assignment—Version 6: Grouped columns are used in Version 6 of a manpower by assignment tracking chart, Figure 28.6. Shaded columns show the head count, by job classification, for each month. Narrow solid columns are used to show actuals for each classification.

28.7 Manpower by Assignment—Version 7: Segmented surface chart and column chart styles are combined in Version 7 of a manpower by assignment tracking chart, Figure 28.7. Planned direct manpower requirements for existing and anticipated business is shown by quarters. A segmented column is used to show actuals to date.

28.8 Manpower by Assignment—Version 8: The graphic portion of Version 8 of a manpower by assignment tracking chart,

Figure 28.8, gives the budget, actuals, and current estimate for total direct manpower. The tabular portion of the chart gives the actual statistics broken down by department.

28.9 Manpower by Assignment—Version 9: The graphic portion of Version 9 of a manpower by assignment tracking chart, Figure 28.9, shows the total number of personnel in terms of planned versus actuals. The actuals are also shown broken down by department. The tabular portion of the chart gives the backup statistics for the graphic portion, plus variance figures and the percent of overtime used. (Also see Section 36 titled *Overtime*.)

28.10 Manpower by Assignment—Version 10: A tabular form of a manpower by assignment tracking chart is shown as Version 10, Figure 28.10. In this example, the budgeted and actual head count is given by department, the total summed at the bottom.

28.11 Manpower by Assignment—Version 11: Direct manpower by project is shown in tabular form in Version 11 of a manpower by assignment chart, Figure 28.11. Statistics are given representing the quarterly head count for each project, and that as a percent of the total for the quarter. In this version, only the actuals, rather than actuals plus original forecast, are given for the period, or periods, up to the reporting date.

28.12 Manpower by Assignment—Version 12: A statistical table is used as Version 12 of a manpower by assignment chart, Figure 28.12. This version of a one-time status report shows planned, actual, and variance labor hours, by function, for the current reporting month and the year to date. Statistics are also given as to the planned and estimated number of labor hours that will be needed to complete the project.

28.13 Manpower by Assignment—Version 13: The one-time status report version of a manpower by assignment chart, Figure 28.13, utilizes graphics to portray the percentage that manning has been accomplished according to the plan. The right-hand side of the chart presents the statistics for planned and actual manning, the total broken down as to direct and indirect.

28.14 Manpower by Assignment—Version 14: A matrix format is used as Version 14 of a manpower by assignment chart, Figure 28.14. The quantity of planned and actual personnel for one point in time is shown by organization unit (left-hand vertical register) and job classification (top horizontal register). The most significant problem in this example has been circled.

28.15 Manpower by Assignment—Version 15: A one-time status report using segmented columns is shown as Version 15 of a manpower by assignment chart, Figure 28.15. The columns in this example, representing separate organization units, are segmented as to direct and indirect personnel.

28.16 Manpower by Assignment—Version 16: The personnel count covering a ten-year time span is displayed as Version 16 of a manpower by assignment chart, Figure 28.16. Each column in this example is segmented to show the proportions of administrative, manufacturing and support, and engineering personnel.

28.17 Manpower by Assignment—Version 17: An organization chart is used as the framework for displaying manpower figures in Version 17 of a manpower by assignment chart, Figure 28.17. This example shows the direct and indirect head count by organization unit for one point in time. A summary is shown as a footnote to the chart.

28.18 Manpower by Assignment—Version 18: Direct and indirect head count figures are shown for one point in time in the "pie" chart version of a manpower by assignment chart, Figure 28.18. The circle in this example is segmented to show manpower in terms of organization unit.

28.19 Manpower by Assignment—Version 19: The location and number of repairmen are shown on the map format used as Version 19 of a manpower by assignment chart, Figure 28.19.

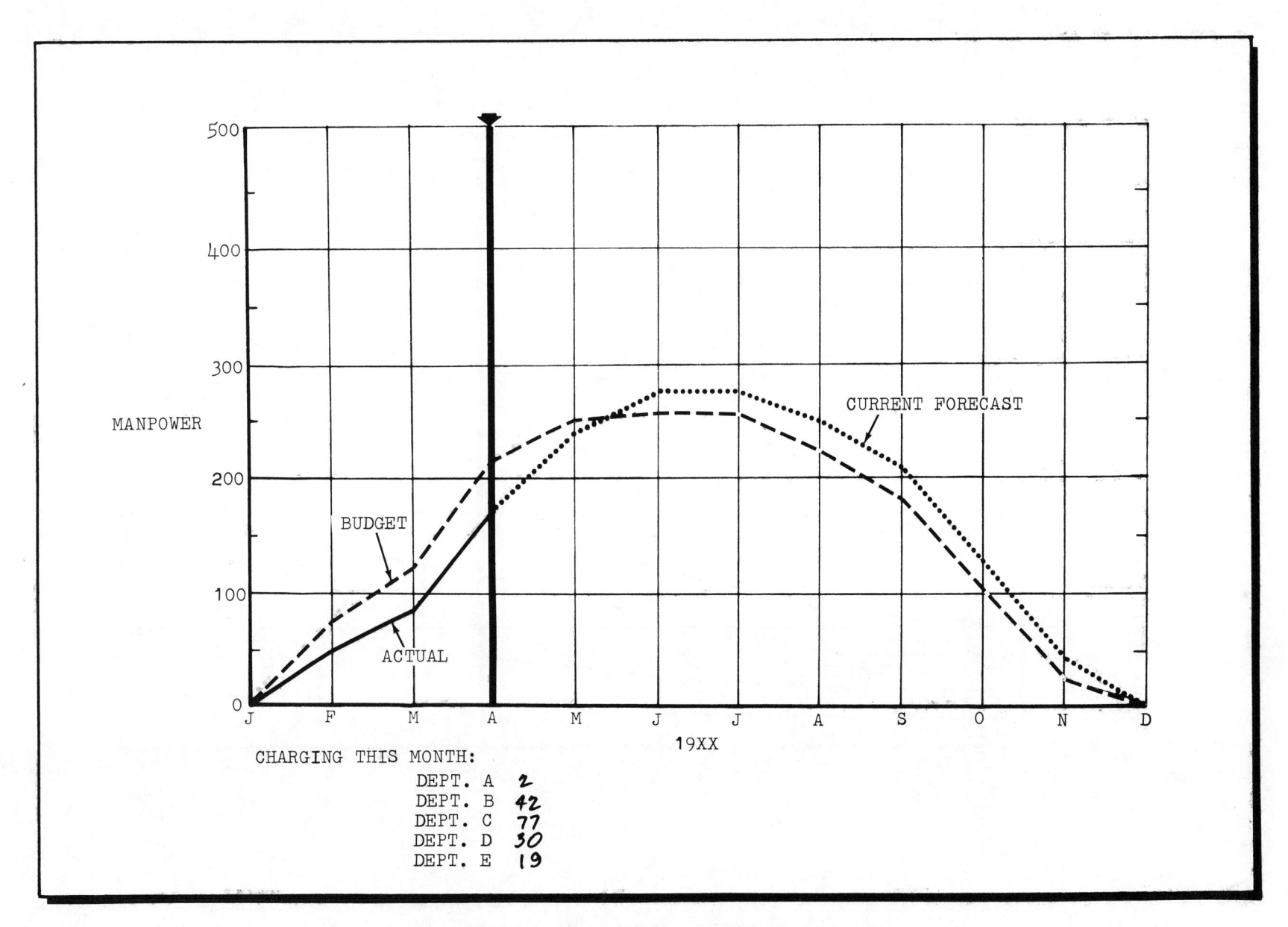

Figure 28.1   Manpower by Assignment—Version 1

305

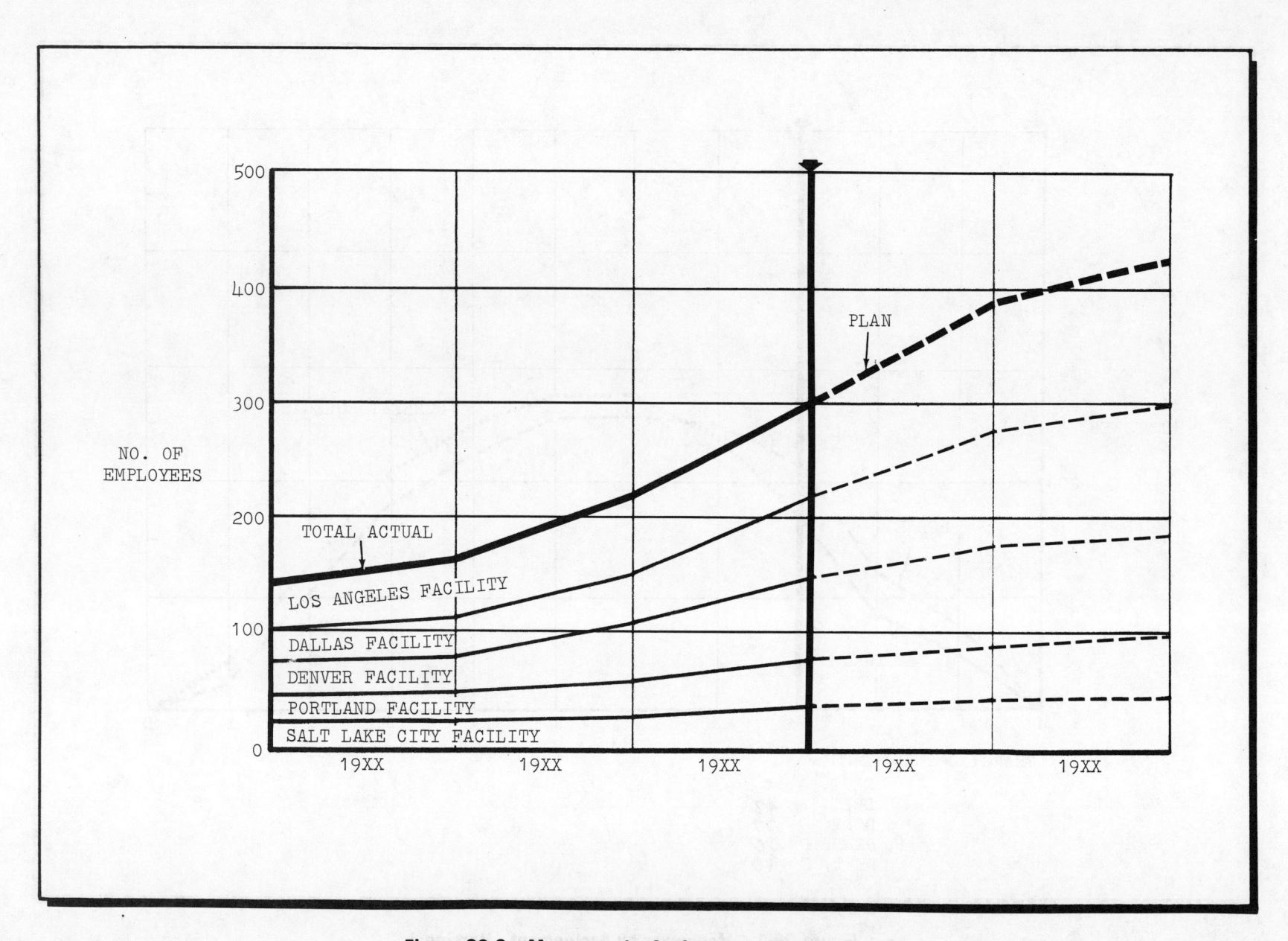

Figure 28.2 Manpower by Assignment—Version 2

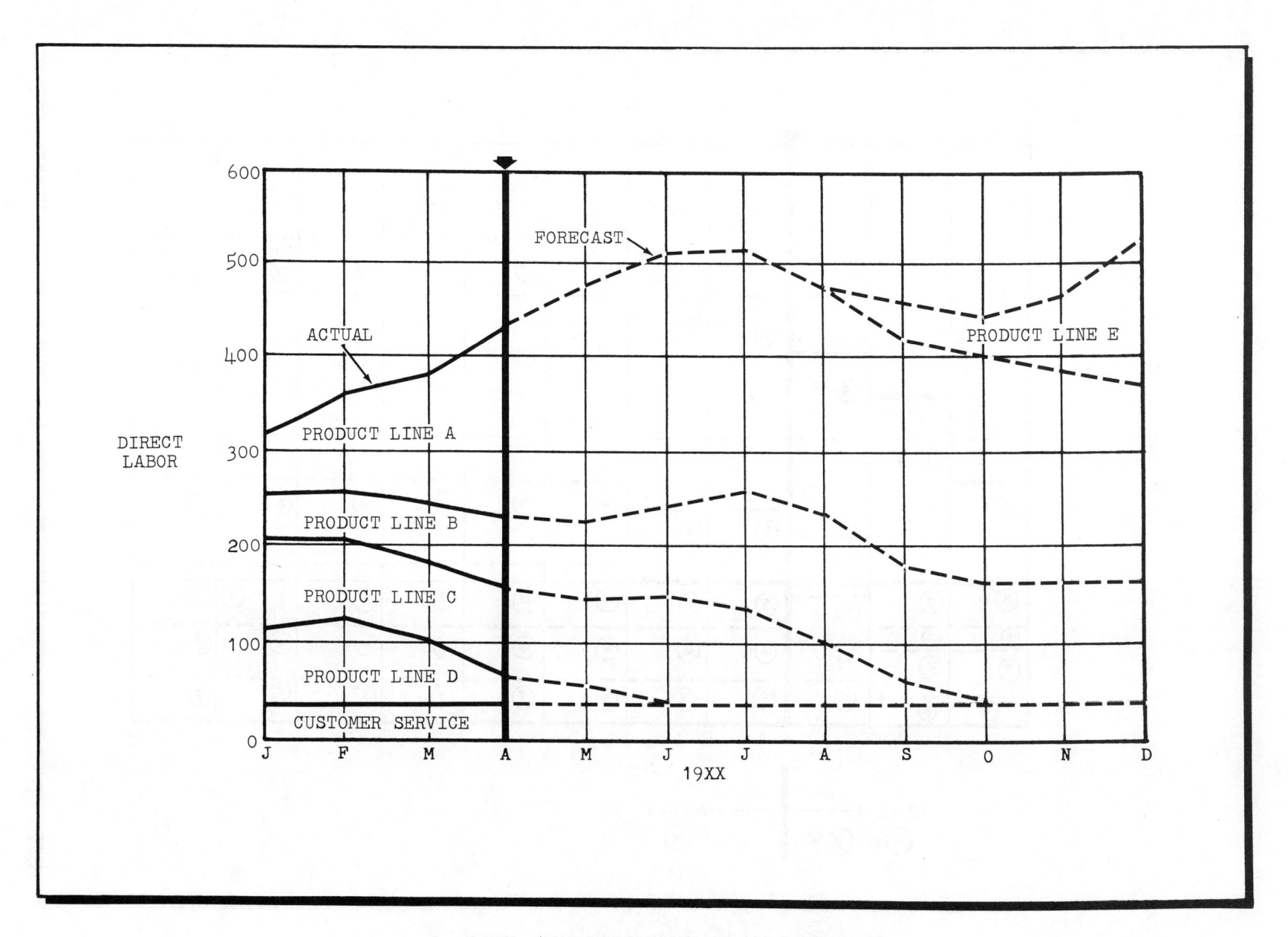

Figure 28.3 Manpower by Assignment—Version 3

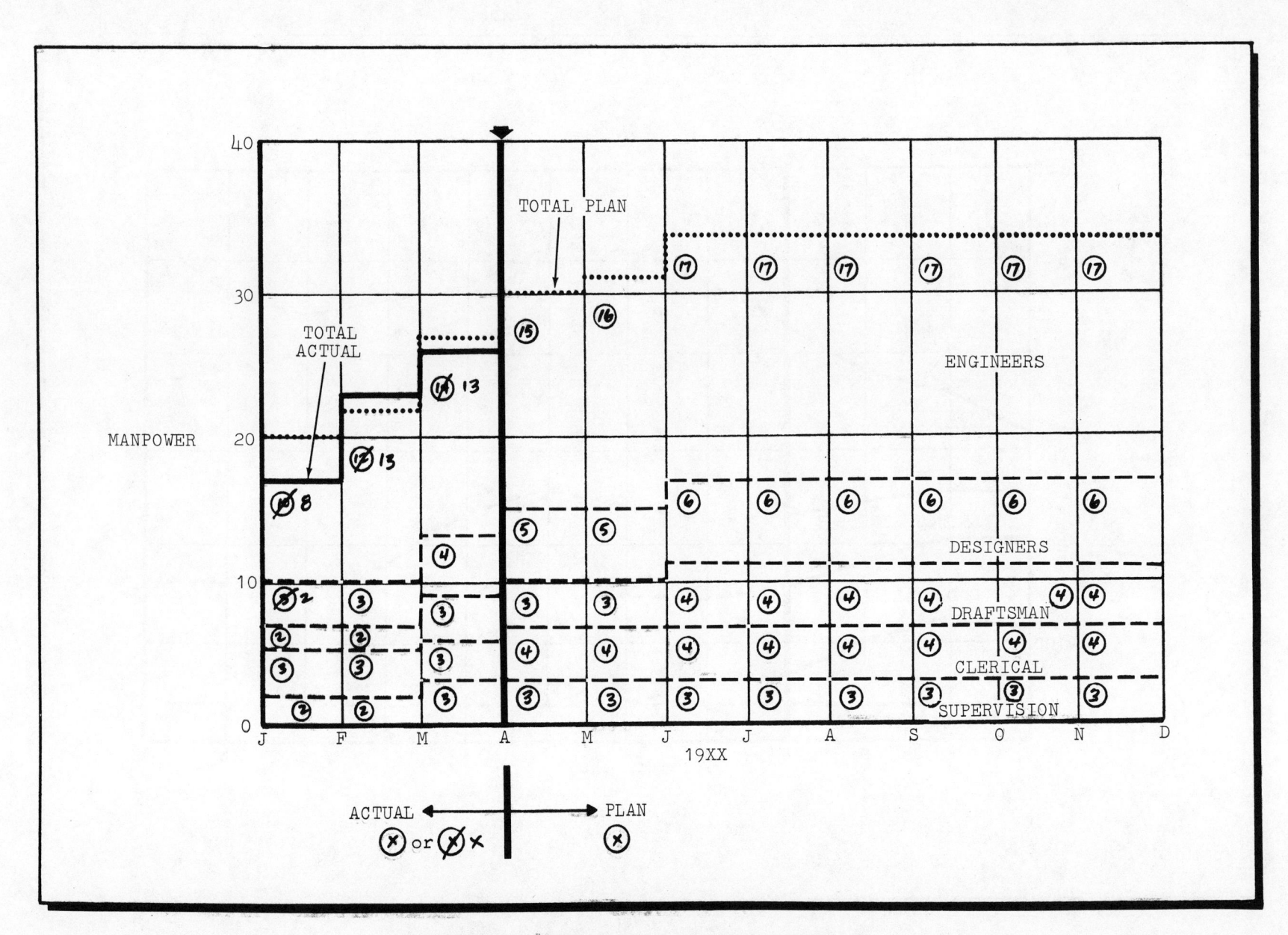

Figure 28.4 Manpower by Assignment—Version 4

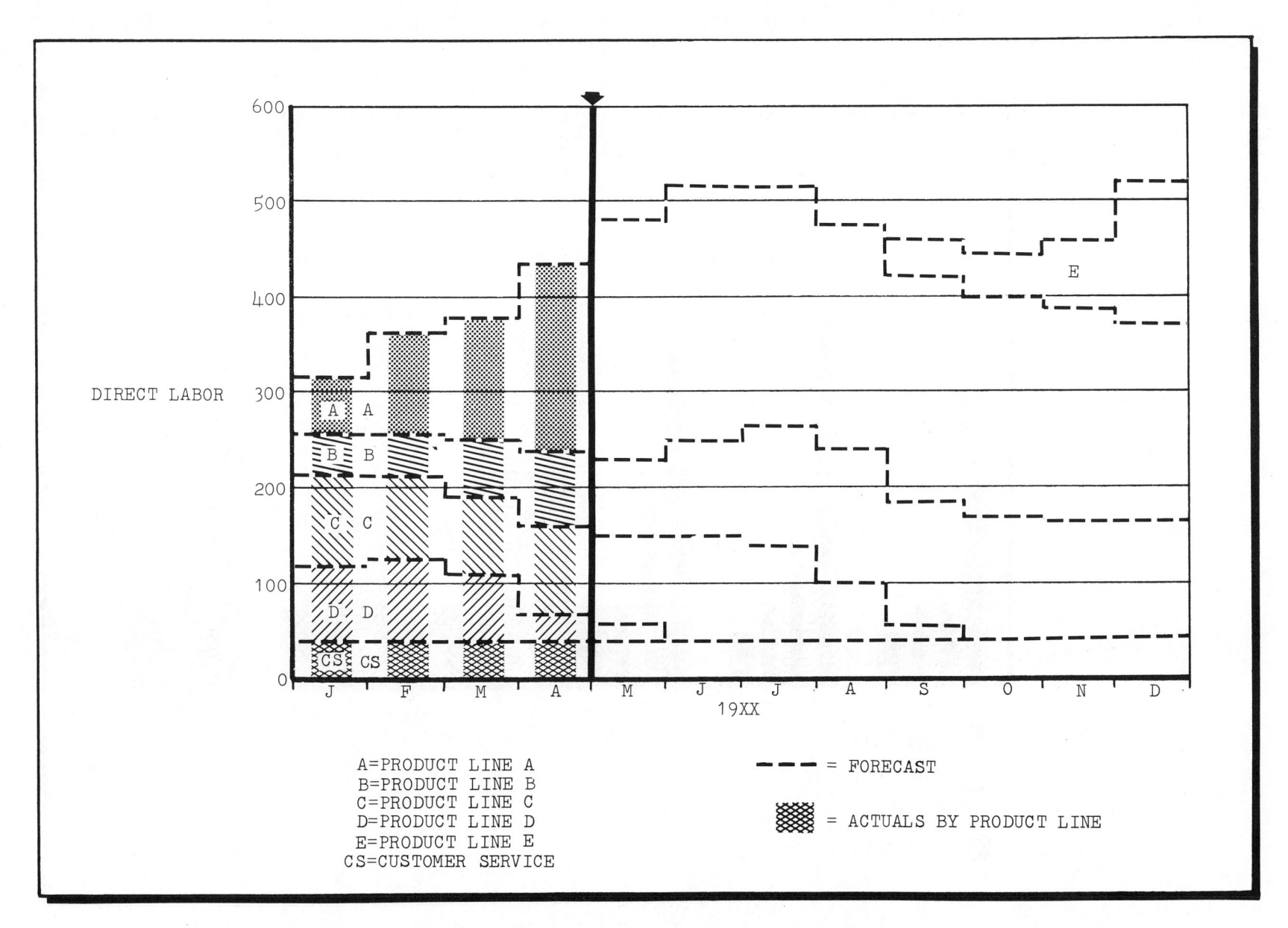

Figure 28.5 Manpower by Assignment—Version 5

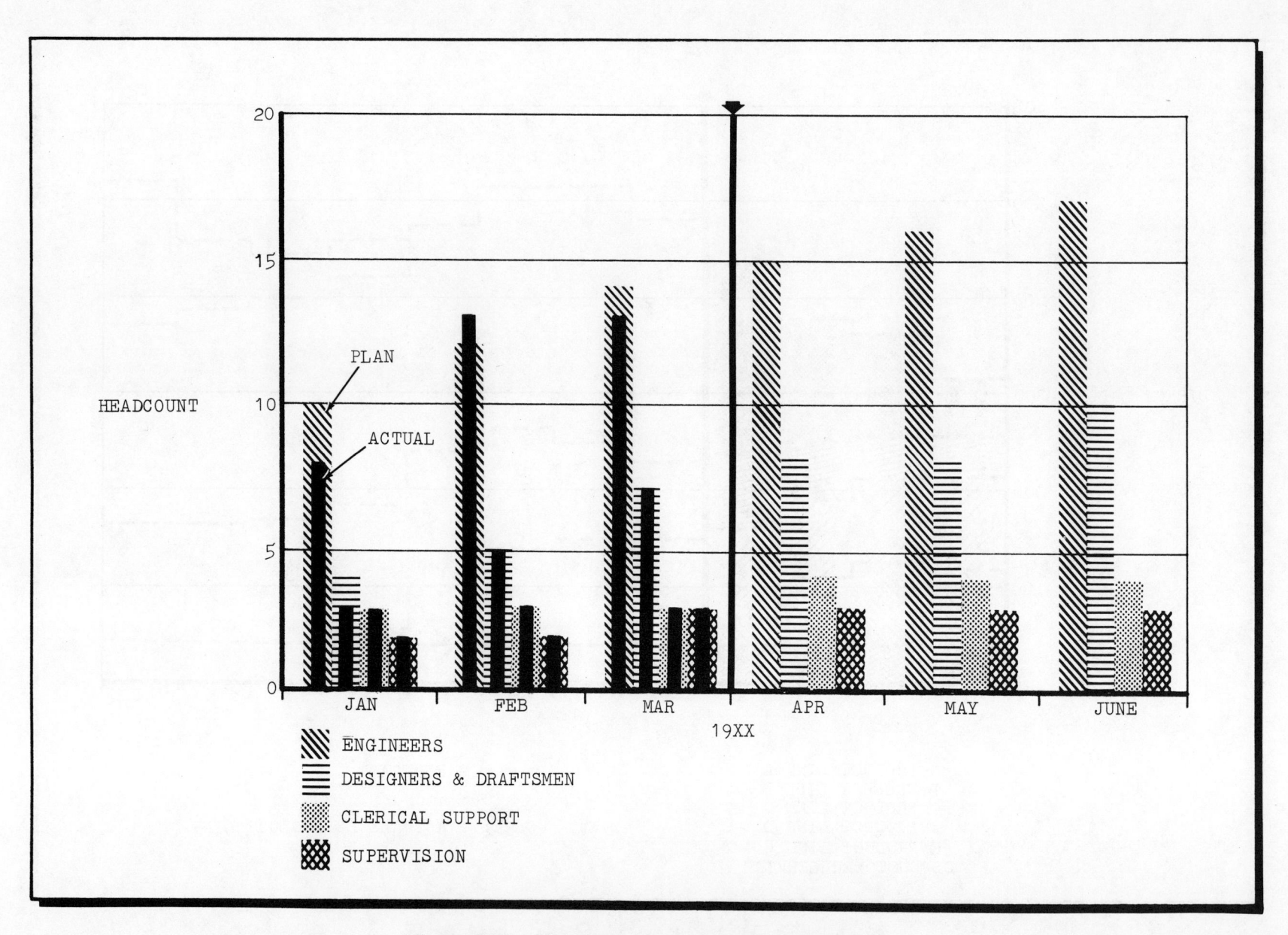

Figure 28.6 Manpower by Assignment—Version 6

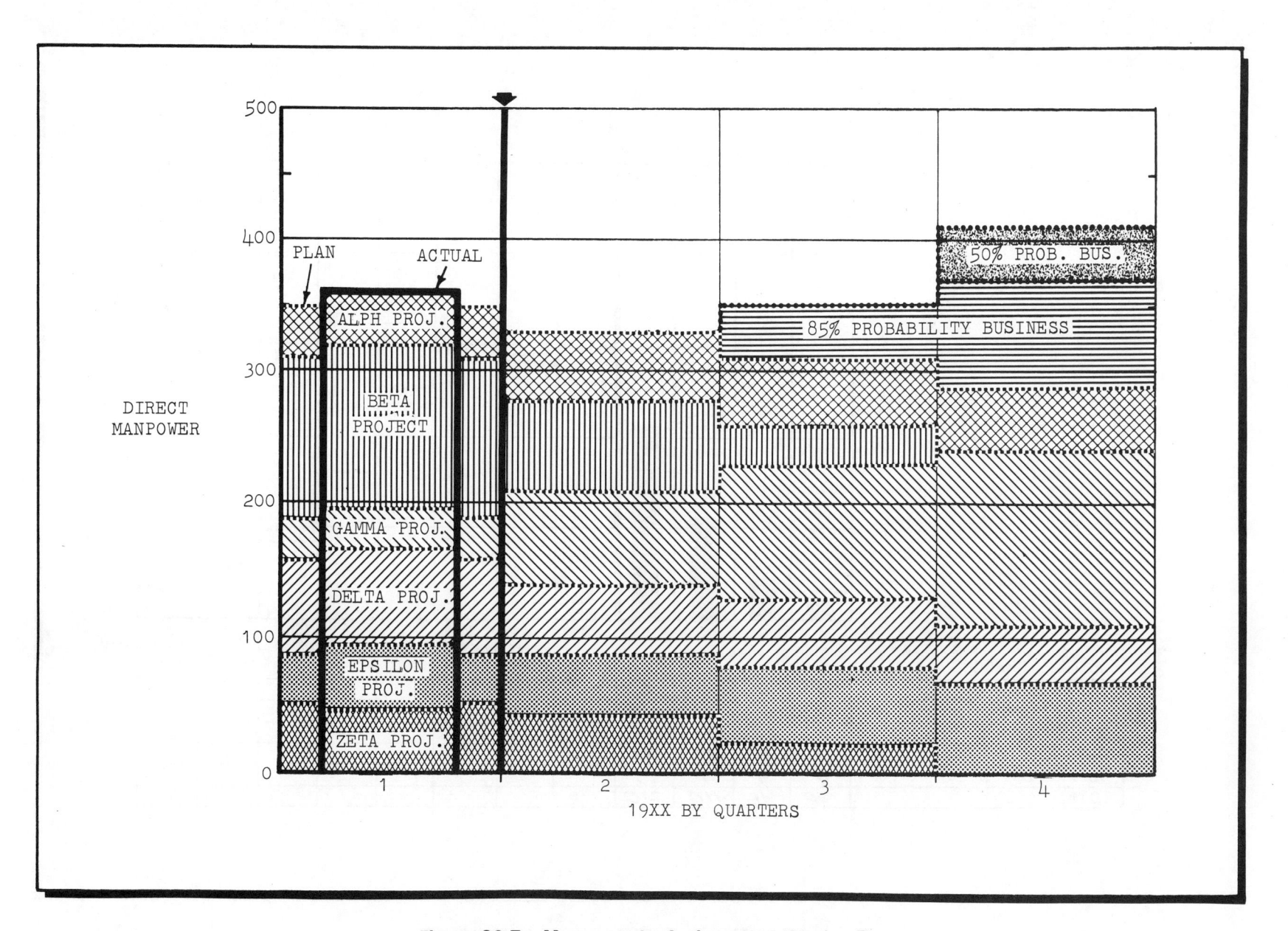

Figure 28.7 Manpower by Assignment—Version 7

DIRECT MANPOWER

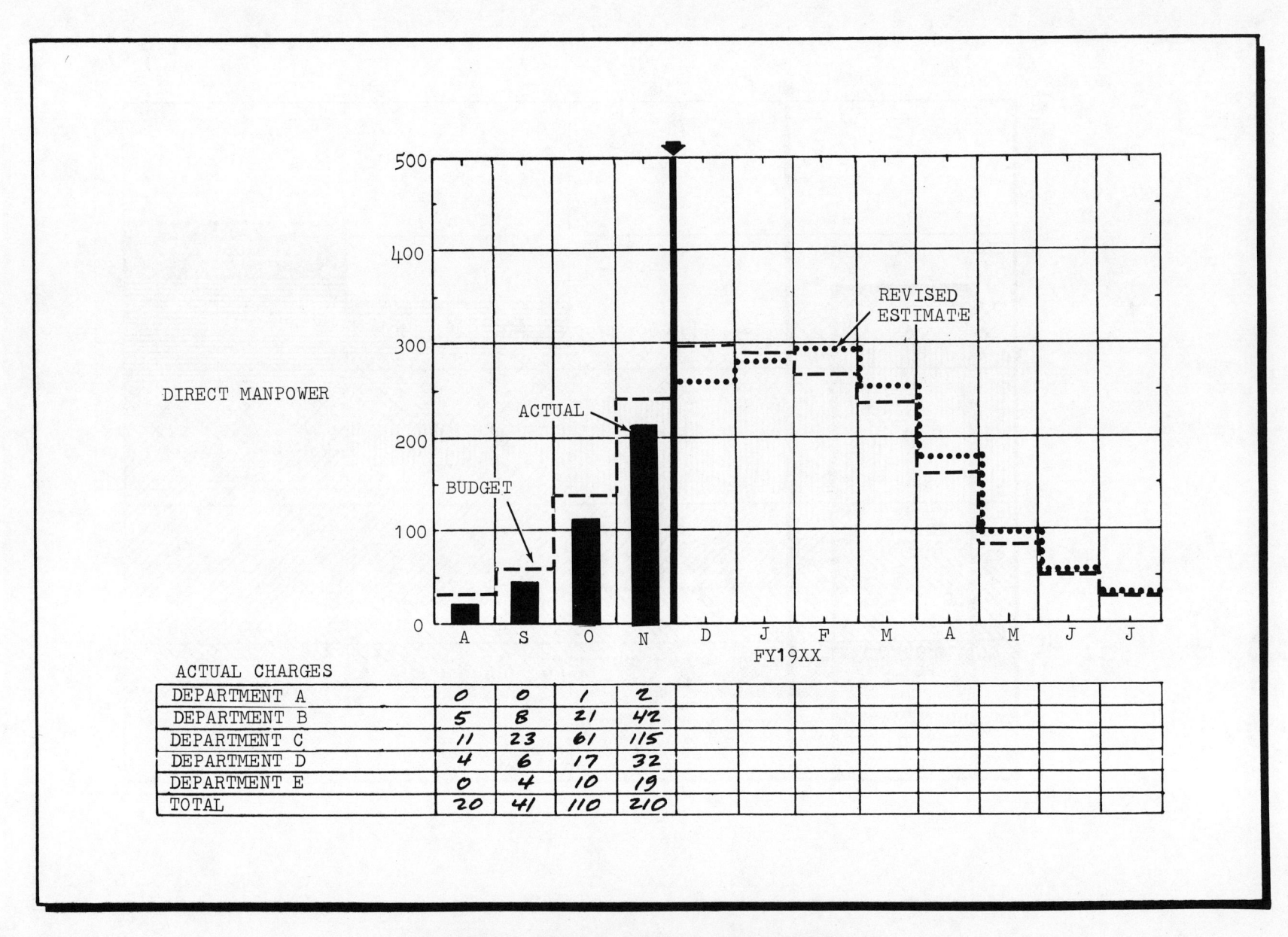

ACTUAL CHARGES												
DEPARTMENT A	0	0	1	2								
DEPARTMENT B	5	8	21	42								
DEPARTMENT C	11	23	61	115								
DEPARTMENT D	4	6	17	32								
DEPARTMENT E	0	4	10	19								
TOTAL	20	41	110	210								

Figure 28.8 Manpower by Assignment—Version 8

312

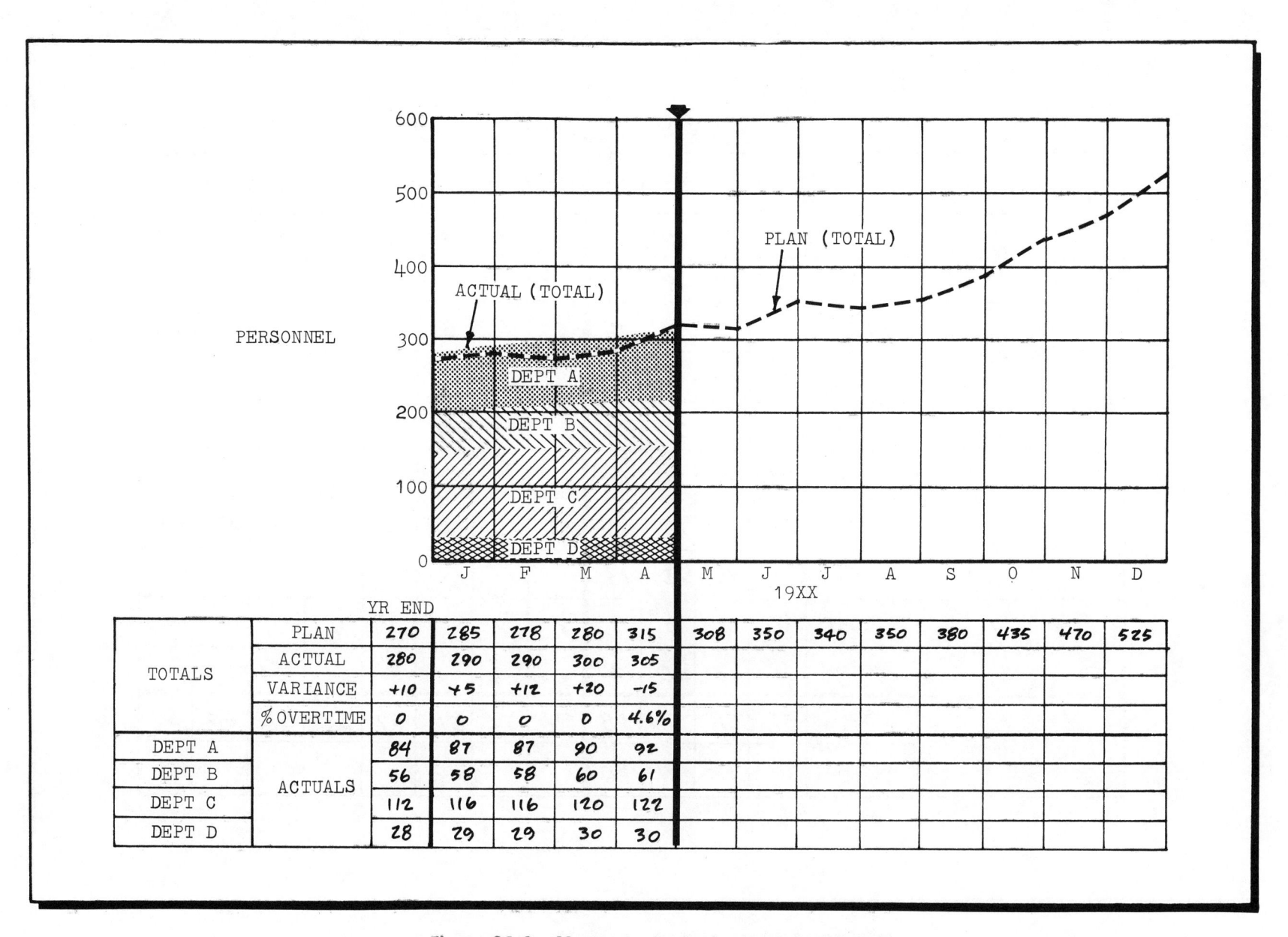

		YR END												
TOTALS	PLAN	270	285	278	280	315	308	350	340	350	380	435	470	525
	ACTUAL	280	290	290	300	305								
	VARIANCE	+10	+5	+12	+20	-15								
	% OVERTIME	0	0	0	0	4.6%								
DEPT A	ACTUALS	84	87	87	90	92								
DEPT B		56	58	58	60	61								
DEPT C		112	116	116	120	122								
DEPT D		28	29	29	30	30								

Figure 28.9 Manpower by Assignment—Version 9

HEADCOUNT BY DEPARTMENT		19XX											
		J	F	M	A	M	J	J	A	S	O	N	D
DEPT 100	BUDGET	10	10	10	9	8	7	7	8	9	10	11	11
	ACTUAL	8	9	9	9								
DEPT 200	BUDGET	5	5	5	5	5	5	5	5	5	5	5	5
	ACTUAL	4	4	5	5								
DEPT 300	BUDGET	21	21	22	22	21	20	19	19	20	21	22	22
	ACTUAL	25	24	24	24								
DEPT 400	BUDGET	13	13	13	13	12	12	12	12	13	13	13	13
	ACTUAL	13	13	13	13								
DEPT 500	BUDGET	9	9	9	9	8	8	8	8	9	9	9	9
	ACTUAL	11	10	10	9								
TOTAL	BUDGET	58	58	59	58	54	52	51	52	56	58	60	60
	ACTUAL	61	60	61	60								

Figure 28.10 Manpower by Assignment—Version 10

	DIRECT MANPOWER 19XX							
PROJECT	1ST QUARTER		2ND QUARTER		3RD QUARTER		4TH QUARTER	
	HEADCOUNT	%	HEADCOUNT	%	HEADCOUNT	%	HEADCOUNT	%
ALPHA	38	10.6	50	15.2	50	14.3	50	12.2
BETA	122	34.1	70	21.2	30	8.6	0	0
GAMMA	30	8.4	70	21.2	100	28.6	130	31.7
DELTA	72	20.1	50	15.2	50	14.3	40.	9.8
EPSILON	50	14.0	50	15.2	60	17.1	70	17.0
ZETA	46	12.8	40	12.0	20	5.7	0	0
TOTAL-FIRM BUS.	358	100.0%	330	100.0%	310	88.6%	290	70.7%
85% PROBABLE	0	0	0	0	40	11.4	80	19.5
50% PROBABLE	0	0	0	0	0	0	40	9.8
TOTAL	358	100.0%	330	100.0%	350	100.0%	410	100.0%

ACTUAL ←→ FORECAST

Figure 28.11　Manpower by Assignment—Version 11

STATUS AS OF _____

FUNCTION	LABOR HOURS								
	THIS MONTH			PROJECT TO DATE			EST AT COMPLETION		
	PLAN	ACTUAL	VAR	PLAN	ACTUAL	VAR	PLAN	EST.ACT	EST.VAR
ENGINEERING DESIGN	510	480	-30	3570	3450	-120	5610	5500	-110
PROTOTYPE FABRICATION	860	910	+50	4300	4870	+570	6020	7000	+980
PROTOTYPE ASSEMBLY	774	780	+6	2322	2320	-2	3870	3870	0
UNIT TEST	258	275	+17	774	800	+26	1290	1350	+60
SYSTEM TEST	280	210	-70	560	500	-60	840	750	-90
PROJECT CONTROL	340	340	0	2380	2380	0	3740	3740	0
TOTAL	3022	2995	-27	13906	14320	+414	21370	22210	+840

Figure 28.12 Manpower by Assignment—Version 12

STATUS AS OF ____________

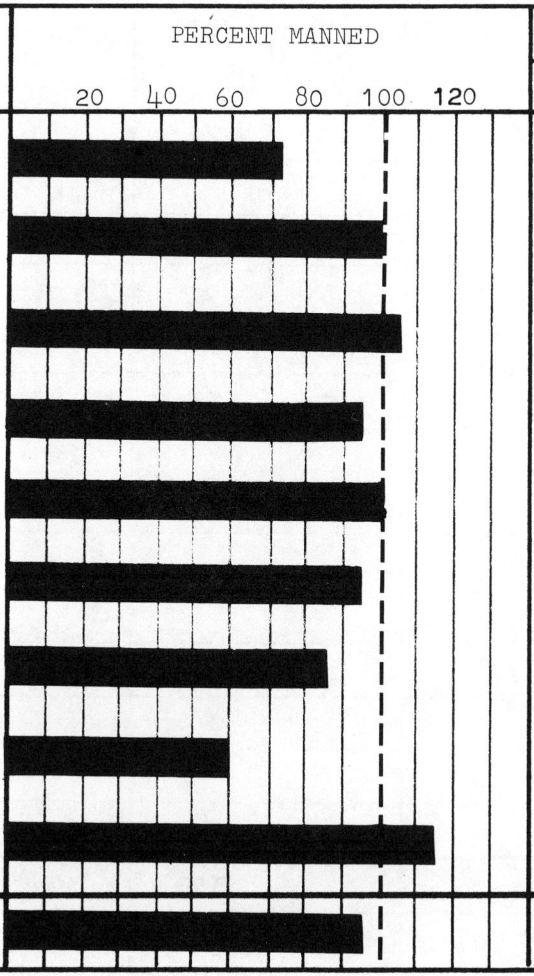

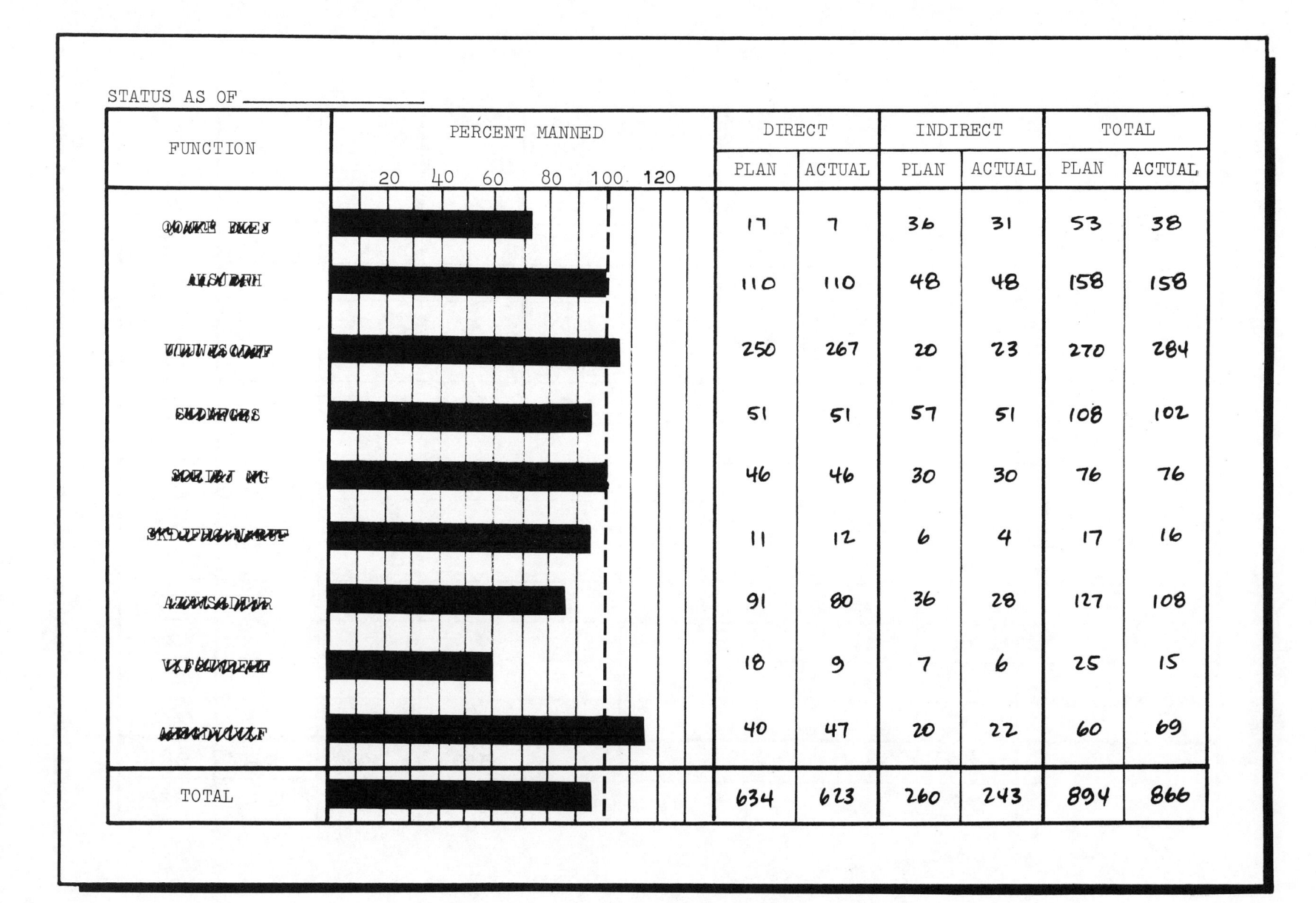

PERCENT MANNED
20
40
60
80
100
120

FUNCTION	DIRECT PLAN	DIRECT ACTUAL	INDIRECT PLAN	INDIRECT ACTUAL	TOTAL PLAN	TOTAL ACTUAL
[illegible]	17	7	36	31	53	38
[illegible]	110	110	48	48	158	158
[illegible]	250	267	20	23	270	284
[illegible]	51	51	57	51	108	102
[illegible]	46	46	30	30	76	76
[illegible]	11	12	6	4	17	16
[illegible]	91	80	36	28	127	108
[illegible]	18	9	7	6	25	15
[illegible]	40	47	20	22	60	69
TOTAL	634	623	260	243	894	866

Figure 28.13 Manpower by Assignment—Version 13

STATUS AS OF _____

ORGANIZATION / CLASSIFICATION	P/A	MANAGEMENT	OFFICE & CLERICAL	SC'NTISTS & RESEARCH ENG'RS	DSNERS & DRFTSMEN	TOOL MAKERS & MACH'NSTS	FABS & ASSMBLRS	QUAL & TEST ENG'RS	LABORERS	TOTAL
GENERAL MANAGER AND STAFF	P	4	6							10
GENERAL MANAGER AND STAFF	A	4	6							10
ENGINEERING	P	23	43	37	115		26	11		255
ENGINEERING	A	22	42	29	116		27	10		246
MANUFACTURING	P	32	58			17	283		4	394
MANUFACTURING	A	31	56			15	281		4	387
QUALITY CONTROL	P	4	11	1				28		44
QUALITY CONTROL	A	4	10	1				29		44
FINANCE	P	5	29							34
FINANCE	A	5	28							33
SALES	P	4	25							29
SALES	A	4	23							27
ADMINISTRATION	P	16	182							216
ADMINISTRATION	A	15	178							211
TOTAL	P	88	354	38	115	17	309	39	22	982
TOTAL	A	85	343	30	116	15	308	39	22	958

P = PLAN
A = ACTUAL

Figure 28.14 Manpower by Assignment—Version 14

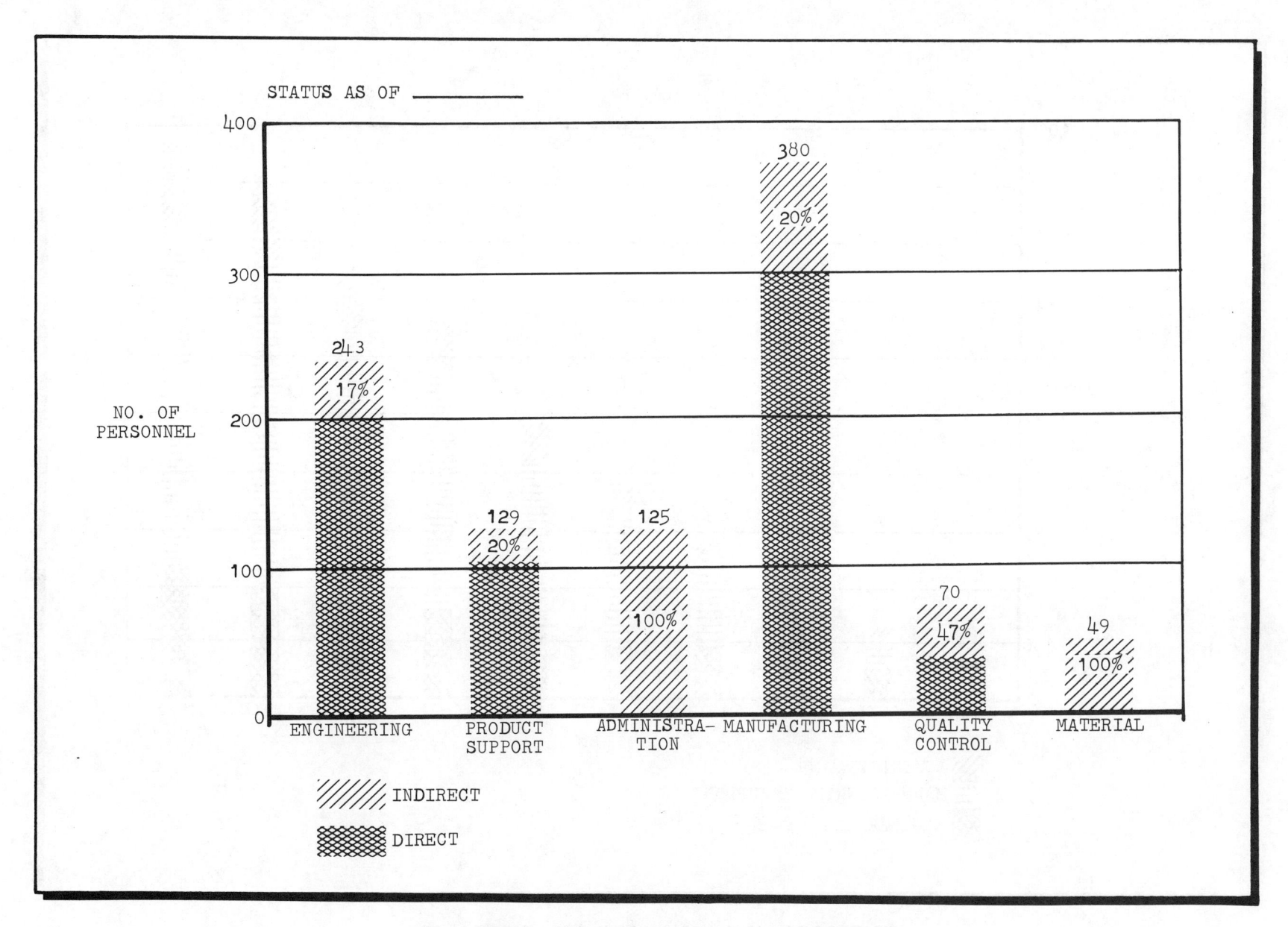

Figure 28.15 Manpower by Assignment—Version 15

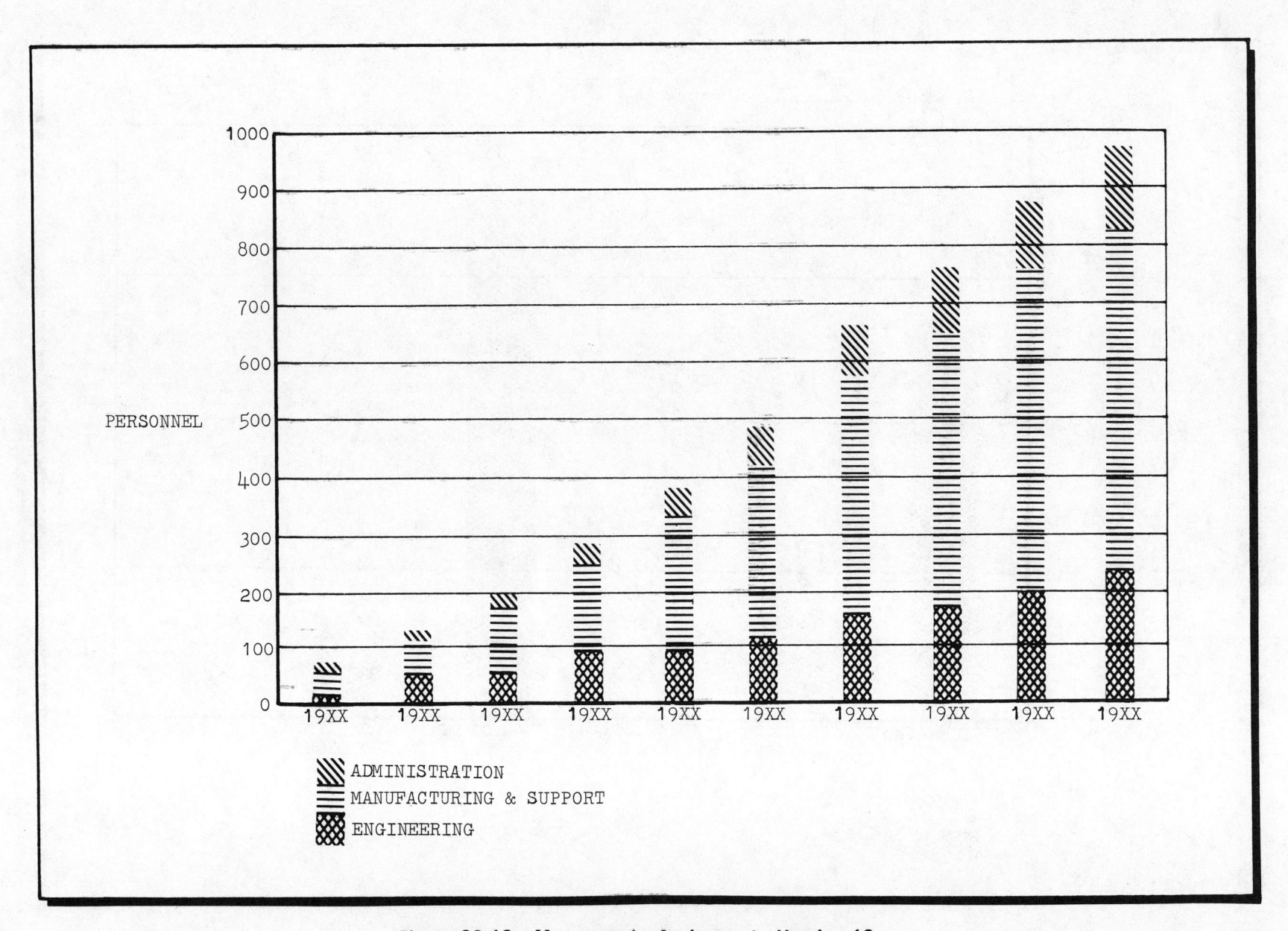

Figure 28.16 Manpower by Assignment—Version 16

MANPOWER STATUS AS OF _____

```
                    ┌─────────────────┐
                    │ GENERAL MANAGER │
                    ├─────────────────┤
                    │ 0 DIRECT        │
                    │ 3 INDIRECT      │
                    └─────────────────┘
```

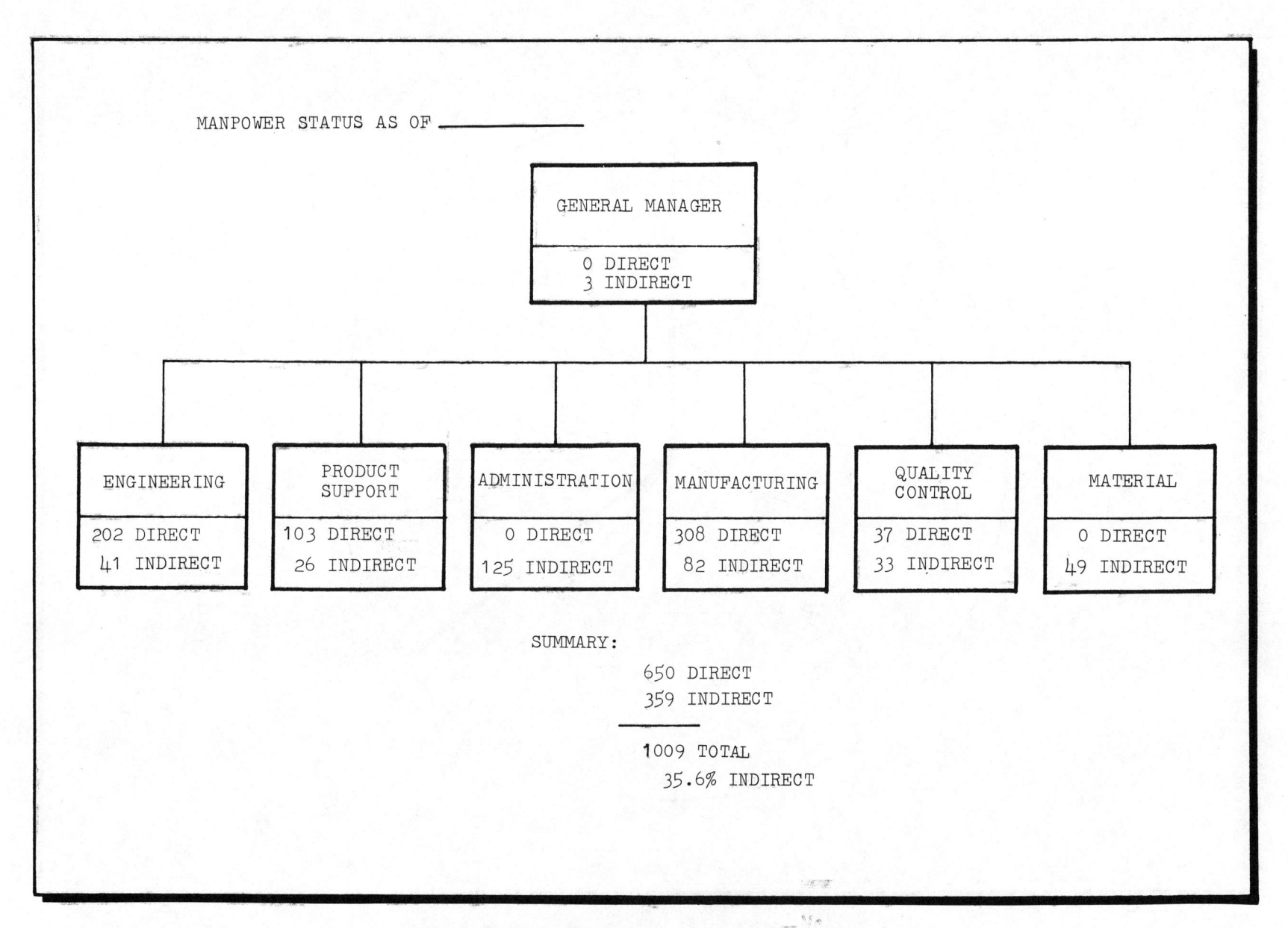

ENGINEERING	PRODUCT SUPPORT	ADMINISTRATION	MANUFACTURING	QUALITY CONTROL	MATERIAL
202 DIRECT	103 DIRECT	0 DIRECT	308 DIRECT	37 DIRECT	0 DIRECT
41 INDIRECT	26 INDIRECT	125 INDIRECT	82 INDIRECT	33 INDIRECT	49 INDIRECT

SUMMARY:

    650 DIRECT
    359 INDIRECT
    ―――――
    1009 TOTAL
    35.6% INDIRECT

Figure 28.17   Manpower by Assignment—Version 17

DIRECT 64.8% | INDIRECT 35.2%

ENGINEERING
202

MANAGEMENT &
ADMINISTRATION
215

PRODUCT SUPPORT
103

FINANCE
37

SALES
28

PERSONNEL 22

MATERIAL
49

MANUFACTURING
303

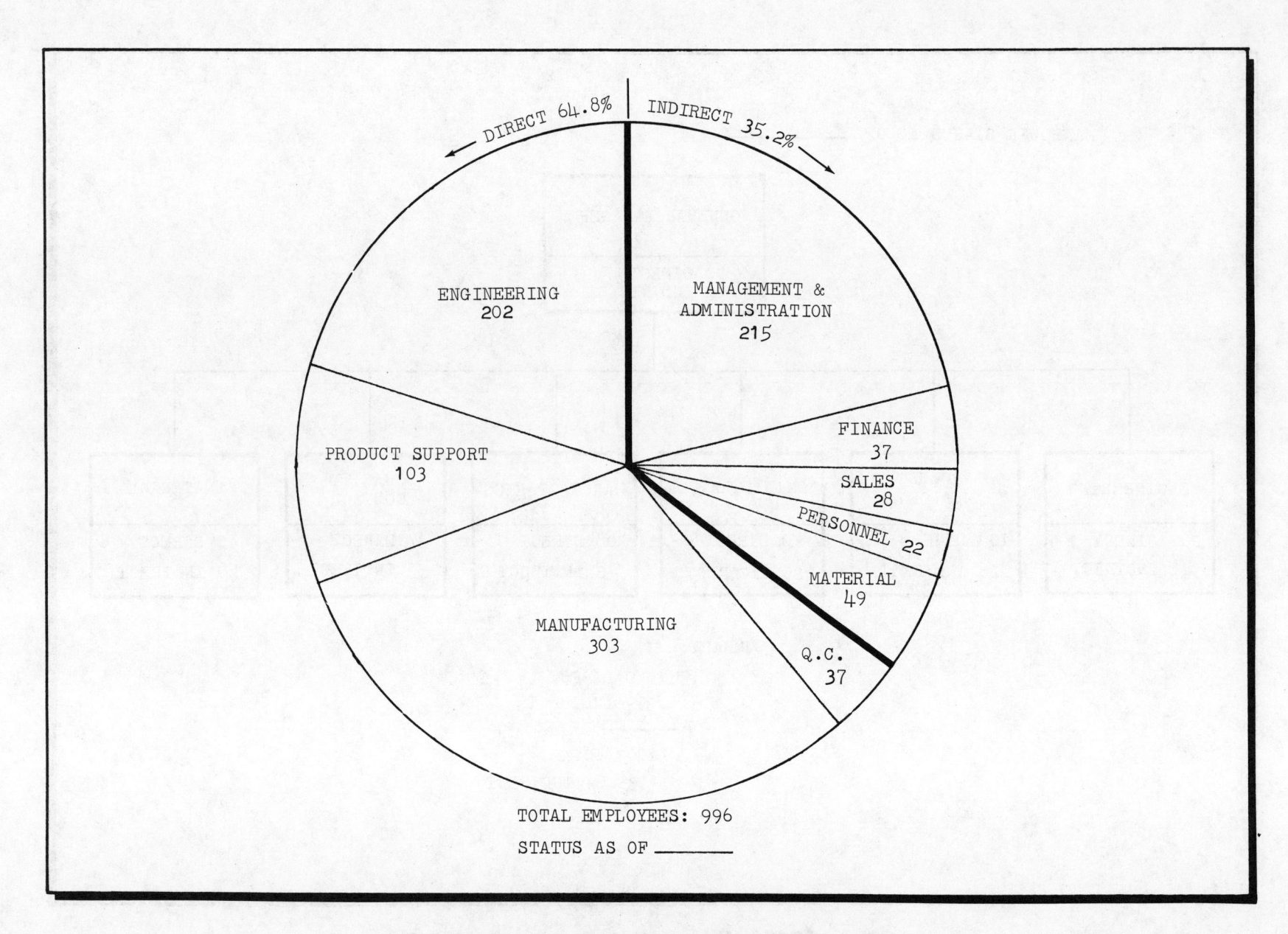

Q.C.
37

TOTAL EMPLOYEES: 996
STATUS AS OF _____

Figure 28.18   Manpower by Assignment—Version 18

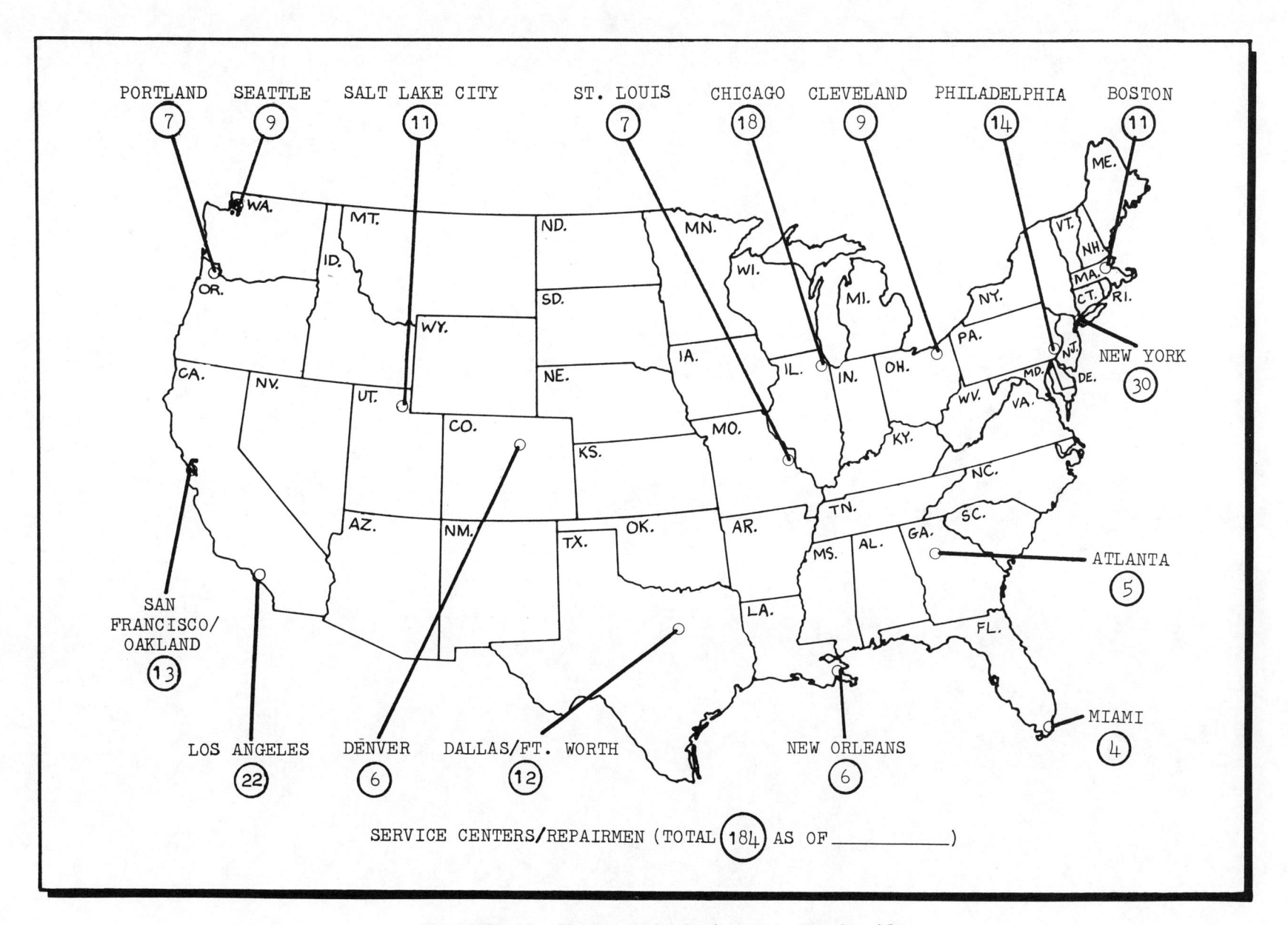

PORTLAND (7) SEATTLE (9) SALT LAKE CITY (11) ST. LOUIS (7) CHICAGO (18) CLEVELAND (9) PHILADELPHIA (14) BOSTON (11)

NEW YORK (30)

ATLANTA (5)

MIAMI (4)

SAN FRANCISCO/OAKLAND (13)

LOS ANGELES (22) DENVER (6) DALLAS/FT. WORTH (12) NEW ORLEANS (6)

SERVICE CENTERS/REPAIRMEN (TOTAL (184) AS OF _____)

Figure 28.19   Manpower by Assignment—Version 19

29.0 MANPOWER BY EXPERIENCE

Charts that show manpower in terms of experience are covered in this section. The subject matter of *experience* does not lend itself well to tracking type formats. Also see manpower sections 27.0, 28.0, and 30.0 through 32.0.

29.1 Manpower by Experience—Version 1: Version 1 of a manpower by experience chart, Figure 29.1, is a frequency distribution style of chart. The distribution of the number of employees in relation to years of service is shown in step line form.

This chart could be augmented by adding, in call-out or note form, the central tendencies: mode, mean, and median.

29.2 Manpower by Experience—Version 2: The average years of experience of employees, by discipline, are shown in Version 2 of a manpower by experience chart, Figure 29.2. The number and type of advanced degrees are also given, in note form, in this example. As with Version 1, this example is a non-tracking style of chart, showing status for one point in time.

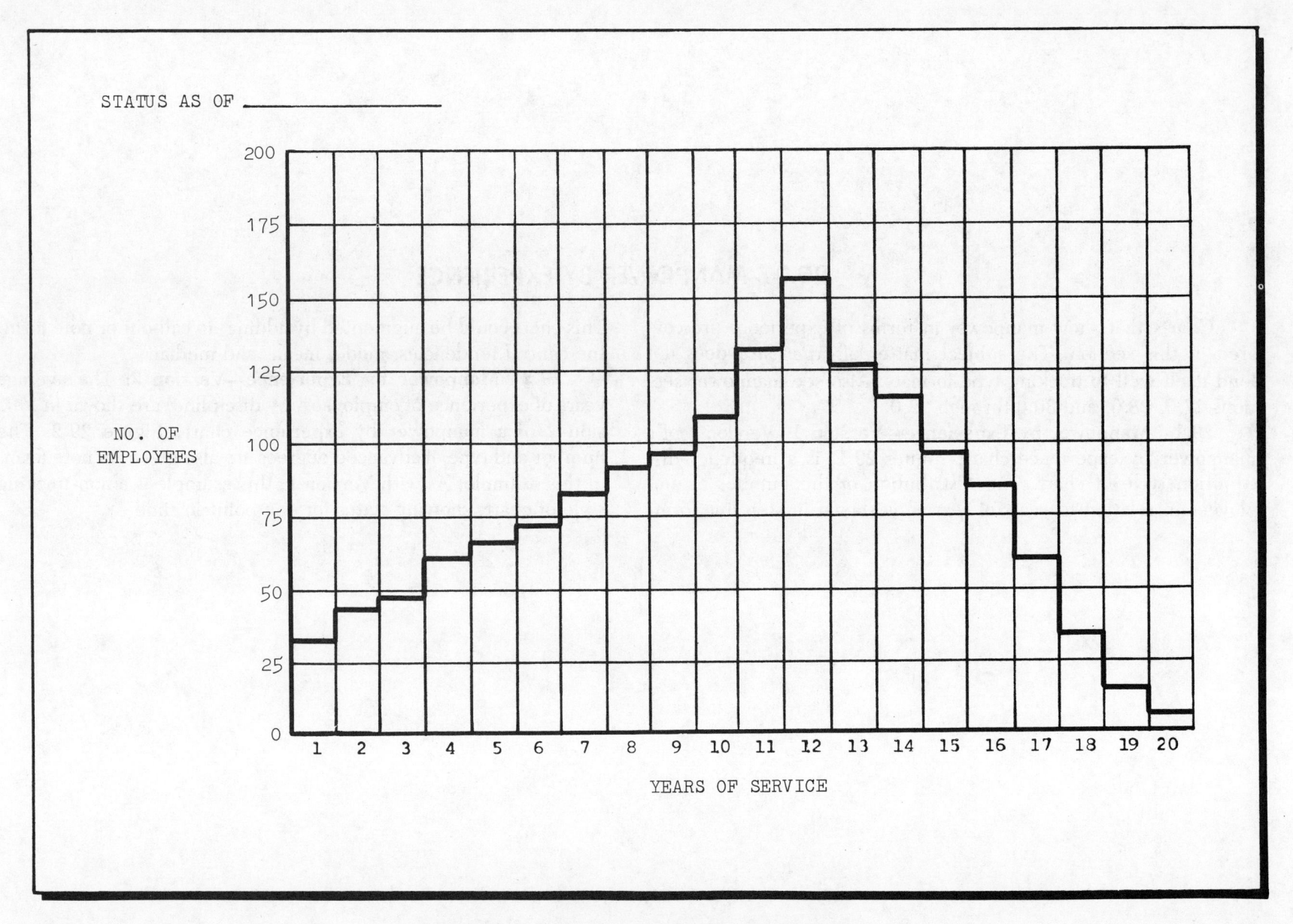

Figure 29.1   Manpower by Experience—Version 1

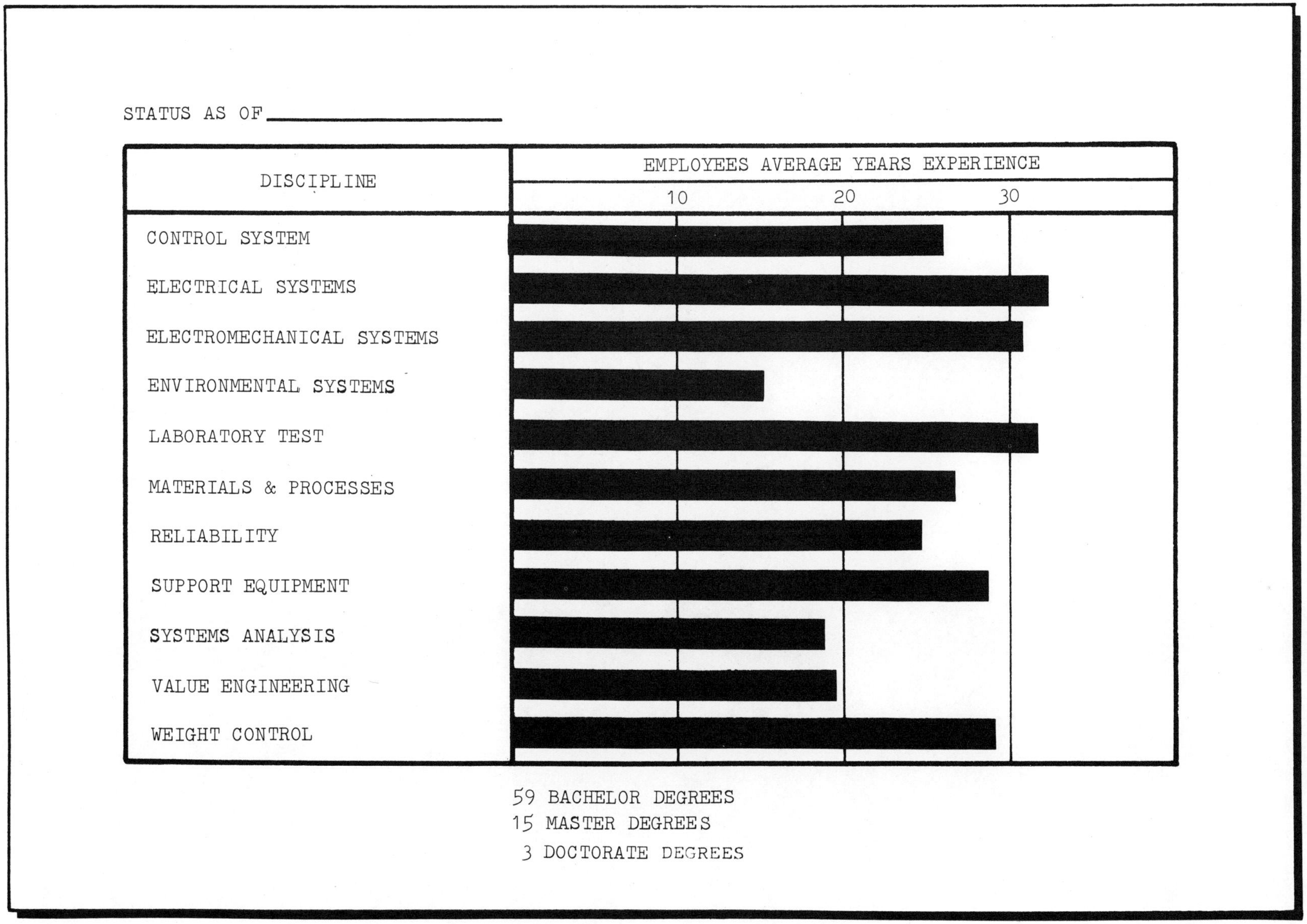

STATUS AS OF _____

DISCIPLINE	EMPLOYEES AVERAGE YEARS EXPERIENCE
	10　　　20　　　30
CONTROL SYSTEM	
ELECTRICAL SYSTEMS	
ELECTROMECHANICAL SYSTEMS	
ENVIRONMENTAL SYSTEMS	
LABORATORY TEST	
MATERIALS & PROCESSES	
RELIABILITY	
SUPPORT EQUIPMENT	
SYSTEMS ANALYSIS	
VALUE ENGINEERING	
WEIGHT CONTROL	

59 BACHELOR DEGREES
15 MASTER DEGREES
3 DOCTORATE DEGREES

Figure 29.2　Manpower by Experience—Version 2

30.0 MANPOWER SUMMARIES

Charts that display various aspects of manpower (personnel, employees, man-hours, head count, etc.), usually in relationship to a plan, or budget, or forecast, or authorized level, are shown in this section. Also see manpower sections 27.0 through 29.0, and 31.0 and 32.0. For labor hours in terms of dollars, see Section 3.0, *Budget–Detail*.

30.1 Manpower Summary—Version 1: A simple version of a manpower summary tracking chart is shown as Version 1, Figure 30.1. The authorized level for personnel head count is shown with a dashed line. Actual head count to date is shown with a solid line.

30.2 Manpower Summary—Version 2: Column and step line chart styles have been combined in Version 2 of a manpower summary tracking chart, Figure 30.2. A dashed step line shows the authorized level of manpower. The solid columns show actuals to date.

30.3 Manpower Summary—Version 3: A chart where man-hours are plotted on a cumulative basis is shown as Version 3 of a manpower summary tracking chart, Figure 30.3. The budget, in this example, is shown with a dashed line, and actuals to date are shown with a solid line. The delta on the right-hand side of the grid indicates the current estimated man-hours at completion.

30.4 Manpower Summary—Version 4: Changing conditions often dictate that an original plan be periodically examined and, if necessary, revised. Version 4 of a manpower summary tracking chart, Figure 30.4, displays the original manpower budget with a dashed line, actuals to date with a solid line, and the current revised estimate to complete with a dotted line.

30.5 Manpower Summary—Version 5: Version 5 of a manpower summary tracking chart, Figure 30.5, is similar to Version 4 except that shading has been added. In this example, the shading covers both the actuals to date and the revised estimate portion of the ensuing months. The disadvantage of this style of chart is that the application and reapplication of the shading for each new reporting date is a time-consuming task.

30.6 Manpower Summary—Version 6: Six years of employment activity can be seen on the format used as Version 6 of a manpower summary tracking chart, Figure 30.6. Actuals for the previous four years are seen on the left-hand grid. The center grid displays the forecast and the actuals for the current year, while the right-hand grid shows the forecast for the coming year by quarters.

30.7 Manpower Summary—Version 7: Total manpower, together with those portions of the total that are direct and indirect, are shown in Version 7 of a manpower summary tracking chart, Figure 30.7. The plans are shown with dashed lines. The direct and indirect manpower segments are shaded.

30.8 Manpower Summary—Version 8: Two separate grids are used in Version 8 of a manpower summary tracking chart, Figure 30.8. The left-hand grid displays the planned and actual number of direct changing employees. The right-hand grid shows the indirect.

30.9 Manpower Summary—Version 9: A format that can be used when manloading a small project with specific people is shown as Version 9 of a manpower summary tracking chart, Figure 30.9. Bars, each identified as to an individual, are plotted according to date. A solid, inverted delta indicates the actual start date, and shading shows the period when each individual is actually charging to the project.

30.10 Manpower Summary—Version 10: The graphic portion of Version 10 of a manpower summary tracking chart, Figure 30.10, shows the planned and actual number of indirect and total employees, by month. The table gives the ratio of indirect employees to the total.

30.11 Manpower Summary—Version 11: As with Version 10, statistics are combined with graphics in Version 11 of a manpower summary tracking chart, Figure 30.11. The actual and forecasted numbers of employees are plotted on the graph and are given in statistical form in the table, as well. The variance statistics are also given in the table.

30.12 Manpower Summary—Version 12: The tabular portion of Version 12 of a manpower summary tracking chart, Figure 20.12, lists man-hour statistics on both a per week and a cumulative basis. The graphic portion of the chart displays the budgeted and actual weekly figures.

30.13 Manpower Summary—Version 13: The number of forecasted and actual employees in terms of direct and indirect charging is shown in both graphic and tabular form in Version 13 of a manpower summary chart, Figure 30.13. The table also gives the percentage figures for the ratio of indirect to total employees for each month.

30.14 Manpower Summary—Version 14: The status report version of a manpower summary chart, Figure 30.14, can be used as a tracking chart by adding new figures and reversing the year-end estimate each month. Planned, actual, and variance man-hour statistics are given on both a monthly and year-to-date basis.

30.15 Manpower Summary—Version 15: A format that displays employment figures over a ten-year time span is shown as Version 15 of a manpower summary chart, Figure 30.15.

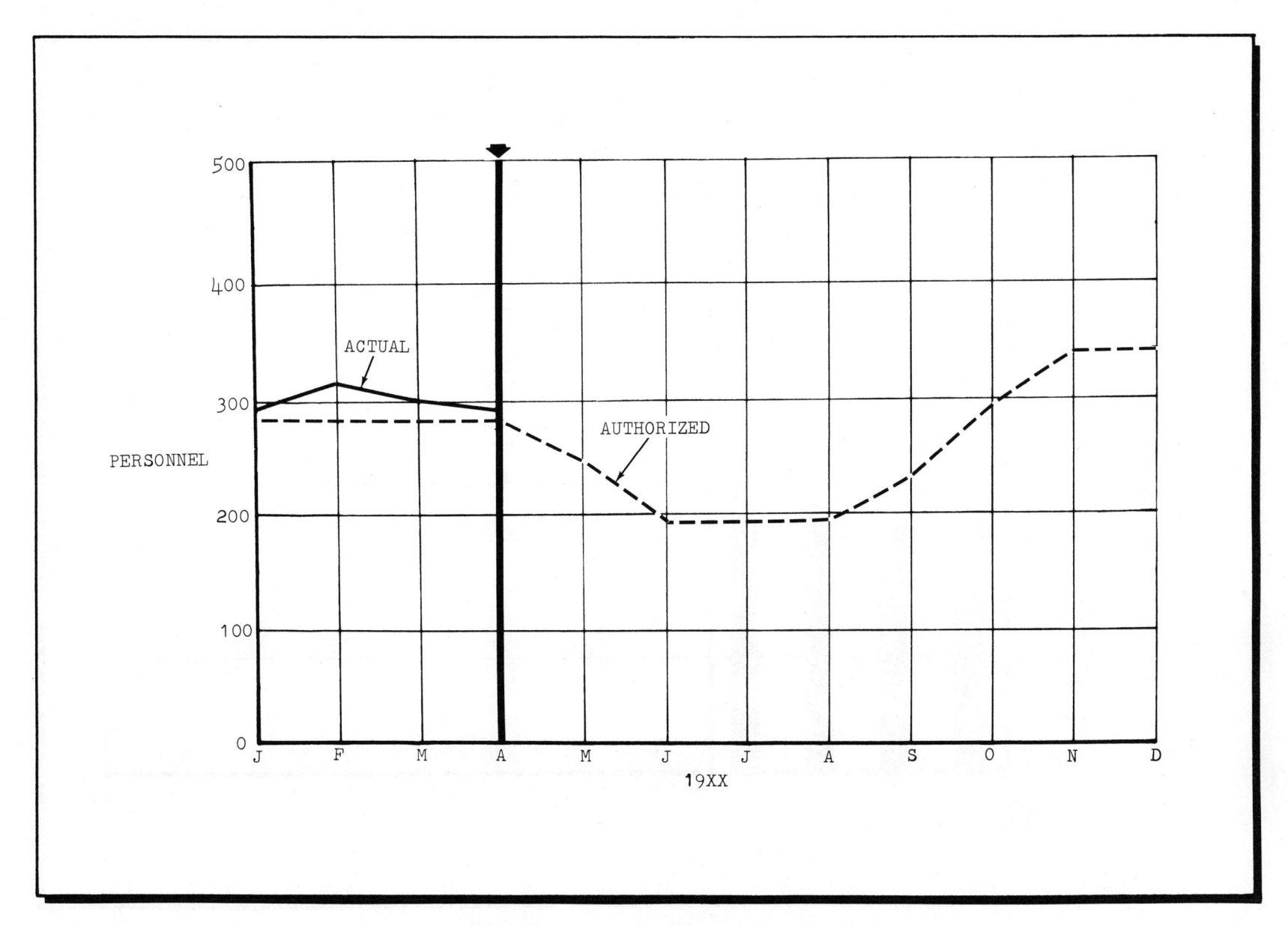

Figure 30.1 Manpower Summary—Version 1

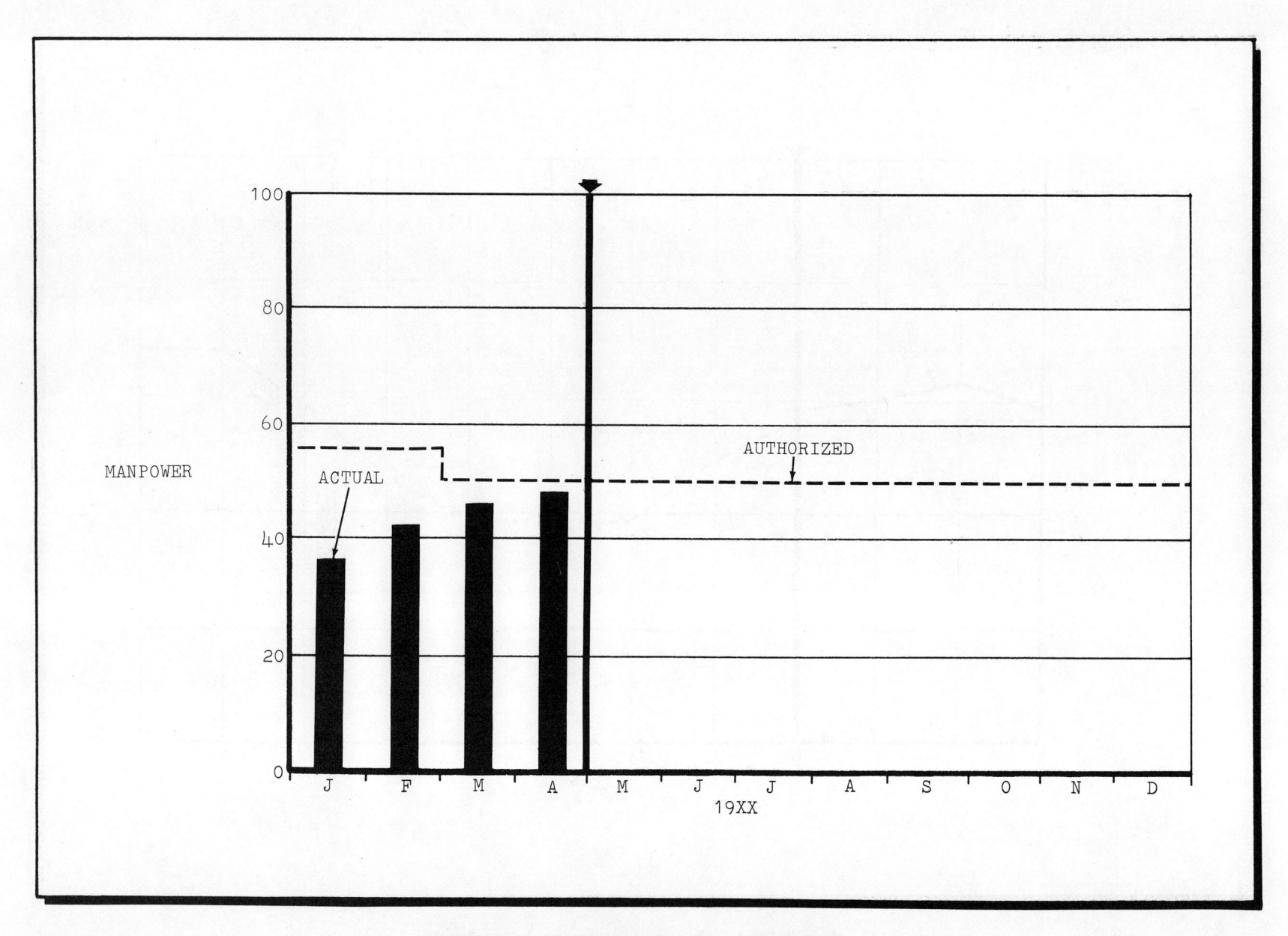

Figure 30.2   Manpower Summary—Version 2

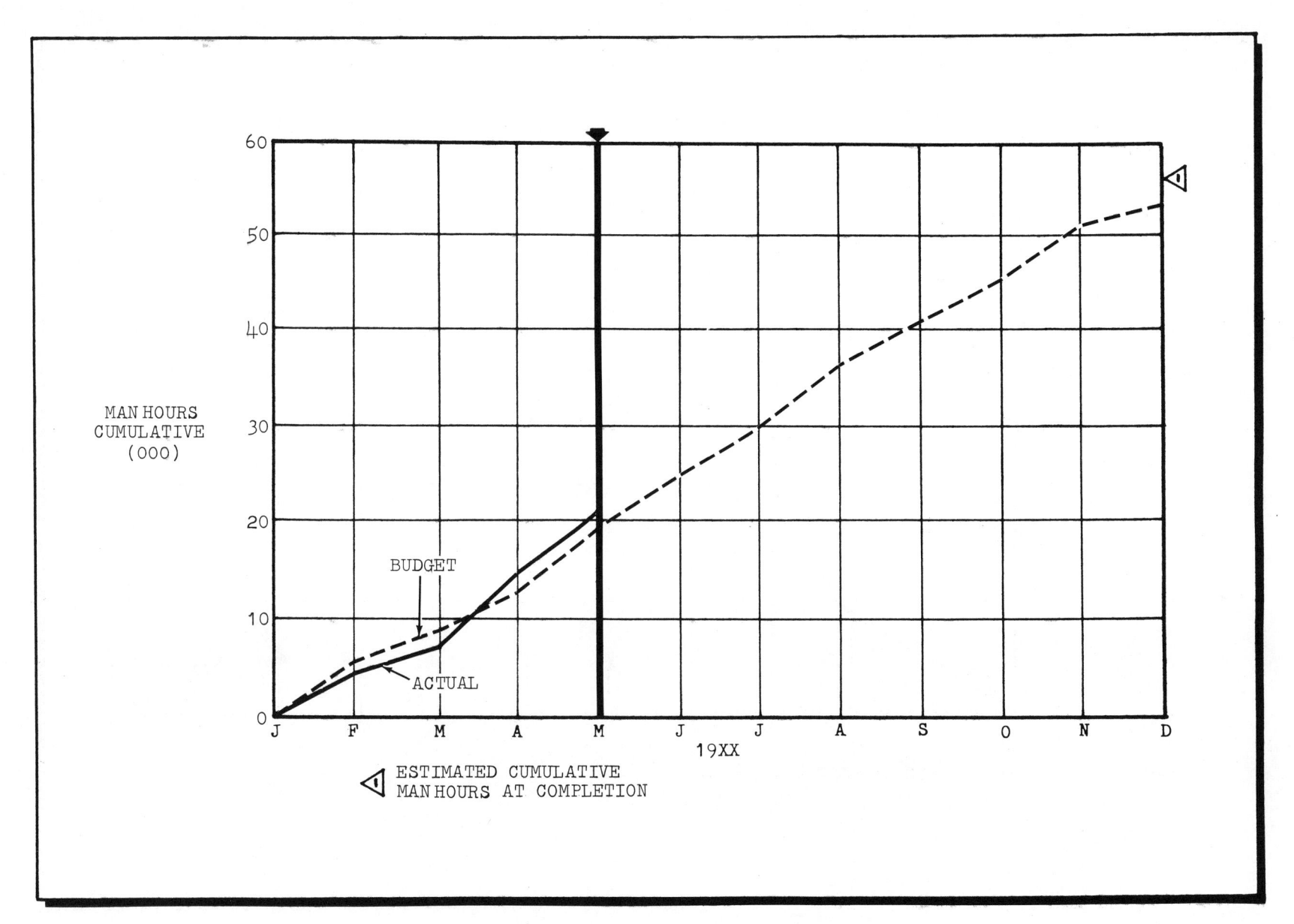

Figure 30.3   Manpower Summary—Version 3

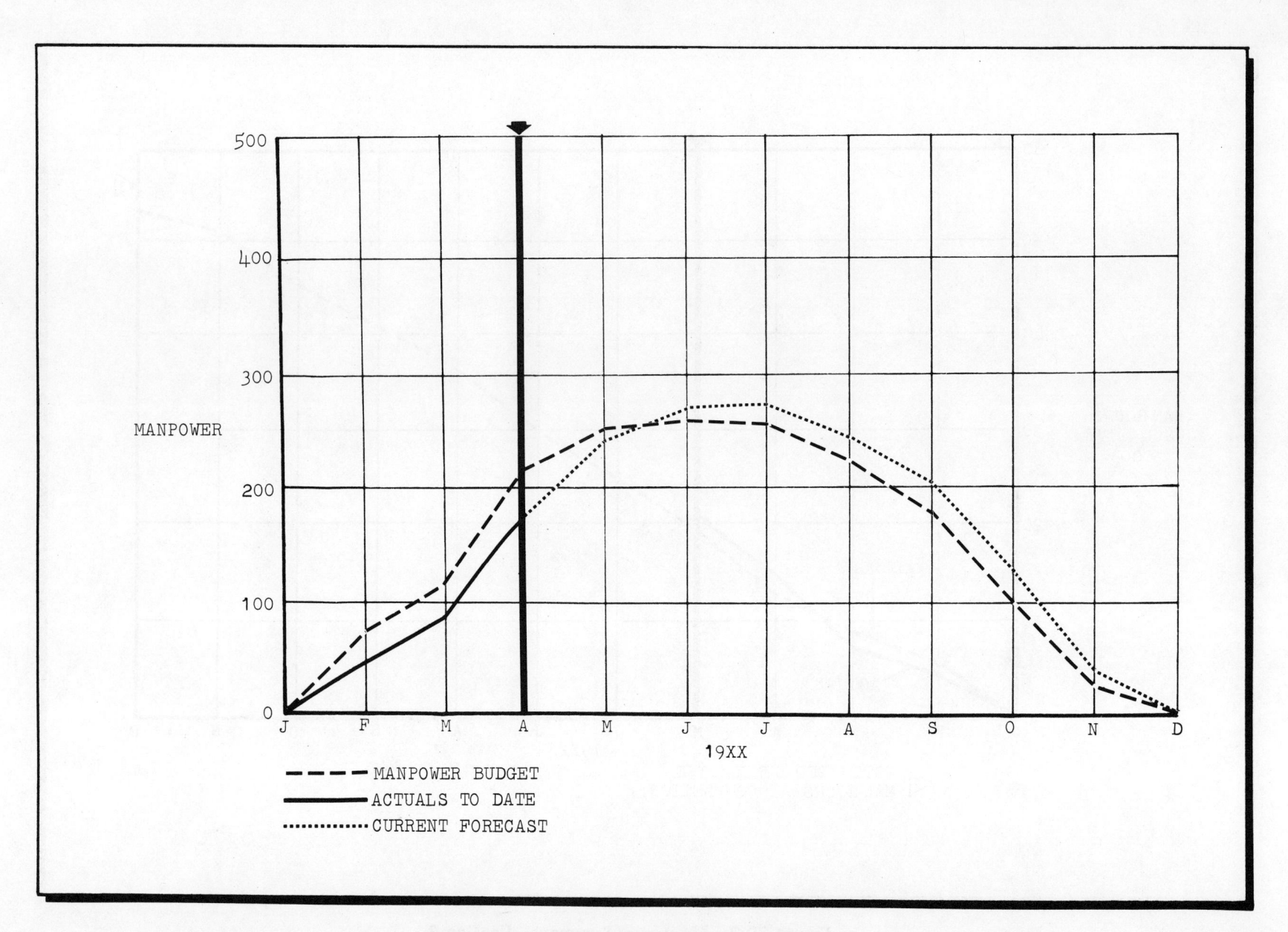

Figure 30.4 Manpower Summary—Version 4

334

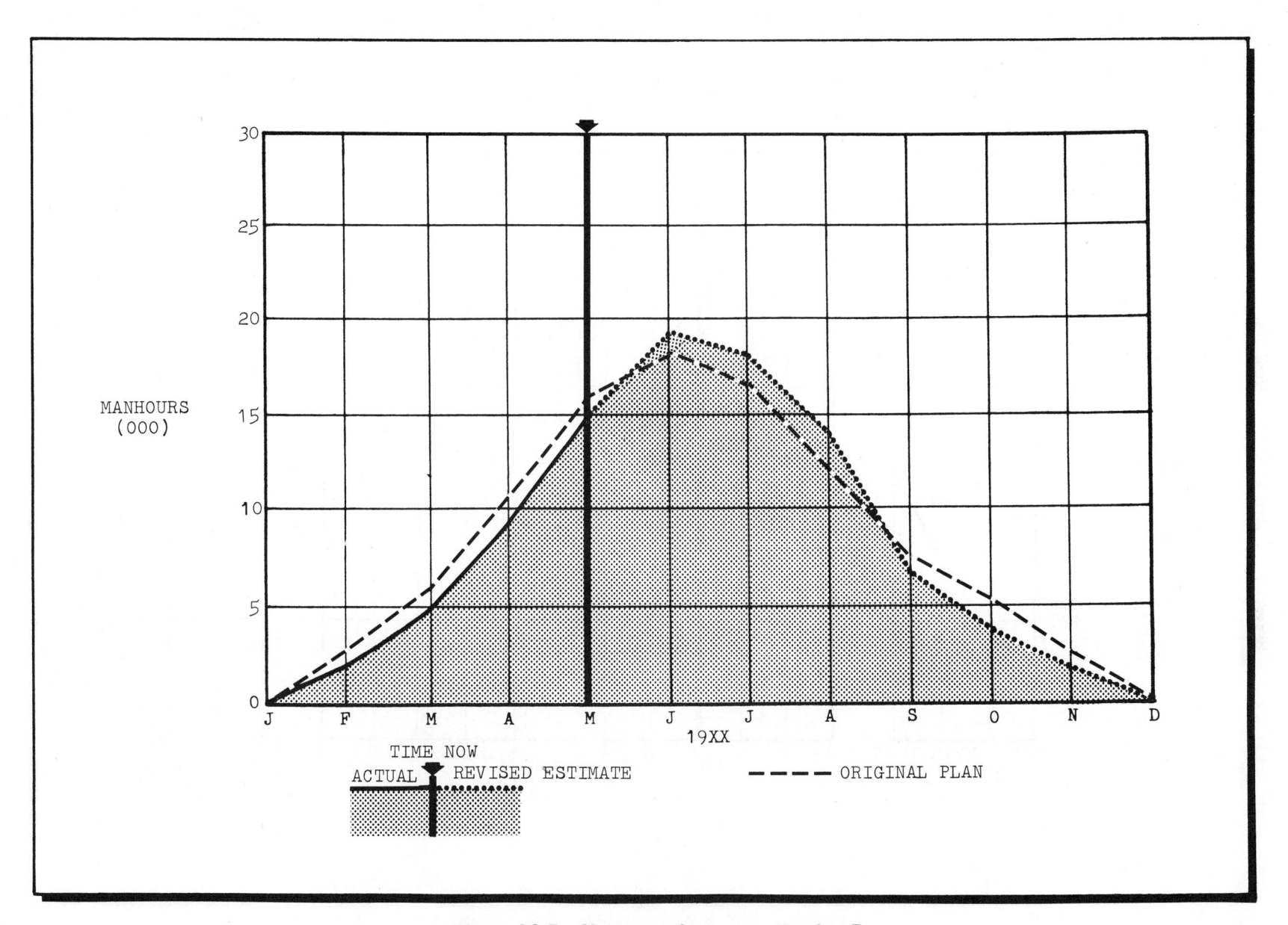

Figure 30.5 Manpower Summary—Version 5

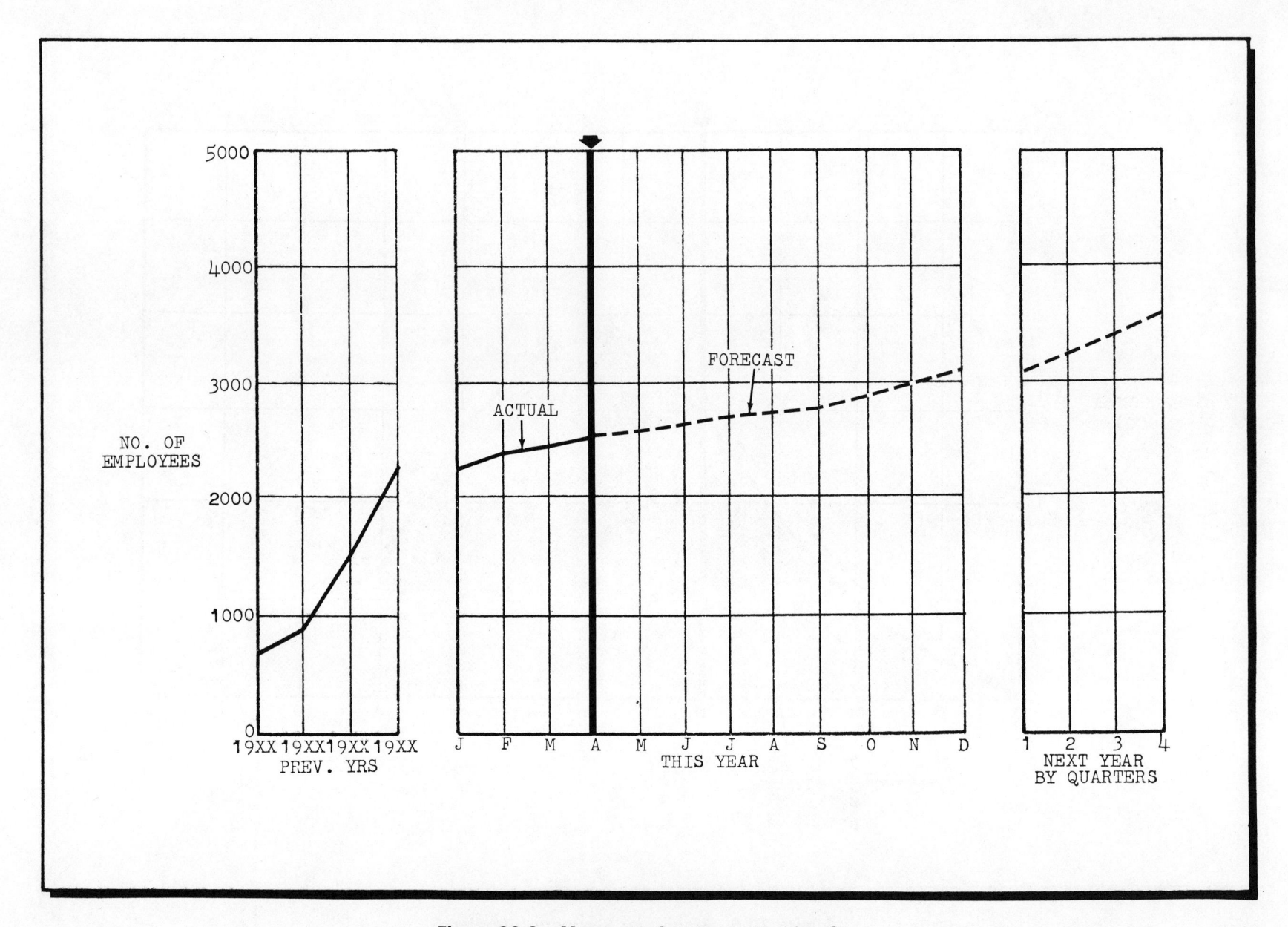

Figure 30.6 Manpower Summary—Version 6

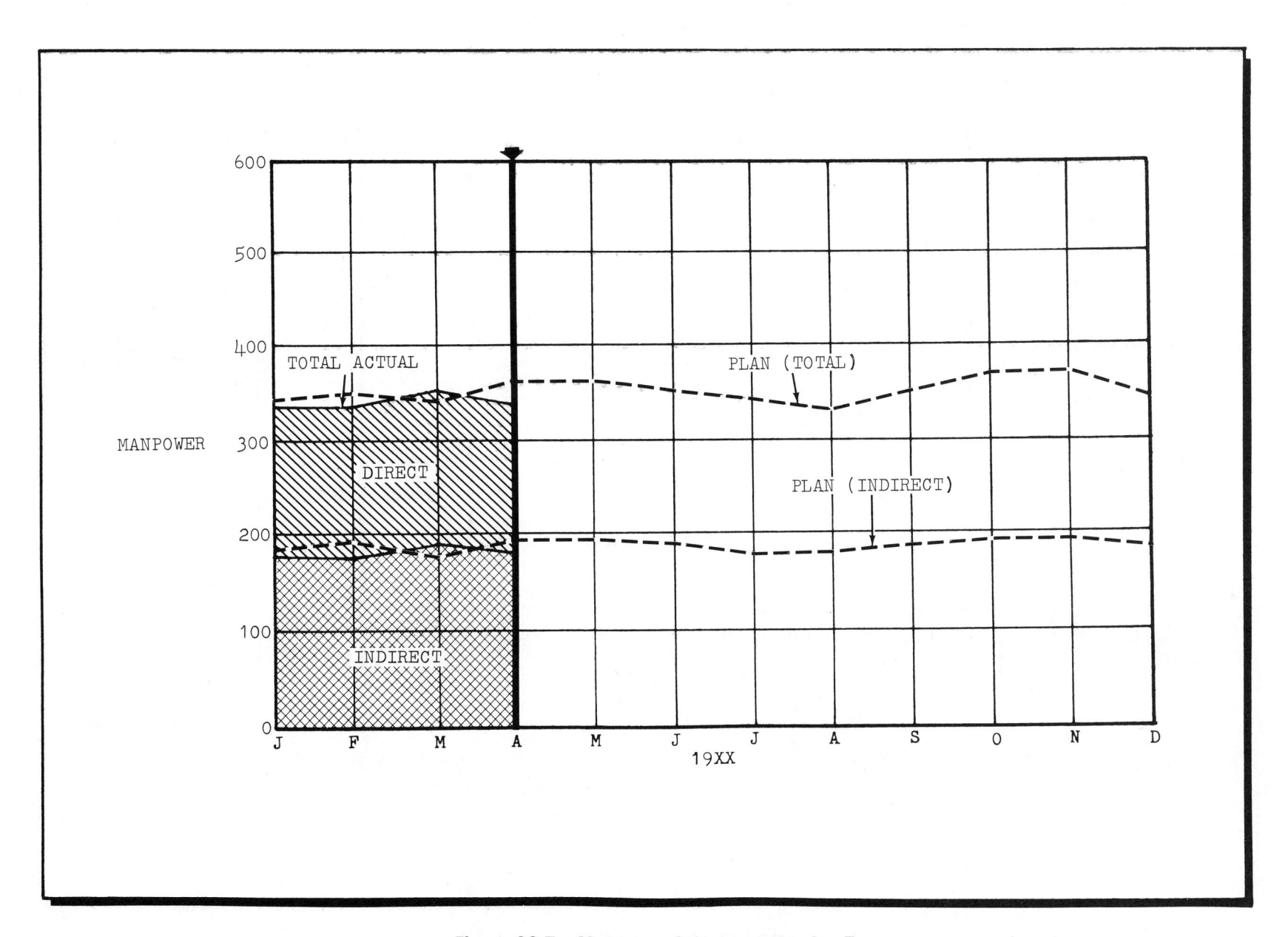

Figure 30.7 Manpower Summary—Version 7

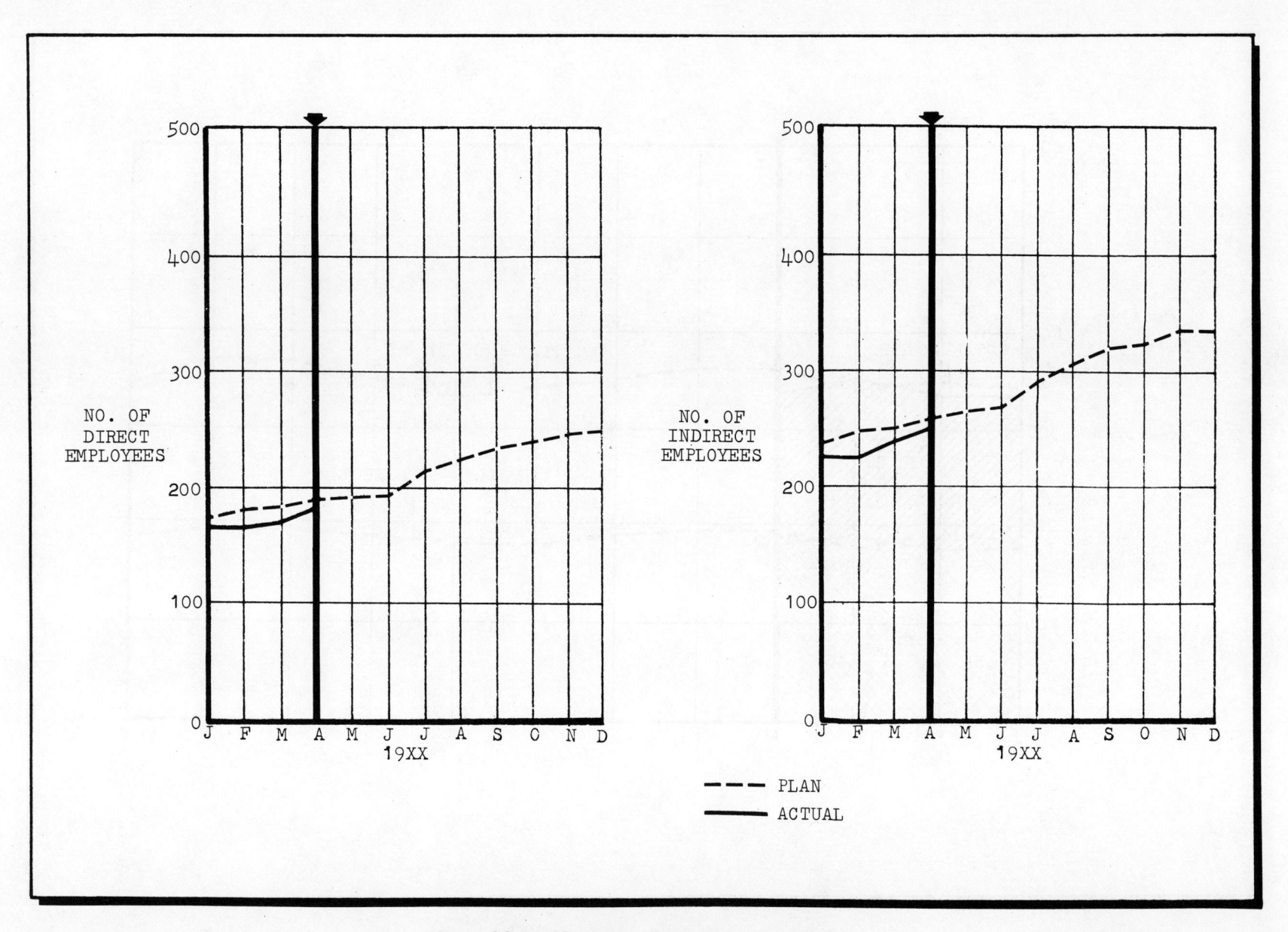

Figure 30.8   Manpower Summary—Version 8

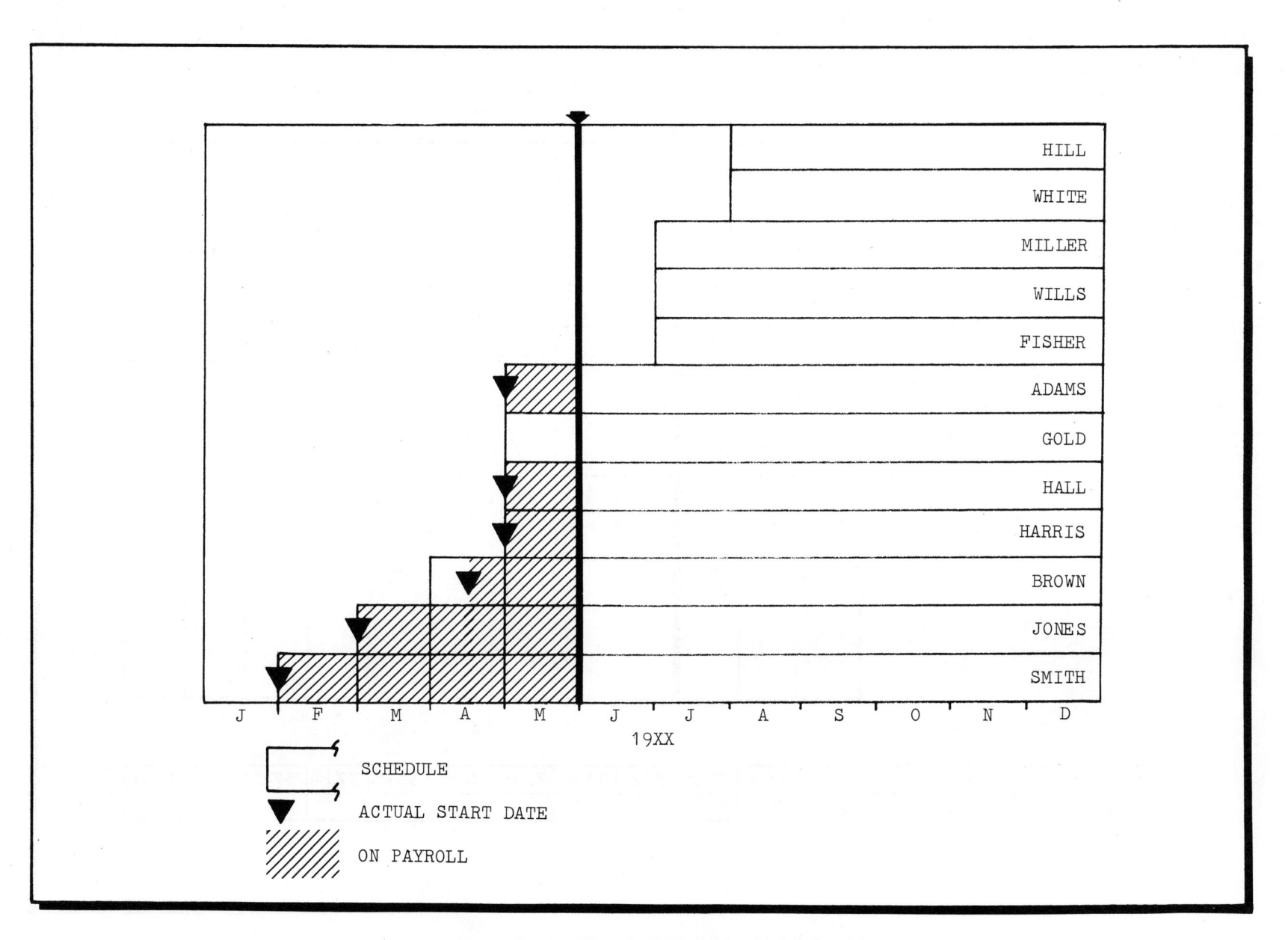

Figure 30.9 Manpower Summary—Version 9

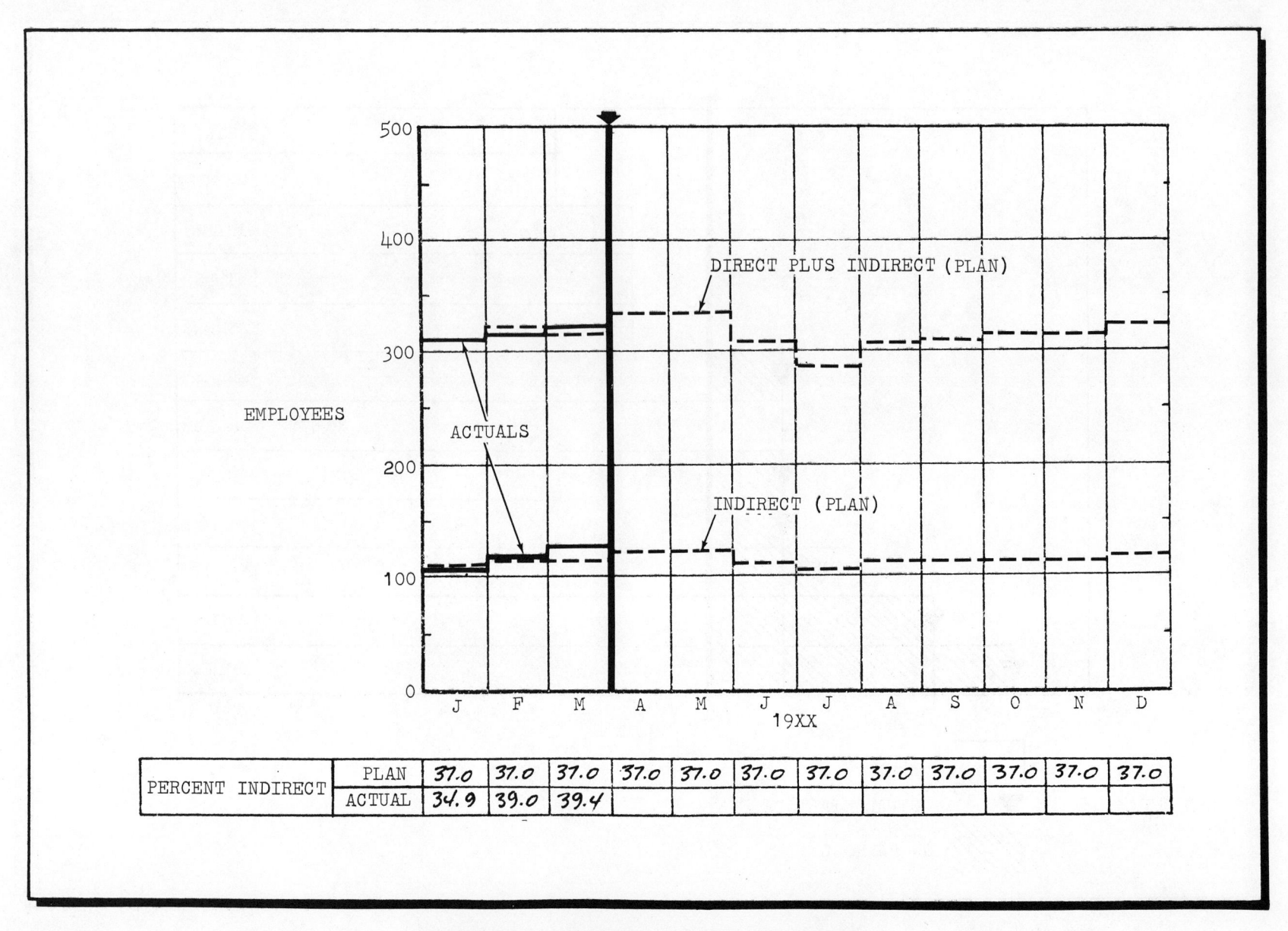

PERCENT INDIRECT	PLAN	37.0	37.0	37.0	37.0	37.0	37.0	37.0	37.0	37.0	37.0	37.0	37.0
	ACTUAL	34.9	39.0	39.4									

Figure 30.10 Manpower Summary—Version 10

NO. OF EMPLOYEES

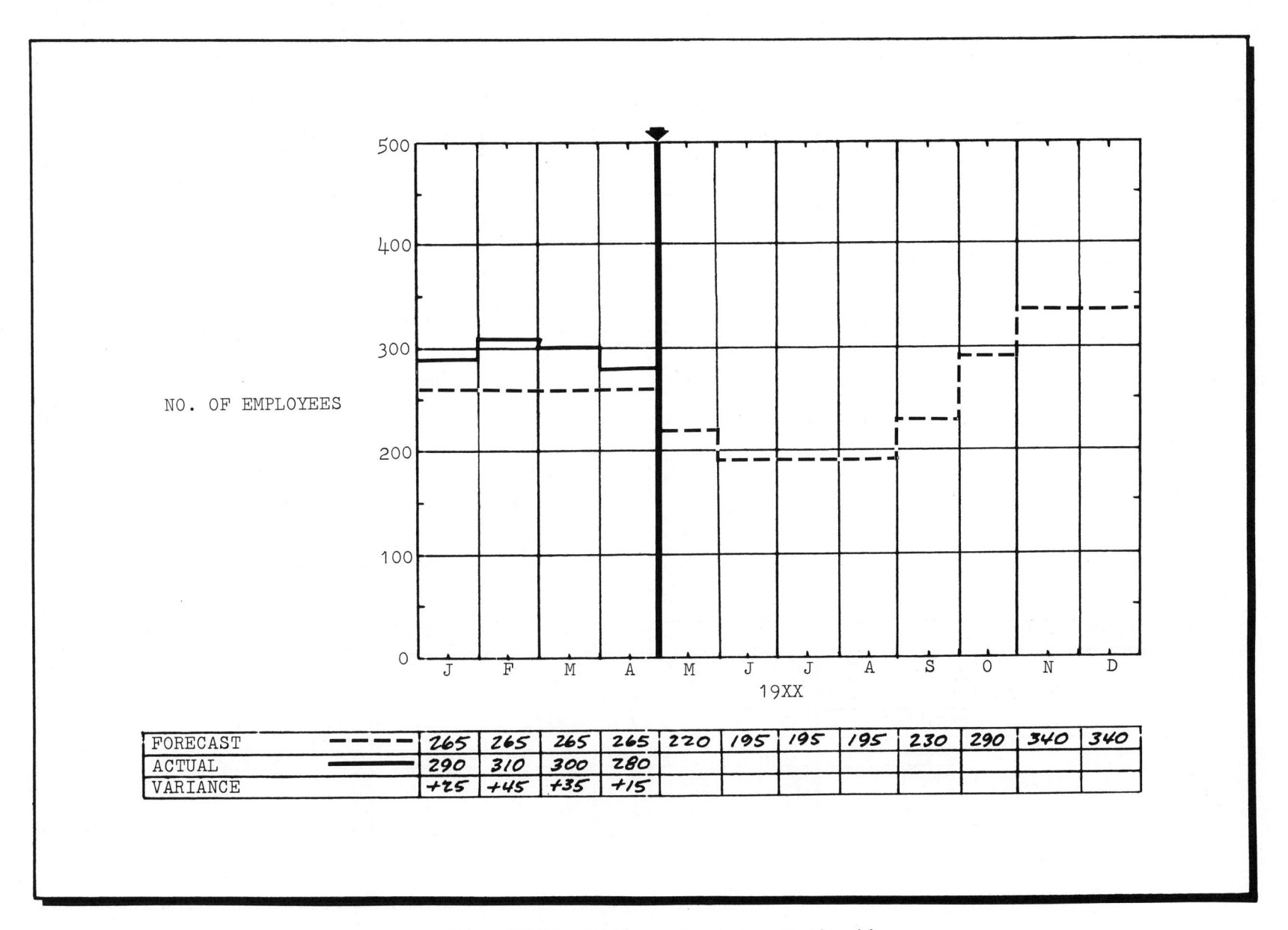

		J	F	M	A	M	J	J	A	S	O	N	D
FORECAST	-----	265	265	265	265	220	195	195	195	230	290	340	340
ACTUAL	———	290	310	300	280								
VARIANCE		+25	+45	+35	+15								

Figure 30.11   Manpower Summary—Version 11

341

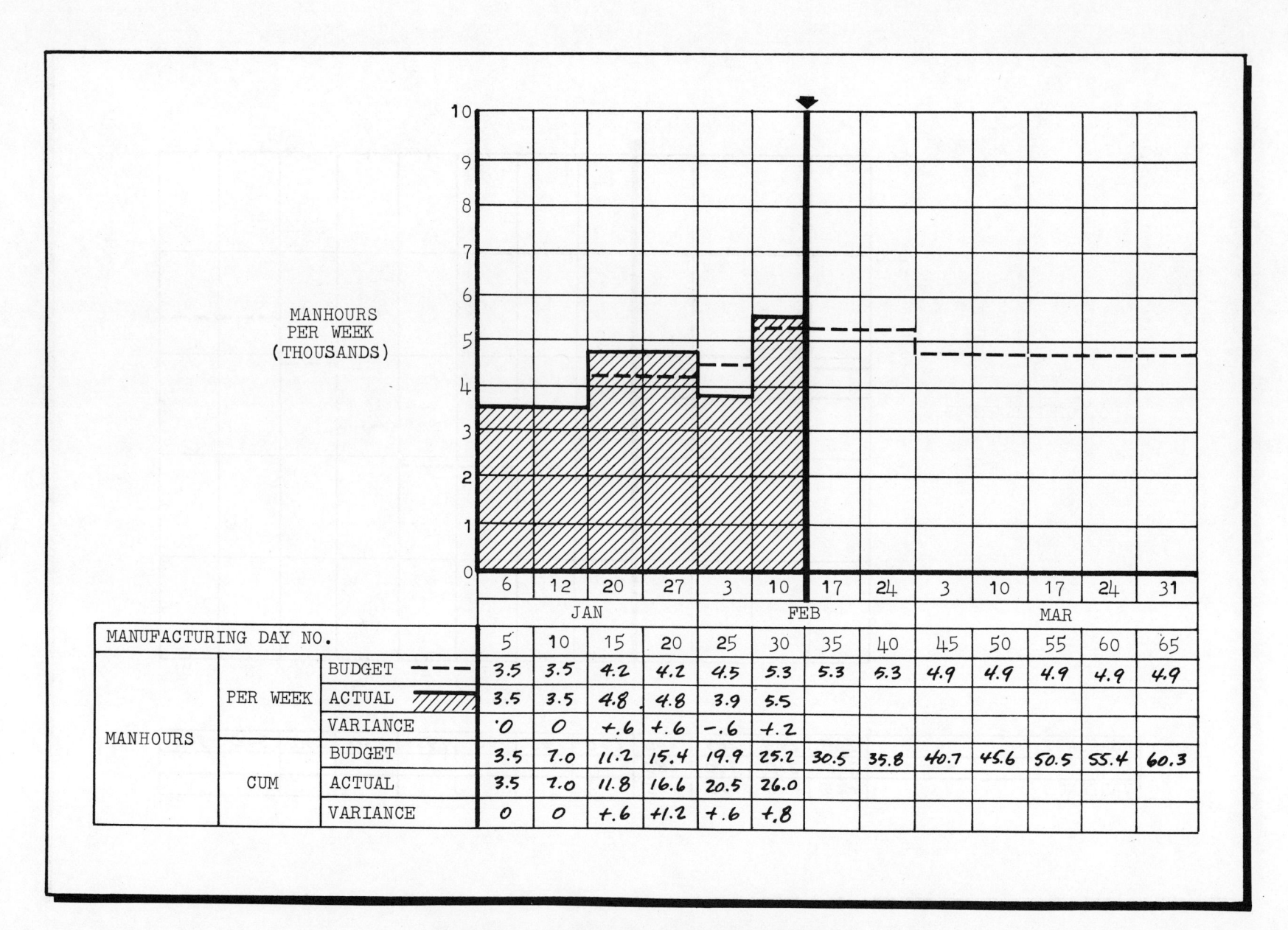

				5	10	15	20	25	30	35	40	45	50	55	60	65
MANUFACTURING DAY NO.																
MANHOURS	PER WEEK	BUDGET	----	3.5	3.5	4.2	4.2	4.5	5.3	5.3	5.3	4.9	4.9	4.9	4.9	4.9
		ACTUAL	▧	3.5	3.5	4.8	4.8	3.9	5.5							
		VARIANCE		0	0	+.6	+.6	-.6	+.2							
	CUM	BUDGET		3.5	7.0	11.2	15.4	19.9	25.2	30.5	35.8	40.7	45.6	50.5	55.4	60.3
		ACTUAL		3.5	7.0	11.8	16.6	20.5	26.0							
		VARIANCE		0	0	+.6	+1.2	+.6	+.8							

Figure 30.12 Manpower Summary—Version 12

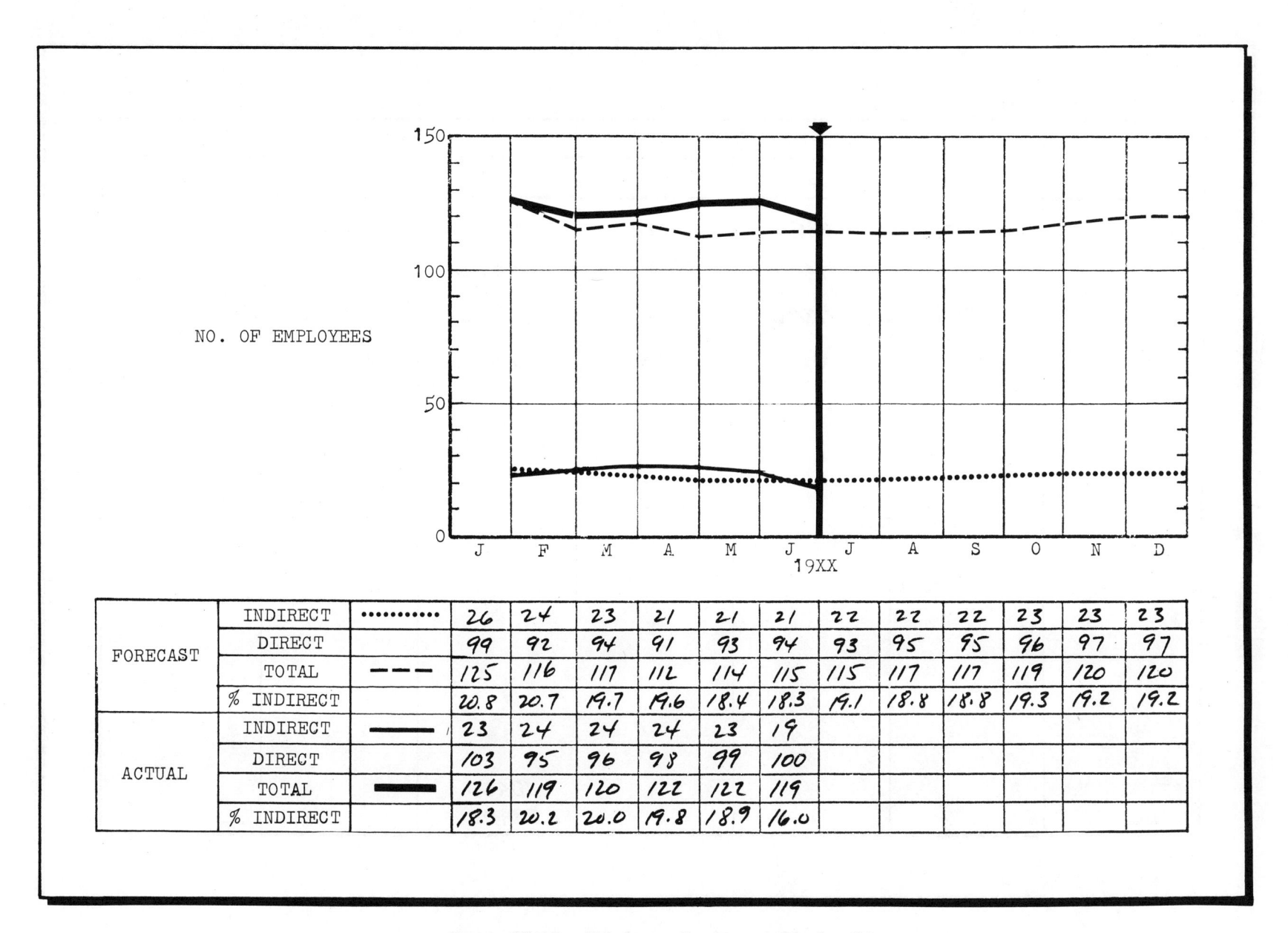

			J	F	M	A	M	J	J	A	S	O	N	D
FORECAST	INDIRECT	··········	26	24	23	21	21	21	22	22	22	23	23	23
	DIRECT		99	92	94	91	93	94	93	95	95	96	97	97
	TOTAL	– – –	125	116	117	112	114	115	115	117	117	119	120	120
	% INDIRECT		20.8	20.7	19.7	19.6	18.4	18.3	19.1	18.8	18.8	19.3	19.2	19.2
ACTUAL	INDIRECT	———	23	24	24	24	23	19						
	DIRECT		103	95	96	98	99	100						
	TOTAL	▬▬▬	126	119	120	122	122	119						
	% INDIRECT		18.3	20.2	20.0	19.8	18.9	16.0						

Figure 30.13 Manpower Summary—Version 13

STATUS THROUGH __APRIL__

MONTH	MANHOURS-PER MONTH			MANHOURS-YTD		
	PLAN	ACTUAL	(OVER)UNDER	PLAN	ACTUAL	(OVER)UNDER
JAN	7052	6880	178	7052	6880	178
FEB	7224	7396	(178)	14276	14276	—
MAR	7396	7396	—	21672	21672	—
APR	7740	8084	(344)	29412	29766	(344)
YEAR END: ORIGINAL PLAN REVISED EST				78400 79400		

Figure 30.14 Manpower Summary—Version 14

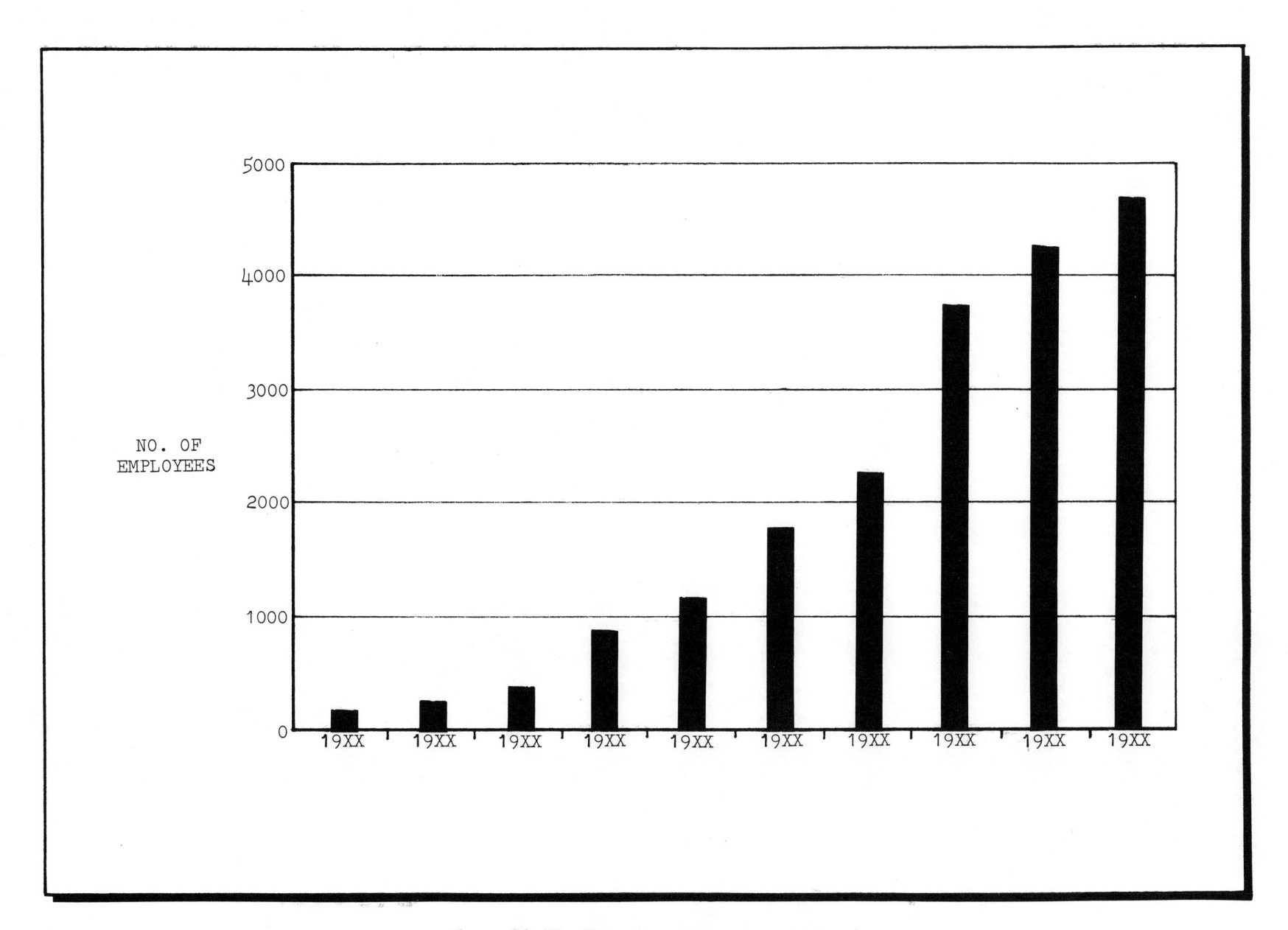

Figure 30.15 Manpower Summary—Version 15

31.0 MANPOWER TURNOVER

Charts that show manpower in terms of the number of employees hired as replacements for those who have left during a specific time period are shown in this section. Also see manpower sections 27.0 through 30.0, and 32.0.

31.1 Manpower Turnover—Version 1: The current employee turnover rate is compared to that of the previous year in Version 1 of a manpower turnover tracking chart, Figure 31.1. Turnover rate is the ratio of the number of replacements hired to the number of employees in the average work force.

31.2 Manpower Turnover—Version 2: Column chart and step line chart styles are used to show the authorized and actual total month-end work force in the graphic portion of Version 2 of a manpower turnover tracking chart, Figure 31.2. The table gives the backup statistics for the graph.

31.3 Manpower Turnover—Version 3: Version 3 of a manpower turnover tracking chart, Figure 31.3, is a table that tracks the total work force in terms of additions and deletions each month. The month-end figure is tracked against the authorized work force. The bottom line of the table gives the monthly turnover rate.

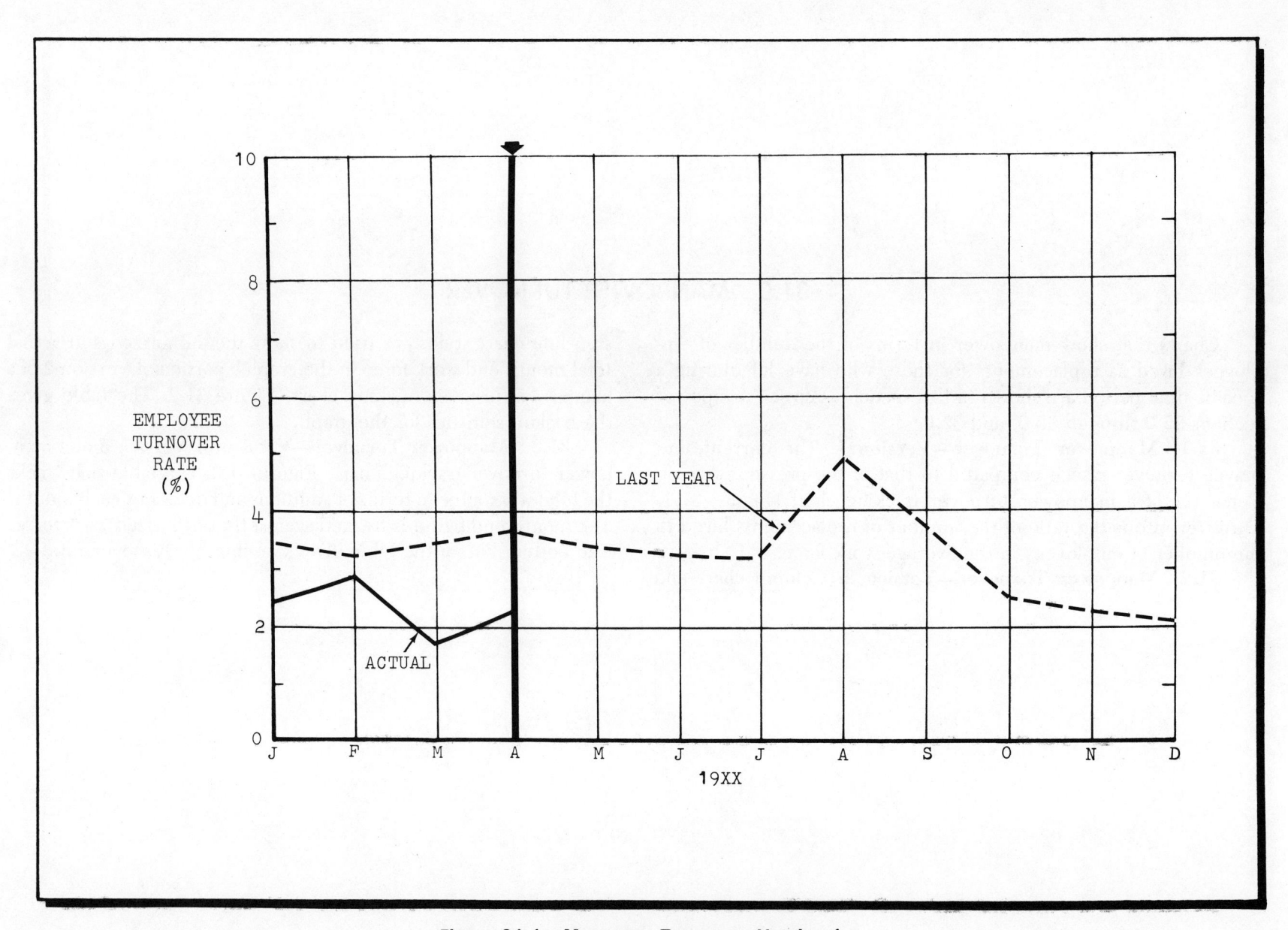

Figure 31.1 Manpower Turnover—Version 1

WORK FORCE-START OF MONTH	176	176	176	179	186							
ADDITIONS	+4	+5	+6	+11								
DELETIONS	-4	-5	-3	-4								
WORK FORCE-END OF MO. ■	176	176	179	186								
WORK FORCE-AUTHORIZED — —	176	176	180	185	190	190	190	185	180	175	175	175
VARIANCE	0	0	-1	+1								

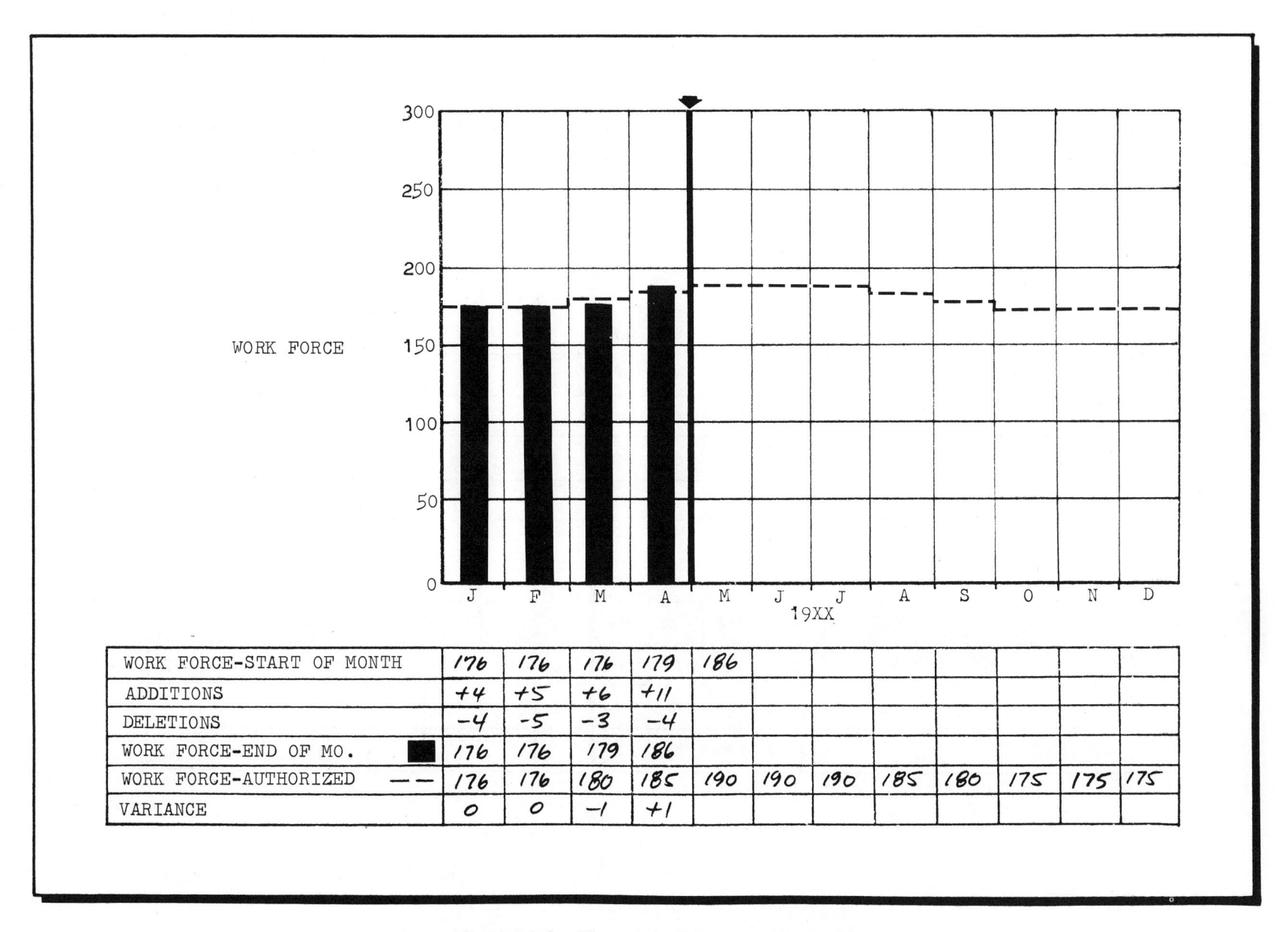

Figure 31.2 Manpower Turnover—Version 2

					19XX							
	J	F	M	A	M	J	J	A	S	O	N	D
WORK FORCE-START OF MONTH	176	176	176	179	186							
NEW HIRES (REPLACEMENTS)	+4	+5	+3	+4								
NEW HIRES (TO INCREASE W.F.)	0	0	+3	+6								
RETURNEES FROM LEAVES*	0	0	0	+1								
RESIGNATIONS	0	-2	-1	0								
LAYOFFS	0	0	0	0								
DISCHARGES	-2	-1	0	-2								
RETIREMENTS	-2	-1	0	-2								
LEAVES OF ABSENCE*	0	0	0	0								
DEATHS	0	-1	0	0								
WORK FORCE-END OF MONTH	176	176	179	186								
AUTHORIZED WORK FORCE	176	176	180	185	190	190	190	185	180	175	175	175
VARIANCE	0	0	-1	-1								
TURNOVER RATE	2.3%	2.8%	1.7%	2.2%								

*MORE THAN 17 DAYS

Figure 31.3 Manpower Turnover—Version 3

32.0 MANPOWER VERSUS WORKLOAD

Charts that display manpower in relationship to workload requirements are shown in this section. Also see manpower sections 27.0 through 31.0.

32.1 Manpower Versus Workload—Version 1: In Version 1 of a manpower versus workload tracking chart, Figure 32.1, available manpower is shown with a dotted line and required man-hours are shown with a dashed line. Plottings to the left of the time-now line are actuals, and plotting to the right represent the forecast. In this example, the man-hours required to date in excess of those available are shown to have been subcontracted.

32.2 Manpower Versus Workload—Version 2: Paired columns in Version 2 of a manpower versus workload tracking chart, Figure 32.2., display anticipated and actual workload. A dashed step line shows available manpower. The plottings can be read either in terms of man-hours per month (left-hand scale) or men per month (right-hand scale).

32.3 Manpower Versus Workload—Version 3: Available man-hours in Version 3 of a manpower versus workload tracking chart, Figure 32.3, are segmented as to first shift, second shift, and premium time. The anticipated workload, shown with a stepped dotted line, is seen to eventually require time from all three categories. Actual man-hours used to date are shown with a stepped solid line.

32.4 Manpower Versus Workload—Version 4: Version 4 of a manpower versus workload tracking chart, Figure 32.4, uses two grids. The left-hand grid shows the workload in terms of the number of units per month. The right-hand grid shows the number of employees required to produce the units.

32.5 Manpower Versus Workload—Version 5: Three separate grids are used in Version 5 of a manpower versus workload tracking chart, Figure 32.5. The left-hand grid displays the workload in terms of quantity of units per month. The right-hand grid shows, in step line style, the planned and actual number of employees, the total segmented as to the portions which are direct, indirect, and overhead. The center grid displays a measure of efficiency: the number of units produced per direct labor employee and per total employee.

32.6 Manpower Versus Workload—Version 6: Statistics are combined with graphics in Version 6 of a manpower versus workload tracking chart, Figure 32.6. The graphics, in this example, are plotted on a cumulative basis. The table displays the scheduled and actual quantity of production units, the scheduled and actual man-hour requirements, and the anticipated and actually used portion of available man-hours.

32.7 Manpower Versus Workload—Version 7: The combined statistical table/graphic display shown as Version 7 of a manpower versus workload tracking chart, Figure 32.7, shows man-hours on a monthly basis. In the graphic portion of the chart, step lines are used to show the estimated requirement in relationship to the anticipated available man-hours. Actual man-hours used are shown with solid columns. The table gives the backup statistics for the graph, plus itemizes the requirements that are in excess of availability, noting that this excess may be either subcontracted or allocated to a second shift.

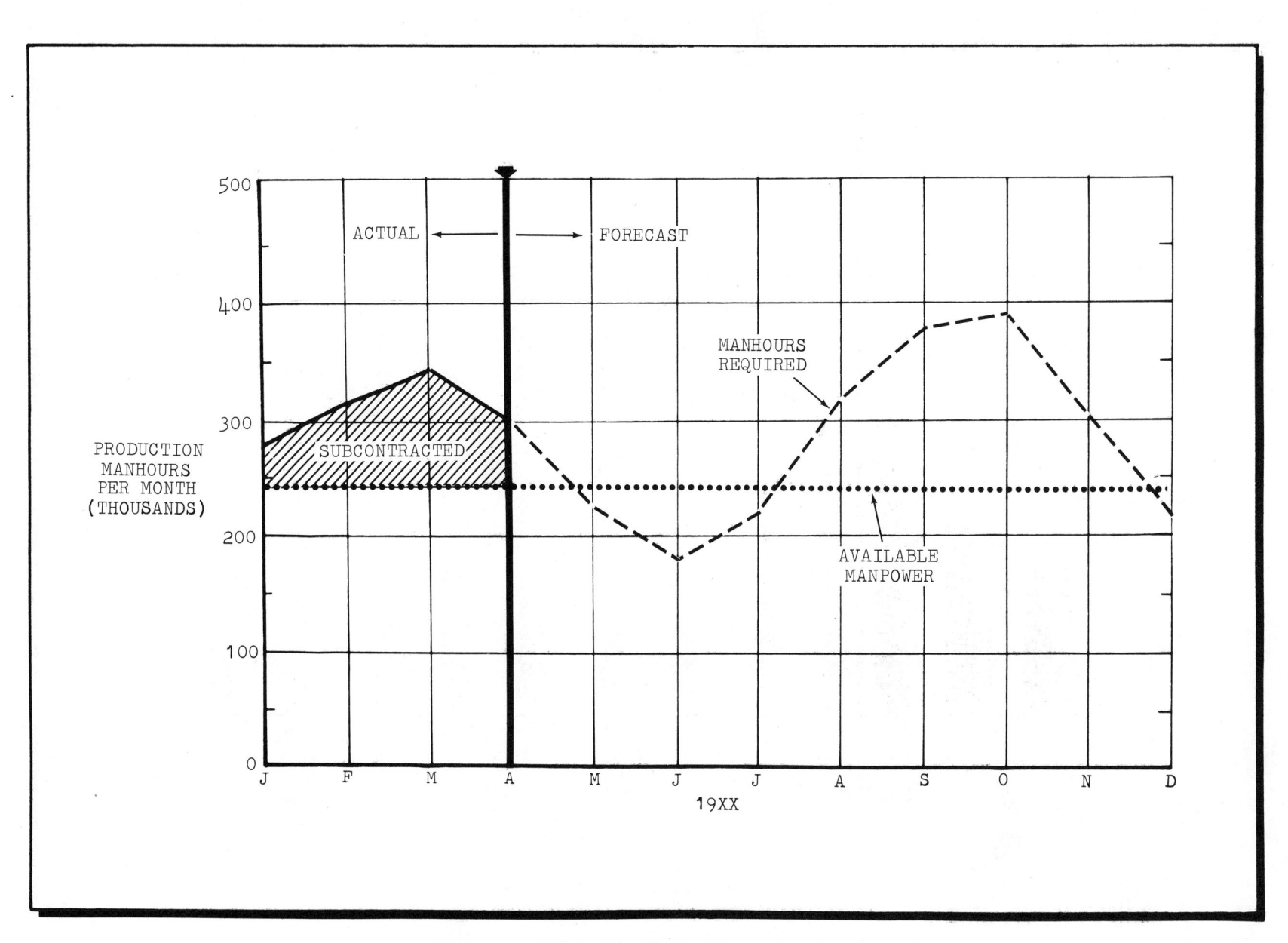

Figure 32.1 Manpower Versus Workload—Version 1

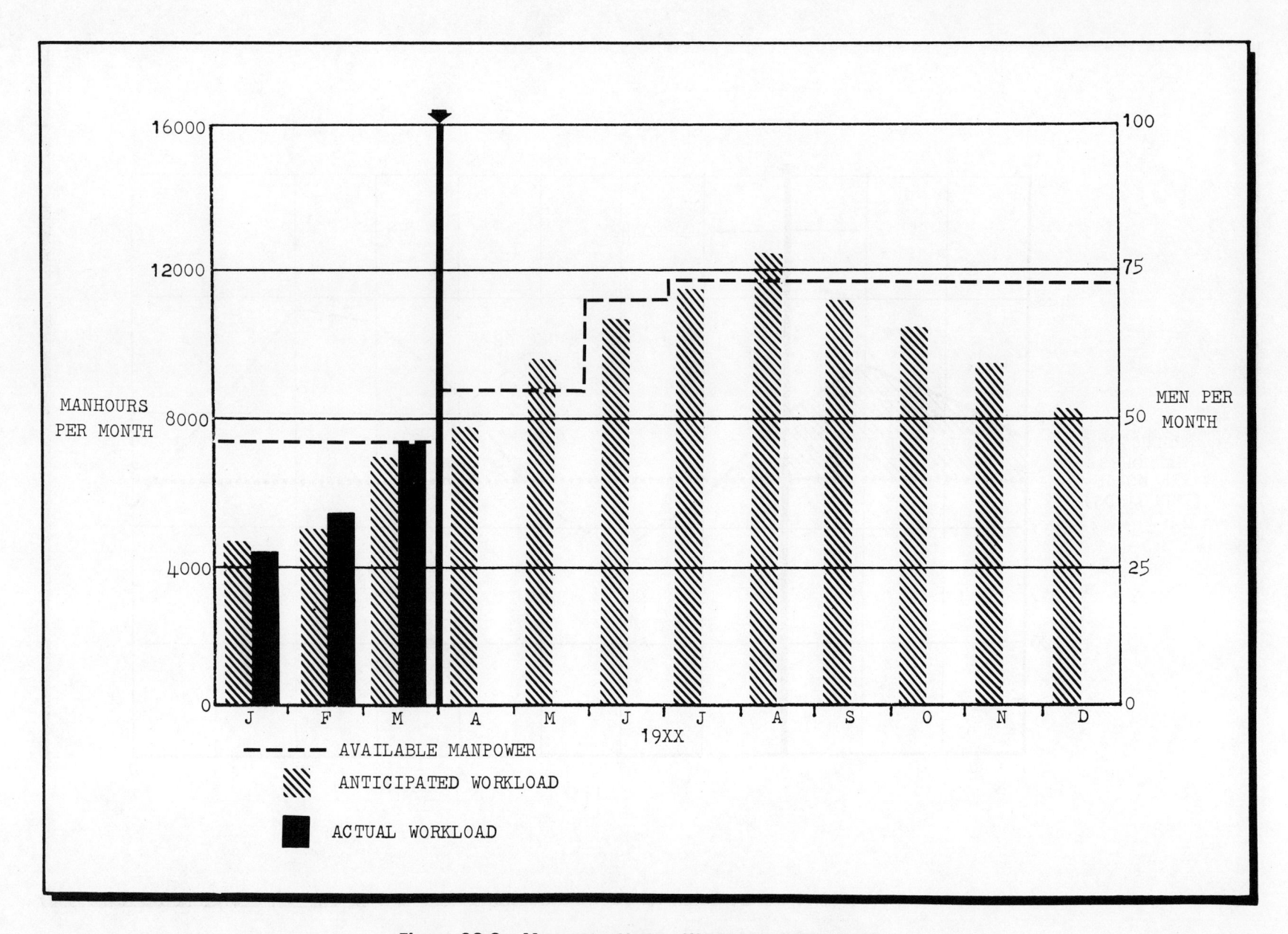

Figure 32.2 Manpower Versus Workload—Version 2

354

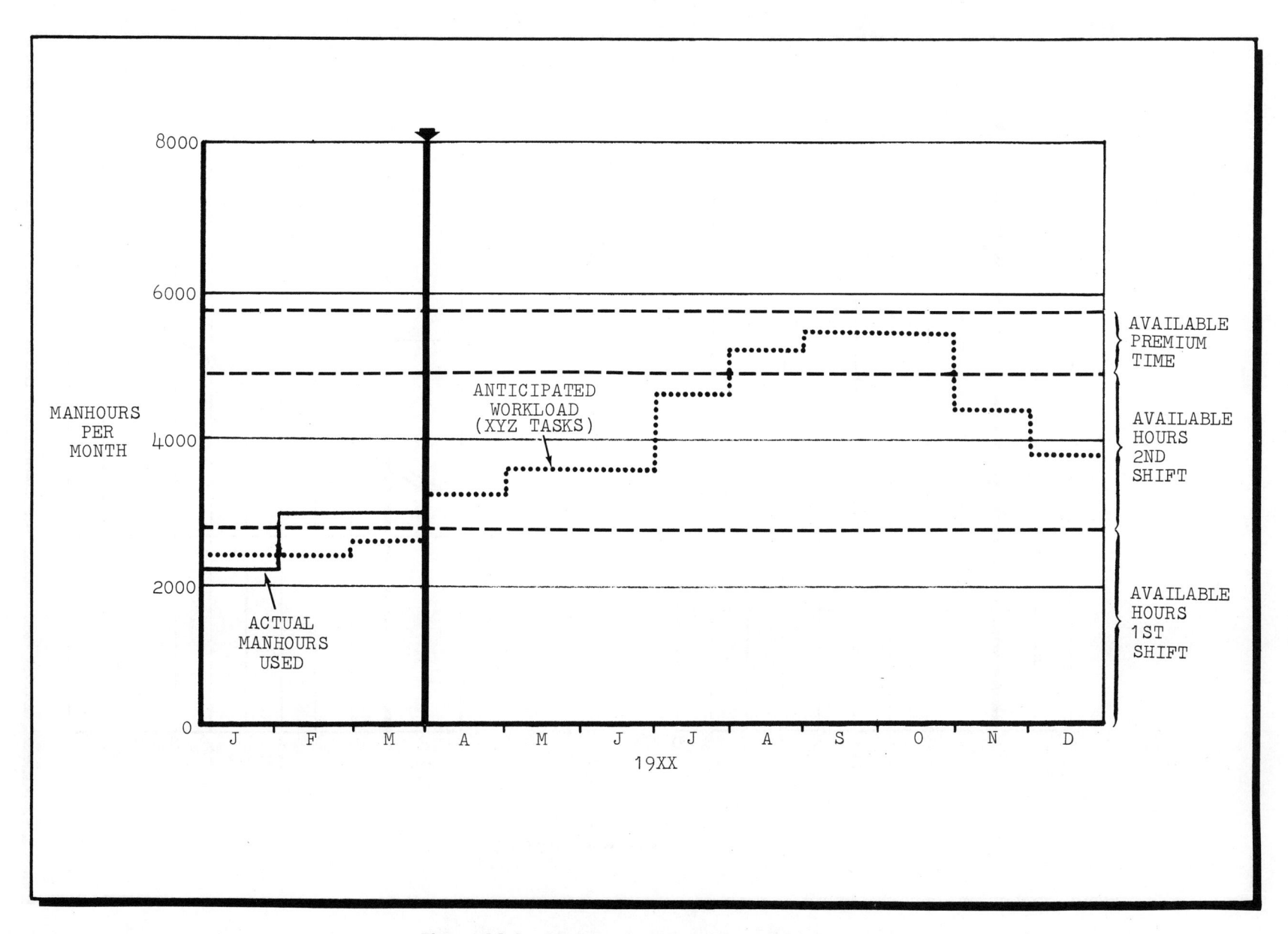

Figure 32.3   Manpower Versus Workload—Version 3

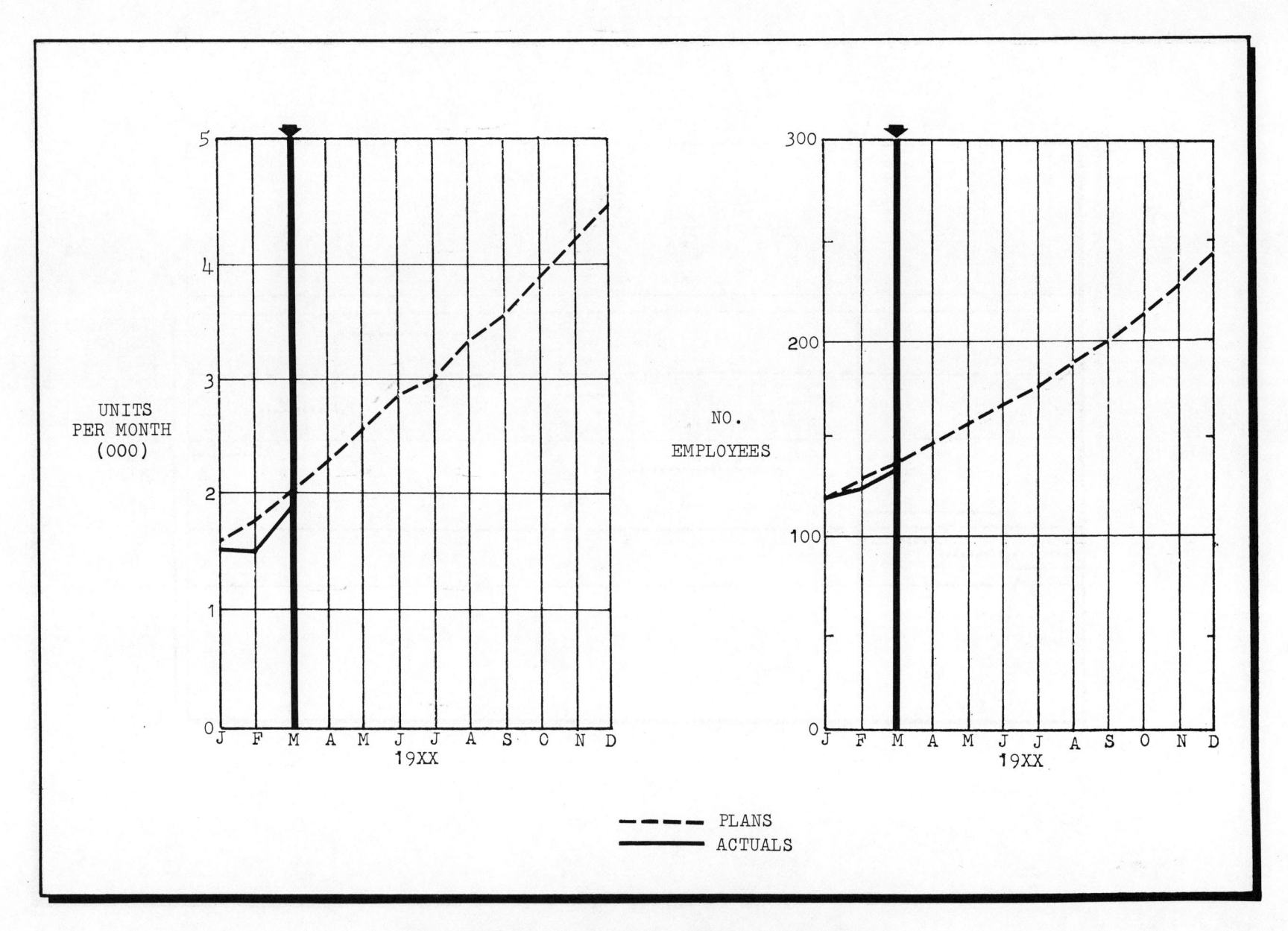

Figure 32.4   Manpower Versus Workload—Version 4

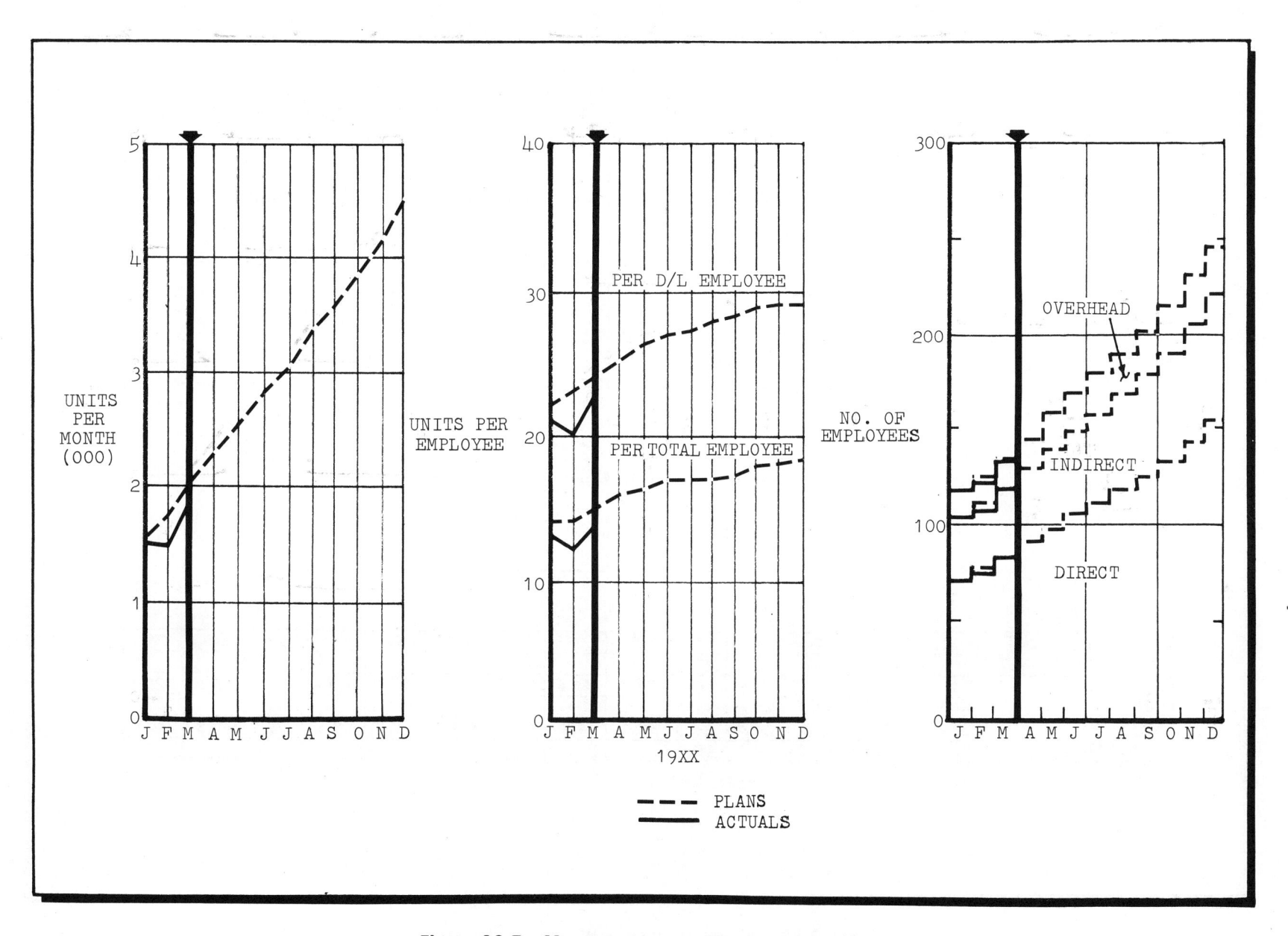

Figure 32.5 Manpower Versus Workload—Version 5

MANHOURS
CUMULATIVE
(THOUSANDS)

CUMULATIVE													
QUANTITY OF PRODUCTION UNITS	SCHEDULED	2	4	7	10	14	19	25	32	41	50	55	58
	ACTUAL	2	4	7									
MANHOURS REQUIRED	PER SCHED	10.4	20.4	34.5	48.0	65.6	86.6	110.6	137.2	169.6	201.1	218.6	229.1
	ACTUAL	11.0	21.2	35.0									
MANHOURS AVAILABLE	ANTICIPATED	11.5	24.0	39.5	58.0	76.5	97.5	118.5	139.5	159.5	174.5	189.5	204.5
	USED	11.0	21.2	35.0									

– – – ESTIMATED REQUIRED
– · – · – ANTICIPATED AVAILABLE
——— USED

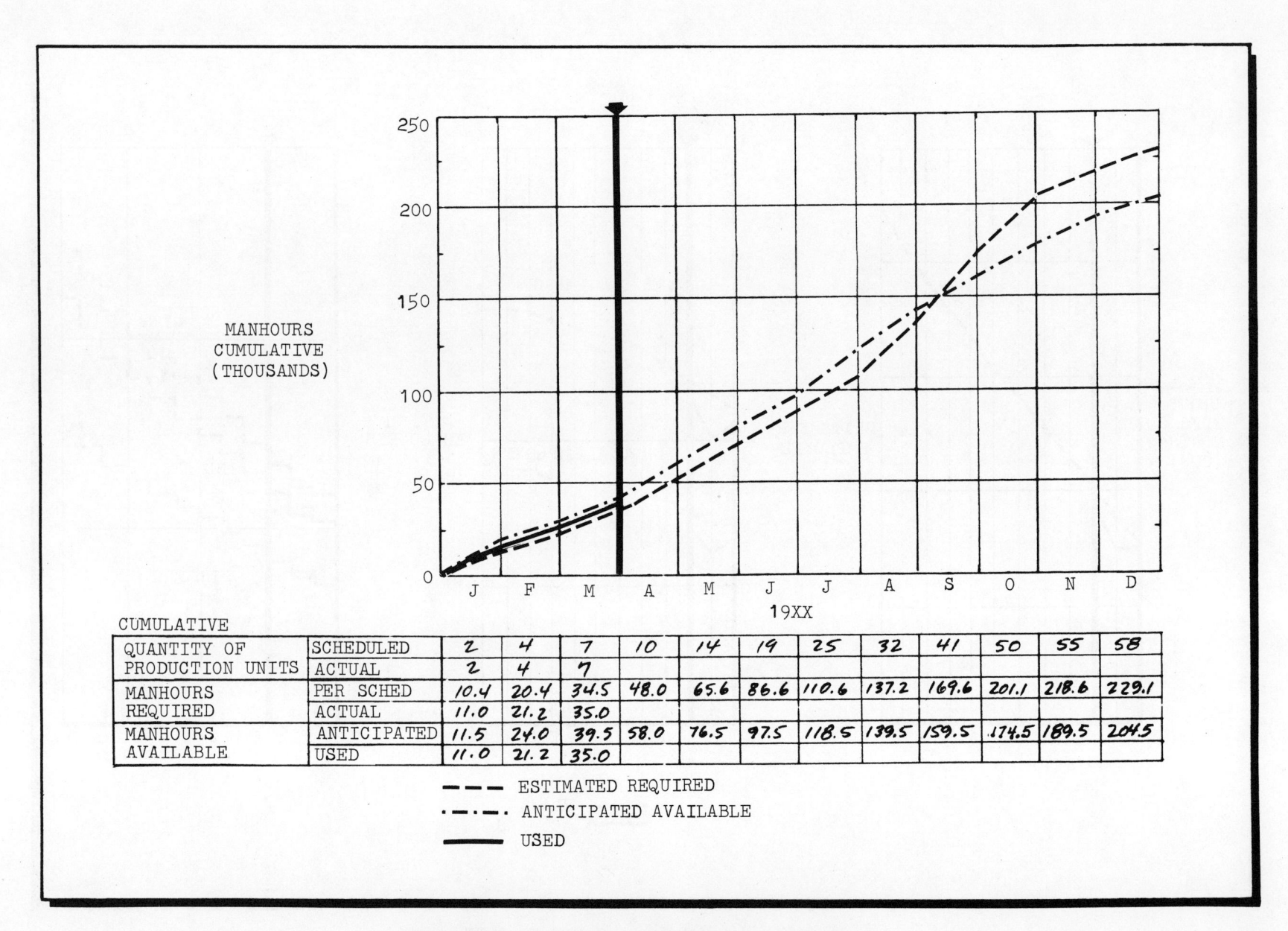

Figure 32.6   Manpower Versus Workload—Version 6

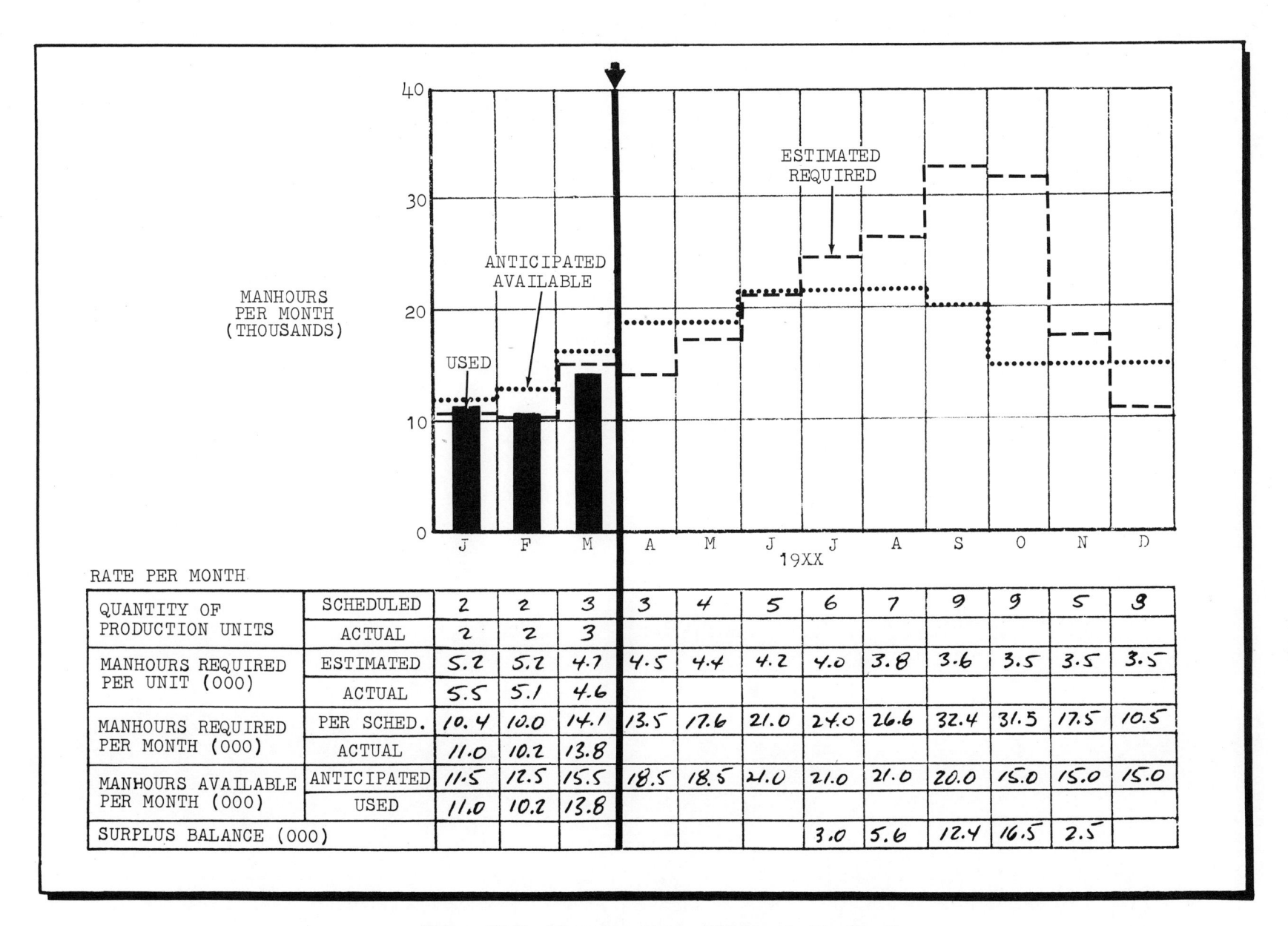

RATE PER MONTH													
QUANTITY OF PRODUCTION UNITS	SCHEDULED	2	2	3	3	4	5	6	7	9	9	5	3
	ACTUAL	2	2	3									
MANHOURS REQUIRED PER UNIT (000)	ESTIMATED	5.2	5.2	4.7	4.5	4.4	4.2	4.0	3.8	3.6	3.5	3.5	3.5
	ACTUAL	5.5	5.1	4.6									
MANHOURS REQUIRED PER MONTH (000)	PER SCHED.	10.4	10.0	14.1	13.5	17.6	21.0	24.0	26.6	32.4	31.5	17.5	10.5
	ACTUAL	11.0	10.2	13.8									
MANHOURS AVAILABLE PER MONTH (000)	ANTICIPATED	11.5	12.5	15.5	18.5	18.5	21.0	21.0	21.0	20.0	15.0	15.0	15.0
	USED	11.0	10.2	13.8									
SURPLUS BALANCE (000)								3.0	5.6	12.4	16.5	2.5	

Figure 32.7 Manpower Versus Workload—Version 7

33.0 NET PROFITS TO TANGIBLE NET WORTH

The rate of return for invested capital is an important measurement of an enterprise's operations. Charts for showing the ratio of net profits (the profit remaining after all costs, including taxes, have been deducted) to tangible net worth (net worth less the value of intangible assets . . . goodwill, organization costs, etc.) are displayed in this section.

33.1 Net Profits to Tangible Net Worth—Version 1: A basic method for illustrating the percentage of net profits to tangible net worth is shown as Version 1, Figure 33.1. The goal in this example, shown with a dashed line, is in terms of an "industry average." Such averages, which vary widely according to industry, can often be obtained from banks or trade associations. The actual performance in this example is plotted using a solid line.

33.2 Net Profits to Tangible Net Worth—Version 2: A step line chart style has been combined with a column chart style to display the ratio of net profits to tangible net worth in Version 2, Figure 33.2. The current year's goal and the past year's actual performance are both shown in step line form. The current year's actual performance, up to the reporting date (through April in this example), is shown with solid columns.

33.3 Net Profits to Tangible Net Worth—Version 3: A method for displaying the performance of multiple divisions in terms of the ratio of net profits to tangible net worth is shown as Version 3, Figure 33.3 In this example, the performances of three separate divisions are compared, a dashed line representing the goal and a solid line representing the actual percentage.

33.4 Net Profits to Tangible Net Worth—Version 4: A statistical table has been combined with graphics in Version 4 of a net profits to tangible net worth tracking chart, Figure 33.4. The graph shows the goal in dashed line form and actuals with solid columns. In the table, statistics are shown for net profits, tangible net worth, and the actual and planned ratio of net profits to tangible net worth.

33.5 Net Profits to Tangible Net Worth—Version 5: A tabular version of a net profits to tangible net worth tracking chart is shown in Figure 33.5. Given are the statistics for actual net profits, actual net worth, and the ratio of net profits to tangible net worth in terms of the goal, the actual performance, and the variance between these latter two statistics.

33.6 Net Profits to Tangible Net Worth—Version 6: Version 6 of a net profits to tangible net worth chart, Figure 33.6, is in the form of a one-time status report. One of the disadvantages of this style of chart is that it must be completely redone for each new reporting date.

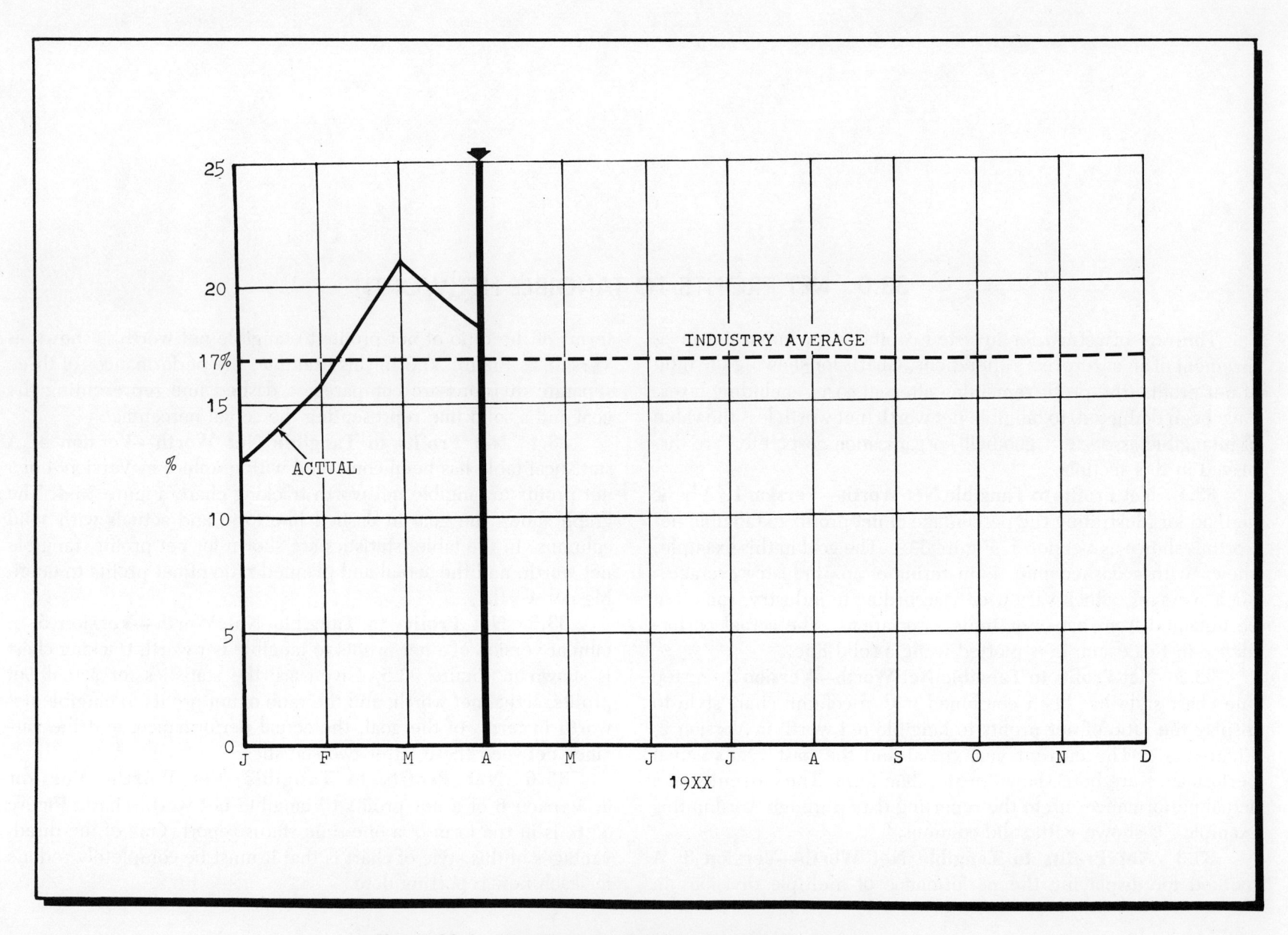

Figure 33.1   Net Profits to Tangible Net Worth—Version 1

362

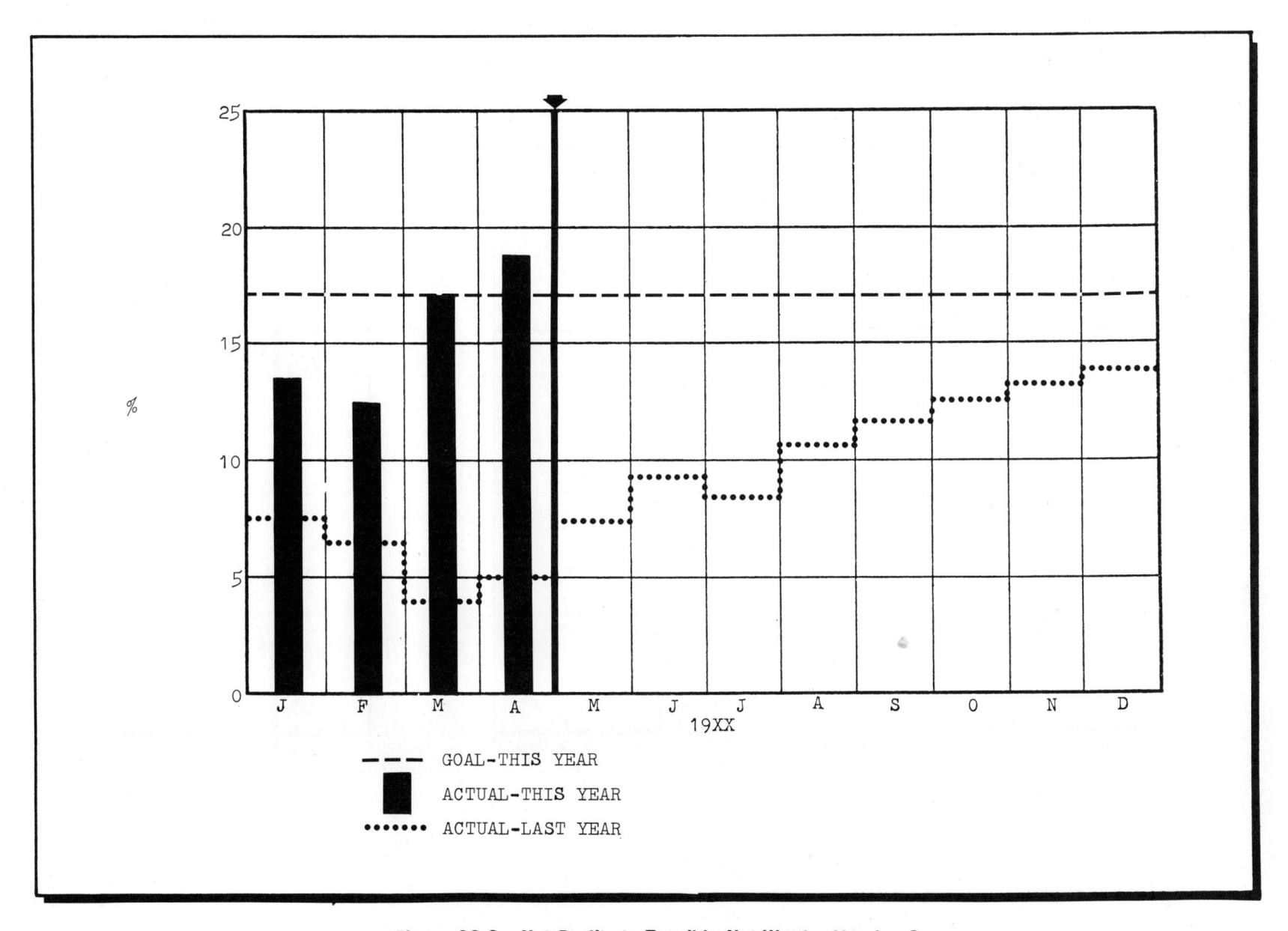

Figure 33.2 Net Profits to Tangible Net Worth—Version 2

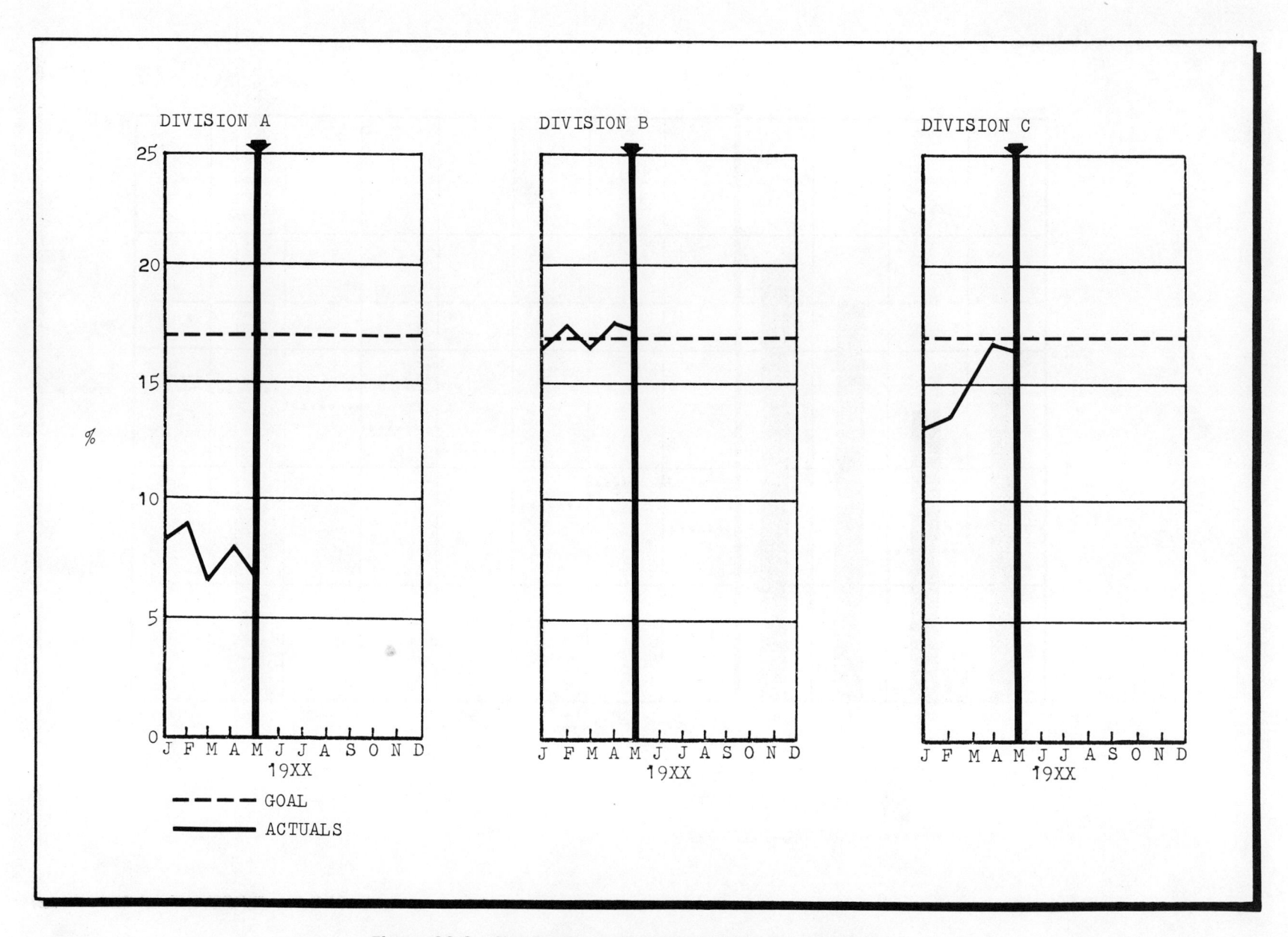

Figure 33.3 Net Profits to Tangible Net Worth—Version 3

NET PROFIT AFTER TAXES (NP) $000		3.7	5.5	6.9								
TANGIBLE NET WORTH (TNW) $000		30.9	34.4	32.9								
RATIO-NP TO TNW %	ACT. ■	12.0	16.0	21.0								
	GOAL ·····	17.0	17.0	17.0	17.0	17.0	17.0	17.0	17.0	17.0	17.0	17.0

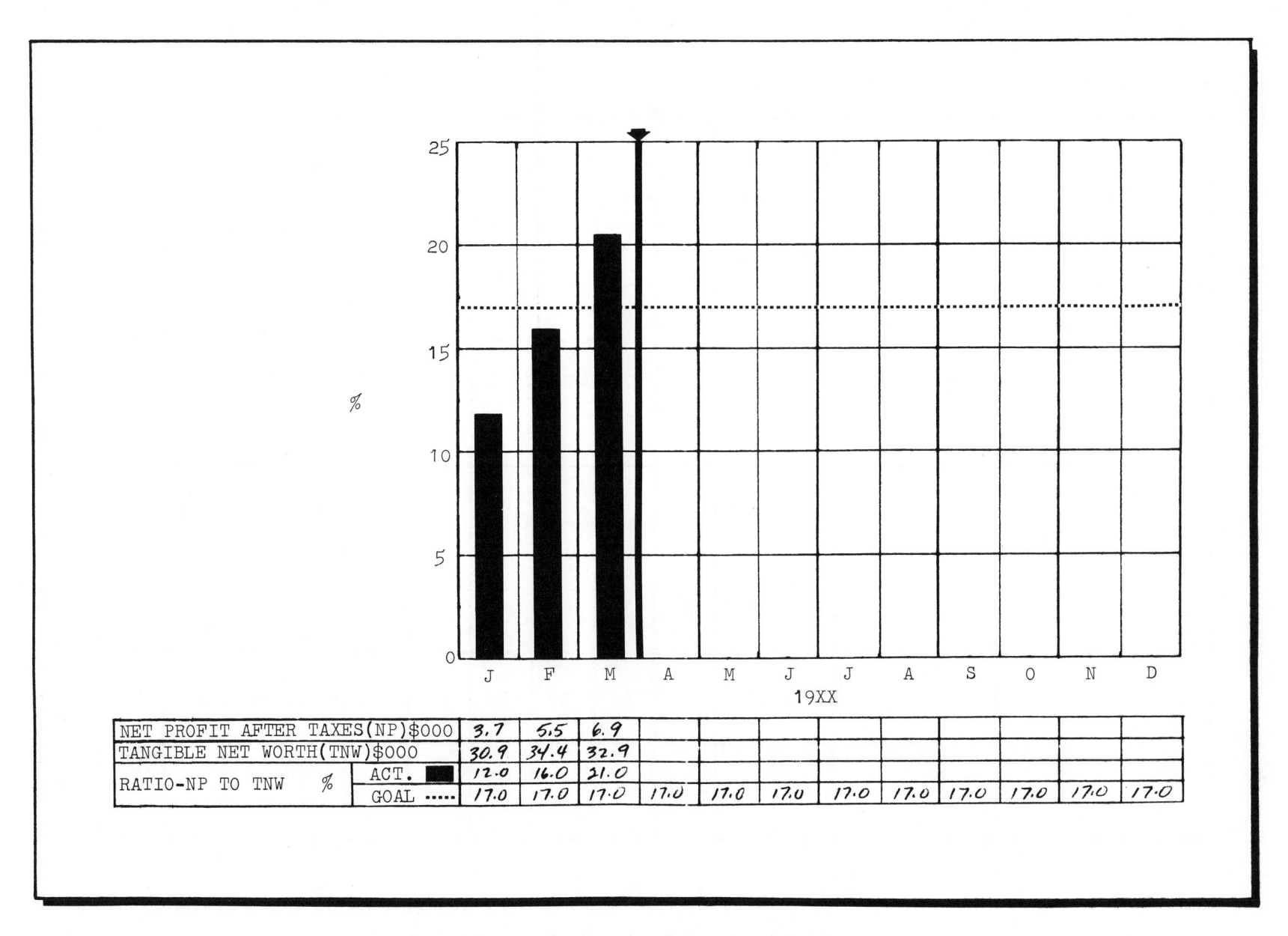

Figure 33.4 Net Profits to Tangible Net Worth—Version 4

ITEM		19XX											
		J	F	M	A	M	J	J	A	S	O	N	D
NET PROFIT AFTER TAXES (NP) $000		3.7	5.5	6.9									
NET WORTH $000		32.0	35.5	34.0									
LESS INTANGIBLE ASSETS $000		1.1	1.1	1.1									
TANGIBLE NET WORTH (TNW) $000		30.9	34.4	32.9									
PERCENTAGE NP TO TNW	ACTUAL	12.0	16.0	21.0									
	GOAL	17.0	17.0	17.0	17.0	17.0	17.0	17.0	17.0	17.0	17.0	17.0	17.0
	VARIANCE	-5.0	-1.0	+4.0									

Figure 33.5 Net Profits to Tangible Net Worth—Version 5

STATUS AS OF __June__

ITEM	PLAN	ACTUAL	VARIANCE
NET PROFITS (NP) $000	5.6	6.9	+1.3
TANGIBLE NET WORTH (TNW) $000	33.0	32.9	−.1
RATIO-NP TO TNW	17%	21%	+4%

Figure 33.6 Net Profits to Tangible Net Worth—Version 6

34.0 NET SALES TO INVENTORY

Charts in this section display the multiple of net sales to inventory. Such a multiple, which shows the number of times inventory is turned over during a specific time period, varies widely from one business to the next. Averages for a given business category can usually be obtained from banks and trade associations.

Net sales are gross sales minus returns and allowances. Inventory for wholesalers or retailers consists of all stock on hand. For manufacturers, inventory consists of all finished goods and all raw and partially completed materials. Also see Section 25.0, *Inventory*.

34.1 Net sales to Inventory—Version 1: A simple version of a net sales to inventory tracking chart is shown in Figure 34.1. In this example, the multiple of actual annualized net sales to inventory (solid line) is compared against an industry average (dashed line).

34.2 Net Sales to Inventory—Version 2: Version 2 of a net sales to inventory tracking chart, Figure 34.2, measures the current year's actuals against the previous year's performance. This particular example shows a seasonal fluctuation in the previous year's figures. Also, an arrowhead has been used to draw attention to the fact that the amount scale does not start with zero.

34.3 Net Sales to Inventory—Version 3: Several chart techniques have been combined in Version 3 of a net sales to inventory tracking chart, Figure 34.3. The statistical table presents the monthly and annualized net sales figures, the value of the inventory, and the multiple of net sales to inventory. This latter set of statistics is also shown on the graphic part of the chart in solid column form, compared against an "industry average" (dashed line).

34.4 Net Sales to Inventory—Version 4: A non-graphic version of a net sales to inventory tracking chart is shown as Version 4, Figure 34.4. In this example, net sales figures are given both in terms of monthly and annualized statistics. The annualized statistics are divided by the inventory value statistics to give the actual multiple of net sales to inventory.

34.5 Net Sales to Inventory—Version 5: Version 5 of a net sales to inventory chart, Figure 34.5, is in the form of a one-time status report. Planned, actual, and variance figures are given for monthly and annualized sales, inventory value, and the multiple of net sales to inventory.

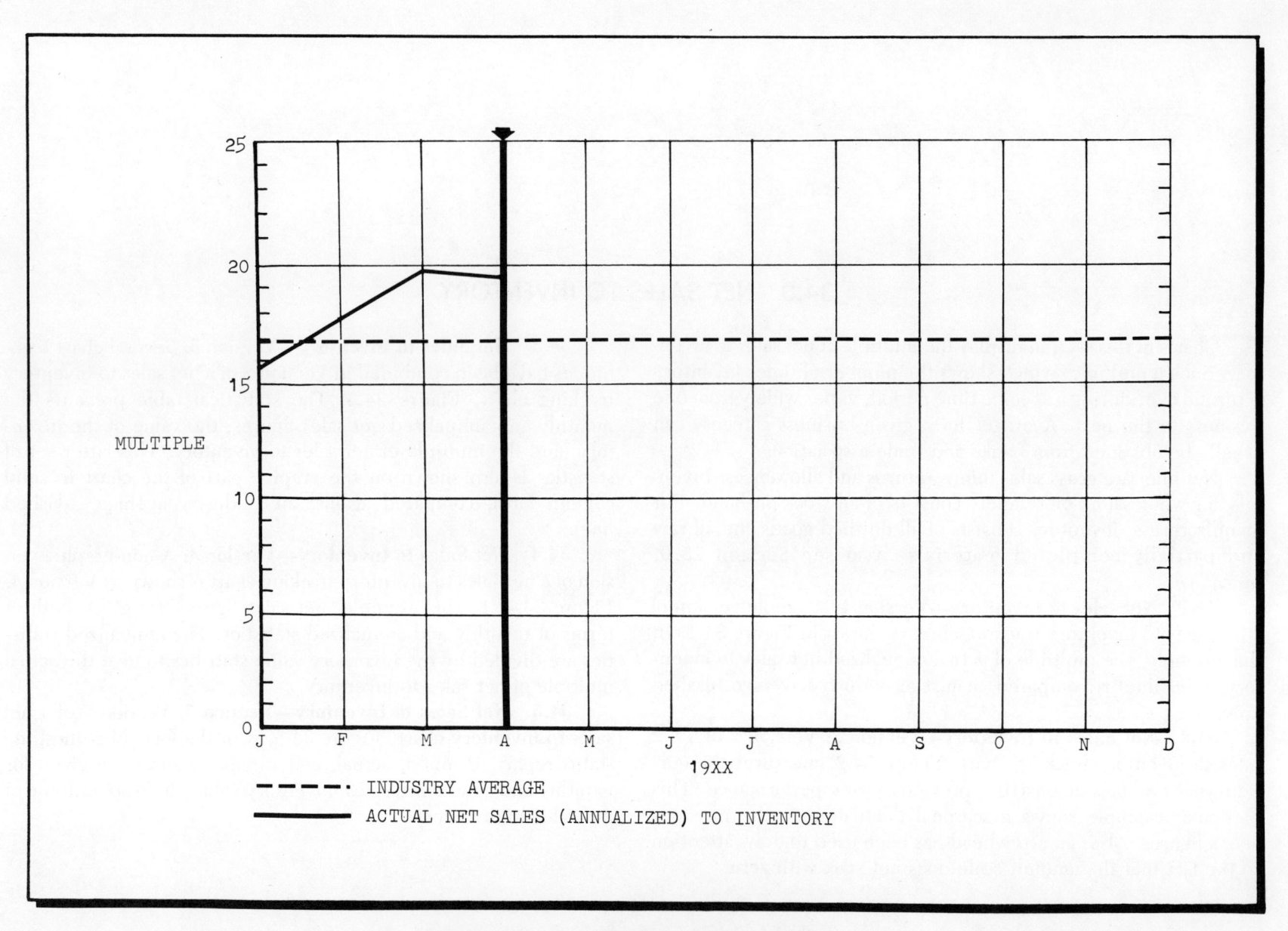

Figure 34.1 Net Sales to Inventory—Version 1

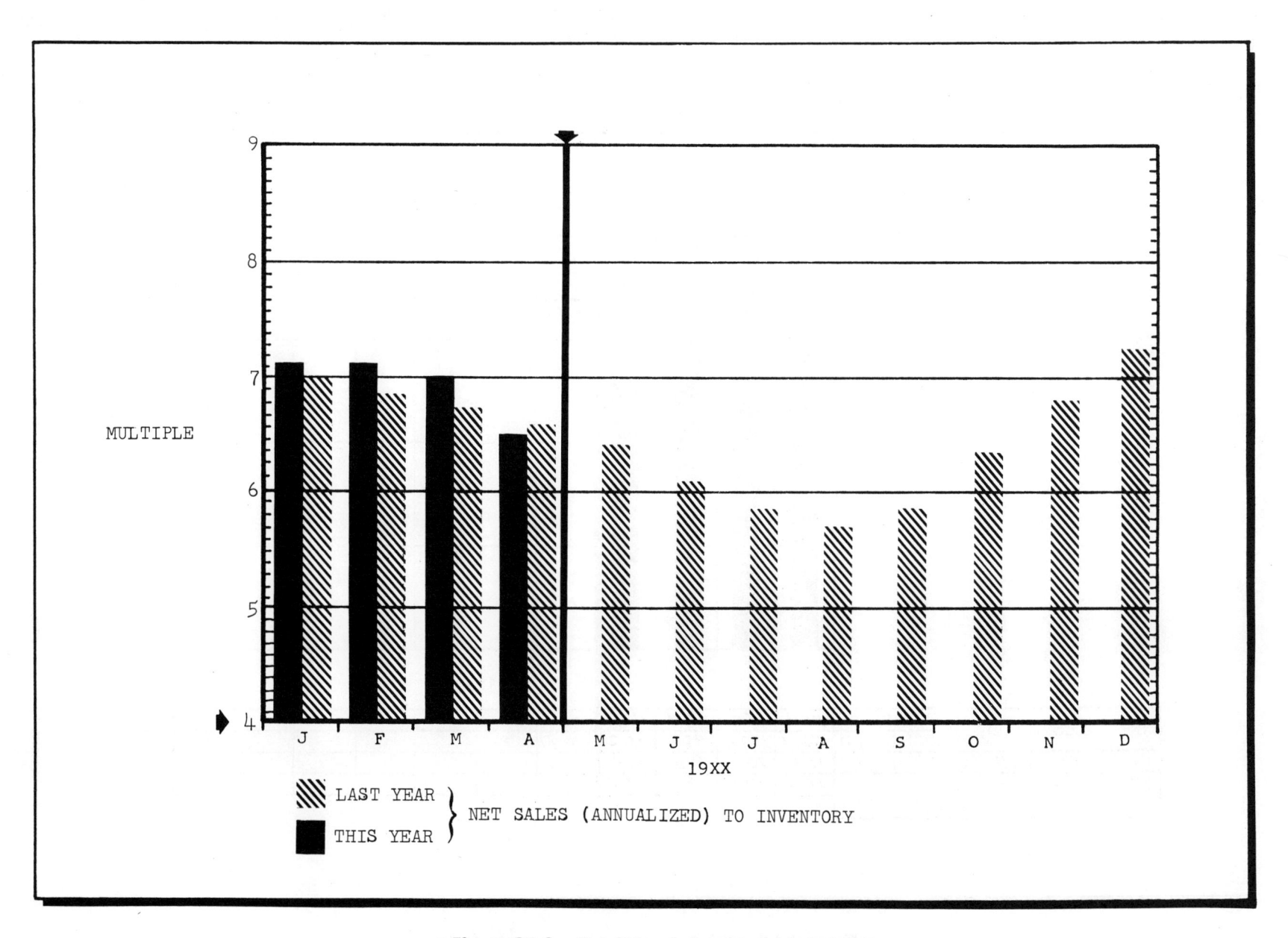

Figure 34.2 Net Sales to Inventory—Version 2

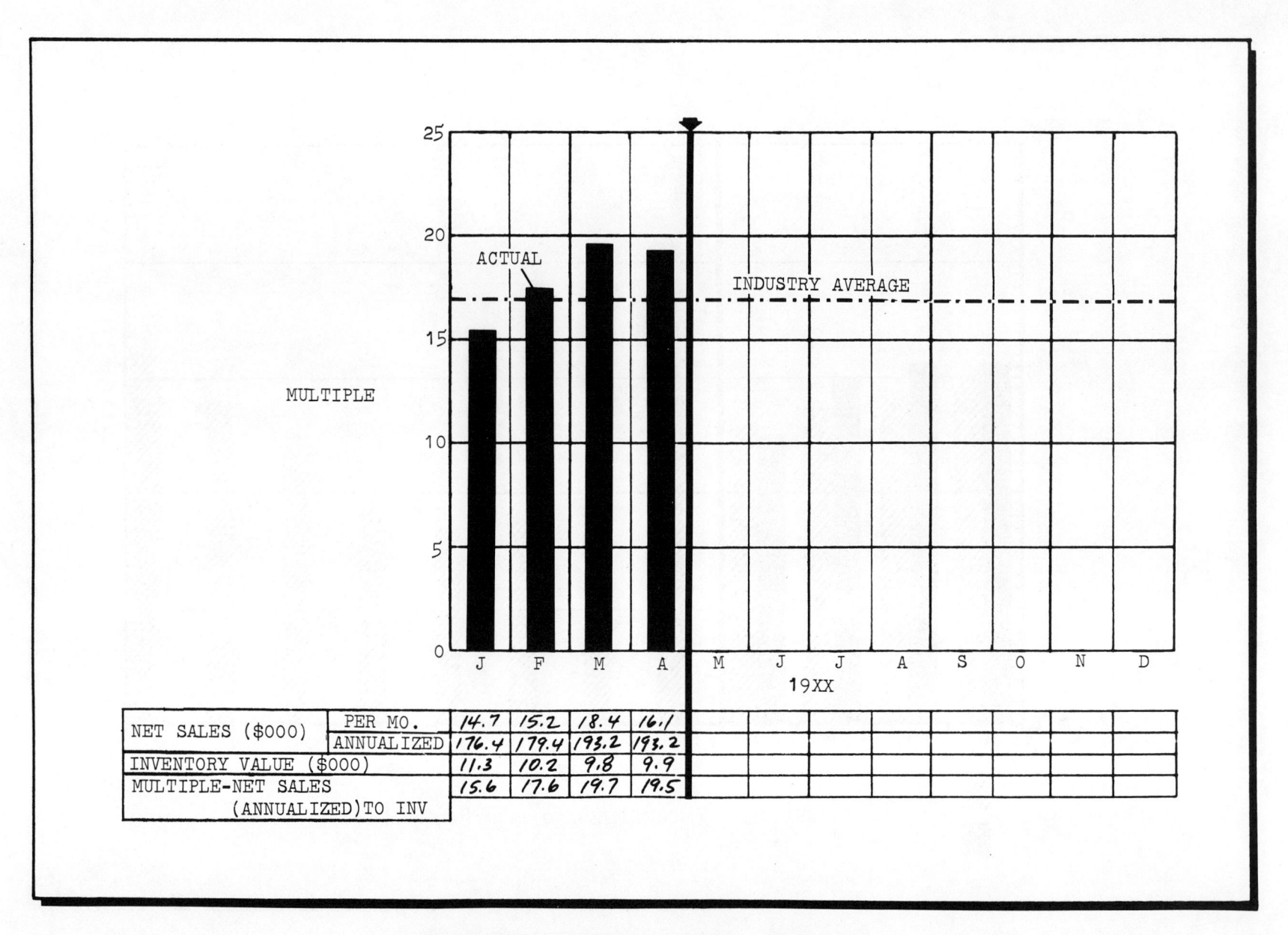

Figure 34.3 Net Sales to Inventory—Version 3

ITEM		19XX											
		J	F	M	A	M	J	J	A	S	O	N	D
NET SALES ($000)	PER MO.	14.7	15.2	18.4	16.1								
	ANNUALIZED	176.4	179.4	193.2	193.2								
INVENTORY VALUE ($000)		11.3	10.2	9.8	9.9								
MULTIPLE— NET SALES (ANNUALIZED) TO INVENTORY	ACTUAL	15.6	17.6	19.7	19.5								
	INDUSTY AVERAGE	17.0	17.0	17.0	17.0	17.0	17.0	17.0	17.0	17.0	17.0	17.0	17.0
	VARIANCE	-1.4	+.6	+2.7	+2.5								

Figure 34.4   Net Sales to Inventory—Version 4

STATUS AS OF __April 15__

ITEM	PLAN	ACTUAL	VARIANCE
NET SALES-THIS MONTH ($000)	14.0	16.1	+2.1
NET SALES-ANNUALIZED ($000)	187.0	193.2	+6.2
INVENTORY VALUE ($000)	11.0	9.9	−1.1
MULTIPLE-NET SALES (ANNUALIZED) TO INVENTORY	17.0*	19.5	+2.5

*INDUSTRY AVERAGE

Figure 34.5 Net Sales to Inventory—Version 5

35.0 OVERHAUL AND REPAIR

Charts that display the status of overhaul and repair activities are shown in this section. Also see Section 26.0, *Maintenance*.

35.1 Overhaul and Repair—Version 1: Version 1 of an overhaul and repair tracking chart, Figure 35.1, shows returns (of units of equipment or systems, etc.) as a percentage of the total number of items that are in use. The downward slope of both the forecast and actuals in the example might be a reflection of a new product in use where in its early stages more problems are expected.

35.2 Overhaul and Repair—Version 2: Backlog, the quantity of items on hand awaiting overhaul or repair, is the factor examined in Version 2 of an overhaul and repair tracking chart, Figure 35.2. The actual month-end backlog is plotted with a solid line and is in register with the left-hand scale. Backlog as a percent of the number of units or items in use is plotted with a dotted line and is in register with the right-hand scale.

35.3 Overhaul and Repair—Version 3: Version 3 of an overhaul and repair tracking chart, Figure 35.3, tracks activity in terms of the quantity of units processed per month. In this example, the actual scheduled overhauls and the actual scheduled overhauls plus unscheduled repairs are compared against a forecasted workload.

35.4 Overhaul and Repair—Version 4: Version 4 of an overhaul and repair tracking chart, Figure 35.4, shows the quantity of units on a cumulative basis. Forecasts of O and R workload are often made on the basis of the number of units in use. Both factors, together with actual overhauls and repairs to date, are shown on the chart.

35.5 Overhaul and Repair—Version 5: The cumulative quantities of overhaul and repair work received (dashed line) are compared with the cumulative quantity of work shipped (solid line) in Version 5, Figure 35.5. The vertical distance between the two lines shows the quantity in process, and the horizontal distance shows the cycle time.

35.6 Overhaul and Repair—Version 6: Three factors are shown in Version 6 of an overhaul and repair tracking chart, Figure 35.6. In this example, actual shipments are shown in relationship to planned shipments, and the actual month-end backlog is also given.

35.7 Overhaul and Repair—Version 7: Version 7 of an overhaul and repair tracking chart, Figure 35.7, is identical to Version 6 except that shading has been added to better illustrate the backlog portion of the chart.

35.8 Overhaul and Repair—Version 8: A surface chart technique is used in Version 8 of an overhaul and repair tracking chart, Figure 35.8. The total quantity of items in process is segmented as to units overhauled or repaired and shipped, the backlog balance, and the units received each month for overhaul and repair. The dotted line indicates the month-end backlog.

35.9 Overhaul and Repair—Version 9: The overhaul and repair activities of three different models are compared in Version 9, Figure 35.9. For each model the month-end backlog is given, as well as the quantity of received units and shipped units, the latter in relationship to a forecast of shipments.

35.10 Overhaul and Repair—Version 10: The graphic portion of Figure 35.10 shows the total quantity of overhaul and repair in-process units segmented as to those overhauled, repaired, and shipped each month, the backlog balance, and the units received during each month. The statistics at the bottom of the chart give the average turnaround days between receipt and shipment of the units.

35.11 Overhaul and Repair—Version 11: Version 11 of an overhaul and repair tracking chart, Figure 35.11, displays actual shipments to date with solid columns, comparing these to planned shipments which are shown with a dashed step line. The month-end backlog portion of the chart is shaded, while the average turnaround time statistics are given at the bottom of the chart.

35.12 Overhaul and Repair—Version 12: Version 12 of an overhaul and repair tracking chart, Figure 35.12, displays units received and units shipped in column chart form, and the actual and forecasted month-end backlog in line chart form. The backup statistics are given in the tabular portion of the chart.

35.13 Overhaul and Repair—Version 13: Two separate graphic charts and a statistical table are combined in Version 13 of an overhaul and repair tracking chart, Figure 35.13. The top grid shows the quantity of units actually received and shipped compared against an anticipated level of receipts and shipments. The lower grid uses columns to show the month-end backlog. Backup statistics are given in the table.

35.14 Overhaul and Repair—Version 14: A key feature of Version 14 of an overhaul and repair tracking chart, Figure 35.14, is that the age of the backlog (the number of days the units have been in-house) is given. The graphic portion of the chart plots the backlog and the received/shipped figures to the center of the grid spaces for each month.

35.15 Overhaul and Repair—Version 15: A one-time status report version of an overhaul and repair chart is shown as Version 15, Figure 35.15. In this example, statistics are given for each unit in terms of the beginning backlog balance, the receipts and shipments made during the month, the month-end backlog, the turnaround days for the current and previous months so these figures can be compared, and the age of the backlog.

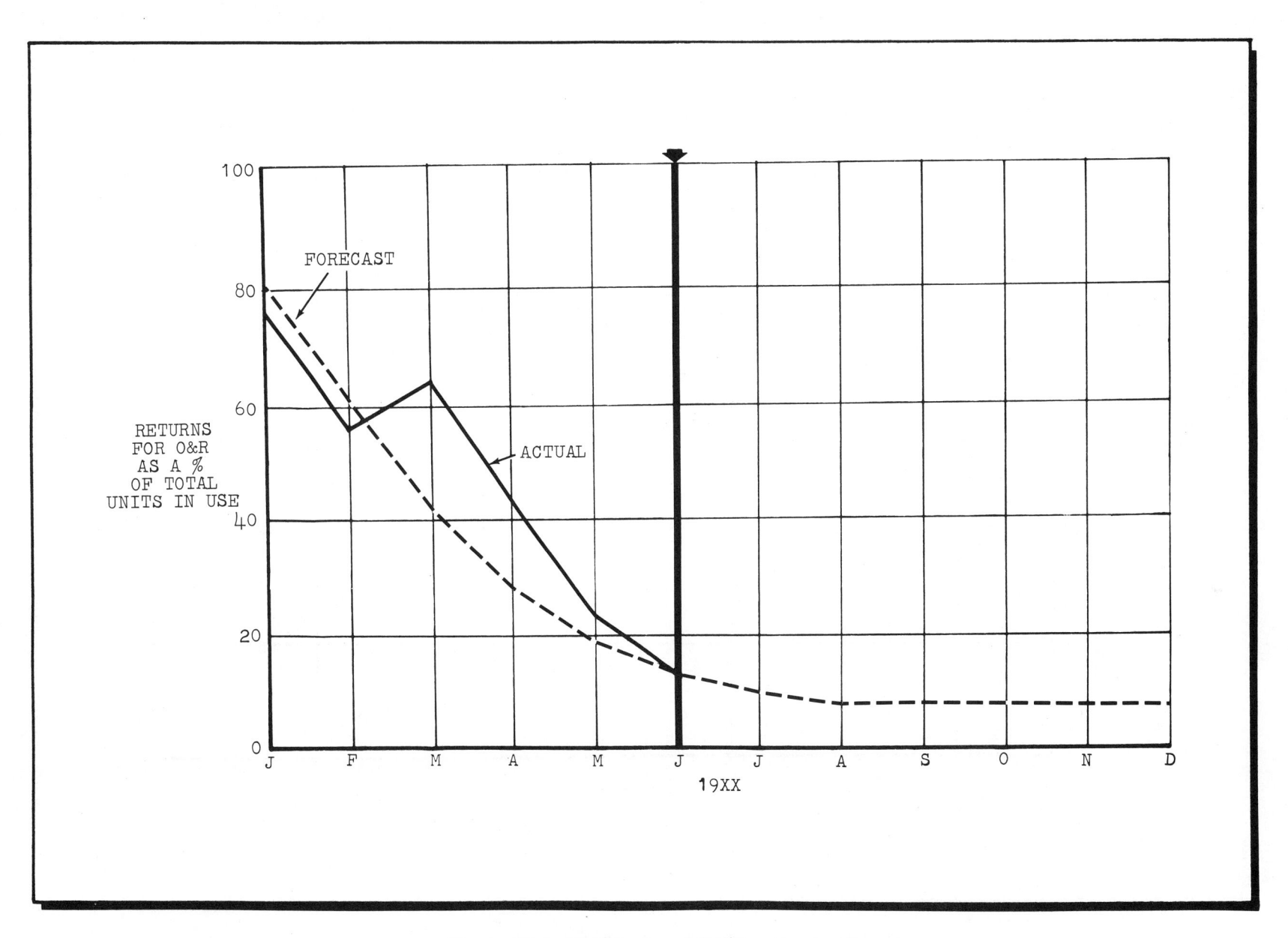

Figure 35.1 Overhaul and Repair—Version 1

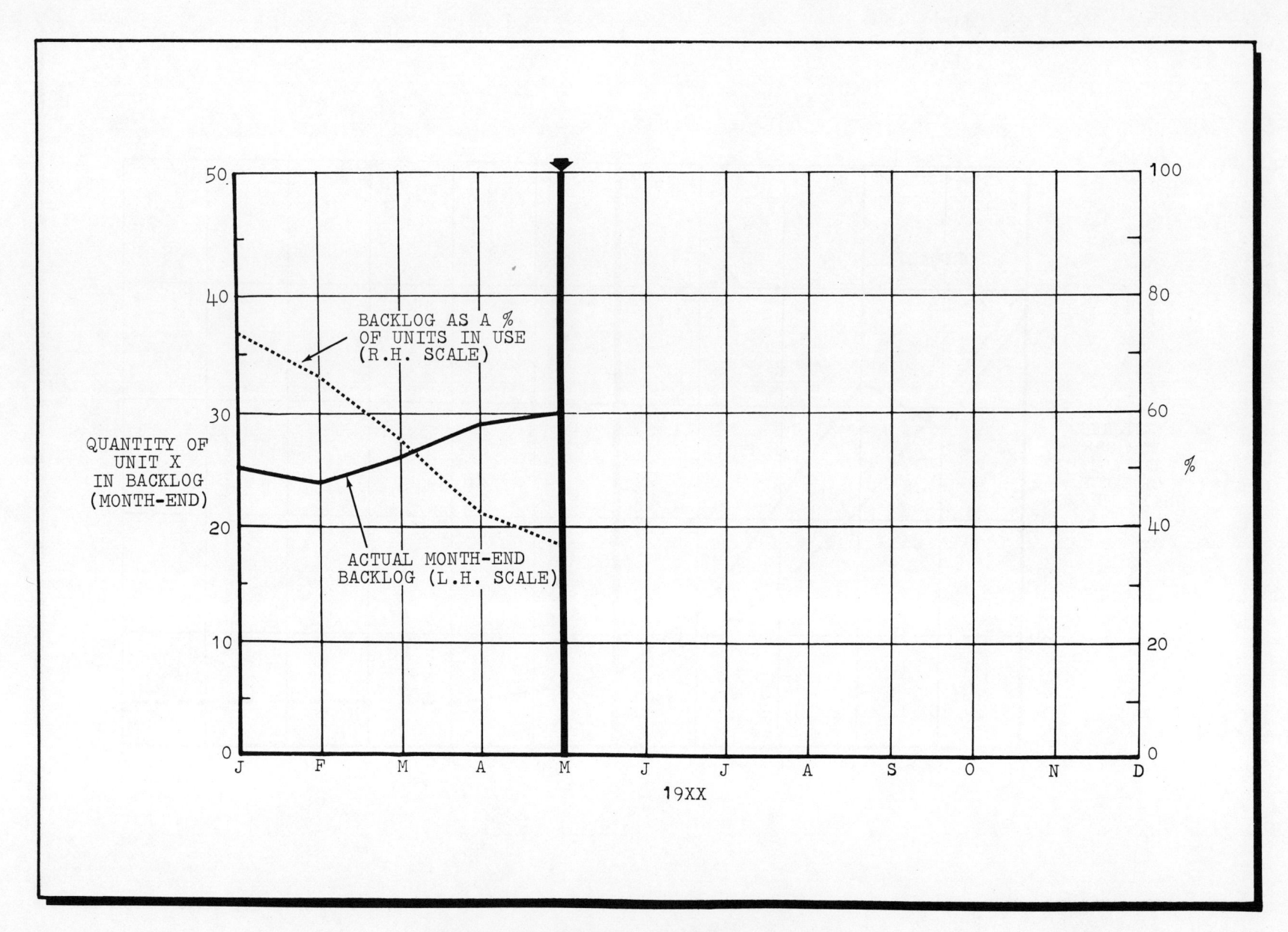

Figure 35.2 Overhaul and Repair—Version 2

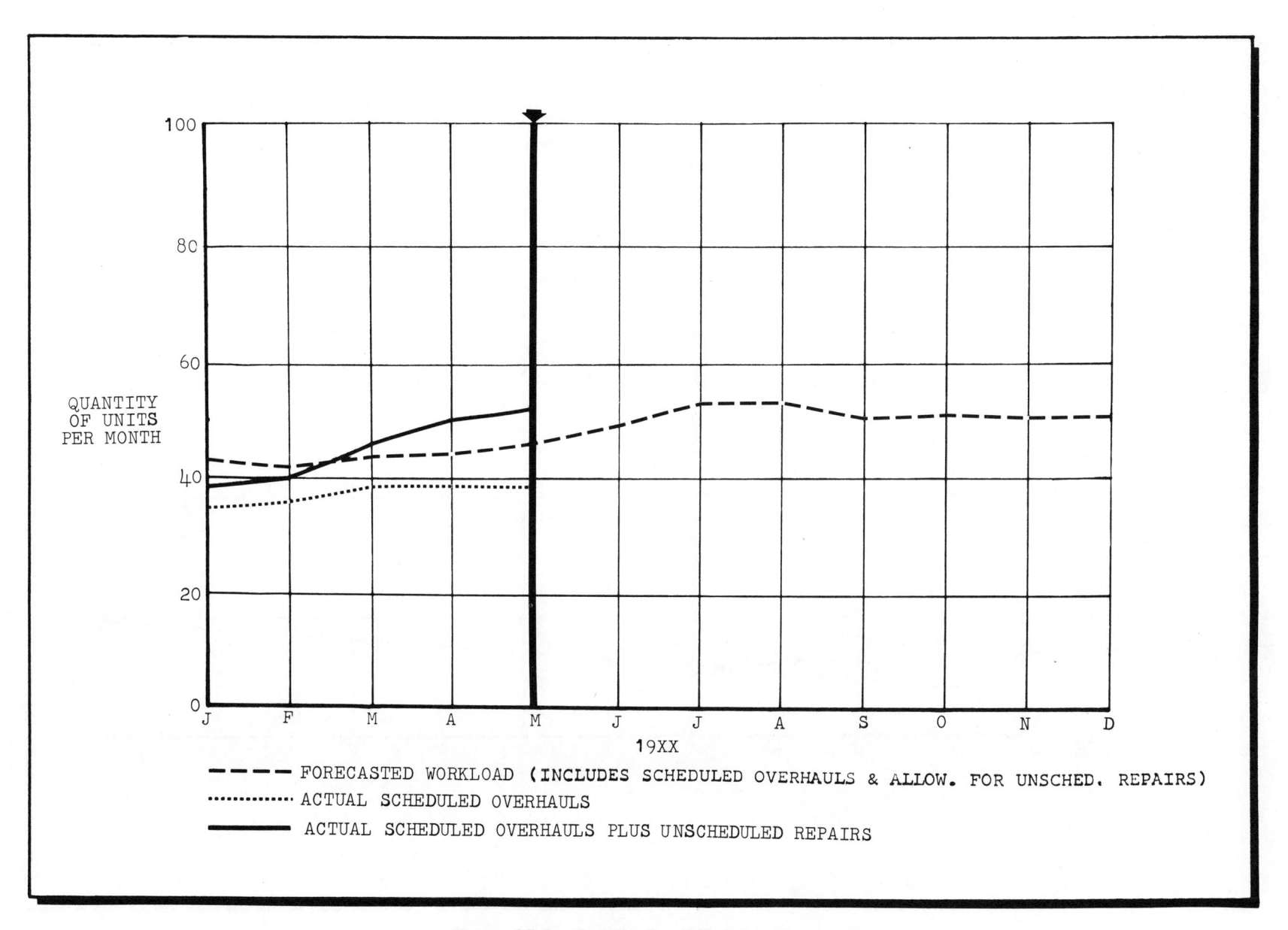

Figure 35.3 Overhaul and Repair—Version 3

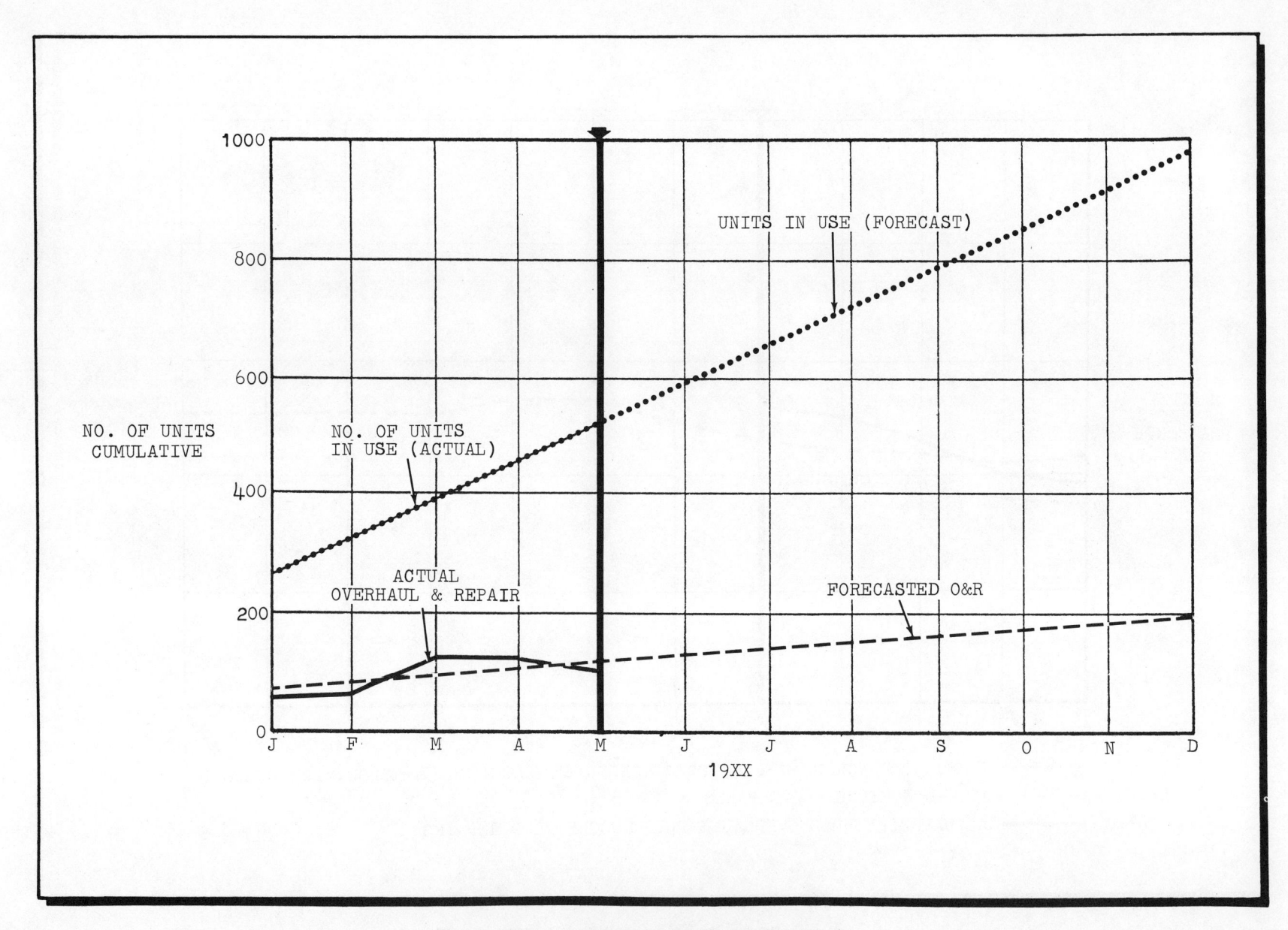

Figure 35.4 Overhaul and Repair—Version 4

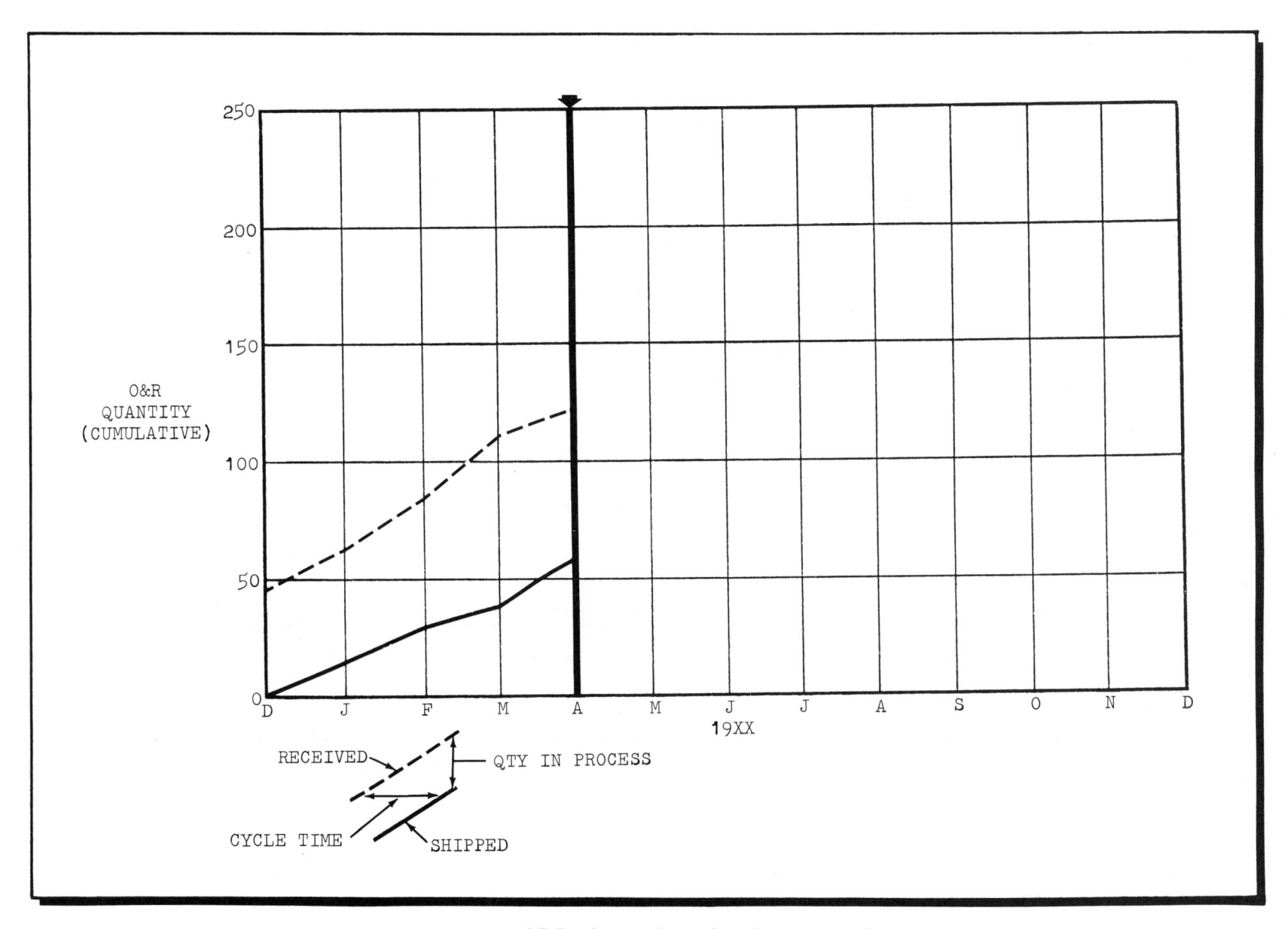

Figure 35.5 Overhaul and Repair—Version 5

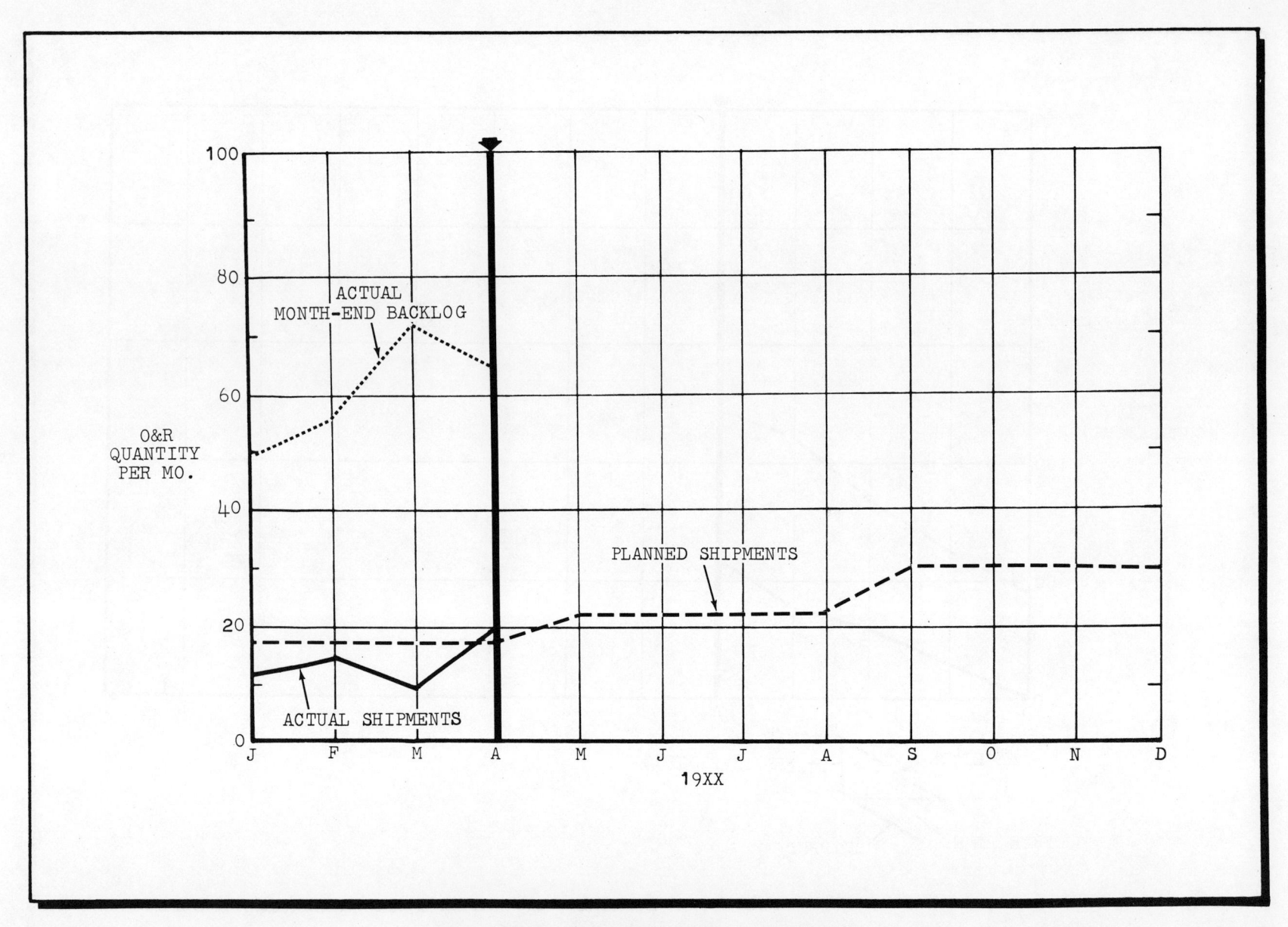

Figure 35.6 Overhaul and Repair—Version 6

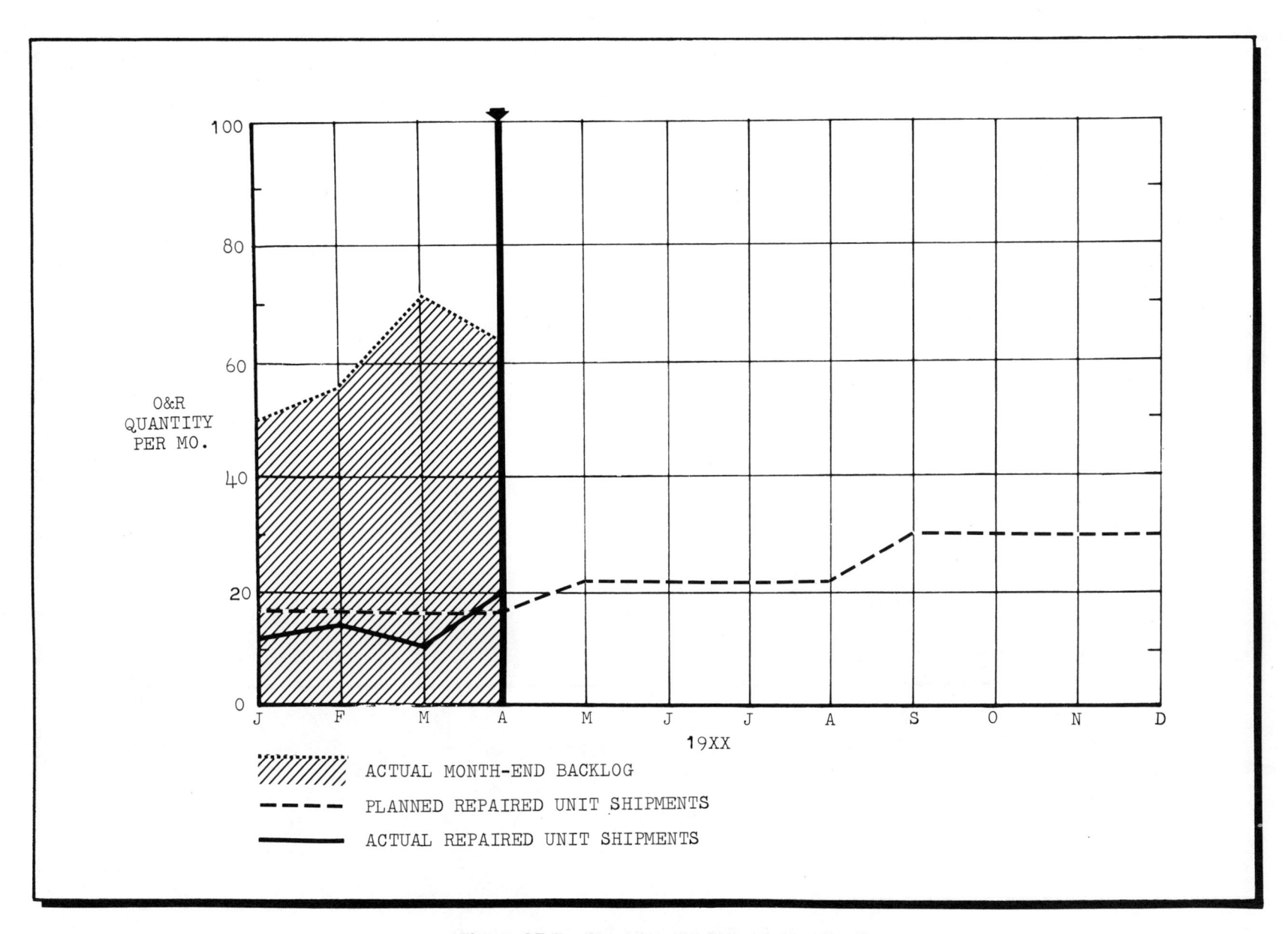

Figure 35.7 Overhaul and Repair—Version 7

383

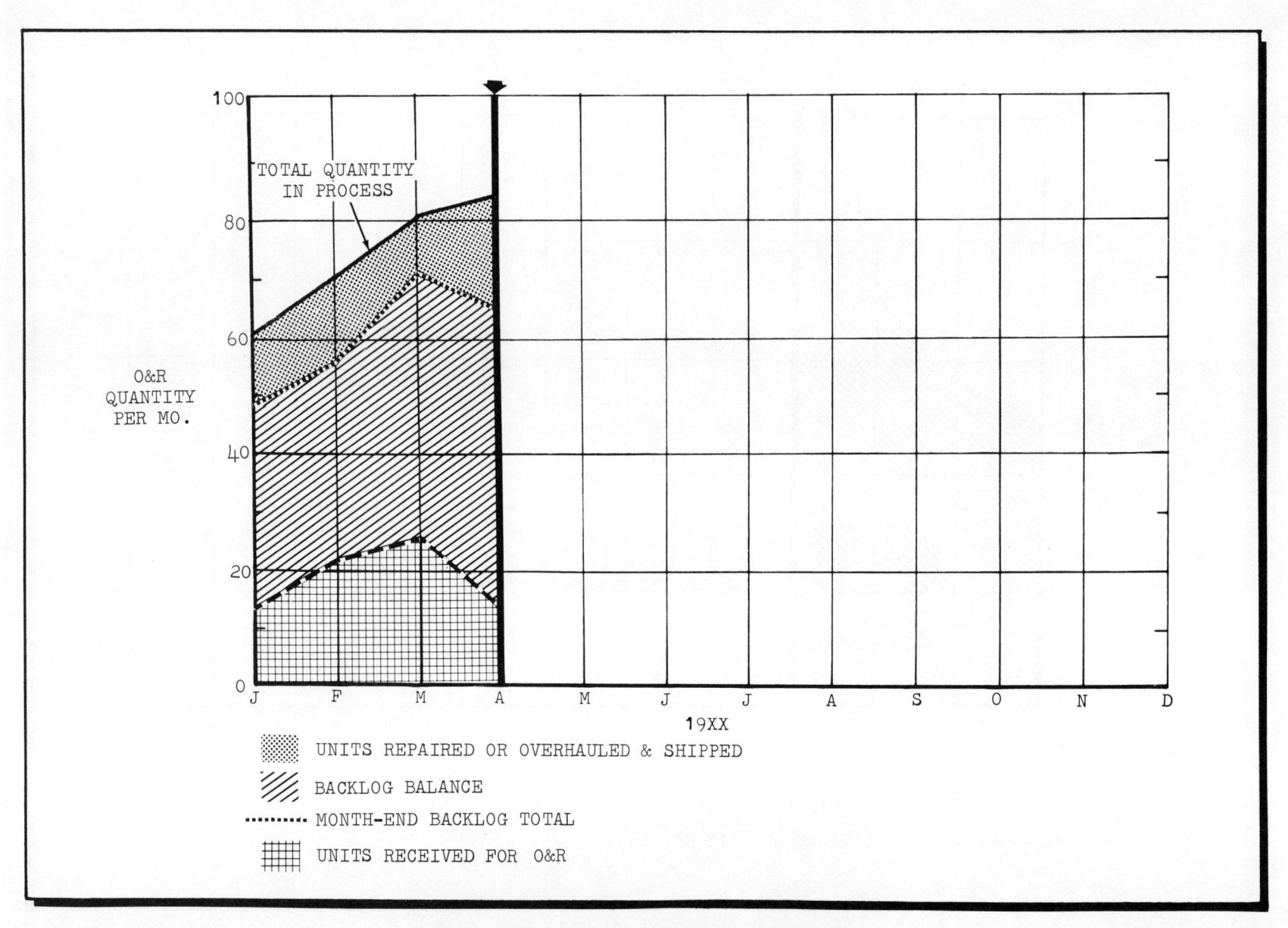

Figure 35.8 Overhaul and Repair—Version 8

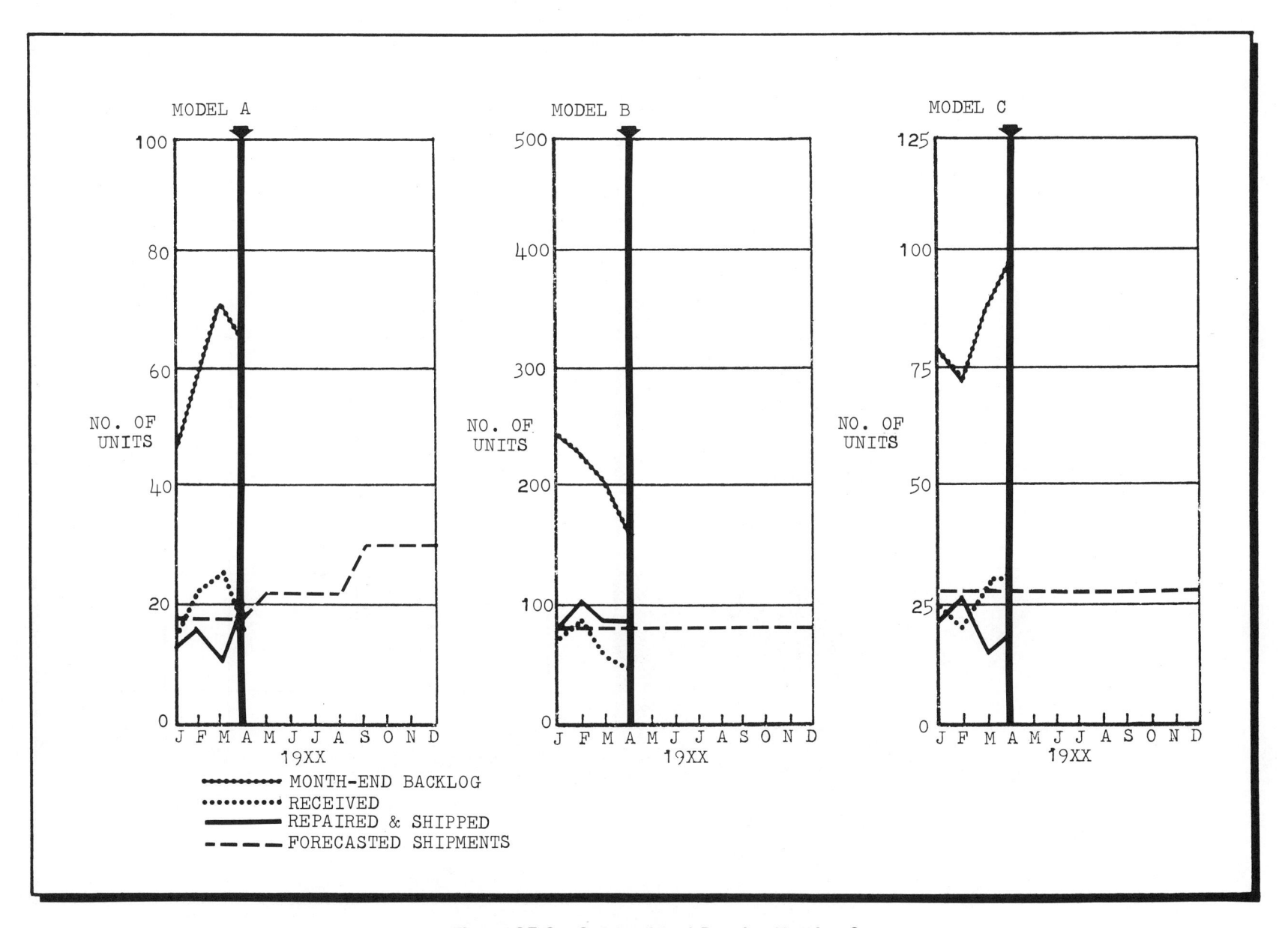

Figure 35.9 Overhaul and Repair—Version 9

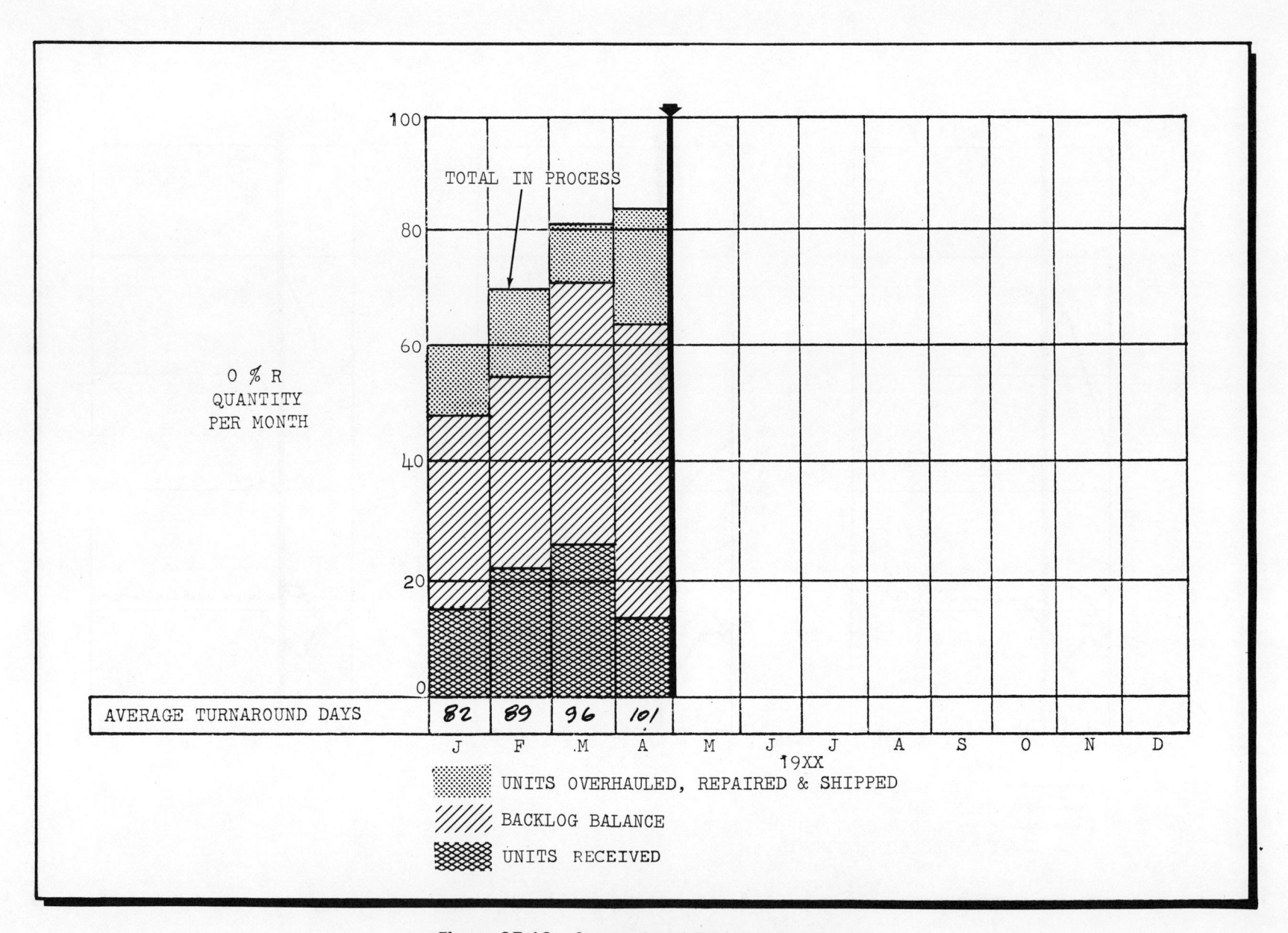

Figure 35.10 Overhaul and Repair—Version 10

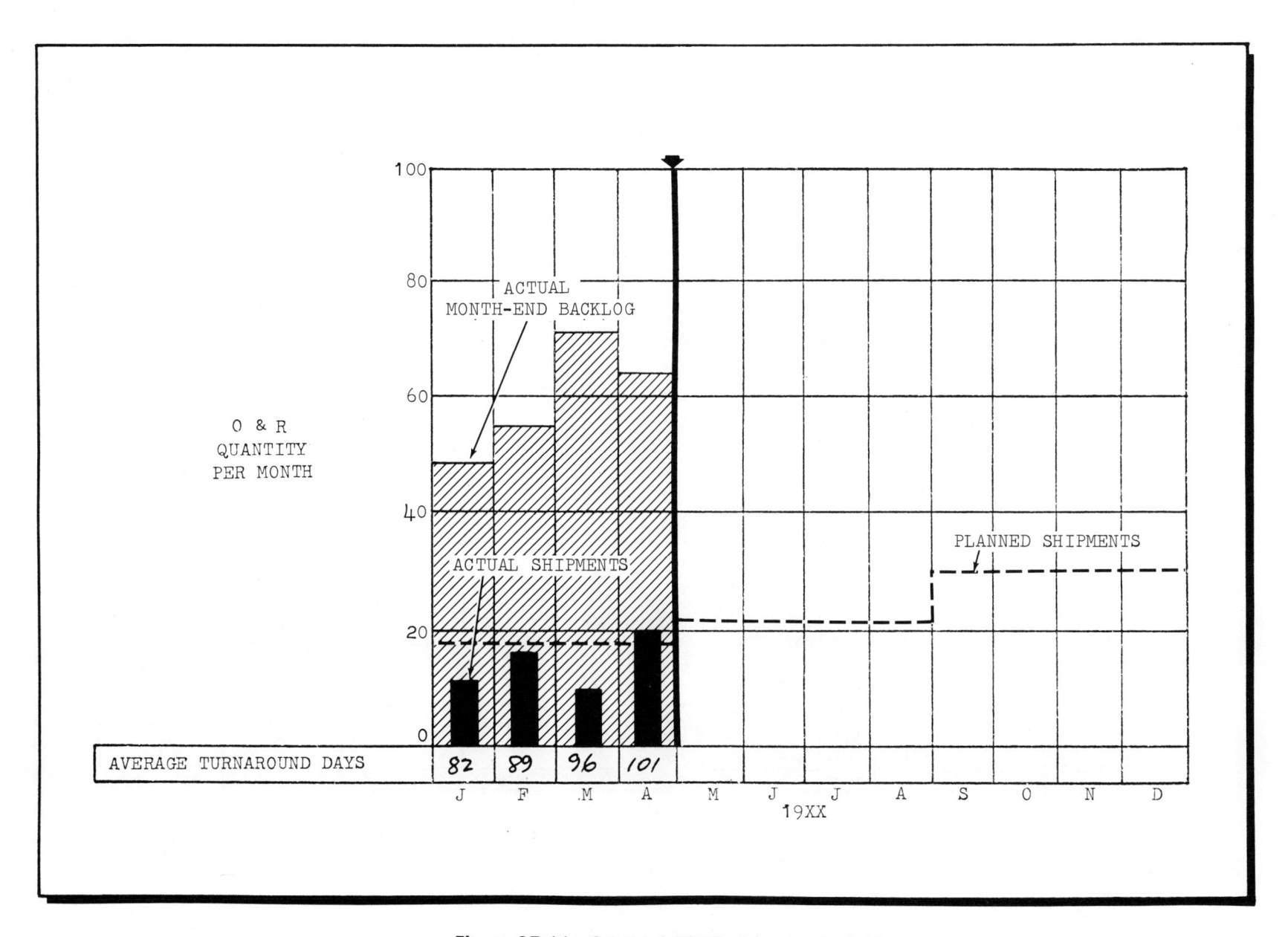

Figure 35.11 Overhaul and Repair—Version 11

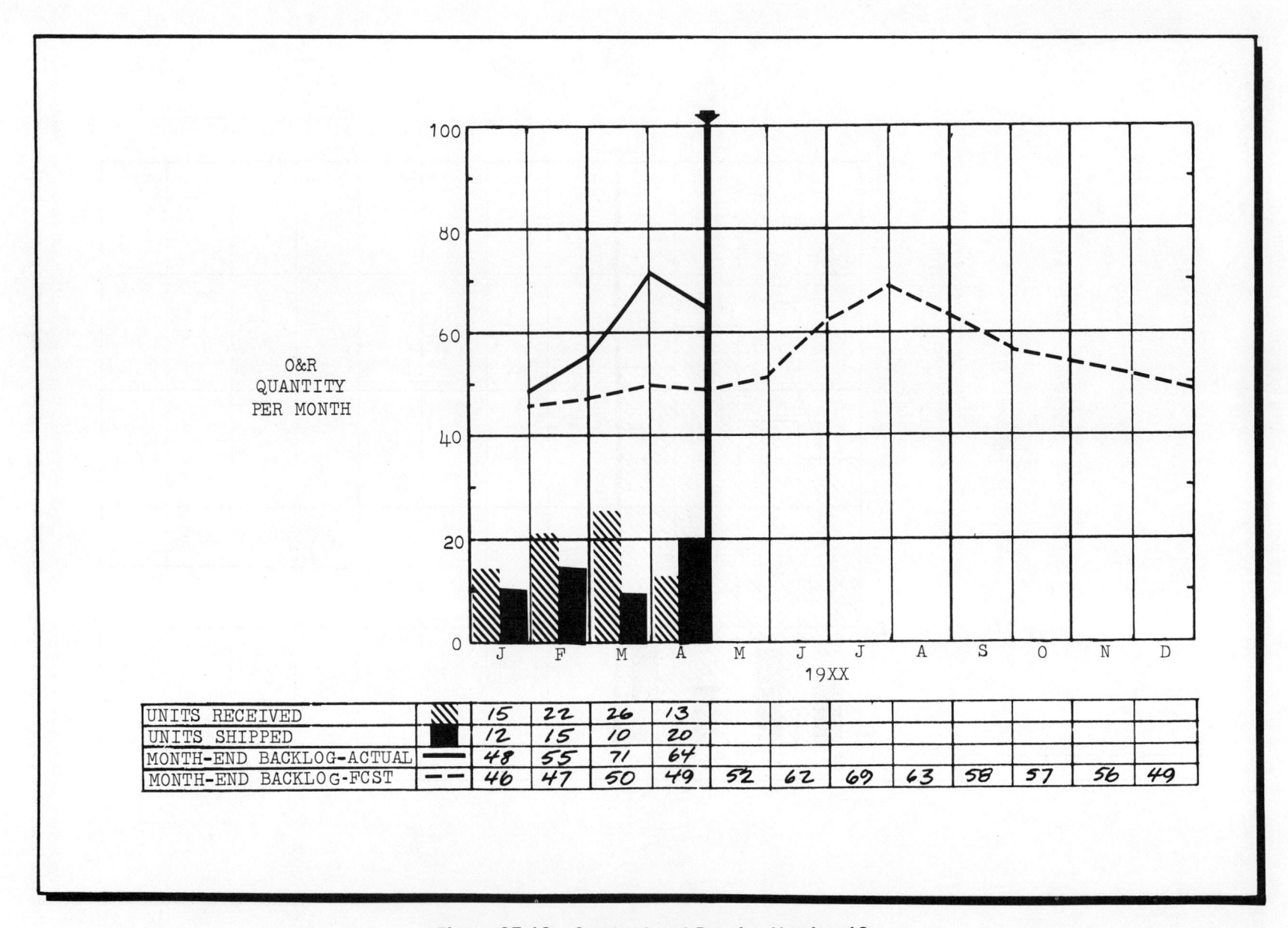

UNITS RECEIVED	▨	15	22	26	13								
UNITS SHIPPED	■	12	15	10	20								
MONTH-END BACKLOG-ACTUAL	——	48	55	71	64								
MONTH-END BACKLOG-FCST	— —	46	47	50	49	52	62	69	63	58	57	56	49

Figure 35.12 Overhaul and Repair—Version 12

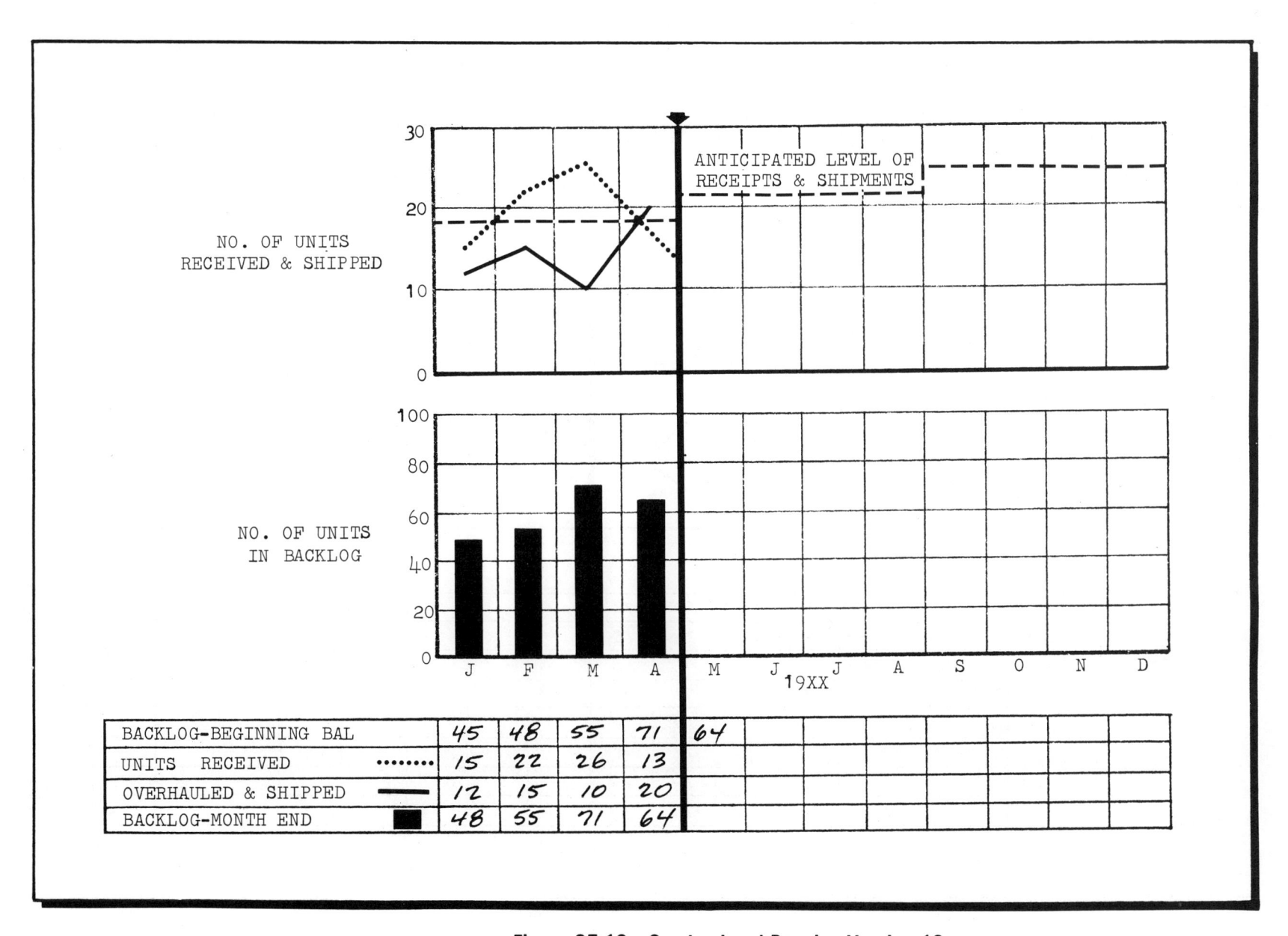

BACKLOG—BEGINNING BAL		45	48	55	71	64							
UNITS RECEIVED		15	22	26	13								
OVERHAULED & SHIPPED ———		12	15	10	20								
BACKLOG—MONTH END ■		48	55	71	64								

Figure 35.13 Overhaul and Repair—Version 13

O & R
QUANTITY PER MO.

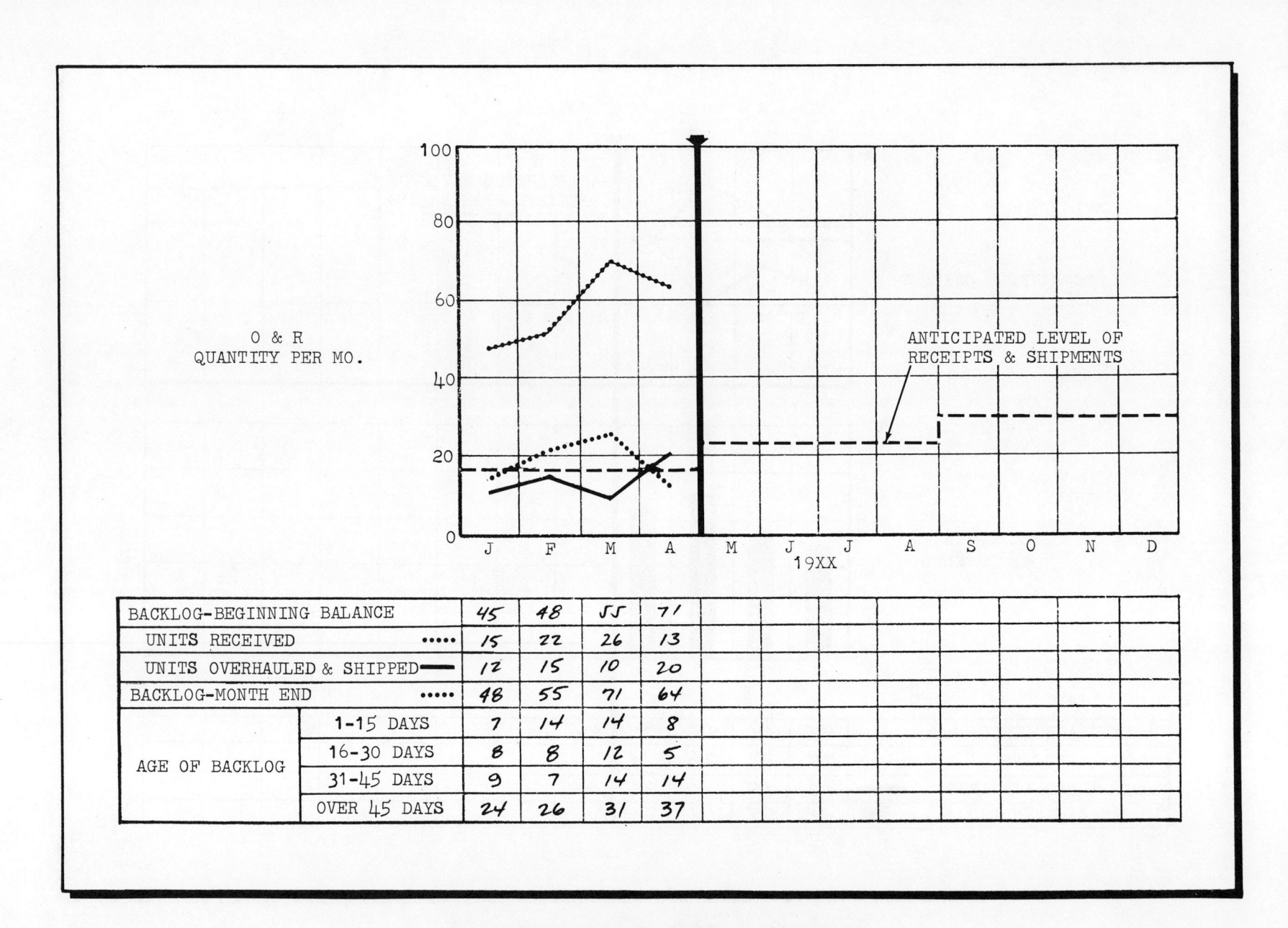

ANTICIPATED LEVEL OF
RECEIPTS & SHIPMENTS

19XX

		J	F	M	A	M	J	J	A	S	O	N	D
BACKLOG—BEGINNING BALANCE		45	48	55	71								
UNITS RECEIVED		15	22	26	13								
UNITS OVERHAULED & SHIPPED ———		12	15	10	20								
BACKLOG—MONTH END		48	55	71	64								
AGE OF BACKLOG	1–15 DAYS	7	14	14	8								
	16–30 DAYS	8	8	12	5								
	31–45 DAYS	9	7	14	14								
	OVER 45 DAYS	24	26	31	37								

Figure 35.14   Overhaul and Repair—Version 14

STATUS AS OF _____

UNIT	BACKLOG BEGIN-NING BAL.	RECEIPTS	SHIP-MENTS	BACKLOG MONTH-END	TURNAROUND DAYS		AGE OF BACKLOG (NO. OF DAYS IN-HOUSE)			
					LAST MO	THIS MO	1-15	16-30	31-45	OVER 45
A	10	10	15	5	19	17	5	0	0	0
B	27	13	23	17	38	34	8	5	4	0
C	3	9	9	3	11	11	3	0	0	0
D	33	15	14	34	58	60	8	7	7	12
E	18	15	20	13	34	29	10	3	0	0
F	45	15	12	48	75	82	7	8	9	24
G	17	14	21	10	30	26	8	2	0	0

Figure 35.15 Overhaul and Repair—Version 15

36.0 OVERTIME

Charts that display overtime in terms of its percentage to straight time, and in terms of hours and dollars, are shown in this section.

36.1 Overtime—Version 1: A method for displaying actual versus authorized overtime as a percent of straight time is shown in Version 1 of an overtime tracking chart, Figure 36.1. Overtime is usually considered an emergency measure and is not planned for over a long period of time. In the example, it is authorized only for the month following the reporting date.

36.2 Overtime—Version 2: Version 2 of an overtime tracking chart, Figure 36.2, displays actual straight-time hours plus actual total hours, the net difference between these two plottings being the overtime used. Tracking is against total budgeted hours.

36.3 Overtime—Version 3: The same style chart used in Version 2 is applied to Version 3 of an overtime tracking chart, Figure 36.3. In this example, though, tracking is on the basis of costs.

36.4 Overtime—Version 4: Dual amount scales are used in Version 4 of an overtime tracking chart, Figure 36.4. The lower plottings show actual straight time and total hours tracked against budgeted hours, all in register with the left-hand scale. The upper plottings are in terms of costs and are related to the right-hand amount scale.

36.5 Overtime—Version 5: Overtime is tracked in terms of dollars in Version 5 of an overtime tracking chart, Figure 36.5. Paired columns are used in the graphic portion of the chart, with the left-hand column for each month representing budgeted dollars, and the right-hand segmented columns showing straight time plus overtime dollars. The backup for the graphics is given in the tabular portion of the chart.

36.6 Overtime—Version 6: In the graphic portion of Version 6 of an overtime tracking chart, Figure 36.6, the total authorized overtime hours are shown on a monthly basis. Actuals, shown with solid columns, are plotted on a weekly basis but cumulated by the month. The plotting for the first week in April, for instance, shows approximately half the authorized overtime for the month already used with three weeks remaining. The tabular portion of this example gives the percent overtime to straight time for each month.

36.7 Overtime—Version 7: Version 7 of an overtime tracking chart, Figure 36.7, is similar to Version 6 except in this example additional statistics are given in the tabular portion of the chart. In addition to the percent of overtime to straight-time statistics, the actual straight-time hours and the budgeted, actual, and variance overtime hours are given.

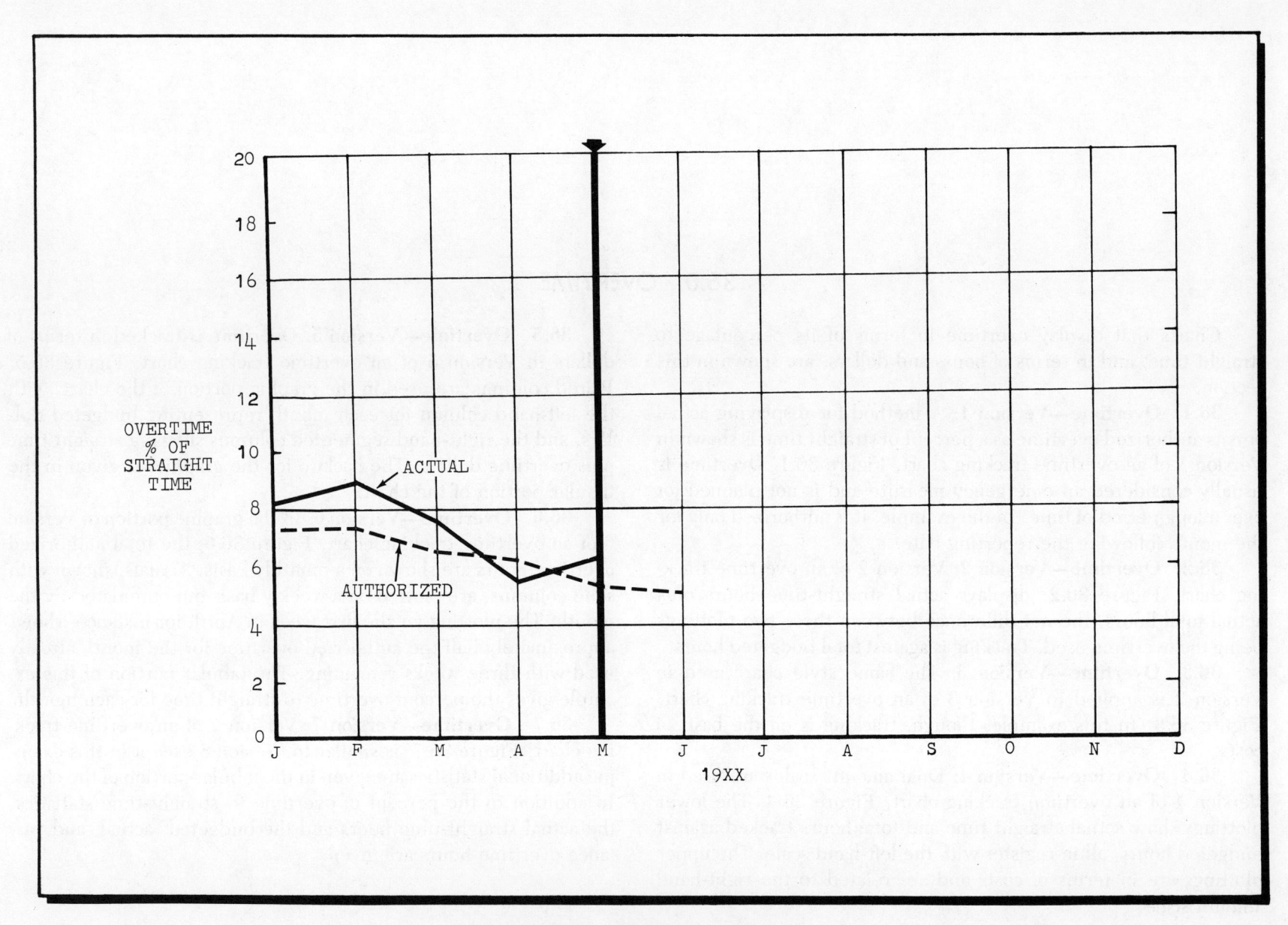

Figure 36.1　Overtime—Version 1

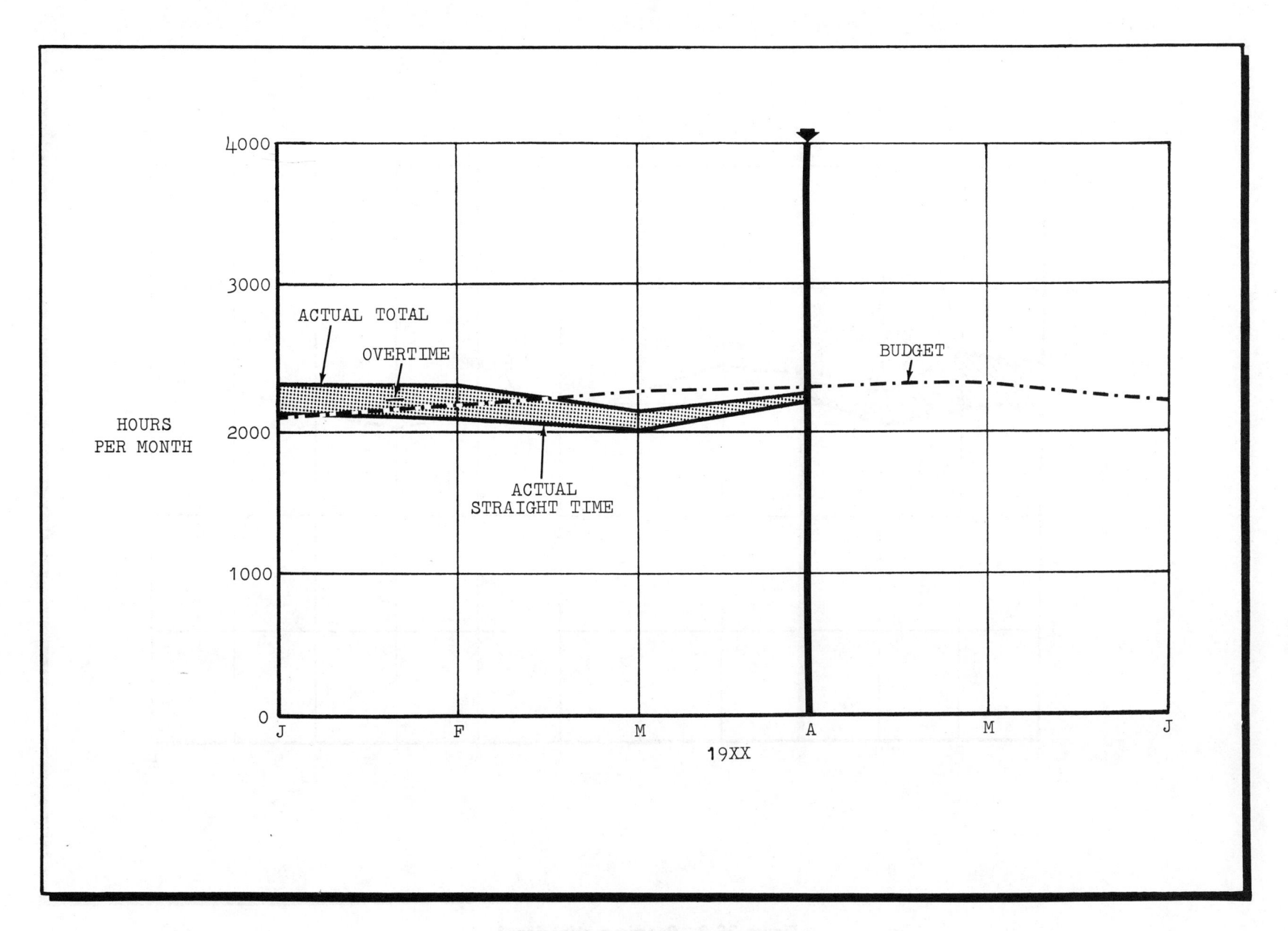

Figure 36.2   Overtime—Version 2

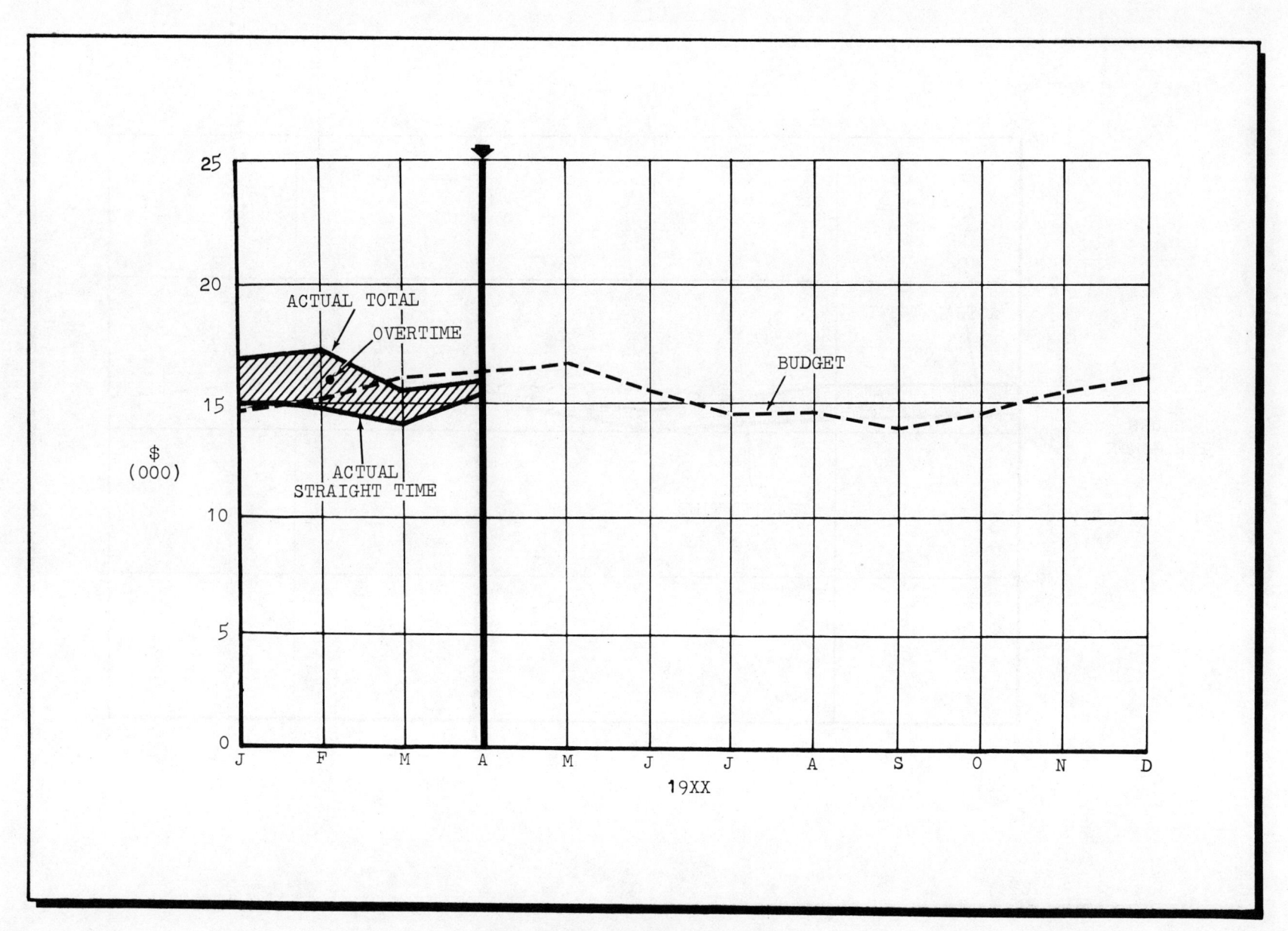

Figure 36.3   Overtime—Version 3

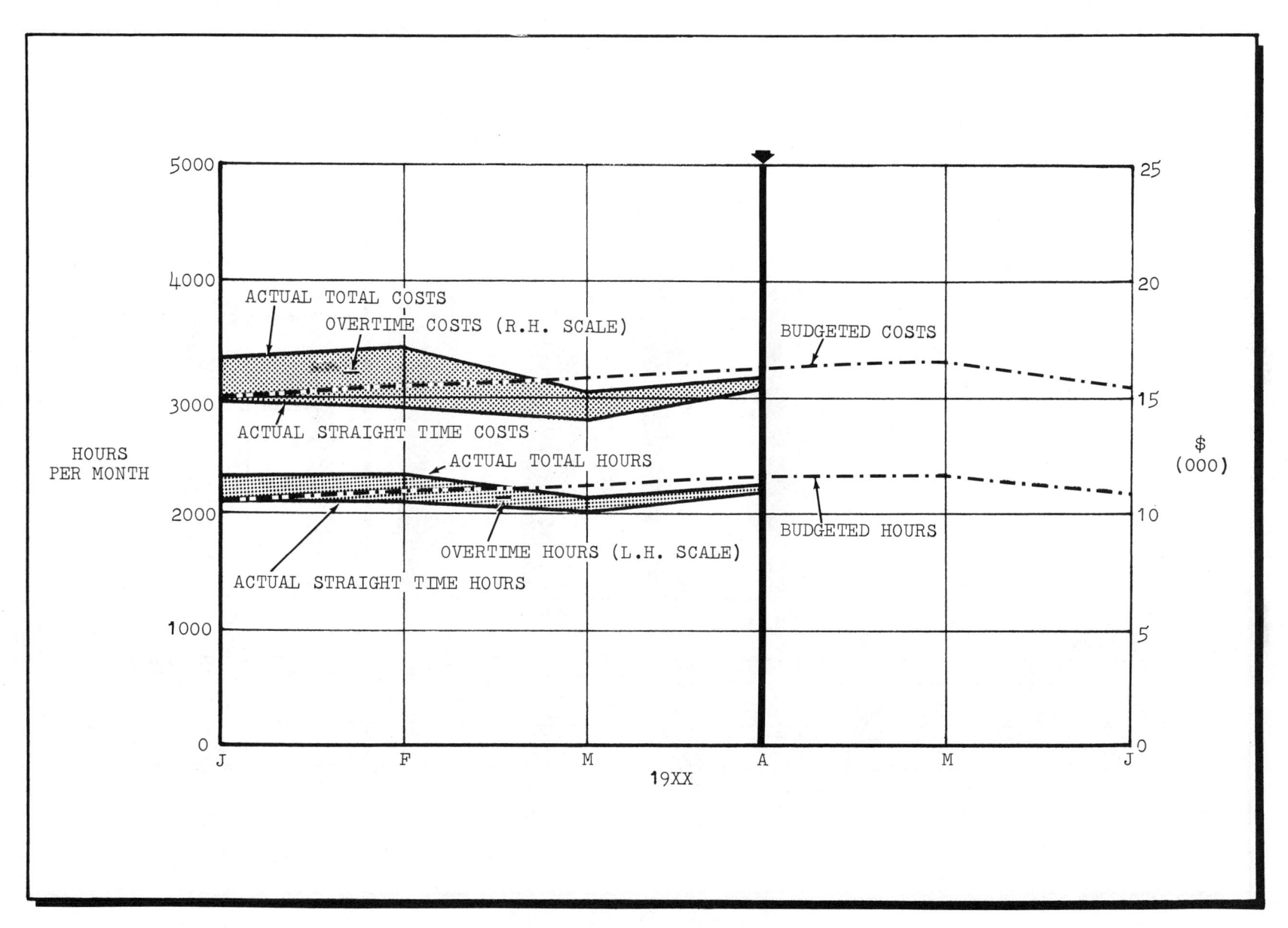

Figure 36.4 Overtime—Version 4

$ (000)
PER MONTH

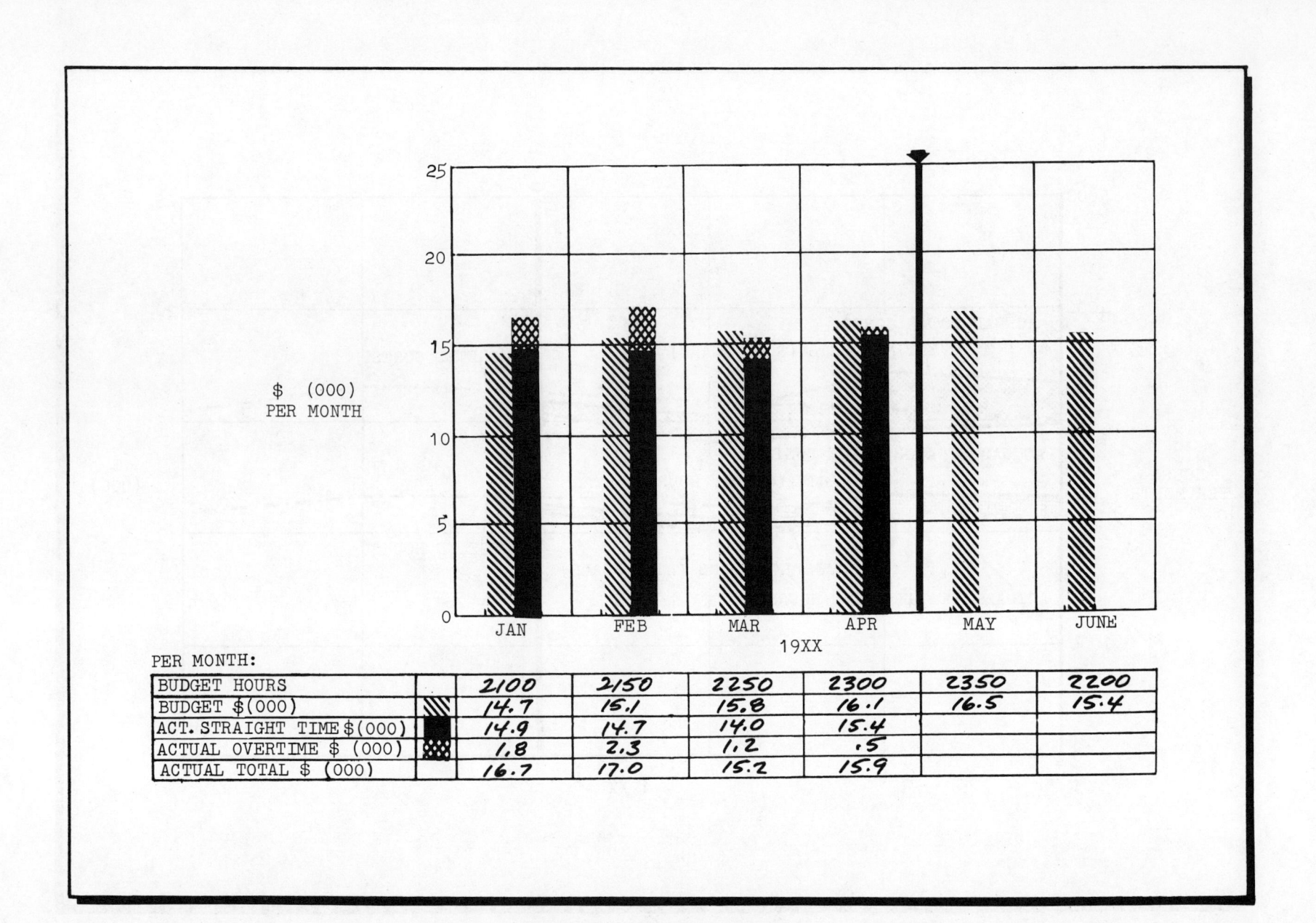

PER MONTH:							
BUDGET HOURS		2100	2150	2250	2300	2350	2200
BUDGET $(000)	▨	14.7	15.1	15.8	16.1	16.5	15.4
ACT. STRAIGHT TIME $(000)	■	14.9	14.7	14.0	15.4		
ACTUAL OVERTIME $ (000)	▩	1.8	2.3	1.2	.5		
ACTUAL TOTAL $ (000)		16.7	17.0	15.2	15.9		

Figure 36.5   Overtime—Version 5

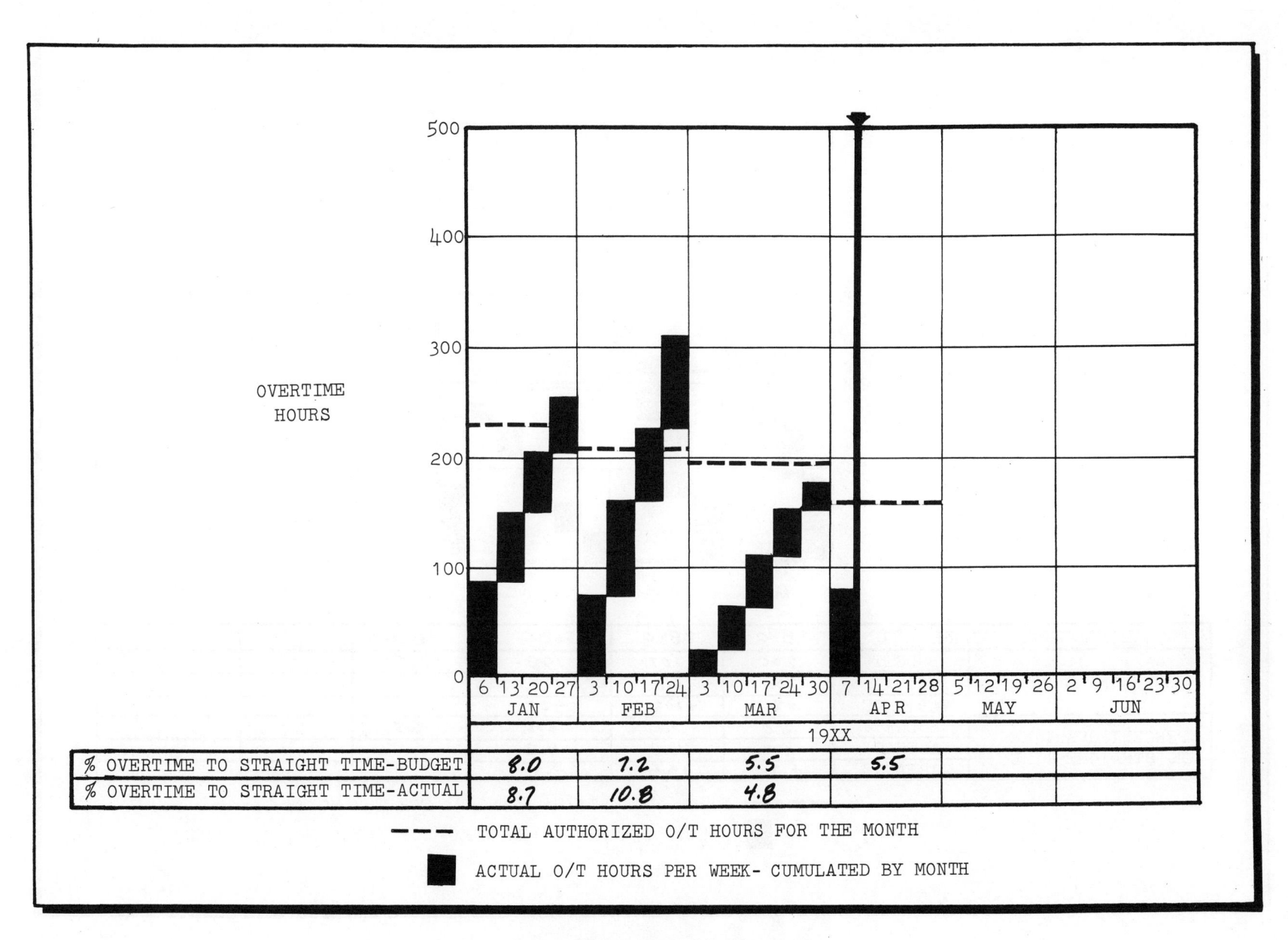

Figure 36.6 Overtime—Version 6

399

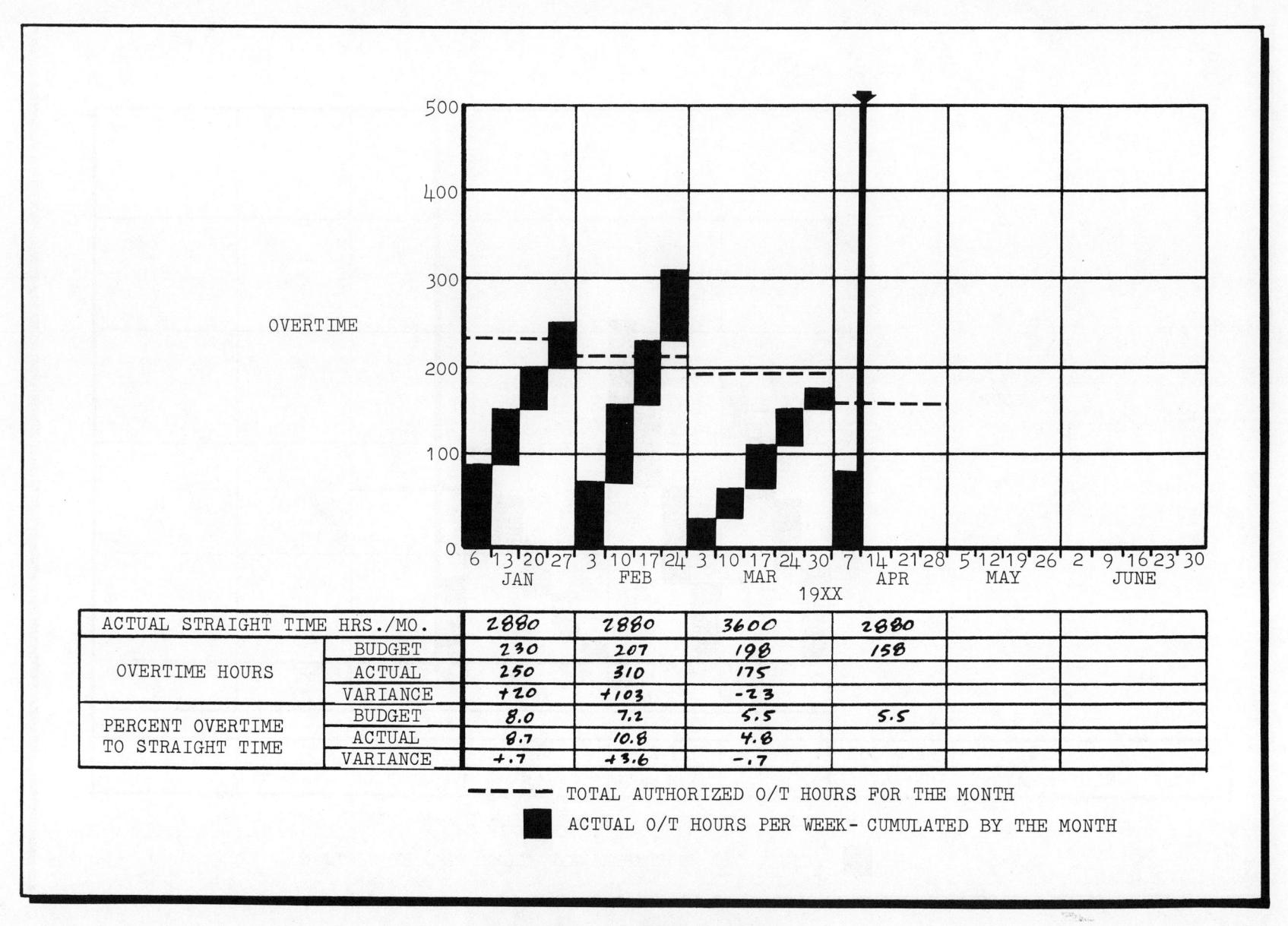

ACTUAL STRAIGHT TIME HRS./MO.		2880	2880	3600	2880		
OVERTIME HOURS	BUDGET	230	207	198	158		
	ACTUAL	250	310	175			
	VARIANCE	+20	+103	-23			
PERCENT OVERTIME TO STRAIGHT TIME	BUDGET	8.0	7.2	5.5	5.5		
	ACTUAL	8.7	10.8	4.8			
	VARIANCE	+.7	+3.6	-.7			

- - - - TOTAL AUTHORIZED O/T HOURS FOR THE MONTH

■ ACTUAL O/T HOURS PER WEEK - CUMULATED BY THE MONTH

Figure 36.7 Overtime—Version 7

37.0 PERCENT RETURN ON GROSS ASSETS

One of the most essential financial ratios is the percent return on gross assets, sometimes referred to as return on investment. Examples of charts that display this ratio, the product of gross assets turnover and earnings as a percent of sales, are included in this section. Also see Section 23.0, *Gross Assets* and 24.0, *Gross Assets Turnover*.

37.1 Percent Return on Gross Assets—Version 1: Figure 37.1 presents a simplified version of a percent return on gross assets chart. In this example, a 20% return is specified as a goal. Actuals are plotted both in terms of monthly and year-to-date average statistics.

37.2 Percent Return on Gross Assets—Version 2: Version 2 of a percent return on gross assets chart, Figure 37.2, is identical to Version 1, except that the data have been plotted, in this example, in semi-logarithmic format.

37.3 Percent Return on Gross Assets—Version 3: A column chart version of a percent return on gross assets chart is shown in Figure 37.3. A paired column chart of this nature is usually considered to be more difficult to interpret than the line curve type shown in Versions 1 and 2.

37.4 Percent Return on Gross Assets—Version 4: In some situations, it is useful to show the current percentage return on gross assets in relationship to past performance and in terms of what is forecast for the next year. An approach for doing this is shown in step line form in Figure 37.4.

37.5 Percent Return on Gross Assets—Version 5: Version 5 of a percent return on gross assets chart, Figure 37.5, is identical to Version 4 except this one is shown in line curve form and is plotted as point data.

37.6 Percent Return on Gross Assets—Version 6: Version 6 of a percent return on gross assets chart, Figure 37.6, is a simple column chart which shows the general trend covering a ten-year period. In this example, no goal or plan is shown, so the only information that can be interpreted is the current year's performance in relationship to previous years.

37.7 Percent Return on Gross Assets—Version 7: A method for comparing a company's overall performance in relationship to competitors is shown in Figure 37.7. In this example, Competitor A has been declining in the past several years in terms of performance in managing assets and costs, whereas Competitor B has been improving. The example, as shown, is not set up for tracking purposes.

37.8 Percent Return on Gross Assets—Version 8: The percent return on gross assets chart shown as Version 8, Figure 37.8, is in terms of the current year's plan and actual performance compared to the previous year's actual performance and the coming year's forecast. The current year's actual columns are overlapped on the plan columns so as to not obliterate the plan when exceeded by actual performance (second quarter).

37.9 Percent Return on Gross Assets—Version 9: Statistics are added to a graphic layout of percent return on gross assets in Figure 37.9. In the graphic portion, a goal of 20% return on gross assets is indicated by a dash line. The performance, in terms of monthly and year-to-date statistics, is shown in both graphic and statistical form.

37.10 Percent Return on Gross Assets—Version 10: Five separate lines of statistics are used on the combination graph and statistical table shown as Version 10 of a percent return on gross assets chart, Figure 37.10. The table shows planned and actual performance on both a monthly and a year-to-date basis, with the year-to-date variances also given for each reporting date. The year-to-date planned and actual performance figures are also plotted on the graph.

37.11 Percent Return on Gross Assets—Version 11: A statistical table showing percent return on gross assets is displayed as Version 11, Figure 37.11. Planned, actual, and variance statistics are shown on both a monthly and a year-to-date basis.

37.12 Percent Return on Gross Assets—Version 12: A "box score" type status report is shown as Version 12, Figure 37.12. In this example, the variance relative to earnings as a percent of sales indicates that the reason for the low return on gross assets involves the management of costs rather than the management of assets.

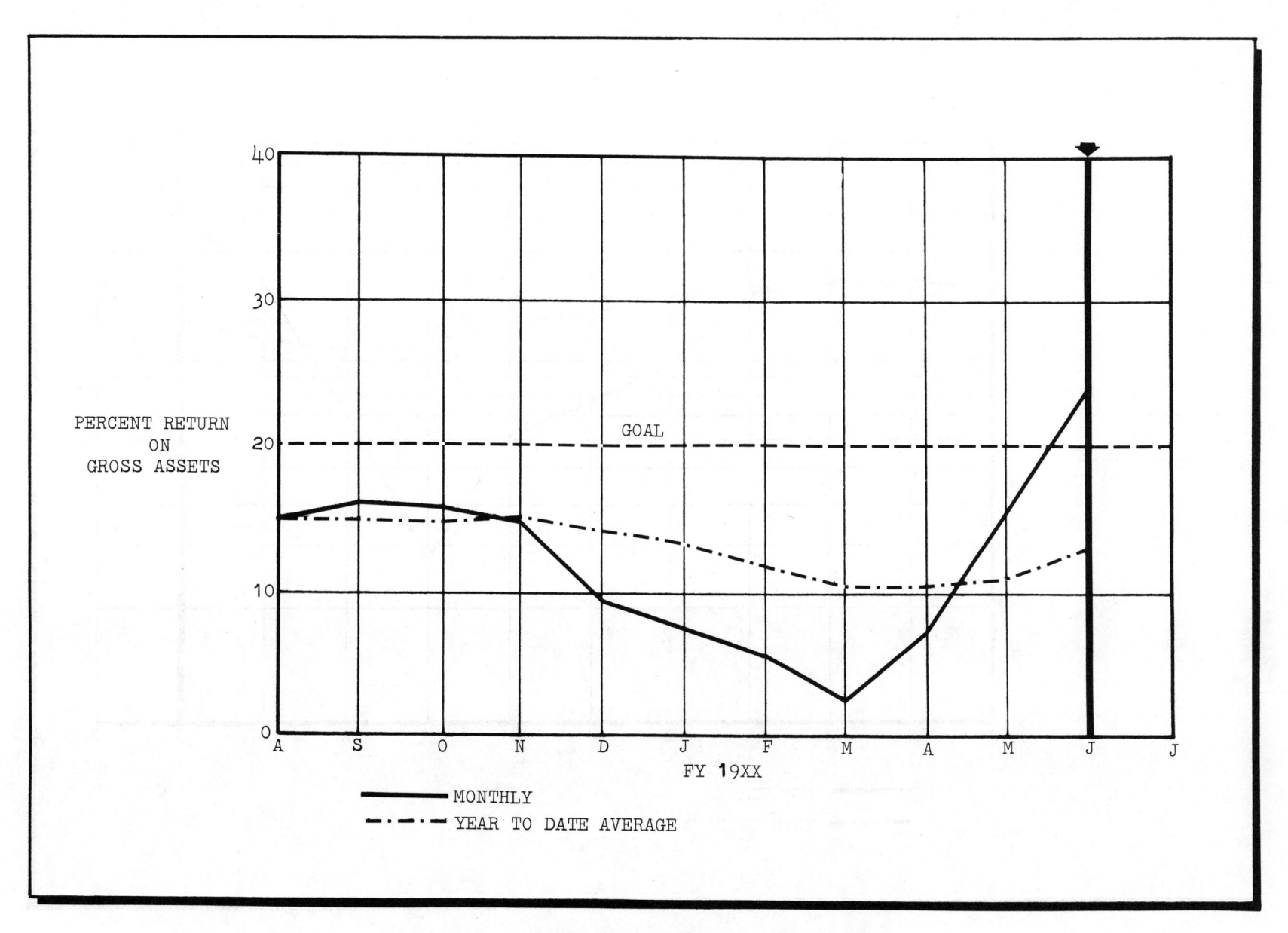

Figure 37.1   Percent Return on Gross Assets—Version 1

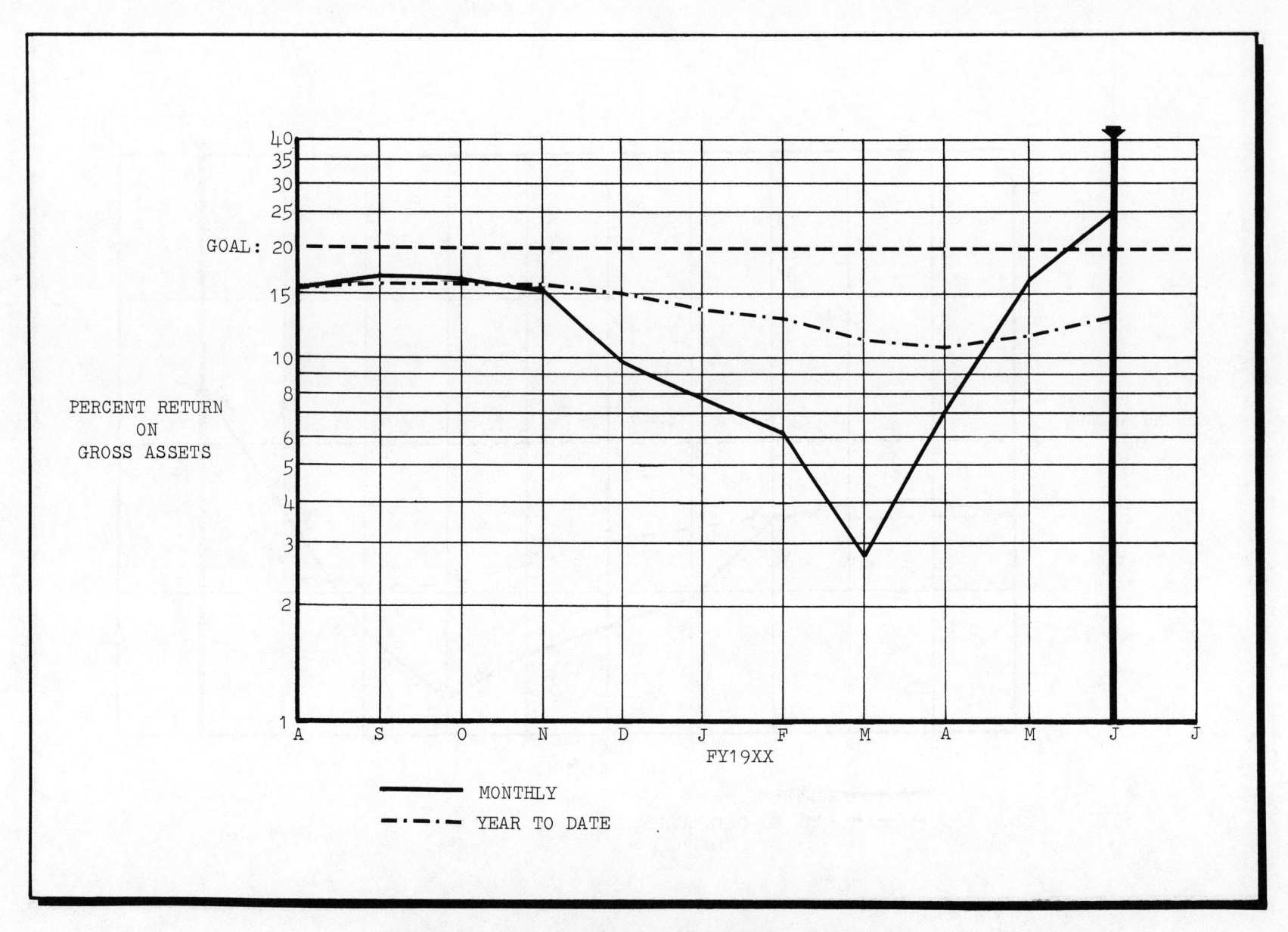

Figure 37.2 Percent Return on Gross Assets—Version 2

404

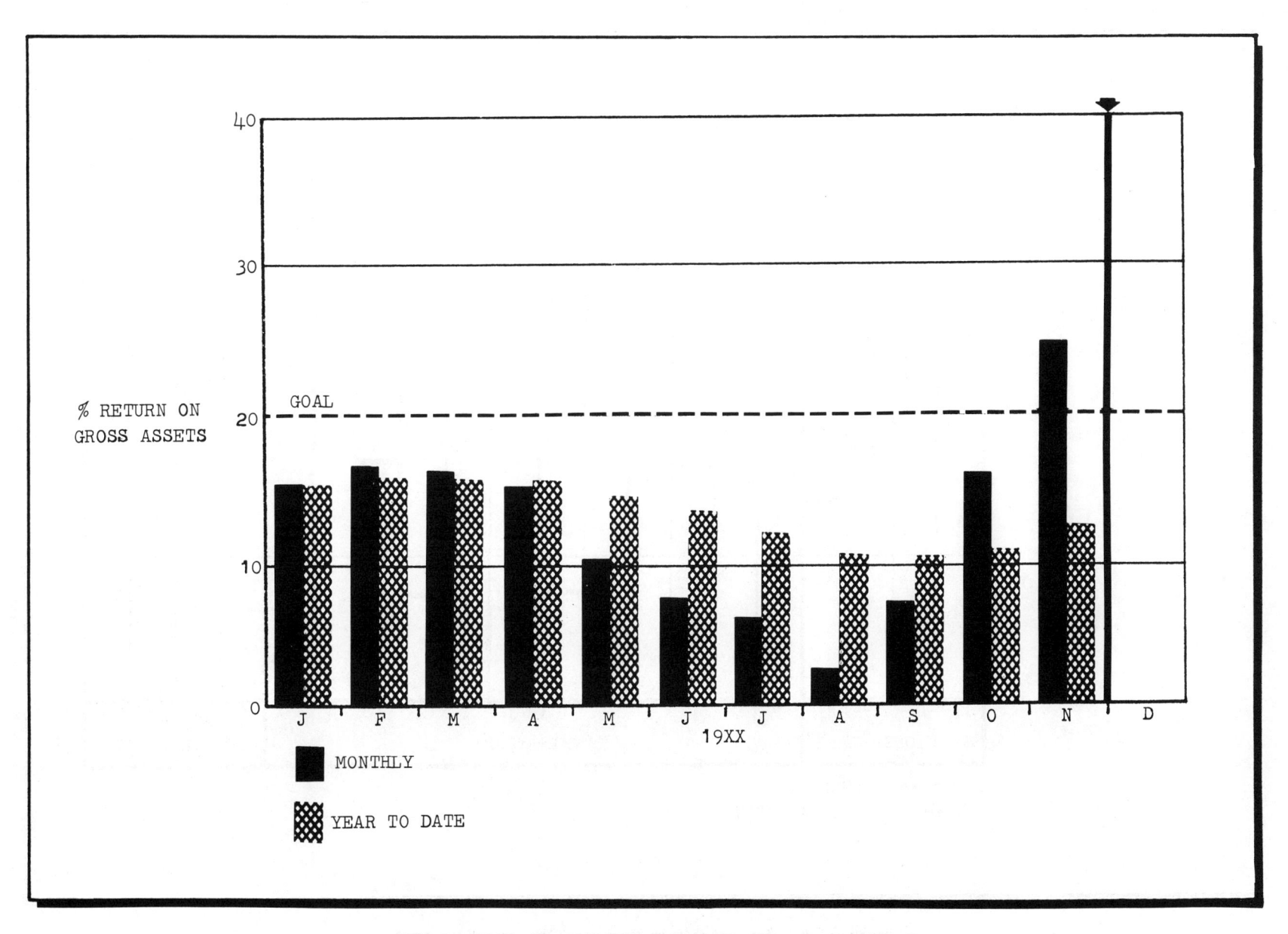

Figure 37.3 Percent Return on Gross Assets—Version 3

405

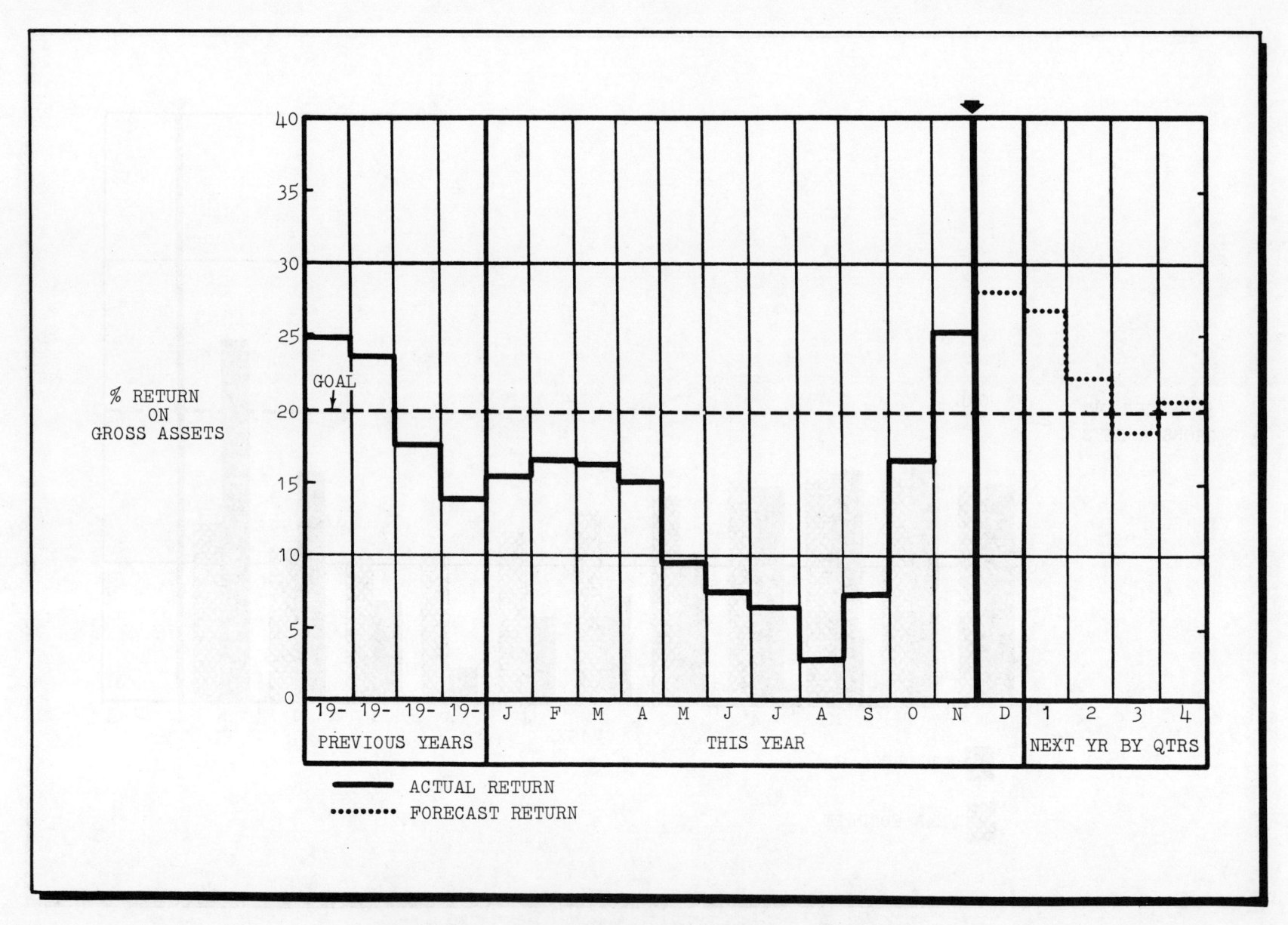

Figure 37.4 Percent Return on Gross Assets—Version 4

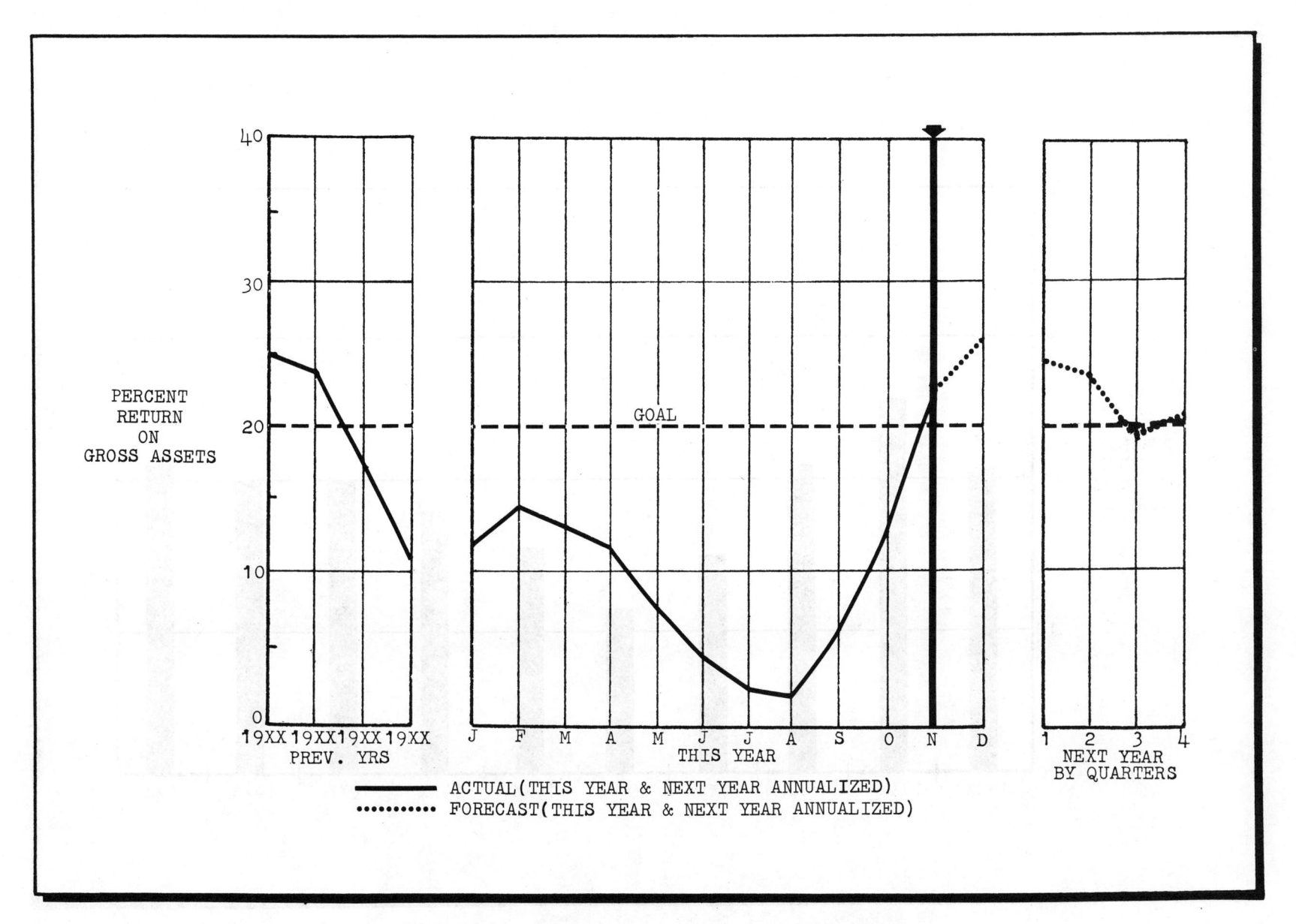

Figure 37.5   Percent Return on Gross Assets—Version 5

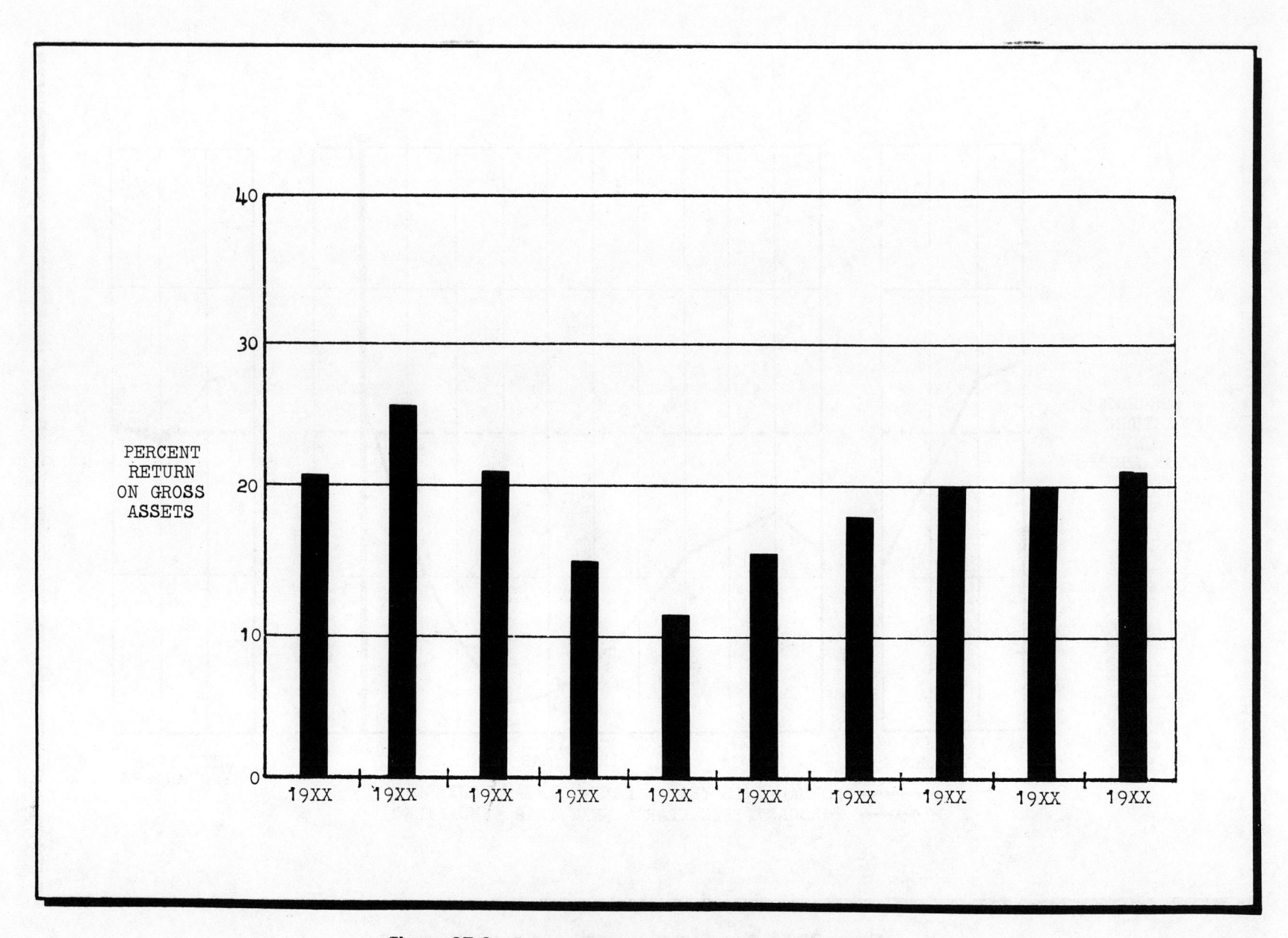

Figure 37.6 Percent Return on Gross Assets—Version 6

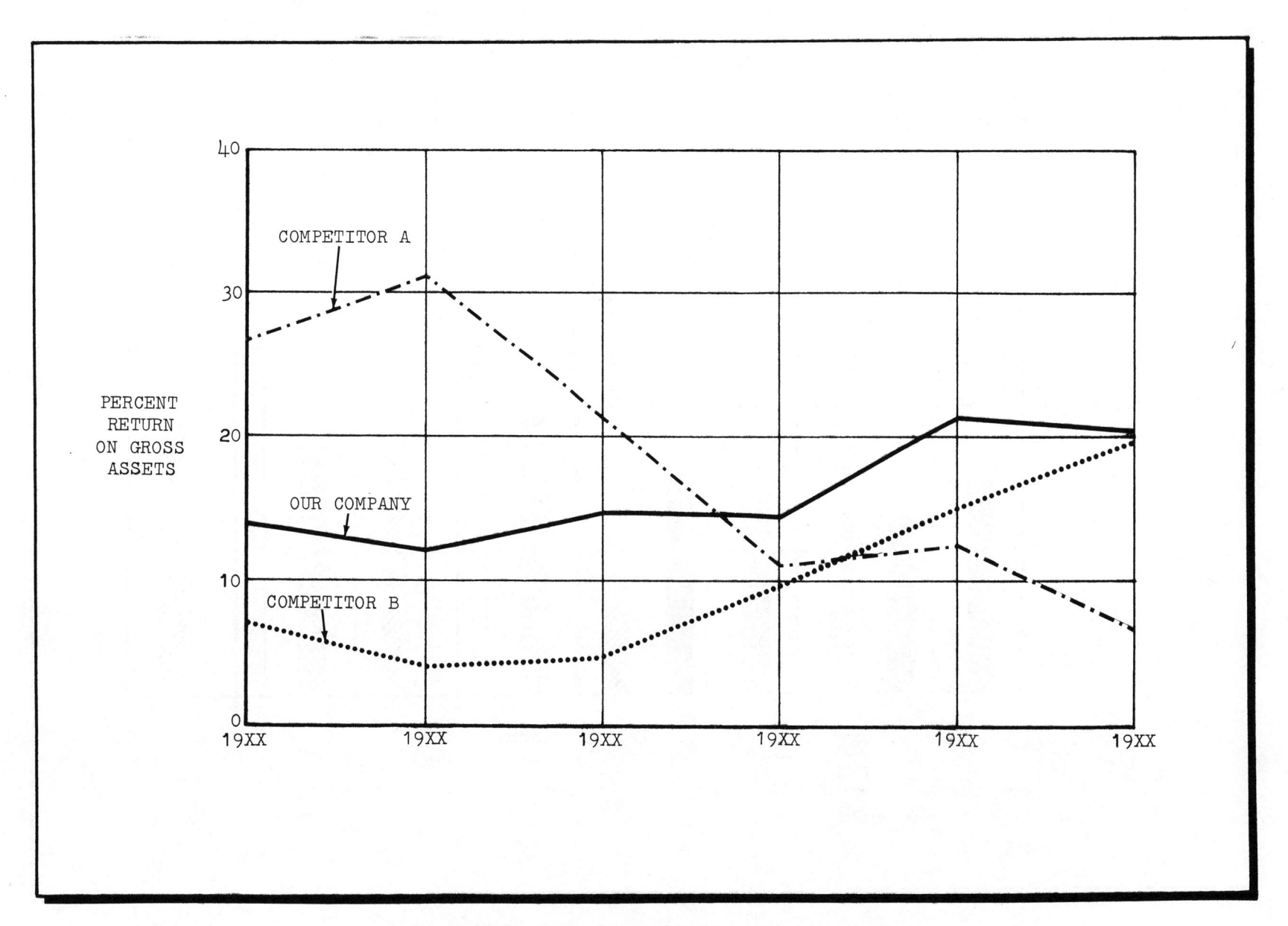

Figure 37.7 Percent Return on Gross Assets—Version 7

409

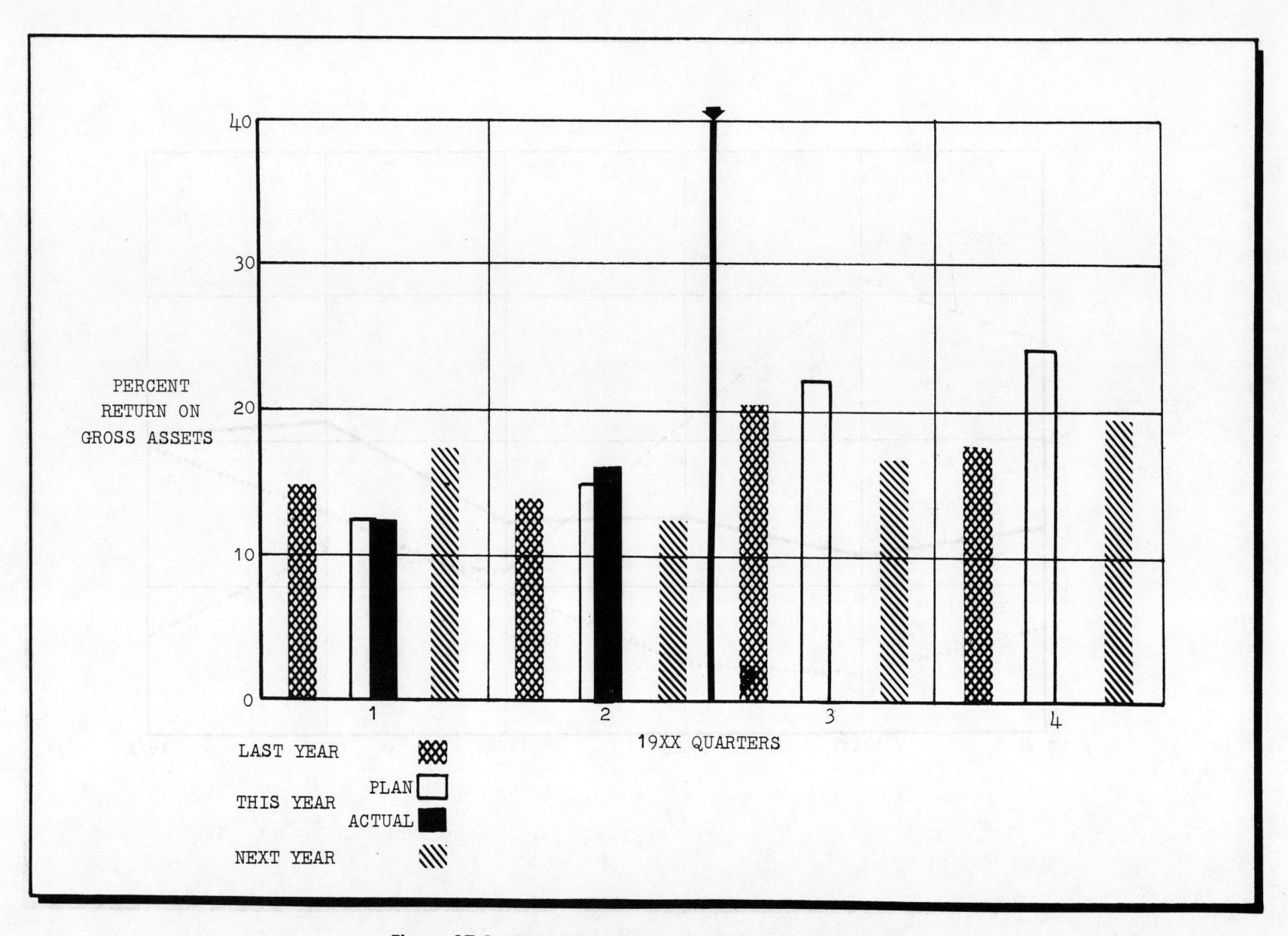

Figure 37.8 Percent Return on Gross Assets—Version 8

PERCENT RETURN
ON
GROSS ASSETS

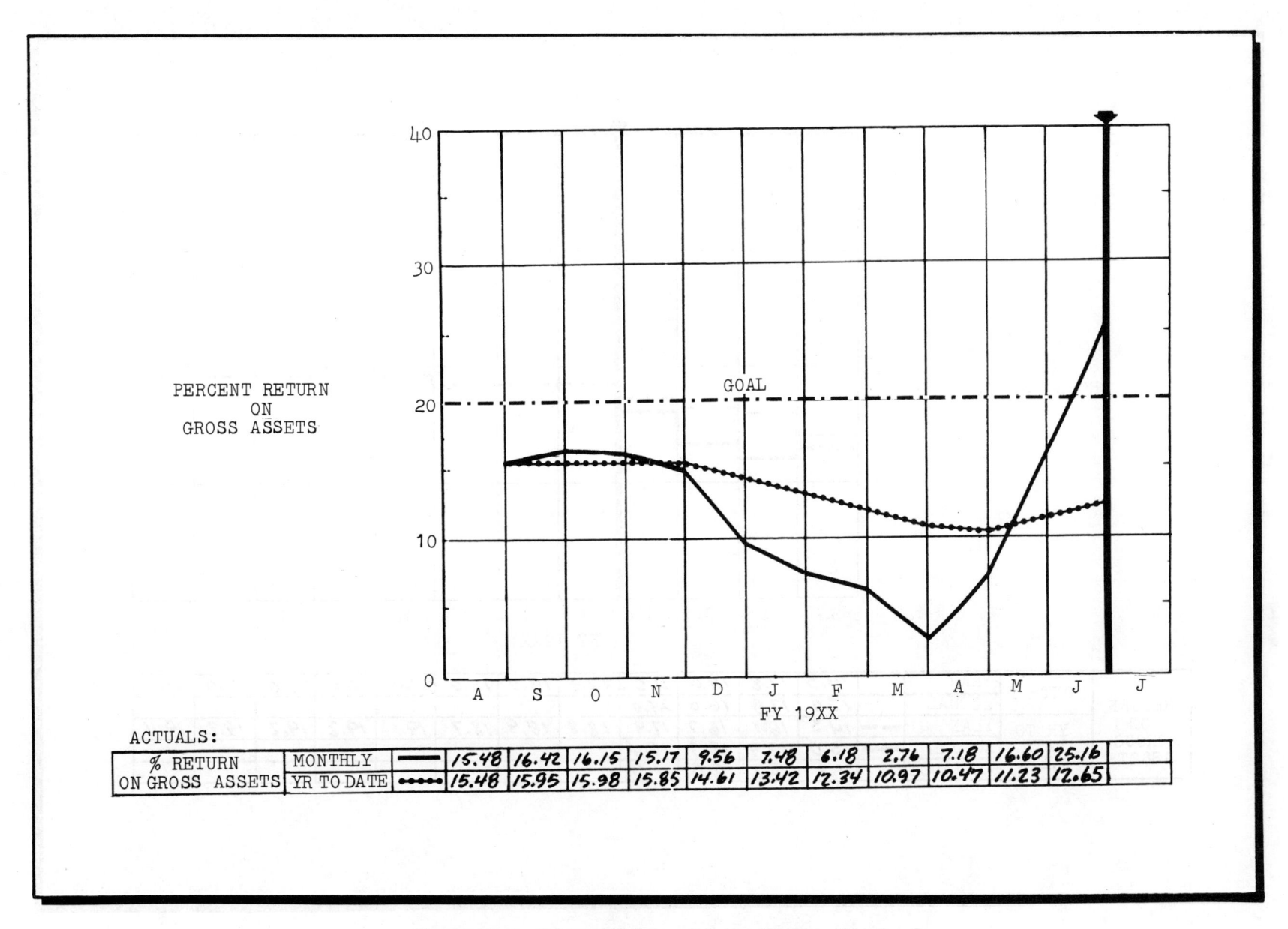

GOAL

FY 19XX

ACTUALS:

% RETURN ON GROSS ASSETS		A	S	O	N	D	J	F	M	A	M	J
	MONTHLY	15.48	16.42	16.15	15.17	9.56	7.48	6.18	2.76	7.18	16.60	25.16
	YR TO DATE	15.48	15.95	15.98	15.85	14.61	13.42	12.34	10.97	10.47	11.23	12.65

Figure 37.9 Percent Return on Gross Assets—Version 9

% RETURN ON GROSS ASSETS	MONTHLY	PLAN		14.3	17.8	18.0	21.5	22.5	19.0	18.0	21.4	20.0	20.0	19.0	21.0
		ACTUAL		13.0	12.8	16.0	24.0								
	YR TO DATE AVER.	PLAN	-- --	14.3	16.1	16.7	17.9	18.8	18.9	18.7	19.1	19.2	19.2	19.2	19.4
		ACTUAL	——	13.0	12.9	13.9	16.4								
		VARIANCE		1.3	3.2	2.8	1.5								

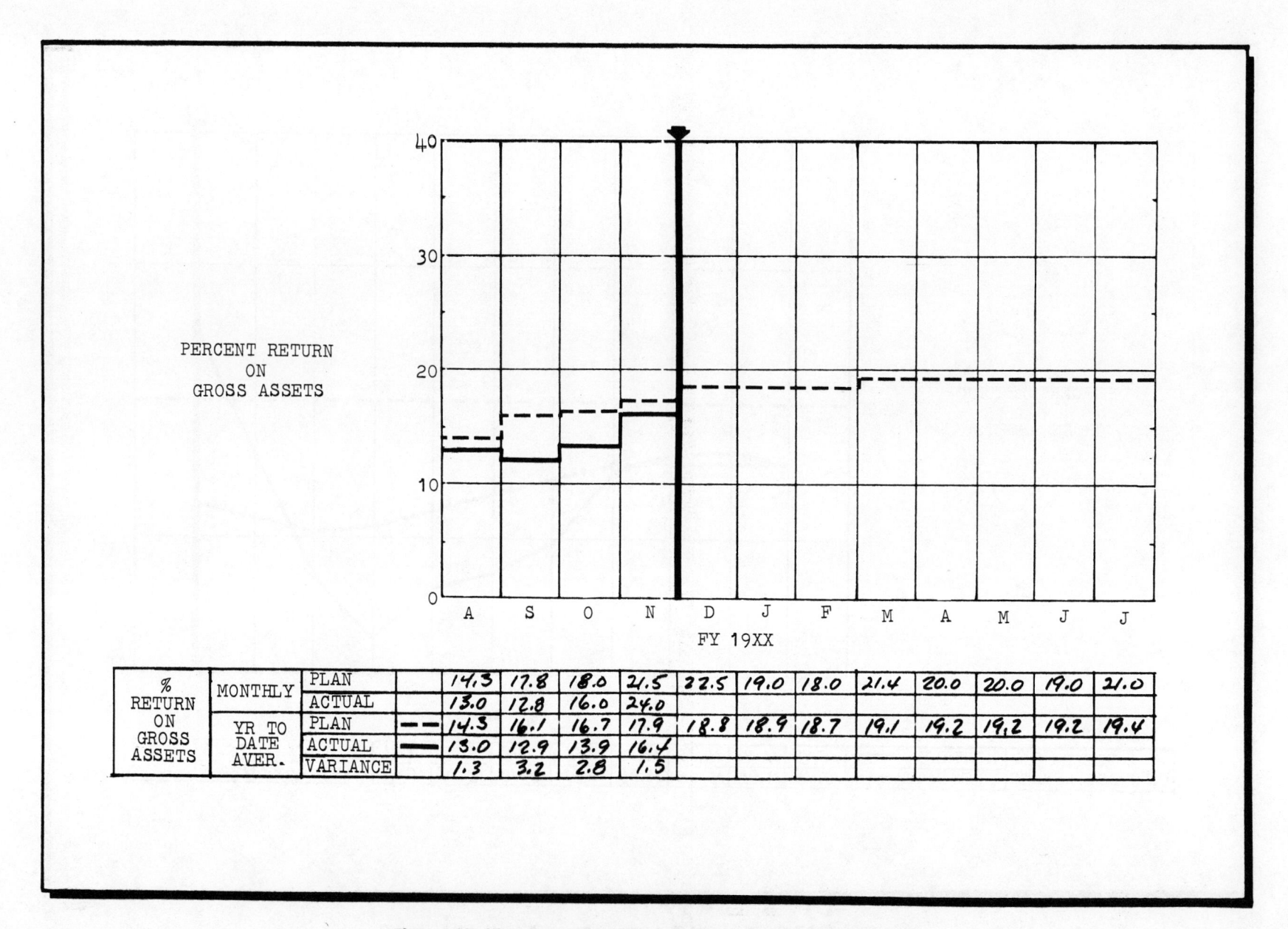

Figure 37.10   Percent Return on Gross Assets—Version 10

		A	S	O	N	D	J	F	M	A	M	J	J
	PLAN	14.3	17.8	18.0	21.5	22.5	19.0	18.0	21.4	20.0	20.0	19.0	21.0
% RETURN MONTHLY	ACTUAL	13.0	12.8	16.0	24.0								
	VARIANCE	-1.3	-5.0	-2.0	+2.5								
	PLAN	14.3	16.1	16.7	17.9	18.8	18.9	18.7	19.1	19.2	19.2	19.2	19.4
% RETURN YEAR TO DATE	ACTUAL	13.0	12.9	13.9	16.4								
	VARIANCE	-1.3	-3.2	-2.8	-1.5								

FY19XX

Figure 37.11 Percent Return on Gross Assets—Version 11

ITEM		STATUS AS OF __JUNE 30__		
		PLAN	ACTUAL	VARIANCE
GROSS ASSET TURNOVER	MONTHLY	1.58	1.58	
	YEAR TO DATE	1.73	1.73	
EARNINGS AS PERCENT OF SALES	MONTHLY	9.60	6.30	−3.30
	YEAR TO DATE	9.16	8.36	−.80
PERCENT RETURN ON GROSS ASSETS	MONTHLY	15.17	9.95	−5.22
	YEAR TO DATE	15.85	14.46	−1.39

Figure 37.12   Percent Return on Gross Assets—Version 12

38.0 PROBLEMS AND ACTIONS

Charts which highlight problems and corrective actions are shown in this section. They are usually "word" style charts and are used to draw special attention to serious deviations from normal operations, being extracted from the regular plan and control system documentation. Problem/action charts are sometimes titled *Problem Report*, *Critical Items*, *Hot Line Report*, *Bottlenecks*, *Problem Hit Parade*, *Red Flag Report*, etc.

38.1 Problems and Actions—Version 1: A simple type of problem/action report is shown as Version 1, Figure 38.1. Space is left to add new problems and actions on subsequent reports. Problems described in previous reports are left on the chart and lightly crossed out when disposed of. Most users feel that charts that name individuals rather than organization units as having corrective action responsibility are more effective.

38.2 Problems and Actions—Version 2: Two additional columns of data are added in Version 2 of a problems and actions chart, Figure 38.2. In addition to listing the problems, actions, responsibilities, and due dates as was done in Version 1, a column for describing each problem's impact has been added together with a column where arrowheads are used to indicate new entries since the previous report.

38.3 Problems and Actions—Version 3: Columns that track corrective action progress are used in Version 3 of a problems and actions chart, Figure 38.3. In addition to a get-well date, the date that action was assigned is listed. Also, columns are provided to list the number of days the action is behind schedule, if that is the case, and for listing the date of completion. A column for identifying problems as to criticality is also provided.

38.4 Problems and Actions—Version 4: A format for reporting a single problem is shown as Version 4, Figure 38.4. Space is provided for a brief description of the problem, a discussion of its effect, and a listing of one of several corrective actions. Space is provided at the bottom of the chart for showing assigned responsibility and solution date.

38.5 Problems and Actions—Version 5: A status chart that begins by citing a current major achievement before listing a major problem is shown as Version 5, Figure 38.5. The problem listed is expanded upon by describing its impact, the corrective action required and get-well date, and progress to date.

38.6 Problems and Actions—Version 6: A problem/action chart emphasizing financial considerations is shown as Version 6, Figure 38.6. The upper left-hand corner of the chart presents a brief financial projection which indicates a potential loss. The problem causing this is described in the upper right-hand portion of the chart, and remedial actions, responsibilities, and due dates are listed on the lower half of the chart.

38.7 Problems and Actions—Version 7: A problem/action chart that highlights schedule performance problems is shown as

Version 7, Figure 38.7. Only schedule performance *problems* are listed on this style of chart.

38.8 Problems and Actions—Version 8: Technical problems are emphasized on Version 8 of a problems and actions chart, Figure 38.8. Problems, only, are listed together with the target value, indicated value, and variance for each item. Columns are also provided for listing the action assignee and the recovery date for each problem.

STATUS AS OF __JUNE 1__

PROBLEM	ACTION	INDIVIDUAL RESPONSIBLE	GET-WELL DATE
~~NUMEROUS DESIGN ERRORS~~	~~SET UP A DESIGN CLEAN-UP TEAM~~	~~SMITH~~	~~MAY 28~~ COMPLETED
PLASTIC PARTS AVAILABILITY IN JEOPARDY	DEVELOP ALTERNATE SOURCE	JONES	JUNE 12

Figure 38.1 Problems and Actions—Version 1

STATUS AS OF __AUGUST 15__

CRITICAL PROBLEM	IMPACT	ACTION	RESPONSI-BILITY	DUE	NEW ◀
~~FIELD UNIT LACKING VITAL SPARE PARTS~~	~~CUSTOMER DISSATIS-FACTION WITH PROMISED SERVICE~~	~~MAKE UP SPECIAL RUSH SHIPMENT~~	~~JONES~~	~~AUG 6~~ COMPLETED AUG 6	
PRODUCTION LINE PURCHASED PARTS SHORTAGE	WILL HALT PRODUCTION LINE	SHORT RANGE: DIVERT NEEDED PARTS FROM O&R STOCK	BROWN	AUG 10	
		LONG RANGE: DEVELOP IMPROVED INVENTORY SYSTEM	HALL	SEPT 30	
USER MANUALS NEED UPDATING	COULD DELAY CUSTOMER ACCEPTANCE OF HARDWARE	SUBCONTRACT MANUAL UPDATING ON RUSH BASIS	MARTIN	AUG 18	◀

Figure 38.2   Problems and Actions—Version 2

STATUS AS OF JUNE 7

CRITICAL ITEM	CODE *	ACTION	ASSIGN TO	DATE ASSIGNED	GET-WELL DATE	DAYS BEHIND	DATE COMPLETE
RELIABILITY DEMO. IS 230 HOURS MTBF INSTEAD OF 275, PER SPEC. COULD RESULT IN $20,000 INCENTIVE LOSS	1	CHANGE COMPONENT #103 TO #103 MOD. A	SMITH	6/1	6/15		6/5
REPAIR BACKLOG DOUBLED PAST 2 WEEKS	2	DIVERT EXCESS WORKLOAD TO L.A. PLANT	JONES	6/1	6/3	4	
TEST SPECIFICATION FROM DENVER MISSING	3	(1) TRACE ON EXPEDITED BASIS. (2) REQUEST RUSH BACK-UP COPY	MOLLS	6/7	6/14		

*CRITICALITY CODE: 1 = CRITICAL PROBLEM   2 = MAJOR   3 = MINOR

Figure 38.3 Problems and Actions—Version 3

REPORT DATE __AUGUST 1__

```
BRIEF DESCRIPTION OF PROBLEM:
    UNEXPECTED INCREASE IN XYZ WORKLOAD EXCEEDS SYSTEM TEST CONSOLE CAPACITY
```

```
EFFECT (INCLUDING SCHEDULE & COST IMPACT):
    CURRENT BEHIND-SCHEDULE CONDITION: 2 WEEKS
    BUDGET OVERRUN: $2740
```

```
RECOMMENDED CORRECTIVE ACTION(S):
    1. ACQUIRE NEW CONSOLE (LEAD TIME: 4 WEEKS)
    2. IMMEDIATELY START EXTENDED WORK WEEK TO COVER NEXT 4 WEEKS
```

ASSIGNED RESPONSIBILITY: JOHNSON   DEPT: 10A   SOLUTION DATE: SEPT 1

Figure 38.4   Problems and Actions—Version 4

STATUS AS OF **June 1**

MAJOR ACHIEVEMENT:

TESTS OF FIRST PRODUCTION UNIT SHOW PERFORMANCE EXCEEDING SPECIFICATION BY 8%

MAJOR PROBLEM:

NO CUSTOMER INSPECTOR AT FIELD SITE

IMPACT:

SITUATION IS DELAYING ACCEPTANCE OF FIRST PRODUCTION UNIT & PAYMENT

CORRECTIVE ACTION & GET-WELL DATE:

CUSTOMER MUST ASSIGN FULL TIME INSPECTOR NOW OR DELETE REQUIREMENT -JUNE 15

PROGRESS TO DATE:

MEETING SCHEDULED FOR JUNE 8

Figure 38.5 Problems and Actions—Version 5

STATUS AS OF __JUNE 15__

FINANCIAL PROJECTION			PROBLEM: PRODUCTION DEPARTMENT'S ESTIMATED COST TO COMPLETE HAS RISEN FROM $9,961 TO $14,020.	
SELLING PRICE	$32,460			
EST. COST AT COMPLETION	33,500			
EST. PROFIT (LOSS)	(1,040)	(3.2)%	REASON: CURRENT SPEC. FOR FINE FINISH TOO DIFFICULT TO ACHIEVE WITH EXISTING EQUIPMENT	
PLANNED PROFIT	3,019	9.3%		
EXPENDED & COMMITTED TO DATE	10,063			
REMEDIAL ACTION(S):			RESPONSIBILITY	DUE DATE
(1) ENGINEERING DEPARTMENT EXAMINE SPEC TO SEE IF REQUIREMENT CAN BE EASED WITHOUT SERIOUSLY REDUCING QUALITY OF PRODUCT			HILL	JUNE 20
(2) CONDUCT STUDY OF AVAILABLE FINISHING EQUIPMENT. INITIATE ACQUISITION IF COST-EFFECTIVE			JONES	JUNE 30

Figure 38.6 Problems and Actions—Version 6

STATUS AS OF __7/1__

ITEM	SCHEDULE PROBLEM			ACTION REQUIRED	INDIVIDUAL RESPONSIBLE	RECOVERY DATE
	SCHEDULE	PREDICTED	INDICATED VARIANCE (DAYS)			
~~PART NO. 1XXXXX~~	~~6/10~~	~~6/20~~	~~-10~~	~~PURCHASED PART SHORTAGE. EXPEDITE NEW SHIPMENT~~	~~JOHNSON~~	~~7/1~~ COMPLETE
PART NO. 7XXXX	6/14	6/22	-7	TEST EQUIPMENT BREAKDOWN. REPAIR ON OVERTIME BASIS	MOORE	6/28
PART NO. 11XXX	6/29	7/15	-16	ENGINEERING DRAWING RELEASE TWO WEEKS LATE. SUBCONTRACT 1/2 OF WORKLOAD TO CATCH UP.	WHITE	8/1

Figure 38.7 Problems and Actions—Version 7

STATUS AS OF _June 1_

	TECHNICAL PROBLEM			ACTION ASSIGNED TO	RECOVERY DATE
	TARGET VALUE	INDICATED VALUE	VARIANCE		
WEIGHT (LBS)	1000 ± 25	1105	+105	SMITH	JULY 15
SIZE (CU.FT.)	1.95	2.24	+.29	JONES	JULY 15

Figure 38.8 Problems and Actions—Version 8

39.0 PRODUCT USAGE

Charts that display the extent to which a product of equipment is being used are shown in this section.

39.1 Product Usage—Version 1: A simple version of a product usage tracking chart is shown as Version 1, Figure 39.1. Usage is tracked in this example on the basis of hours per month, with actuals compared against a predicted usage amount.

39.2 Product Usage—Version 2: A method for tracking the usage of a single item is displayed as Version 2 of a product usage chart, Figure 39.2. The total hours per month are segmented to show the portions of in-use hours, avoidable and unavoidable delays, repair, and service.

39.3 Product Usage—Version 3: The usage hours of three different models of a product are compared in Version 3 of a product usage chart, Figure 39.3. The total each month is compared against a predicted usage, which, in this example, is forecasted only one month in advance of use.

39.4 Product Usage—Version 4: A one-time status report version of a product usage chart is shown as Version 4, Figure 39.4. One hundred percent bars for each model, in this example, are segmented to show the percentages of time where each product was put to satisfactory use, unsatisfactory use, or was not used at all.

39.5 Product Usage—Version 5: A segmented circle chart ("pie" chart) is used as Version 5 of a product usage chart, Figure 39.5. In this one-time status report style, the circle is segmented to show the portions of total time a single item of equipment was used, delayed in use, serviced, repaired.

39.6 Product Usage—Version 6: A frequency distribution style of chart is used as Version 6 of a product usage chart, Figure 39.6. In this example, the current year is compared to the previous year in terms of the number of units in use according to the number of years in use.

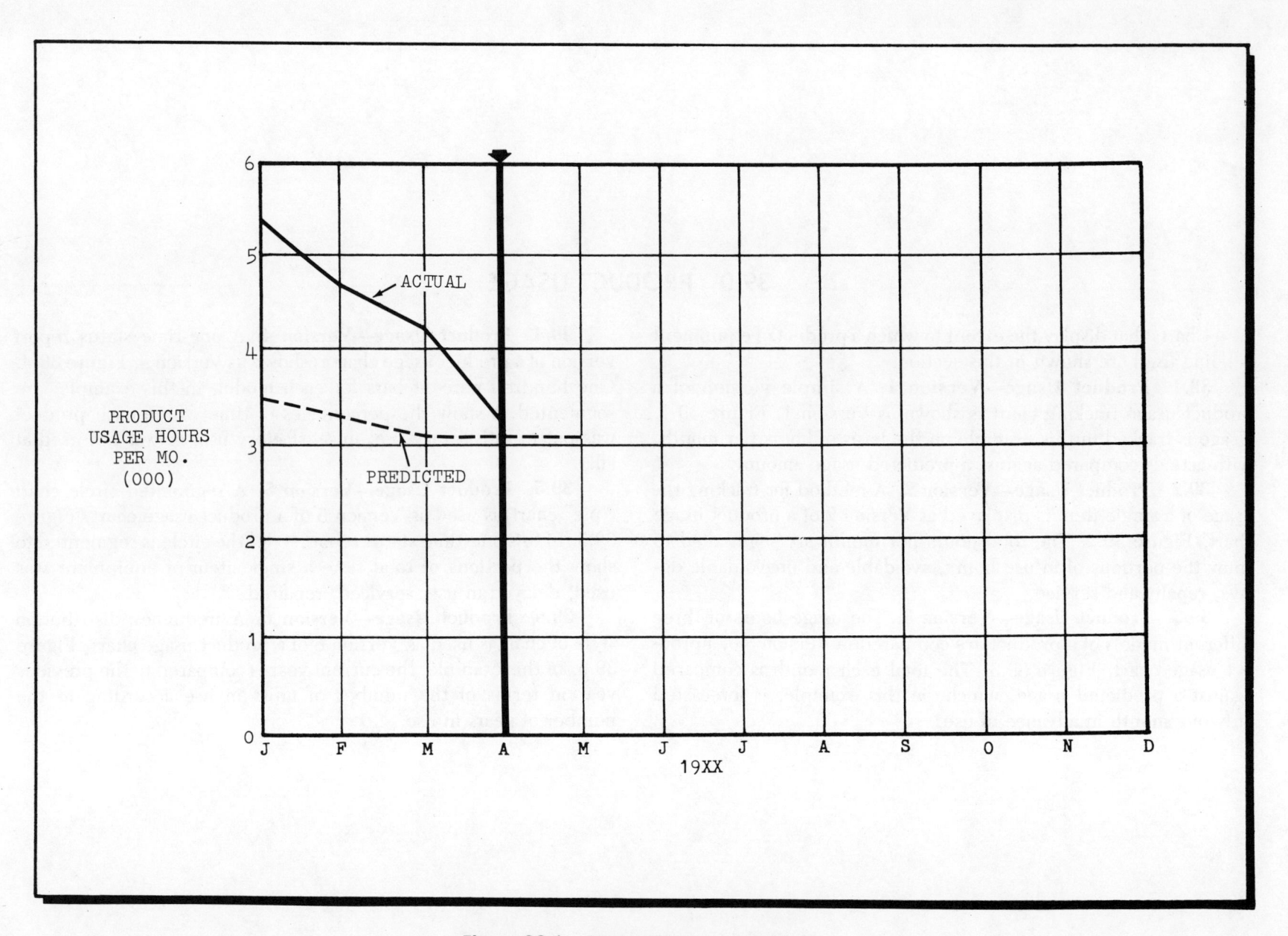

Figure 39.1   Product Usage—Version 1

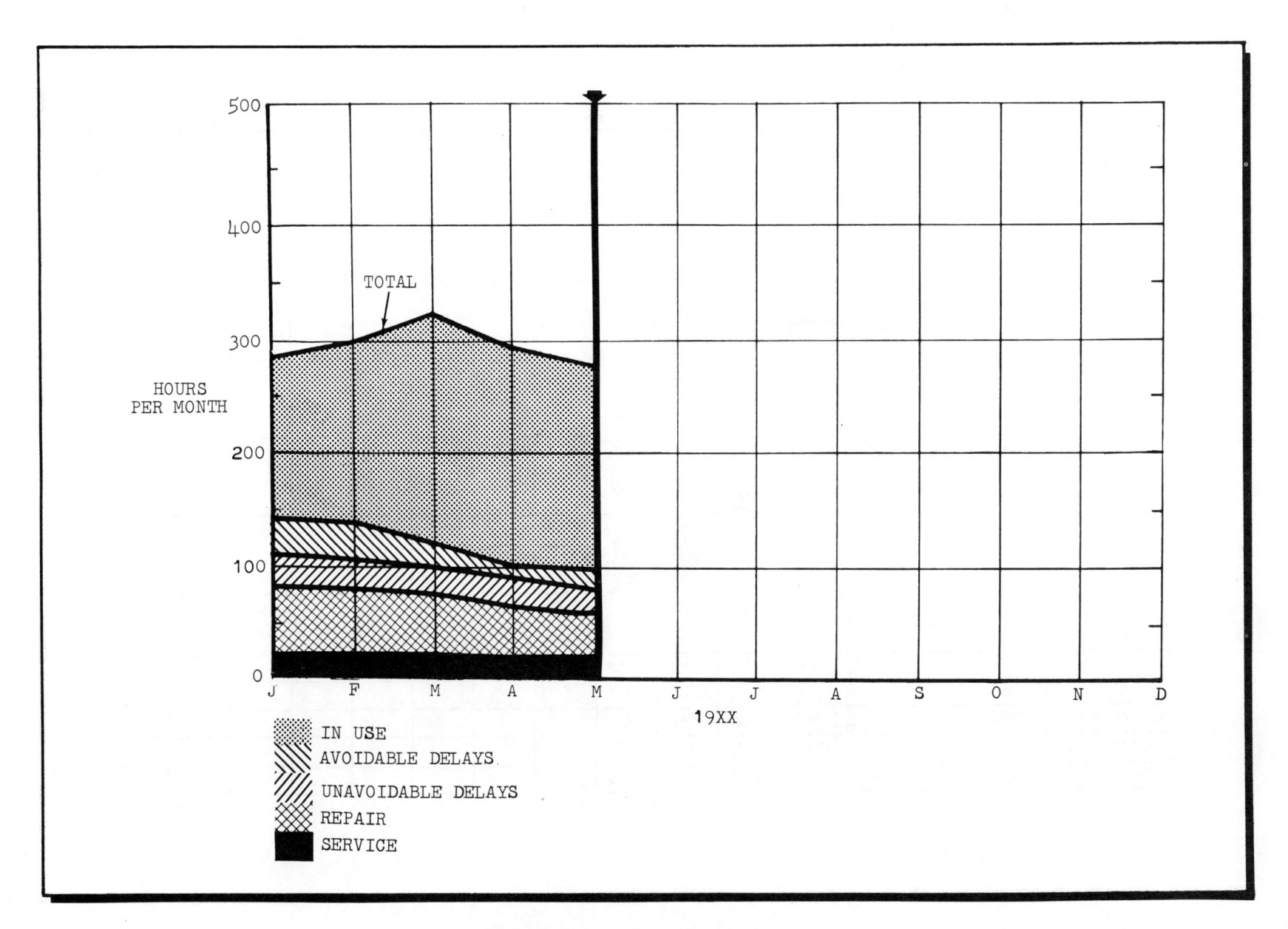

Figure 39.2 Product Usage—Version 2

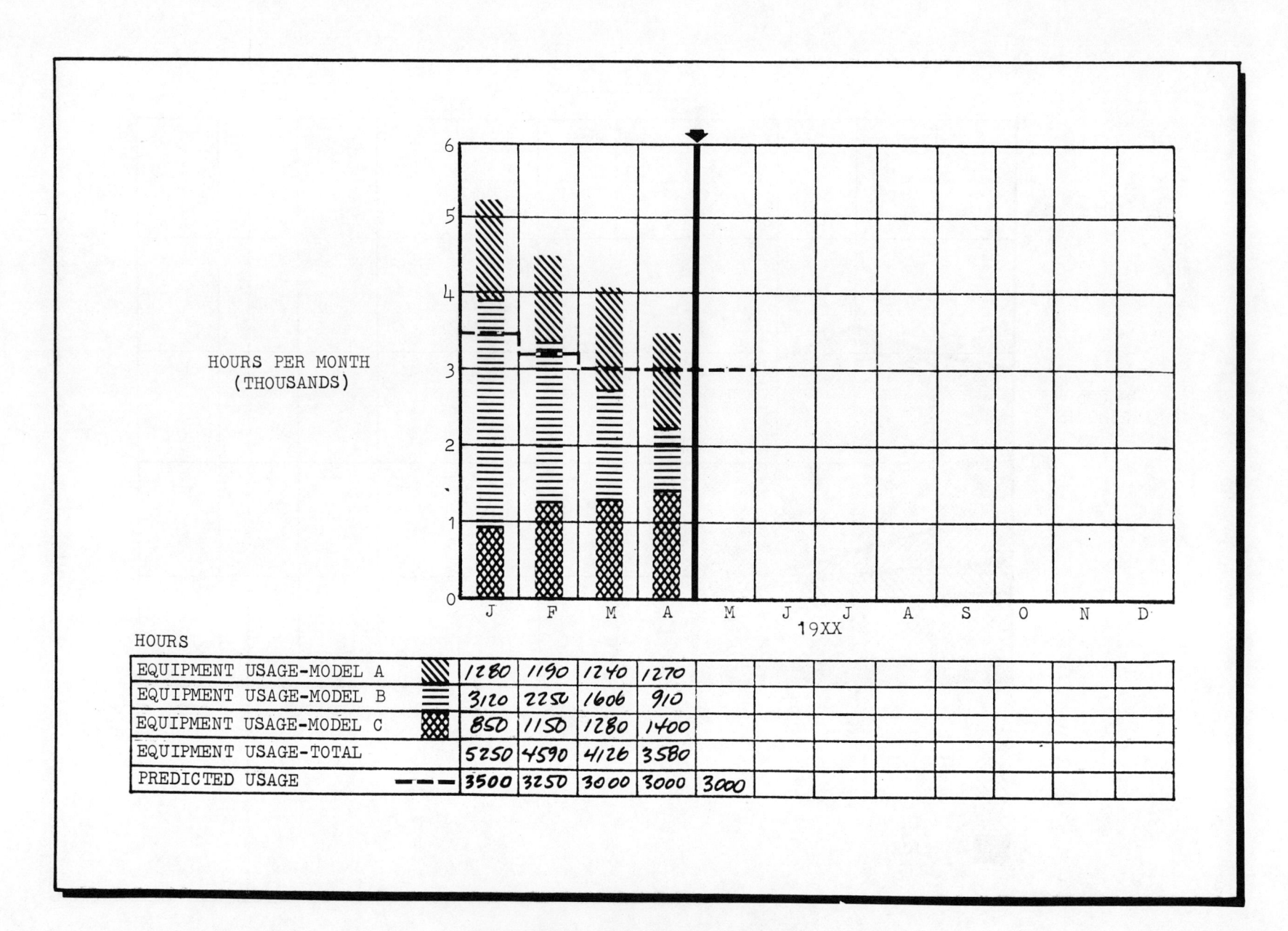

HOURS													
EQUIPMENT USAGE-MODEL A		1280	1190	1240	1270								
EQUIPMENT USAGE-MODEL B		3120	2250	1606	910								
EQUIPMENT USAGE-MODEL C		850	1150	1280	1400								
EQUIPMENT USAGE-TOTAL		5250	4590	4126	3580								
PREDICTED USAGE	---	3500	3250	3000	3000	3000							

Figure 39.3 Product Usage—Version 3

STATUS AS OF _____

ITEM	USAGE AS A % OF TOTAL AVAILABILITY
MODEL A	
MODEL B	
MODEL C	
MODEL D	
MODEL E	
MODEL F	
MODEL G	

////// NOT USED

███ UNSATISFACTORY USAGE

▨▨▨ SATISFACTORY USAGE

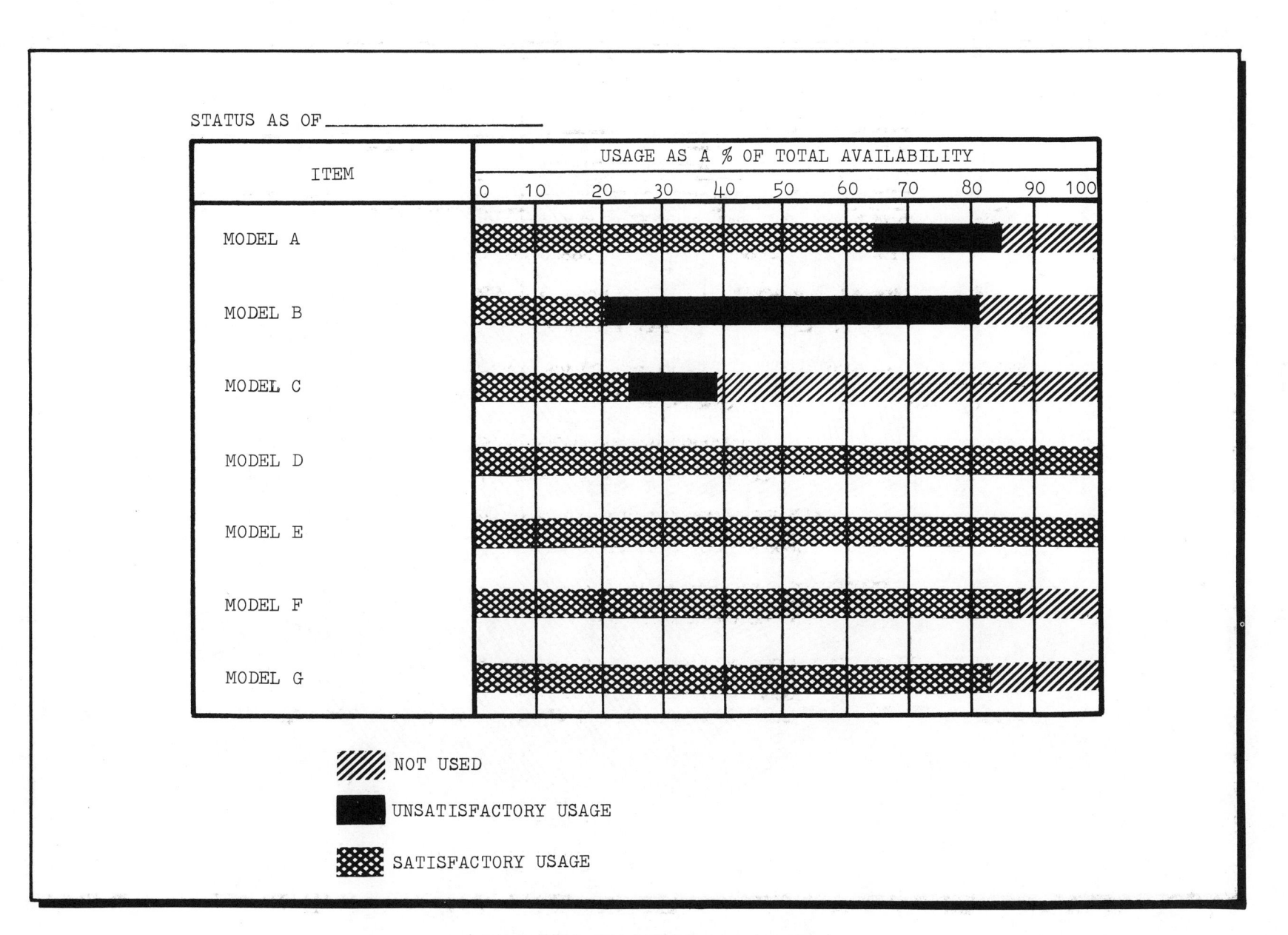

Figure 39.4 Product Usage—Version 4

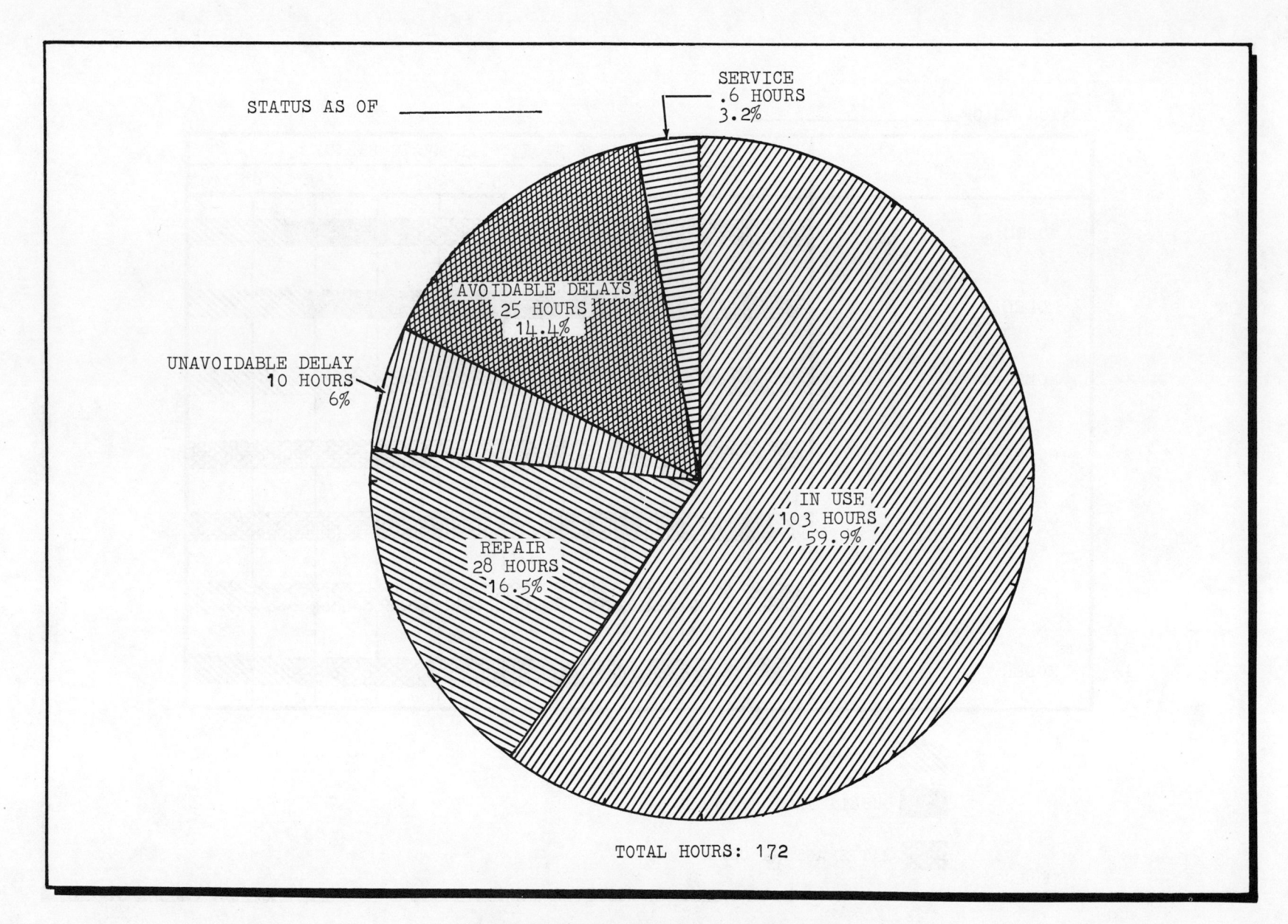

Figure 39.5 Product Usage—Version 5

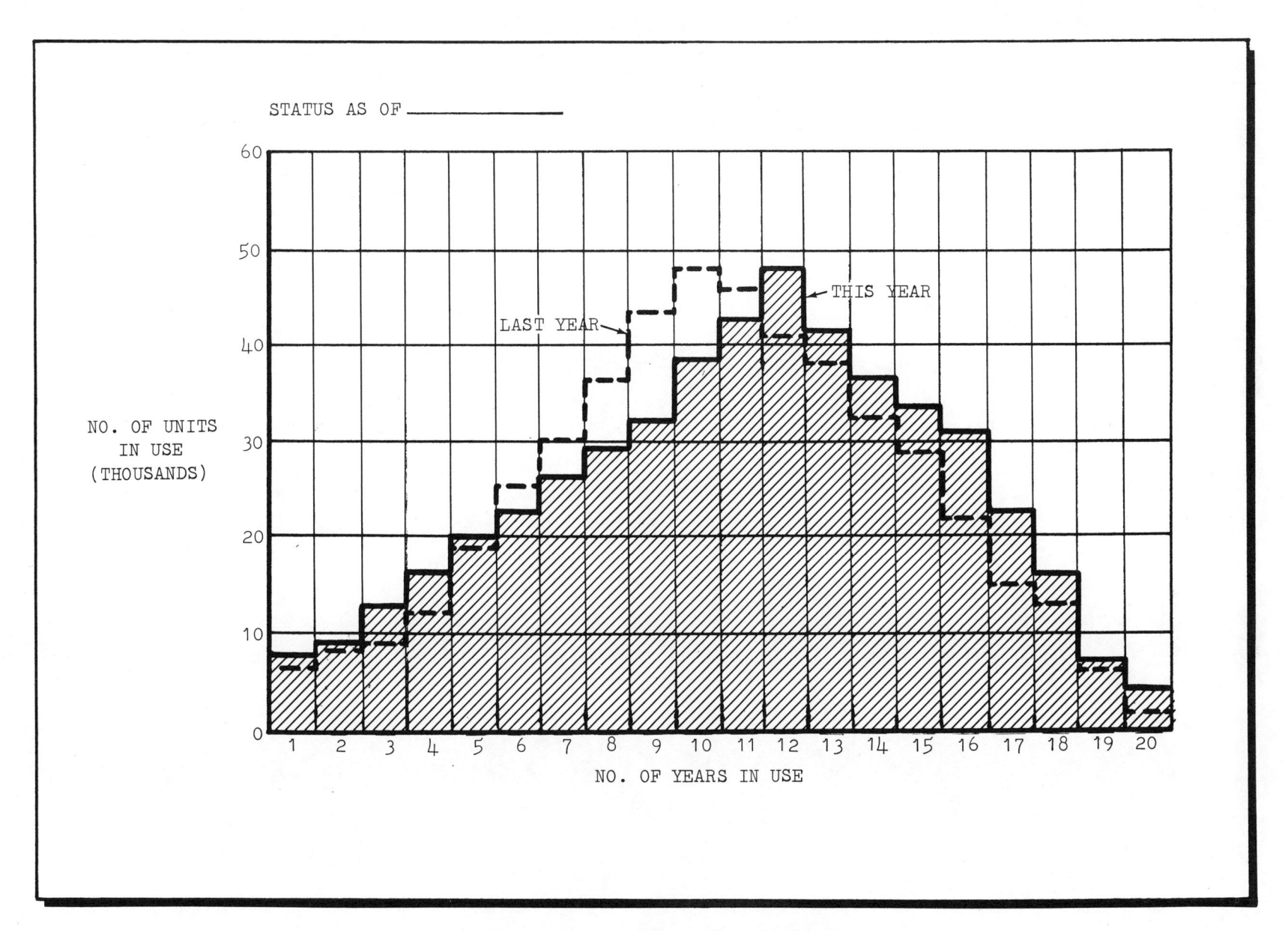

Figure 39.6 Product Usage—Version 6

40.0 PROPOSALS/QUOTATIONS

Charts that show the status of proposals or quotations being prepared and submitted to prospects for the purpose of securing new or follow-on business are shown in this section. In most examples in this section, the terms "proposal" and "quotation" are interchangeable.

40.1 Proposals/Quotations—Version 1: Version 1 of a proposal or quotation tracking chart, Figure 40.1, uses a segmented column technique. Each segmented column shows the dollar value of total on-hand business as well as the value of outstanding quotations for each month. The columns are compared against a goal which has been established by management.

40.2 Proposals/Quotations—Version 2: Version 2 of a proposal or quotation chart, Figure 40.2, displays a method for tracking progress in terms of the number of proposals being prepared each month. The surface chart technique is used to show those portions of the total which are on schedule or delinquent. The total is compared against the total number of proposals prepared each month during the previous year.

40.3 Proposals/Quotations—Version 3: Version 3 of a proposal/quotation chart, Figure 40.3, is similar to Version 2 except that tracking is done in terms of the dollar value of the proposals rather than the quantity. Notes have been added to this example as well, indicating for management the delinquent proposals of highest value and longest duration, together with the identification of the departments responsible for the proposals being past due.

40.4 Proposals/Quotations—Version 4: Delinquent proposals are emphasized in Version 4 of a proposal or quotation tracking chart, Figure 40.4. A surface chart technique is used so that the total can be visually segmented as to the departments responsible for the delay in processing the proposals.

40.5 Proposals/Quotations—Version 5: Segmented columns are plotted in terms of the dollar value of delinquent proposals in Version 5 of a proposal/quotation tracking chart, Figure 40.5. The columns are segmented as to specific projects.

40.6 Proposals/Quotations—Version 6: A great deal of detail is displayed in Version 6 of a proposal/quotation tracking chart, Figure 40.6. The detail, in this instance, makes a complex chart which may be difficult for some people to interpret. The total of proposals being processed each month is subdivided into those portions that were issued to the prospect or requester, those that are in the process of being prepared, and those that are new. Further, the "issued" and "in-process" sections each contain solid columns which indicate those portions of the segments that are past due.

40.7 Proposals/Quotations—Version 7: Delinquent proposals are tracked through the use of a symbol, or "milestone," chart in

Version 7 of a proposal/quotation tracking chart, Figure 40.7. Each proposal is identified as to proposal number, name, value, and department responsible for the delay in its preparation. The graphic portion of the chart displays symbols which indicate the date when the proposal was first due to the prospect and the anticipated slippage date. When each proposal is finally issued the symbols would be darkened.

40.8 Proposals/Quotations—Version 8: A one-time status report which shows delinquent proposals is used as Version 8 of a proposals/quotations tracking chart, Figure 40.8. In this example, each proposal is identified by number, name, number of days that the proposal is past due, and department responsible for the delay in its preparation. The graphic portion of the chart displays the relative value of each proposal to the total value of all those that are delinquent.

40.9 Proposals/Quotations—Version 9: Version 9 of a proposal or quotation chart, Figure 40.9, is a one-time status report. Each delinquent proposal, in this example, is identified as to proposal number, project name, value of the project, number of days the proposal is past due, and department responsible for the delay.

40.10 Proposals/Quotations—Version 10: A statistical table is combined with a graphic chart in Version 10 of a proposal/quotation tracking chart, Figure 40.10. The graphic portion of the chart, in terms of quantity of proposals per month, plots the total number of proposals that are in process and segments that total as to those on schedule versus those that are delinquent. The total is compared against the total processed each month during the previous year. The tabular portion of the chart gives the backup statistics for the graph, plus the dollar value of the proposals being processed.

40.11 Proposals/Quotations—Version 11: A milestone symbol chart is used to display the elements of proposal planning in Version 11 of a proposal/quotation tracking chart, Figure 40.11. Each proposal is identified as to number, estimated value, name of the project leader, and title. Then, each step involved in the proposal process (conference, prepare proposal, submit proposal, expected go-ahead) is scheduled with milestone symbols on the graphic portion of the chart.

40.12 Proposals/Quotations—Version 12: A non-graphic one-time status report version of a proposal/quotation chart is shown as Version 12, Figure 40.12. This is an information type report showing, in this example, the plan for the development of proposals. The information would have to be translated to another format for tracking purposes.

40.13 Proposals/Quotations—Version 13: Version 13 of a proposal/quotation tracking chart, Figure 40.13, concerns itself with the capture rate. The capture rate is the percent of the value of business won in relationship to the value of all proposals submitted on a year-to-date basis. In this example, this year's actual percentages are compared against last year's.

40.14 Proposals/Quotations—Version 14: A great deal of information is displayed in Version 14 of a proposal/quotation tracking chart, Figure 40.14. Each prepared proposal is identified in terms of the proposal number, its title or description, and its estimated value. The graphic portion of the chart displays the evaluation period time span of the open proposal, and the letters "W" and "L" indicate whether a contract was won or lost. The statistics at the bottom of the chart give the monthly and year-to-date dollar values of all submitted proposals, and that portion which has been captured (won). The bottom line gives the year-to-date capture rate.

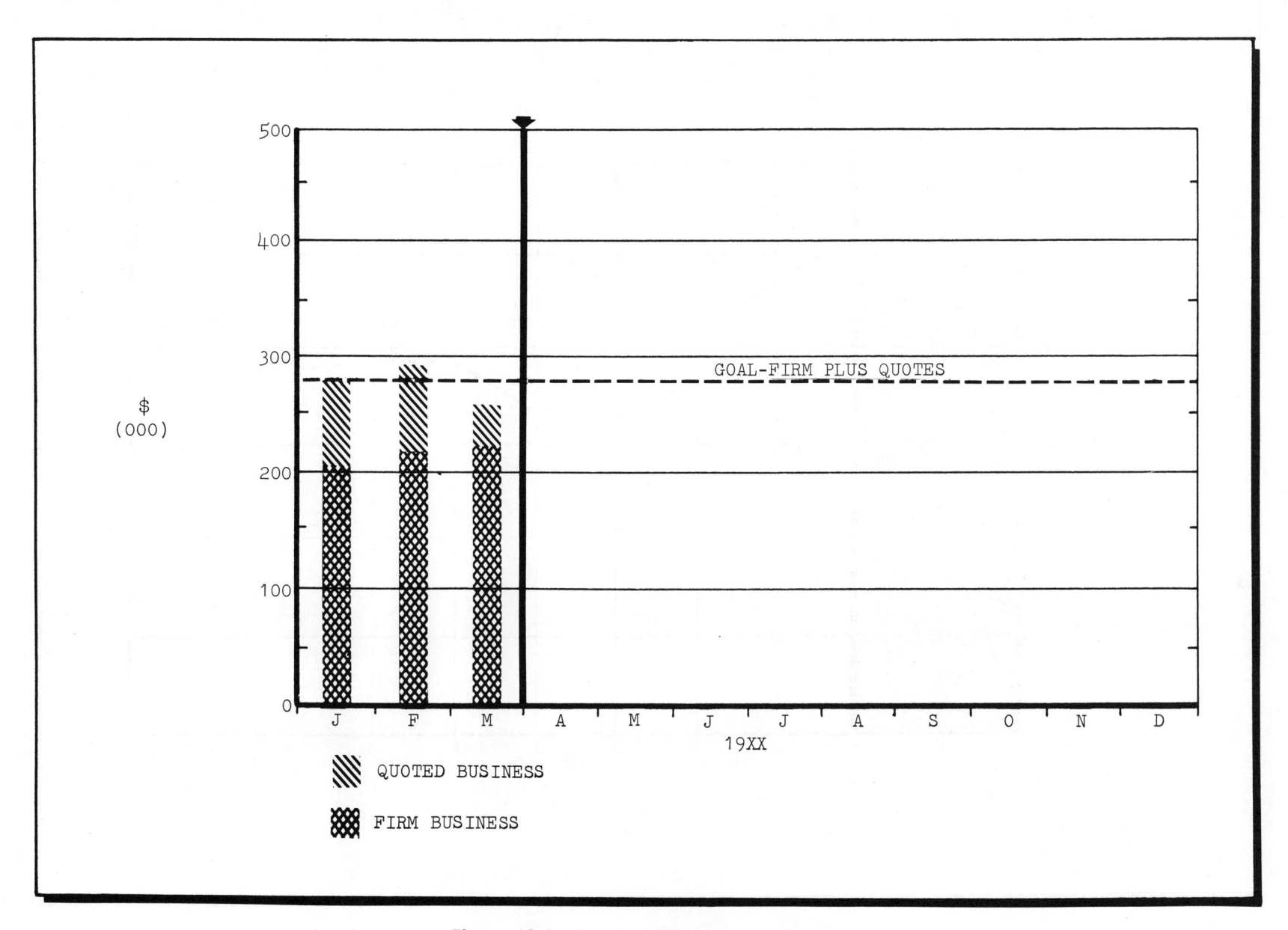

Figure 40.1   Proposals/Quotations—Version 1

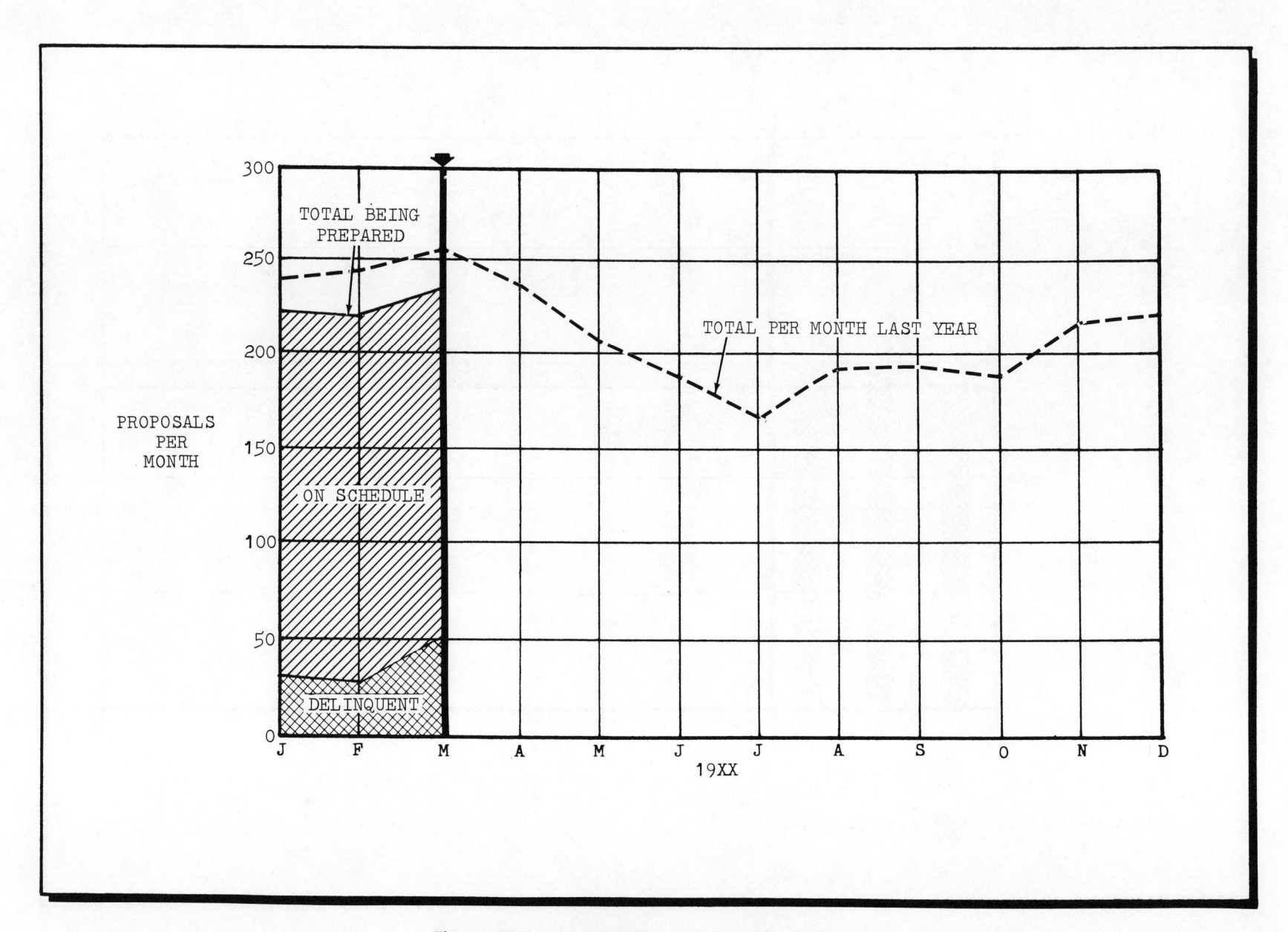

Figure 40.2 Proposals/Quotations—Version 2

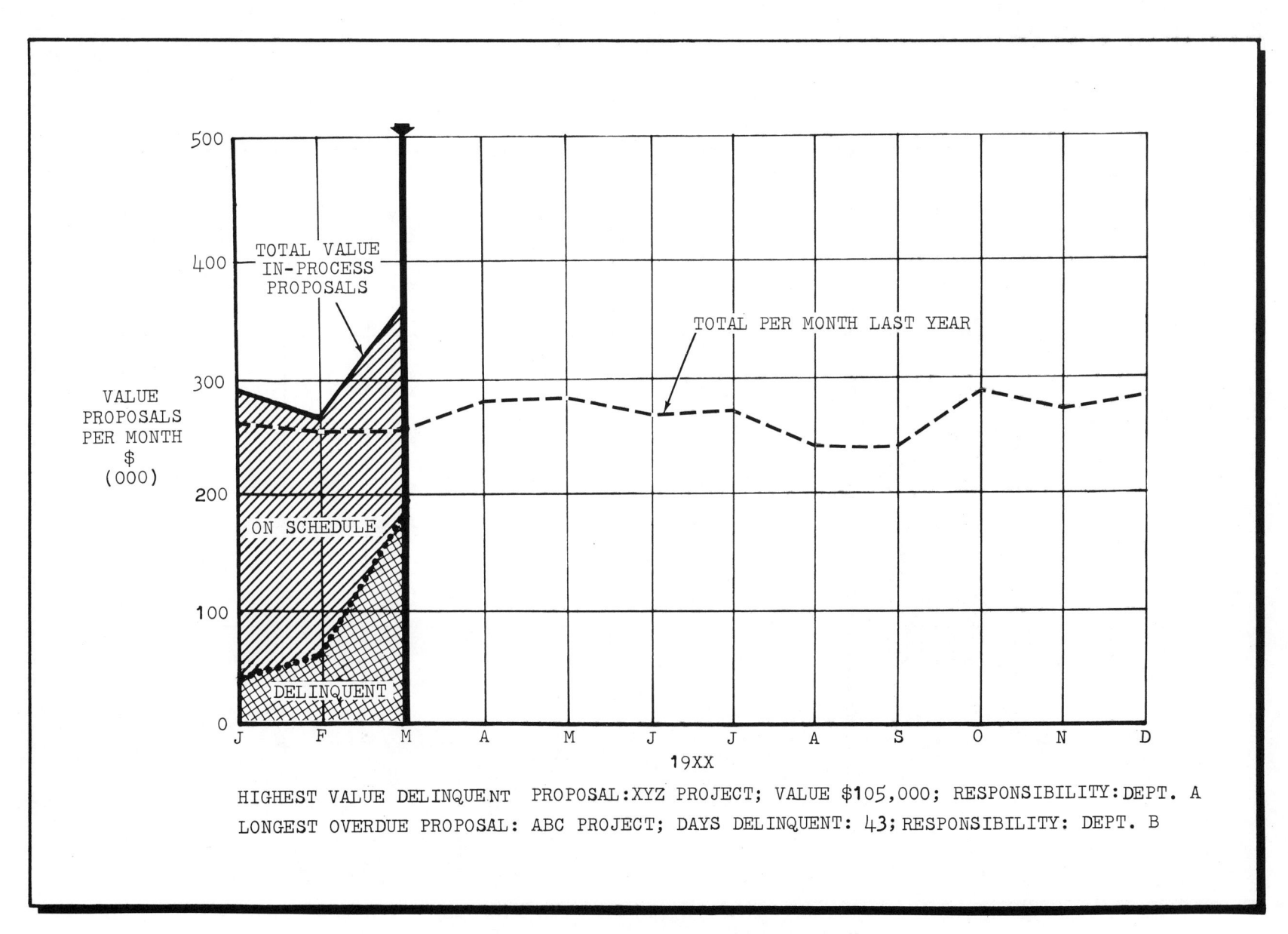

Figure 40.3 Proposals/Quotations—Version 3

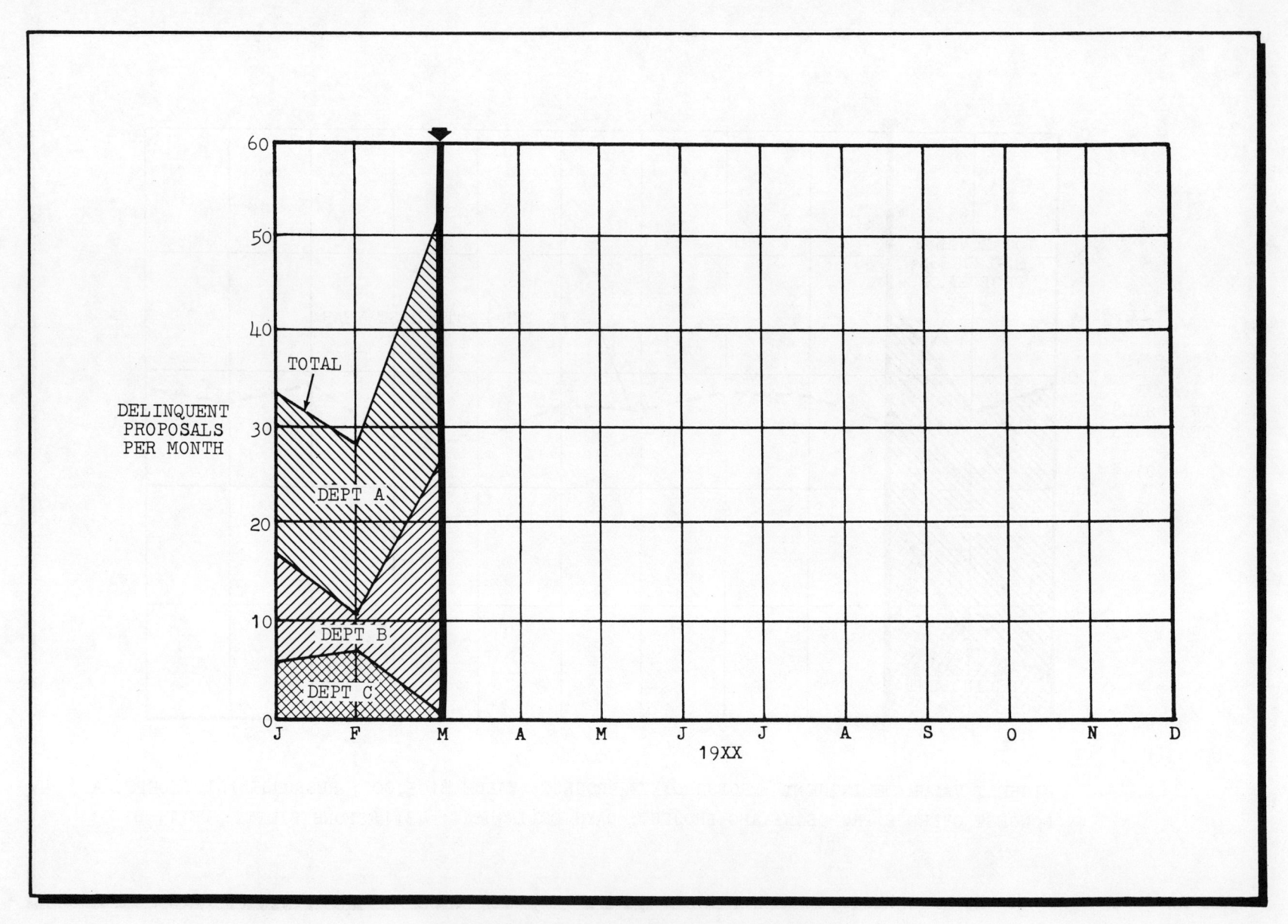

Figure 40.4 Proposals/Quotations—Version 4

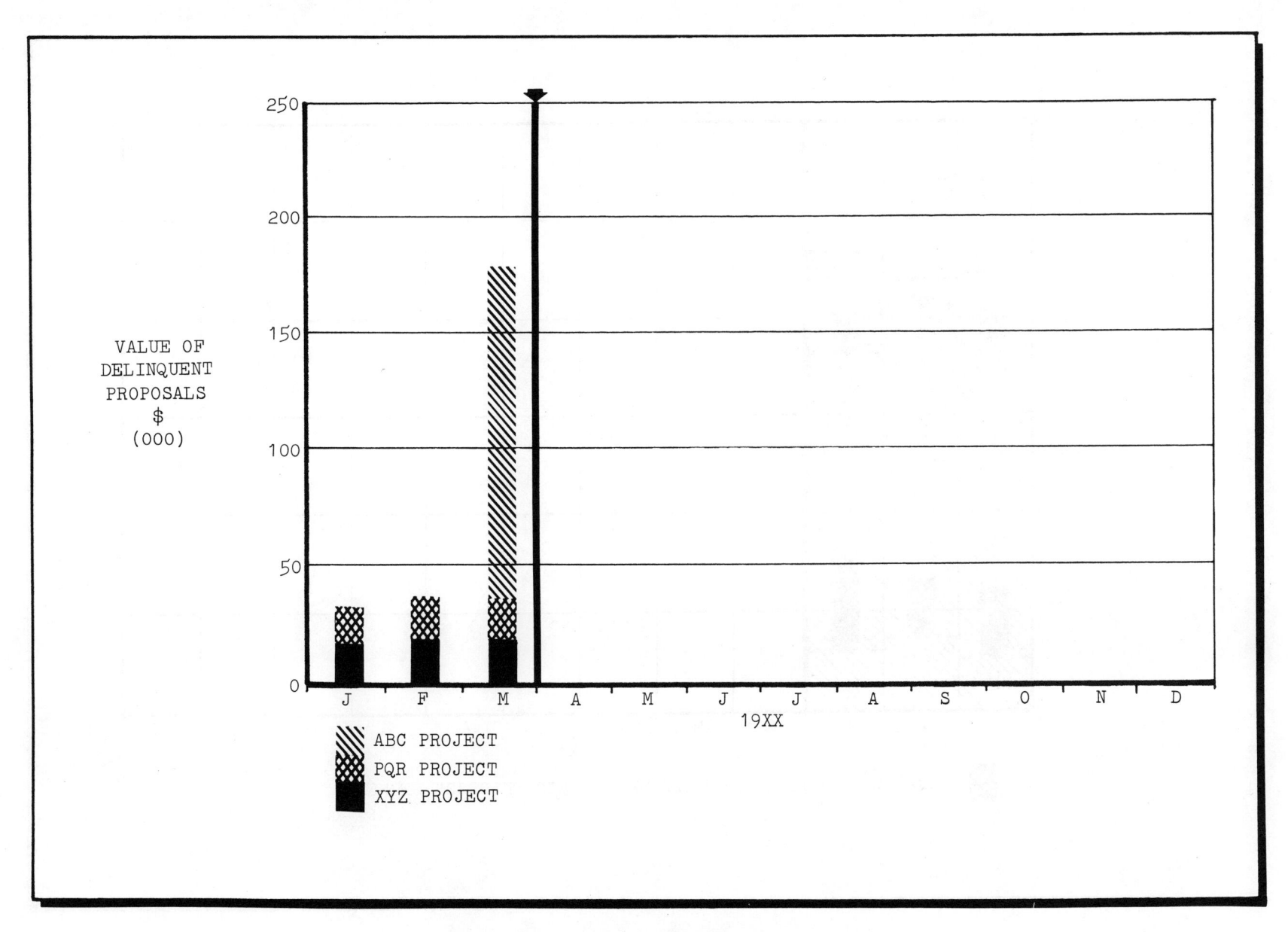

Figure 40.5 Proposals/Quotations—Version 5

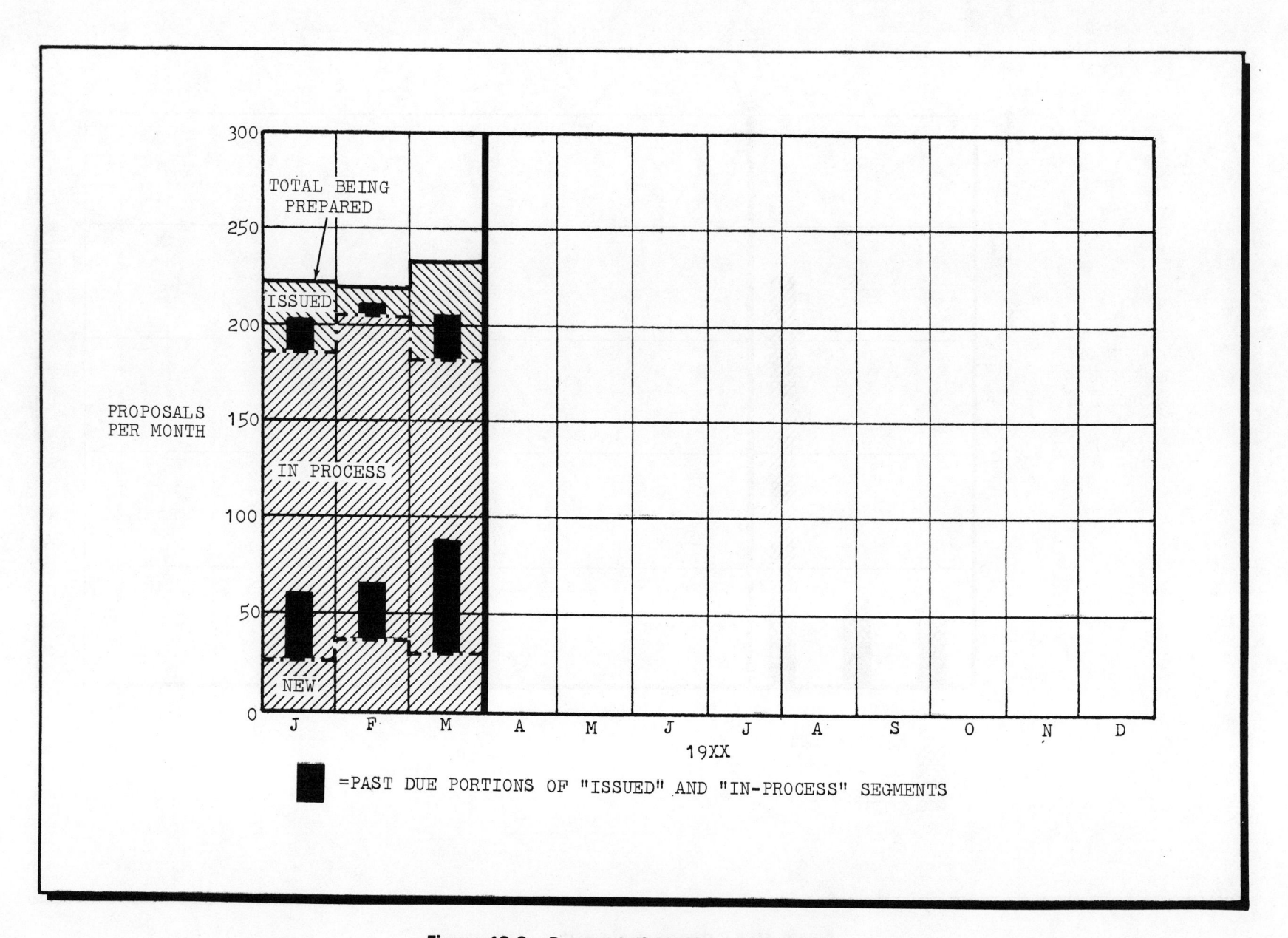

Figure 40.6   Proposals/Quotations—Version 6

DELINQUENT PROPOSALS

PROPOSAL NO.	PROJECT NAME	VALUE ($000)	DEPT RESPONS. FOR DELAY	APRIL					MAY				JUNE			
				1	8	15	22	29	6	13	20	27	3	10	17	24
6412	BFURNSB	43.0	PRICING	△											◇	
5123	WIEURNS	11.0	ENGINEERING			△							◇			
4668	FKDIEEO	2.0	MANUFACTURING					△						◇		
3987	WKDJCVN	80.0	MANUFACTURING							△				◇		
4471	NGJFKDO	17.0	PRICING							△				◇		
4512	OSIEJRHT	102.0	CONTRACTS							△			◇			
8716	UTJGHFD	3.0	CONTRACTS								△		◇			

△ DUE DATE TO PROSPECT
◇ ANTICIPATED SLIPPAGE
◆▲ ACTUAL COMPLETION

Figure 40.7 Proposals/Quotations—Version 7

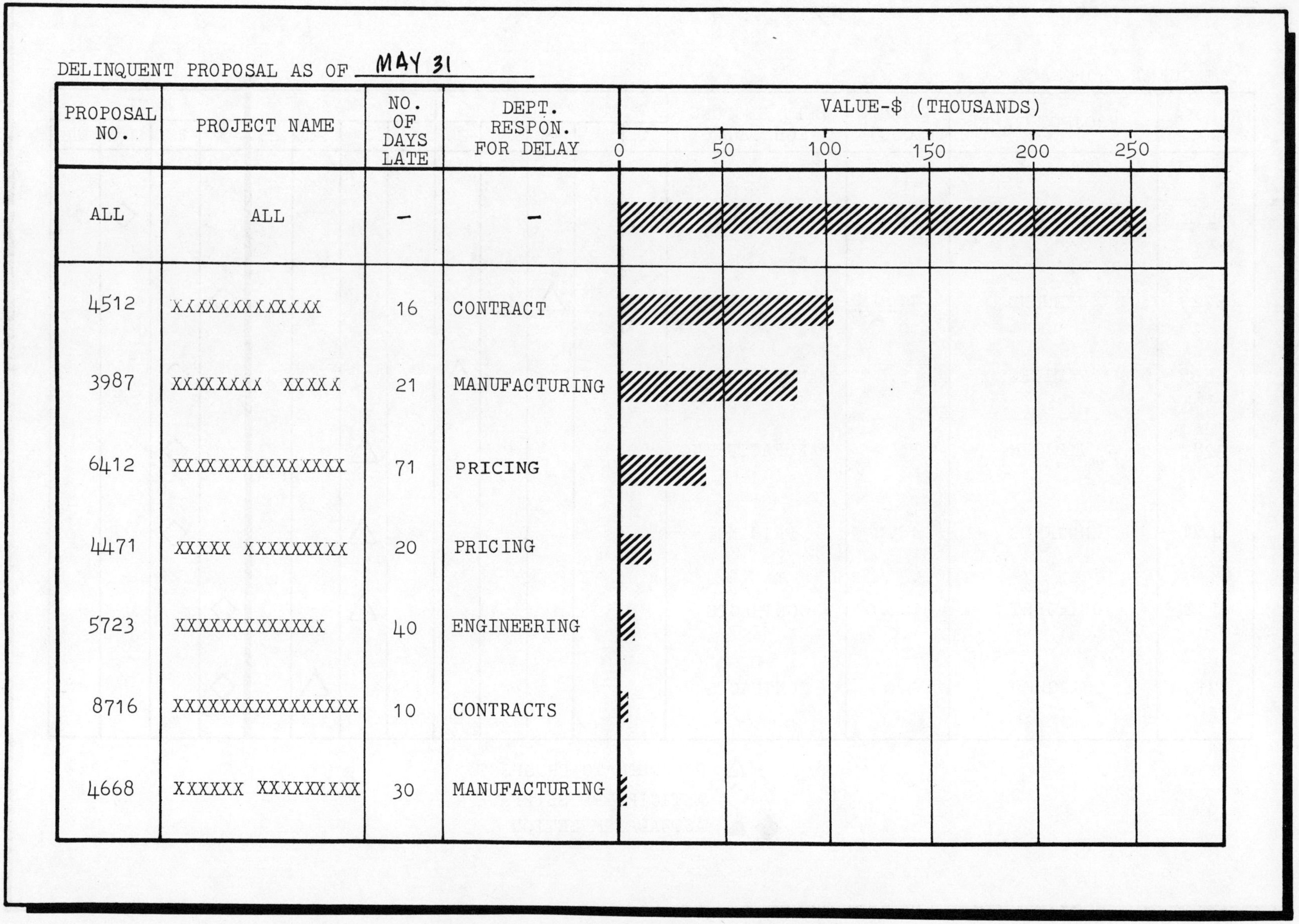

DELINQUENT PROPOSAL AS OF **MAY 31**

PROPOSAL NO.	PROJECT NAME	NO. OF DAYS LATE	DEPT. RESPON. FOR DELAY	VALUE-$ (THOUSANDS)
ALL	ALL	–	–	▨▨▨▨ (~260)
4512	XXXXXXXXXXX	16	CONTRACT	▨▨ (~105)
3987	XXXXXXX XXXX	21	MANUFACTURING	▨▨ (~90)
6412	XXXXXXXXXXXXX	71	PRICING	▨ (~45)
4471	XXXXX XXXXXXXXX	20	PRICING	▨ (~15)
5723	XXXXXXXXXXXX	40	ENGINEERING	▨ (~10)
8716	XXXXXXXXXXXXXX	10	CONTRACTS	▨ (~8)
4668	XXXXXX XXXXXXXXX	30	MANUFACTURING	▨ (~8)

Figure 40.8   Proposals/Quotations—Version 8

DELINQUENT PROPOSALS AS OF __MAY 31__

PROPOSAL NO.	PROJECT NAME	VALUE ($000)	NUMBER OF DAYS LATE	DEPARTMENT RESPONSIBLE FOR DELAY
4512	GFJDKFJGH	102.0	16	CONTRACTS
3987	GHTYRUDFGH	80.0	21	MANUFACTURING
6412	YWODIFJ	43.0	71	PRICING
4471	BNVJDIRUT	17.0	20	PRICING
5123	GDJFJGH SPDL	11.0	40	ENGINEERING
8716	IWODKFJGHS	3.0	10	CONTRACTS
4668	FKGJTHRUE	2.0	30	MANUFACTURING

Figure 40.9 Proposals/Quotations—Version 9

QUANTITY OF PROPOSALS

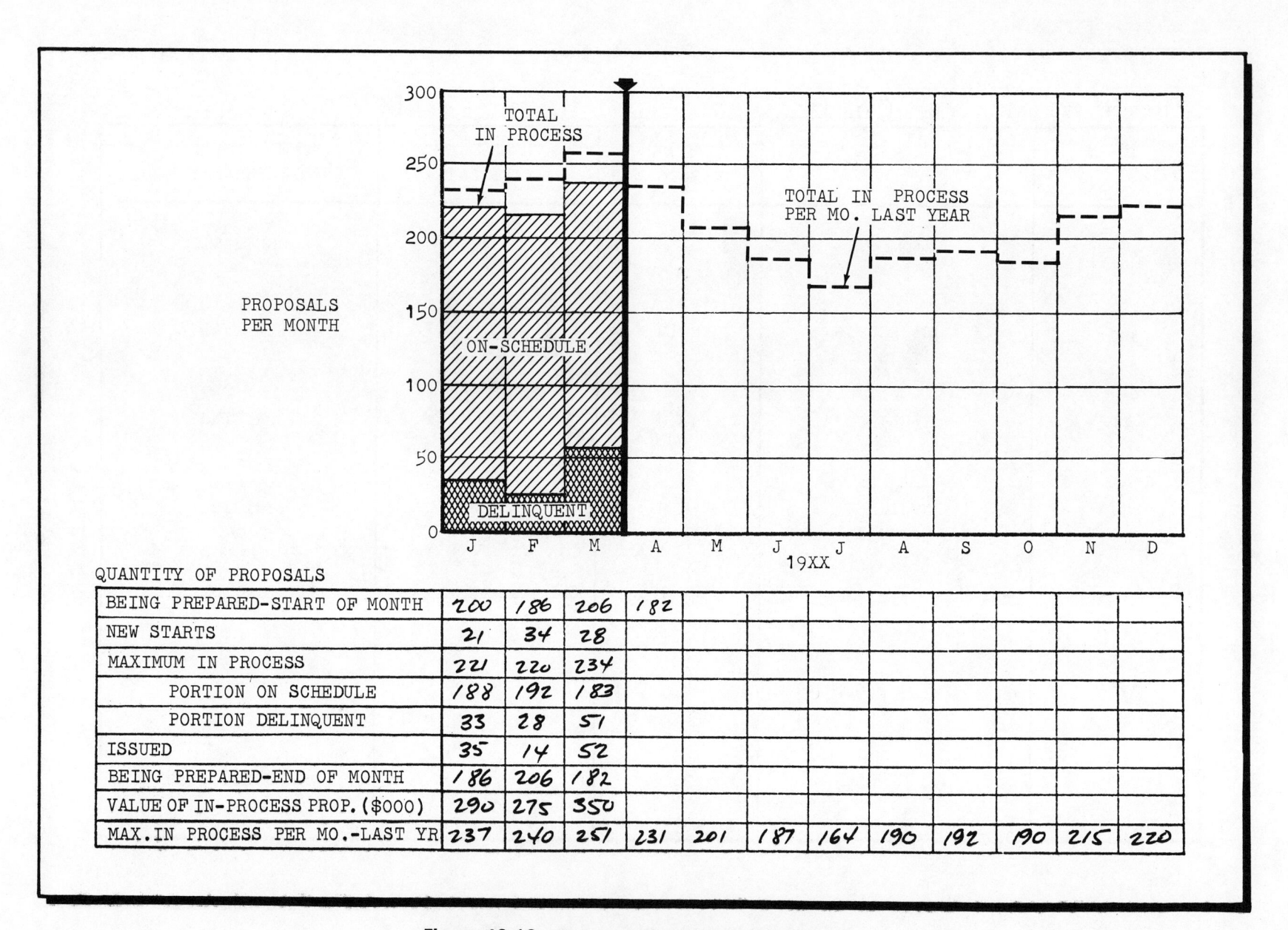

	J	F	M	A	M	J	J	A	S	O	N	D
BEING PREPARED-START OF MONTH	200	186	206	182								
NEW STARTS	21	34	28									
MAXIMUM IN PROCESS	221	220	234									
PORTION ON SCHEDULE	188	192	183									
PORTION DELINQUENT	33	28	51									
ISSUED	35	14	52									
BEING PREPARED-END OF MONTH	186	206	182									
VALUE OF IN-PROCESS PROP. ($000)	290	275	350									
MAX. IN PROCESS PER MO.-LAST YR	237	240	251	231	201	187	164	190	192	190	215	220

Figure 40.10 Proposals/Quotations—Version 10

PROPOSAL NO.	APPROX. VALUE	PROJECT LEADER	DESCRIPTION	JUNE				JULY					AUG			
				3	10	17	24	1	8	15	22	29	5	12	19	26
A-110	127.0	JONES	TRAINING PROGRAM													
			CONFERENCE			▲										
			PREPARE PROPOSAL			▲━━━━━━━━━△										
			SUBMIT PROPOSAL						△							
			EXPECTED GO-AHEAD										△			
A-760	142.0	SMITH	TEST DATA PACKAGE													
			CONFERENCE					△								
			PREPARE PROPOSAL					△━━━━━━━━△								
			SUBMIT PROPOSAL								△					
			EXPECTED GO-AHEAD												△	
C-410	277.0	BROWN	SPARE PARTS													
			CONFERENCE			▲										
			PREPARE PROPOSAL			▲━━━━━━━━━━━━△				◇						
			SUBMIT PROPOSAL							△						
			EXPECTED GO-AHEAD											△		
E-527	248.0	WILLS	FIELD SERVICE													
			CONFERENCE					△								
			PREPARE PROPOSAL					△━━━━━━━━━━━━△								
			SUBMIT PROPOSAL								△					
			EXPECTED GO-AHEAD													△

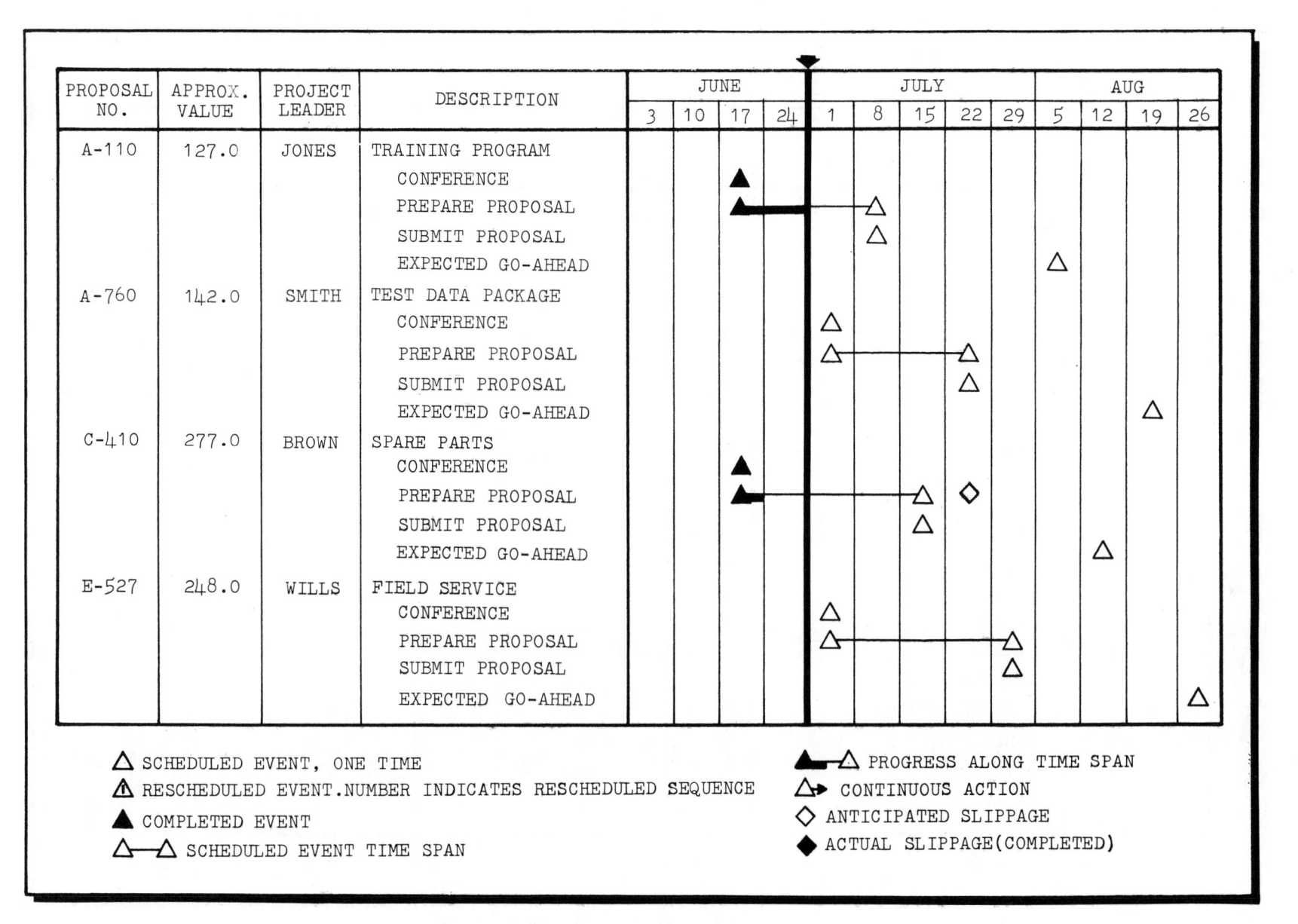

△ SCHEDULED EVENT, ONE TIME
⚠ RESCHEDULED EVENT. NUMBER INDICATES RESCHEDULED SEQUENCE
▲ COMPLETED EVENT
△━△ SCHEDULED EVENT TIME SPAN

▲━△ PROGRESS ALONG TIME SPAN
△▶ CONTINUOUS ACTION
◇ ANTICIPATED SLIPPAGE
◆ ACTUAL SLIPPAGE (COMPLETED)

Figure 40.11 Proposals/Quotations—Version 11

PROPOSAL PLAN AS OF __JUNE 1__

PROPOSAL NO.	DESCRIPTION	DATE	APPROX. PRICE ($000)	SOLIC ITED	UNSOLIC ITED	PROJECT LEADER	PROBABILITY OF A CAPTURE	PROPOSAL PREP. BUDGET ($000)
A-110	TRAINING PROGRAM		127.0	✓		JONES	85%	1.0
	CONFERENCE	6/17						
	PREPARE PROPOSAL	6/17 - 7/8						
	SUBMIT PROPOSAL	7/8						
	EXPECTED GO-AHEAD	8/5						
A-760	TEST DATA PACKAGE		142.0		✓	SMITH	50%	.7
	CONFERENCE	7/1						
	PREPARE PROPOSAL	7/1 - 7/22						
	SUBMIT PROPOSAL	7/22						
	EXPECTED GO-AHEAD	8/19						
C-410	SPARE PARTS		277.0	✓		BROWN	90%	1.6
	CONFERENCE	6/17						
	PREPARE PROPOSAL	6/17 - 7/15						
	SUBMIT PROPOSAL	7/15						
	EXPECTED GO-AHEAD	8/12						
E-527	FIELD SERVICE		248.0		✓	WILLS	35%	1.0
	CONFERENCE	7/1						
	PREPARE PROPOSAL	7/1 - 7/29						
	SUBMIT PROPOSAL	7/29						
	EXPECTED GO-AHEAD	8/26						

Figure 40.12 Proposals/Quotations—Version 12

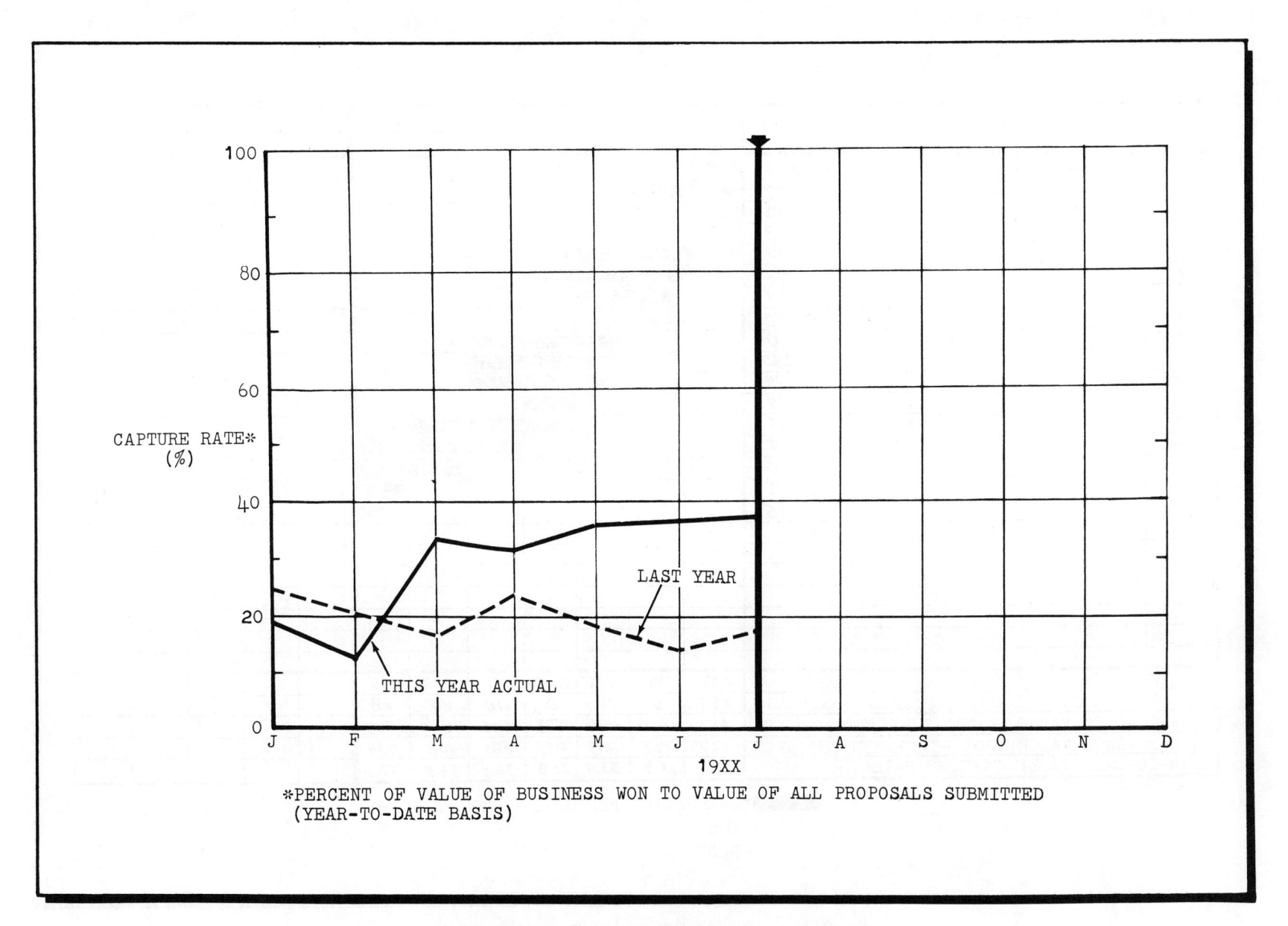

Figure 40.13 Proposals/Quotations—Version 13

SUBMITTED PROPOSALS

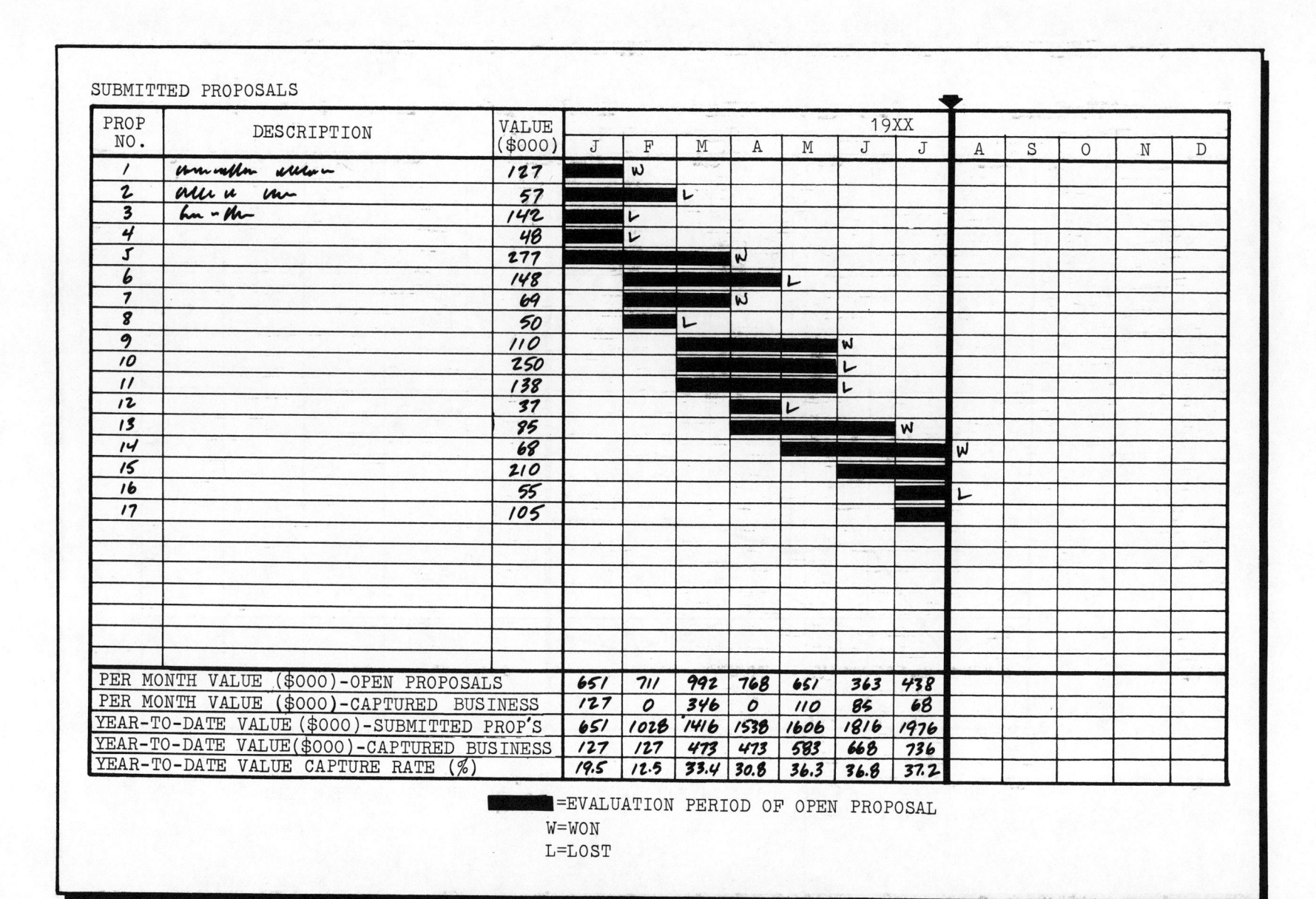

PROP NO.	DESCRIPTION	VALUE ($000)	J	F	M	A	M	J	J	A	S	O	N	D
									19XX					
1		127	▇ W											
2		57	▇▇ L											
3		142	▇ L											
4		48	▇ L											
5		277		▇▇▇ W										
6		148		▇▇▇ L										
7		69		▇▇ W										
8		50		▇ L										
9		110			▇▇▇ W									
10		250			▇▇▇ L									
11		138			▇▇▇ L									
12		37				▇ L								
13		85					▇▇ W							
14		68						▇▇ W						
15		210							▇					
16		55							▇ L					
17		105							▇					
PER MONTH VALUE ($000)-OPEN PROPOSALS			651	711	992	768	651	363	438					
PER MONTH VALUE ($000)-CAPTURED BUSINESS			127	0	346	0	110	85	68					
YEAR-TO-DATE VALUE ($000)-SUBMITTED PROP'S			651	1028	1416	1538	1606	1816	1976					
YEAR-TO-DATE VALUE ($000)-CAPTURED BUSINESS			127	127	473	473	583	668	736					
YEAR-TO-DATE VALUE CAPTURE RATE (%)			19.5	12.5	33.4	30.8	36.3	36.8	37.2					

▇ =EVALUATION PERIOD OF OPEN PROPOSAL
W=WON
L=LOST

Figure 40.14 Proposals/Quotations—Version 14

41.0 QUALITY

Charts that can be used to track and analyze the quality of goods produced are shown in this section. Also see Sections 1.0, *Accuracy* and 43.0, *Reliability*.

41.1 Quality—Version 1: A simple chart for displaying the percentage of goods accepted (via an inspection process, for instance) is illustrated as Version 1 of a quality tracking chart, Figure 41.1. This type of measurement is often referred to as "yield" or "quality yield." This example shows a yield goal of 95%. The amount scale has an arrow to show that it does not start from a zero base.

41.2 Quality—Version 2: Version 2 of a quality chart, Figure 41.2, tracks quality in terms of rejections. Actual rejections in this example are shown in relationship to an "acceptable rate" of rejections. Tracking charts are useful when actuals are tracked against some type of goal such as what is shown. Other goals could be "requirement," or "performance last year," or "industry average."

41.3 Quality—Version 3: Quality is tracked in terms of the average number of defects per unit inspected in Version 3 of a quality tracking chart, Figure 41.3. In this example, the actuals are compared with the average for the previous year.

41.4 Quality—Version 4: Quality is tracked in terms of the monthly quantity of product defects per employee in Version 4 of a quality tracking chart, Figure 41.4. Lacking other comparison criteria, the goal in this example is "zero defects."

41.5 Quality—Version 5: Version 5 of a quality tracking chart, Figure 41.5, is similar to Version 4, except, in this example, the total quality of monthly product defects per employee is segmented according to department. Such a display will enable the chart reader to determine where there is the highest potential for greater improvement.

41.6 Quality—Version 6: In Version 6 of a quality tracking chart, Figure 41.6, the rejection percentage is compared among vendors. The same format could be used to make comparisons between departments or product models.

41.7 Quality—Version 7: Version 1 of a quality tracking chart showed the monthly percent of accepted goods. Version 7, Figure 41.7, shows the same measurement but adds segments that allocate responsibility for the reject portion of the chart, that part between "accepted" and 100%.

41.8 Quality—Version 8: Twin grids are used in Version 8 of a quality tracking chart, Figure 41.8. The left-hand grid shows the total number of parts inspected (solid line) and accepted (dotted line) for each month up to the reporting date. The right-hand grid shows, in percentage form, the disposition of the rejected parts: scrapped or reworked, in this example.

41.9 Quality—Version 9: Three grids are used in Version 9 of a quality tracking chart, Figure 41.9. The left-hand grid shows the monthly quantity of inspected and accepted parts. The center grid shows the rejection rate per month. The right-hand grid shows the charged causes for the rejections for each month.

41.10 Quality—Version 10: Version 10 of a quality tracking chart, Figure 41.10, displays a method for drawing attention to the five most significant product defects for each time period.

41.11 Quality—Version 11: Two styles of charts are used in Version 11 of a quality tracking chart, Figure 41.11. The upper grid utilizes a column chart style to show the percentage of rejected parts per month compared against the average for the previous year. The lower part of the chart uses shading to show the three highest frequency discrepancies for each reporting period.

41.12 Quality—Version 12: Graphics are combined with statistics in Version 12 of a quality tracking chart, Figure 41.12. The column chart shows yield in relationship to a goal. The table gives the statistics for the quantity of parts inspected, and the quantity and percentage of parts accepted and rejected.

41.13 Quality—Version 13: The percent of rejected parts per month is compared with the average for the previous year in the graphic portion of Version 13 of a quality tracking chart, Figure 41.13. The table gives the quantity of parts inspected, the quantity and percentage of parts rejected, and the quantity of rejections by discrepancy type.

41.14 Quality—Version 14: The number of parts inspected and accepted, and the percentage of rejections are shown on two separate grids in Version 14 of a quality tracking chart, Figure 41.14. The table on the right-hand side of the chart gives the current month's statistics broken down, in this example, by department. The breakdown could also be in terms of part number, model, or process (punch press, painting, etc.).

41.15 Quality—Version 15: A statistical table that can be used for tracking purposes is shown in Version 15 of a quality tracking chart, Figure 41.15. The quantity of inspected and rejected parts, and the percentage of rejections are shown on the first three lines. The following eight lines give the quantity of rejections broken down by discrepancy type.

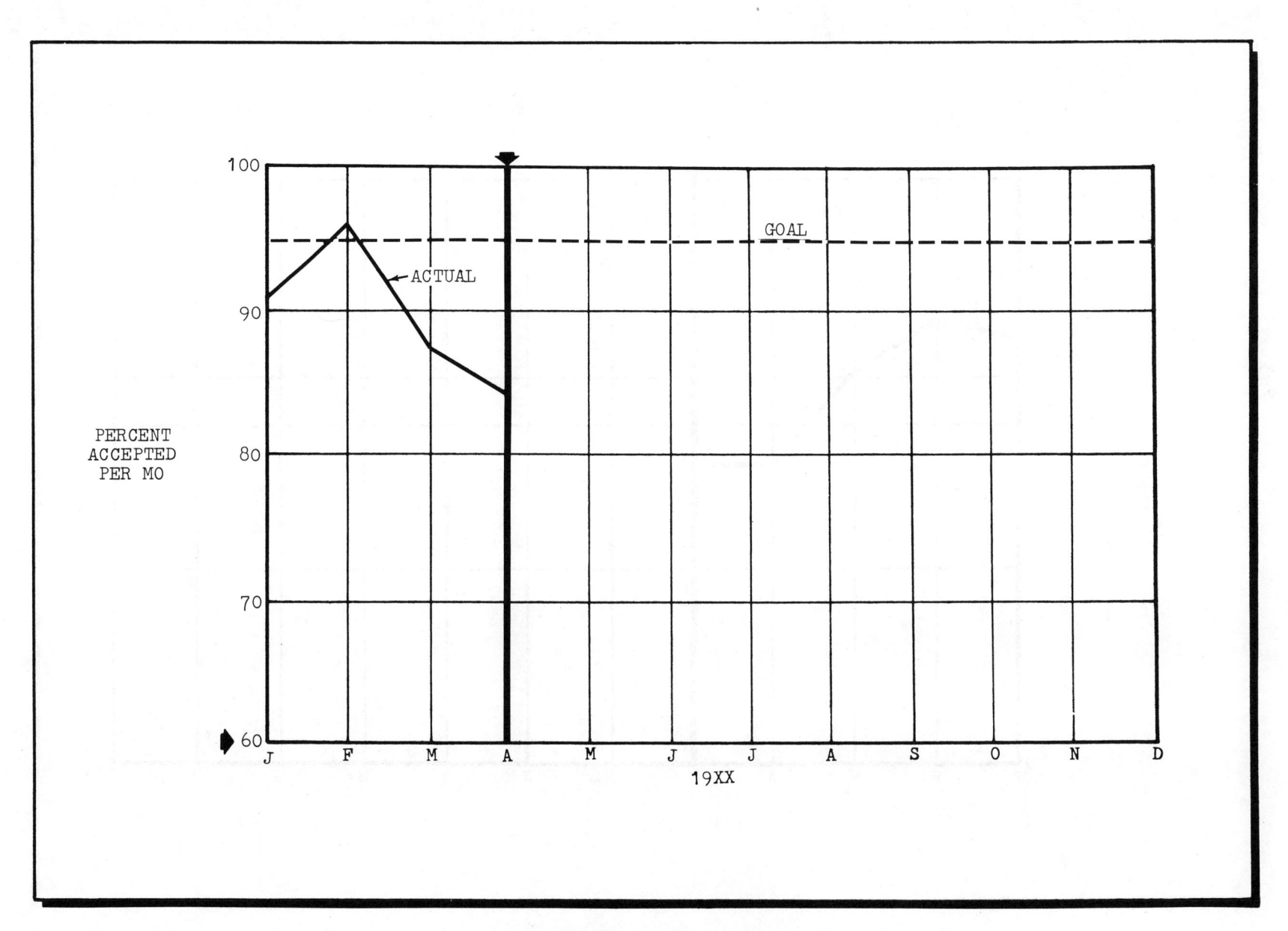

Figure 41.1 Quality—Version 1

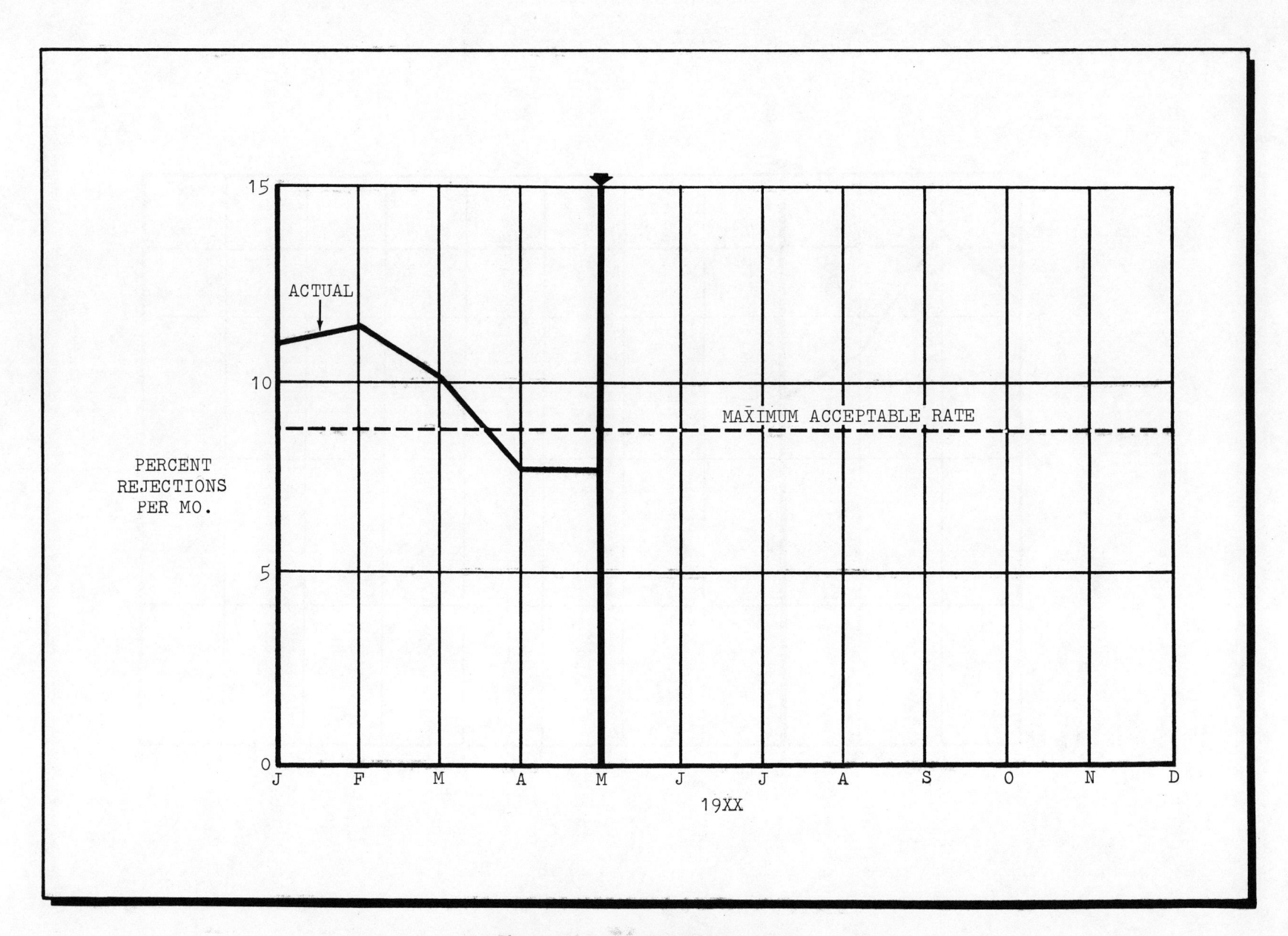

Figure 41.2 Quality—Version 2

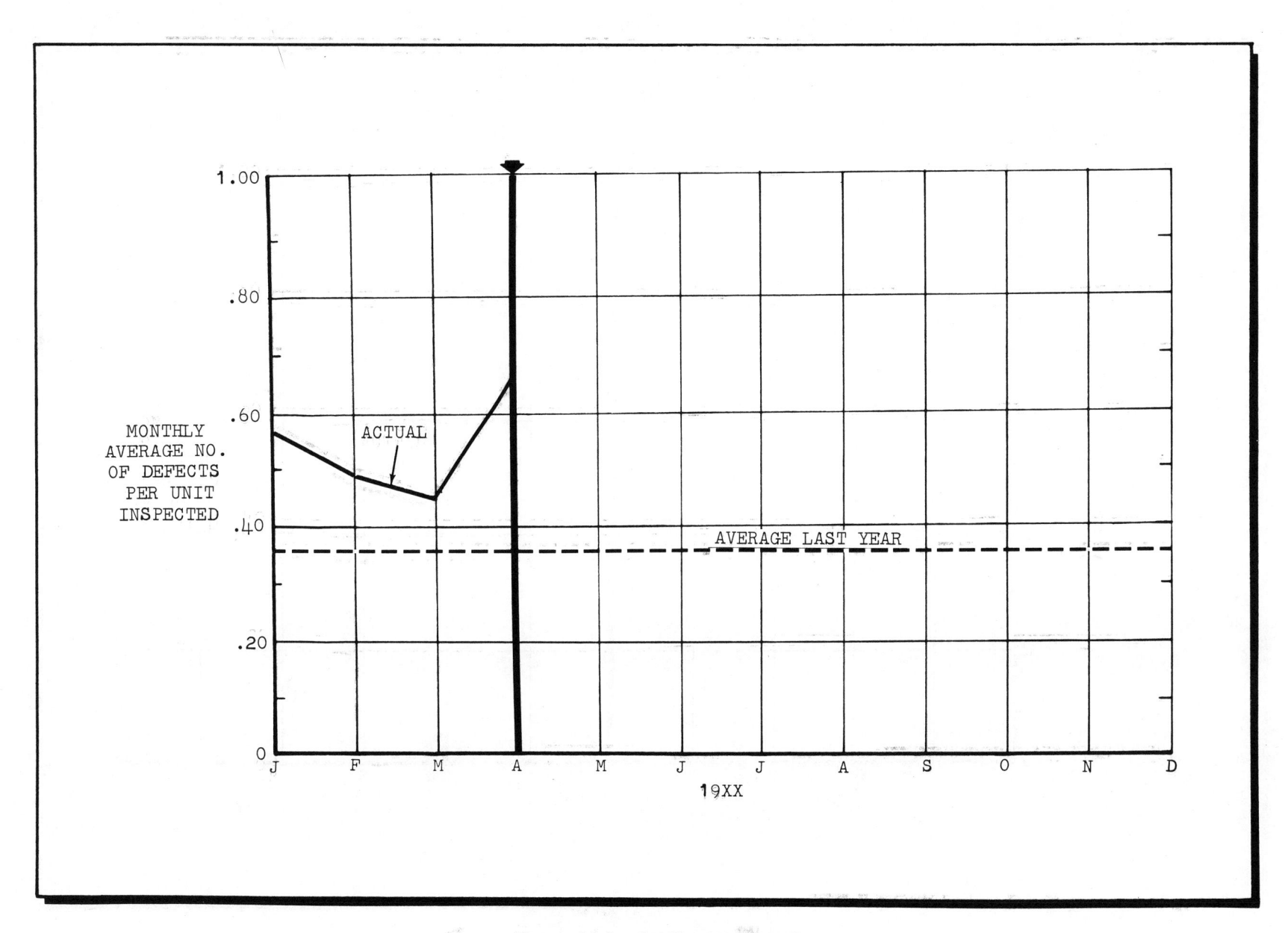

Figure 41.3   Quality—Version 3

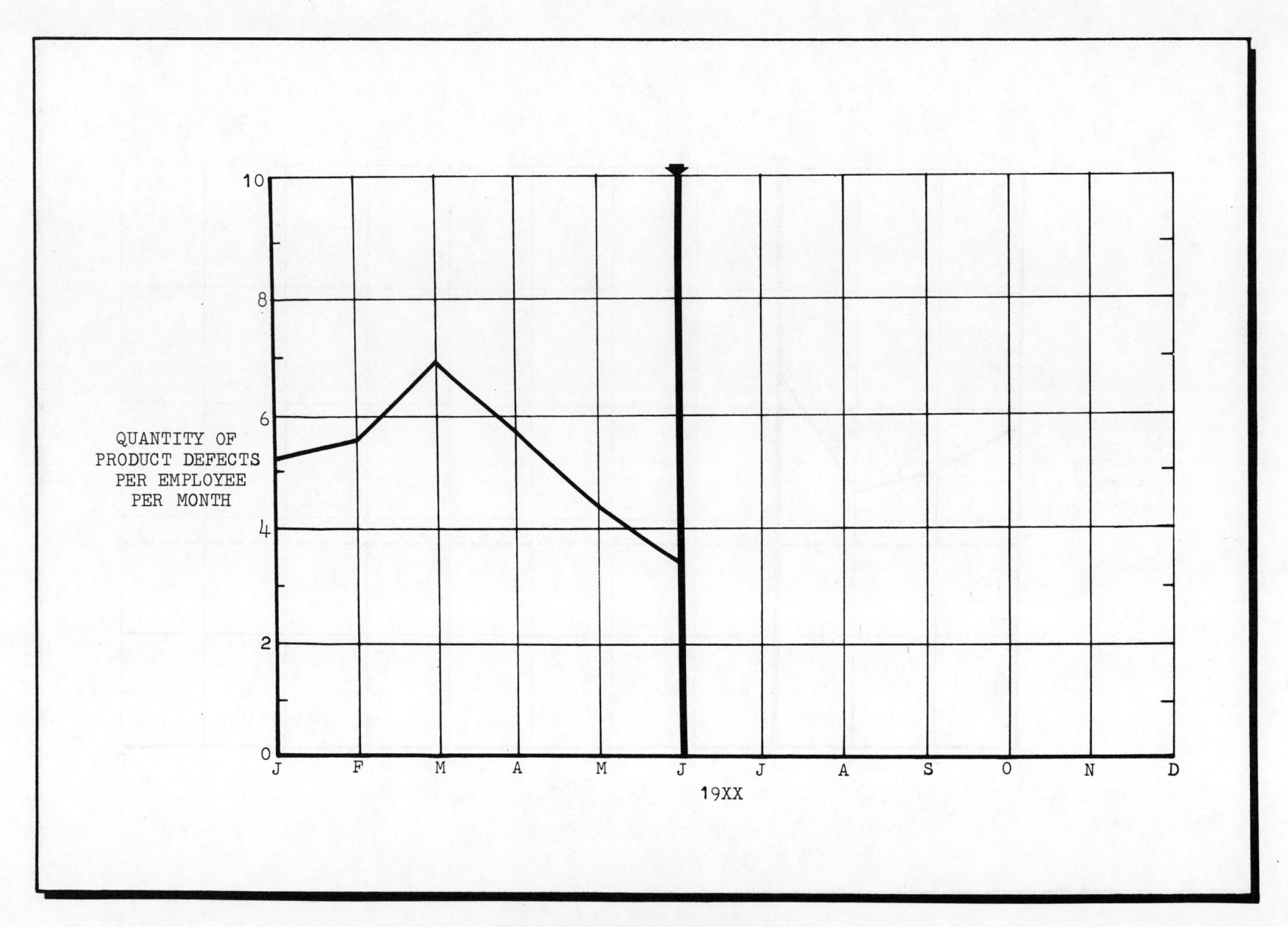

Figure 41.4   Quality—Version 4

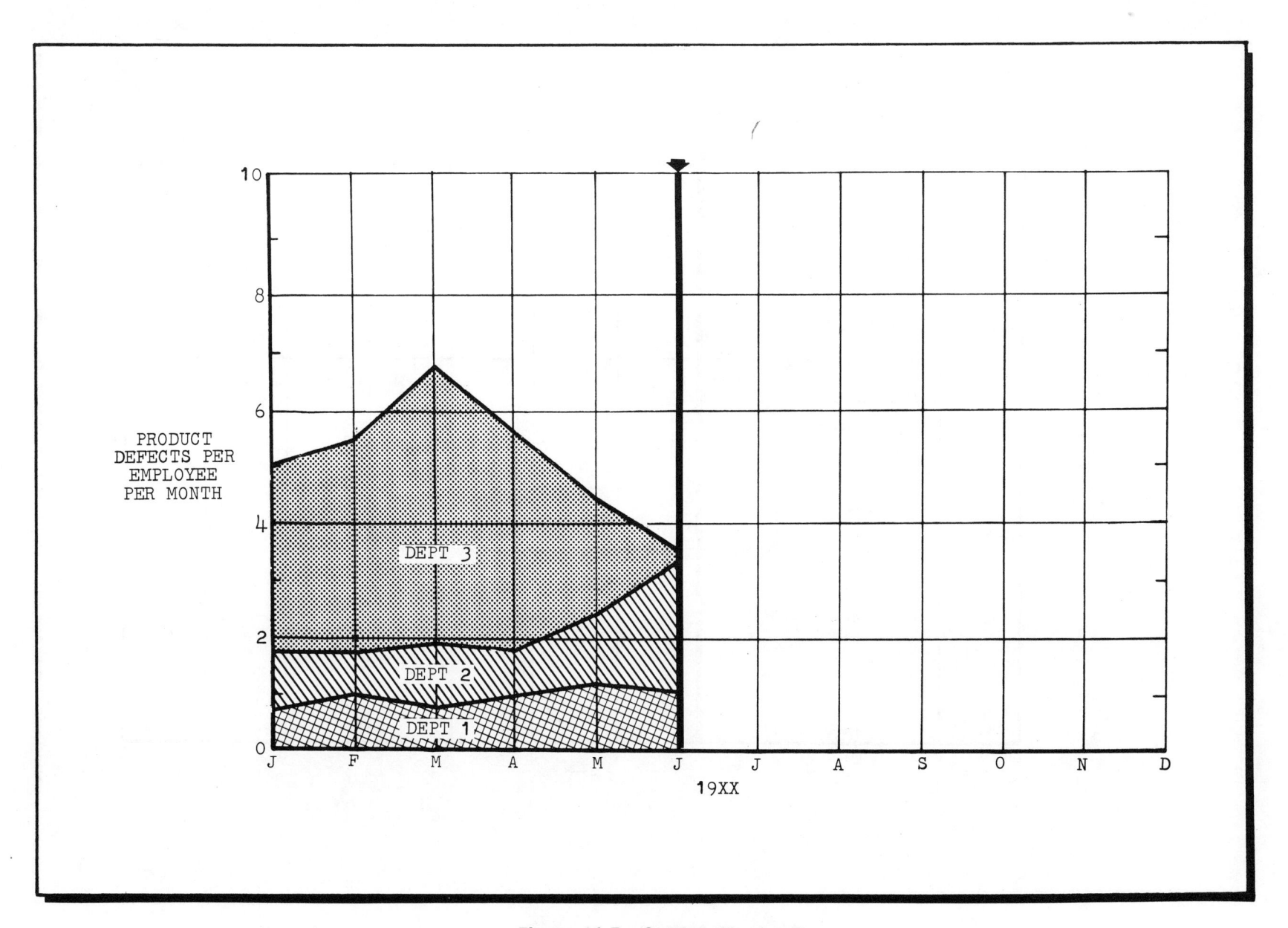

Figure 41.5 Quality—Version 5

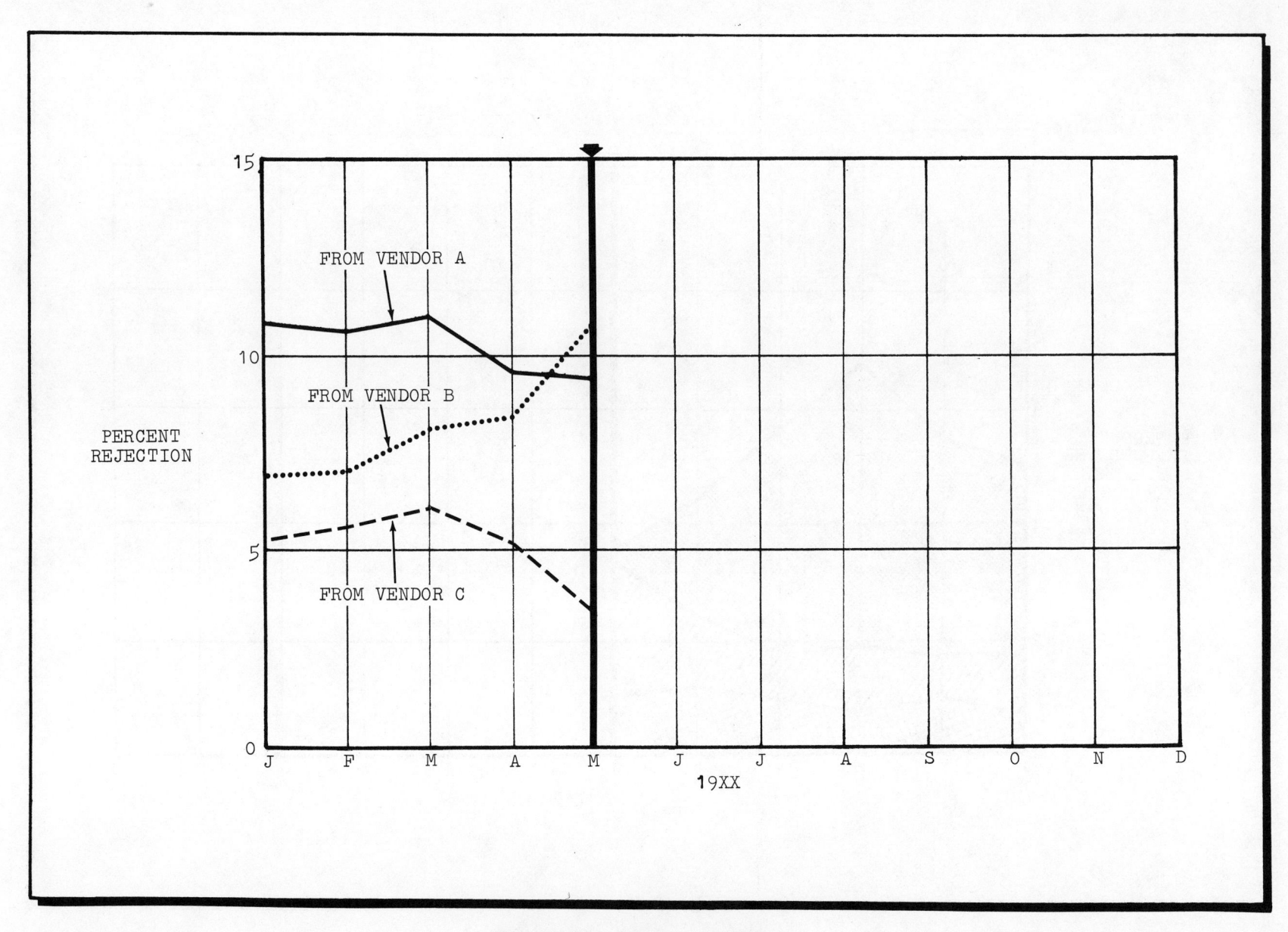

Figure 41.6   Quality—Version 6

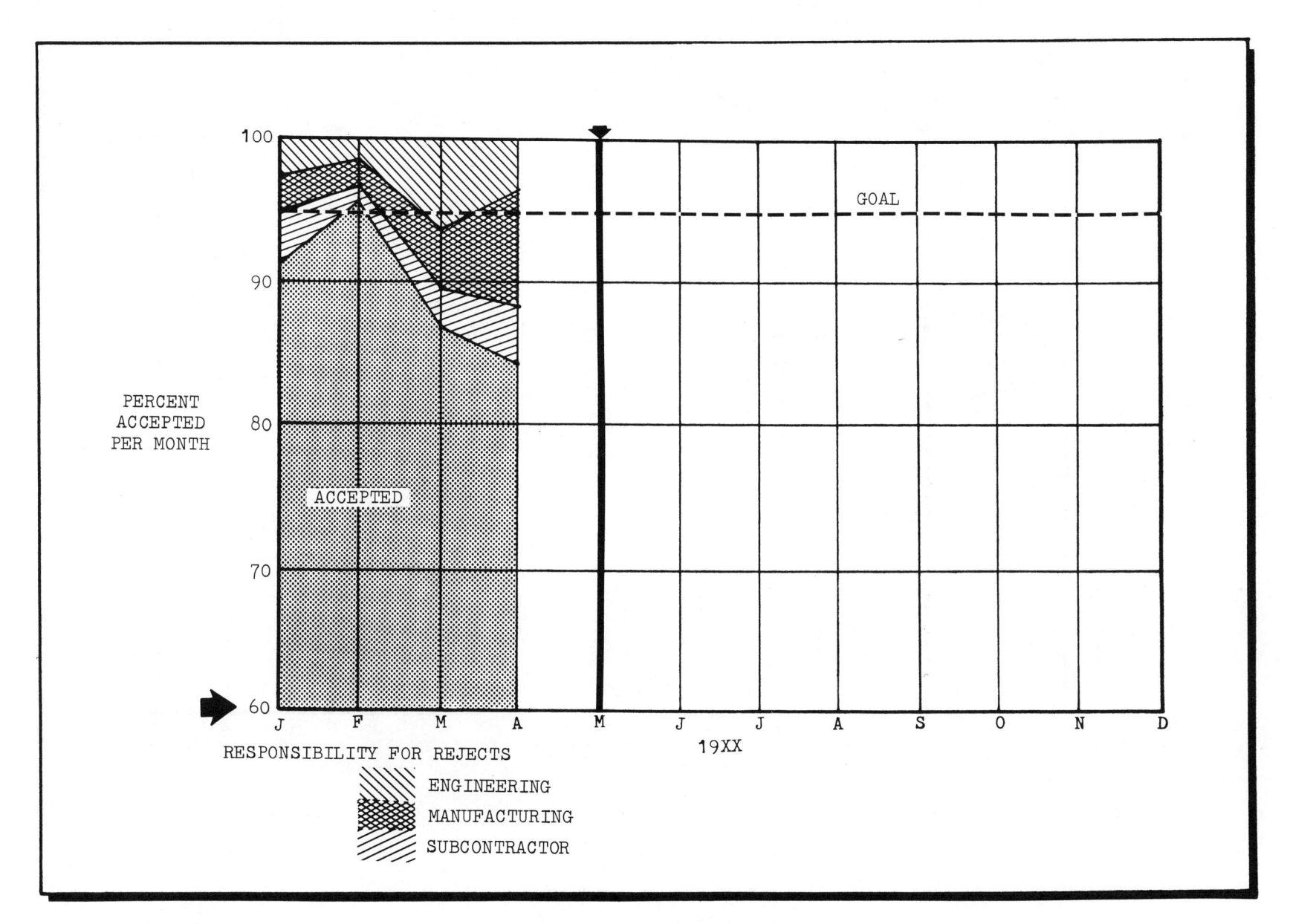

Figure 41.7 Quality—Version 7

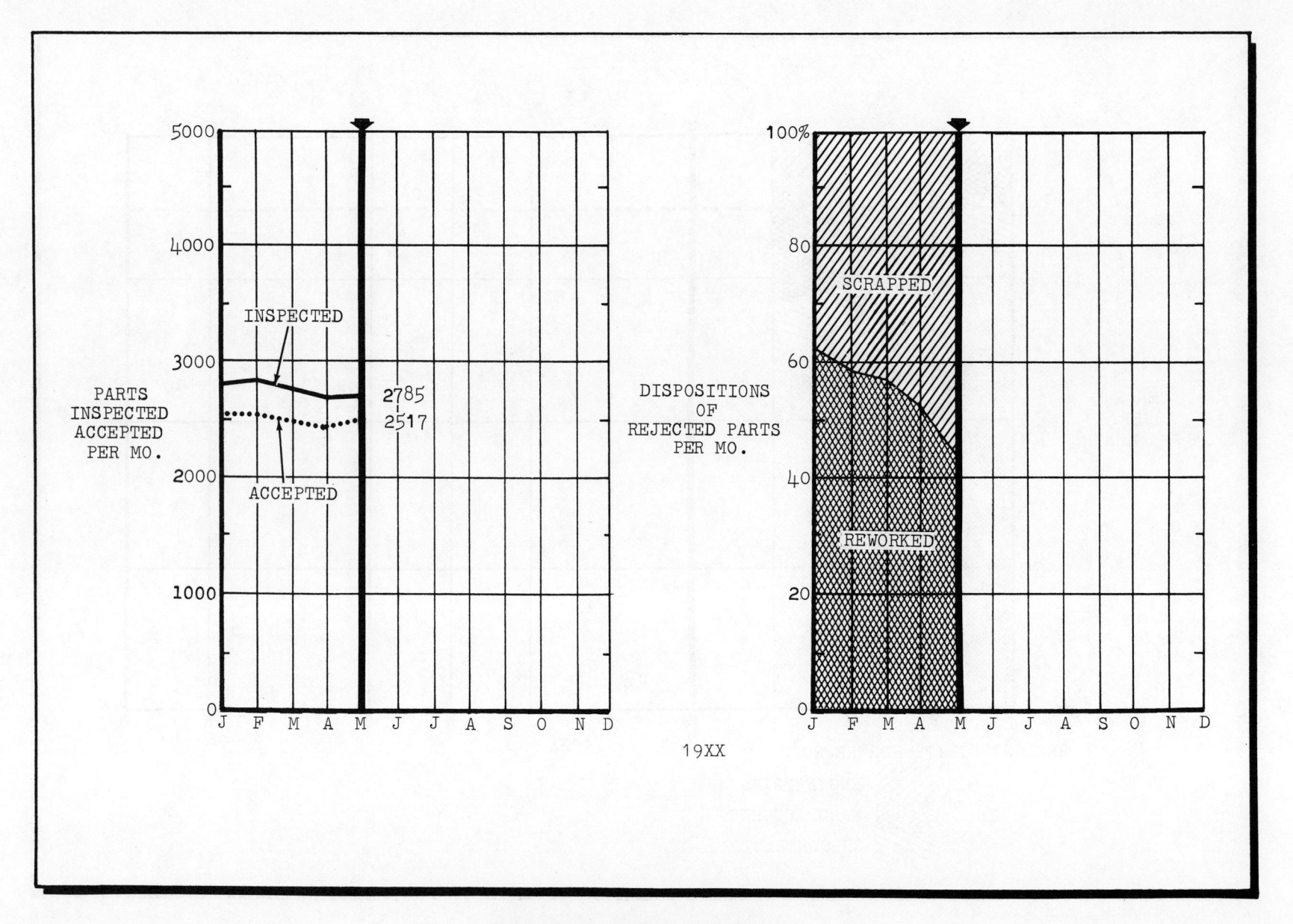

Figure 41.8 Quality—Version 8

458

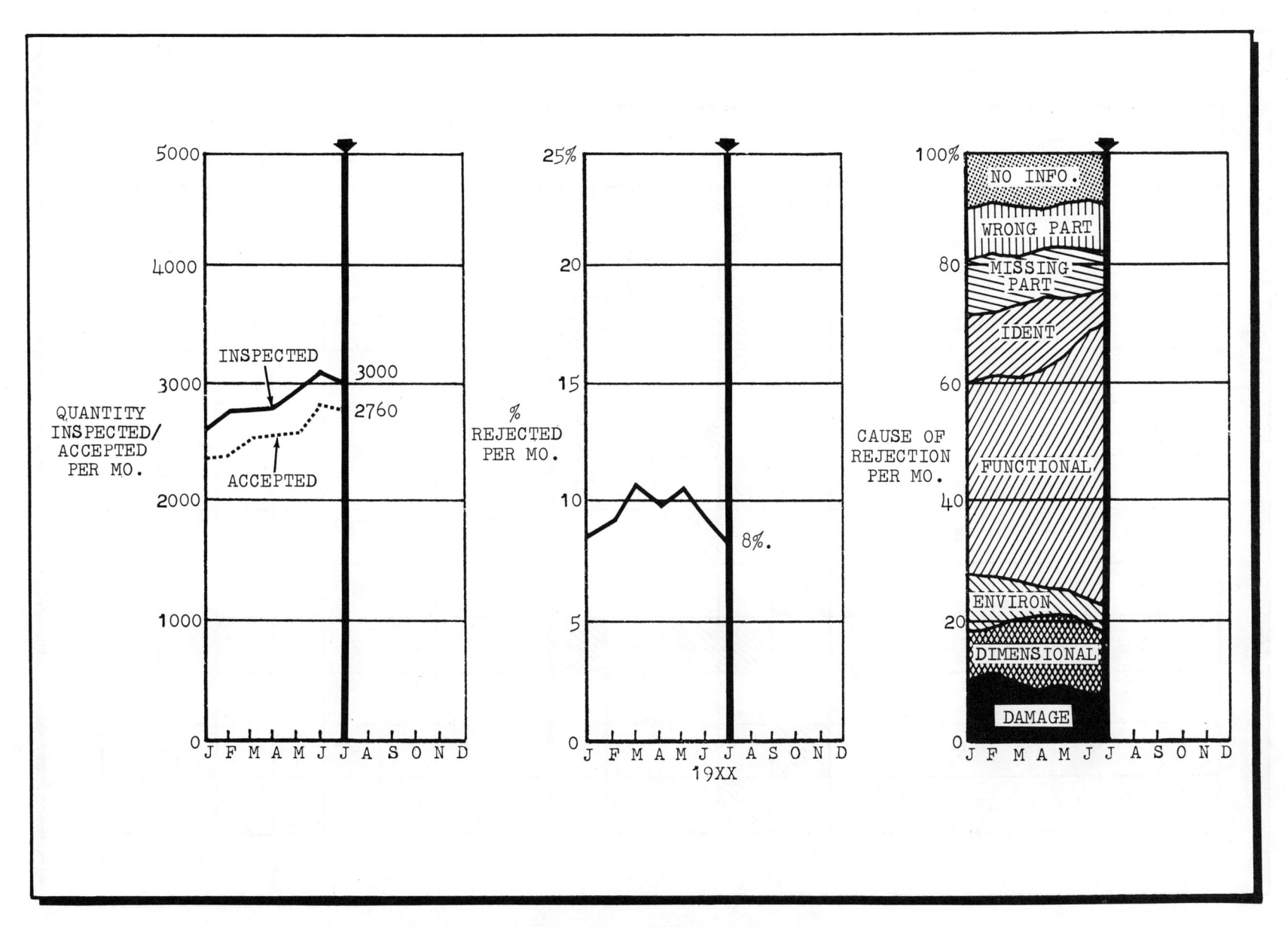

Figure 41.9   Quality—Version 9

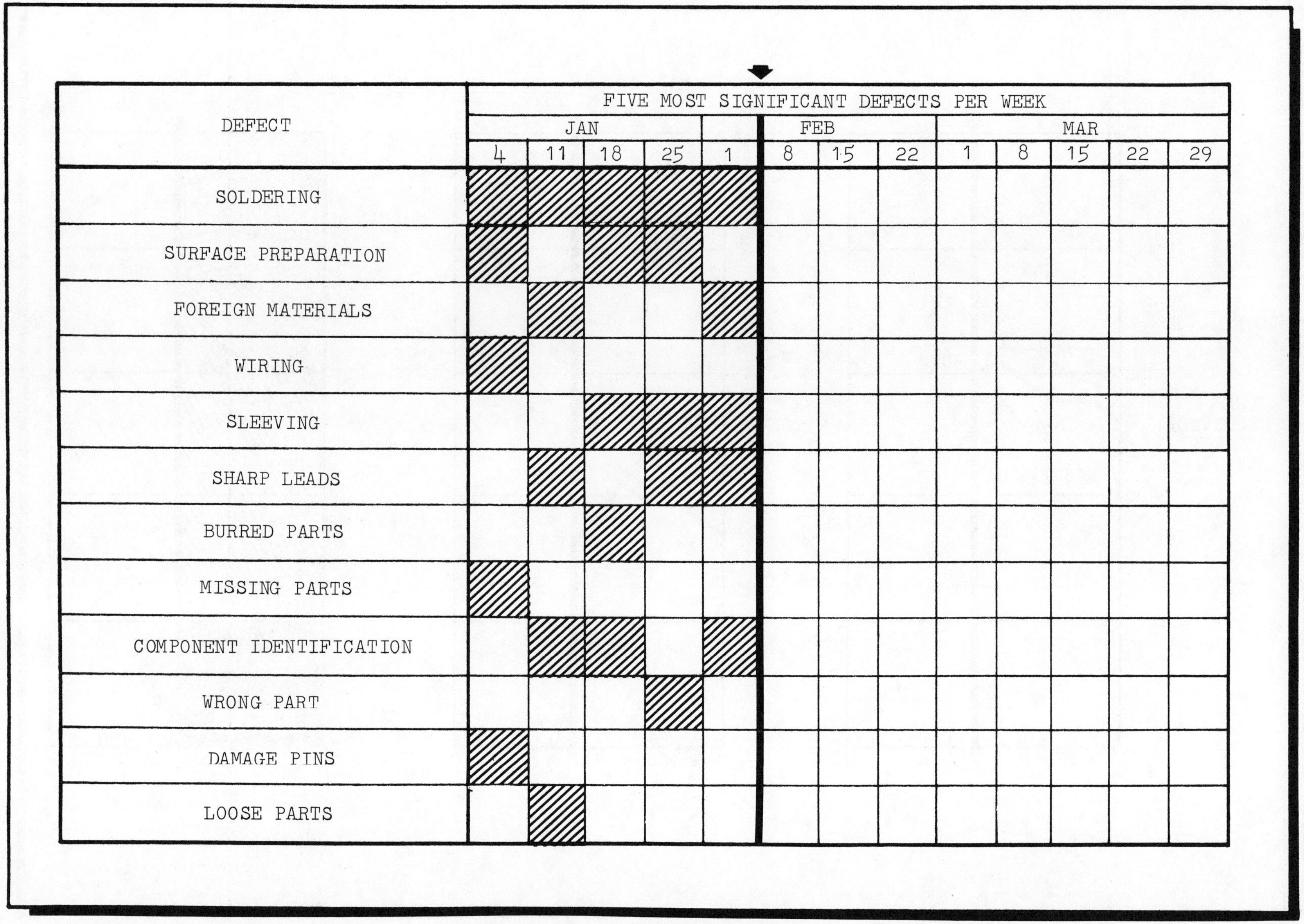

DEFECT	FIVE MOST SIGNIFICANT DEFECTS PER WEEK												
	JAN					FEB			MAR				
	4	11	18	25	1	8	15	22	1	8	15	22	29
SOLDERING	▨	▨	▨	▨	▨								
SURFACE PREPARATION	▨		▨		▨								
FOREIGN MATERIALS		▨		▨									
WIRING	▨												
SLEEVING			▨	▨	▨								
SHARP LEADS		▨		▨	▨								
BURRED PARTS			▨										
MISSING PARTS	▨												
COMPONENT IDENTIFICATION		▨	▨		▨								
WRONG PART				▨									
DAMAGE PINS	▨												
LOOSE PARTS		▨												

Figure 41.10 Quality—Version 10

PERCENT
REJECTED PARTS
PER MO.

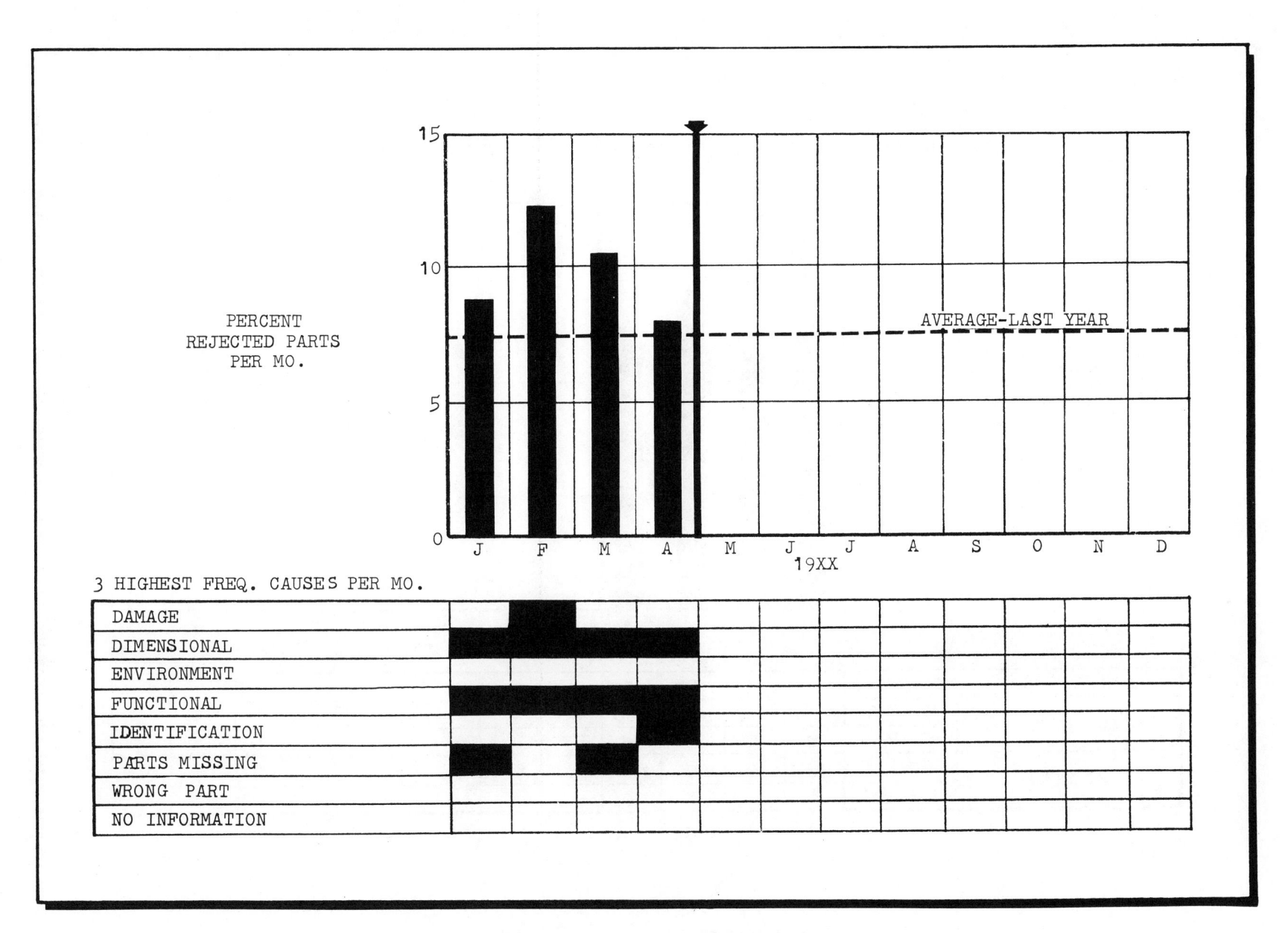

AVERAGE-LAST YEAR

19XX

3 HIGHEST FREQ. CAUSES PER MO.

DAMAGE												
DIMENSIONAL												
ENVIRONMENT												
FUNCTIONAL												
IDENTIFICATION												
PARTS MISSING												
WRONG PART												
NO INFORMATION												

Figure 41.11   Quality—Version 11

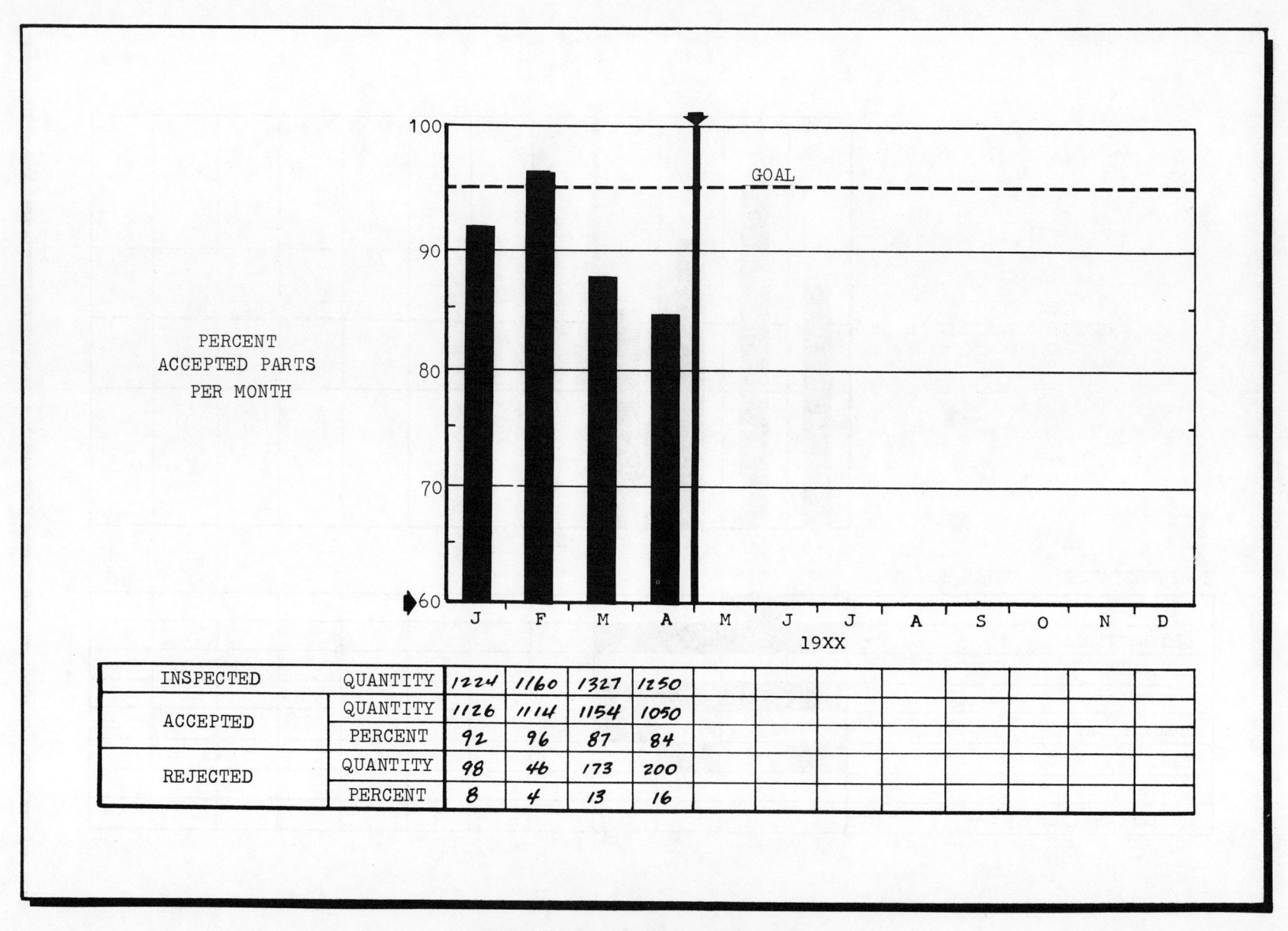

INSPECTED	QUANTITY	1224	1160	1327	1250								
ACCEPTED	QUANTITY	1126	1114	1154	1050								
	PERCENT	92	96	87	84								
REJECTED	QUANTITY	98	46	173	200								
	PERCENT	8	4	13	16								

Figure 41.12   Quality—Version 12

PERCENT REJECTED PARTS PER MONTH

AVERAGE LAST YEAR

19XX

		J	F	M	A	M	J	J	A	S	O	N	D
QUANTITY INSPECTED		1267	1482	1317	1266								
QUANTITY REJECTED		114	182	138	101								
PERCENT REJECTED		9.0	12.3	10.5	8.0								
QUANTITY OF REJECTS BY DISCREPANCY TYPE	DAMAGE	9	24	15	11								
	DIMENSIONAL	38	51	25	19								
	ENVIRONMENT	2	3	1	6								
	FUNCTIONAL	53	82	59	42								
	IDENTIFICATION	0	16	14	16								
	PARTS MISSING	12	5	22	7								
	WRONG PART	0	1	0	0								
	NO INFORMATION	0	0	2	0								

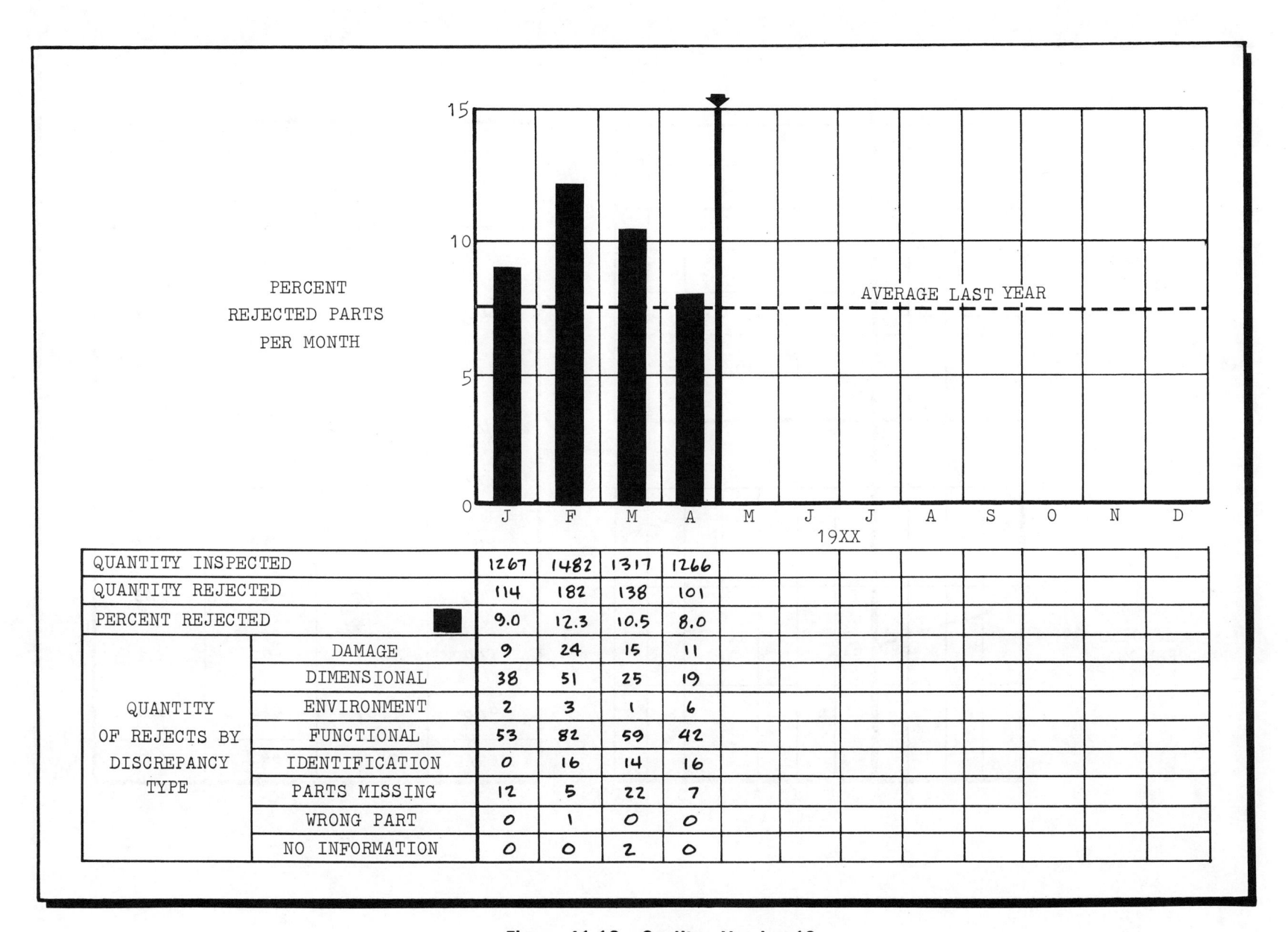

Figure 41.13   Quality—Version 13

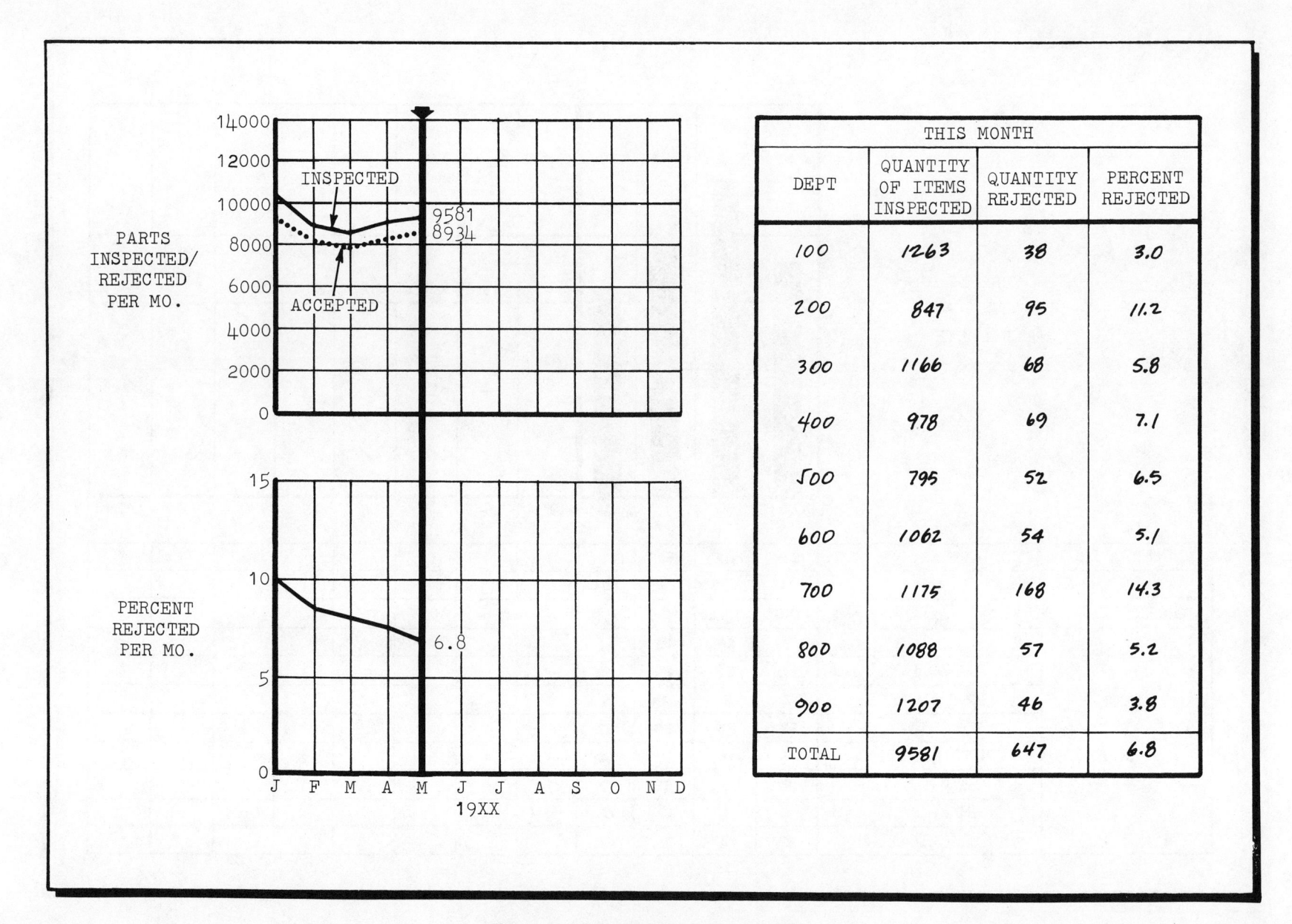

	THIS MONTH		
DEPT	QUANTITY OF ITEMS INSPECTED	QUANTITY REJECTED	PERCENT REJECTED
100	1263	38	3.0
200	847	95	11.2
300	1166	68	5.8
400	978	69	7.1
500	795	52	6.5
600	1062	54	5.1
700	1175	168	14.3
800	1088	57	5.2
900	1207	46	3.8
TOTAL	9581	647	6.8

Figure 41.14   Quality—Version 14

ITEM		19XX											
		J	F	M	A	M	J	J	A	S	O	N	D
QUANTITY INSPECTED		1267	1482	1317	1266								
QUANTITY REJECTED		114	182	138	101								
PERCENT REJECTED		9.0	12.3	10.5	8.0								
QUANTITY OF REJECTS BY DISCREPANCY TYPE	DAMAGE	9	24	15	11								
	DIMENSIONAL	38	51	25	19								
	ENVIRONMENT	2	3	1	6								
	FUNCTIONAL	53	82	59	42								
	IDENTIFICATION	0	16	14	16								
	PARTS MISSING	12	5	22	7								
	WRONG PART	0	1	0	0								
	NO INFORMATION	0	0	2	0								

Figure 41.15 Quality—Version 15

42.0 RECEIVABLES

Charts that display the status of receivables are shown in this section. Also see Section 2.0, *Average Collection Period of Receivables*.

42.1 Receivables—Version 1: A simple version of a receivables tracking chart is shown as Version 1, Figure 42.1. The amount scale is in terms of the dollar value of the receivables. A dashed line is used to show the forecast, and actuals are plotted with a solid line.

42.2 Receivables—Version 2: Total and past due receivables are both tracked in Version 2 of a receivables tracking chart, Figure 42.2. A dashed line and a solid line are used to show the planned and actual dollar amount of receivables. The actual past due receivables to date are shown with ball and line.

42.3 Receivables—Version 3: Version 3 of a receivables tracking chart, Figure 42.3, is identical to Version 2 except a "control level" (dotted line) for the amount of past due receivables has been added. Such control levels are established by management on the basis of past experience and are usually calculated as a percentage of forecasted receivables. When the sum of past due receivables exceeds this level, it indicates the need for special management actions.

42.4 Receivables—Version 4: Segmented columns are combined with step lines in Version 4 of a receivables tracking chart, Figure 42.4. Each total bar, in this example, represents the total receivables for the month. Each bar is also segmented to show that portion of the total that is past due.

42.5 Receivables—Version 5: Version 5 of a receivables chart, Figure 42.5, tracks total and past due receivables by quarters. Plans are in step line form and actuals are in column form.

42.6 Receivables—Version 6: Statistics and graphics are combined in Version 6 of a receivables tracking chart, Figure 42.6. The amount scale on this example is in terms of the percentage of total receivables that are past due . . . over 30 days, on this chart. A dashed line represents the control level for past due receivables, and solid columns are used to show actuals for each month. The tabular portion of the chart contains the backup statistics.

42.7 Receivables—Version 7: Version 7 of a receivables chart, Figure 42.7, examines the status of receivables by major customers. In this particular example, there is no plan, or standard, or forecast, against which actuals can be measured, so its usefulness is limited.

42.8 Receivables—Version 8: Version 8 of a receivables chart, Figure 42.8, examines past due accounts receivable by major customer. Totals and averages are both given on a dollar amount and percentage of total basis. As with Version 7, there is no plan, or goal, against which the actuals can be evaluated.

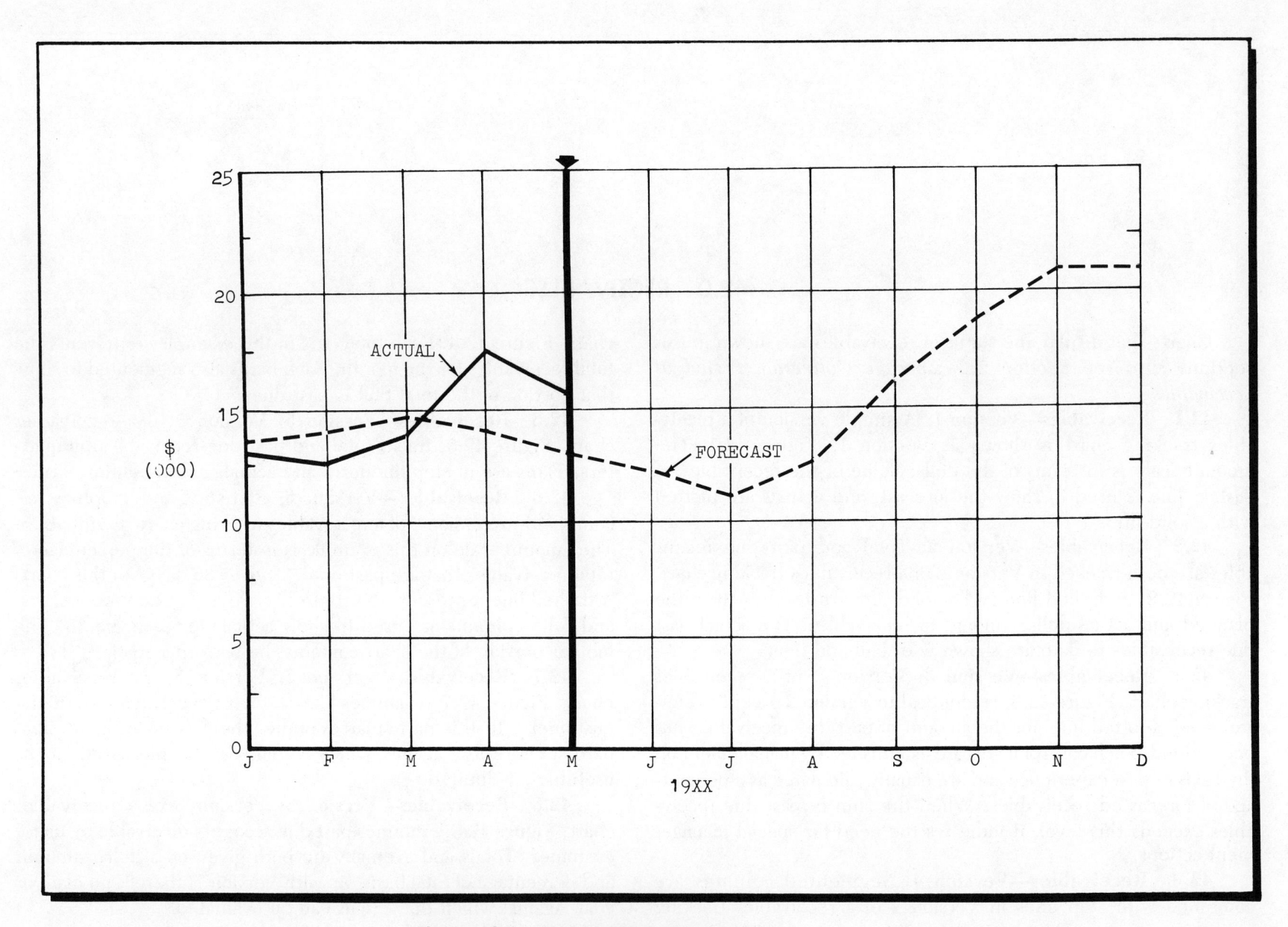

Figure 42.1   Receivables—Version 1

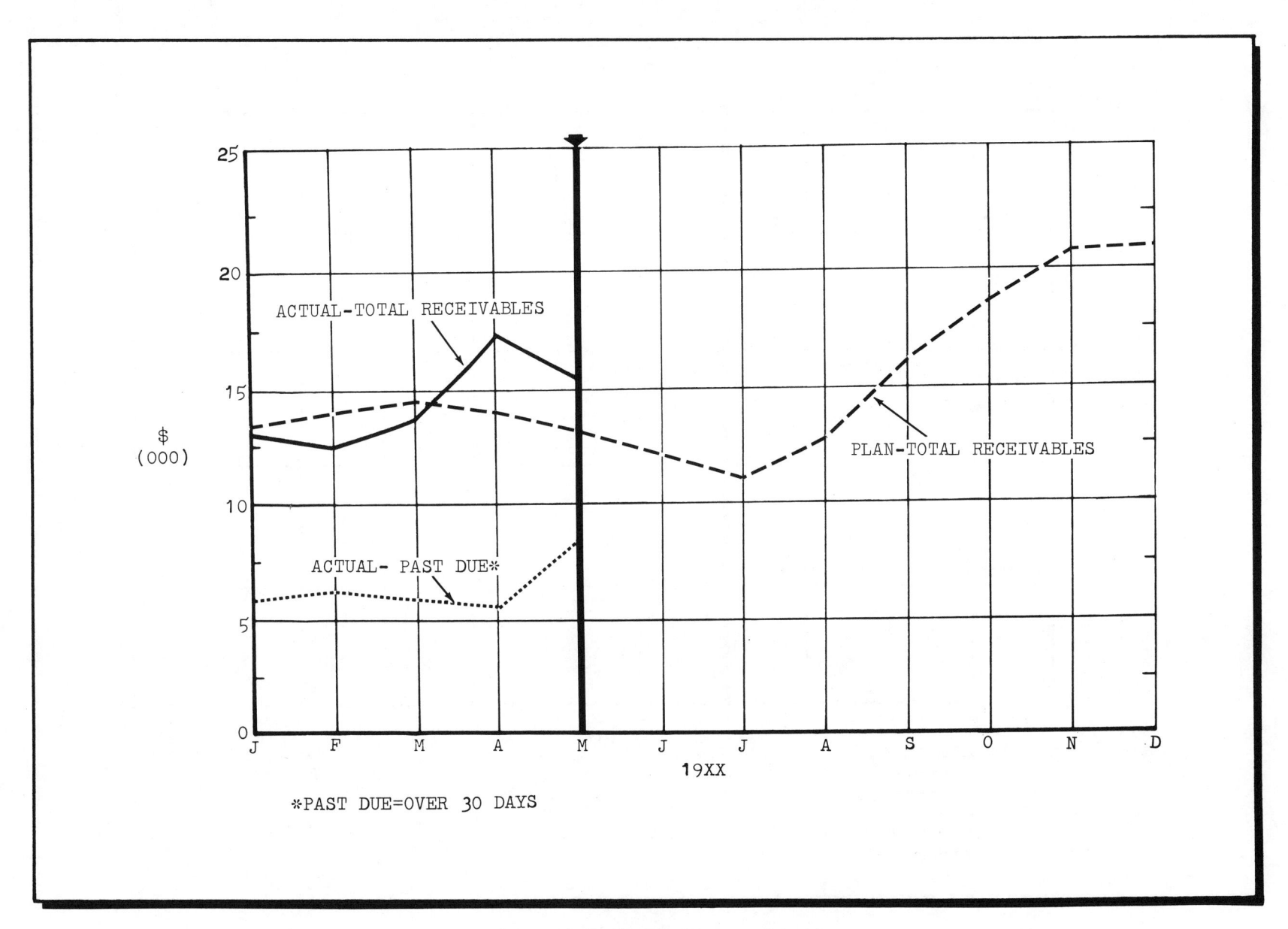

Figure 42.2 Receivables—Version 2

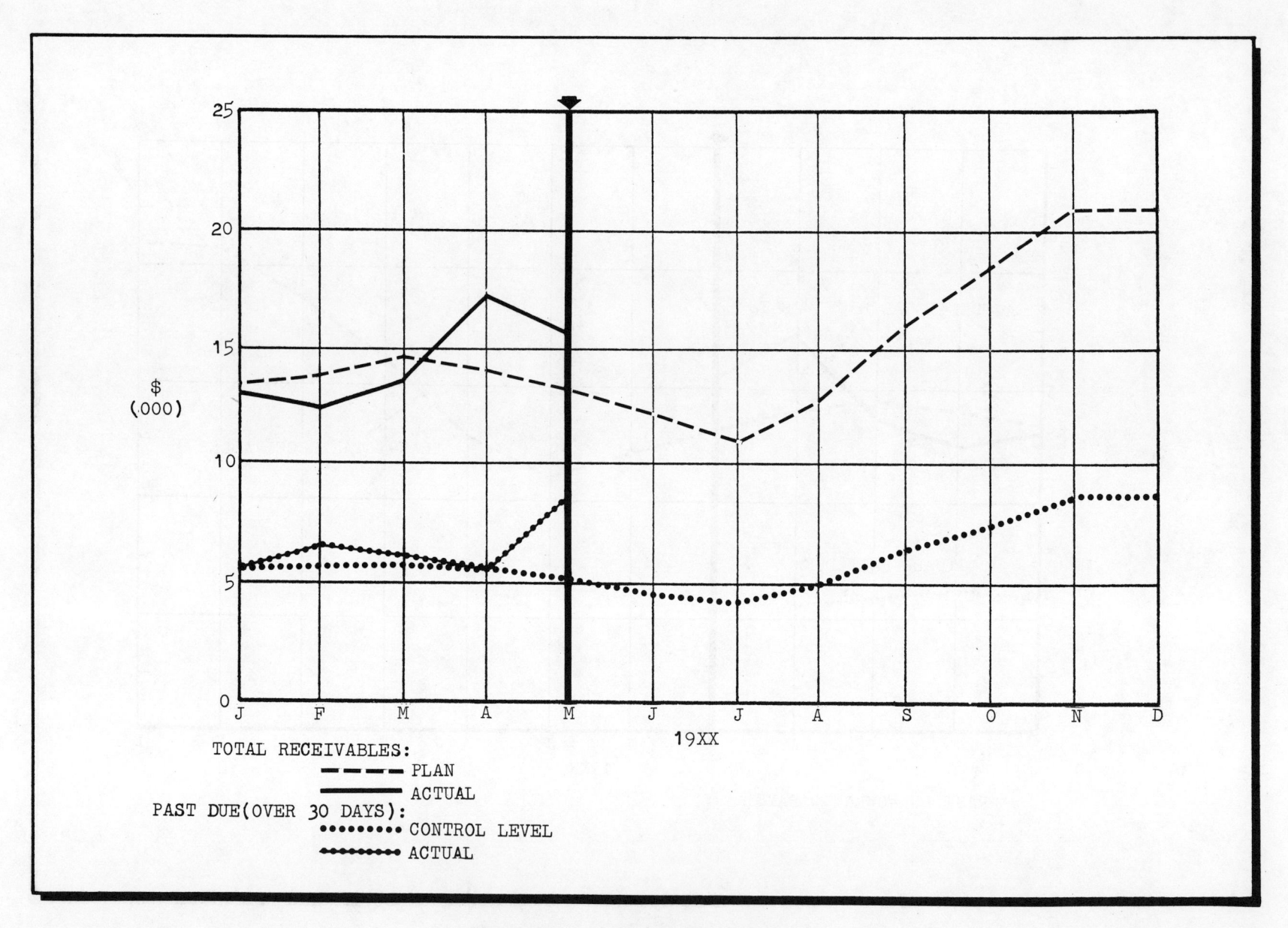

Figure 42.3   Receivables—Version 3

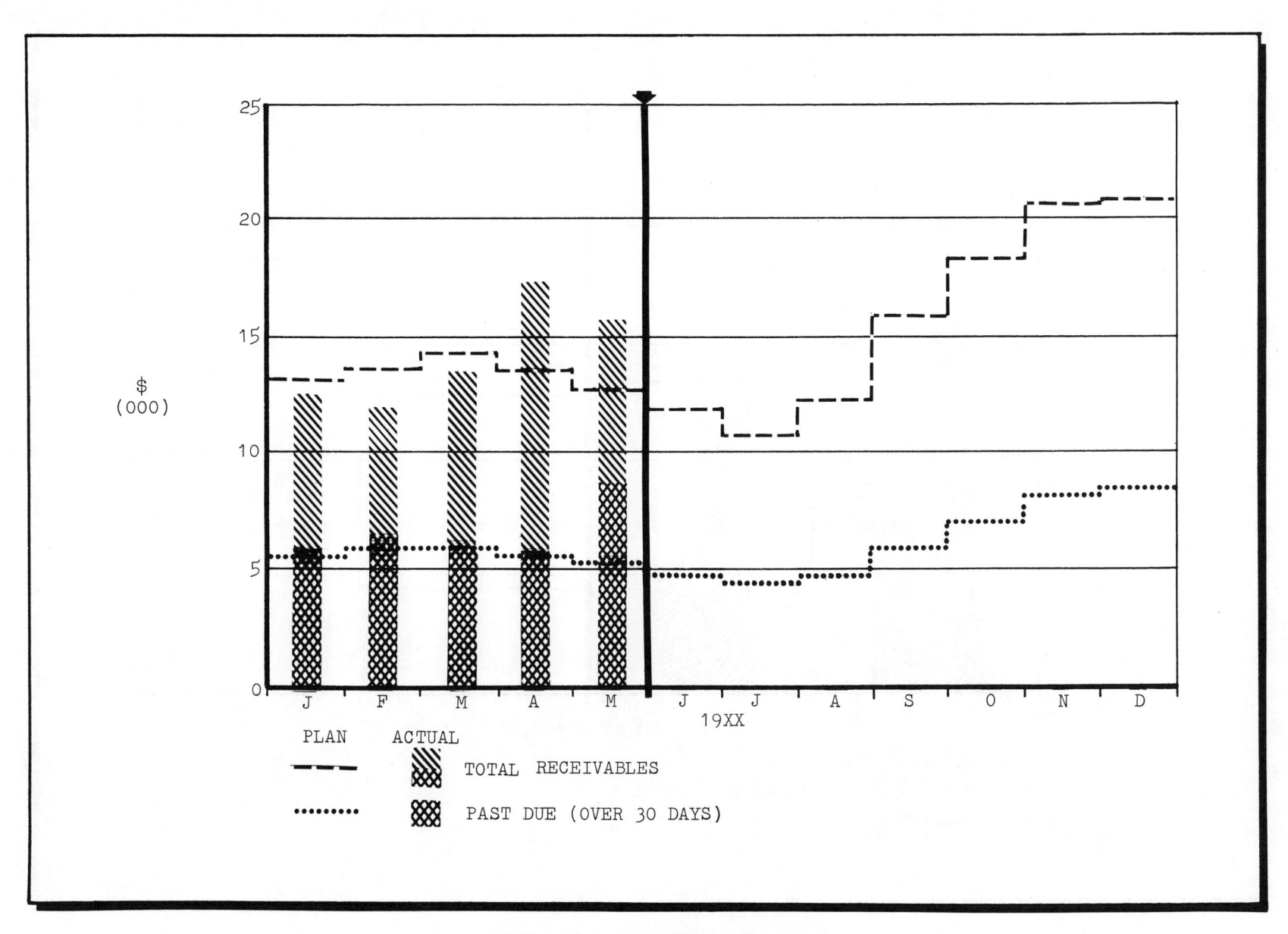

Figure 42.4   Receivables—Version 4

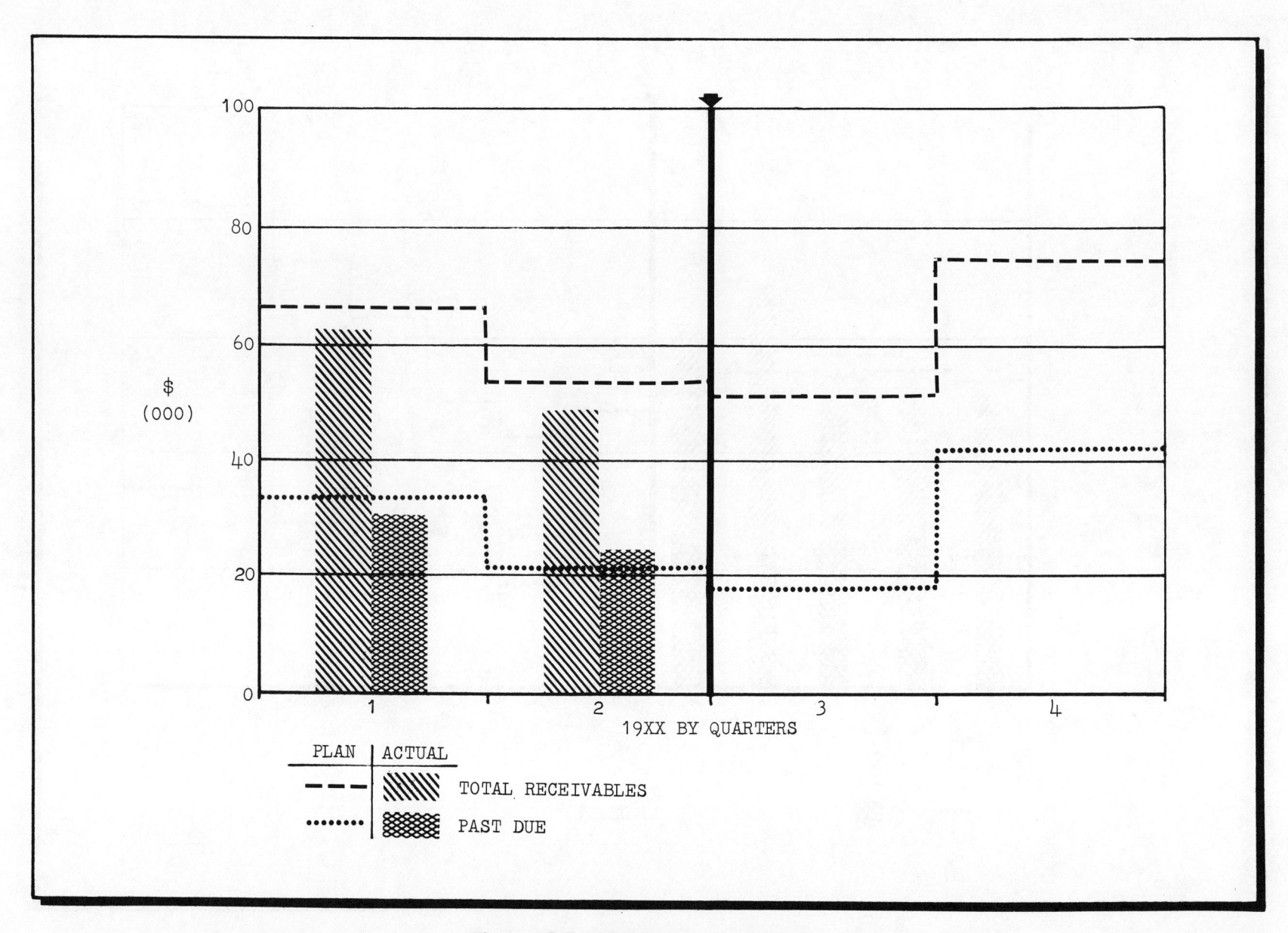

Figure 42.5 Receivables—Version 5

472

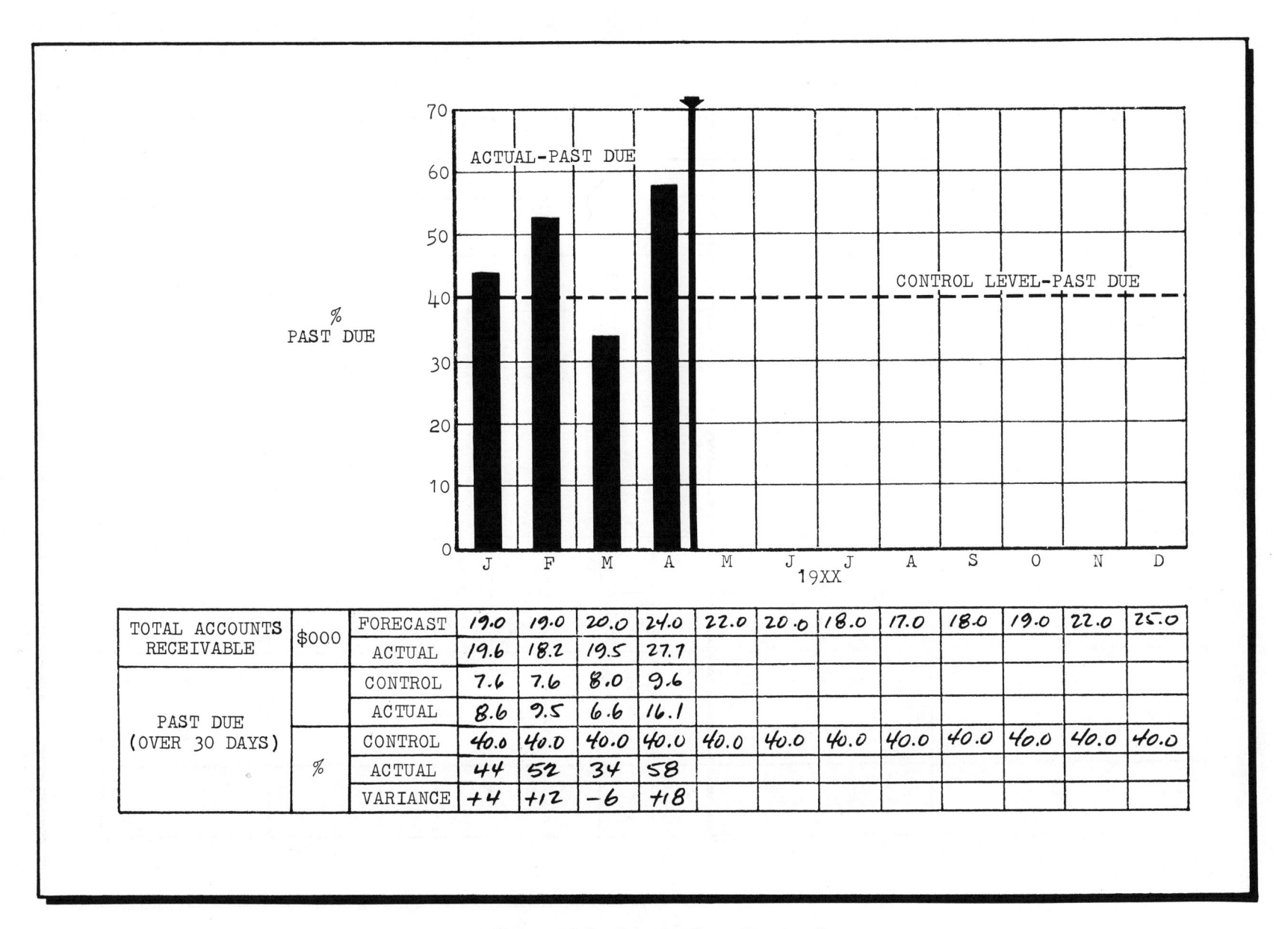

TOTAL ACCOUNTS RECEIVABLE	$000	FORECAST	19.0	19.0	20.0	24.0	22.0	20.0	18.0	17.0	18.0	19.0	22.0	25.0
		ACTUAL	19.6	18.2	19.5	27.7								
PAST DUE (OVER 30 DAYS)		CONTROL	7.6	7.6	8.0	9.6								
		ACTUAL	8.6	9.5	6.6	16.1								
	%	CONTROL	40.0	40.0	40.0	40.0	40.0	40.0	40.0	40.0	40.0	40.0	40.0	40.0
		ACTUAL	44	52	34	58								
		VARIANCE	+4	+12	−6	+18								

Figure 42.6 Receivables—Version 6

TOTAL ACCOUNTS RECEIVABLE ($000)

CUSTOMER	19XX													AVERAGE TO DATE
	J	F	M	A	M	J	J	A	S	O	N	D	
A	6.7	4.1	4.5	7.9									5.8
B	5.4	4.5	5.4	7.6									5.7
C	–	.2	.5	.8									.4
D	.7	.7	.3	1.2									.7
E	.2	.5	.8	1.8									.8
F	.5	.5	.9	1.4									.8
G	.6	1.2	.5	.5									.7
H	–	.8	1.2	.4									.6
I	.8	.8	.4	1.3									.8
MISCL.	4.7	4.9	5.0	4.8									4.9
TOTAL ACCOUNTS REC.BAL.	19.6	18.2	19.5	27.7									21.2

Figure 42.7   Receivables—Version 7

PAST DUE ACCOUNTS RECEIVABLE

CUSTOMER		\$000	J	F	M	A	M	J	J	A	S	O	N	D	AVERAGE TO DATE	AVER % PAST DUE TO TOTAL BY CUSTOMER
A		$000	3.3	2.9	2.2	5.6									3.5	61
B			2.1	2.3	2.0	4.0									2.6	46
C			—	.3	.2	.3									.2	50
D			.2	.3	.2	.5									.3	48
E			.4	.4	.2	.6									.4	55
F			.4	.5	.3	.8									.5	62
G			.4	.4	.2	.6									.4	50
H			—	.2	.2	.4									.2	32
I			.1	.1	—	.2									.1	10
J		$000	1.7	2.1	1.1	3.1									2.0	41
TOTAL PAST DUE	$000		8.6	9.5	6.6	16.1									10.2	
	%		44	52	34	58									48	

Figure 42.8   Receivables—Version 8

43.0 RELIABILITY

Charts that display the status of product reliability in terms of predicted reliability in the design phase, tested or observed reliability in the manufacturing phase, and actual reliability in the operation phase are shown in this section. Also see Sections 1.0, *Accuracy*, 26.0, *Maintenance*, and 41.0, *Quality*.

43.1 Reliability—Version 1: Reliability is tracked, in Version 1 of a reliability chart, Figure 43.1, in terms of failures as a percent of the total number of units in use. Actuals in this example are compared to a goal.

43.2 Reliability—Version 2: A commonly used measurement when examining product reliability is the mean time between failures (MTBF), calculated by dividing the product's hours of use by the number of failures experienced during that time period. Actual MTBF, in this example (Figure 43.2), is tracked against a requirement.

43.3 Reliability—Version 3: In Version 3 of a reliability tracking chart, Figure 43.3, actual MTBF is compared against two factors: a requirement of 260 hours, and a *predicted* mean time between failures.

43.4 Reliability—Version 4: Incentive limits have been added in Version 4 of a reliability tracking chart, Figure 43.4. In this example, the actual mean time between failures is plotted to date and compared against a contractual requirement of 260 hours. When actuals go above the requirement, a bonus, up to a maximum, will be paid. When actuals fall below the 260-hour MTBF requirement, a penalty, up to a maximum, will be assessed.

43.5 Reliability—Version 5: The monthly failure rate per 1000 units is shown both in actual and cumulative average form in Version 5 of a reliability tracking chart, Figure 43.5. Both measurements are compared, in this example, against a maximum limit goal.

43.6 Reliability—Version 6: The measurement criteria used in Version 6 of a reliability tracking chart, Figure 43.6, is the mean time between rejections. Actuals, in column form, are compared against the MTBR of the previous six months, in this example.

43.7 Reliability—Version 7: Column and line chart styles are combined in Version 7 of a reliability tracking chart, Figure 43.7. Columns are used to show the monthly actual mean time between failures. A solid line is used to show actuals in terms of a three-month running average. Both forms of actuals are compared against a goal.

43.8 Reliability—Version 8: The mean time between failures is shown in Version 8 of a reliability tracking chart, Figure 43.8, in terms of the actual and predicted MTBF, and the 90% confidence level range. These three factors are compared against a specification.

43.9 Reliability—Version 9: Columns are used to show actual mean time between failures in Version 9 of a reliability tracking chart, Figure 43.9. The columns in this example are sectioned to show the 90% confidence level lower limit for MTBF.

43.10 Reliability—Version 10: The lower limits of 60% and 90% confidence levels of mean time between failures are compared against a requirement in Version 10 of a reliability tracking chart, Figure 43.10.

43.11 Reliability—Version 11: Reliability in terms of monthly failures per 1000 hours of use is shown in Version 11 of a reliability tracking chart, Figure 43.11. In this version, the location of the failures as to major subsystem is shown.

43.12 Reliability—Version 12: In Version 12 of a reliability chart, Figure 43.12, MTBF (mean time between failures) is tracked in relationship to the number of new model (−2 configuration), old model (−1 configuration), and retrofitted (updated −1 configuration) systems in use. In this example, the purpose of the comparison is to see if there is an improvement in MTBF that is related to an increased number of new or retrofitted systems in use.

43.13 Reliability—Version 13: Monthly failures are shown by criticality classification in Version 13 of a reliability tracking chart, Figure 43.13. In this example, there is no goal against which the failures can be compared.

43.14 Reliability—Version 14: Version 14 of a reliability tracking chart, Figure 43.14, displays a method for showing the percent of monthly yield by test cycle. The ultimate goal would be to achieve 100% (no failures) on the first test, eliminating the need to recycle the unit, system, or equipment through subsequent test cycles.

43.15 Reliability—Version 15: Dual grids are used in Version 15 of a reliability tracking chart, Figure 43.15. The left-hand grid shows the actual mean time between failures per month compared against a requirement of 2500 hours. The right-hand grid shows the actual number of failures per month compared against a maximum allowance of 230.

43.16 Reliability—Version 16: Statistics and graphs are combined in Version 16 of a reliability tracking chart, Figure 43.16. The graphic portion of the chart uses columns to show the actual monthly average number of failures per system with a solid line showing the cumulative average. This latter average could also be shown as a three-month moving average. The table gives the statistics as to the number of systems tested per month, and the monthly and cumulative average figures for the average number of failures per system.

43.17 Reliability—Version 17: The combined statistical and graphic chart shown in Figure 43.17, tracks reliability in terms of the quantity of monthly failures per 1000 units. Failures per 1000 are given as both monthly and year-to-date (cumulative average) figures.

43.18 Reliability—Version 18: The mean time between failures, on a year-to-date basis, is compared against a requirement in the graphic portion of Version 18 of a reliability tracking chart, Figure 43.18. The actuals are plotted as month-end figures. The tabular portion of the chart gives the monthly and year-to-date statistics for test hours, failures, and MTBF hours.

43.19 Reliability—Version 19: Version 19 of a reliability tracking chart, Figure 43.19, is similar to Version 18, except in this example the graphic portion of the chart shows both the monthly and year-to-date figures for mean time between failures.

43.20 Reliability—Version 20: Columns show actual mean time between failures hours per month compared against a specification in Version 20 of a reliability tracking chart, Figure 43.20. The statistical portion of the chart includes a breakdown of failures by cause.

43.21 Reliability—Version 21: In some circumstances, there is an important distinction between *reported* failures and *verified* failures. Both types are plotted in terms of monthly failures per 1000 hours in Version 21 of a reliability tracking chart, Figure

Reliability

43.21. The horizontal scale, in this example, is graduated in terms of usage hours then related to time in the table.

43.22 Reliability—Version 22: A statistical table version of a reliability tracking chart is shown as Version 22, Figure 43.22. In this example, the quantity of failures by part are tracked on a monthly basis.

43.23 Reliability—Version 23: Test hours, failures, and the mean time between failures are shown on both a monthly and cumulative basis in Version 23 of a reliability tracking chart, Figure 43.23. A variation would be to show *operating* rather than *test* hours.

43.24 Reliability—Version 24: Reliability is tracked in terms of the average number of failures per system each month in Version 24, Figure 43.24. In this tabular version of a reliability tracking chart, statistics are given on both a monthly and cumulative (year-to-date) basis.

43.25 Reliability—Version 25: Rejections per month and the mean time between rejections (MTBR) per month are broken down by subsystem in the tabular version of a reliability tracking chart shown in Figure 43.25. System totals are summarized across the bottom of the chart.

43.26 Reliability—Version 26: A format that can be used for a one-time status report is shown as Version 26 of a reliability chart, Figure 43.26. The focus of attention in this example is the mean time between failures statistics on the right-hand side of the table where the variances between actual performances and requirements for separate production units (or systems) can be seen.

43.27 Reliability—Version 27: The status report style of a reliability chart shown as Version 27, Figure 43.27, gives the number of failures for separate parts by malfunction category, with totals for the reporting period given at the bottom. The right-hand side of the table provides space for remarks.

43.28 Reliability—Version 28: The one-time status report version of a reliability chart shown in Figure 43.28 lists the statistics necessary to arrive at the yield percentage displayed in the right-hand column. Low yield percentages are indicators of which systems may be in need of special attention.

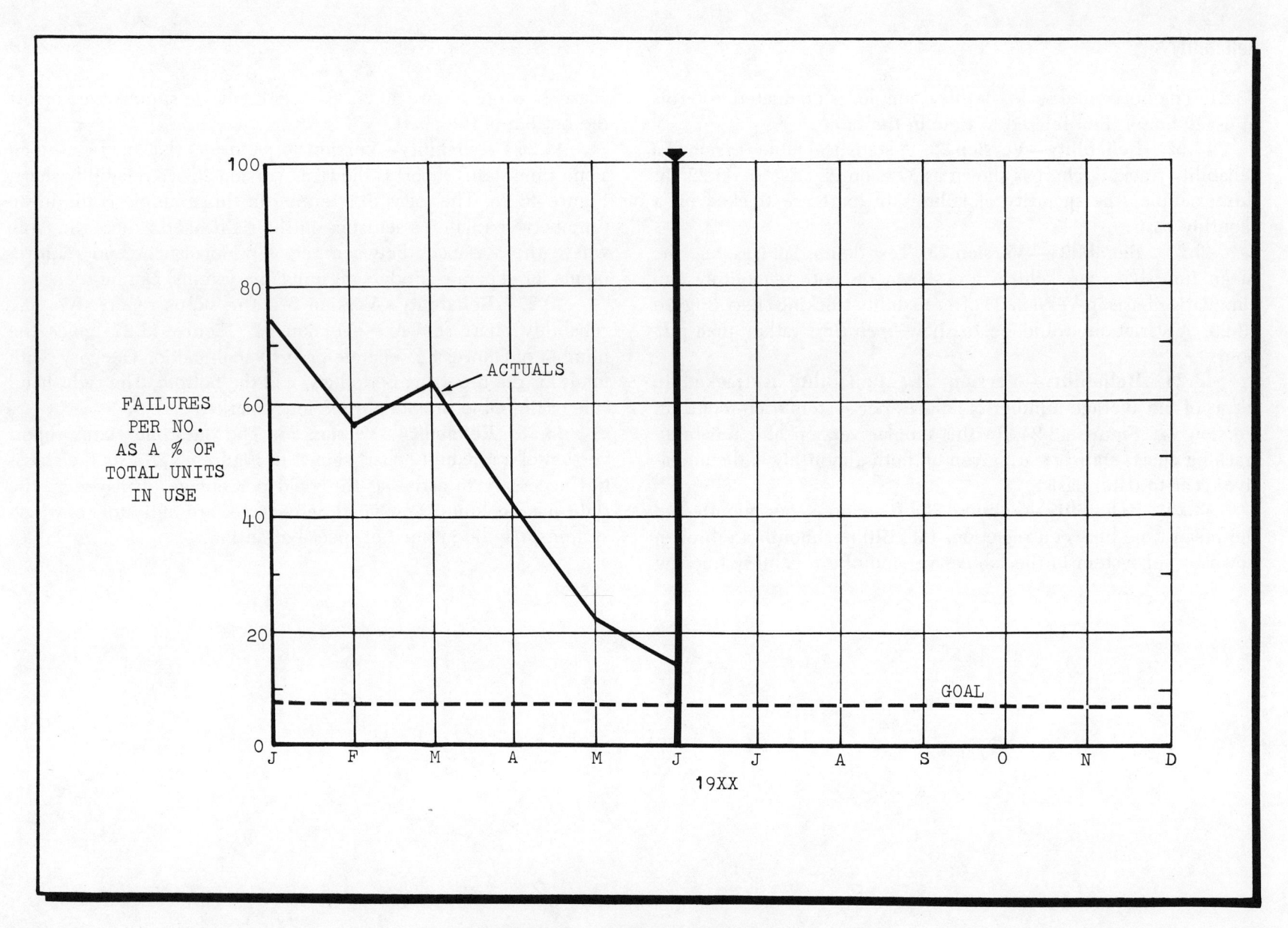

Figure 43.1   Reliability—Version 1

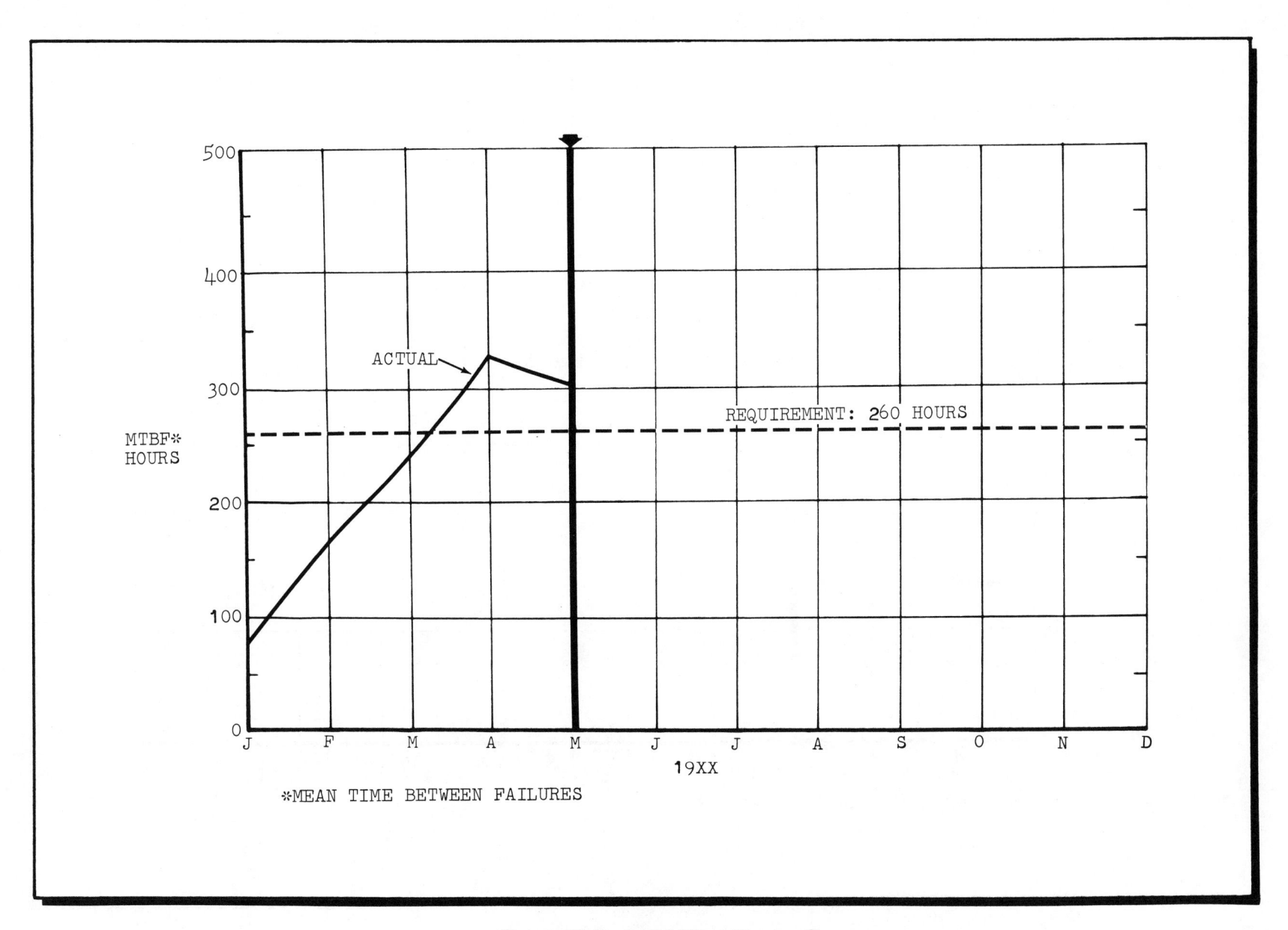

Figure 43.2 Reliability—Version 2

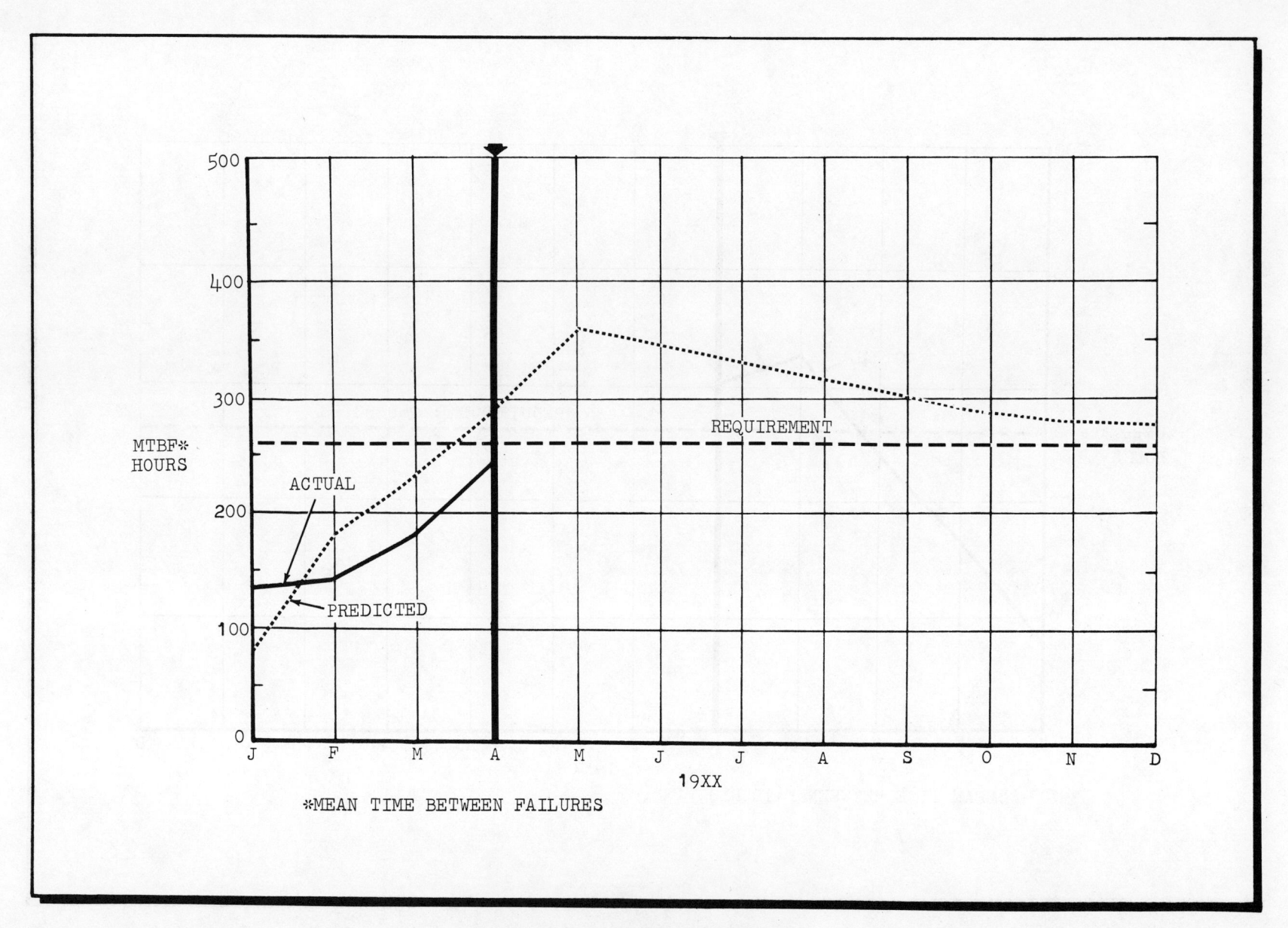

Figure 43.3 Reliability—Version 3

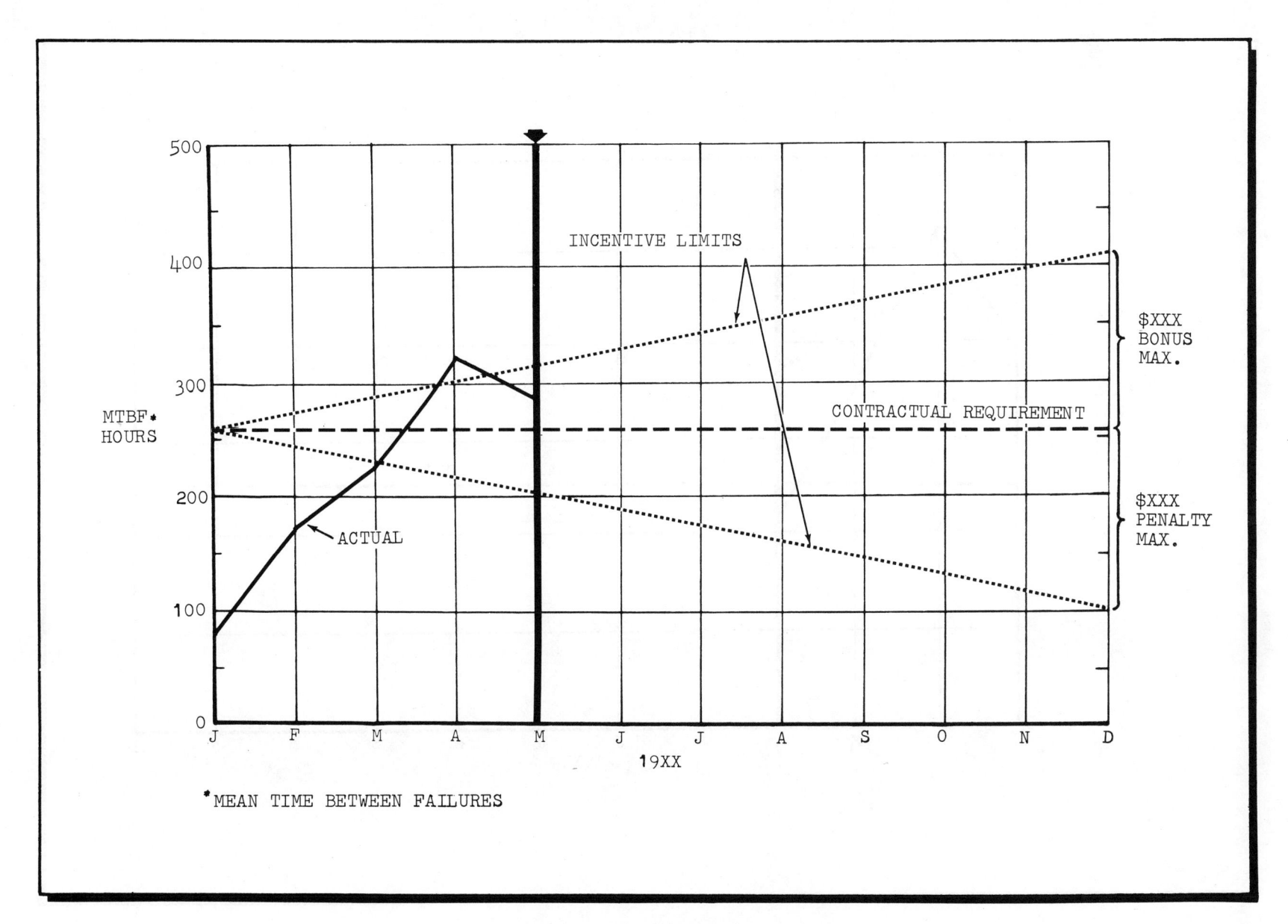

Figure 43.4   Reliability—Version 4

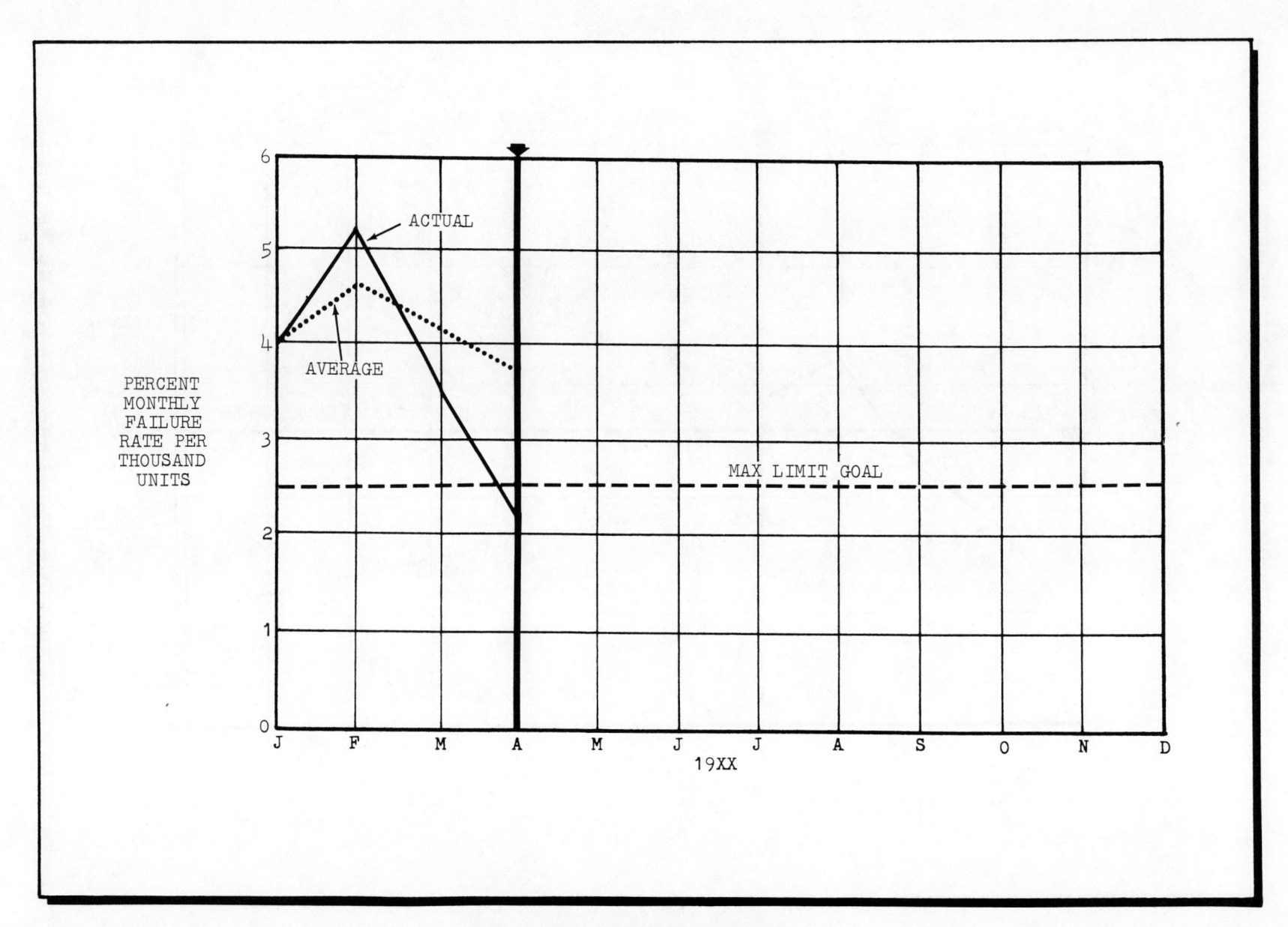

Figure 43.5   Reliability—Version 5

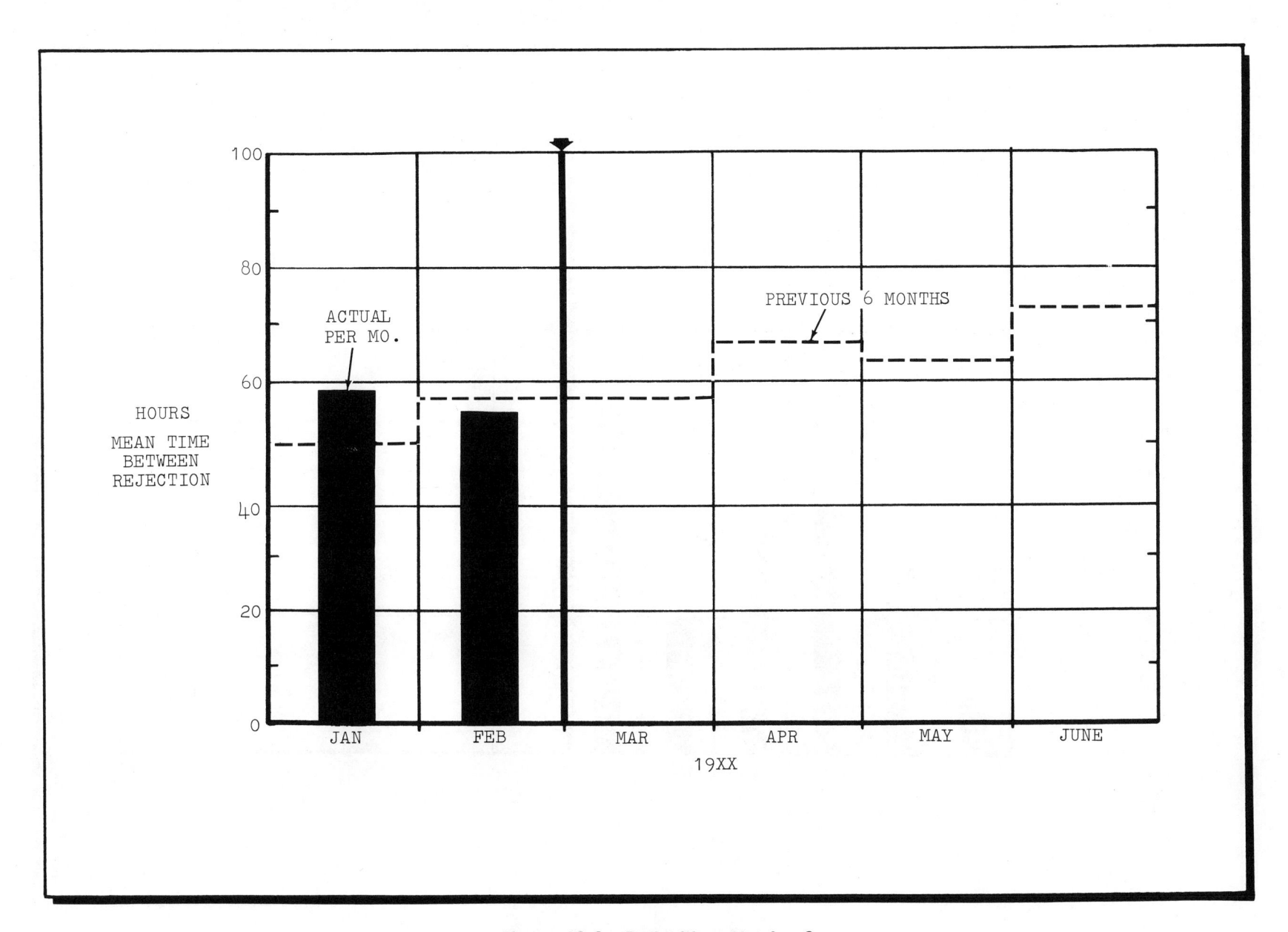

Figure 43.6   Reliability—Version 6

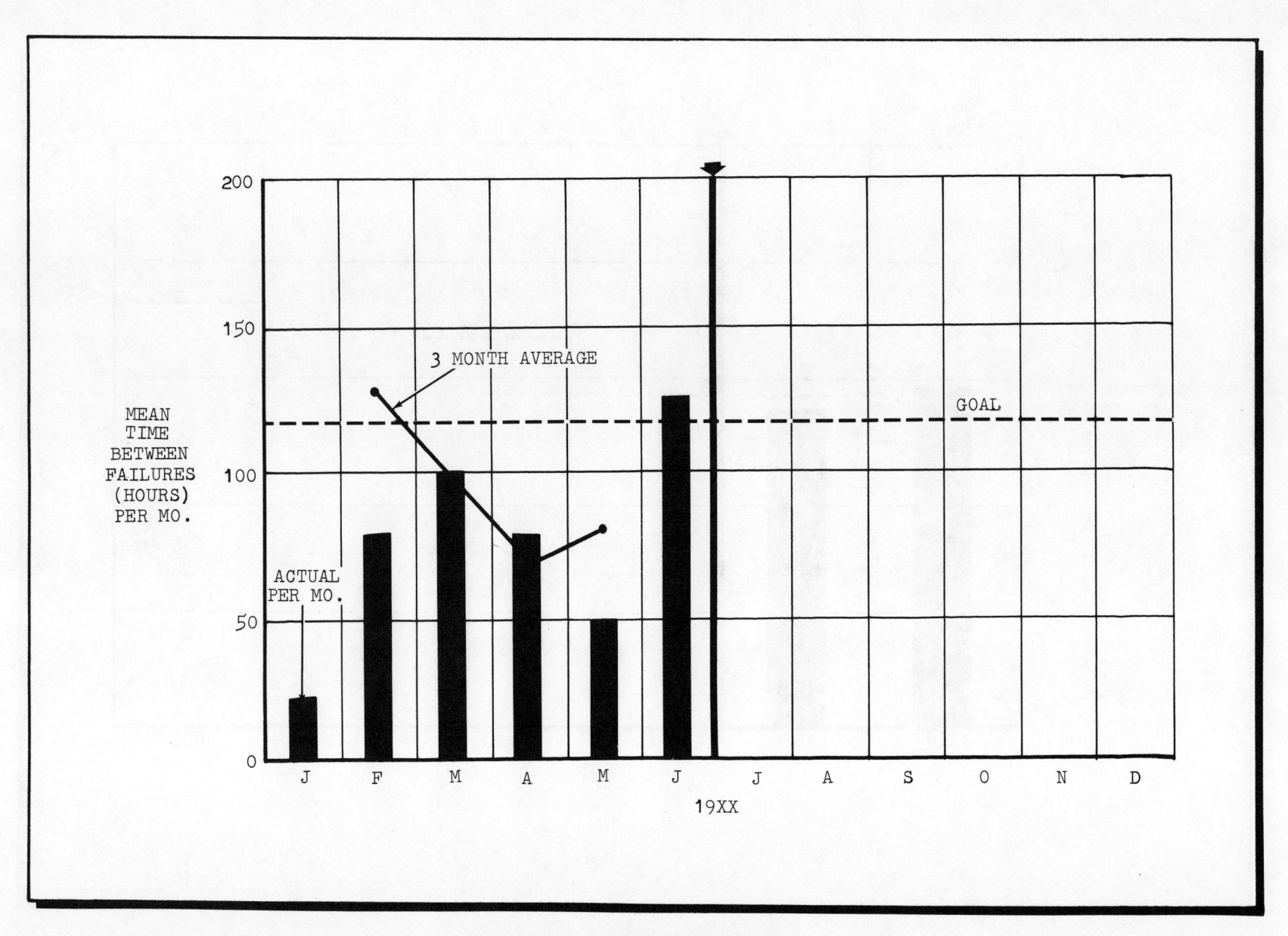

Figure 43.7 Reliability—Version 7

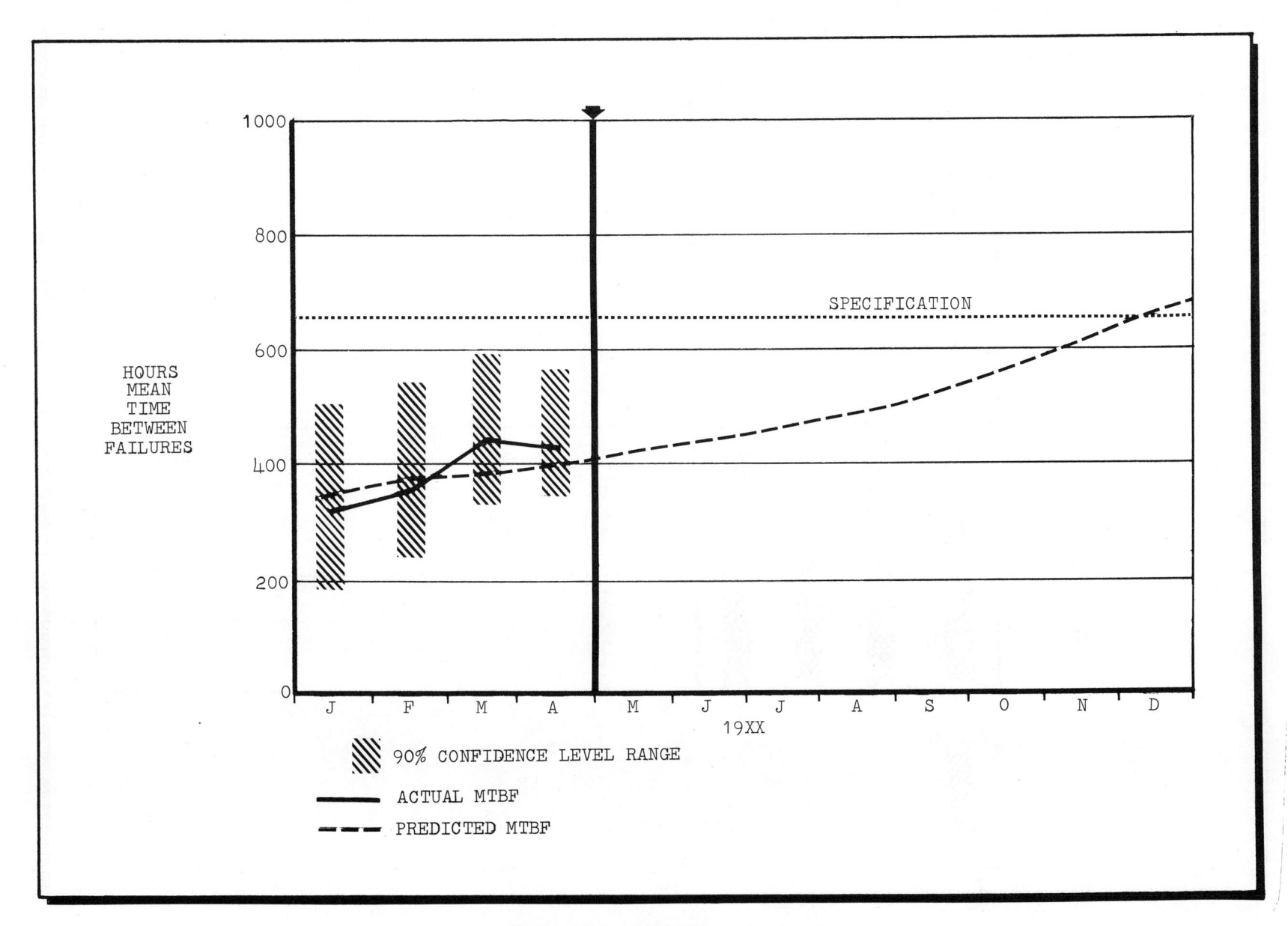

Figure 43.8 Reliability—Version 8

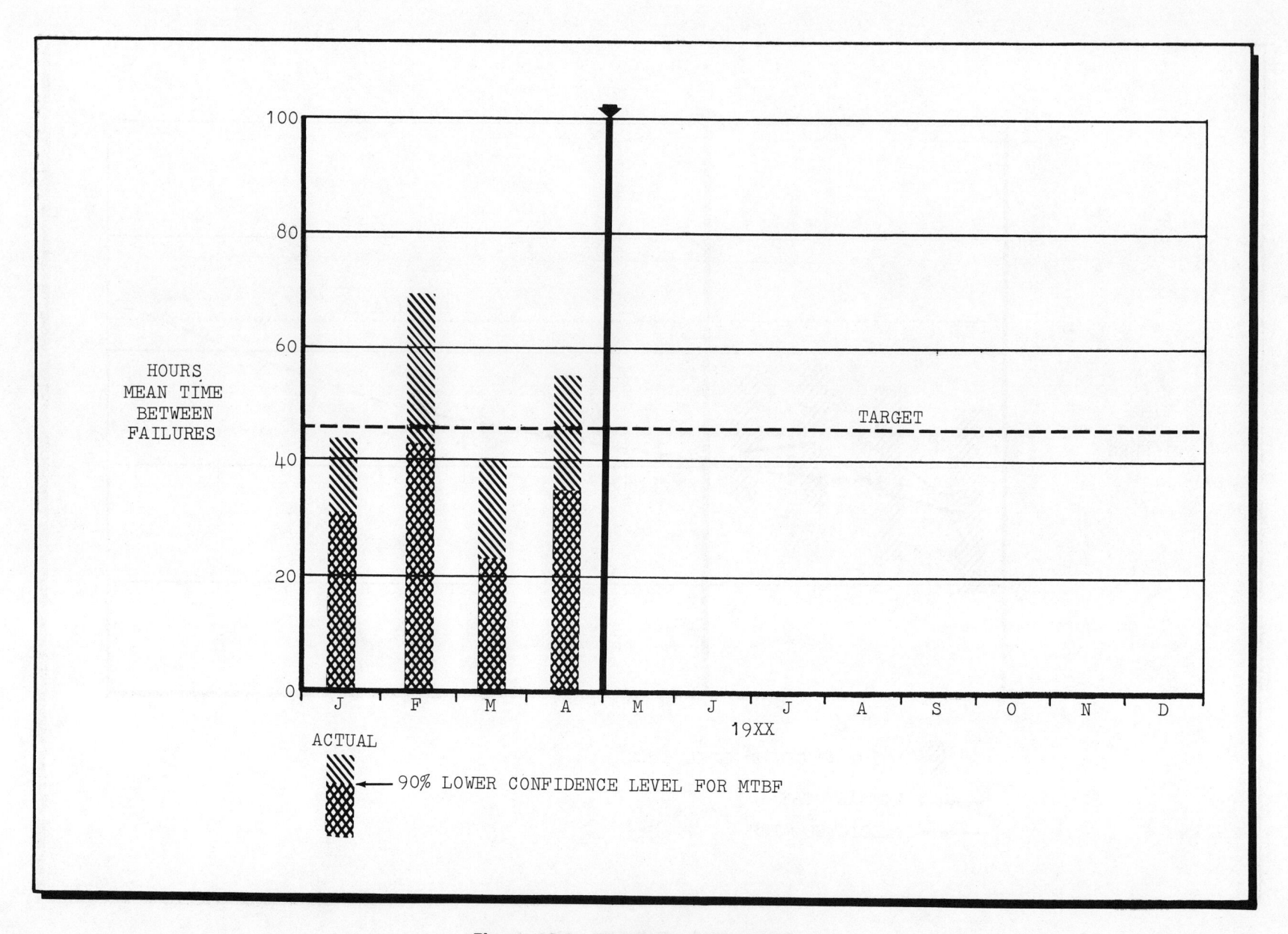

Figure 43.9   Reliability—Version 9

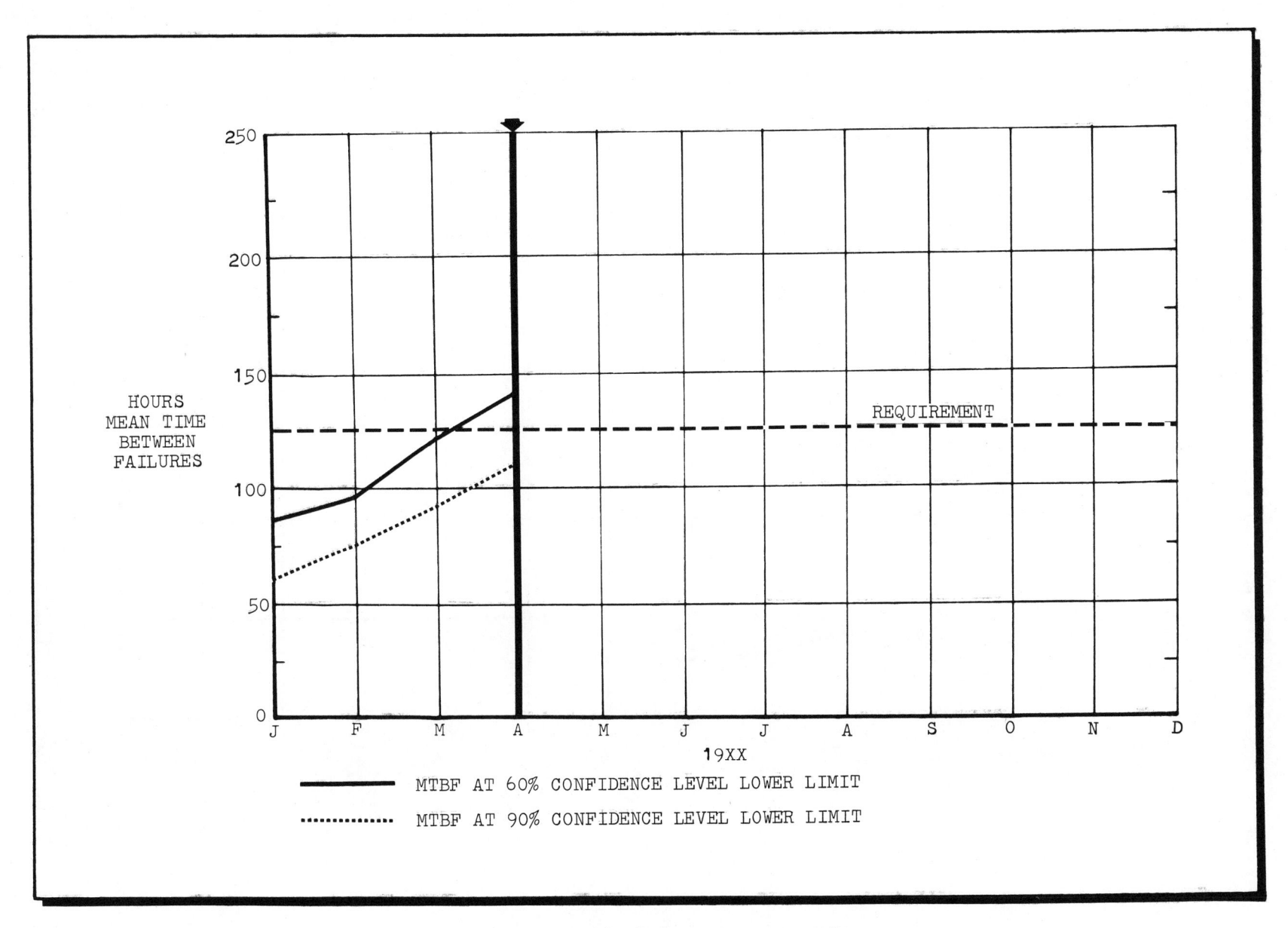

Figure 43.10   Reliability—Version 10

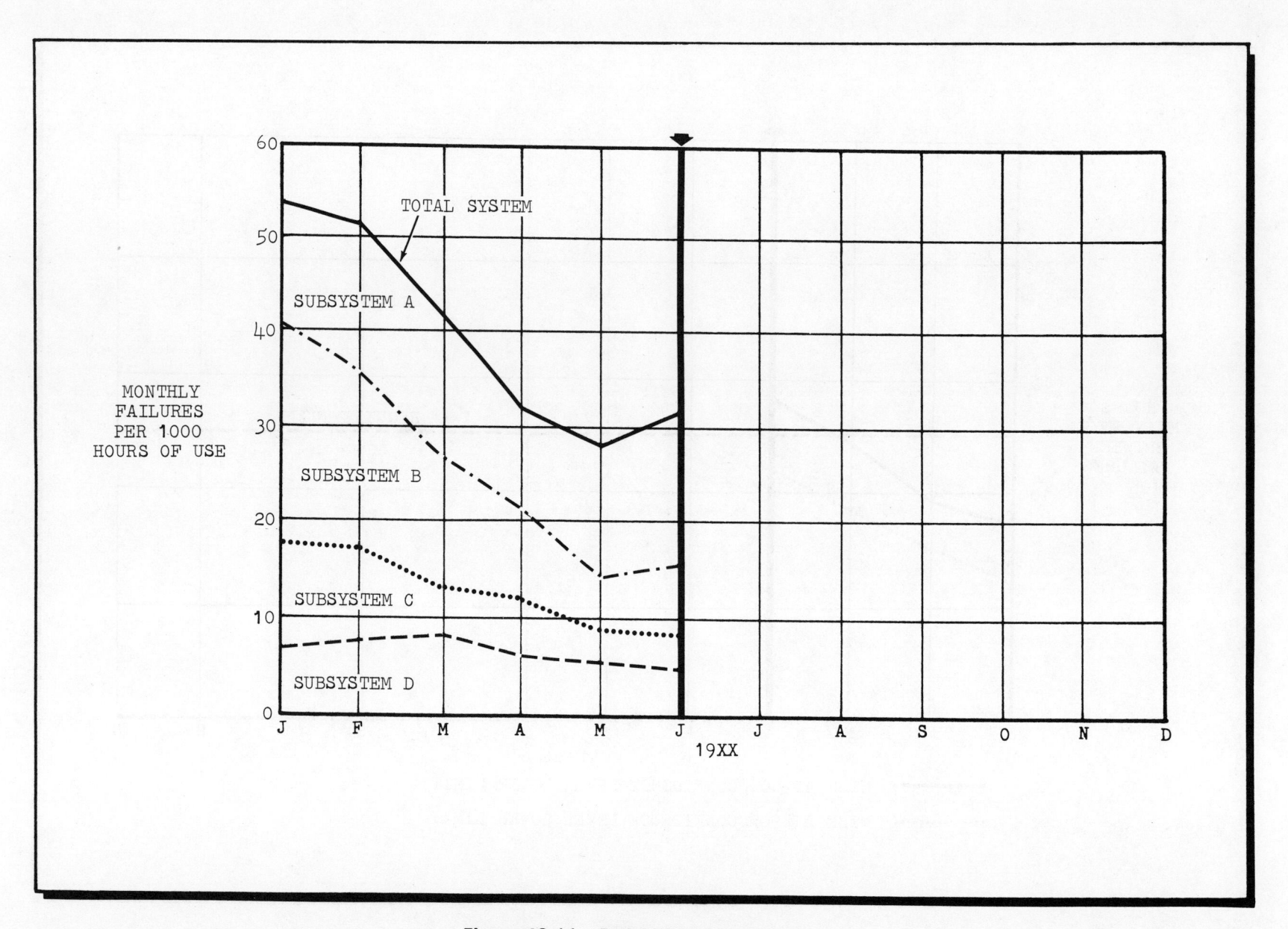

Figure 43.11   Reliability—Version 11

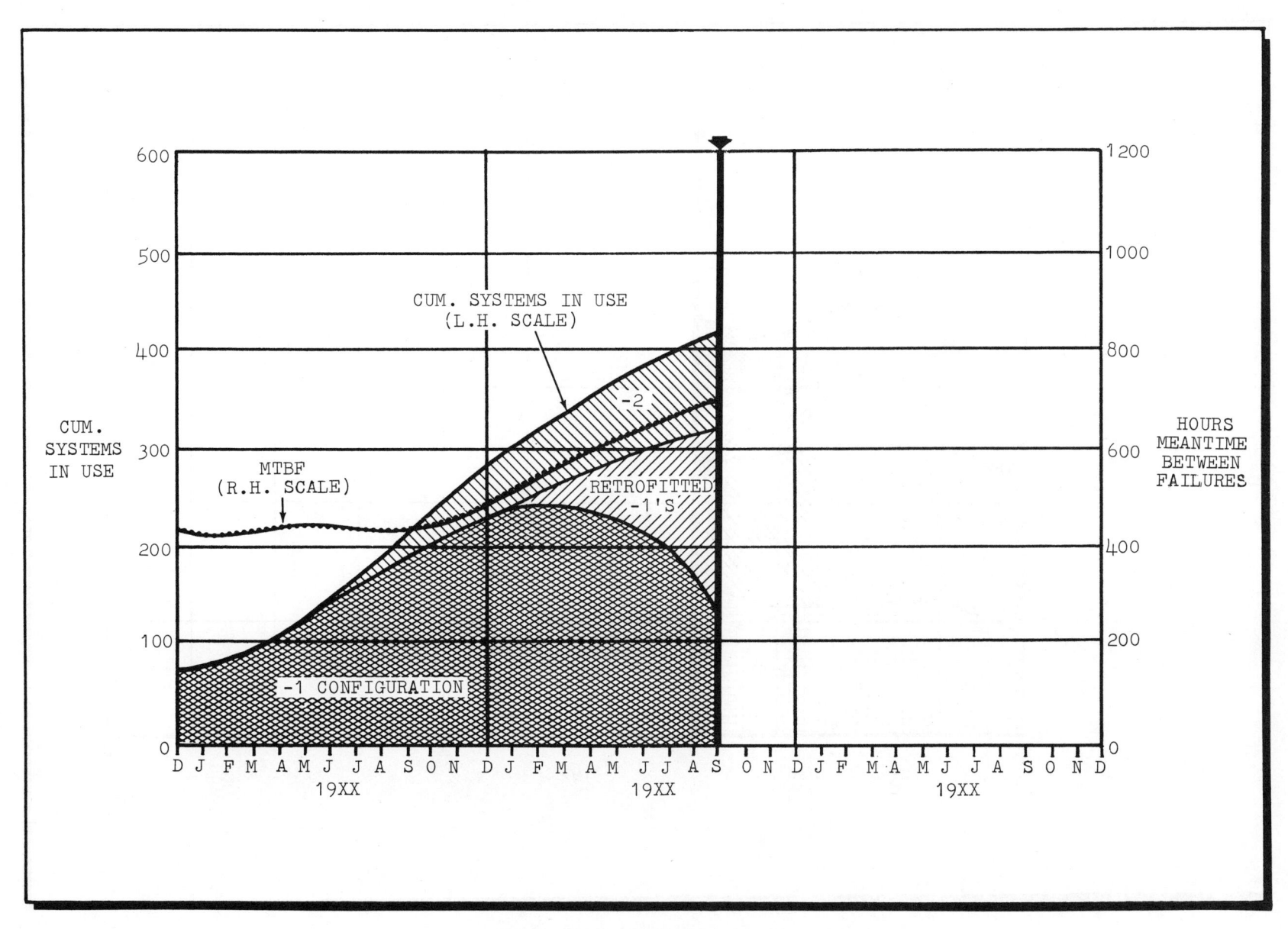

Figure 43.12 Reliability—Version 12

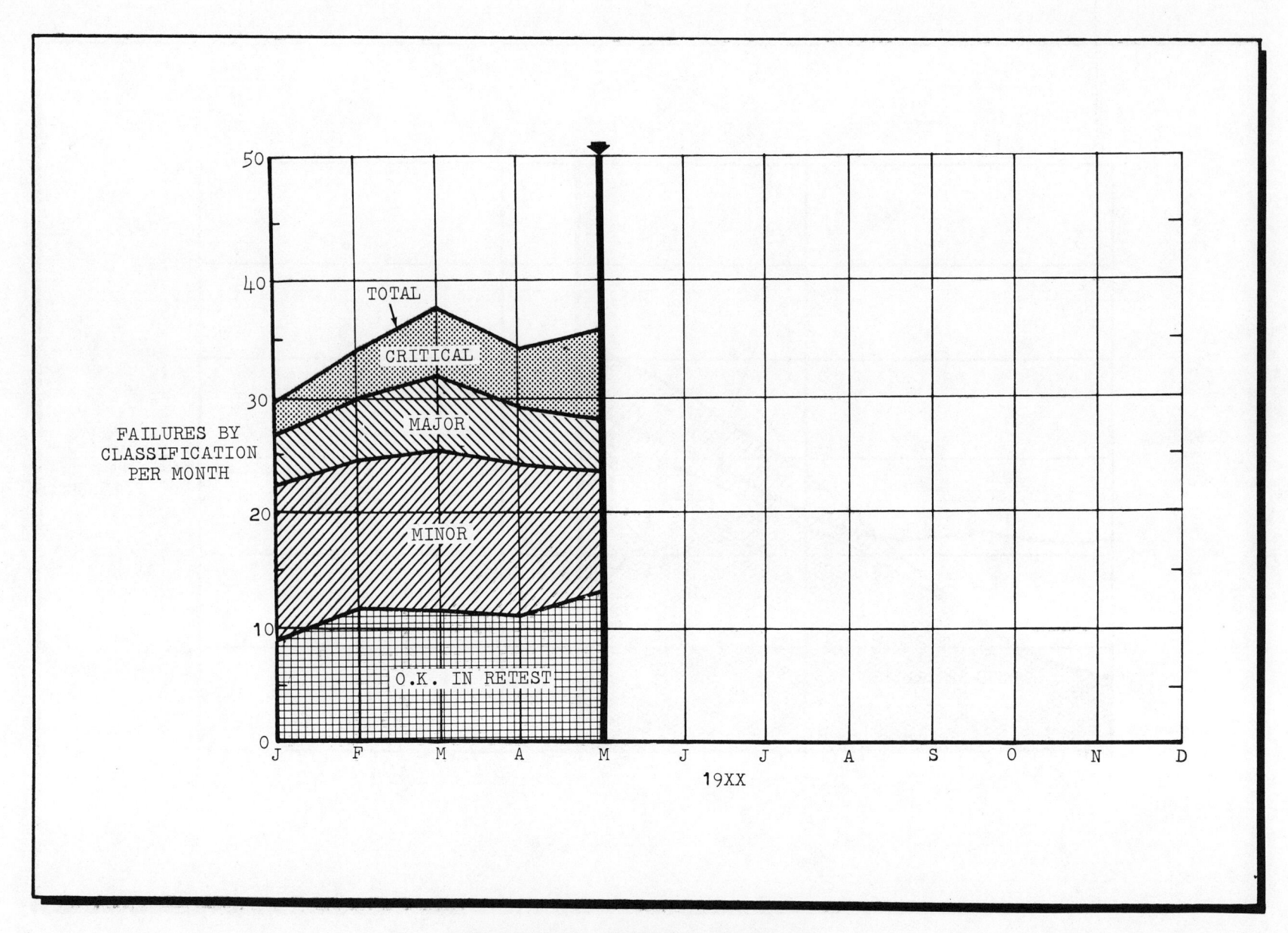

Figure 43.13   Reliability—Version 13

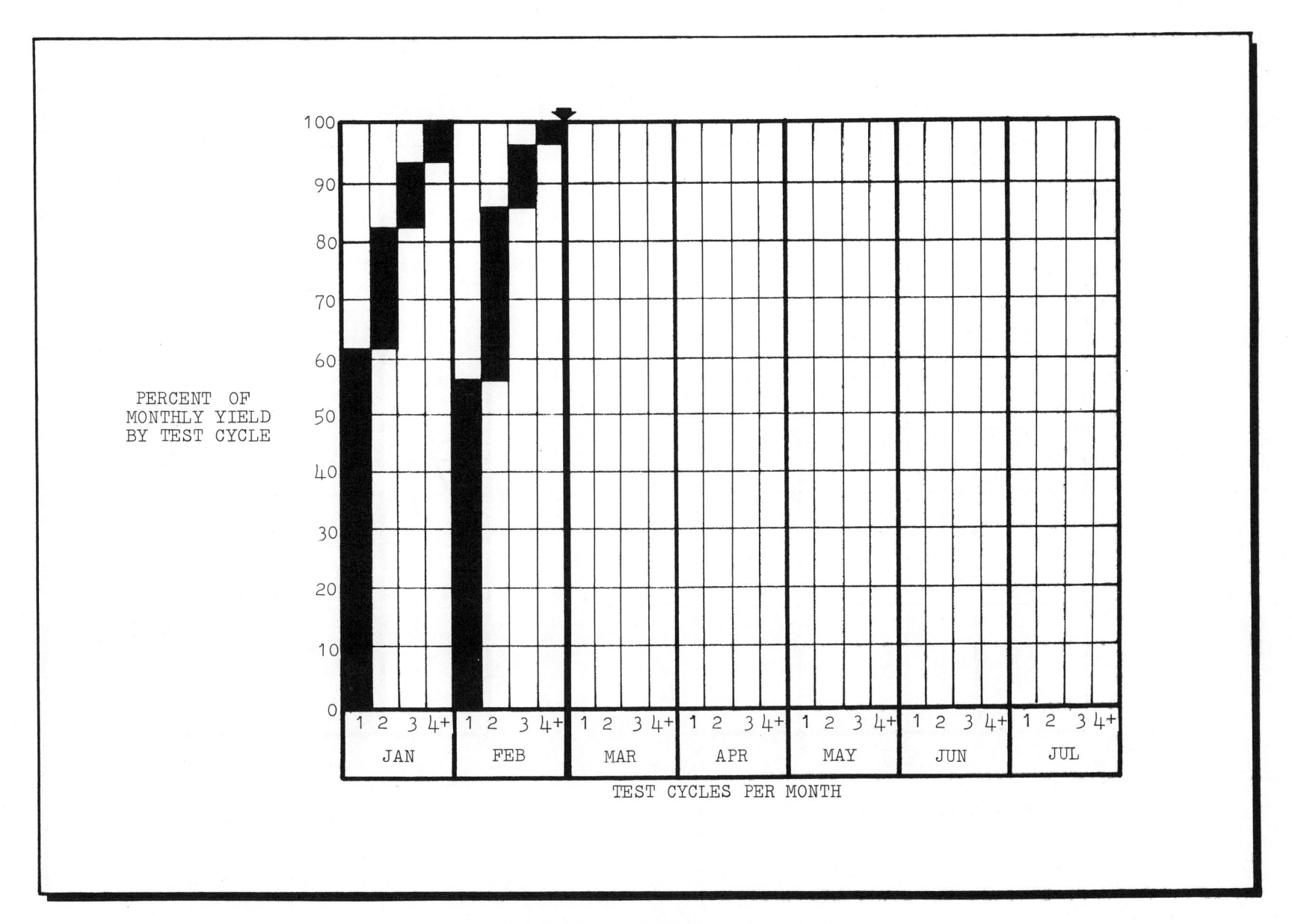

Figure 43.14 Reliability—Version 14

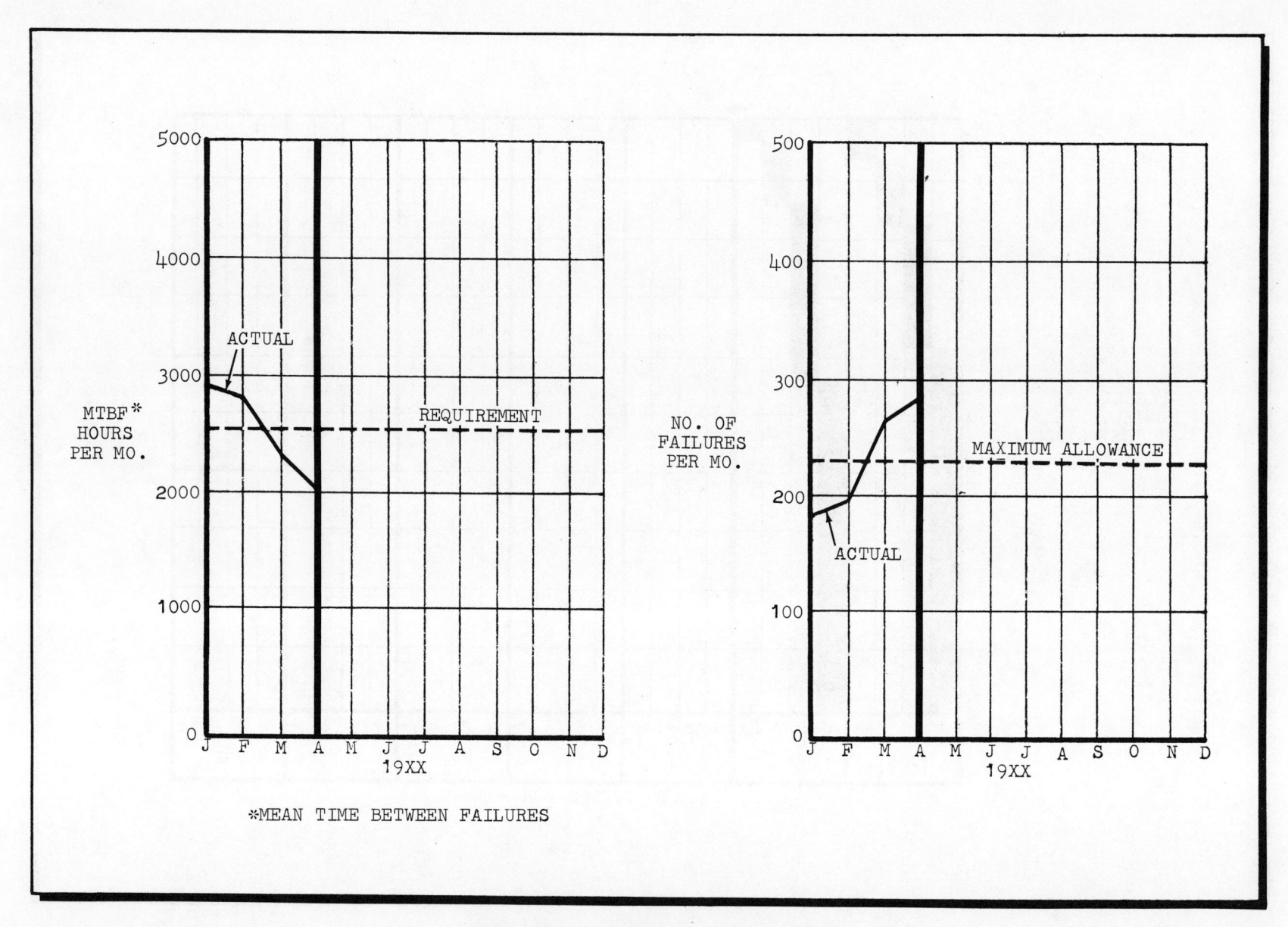

Figure 43.15 Reliability—Version 15

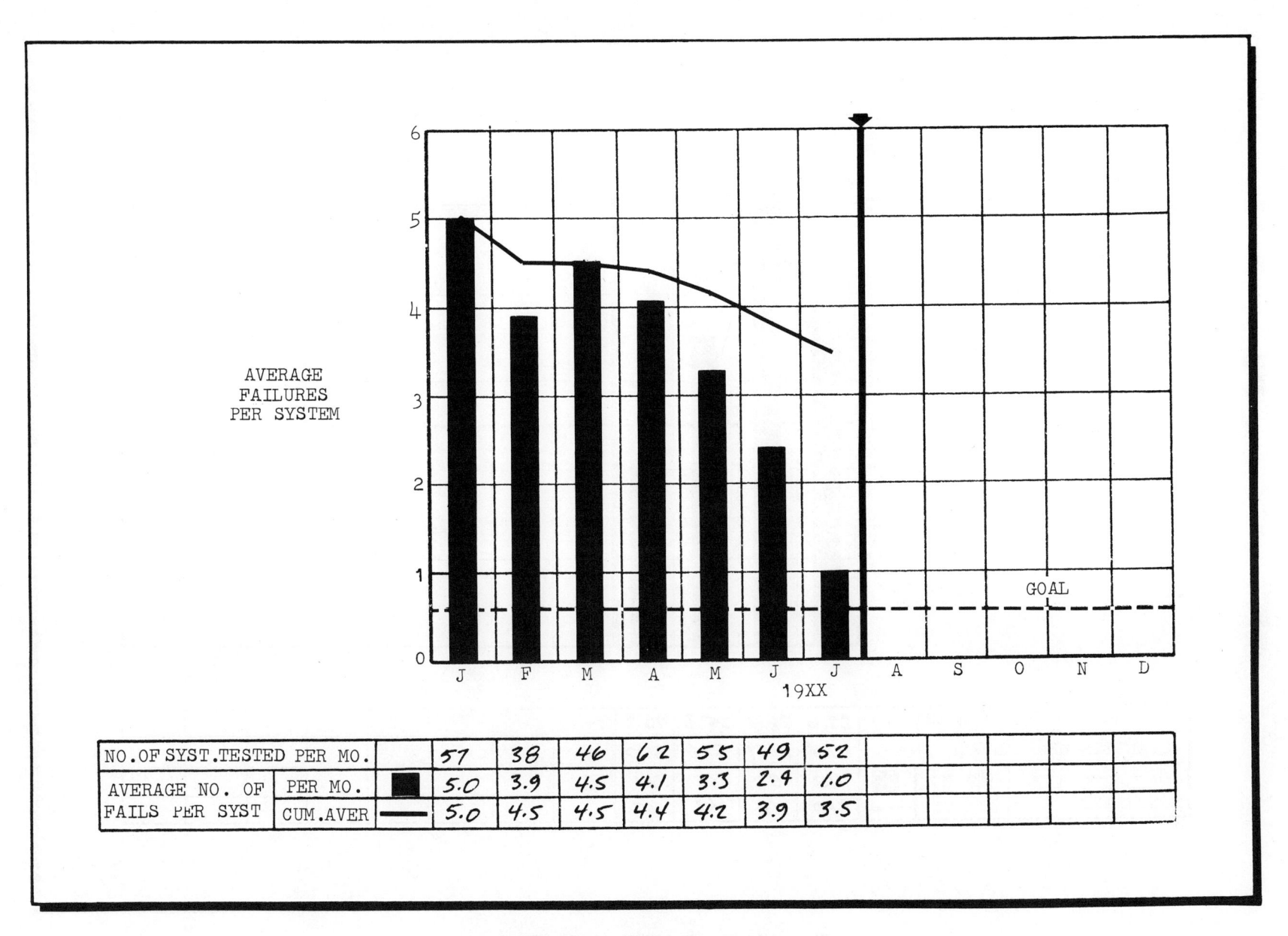

NO. OF SYST. TESTED PER MO.		57	38	46	62	55	49	52					
AVERAGE NO. OF FAILS PER SYST	PER MO. ■	5.0	3.9	4.5	4.1	3.3	2.4	1.0					
	CUM. AVER —	5.0	4.5	4.5	4.4	4.2	3.9	3.5					

Figure 43.16 Reliability—Version 16

MONTHLY FAILURES
PER
THOUSAND UNITS

GOAL

J F M A M J J A S O N D
19XX

QUANTITY OF UNITS (THOUSANDS)			27.6	28.4	25.3	26.2								
QUANTITY OF FAILURES			1104	1477	886	550								
FAILURES PER THOUSAND	PER MO.	■	40	52	35	21								
	YTD AVER	—	40	46	42	37								

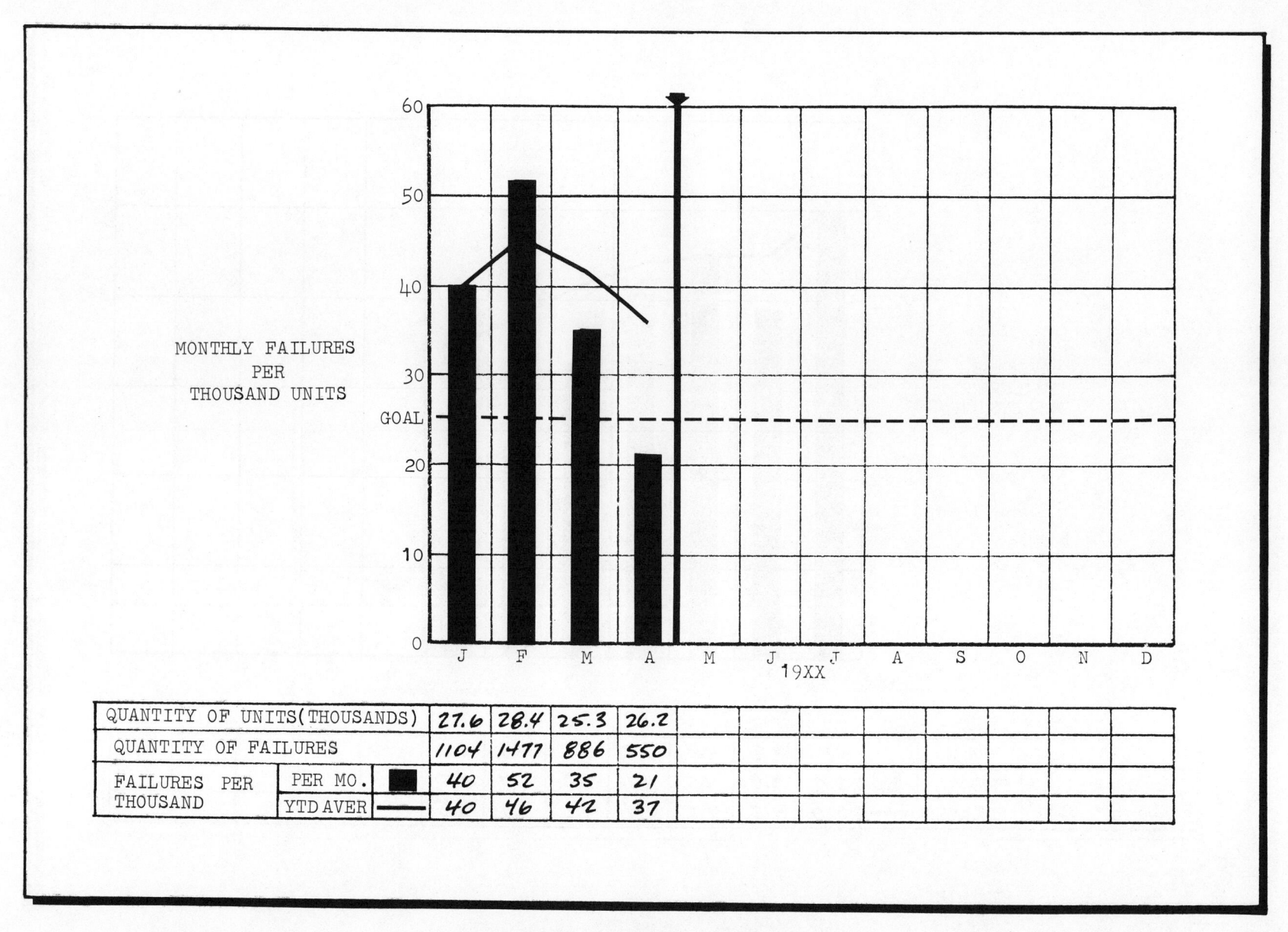

Figure 43.17   Reliability—Version 17

TEST HOURS	PER MO.	628	598	640	610									
	YTD	628	1226	1866	2476									
FAILURES	PER MO.	2	3	0	4									
	YTD	2	5	5	9									
MEANTIME BETWEEN FAILURES (HOURS)	PER MO.	314	199	7640	153									
	YTD	314	245	373	275									

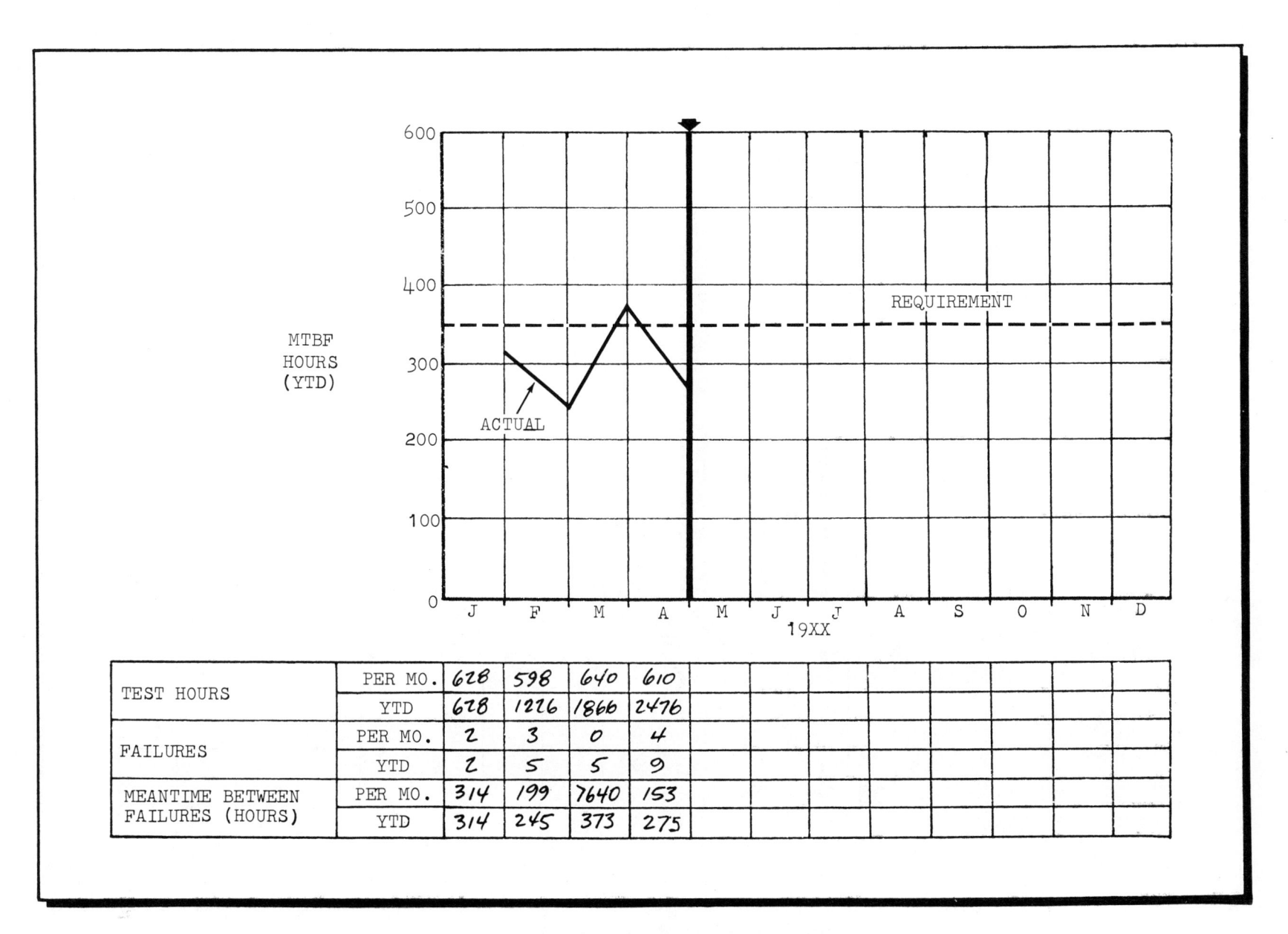

Figure 43.18 Reliability—Version 18

TEST HOURS	PER MO.	628	598	640	610								
	YTD	628	1226	1866	2476								
FAILURES	PER MO.	2	3	0	4								
	YTD	2	5	5	9								
MEAN TIME BETWEEN FAILURES (HOURS)	PER MO. ■	314	199	>640	153								
	YTD. —	314	245	373	275								

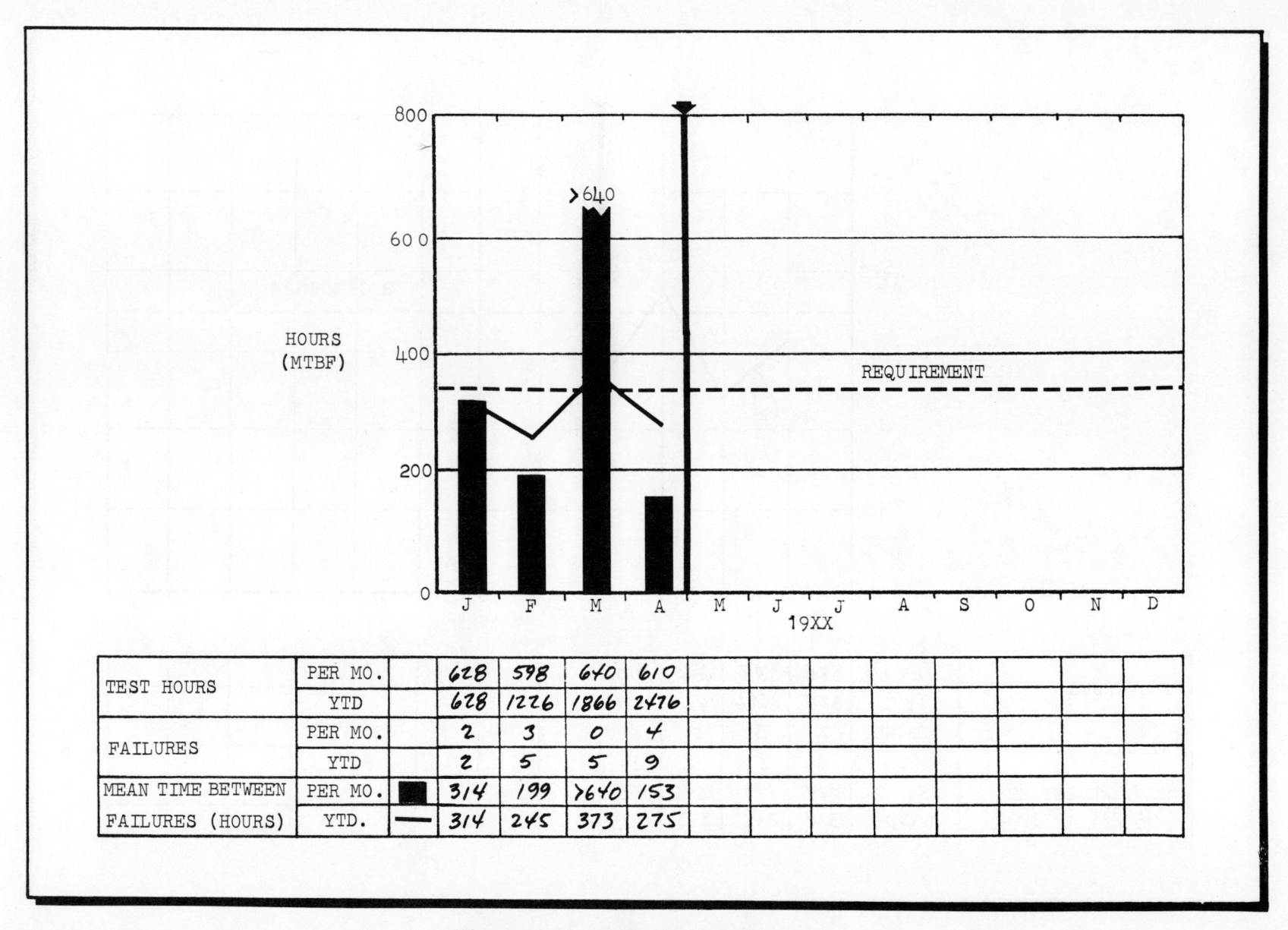

Figure 43.19   Reliability—Version 19

MTBF*
HOURS
PER MO.

REQUIREMENT

J F M A M J J A S O N D
19XX

USAGE HOURS		906	698	798									
FAILURES-CAUSE 1		4	2	1									
FAILURES-CAUSE 2		0	1	0									
FAILURES-CAUSE 3		3	2	3									
TOTAL FAILURES		7	5	4									
HOURS-MTBF*	■	115	138	200									

*MEAN TIME BETWEEN FAILURES

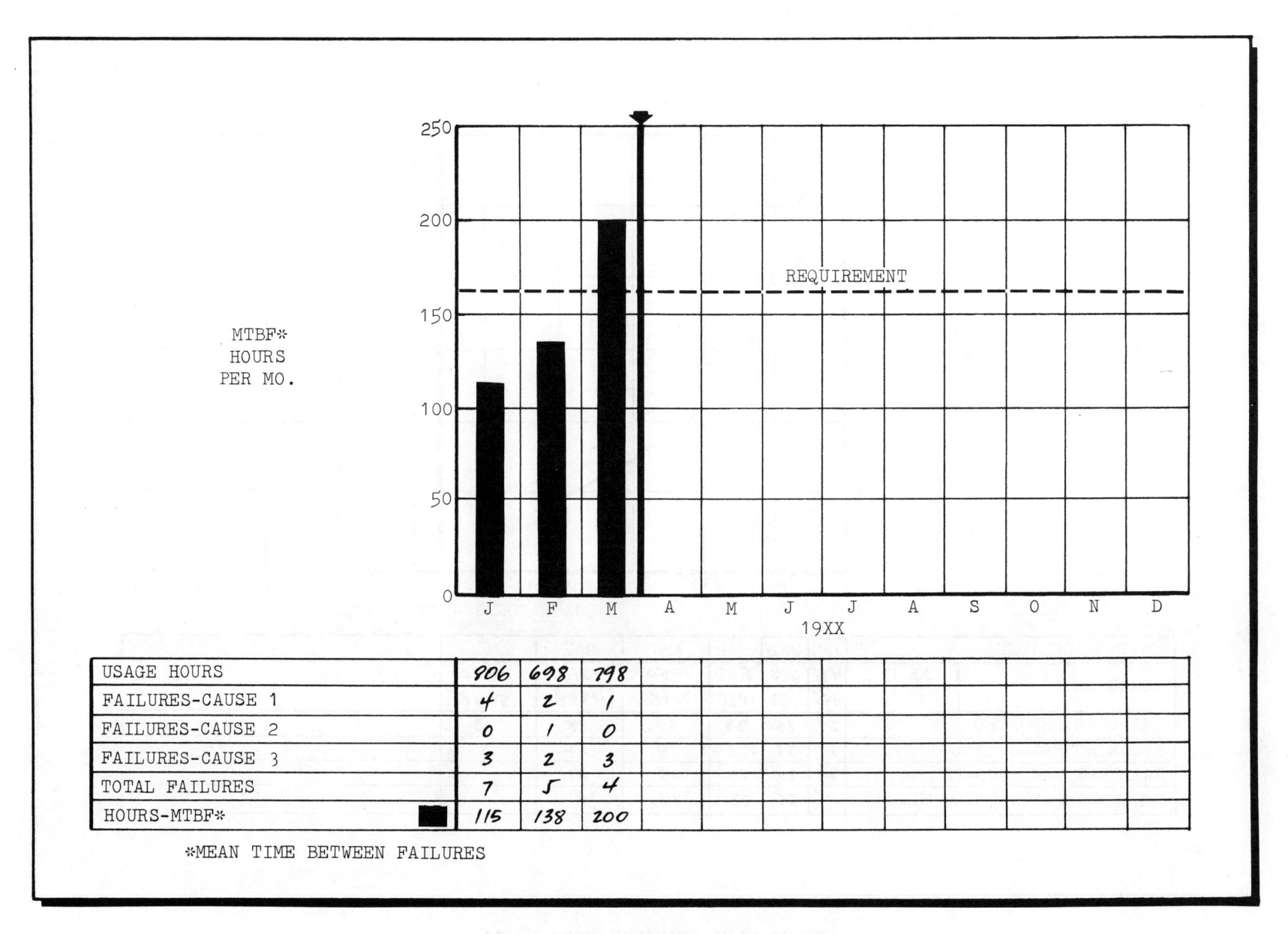

Figure 43.20   Reliability—Version 20

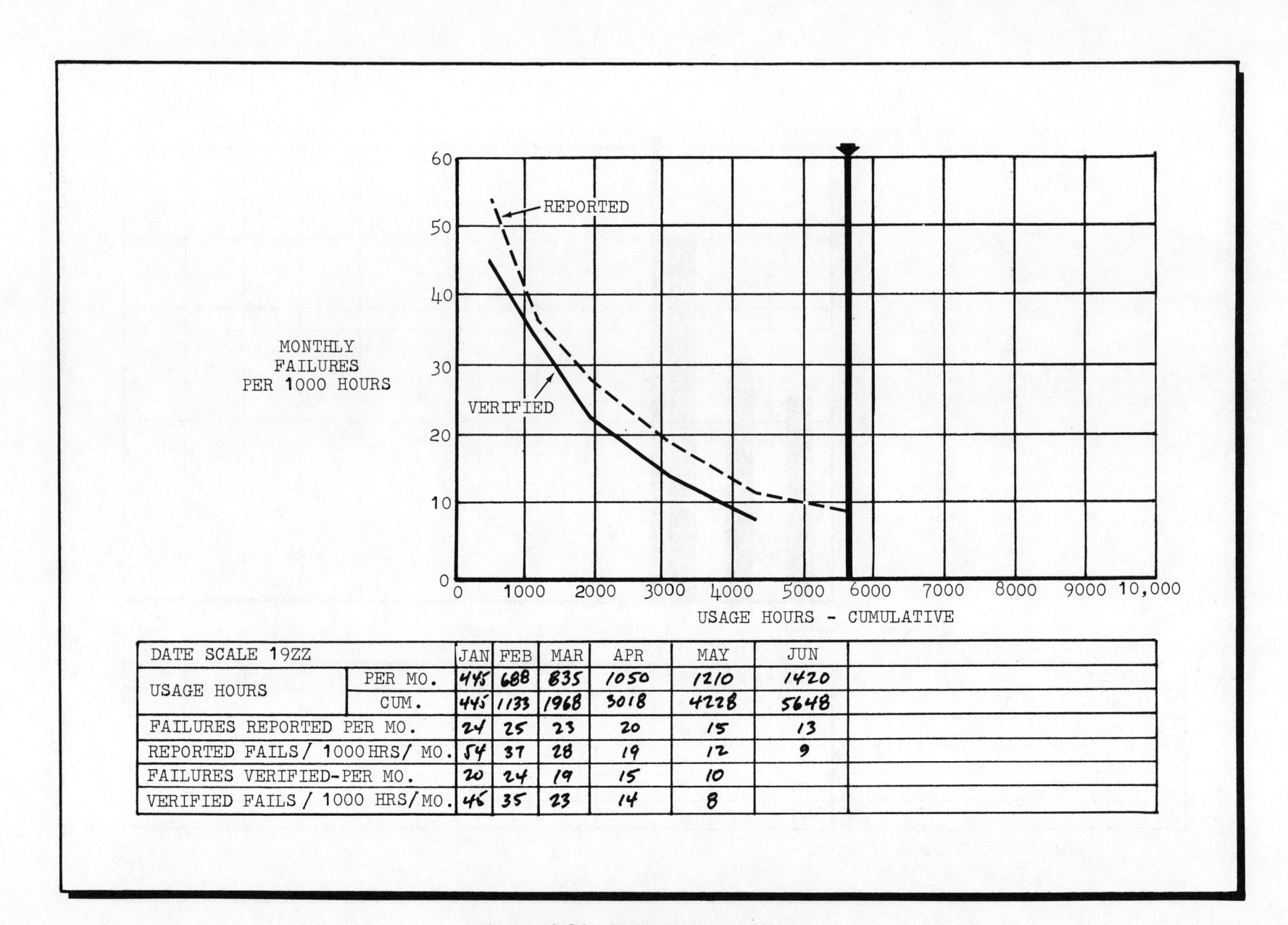

DATE SCALE 19ZZ		JAN	FEB	MAR	APR	MAY	JUN	
USAGE HOURS	PER MO.	445	688	835	1050	1210	1420	
	CUM.	445	1133	1968	3018	4228	5648	
FAILURES REPORTED PER MO.		24	25	23	20	15	13	
REPORTED FAILS / 1000 HRS / MO.		54	37	28	19	12	9	
FAILURES VERIFIED-PER MO.		20	24	19	15	10		
VERIFIED FAILS / 1000 HRS / MO.		46	35	23	14	8		

Figure 43.21 Reliability—Version 21

QUANTITY OF FAILURES BY PART		19XX											
		J	F	M	A	M	J	J	A	S	O	N	D
PART #1	AGSHDJFK	0	1	1	0								
PART #2	TJGMDNSH	2	1	1	2								
PART #3	ODIFUGYRJ	2	1	0	0								
PART #4	JFHGNDMS	8	6	9	10								
PART #5	HEIRUTYWKD	1	2	2	2								
PART #6	SPDLFKGJD	0	0	1	0								
TOTAL		13	11	14	14								

Figure 43.22   Reliability—Version 22

ITEM			19XX											
			J	F	M	A	M	J	J	A	S	O	N	D
TEST HOURS	PER MO		628	598	640	610								
	CUM		628	1226	1866	2476								
FAILURES	PER MO		2	3	0	4								
	CUM		2	5	5	9								
MEAN TIME BETWEEN FAILURES (HOURS)	PER MO		314	199	7640	153								
	CUM		314	245	373	275								

Figure 43.23   Reliability—Version 23

ITEM		19XX											
		J	F	M	A	M	J	J	A	S	O	N	D
SYSTEMS TESTED	PER MO.	57	38	46	62	55	49	52					
	CUM	57	95	141	203	258	307	359					
TOTAL NO. OF FAILURES	PER MO.	285	148	207	254	182	118	52					
	CUM	285	433	640	894	1076	1194	1246					
AVERAGE NO. OF FAILURES PER SYSTEM	PER MO.	5.0	3.9	4.5	4.1	3.3	2.4	1.0					
	CUM AVER.	5.0	4.5	4.5	4.4	4.2	3.9	3.5					

Figure 43.24 Reliability—Version 24

UNIT		19XX											
		JAN		FEB		MAR		APR		MAY		JUN	
		R	MTBR	R	MTBR	R	MTBR	R	MTBR	R	MTBR	R	MTBR
SUBSYSTEM A		6	410	10	310								
SUBSYSTEM B		1	2460	2	1550								
SUBSYSTEM C		4	615	5	620								
SUBSYSTEM D		31	79	38	82								
SUBSYSTEM E		0	—	1	3100								
TOTAL SYSTEM	TOTAL REJECTS PER MO.	42		56									
	MAX. USAGE HRS. PER MO.	2460		3100									
	MTBR-PER MO.	58.6		55.4									
	MTBR-CUM AVER	58.6		57.0									

R=REJECTIONS BY SUBSYSTEM & TOTAL
MTBR=MEAN TIME BETWEEN REJECTION BY SUBSYSTEM

Figure 43.25 Reliability—Version 25

STATUS AS OF _____

ITEM	NO. OF UNITS	TOTAL OPERATING HOURS	TOTAL FAILURES	HOURS (MEANTIME BETWEEN FAILURES)		
				ACTUAL	REQ'MENTS	VARIANCE
AKWUEHRTJGH	27	4286	24	179	140	+39
AKSJDHFG	173	10573	66	160	150	+10
AKSJDHFGA	168	8250	75	110	75	+35
SJDJFHGG	54	3472	3	1157	1500	-343
WIEURYFHG	17	9618	23	418	500	-82
FHGLSKDJFJGHD	280	6500	32	203	180	+23
EROITFJGHSHD	140	2186	11	199	180	+19

Figure 43.26　Reliability—Version 26

STATUS AS OF _____

NO. OF FAILURES BY PART & CATEGORY	MALFUNCTION CATEGORY						REMARKS
	ELECT	MECH	WORKMAN-SHIP	OPERATOR ERROR	OTHER	TOTALS	
PART #1	0	0	0	0	0	0	
PART #2	0	2	0	0	0	2	
PART #3	0	0	0	0	0	0	
PART #4	0	2	6	1	1	10	SPECIAL INVESTIGATION NOW BEING MADE BY JONES
PART #5	2	0	0	0	0	2	
PART #6	0	0	0	0	0	0	
TOTAL	2	4	6	1	1	14	

Figure 43.27   Reliability—Version 27

STATUS-MONTH OF _____

SYSTEM	NO. OF SYSTEMS TESTED	NO. OF SYSTEMS WITH NO FAILURES	NO. OF FAILURES	AVER. FAILURES PER SYSTEM	NO. OF SYSTS CORRECTED BY ADJUSTMENT	NO. OF SYSTEMS ACCEPTED	PERCENT YIELD FOR MO.
SKDJFHGYEYEBHD	146	88	252	1.7	48	136	93.1
SOEIRITUGJGH	27	14	38	1.4	13	27	100.0
SBDBFBGGAY	250	188	180	.7	60	248	99.2
YSYDHFGDBD	187	172	30	.2	15	187	100.0
SGDFWTECDF FGIIUZ	68	46	110	1.6	13	59	86.8
SGDFWTEURUFHFG	47	24	74	.3	20	44	93.6
JSHDHFBGHFYD	15	14	3	.2	1	15	100.0

Figure 43.28 Reliability—Version 28

44.0 REVENUE VERSUS COSTS

Charts that display cost dollars in relationship to revenue dollars are shown in this section. Also see Section 10.0, *Costs as a Percent of Sales*.

44.1 Revenue Versus Costs—Version 1: Forecasted and actual revenue and costs are displayed together in Version 1, Figure 44.1. In this example, the information has been plotted on a rate-per-month basis.

44.2 Revenue Versus Costs—Version 2: In Version 2 of a revenue versus costs tracking chart, Figure 44.2, the amount scale has been expanded so as to more clearly show the differences between planned and actual performance. Also, the costs budget has been revised according to actual revenues so that a more meaningful relationship can be determined between budgeted and actual costs.

44.3 Revenue Versus Costs—Version 3: Version 3 of a revenue versus costs chart, Figure 44.3, is similar to Version 2 except that the space between actual revenue and actual costs has been shaded. Two patterns are used: one for the area where costs are less than revenue, and another for when costs exceed revenue. As with Version 2, an arrowhead is used on the amount scale to draw attention to the fact that it does not begin from a zero base.

44.4 Revenue Versus Costs—Version 4: Column and step line chart styles are combined in Version 4 of a revenue versus costs chart, Figure 44.4. Step lines are used to display plans. Columns are used to show actual performance to date.

44.5 Revenue Versus Costs—Version 5: When planned and actual revenue and costs are graphically compared on a year-to-date (cumulative) basis, the plotting lines have a tendency to run together in the early portions of the date scale. One way of minimizing this is to use a log-log grid as illustrated in Version 5 of a revenue versus costs tracking chart, Figure 44.5.

44.6 Revenue Versus Costs—Version 6: Separate grids for revenue and costs are used in Version 6 of a revenue versus costs tracking chart, Figure 44.6. In both grids, plans are shown with dashed lines and actuals to date are shown with solid lines.

44.7 Revenue Versus Costs—Version 7: Revenue and costs are compared on a multi-year basis in Version 7 of a revenue versus costs tracking chart, Figure 44.7. Actual revenue and costs for four previous years are shown on the left-hand grid. The center grid shows planned and actual performance, and the right-hand grid shows the average monthly revenue forecast and costs budget for the coming year by quarters.

44.8 Revenue Versus Costs—Version 8: The relationship between revenue and costs displayed in Version 8 of a revenue versus costs tracking chart, Figure 44.8, is typical of a newly started business. Money is expended prior to the receipt of revenue. In this example, shading has been added to highlight costs.

44.9 Revenue Versus Costs—Version 9: A statistical table is combined with graphics in Version 9 of a revenue versus costs tracking chart, Figure 44.9. The lines on the graphic portion of this example are plotted to the center of the spaces to correspond with the statistics that are given in the table underneath. An arrowhead has been used on the amount scale to show that it does not begin from zero.

44.10 Revenue Versus Costs—Version 10: Another version of a graphic chart combined with a statistical table is shown as Version 10 of a revenue versus costs tracking chart, Figure 44.10. In this example, the rate-per-month data are plotted in the graphic portion of the chart whereas both rate-per-month and year-to-date statistics are given in the table.

44.11 Revenue Versus Costs—Version 11: A statistical table version of a revenue versus costs tracking chart is shown as Version 11, Figure 44.11. Planned and actual revenue and costs statistics are given on both a monthly and cumulative basis. The costs section of the table gives the original budget and the budget that has been revised to correspond with actual revenue.

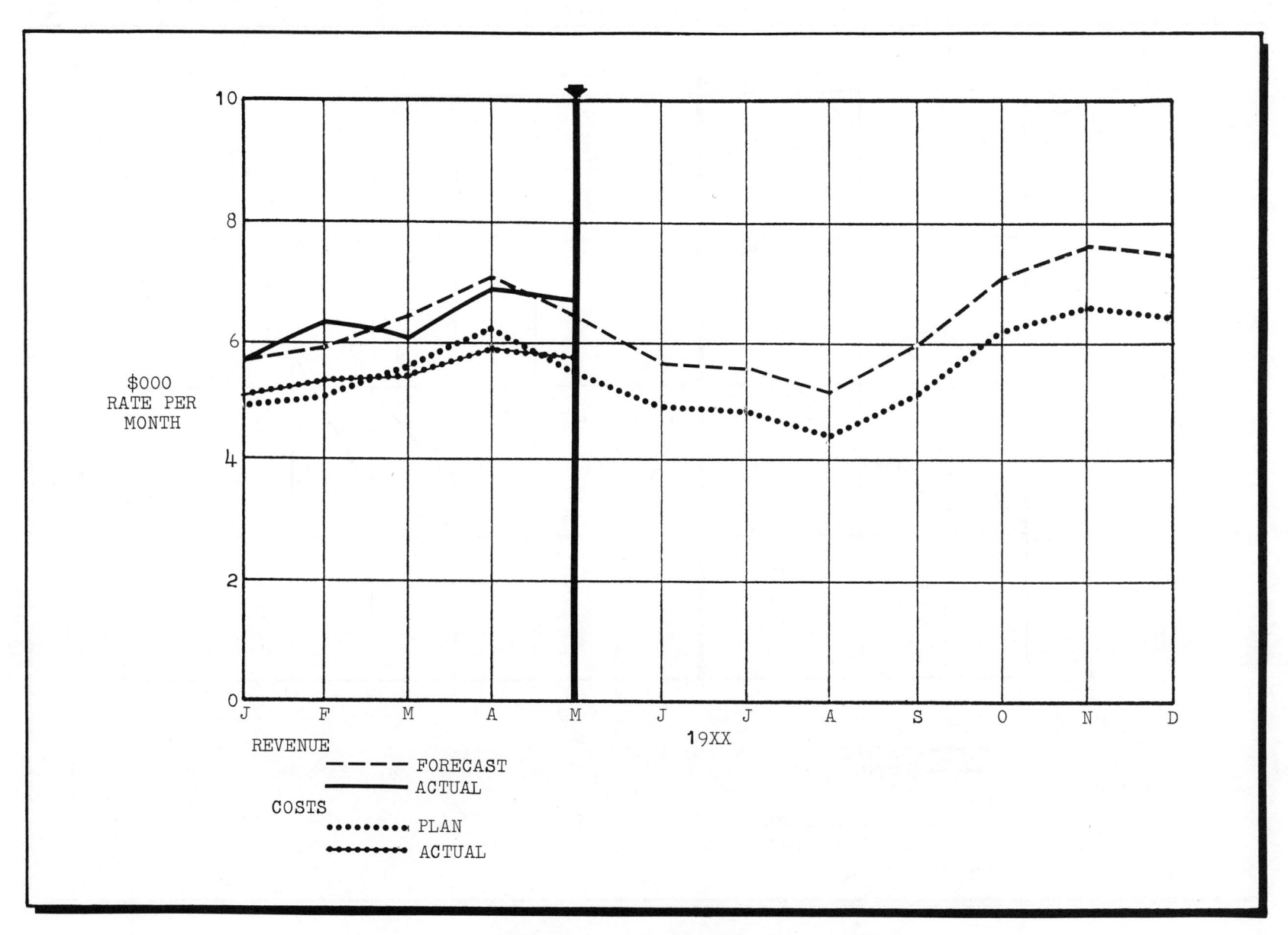

Figure 44.1 Revenue Versus Costs—Version 1

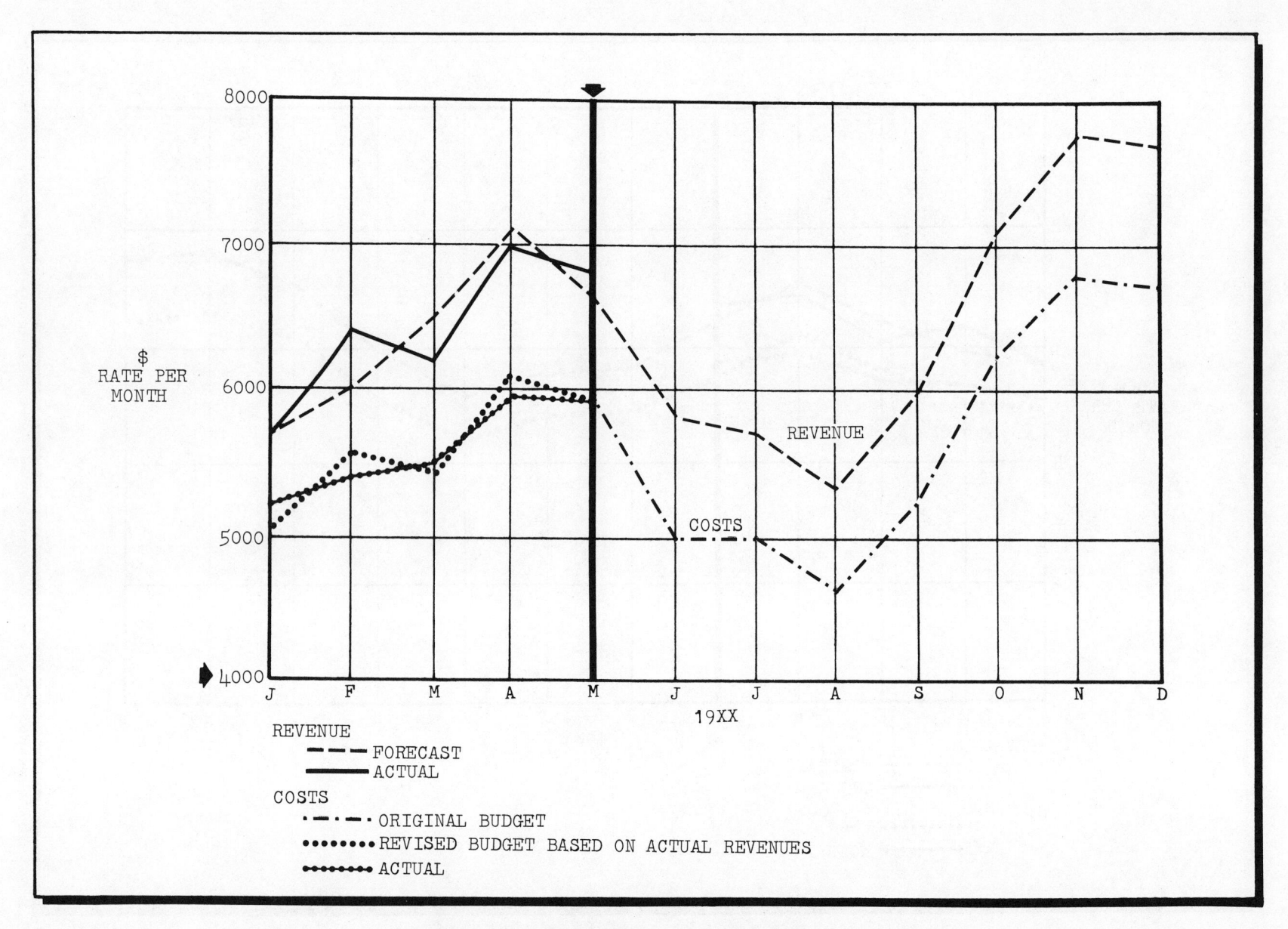

Figure 44.2   Revenue Versus Costs—Version 2

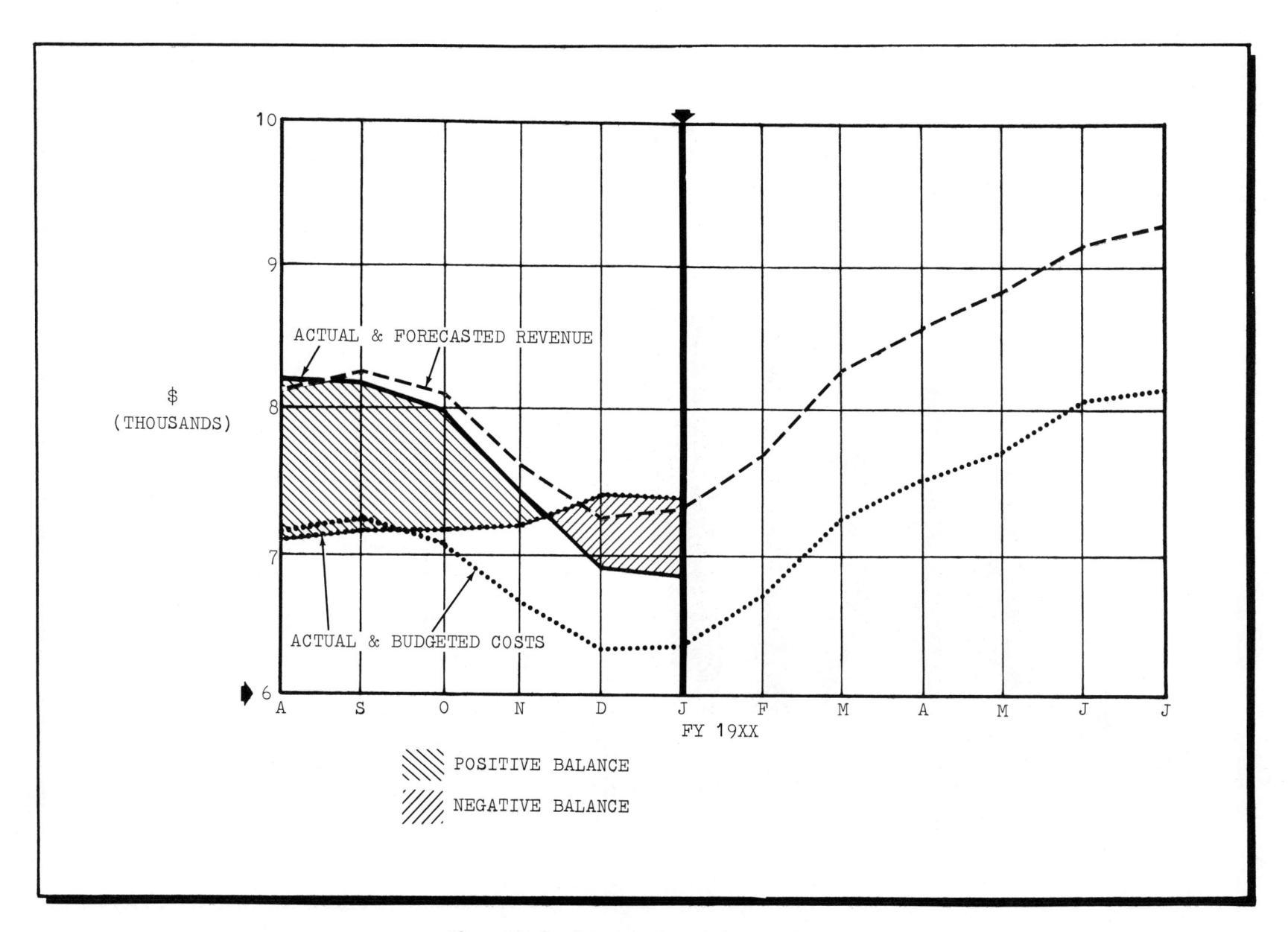

Figure 44.3 Revenue Versus Costs—Version 3

513

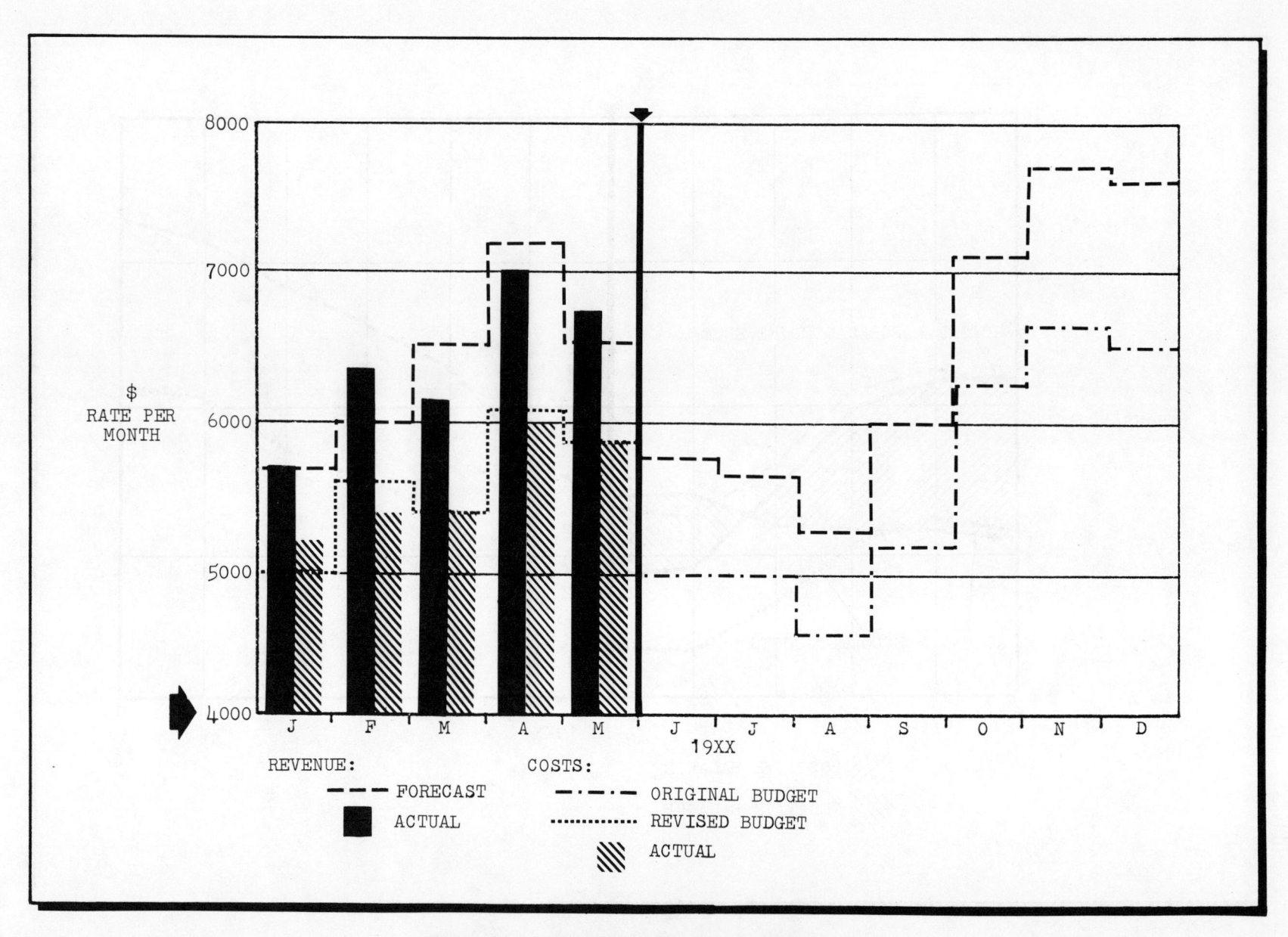

Figure 44.4   Revenue Versus Costs—Version 4

514

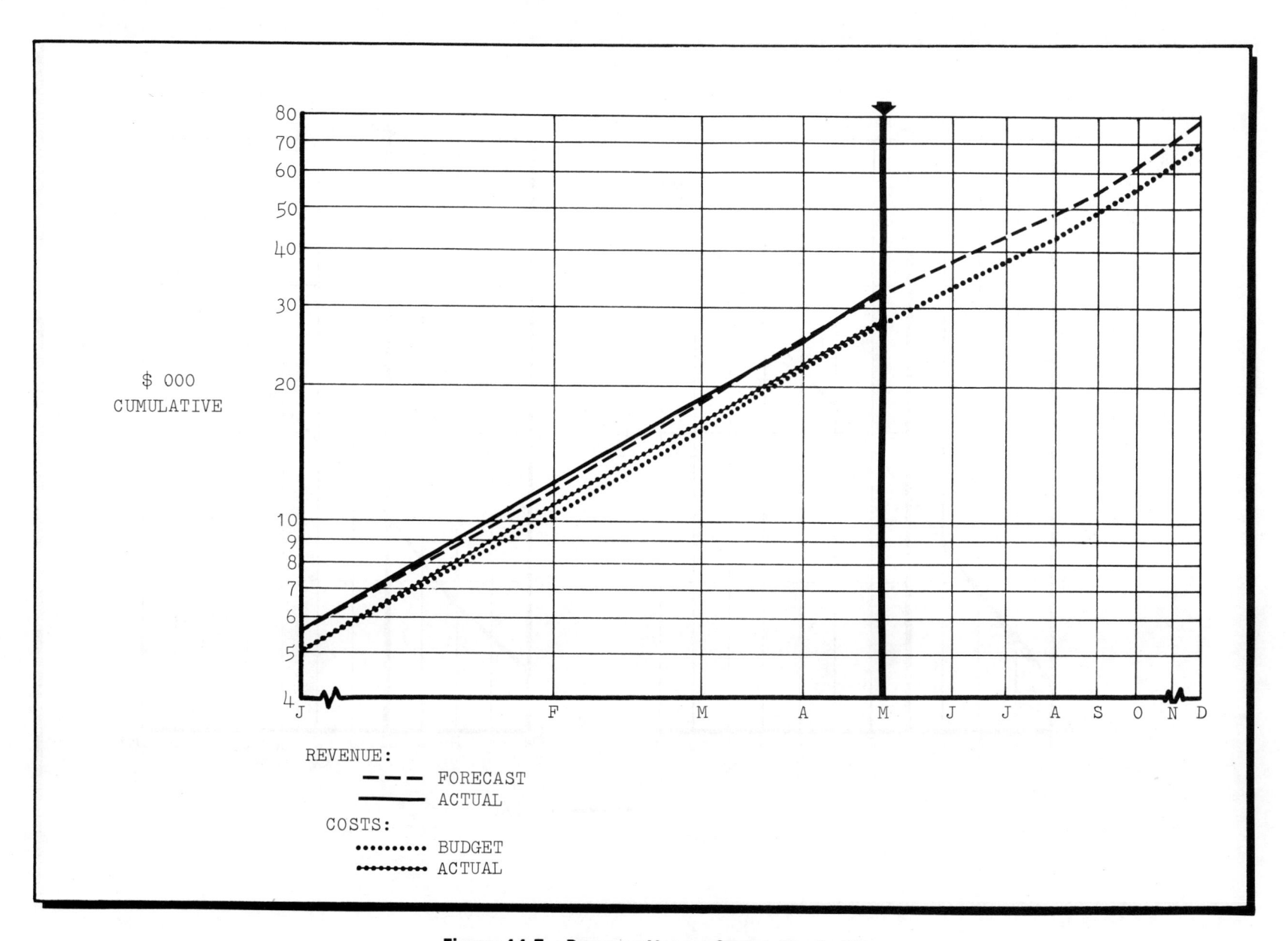

Figure 44.5 Revenue Versus Costs—Version 5

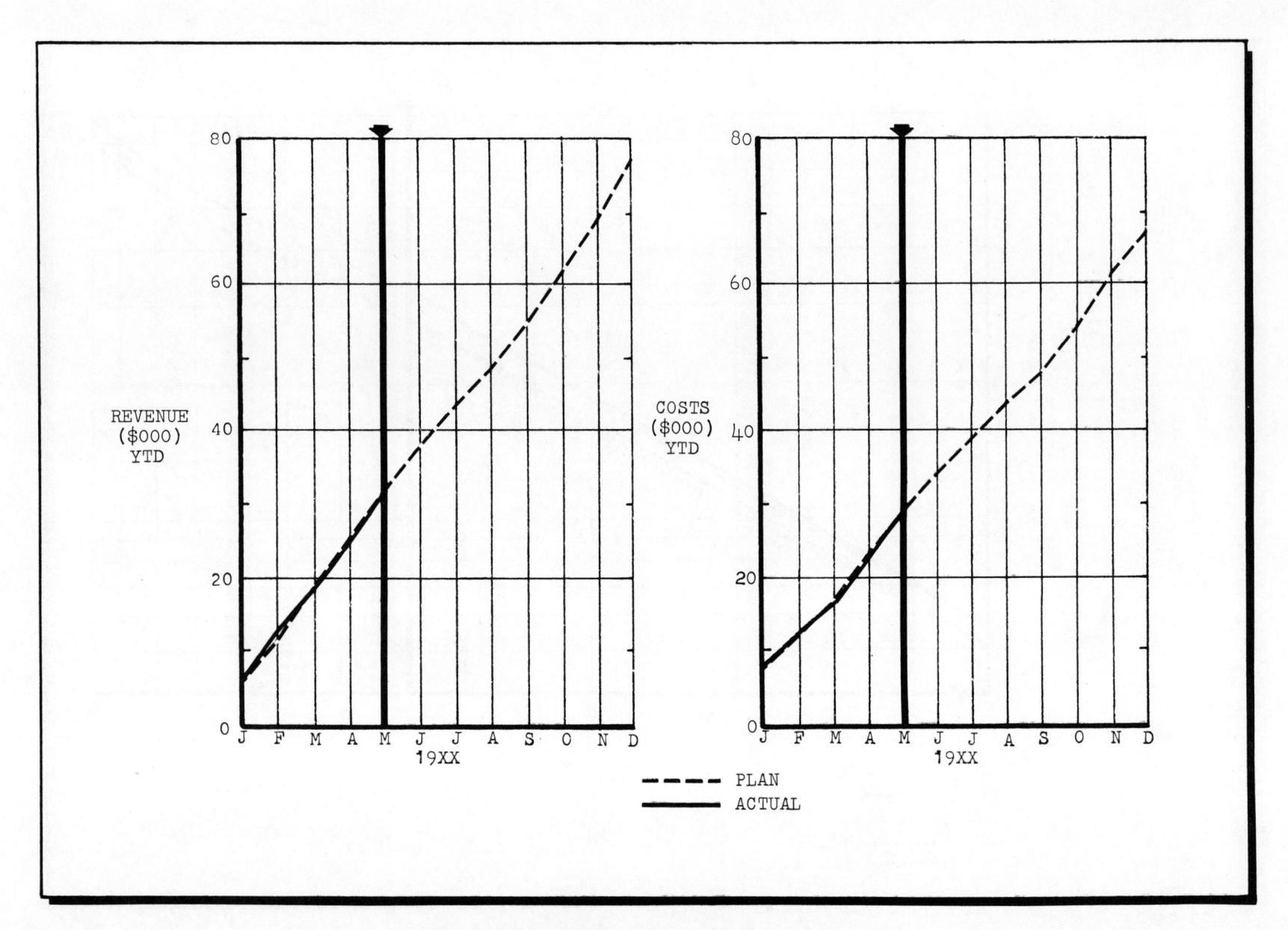

Figure 44.6 Revenue Versus Costs—Version 6

516

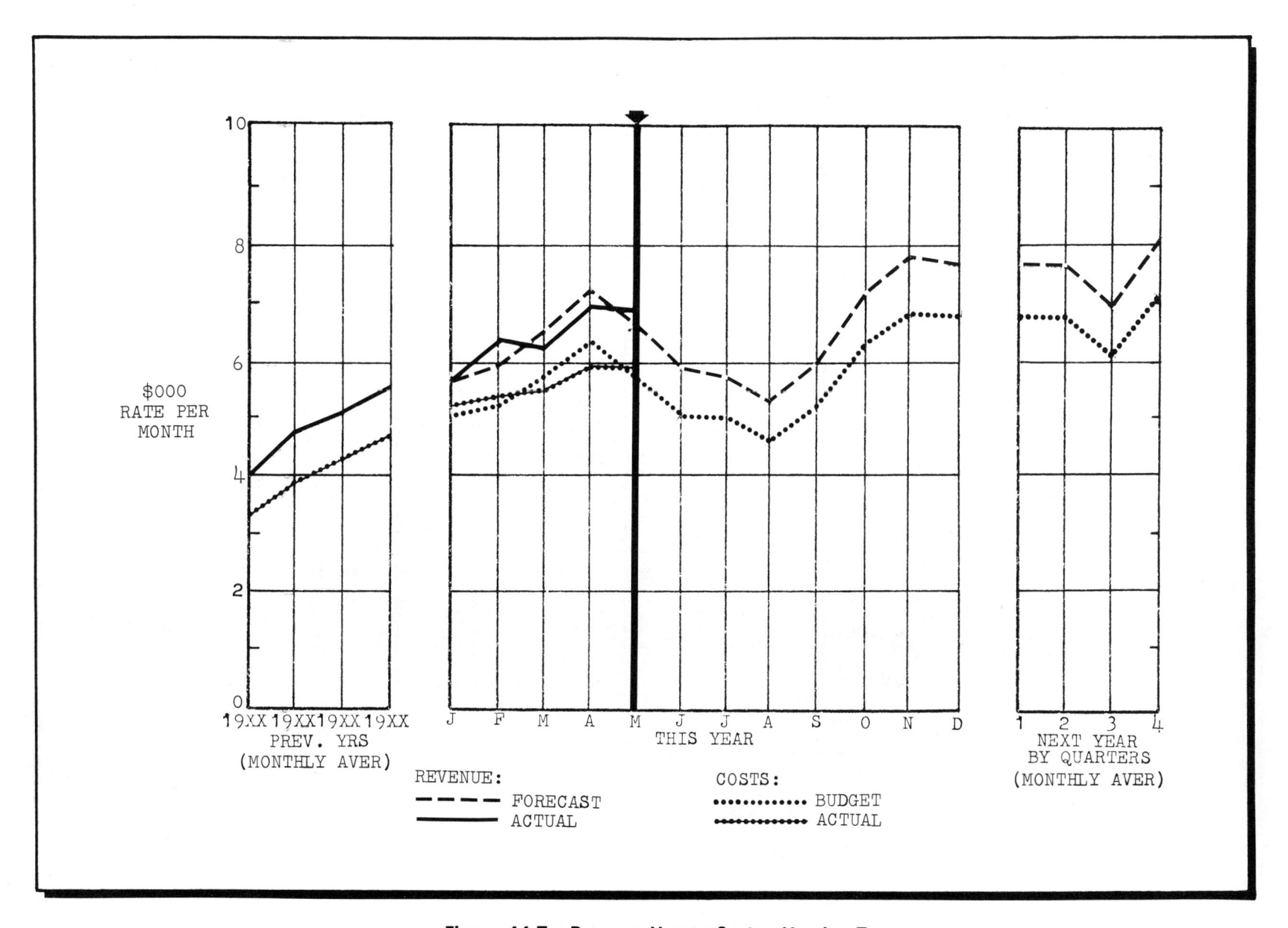

Figure 44.7 Revenue Versus Costs—Version 7

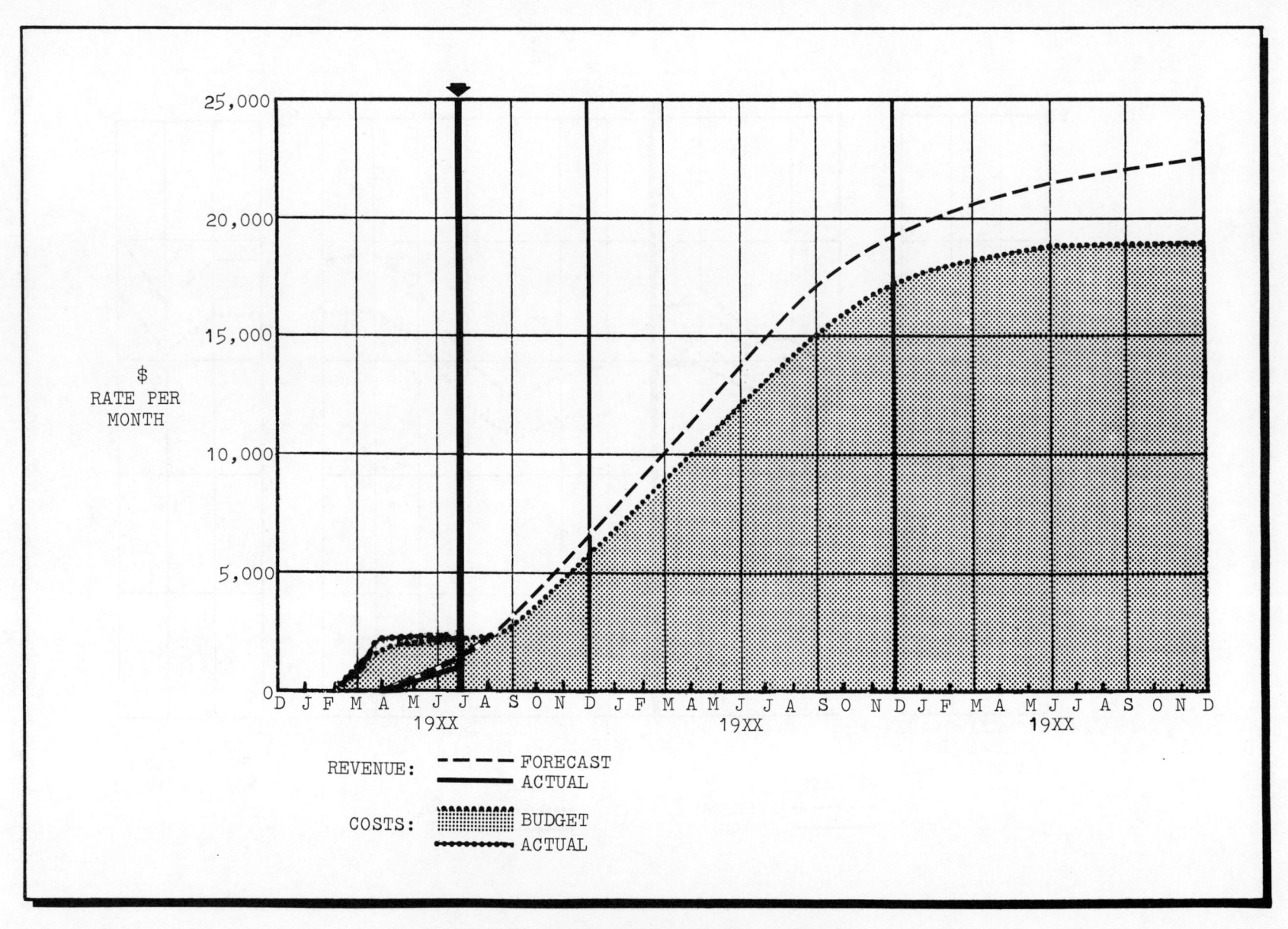

Figure 44.8 Revenue Versus Costs—Version 8

$
(THOUSANDS)
RATE PER MONTH

RATE PER MO.

			J	F	M	A	M	J	J	A	S	O	N	D
REVENUE	FORECAST	– –	5.7	6.0	6.5	7.2	6.6	5.8	5.7	5.3	6.0	7.2	7.8	7.7
	ACTUAL	——	5.7	6.4	6.2	7.0	6.8							
COSTS	BUDGET	–·–	5.0	5.2	5.7	6.3	5.7	5.0	5.0	4.6	5.2	6.3	6.8	6.7
	ACTUAL	•••••	5.2	5.4	5.5	6.0	5.9							
	REV. BUDGET	••••••	5.0	5.6	5.4	6.1	5.9							

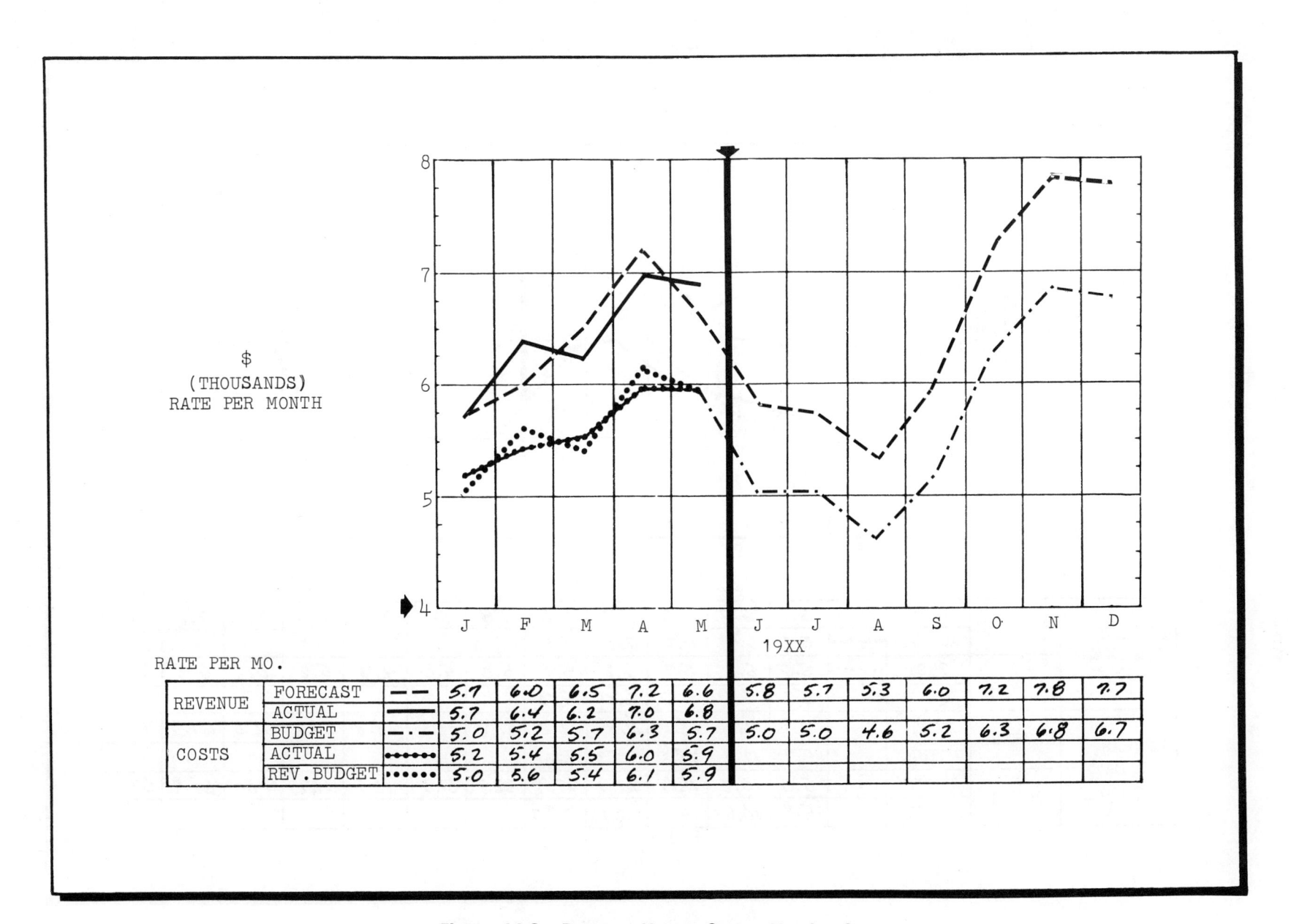

Figure 44.9 Revenue Versus Costs—Version 9

519

RATE PER MONTH $000	REVENUE	FCST	— — —	5.7	6.0	6.5	7.2	6.6	5.8	5.7	5.3	6.0	7.2	7.8	7.7
		ACTUAL	————	5.7	6.4	6.2	7.0	6.8							
	COSTS	FCST	········	5.0	5.2	5.7	6.3	5.7	5.0	5.0	4.6	5.2	6.3	6.8	6.7
		ACTUAL	••••••	5.2	5.4	5.5	6.0	5.9							
YEAR TO DATE $000	REVENUE	FCST		5.7	11.7	18.2	25.4	32.0	37.8	43.5	48.8	54.8	62.0	69.9	77.6
		ACTUAL		5.7	12.1	18.3	25.3	32.1							
	COSTS	FCST		5.0	10.2	15.9	22.2	27.9	32.9	37.9	42.5	47.7	54.0	60.8	67.5
		ACTUAL		5.2	10.6	16.1	22.1	28.0							

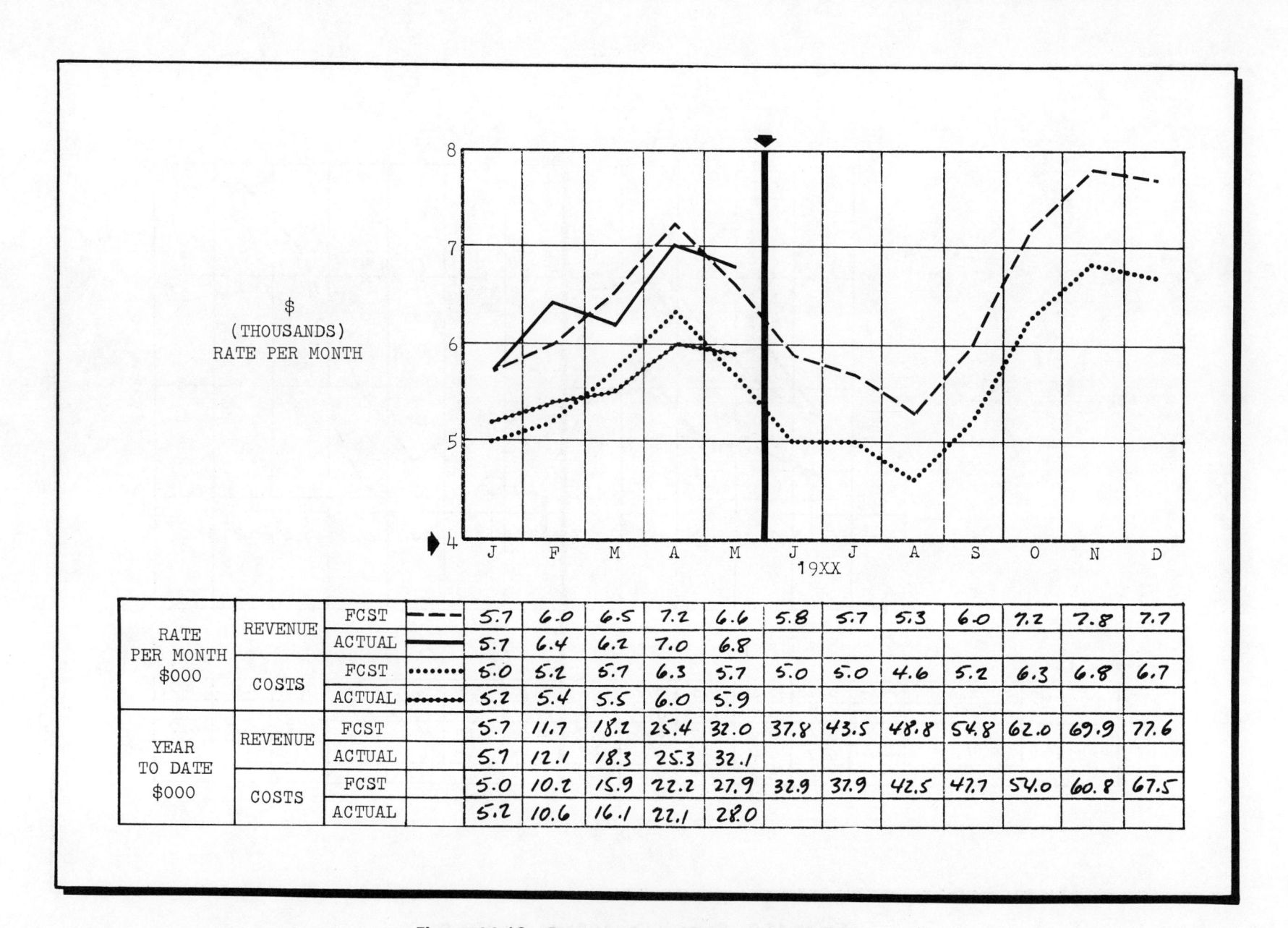

Figure 44.10 Revenue Versus Costs—Version 10

CATEGORY			\multicolumn{12}{c}{19XX}
			J	F	M	A	M	J	J	A	S	O	N	D
REVENUE $ 000	FORECAST	MONTHLY	5.7	6.0	6.5	7.2	6.6	5.8	5.7	5.3	6.0	7.2	7.8	7.7
		YEAR-TO-DATE	5.7	11.7	18.2	25.4	32.0	37.8	43.5	48.8	54.8	62.0	69.9	77.6
	ACTUAL	MONTHLY	5.7	6.4	6.2	7.0	6.8							
		YEAR-TO-DATE	5.7	12.1	18.3	25.3	32.1							
COSTS $ 000	BUDGET	MONTHLY	5.0	5.2	5.7	6.3	5.7	5.0	5.0	4.6	5.2	6.3	6.8	6.7
		YEAR-TO-DATE	5.0	10.2	15.9	22.2	27.9	32.9	37.9	42.5	47.7	54.0	60.8	67.5
	ACTUAL	MONTHLY	5.2	5.4	5.5	6.0	5.9							
		YEAR-TO-DATE	5.2	10.6	16.1	22.1	28.0							
	REVISED BUDGET	MONTHLY	5.0	5.6	5.4	6.1	5.9							
		YEAR-TO-DATE	5.0	10.6	16.0	22.1	28.0							

Figure 44.11 Revenue Versus Costs—Version 11

45.0 SALES

This section contains chart examples that deal with sales in terms of dollars and percentages.

45.1 Sales—Version 1: A simple version of a sales tracking chart is shown in Version 1, Figure 45.1. In this example, cumulative statistics for a year are plotted in terms of the sales plan, or forecast, and the actual sales. The legend is located in the footnote section of this example, together with the value of the current cumulative variance between planned and actual sales.

45.2 Sales—Version 2: Version 2 of a sales chart, Figure 45.2, is identical to Version 1 except that a paired column format is used instead of the line curve style that was used in Version 1.

45.3 Sales—Version 3: In some businesses it is customary to make new annual sales forecasts every quarter of the fiscal year. The chart shown in Figure 45.3 shows the first quarter forecast with a dashed line and the second quarter forecast with a dotted line. Actual sales, up to the reporting date, are shown with a solid line.

45.4 Sales—Version 4: Version 4 of a sales tracking chart, Figure 45.4, shows planned and actual sales together with minimum and maximum limits for management action. When actual sales exceed or fall below these limits, it is an indication for management to take corrective actions. Sales not meeting minimum requirements would require actions to increase sales or to cut back capabilities or capacities. Sales in excess of the maximum limit may exceed the seller's capacity or capability to produce or deliver.

45.5 Sales—Version 5: In normal circumstances, forecasted sales fall into several categories of probability of capture. In Version 5, Figure 45.5, three different categories are shown: firm business, forecasted new business, and "blue sky" business. The shading, in this example, indicates the sales forecast figures are stacked, the top dashed line representing the total plan. Actuals, in this example, are plotted only in terms of the top line . . . total plan.

45.6 Sales—Version 6: In Version 6 of a sales tracking chart, Figure 45.6, the year-end goal of $66,300 is plotted over the total time span. Weekly sales are annualized on a year-to-date basis so as to more easily relate the weekly sales to the year-end goal.

45.7 Sales—Version 7: Planned and actual performance in terms of weekly rate of sales are shown in step line form in Version 7 of a sales tracking chart, Figure 45.7. So that the chart reader's attention can be more easily drawn to unfavorable conditions, whenever actual sales fall under the plan, in this example, that portion of the chart has been shaded.

45.8 Sales—Version 8: A more complicated version of a sales tracking chart than shown in previous versions is displayed in Figure 45.8. Double scales are used in this example, the left-hand scale in terms of monthly sales and the right-hand scale in terms of year-to-date, or cumulative, sales.

45.9 Sales—Version 9: Sales performance in terms of percent deviation from plan is shown in the example in Figure 45.9. Zero represents the plan covering, in this example, the time span of a year. Limit lines for management action also are used. Corrective action is necessary when actuals exceed or fall below the limits.

45.10 Sales—Version 10: Version 10 of a sales tracking chart, Figure 45.10, displays one method for showing the current year's planned and actual sales in relationship to the previous year's sales.

45.11 Sales—Version 11: A method for showing forecasted and actual sales by quarters is displayed as Version 11 of a sales tracking chart, Figure 45.11. In this example, paired columns are used. Actual sales for two previous years are indicated with numerically coded deltas.

45.12 Sales—Version 12: Version 12 of a sales tracking chart, Figure 45.12, is identical to Version 11 except that the sales for the two previous years are shown with dashed step lines rather than with coded deltas.

45.13 Sales—Version 13: A method for showing the current year's forecasted and actual sales in relationship to performance in previous years and for what is forecasted for the coming year is shown as Version 13, Figure 45.13. In this example, the current year's planned and actual sales and the following year's forecasted quarterly sales have both been annualized for easier comparison with performance in previous years.

45.14 Sales—Version 14: A statistical table supplements a graphic chart in Version 14 of a sales tracking chart, Figure 45.14. In this example, three lines of statistics are shown—the cumulative planned sales, the cumulative actual sales, and the variance between those two figures.

45.15 Sales—Version 15: Version 15 of a sales tracking chart, Figure 45.15, is identical to Version 14 except that two additional lines of statistics have been added. These are the planned and actual sales figures in terms of rate per month. The graphic portion of the chart shows cumulative figures, only, as with the previous version.

45.16 Sales—Version 16: Space is provided in the statistical portion of Version 16 of a sales tracking chart, Figure 45.16, for entering each new quarterly forecast as it is made. Actual sales statistics are given as well. The cumulative variance, in this example, is given in terms of the latest forecast, only.

45.17 Sales—Version 17: A combination graph and statistical table shows forecasted and actual sales by category in Version 17 of a sales tracking chart, Figure 45.17. Statistics are given for firm business, new business, and "blue sky" business. Tracking, in this example, is done in terms of total sales, only.

45.18 Sales—Version 18: Version 18 of a sales tracking chart, Figure 45.18, is identical to Version 17 except in this version paired and segmented columns are used. Again, as with Version 17, tracking is done only in terms of total sales.

45.19 Sales—Version 19: Version 19 of a sales tracking chart, Figure 45.19, is identical to Version 17 and 18 except the graphic portion of Version 19 shows rate per month rather than cumulative sales. This form is useful when examining sales in terms of capacity and capability.

45.20 Sales—Version 20: One of the most complex forms of a sales tracking chart is shown in Figure 45.20. In this example, the chart consists of three parts: two graphic and one statistical section. Sales are plotted in graphic form in terms of cumulative sales on one grid, and rate-per-month sales on the other. The statistical portion of the chart shows all the statistics that are plotted, and gives the cumulative variances as well.

45.21 Sales—Version 21: A statistical table designed for tracking sales is shown in Version 21, Figure 45.21. In this particular example, the planned and actual sales statistics are broken down by the categories of firm business, new business, "blue sky" business, and totals. A check mark has been used, in this example, to draw the chart reader's attention to the most significant unfavorable condition.

Sales

45.22 Sales—Version 22: A segmented circle chart ("pie" chart) is used to show sales by major customer in Version 22 of a sales chart, Figure 45.22. This is a one-scale chart and is not useful for tracking purposes.

45.23 Sales—Version 23: Another version of a segmented circle chart is shown as Version 23, Figure 45.23. This example shows sales for one particular point in time in terms of product lines.

45.24 Sales—Version 24: Version 24 of a sales chart, Figure 45.24, is a two-scale chart showing the mix of product line sales covering a ten-year period. Like the "pie" chart, this example is not a tracking chart and is useful primarily for information, or trend-indicating, purposes.

45.25 Sales—Version 25: A commonly used trend-indicating, non-tracking chart is shown in Version 25, Figure 45.25. This is a column chart covering a ten-year segment of time. Each column, in this example, is segmented into two portions, hardware sales and service sales. This example shows that service sales have increased more significantly than hardware sales. An alternate to this type of chart would be to segment the columns as to government and non-government business, or according to other similar factors.

45.26 Sales—Version 26: Another type of trend-indicating, non-tracking chart is shown as Version 26, Figure 45.26. In this example, existing firm and prospective sales are stacked on a rate-per-month basis. This type of information chart can be useful when examining business in terms of capacities and capabilities.

45.27 Sales—Version 27: A non-tracking statistical table and a graph are combined in Version 27 of a sales chart, Figure 45.27. Sales are shown in segmented columns, by quarters, and statistical backup data, by customer and prospect, are provided in the table on the right-hand portion of the chart.

45.28 Sales—Version 28: A "box score" type of one-time status report is shown as Version 28, Figure 45.28. In this example, status for a given point in time is given in terms of planned and actual sales and the variance between these two factors.

45.29 Sales—Version 29: A more complicated style of box score is shown in Version 29 of a sales chart, Figure 45.29. A check mark is used, in this example, to draw the chart reader's attention to the most unfavorable condition. The disadvantage of this style of chart is that it must be completely redone for each new reporting period.

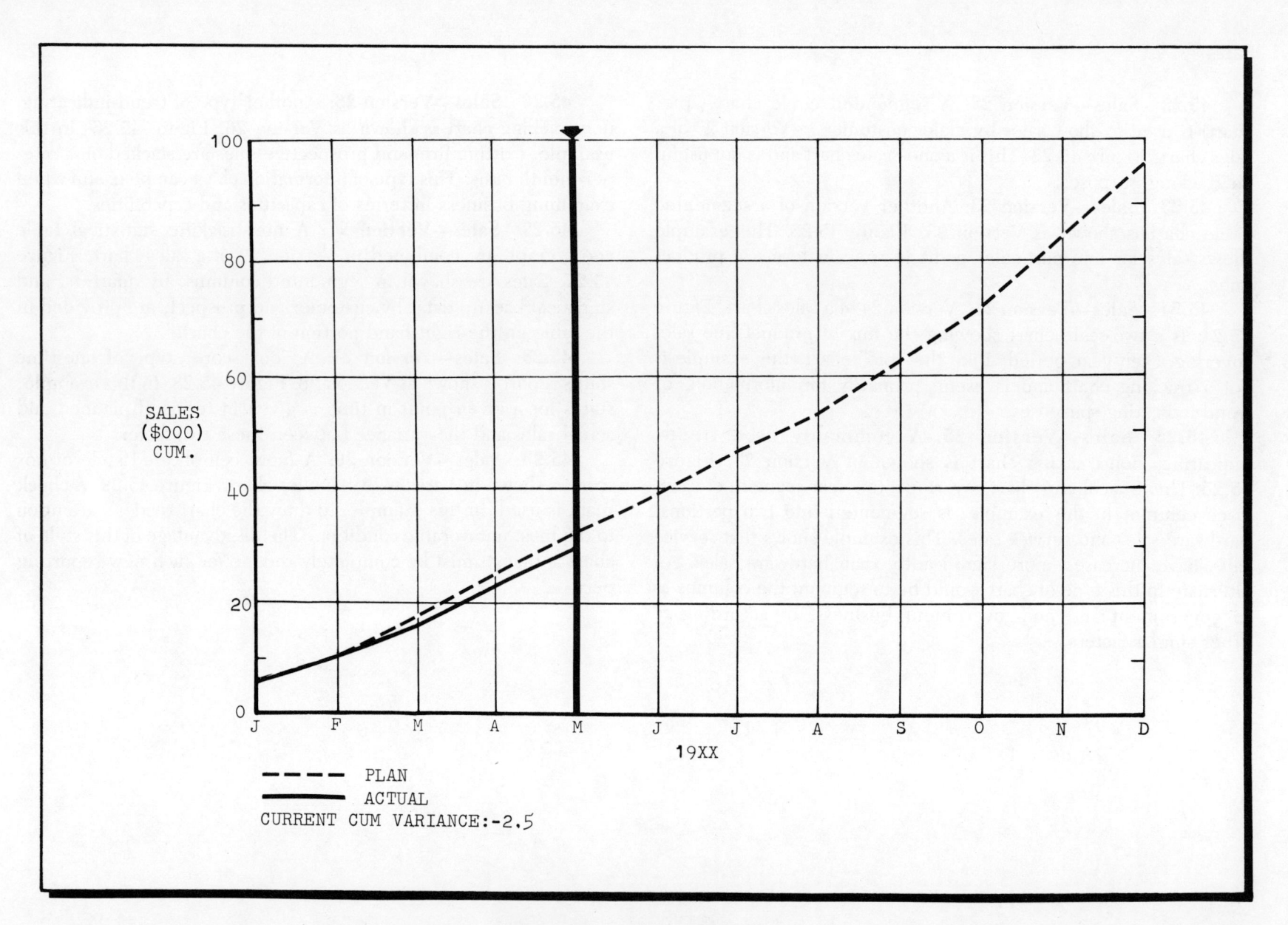

Figure 45.1   Sales—Version 1

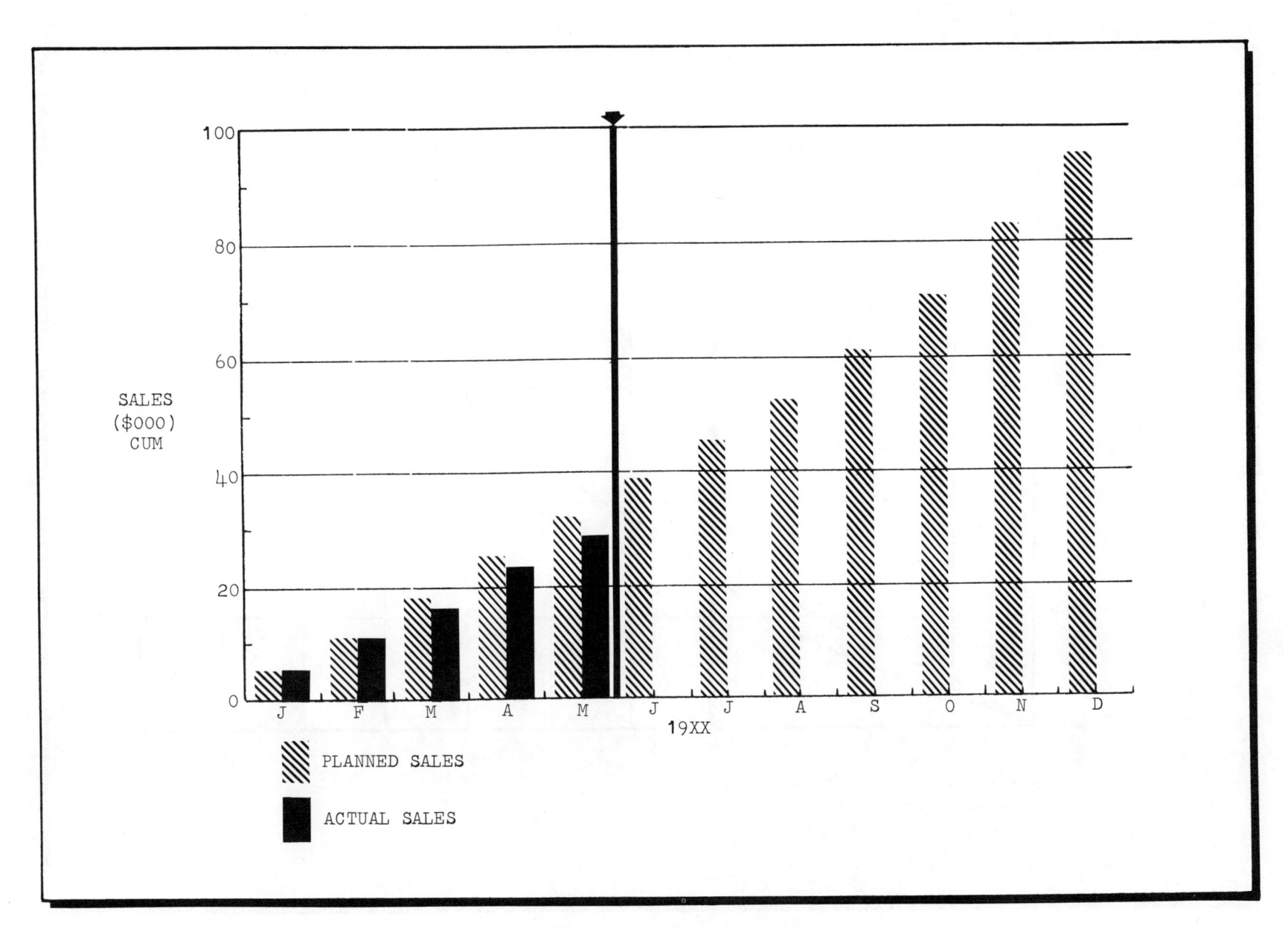

Figure 45.2   Sales—Version 2

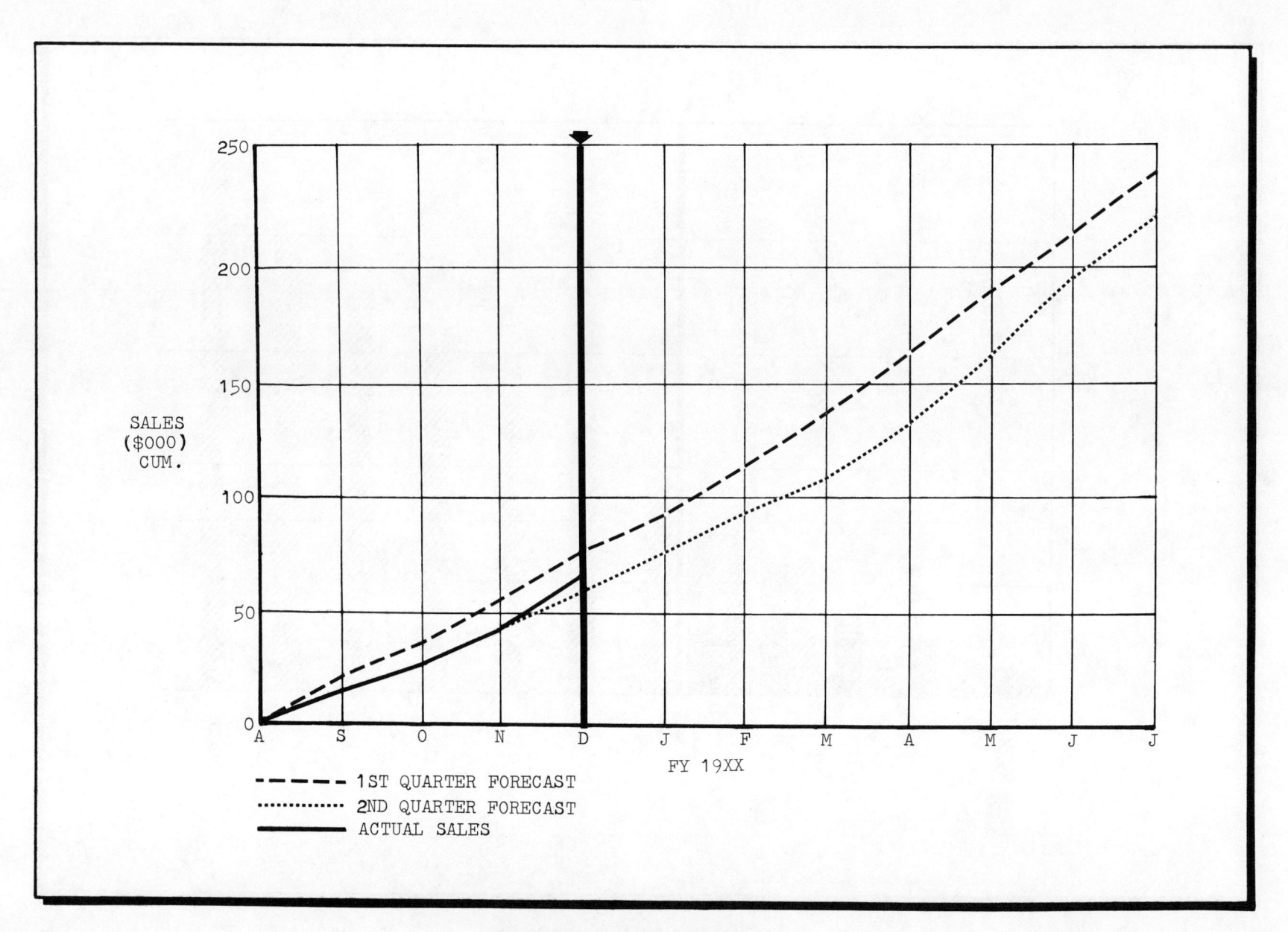

Figure 45.3 Sales—Version 3

528

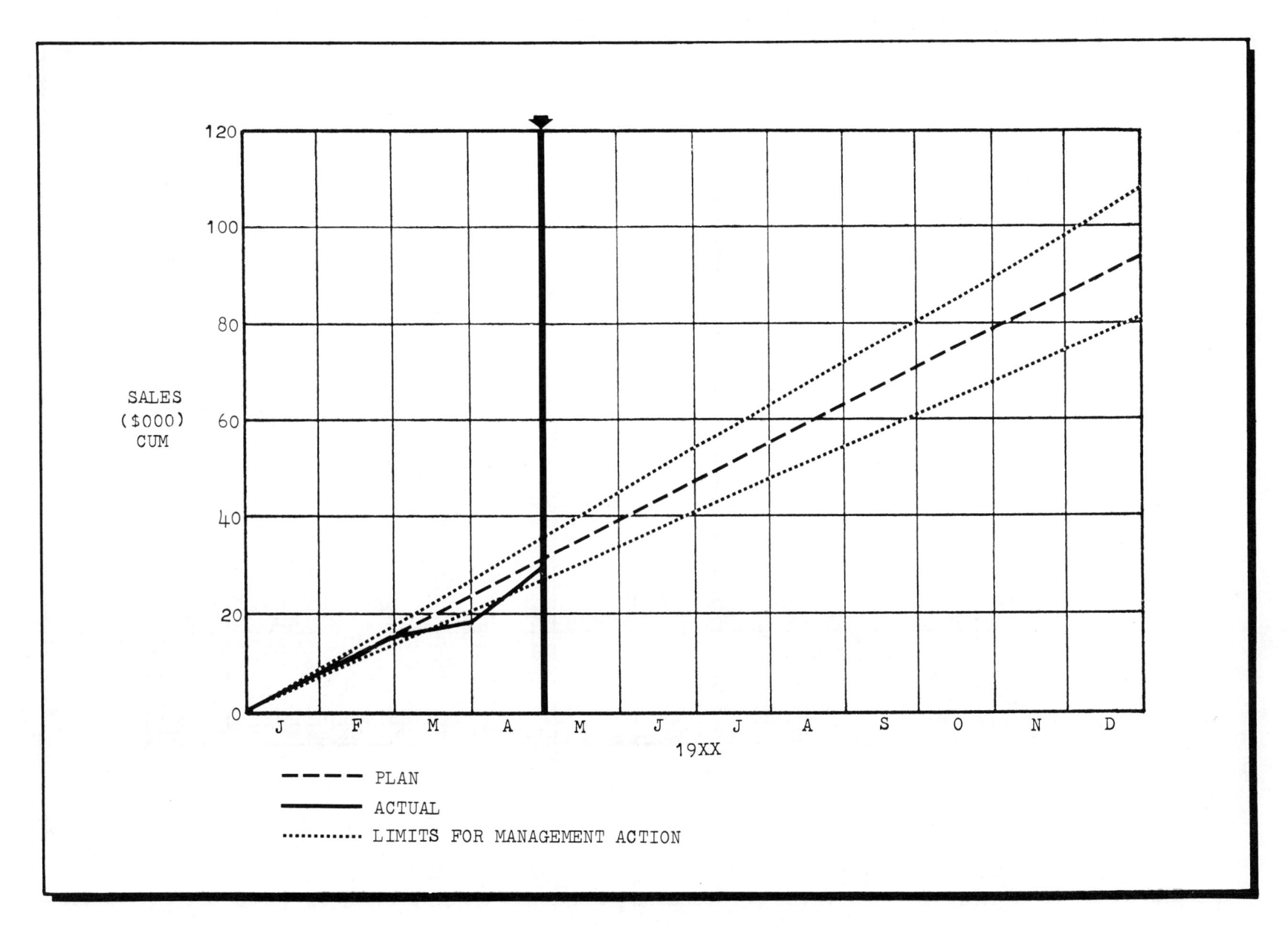

Figure 45.4 Sales—Version 4

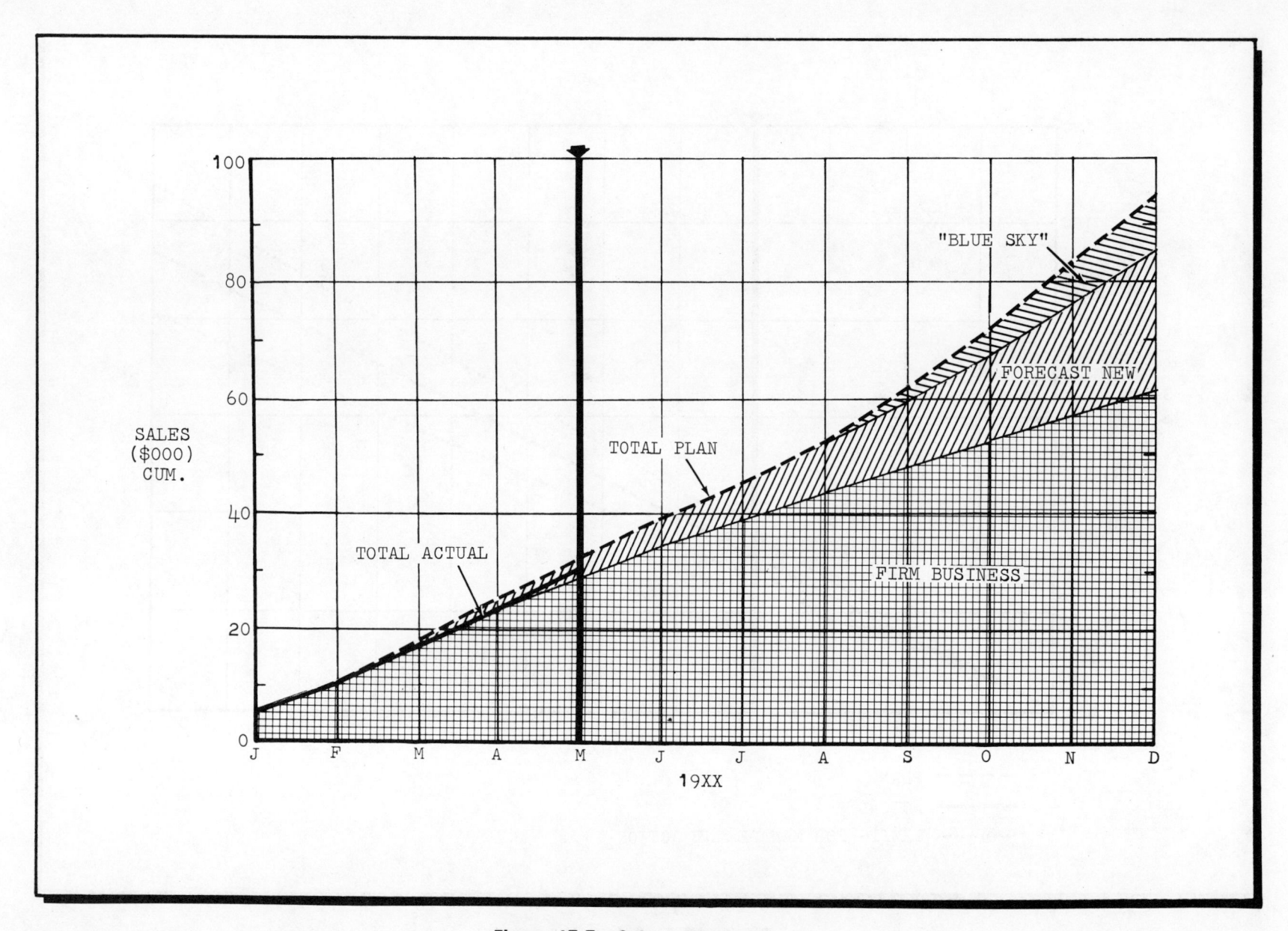

Figure 45.5   Sales—Version 5

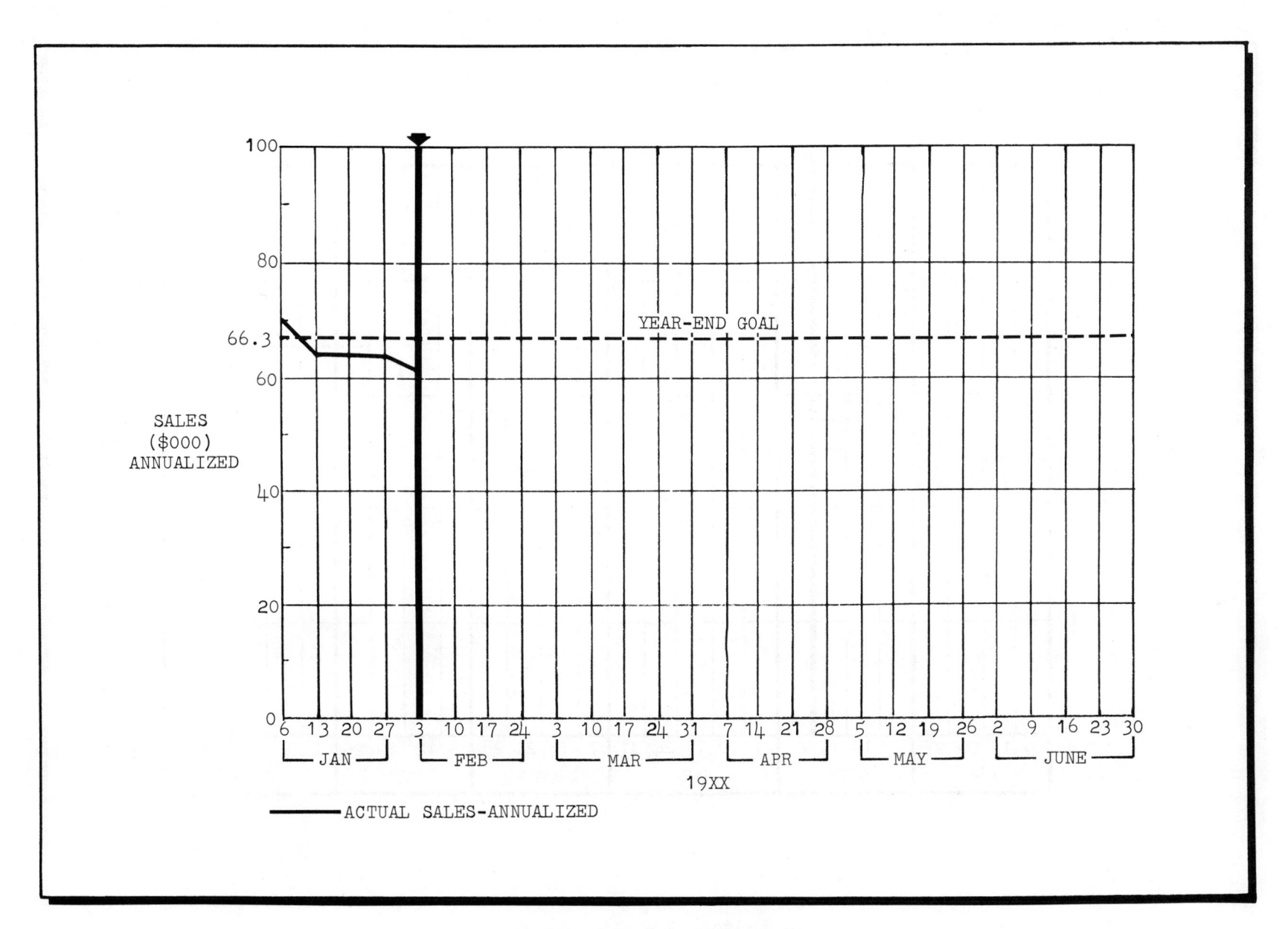

Figure 45.6 Sales—Version 6

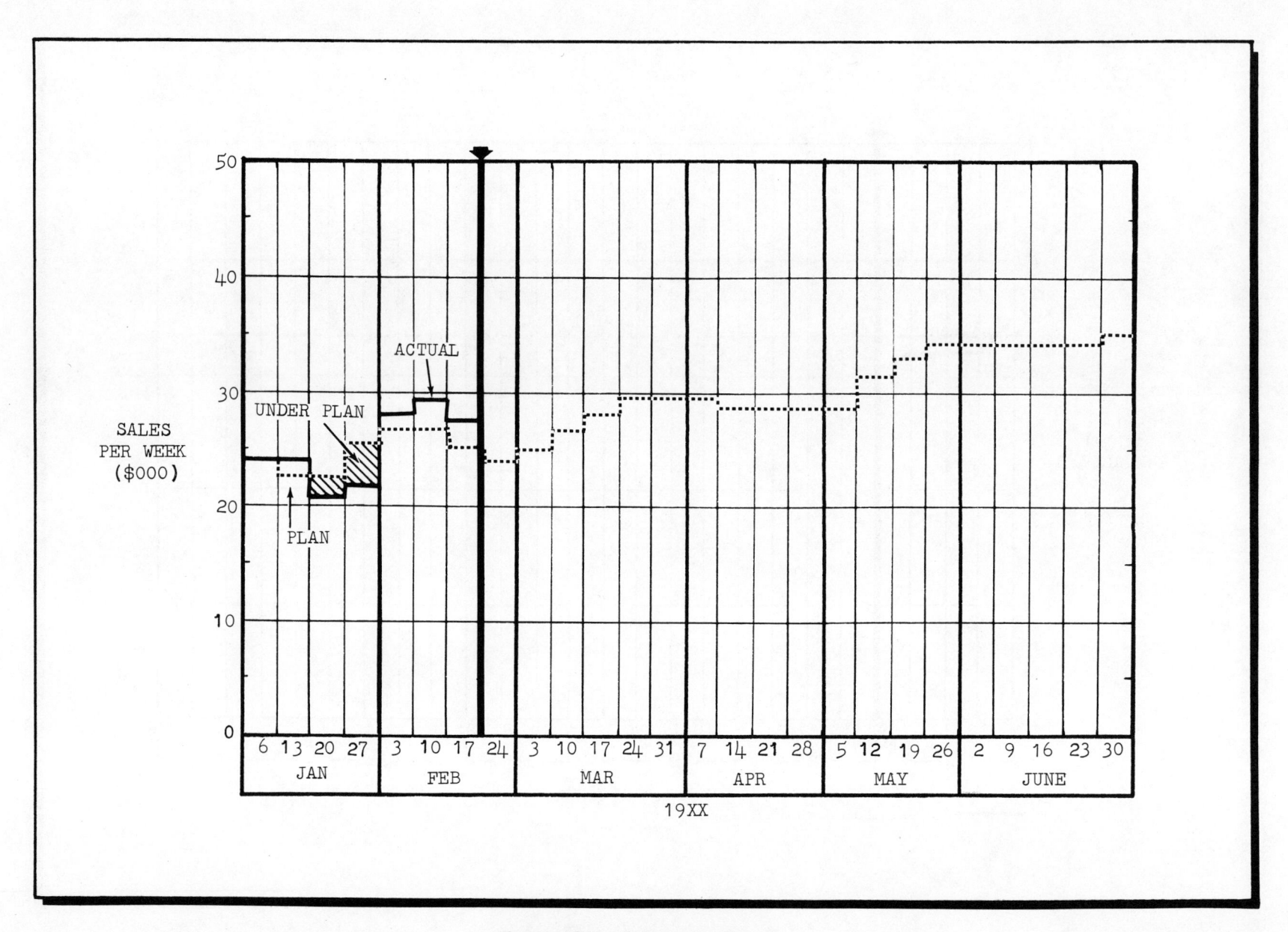

Figure 45.7 Sales—Version 7

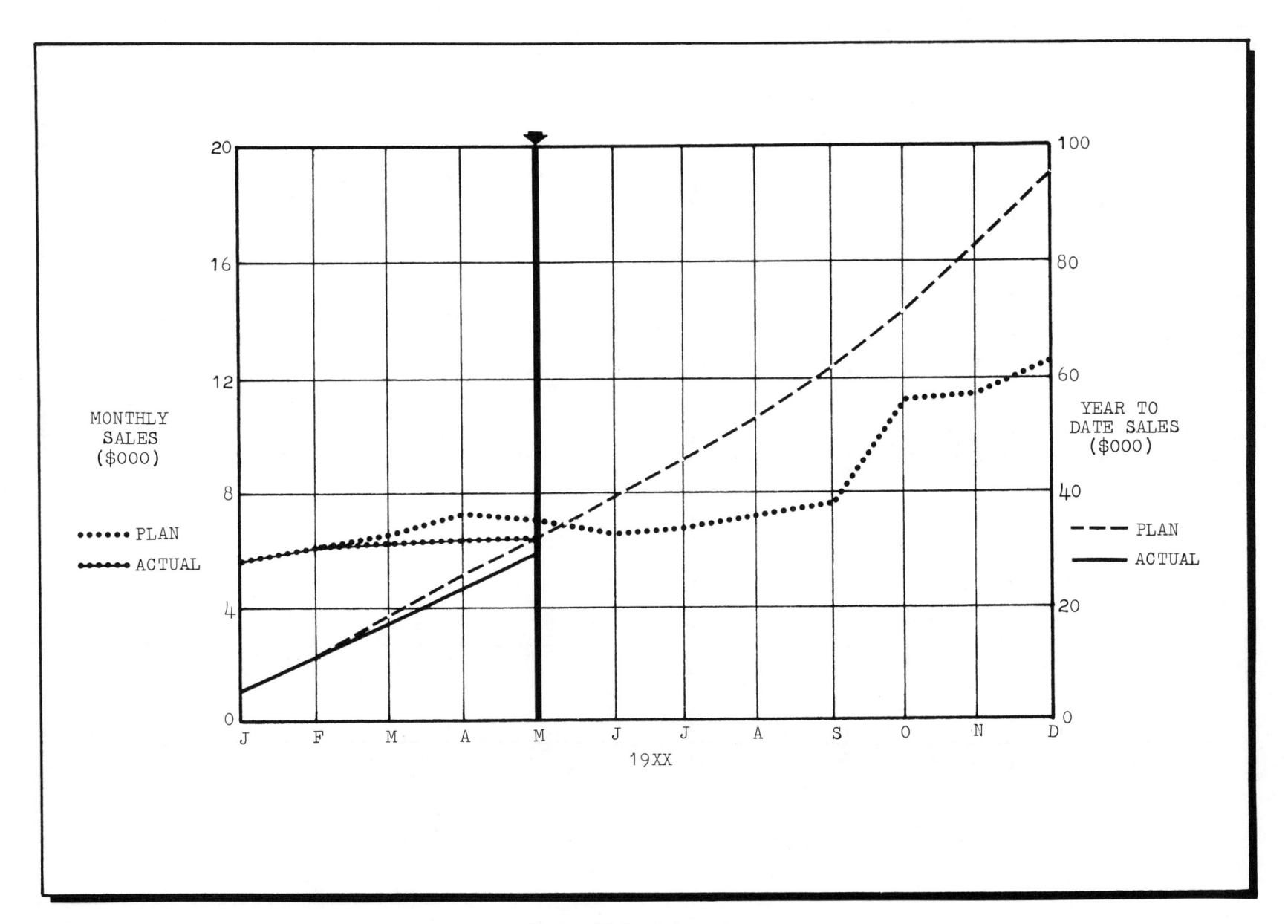

Figure 45.8   Sales—Version 8

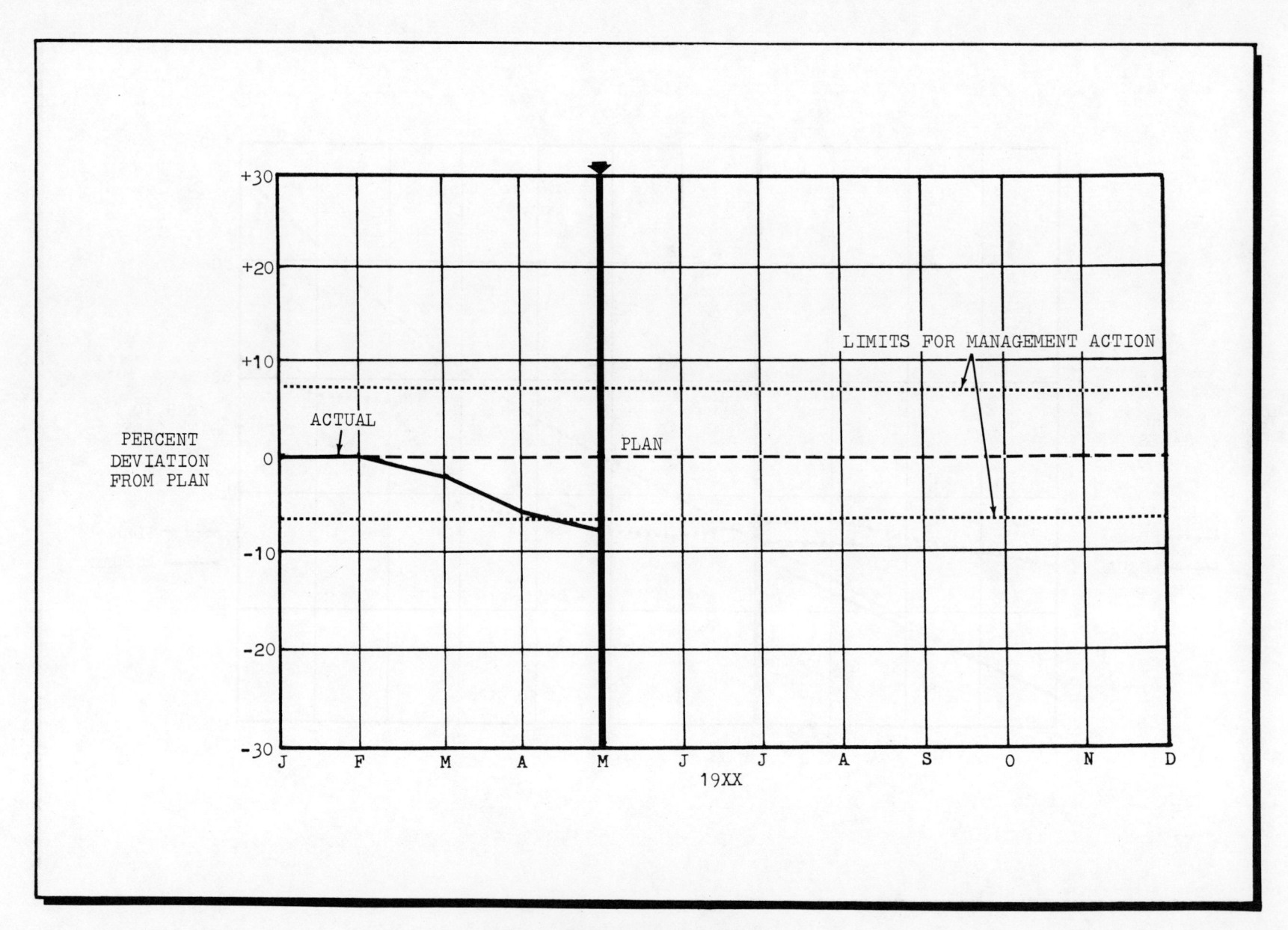

Figure 45.9 Sales—Version 9

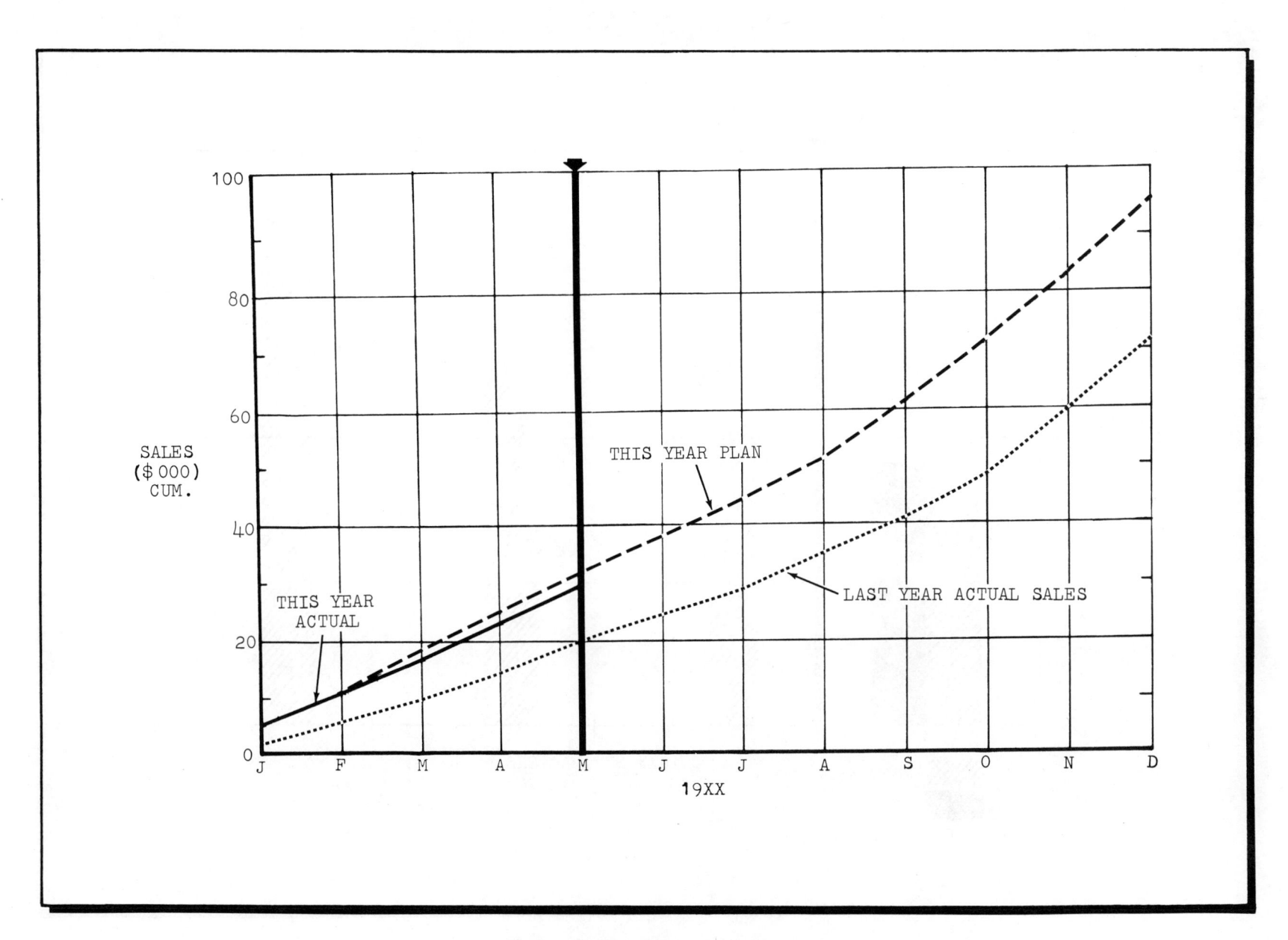

Figure 45.10   Sales—Version 10

QUARTERLY SALES ($000)

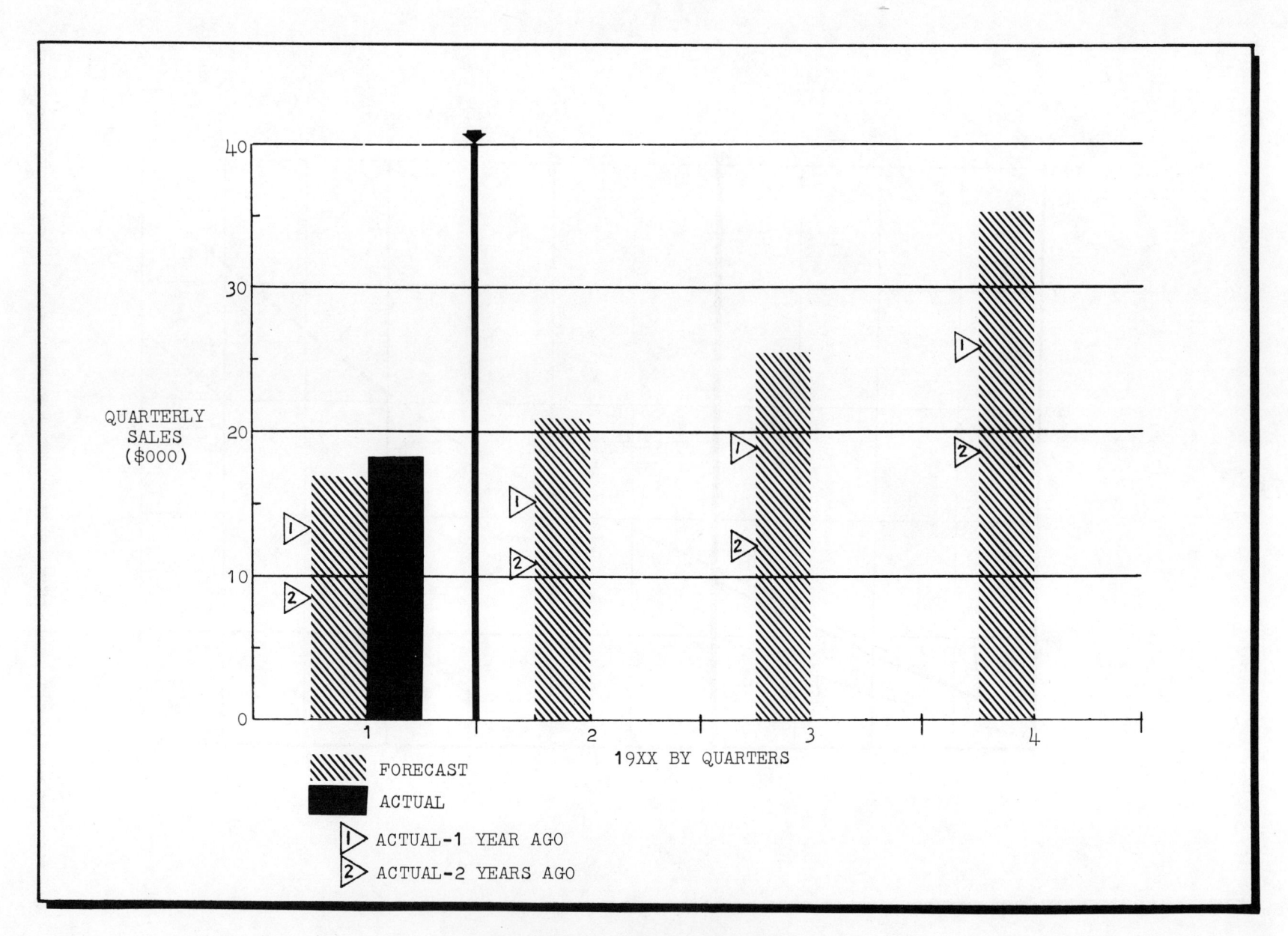

19XX BY QUARTERS

▨ FORECAST
■ ACTUAL
▷1 ACTUAL—1 YEAR AGO
▷2 ACTUAL—2 YEARS AGO

Figure 45.11   Sales—Version 11

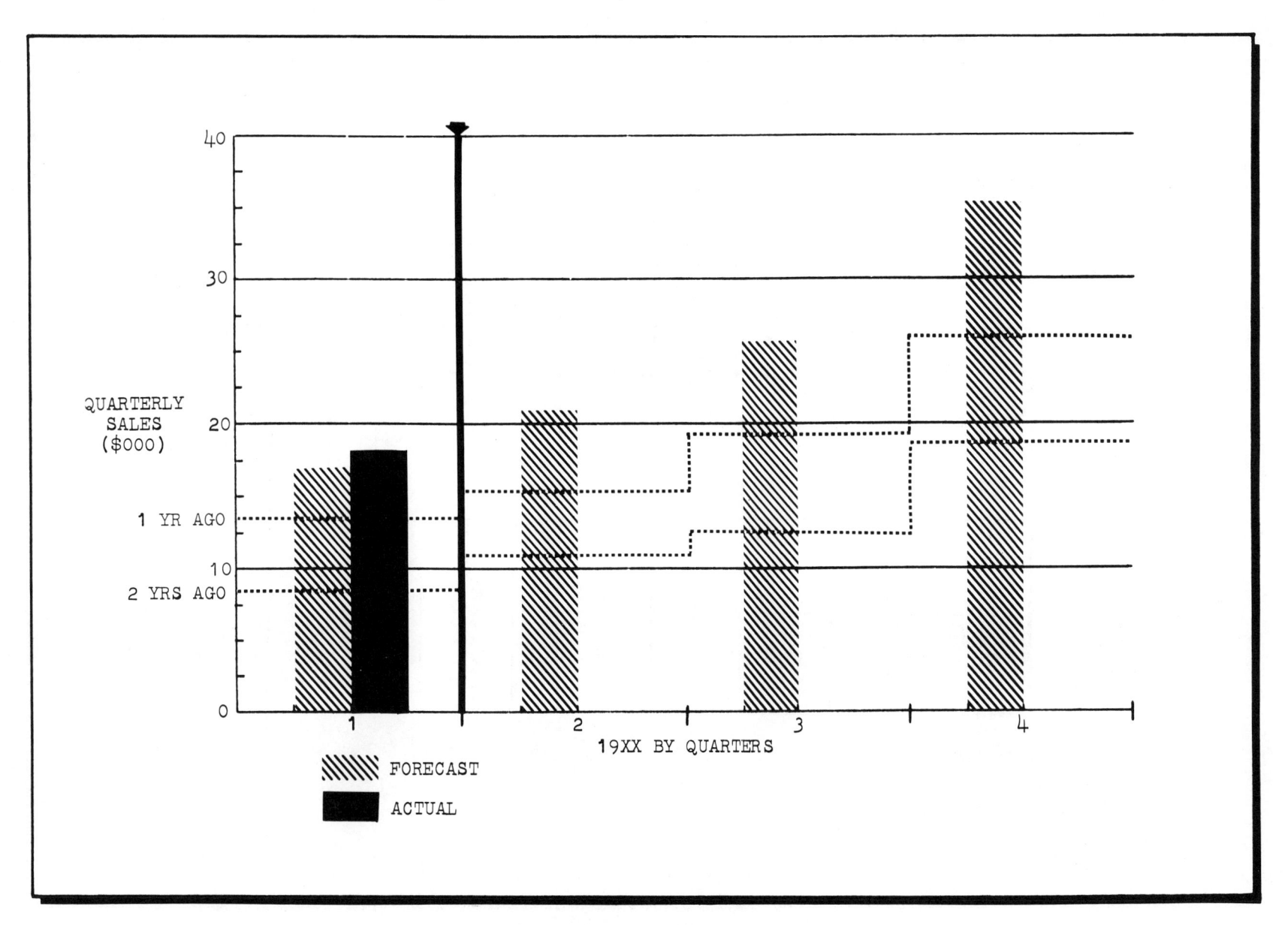

Figure 45.12   Sales—Version 12

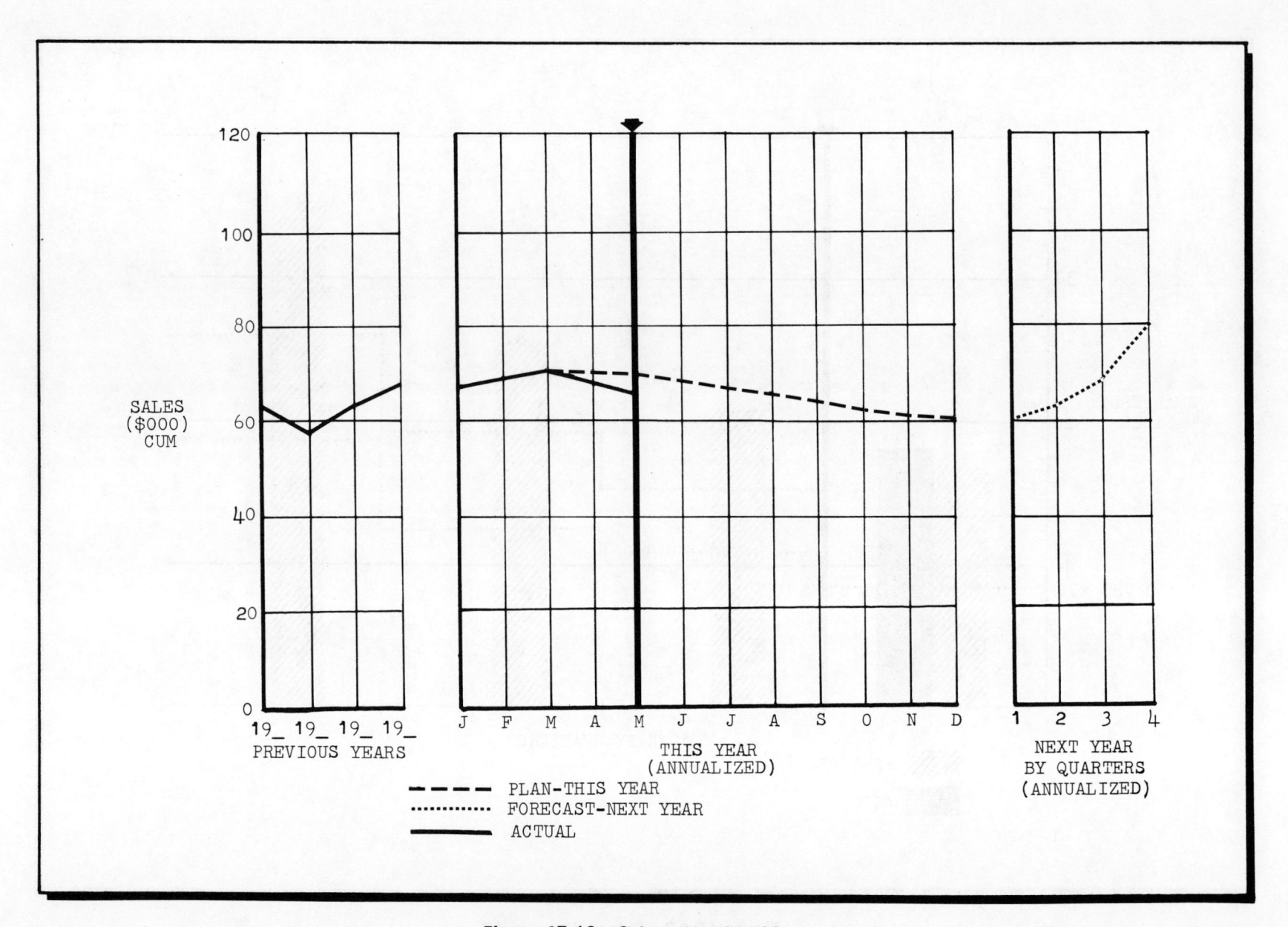

Figure 45.13 Sales—Version 13

538

SALES
($000)
CUM

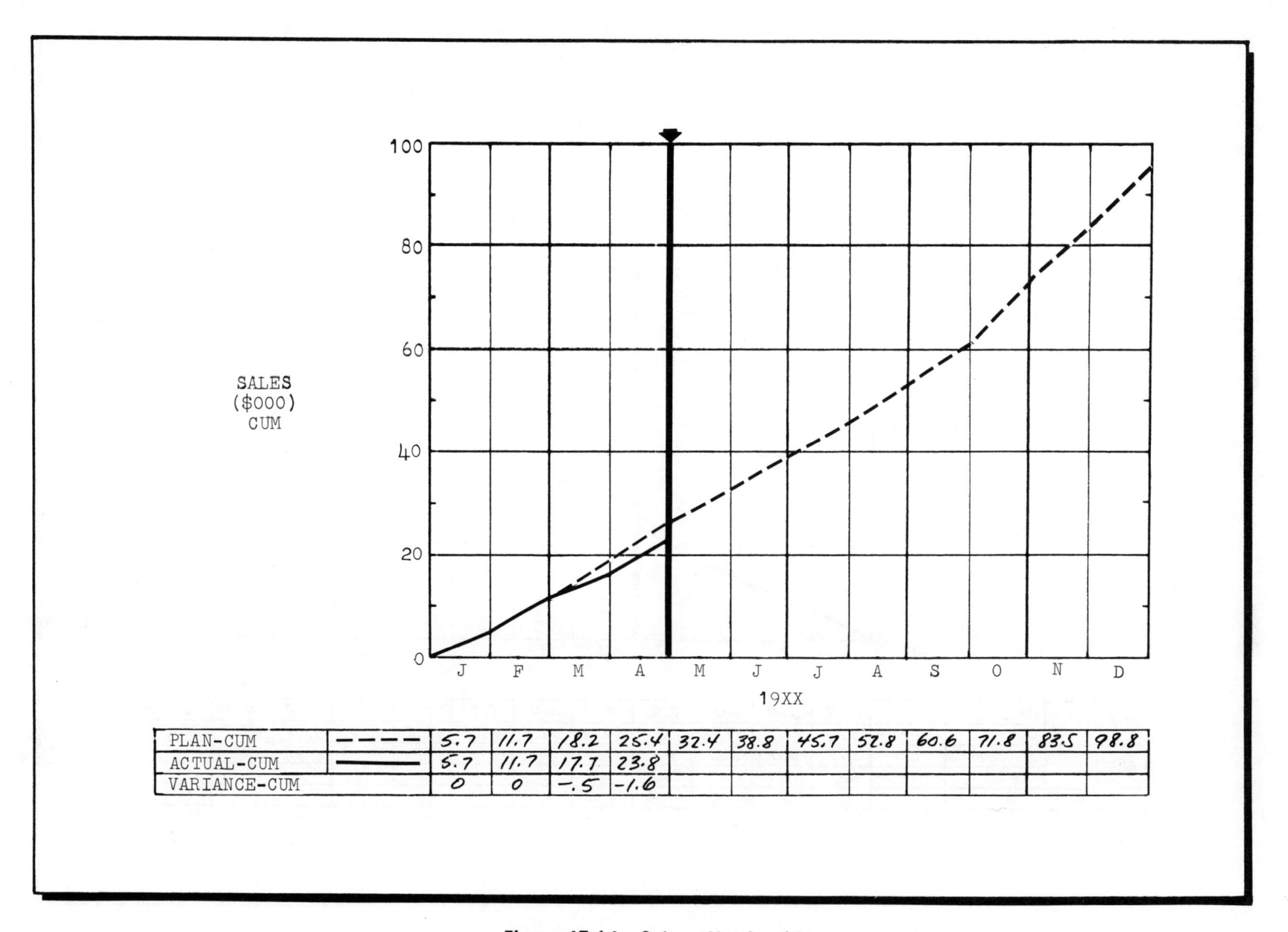

		J	F	M	A	M	J	J	A	S	O	N	D
PLAN-CUM	– – –	5.7	11.7	18.2	25.4	32.4	38.8	45.7	52.8	60.6	71.8	83.5	98.8
ACTUAL-CUM	——	5.7	11.7	17.7	23.8								
VARIANCE-CUM		0	0	-.5	-1.6								

Figure 45.14 Sales—Version 14

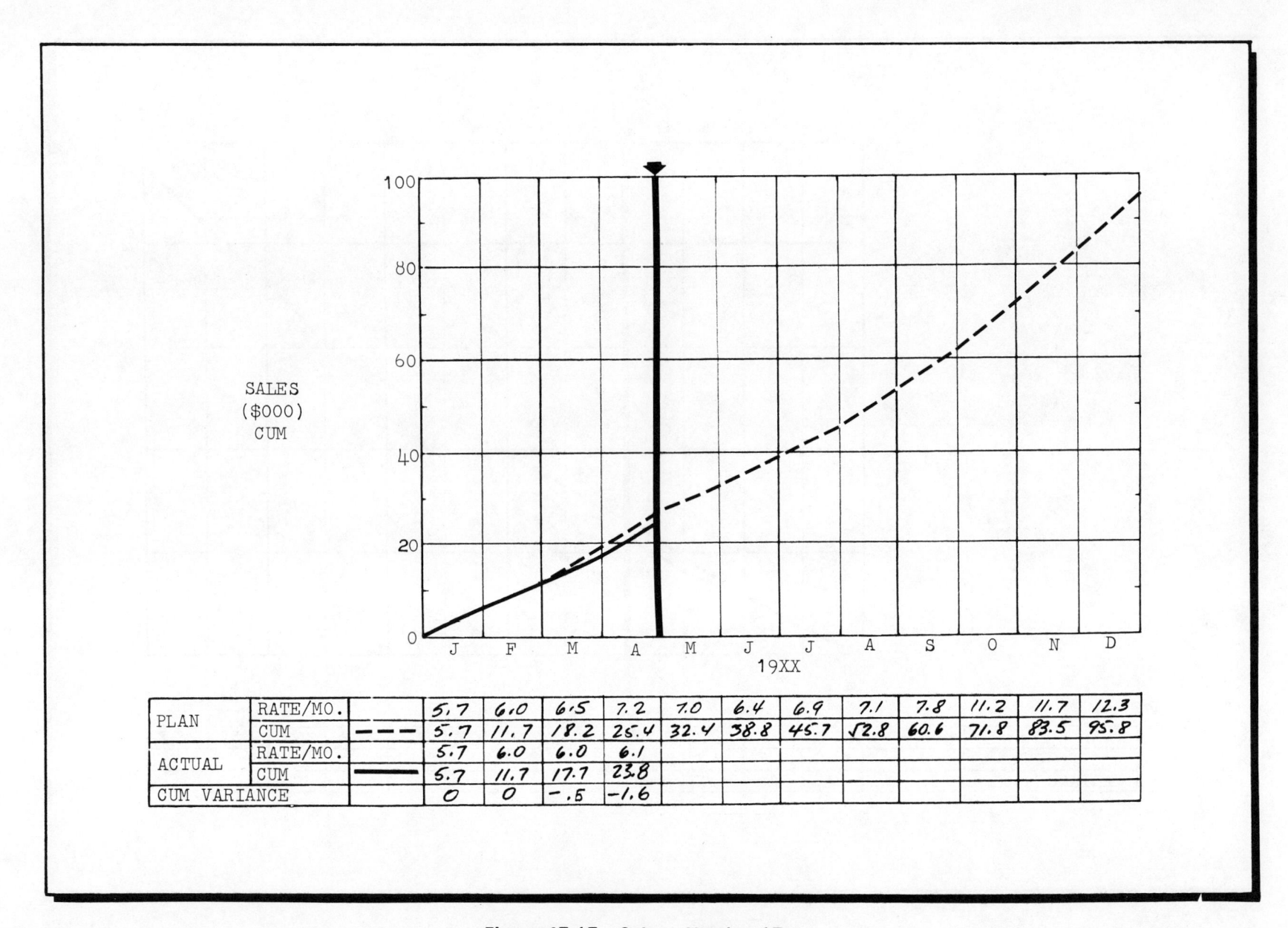

PLAN	RATE/MO.		5.7	6.0	6.5	7.2	7.0	6.4	6.9	7.1	7.8	11.2	11.7	12.3
	CUM	– – – –	5.7	11.7	18.2	25.4	32.4	38.8	45.7	52.8	60.6	71.8	83.5	95.8
ACTUAL	RATE/MO.		5.7	6.0	6.0	6.1								
	CUM	————	5.7	11.7	17.7	23.8								
CUM VARIANCE			0	0	-.5	-1.6								

Figure 45.15   Sales—Version 15

CUMULATIVE

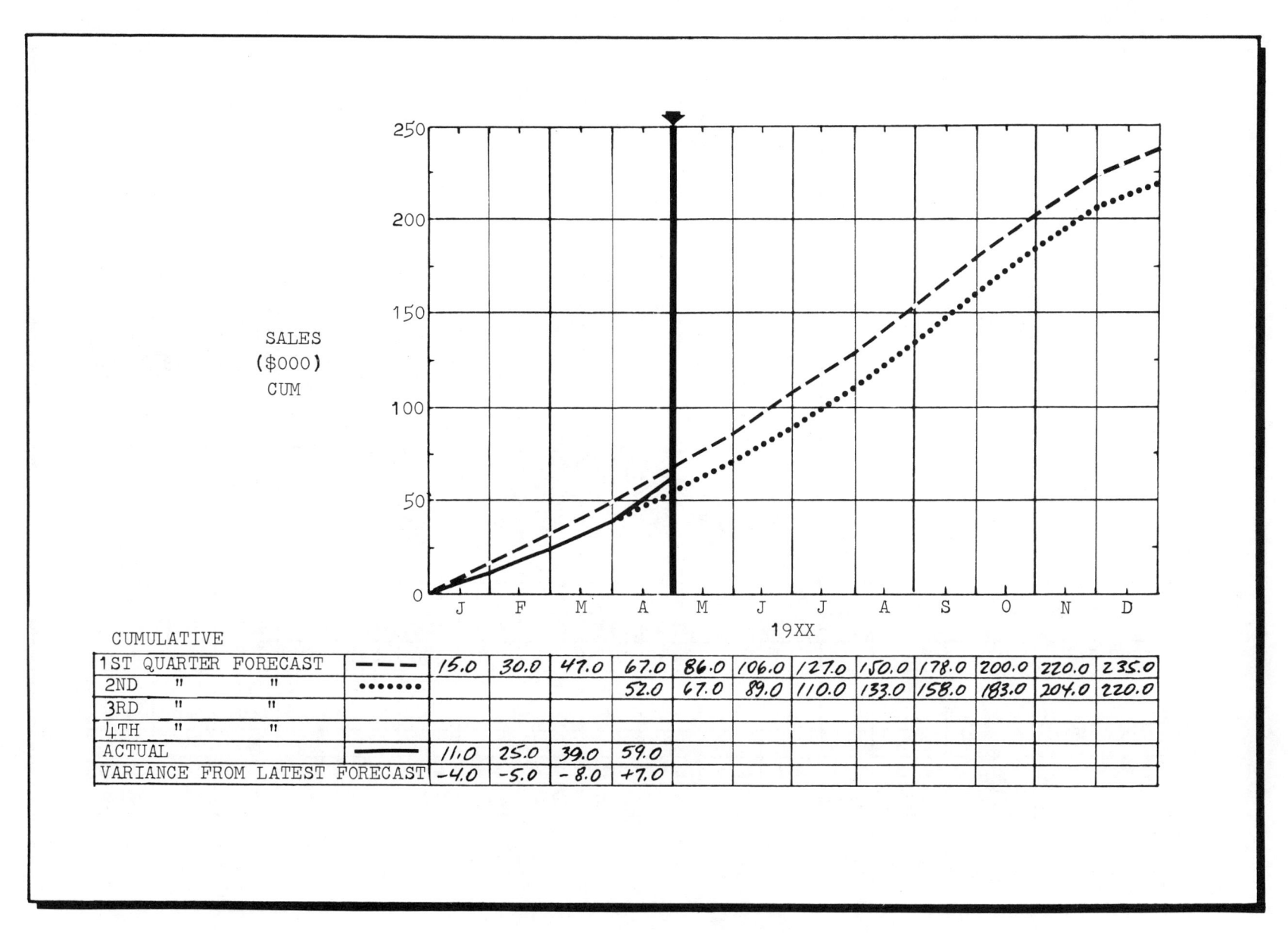

		J	F	M	A	M	J	J	A	S	O	N	D
1ST QUARTER FORECAST	— — —	15.0	30.0	47.0	67.0	86.0	106.0	127.0	150.0	178.0	200.0	220.0	235.0
2ND " "	• • • • • •				52.0	67.0	89.0	110.0	133.0	158.0	183.0	204.0	220.0
3RD " "													
4TH " "													
ACTUAL	————	11.0	25.0	39.0	59.0								
VARIANCE FROM LATEST FORECAST		-4.0	-5.0	-8.0	+7.0								

Figure 45.16 Sales—Version 16

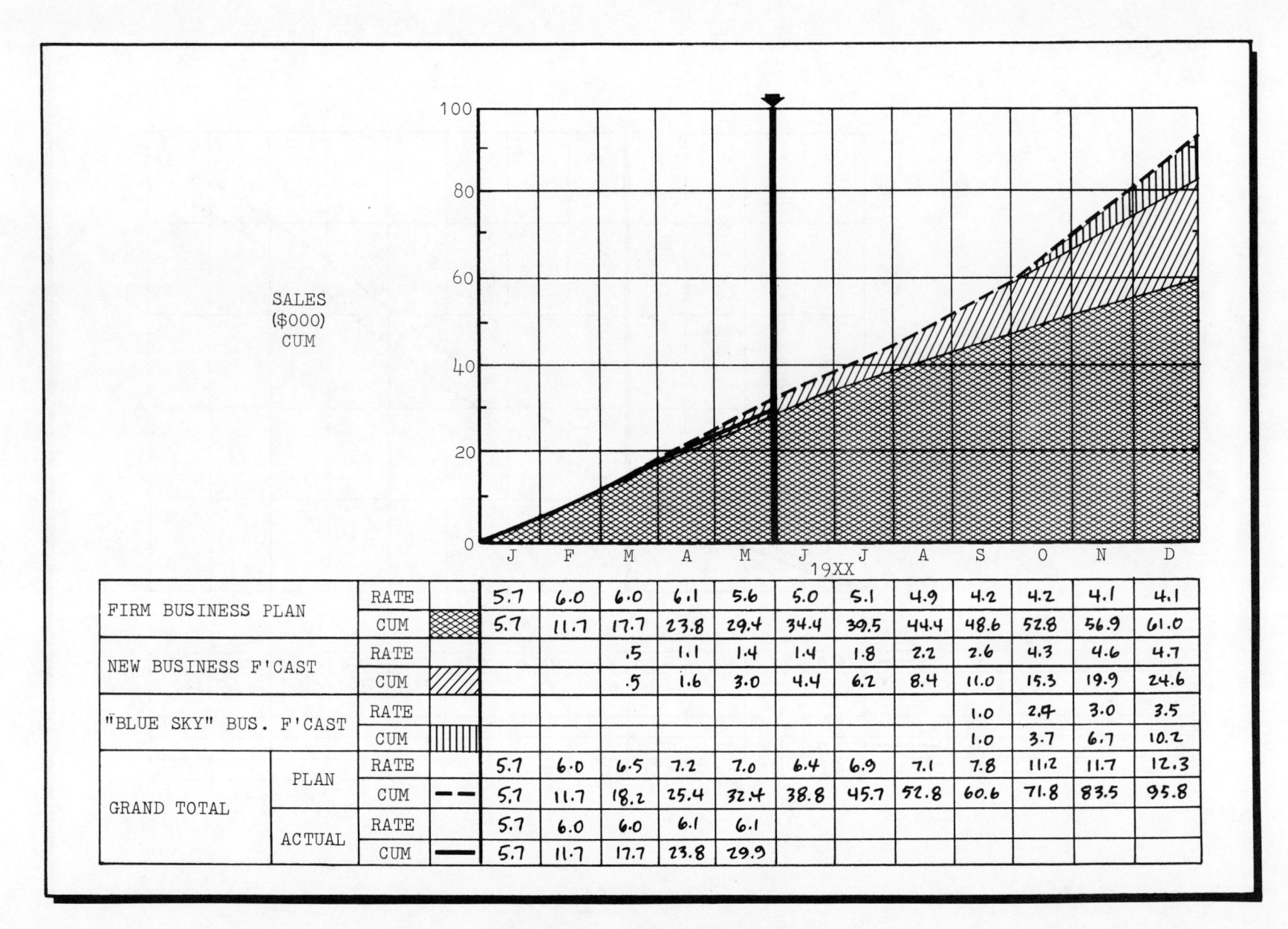

			J	F	M	A	M	J	J	A	S	O	N	D
FIRM BUSINESS PLAN		RATE	5.7	6.0	6.0	6.1	5.6	5.0	5.1	4.9	4.2	4.2	4.1	4.1
		CUM	5.7	11.7	17.7	23.8	29.4	34.4	39.5	44.4	48.6	52.8	56.9	61.0
NEW BUSINESS F'CAST		RATE			.5	1.1	1.4	1.4	1.8	2.2	2.6	4.3	4.6	4.7
		CUM			.5	1.6	3.0	4.4	6.2	8.4	11.0	15.3	19.9	24.6
"BLUE SKY" BUS. F'CAST		RATE										1.0	2.7	3.0	3.5
		CUM										1.0	3.7	6.7	10.2
GRAND TOTAL	PLAN	RATE	5.7	6.0	6.5	7.2	7.0	6.4	6.9	7.1	7.8	11.2	11.7	12.3
		CUM	5.7	11.7	18.2	25.4	32.4	38.8	45.7	52.8	60.6	71.8	83.5	95.8
	ACTUAL	RATE	5.7	6.0	6.0	6.1	6.1							
		CUM	5.7	11.7	17.7	23.8	29.9							

Figure 45.17   Sales—Version 17

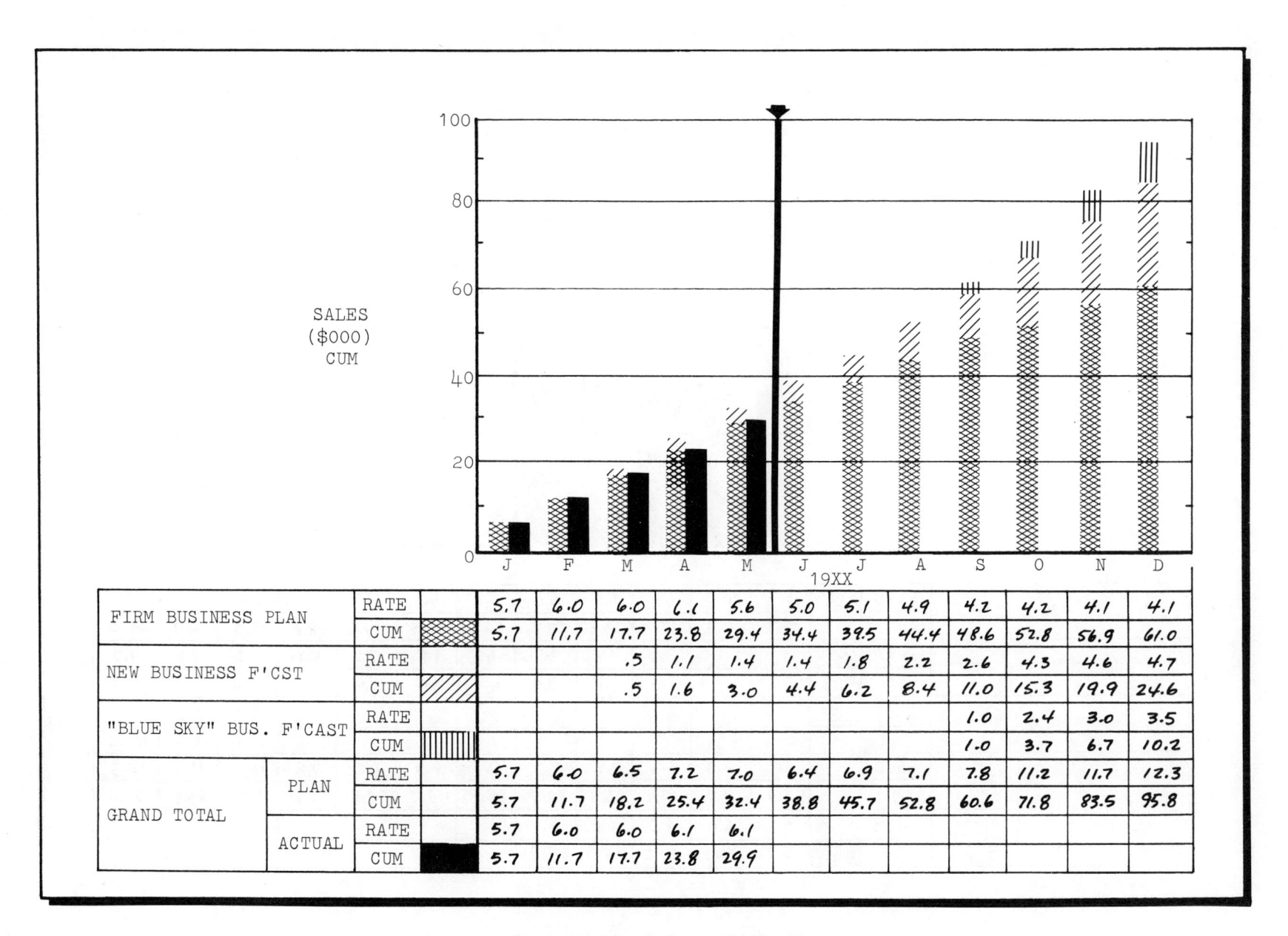

			J	F	M	A	M	J	J	A	S	O	N	D
FIRM BUSINESS PLAN		RATE	5.7	6.0	6.0	6.1	5.6	5.0	5.1	4.9	4.2	4.2	4.1	4.1
		CUM	5.7	11.7	17.7	23.8	29.4	34.4	39.5	44.4	48.6	52.8	56.9	61.0
NEW BUSINESS F'CST		RATE			.5	1.1	1.4	1.4	1.8	2.2	2.6	4.3	4.6	4.7
		CUM			.5	1.6	3.0	4.4	6.2	8.4	11.0	15.3	19.9	24.6
"BLUE SKY" BUS. F'CAST		RATE									1.0	2.4	3.0	3.5
		CUM									1.0	3.7	6.7	10.2
GRAND TOTAL	PLAN	RATE	5.7	6.0	6.5	7.2	7.0	6.4	6.9	7.1	7.8	11.2	11.7	12.3
		CUM	5.7	11.7	18.2	25.4	32.4	38.8	45.7	52.8	60.6	71.8	83.5	95.8
	ACTUAL	RATE	5.7	6.0	6.0	6.1	6.1							
		CUM	5.7	11.7	17.7	23.8	29.9							

Figure 45.18 Sales—Version 18

SALES
($000)
RATE PER MONTH

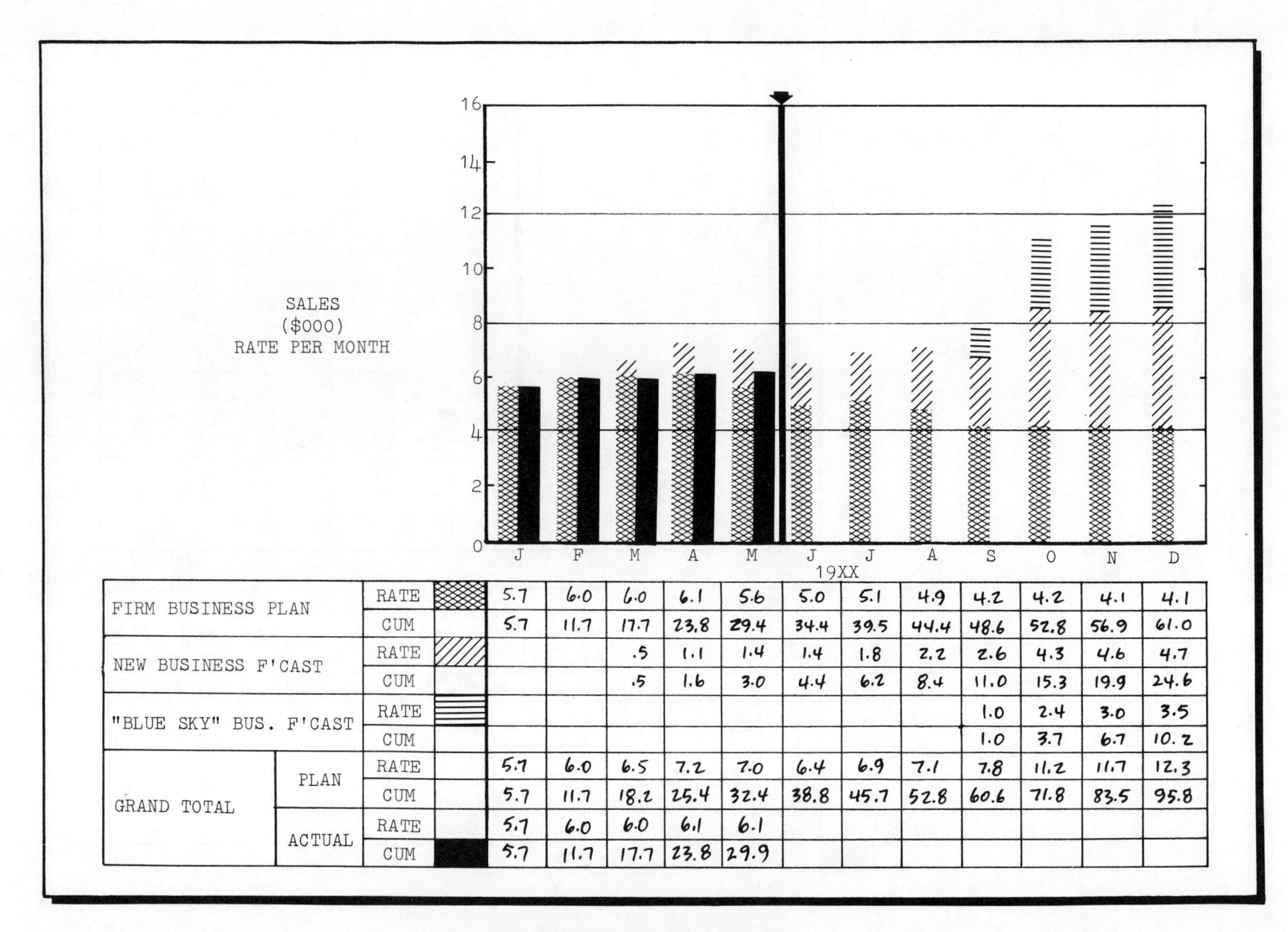

				J	F	M	A	M	J	J	A	S	O	N	D
FIRM BUSINESS PLAN		RATE	▦	5.7	6.0	6.0	6.1	5.6	5.0	5.1	4.9	4.2	4.2	4.1	4.1
		CUM		5.7	11.7	17.7	23.8	29.4	34.4	39.5	44.4	48.6	52.8	56.9	61.0
NEW BUSINESS F'CAST		RATE	▨			.5	1.1	1.4	1.4	1.8	2.2	2.6	4.3	4.6	4.7
		CUM				.5	1.6	3.0	4.4	6.2	8.4	11.0	15.3	19.9	24.6
"BLUE SKY" BUS. F'CAST		RATE	≡									1.0	2.4	3.0	3.5
		CUM										1.0	3.7	6.7	10.2
GRAND TOTAL	PLAN	RATE		5.7	6.0	6.5	7.2	7.0	6.4	6.9	7.1	7.8	11.2	11.7	12.3
		CUM		5.7	11.7	18.2	25.4	32.4	38.8	45.7	52.8	60.6	71.8	83.5	95.8
	ACTUAL	RATE		5.7	6.0	6.0	6.1	6.1							
		CUM	■	5.7	11.7	17.7	23.8	29.9							

Figure 45.19   Sales—Version 19

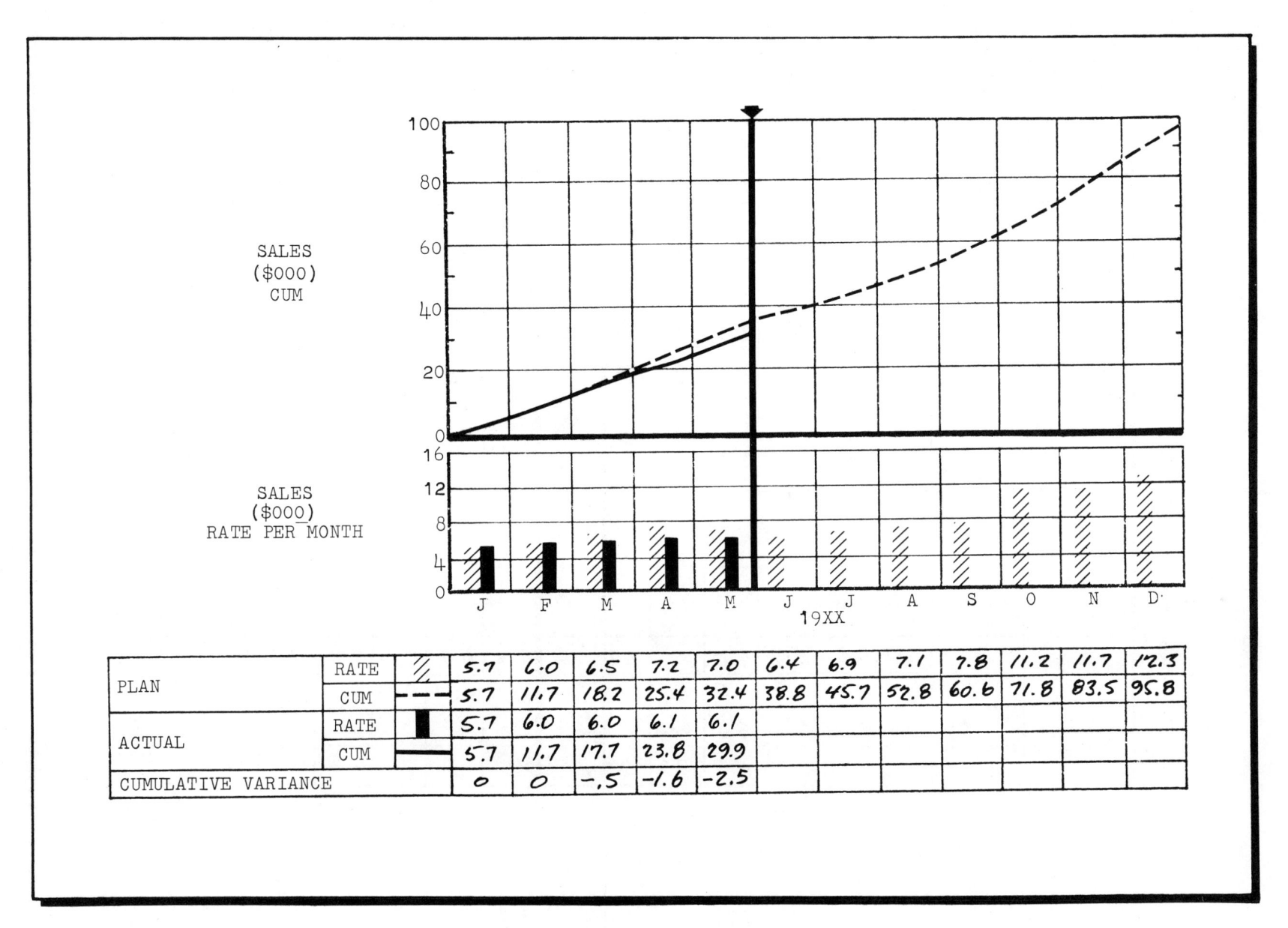

			J	F	M	A	M	J	J	A	S	O	N	D
PLAN	RATE	▨	5.7	6.0	6.5	7.2	7.0	6.4	6.9	7.1	7.8	11.2	11.7	12.3
	CUM	---	5.7	11.7	18.2	25.4	32.4	38.8	45.7	52.8	60.6	71.8	83.5	95.8
ACTUAL	RATE	▮	5.7	6.0	6.0	6.1	6.1							
	CUM	—	5.7	11.7	17.7	23.8	29.9							
CUMULATIVE VARIANCE			0	0	-.5	-1.6	-2.5							

Figure 45.20 Sales—Version 20

CATEGORY ($000)			19XX											
			J	F	M	A	M	J	J	A	S	O	N	D
FIRM BUSINESS	PLAN	RATE/MO	5.7	6.0	6.0	6.1	5.6	5.0	5.1	4.9	4.2	4.2	4.1	4.1
		CUM	5.7	11.7	17.7	23.8	29.4	34.4	39.5	44.4	48.6	52.8	56.9	61.0
	ACTUAL	RATE/MO	5.7	6.0	6.0	6.1	5.6							
		CUM	5.7	11.7	17.7	23.8	29.4							
NEW BUSINESS	FCST	RATE/MO			.5	1.1	1.4	1.4	1.8	2.2	2.6	4.3	4.6	4.7
		CUM			.5	1.6	3.0	4.4	6.2	8.4	11.0	15.3	19.9	24.6
	ACTUAL	RATE/MO			0	0	.5							
		CUM			0	0	.5							
"BLUE SKY" BUSINESS	FCST	RATE/MO									1.0	2.4	3.0	3.5
		CUM									1.0	3.7	6.7	10.2
	ACTUAL	RATE/MO												
		CUM												
GRAND TOTAL	PLAN	RATE/MO	5.7	6.0	6.5	7.2	7.0	6.4	6.9	7.1	7.8	11.2	11.7	12.3
		CUM	5.7	11.7	18.2	25.4	32.4	38.8	45.7	52.8	60.6	71.8	83.5	95.8
	ACTUAL	RATE/MO	5.7	6.0	6.0	6.1	6.1							
		CUM	5.7	11.7	17.7	23.8	29.9							

Figure 45.21 Sales—Version 21

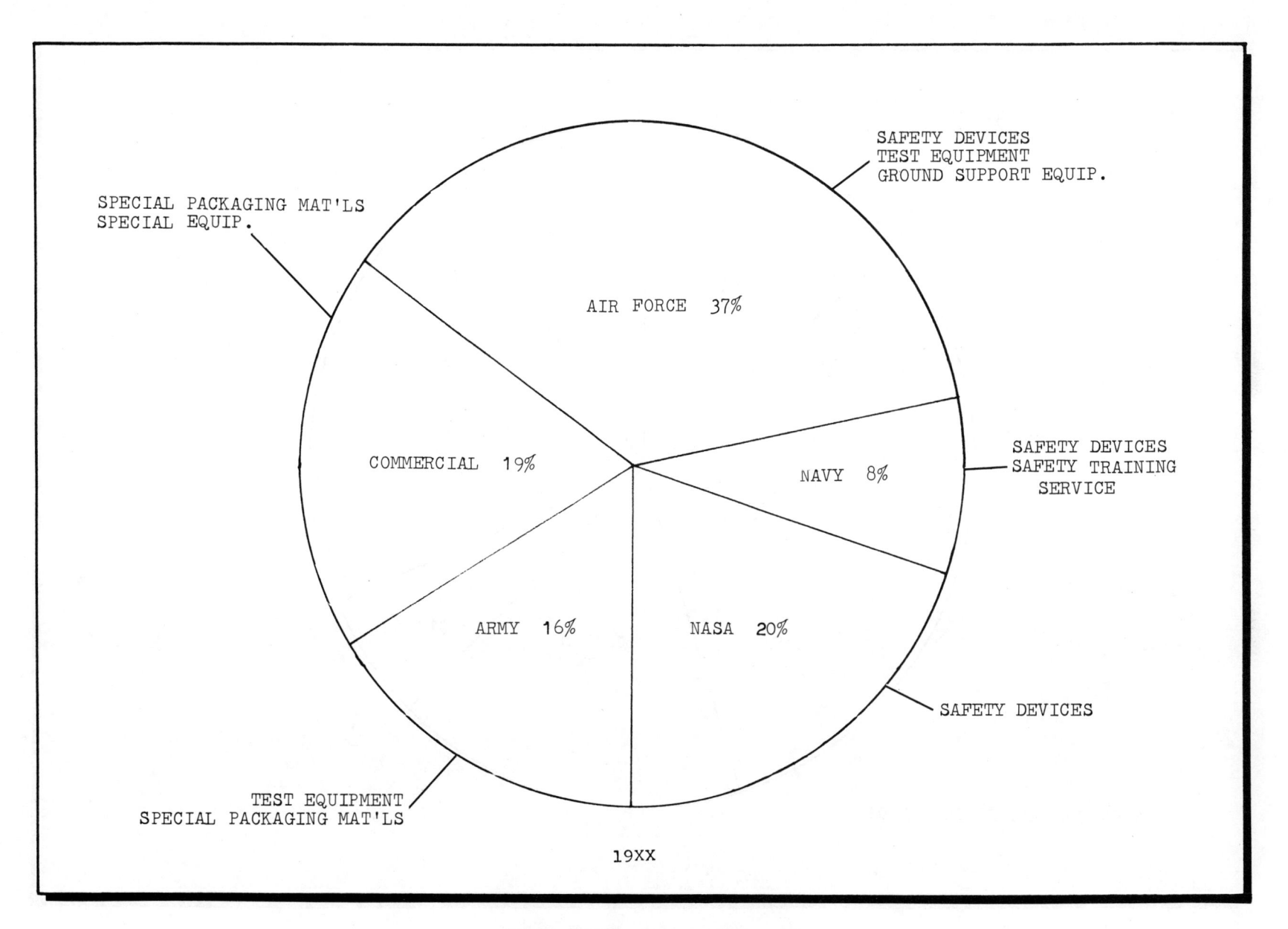

SAFETY DEVICES
TEST EQUIPMENT
GROUND SUPPORT EQUIP.

SPECIAL PACKAGING MAT'LS
SPECIAL EQUIP.

AIR FORCE 37%

COMMERCIAL 19%

NAVY 8%

SAFETY DEVICES
SAFETY TRAINING
SERVICE

ARMY 16%

NASA 20%

SAFETY DEVICES

TEST EQUIPMENT
SPECIAL PACKAGING MAT'LS

19XX

Figure 45.22   Sales—Version 22

CONFERENCE
TABLES
14%
$25.0

CREDENZAS
10%
$17.9

DESKS
22%
$39.3

FILE CABINETS
31%
$55.3

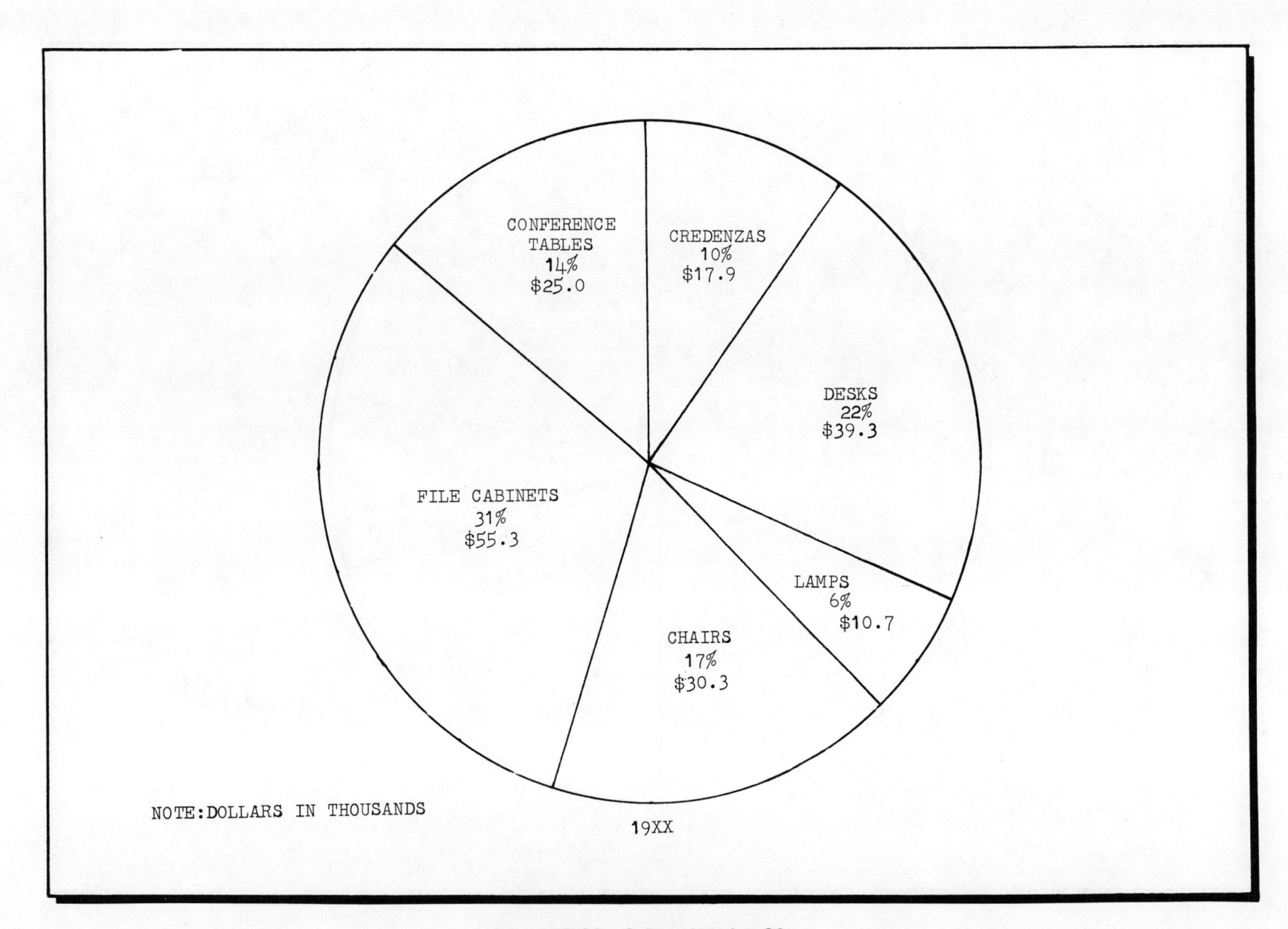

LAMPS
6%
$10.7

CHAIRS
17%
$30.3

NOTE: DOLLARS IN THOUSANDS

19XX

Figure 45.23   Sales—Version 23

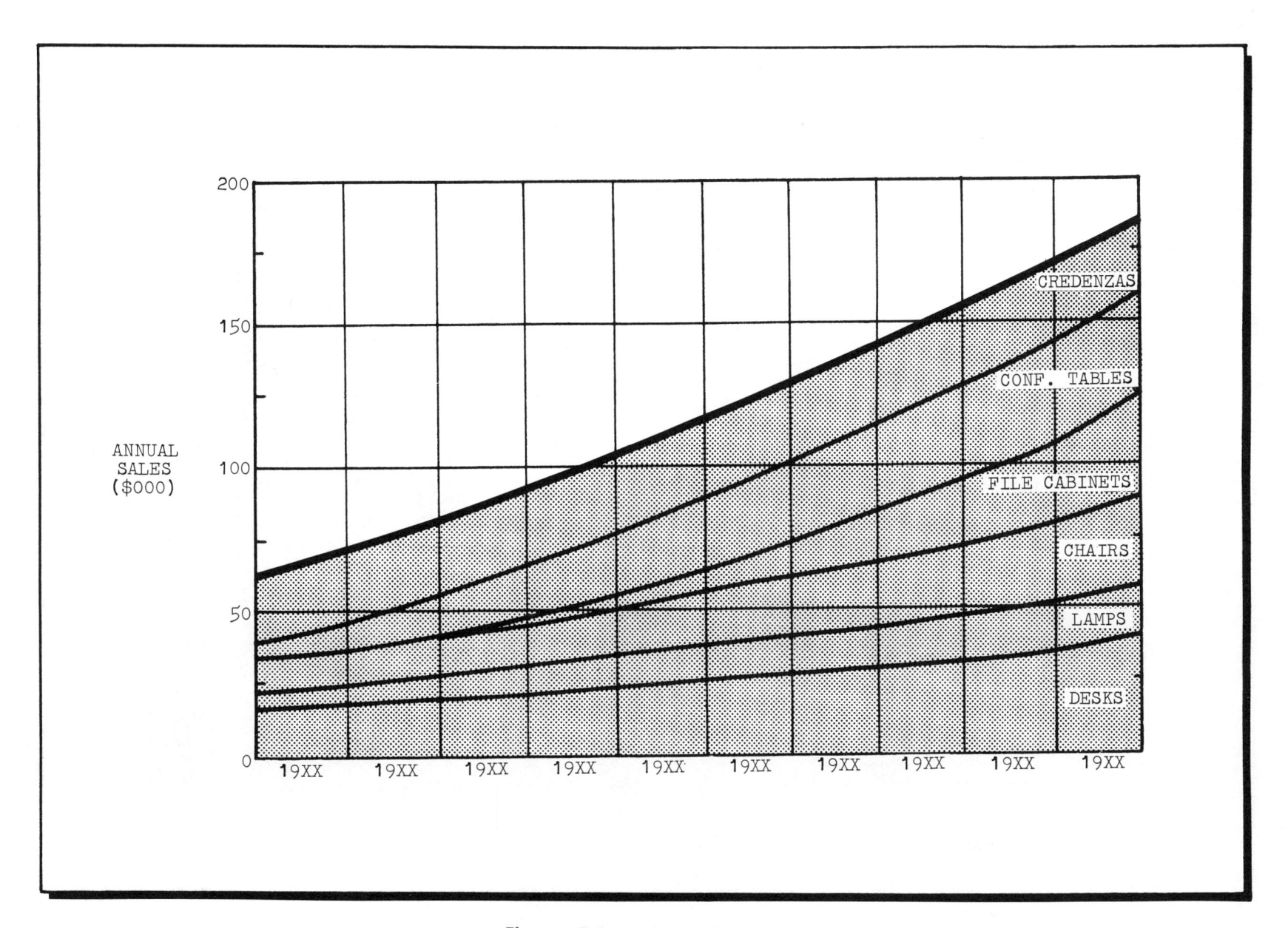

Figure 45.24   Sales—Version 24

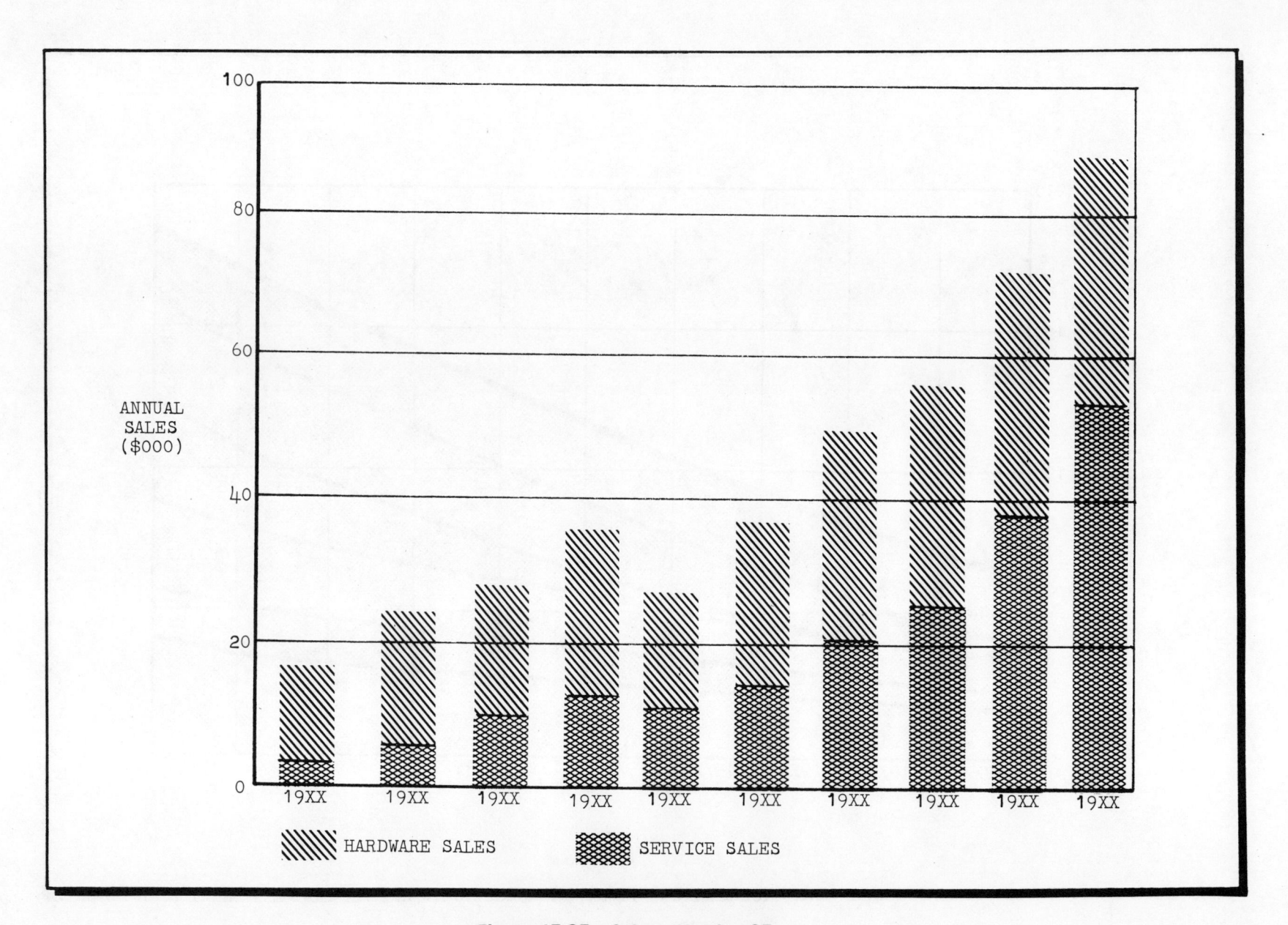

Figure 45.25   Sales—Version 25

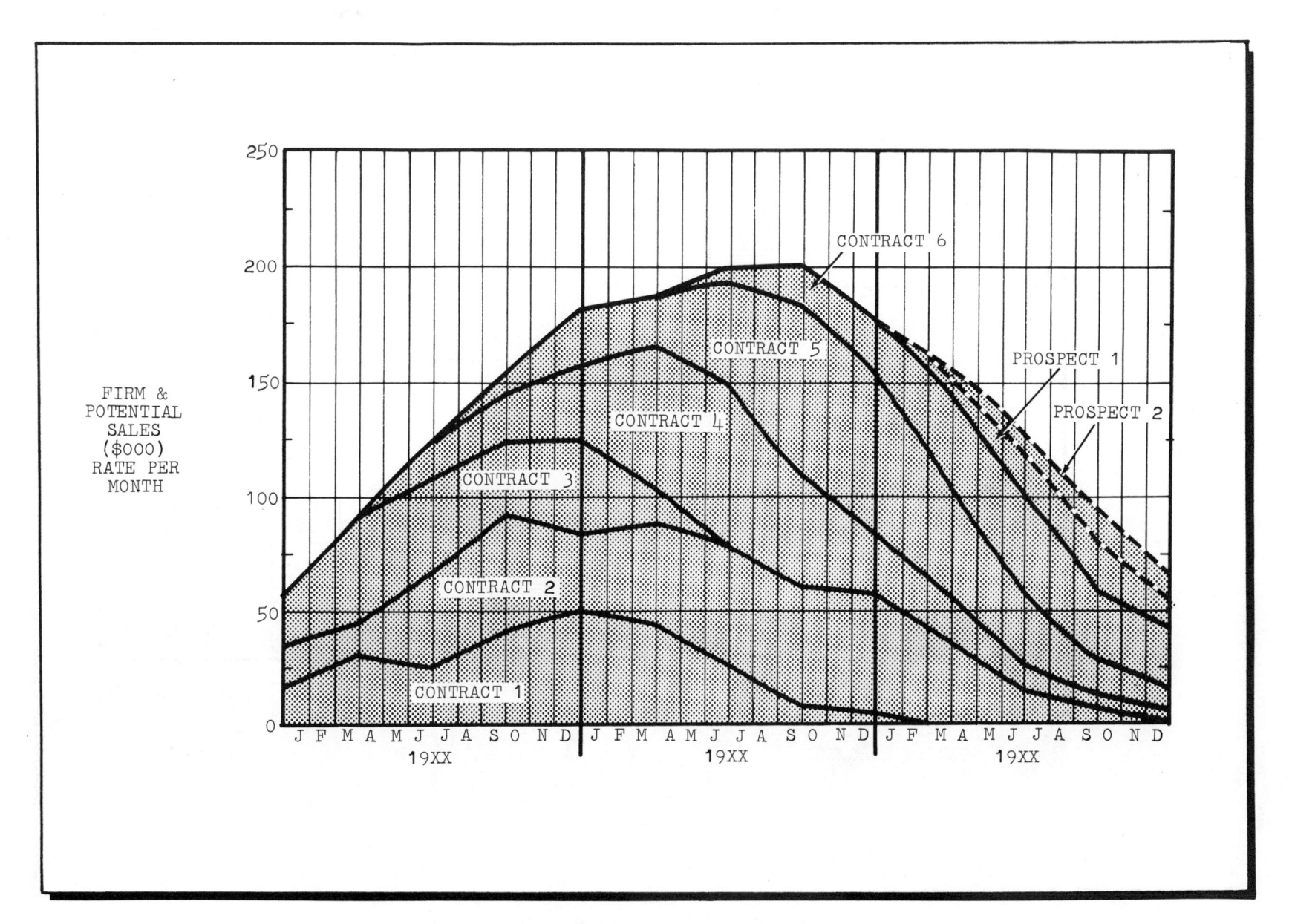

Figure 45.26   Sales—Version 26

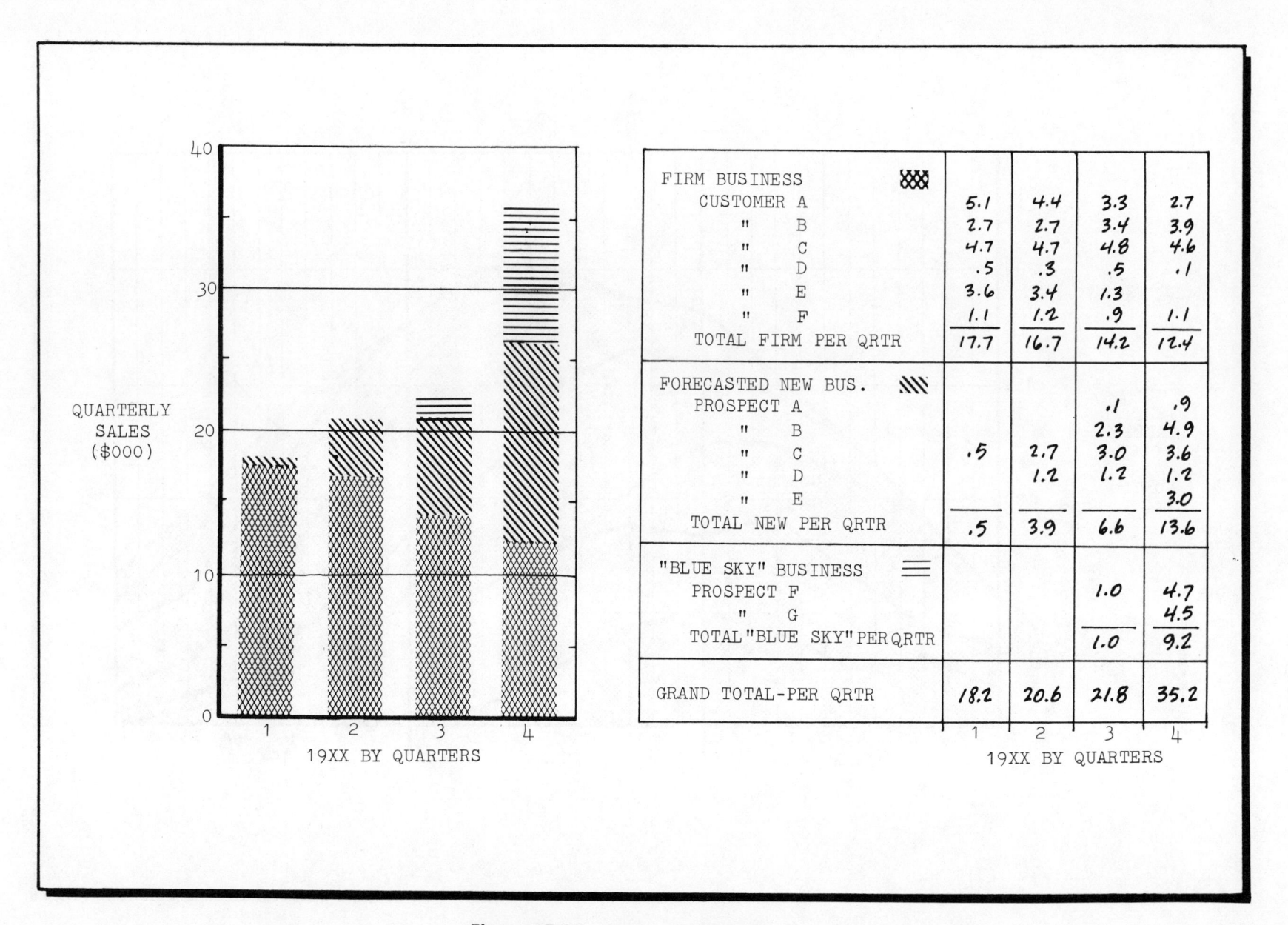

	1	2	3	4
FIRM BUSINESS ▨				
CUSTOMER A	5.1	4.4	3.3	2.7
" B	2.7	2.7	3.4	3.9
" C	4.7	4.7	4.8	4.6
" D	.5	.3	.5	.1
" E	3.6	3.4	1.3	
" F	1.1	1.2	.9	1.1
TOTAL FIRM PER QRTR	17.7	16.7	14.2	12.4
FORECASTED NEW BUS. ▨				
PROSPECT A			.1	.9
" B			2.3	4.9
" C	.5	2.7	3.0	3.6
" D		1.2	1.2	1.2
" E				3.0
TOTAL NEW PER QRTR	.5	3.9	6.6	13.6
"BLUE SKY" BUSINESS ≡				
PROSPECT F			1.0	4.7
" G				4.5
TOTAL "BLUE SKY" PER QRTR			1.0	9.2
GRAND TOTAL-PER QRTR	18.2	20.6	21.8	35.2

19XX BY QUARTERS

QUARTERLY SALES ($000) — 19XX BY QUARTERS

Figure 45.27 Sales—Version 27

ITEM ($000)	STATUS AS OF JUNE 1		
	PLANNED SALES	ACTUAL SALES	VARIANCE
FIRM BUSINESS	$29.4	$29.4	0
NEW BUSINESS	3.0	.5	$-2.5
"BLUE SKY" BUSINESS	0	0	0
TOTAL	$32.4	$29.9	$-2.5

Figure 45.28   Sales—Version 28

STATUS AS OF **JUNE 1**

SALES ($000)	STATUS THIS MONTH			CUM STATUS TO DATE			EST. YEAR END POSITIONS		
	PLAN	ACTUAL	VAR.	PLAN	ACTUAL	VAR.	PLAN	ACTUAL	VAR.
DESKS	$3.3	$3.3	0	$19.7	$19.7	0	$39.3	$39.3	0
LAMPS	.9	.8	$-.1	5.4	5.2	$-.2	10.7	10.7	0
CHAIRS	2.5	2.5	0	15.2	15.2	0	30.3	30.3	0
FILE CABINETS	4.6	2.0	-2.6	27.7	21.0	-6.7	55.3	45.0	$-10.3 ✓
CONFERENCE TABLES	2.1	3.0	+.9	12.5	13.5	+1.0	25.0	27.0	+2.0
CREDENZAS	1.5	1.5	0	9.0	9.0	0	17.9	17.9	0
TOTAL	$14.9	$13.1	$-1.8	$89.5	$83.6	$-5.9	$178.5	$170.2	$-8.3

Figure 45.29   Sales—Version 29

46.0 SALES BACKLOG

Examples of charts that display the status of the backlog of sales are shown in this section.

46.1 Sales Backlog—Version 1: An example of a simple sales backlog tracking chart is shown as Version 1, Figure 46.1. Two factors are displayed in this example. First, there is the forecasted month-end backlog which has been established on the basis of an existing backlog, then adjusted each month by forecasted new sales and planned shipments. Against this base line the actual month-end backlog (solid line) is displayed.

46.2 Sales Backlog—Version 2: The monitoring of sales backlog in terms of new orders as a percent of backlog is shown in Version 2, Figure 46.2. The dashed line represents the forecast, and the solid line represents actuals.

46.3 Sales Backlog—Version 3: The month-end backlog and the two elements that control the backlog, new orders and shipments, are shown together in Version 3 of a sales backlog chart, Figure 46.3. In this example, forecasts, or plans, are not shown. The information that is imparted by the chart is that the fluctuations in the backlog can be related directly to the fluctuations in new orders and/or shipments.

46.4 Sales Backlog—Version 4: Version 4 of a sales backlog chart, Figure 46.4, is similar to Version 3 except that in Version 4 the month-end backlog is shown in the form of columns. In addition, a line has also been added in this example to show the average month-end backlog of the previous year.

46.5 Sales Backlog—Version 5: Version 5 of a sales backlog chart, Figure 46.5, shows the month-end backlog in column form, and shows new orders and shipments plotted on a cumulative basis. As with Versions 3 and 4, plans and forecasts are not shown in this example. The information that the chart imparts is primarily the fluctuations in new orders and shipments and the effect they have on the backlog.

46.6 Sales Backlog—Version 6: A table of statistics has been combined with a graphic chart in Version 6 of a sales backlog chart, Figure 46.6. In this example, the statistical table shows the backlog at the start of the month, the new orders for that month, the sum of the existing backlog and the new orders, the shipments that have been made for the month, which are then subtracted from the backlog, plus new orders to give the month-end backlog.

46.7 Sales Backlog—Version 7: In Version 7 of a sales backlog tracking chart, Figure 46.7, new orders, shipments, and the month-end backlog are all shown in terms of forecasted and actual performance. Under normal circumstances, new orders and shipments would, statistically, be very similar to each other and if plotted on the same grid there would be a tendency for the lines to overlap making the chart difficult to interpret. For this reason,

Version 7 utilizes two grids to separately show these two related factors.

46.8 Sales Backlog—Version 8: The most complex version of a sales backlog tracking chart in this section is shown as Version 8, Figure 46.8. The table contains nine lines of data showing forecasted, actual, and variance statistics related to new orders, shipments, and month-end backlog. These statistics are plotted on two separate grids. This much information packed into such a confined space makes the graphic legibility not as good as where just the graphs are used, as in Version 7.

46.9 Sales Backlog—Version 9: An example of a statistical table that can be used for tracking sales backlog is shown as Version 9, Figure 46.9. Forecasted, actual, and variance statistics are shown in terms of new orders, shipments, and the resulting month-end backlog.

46.10 Sales Backlog—Version 10: A detailed version of a statistical table showing sales backlog factors is shown as Version 10, Figure 46.10. Forecasted, actual, and variance statistics are given for new orders, shipments, and for the backlog. Statistics for new orders as a percent of backlog are given, as well. To help direct the chart reader's attention to the most essential statistic on the chart, a circle has been used in this example.

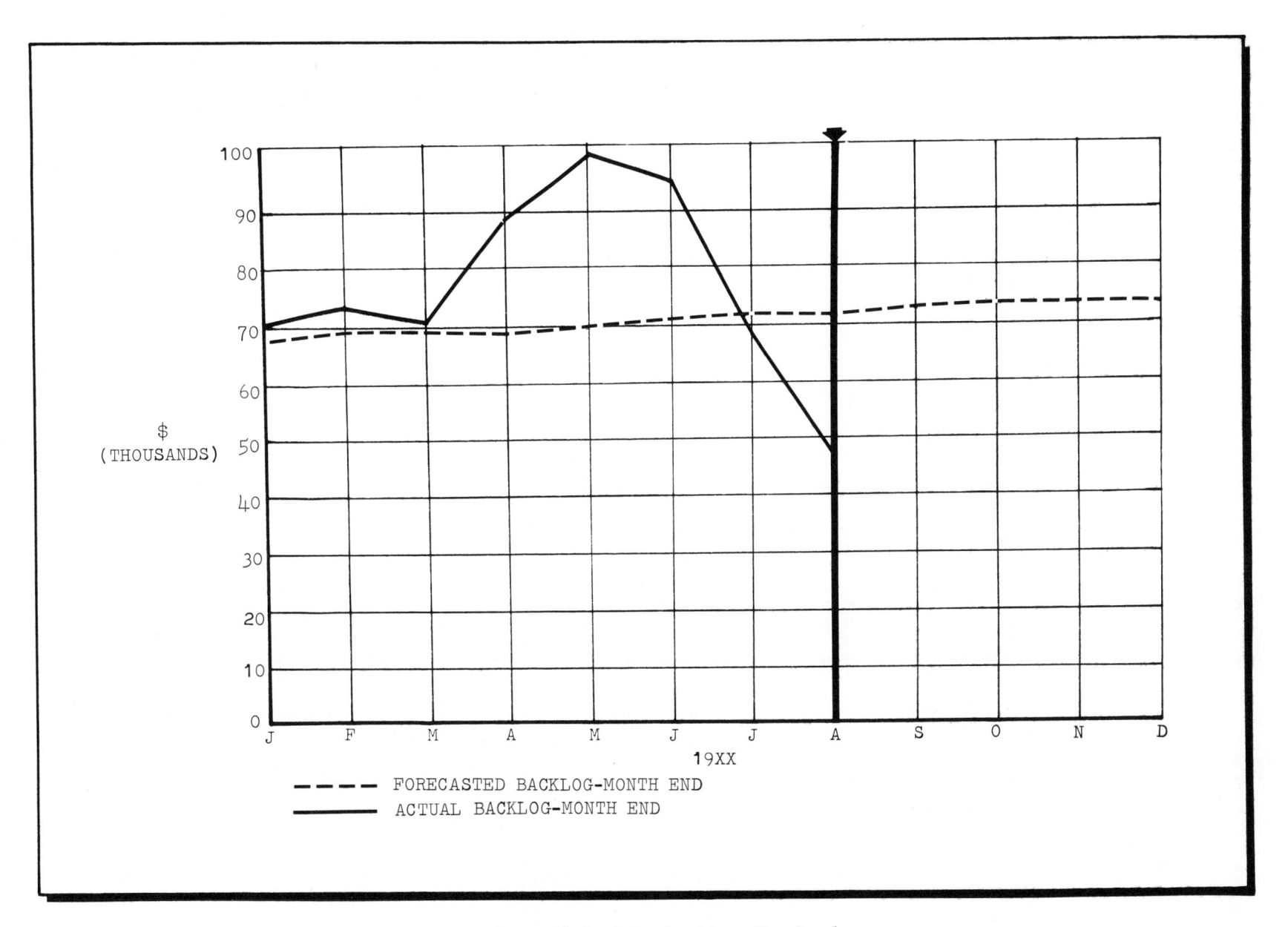

Figure 46.1   Sales Backlog—Version 1

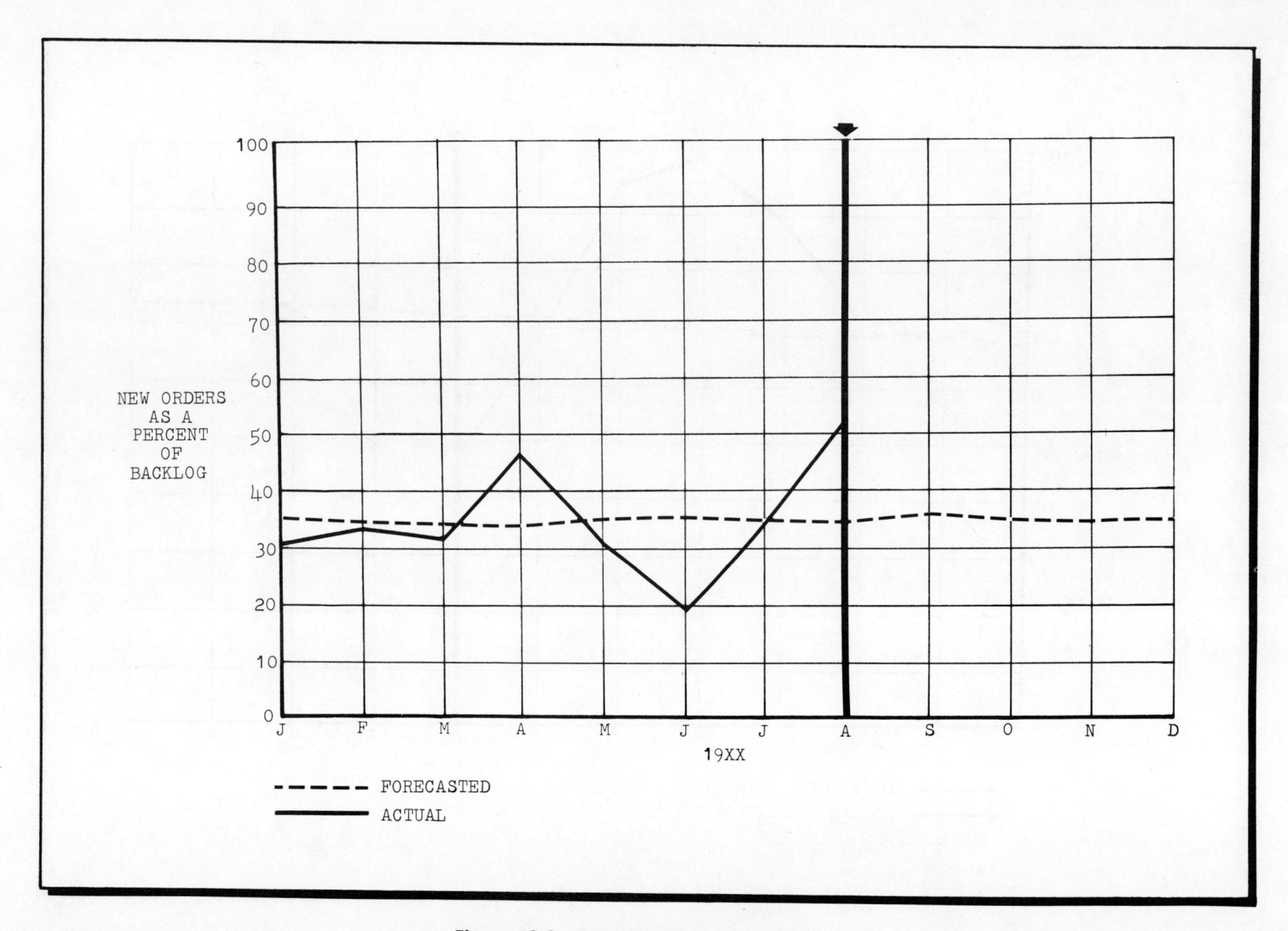

Figure 46.2   Sales Backlog—Version 2

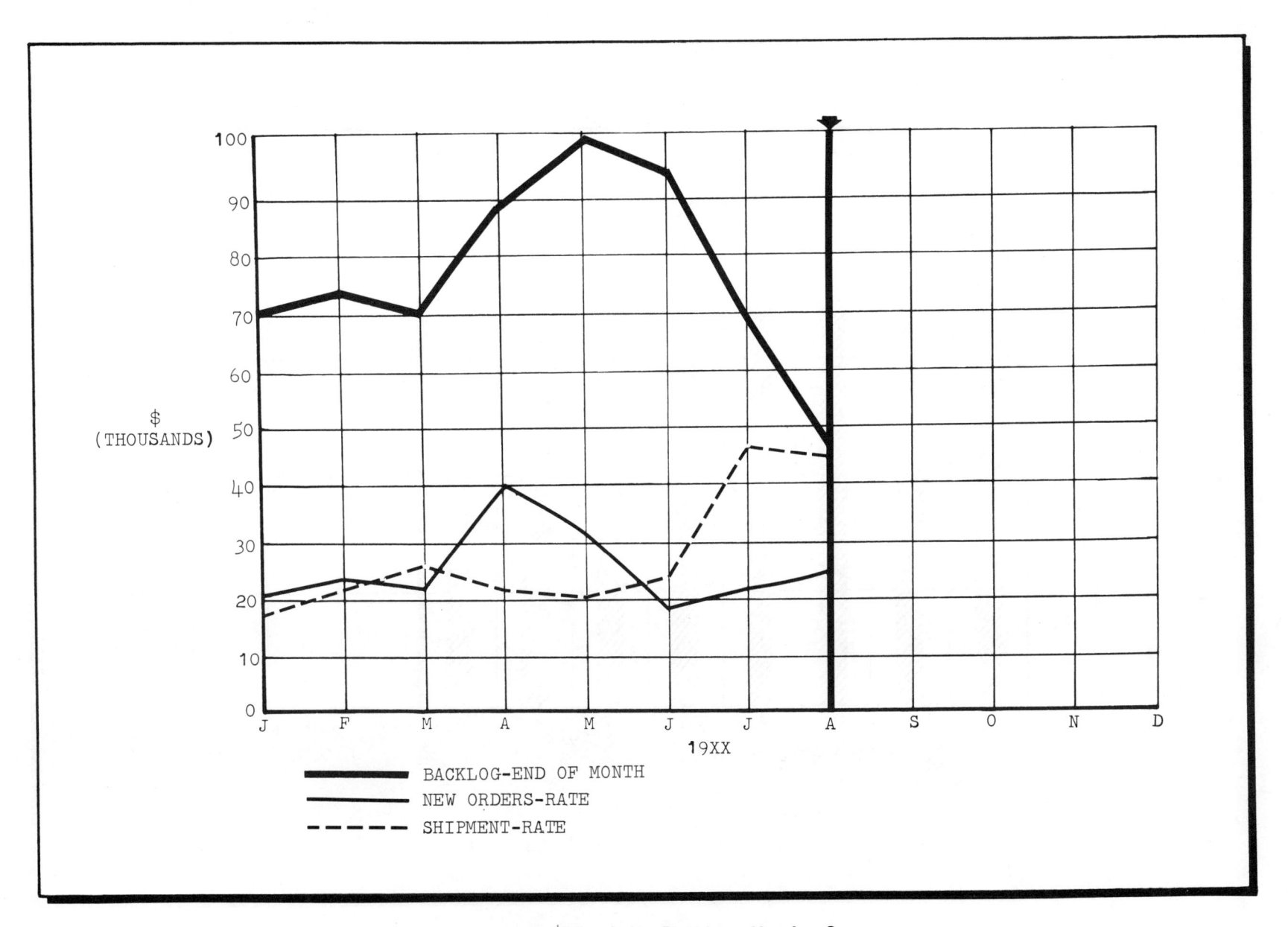

Figure 46.3 Sales Backlog—Version 3

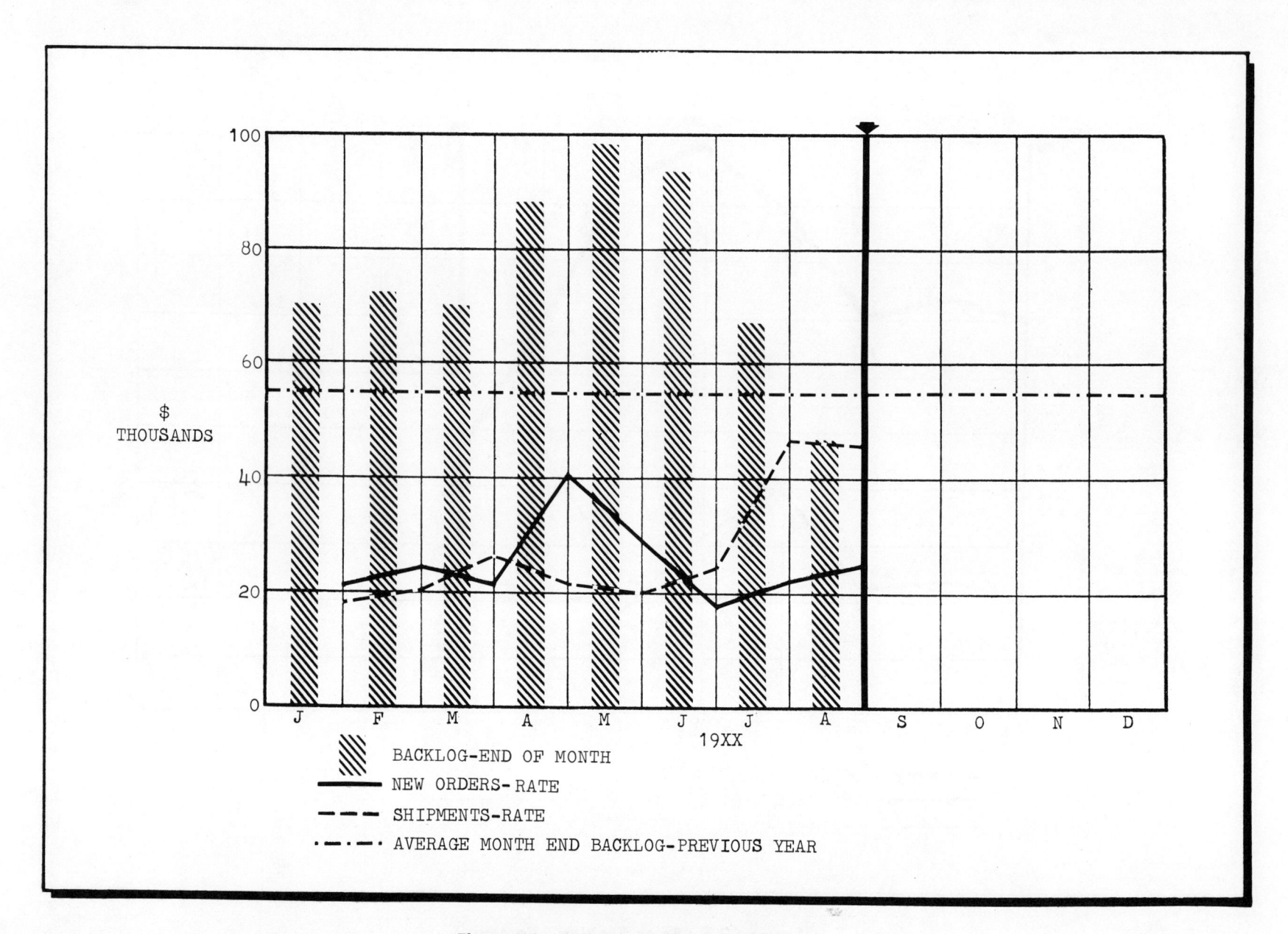

Figure 46.4 Sales Backlog—Version 4

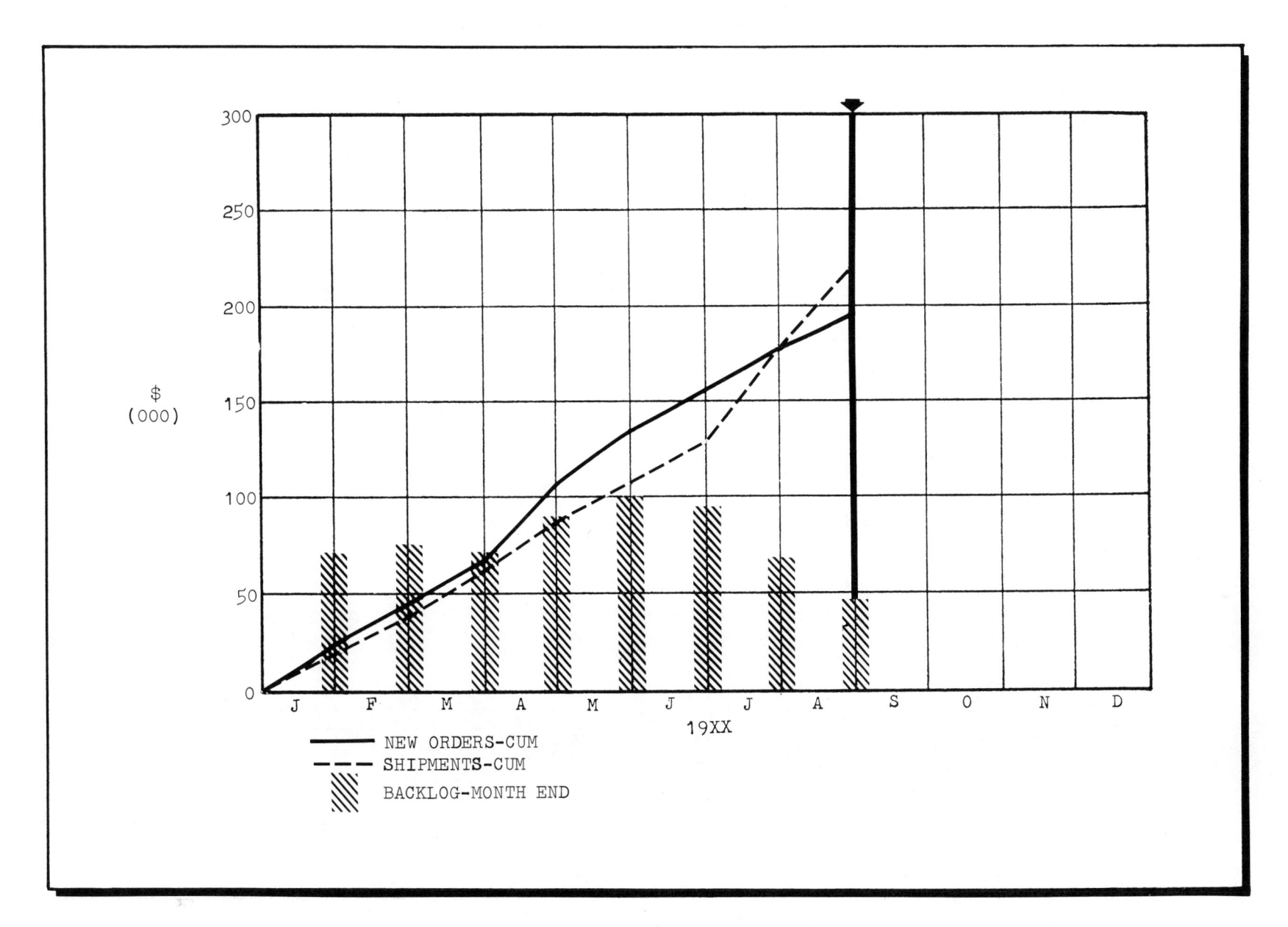

Figure 46.5 Sales Backlog—Version 5

BACKLOG-START OF MO.		67	70	73	70	89	99	94	68				
NEW ORDERS-RATE/MO.	———	21	23	22	40	30	18	21	24				
BACKLOG PLUS NEW		88	93	95	110	119	117	115	92				
SHIPMENTS-RATE/MO.	....	18	20	25	21	20	23	47	45				
BACKLOG-END OF MO.	▬▬▬	70	73	70	89	99	94	68	47				

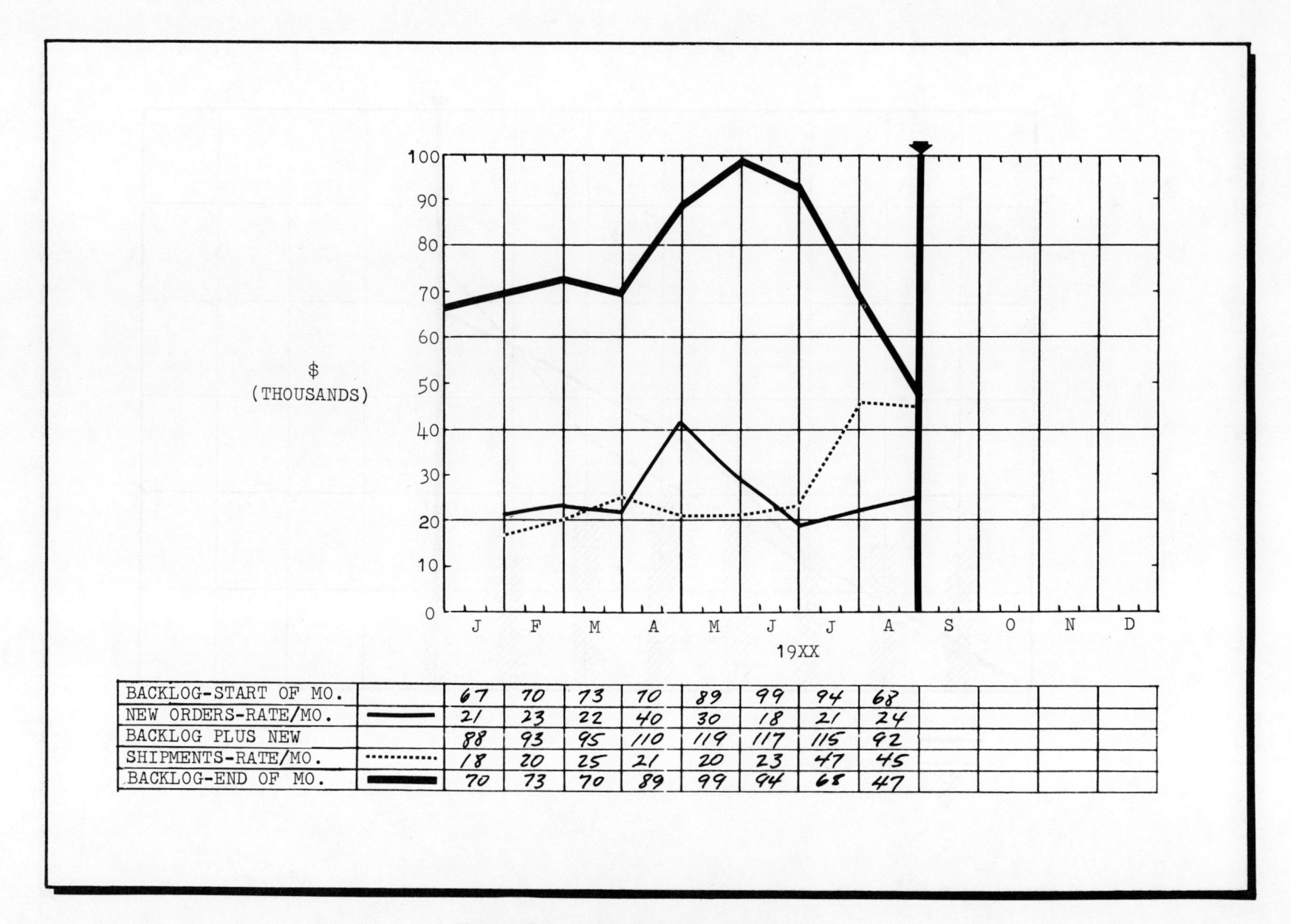

Figure 46.6   Sales Backlog—Version 6

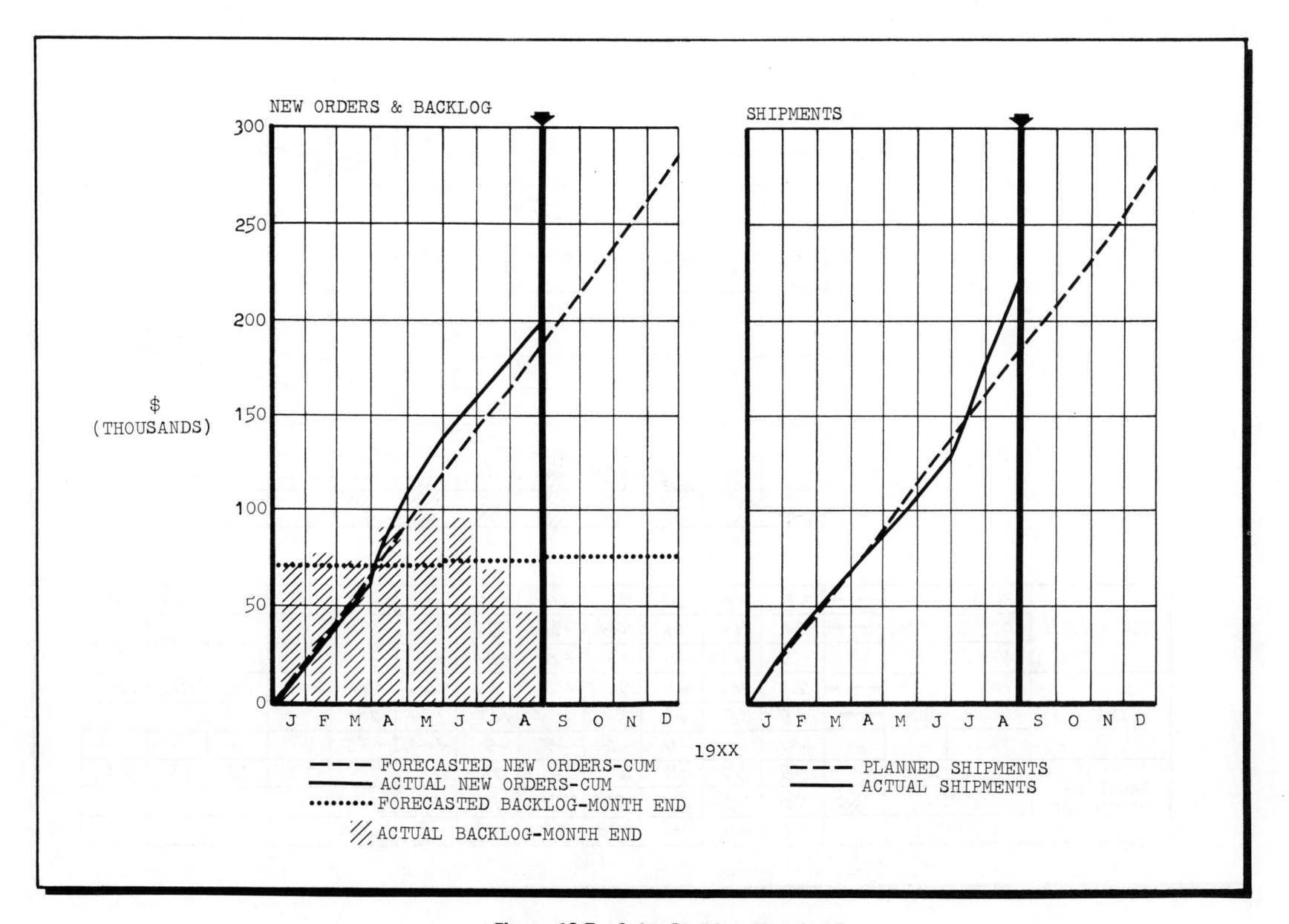

Figure 46.7 Sales Backlog—Version 7

563

			J	F	M	A	M	J	J	A	S	O	N	D
NEW ORDERS	FCST	----- CUM.	23	46	69	92	116	140	164	188	213	238	263	288
	ACTUAL		21	44	66	106	136	154	175	198				
	VAR.		-2	-2	-3	+14	+20	+14	+11	+10				
SHIPMENTS	FCST	----- CUM.	22	44	67	90	113	136	160	184	208	232	257	282
	ACTUAL		18	38	63	84	104	127	174	219				
	VAR.		-4	-6	-4	-6	-9	-9	+14	+35				
BACKLOG—MONTH-END	FORECAST	········	68	69	69	69	70	71	71	71	72	73	73	73
	ACTUAL	▨	70	73	70	89	99	94	68	47				
	VARIANCE		+2	+14	+1	+20	+29	+23	-3	-24				

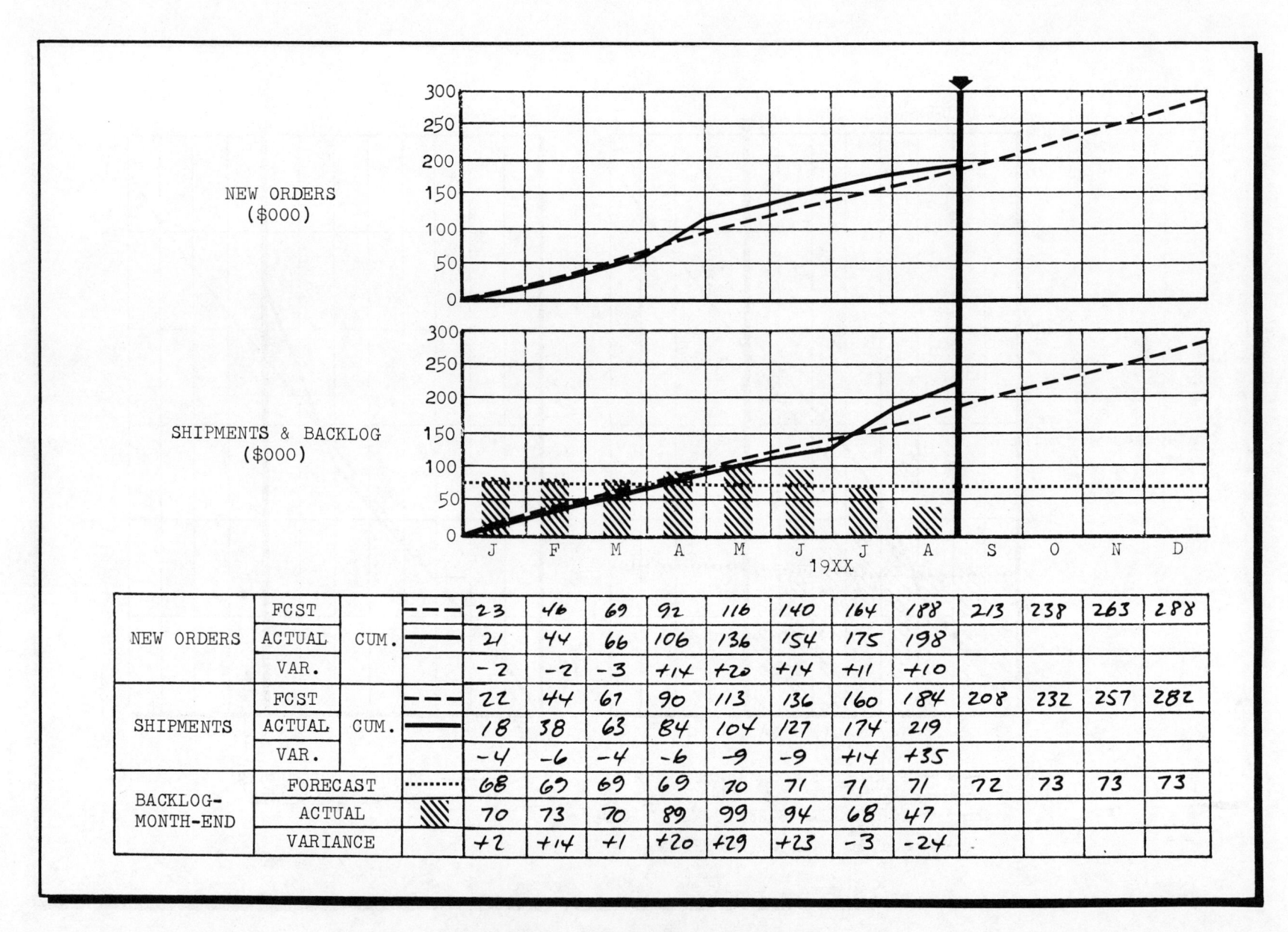

Figure 46.8 Sales Backlog—Version 8

ITEM ($000)			\multicolumn{12}{c}{19__}											
			J	F	M	A	M	J	J	A	S	O	N	D
NEW ORDERS	F'CAST	CUM	23	46	69	92	116	140	164	188	213	238	263	288
	ACTUAL		21	44	66	106	136	154	175	198				
	VAR.		-2	-2	-3	+14	+20	+14	+11	+10				
SHIPMENTS	F'CAST	CUM	22	44	67	90	113	136	160	184	208	232	257	282
	ACTUAL		18	38	63	84	104	127	174	219				
	VAR.		-4	-6	-4	-6	-9	-9	+14	+35				
BACKLOG— MONTH END	FORECAST		68	69	69	69	70	71	71	71	72	73	73	73
	ACTUAL		70	73	70	89	99	94	69	47				
	VARIANCE		+2	+4	+1	+20	+29	+23	-3	-24				

Figure 46.9 Sales Backlog—Version 9

	FACTOR		19XX											
			J	F	M	A	M	J	J	A	S	O	N	D
F O R E C A S T E D	BACKLOG-START OF MONTH		67	68	69	69	69	70	71	71	71	72	73	73
	NEW ORDERS	RATE	23	23	23	23	24	24	24	24	25	25	25	25
		CUM	23	46	69	92	116	140	164	188	213	238	263	288
	BACKLOG+NEW ORDERS FOR MO.		90	91	92	92	93	94	95	95	96	97	98	98
	SHIPMENTS	RATE	22	22	23	23	23	23	24	24	24	24	25	25
		CUM	22	44	67	90	113	136	160	184	208	232	257	282
	BACKLOG-END OF MONTH		68	69	69	69	70	71	71	71	72	73	73	73
	NEW ORDERS AS % OF BACKLOG		34%	33%	33%	33%	34%	34%	34%	34%	35%	34%	34%	34%
A C T U A L S	BACKLOG-START OF MONTH		67	70	73	70	89	99	94	68	47			
	NEW ORDERS	RATE	21	23	22	40	30	18	21	24				
		CUM	21	44	66	106	136	154	175	198				
	BACKLOG+NEW ORDERS FOR MO.		88	93	95	110	119	117	115	92				
	SHIPMENTS	RATE	18	20	25	21	20	23	47	45				
		CUM	18	38	63	84	104	127	174	219				
	BACKLOG-END OF MONTH		70	73	70	89	99	94	68	47				
	NEW ORDERS AS % OF BACKLOG		30%	32%	31%	45%	30%	19%	31%	51%				
V A R I A N C E	NEW ORDERS	CUM	-2	-2	-3	+14	+20	+14	+11	+10				
	SHIPMENTS	CUM	-4	-6	-4	-6	-9	-9	+14	+35				
	BACKLOG-END OF MONTH		+2	+4	+1	+20	+29	+23	-3	(-24)				
	NEW ORDERS AS % OF BACKLOG		-4%	-1%	-2%	+12%	-4%	-15%	-3%	+17%				

NOTE: ALL DOLLARS IN THOUSANDS

Figure 46.10 Sales Backlog—Version 10

47.0 SALES EFFORT

Methods for using charts to monitor sales activity are shown in this section. Also see Sections 40.0, *Proposals/Quotations*, 45.0, *Sales*, 46.0, *Sales Backlog*, and 48.0, *Sales per Employee*.

47.1 Sales Effort—Version 1: Two amount scales are used in Version 1 of a sales effort tracking chart, Figure 47.1. The left-hand scale is in terms of monthly sales. The right-hand scale is in terms of the number of sales calls per month. Actual sales calls are plotted in relationship to a quota.

47.2 Sales Effort—Version 2: Sales calls per month and monthly sales dollars are shown on separate grids in Version 2 of a sales effort tracking chart, Figure 47.2. Actual sales calls are plotted in relationship with a quota on the left-hand grid. Actual sales are shown on the right-hand grid so the results of the sales calls activity can be seen.

47.3 Sales Effort—Version 3: A method for comparing the performance of individual salesmen is shown in Version 3 of a sales effort chart, Figure 47.3. This is a one-time status report style of chart. The bars must be extended and the goal changed for each new reporting date.

47.4 Sales Effort—Version 4: A symbol chart style is used in Version 4 of a sales effort tracking chart, Figure 47.4. In this example, ten top prospects have been listed in the left-hand column, followed by the names of the salesmen responsible for the prospects. The graphic portion of the chart utilizes symbols to record scheduled and actual contacts with the prospect made by the salesman, with a space for comments on the right-hand side of the chart.

47.5 Sales Effort—Version 5: The performance of five separate departments is compared in Version 5 of a sales effort tracking chart, Figure 47.5. The weekly sales quota for each department is shown, and performance is measured in terms of the percent deviation from plan for each department in the graphic portion of the chart.

47.6 Sales Effort—Version 6: A statistical table is combined with a graphic chart to monitor the activities of an individual salesman in Version 6 of a sales effort tracking chart, Figure 47.6. The graphic portion of the chart in this example displays the actual number of sales calls made in relationship to a plan. The table shows sales dollars on both a weekly and cumulative basis.

47.7 Sales Effort—Version 7: Monthly sales and sales calls per month are shown on separate grids in Version 7 of a sales effort tracking chart, Figure 47.7. The planned and actual statistical backup for both of these factors are given in the tabular portion of the chart.

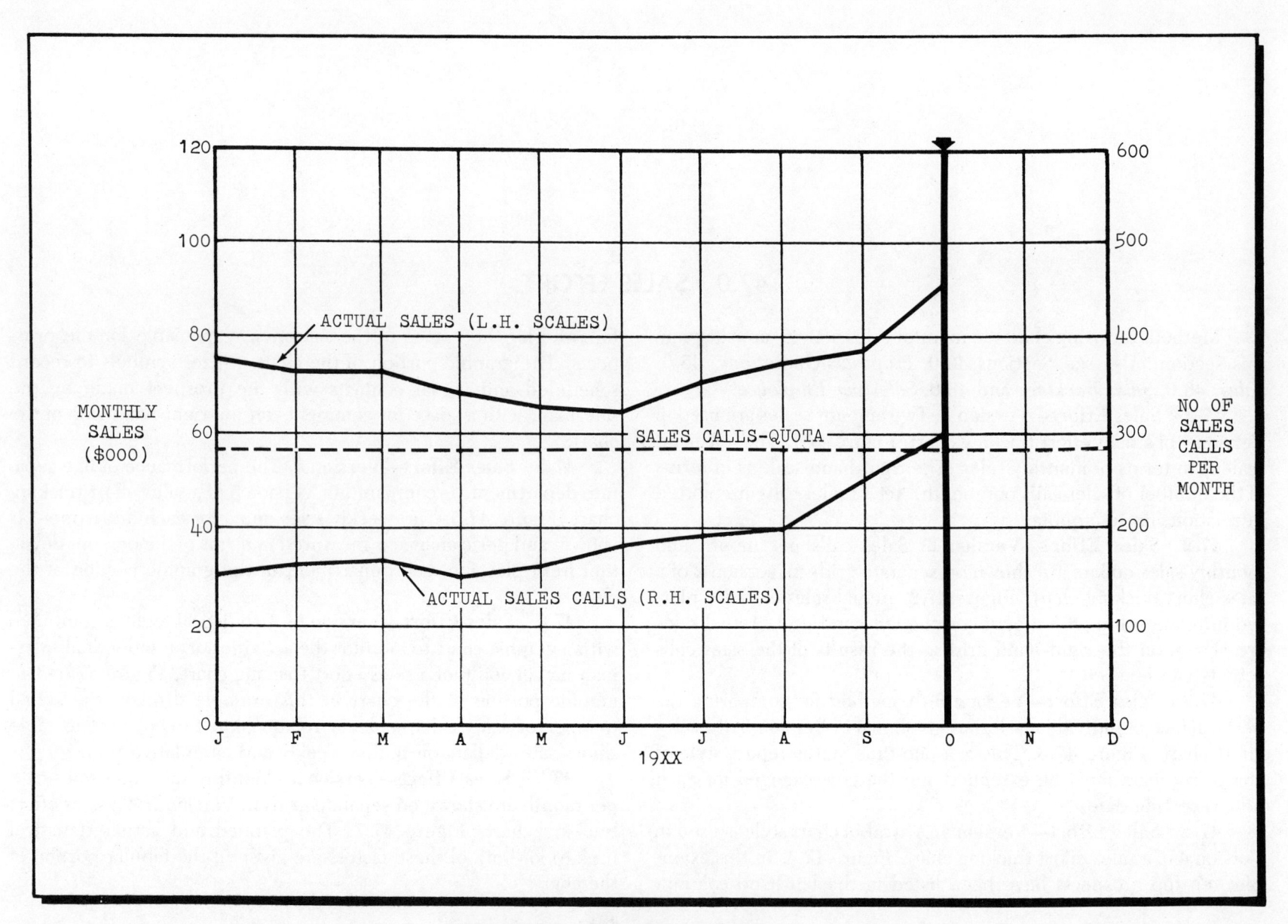

Figure 47.1 Sales Effort—Version 1

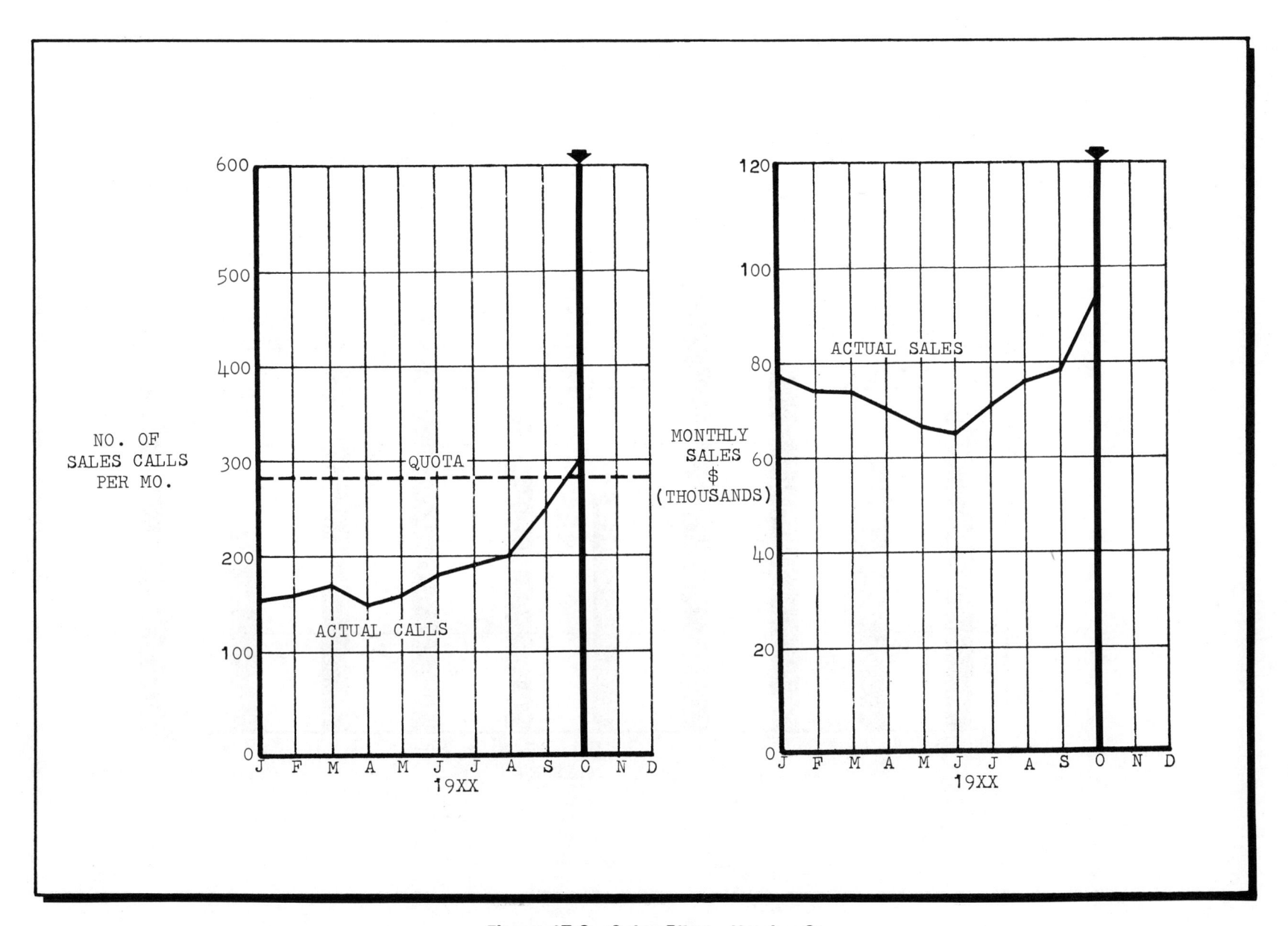

Figure 47.2 Sales Effort—Version 2

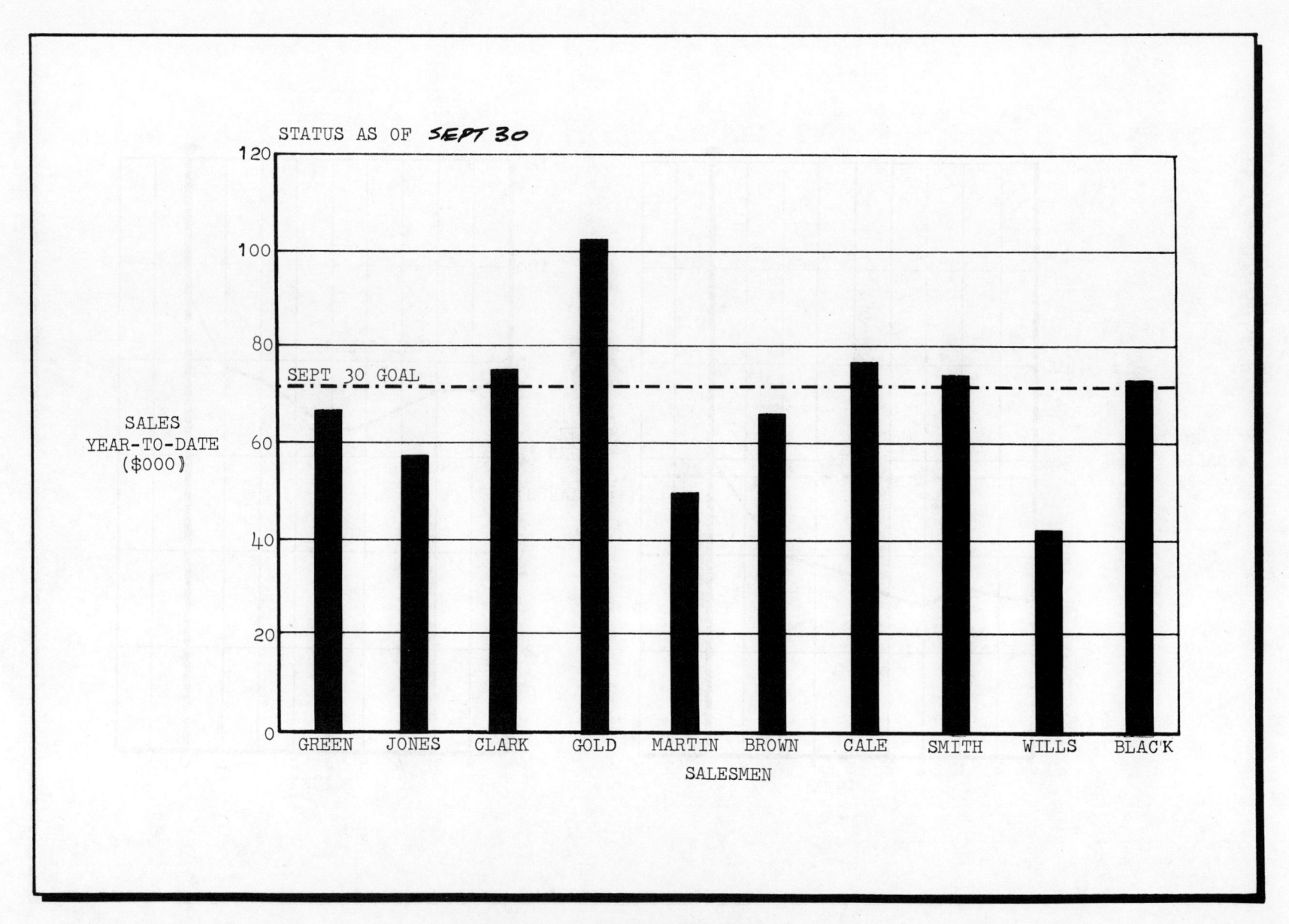

Figure 47.3   Sales Effort—Version 3

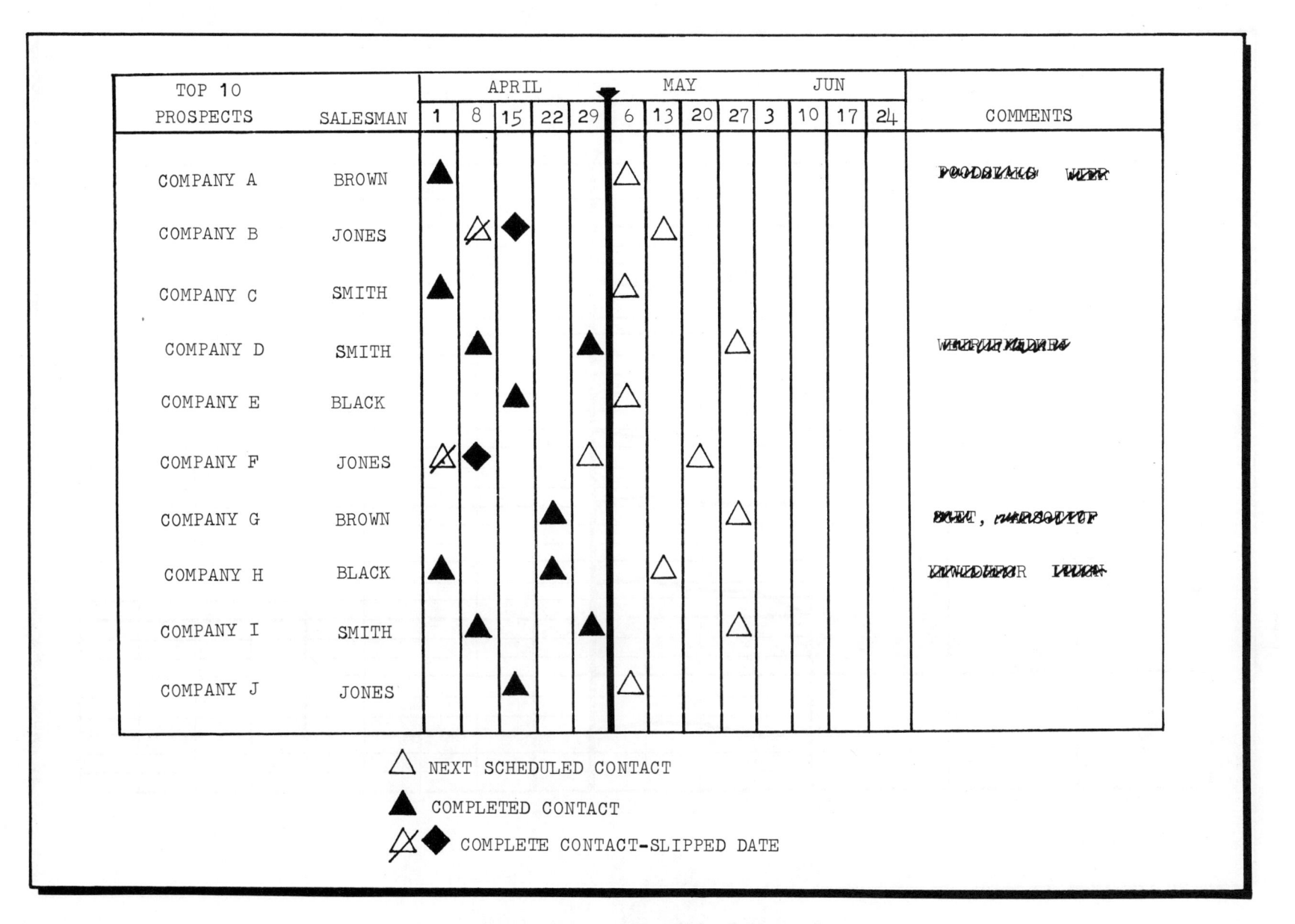

TOP 10 PROSPECTS	SALESMAN	APRIL 1	8	15	22	29	MAY 6	13	20	27	JUN 3	10	17	24	COMMENTS
COMPANY A	BROWN	▲					△								~~POODBIALG WLER~~
COMPANY B	JONES		⟁	◆				△							
COMPANY C	SMITH	▲					△								
COMPANY D	SMITH			▲		▲				△					~~WRPUT XIDRES~~
COMPANY E	BLACK			▲			△								
COMPANY F	JONES	⟁	◆			△			△						
COMPANY G	BROWN				▲					△					~~BCET, MARSOATF~~
COMPANY H	BLACK	▲			▲			△							~~DMIDAPR LUA~~
COMPANY I	SMITH			▲		▲				△					
COMPANY J	JONES			▲			△								

△ NEXT SCHEDULED CONTACT
▲ COMPLETED CONTACT
⟁ ◆ COMPLETE CONTACT-SLIPPED DATE

Figure 47.4   Sales Effort—Version 4

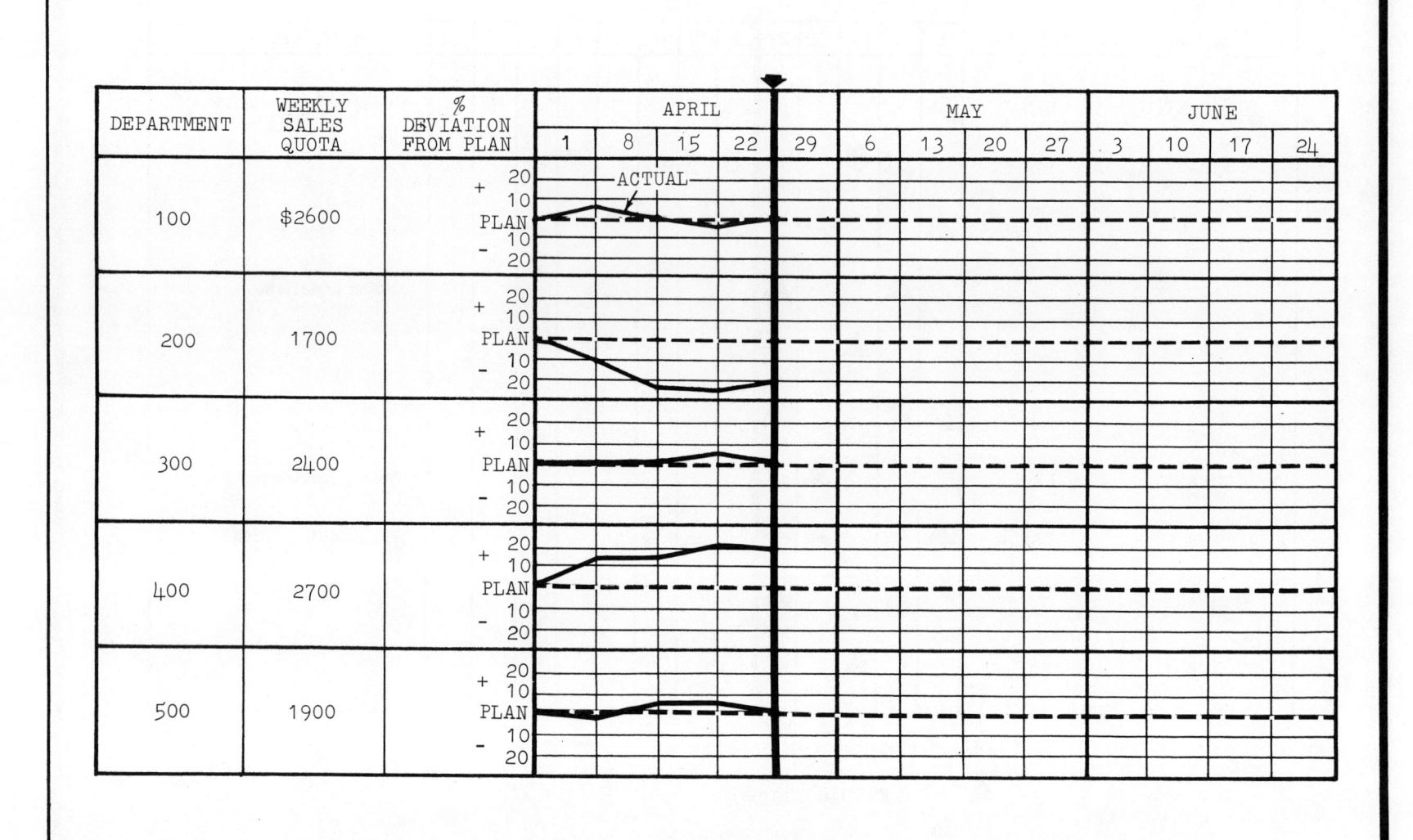

DEPARTMENT	WEEKLY SALES QUOTA	% DEVIATION FROM PLAN	APRIL					MAY				JUNE			
			1	8	15	22	29	6	13	20	27	3	10	17	24
100	$2600	+20 +10 PLAN −10 −20	ACTUAL												
200	1700	+20 +10 PLAN −10 −20													
300	2400	+20 +10 PLAN −10 −20													
400	2700	+20 +10 PLAN −10 −20													
500	1900	+20 +10 PLAN −10 −20													

Figure 47.5   Sales Effort—Version 5

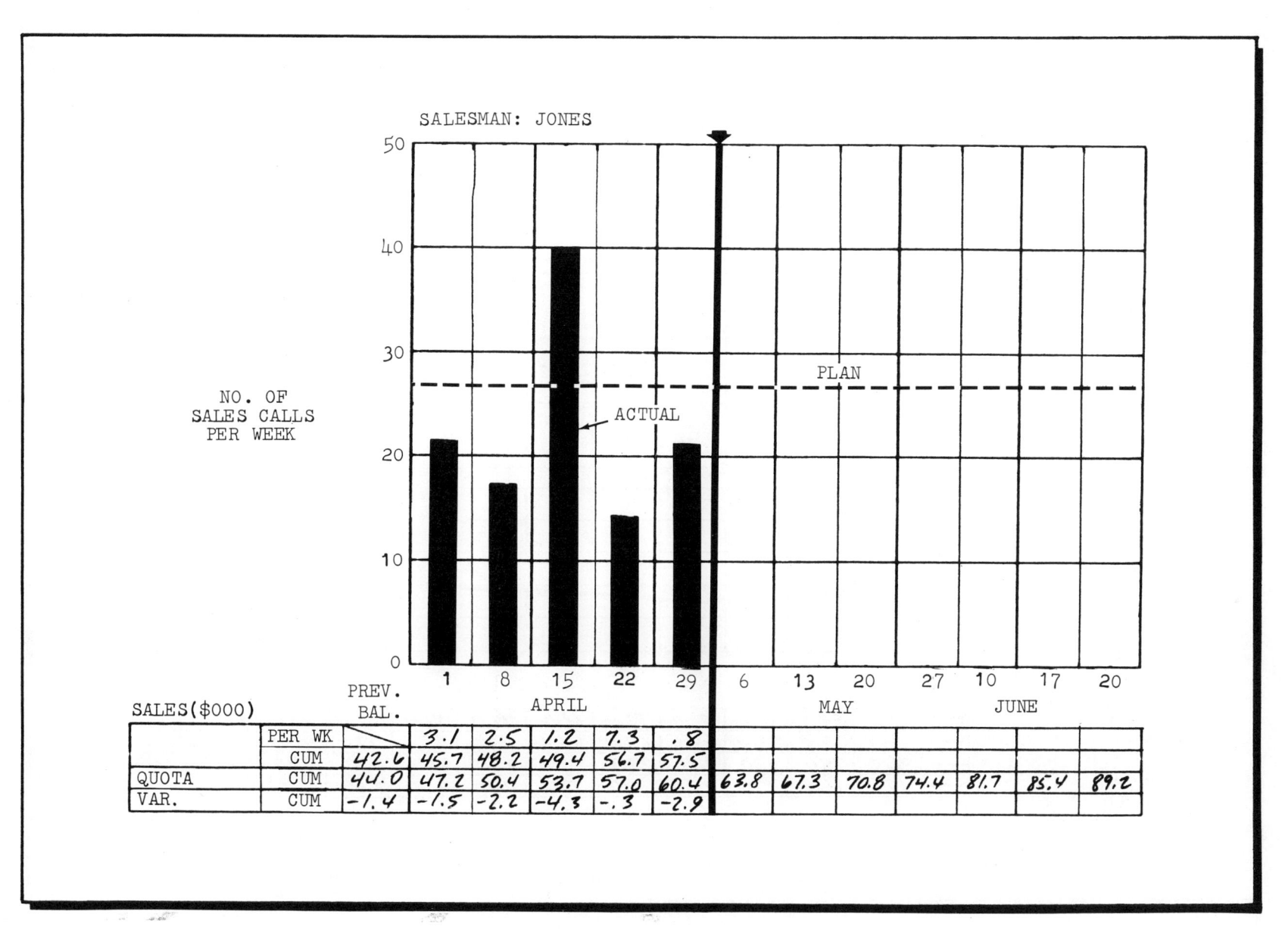

Figure 47.6 Sales Effort—Version 6

SALES ($000)		PREV. BAL.	1	8	15	22	29	6	13	20	27	10	17	20
	PER WK		3.1	2.5	1.2	7.3	.8							
	CUM	42.6	45.7	48.2	49.4	56.7	57.5							
QUOTA	CUM	44.0	47.2	50.4	53.7	57.0	60.4	63.8	67.3	70.8	74.4	81.7	85.4	89.2
VAR.	CUM	-1.4	-1.5	-2.2	-4.3	-.3	-2.9							

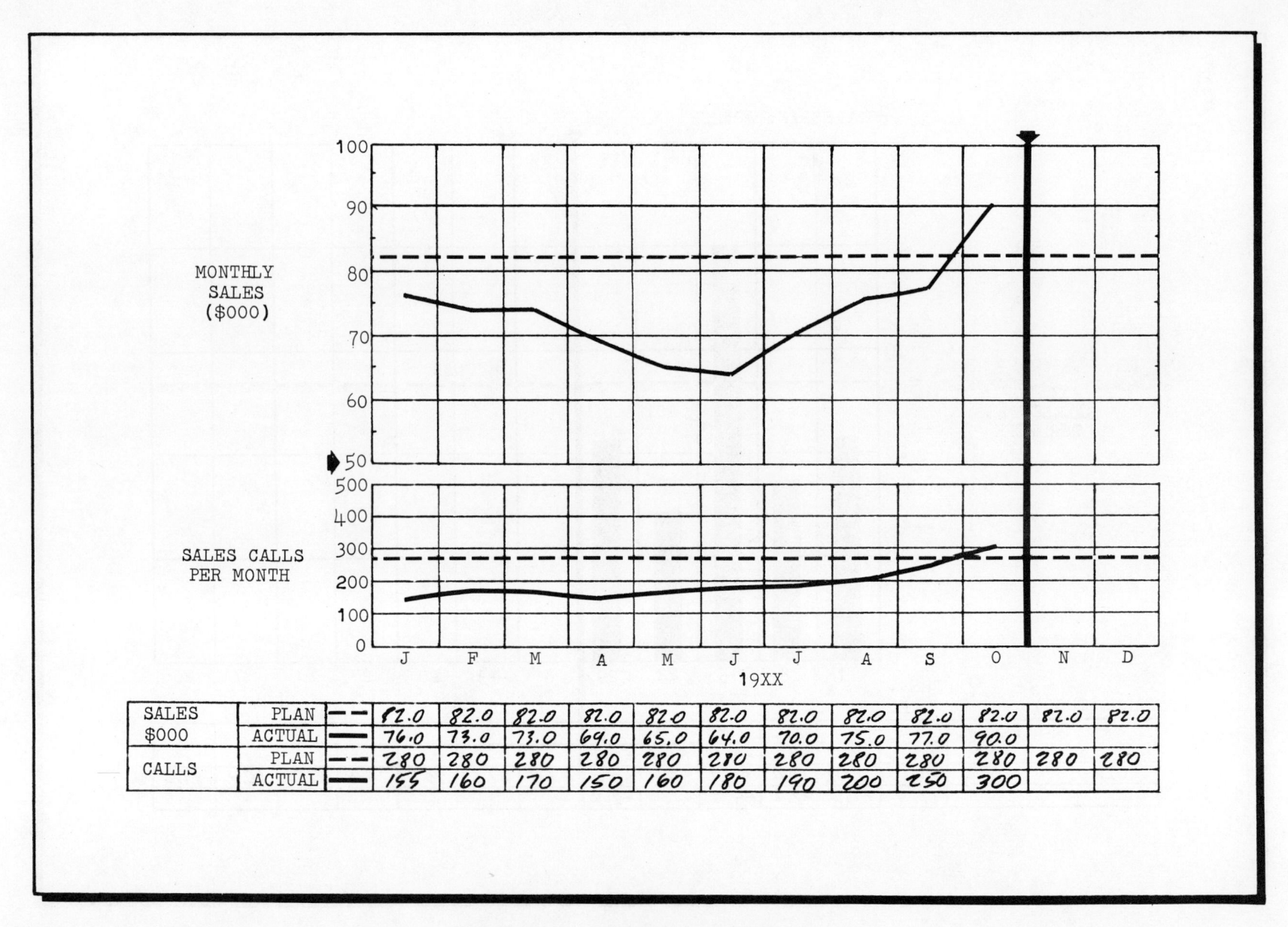

SALES	PLAN	--	82.0	82.0	82.0	82.0	82.0	82.0	82.0	82.0	82.0	82.0	82.0	82.0
$000	ACTUAL	—	76.0	73.0	73.0	64.0	65.0	64.0	70.0	75.0	77.0	90.0		
CALLS	PLAN	--	280	280	280	280	280	280	280	280	280	280	280	280
	ACTUAL	—	155	160	170	150	160	180	190	200	250	300		

Figure 47.7   Sales Effort—Version 7

48.0 SALES PER EMPLOYEE

Some enterprises examine their sales in terms of the number of their employees as one measure of performance. This section contains examples of charts that can be used for this purpose. Also see Sections 45.0, *Sales*, 46.0, *Sales Backlog*, and 47.0, *Sales Effort*.

48.1 Sales per Employee—Version 1: A simple version of a sales per employee tracking chart is shown as Version 1, Figure 48.1. The goal in this example has been set at $17,000 in annual sales for each employee. Actuals have been plotted in terms of monthly sales, annualized, then divided by the number of employees.

48.2 Sales per Employee—Version 2: Version 2 of a sales per employee tracking chart, Figure 48.2, is identical to Version 1, except in this example columns have been used, instead of a line curve, to show actual status.

48.3 Sales per Employee—Version 3: Sales per employee shown in terms of the percentage deviation from the plan is shown as Version 3, Figure 48.3. The center, dashed line represents the plan, and deviations are plotted in relationship to that center line.

48.4 Sales per Employee—Version 4: Version 4 of a sales per employee tracking chart, Figure 48.4, is a percent deviation from plan style chart, as was Version 3. In this example, columns are used to show actual status.

48.5 Sales per Employee—Version 5: The current year's plan and actual performance related to annual sales per employee are shown in this example, Figure 48.5, in relationship to performance in two previous years.

48.6 Sales per Employee—Version 6: In Version 6 of a sales per employee tracking chart, Figure 48.6, planned and actual performance are shown in paired column chart form, by quarters. The previous year's sales per employee performance is shown in the form of a dashed step line.

48.7 Sales per Employee—Version 7: A multi-year version of a sales per employee tracking chart is shown as Version 7, Figure 48.7. The annual sales per employee for four previous years are shown in the left-hand portion of the chart. The current, annualized sales per employee are shown, by month and on a tracking basis, in the center portion of the chart. The right-hand portion of the chart shows the projected sales per employee by quarter for the coming year.

48.8 Sales per Employee—Version 8: Paired charts are used in Version 8 of a sales per employee tracking chart, Figure 48.8, to show three separate factors: sales, employment, and annual sales per employee. Planned and actual employment and planned and actual sales, on a cumulative basis, are both shown in line curve form on the left-hand grid. The annual sales per employee is shown on the right-hand grid.

48.9 Sales per Employee—Version 9: Graphics have been

combined with a statistical table in Version 9 of a sales per employee tracking chart, Figure 48.9. Forecasted and actual annualized sales per employee statistics are given in the table, and are plotted on the graph, as well. The table also provides the variance between these two statistics in terms of dollars and percentages.

48.10 Sales per Employee—Version 10: Nine lines of statistical data are shown in conjunction with a graphic display in Version 10 of a sales per employee tracking chart, Figure 48.10. Forecasted, actual, and variance statistics are given in the table for cumulative sales, number of employees, and annualized sales per employee. The annualized sales per employee figures, which are on a year-to-date basis, are also plotted on the graphic portion of the chart.

48.11 Sales per Employee—Version 11: A method for tracking sales per employee utilizing a statistical table is shown as Version 11, Figure 48.11. In this table forecasted, actual, and variance statistics are given for cumulative sales, number of employees, and annualized sales per employee.

48.12 Sales per Employee—Version 12: A box score style of one-time status report is shown as Version 12 of a sales per employee chart, Figure 48.12. In this example, statistics are given, by quarters, for the current year and for two previous years. Forecasted, actual, and variance figures are provided for the current year. In this example, the statistics show sales per employee figures with, and without, overtime factors.

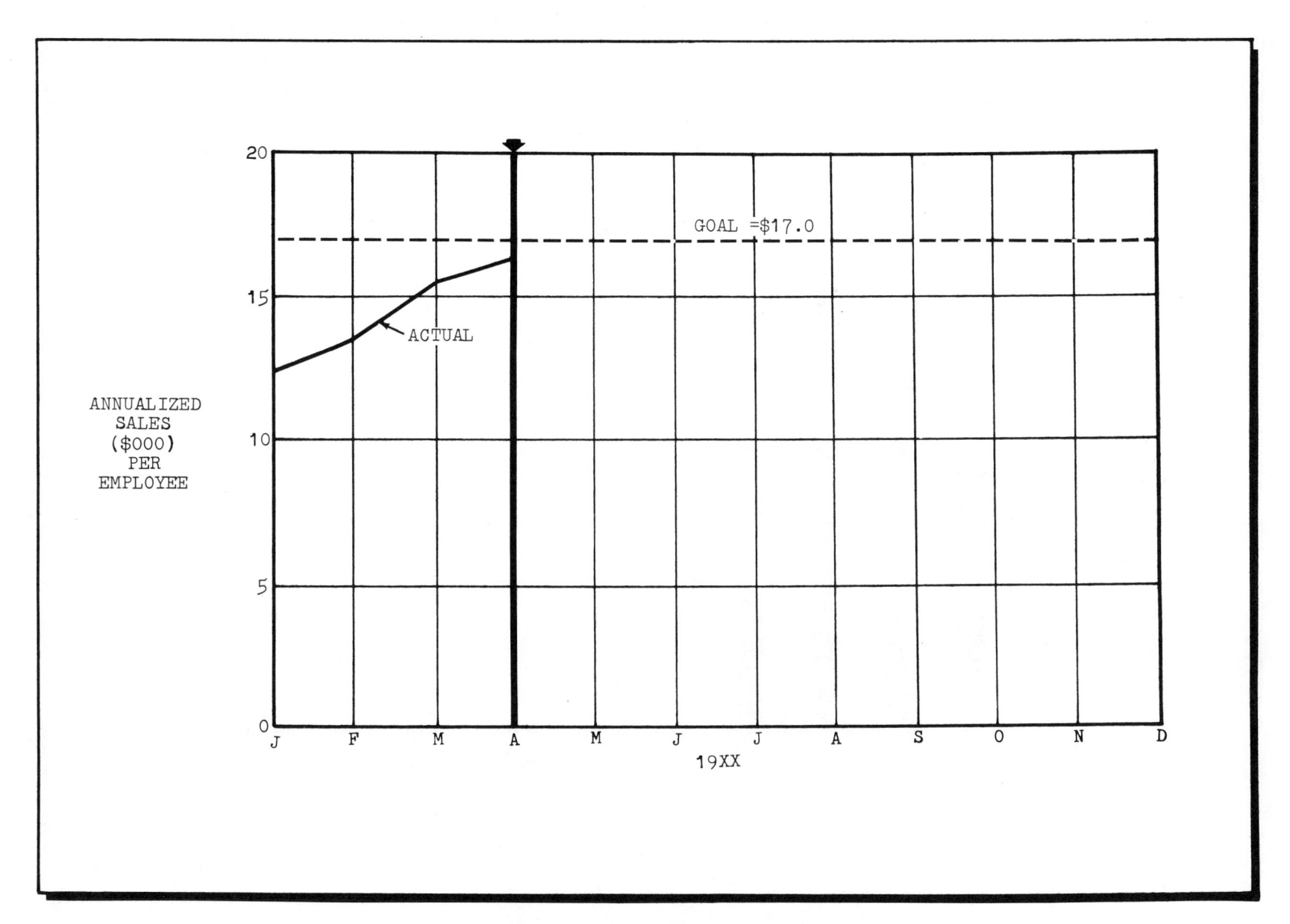

Figure 48.1　Sales per Employee—Version 1

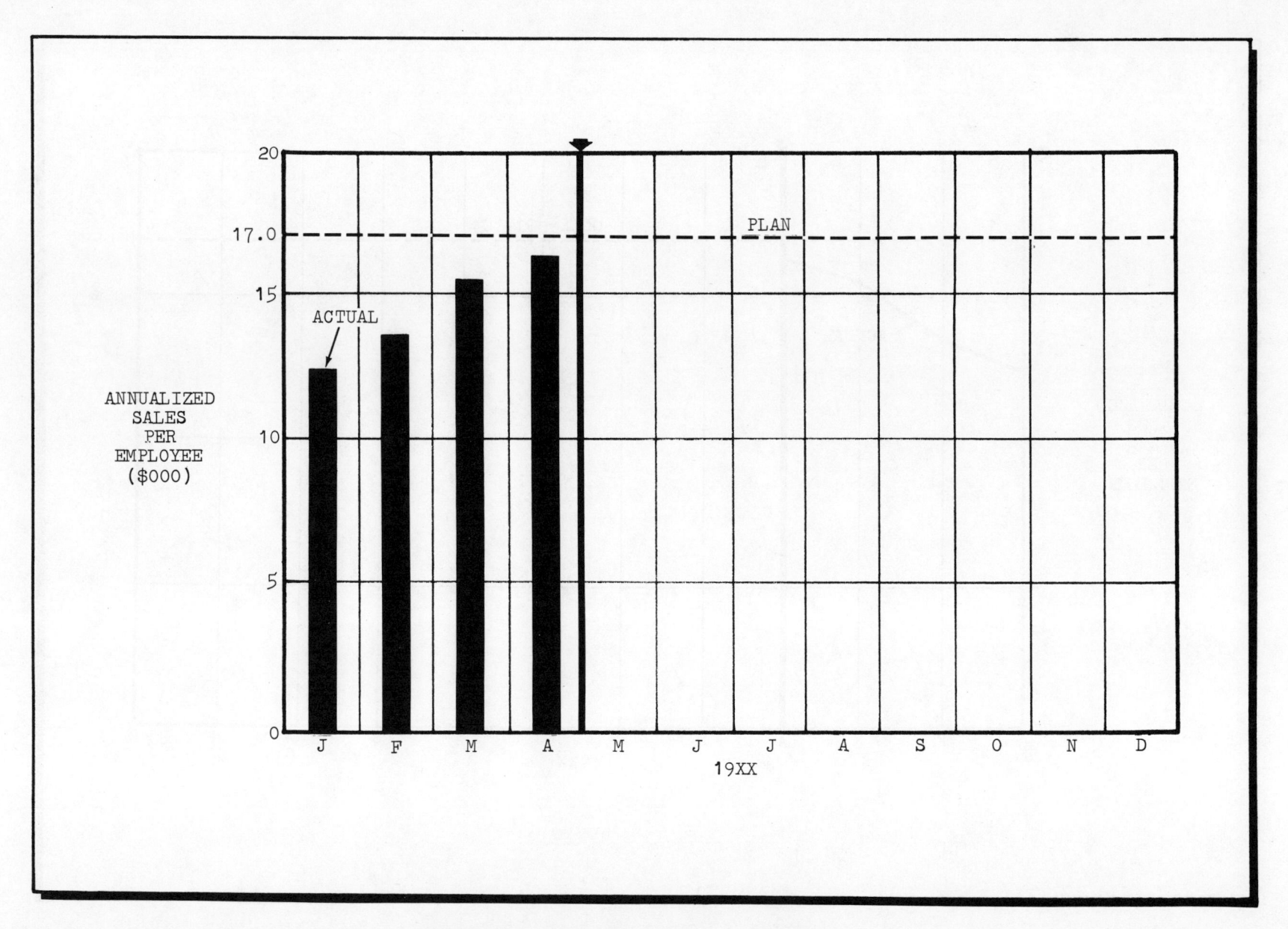

Figure 48.2   Sales per Employee—Version 2

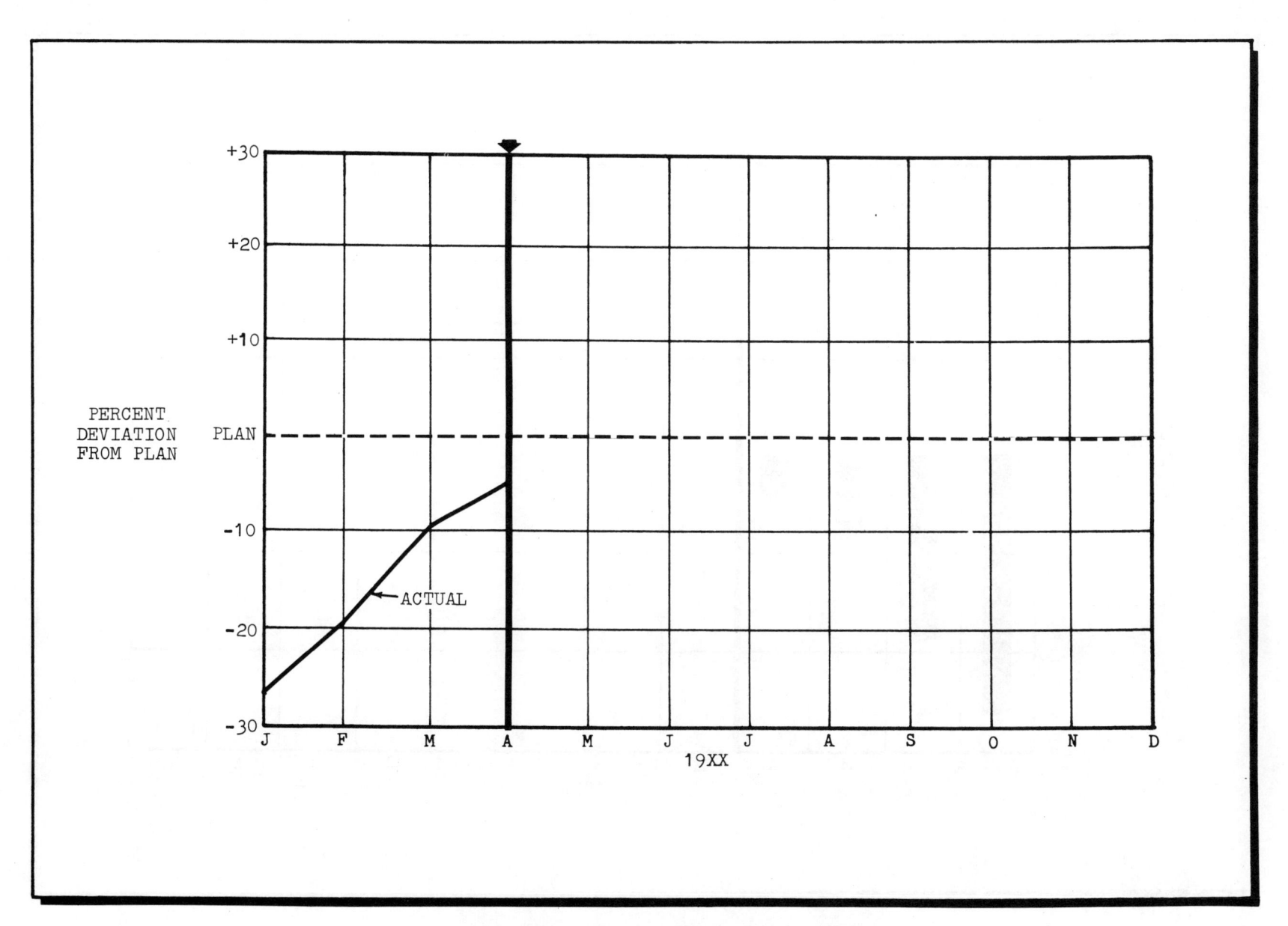

Figure 48.3　Sales per Employee—Version 3

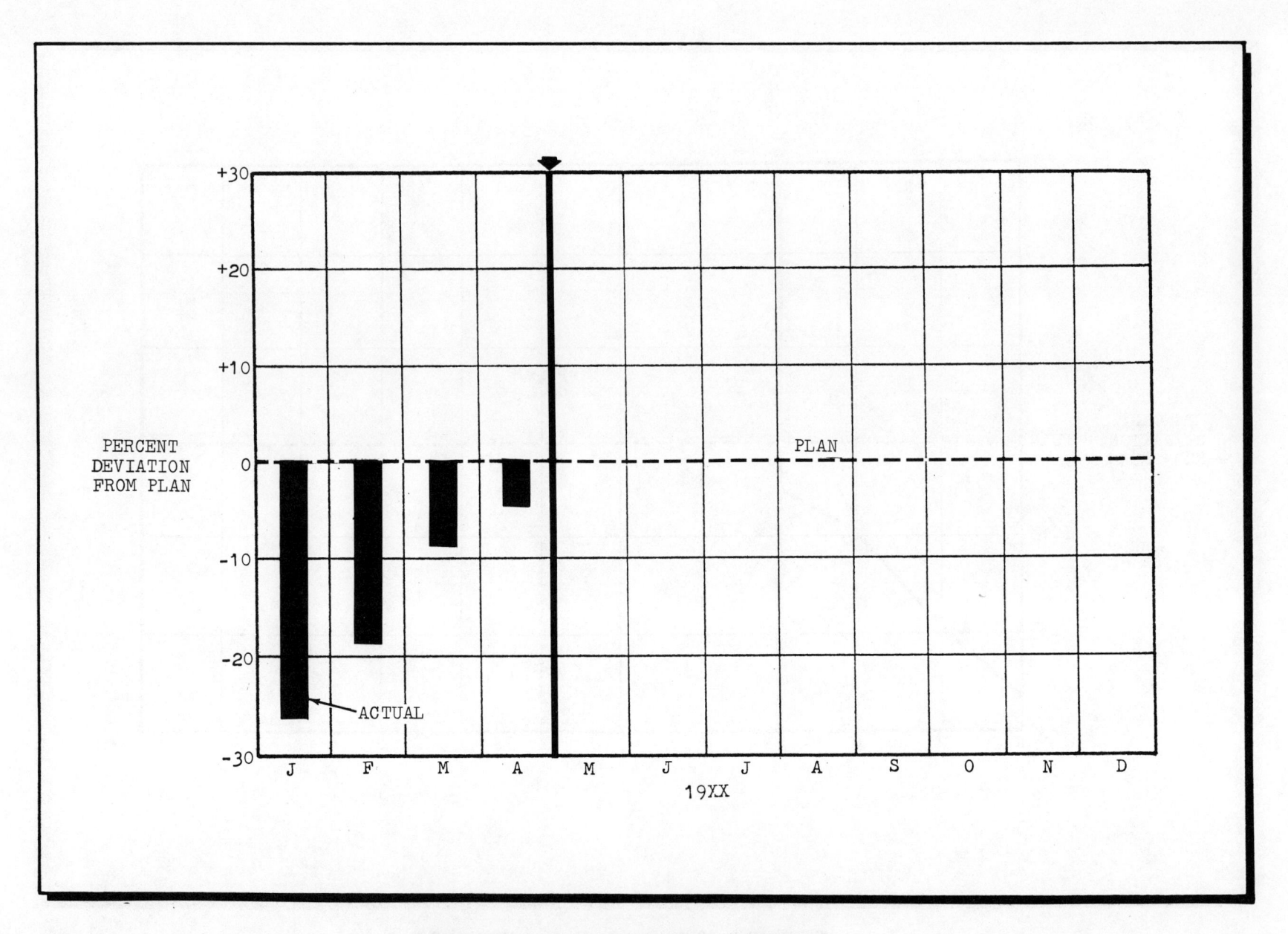

Figure 48.4 Sales per Employee—Version 4

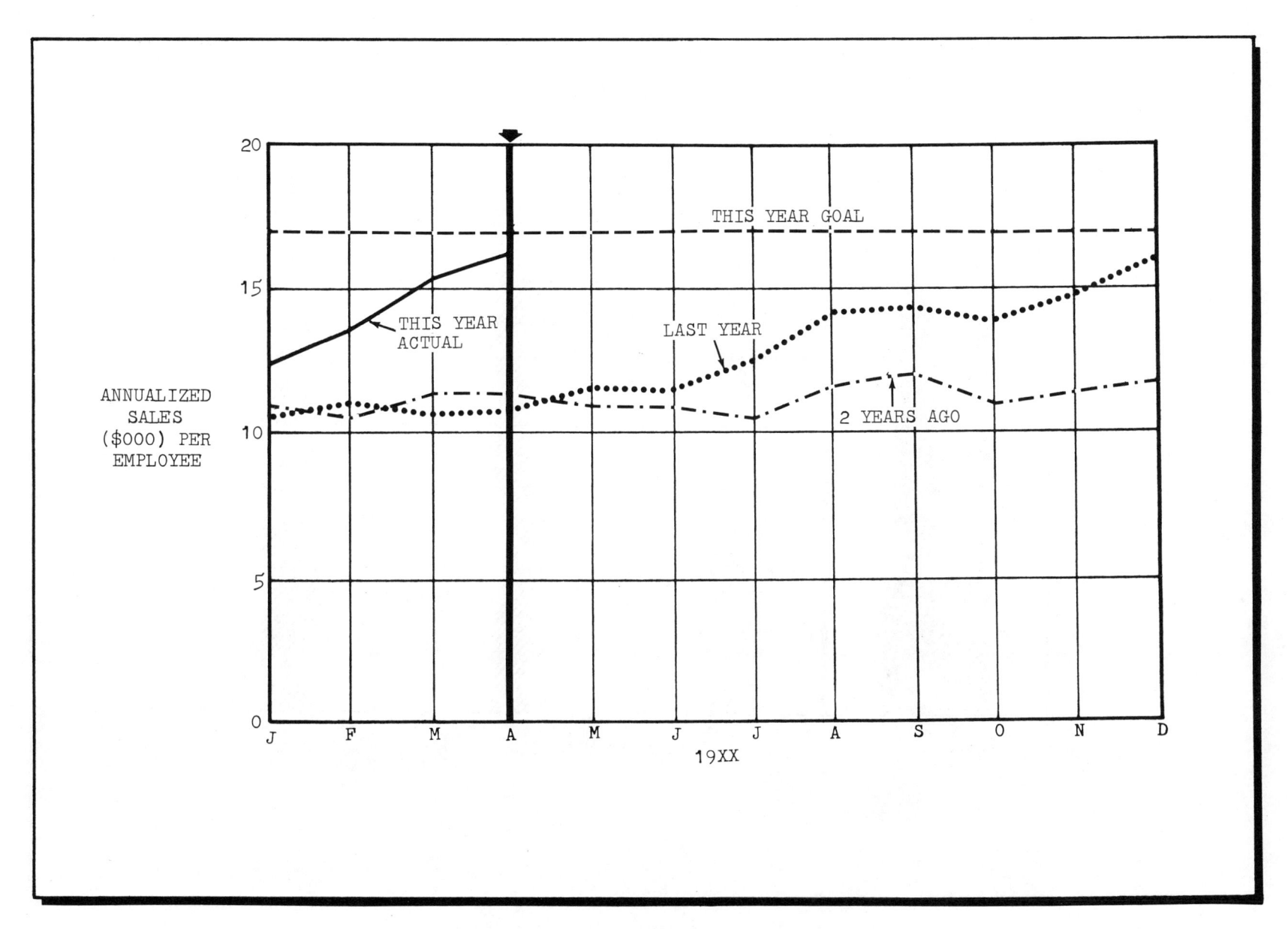

Figure 48.5   Sales per Employee—Version 5

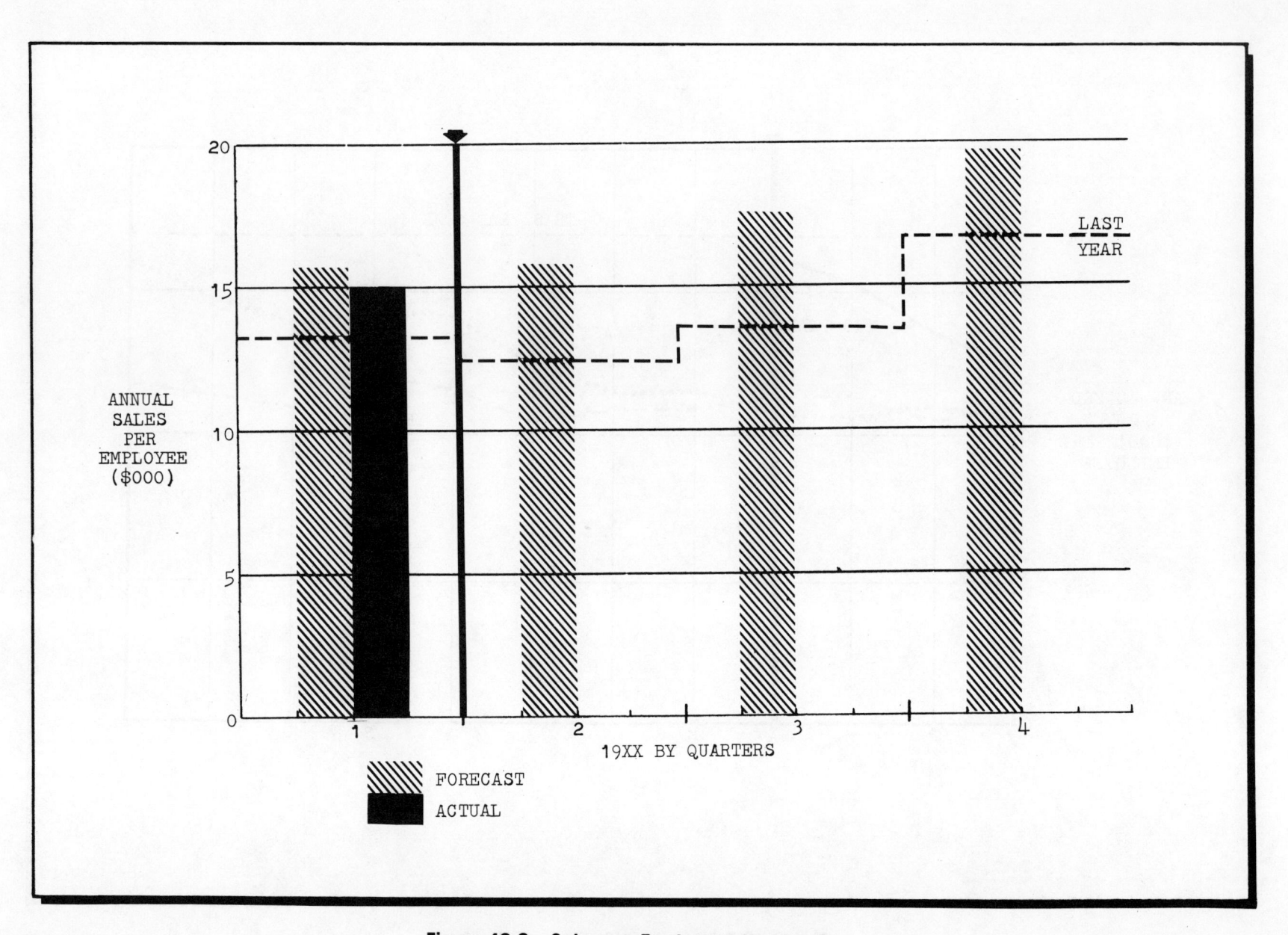

Figure 48.6   Sales per Employee—Version 6

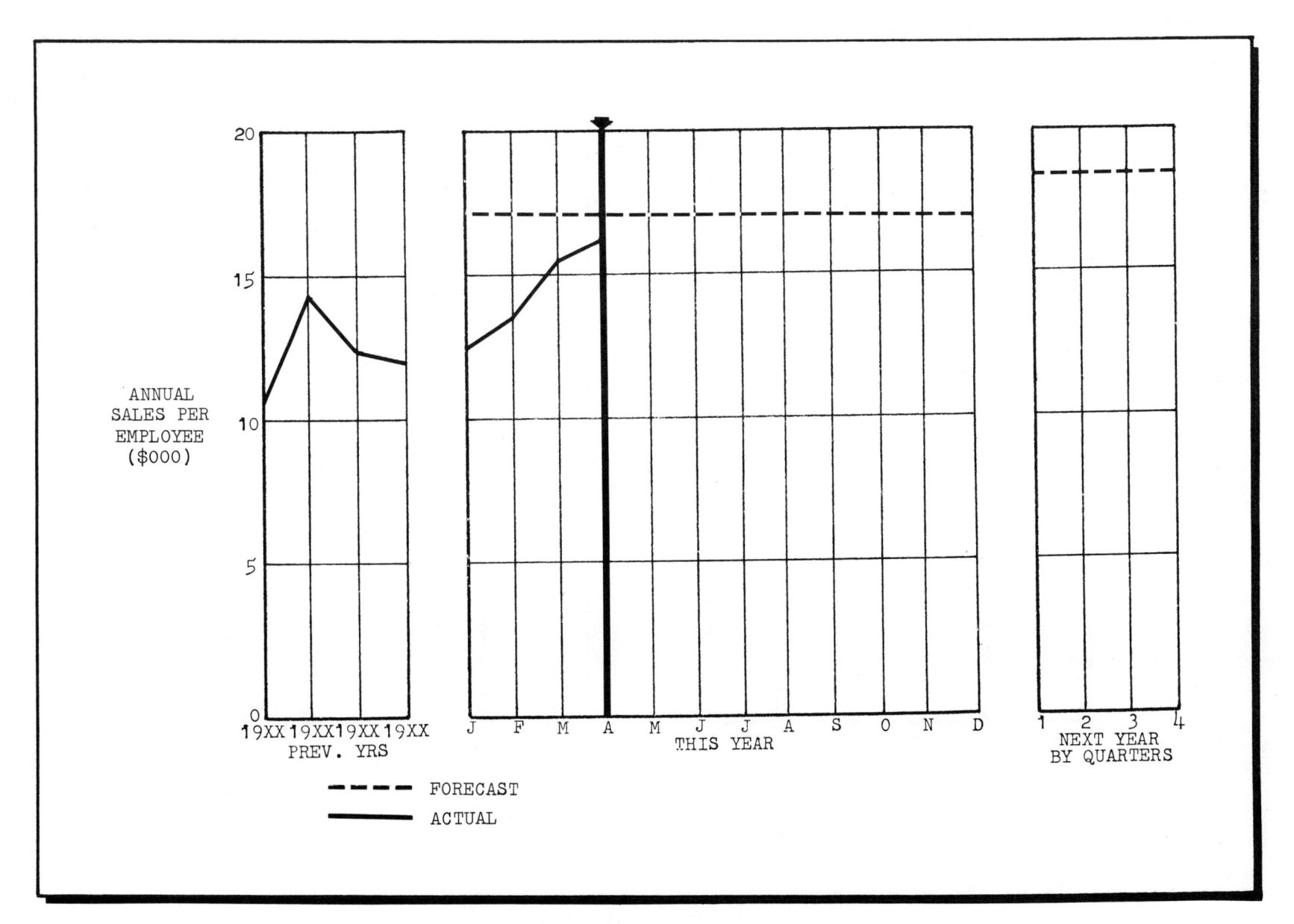

Figure 48.7 Sales per Employee—Version 7

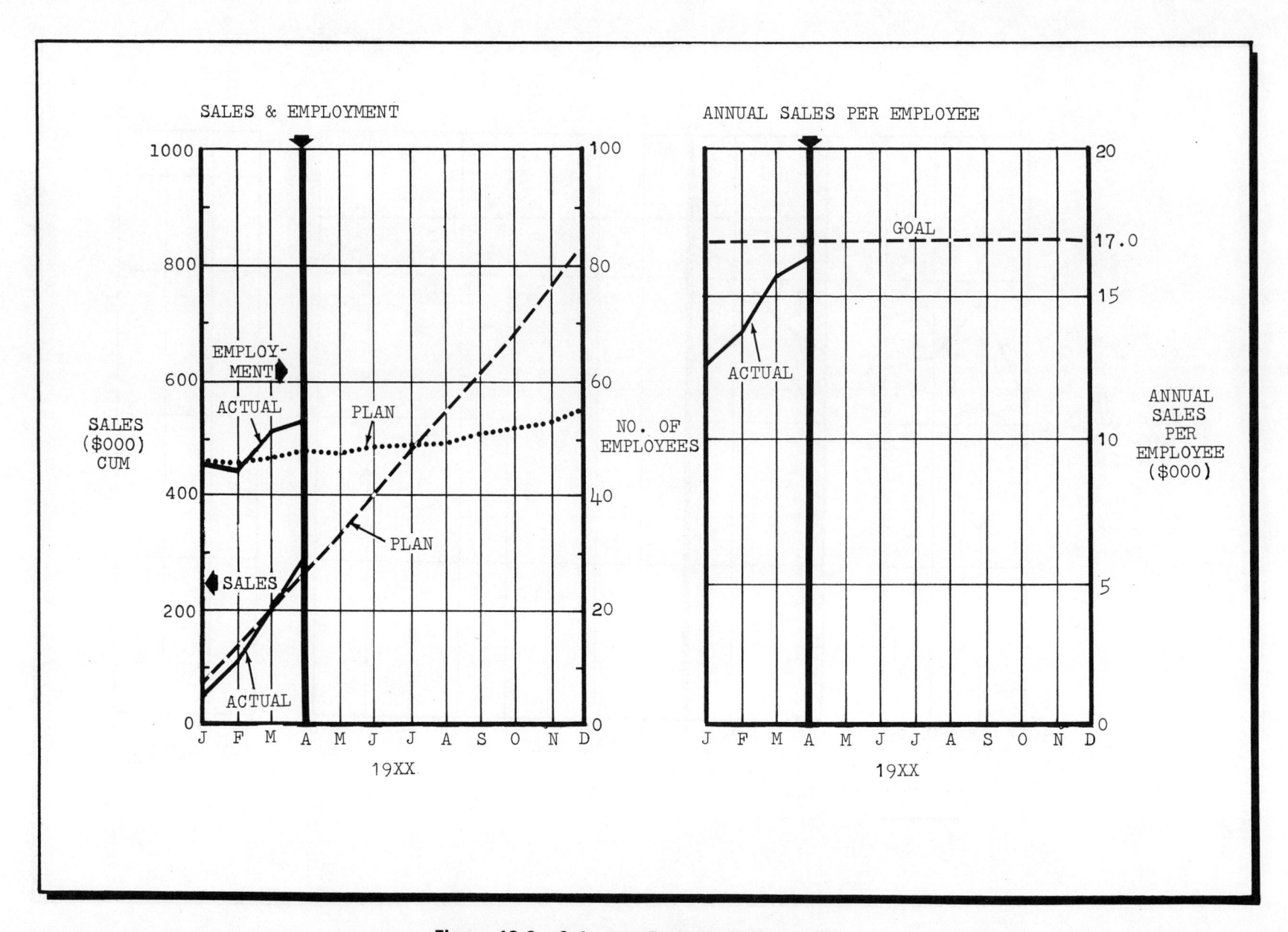

Figure 48.8 Sales per Employee—Version 8

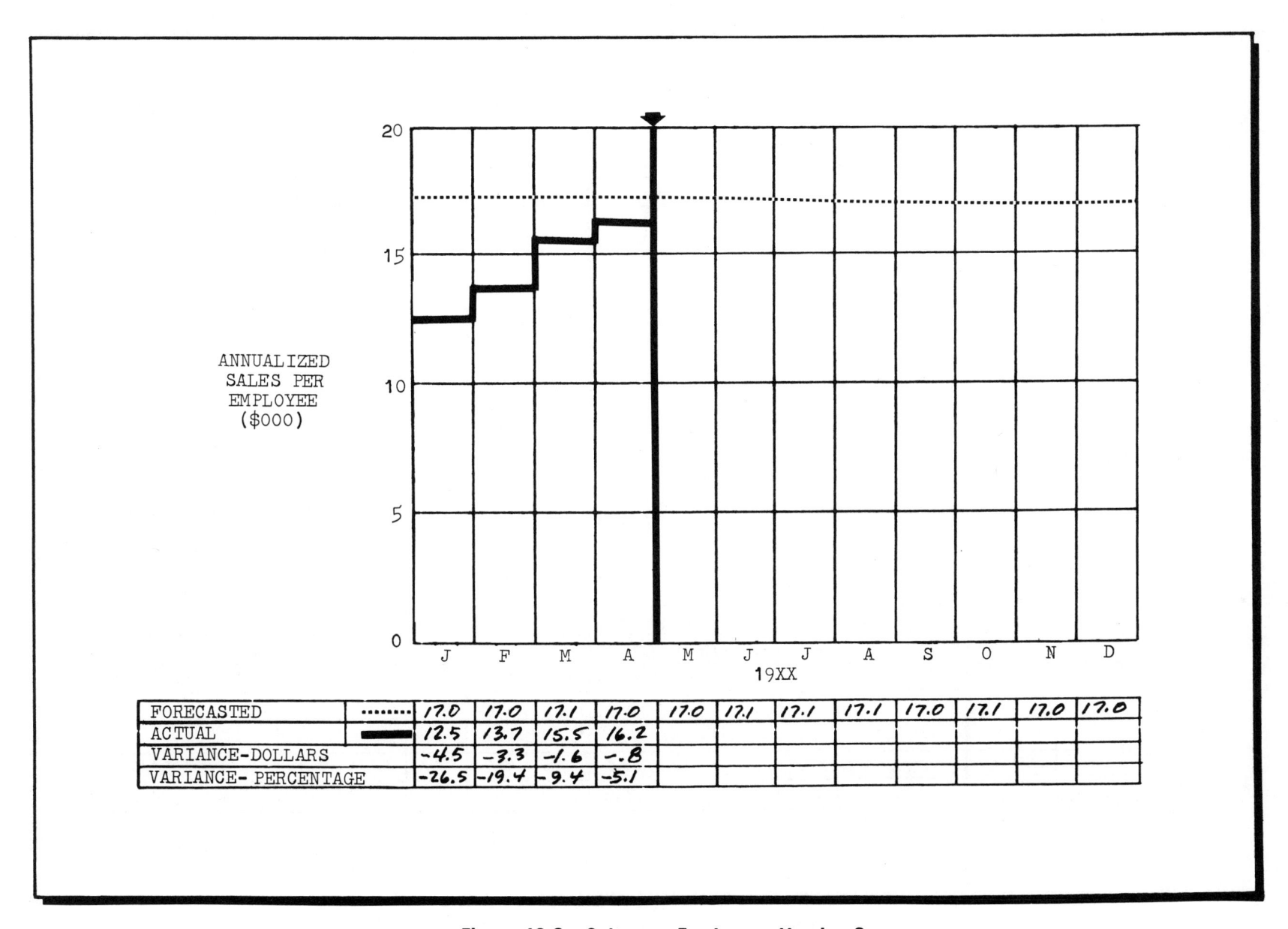

		J	F	M	A	M	J	J	A	S	O	N	D
FORECASTED	········	17.0	17.0	17.1	17.0	17.0	17.1	17.1	17.1	17.0	17.1	17.0	17.0
ACTUAL	▬▬▬	12.5	13.7	15.5	16.2								
VARIANCE-DOLLARS		-4.5	-3.3	-1.6	-.8								
VARIANCE- PERCENTAGE		-26.5	-19.4	-9.4	-5.1								

Figure 48.9 Sales per Employee—Version 9

ANNUAL SALES PER EMPLOYEE ($000)

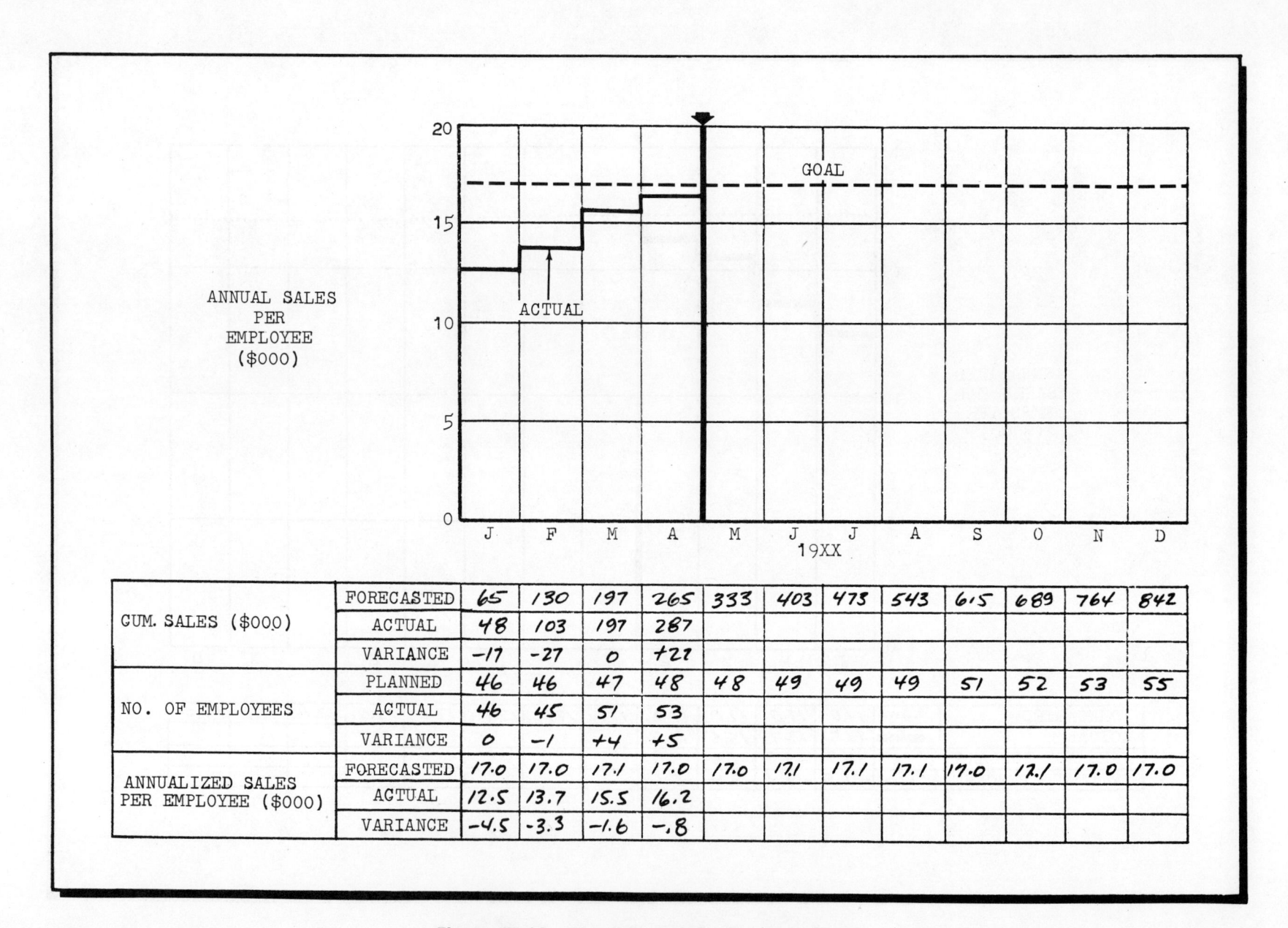

[Chart showing actual vs goal, J–D 19XX, actual stepping up from ~12.5 to ~16.2 through April, goal line at ~17]

		J	F	M	A	M	J	J	A	S	O	N	D
CUM. SALES ($000)	FORECASTED	65	130	197	265	333	403	473	543	615	689	764	842
	ACTUAL	48	103	197	287								
	VARIANCE	−17	−27	0	+22								
NO. OF EMPLOYEES	PLANNED	46	46	47	48	48	49	49	49	51	52	53	55
	ACTUAL	46	45	51	53								
	VARIANCE	0	−1	+4	+5								
ANNUALIZED SALES PER EMPLOYEE ($000)	FORECASTED	17.0	17.0	17.1	17.0	17.0	17.1	17.1	17.1	17.0	17.1	17.0	17.0
	ACTUAL	12.5	13.7	15.5	16.2								
	VARIANCE	−4.5	−3.3	−1.6	−.8								

Figure 48.10 Sales per Employee—Version 10

FACTOR		J	F	M	A	19XX M	J	J	A	S	O	N	D
CUM SALES ($000)	FORECAST	65	130	197	265	333	403	473	543	615	689	764	842
	ACTUAL	48	103	197	287								
	VARIANCE	-17	-27	0	+22								
NUMBER OF EMPLOYEES	FORECAST	46	46	47	48	48	49	49	49	51	52	53	55
	ACTUAL	46	45	51	53								
	VARIANCE	0	-1	+4	+5								
ANNUALIZED SALES PER EMPLOYEE ($000)	FORECAST	17.0	17.0	17.1	17.0	17.0	17.1	17.1	17.1	17.0	17.1	17.0	17.0
	ACTUAL	12.5	13.7	15.5	16.2								
	VAR.-$	-4.5	-3.3	-1.6	-.8								
	VAR.-%	-26.5	-19.4	-9.4	-5.1								

Figure 48.11 Sales per Employee—Version 11

STATUS AS OF <u>FIRST QUARTER</u>   (1)

QUARTER	2 YEARS AGO(2)	LAST YEAR(2)	THIS YEAR		
			FORECAST(3)	ACTUAL	VARIANCE
1	12.2	13.0	15.5	15.0	-.5
2	11.7	12.3	15.6		
3	13.1	13.5	17.4		
4	12.2	16.8	19.7		
AVERAGE	12.3	13.9	17.1		
AVERAGE (EXCLUDING OVERTIME)	13.3	15.0	18.0		

NOTES:
(1) ALL FIGURES ANNUALIZED ($000)
(2) INCLUDES 8% OVERTIME
(3) INCLUDES 5% OVERTIME

Figure 48.12   Sales per Employee—Version 12

49.0 SCHEDULE, COST, AND TECHNICAL PERFORMANCE

In monitoring progress, it is useful to examine schedule performance, cost performance, and technical performance in relationship to each other. Charts that display this much information are usually considered to be "busy" or "cluttered," a circumstance difficult to avoid. Charts that display these three performance factors are shown in this section.

49.1 Schedule, Cost, and Technical Performance—Version 1: In circumstances where there is only a single technical factor to monitor, a trio of deviation-from-plan style of charts can be used to track schedule, cost, and technical performance as shown in Version 1, Figure 49.1. On all three grids a solid line shows progress to date. Dashed lines show the upper and lower limits which, when exceeded, call for special actions. A dotted line shows the minimum value allowed for reliability performance.

49.2 Schedule, Cost, and Technical Performance—Version 2: Multiple technical parameters can be summarized with schedule and cost performance information in Version 2 of a schedule, cost, and technical performance tracking chart, Figure 49.2. A solid, straight line down the center of each grid indicates performance within planned limits. When the solid line goes above or below the center it indicates that performance is above or below plans or budgets, or beyond tolerance limits for technical characteristics.

49.3 Schedule, Cost, and Technical Performance—Version 3: Check marks are used to indicate status in Version 3 of a schedule, cost, and technical performance tracking chart, Figure 49.3. Check marks within the clear area of each grid indicate favorable performance. Check marks in the shaded portion of each grid indicate unfavorable conditions.

49.4 Schedule, Cost, and Technical Performance—Version 4: Version 4 of a schedule, cost, and technical performance tracking chart, Figure 49.4, is similar to Version 3 except in this version statistics are used instead of check marks. Further, the category titles are augmented by requirement information.

49.5 Schedule, Cost, and Technical Performance—Version 5: A complex version of a schedule, cost, and technical performance chart is shown as Version 5, Figure 49.5. The graphic portion of the chart displays schedule and cost data including the value of completed work. To correlate schedules to costs, the cumulative cost amount scale is in register with the schedule curves. A table gives the targeted and expected technical performance values and relates deviations as to their impact on the schedule and on costs.

49.6 Schedule, Cost, and Technical Performance—Version 6: A tabular type tracking chart is shown as Version 6 of a schedule, cost, and technical performance chart, Figure 49.6. In this example, planned and actual schedule and cost performance data are given on a cumulative basis. Predicted and current value data are given for each of the technical parameters. A check mark system is used to indicate the most critical problem at the time of the report.

49.7 Schedule, Cost, and Technical Performance—Version 7: Version 7 of a schedule, cost, and technical performance chart, Figure 49.7, is a simple version of a one-time status report. Status is given for schedule, cost, and technical factors as to performance for the current month. Space is provided on the right-hand side of the table for remarks or analyses.

49.8 Schedule, Cost, and Technical Performance—Version 8: The one-time status report shown as Version 8, Figure 49.8, gives detailed schedule and cost data for the current month, the year to date, and the expected position at completion. Technical performance information is given only on an exception basis.

49.9 Schedule, Cost, and Technical Performance—Version 9: A detailed version of a one-time schedule, cost, and technical performance status chart is shown as Version 9, Figure 49.9. To aid in interpreting the chart, circles are used in this example to emphasize critical areas of concern.

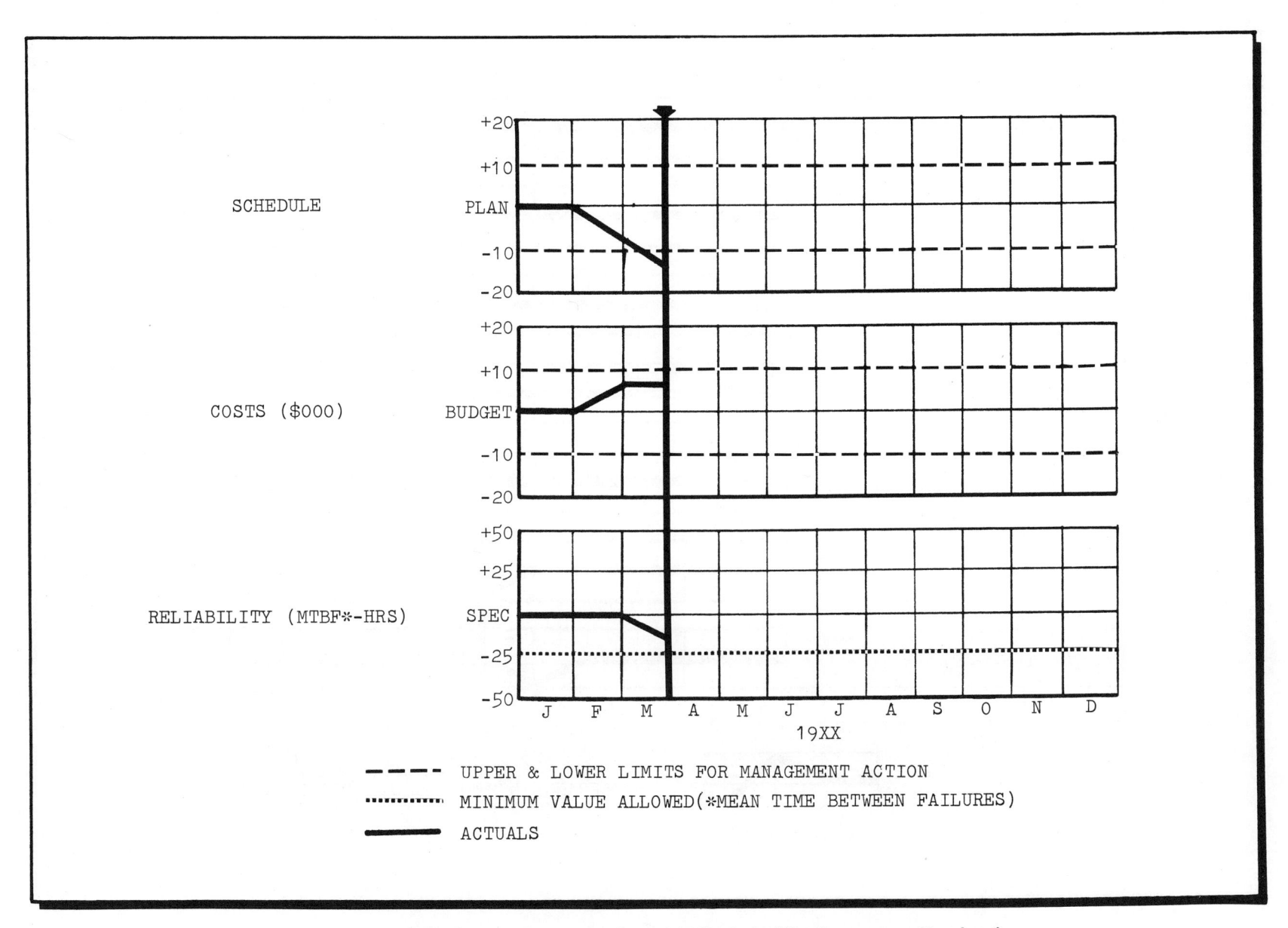

Figure 49.1 Schedule, Cost, and Technical Performance—Version 1

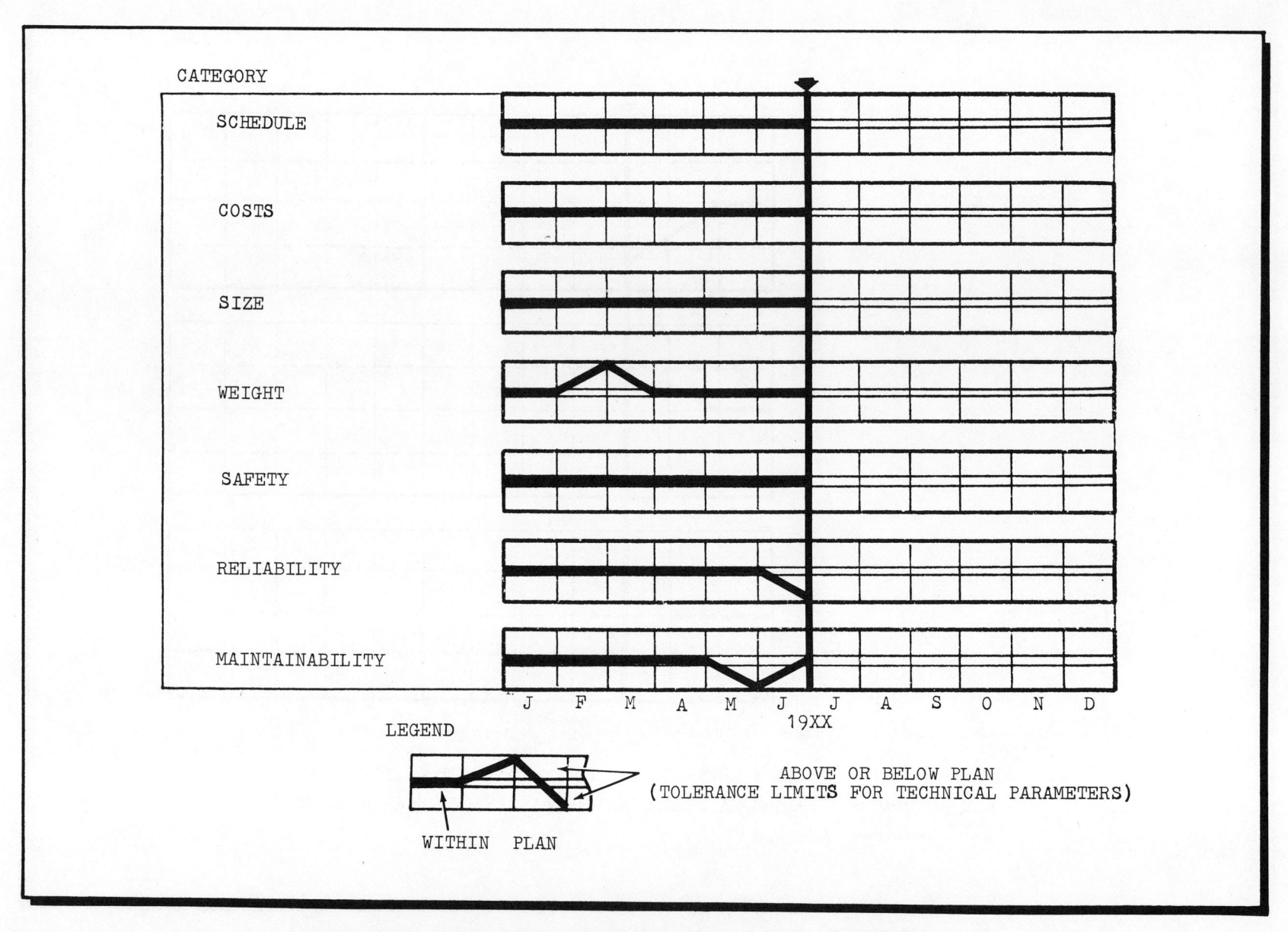

Figure 49.2 Schedule, Cost, and Technical Performance—Version 2

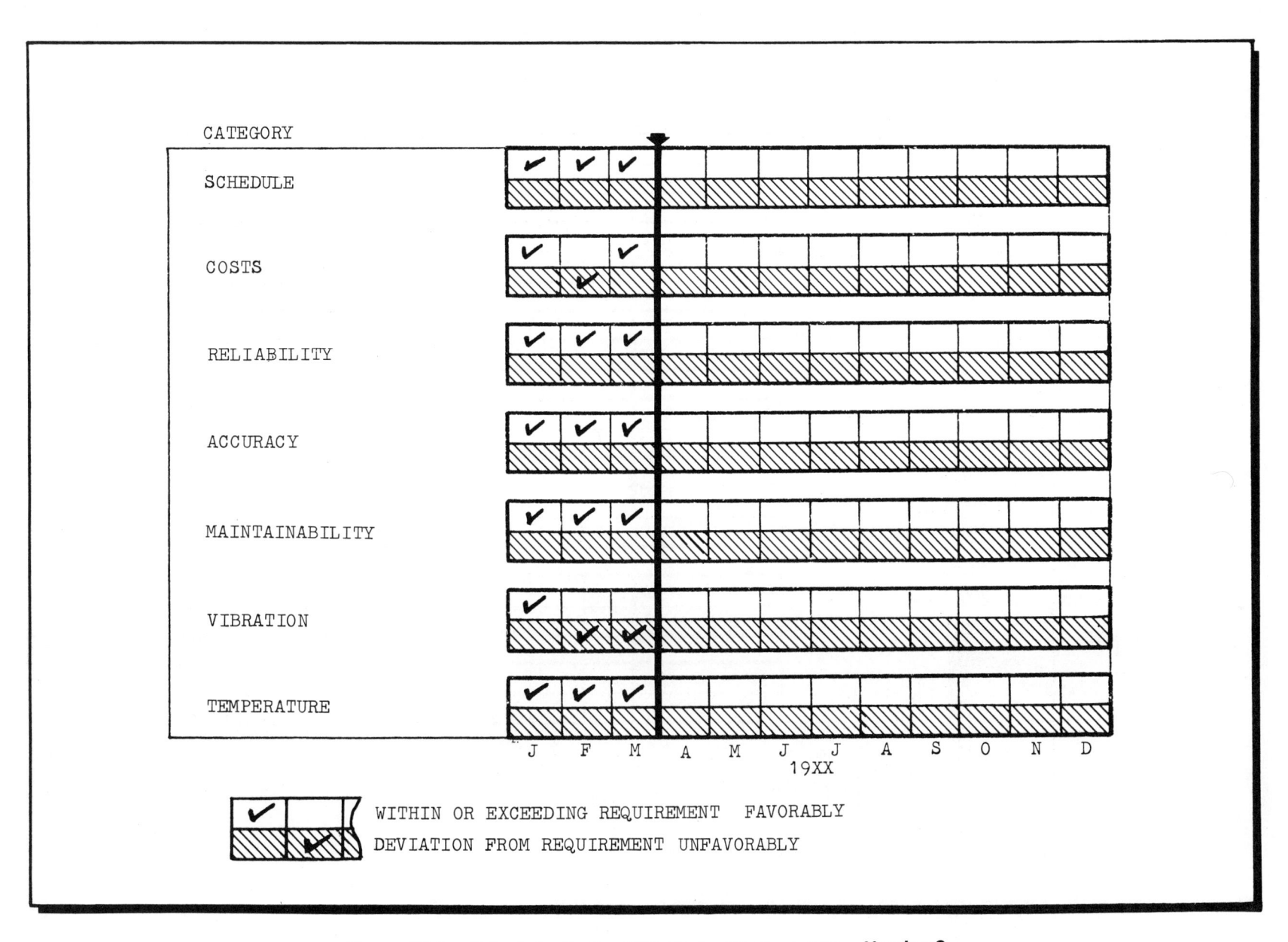

Figure 49.3 Schedule, Cost, and Technical Performance—Version 3

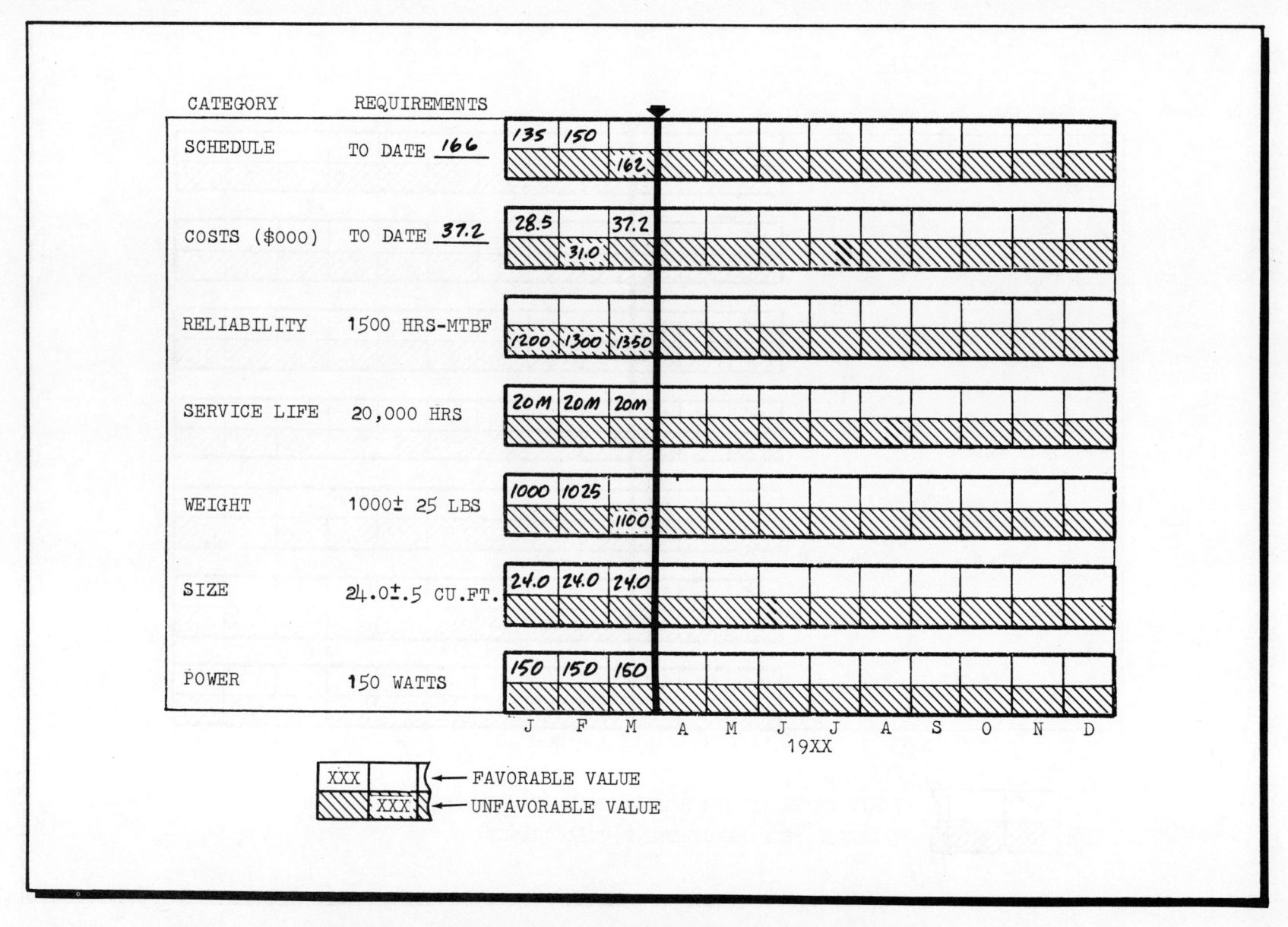

CATEGORY	REQUIREMENTS													
SCHEDULE	TO DATE 166	135	150	162										
COSTS ($000)	TO DATE 37.2	28.5	31.0	37.2										
RELIABILITY	1500 HRS-MTBF	1200	1300	1350										
SERVICE LIFE	20,000 HRS	20M	20M	20M										
WEIGHT	1000 ± 25 LBS	1000	1025	1100										
SIZE	24.0 ± .5 CU.FT.	24.0	24.0	24.0										
POWER	150 WATTS	150	150	150										
		J	F	M	A	M	J	J	A	S	O	N	D	
							19XX							

XXX ← FAVORABLE VALUE
XXX ← UNFAVORABLE VALUE

Figure 49.4   Schedule, Cost, and Technical Performance—Version 4

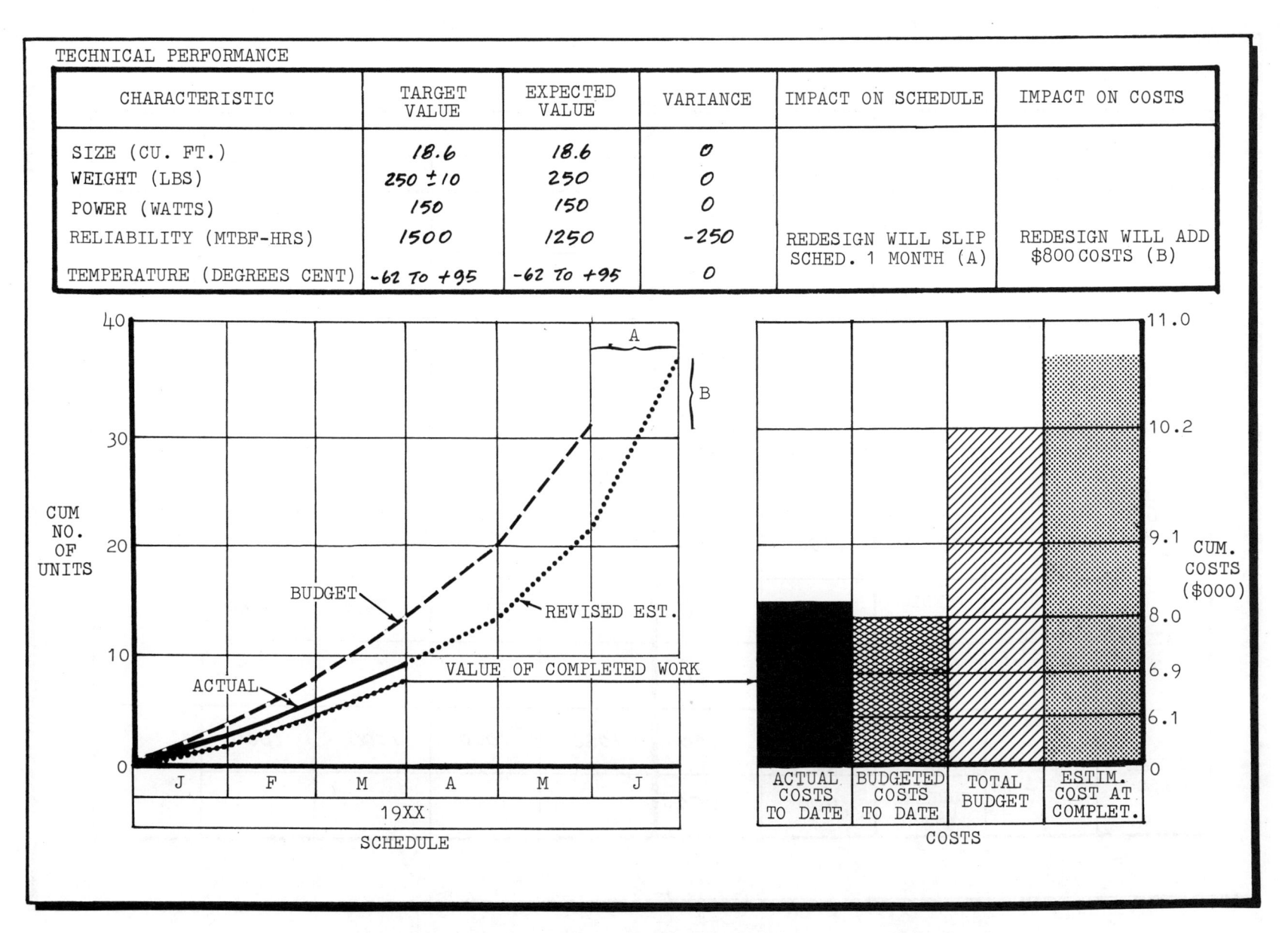

TECHNICAL PERFORMANCE					
CHARACTERISTIC	TARGET VALUE	EXPECTED VALUE	VARIANCE	IMPACT ON SCHEDULE	IMPACT ON COSTS
SIZE (CU. FT.)	18.6	18.6	0		
WEIGHT (LBS)	250 ±10	250	0		
POWER (WATTS)	150	150	0		
RELIABILITY (MTBF-HRS)	1500	1250	-250	REDESIGN WILL SLIP SCHED. 1 MONTH (A)	REDESIGN WILL ADD $800 COSTS (B)
TEMPERATURE (DEGREES CENT)	-62 TO +95	-62 TO +95	0		

Figure 49.5 Schedule, cost, and Technical Performance—Version 5

CATEGORY			19XX						MOST CRITICAL (✓)
			J	F	M	A	M	J	
SCHEDULE		CUM PLAN	150	175	200	225	250	275	
		CUM ACTUAL	149	175					
COSTS ($000)		CUM BUDGET	56.3	65.5	72.5	86.4	97.1	105.3	
		CUM ACTUAL	57.1	66.1					
RELIABILITY (MTBF-HRS)	SPEC 1500	PREDICTION	1200	1300	1400	1500	1500	1500	✓
		CURRENT VALUE	1100	1100					
SIZE (CU.FT.)	SPEC 24.0 ± .5	PREDICTION	26.0	26.0	25.0	24.0	24.0	24.0	
		CURRENT VALUE	26.0	25.0					
WEIGHT (LBS)	SPEC. 1000 ± 25	PREDICTION	1100	1100	1050	1000	1000	1000	
		CURRENT VALUE	1100	1050					

Figure 49.6 Schedule, Cost, and Technical Performance—Version 6

STATUS AS OF _____

FACTOR	THIS MONTH			ANALYSIS
	PLAN OR REQUIREMENT	ACTUAL	VARIANCE	
SCHEDULE:				
UNIT A	101	101	0	
UNIT B	112	110	-2	
UNIT C	117	117	0	
COSTS ($000)				
TOTAL	87.0	85.5	-1.5	
TECHNICAL PERFORMANCE				
WEIGHT (LBS)	1000±25	1150	+150	RE-EVLUATION NOW IN WORK (JONES)
SIZE (CU.FT.)	24.0±.5	26.3	+2.3	
RELIABILITY (MTBF-HRS)	1500	1500	0	
SERVICE LIFE (YRS)	3	3	0	

Figure 49.7 Schedule, Cost, and Technical Performance—Version 7

STATUS AS OF _____

ITEM		SCHEDULE			COSTS($000)			TECHNICAL PERFORMANCE
		PLAN	ACTUAL	VAR	BUDGET	ACTUAL	VAR	CRITICAL FACTOR
UNIT 1	THIS MO.	12	12	0	22.1	22.0	-.1	NONE
	TO DATE	57	57	0	104.9	104.9	0	
	AT COMPL.	143	143	0	212.0	212.0	0	
UNIT 2	THIS MO.	103	103	0	51.0	51.0	0	NONE
	TO DATE	210	210	0	104.0	104.0	0	
	AT COMPL.	312	312	0	203.1	203.1	0	
UNIT 3	THIS MO.	12	6	-6	75.6	37.8	-37.8	RELIABILITY TESTS 200 HOURS BELOW SPEC. REDESIGN WILL CAUSE $107,000 OVERRUN.
	TO DATE	36	13	-23	226.8	81.9	-144.9	
	AT COMP.	110	110	0	693.0	800.0	+107.0	
UNIT 4	THIS MO.	10	10	0	16.0	16.0	0	NONE
	TO DATE	42	42	0	58.3	58.3	0	
	AT COMPL.	44	44	0	61.0	61.0	0	
UNIT 5	THIS MO.	52	52	0	106.5	107.4	+.9	NONE
	TO DATE	52	52	0	106.5	107.4	+.9	
	AT COMPL.	100	100	0	204.0	204.0	0	

Figure 49.8 Schedule, Cost, and Technical Performance—Version 8

STATUS AS OF _____

ITEM	SCHEDULE				COST ($000)					TECHNICAL PERFORMANCE			
	MILESTONE	SCHED DATE	EXP DATE	VAR. (WKS)	TO DATE			AT COMPLETION			CHARACTERISTIC	SPEC	EXP	VAR
					VAL	ACT	VAR	BUD	EXP	VAR				
ABC SYSTEM	PROCUREMENT COMPLETE	1 APR	7 APR	+1.0	42.8	41.5	-1.3	127.0	125.0	-2.0	SIZE (CU.FT)	24.0	24.0	0
											WEIGHT (LBS)	1000±25	1000	0
	SUBASSEMBLY A COMPLETE	4 APR	4 APR	0							POWER (WATTS)	150	150	0
											STOR. LIFE (YRS)	3	3	0
											RELIABILITY (MTBF-HRS)	1500	1500	0
XYZ SYSTEM	ENGINEERING DRAWINGS COMPLETE	1 APR	1 APR	0	28.3	34.5	+6.2	123.0	133.0	(+10.0)	SIZE (CU.FT.)	18.6	18.6	0
											WEIGHT (LBS)	800±20	800	0
	BREADBOARD COMPLETE	6 APR	20 APR	+2.0							POWER (WATTS)	150	150	0
											TEMP (DEG. C)	-62 to +95	-62 to +95	0
											RELIABILITY (MTBF-HRS)	1500	1270	(-230)
FIELD TESTING UNIT	DETAILED SPECIFICATIONS COMPLETE	4 APR	4 APR	0	6.3	6.2	-.1	57.4	57.4	0	SIZE (CU.FT)	10	10	0
											WEIGHT (LBS)	470±15	480	+10
											POWER (WATTS)	150	150	0
											SER. LIFE (YRS)	10	10	0
TRAINING	COURSE OUTLINE COMPLETE	1 APR	25 MAR	-1.0	4.1	3.9	-.2	9.5	9.5	0	NOT APPLICABLE			
	TRAINING AIDS DESIGNED	4 APR	4 APR	0										

CRITICAL ITEMS CIRCLED (XXX)

Figure 49.9 Schedule, Cost, and Technical Performance—Version 9

50.0 SCHEDULE AND COSTS

In controlling an activity, it can be essential to monitor expenditures in relationship to work accomplishment. Charts that relate costs to schedule compliance are shown in this section. Also see Section 49.0, *Schedule, Cost, and Technical Performance*.

50.1 Schedule and Costs—Version 1: One of the most fundamental ways for displaying schedule and cost data is shown as Version 1, Figure 50.1. The left-hand grid in this example shows planned and actual schedule performance. The right-hand grid displays planned and actual cost performance. This approach shows trends but lacks precision.

50.2 Schedule and Costs—Version 2: In Version 2 of a schedule and costs tracking chart, Figure 50.2, budgeted and actual costs are shown together with a revised estimate to complete. To this has been added "value of completed work." Costs have been related to schedule performance, in this latter measurement, by attaching a dollar value to the work completed using the original cost estimates.

50.3 Schedule and Costs—Version 3: Version 3 of a schedule and costs tracking chart, Figure 50.3, is plotted on the basis of month-end position. In this example, the cumulated variance between actual expenditures and the value of completed work is shown on the grid. This example also graphically portrays an anticipated schedule slippage.

50.4 Schedule and Costs—Version 4: Grouped columns are used in Version 4 of a schedule and costs tracking chart, Figure 50.4. The columns show, for each month, budgeted and actual costs, and the dollar value of completed work. The delta is positioned on the grid to show both the estimated date of completion and cost at completion.

50.5 Schedule and Costs—Version 5: Two chart styles are used to show the relationship of costs to schedule compliance in Version 5, Figure 50.5. The left-hand grid shows the cumulative number of scheduled and actual units. The right-hand grid displays dollars and is scaled to match the unit quantities. A horizontal line drawn from actual units completed to date to the cost scale shows the value of work completed to be less, in this example, than the amount of money already spent.

50.6 Schedule and Costs—Version 6: The amount scale in Version 6 of a schedule and costs tracking chart, Figure 50.6, is in terms of 100 percent. The percentages of total units scheduled and completed to date, and the percentages of budgeted and actual costs to date are shown. This example shows the activity to be seriously behind schedule and over-expended.

50.7 Schedule and Costs—Version 7: A deviation from plan style of chart is used as Version 7 of a schedule and costs tracking chart, Figure 50.7. Schedule variances are shown with a solid line and are in register with the left-hand amount scale. Cost variances, shown with a dotted line, are in register with the right-hand scale. A variation would be to have the left-hand scale in terms of percentage deviation rather than cost deviation.

50.8 Schedule and Costs—Version 8: A method for displaying schedule and cost information for a multi-task project is shown in Version 8, Figure 50.8. The symbol chart displays major milestone activity. The budgeted and actual costs are shown on the lower grid in register with the milestones.

50.9 Schedule and Costs—Version 9: Milestone symbols, in terms of task completions, are plotted according to date and in relationship to budget on Version 9 of a schedule and costs tracking chart, Figure 50.9.

50.10 Schedule and Costs—Version 10: Version 10 of a schedule and costs tracking chart, Figure 50.10, shows how a summary type network can be combined with a cost chart. Progress on the network is shown by shading completed portions of the network's activity lines. Costs are displayed on a cumulative basis with the budget shown with a dashed line and actuals to date shown with a solid line.

50.11 Schedule and Costs—Version 11: Statistics are combined with graphics in Version 11 of a schedule and costs tracking chart, Figure 50.11. The cumulative budgeted and actual cost data, and the value of completed work are all plotted on the graphic portion of the chart with the statistical backup given in the table. The table also gives the monthly rate figures and the scheduled and completed quantity of units on a per month and cumulative basis.

50.12 Schedule and Costs—Version 12: Scheduled and actual units and budgeted and actual costs, all on a cumulative basis, are given as statistics in the top portion of Version 12 of a schedule and costs tracking chart, Figure 50.12. The graphic portion of the chart first displays units delivered scaled according to date: when they *should* have been delivered. Costs to date are also plotted on the basis of date: when they *should* have been spent. This method graphically portrays the imbalance between schedule and costs.

50.13 Schedule and Costs—Version 13: A statistical table style is used as a one-time status report version of a schedule and costs chart, Figure 50.13. Scheduled, actual, and variance statistics for year-to-date deliveries are given first followed by year-to-date costs on a budget, actual, and variance basis. The final section provides a cost/schedule analysis. The unit cost is given first followed by a figure representing the value of the delivery variance items (unit cost × delivery variance). This figure is compared against the actual budget variance, the result being the net cost position (final column).

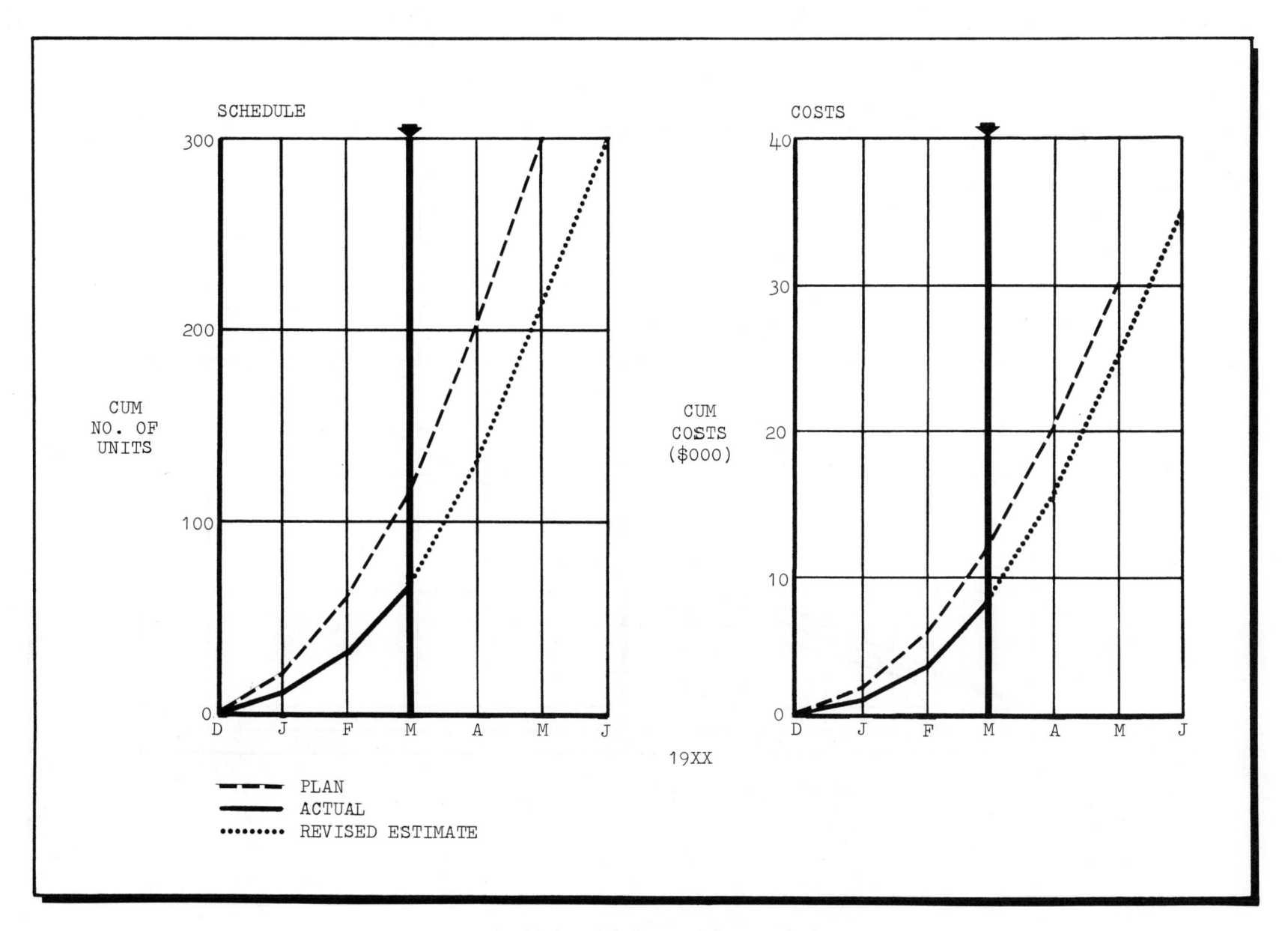

Figure 50.1 Schedule and Costs—Version 1

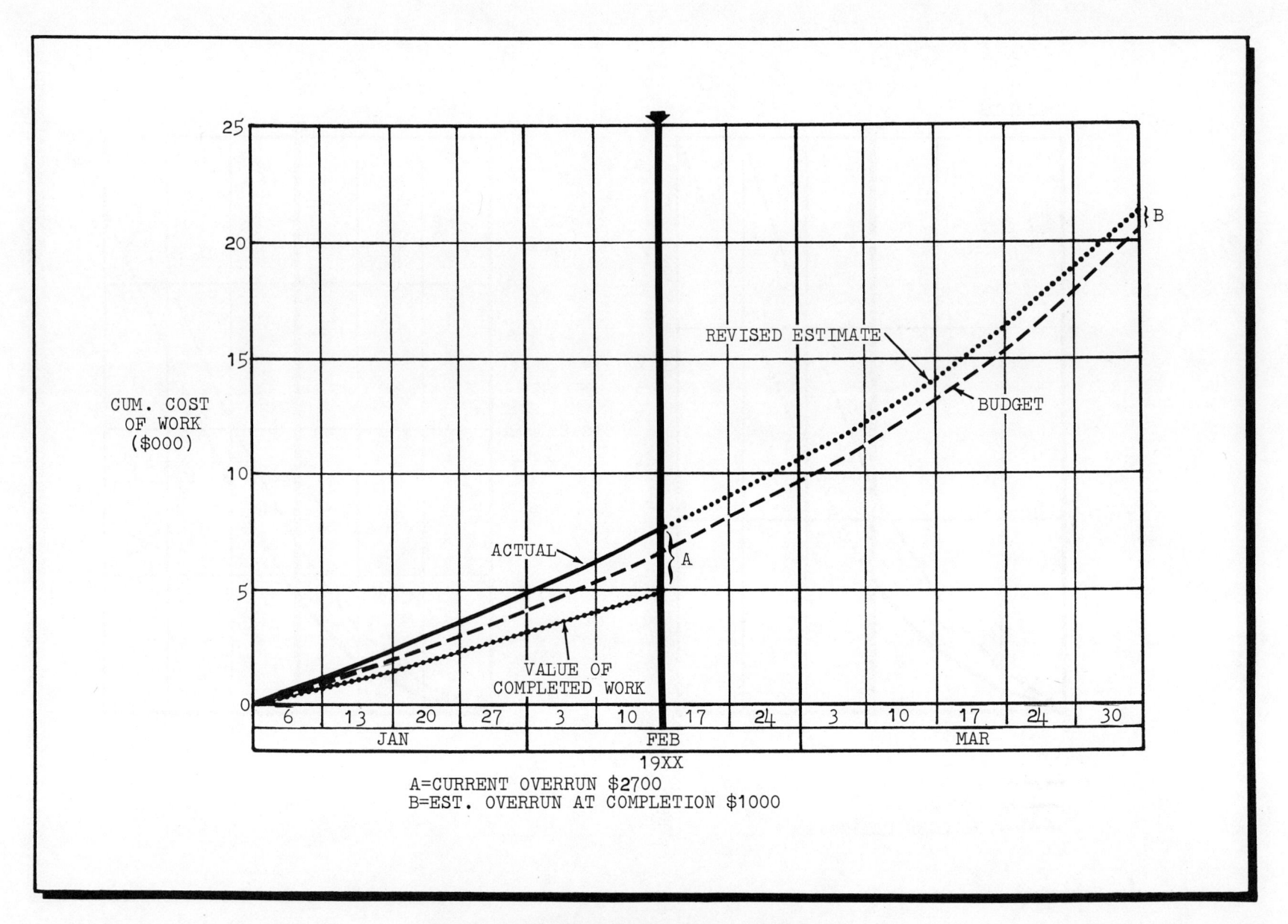

Figure 50.2 Schedule and Costs—Version 2

A = CURRENT OVERRUN $2700
B = EST. OVERRUN AT COMPLETION $1000

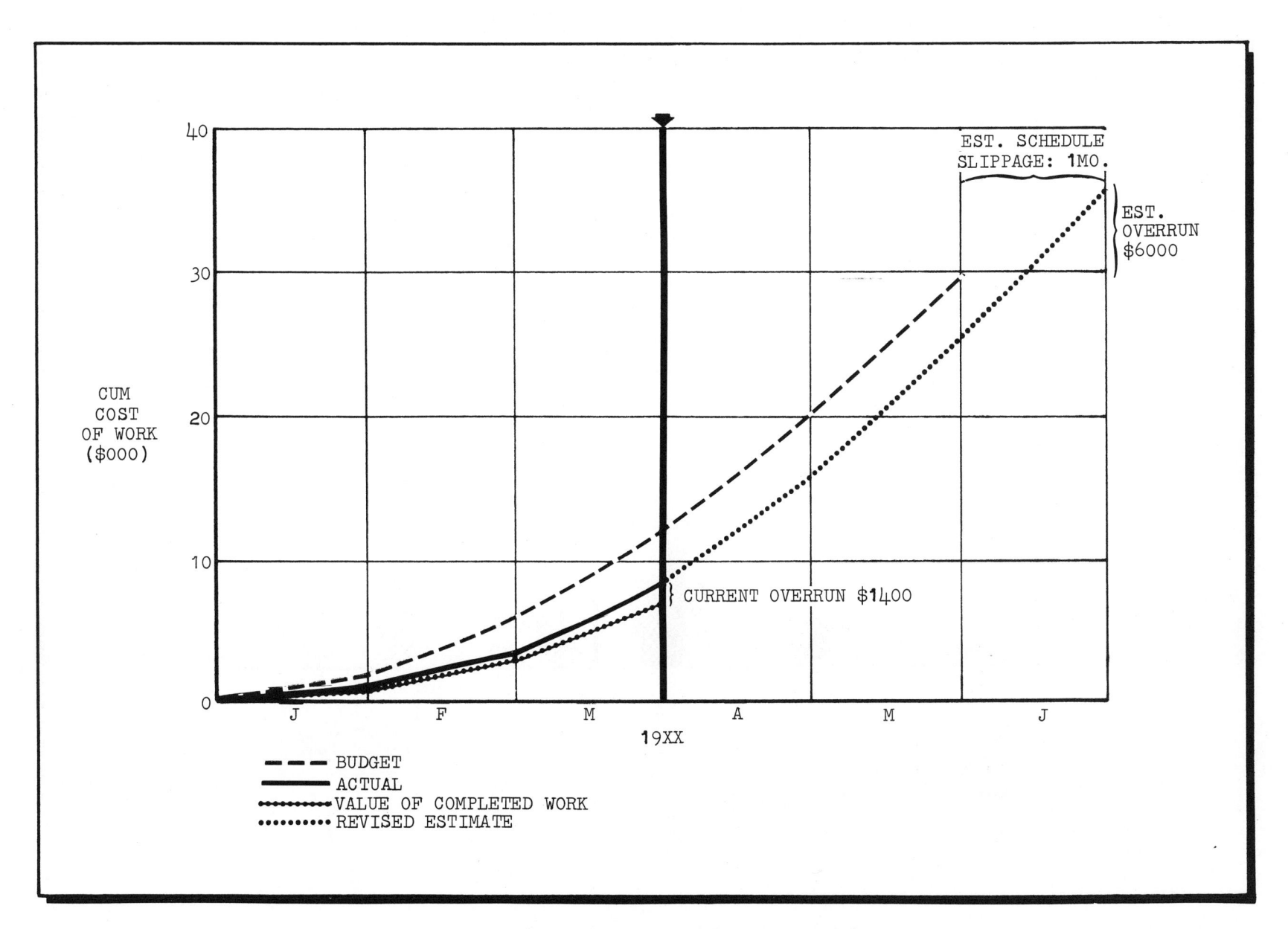

Figure 50.3 Schedule and Costs—Version 3

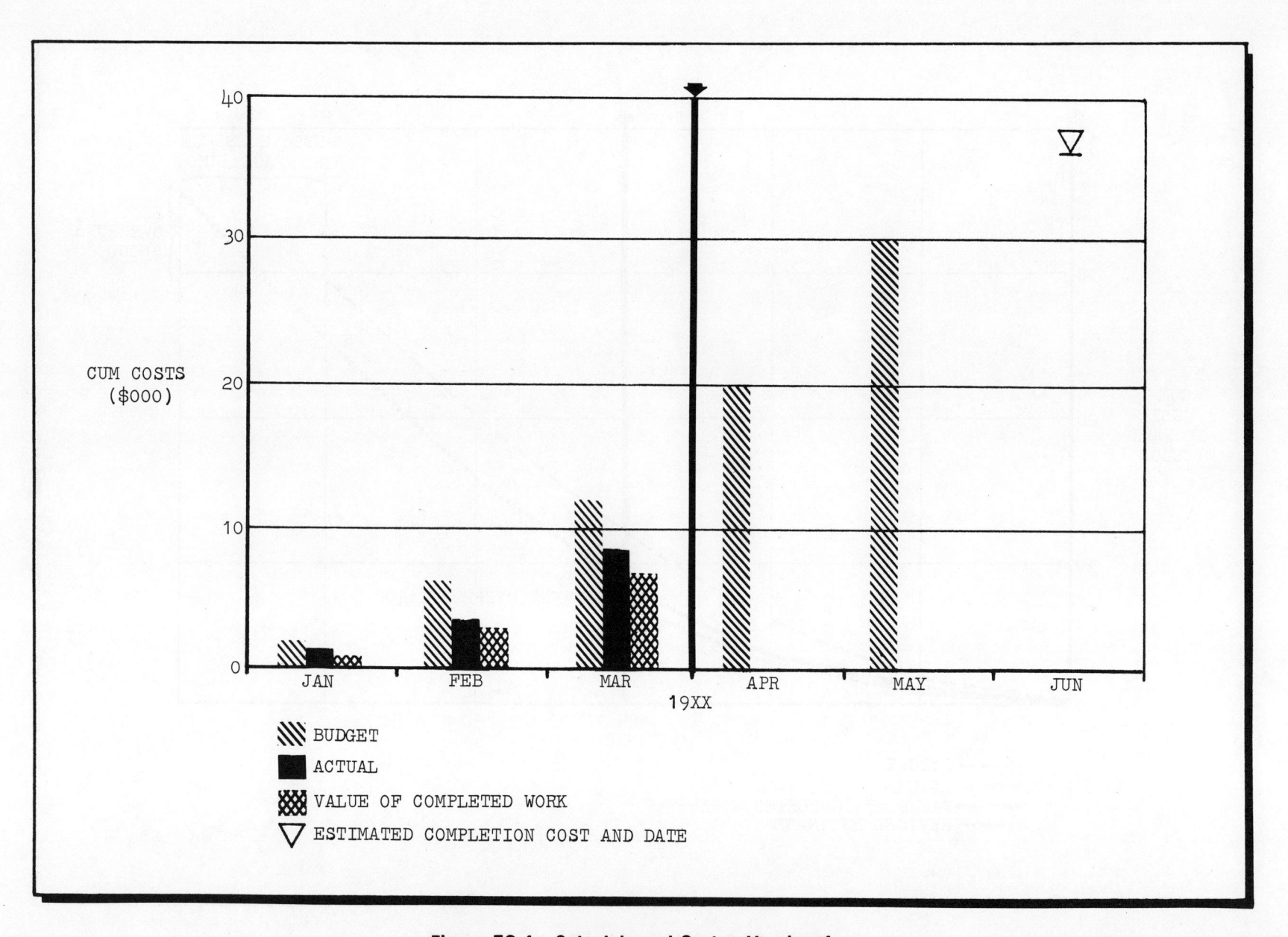

Figure 50.4   Schedule and Costs—Version 4

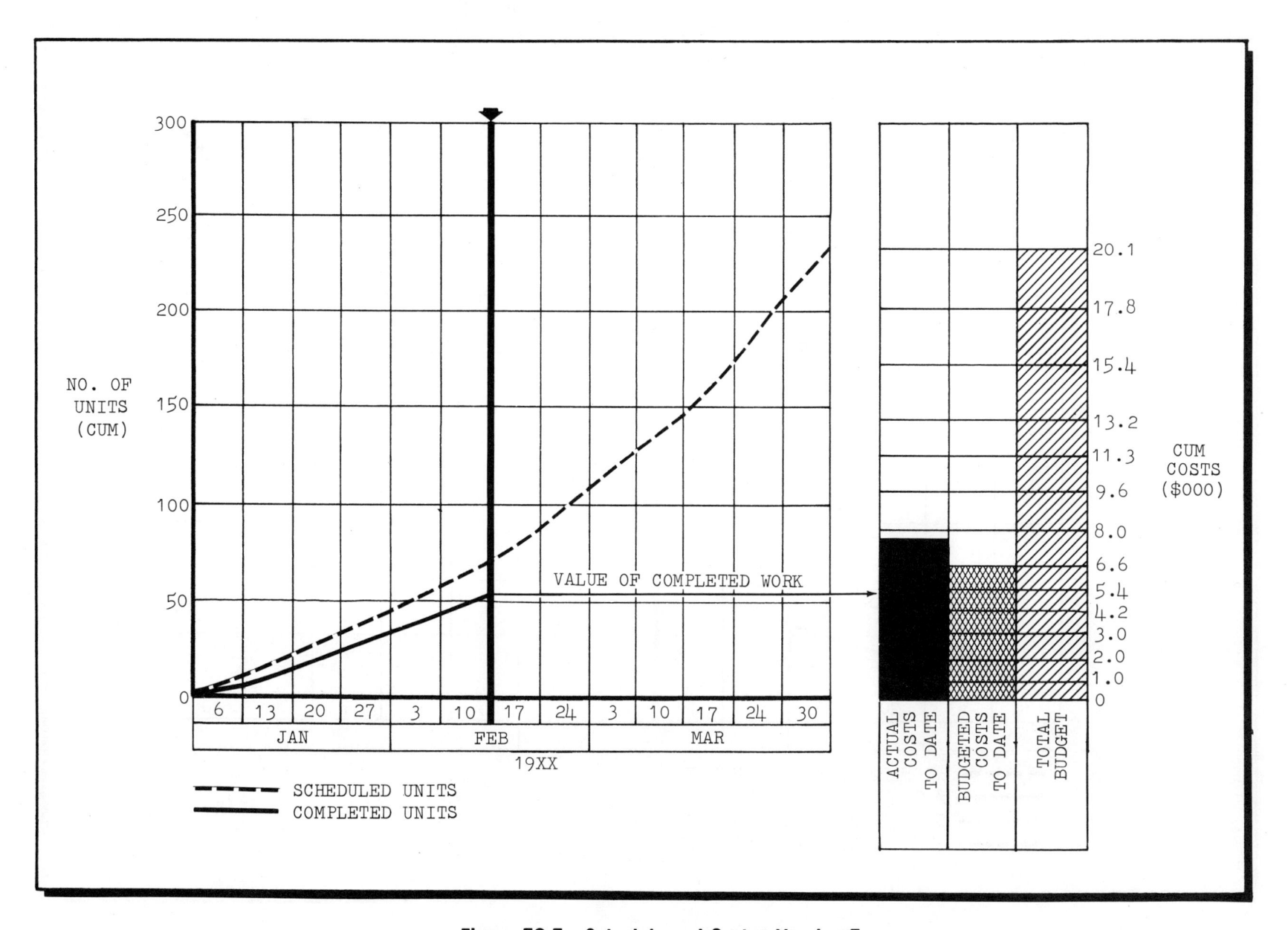

Figure 50.5 Schedule and Costs—Version 5

607

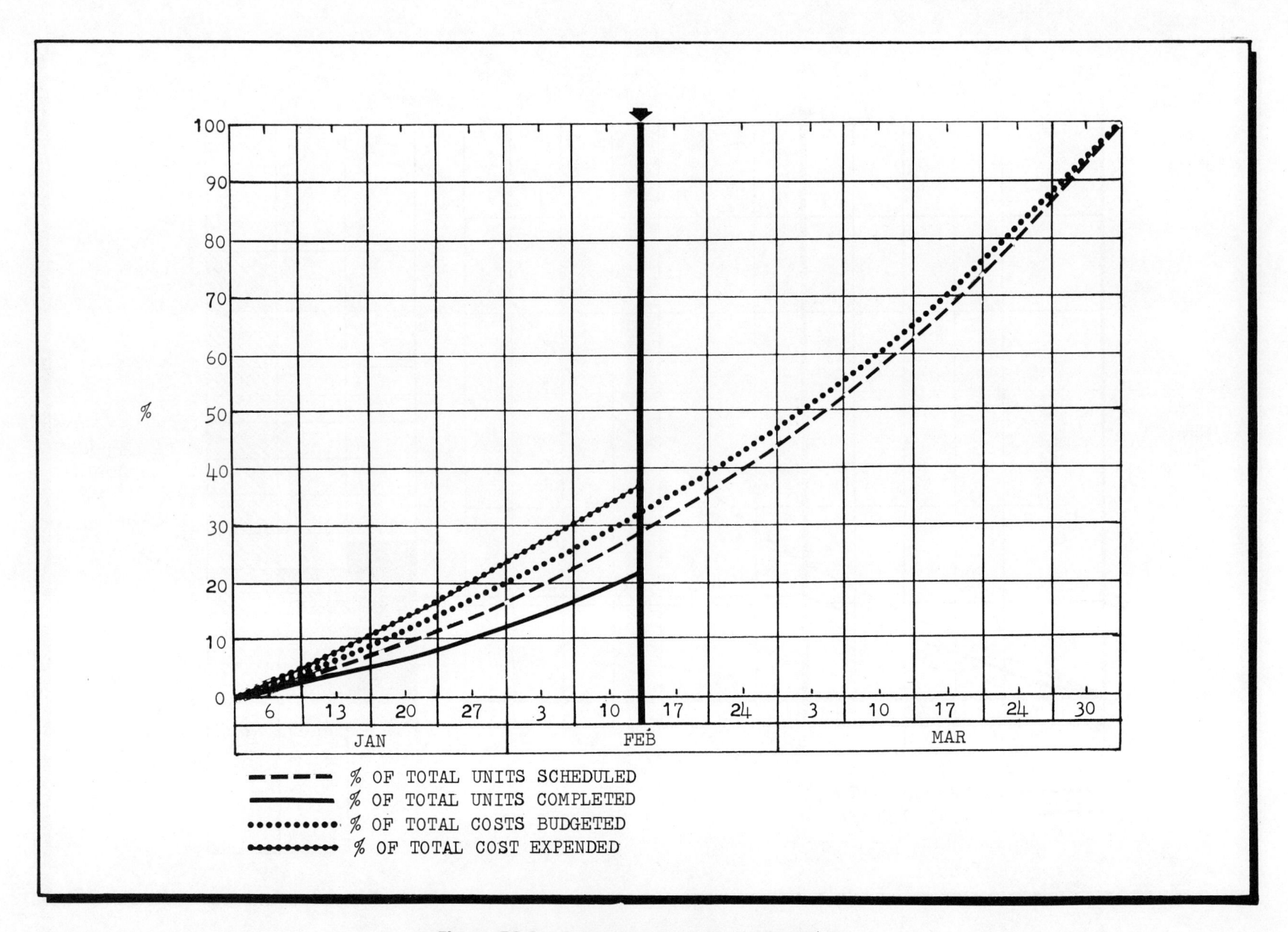

Figure 50.6 Schedule and Costs—Version 6

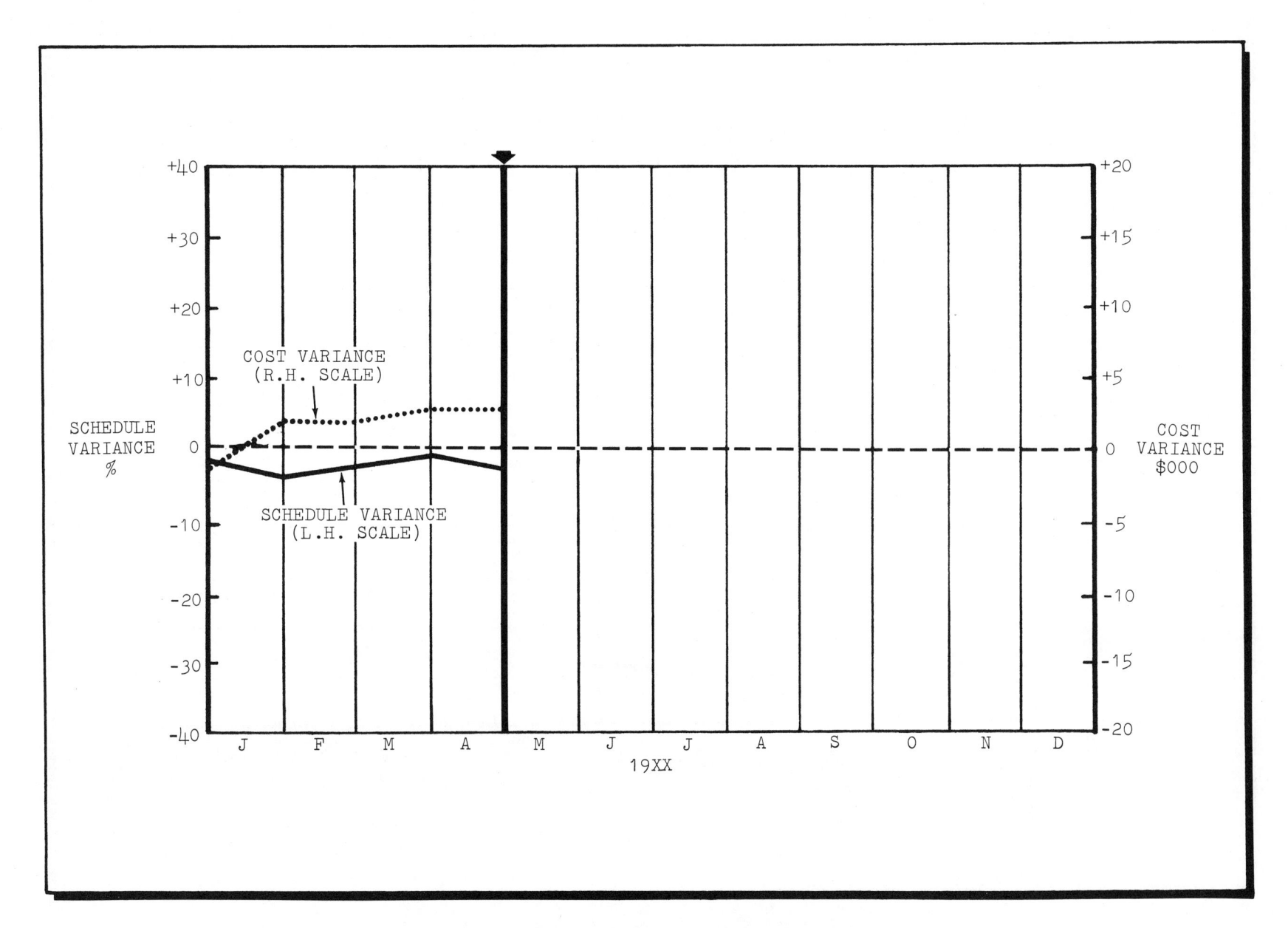

Figure 50.7 Schedule and Costs—Version 7

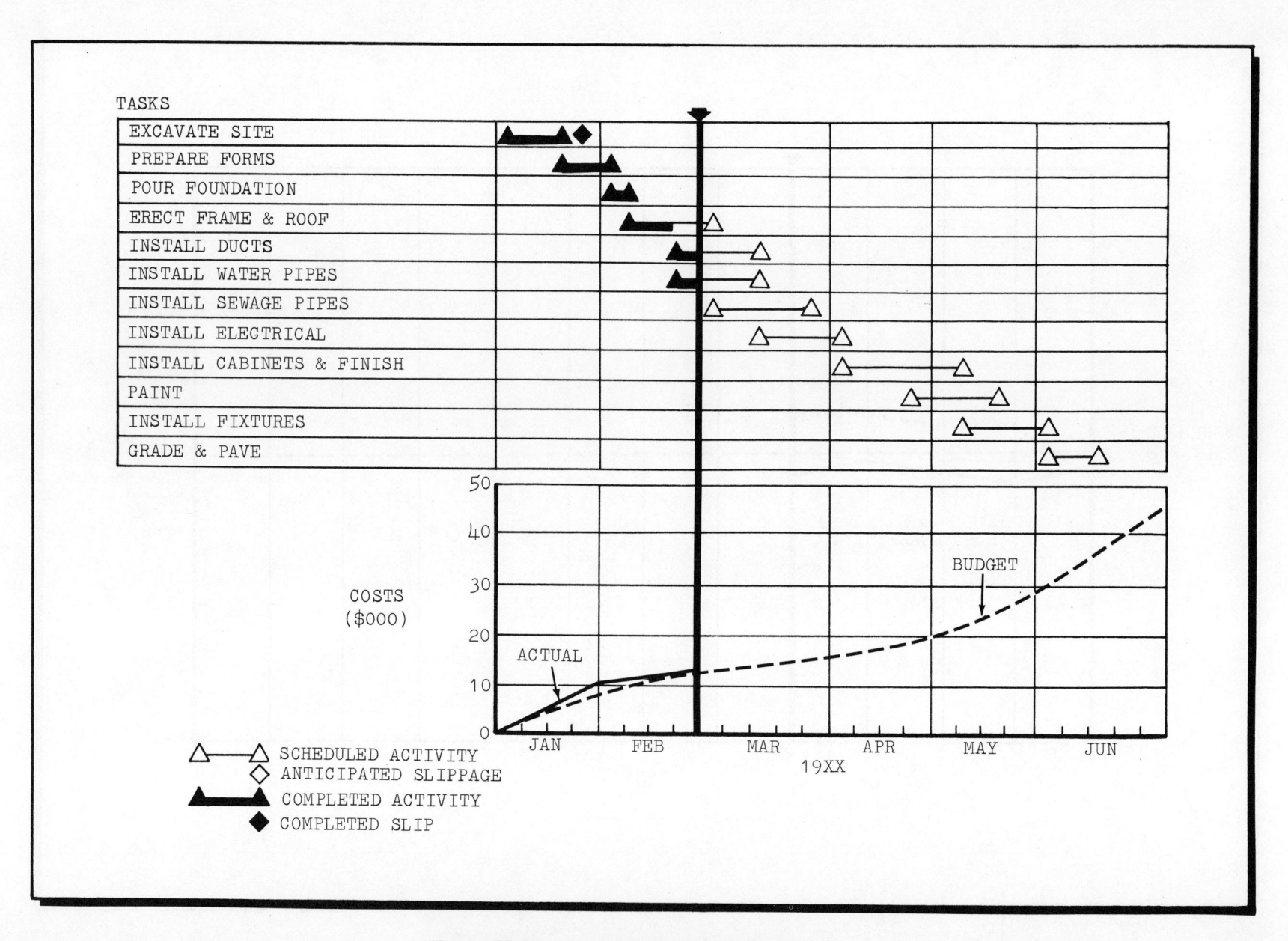

Figure 50.8 Schedule and Costs—Version 8

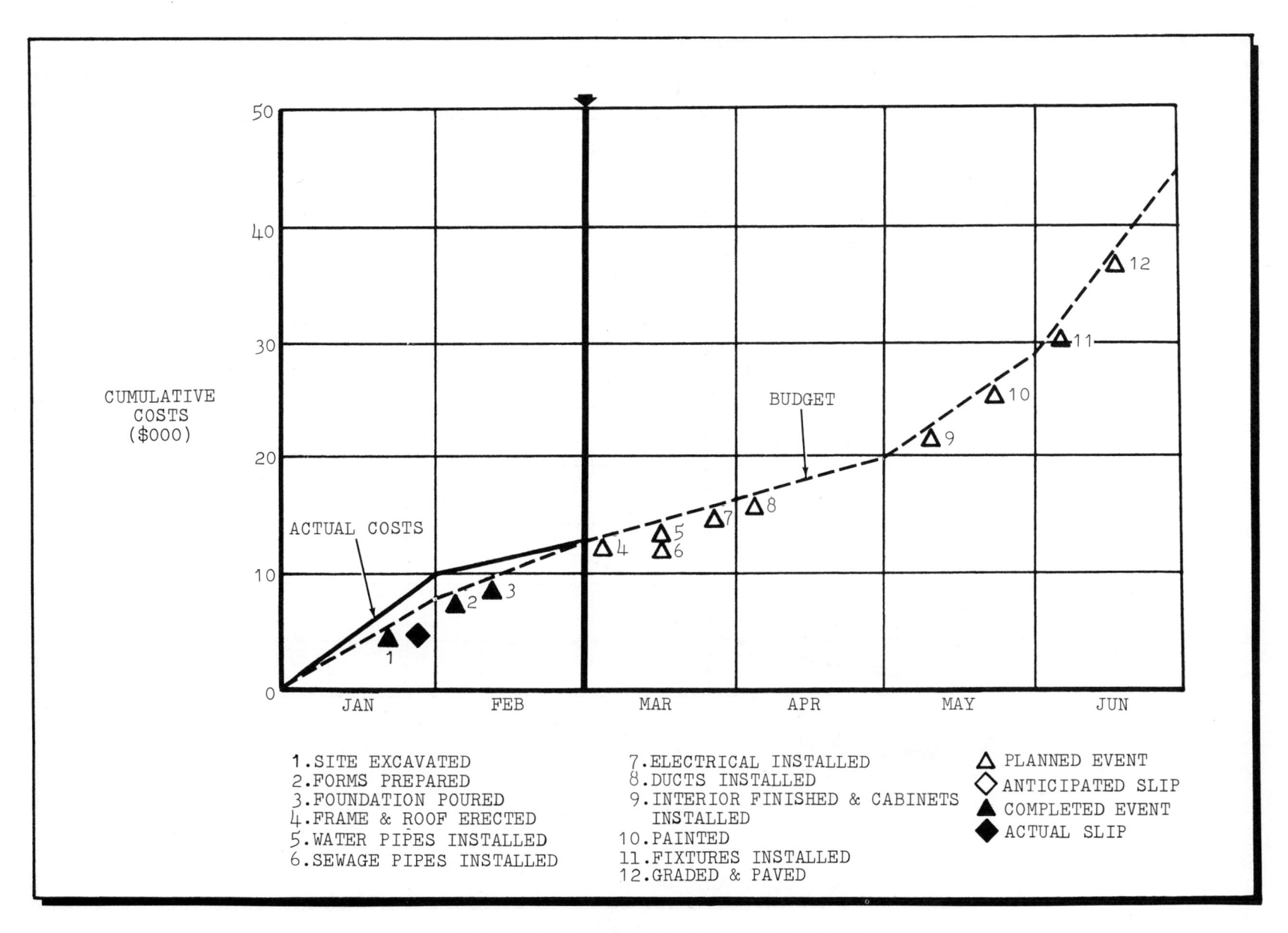

Figure 50.9 Schedule and Costs—Version 9

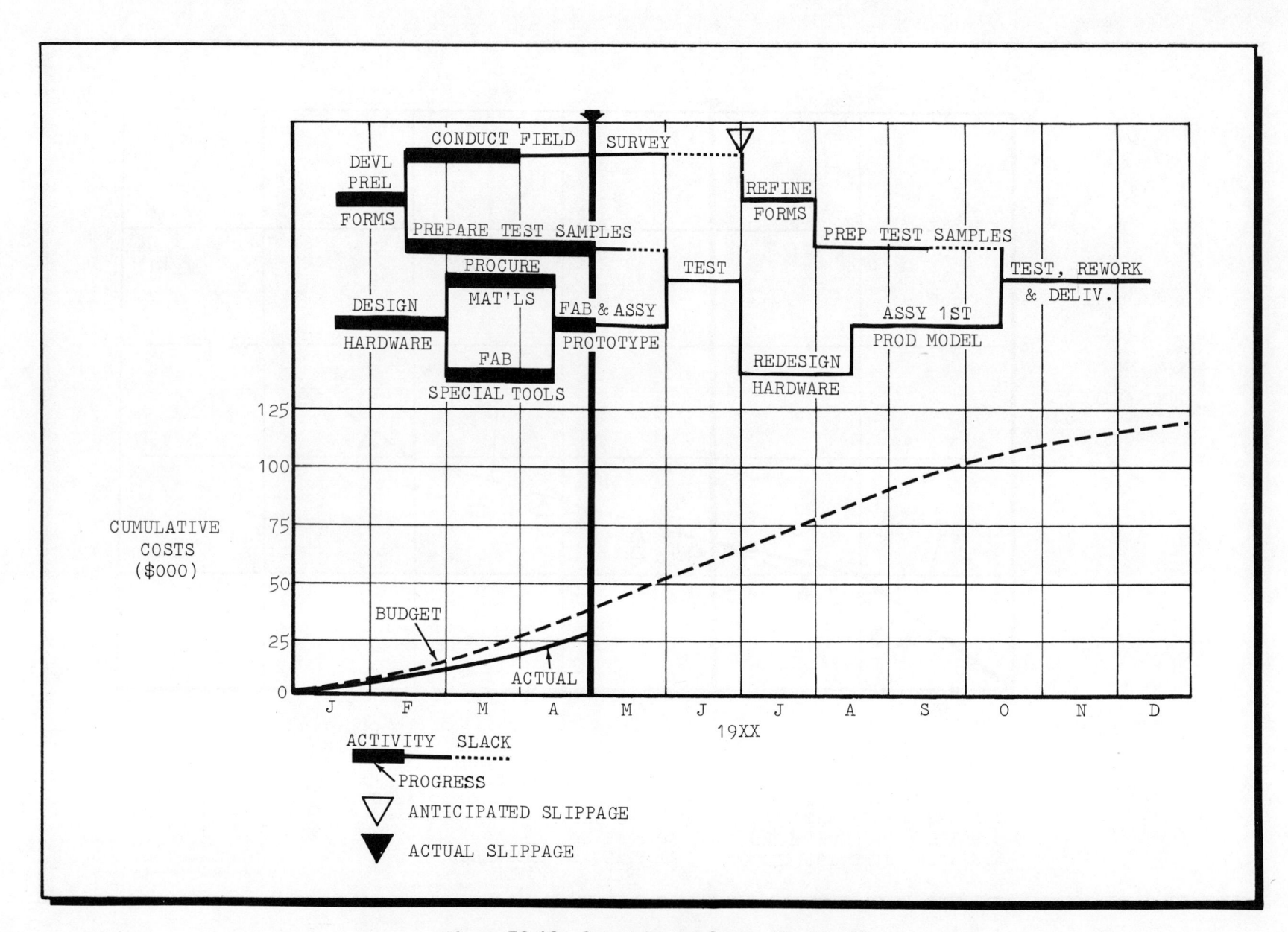

Figure 50.10 Schedule and Costs—Version 10

SCHEDULED UNITS	PER MO.		10	10	11	12	13	14	16	18	20	23	26	29	31
	CUM		10	20	31	43	56	70	86	104	124	147	173	202	233
COMPLETED UNITS	PER MO.		7	8	8	9	10	10							
	CUM		7	15	23	32	42	52							
BUDGETED COSTS ($000)	PER MO.		1.0	1.0	1.1	1.1	1.2	1.3	1.4	1.5	1.7	1.9	2.2	2.4	2.6
	CUM	– –	1.0	2.0	3.1	4.2	5.4	6.7	8.1	9.6	11.3	13.2	15.4	17.8	20.4
ACTUAL COSTS ($000)	PER MO.		1.2	1.2	1.2	1.4	1.4	1.3							
	CUM	——	1.2	2.4	3.6	5.0	6.4	7.7							
VALUE OF COMPLETE WORK ($000)	PER MO.		.7	.8	.8	.9	.9	.9							
	CUM	······	.7	1.5	2.3	3.2	4.1	5.0							

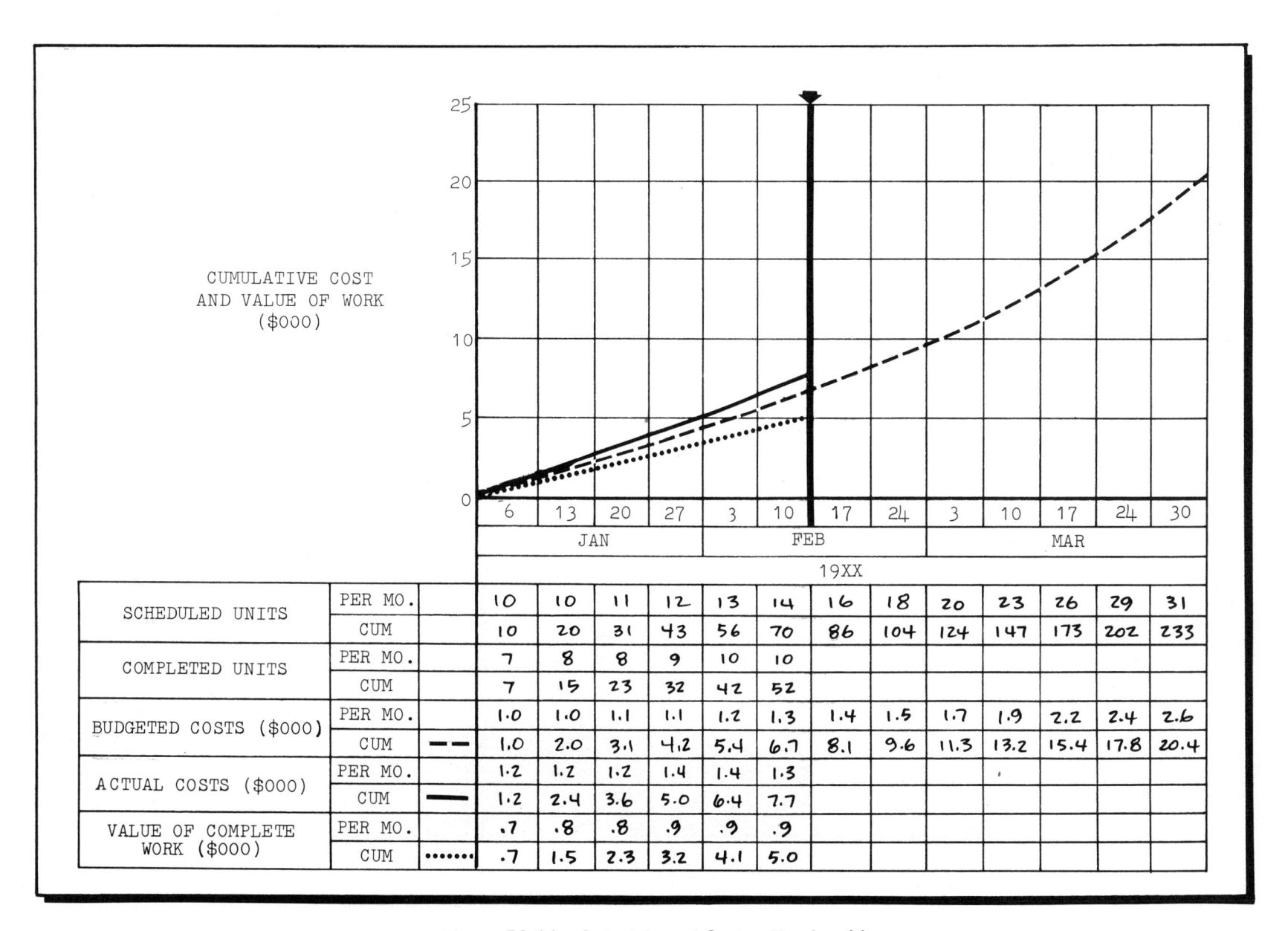

Figure 50.11 Schedule and Costs—Version 11

ITEMS (CUMULATIVE)	19XX						1ST QUARTER						
	JAN				FEB				MAR				
	6	13	20	27	3	10	17	24	3	10	17	24	30
SCHEDULED UNITS	10	20	31	43	56	70	86	104	124	147	173	202	233
COMPLETED UNITS	7	15	23	32	42	52							
BUDGETED COSTS ($000)	1.0	2.0	3.1	4.2	5.4	6.7	8.1	9.6	11.3	13.2	15.4	17.8	20.4
ACTUAL COSTS ($000)	1.2	2.4	3.6	5.0	6.4	7.7							
UNITS COMPLETED TO DATE RELATED TO SCHEDULE													
COSTS TO DATE RELATED TO BUDGET DATE													

Figure 50.12 Schedule and Costs—Version 12

STATUS AS OF _____

PRODUCT	DELIVERIES-YTD			COSTS-YTD ($)			COST/SCHED. ANALYSIS ($)			
	SCHED	ACTUAL	VAR	BUDGET	ACT	VAR	UNIT COST	VALUE OF DELIVERY VAR	ACTUAL COST VAR	NET COST POSITION
~~	100	95	−5	1000	950	−50	10	−50	−50	0
~~	100	100	0	1000	1000	0	10	0	0	0
~~	300	322	+22	4200	4508	+308	14	+308	+308	0
~~	175	180	+5	1050	1260	+210	6	+30	+210	+180
~~	410	410	0	4510	4410	−100	11	0	−100	−100
~~	150	150	0	1500	1500	0	10	0	0	0
~~	260	260	0	2080	2080	0	8	0	0	0
~~	240	230	−10	2880	2875	−5	12	−120	−5	+115

Figure 50.13 Schedule and Costs—Version 13

51.0 SCHEDULES—END ITEM—MULTIPLE PRODUCTS

End item schedules are those that deal with the production of items on a repetitive basis and which consider only one factor in the item's life cycle ("delivery" or "sales" or "completion," for instance). This section is concerned with end item schedule formats that display plans and progress relative to two or more types of items. Also see section 52.0, *Schedules–End Item–Single Product Type*.

51.1 Schedule—End Item—Multiple Products—Version 1: Progress relating to several types of units (multiple products or services) can be shown on the same chart as illustrated in Figure 51.1. In this example, multiple amount scales are used.

51.2 Schedule—End Item—Multiple Products—Version 2: Comparison of schedule performance such as between departments or divisions of an enterprise, or between product types, can be made utilizing side-by-side charts as shown in Figure 51.2. Notations as to variance, as shown in this example, can be added to aid the viewer in more quickly determining precise performance.

51.3 Schedule—End Item—Multiple Products—Version 3: Deviation charts normally require a minimum amount of vertical space. For this reason they lend themselves well to "stacking," such as shown in Figure 51.3, permitting the comparison of multiple item types.

51.4 Schedule—End Item—Multiple Products—Version 4: A daily schedule with a statistical breakdown of item types is shown in Figure 51.4. Since the statistics for the schedule are not given in this example, the net variance between total scheduled and total actual performance is pointed out on the chart.

51.5 Schedule—End Item—Multiple Products—Version 5: Version 5 of an end item schedule shown in Figure 51.5 displays a method of showing status of a set of related items, such as the separate elements of a program or project. Different amount scales are used for each element, but all are proportioned to the same time scale. This is a highly visible method for showing status of multiple items, but it is not flexible when it comes to accommodating schedule changes.

51.6 Schedule—End Item—Multiple Products—Version 6: A milestone chart method for showing schedules and performance for multiple products or services is presented in Figure 51.6. To avoid confusion when multiple schedule items are shown on the same line, a separate line has been provided for entering "slippage" symbols if they are needed. Using a single line for multiple schedule quantities, as shown in this example, is practical when there are only relatively few items.

51.7 Schedule—End Item—Multiple Products—Version 7: A statistical table sometimes called a "delivery digest" or "schedule digest" is shown in Figure 51.7. The format and the amount of detail presented in this type of chart puts it more in the category of an analytical report. It is still a progress tracking chart, however, comparing schedule to actual performance over a time span.

51.8 Schedule—End Item—Multiple Products—Version 8: Another method for monitoring schedule compliance on several related items or on separate segments of an enterprise is shown in Version 8 of an end item schedule for multiple products (Figure 51.8). If more than three or four items are to be compared in this manner, some of the statistics, such as scheduled and actual rates, could be eliminated from the table.

51.9 Schedule—End Item—Multiple Products—Version 9: Another approach for comparing schedule performance of multiple products (multiple items that make up a set, for instance) is shown in Figure 51.9. Either cumulative data (as shown) or data based on rate-per-time period could be used.

51.10 Schedule—End Item—Multiple Products—Version 10: Version 10, Figure 51.10, is virtually identical to Version 9 except that space has been provided for explanatory remarks for each line item.

51.11 Schedule—End Item—Multiple Products—Version 11: Version 11 of an end item schedule is shown in Figure 51.11. Often called a "box score," this form is not considered to be a progress tracking chart inasmuch as it does not show historical and/or forecasted values, and it must be redone, rather than merely updated, for each reporting period.

51.12 Schedule—End Item—Multiple Products—Version 12: Another form of a "box score" is shown in Figure 51.12. Instead of showing net cumulative variance as on the previous version, this statistical table provides space for explanatory remarks.

51.13 Schedule—End Item—Multiple Products—Version 13: Version 13 of an end item schedule for multiple products, Figure 51.13, is another "box score" type statistical table. This version differs from the previously described versions in that it provides space for differentiating between the schedule and what is actually due (including past due items) for a given reporting period. A column for posting a recovery date is also provided.

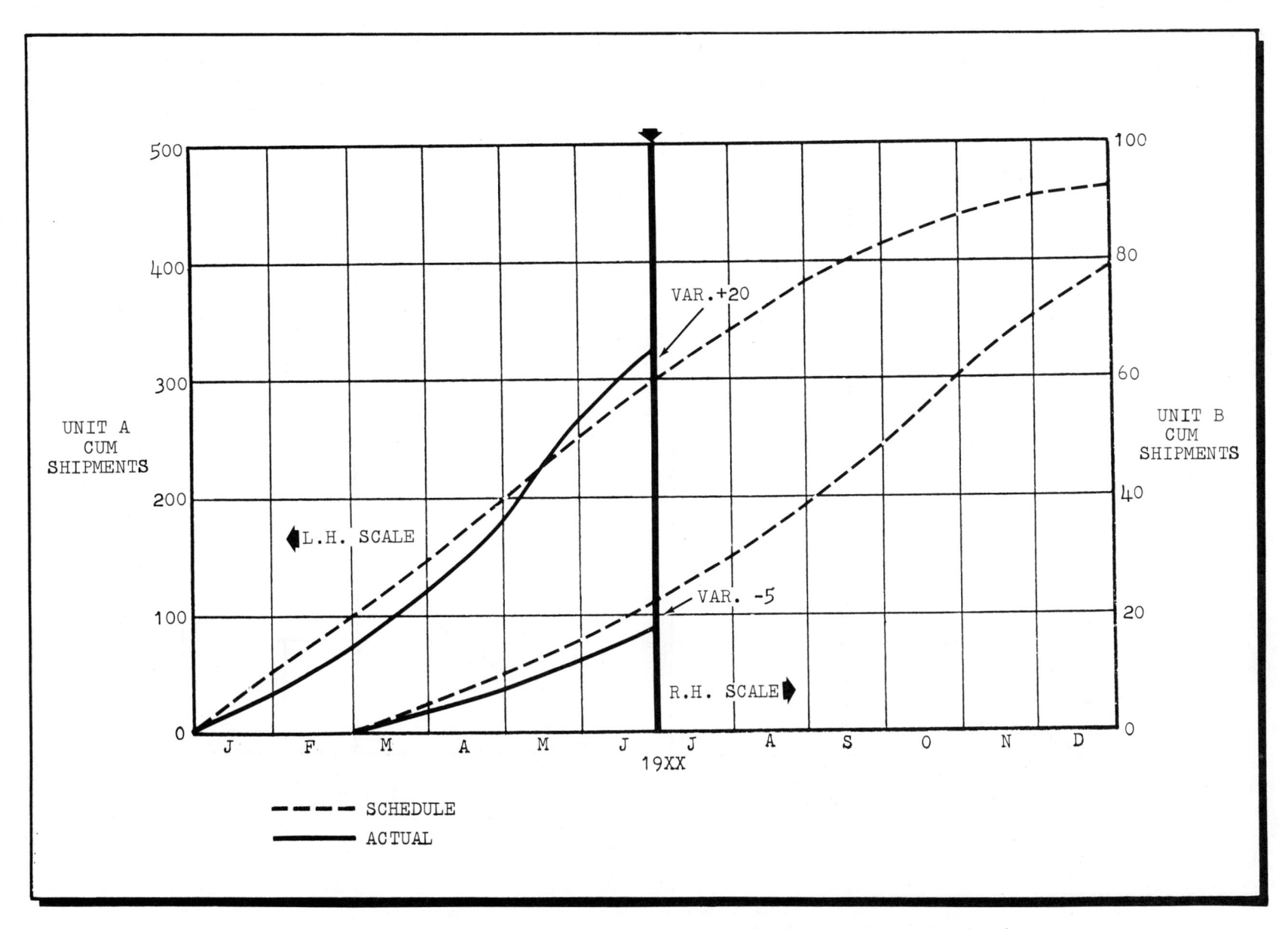

Figure 51.1 Schedule—End Item—Multiple Products—Version 1

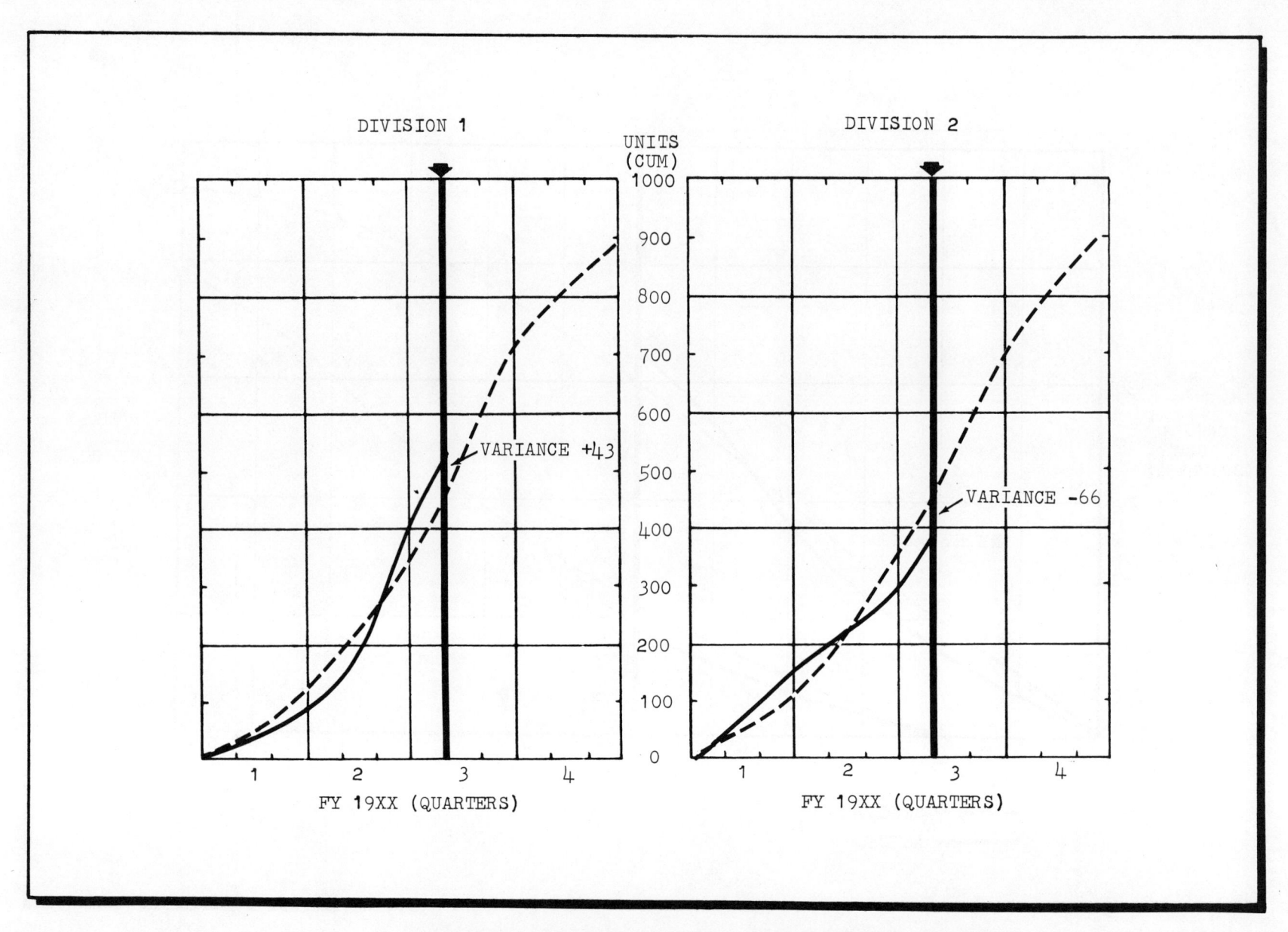

Figure 51.2 Schedule—End Item—Multiple Products—Version 2

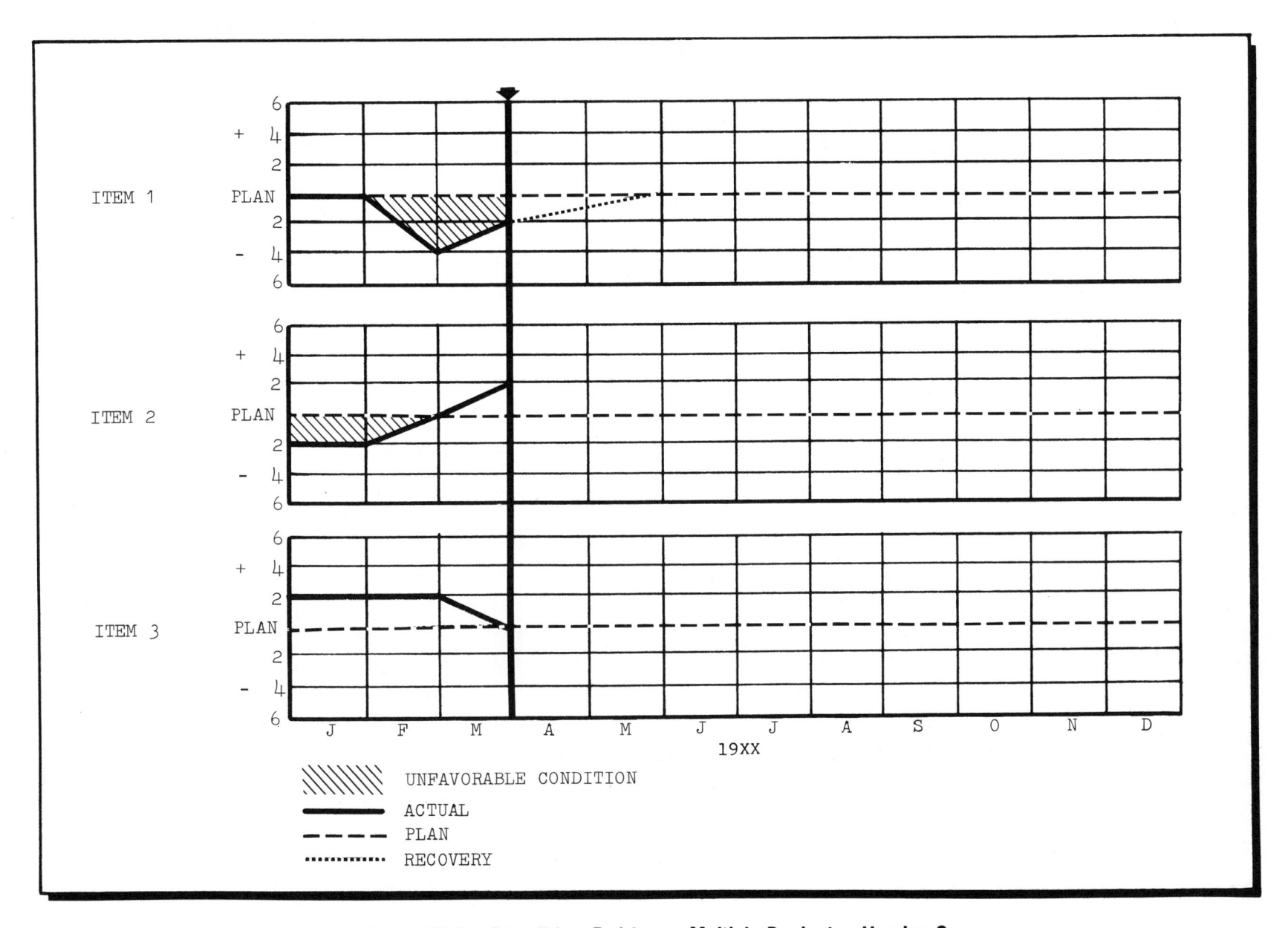

Figure 51.3 Schedule—End Item—Multiple Products—Version 3

TOTAL ITEMS
SHIPPED
(CUMULATIVE)

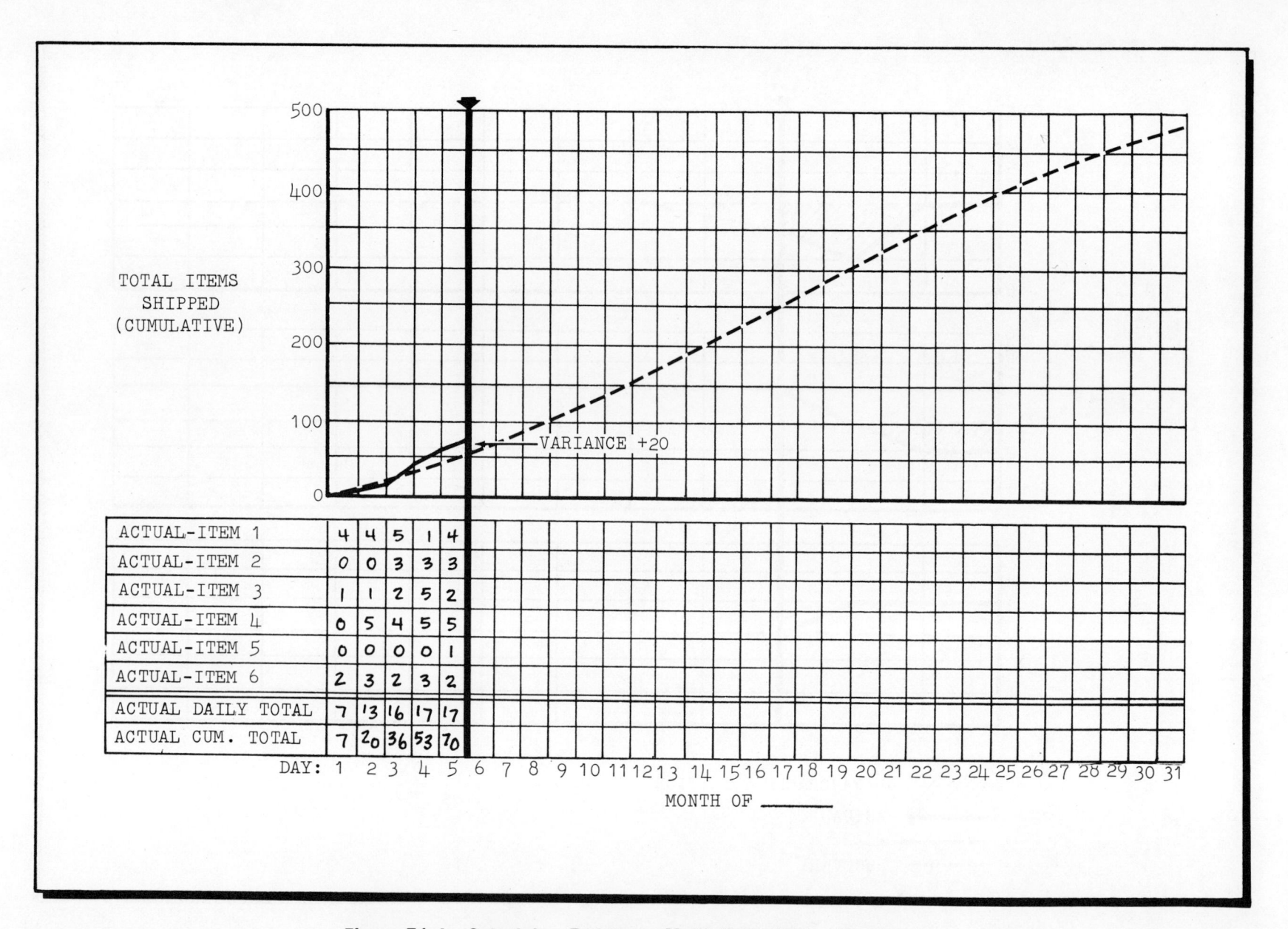

VARIANCE +20

ACTUAL-ITEM 1	4	4	5	1	4
ACTUAL-ITEM 2	0	0	3	3	3
ACTUAL-ITEM 3	1	1	2	5	2
ACTUAL-ITEM 4	0	5	4	5	5
ACTUAL-ITEM 5	0	0	0	0	1
ACTUAL-ITEM 6	2	3	2	3	2
ACTUAL DAILY TOTAL	7	13	16	17	17
ACTUAL CUM. TOTAL	7	20	36	53	70

DAY: 1 2 3 4 5 6 7 8 9 10 11 12 13 14 15 16 17 18 19 20 21 22 23 24 25 26 27 28 29 30 31

MONTH OF _____

Figure 51.4   Schedule—End Item—Multiple Products—Version 4

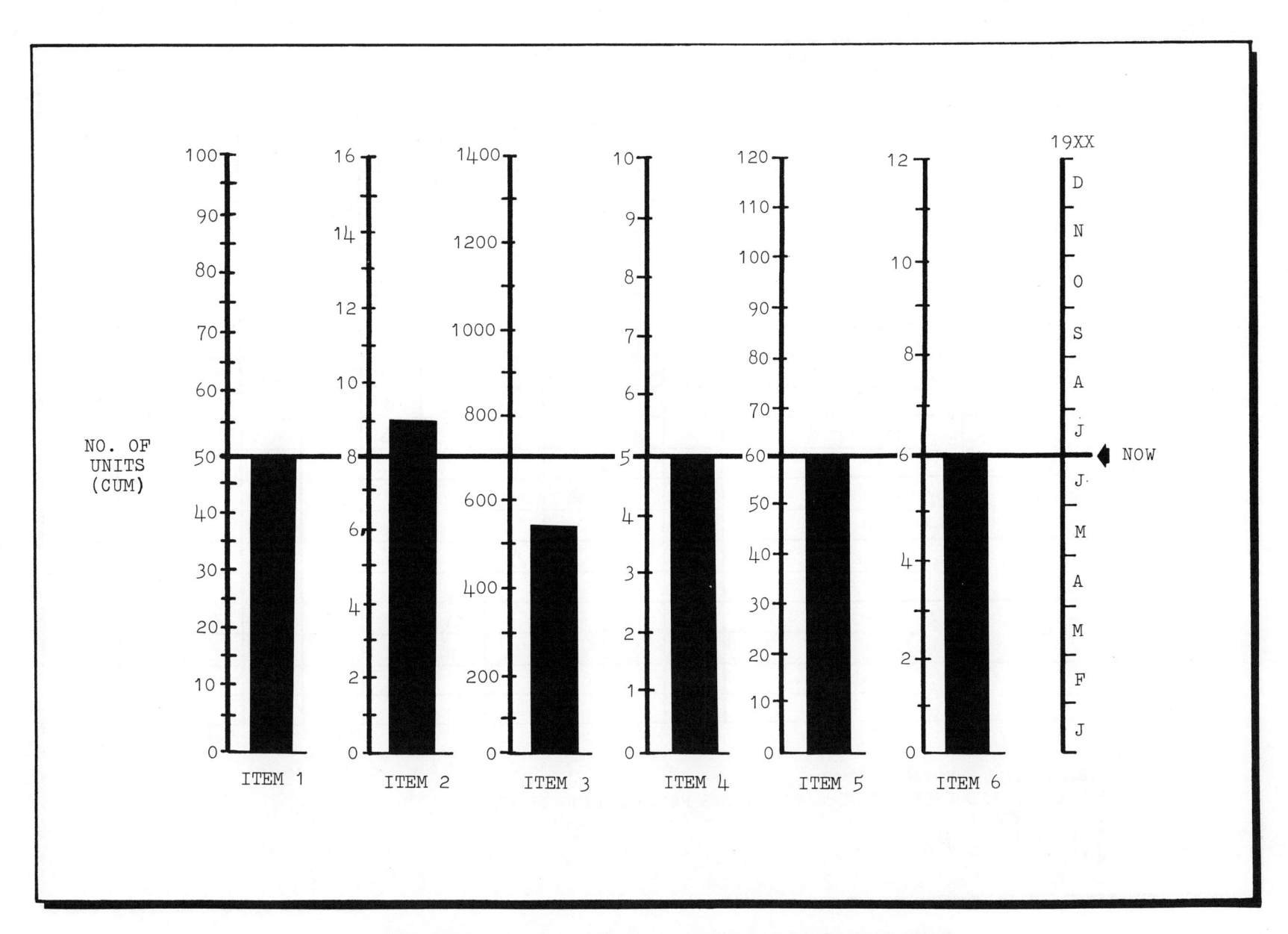

Figure 51.5 Schedule—End Item—Multiple Products—Version 5

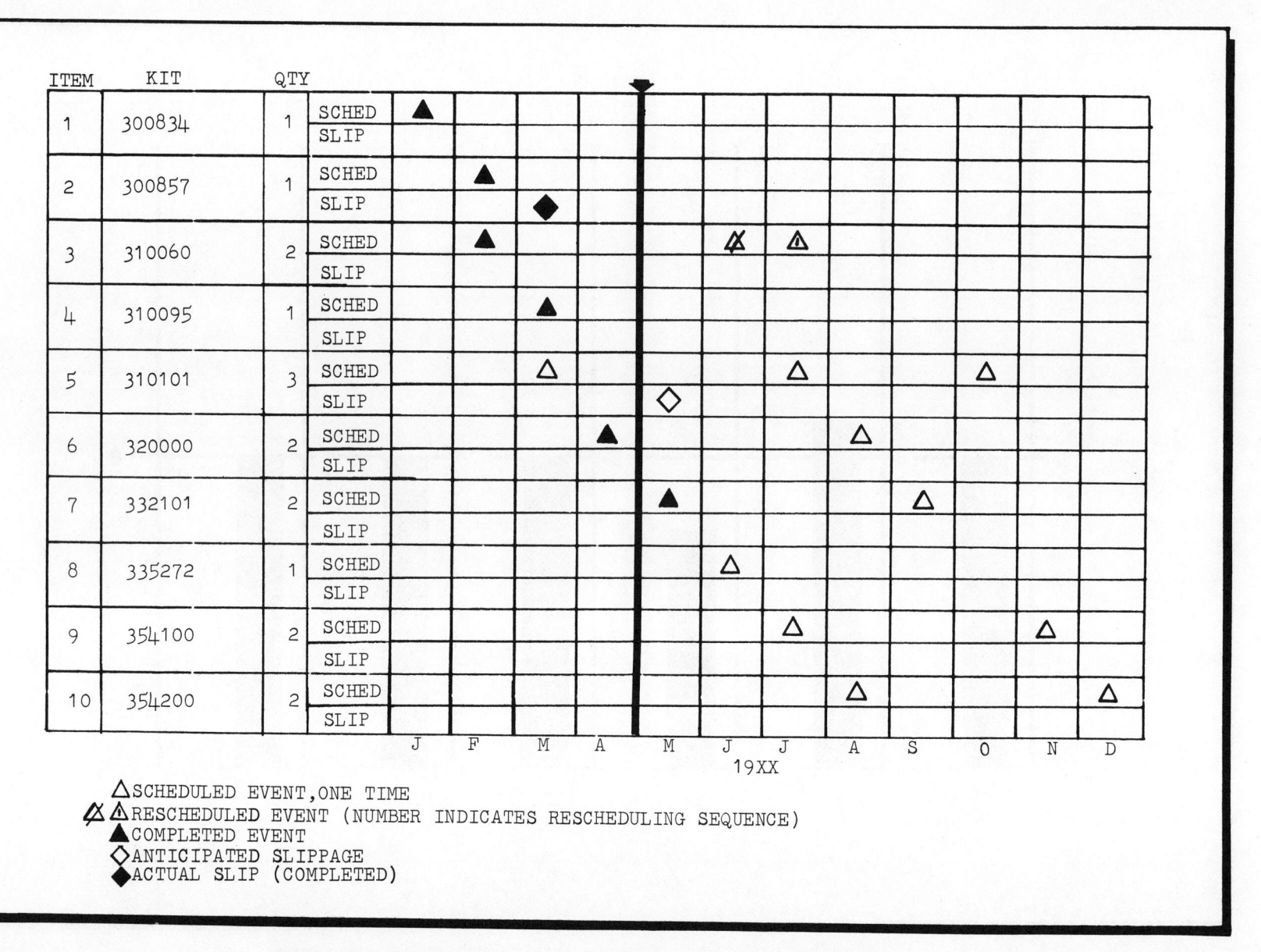

ITEM	KIT	QTY		J	F	M	A	M	J	J	A	S	O	N	D
1	300834	1	SCHED	▲											
			SLIP												
2	300857	1	SCHED		▲										
			SLIP			◆									
3	310060	2	SCHED		▲				⟁	△					
			SLIP												
4	310095	1	SCHED			▲									
			SLIP												
5	310101	3	SCHED			△				△		△			
			SLIP					◇							
6	320000	2	SCHED				▲			△					
			SLIP												
7	332101	2	SCHED				▲				△				
			SLIP												
8	335272	1	SCHED					△							
			SLIP												
9	354100	2	SCHED							△				△	
			SLIP												
10	354200	2	SCHED								△				△
			SLIP												

19XX

△ SCHEDULED EVENT, ONE TIME
⟁ △ RESCHEDULED EVENT (NUMBER INDICATES RESCHEDULING SEQUENCE)
▲ COMPLETED EVENT
◇ ANTICIPATED SLIPPAGE
◆ ACTUAL SLIP (COMPLETED)

Figure 51.6 Schedule—End Item—Multiple Products—Version 6

CONTRACT ITEM	CUM STATUS END OF JULY		AUGUST ACTUALS (WEEKLY/CUM)					CUM TOTAL THROUGH AUGUST		EST VARIANCE AT END OF AUGUST
	SCHED	ACT	2	9	16	23	30	SCHED	EST	
INERTIAL NAVIGATION SYSTEM A	312	343	0/343	1/344	3/347			358	359	+1
INERTIAL NAVIGATION SYSTEM B	49	47	2/49	0/49	0/49			59	55	−4
PLATFORM	73	118	2/120	0/120	0/120			87	120	+33
CONTROL UNIT	58	48	5/53	5/58	5/63			68	70	+2
COMPUTER	65	69	2/71	1/72	2/74			71	76	+5
LINE TEST SET	31	28	0/28	0/28	0/28			31	31	0
PLATFORM TEST BENCH	10	10	0/10	0/10	0/10			10	10	0
ELECTRONIC TEST BENCH	9	9	0/9	0/9	0/9			9	9	0
LINE ANALYZER	5	1	0/1	1/2	1/3			5	4	−1

Figure 51.7 Schedule—End Item—Multiple Products—Version 7

		J	F	M	A	M	J	J	A	S	O	N	D
PLATFORM TEST BENCH	SCHED. RATE	1	2	2	2	3	0	0	0	2	0	6	4
	ACT. RATE	2	0	2	0	0	0	3					
	SCHED. CUM	1	3	5	7	10	10	10	10	12	12	18	22
	ACT. CUM	2	2	4	4	4	4	7					
	CUM. VAR.	+1	-1	-1	-3	-6	-6	-3					
	RECOVERY								3				
ELECTRONIC TEST BENCH	SCHED. RATE	1	3	2	3	1	0	0					
	ACT. RATE	0	2	3	3	0	2	0					
	SCHED. CUM	1	4	6	9	10	10	10					
	ACT CUM	0	2	5	8	8	10	10					
	CUM. VAR.	-1	-2	-1	-1	-2	0	0					
	RECOVERY												

19XX

Figure 51.8 Schedule—End Item—Multiple Products—Version 8

PART NO.	CUMULATIVE STATUS					▼								
AX 323	SCHEDULE	0	3	5	10	14	18	20						
	ACTUAL	0	2	4	8									
	VARIANCE	0	-1	-1	-2									
AX 324	SCHEDULE	1	2	4	8	13	18	23	28	32	36	37	38	
	ACTUAL	0	3	5	8									
	VARIANCE	-1	+1	+1	0									
AX 325	SCHEDULE	0	0	3	6	9	12	15	18	21	24	27	30	
	ACTUAL	0	0	3	5									
	VARIANCE	0	0	0	-1									
AX 326	SCHEDULE	2	4	6	9	12	15	19	23	28	28	28	29	
	ACTUAL	2	4	6	9									
	VARIANCE	0	0	0	0									
AX 327	SCHEDULE	1	3	5	7	10	15	20	25	30	35	40	42	
	ACTUAL	0	0	0	0									
	VARIANCE	-1	-3	-5	-7									
		J	F	M	A	M	J	J	A	S	O	N	D	
						19XX								

Figure 51.9 Schedule—End Item—Multiple Products—Version 9

PART NO.	CUM STATUS	J	F	M	A	M	J	J	A	S	O	N	D	REMARKS
AX 323	SCHED	0	3	5	10	14	18	20						EXPECT TO BE ON SCHEDULE BY MAY 15
	ACT	0	2	4	8									
	VAR	0	-1	-1	-2									
AX 324	SCHED	1	2	4	8	13	18	23	28	32	36	37	38	
	ACT	0	3	5	8									
	VAR	-1	+1	+1	0									
AX 325	SCHED	0	0	3	6	9	12	15	18	21	24	27	30	BEHIND SCHEDULE UNIT IS IN SHIPPING DEPT
	ACT	0	0	3	5									
	VAR	0	0	0	-1									
AX 326	SCHED	2	4	6	9	12	15	19	23	28	28	28	29	
	ACT	2	4	6	9									
	VAR	0	0	0	0									
AX 327	SCHED	1	3	5	7	10	15	20	25	30	35	40	42	WAITING FOR SUB-ASSEMBLY FROM DEPT. Y
	ACT	0	0	0	0									
	VAR	0	-3	-5	-7									

19XX

Figure 51.10 Schedule—End Item—Multiple Products—Version 10

STATUS THROUGH **JUNE**

LOT NUMBER	CUSTOMER	SCHEDULE CUM	ACTUAL CUM	NET VARIANCE CUM
6579		95	95	0
6580		43	42	-1
6581		27	26	-1
6582		85	81	-4
6583		CANCELLED		
6584		361	359	-2
6585		20	20	0
6586		159	156	-3
6587		25	25	0
	TOTALS	815	804	-11

Figure 51.11 Schedule—End Item—Multiple Products—Version 11

STATUS THROUGH __JUNE___

PURCHASE ORDER NO.	QUANTITY ORDERED	QUANTITY SHIPPED	REMARKS
H-6441	36	36	COMPLETE
I-338175	138	138	COMPLETE
I-89903	140	0	DELIVERIES BEING HELD PENDING CUSTOMER APPROVAL OF CHANGES
I-62361 (WITH ADD-ON)	28	20	ADD-ON OF 8 TO BE DELIVERED BY JULY 10
C-N383-82040A	199	199	COMPLETE
H-64575	14	14	COMPLETE

Figure 51.12 Schedule—End Item—Multiple Products—Version 12

STATUS THROUGH __DECEMBER__

PART NO.	SCHEDULED THIS MONTH	DUE THIS MONTH*	ACTUAL THIS MONTH	CUM VARIANCE	RECOVERY DATE
A-764	380	380	380	0	
C-15621	172	172	170	-2	JAN 15
M-1011	58	65	65	0	
MC-68	10	10	10	0	
43721	460	520	500	-20	FEB 1
6988	180	180	180	0	
7161	240	240	230	-10	JAN 10
8225	18	32	32	0	
8870	40	40	40	0	

* INCLUDES PAST DUE PARTS

Figure 51.13 Schedule—End Item—Multiple Products—Version 13

52.0 SCHEDULES—END ITEM—SINGLE PRODUCT TYPE

Schedules that deal with the production of items on a repetitive basis and which consider only one factor in the item's life cycle such as "delivery" or "sales" or "completion," for instance, are called end item schedules. This section is concerned with end item schedules that involve single product types. Section 51.0 displays end item schedules that deal with multiple product types.

52.1 Schedule—End Item—Single Product Type—Version 1: The most simple version of an end item schedule designed for a single product type is shown in Figure 52.1. In this example, plotted in terms of cumulative (year-to-date) deliveries, there are no grid lines nor statistics. This type is considered primarily as a trend-indicating chart. It is, nevertheless, in the category of progress tracking charts for it presents both the plan (schedule) and the actual performance against that plan over a time span.

52.2 Schedule—End Item—Single Product Type—Version 2: The same data shown on Version 1 of the end item schedule chart can be plotted in terms of rate-per-time segment instead of cumulative. This is shown in Version 2, Figure 52.2. It is usually good practice to label, or otherwise explain, unusual occurrences in the plotted data. In the example, the reason for the dip in the actual performance line is explained by the label as due to a labor dispute.

52.3 Schedule—End Item—Single Product Type—Version 3: In Figure 52.3, numeric figures indicating scheduled and actual amounts have been added to the basic trend chart to aid the viewer in reading the chart. In the example, a "recovery" plan has also been added. This is a plan supplementary to the original schedule indicating when, and at what rate, a return (recovery) to the original plan is expected. A rescheduling could be handled in a similar fashion.

52.4 Schedule—End Item—Single Product Type—Version 4: A variation of a recovery plan is to show a behind-schedule condition in terms of delinquent items as illustrated in Figure 52.4. This approach has the disadvantage of often being misunderstood because the same amount scale is used in one instance as a positive number (items delivered) and in the other as a negative number (items *not* delivered).

52.5 Schedule—End Item—Single Product Type—Version 5: In Version 5 (Figure 52.5) of an end item schedule, the numeric value of the net variance between the plan and the actual performance (-20) is called out. This approach is considered by many as preferable to Version 3 where the chart viewer must do mental arithmetic to determine the variance between the plan and actual performance.

52.6 Schedule—End Item—Single Product Type—Version 6: Factors other than schedule and actual performance data are often imposed on chart makers. Version 6, Figure 52.6, shows how one such factor (a customer-imposed restriction, in this case) can be handled.

52.7 Schedule—End Item—Single Product Type—Version 7: In cases where a production schedule does not coincide with orders that are on hand (where a "cushion" is desirable, for instance), both factors can be shown on the chart. An example is illustrated in Figure 52.7.

52.8 Schedule—End Item—Single Product Type—Version 8: A full grid is used in Version 8, Figure 52.8. Also, the clutter of identifying lines on the plotted area of a chart is eliminated by utilizing a key (legend) in lieu of call-outs. The net variance as of the reporting date (end of June in this example) is also given. Additional information could also be added to the legend by inserting the scheduled and actual performance statistics for the reporting period.

52.9 Schedule—End Item—Single Product Type—Version 9: Another method for displaying schedule status is shown in Figure 52.9. In this example, items are examined from the standpoint of the percent that have been delivered on time. A "minimum goal" line or "limit line for management action" can also be added as shown in the example.

52.10 Schedule—End Item—Single Product Type—Version 10: A single line of statistics added to the basic end item schedule chart presents the cumulative variance between the schedule and actual performance for each time segment. In the example shown in Figure 52.10, the statistics are lined up in register with the graph.

52.11 Schedule—End Item—Single Product Type—Version 11: Two elements of statistical data are carried with the graphic material in Version 11, Figure 52.11. These are the cumulative statistics for both the schedule and the actual performance. The legend for these two items plus the key for the recovery plan are also shown, although the actual statistics for this latter plan are not shown in this version. To ease the problem of mental arithmetic, the net cumulative variance for the current reporting period is displayed in the chart's note section.

52.12 Schedule—End Item—Single Product Type—Version 12: Version 12 of an end item schedule, Figure 52.12, differs from Version 11 in that an additional line of statistical data has been added. The net cumulative variance for each reporting period is given, thus eliminating the need for periodically expunging the single statistic given in note form on the previous version.

52.13 Schedule—End Item—Single Product Type—Version 13: Accountability for delinquent items is shown on Version 13 of an end item schedule chart, Figure 52.13. This approach enables the viewer to determine what corrective actions are required to return shipments to an on-schedule position.

52.14 Schedule—End Item—Single Product Type—Version 14: Four lines of statistical data are used in Version 14, Figure 52.14. The scheduled and actual performance statistics are given in terms of both rate-per-month and cumulative, although only the cumulative data are plotted in graphic form. The net cumulative variance between the scheduled and actual performance is shown in note form.

52.15 Schedule—End Item—Single Product Type—Version 15: Version 15 of an end item schedule chart is shown in Figure 52.15. This is identical to Version 14 except that the net cumulative variance statistics are shown for each reporting period rather than as a note covering the current reporting period, only.

52.16 Schedule—End Item—Single Product Type—Version 16: Six lines of statistical data are presented with the graphic end item schedule chart shown in Figure 52.16. In this version, the statistics for the recovery rate have been added to the other statistics that were included in Version 15.

52.17 Schedule—End Item—Single Product Type—

Schedules—End Item—Single Product Type

Version 17: In Version 17 of an end item schedule, as shown in Figure 52.17, seven lines of statistical data are presented together with the graphic plot of cumulative data. This version differs from the previously shown Version 16 in that the cumulative statistics for the recovery schedule have been added.

52.18 Schedule—End Item—Single Product Type—Version 18: A variation of the previously displayed combination graphic chart/statistical table has the table to the side of the plotted data, as shown in Figure 52.18, rather than underneath.

52.19 Schedule—End Item—Single Product Type—Version 19: Version 19 of an end item schedule, Figure 52.19, is identical to Version 17 except that shading has been added. The shading, in this example, highlights the surplus and deficit variances between the plan and the actual and projected performance.

52.20 Schedule—End Item—Single Product Type—Version 20: In Version 20, Figure 52.20, the features of both line and surface charts have been combined. In this example, the shading highlights actual performance leaving the unshaded deficit portion between the schedule and actual performance standing out by contrast.

52.21 Schedule—End Item—Single Product Type—Version 21: In Version 21 of an end item schedule chart (Figure 52.21), the cumulative plan, actual, and recovery data have been plotted in step form. As with the previously described Version 20, the actual performance data have been shaded. In this format, there is less visual distortion of the April data than that in Version 20.

52.22 Schedule—End Item—Single Product Type—Version 22: Version 22, Figure 52.22, is the most complex version of an end item schedule presented in this series. In addition to carrying a full complement of statistical data, both cumulative and rate-per-time segment data have been plotted on separate, but date-registered, grids.

52.23 Schedule—End Item—Single Product Type—Version 23: The number of deliveries in terms of rate-per-month instead of cumulative quantities is displayed in Version 23 of an end item schedule chart (Figure 52.23). In this column chart version, six lines of statistics are also used.

52.24 Schedule—End Item—Single Product Type—Version 24: Version 24 of an end item schedule chart, Figure 52.24, differs from Version 23 only in that different types of columns are used. In any type of column chart it is useful to use a technique where the plotting of the actual performance data does not totally obliterate the plan.

52.25 Schedule—End Item—Single Product Type—Version 25: Version 25, Figure 52.25, combines a column chart with a step line chart. It can be noted that even after the actual performance columns have been, or will have been, inserted, the original schedule and recovery plan will still be visible.

52.26 Schedule—End Item—Single Product Type—Version 26: Version 26 of an end item schedule chart, Figure 52.26, differs from Version 25 only in that shading has been added to the schedule and recovery plan data in order to make them more visible.

52.27 Schedule—End Item—Single Product Type—Version 27: An end item schedule in the form of a deviation chart is shown in Figure 52.27. Only the cumulative surplus and deficit variances from plan (center line) are plotted on this type of chart. The visual impact of this chart could be further enhanced through color coding: green for the surplus (above the line) delivery, and red for the deficit (below the line).

52.28 Schedule—End Item—Single Product Type—Version 28: A deviation chart which displays upper and lower limit lines for management action is shown in Figure 52.28. In this example, the area that falls within the limits has been shaded in order to aid in chart interpretation.

52.29 Schedule—End Item—Single Product Type—Version 29: Version 29 of an end item schedule chart, Figure 52.29, combines a simple-to-read deviation chart with a table of statistics. The deviation type chart is especially useful when dealing with large quantities of deliverable items. If the chart viewer notes an unfavorable condition on the deviation chart, such as shown in this example, he has the option to study the statistics for a more precise evaluation.

52.30 Schedule—End Item—Single Product Type—Version 30: A milestone type end item schedule chart is shown in Figure 52.30. The itemized list of "deliverables" on the left can be in terms of single units by serial number (as shown), or can be in terms of groups of units such as "lot number." The milestone type of chart is normally used for in-process schedules where time spans are involved.

52.31 Schedule—End Item—Single Product Type—Version 31: Version 31, Figure 52.31, shows an end item schedule totally in terms of a statistical table. Six lines of data are used and, as with previously described graphic versions, progress can be tracked on this chart.

52.32 Schedule—End Item—Single Product Type—Version 32. Version 32 of an end item schedule, Figure 52.32, is identical to Version 31 except that an additional line of statistical data has been added: the scheduled recovery in terms of cumulative deliveries.

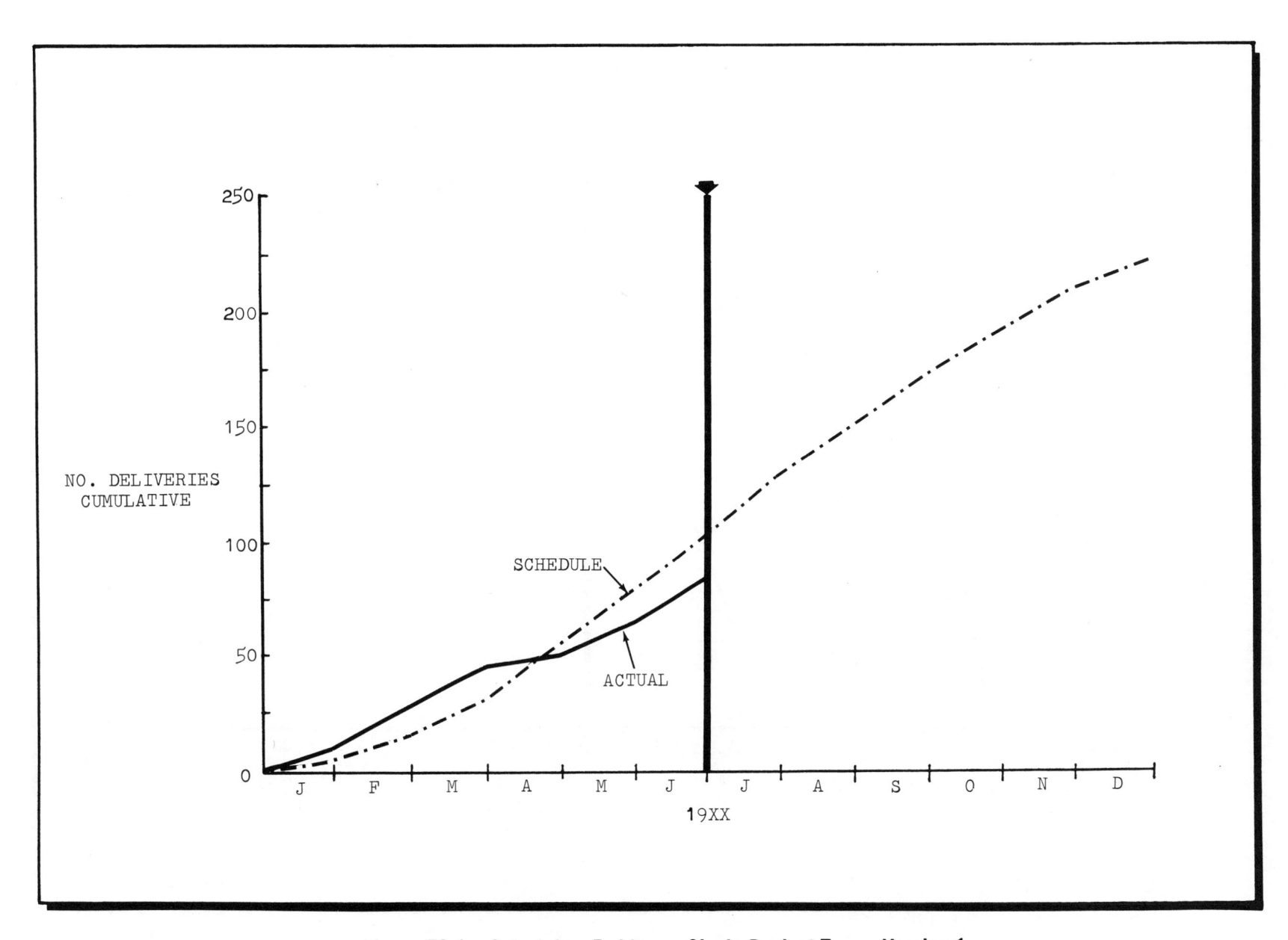

Figure 52.1   Schedule—End Item—Single Product Type—Version 1

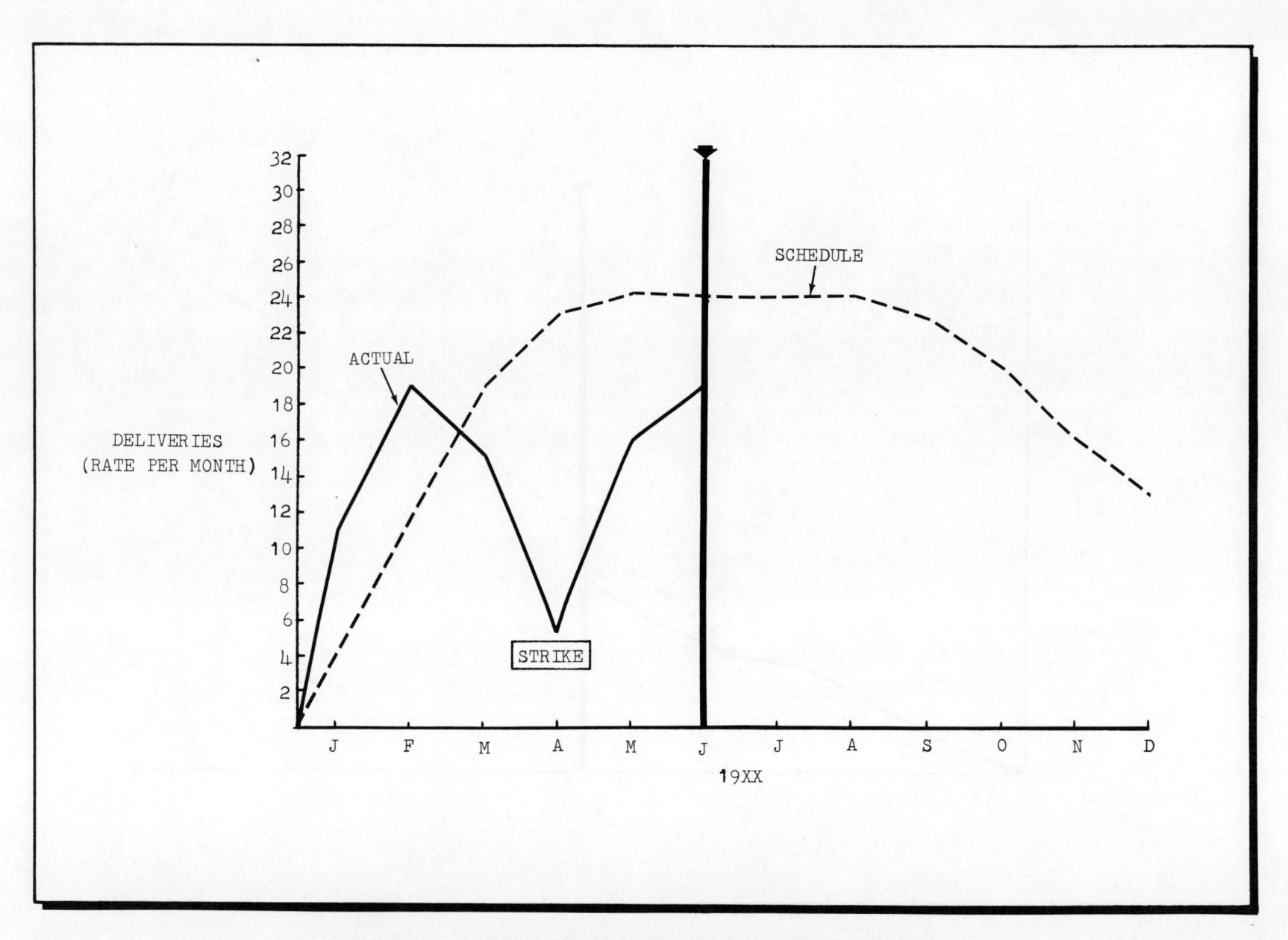

Figure 52.2 Schedule—End Item—Single Product Type—Version 2

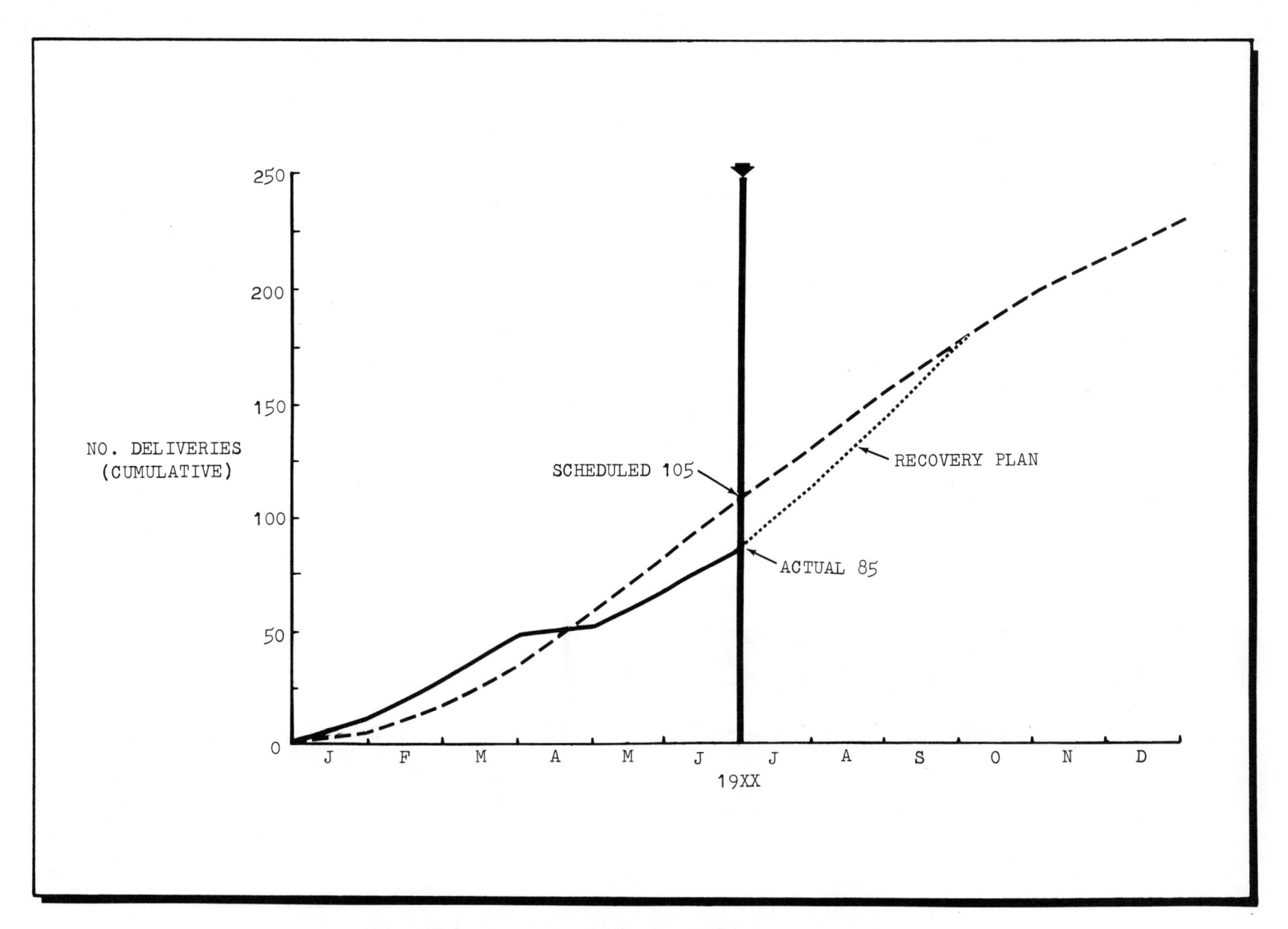

Figure 52.3 Schedule—End Item—Single Product Type—Version 3

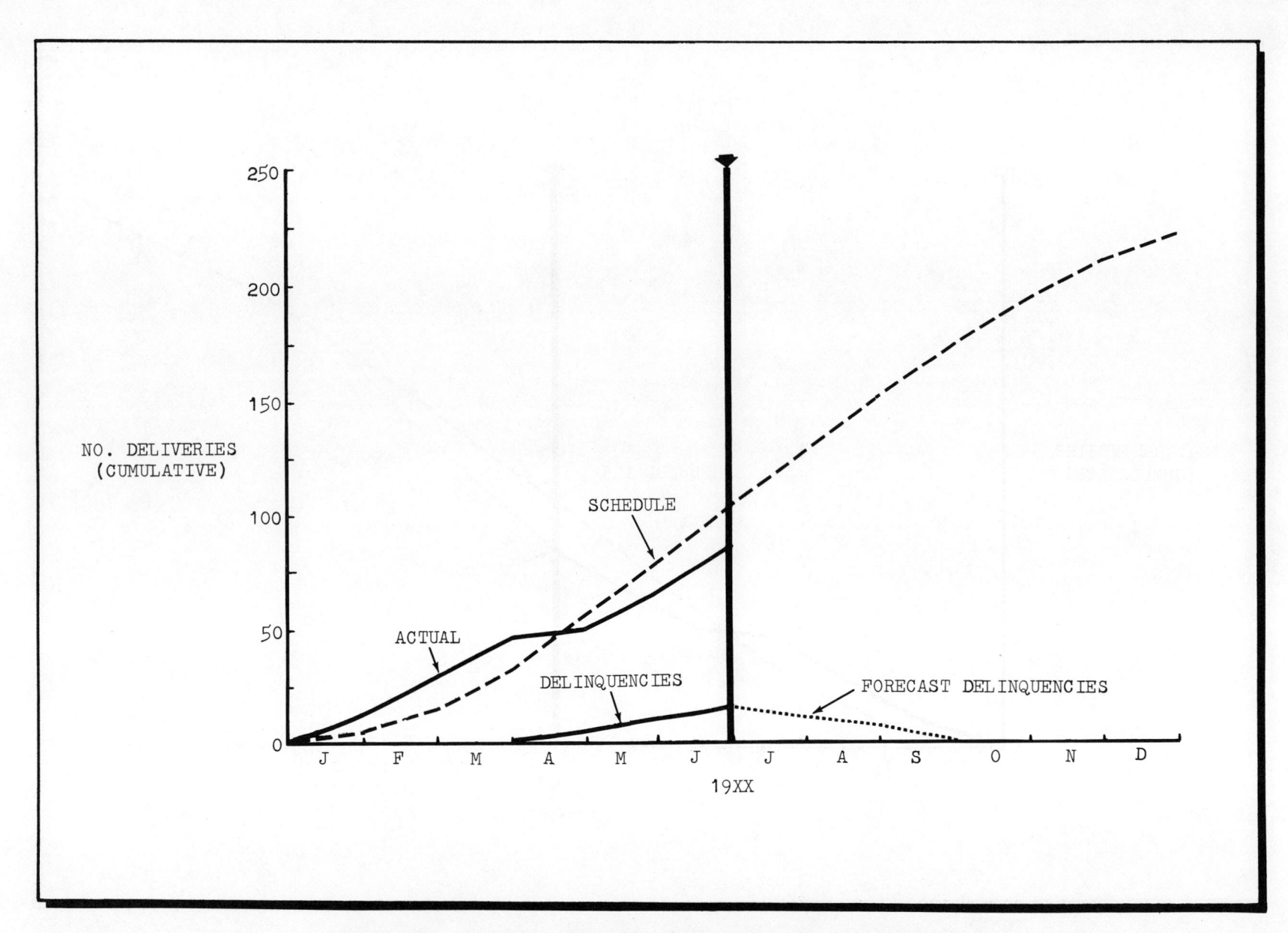

Figure 52.4   Schedule—End Item—Single Product Type—Version 4

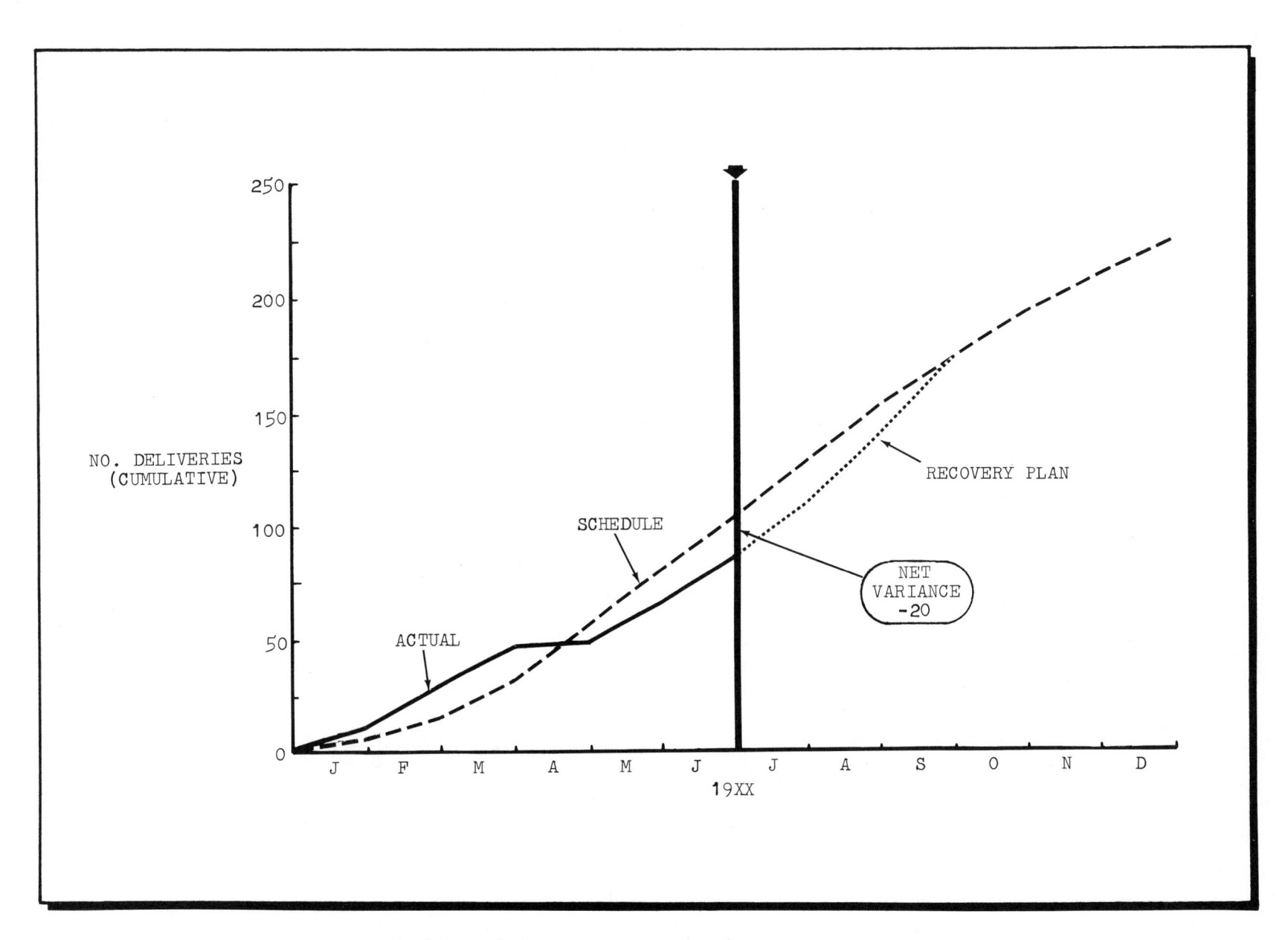

Figure 52.5   Schedule—End Item—Single Product Type—Version 5

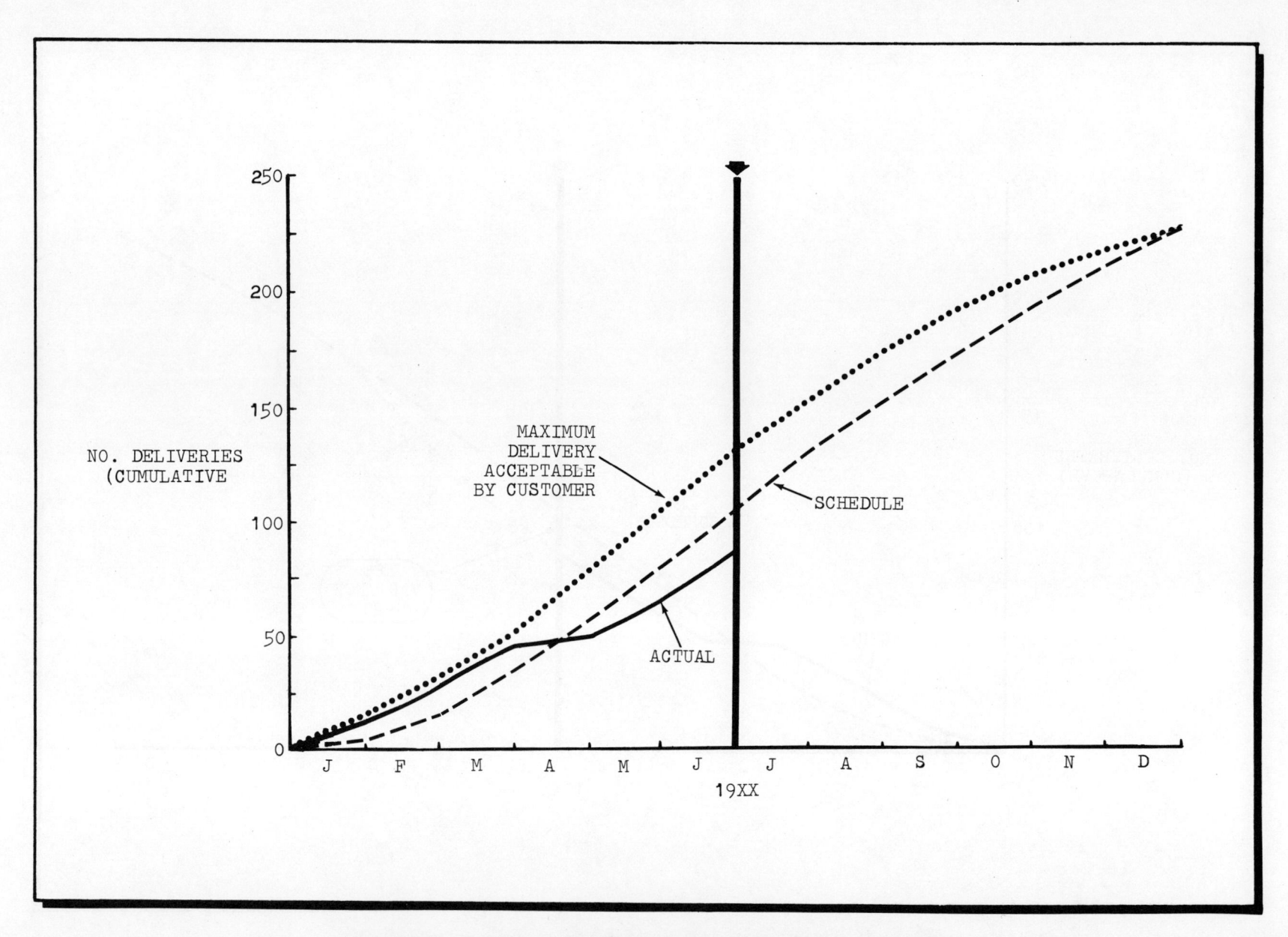

Figure 52.6   Schedule—End Item—Single Product Type—Version 6

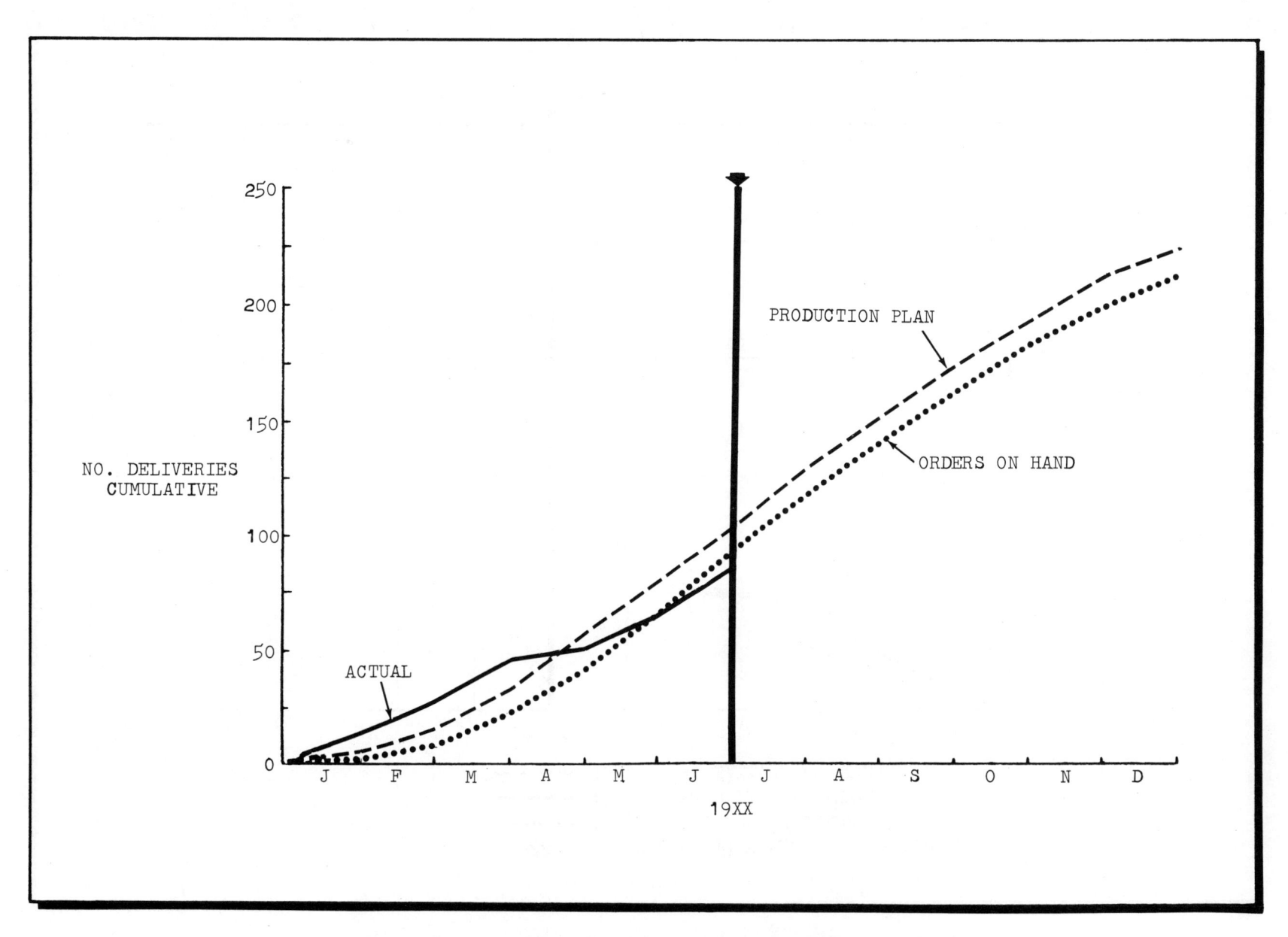

Figure 52.7 Schedule—End Item—Single Product Type—Version 7

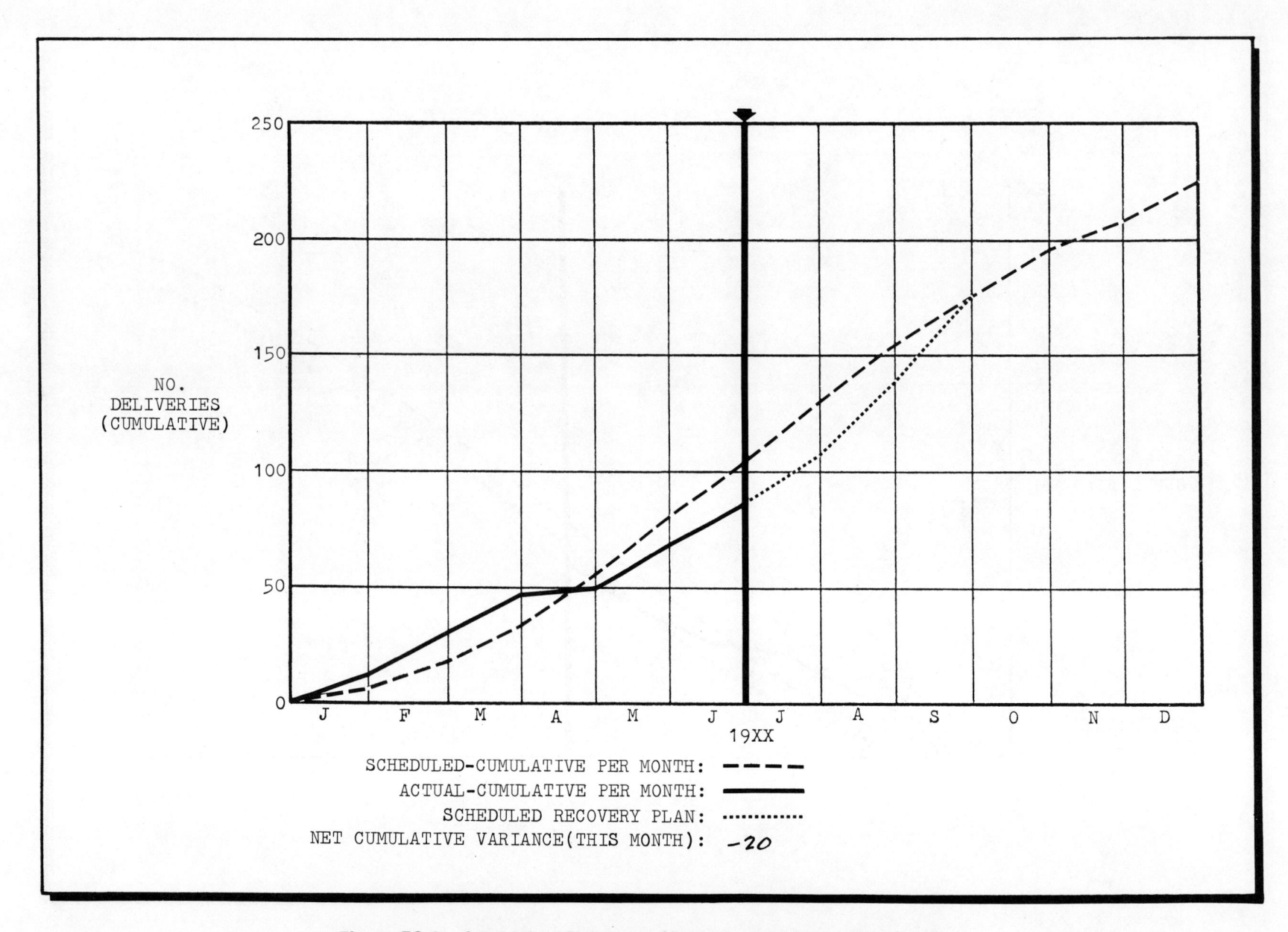

Figure 52.8   Schedule—End Item—Single Product Type—Version 8

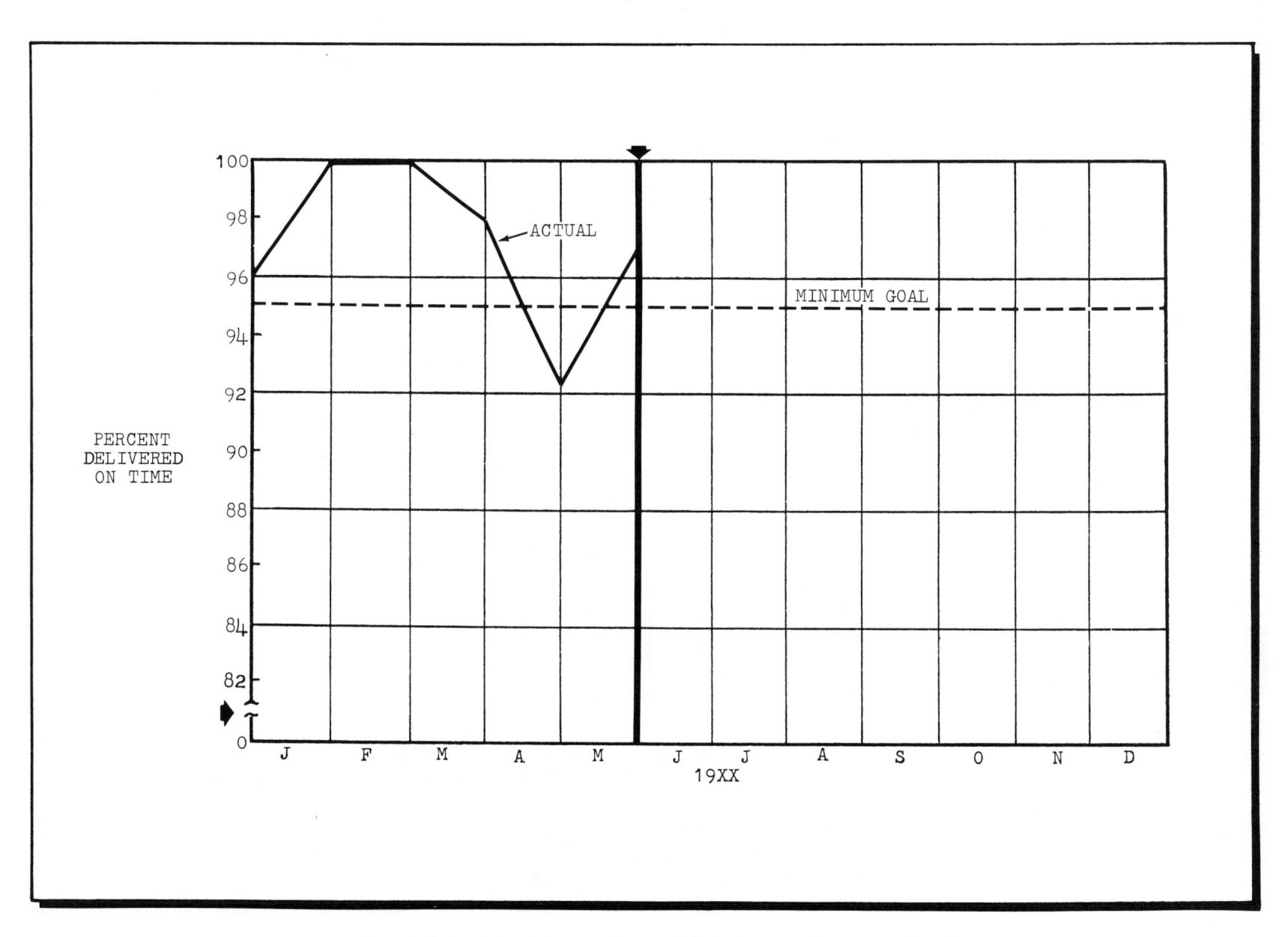

Figure 52.9 Schedule—End Item—Single Product Type—Version 9

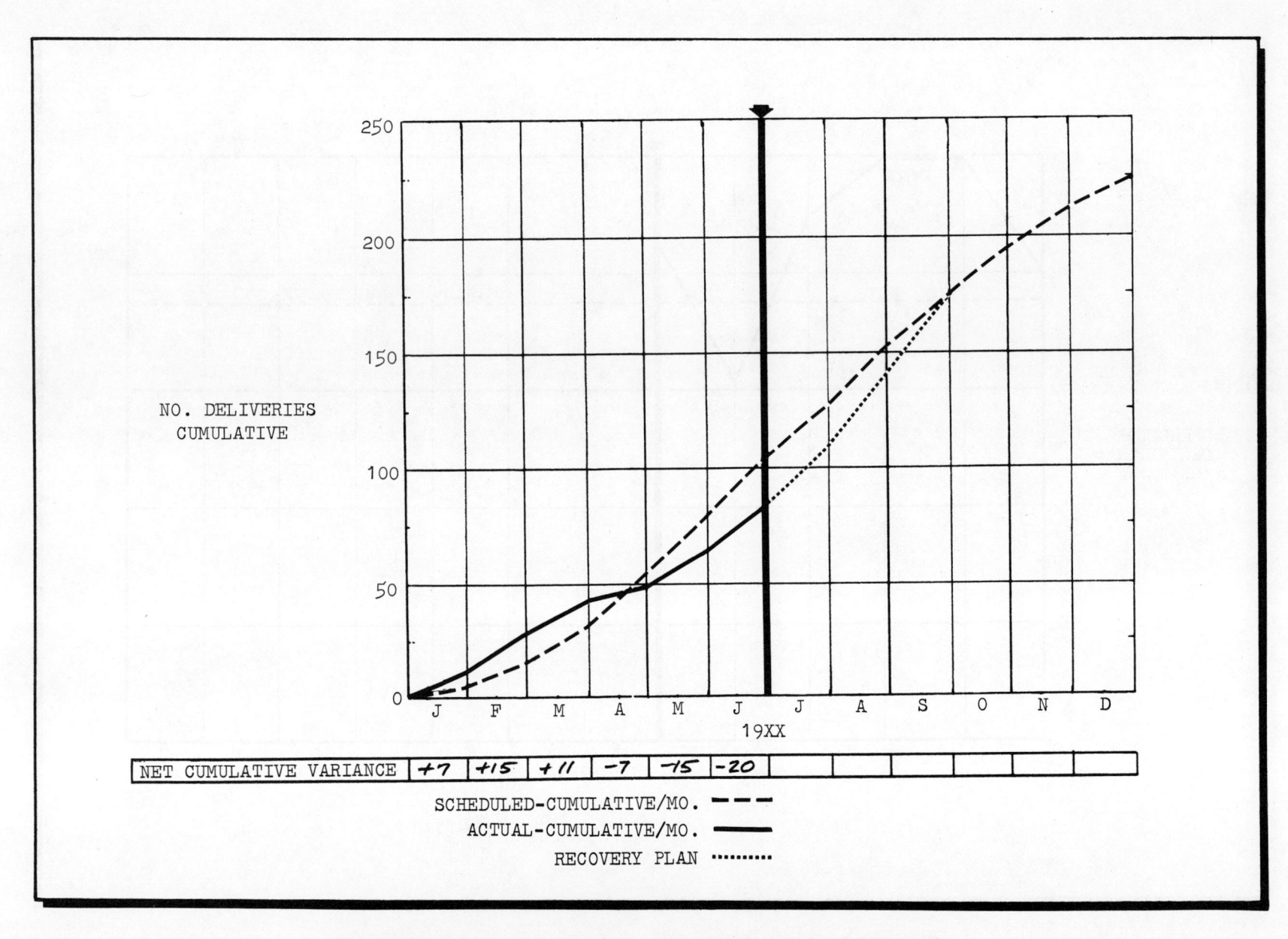

Figure 52.10   Schedule—End Item—Single Product Type—Version 10

NO. DELIVERIES
(CUMULATIVE)

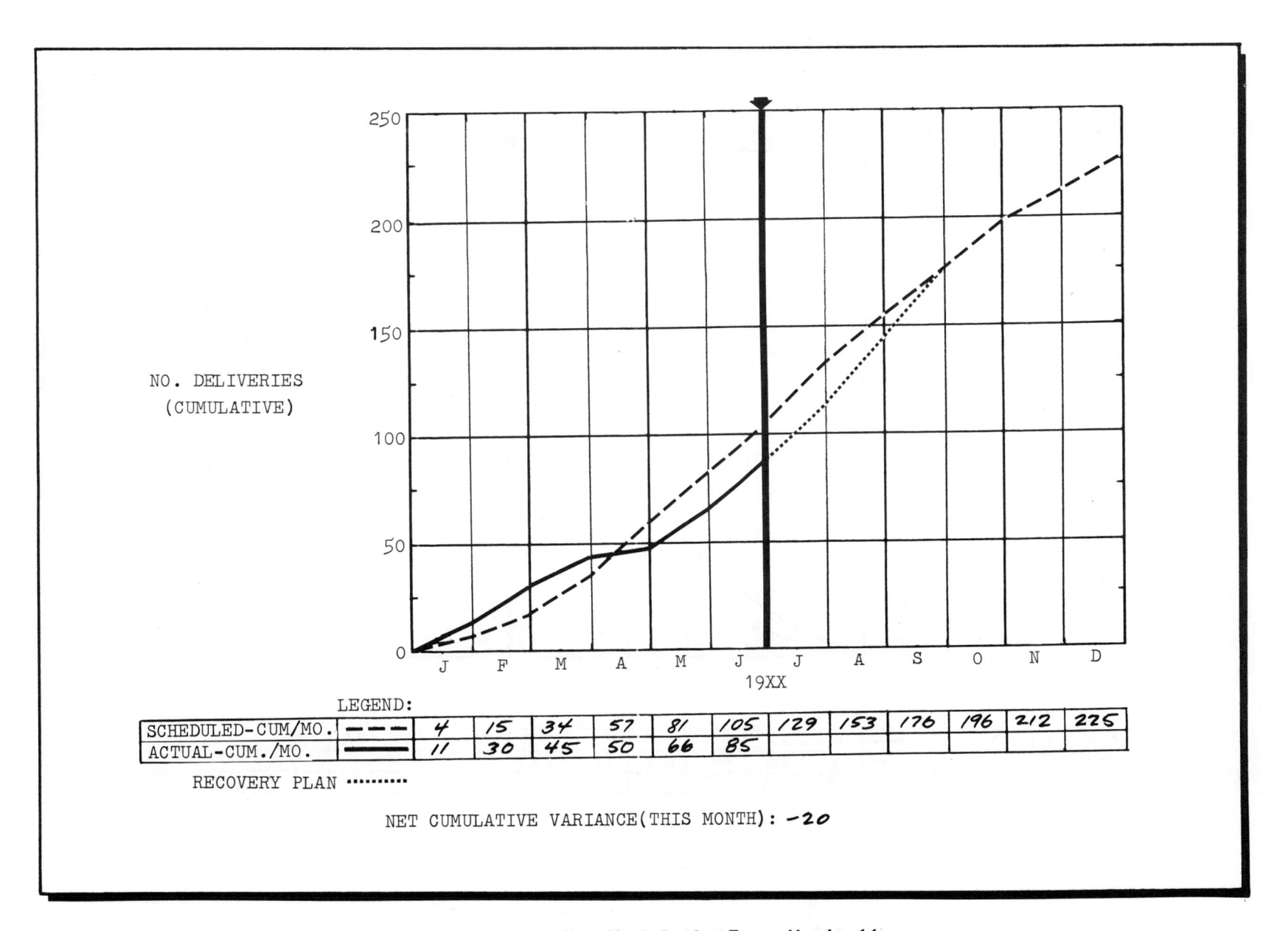

LEGEND:

SCHEDULED-CUM/MO. ----	4	15	34	57	81	105	129	153	176	196	212	225
ACTUAL-CUM./MO. ────	11	30	45	50	66	85						

RECOVERY PLAN ··········

NET CUMULATIVE VARIANCE (THIS MONTH): **-20**

Figure 52.11 Schedule—End Item—Single Product Type—Version 11

647

NO. DELIVERIES
(CUMULATIVE)

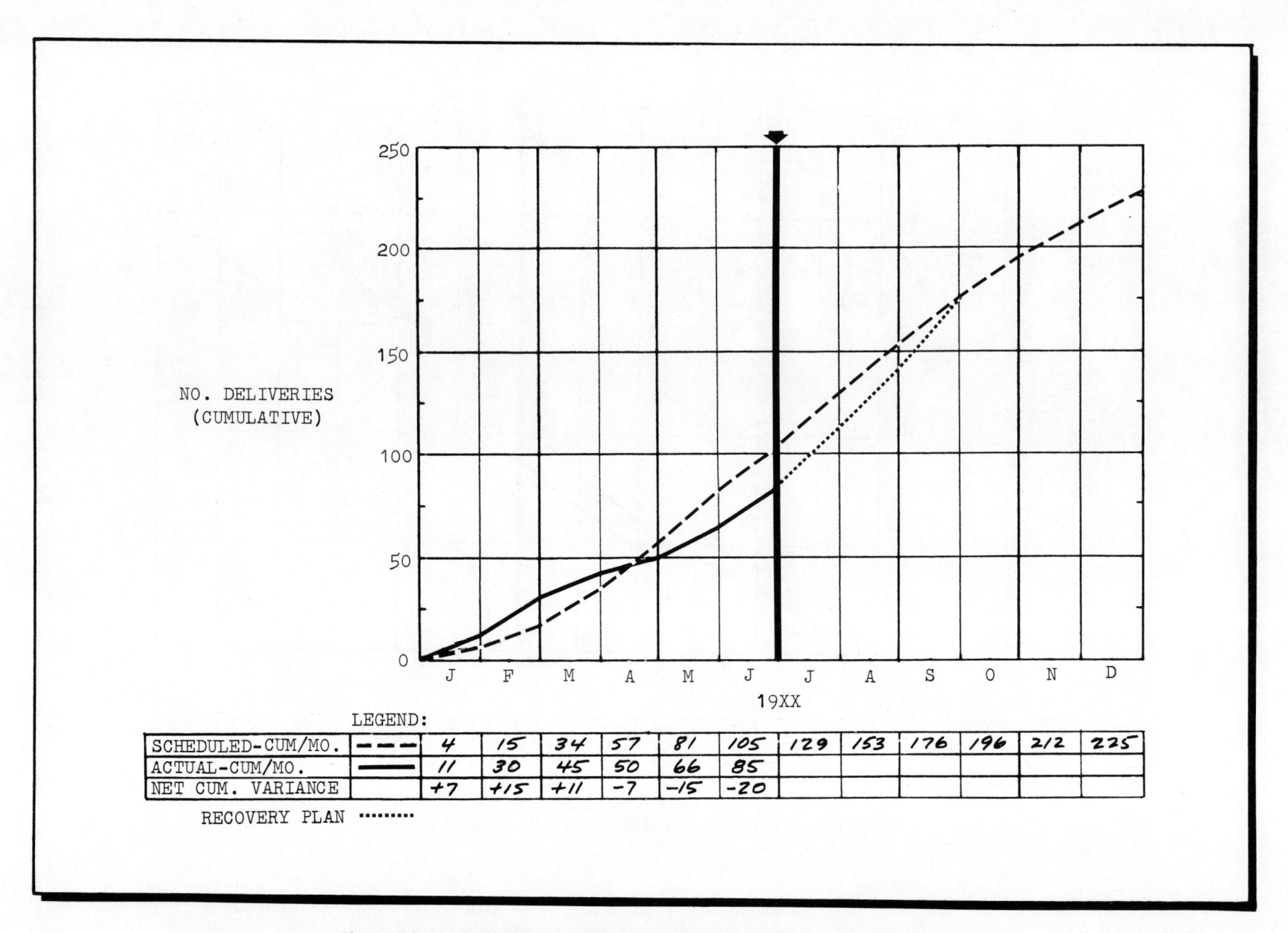

LEGEND:

		J	F	M	A	M	J	J	A	S	O	N	D
SCHEDULED-CUM/MO.	----	4	15	34	57	81	105	129	153	176	196	212	225
ACTUAL-CUM/MO.	——	11	30	45	50	66	85						
NET CUM. VARIANCE		+7	+15	+11	-7	-15	-20						

RECOVERY PLAN ·········

Figure 52.12 Schedule—End Item—Single Product Type—Version 12

SHIPPED
(CUMULATIVE)

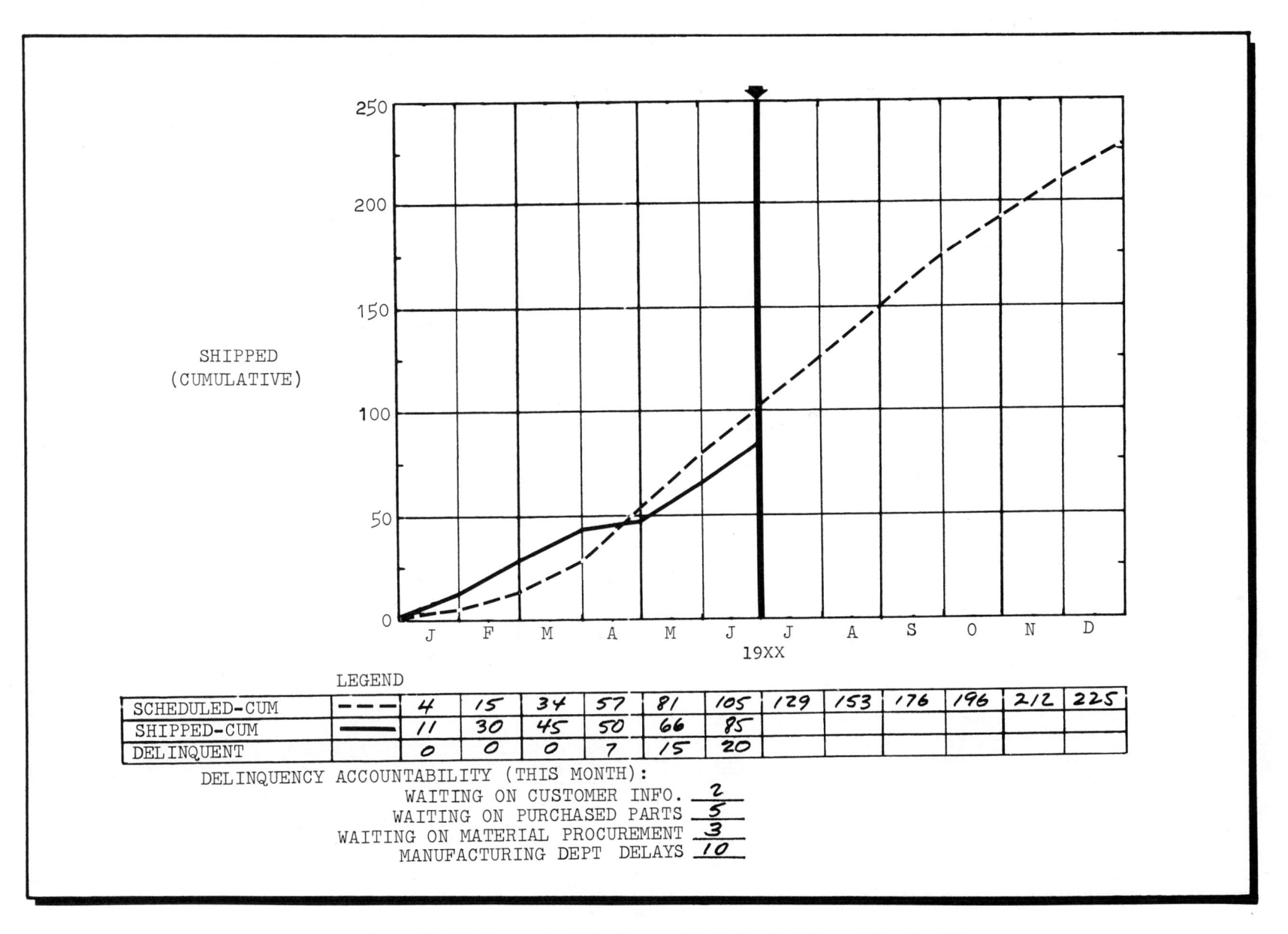

LEGEND													
SCHEDULED-CUM	-----	4	15	34	57	81	105	129	153	176	196	212	225
SHIPPED-CUM	———	11	30	45	50	66	85						
DELINQUENT		0	0	0	7	15	20						

DELINQUENCY ACCOUNTABILITY (THIS MONTH):
WAITING ON CUSTOMER INFO. 2
WAITING ON PURCHASED PARTS 5
WAITING ON MATERIAL PROCUREMENT 3
MANUFACTURING DEPT DELAYS 10

Figure 52.13 Schedule—End Item—Single Product Type—Version 13

NO. DELIVERIES
(CUMULATIVE)

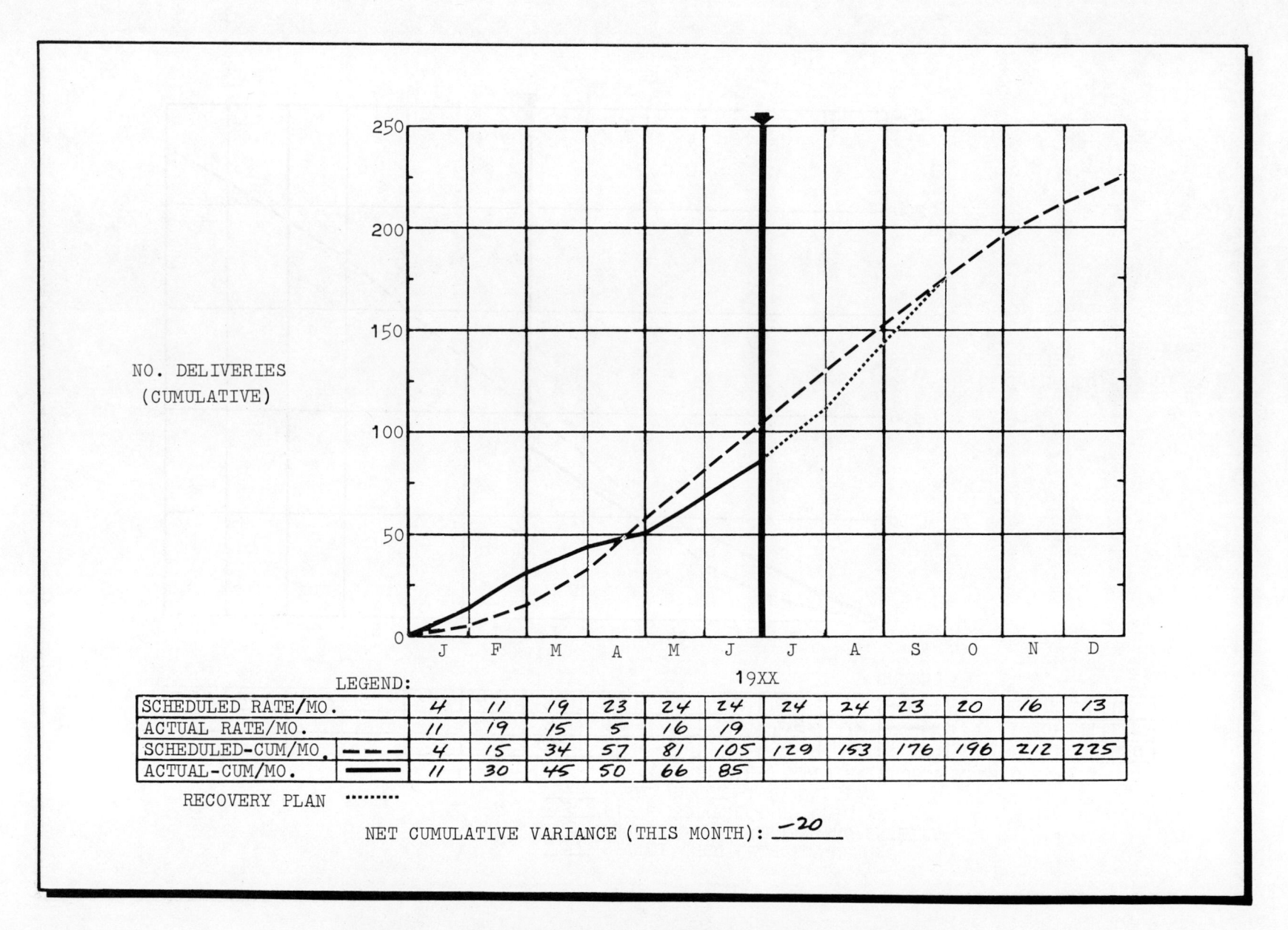

                    J F M A M J J A S O N D
                              19XX

LEGEND:

SCHEDULED RATE/MO.		4	11	19	23	24	24	24	24	23	20	16	13
ACTUAL RATE/MO.		11	19	15	5	16	19						
SCHEDULED-CUM/MO.	- - - -	4	15	34	57	81	105	129	153	176	196	212	225
ACTUAL-CUM/MO.	———	11	30	45	50	66	85						

RECOVERY PLAN ....

NET CUMULATIVE VARIANCE (THIS MONTH): ___-20___

Figure 52.14   Schedule—End Item—Single Product Type—Version 14

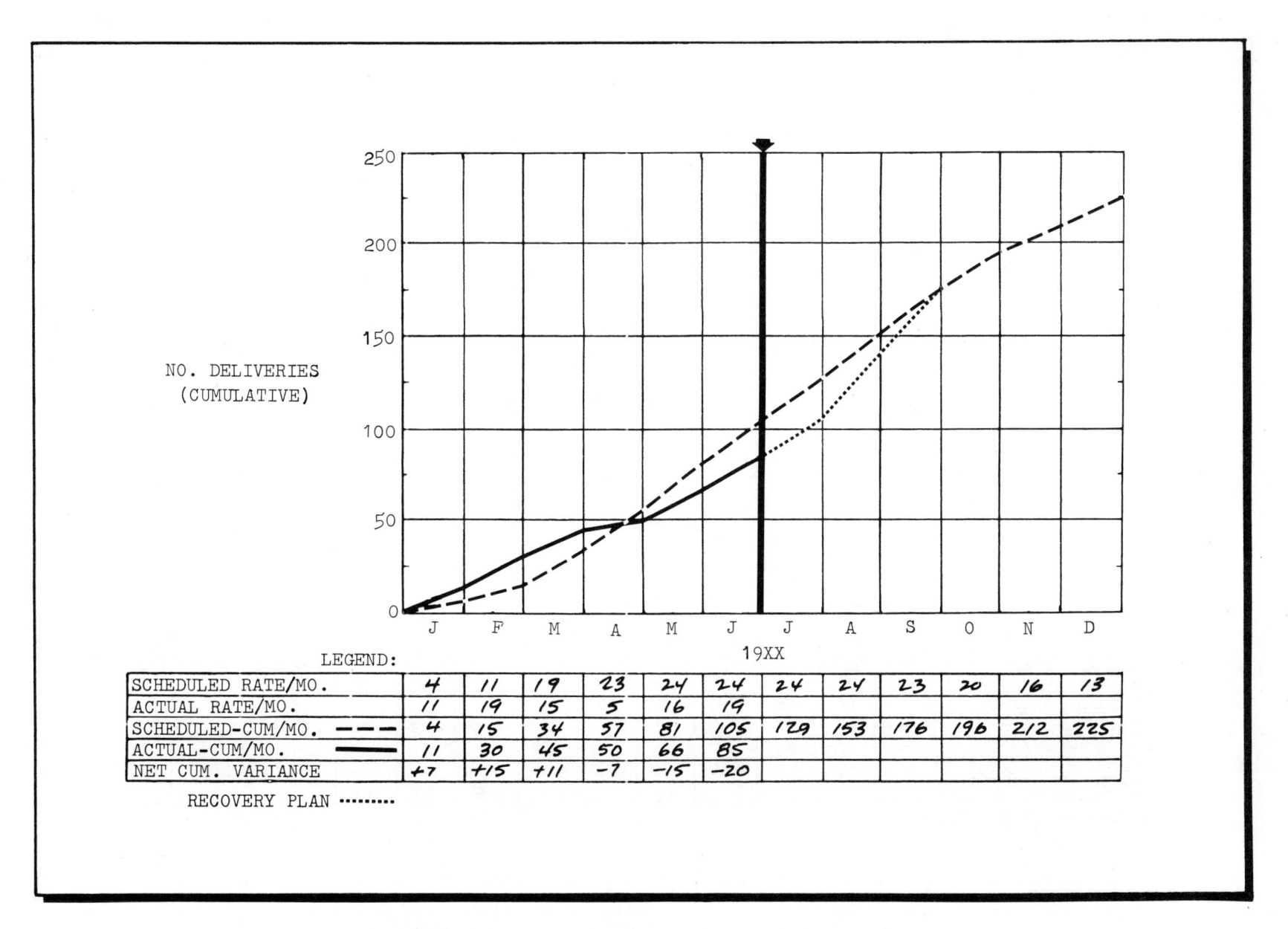

	J	F	M	A	M	J	J	A	S	O	N	D
SCHEDULED RATE/MO.	4	11	19	23	24	24	24	24	23	20	16	13
ACTUAL RATE/MO.	11	19	15	5	16	19						
SCHEDULED-CUM/MO. ----	4	15	34	57	81	105	129	153	176	196	212	225
ACTUAL-CUM/MO. ——	11	30	45	50	66	85						
NET CUM. VARIANCE	+7	+15	+11	-7	-15	-20						

RECOVERY PLAN ··········

Figure 52.15 Schedule—End Item—Single Product Type—Version 15

NO. DELIVERIES
(CUMULATIVE)

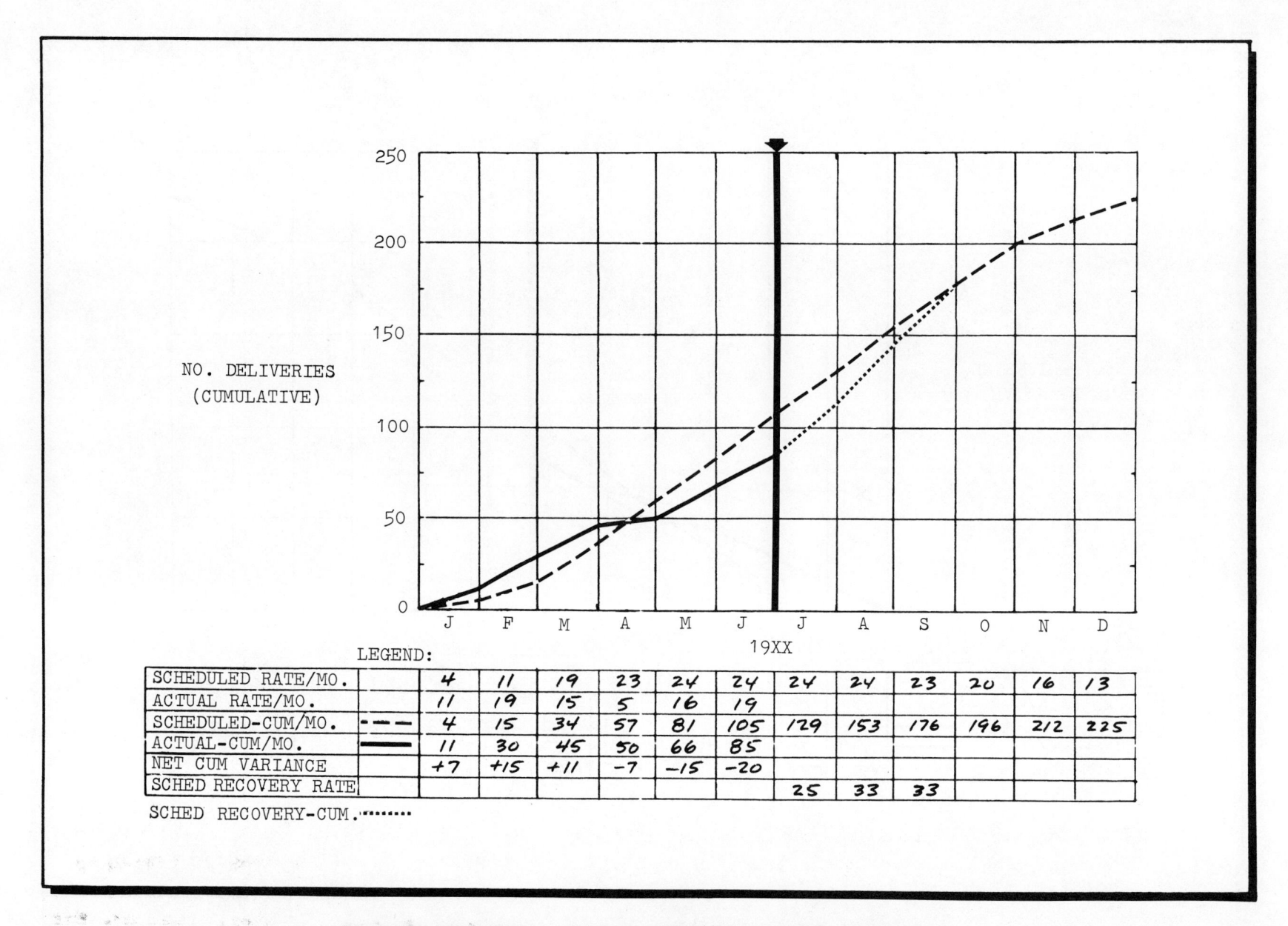

LEGEND:

SCHEDULED RATE/MO.		4	11	19	23	24	24	24	24	23	20	16	13
ACTUAL RATE/MO.		11	19	15	5	16	19						
SCHEDULED-CUM/MO.	- - -	4	15	34	57	81	105	129	153	176	196	212	225
ACTUAL-CUM/MO.	———	11	30	45	50	66	85						
NET CUM VARIANCE		+7	+15	+11	-7	-15	-20						
SCHED RECOVERY RATE								25	33	33			

SCHED RECOVERY-CUM. ·········

Figure 52.16 Schedule—End Item—Single Product Type—Version 16

NO. DELIVERIES
(CUMULATIVE)

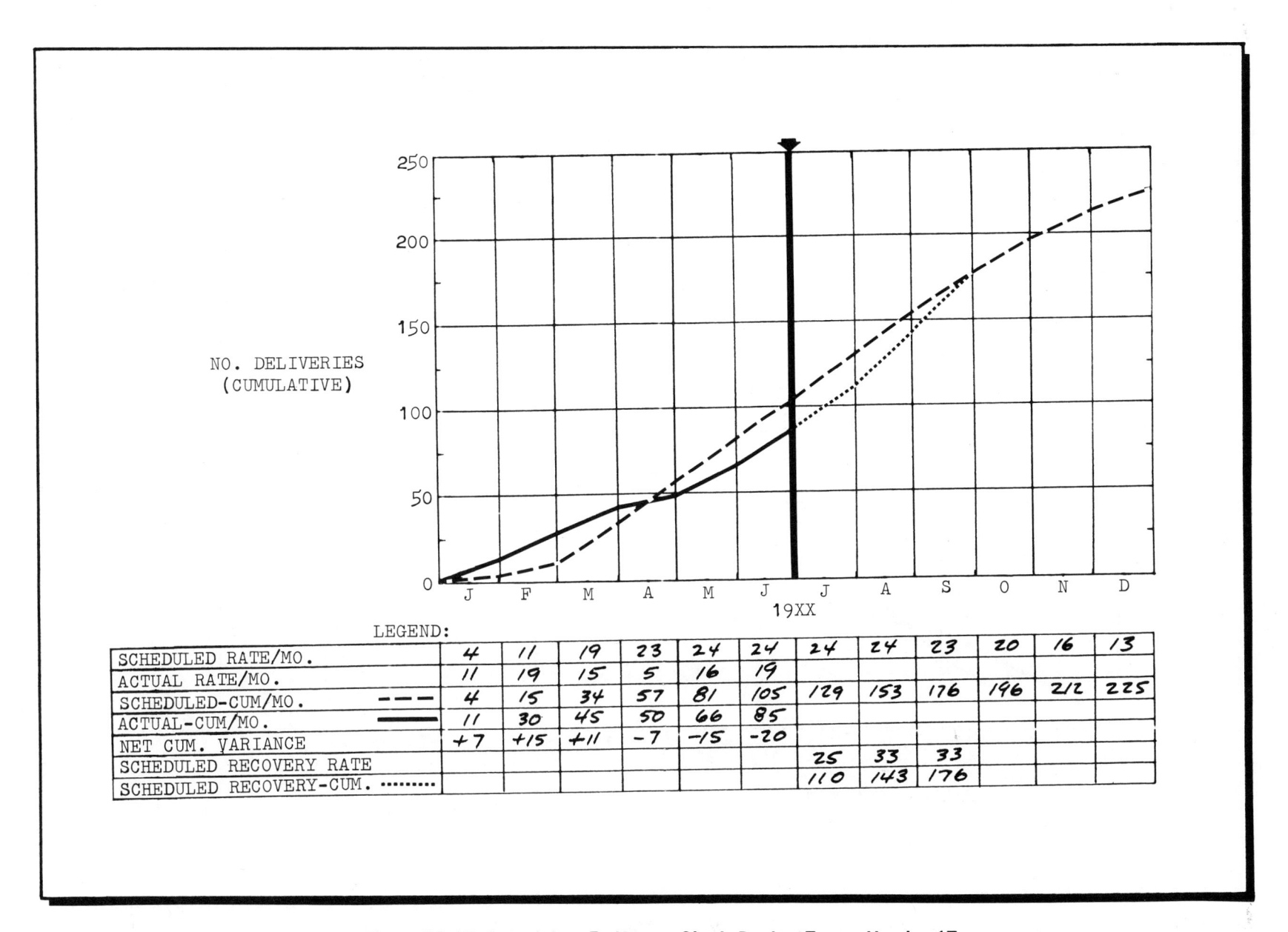

LEGEND:												
SCHEDULED RATE/MO.		4	11	19	23	24	24	24	24	23	20	16	13
ACTUAL RATE/MO.		11	19	15	5	16	19						
SCHEDULED-CUM/MO.	– – –	4	15	34	57	81	105	129	153	176	196	212	225
ACTUAL-CUM/MO.	———	11	30	45	50	66	85						
NET CUM. VARIANCE		+7	+15	+11	−7	−15	−20						
SCHEDULED RECOVERY RATE								25	33	33			
SCHEDULED RECOVERY-CUM.	········							110	143	176			

Figure 52.17 Schedule—End Item—Single Product Type—Version 17

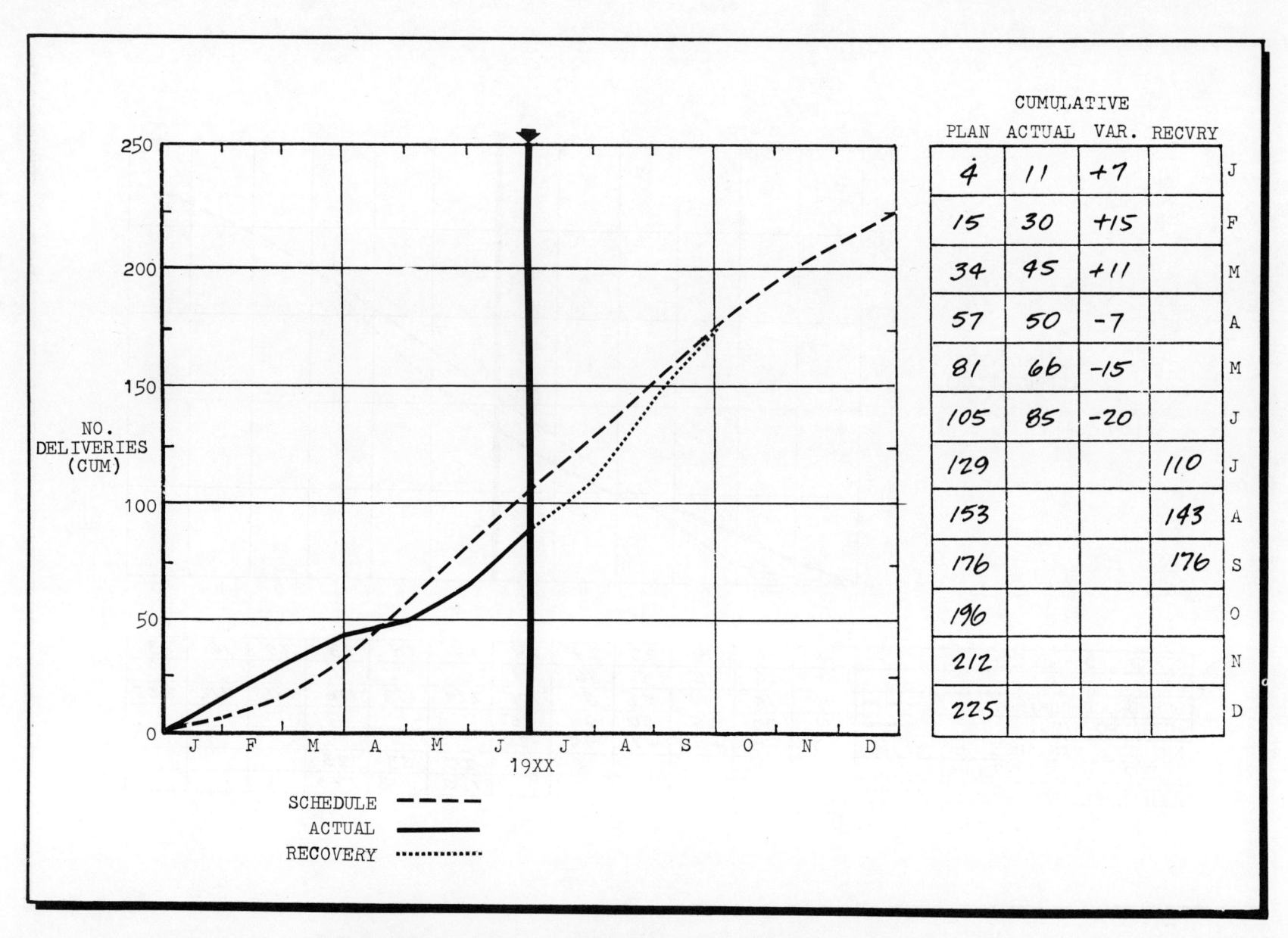

CUMULATIVE				
PLAN	ACTUAL	VAR.	RECVRY	
4	11	+7		J
15	30	+15		F
34	45	+11		M
57	50	-7		A
81	66	-15		M
105	85	-20		J
129			110	J
153			143	A
176			176	S
196				O
212				N
225				D

Figure 52.18 Schedule—End Item—Single Product Type—Version 18

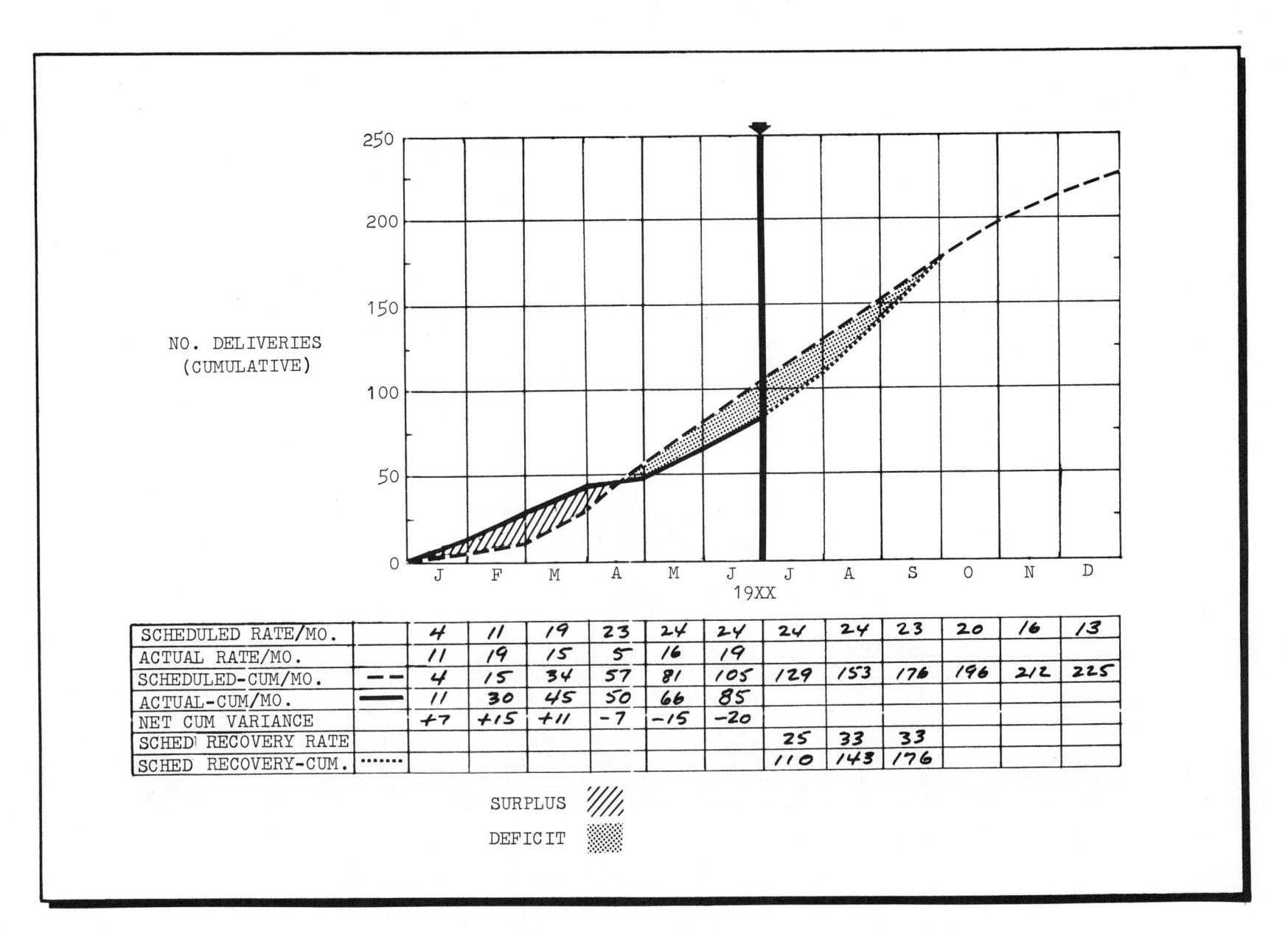

		J	F	M	A	M	J	J	A	S	O	N	D
SCHEDULED RATE/MO.		4	11	19	23	24	24	24	24	23	20	16	13
ACTUAL RATE/MO.		11	19	15	5	16	19						
SCHEDULED-CUM/MO.	– –	4	15	34	57	81	105	129	153	176	196	212	225
ACTUAL-CUM/MO.	——	11	30	45	50	66	85						
NET CUM VARIANCE		+7	+15	+11	-7	-15	-20						
SCHED RECOVERY RATE								25	33	33			
SCHED RECOVERY-CUM.	·······							110	143	176			

SURPLUS ////
DEFICIT ░░░

Figure 52.19   Schedule—End Item—Single Product Type—Version 19

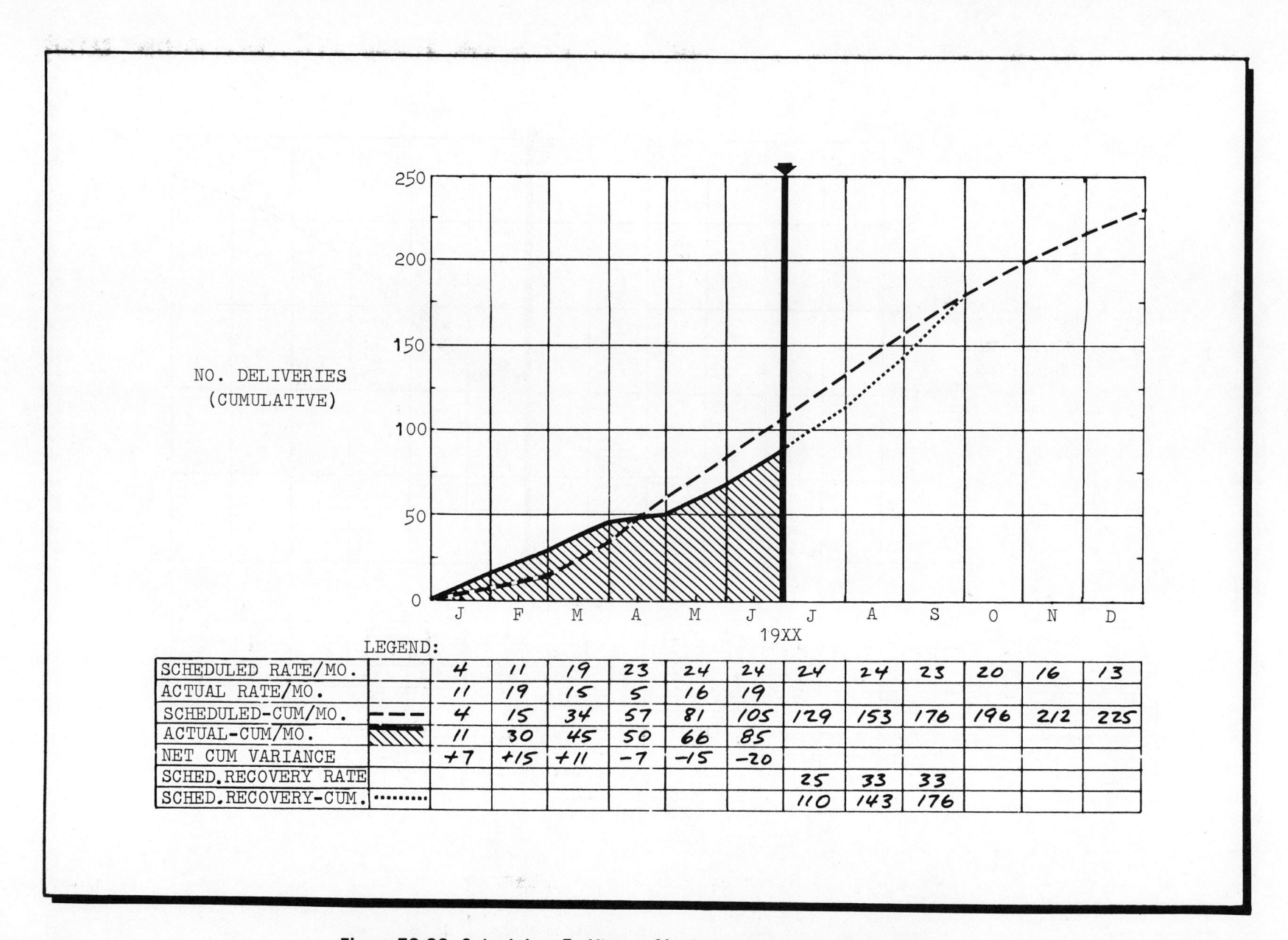

LEGEND:												
SCHEDULED RATE/MO.		4	11	19	23	24	24	24	24	23	20	16	13
ACTUAL RATE/MO.		11	19	15	5	16	19						
SCHEDULED-CUM/MO.	– – –	4	15	34	57	81	105	129	153	176	196	212	225
ACTUAL-CUM/MO.	▨	11	30	45	50	66	85						
NET CUM VARIANCE		+7	+15	+11	−7	−15	−20						
SCHED. RECOVERY RATE								25	33	33			
SCHED. RECOVERY-CUM.	········							110	143	176			

Figure 52.20 Schedule—End Item—Single Product Type—Version 20

NO. DELIVERIES
(CUMULATIVE)

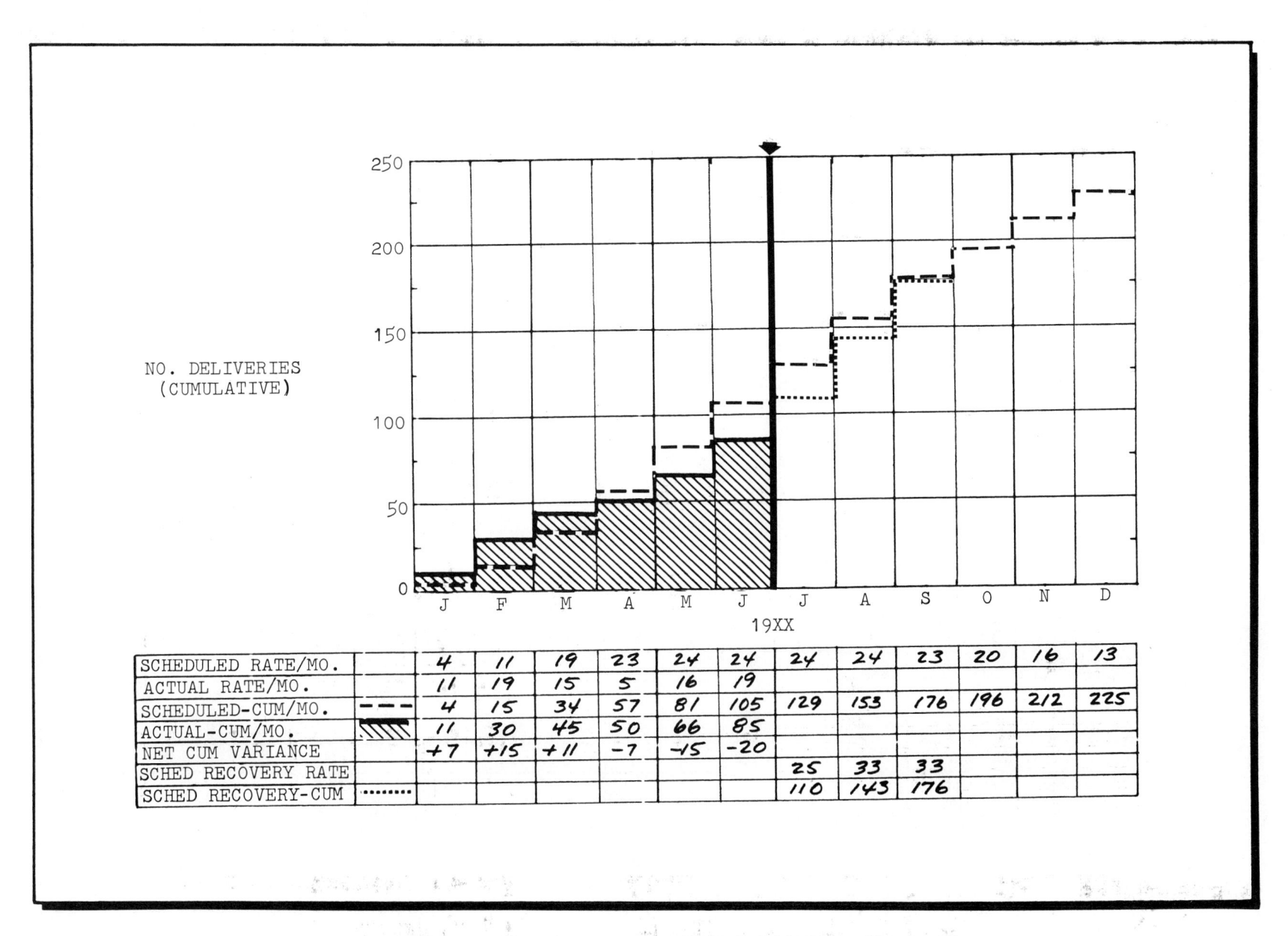

		J	F	M	A	M	J	J	A	S	O	N	D
SCHEDULED RATE/MO.			4	11	19	23	24	24	24	24	23	20	16	13
ACTUAL RATE/MO.			11	19	15	5	16	19						
SCHEDULED-CUM/MO.	---		4	15	34	57	81	105	129	153	176	196	212	225
ACTUAL-CUM/MO.	▨		11	30	45	50	66	85						
NET CUM VARIANCE			+7	+15	+11	-7	-15	-20						
SCHED RECOVERY RATE									25	33	33			
SCHED RECOVERY-CUM	······								110	143	176			

Figure 52.21 Schedule—End Item—Single Product Type—Version 21

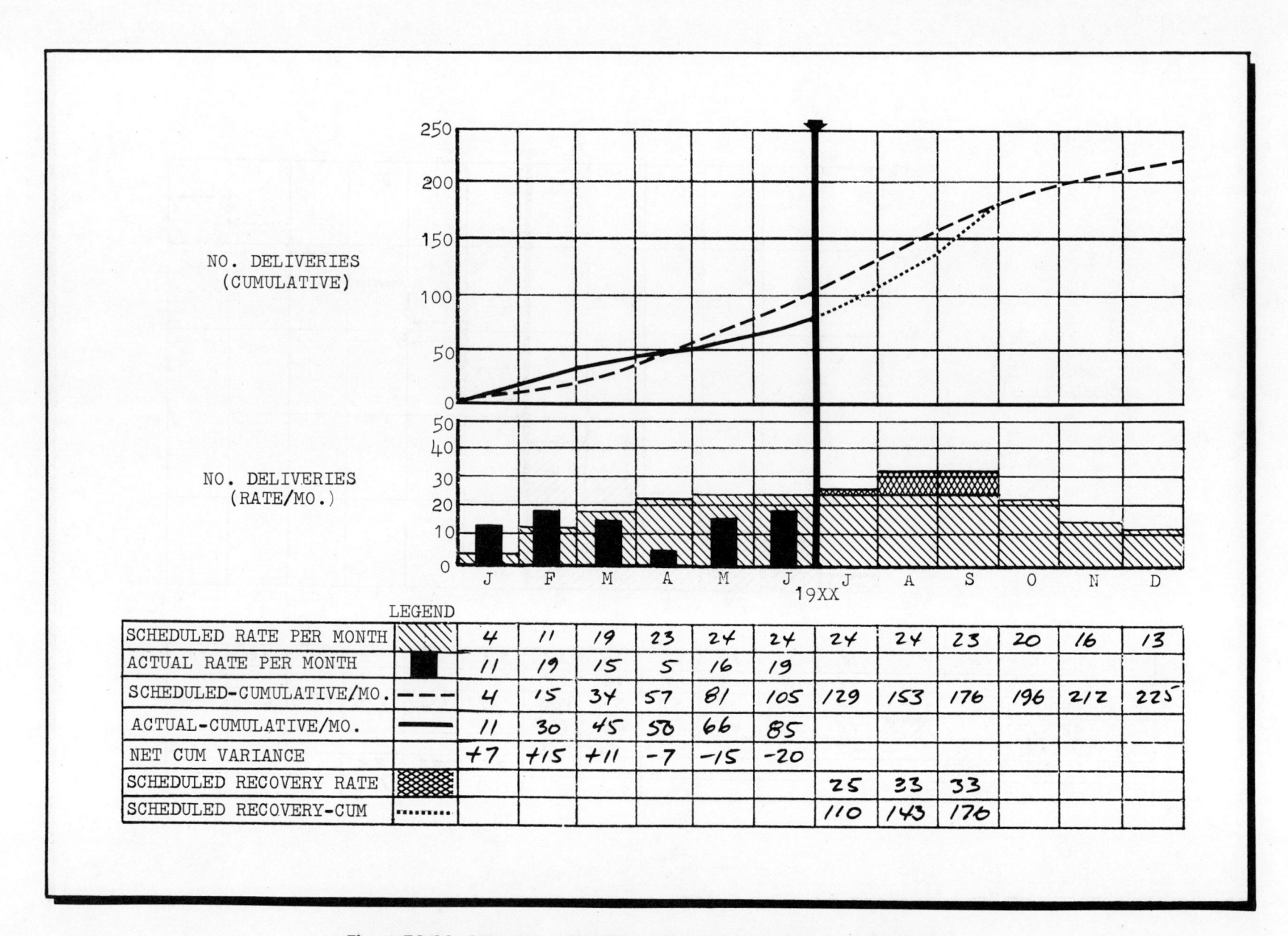

LEGEND												
SCHEDULED RATE PER MONTH ▨	4	11	19	23	24	24	24	24	23	20	16	13
ACTUAL RATE PER MONTH ■	11	19	15	5	16	19						
SCHEDULED-CUMULATIVE/MO. ----	4	15	34	57	81	105	129	153	176	196	212	225
ACTUAL-CUMULATIVE/MO. ——	11	30	45	50	66	85						
NET CUM VARIANCE	+7	+15	+11	-7	-15	-20						
SCHEDULED RECOVERY RATE ▦							25	33	33			
SCHEDULED RECOVERY-CUM ⋯⋯							110	143	176			

Figure 52.22 Schedule—End Item—Single Product Type—Version 22

NO. DELIVERIES
(RATE PER MONTH)

LEGEND:

		J	F	M	A	M	J	J	A	S	O	N	D
SCHEDULED RATE/MO.	▨	4	11	19	23	24	24	24	24	23	20	16	13
ACTUAL RATE/MO.	■	11	19	15	5	16	19						
SCHEDULED-CUM/MO.		4	15	34	57	81	105	129	153	176	196	212	225
ACTUAL-CUM/MO.		11	30	45	50	66	85						
NET CUM. VARIANCE		+7	+15	+11	-7	-15	-20						
SCHED. RECOVERY RATE.	▩							25	33	33			

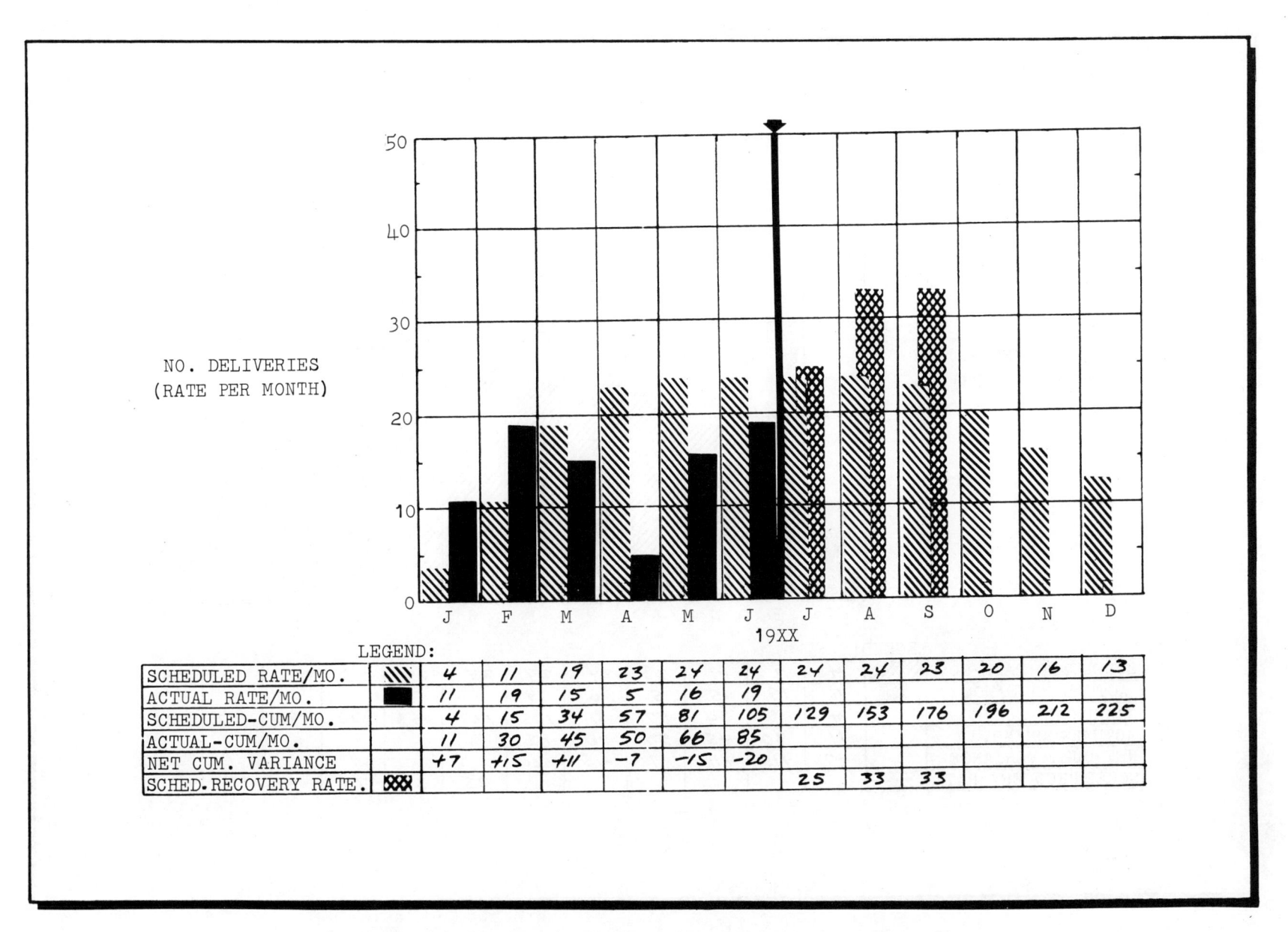

Figure 52.23 Schedule—End Item—Single Product Type—Version 23

NO. DELIVERIES
(RATE PER MONTH)

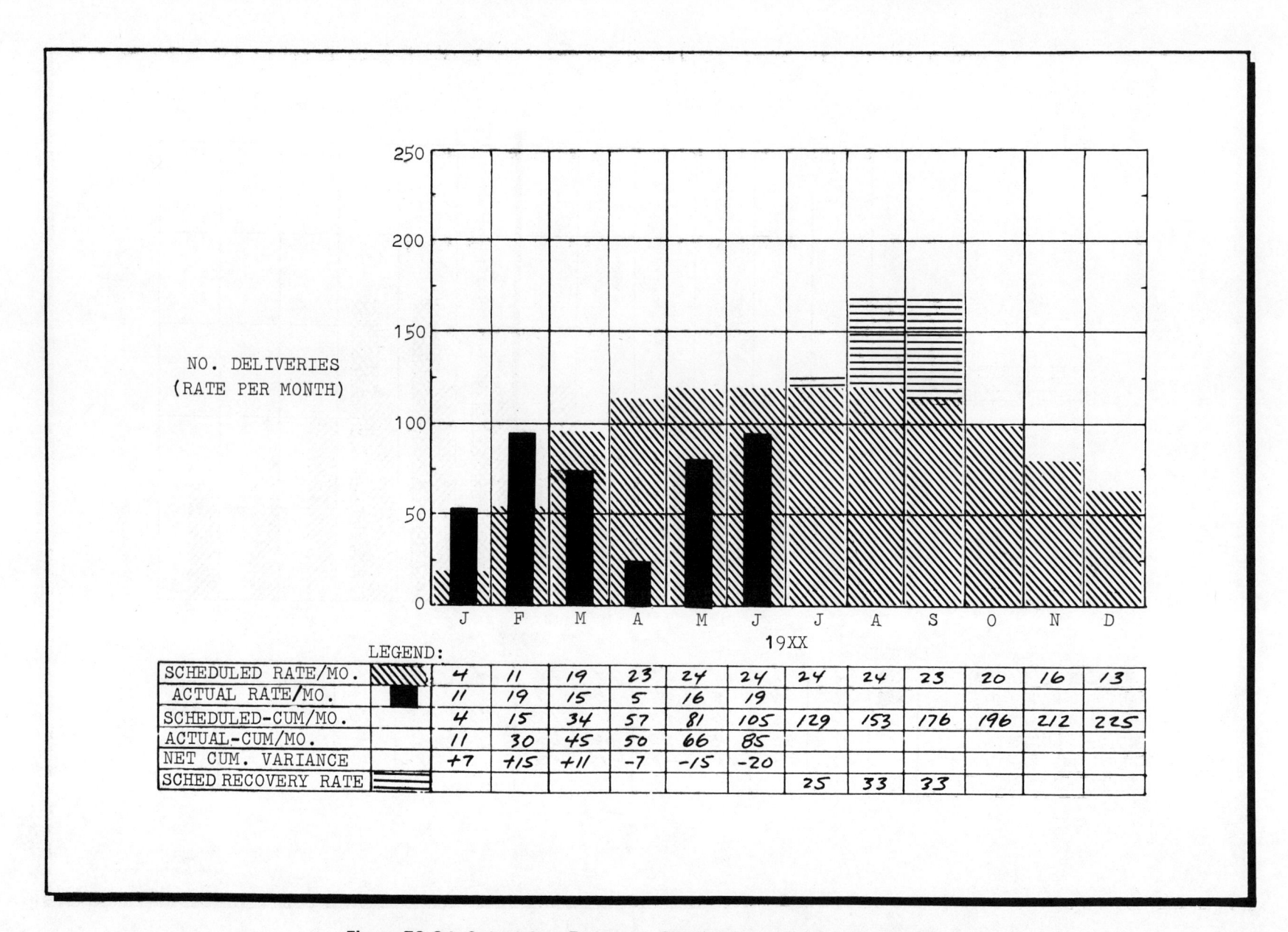

LEGEND:												
SCHEDULED RATE/MO.		4	11	19	23	24	24	24	24	23	20	16	13
ACTUAL RATE/MO.		11	19	15	5	16	19						
SCHEDULED-CUM/MO.		4	15	34	57	81	105	129	153	176	196	212	225
ACTUAL-CUM/MO.		11	30	45	50	66	85						
NET CUM. VARIANCE		+7	+15	+11	-7	-15	-20						
SCHED RECOVERY RATE								25	33	33			

Figure 52.24 Schedule—End Item—Single Product Type—Version 24

NO. DELIVERIES
(RATE PER MONTH)

LEGEND:

		J	F	M	A	M	J	J	A	S	O	N	D
SCHEDULED RATE/MO.	— — —	4	11	19	23	24	24	24	24	23	20	16	13
ACTUAL RATE/MO.	■	11	19	15	5	16	19						
SCHEDULED-CUM/MO.		4	15	34	57	81	105	129	153	176	196	212	225
ACTUAL-CUM/MO.		11	30	45	50	66	85						
NET CUM VARIANCE		+7	+15	+11	-7	-15	-20						
SCHEDULED RECOVERY RATE	....							25	33	33			

Figure 52.25 Schedule—End Item—Single Product Type—Version 25

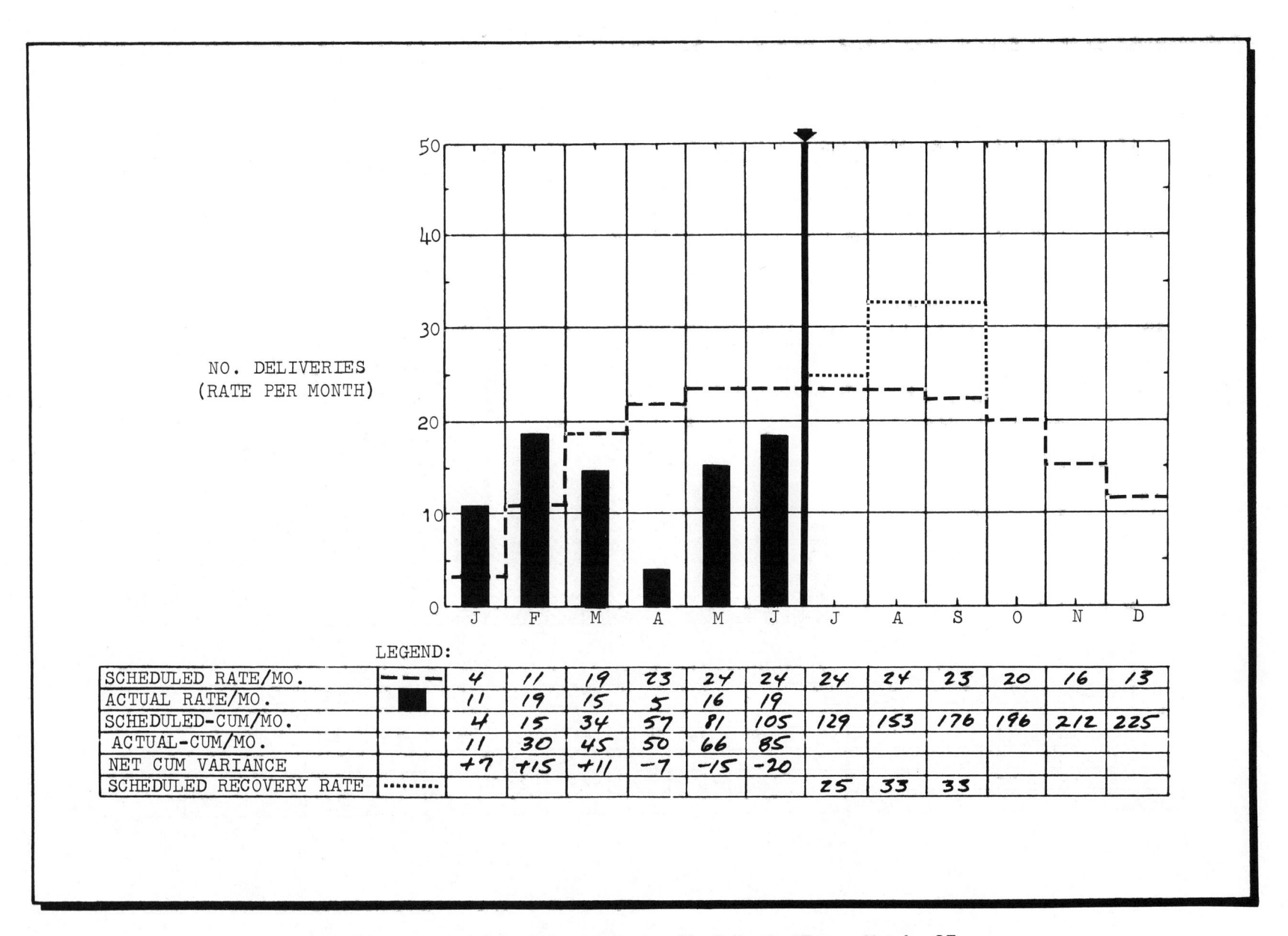

NO. DELIVERIES
(RATE PER MONTH)

		J	F	M	A	M	J	J	A	S	O	N	D
SCHEDULED RATE/MO.	▨	4	11	19	23	24	24	24	24	23	20	16	13
ACTUAL RATE/MO.	■	11	19	15	5	16	19						
SCHEDULED-CUM/MO.		4	15	34	57	81	105	129	153	176	196	212	225
ACTUAL-CUM/MO.		11	30	45	50	66	85						
NET CUM VARIANCE		+7	+15	+11	-7	-15	-20						
SCHEDULED RECOVERY RATE	▩							25	33	33			

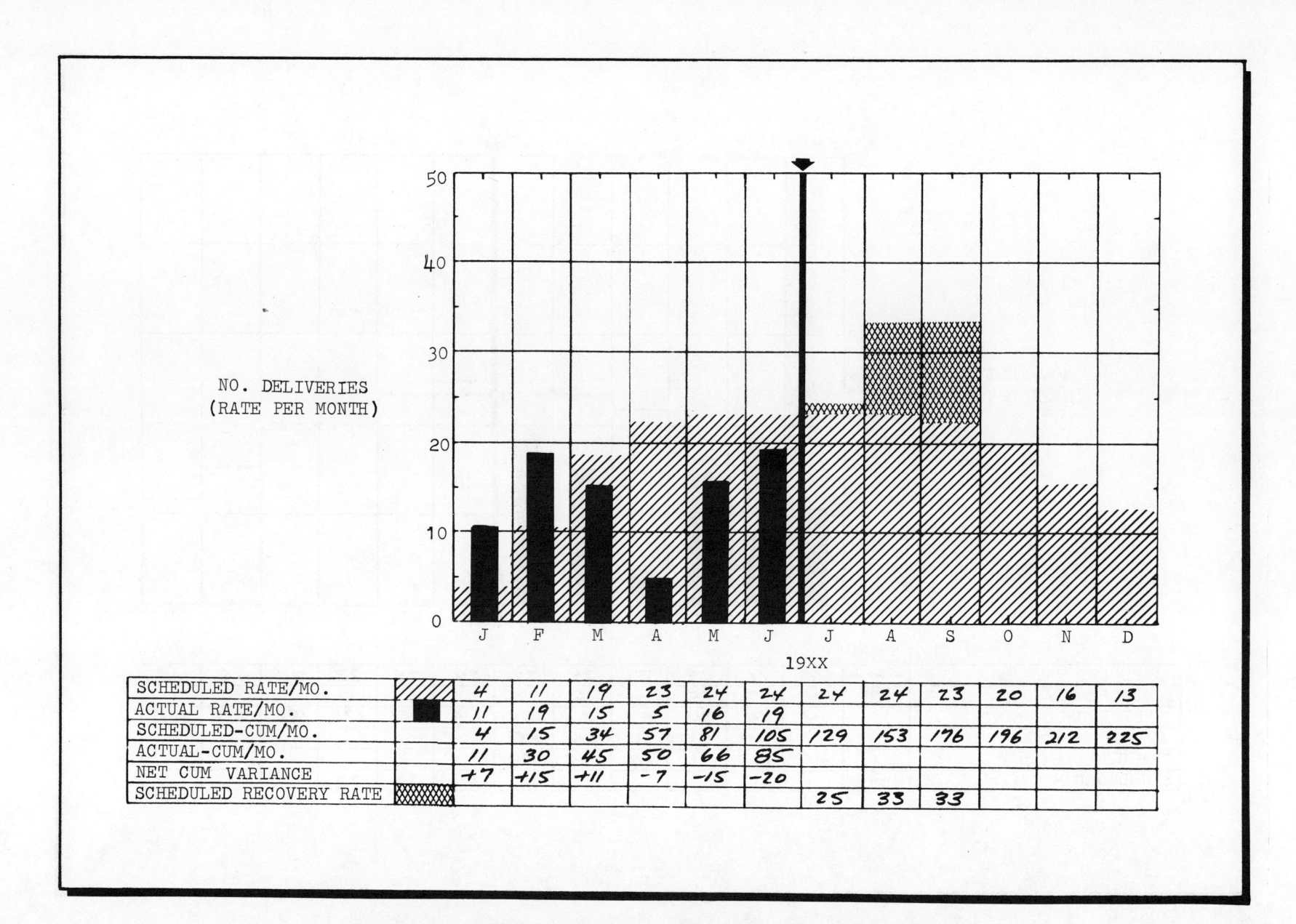

Figure 52.26 Schedule—End Item—Single Product Type—Version 26

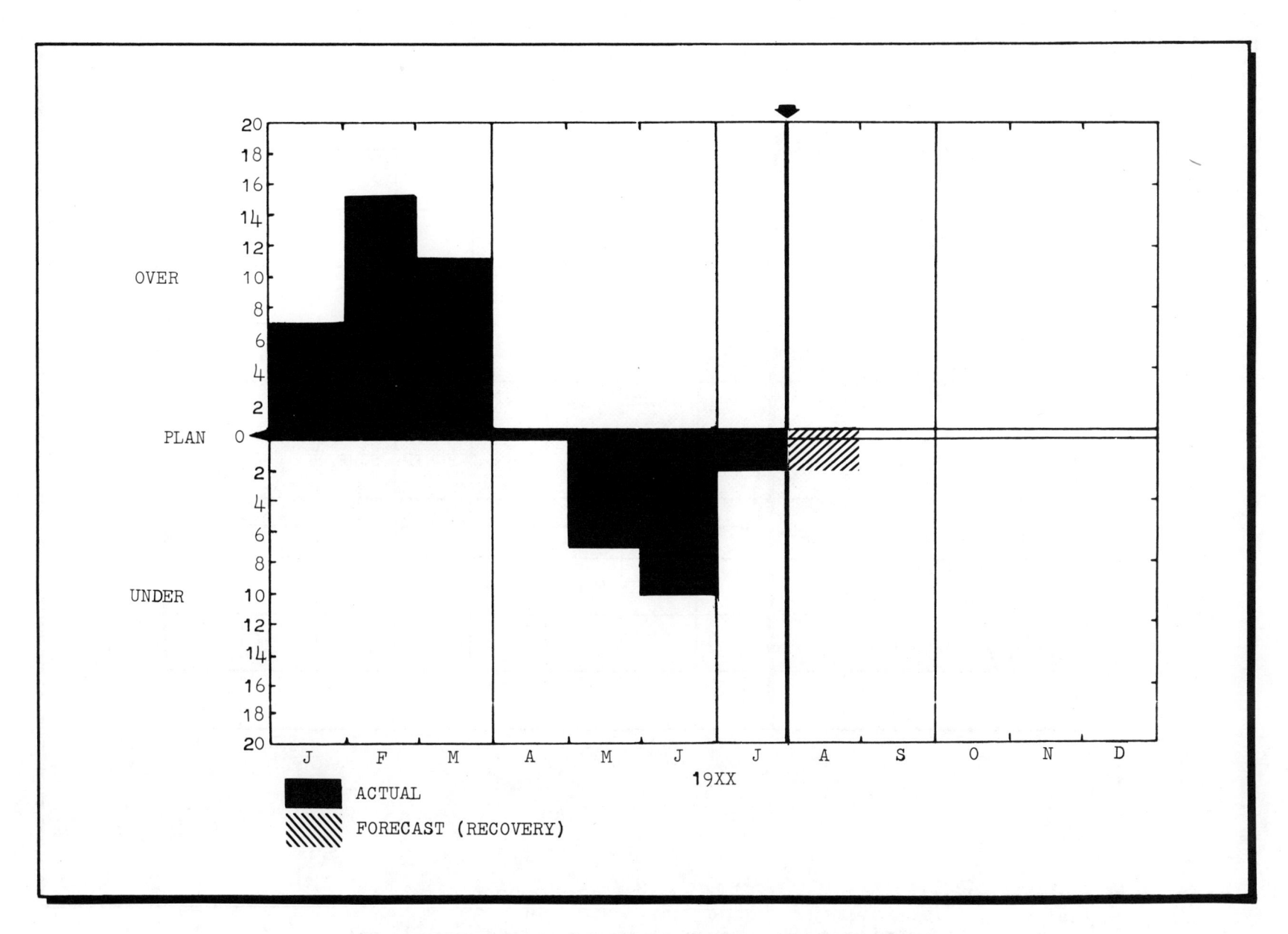

Figure 52.27 Schedule—End Item—Single Product Type—Version 27

Figure 52.28 Schedule—End Item—Single Product Type—Version 28

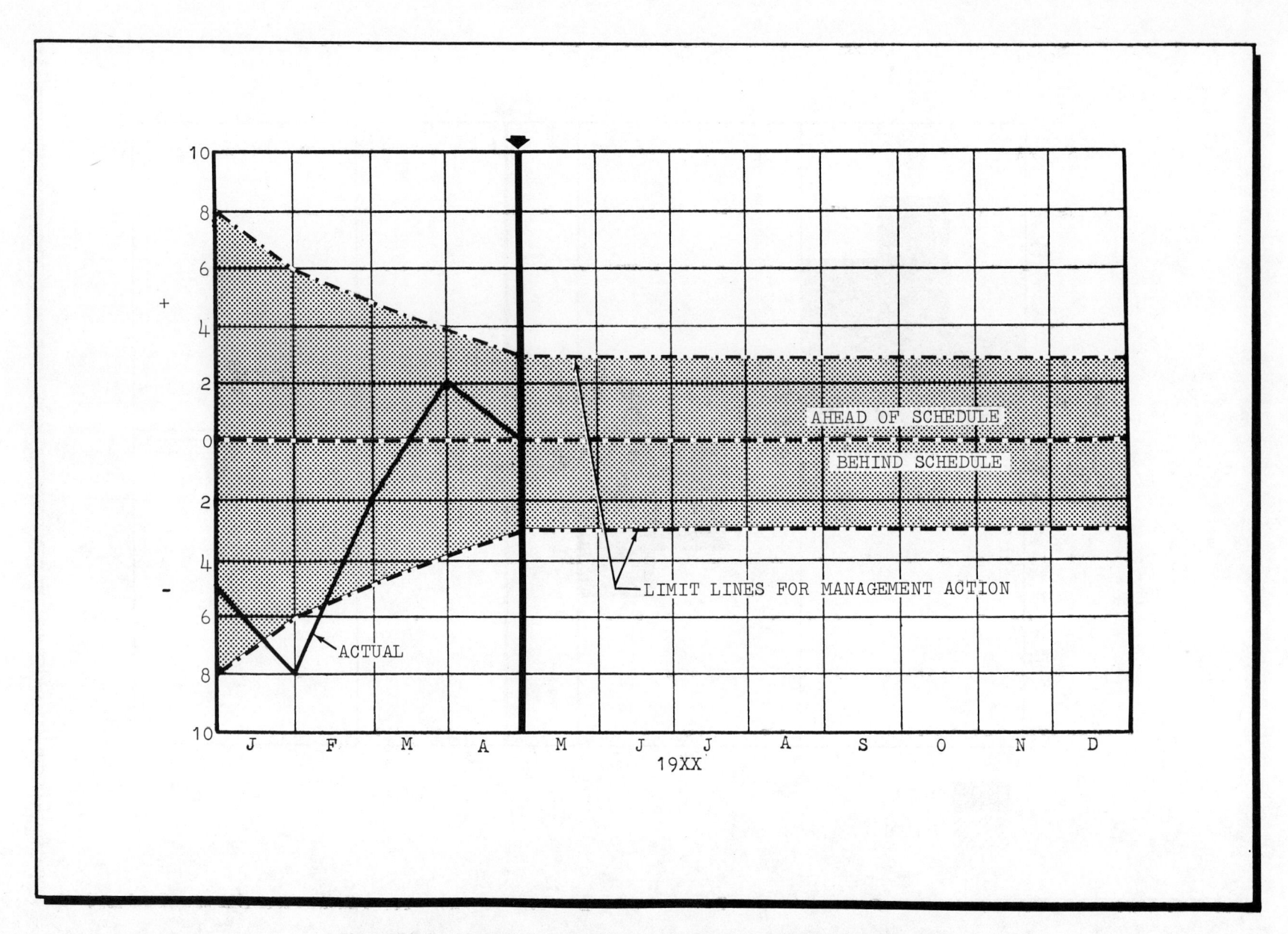

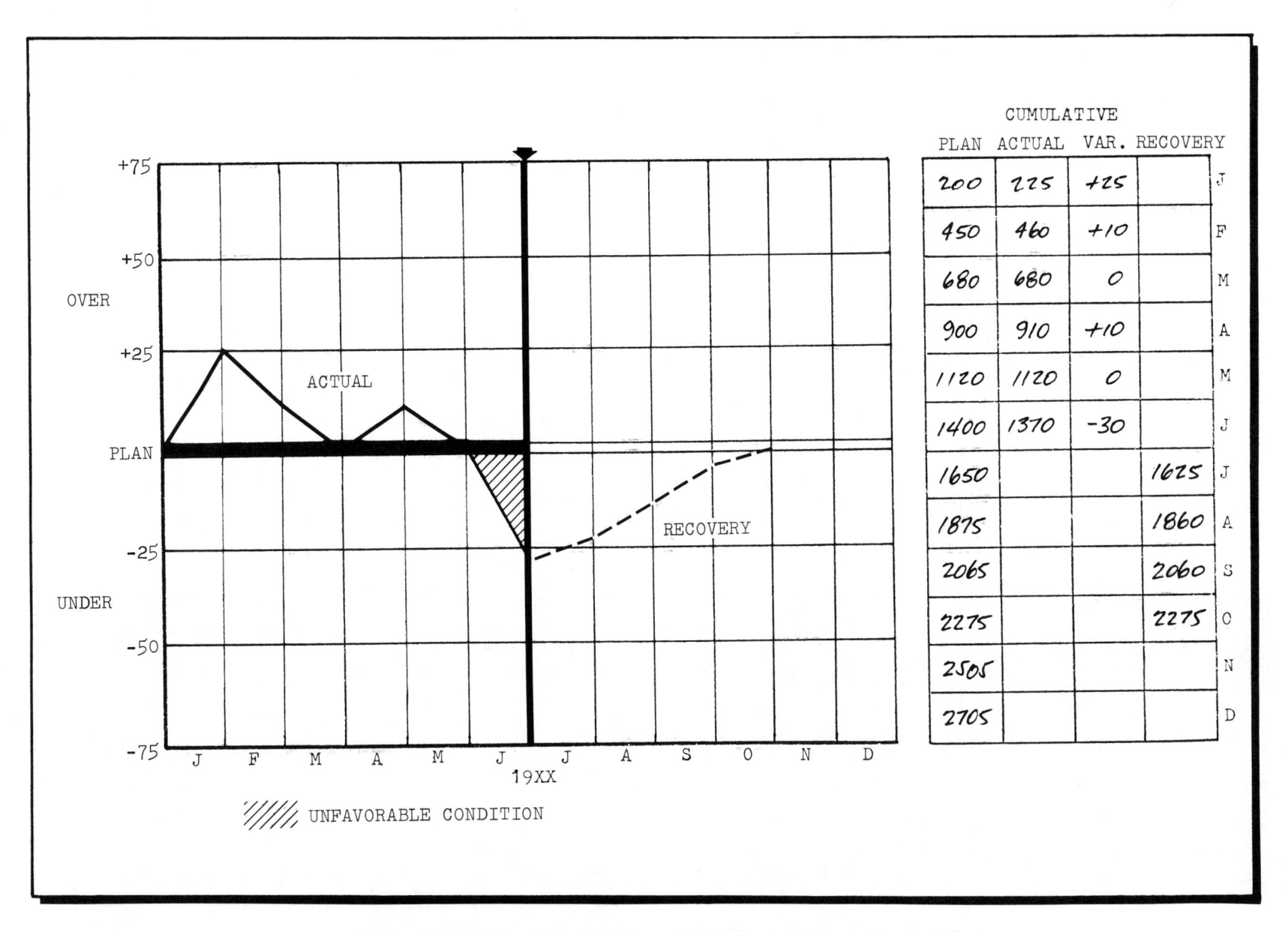

CUMULATIVE				
PLAN	ACTUAL	VAR.	RECOVERY	
200	225	+25		J
450	460	+10		F
680	680	0		M
900	910	+10		A
1120	1120	0		M
1400	1370	-30		J
1650			1625	J
1875			1860	A
2065			2060	S
2275			2275	O
2505				N
2705				D

Figure 52.29   Schedule—End Item—Single Product Type—Version 29

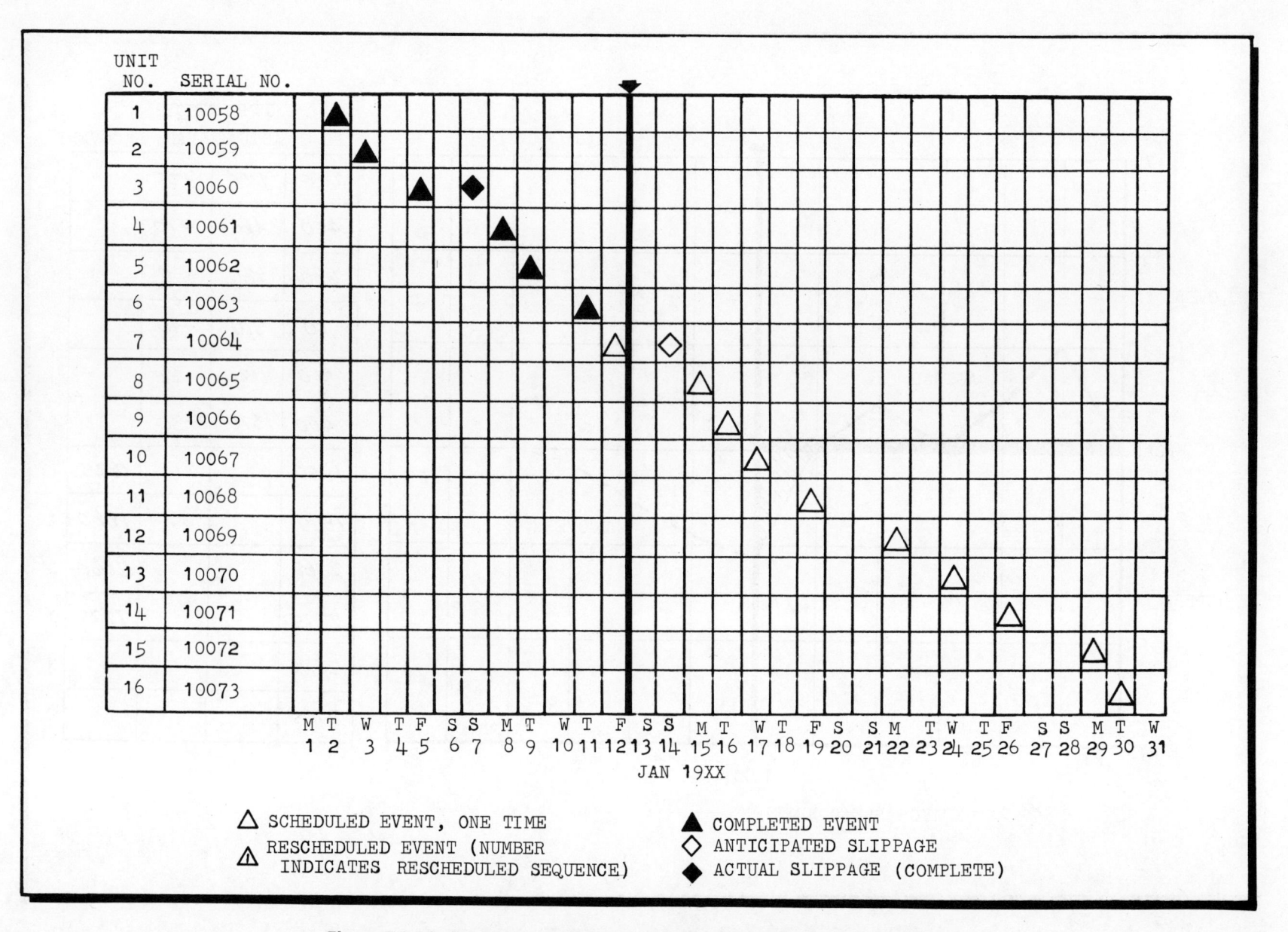

Figure 52.30 Schedule—End Item—Single Product Type—Version 30

666

	J	F	M	A	M	J	J	A	S	O	N	D
SCHEDULED RATE PER MO.	4	11	19	23	24	24	24	24	23	20	16	13
ACTUAL RATE PER MO.	11	19	15	5	16	19						
SCHEDULED-CUMULATIVE/MO	4	15	34	57	81	105	129	153	176	196	212	225
ACTUAL-CUMULATIVE/MO	11	30	45	50	66	85						
NET CUM. VARIANCE	+7	+15	+11	-7	-15	-20						
SCHEDULED RECOVERY RATE							25	33	33			

19XX

Figure 52.31 Schedule—End Item—Single Product Type—Version 31

	J	F	M	A	M	J	J	A	S	O	N	D
SCHEDULED RATE PER MONTH	4	11	19	23	24	24	24	24	23	20	16	13
ACTUAL RATE PER MONTH	11	19	15	5	16	19						
SCHEDULED-CUMULATIVE/MO	4	15	34	57	81	105	129	153	176	196	212	225
ACTUAL-CUMULATIVE/MO	11	30	45	50	66	85						
NET CUM VARIANCE	+7	+15	+11	-7	-15	-20						
SCHEDULED RECOVERY RATE							25	33	33			
SCHEDULED RECOVERY-CUM.							110	143	176			

19XX

Figure 52.32 Schedule—End Item—Single Product Type—Version 32

53.0 SCHEDULES—FIRST OR SINGLE ARTICLE

This section contains charts designed to display schedule status for non-repetitive types of activities. These are sometimes referred to as "first article schedules" or "first unit schedules" and are applicable to programs or projects that have a single, one-time objective. The product of such an activity can be either a hard goods product, such as a prototype or first production unit, or it can be a software product such as a report or a data processing program. Examples of non-repetitive type activities that fall into this category include the construction of a building, the study of some portion of an enterprise's operations for the purpose of developing improvements, and research and development projects.

53.1 Schedule—First or Single Article—Version 1: A simple method for graphically displaying first or single unit schedule status is shown in Figure 53.1. This type of chart is often called a milestone chart (see Section 6.0 for a detailed description of milestone chart symbols). The style that is shown in the example is an event-oriented type, one that deals with a single point in time such as starting or completing an activity.

53.2 Schedule—First or Single Article—Version 2: A combination event/activity milestone chart is shown in Figure 53.2. The first and last items in the example chart (Contract Award and Deliver First Production Unit) are events. The rest of the items are activities that require a span of time for their completion. In the example, all events and activities, except one, are on schedule as of the report date of the end of April of the first year. The third item, Prepare and Release Specifications, is shown to be one month behind schedule, and the diamond symbol indicates that it is anticipated that the activity's completion will slip schedule by one month.

53.3 Schedule—First or Single Article—Version 3: Information other than titles of events and activities can be given in the non-graphic portion of a schedule chart, as illustrated in Figure 53.3. In this example, task numbers are first given. Such codes, in a total control system, could also be related to other management control elements such as cost control and work assignment control. The chart also lists, in this example, the name of the person, or persons, in charge of each task so that responsibility for performance can more readily be ascertained by the chart reader.

53.4 Schedule—First or Single Article—Version 4: Figure 53.4 shows an example of a first or single unit schedule which provides space for an analytical commentary. This space can be used to provide general comments and explanations of exceptions to schedule compliance that are disclosed on the graphic portion of the chart.

53.5 Schedule—First or Single Article—Version 5: Version 5 of a first or single unit schedule, Figure 53.5, is identical to Version 4 except that an extra column has been added to the right-hand side of the chart for a symbol to indicate which analysis item is new since the previous report. Each time this type of chart is updated, more information is added to it, and a column such as shown can be useful in focusing the chart reader's attention on the item or problem which is of immediate concern.

53.6 Schedule—First or Single Article—Version 6: A statistical table has been combined with the milestone chart in Figure 53.6. In this example, the graphic portion of the chart provides a general indication of schedule and performance. The statistical table provides precise dates and variances. The disadvantage of this style of chart is that when a number of milestones are stacked in the same time segment, the statistical portion of such a chart can become very cluttered.

53.7 Schedule—First or Single Article—Version 7: A version of a first or single article schedule that is sometimes called a phasing chart is shown in Figure 53.7. In a phasing chart such as this, multiple levels of detail are presented. In the example, the top part of the chart, in bar graph form, presents the main project phases. The milestone chart below it presents a more detailed list of the activities that are related to those phases.

53.8 Schedule—First or Single Article—Version 8: Another version of a phasing chart is shown in Figure 53.8. In this approach, a single bar with arrows is used to pinpoint phase events.

53.9 Schedule—First or Single Article—Version 9: In any program or project involving the development of a first or single article, the relationships between the various tasks are usually significant. There is normally a critical sequence of events that involves some of the tasks and not others. In many instances, this sequence is based on the fact that there is little if any slack, or cushion, in the time allotted to complete the tasks. Figure 53.9 displays an approach to portraying a critical path by tying together certain tasks where the planning has indicated that slippages would have an adverse impact on the total project.

53.10 Schedule—First or Single Article—Version 10: If a number of milestones were stacked vertically in the same time segment, it is sometimes difficult from a graphics standpoint to draw a connecting critical path such as was shown on Version 9. Version 10, Figure 53.10, shows an alternate approach. In this case, events are heavily underlined to signify criticality. The disadvantage of this approach is that continuity of critical events is not apparent.

53.11 Schedule—First or Single Article—Version 11: A simple approach to symbols is used in a first or single article schedule shown as Version 11, Figure 53.11. Circles represent scheduled events, and the chart is updated by merely crossing out those events that have been completed.

53.12 Schedule—First or Single Article—Version 12: Another approach for showing planned and actual status of a first or single article schedule is shown in Figure 53.12. In this example, a step line approach is used. The dashed line represents the plan, a solid vertical line represents completions. A simple method for showing slipped or rescheduled events is used.

53.13 Schedule—First or Single Article—Version 13: Sometimes it is necessary to show two or more schedule factors on a single chart. Figure 53.13 shows an example of one way this can be accomplished. The circles in this example represent what can be considered as an "internal" schedule. The dashed step line represents delivery that is required by the customer. This might be a contract commitment. The difference between the two points (the circle and the line) in this example represents the production "cushion." This particular approach enables better interpretation of the impact of slippages. For instance, the second milestone in this example is shown to have slipped, but its impact apparently is not significant because it has not slipped beyond the customer required delivery date.

53.14 Schedule—First or Single Article—Version 14: A bar and symbol version of a first or single article schedule is shown in

Schedules—First or Single Article

Figure 53.14. In this example, inverted deltas are used to indicate scheduled dates of one-time events. Bars are used to signify activities that extend over a time span. In any chart of this nature, the graphic purpose is to try and focus the attention of the chart reader to only those items that remain behind schedule, such as the third item in the example, Prepare Electric Drawings.

53.15 Schedule—First or Single Article—Version 15: A typewritten version of a first or single article schedule is shown in Figure 53.15. In this example, the letter P represents the plan (schedule), and the letter O represents anticipated slippages. Completed events and completed portions of activities are crossed out.

53.16 Schedule—First or Single Article—Version 16: Separate lines have been provided for scheduled and actual performance symbols on Version 16 of a first or single article schedule, Figure 53.16. In this example, letters are used to signify control points.

53.17 Schedule—First or Single Article—Version 17: Another version of a multiple line entry first or single article schedule is shown in Figure 53.17. In this example, three scheduling points are entered: the optimistic date, the most likely date, and the pessimistic date. A solid delta is used to indicate the actual completion date.

53.18 Schedule—First or Single Article—Version 18: In those instances where it is desirable to show the separate processing steps required for a single task, a chart such as shown in Figure 53.18 can be used. In this example, three separate processing events are shown, each on separate lines with individual symbols. Shading indicates completion of the tasks, and a dashed line is used to show schedule slippages.

53.19 Schedule—First or Single Article—Version 19: Another method for showing multiple processes related to individual tasks is shown in Version 19 of a first or single article schedule, Figure 53.19. In this example segmented bars are used, each separately shaded segment representing a different process. Progress is indicated using chart tape at the bottom of each bar, applied in such a manner that the separate processing segments can still be identified. The tape could also be run through the center of each bar. Inverted deltas are used to show rescheduled completion points for each separate process, such as illustrated with item 4 of the example. Attempting to try and show slippages in terms of activity time spans would be impractical from a graphic standpoint on this type of chart.

53.20 Schedule—First or Single Article—Version 20: A method of showing a significant number of separate processing steps for each separate activity or task is shown in Figure 53.20. This approach has the disadvantage of becoming extremely cluttered and difficult to interpret when slippages of one process extend beyond the symbol for the succeeding process, or processes. It is an approach that is best to use only when it is felt that the function being scheduled is relatively stable and not likely to depart significantly from the plan.

53.21 Schedule—First or Single Article—Version 21: Networks are usually thought of as planning tools from which control charts are derived. A normal practice, for instance, is to extract key milestones from a detailed network and construct a milestone type tracking chart for management control purposes. If small and relatively uncomplicated, the network, itself, can sometimes be used as a tracking chart. An example of this is shown in Figure 53.21. In this example, both events and activities are shown. Progress is noted in terms of crossing out completed events. Networks that are not time-oriented (drawn in relationship to a time scale) are easier to interpret if some type of graphic technique, such as an arrow, is used to point out problems or anomalies.

53.22 Schedule—First or Single Article—Version 22: A time-oriented network tracking chart is shown in Figure 53.22.

Because the network is time-related through the use of a time scale, the connecting lines between events are vertical except where there is slack time involved. In those cases, the lines slant making the slack, or cushion, more apparent. This example shows the Conduct Field Survey activity as behind schedule by one month, but because of the slack this slippage (diamond symbol) has no deleterious impact on the overall project.

53.23 Schedule—First or Single Article—Version 23: Version 23 of a first or single article schedule, Figure 53.23, is similar to Version 22 except that the event symbols for starting and completing activities have been omitted from this version. A further difference is that the dotted slack line is shown as an extension of the horizontal activity line. As with Version 22, progress is shown utilizing chart tape placed along the activity lines.

53.24 Schedule—First or Single Article—Version 24: An event-oriented network is shown in Figure 53.24. It shows tasks in terms of "start" or "complete," only. As with Versions 22 and 23, it is time-oriented, with a time scale, thus permitting the use of a time-now line signifying the reporting date. In this example, completed events are simply crossed off. Another feature of this example is that the critical path connecting events most critical to the completion of the project is indicated with a heavy line. If a slippage was to occur on any event on this pathway, it would have a significant impact on the project as a whole.

53.25 Schedule—First or Single Article—Version 25: Activities, rather than events, are identified in all but the first call-out label on the network shown in Figure 53.25. Progress is indicated in terms of using chart tape on the task label.

53.26 Schedule—First or Single Article—Version 26: The concepts of networks and milestone charts are combined in Figure 53.26. This approach tends to become extremely complicated when there are a great number of events and activities being tracked. In this particular example, slippages are shown only for a given set of processes. If the attempt was to show slippages for each separate process (Final Assembly, Unit Test, etc.), the chart would become too difficult to interpret.

53.27 Schedule—First or Single Article—Version 27: Version 27 of a first or single article schedule, Figure 53.27, is identical to Version 26 except that bars and symbols are used. Inverted deltas, with code numbers, are used in this example to signify processing events. Progress is shown by shading the bar.

53.28 Schedule—First or Single Article—Version 28: The monitoring of the release of a large number of engineering drawings required for a first or single article can be accomplished with a format such as shown in Version 28, Figure 53.28. The milestone chart on the left-hand side tracks the time span when drawings are to be released. The line curve chart on the right tracks the cumulative quantity of released drawings.

53.29 Schedule—First or Single Article—Version 29: Line of balance charts are usually thought of as applicable only to production scheduling. In a modified form, the technique can be used for first or single article schedules. An example of this is shown in Figure 53.29. The plan, in terms of activity set-back, is shown at the bottom of the chart. The time spans for each work element are then transferred to the schedule in terms of percentages. Task 1, for instance (Analyze Department A), has a time span from the first of January to the middle of February during which time that task should have been completed 100 percent. This is translated to the schedule chart in the form of a straight line that goes from 0 to 100 percent in that same time frame. The progress chart is constructed by drawing imaginary horizontal lines across from the schedule chart to the progress chart using, as reference points, the intersections of the time-now line with the individual task schedule lines. This gives, for the reporting period, the line of balance for each

Schedules—First or Single Article

separate task. The bar for each task is constructed on the basis of the percentage of work completed. The differences between the bars and the line of balance provide current status to the chart reader.

53.30 Schedule—First or Single Article—Version 30: In Version 30 of a first or single article schedule, Figure 53.30, the plan is depicted in work flow form. Each work element, then, is projected to the right in line bar form, the single line bar covering the time span for that particular task. Each bar line is divided into segments totalling 100 percent. Progress for each reporting period is shown as a percentage completion for each task. An alternate version of this chart could omit the graphic portrayal of the plan, using call-outs, only.

53.31 Schedule—First or Single Article—Version 31: A deviation chart technique is used for showing first or single article schedule status in Figure 53.31. This is an approach that can be taken if there are a relatively few individual tasks. In the example shown, there are six separate tasks. Miniature deviation charts for each task are in bar chart form, the bar lengths according to scheduled time spans. Deviation is shown in terms of weeks ahead of or behind schedule.

53.32 Schedule—First or Single Article—Version 32: A statistical table version of a first or single article schedule is shown in Figure 53.32. In this example, three separate lines are provided for each task: scheduled completion date, forecast, actual completion date. This type of chart is not as readily interpreted as are the more graphic versions.

53.33 Schedule—First or Single Article—Version 33: A "box score" type of first or single article schedule report is shown in Figure 53.33. This report has been set up in such a way as to draw the chart reader's eyes to the exceptions in the plan. The problem with this style of report is that it normally has to be completely redone for each new reporting period.

53.34 Schedule—First or Single Article—Version 34: Another version of a box score is shown in Figure 53.34. This report is similar to Version 33 except that an analysis section has been added so that explanations and other information can be presented.

53.35 Schedule—First or Single Article—Version 35: This box score type of first or single article schedule report, Figure 53.35, is similar to Versions 33 and 34 except that schedules and completions are in terms of percentages.

53.36 Schedule—First or Single Article—Version 36: The box score type of first or single article schedule report shown in Figure 53.36 reports schedule changes such as slippages or rescheduled events or activities. The impact of these changes on the total project is indicated with a symbol, the purpose of which is to focus the chart reader's attention on those elements that require management action or attention.

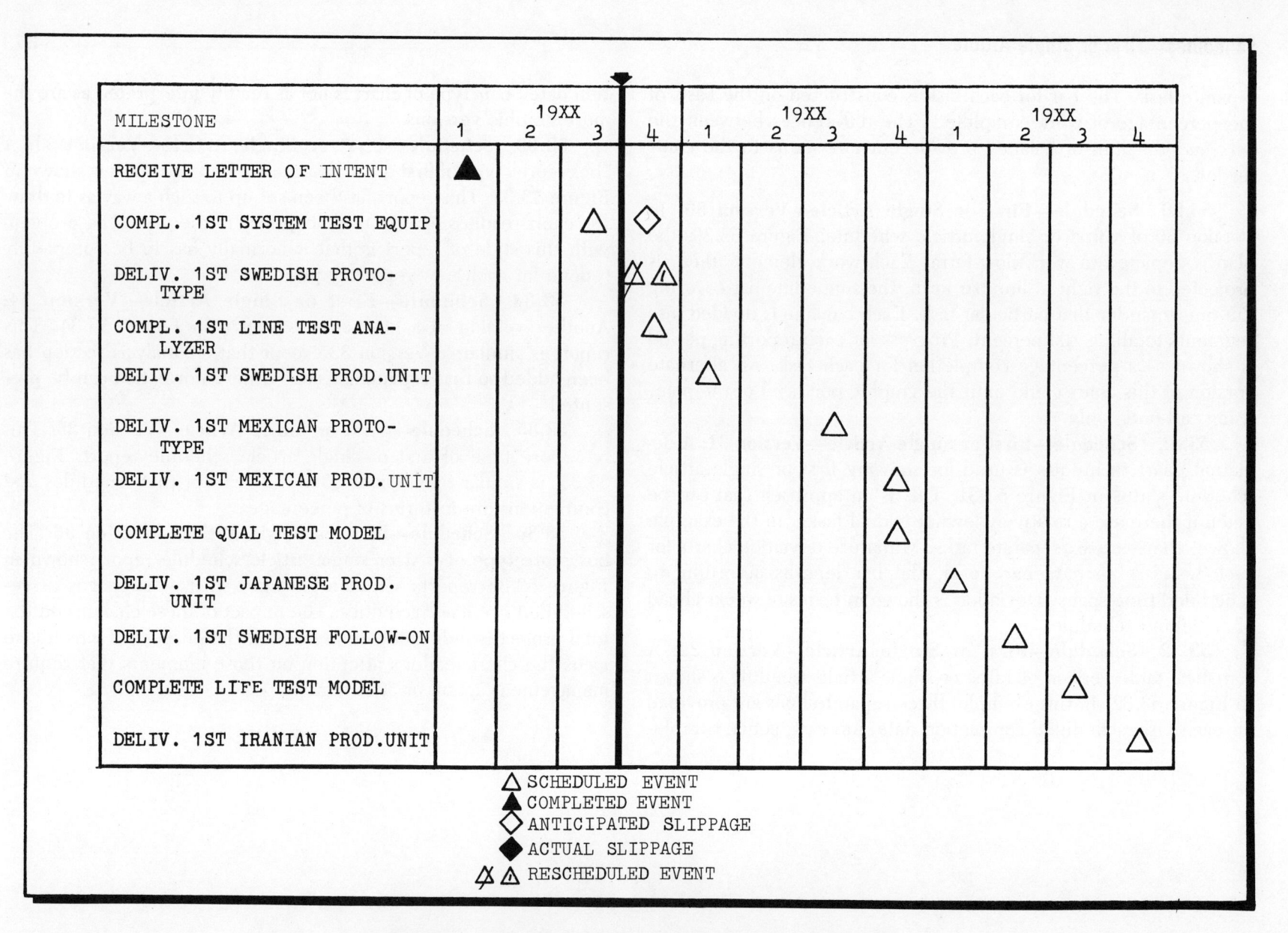

MILESTONE	19XX 1	2	3	4	19XX 1	2	3	4	19XX 1	2	3	4
RECEIVE LETTER OF INTENT	▲											
COMPL. 1ST SYSTEM TEST EQUIP			△	◇								
DELIV. 1ST SWEDISH PROTO-TYPE				⚡△								
COMPL. 1ST LINE TEST ANA-LYZER				△								
DELIV. 1ST SWEDISH PROD. UNIT					△							
DELIV. 1ST MEXICAN PROTO-TYPE							△					
DELIV. 1ST MEXICAN PROD. UNIT								△				
COMPLETE QUAL TEST MODEL								△				
DELIV. 1ST JAPANESE PROD. UNIT									△			
DELIV. 1ST SWEDISH FOLLOW-ON										△		
COMPLETE LIFE TEST MODEL											△	
DELIV. 1ST IRANIAN PROD. UNIT												△

△ SCHEDULED EVENT
▲ COMPLETED EVENT
◇ ANTICIPATED SLIPPAGE
◆ ACTUAL SLIPPAGE
⚡△ RESCHEDULED EVENT

Figure 53.1　Schedule—First or Single Article—Version 1

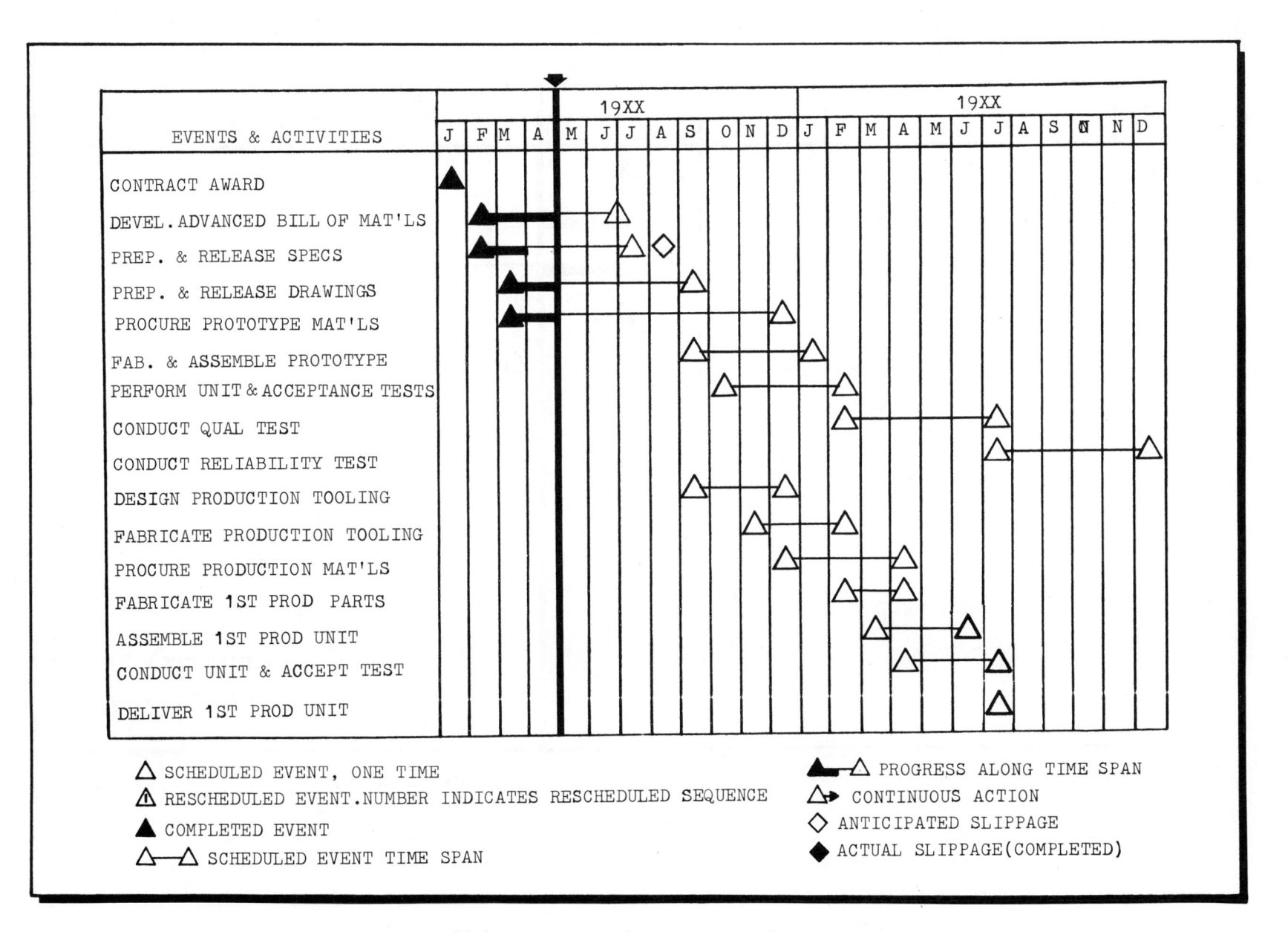

Figure 53.2 Schedule—First or Single Article—Version 2

TASK NO.	TASK	PERSON IN CHARGE	WEEK NO											
			1	2	3	4	5	6	7	8	9	10	11	12
1001	DEVELOP PROJECT PLAN	JONES	▲—▲											
1002	ANALYZE DEPT X	SMITH		▲—————△										
1003	ANALYZE DEPT Y	JONES		▲———————△										
1004	ANALYZE DEPT Z	BROWN		▲————△ ◇										
1005	FLOWCHART EXIST'G SYSTEM	SMITH				△————————△								
1006	ANALYZE FILE STRUCTURE	JONES				△————————————△								
1007	DEFINE NEW REQ'MENTS	BROWN					△————————△							
1008	FLOWCHART NEW SYSTEM	SMITH						△————————△						
1009	PREP. INPUT/OUTPUT FORMS	JONES/BROWN							△————————△					
1010	ANALYZE COSTS/BENEFITS	SMITH								△————————△				
1011	PREP. IMPLEMENT'N PLAN	JONES									△————————△			
1012	WRITE FINAL REPORT	SMITH/BROWN									△————————————————△			

△ SCHEDULED EVENT, ONE TIME
⚠ RESCHEDULED EVENT. NUMBER INDICATES RESCHEDULED SEQUENCE
▲ COMPLETED EVENT
△—△ SCHEDULED EVENT TIME SPAN

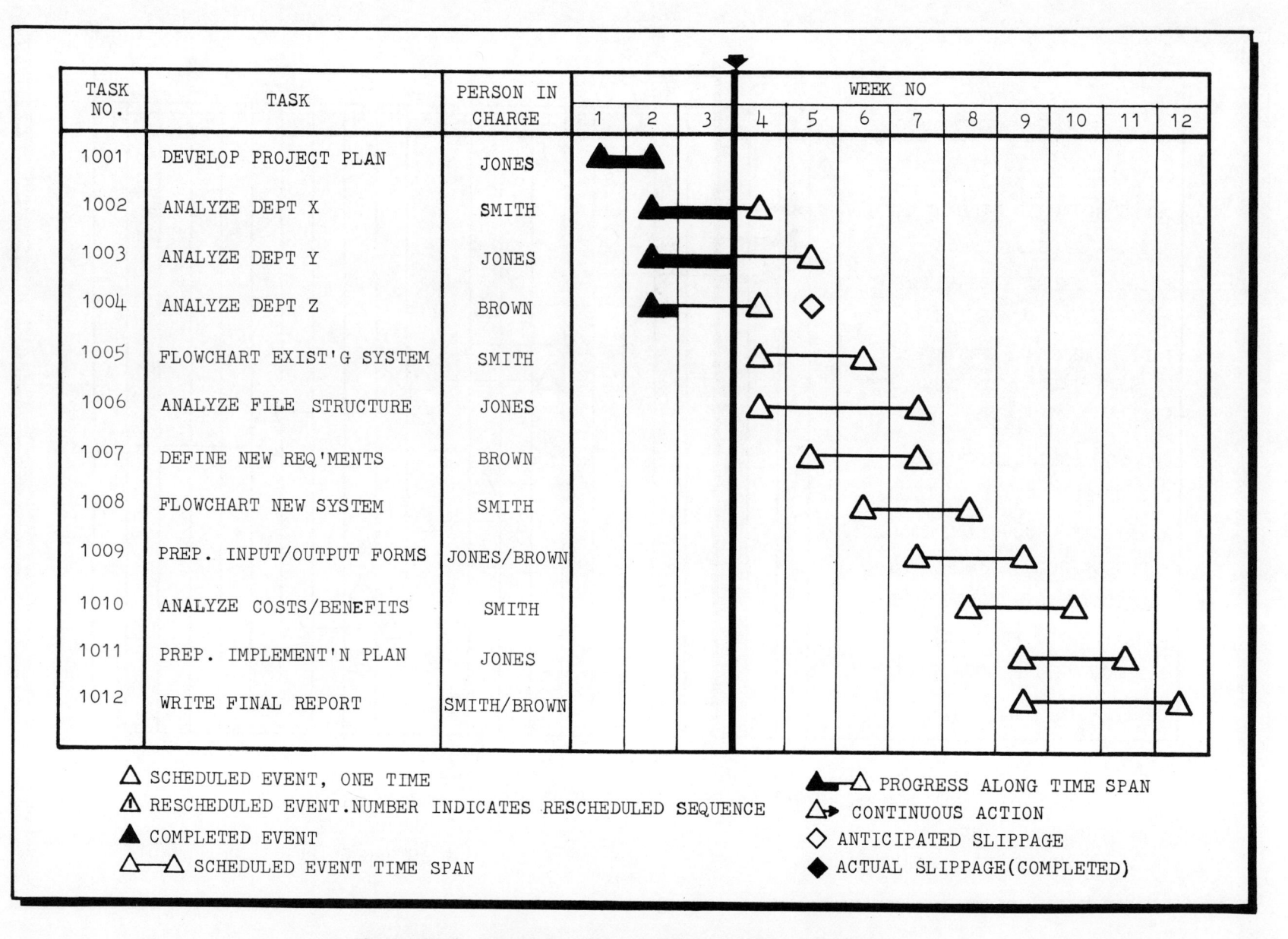

▲—△ PROGRESS ALONG TIME SPAN
△→ CONTINUOUS ACTION
◇ ANTICIPATED SLIPPAGE
◆ ACTUAL SLIPPAGE (COMPLETED)

Figure 53.3   Schedule—First or Single Article—Version 3

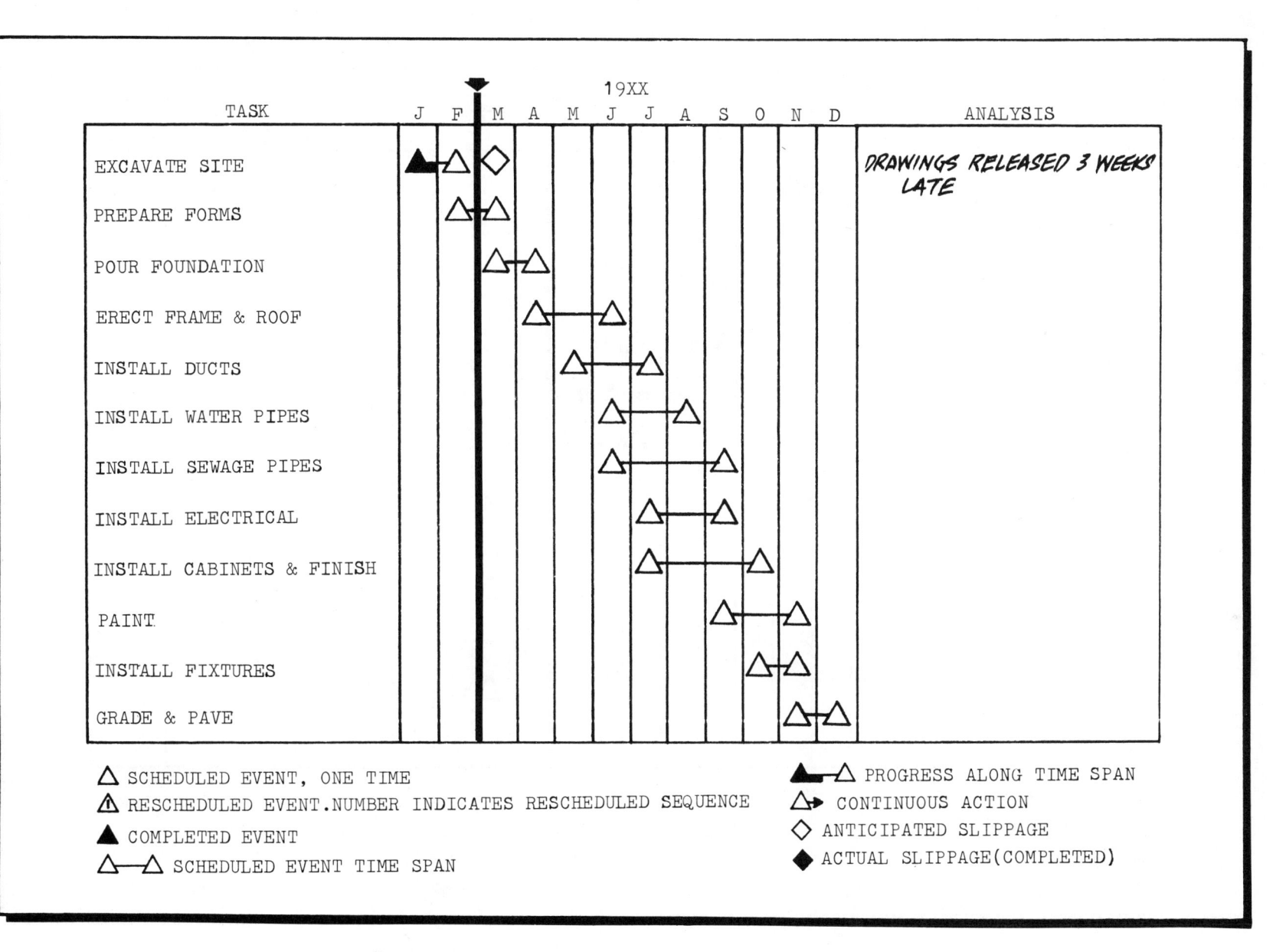

Figure 53.4 Schedule—First or Single Article—Version 4

TASK	19XX J F M A M J J A S O N D	ANALYSIS	NEW SINCE LAST REPORT
EXCAVATE SITE	▲—▲ ◆	DRAWINGS RELEASED 3 WEEKS LATE	
PREPARE FORMS	▲—▲		
POUR FOUNDATION	▲—▲ ◆	DELAY DUE TO STRIKE	
ERECT FRAME & ROOF	▲—▲—▲¹	RESCHEDULED BECAUSE OF DELAYS CAUSED BY STRIKE	
INSTALL DUCTS	▲—▲—▲¹	RESCHEDULED BECAUSE OF STRIKE	
INSTALL WATER PIPES	▲—▲		
INSTALL SEWAGE PIPES	▲—————△ ◇	TWO WEEKS DELAY DUE TO MAT'L SHORTAGE	◆
INSTALL ELECTRICAL	▲——△		
INSTALL CABINETS & FINISH	▲——△	ONE WEEK DELAY IN START NOW ON SCHEDULE	
PAINT	△——△		
INSTALL FIXTURES	△△		
GRADE & PAVE	△△		

△ SCHEDULED EVENT, ONE TIME
⚠ RESCHEDULED EVENT. NUMBER INDICATES RESCHEDULED SEQUENCE
▲ COMPLETED EVENT
△—△ SCHEDULED EVENT TIME SPAN
▲—△ PROGRESS ALONG TIME SPAN
△→ CONTINUOUS ACTION
◇ ANTICIPATED SLIPPAGE
◆ ACTUAL SLIPPAGE (COMPLETED)

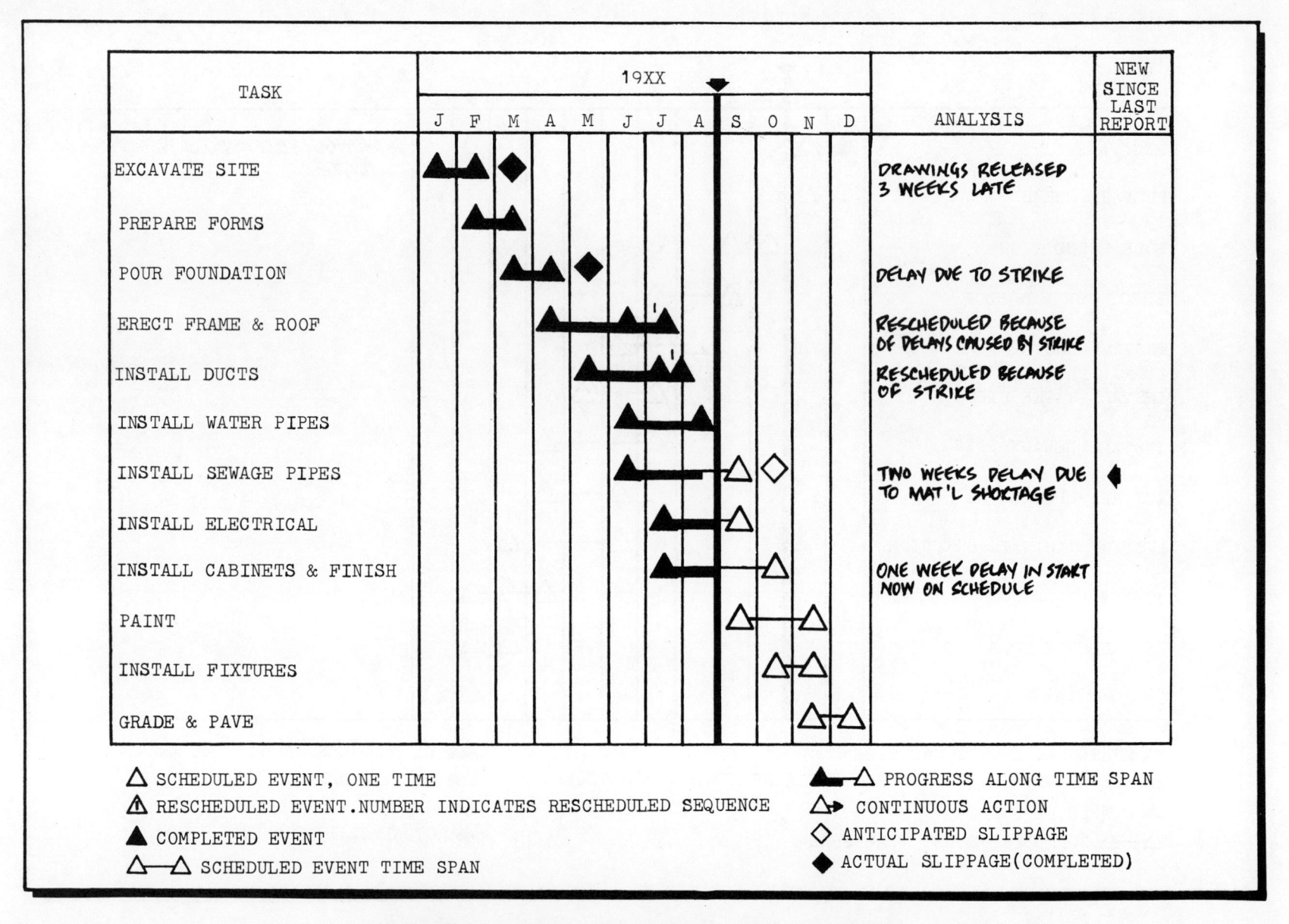

Figure 53.5 Schedule—First or Single Article—Version 5

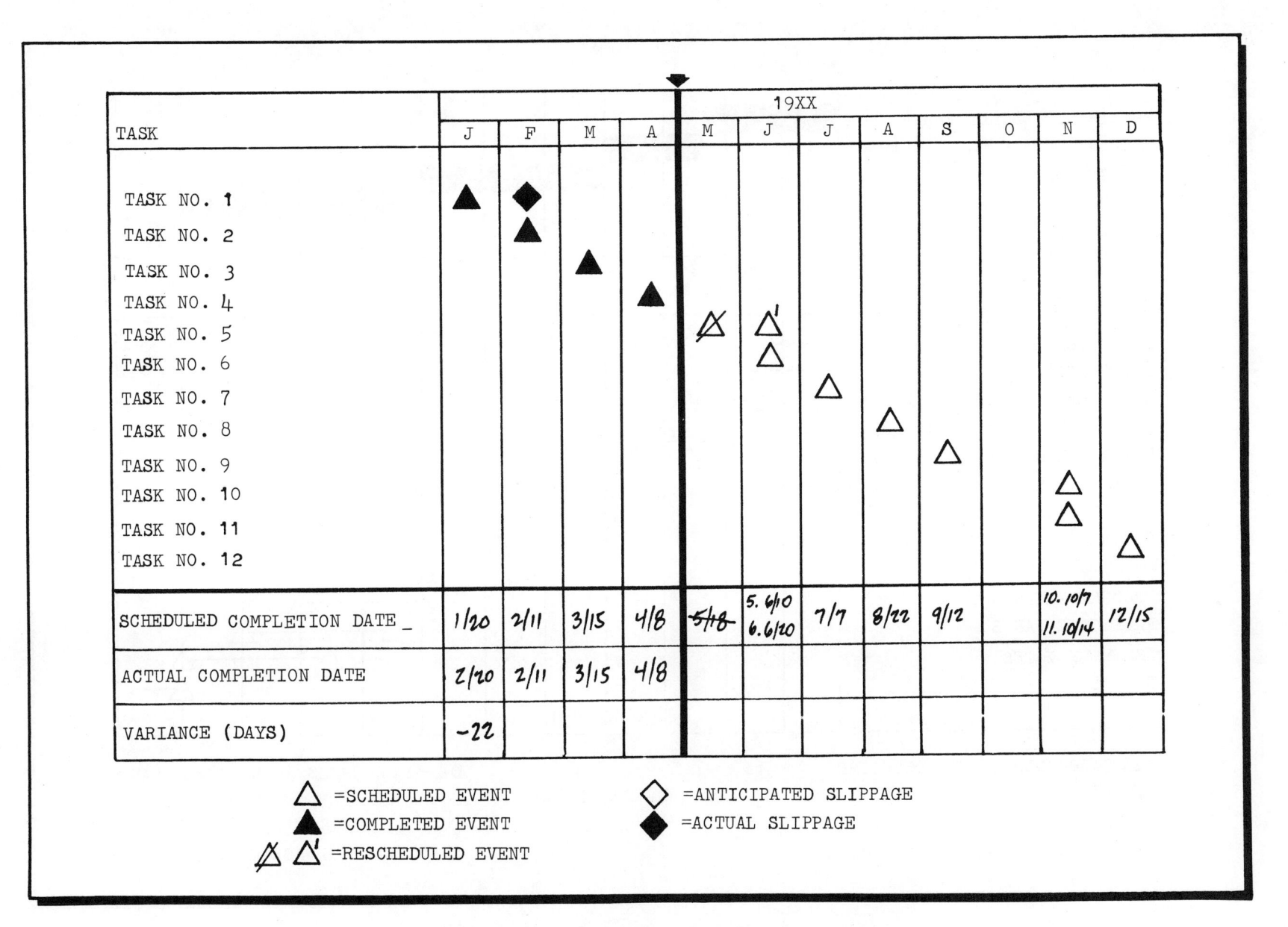

TASK	J	F	M	A	M	J	J	A	S	O	N	D
												19XX
TASK NO. 1	▲	◆										
TASK NO. 2		▲										
TASK NO. 3			▲									
TASK NO. 4				▲								
TASK NO. 5					⚠	△'						
TASK NO. 6						△						
TASK NO. 7							△					
TASK NO. 8								△				
TASK NO. 9									△			
TASK NO. 10											△	
TASK NO. 11											△	
TASK NO. 12												△
SCHEDULED COMPLETION DATE	1/20	2/11	3/15	4/8	5/8	5. 6/10 6. 6/20	7/7	8/22	9/12		10. 10/7 11. 10/14	12/15
ACTUAL COMPLETION DATE	2/20	2/11	3/15	4/8								
VARIANCE (DAYS)	−22											

△ = SCHEDULED EVENT
▲ = COMPLETED EVENT
⚠ △' = RESCHEDULED EVENT
◇ = ANTICIPATED SLIPPAGE
◆ = ACTUAL SLIPPAGE

Figure 53.6 Schedule—First or Single Article—Version 6

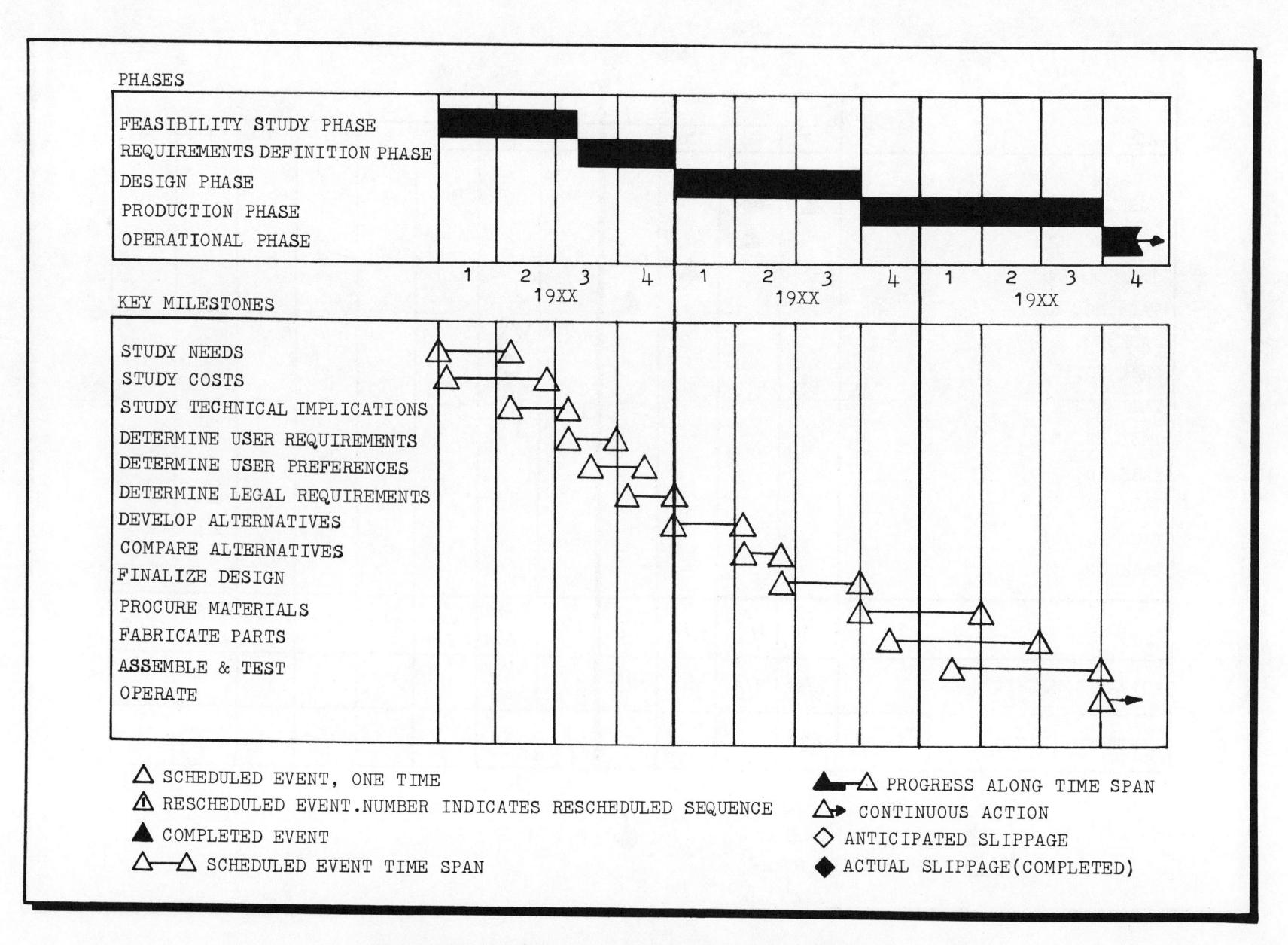

Figure 53.7 Schedule—First or Single Article—Version 7

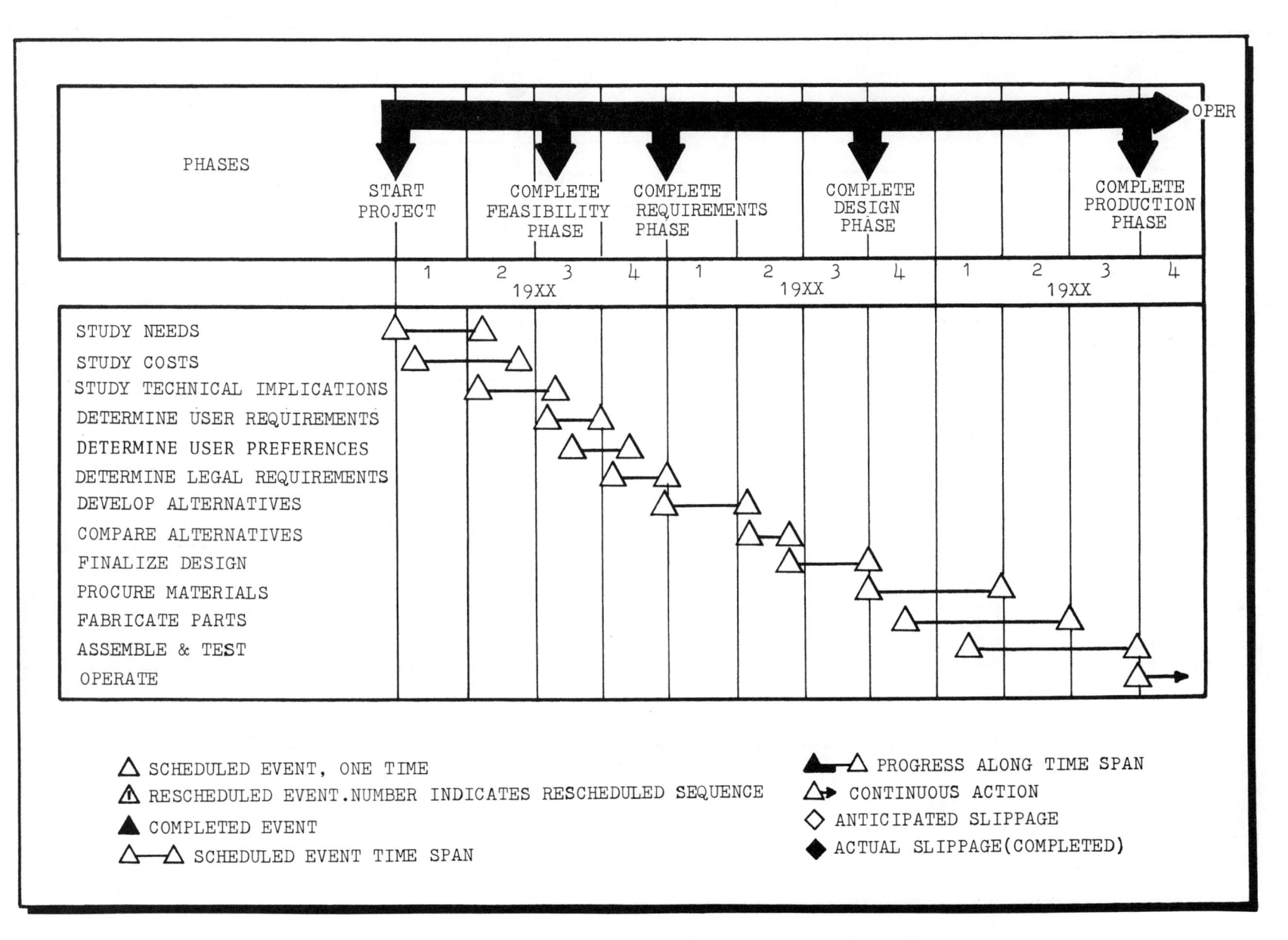

Figure 53.8 Schedule—First or Single Article—Version 8

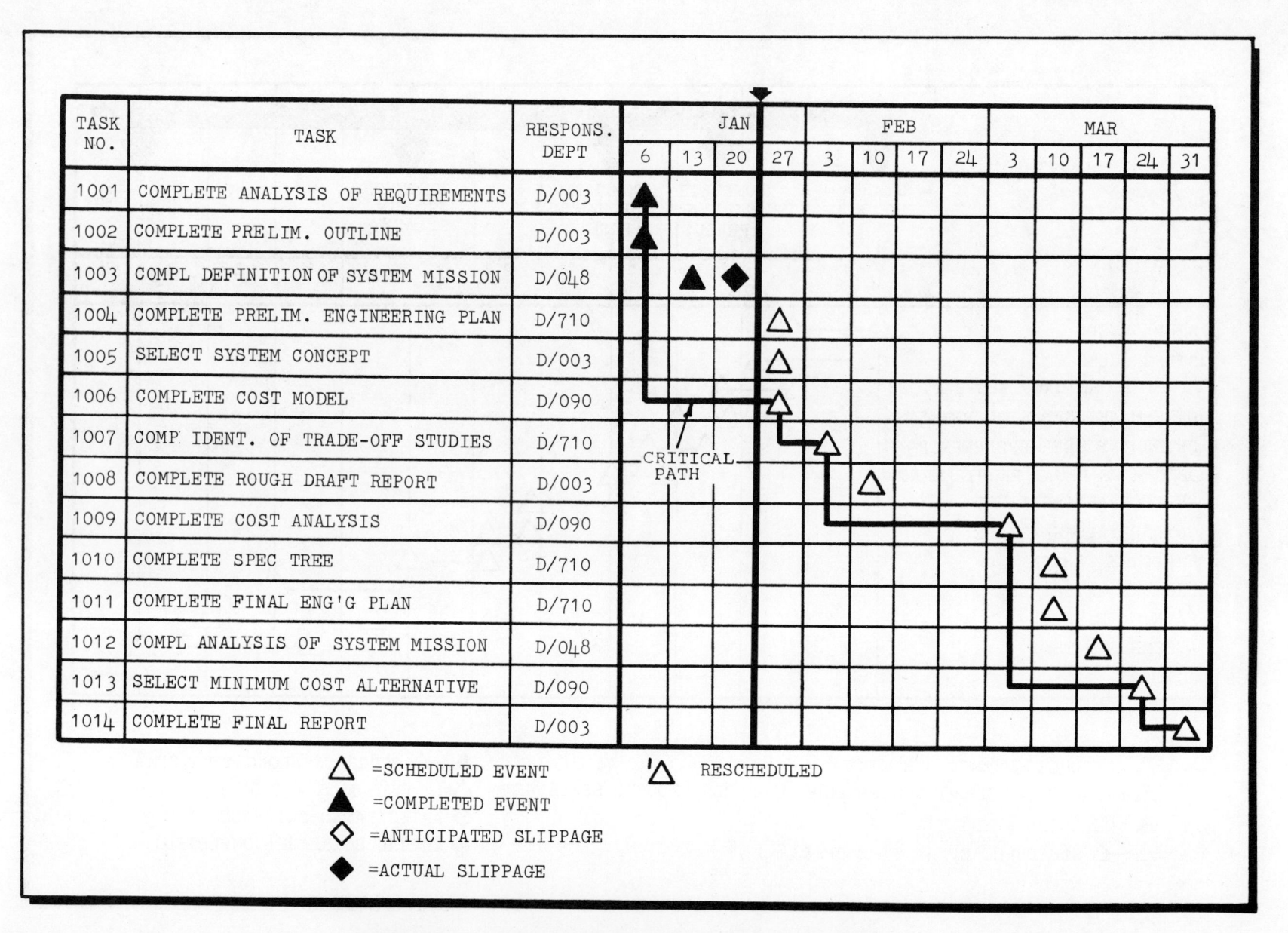

TASK NO.	TASK	RESPONS. DEPT	JAN				FEB				MAR				
			6	13	20	27	3	10	17	24	3	10	17	24	31
1001	COMPLETE ANALYSIS OF REQUIREMENTS	D/003	▲												
1002	COMPLETE PRELIM. OUTLINE	D/003	▲												
1003	COMPL DEFINITION OF SYSTEM MISSION	D/048		▲	◆										
1004	COMPLETE PRELIM. ENGINEERING PLAN	D/710				△									
1005	SELECT SYSTEM CONCEPT	D/003				△									
1006	COMPLETE COST MODEL	D/090				△									
1007	COMP. IDENT. OF TRADE-OFF STUDIES	D/710					△								
1008	COMPLETE ROUGH DRAFT REPORT	D/003						△							
1009	COMPLETE COST ANALYSIS	D/090									△				
1010	COMPLETE SPEC TREE	D/710										△			
1011	COMPLETE FINAL ENG'G PLAN	D/710										△			
1012	COMPL ANALYSIS OF SYSTEM MISSION	D/048											△		
1013	SELECT MINIMUM COST ALTERNATIVE	D/090												△	
1014	COMPLETE FINAL REPORT	D/003													△

△ = SCHEDULED EVENT   '△ RESCHEDULED
▲ = COMPLETED EVENT
◇ = ANTICIPATED SLIPPAGE
◆ = ACTUAL SLIPPAGE

Figure 53.9 Schedule—First or Single Article—Version 9

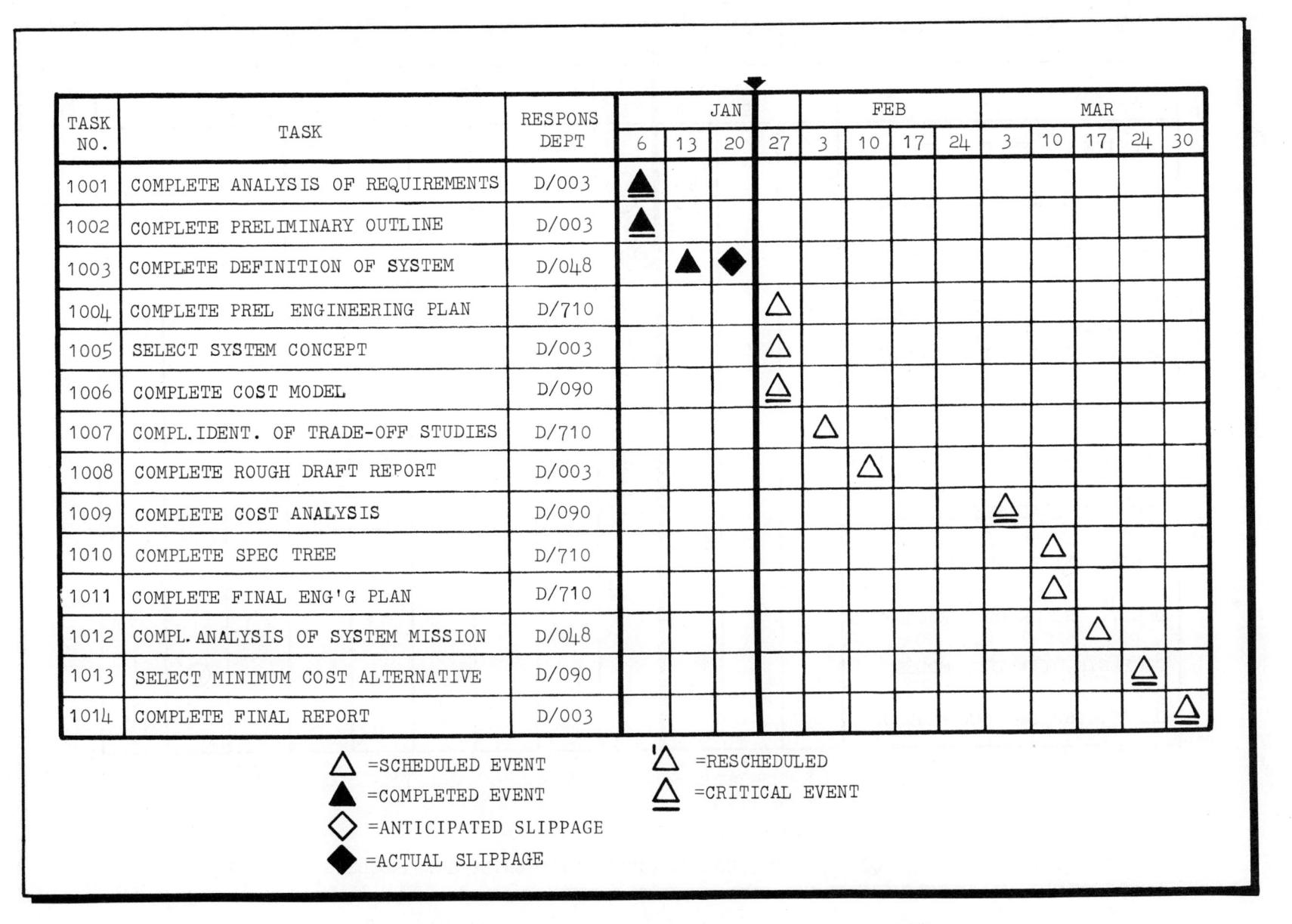

TASK NO.	TASK	RESPONS DEPT	JAN 6	13	20	27	FEB 3	10	17	24	MAR 3	10	17	24	30
1001	COMPLETE ANALYSIS OF REQUIREMENTS	D/003	▲												
1002	COMPLETE PRELIMINARY OUTLINE	D/003	▲												
1003	COMPLETE DEFINITION OF SYSTEM	D/048			▲	◆									
1004	COMPLETE PREL ENGINEERING PLAN	D/710				△									
1005	SELECT SYSTEM CONCEPT	D/003				△									
1006	COMPLETE COST MODEL	D/090				△									
1007	COMPL. IDENT. OF TRADE-OFF STUDIES	D/710					△								
1008	COMPLETE ROUGH DRAFT REPORT	D/003						△							
1009	COMPLETE COST ANALYSIS	D/090									△				
1010	COMPLETE SPEC TREE	D/710										△			
1011	COMPLETE FINAL ENG'G PLAN	D/710										△			
1012	COMPL. ANALYSIS OF SYSTEM MISSION	D/048											△		
1013	SELECT MINIMUM COST ALTERNATIVE	D/090												△	
1014	COMPLETE FINAL REPORT	D/003													△

△ = SCHEDULED EVENT
▲ = COMPLETED EVENT
◇ = ANTICIPATED SLIPPAGE
◆ = ACTUAL SLIPPAGE
'△ = RESCHEDULED
△ = CRITICAL EVENT

Figure 53.10   Schedule—First or Single Article—Version 10

MILESTONE	1	19XX 2 3	4	1	19XX 2 3	4	1	19XX 2 3	4
RECEIVE LETTER OF INTENT	∅								
COMPL. 1ST SYSTEM TEST EQUIP		⊗--○							
DELIV. 1ST SWEDISH PROTOTYPE		⊗·○¹							
COMPL. 1ST LINE TEST ANALYZER			○						
DELIV. 1ST SWEDISH PROD. UNIT				○					
DELIV. 1ST MEXICAN PROTOTYPE					○				
DELIV. 1ST MEXICAN PROD. UNIT						○			
COMPLETE QUAL TEST MODEL						○			
DELIV. 1ST JAPANESE PROD. UNIT							○		
DELIV. 1ST SWEDISH FOLLOW-ON								○	
COMPLETE LIFE TEST MODEL									○
DELIV. 1ST IRANIAN PROD. UNIT									○

○ = SCHEDULED
∅ = COMPLETED
⊗---○ = TIME SLIP
⊗--ⁿ○ = RESCHEDULED (NUMBER INDICATES RESCHEDULING SEQUENCE)

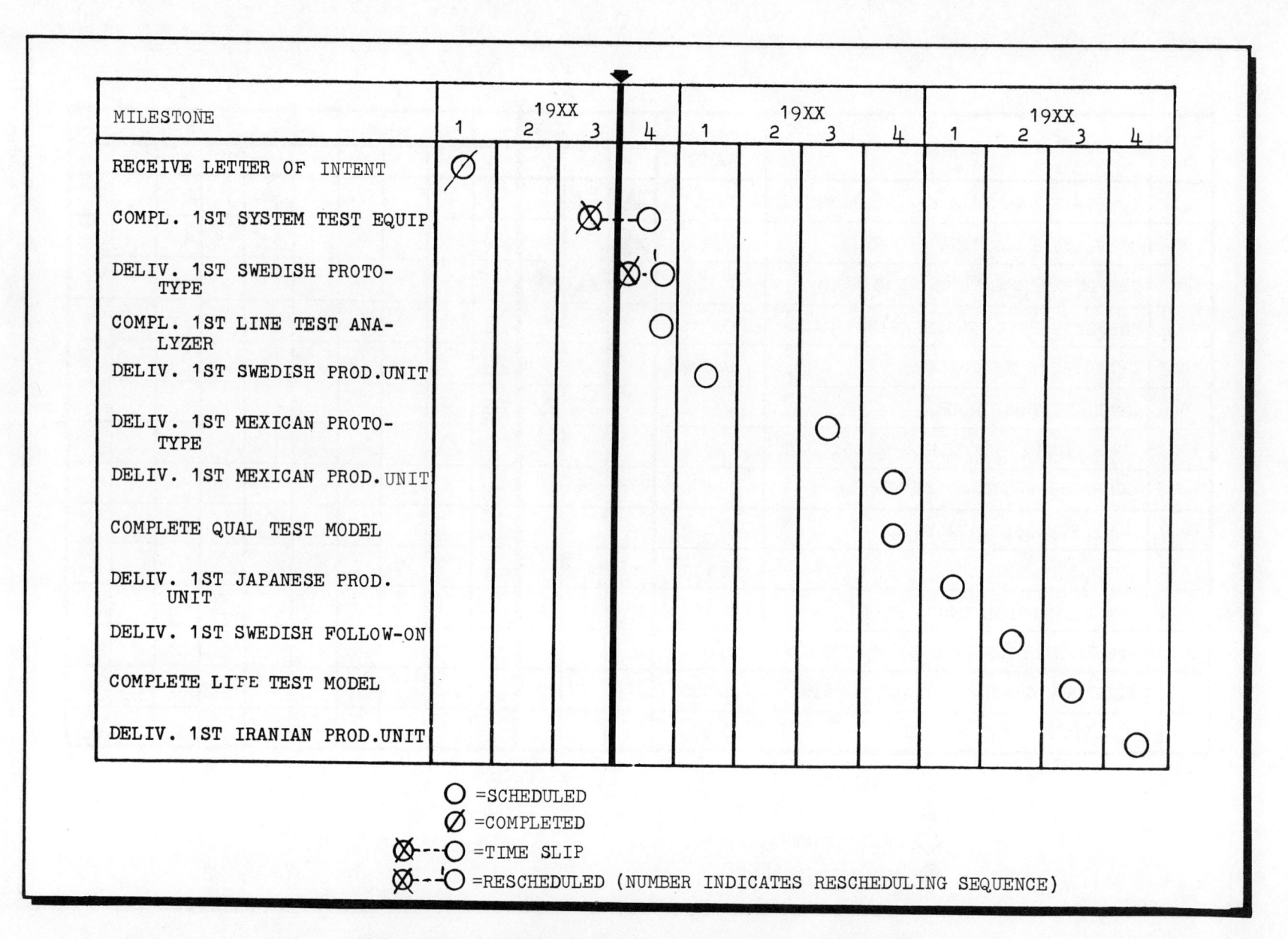

Figure 53.11 Schedule—First or Single Article—Version 11

MILESTONE	19XX 1 2 3 4	19XX 1 2 3 4	19XX 1 2 3 4
RECEIVE LETTER OF INTENT			
COMPL. 1ST SYSTEM TEST EQUIP.			
DELIV. 1ST SWEDISH PROTO-TYPE			
COMPL. 1ST LINE TEST ANA-LYZER			
DELIV. 1ST SWEDISH PROD. UNIT			
DELIV. 1ST MEXICAN PROTO-TYPE			
DELIV. 1ST MEXICAN PROD. UNIT			
COMPLETE QUAL TEST MODEL			
DELIV. 1ST JAPANESE PROD. UNIT			
DELIV. 1ST SWEDISH FOLLOW-ON			
COMPLETE LIFE TEST MODEL			
DELIV. 1ST IRANIAN PROD. UNIT			

| = PLAN
▮ = COMPLETE
|····| = SLIPPED SCHEDULE
|→| = RESCHEDULED

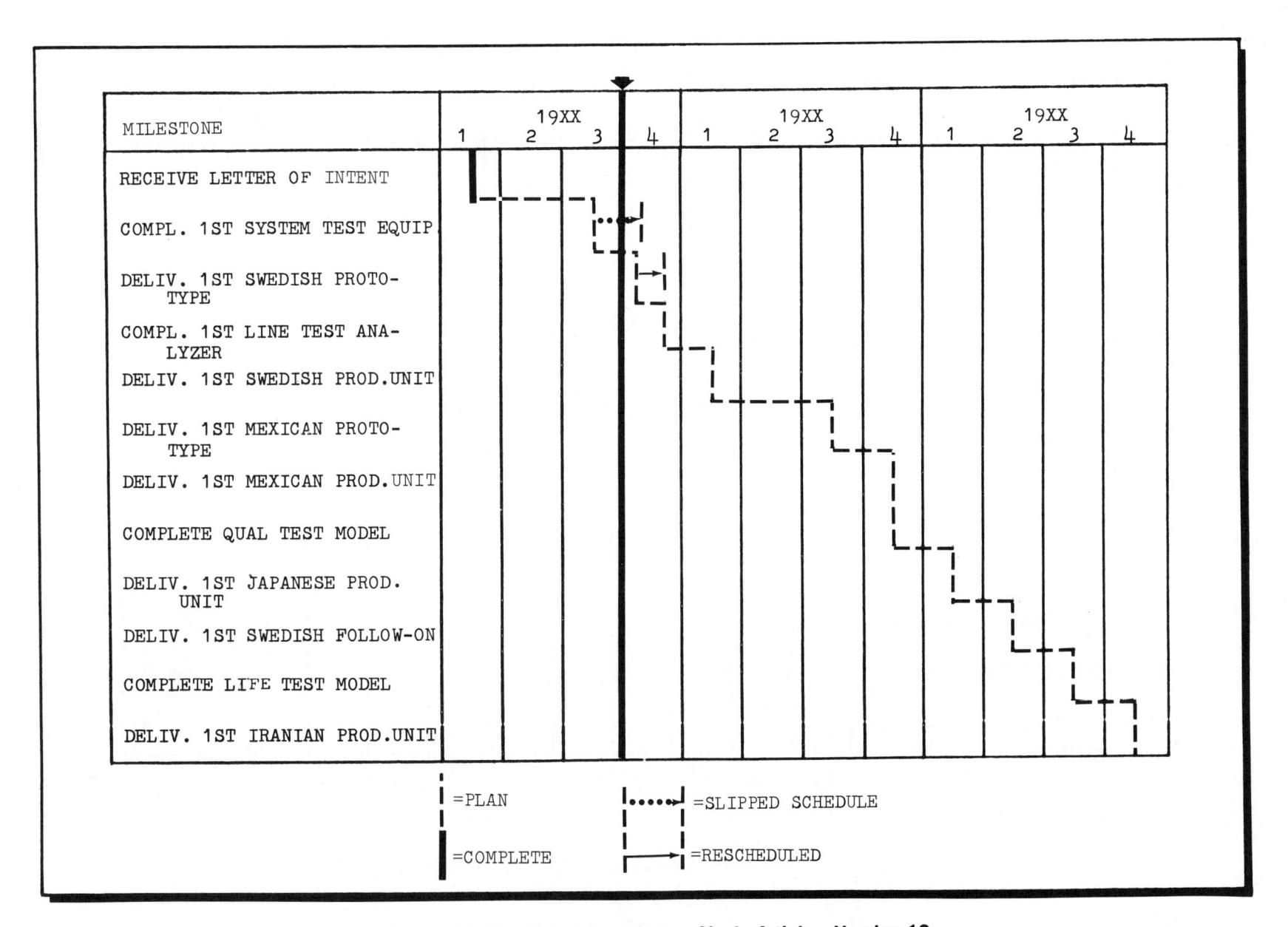

Figure 53.12 Schedule—First or Single Article—Version 12

MILESTONE	19XX 1 2 3 4	19XX 1 2 3 4	19XX 1 2 3 4
RECEIVE LETTER OF INTENT	∅		
COMPL. 1ST SYSTEM TEST EQUIP	⊗--○		
DELIV. 1ST SWEDISH PROTOTYPE	⊗¹--○	← DELIVERY REQUIRED BY CUSTOMER	
COMPL. 1ST LINE TEST ANALYZER	○		
DELIV. 1ST SWEDISH PROD.UNIT		○	
DELIV. 1ST MEXICAN PROTOTYPE		○	
DELIV. 1ST MEXICAN PROD.UNIT		○	
COMPLETE QUAL TEST MODEL		○	
DELIV. 1ST JAPANESE PROD. UNIT			○
DELIV. 1ST SWEDISH FOLLOW-ON			○
COMPLETE LIFE TEST MODEL			○
DELIV. 1ST IRANIAN PROD.UNIT			○

○ = SCHEDULED
∅ = COMPLETED
⊗--○ = TIME SLIP
⊗--○' = RESCHEDULED (NUMBER INDICATES RESCHEDULING SEQUENCE)

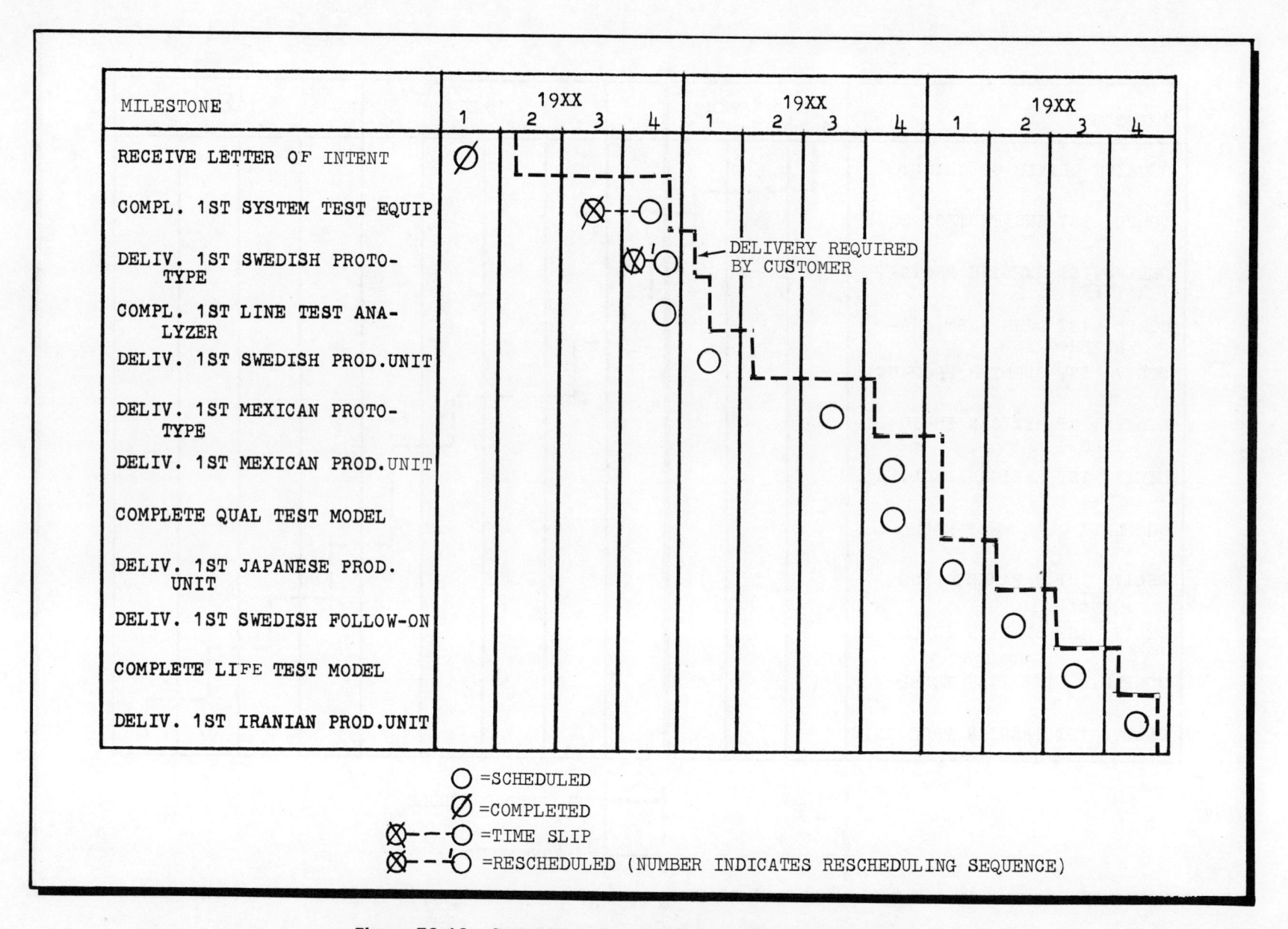

Figure 53.13 Schedule—First or Single Article—Version 13

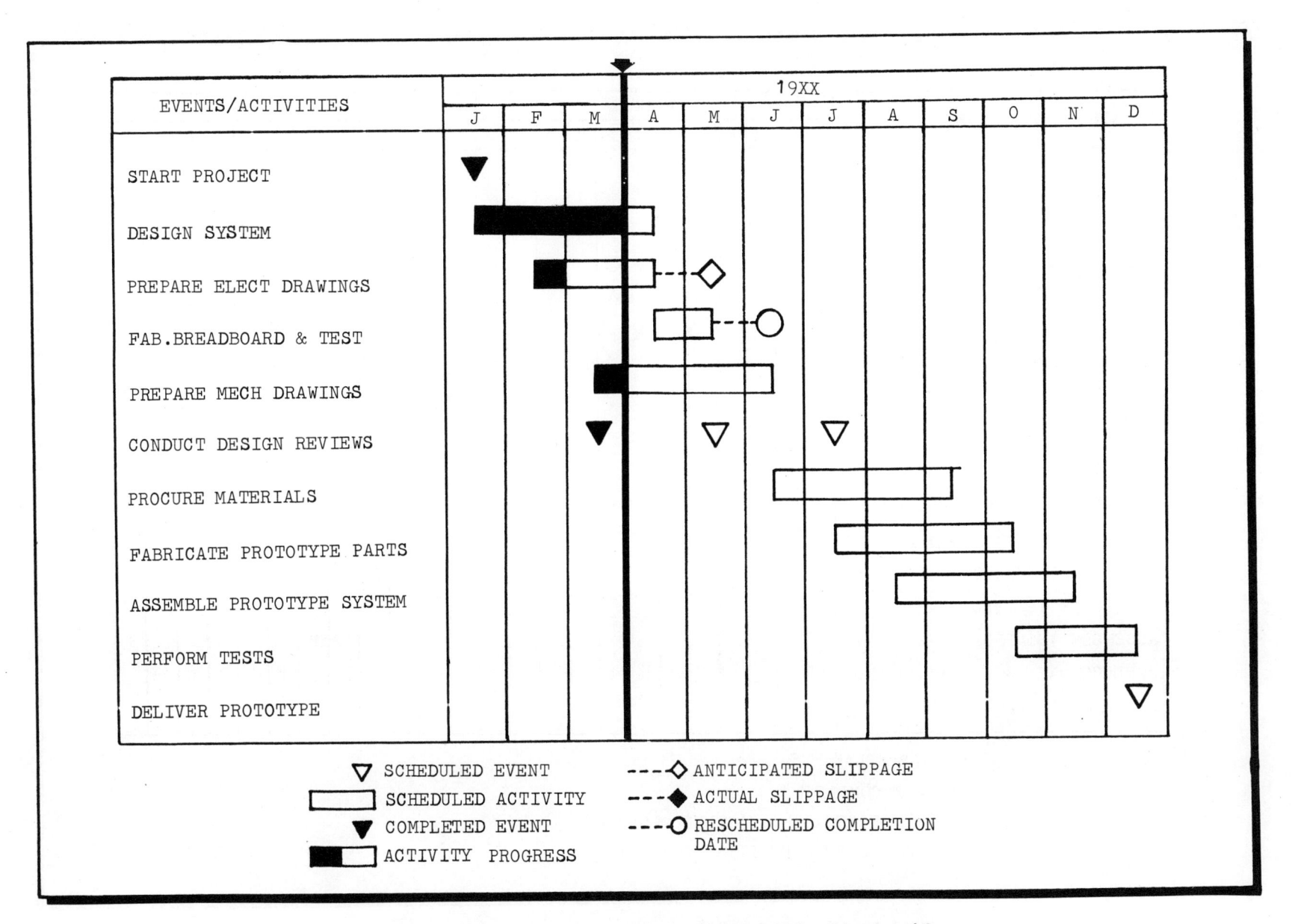

Figure 53.14 Schedule—First or Single Article—Version 14

EVENTS & ACTIVITIES	19XX J F M A M J J A S O N D	19XX J F M A M J J A S O N D
CONTRACT AWARD	P̸	
DEVEL. ADVANCED BILL OF MAT'LS	P̸P̸P̸P̸P̸P̸PPPPP	
PREP. & RELEASE SPECS	P̸P̸P̸PPPPPPPP--O	
PREP & RELEASE DRAWINGS	P̸P̸P̸PPPPPPPPPPP	
PROCURE PROTOTYPE MATERIALS	P̸P̸P̸PPPPPPPPPPPPPPPPP PP	
FAB & ASSEMBLE PROTOTYPE	PPPPPPPPPPP	
PERFORM UNIT & ACCEPT TESTS	PPPPPPPPPP	
CONDUCT QUAL TEST	PPPPPPPPPPPPPP	
CONDUCT RELIABILITY TEST		PP PPPPPPPPPPPP
DESIGN PRODUCTION TOOLING	PPPPPPPPP	
FAB PRODUCTION TOOLING	PPPPPPPPP	
PROCURE PRODUCTION MAT'LS		PPPPPPPPPP
FABRICATE 1ST PROD PARTS		PPPPPP
ASSEMBLE 1ST PROD UNIT		PPPPPPPPP
CONDUCT UNIT & ACCEPT TEST		PPPPPPPPP
DELIVER 1ST PROD UNIT		P

PPP = PLAN

P̸ = COMPLETED

--O = FORECASTED SLIPPED DELIVERY

--Ø = SLIPPED DELIVERY COMPLETED

Figure 53.15 Schedule—First or Single Article—Version 15

MILESTONES	J	F	M	A	M	19XX J	J	A	S	O	N	D
ESTABLISH POLICIES:												
CHANGE CONTROL	S A											
CONFIGURATION MANAGEMENT			S A									
BLOCK SCHEDULING				S	A S							
CHANGE EFFECTIVITY						F						
PART NO. RE-IDENTIFICATION					S	F̸	F					
COMPLETE PROCEDURES:												
CONFIGURATION CONTROL						S						
CLASS I CHANGE							S					
CLASS II CHANGE							S̸	S				
SERIALIZATION								S				
TEST EQUIPMENT									S			
VENDOR CHANGE CONTROL										S		
DESIGN REVIEWS										S		
CHANGE PACKAGING											S	

S=SCHEDULE
A=ACTUAL
S̸=PREVIOUS SCHEDULE
F=FORECAST
F̸=PREVIOUS FORECAST

Figure 53.16 Schedule—First or Single Article—Version 16

MILESTONES	\multicolumn{12}{c}{19XX}
	J	F	M	A	M	J	J	A	S	O	N	D
ESTABLISH POLICIES:												
CHANGE CONTROL	O L ▲	P										
CONFIGURATION MANAGEMENT			O L ▲	P								
BLOCK SCHEDULING				O	L P ▲							
CHANGE EFFECTIVITY					O L	P						
PART NO. RE-IDENTIFICATION					O L		P					
COMPLETE PROCEDURES:												
CONFIGURATION CONTROL						O L	P					
CLASS I CHANGE						O	L P					
CLASS II CHANGE							O L	P				
SERIALIZATION							O	L	P			
TEST EQUIPMENT								O	L	P		
VENDOR CHANGE CONTROL										O L	P	
DESIGN REVIEWS									O	L P		
CHANGE PACKAGING											O L	P

O = OPTIMISTIC
L = MOST LIKELY
P = PESSIMISTIC
▲ = ACTUAL

Figure 53.17   Schedule—First or Single Article—Version 17

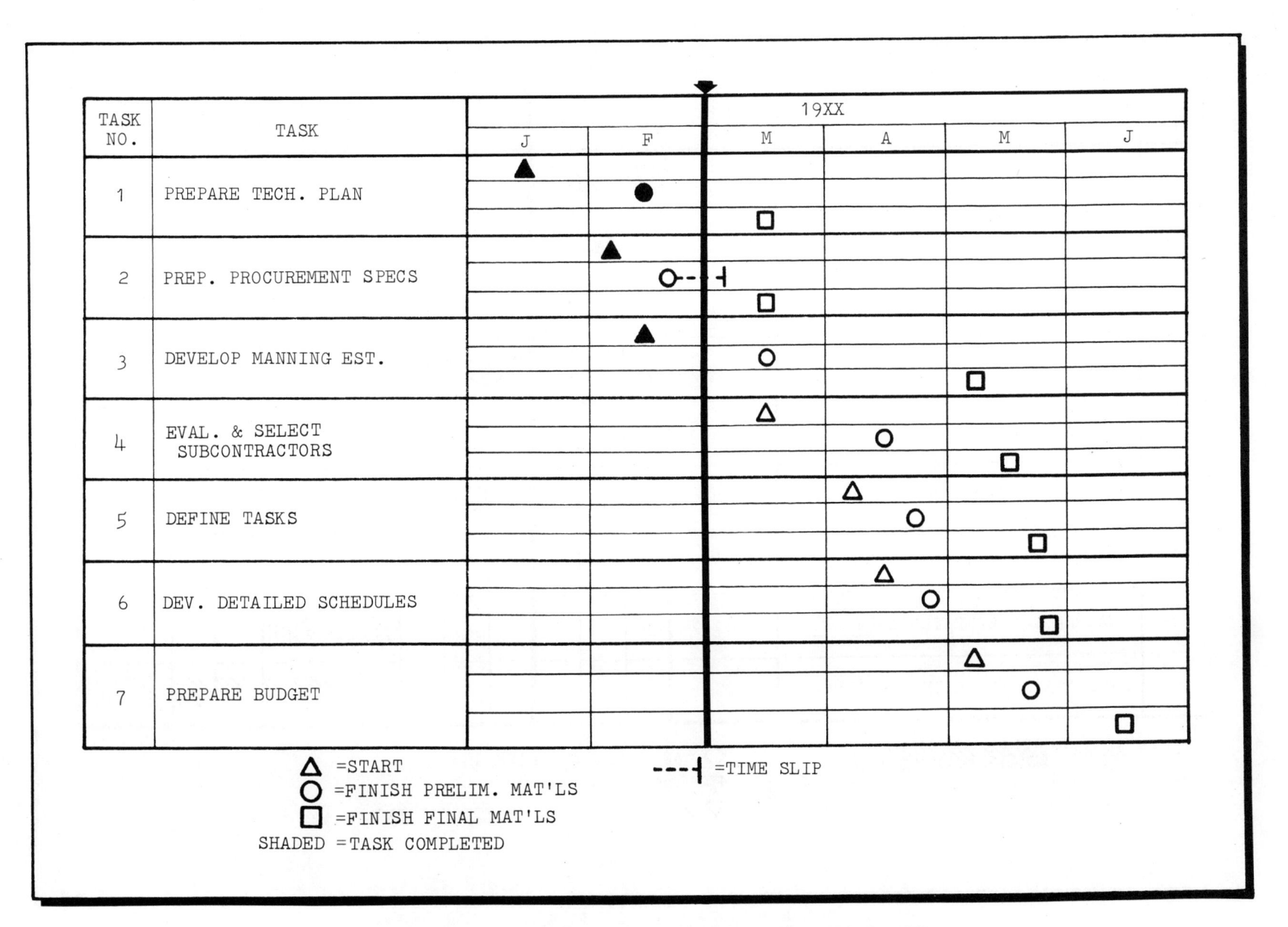

TASK NO.	TASK	J	F	M	A	M	J
				19XX			
1	PREPARE TECH. PLAN	▲	●	☐			
2	PREP. PROCUREMENT SPECS		▲	○--┤ ☐			
3	DEVELOP MANNING EST.		▲	○		☐	
4	EVAL. & SELECT SUBCONTRACTORS			△	○ ☐		
5	DEFINE TASKS			△	○ ☐		
6	DEV. DETAILED SCHEDULES				△ ○ ☐		
7	PREPARE BUDGET					△ ○	☐

△ =START
○ =FINISH PRELIM. MAT'LS
☐ =FINISH FINAL MAT'LS
SHADED =TASK COMPLETED
---┤ =TIME SLIP

Figure 53.18 Schedule—First or Single Article—Version 18

ITEM NO.	TASK	CONTROL NO.	JAN				FEB				MAR				
			6	13	20	27	3	10	17	24	3	10	17	24	31
1	REARRANGE PRODUCTION CONTROL	1200-5													
2	REARRANGE RECEIVING AREA	1200-4					◇								
3	REARRANGE FOREMAN'S OFFICE	1200-7													
4	RELOCATE REWORK SECTION	1200-9						▽	▽	▽					
5	RELOCATE TOOL CRIB	1200-3													
6	RELOCATE SUB-ASSEMBLY SECTION	1200-1													
7	RELOCATE ELECTRICAL SECTION	1200-8													
8	REARRANGE INSPECTION AREA	1200-2													
9	RELOCATE FINAL ASSEMBLY AREA	1200-6													

CLEAR AREA — PROGRESS — CONSTRUCTION — MOVE

◇ = ANTICIPATED SLIPPAGE
◆ = ACTUAL SLIPPAGE
▽ = RESCHEDULED COMPLETION POINT

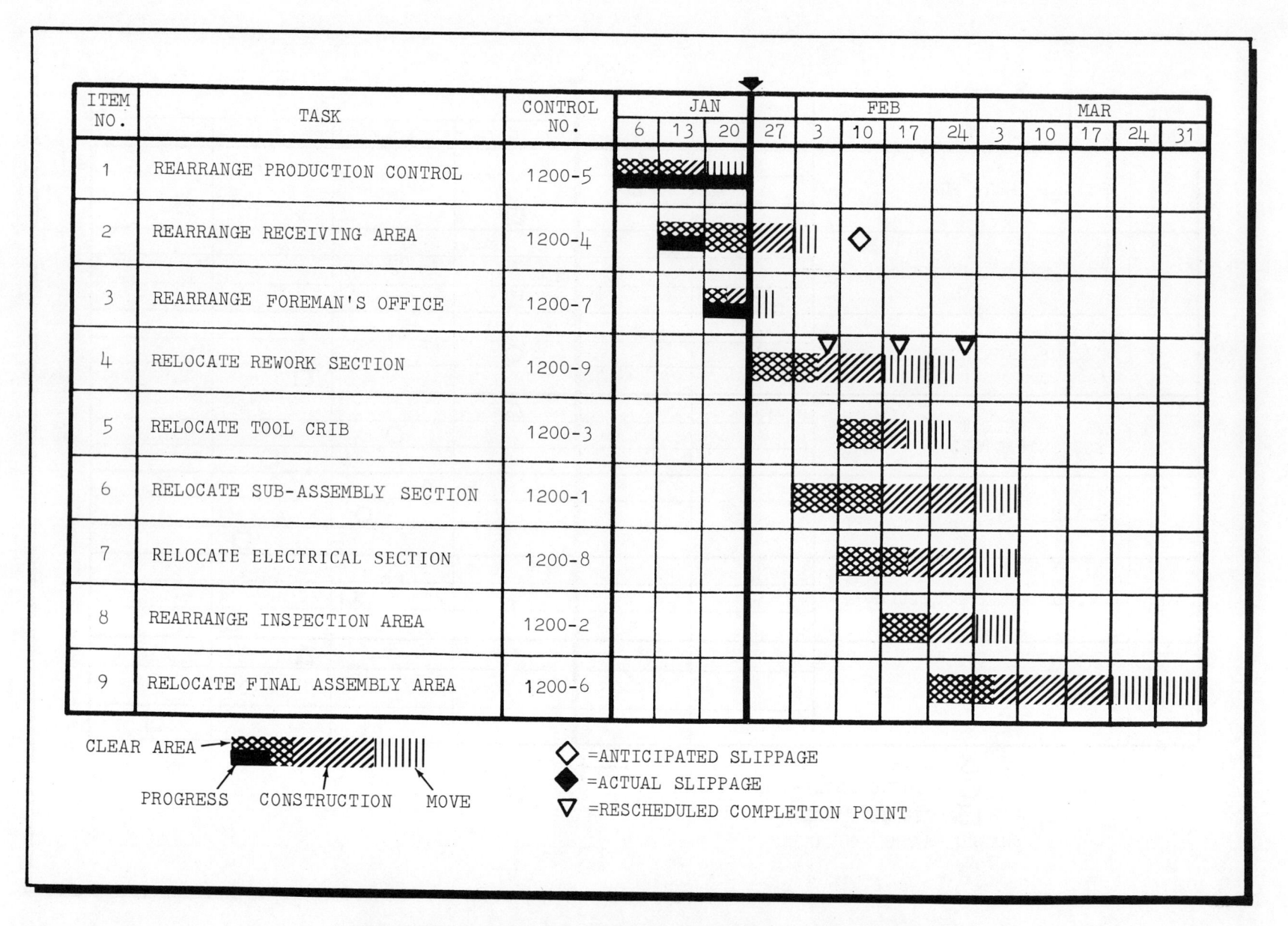

Figure 53.19 Schedule—First or Single Article—Version 19

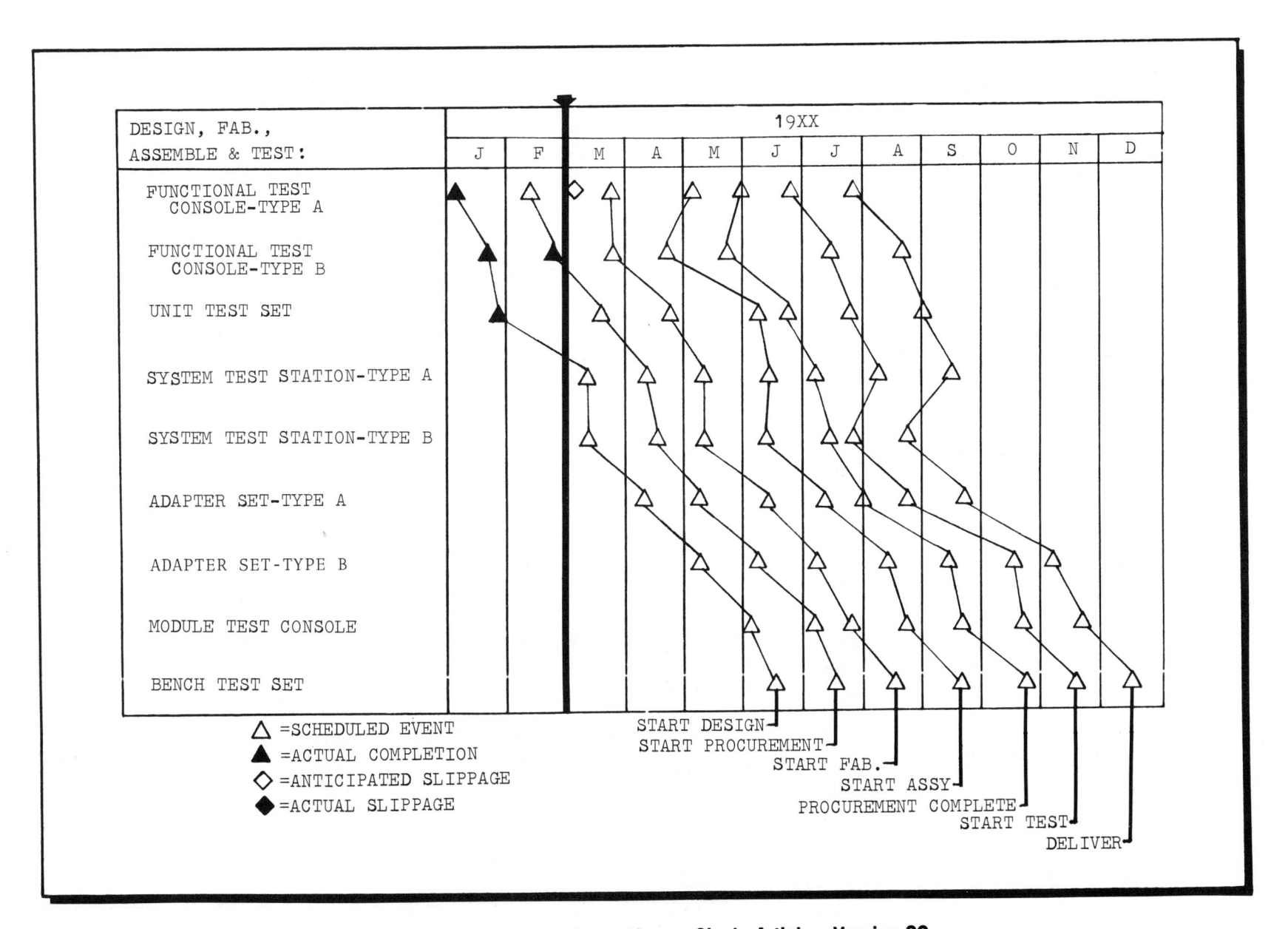

Figure 53.20 Schedule—First or Single Article—Version 20

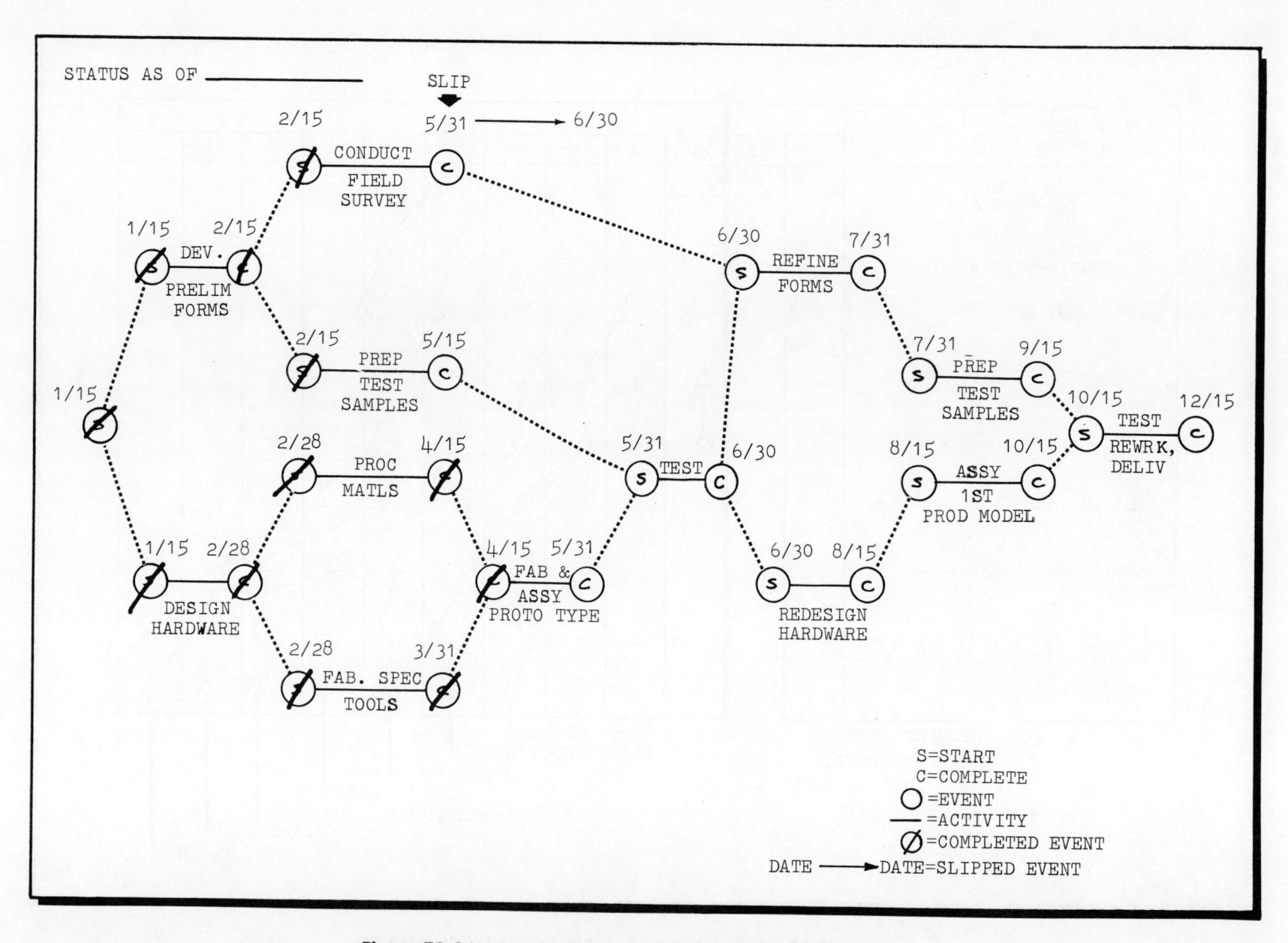

Figure 53.21 Schedule—First or Single Article—Version 21

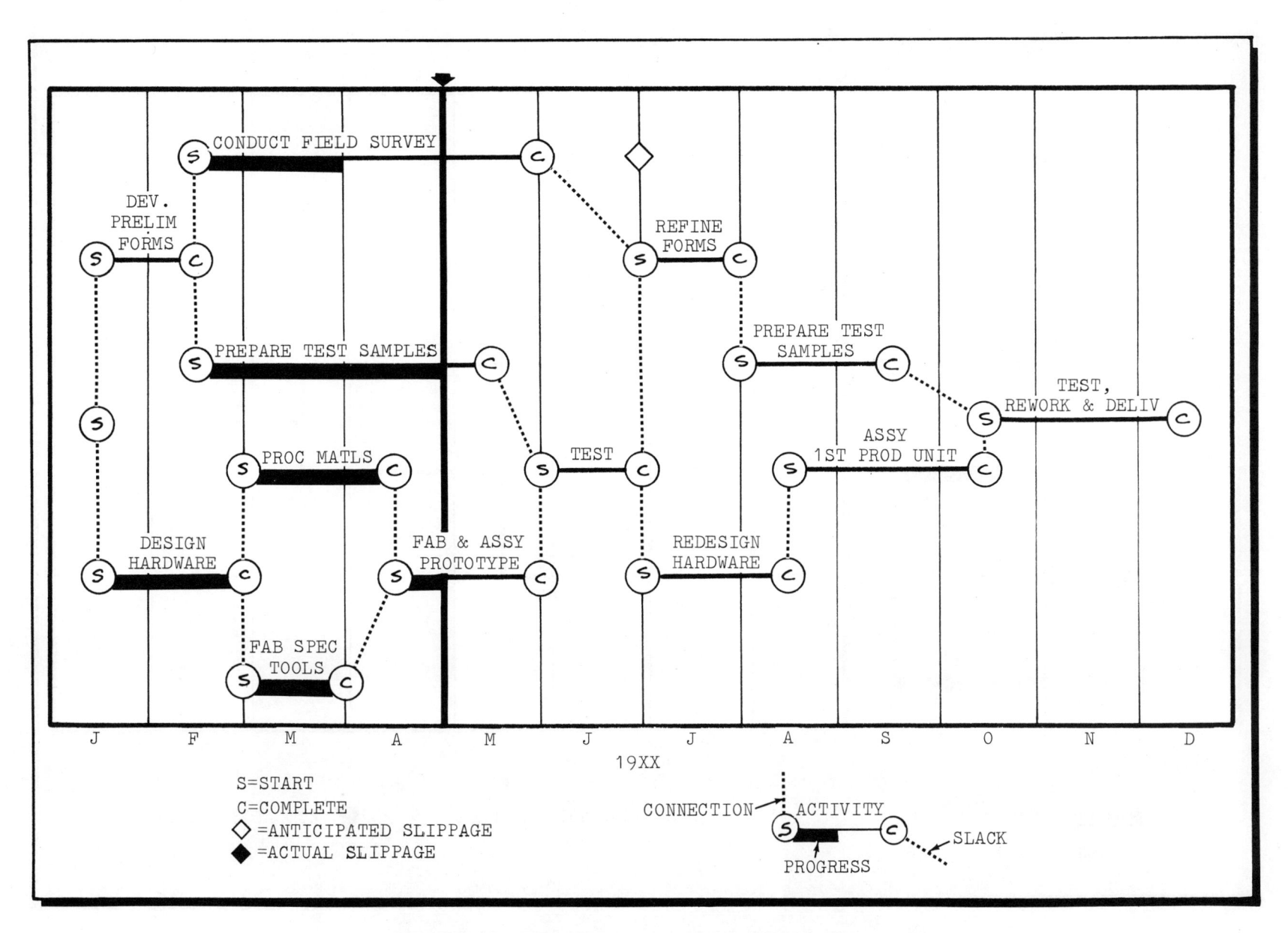

Figure 53.22 Schedule—First or Single Article—Version 22

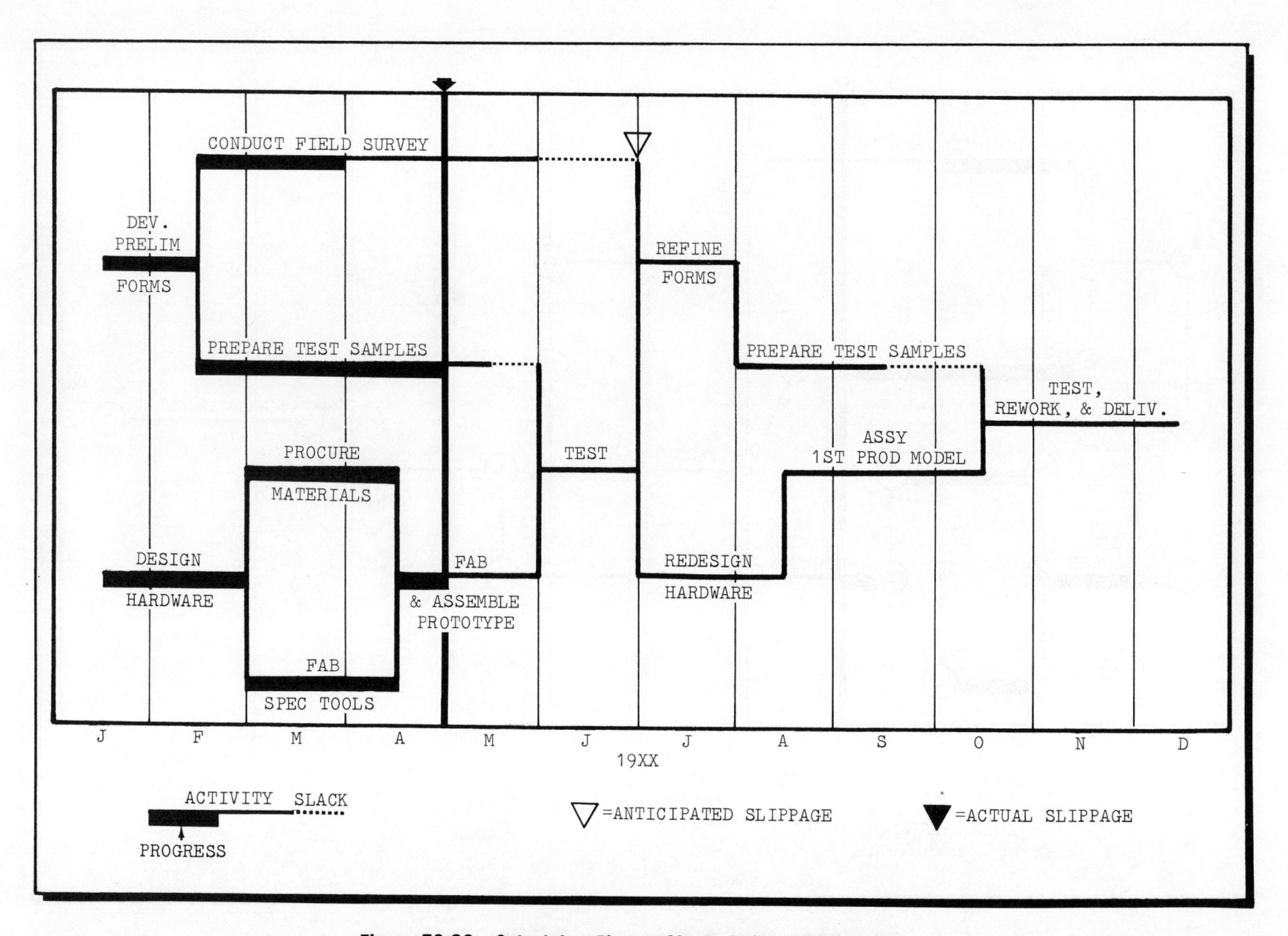

Figure 53.23 Schedule—First or Single Article—Version 23

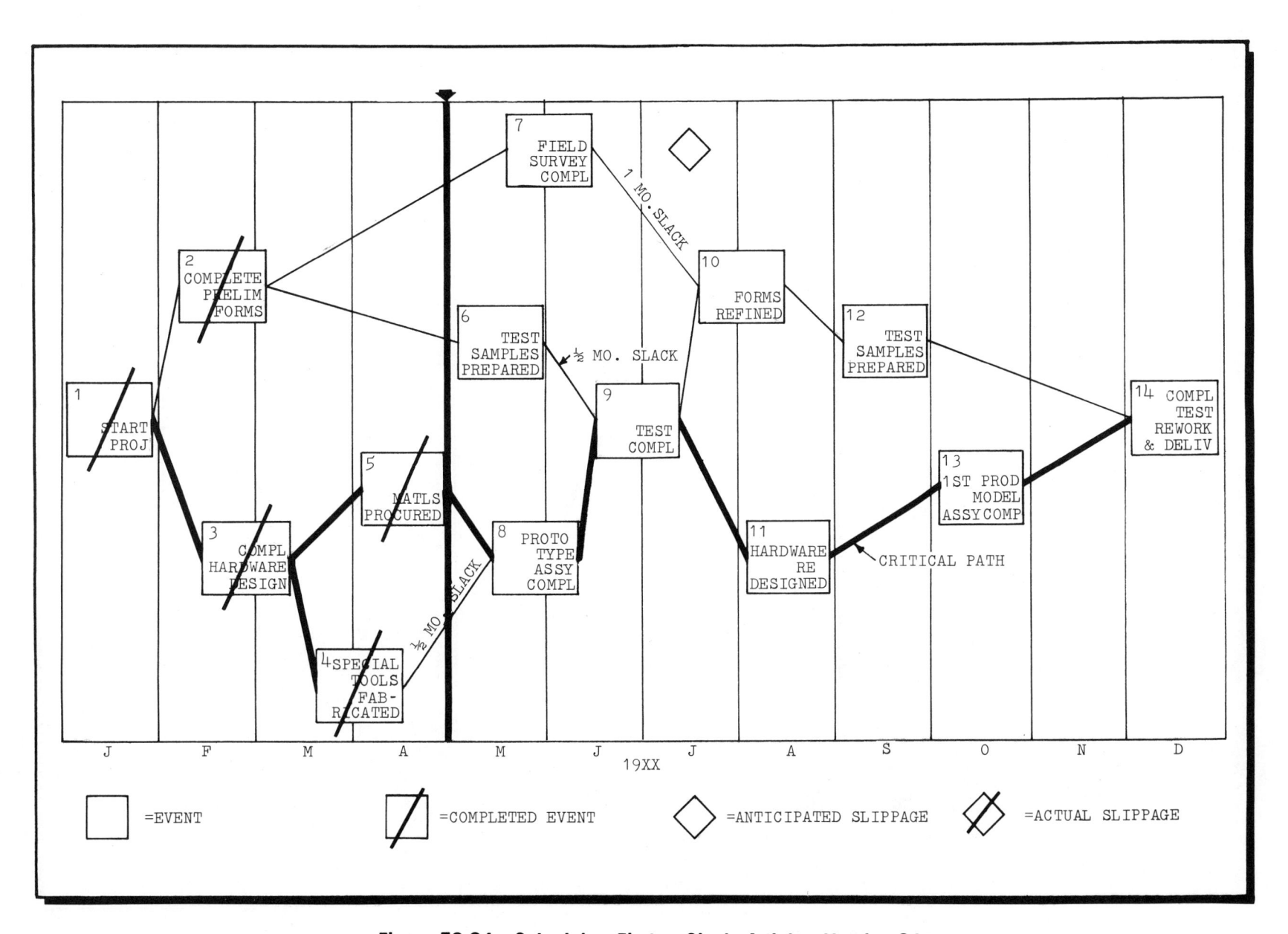

Figure 53.24 Schedule—First or Single Article—Version 24

697

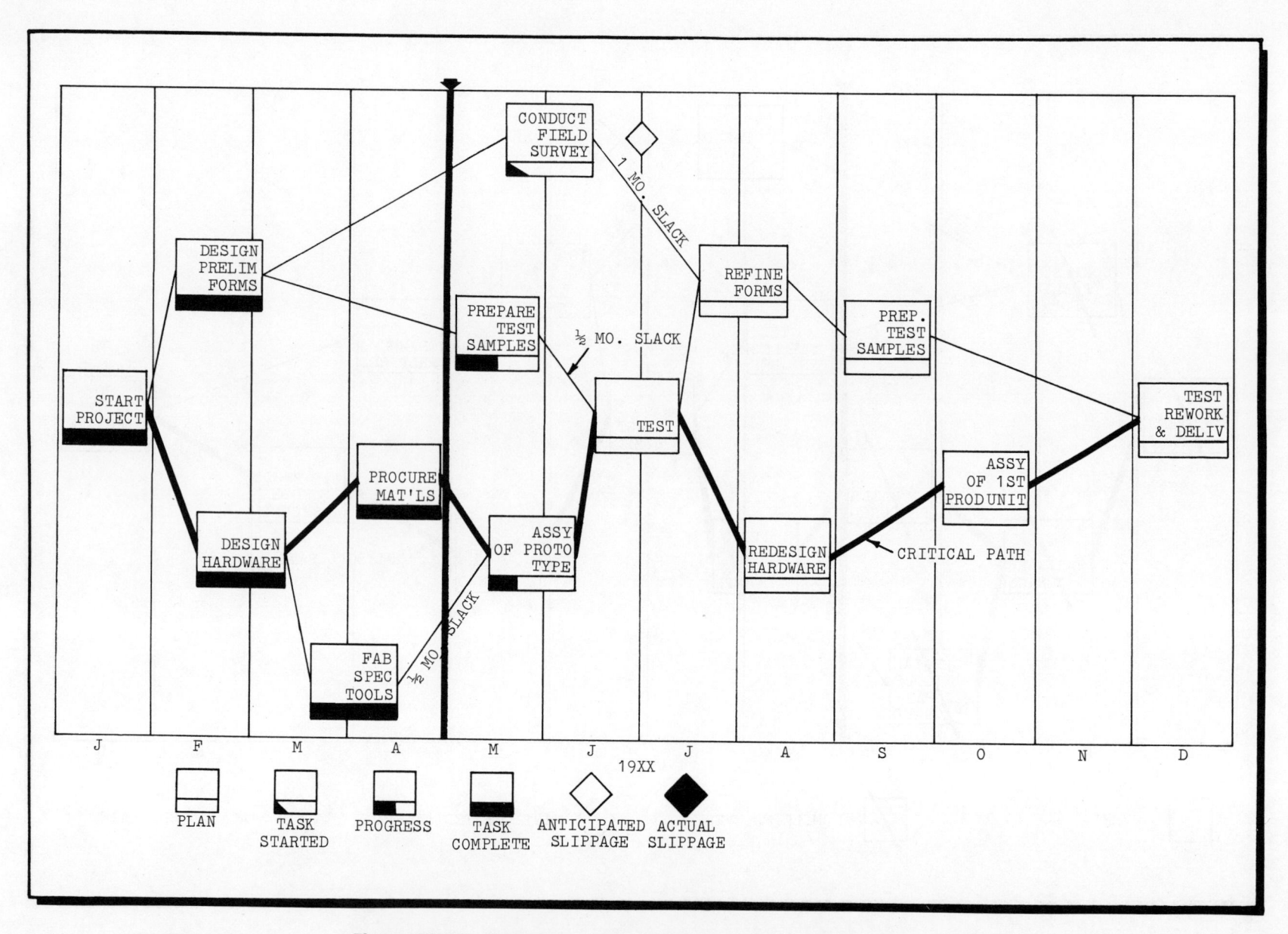

Figure 53.25 Schedule—First or Single Article—Version 25

698

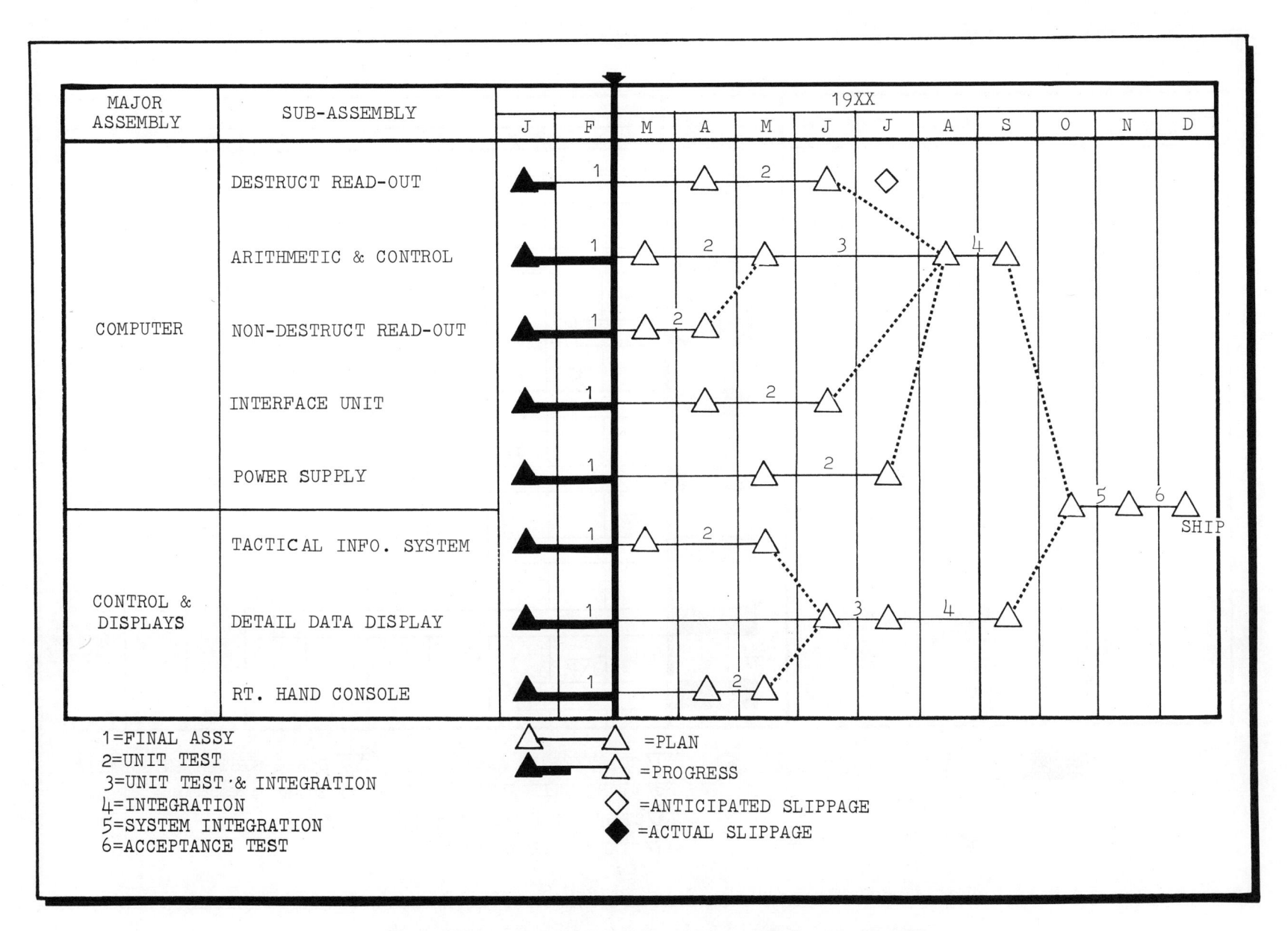

MAJOR ASSEMBLY	SUB-ASSEMBLY	19XX											
		J	F	M	A	M	J	J	A	S	O	N	D
COMPUTER	DESTRUCT READ-OUT												
	ARITHMETIC & CONTROL												
	NON-DESTRUCT READ-OUT												
	INTERFACE UNIT												
	POWER SUPPLY												
CONTROL & DISPLAYS	TACTICAL INFO. SYSTEM												
	DETAIL DATA DISPLAY												
	RT. HAND CONSOLE												

1 = FINAL ASSY
2 = UNIT TEST
3 = UNIT TEST & INTEGRATION
4 = INTEGRATION
5 = SYSTEM INTEGRATION
6 = ACCEPTANCE TEST

△——△ = PLAN
▲——△ = PROGRESS
◇ = ANTICIPATED SLIPPAGE
◆ = ACTUAL SLIPPAGE

Figure 53.26 Schedule—First or Single Article—Version 26

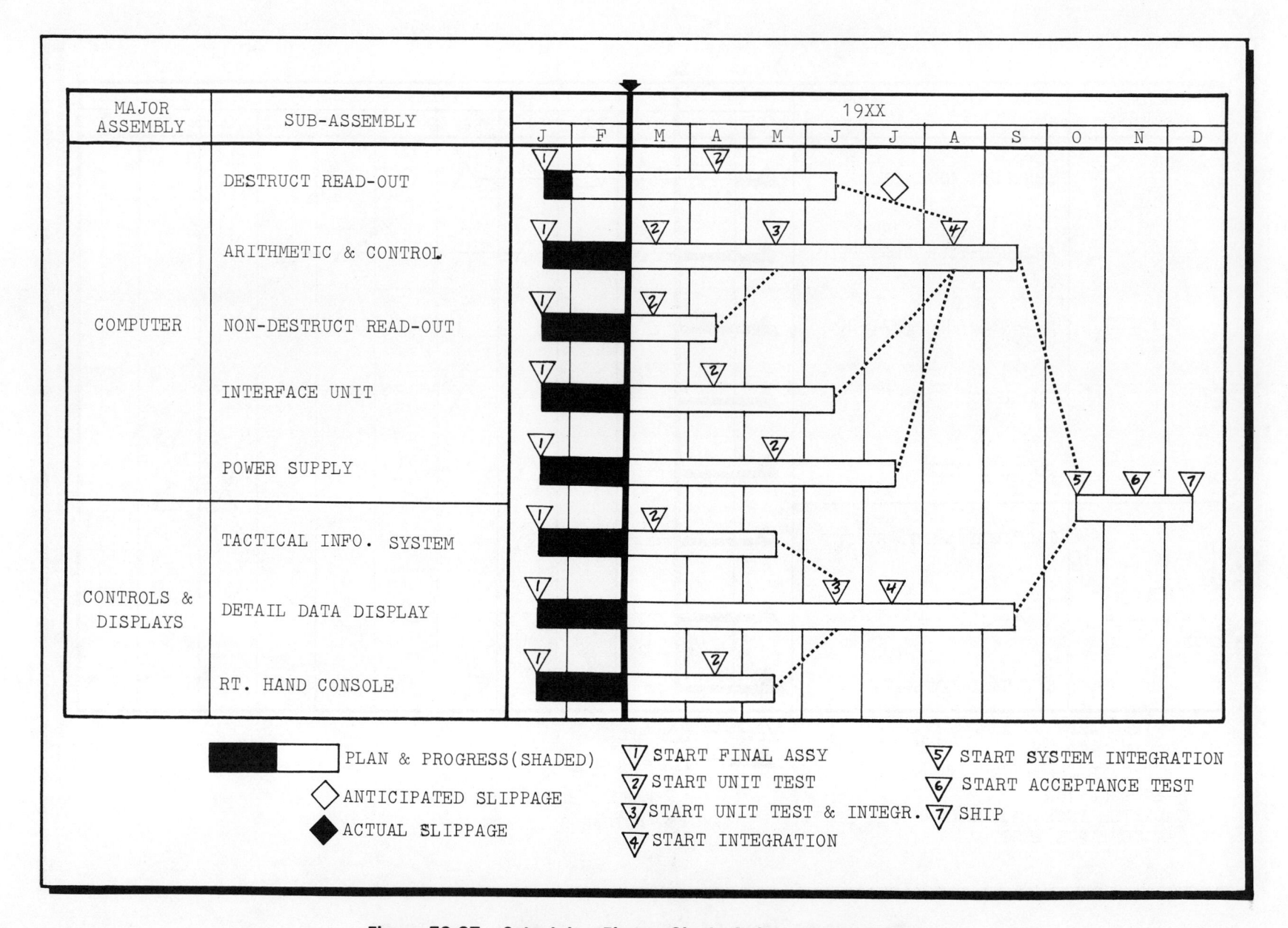

Figure 53.27 Schedule—First or Single Article—Version 27

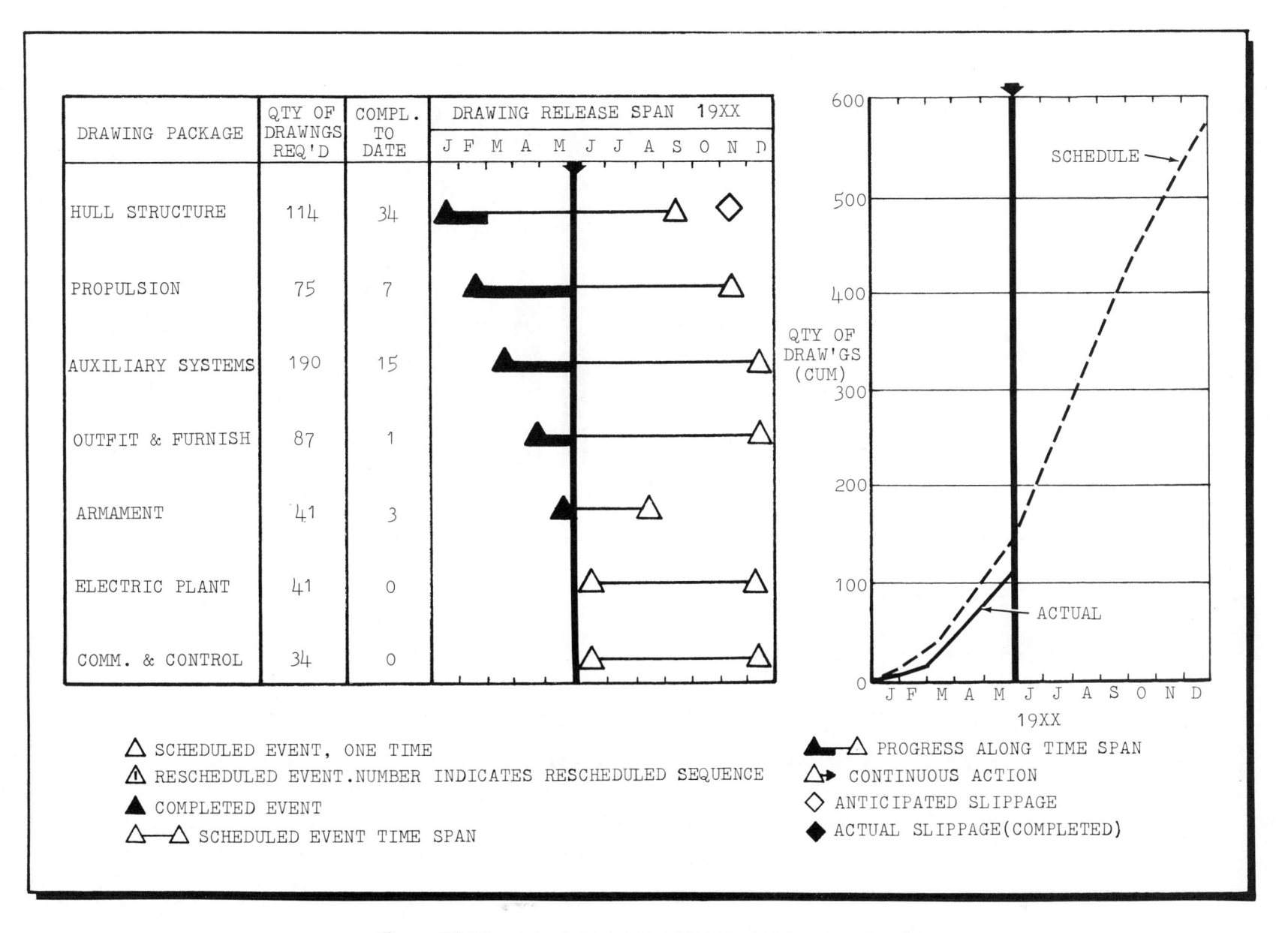

Figure 53.28 Schedule—First or Single Article—Version 28

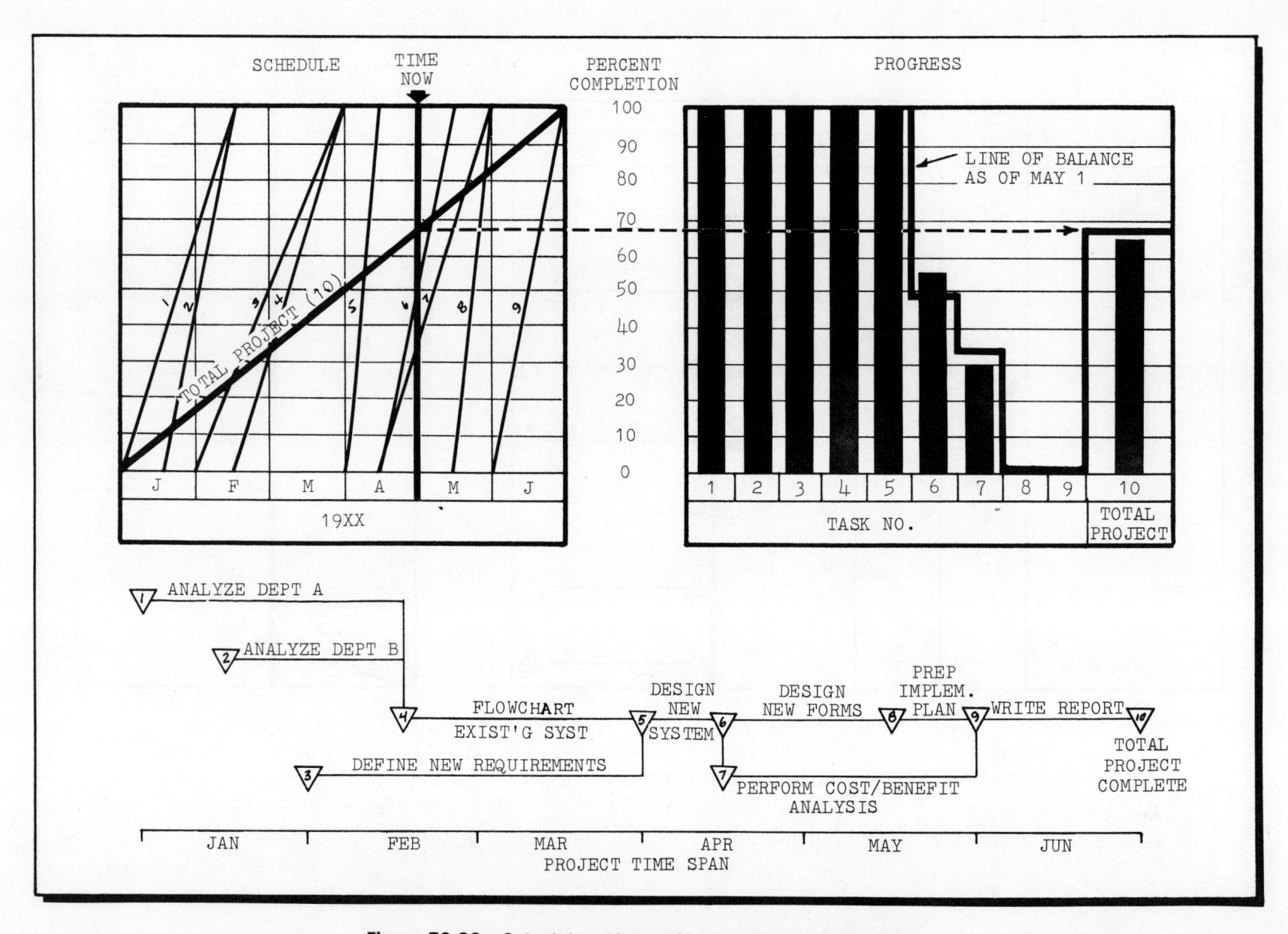

Figure 53.29 Schedule—First or Single Article—Version 29

702

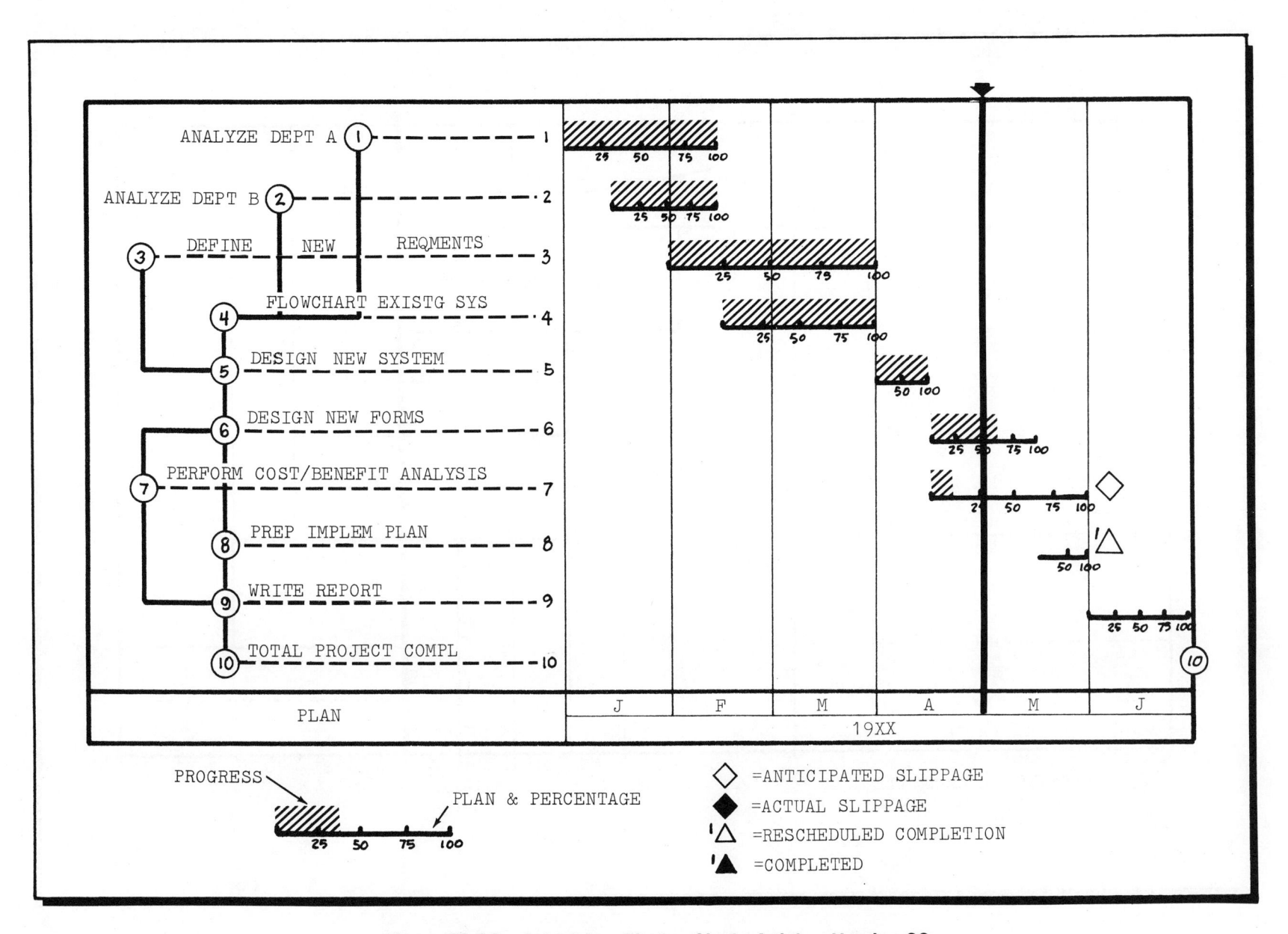

Figure 53.30 Schedule—First or Single Article—Version 30

703

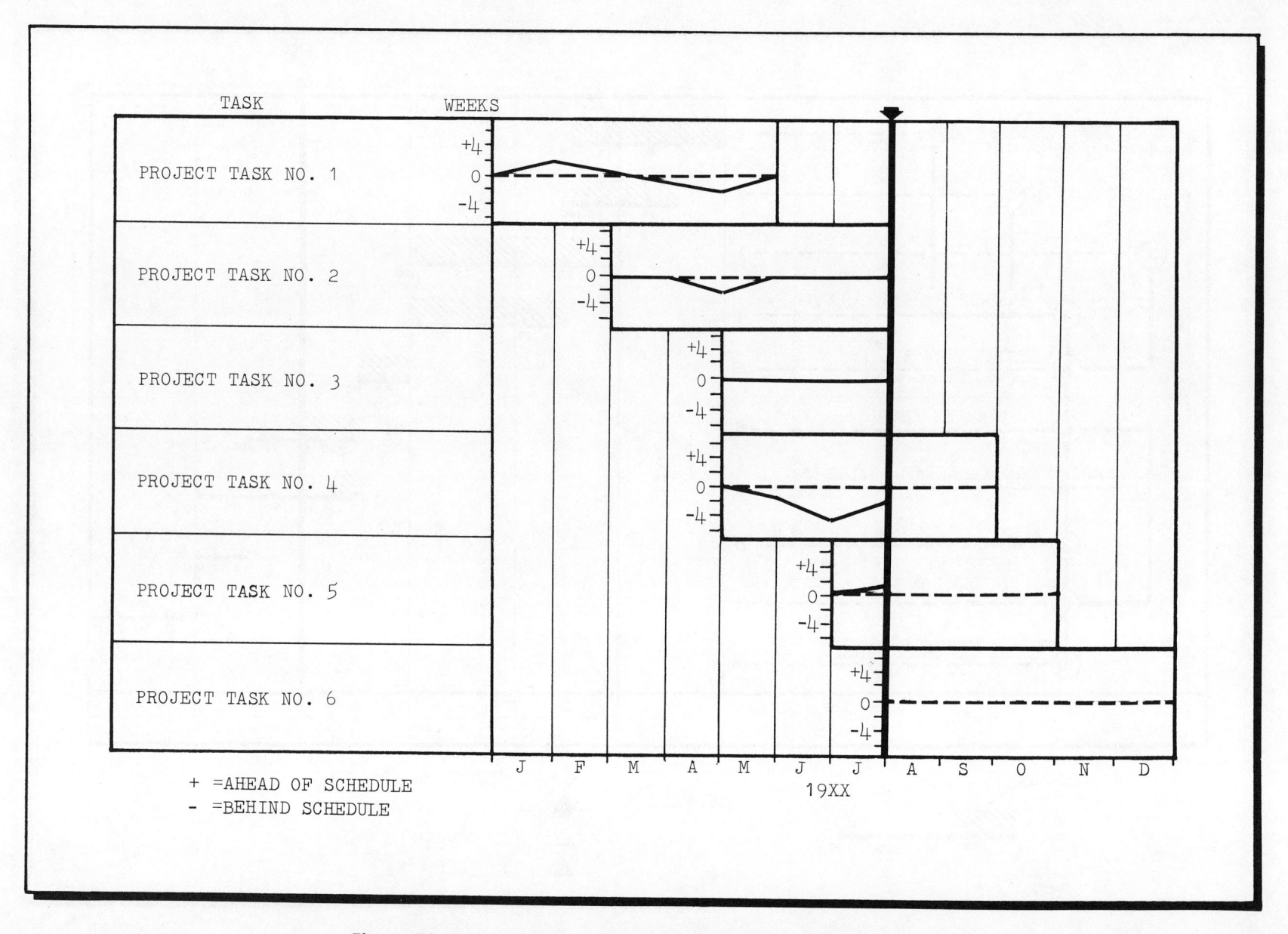

Figure 53.31   Schedule—First or Single Article—Version 31

704

TASK NO.	TASK		19XX					
			J	F	M	A	M	J
1	PREPARE TECH PLANS	S	1/10					
		F						
		A	1/10					
2	PREP. PROCUREMENT SPECS	S		2/10				
		F		2/15				
		A		2/16				
3	DEVELOP MANNING EST.	S		2/20				
		F		2/25				
		A			3/5			
4	EVAL. & SELECT SUBCONTRACTORS	S			3/15			
		F						
		A						
5	DEFINE TASKS	S				4/12		
		F						
		A						
6	DEV. DETAILED SCHEDULES	S					5/22	
		F						
		A						
7	PREPARE BUDGET	S						6/5
		F						
		A						

S=SCHEDULED COMPLETION DATE
F=FORECASTED SLIPPAGE DATE
A=ACTUAL COMPLETION DATE

Figure 53.32 Schedule—First or Single Article—Version 32

STATUS AS OF MAY 31

EVENT/ACTIVITY	SCHEDULED COMPLETION DATE	ACTUAL (ANTICIPATED) COMPLETION DATE	ACTUAL VARIANCE (DAYS)*	PREDICTED VARIANCE (DAYS)*
EXCAVATE SITE	2/15	2/15		
PREPARE FORMS	3/15	3/20	-5	
POUR FOUNDATION	4/15	4/15		
ERECT FRAME & ROOF	6/15	(6/30)		-15
INSTALL DUCTS	7/15	(7/30)		-15
INSTALL WATER PIPES	8/15	(8/15)		
INSTALL SEWAGE PIPES	9/15	(9/15)		
INSTALL ELECTRICAL	9/15	(9/15)		
INSTALL CABINETS & FINISH	10/15	(10/15)		
PAINT	11/15	(11/15)		
INSTALL FIXTURES	11/15	(11/15)		
GRADE & PAVE	12/15	(12/15)		

* + = AHEAD OF SCHEDULE
   - = BEHIND SCHEDULE

Figure 53.33 Schedule—First or Single Article—Version 33

STATUS AS OF: 4/30

WORK ORDER NO.	DESCRIPTION	DEPT.	SCHEDULE DATE	ACTUAL DATE	FORECAST SLIPPAGE (DAYS)	ANALYSIS
10522	COMPLETE SYSTEM DESIGN	D/103	4/10	4/10		
10523	COMPLETE ELECT DRAWINGS	D/103	4/25	4/25		
10524	COMPLETE BREADBOARD MODEL	D/018	5/15		10	STANDARD PARTS NOT IN STOCK
10525	TEST	D/030	5/25		5	
10526	COMPLETE MECH DRAWINGS	D/103	6/10			
10527	COMPL. MAT'L PROCUREMENT	D/080	9/15			
10528	COMPL. PROTOTYPE PARTS	D/003	10/10			
10529	COMPL. PROTOTYPE ASSY	D/018	11/15			
10530	COMPLETE SYSTEM TEST	D/030	12/10			
10531	DELIVER	D/075	12/15			

Figure 53.34 Schedule—First or Single Article—Version 34

STATUS AS OF __MAY 1__

TASK NO.	TASK NAME	ANALYST	% COMPLETE: SCHEDULED	% COMPLETE: ACTUAL	% VARIANCE	PROBLEM
1	ANALYZE DEPT A	JONES	100	100		
2	ANALYZE DEPT B	SMITH	100	100		
3	DEFINE NEW REQUIREMENTS	BROWN	100	100		
4	FLOWCHART EXIST'G SYSTEM	JONES	100	100		
5	DESIGN NEW SYSTEM	BROWN	100	100		
6	DESIGN NEW FORMS	SMITH	48	55	+7	
7	PERFORM COST/BENEFIT ANALYSIS	JONES	33	20	-13	COST DATA FROM DEPT. B LATE IN ARRIVING
8	PREPARE IMPLEM. PLAN	BROWN	0	0		
9	WRITE REPORT	ALL	0	0		
10	TOTAL PROJECT	—	65	64	-1	

Figure 53.35 Schedule—First or Single Article—Version 35

STATUS AS OF **Feb 15**

NO.	MILESTONE	SCHEDULE CHANGE		IMPACT ●			REMARKS
		FROM	TO	NONE	MINOR	MAJOR	
1	PREPARE TECHNICAL PLANS						
2	PREP. PROCUREMENT SPECS	2/10	2/20	●			
3	DEVEL. MANNING EST.						
4	EVAL. & SELECT SUBCONTRACTORS	3/15	4/15			●	UNLESS MORE MANPOWER APPLIED TO THIS TASK, ENTIRE PROJECT WILL SLIP ONE MONTH
5	DEFINE TASKS						
6	DEVELOP DETAILED SCHEDULES						
7	PREPARE BUDGET						

Figure 53.36 Schedule—First or Single Article—Version 36

54.0 SCHEDULES—IN-PROCESS

Charts that display status in terms of the separate processing steps required to produce end items on a repetitive basis are called "in-process" schedules. The concern of this type of chart is to display the status of work accomplished throughout, or at key points in, the process cycle. Since a number of factors are shown on in-process scheduled charts, they are usually more complex than end-item schedule charts.

54.1 Schedule—In-Process—Version 1: One of the more commonly used versions of an in-process schedule is shown in Figure 54.1. In this example, each bar represents a complete cycle of process necessary to produce a single production unit or production lot. Each bar in this version is subdivided into three processing steps: fabrication and assembly, unit test, and system test. Shading is used to show work completed up to the report date (the end of February in this example). Units 128 through 135 are on schedule with the exceptions of unit 131, which is ahead of schedule, and unit 129, which is behind schedule by one week. In this example, since an anticipated slippage symbol is not used in conjunction with unit 129, it can be assumed that though the unit is currently behind schedule, it is still expected to be completed on time.

54.2 Schedule—In-Process—Version 2: The in-process schedule shown in Figure 54.2 is identical to Version 1 except for the method of showing progress. In the Version 2 example, chart tape is used to show progress. This is normally a more expeditious method than that of shading. In both Versions, 1 and 2, it should be noted that the processing numbers on each bar are still visible after tapes or shading have been applied. This approach enhances the usefulness of the charts.

54.3 Schedule—In-Process—Version 3: The bars are shade coded on the in-process schedule shown in Figure 54.3 to differentiate between the three separate processing steps displayed in this example. Progress is shown by using chart tape through the center of each bar. Even after the tape has been applied, the chart reader can still distinguish the separate segments on the bars. Also in this example, an inverted delta is used to show points of actual completion.

54.4 Schedule—In-Process—Version 4: Version 4 of an in-process schedule, Figure 54.4, shows an example of a chart constructed to display a significant number of individual processing steps in a cycle. In the example, nine separate processing steps are shown. Diamonds are used to show anticipated and actual slippages for each cycle. It would be impractical, on this style chart, to attempt to graphically portray slippages for each of the individual bar segments (processing steps).

In the example, Volumes I, II, and IV have been completed. Volume II was completed a half a week behind schedule, and Volume IV was completed one week ahead of schedule. The status of Volume III shows it to be behind schedule by a week and a half, and the diamond symbol shows that it is anticipated that it will slip its schedule by one week. Volumes V through XIII are shown to be in work and on schedule.

54.5 Schedule—In-Process—Version 5: A different method of showing a significant number of separate processing steps is shown in Figure 54.5. Positions A, B, C, D, and E, in the example, could represent separate stations on an assembly line. Precise definitions could be added to the footnote section of the chart. Progress is shown using chart tape. In this example, all production units have been shipped or are on schedule except production unit (or production lot number) 3.

54.6 Schedule—In-Process—Version 6: Graphics and statistics have been combined in Version 6 of an in-process schedule, Figure 54.6. In this example, production quantities for each lot number vary. Actual status in terms of cumulative scheduled versus cumulative actual shipments, and the net variance between these two numbers, can be read directly from the statistical portion of the chart.

54.7 Schedule—In-Process—Version 7: Another method for combining graphics and statistics is shown in Figure 54.7. In this example, cumulative schedule and actual performance statistics, and the variance between these two numbers, are shown for each production lot number. The example shows that as of the reporting date (end of August), production lot number 104 is a half month behind schedule and its completion is expected to slip a half a month to the middle of September. The statistics to the right of the graphic portion of the chart show this as being 100 units behind schedule.

54.8 Schedule—In-Process—Version 8: In many instances, the separate processing steps required to produce a given item overlap. The in-process schedule shown in Figure 54.8 shows one approach to overcoming this problem from a graphics standpoint. In this example, the inverted deltas are used to show the start of each of the separate processing steps.

54.9 Schedule—In-Process—Version 9: Another approach to showing separate processing steps that overlap is shown in Version 9 of an in-process schedule, Figure 54.9. In the example, separate bars are used for the three separate processing steps: procurement of parts, assembly, and test. Shading is used to show status.

54.10 Schedule—In-Process—Version 10: Version 10 of an in-process schedule, Figure 54.10, is identical to Version 9 except that deltas and bars are used instead of bars, alone. Anticipated and actual slippages are shown through the use of diamonds.

54.11 Schedule—In-Process—Version 11: Another approach to showing overlapping processing steps is displayed in Figure 54.11. In this example, different symbols are used for each processing step. This approach eliminates the need for the alpha code that was necessary on the previously shown Version 10; however, multiple symbols of this nature sometimes confuse, rather than help, the chart reader.

54.12 Schedule—In-Process—Version 12: A typewritten version of an in-process schedule is shown in Figure 54.12. In this example, the letter P is used to represent the "procure parts" process, the letter A for "assembly," and the letter T for "test." Slippages are shown with the letter O. Completions are shown by crossing out letters.

54.13 Schedule—In-Process—Version 13: A complex style of an in-process schedule is shown as Version 13, Figure 54.13. In this example, the processing steps are shown in the left-hand column while the plan, itself, is in segmented bar form and is coded in terms of production lot numbers. Black chart tape is used to show progress. In this example, all processes are shown to be on schedule as of the end of the week of January 20, except process number 4 where production lot number 3 is shown to be a half a week behind schedule.

54.14 Schedule—In-Process—Version 14: For some applications, such as when production units are grouped into lots, a step line style of chart can sometimes be used. An example of one is shown in Figure 54.14. Each of the four lines shown in this example is coded differently for each of the separate processing events: start fabrication, start assembly, start test, and ship. Status is shown by shading that portion of the plan that is complete. Diamonds are used to show anticipated and actual slippages from schedule.

54.15 Schedule—In-Process—Version 15: Figure 54.15 shows a curve line chart approach to an in-process schedule. The method for displaying actual accomplishment in relationship to the plan, in this example, departs from normal practice. In this method, the solid line representing actual accomplishment is plotted directly on top of the plan line, and its progress along that line is in terms of the quality scale, only, indicating the number of units actually completed as of the reporting date. In the example, the "start fabrication" and "start assembly" events are seen to be on schedule. The "start test" event is behind schedule, the plan calling for approximately 84 units as of the reporting date whereas only approximately 80 items have actually been started. Regarding shipments, the example shows 60 should have been shipped as of the reporting date whereas only 40 have actually been shipped. A disadvantage of this style of updating is that historical performance cannot be graphically seen.

54.16 Schedule—In-Process—Version 16: A highly regarded type of in-process schedule is shown in Figure 54.16. It is commonly called a "line of balance" chart, and it consists of three elements:

a. A production set-back chart which graphically depicts the work flow in terms of lead time requirements.
b. A cumulative deliveries chart displaying scheduled and actual deliveries of the end product.
c. A progress chart where current status of each process is displayed in bar chart form against a "line of balance" plotted new for each reporting period (July 1, in the example).

Each bar on the progress chart corresponds directly with one of the processing elements on the production set-back chart. The line of balance is constructed for each reporting period in the following manner: The lead time for each element is picked off from the production set-back chart. (In the case of process 1, "Fab. Parts," in the example, this is 32 days.) The lead time for each element process is plotted to the right of the "time-now" line on the cumulative deliveries chart. Then, vertical lines are drawn until they intersect with the schedule line. From these points horizontal lines are drawn to the right, giving the line of balance for each work element process.

In interpreting status from the progress chart, it is normal to start at the right-hand side (process 11 in the example). In the example, shipments are behind schedule by 4 units (also discernible on the cumulative deliveries chart). Working to the left, it can be seen that the cause for the behind-schedule condition appears to be process 2, Purchase Parts, the earliest item on the work flow which reflects a behind-schedule status.

54.17 Schedule—In-Process—Version 17: The line of balance chart shown as Version 17, Figure 54.17, is identical to Version 16 except that the separate processing categories (such as purchasing, fabrication, assembly) have been individually coded. This has been done to more easily relate the process elements on the production set-back portion of the chart to their corresponding bars on the progress chart.

54.18 Schedule—In-Process—Version 18: The line of balance chart shown in Figure 54.18 is similar to those shown as Versions 16 and 17. Added to this version is the quantities breakdown shown in the lower left-hand corner of the chart. In this example, the cumulative schedule and progress charts show status to be five units behind schedule as of the reporting date of May 1. Examination of the progress chart shows that the problem is apparently in the test area, the earliest part of the process cycle showing a behind-schedule position.

54.19 Schedule—In-Process—Version 19: A unique method of displaying in-process plans and status is shown in Figure 54.19. In this approach, bars are constructed on the basis of a work flow diagram as with the previously shown line of balance charts. Each bar represents a separate process step. The length of the bar is based on the overall schedule, but each bar is segmented according to its own separate quantity requirement. In the example, for instance, 280 separate purchased parts are required to produce 40 units. Progress is shown using chart tape laid out to show the actual number of units that have been completed in each of the separate processes at the time of the report.

54.20 Schedule—In-Process—Version 20: Version 20 of an in-process schedule, Figure 54.20, is identical to Version 19 except that instead of showing the work flow diagram, the process elements are listed by name, together with their lead times, quantities required for each unit, and the total quantities scheduled.

54.21 Schedule—In-Process—Version 21: Individual line charts can be used to show each of the separate processes required to produce a single type of end product. An example of this is shown in Figure 54.21. In this example, each of the eight separate processes is on schedule except "Sub-Assembly A" and "Inspect." Flags or arrows could be used to highlight the behind-schedule portions of the chart to more quickly draw the chart reader's eyes to the problems.

54.22 Schedule—In-Process—Version 22: Separate "deviation from plan" charts can be used to show the status relative to the individual processes required to produce a given end item. An example of this is shown in Figure 54.22. Behind-schedule positions can usually be recognized more readily on this type of chart than on that shown in Version 21.

54.23 Schedule—In-Process—Version 23: A totally statistical method for showing in-process schedule plans and actual progress is shown as Version 23, Figure 54.23. In a detailed chart of this nature, it is usually best to emphasize anomalies. In this example, the behind-schedule condition in process 4 is emphasized by showing the statistic (-72) in heavy numerals.

54.24 Schedule—In-Process—Version 24: If there are a relatively few processing steps in a cycle, a full complement of statistics can be shown in table form as illustrated in Version 24 of an in-process schedule, Figure 54.24. In this example, scheduled and actual performance are shown in terms of rate and cumulative statistics. The cum. variance is also shown, as well as a recovery plan. The example shows the system test to be behind schedule by one unit, and recovery is expected during the week following the report date.

54.25 Schedule—In-Process—Version 25: A "box score" version of an in-process schedule is shown in Figure 54.25. This table is constructed so as to quickly focus the chart reader's attention on the problem. In this example, process number 3 is shown to be two units behind schedule, with an anticipated recovery date of February 10. This type of chart has the advantage of quickly showing status in terms of problems, but it has the disadvantage of having to be totally redone for each reporting period.

54.26 Schedule—In-Process—Version 26: Another version of a box score is shown in Figure 54.26. This is identical to Version 25 except that status is shown in terms of percentages rather than quantities of units scheduled and completed. This approach is sometimes useful when dealing with high production quantities.

54.27 Schedule—In-Process—Version 27: The box score

Schedules—In-Process

style of in-process schedule shown in Figure 54.27 uses parts, or units, in the left-hand column rather than processing steps, as was used on the previous box score versions. The processing steps, themselves (sheet metal, weld, etc.), are shown to the right of each part. This example shows stock number A-500-3 to be behind schedule in process steps 2 through 5. The most critical behind-schedule portion of the total process (weld) is check-marked to more readily lead the chart reader's eyes to this portion of the table.

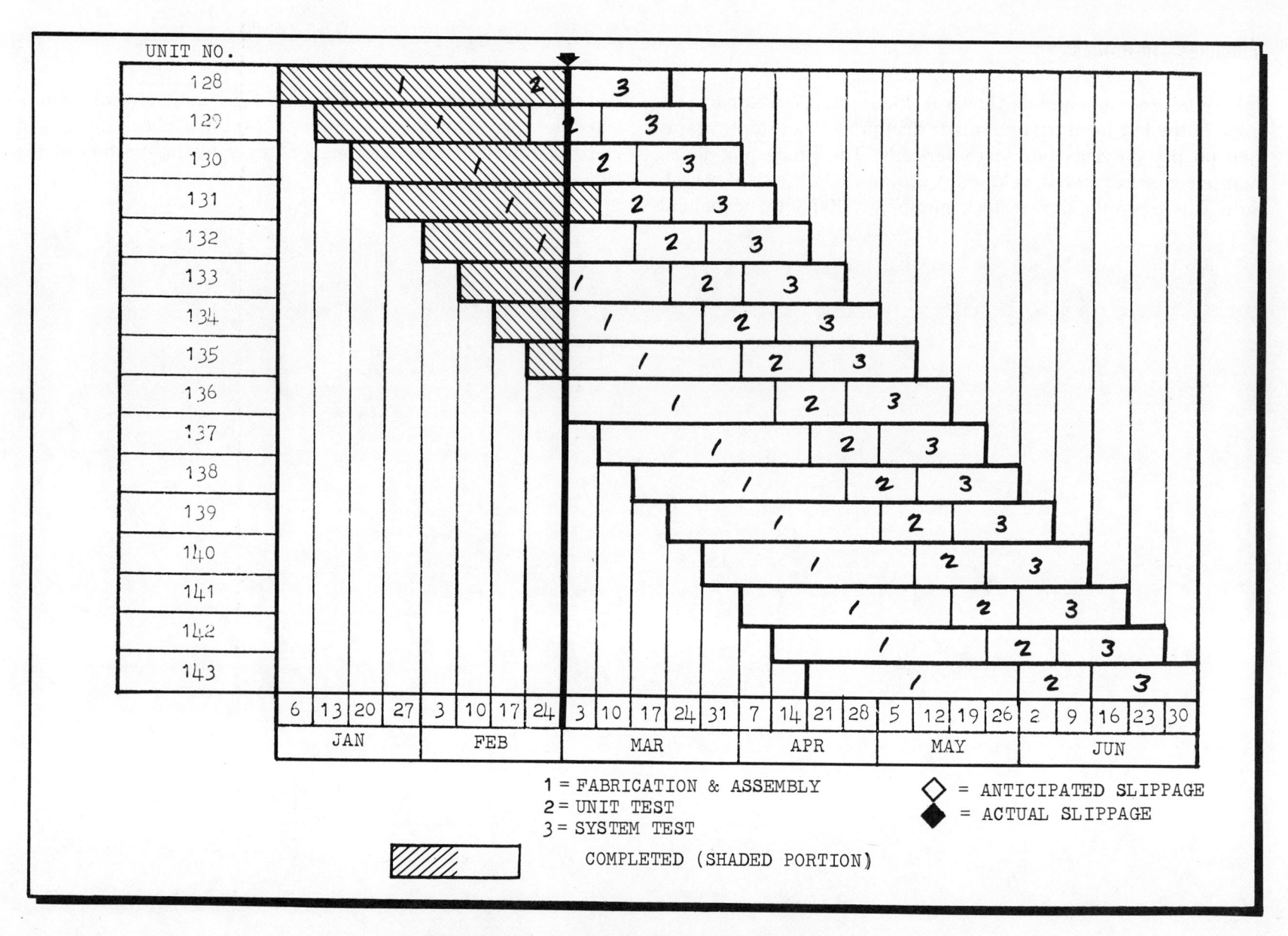

Figure 54.1 Schedule—In-Process—Version 1

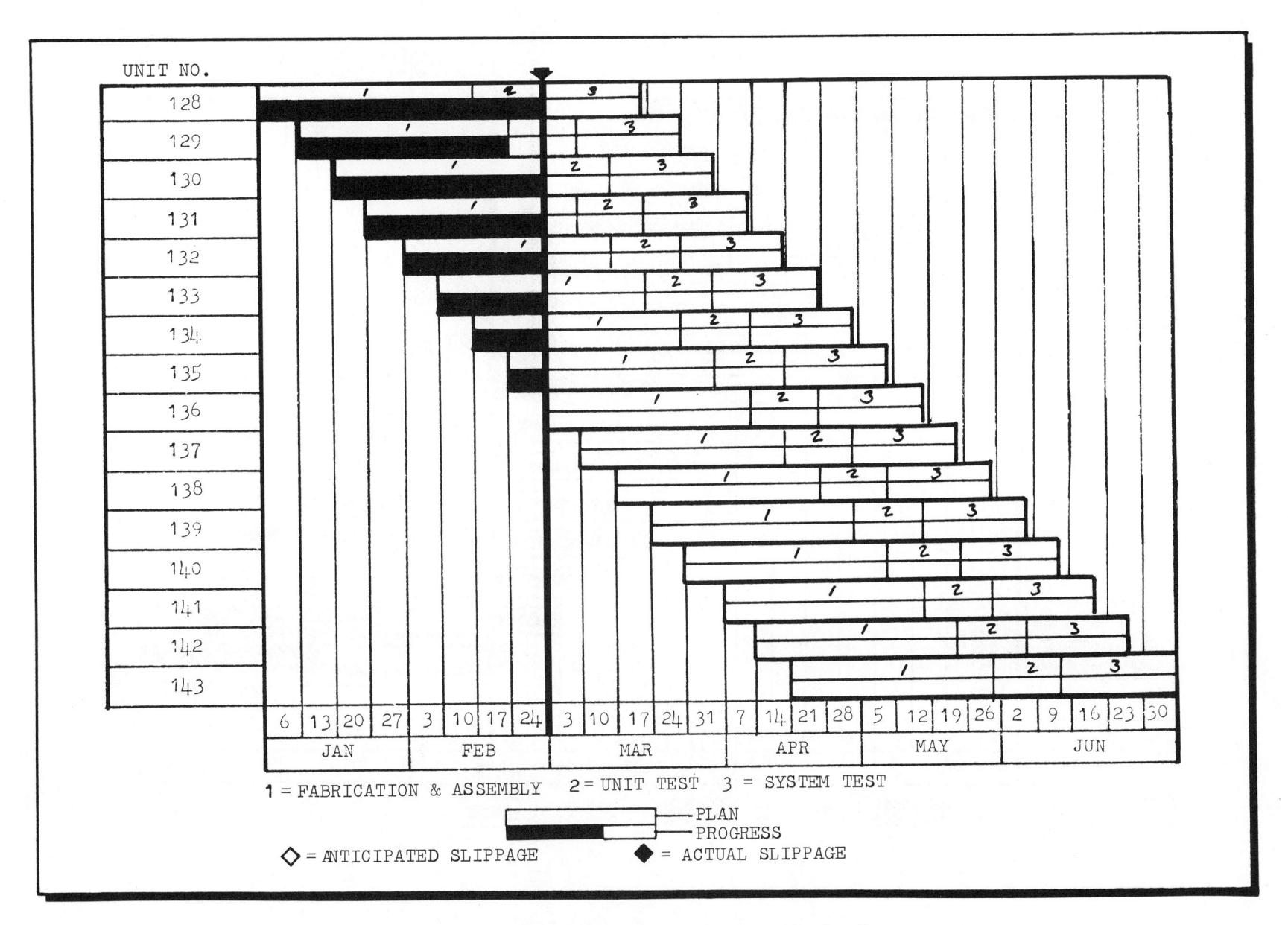

Figure 54.2　Schedule—In-Process—Version 2

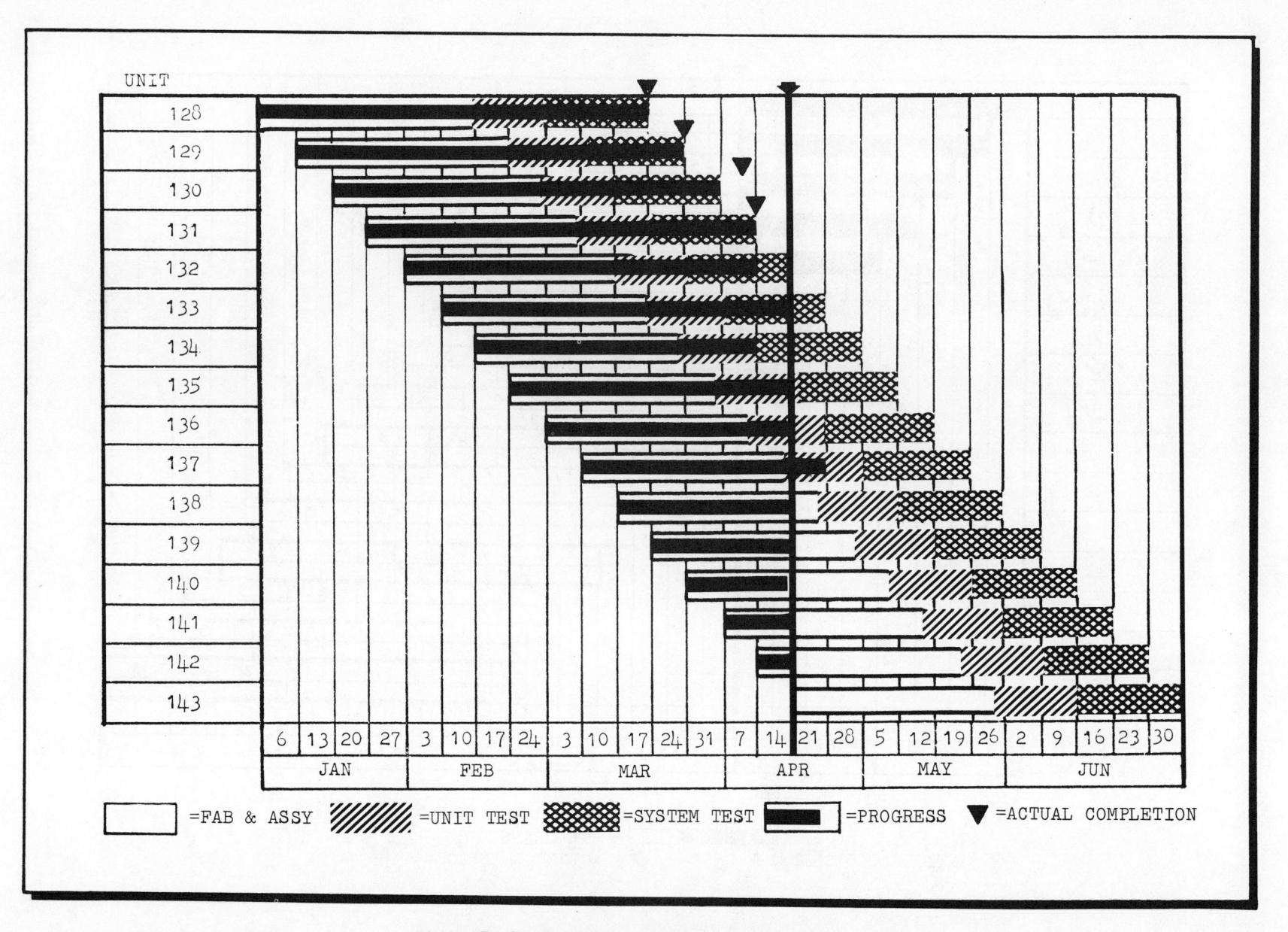

Figure 54.3   Schedule—In-Process—Version 3

718

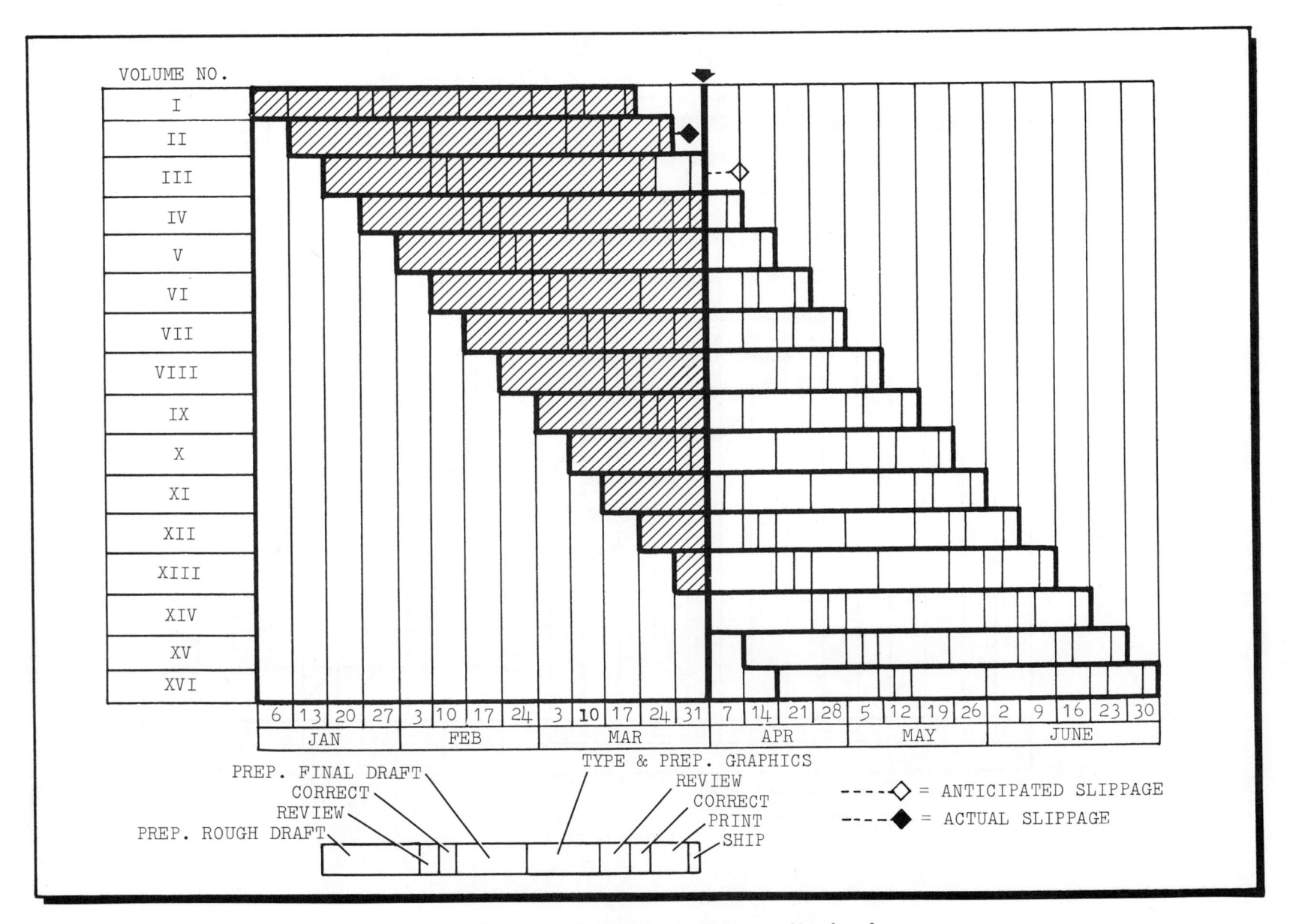

Figure 54.4 Schedule—In-Process—Version 4

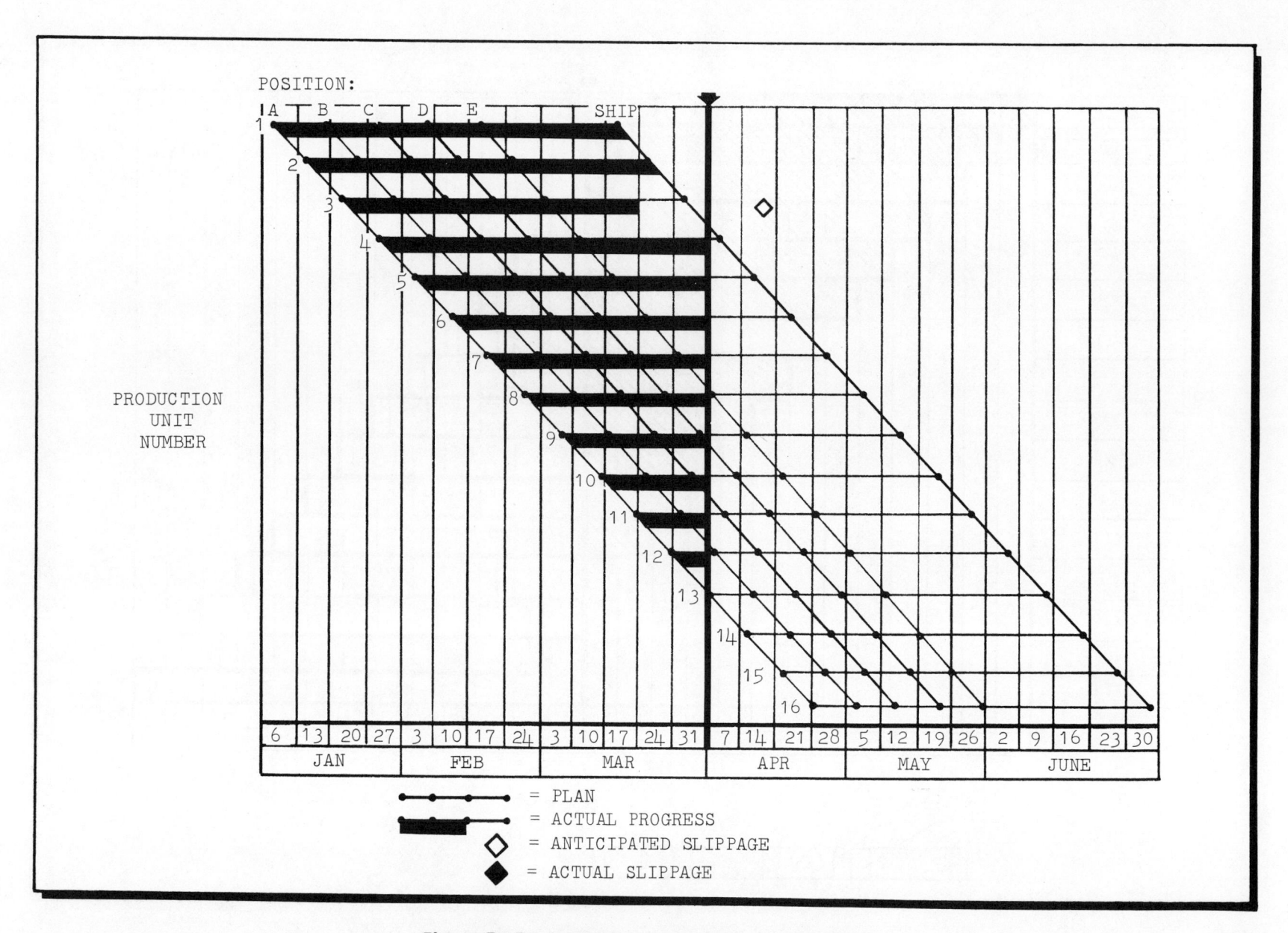

Figure 54.5   Schedule—In-Process—Version 5

720

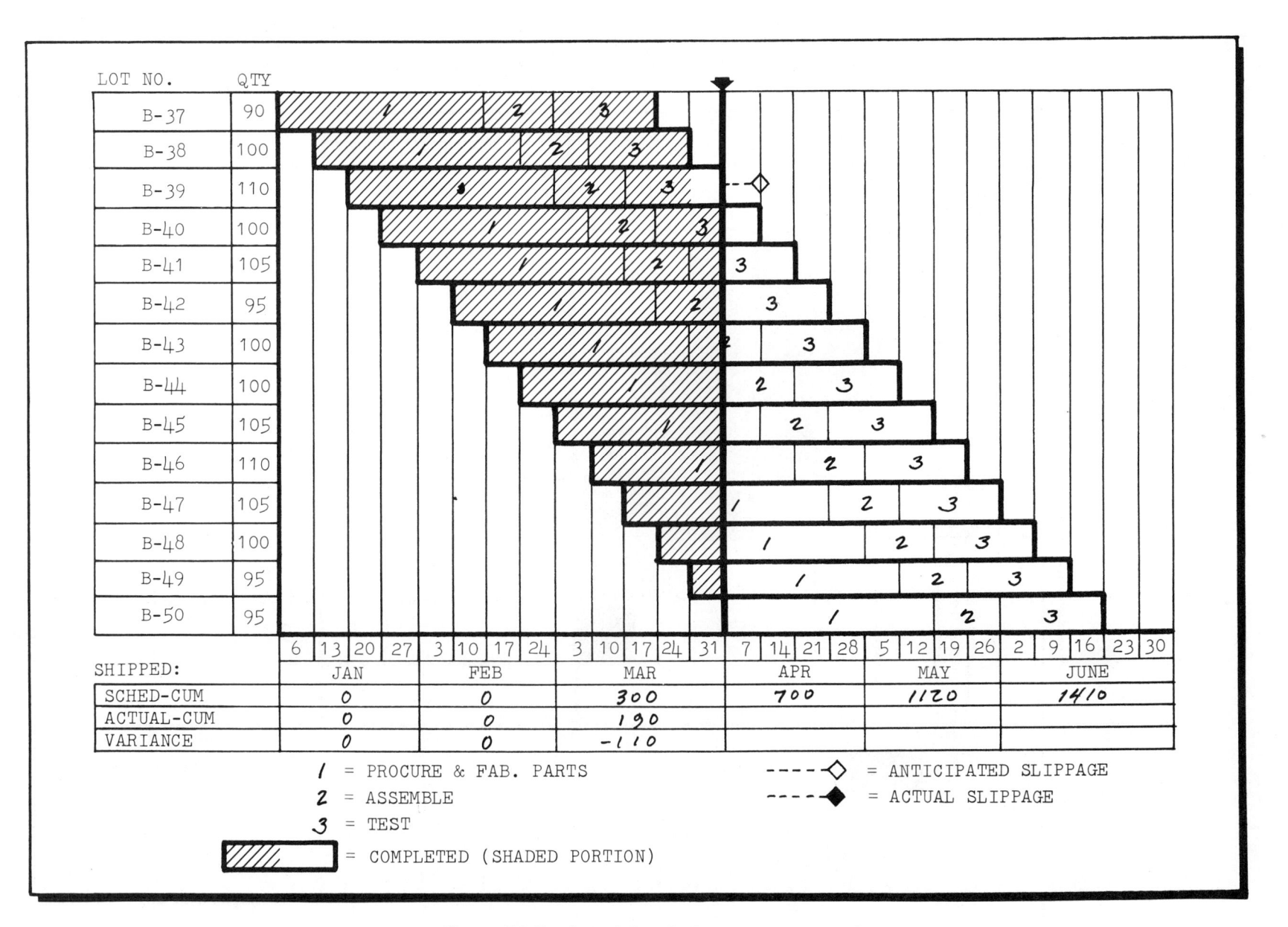

LOT NO.	QTY
B-37	90
B-38	100
B-39	110
B-40	100
B-41	105
B-42	95
B-43	100
B-44	100
B-45	105
B-46	110
B-47	105
B-48	100
B-49	95
B-50	95

SHIPPED:	JAN	FEB	MAR	APR	MAY	JUNE
SCHED-CUM	0	0	300	700	1120	1410
ACTUAL-CUM	0	0	190			
VARIANCE	0	0	-110			

1 = PROCURE & FAB. PARTS
2 = ASSEMBLE
3 = TEST
◇ (dashed) = ANTICIPATED SLIPPAGE
◆ (dashed) = ACTUAL SLIPPAGE
▨ = COMPLETED (SHADED PORTION)

Figure 54.6 Schedule—In-Process—Version 6

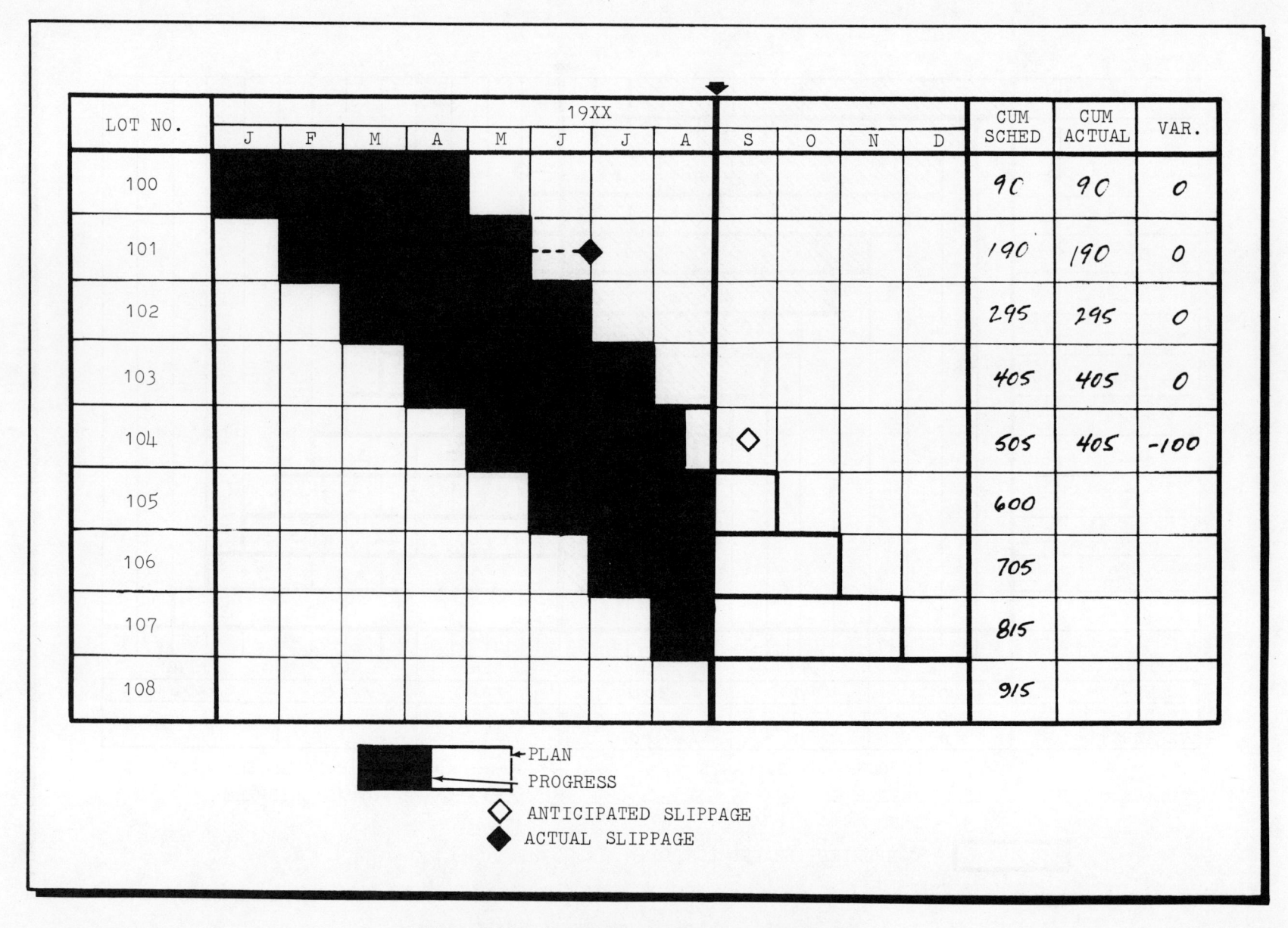

LOT NO.	19XX												CUM SCHED	CUM ACTUAL	VAR.
	J	F	M	A	M	J	J	A	S	O	N	D			
100													90	90	0
101							◆						190	190	0
102													295	295	0
103													405	405	0
104									◇				505	405	-100
105													600		
106													705		
107													815		
108													915		

◻ PLAN
◼ PROGRESS
◇ ANTICIPATED SLIPPAGE
◆ ACTUAL SLIPPAGE

Figure 54.7   Schedule—In-Process—Version 7

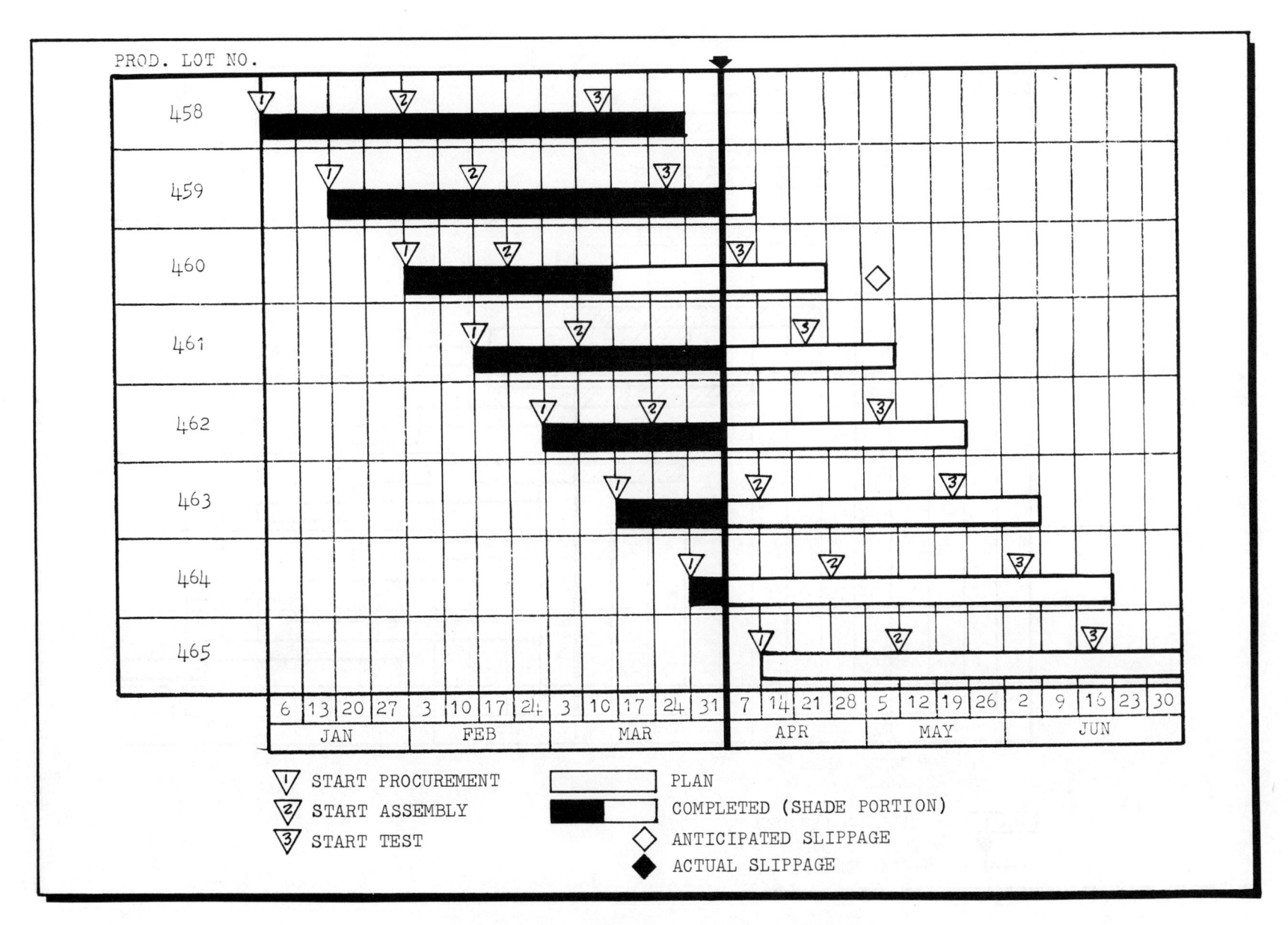

Figure 54.8 Schedule—In-Process—Version 8

723

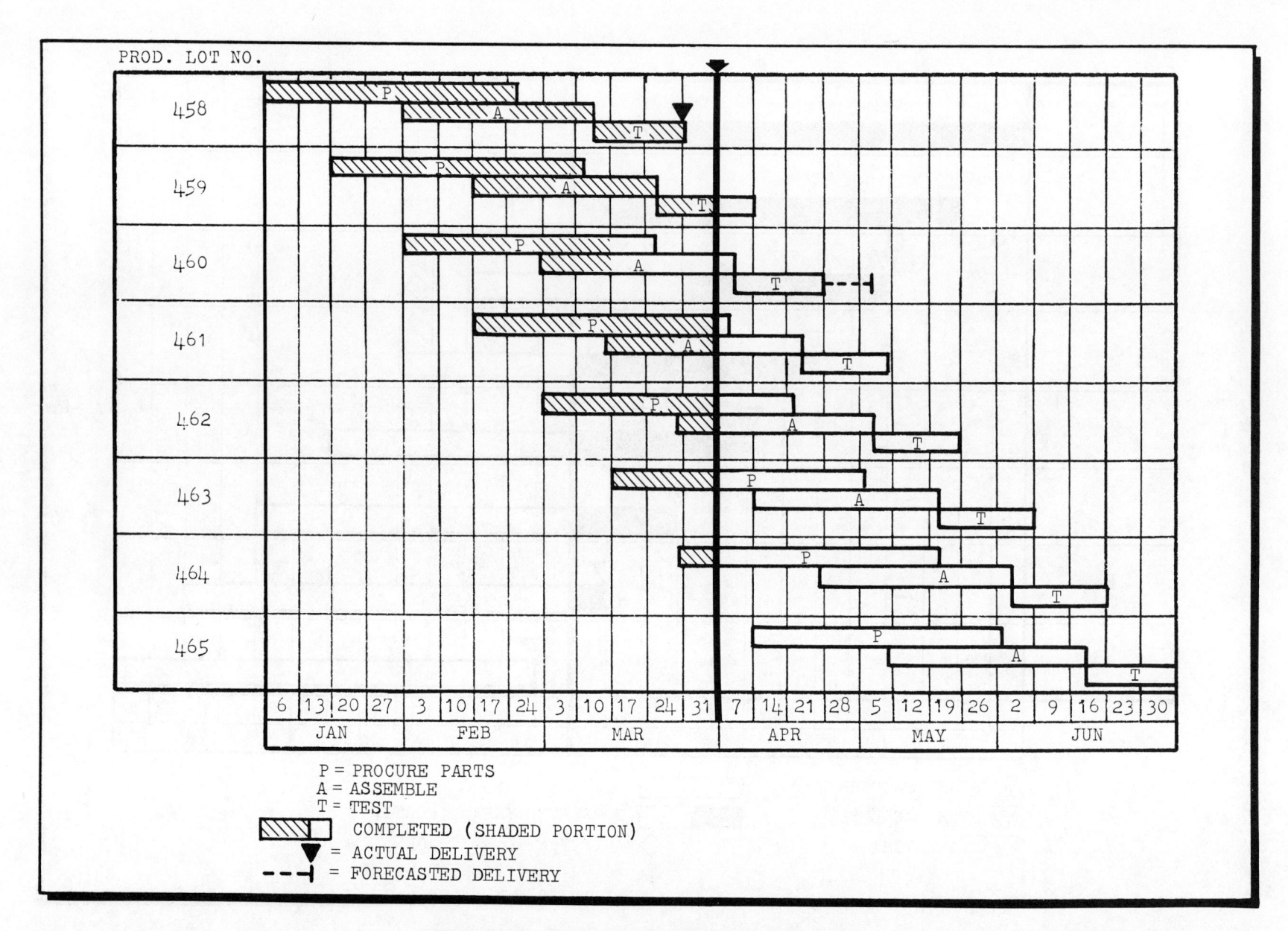

Figure 54.9 Schedule—In-Process—Version 9

724

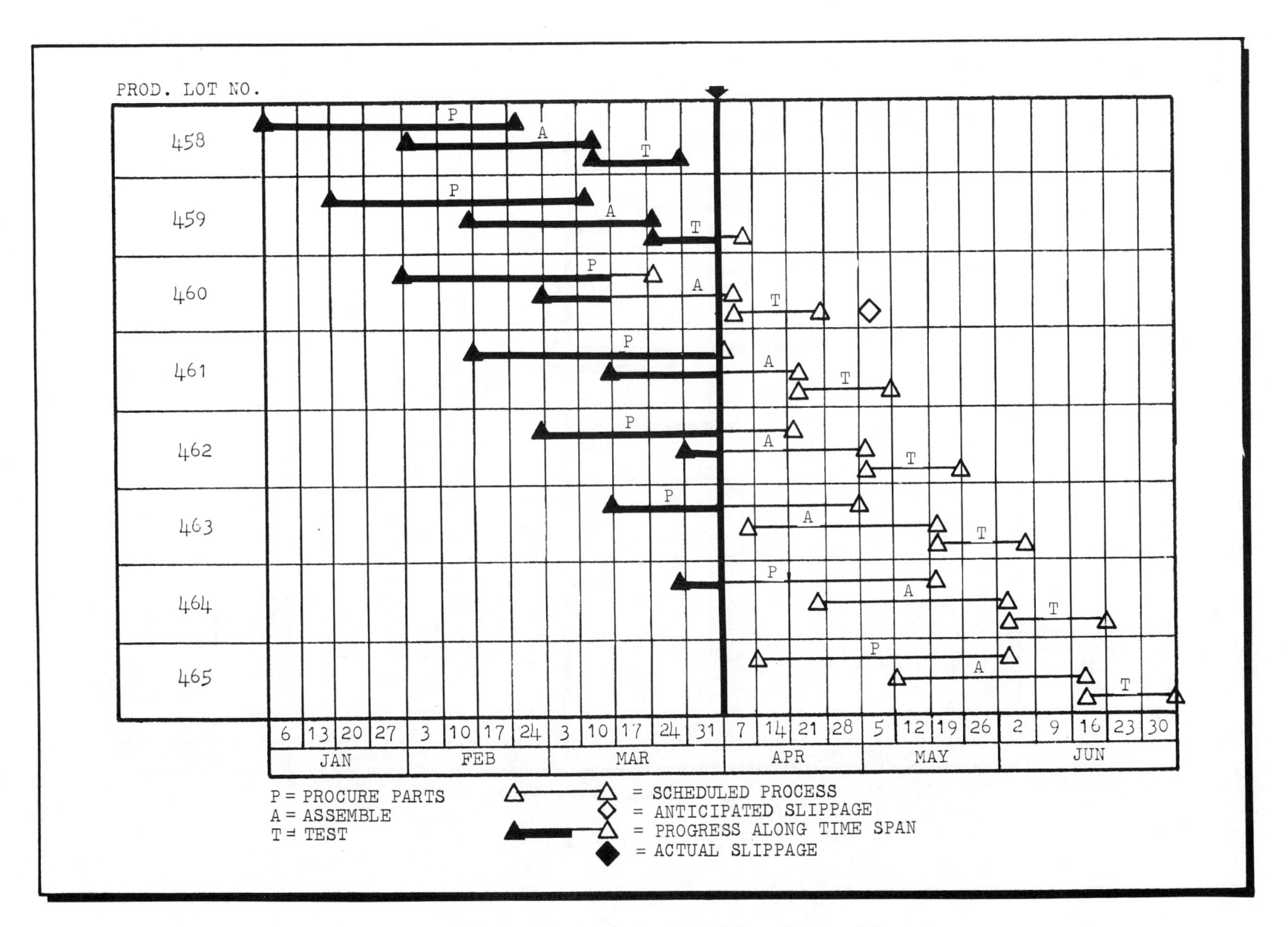

Figure 54.10 Schedule—In-Process—Version 10

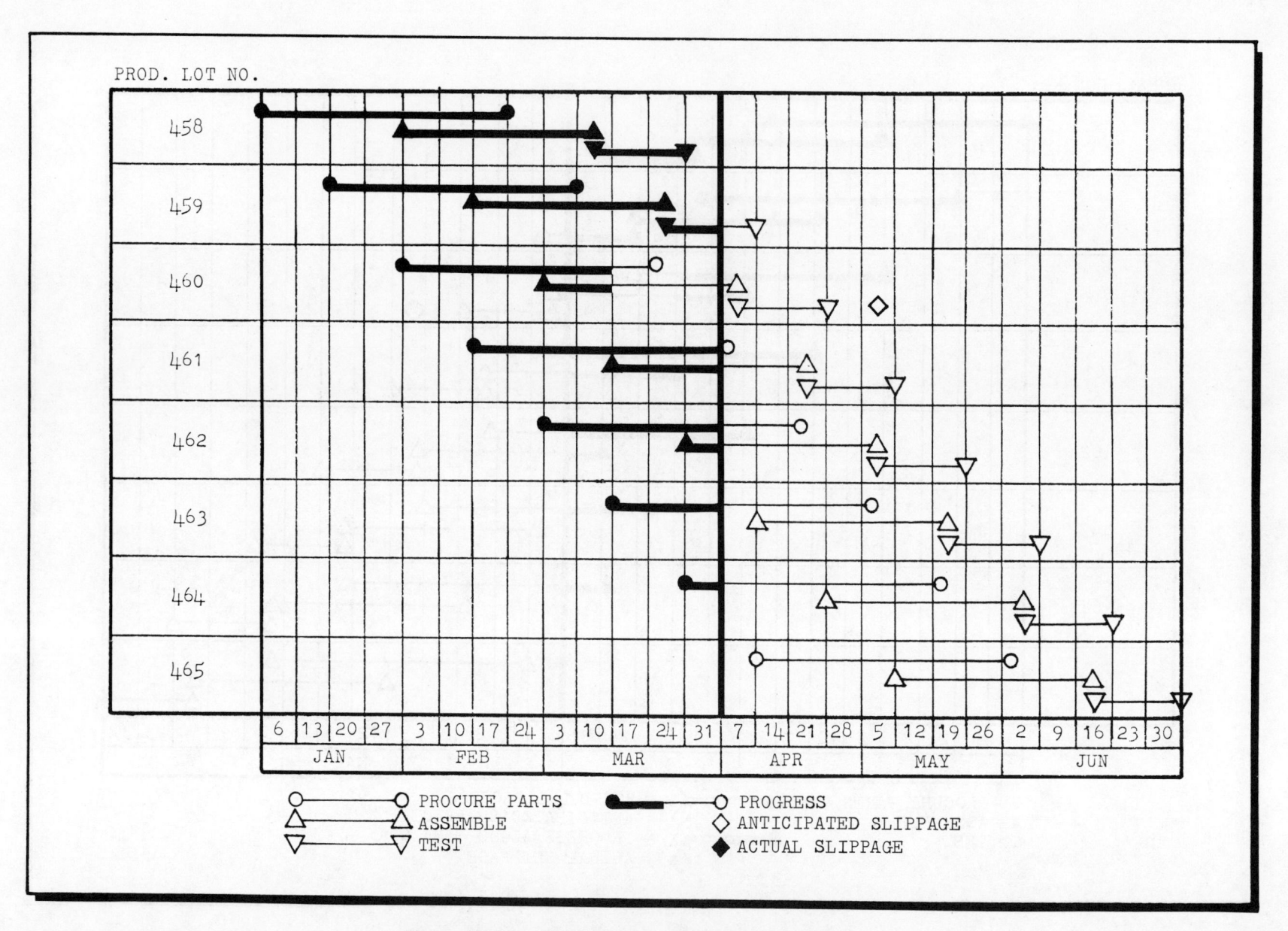

Figure 54.11 Schedule—In-Process—Version 11

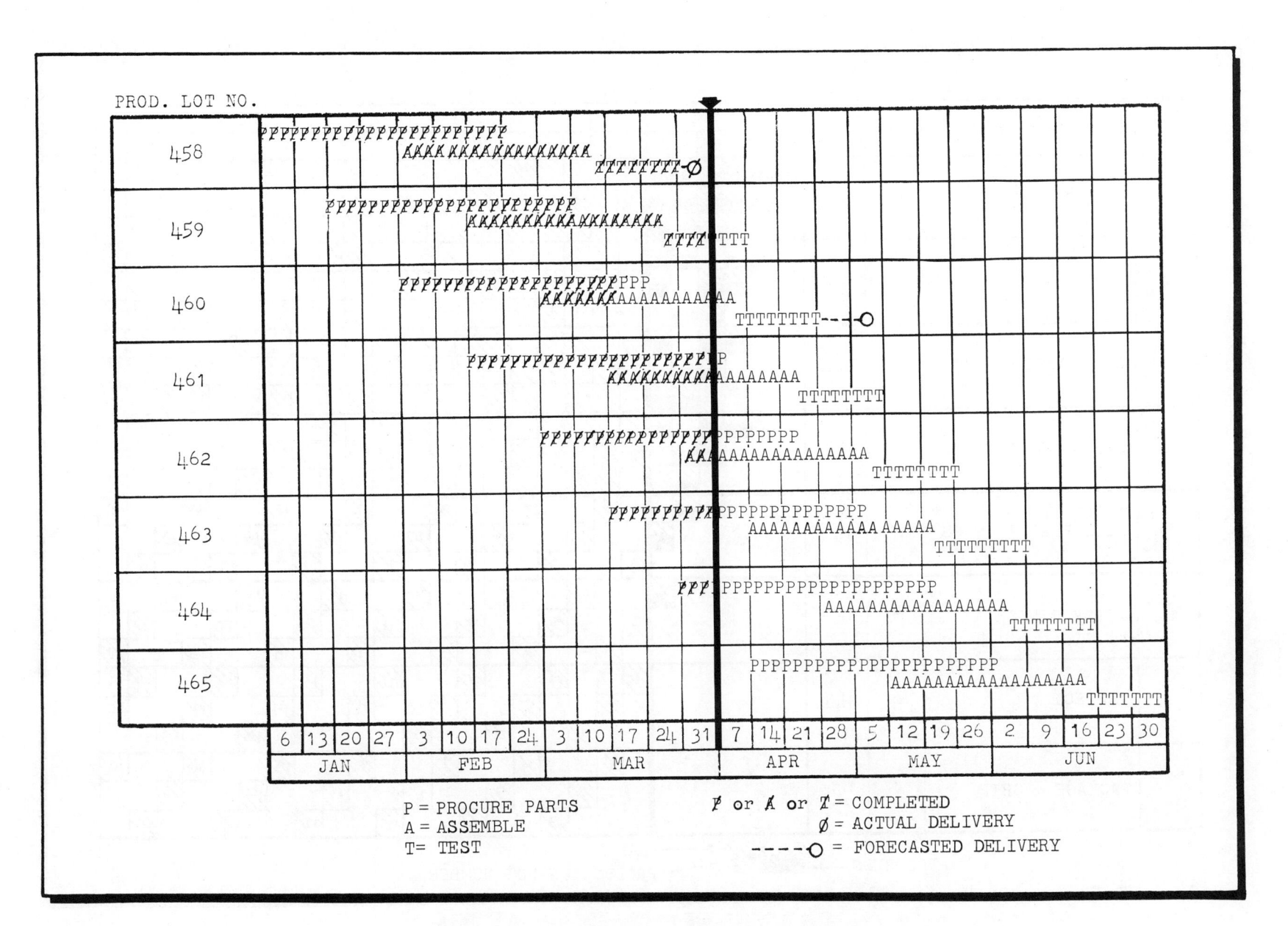

Figure 54.12 Schedule—In-Process—Version 12

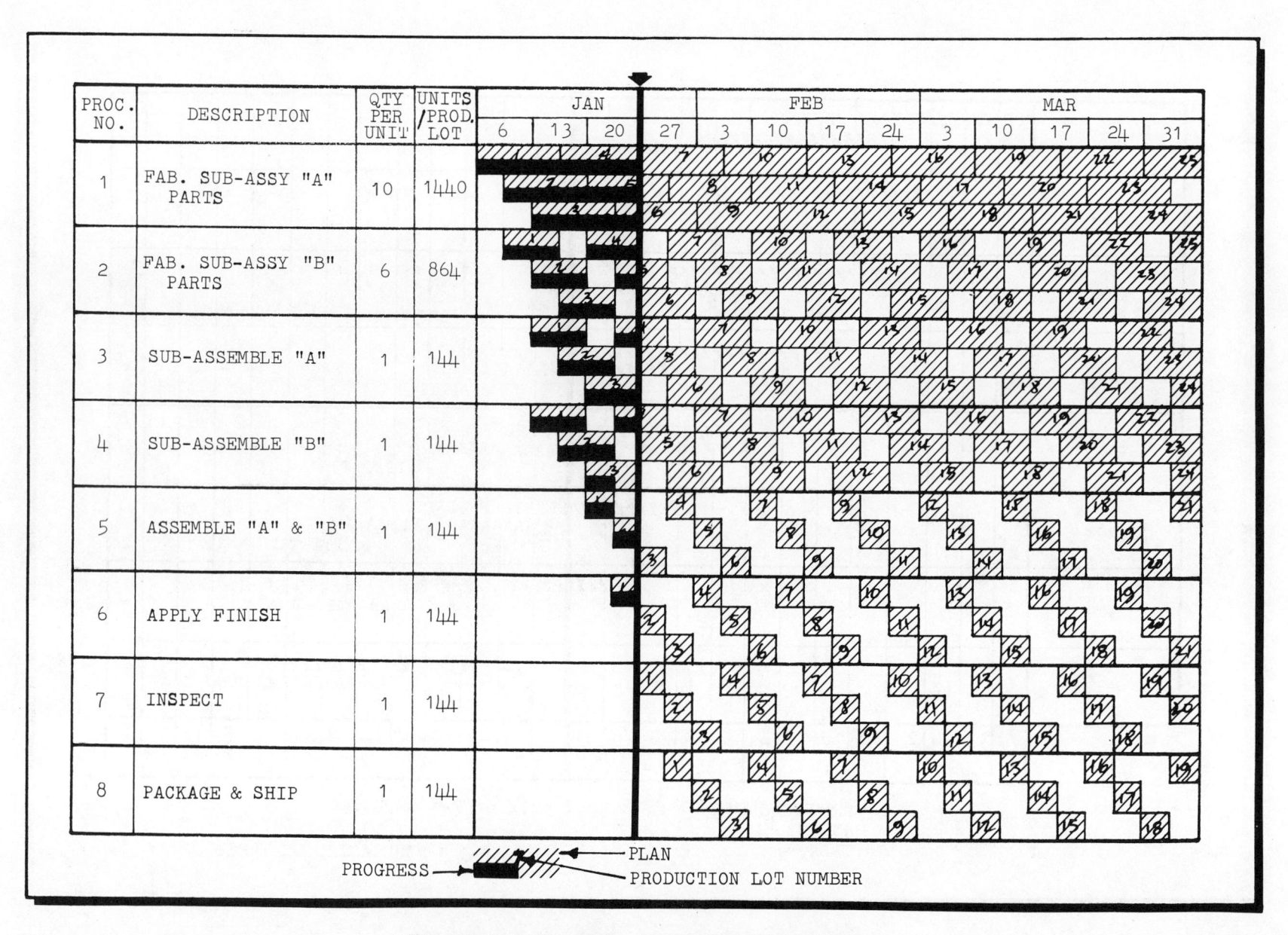

PROC. NO.	DESCRIPTION	QTY PER UNIT	UNITS /PROD. LOT	JAN				FEB				MAR				
				6	13	20	27	3	10	17	24	3	10	17	24	31
1	FAB. SUB-ASSY "A" PARTS	10	1440													
2	FAB. SUB-ASSY "B" PARTS	6	864													
3	SUB-ASSEMBLE "A"	1	144													
4	SUB-ASSEMBLE "B"	1	144													
5	ASSEMBLE "A" & "B"	1	144													
6	APPLY FINISH	1	144													
7	INSPECT	1	144													
8	PACKAGE & SHIP	1	144													

PROGRESS ▬ ▨ ◀— PLAN
PRODUCTION LOT NUMBER

Figure 54.13　Schedule—In-Process—Version 13

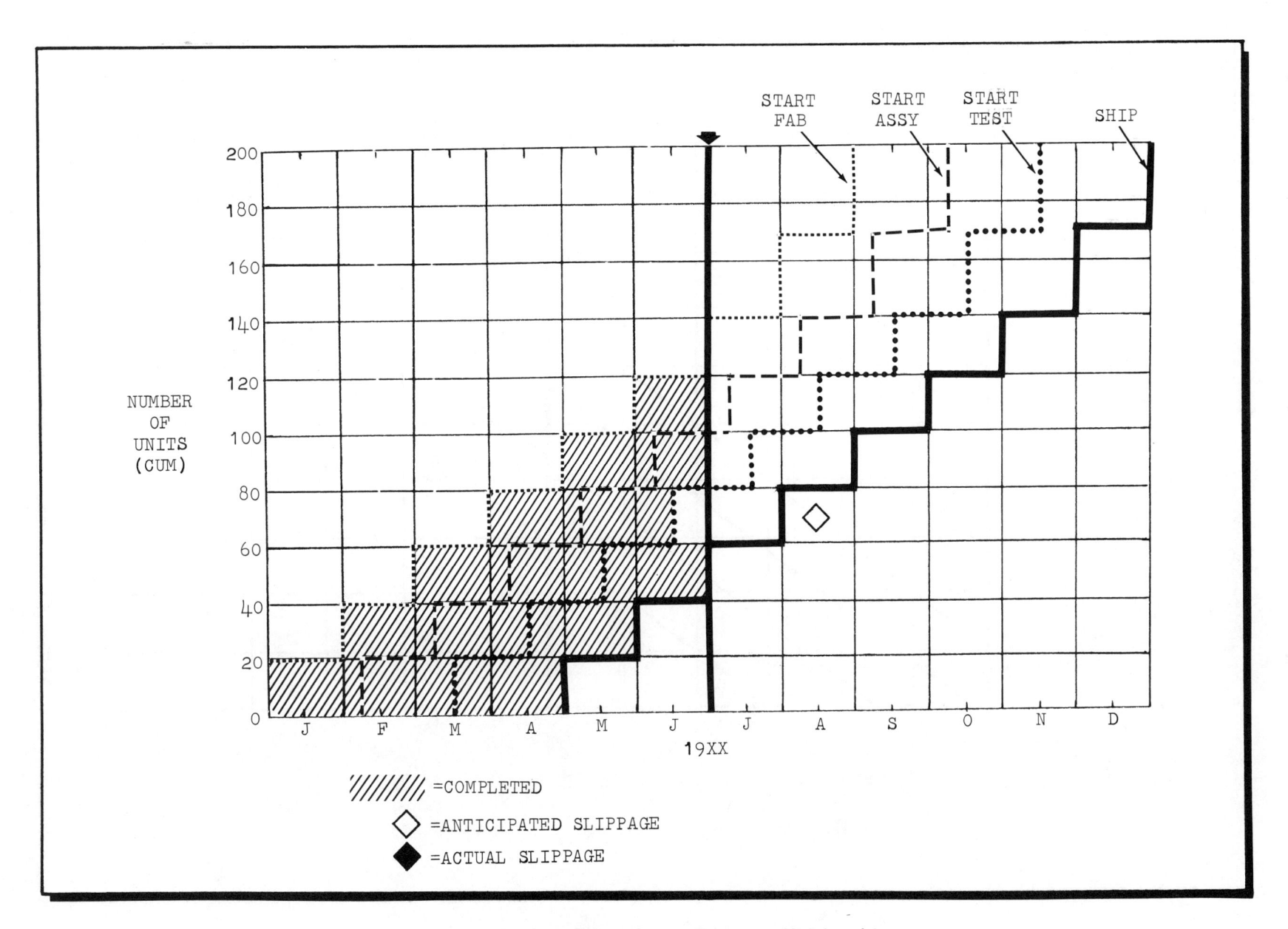

Figure 54.14   Schedule—In-Process—Version 14

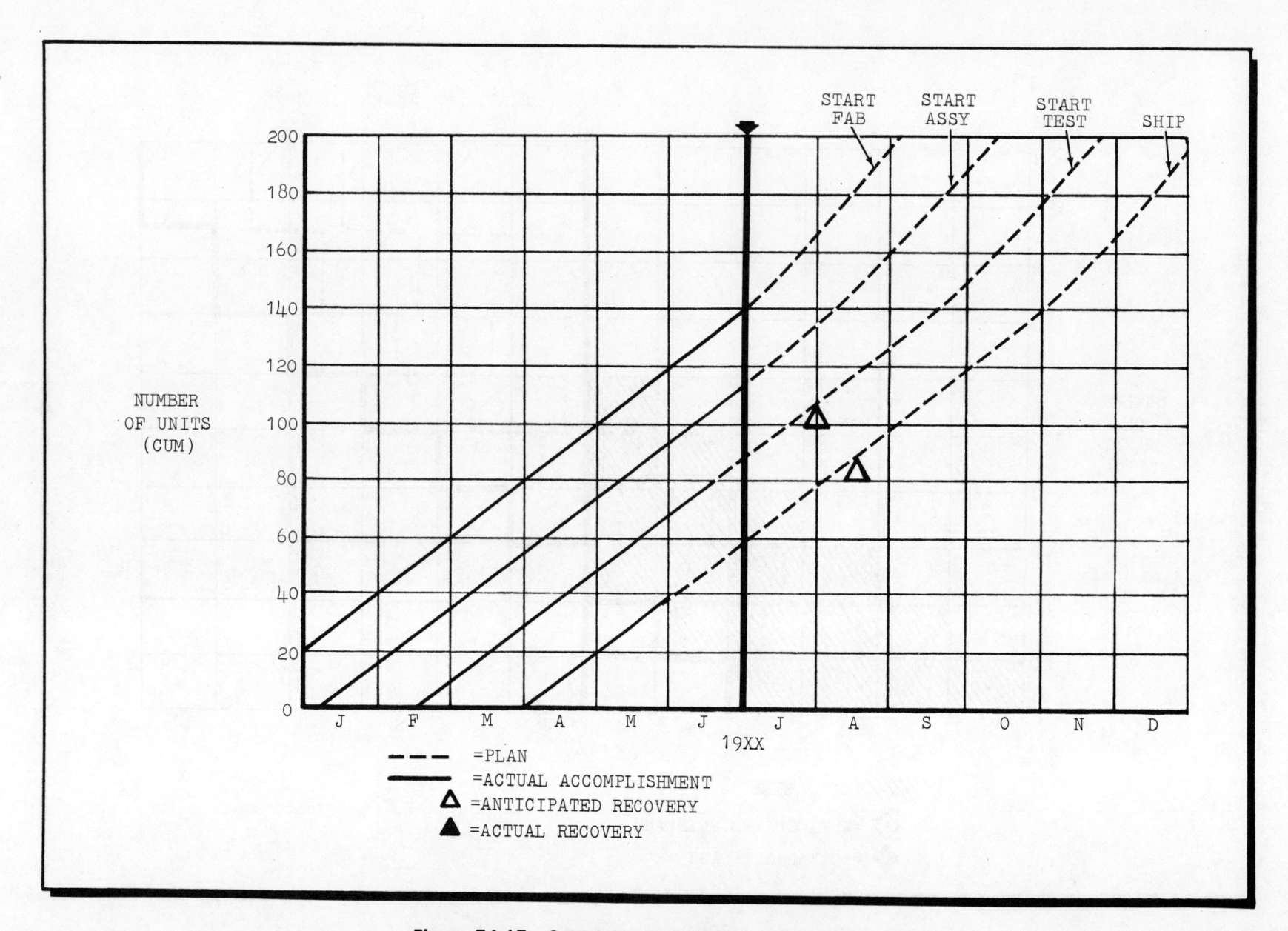

Figure 54.15   Schedule—In-Process—Version 15

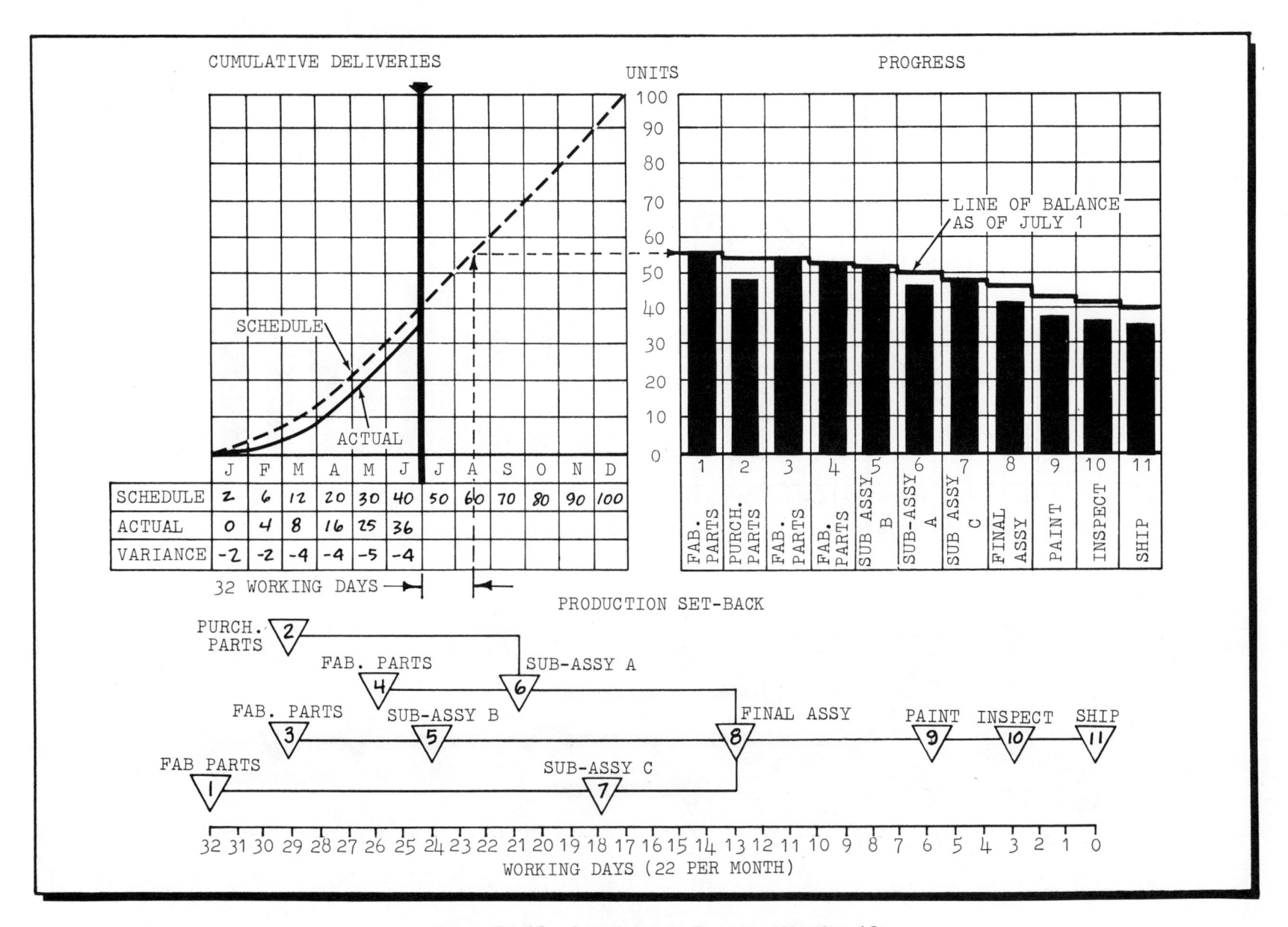

Figure 54.16 Schedule—In-Process—Version 16

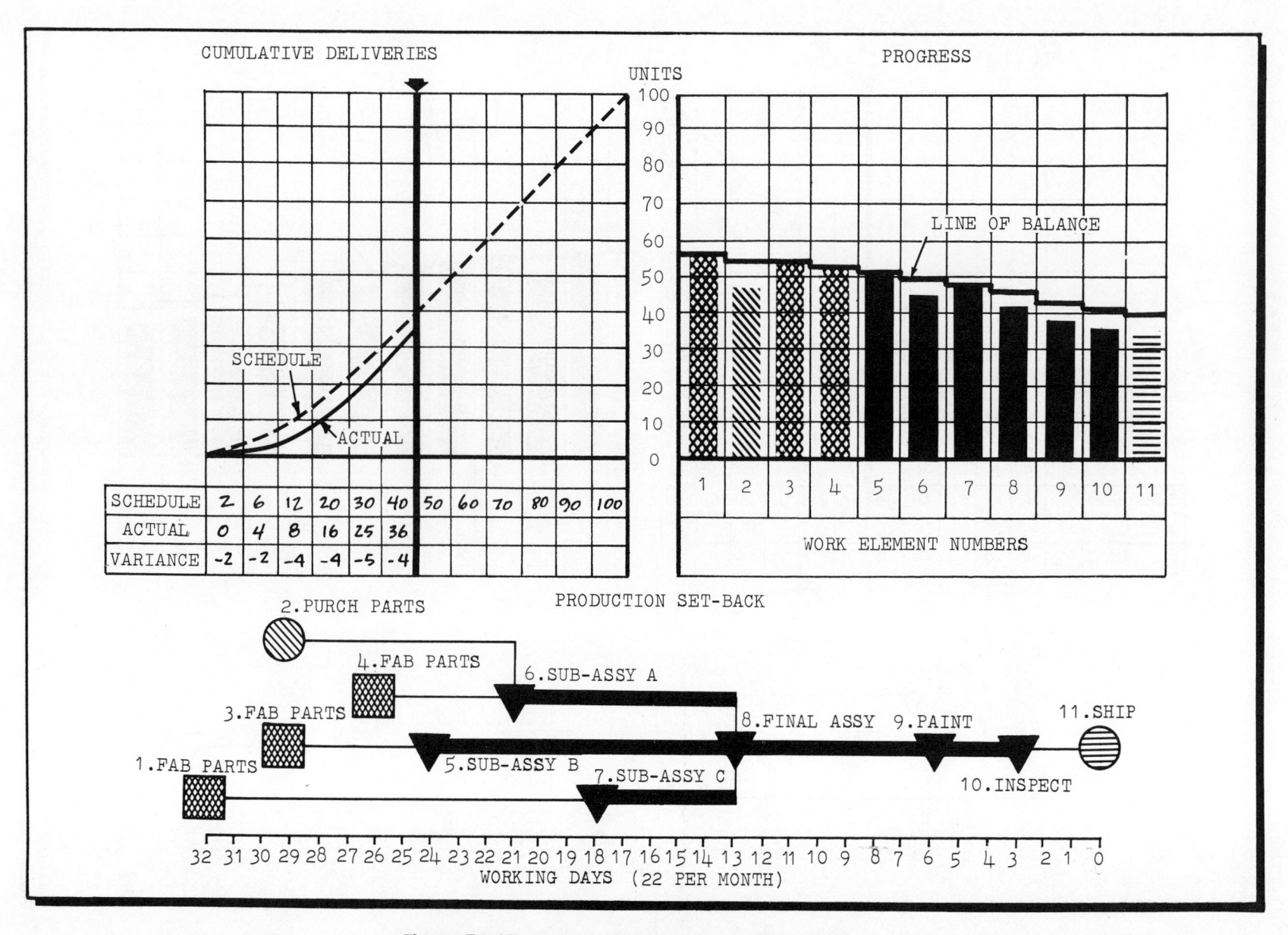

Figure 54.17 Schedule—In-Process—Version 17

CUMULATIVE DELIVERIES

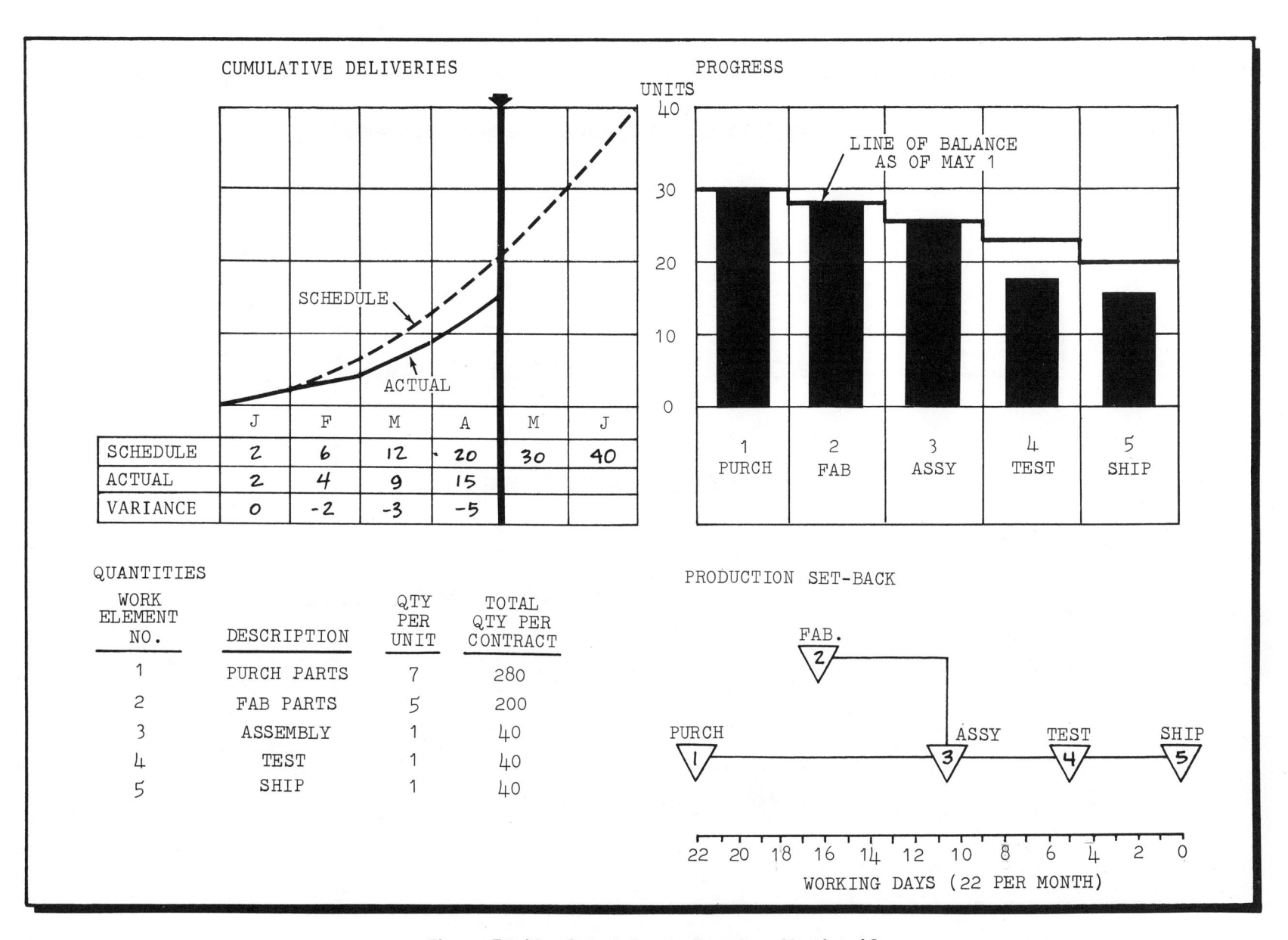

	J	F	M	A	M	J
SCHEDULE	2	6	12	20	30	40
ACTUAL	2	4	9	15		
VARIANCE	0	-2	-3	-5		

PROGRESS

LINE OF BALANCE AS OF MAY 1

1 PURCH — 2 FAB — 3 ASSY — 4 TEST — 5 SHIP

QUANTITIES

WORK ELEMENT NO.	DESCRIPTION	QTY PER UNIT	TOTAL QTY PER CONTRACT
1	PURCH PARTS	7	280
2	FAB PARTS	5	200
3	ASSEMBLY	1	40
4	TEST	1	40
5	SHIP	1	40

PRODUCTION SET-BACK

PURCH (1) — ASSY (3) — TEST (4) — SHIP (5); FAB (2) feeds into ASSY (3)

WORKING DAYS (22 PER MONTH): 22 20 18 16 14 12 10 8 6 4 2 0

Figure 54.18 Schedule—In-Process—Version 18

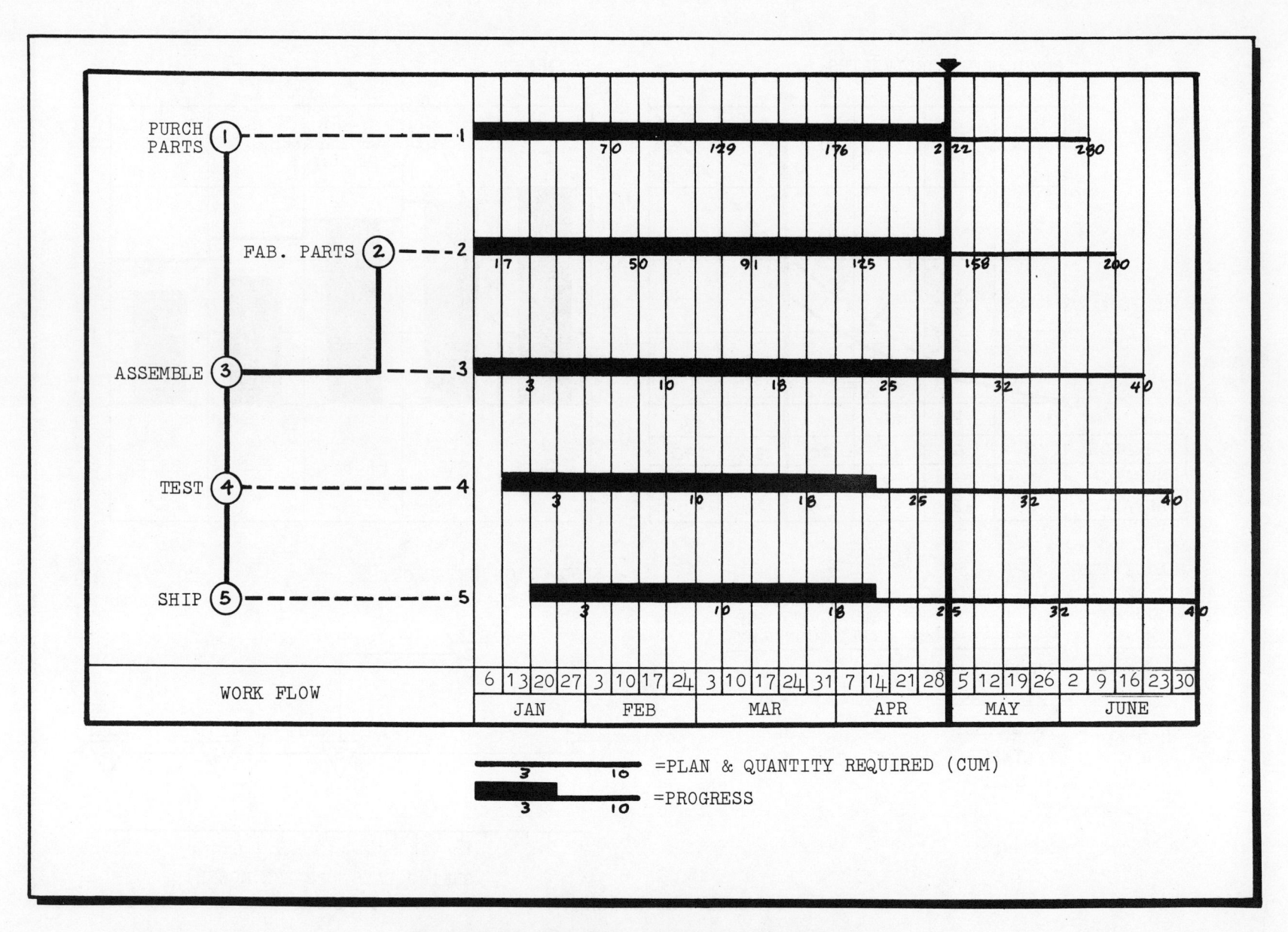

Figure 54.19 Schedule—In-Process—Version 19

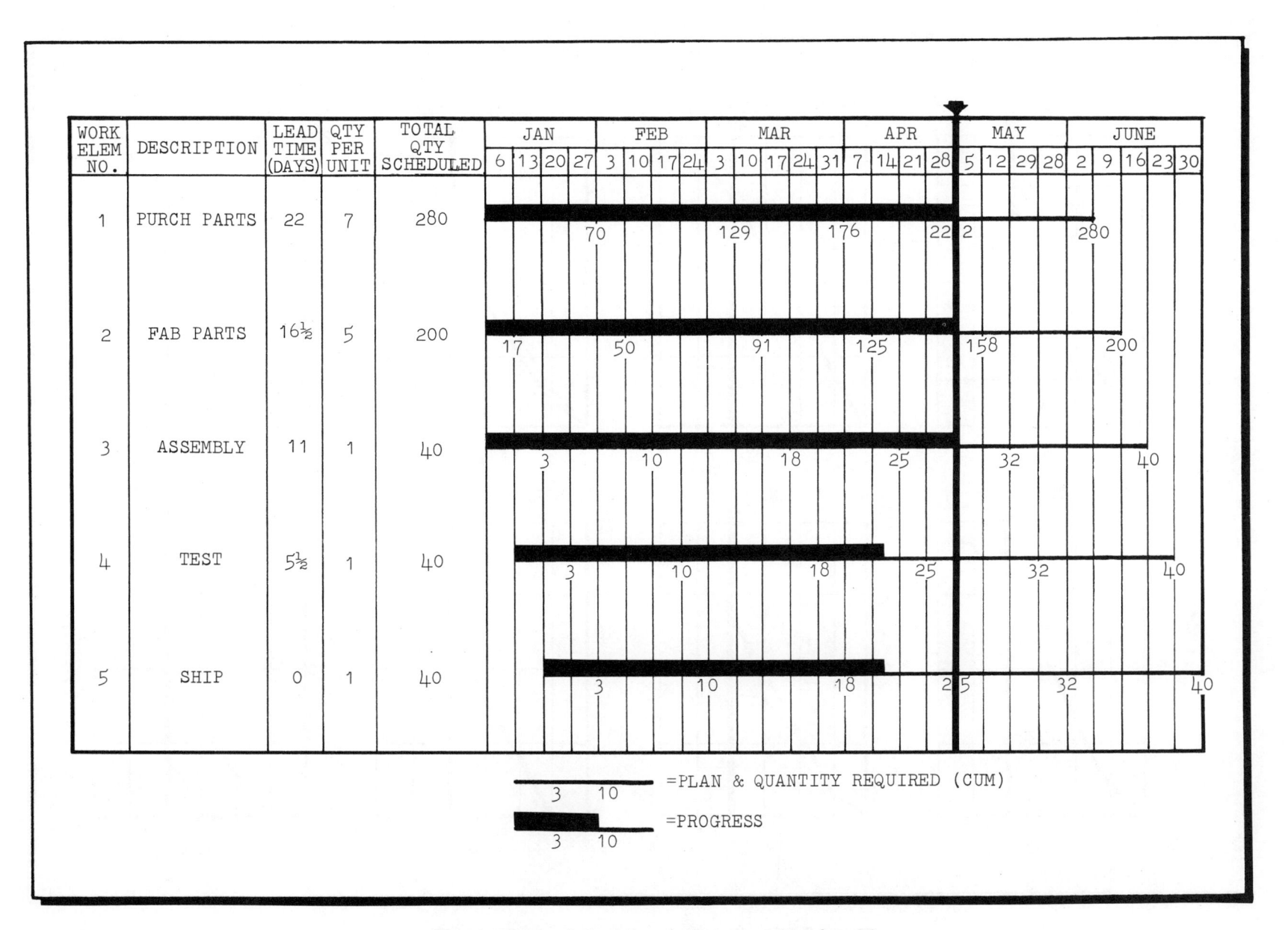

WORK ELEM NO.	DESCRIPTION	LEAD TIME (DAYS)	QTY PER UNIT	TOTAL QTY SCHEDULED	JAN 6	13	20	27	FEB 3	10	17	24	MAR 3	10	17	24	31	APR 7	14	21	28	MAY 5	12	29	28	JUNE 2	9	16	23	30
1	PURCH PARTS	22	7	280						70				129				176			222			280						
2	FAB PARTS	16½	5	200			17			50				91				125				158			200					
3	ASSEMBLY	11	1	40				3		10				18				25				32			40					
4	TEST	5½	1	40				3		10				18				25				32			40					
5	SHIP	0	1	40				3		10				18				25				32			40					

▬▬▬ = PLAN & QUANTITY REQUIRED (CUM)

▬▬▬ = PROGRESS

Figure 54.20 Schedule—In-Process—Version 20

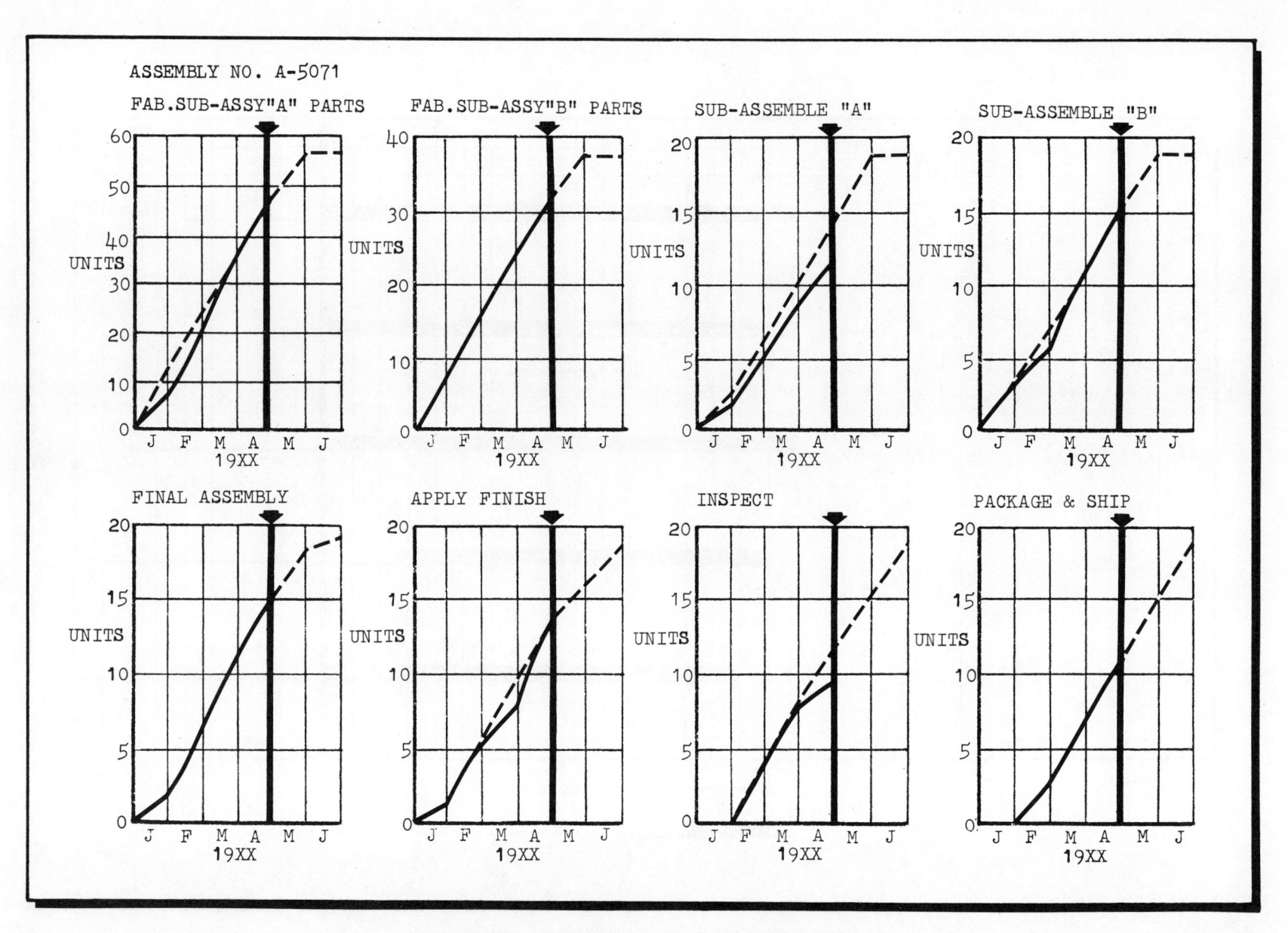

Figure 54.21 Schedule—In-Process—Version 21

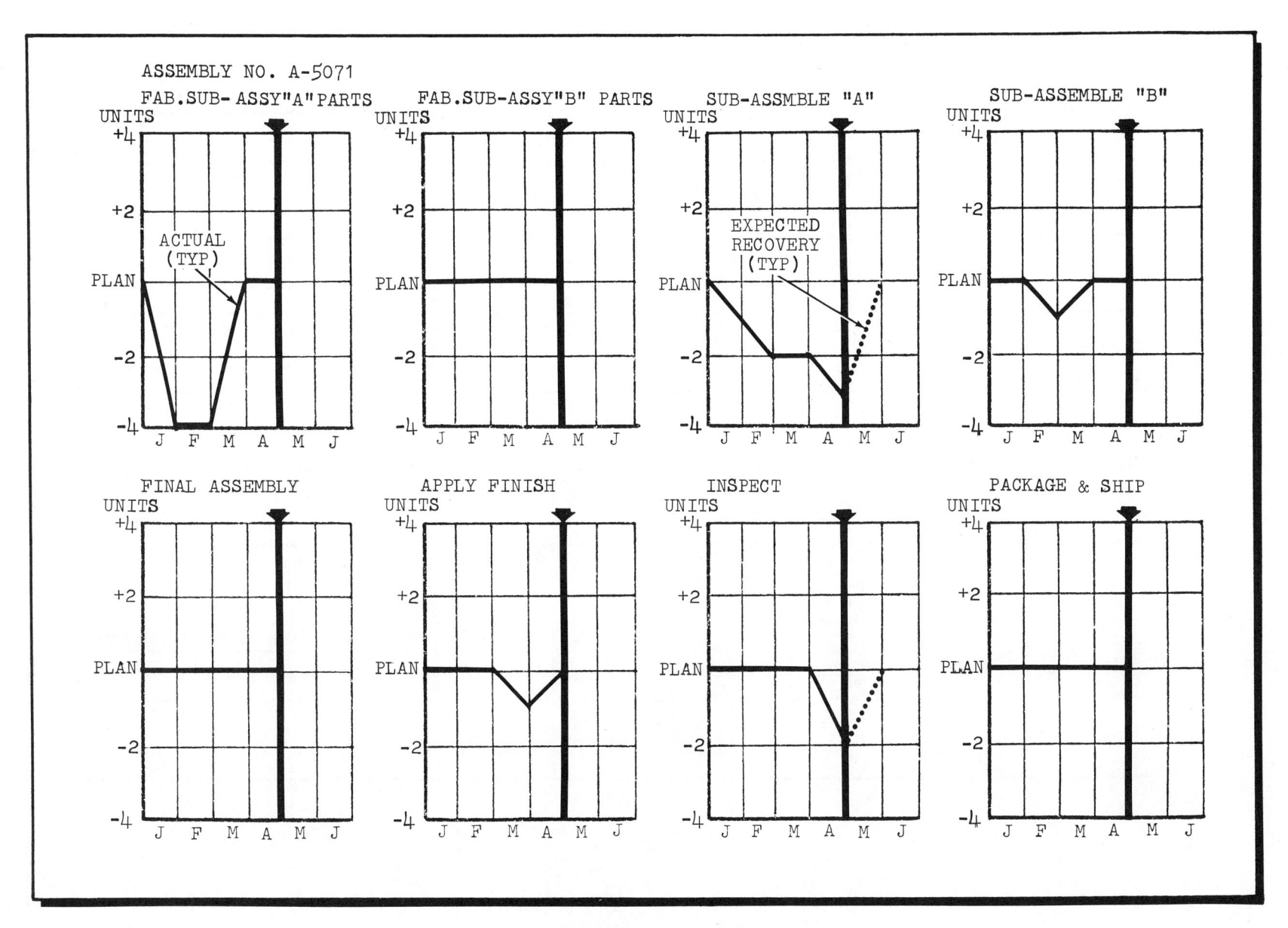

Figure 54.22 Schedule—In-Process—Version 22

PROC. NO	DESCRIPTION		JAN			FEB				MAR				
			6	13	20	27	3	10	17	24	3	10	17	24	31
1	FAB. SUB-ASSY "A" PARTS	S		2880	5760	8640	11520	14400	17280	20160	23040	25920	28800	31680	34560
		A		2880	5760										
		V													
2	FAB. SUB-ASSY "B" PARTS	S		1728	3456	5184	6912	8640	10368	12096	13824	15552	17280	19008	20736
		A		1728	3456										
		V													
3	SUB-ASSEMBLE "A"	S		144	432	720	1008	1296	1584	1872	2160	2448	2736	3024	3312
		A		144	432										
		V													
4	SUB-ASSEMBLE "B"	S		144	432	720	1008	1296	1584	1872	2160	2448	2736	3024	3312
		A		144	360										
		V			-72										
5	ASSEMBLE "A" & "B"	S			288	576	864	1152	1440	1728	2016	2304	2592	2880	3168
		A			288										
		V													
6	APPLY FINISH	S			144	432	720	1008	1296	1584	1872	2160	2448	2736	3024
		A			144										
		V													
7	INSPECT	S				288	576	864	1152	1440	1728	2016	2304	2592	2880
		A													
		V													
8	PACKAGE & SHIP	S				144	432	720	1008	1296	1584	1872	2160	2448	2736
		A													
		V													

S = CUM. SCHEDULE
A = CUM ACTUAL
V = VARIANCE

Figure 54.23 Schedule—In-Process—Version 23

		3	10	17	24	3	10	17	24	31	7	14	21	28	5	12	19	26	2	9	16	23	30
	SCHED. RATE	1	1	1	1	1	1	1	1	1	1	1	1	1	1	1							
	ACTUAL RATE	1	1	1	1	1	1	1	1														
FABRICATE & ASSEMBLE	SCHED. CUM	1	2	3	4	5	6	7	8	9	10	11	12	13	14	15	16						
	ACTUAL CUM	1	2	3	4	5	6	7	8														
	CUM. VARIANCE																						
	RECOVERY																						
	SCHED. RATE				1	1	1	1	1	1	1	1	1	1	1	1	1	1	1	1			
	ACTUAL RATE				1	1	1	1	1	1													
UNIT TEST	SCHED. CUM				1	2	3	4	5	6	7	8	9	10	11	12	13	14	15	16			
	ACTUAL CUM				1	2	3	4	5	6													
	CUM. VARIANCE																						
	RECOVERY																						
	SCHED. RATE							1	1	1	1	1	1	1	1	1	1	1	1	1	1	1	1
	ACTUAL RATE							1	1	0													
SYSTEM TEST	SCHED. CUM							1	2	3	4	5	6	7	8	9	10	11	12	13	14	15	16
	ACTUAL CUM							1	2	2													
	CUM. VARIANCE									−1													
	RECOVERY										1												
		FEB				MAR					APR				MAY				JUNE				

Figure 54.24 Schedule—In-Process—Version 24

STATUS AS OF **FEB 1**

PROCESS NO.	PROCESS	DEPT	CUM QTY SCHEDULED	CUM QTY COMPLETED	VARIANCE	ANTICIPATED RECOVERY DATE
1	PURCHASE PARTS	D/27	70	70		
2	FABRICATE PARTS	D/40	42	42		
3	ASSEMBLE	D/51	7	5	-2	FEB 10
4	TEST	D/30	5	5		
5	PACKAGE & SHIP	D/80	3	3		

ANALYSIS: MAJOR ASSEMBLY FIXTURE DOWN FOR REPAIRS; IS BEING REPAIRED ON 3 SHIFT BASIS.

Figure 54.25 Schedule—In-Process—Version 25

STATUS AS OF **FEB 1** ORDER NO. **51233**

PROCESS NO.	PROCESS	DEPT	PERCENT COMPLETE: SCHEDULE	PERCENT COMPLETE: ACTUAL	VARIANCE	ANTICIPATED RECOVERY DATE
1	PURCHASE PARTS	D/27	25%	25%		
2	FABRICATE PARTS	D/40	21%	21%		
3	ASSEMBLE	D/51	17%	12%	-5%	FEB 10
4	TEST	D/30	12%	12%		
5	PACKAGE & SHIP	D/80	7%	7%		

Figure 54.26 Schedule—In-Process—Version 26

STATUS AS OF **FEB 1**

STOCK NO.	PART NAME	1 SHEET METAL			2 WELD			3 ASSEMBLE			4 PAINT			5 PACK & SHIP		
		CUM SCH	CUM ACT	VAR	CUM SCH	CUM ACT	VAR	CUM SCH	CUM ACT	VAR	CUM SCH	CUM ACT	VAR	CUM SCH	CUM ACT	VAR
A-500-1	2 DR. CABINET-VERTICAL	72	72		58	58		43	43		31	31		21	21	
A-500-2	3 DR. CABINET-VERTICAL	108	108		85	85		63	63		47	47		32	32	
A-500-3	4-DR. CABINET-VERTICAL	50	50		40	25	✓ -15	30	20	-10	21	16	-5	15	12	-3
A-500-4	5-DR. CABINET-VERTICAL	36	36		28	28		22	22		15	15		11	11	
A-500-5	3 DR. CABINET-HORIZONTAL	86	86		68	68		52	52		36	36		25	25	
A-500-6	4 DR. CABINET-HORIZONTAL	72	72		58	58		43	43		31	31		21	21	

Figure 54.27   Schedule—In-Process—Version 27

55.0 TANGIBLE NET WORTH TURNOVER

Net sales divided by tangible net worth (net worth less the value of intangible assets . . . goodwill, organization costs, etc.) produces the tangible net worth turnover rate. This is an approach to determining how actively capital is being put to work. Charts that illustrate the turnover of tangible net worth are shown in this section.

55.1 Tangible Net Worth Turnover—Version 1: A simple version of a tangible net worth turnover tracking chart is shown as Version 1, Figure 55.1. In this example, the plan is shown with a dashed line and actuals to date are shown with a solid line. The plotting is on the basis of a monthly examination of the number of turns per year. This is calculated by annualizing the monthly sales, and dividing that figure by the tangible net worth.

55.2 Tangible Net Worth Turnover—Version 2: Version 2 of a tangible net worth turnover tracking chart, Figure 55.2, is identical to Version 1 except, in this example, paired columns are used. The hatched columns represent the plan and solid columns display actuals to date.

55.3 Tangible Net Worth Turnover—Version 3: A format for displaying data on a multi-year basis is used as Version 3 of a tangible net worth turnover tracking chart, Figure 55.3. The number of actual turns per year for four previous years is shown on the left-hand grid. The center grid shows the current year's forecast and actuals (annualized) to date, while the right-hand grid shows the forecast for the coming year by quarters.

55.4 Tangible Net Worth Turnover—Version 4: The table in Version 4 of a tangible net worth turnover tracking chart, Figure 55.4, gives the statistics for planned and actual annualized net sales, tangible net worth, and the tangible net worth turnover. The graphic portion of the chart uses paired columns to display the turnover rate.

55.5 Tangible Net Worth Turnover—Version 5: A statistical table version of a tangible net worth turnover tracking chart is shown in Figure 55.5. In this example, planned and actual statistics for net sales, net worth, tangible net worth, and tangible net worth turnover are given.

55.6 Tangible Net Worth Turnover—Version 6: A one-time status report version of a tangible net worth turnover chart is shown in Figure 55.6. Figures that display the plan, actuals, and variances are given in tabular form for the turnover rate, and for the sales and net worth backup, as well.

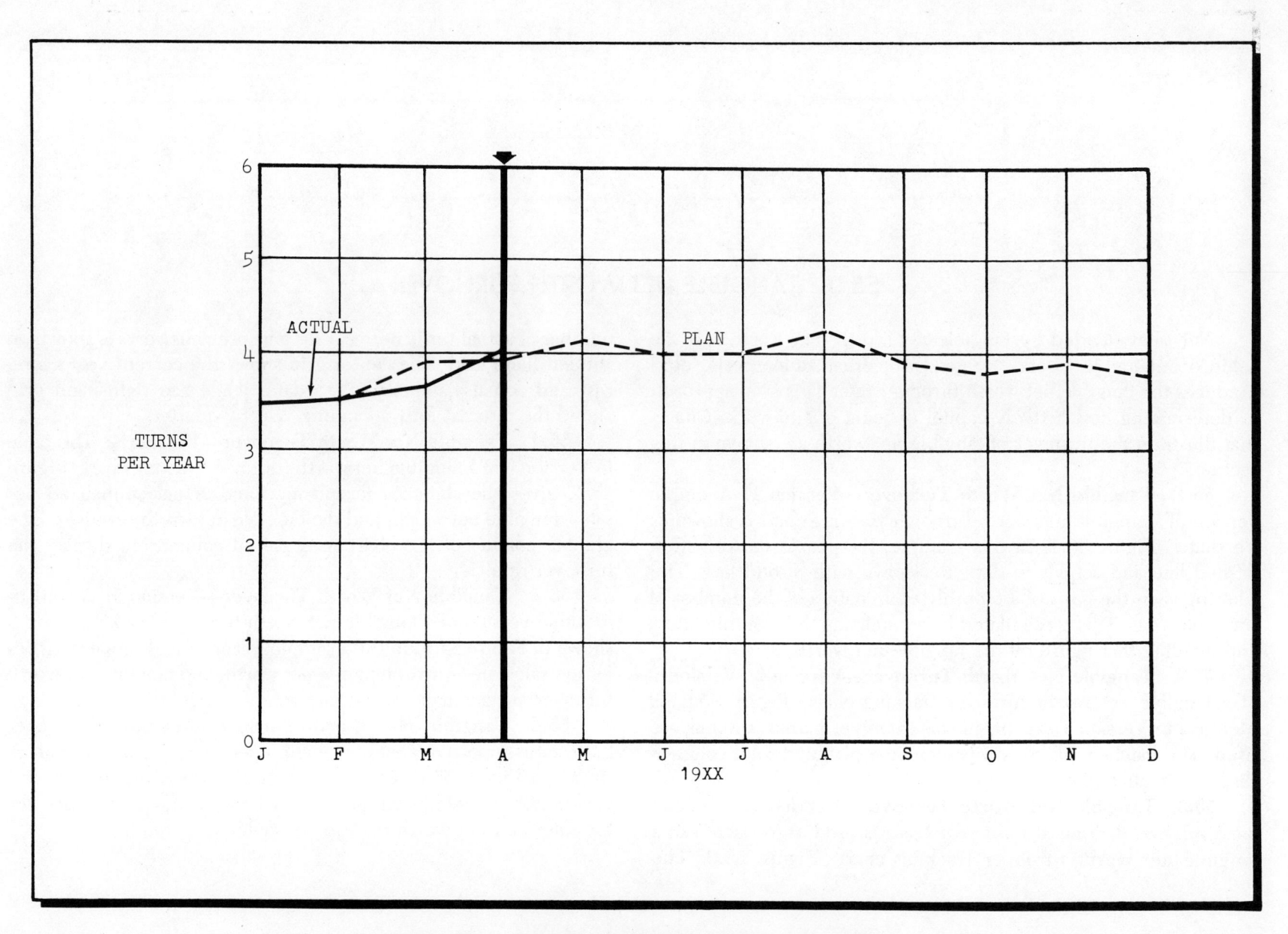

Figure 55.1 Tangible Net Worth Turnover—Version 1

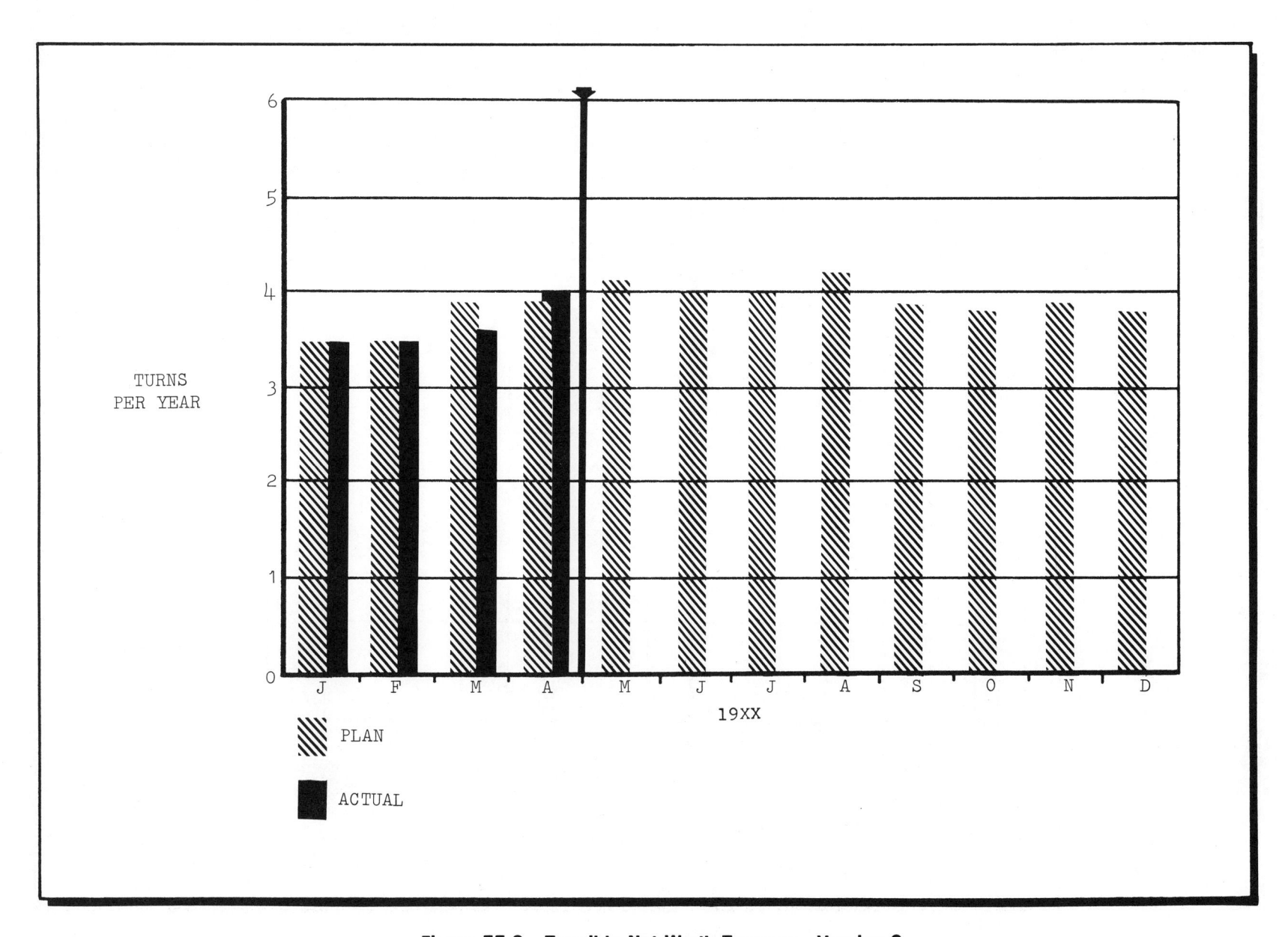

Figure 55.2 Tangible Net Worth Turnover—Version 2

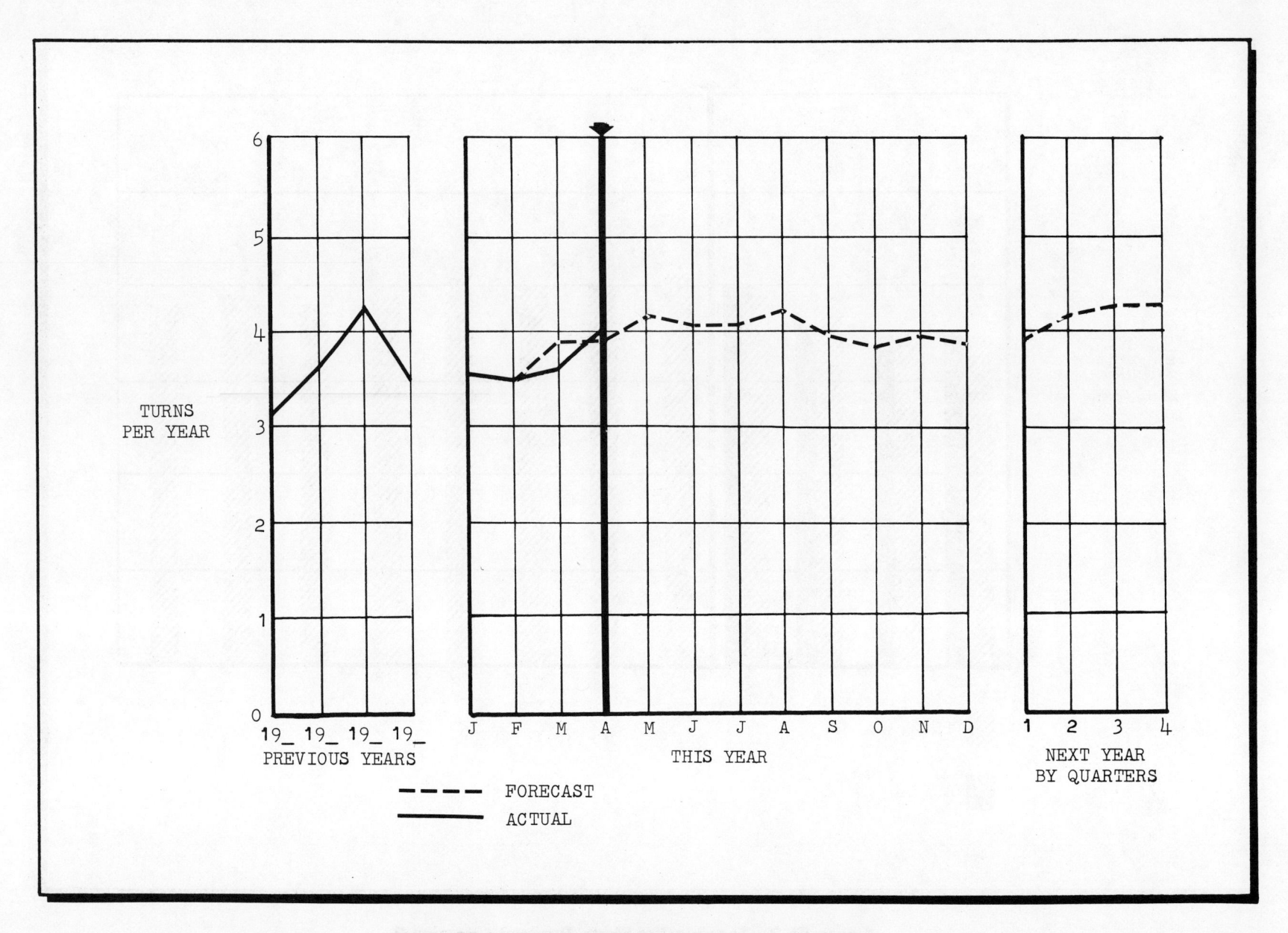

Figure 55.3 Tangible Net Worth Turnover—Version 3

TURNS
PER YEAR

			J	F	M	A	M	J	J	A	S	O	N	D
NET SALES ANNUALIZED—$000	PLAN		108.0	114.0	120.0	126.0	130.0	128.0	123.0	120.0	120.0	122.0	127.0	130.0
	ACTUAL		108.0	120.0	128.0	132.0								
TANGIBLE NET WORTH—$000	PLAN		30.9	32.9	30.9	32.0	32.0	31.9	30.9	28.9	30.9	31.9	32.9	33.9
	ACTUAL		30.9	34.4	32.9	33.1								
TANGIBLE NET WORTH TURNOVER	PLAN	▨	3.5	3.5	3.9	3.9	4.1	4.0	4.0	4.2	3.9	3.8	3.9	3.8
	ACTUAL	■	3.5	3.5	3.6	4.0								

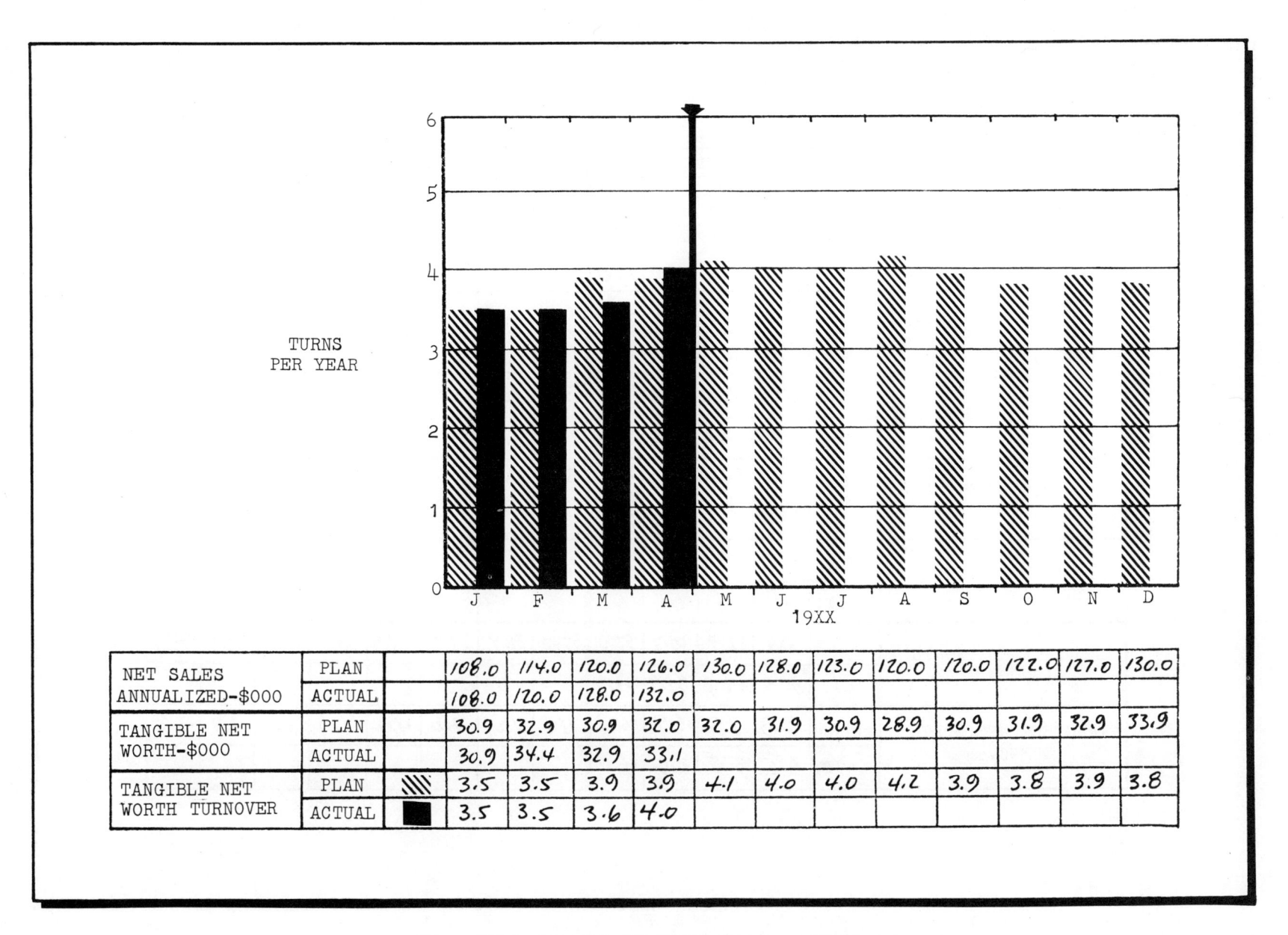

Figure 55.4 Tangible Net Worth Turnover—Version 4

ITEM			\multicolumn{12}{c}{19XX}
			J	F	M	A	M	J	J	A	S	O	N	D
NET SALES ($000)	PER MONTH	PLAN	9.0	10.0	11.0	12.0	12.0	10.0	8.0	8.0	10.0	12.0	14.0	14.0
		ACT.	9.0	11.0	12.0	12.0								
	YEAR TO DATE	PLAN	9.0	19.0	30.0	42.0	54.0	64.0	72.0	80.0	90.0	102.0	116.0	130.0
		ACT.	9.0	20.0	32.0	44.0								
	ANNUALIZED	PLAN	108.0	114.0	120.0	126.0	130.0	128.0	123.0	120.0	120.0	122.0	127.0	130.0
		ACT.	108.0	120.0	128.0	132.0								
NET WORTH ($000)		PLAN	32.0	34.0	32.0	33.1	33.1	33.0	32.0	30.0	32.0	33.0	34.0	35.0
		ACT.	32.0	35.5	34.0	34.2								
MINUS INTANGIBLE ASSETS ($000)		PLAN	1.1	1.1	1.1	1.1	1.1	1.1	1.1	1.1	1.1	1.1	1.1	1.1
		ACT.	1.1	1.1	1.1	1.1								
TANGIBLE NET WORTH ($000)		PLAN	30.9	32.9	30.9	32.0	32.0	31.9	30.9	28.9	30.9	31.9	32.9	33.9
		ACT.	30.9	34.4	32.9	33.1								
TANGIBLE NET WORTH TURNOVER		PLAN	3.5	3.5	3.9	3.7	4.1	4.0	4.0	4.2	3.9	3.8	3.9	3.8
		ACT.	3.5	3.5	3.6	4.0								

Figure 55.5 Tangible Net Worth Turnover—Version 5

STATUS AS OF _____

ITEM		PLAN	ACTUAL	VARIANCE
NET SALES ($000)	PER MONTH	12.0	12.0	0
	YEAR TO DATE	42.0	44.0	+2
	ANNUALIZED	126.0	132.0	+6
NET WORTH ($000)		33.1	34.2	+1.1
MINUS INTANGIBLE ASSETS ($000)		1.1	1.1	0
TANGIBLE NET WORTH ($000)		32.0	33.1	+1.1
TANGIBLE NET WORTH TURNOVER		3.9	4.0	+.1

Figure 55.6 Tangible Net Worth Turnover—Version 6

56.0 TECHNICAL PERFORMANCE SUMMARIES

Charts that display summaries of technical performance progress of a product while it is being designed, tested, or used are shown in this section. Also see Sections 1.0, *Accuracy*, 43.0, *Reliability*, and 49.0, *Schedule, Cost, and Technical Performance*.

56.1 Technical Performance Summary—Version 1: Technical performance trends for three factors (accuracy, weight, and temperature) are displayed in deviation-from-specification form in Version 1 of a technical performance summary chart, Figure 56.1. Upper and lower tolerance limits are shown as dashed lines on each grid.

56.2 Technical Performance Summary—Version 2: Seven separate technical performance categories are displayed in Version 2, Figure 56.2. A straight, solid line indicates that an individual product characteristic is predicted to perform (design stage), or is actually performing (test or usage phase), within specified limits. Deviations from specifications are indicated with the solid line going above or below the center of the grid.

56.3 Technical Performance Summary—Version 3: Technical parameters are recorded on an exception reporting style basis in Version 3 of a technical performance summary chart, Figure 56.3. Monthly performances within specified limits are recorded as check marks in the "A" section of each grid. Out-of-spec performances are recorded in the "B" section.

56.4 Technical Performance Summary—Version 4: Version 4 of a technical performance summary tracking chart, Figure 56.4, is similar to Version 3 except that actual performance figures are recorded in this version instead of check marks.

56.5 Technical Performance Summary—Version 5: A one-time status report version of a technical performance summary chart is shown in Figure 56.5. Various design parameters, in this example, are examined in terms of target value, limits, current value, variance, and the current predicted final value. A check mark is used to more readily draw attention to those parameters that are out of specified limits.

56.6 Technical Performance Summary—Version 6: A one-time status report that compares specified performance of various product characteristics with those of the current and previous months, and which gives a prediction of final values, is shown as Version 6 of a technical performance summary chart, Figure 56.6.

56.7 Technical Performance Summary—Version 7: Current performances relative to a number of product characteristics are compared with goals in Version 7 of a technical performance summary chart, Figure 56.7. Space is also provided to record a criticality code and enter remarks.

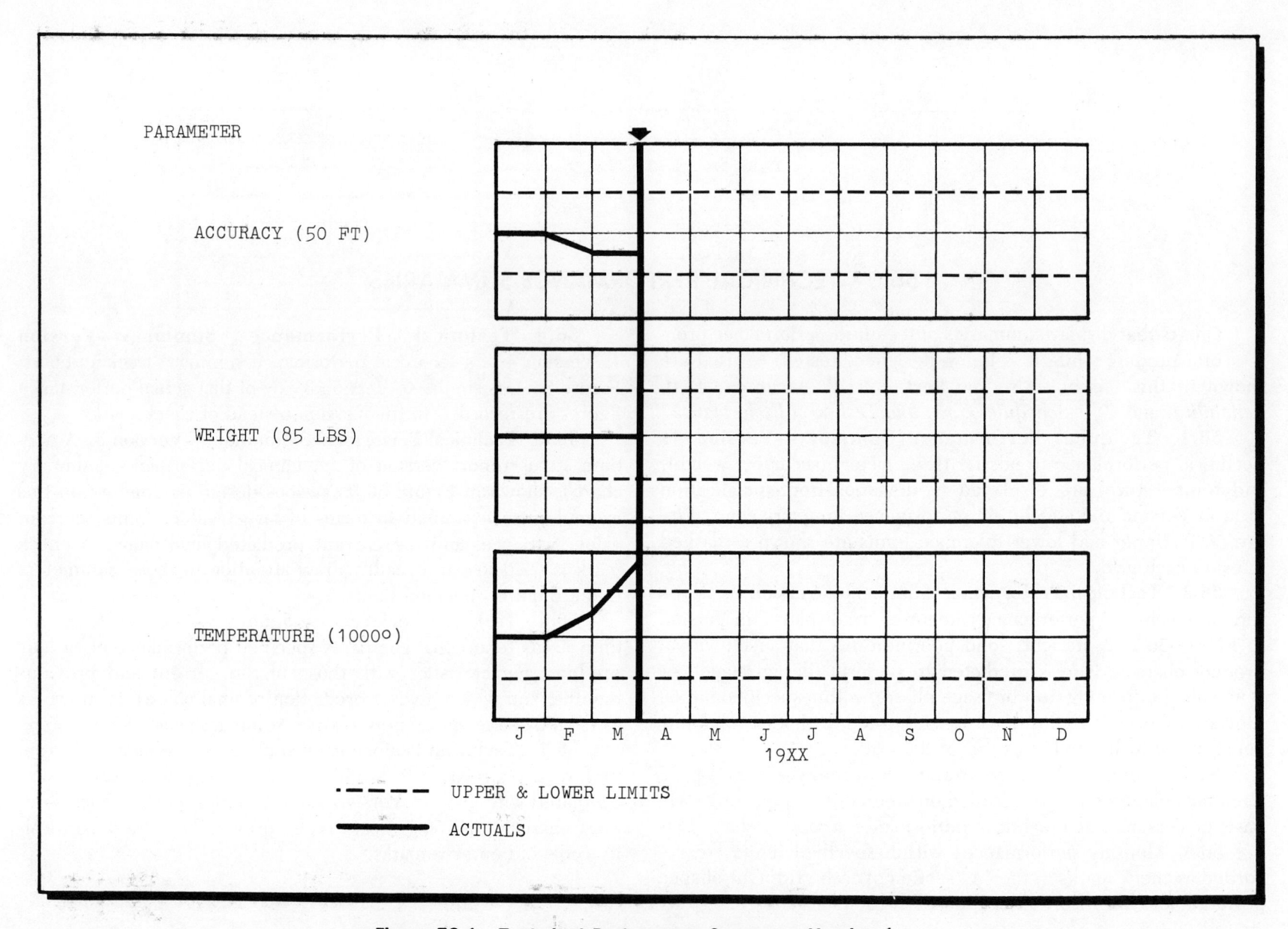

Figure 56.1 Technical Performance Summary—Version 1

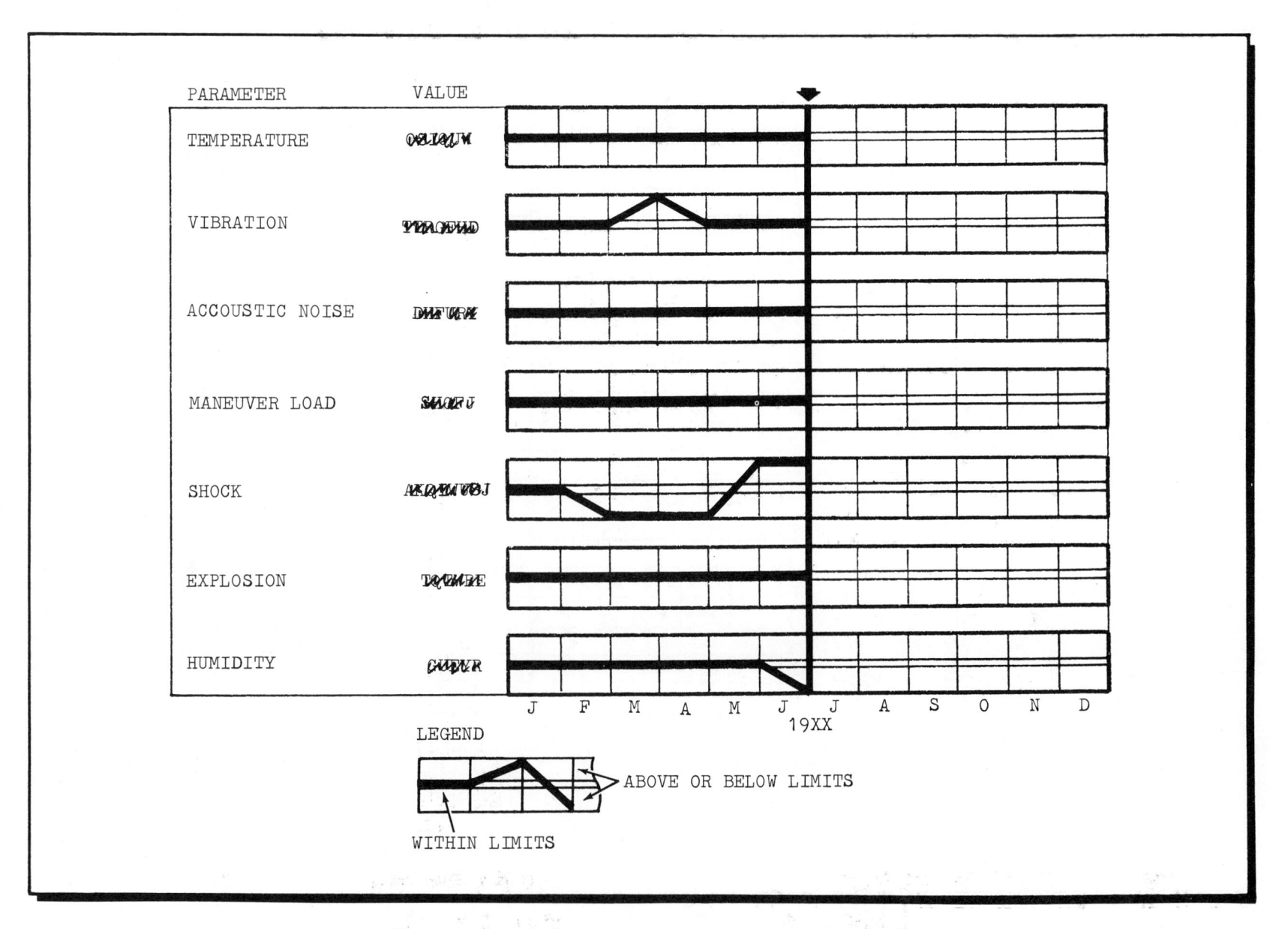

Figure 56.2 Technical Performance Summary—Version 2

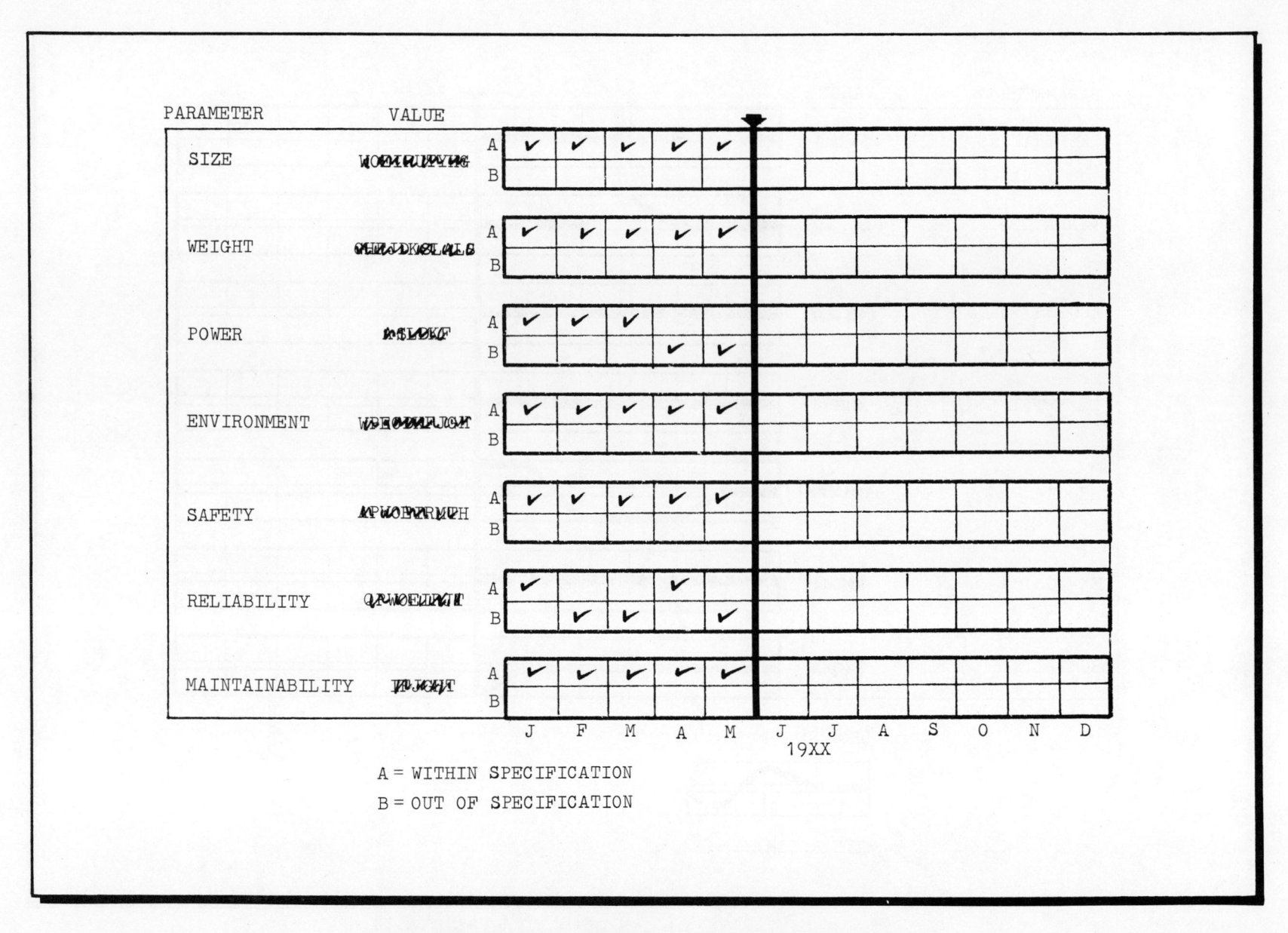

Figure 56.3 Technical Performance Summary—Version 3

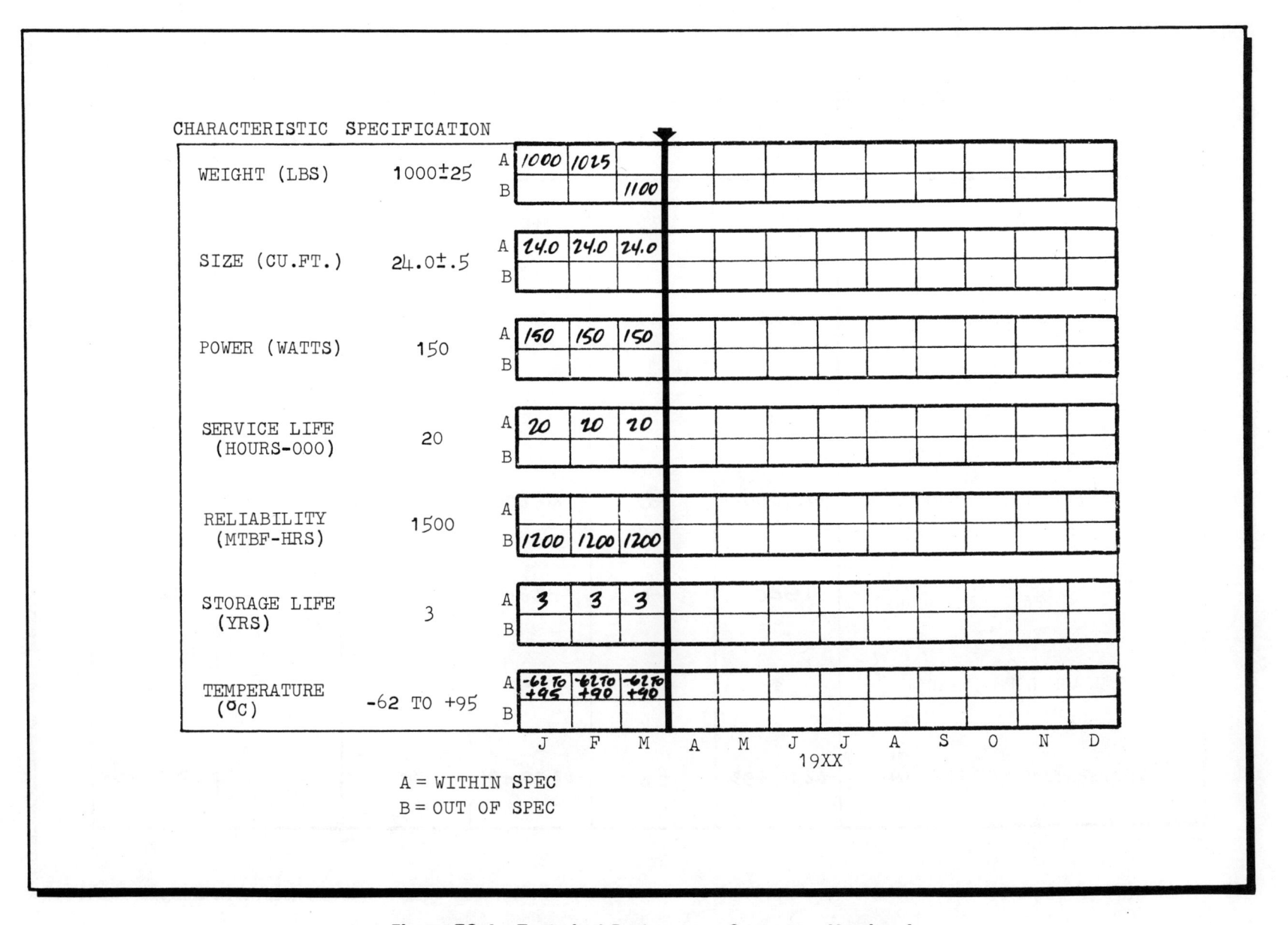

CHARACTERISTIC	SPECIFICATION		J	F	M	A	M	J	J	A	S	O	N	D
WEIGHT (LBS)	1000±25	A	1000	1025										
		B			1100									
SIZE (CU.FT.)	24.0±.5	A	24.0	24.0	24.0									
		B												
POWER (WATTS)	150	A	150	150	150									
		B												
SERVICE LIFE (HOURS-000)	20	A	20	20	20									
		B												
RELIABILITY (MTBF-HRS)	1500	A												
		B	1200	1200	1200									
STORAGE LIFE (YRS)	3	A	3	3	3									
		B												
TEMPERATURE (°C)	−62 TO +95	A	−62 TO +95	−62 TO +90	−62 TO +90									
		B												

19XX

A = WITHIN SPEC
B = OUT OF SPEC

Figure 56.4 Technical Performance Summary—Version 4

DESIGN PARAMETER STATUS AS OF _____

PARAMETER	TARGET VALUE	LIMITS	CURRENT VALUE	VARIANCE	OUT OF SPEC (✔)	CURRENT PREDICTED FINAL VALUE
WEIGHT (LBS)	1000	±25	1100	+75	✔	1050
SIZE (CU.FT.)	24.0	±.5	24.0	0		24.0
POWER (WATTS)	150	—	150	0		150
SERVICE LIFE (HOURS)	20,000	-0	20,000	0		20,000
RELIABILITY (MEAN TIME BETWEEN FAILURES- HOURS)	1500	-0	1350	-150	✔	1600
STORAGE LIFE (YEARS)	3	-0	3	0		3
TEMPERATURE (DEGREES C)	-62 TO +95	±2	-62 TO +95	0		-62 TO +95

Figure 56.5 Technical Performance Summary—Version 5

STATUS AS OF

CHARACTERISTIC	SPEC	LAST MONTH		THIS MONTH		PREDICTED FINAL	
		VALUE	OVER/UNDER	VALUE	OVER/UNDER	VALUE	OVER/UNDER
SPEED (MPH)	500	450	−50	475	−25	500	0
RANGE (MILES)	3000	3000	0	3000	0	3000	0
PAYLOAD (LB)	27,000	25,000	−2000	24,000	−3000	26,000	−1000
FUEL CAPACITY (GALLONS)	15,000	15,500	+500	15,500	+500	15,500	+500
RELIABILITY (MTBF-HOURS)	1800	1800	0	1800	0	1800	0
ALTITUDE (FEET)	−100 TO +70,000	−100 TO +70,000	0	−100 TO +70,000	0	−100 TO +70,000	0

Figure 56.6 Technical Performance Summary—Version 6

STATUS AS OF _____

CHARACTERISTIC	AGREED-TO GOALS		CURRENT PERFORMANCE		CRITIC-ALITY CODE*	REMARKS
	ORIGINAL REQUIREMENT	CURRENT REQUIREMENT	PREDICTION	ACTUALLY ACHIEVED		
WEIGHT (LBS)	1000	1000	1050	1100	B	
SIZE (CU.FT.)	24.0	24.0	24.0	24.0	A	
POWER (WATTS)	150	150	150	150	A	
SERVICE LIFE (HOURS)	22,000	20,000	20,000	20,000	A	
RELIABILITY (MTBF-HRS)	1600	1500	1400	1350	C	SPECIAL ANALYSIS TO BE COMPLETED THIS WEEK
STORAGE LIFE (YEARS)	3	3	3	3	A	
TEMPERATURE (DEGREE C)	-62 TO +95	-62 TO +95	-62 TO +95	-62 TO +95	A	

*A = NO PROBLEM
B = MINOR PROBLEM
C = MAJOR PROBLEM

Figure 56.7 Technical Performance Summary—Version 7

57.0 UNIT COST/TIME

Charts that display performance in terms of the time or cost required to produce a single unit are shown in this section. The amount scale on this type of chart can be in terms of dollars, minutes, hours, days, months, or percentage of dollars or time. Such charts offer one method of gauging productivity and learning.

57.1 Unit Cost/Time—Version 1: A simple version of a chart that can be used for tracking performance relative to unit cost is shown in Figure 57.1. This example shows that it is anticipated that, over a period of time, there will be a reduction in unit costs, probably due to learning, or a reduction in material costs, or the acquisition of improved tools or equipment, or a combination of these factors. The anticipated reduction is shown with a dashed line. Actual unit costs to date are shown with a solid line. An arrowhead has been used in this example to emphasize that the amount scale does not start with zero.

57.2 Unit Cost/Time—Version 2: Improvement is shown in terms of the percent reduction in unit cost in Version 2, Figure 57.2. In this example, the actual unit cost percentage (solid line with shading) exceeded the forecast (dashed line) for January. As with Version 1, an arrowhead has been used on the amount scale to highlight the fact that it does not start from a zero base.

57.3 Unit Cost/Time—Version 3: The amount scale is in terms of units per direct labor hour in Version 3, Figure 57.3. As with the previous two versions, an arrowhead has been used to indicate that the amount scale does not start with zero.

57.4 Unit Cost/Time—Version 4: A method for showing the time (hours) required to manufacture a single unit is displayed in Version 4, Figure 57.4. This example shows actual performance (solid columns) for the current year to date (through March) and for the previous four years. The forecast for the current year and for the coming year is shown with a dashed line.

57.5 Unit Cost/Time—Version 5: Version 5 of a unit cost tracking chart, Figure 57.5, shows a method for breaking down the cost into two or more elements. In this example, actual costs of direct labor plus material are exceeding the plan, whereas the costs of material, alone, are lower than planned. This would indicate a problem in the direct labor portion of the unit cost.

57.6 Unit Cost/Time—Version 6: A log-log grid is used in Version 6, Figure 57.6. In this example, both cumulative and unit costs are plotted in terms of planned and actual performance. A target is used to indicate the cumulative average cost at the completion of 30 units. The vertical (amount) scale is in dollars, and the horizontal scale is in numbers of units rather than time. A time or data scale could be added to correspond with the quantity of units (see Version 7).

57.7 Unit Cost/Time—Version 7: Version 7 of a unit cost

tracking chart, Figure 57.7, shows the use of double scales on the horizontal axis of the grid. One scale is in terms of the quantity of production units. The second scale, in register with the first rather than time, gives the delivery dates. The example chart also shows the use of a call-out flag. In this case, it explains that the installation of new and, apparently, more efficient machinery is the cause of the sudden dip in both forecasted and actual unit costs.

57.8 Unit Cost/Time—Version 8: Two grids are used in Version 8, Figure 57.8, both keyed to the same date scale. The top grid displays the planned and actual quantity of units produced each month. The bottom grid shows the planned and actual costs per unit broken down in terms of material costs, direct labor costs, and overhead.

57.9 Unit Cost/Time—Version 9: A method for comparing performance or alternatives, such as unit types, divisions, or manufacturing methods, is shown in Version 9, Figure 57.9. This example compares three items in terms of hours per unit. The amount scale could also be in terms of costs per unit or percent reduction in cost per unit.

57.10 Unit Cost/Time—Version 10: A statistical table has been combined with a graphic display in Version 10 of a unit cost tracking chart, Figure 57.10. Both the table and the graphic portion of the chart display data relative to budgeted and actual unit costs. In addition, the table also gives the monthly variance between these two figures.

57.11 Unit Cost/Time—Version 11: Five lines of statistics are combined with a graphic chart in Version 11 of a unit cost tracking chart, Figure 57.11. The table gives the production lot number according to the date when each lot is scheduled for delivery. Lot quantities are also given in the table in terms of both lot and cumulative quantities. Forecasted and actual unit costs are given in both tabular and graphic form. An arrowhead is used to emphasize that the amount scale does not start from a zero base.

57.12 Unit Cost/Time—Version 12: Version 12 of a unit cost tracking chart, Figure 57.12, is similar to Version 11 except that the horizontal scale is spaced according to production lot numbers rather than calendar date. The graphic portion of Version 12 uses a stepped line to represent the forecast and solid columns to show actual unit costs.

57.13 Unit Cost/Time—Version 13: A unit cost tracking chart in the form of a statistical table is shown as Version 13, Figure 57.13. In this example, the production lot numbers are given according to delivery date. Each lot is further described as to quantity, followed by the unit cost in terms of forecast, actual, and variance.

57.14 Unit Cost/Time—Version 14: A one-time status report version of a unit cost chart is shown in Figure 57.14. In this example, the detailed and total unit cost factors are given in terms of what has been forecasted and what has been accomplished. A check mark has been used to indicate the most significant problem.

57.15 Unit Cost/Time—Version 15: A method for comparing the current year's performance in relationship to that of previous years relative to required manufacturing hours per unit is shown in Figure 57.15. This style of non-tracking chart is sometimes referred to as a "set-back" chart.

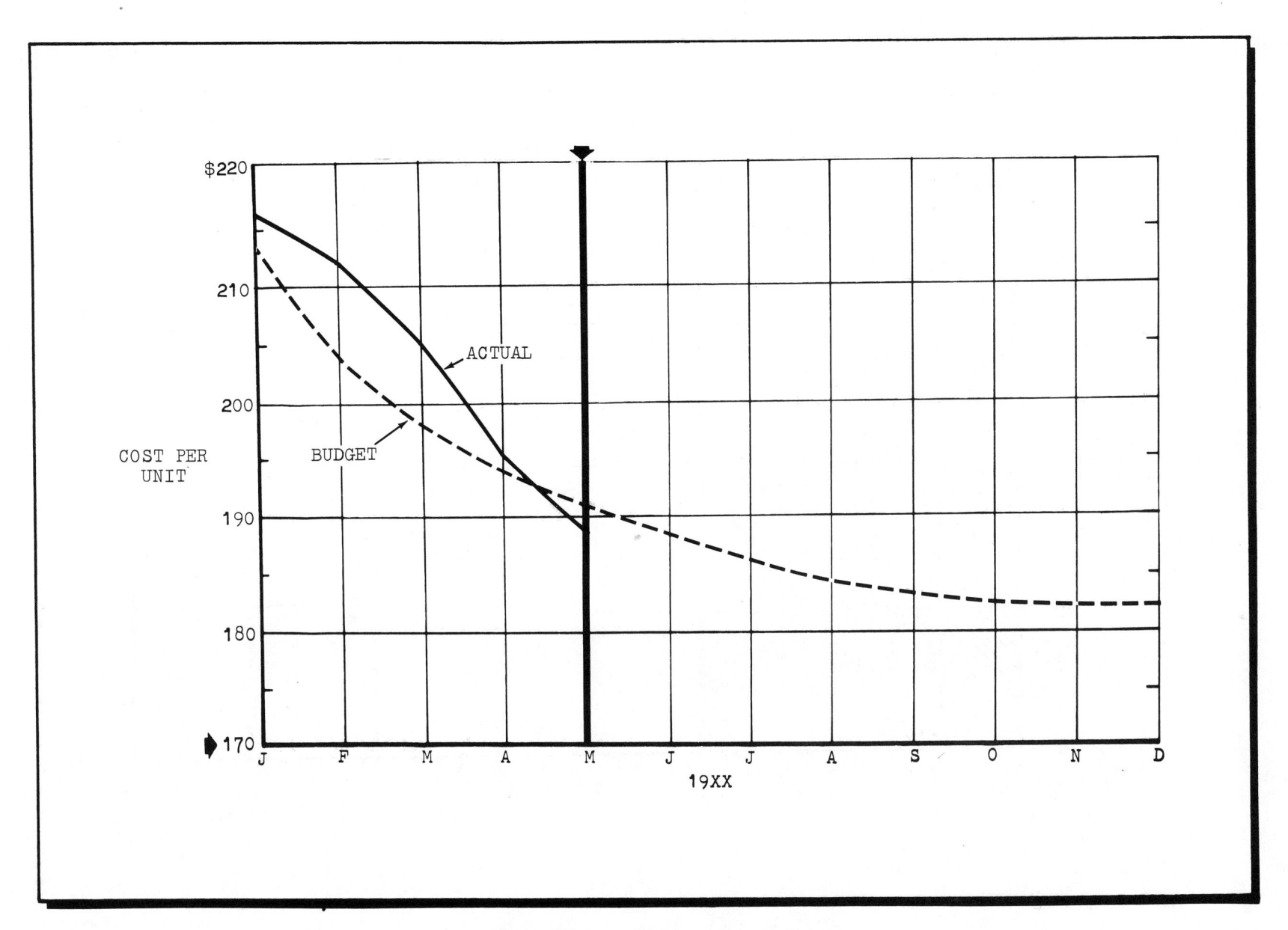

Figure 57.1   Unit Cost/Time—Version 1

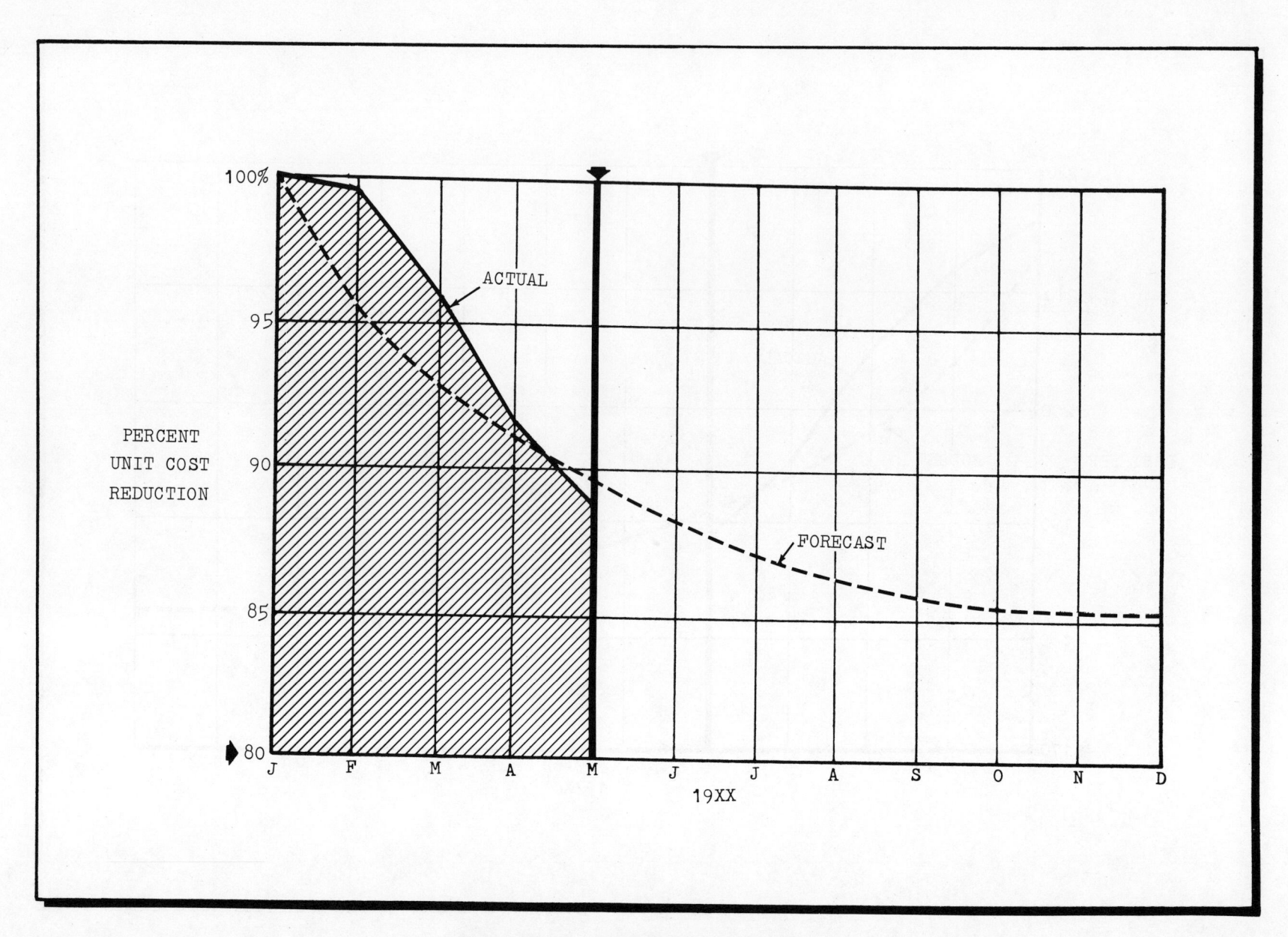

Figure 57.2   Unit Cost/Time—Version 2

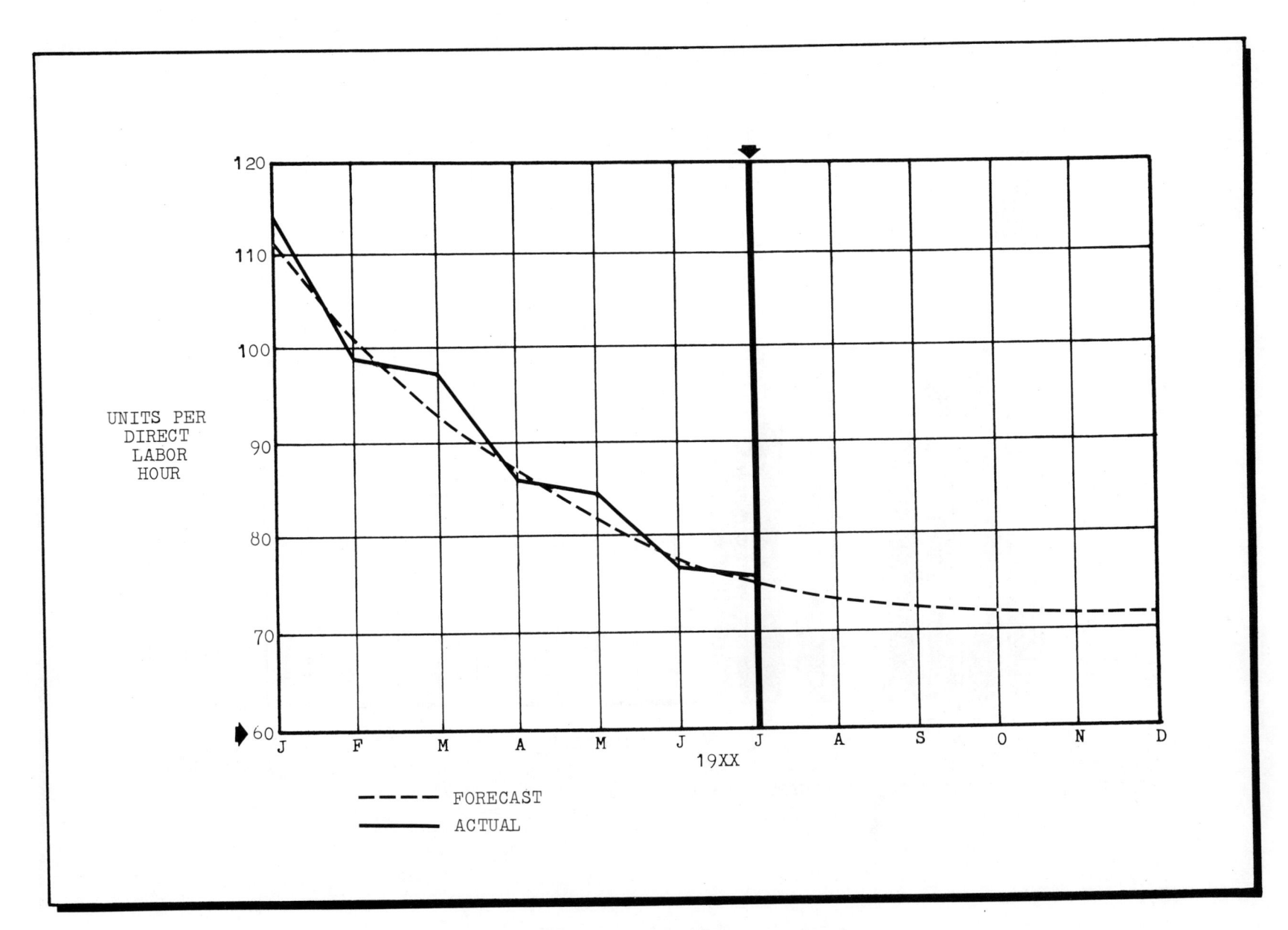

Figure 57.3 Unit Cost/Time—Version 3

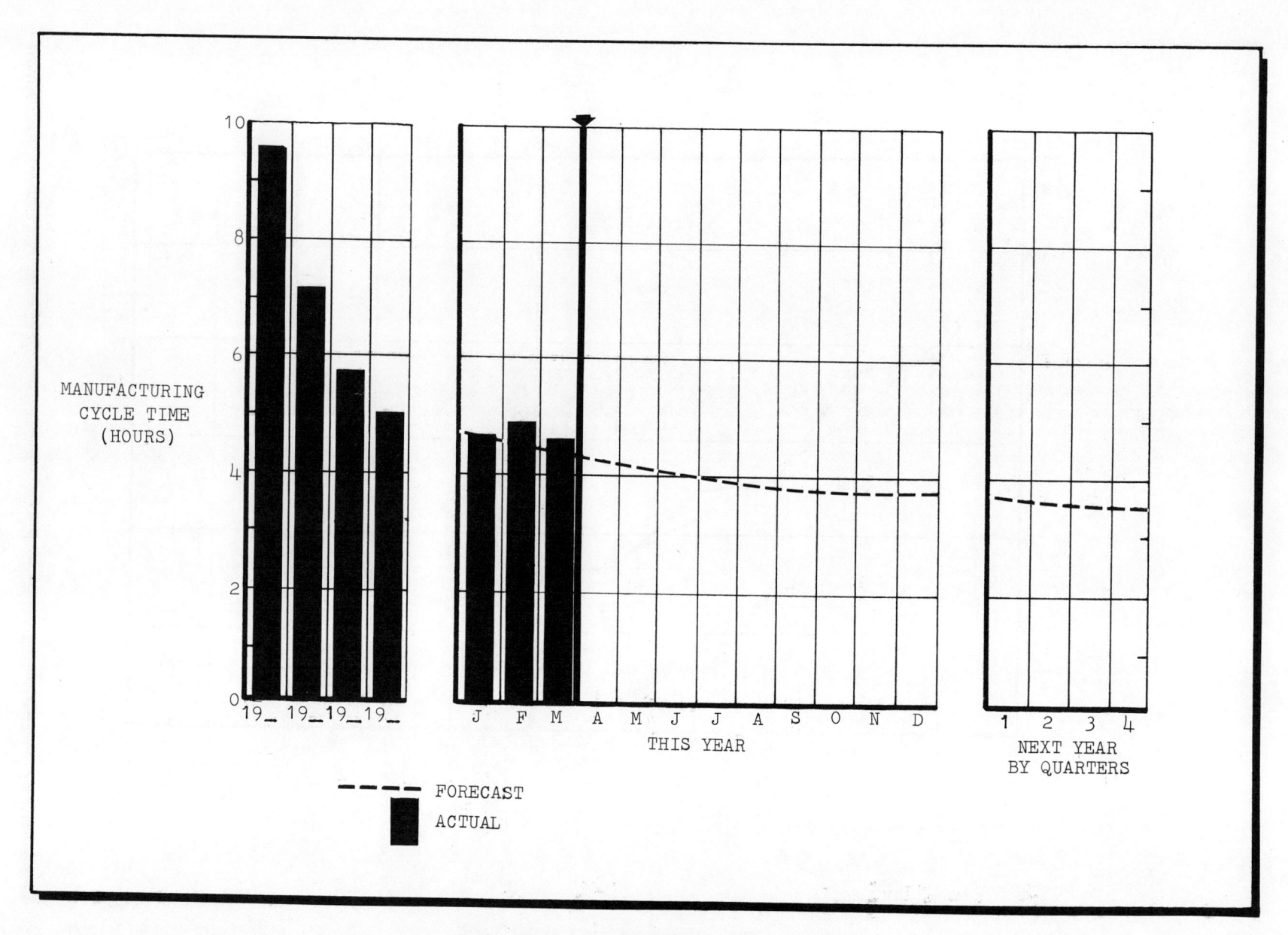

Figure 57.4　Unit Cost/Time—Version 4

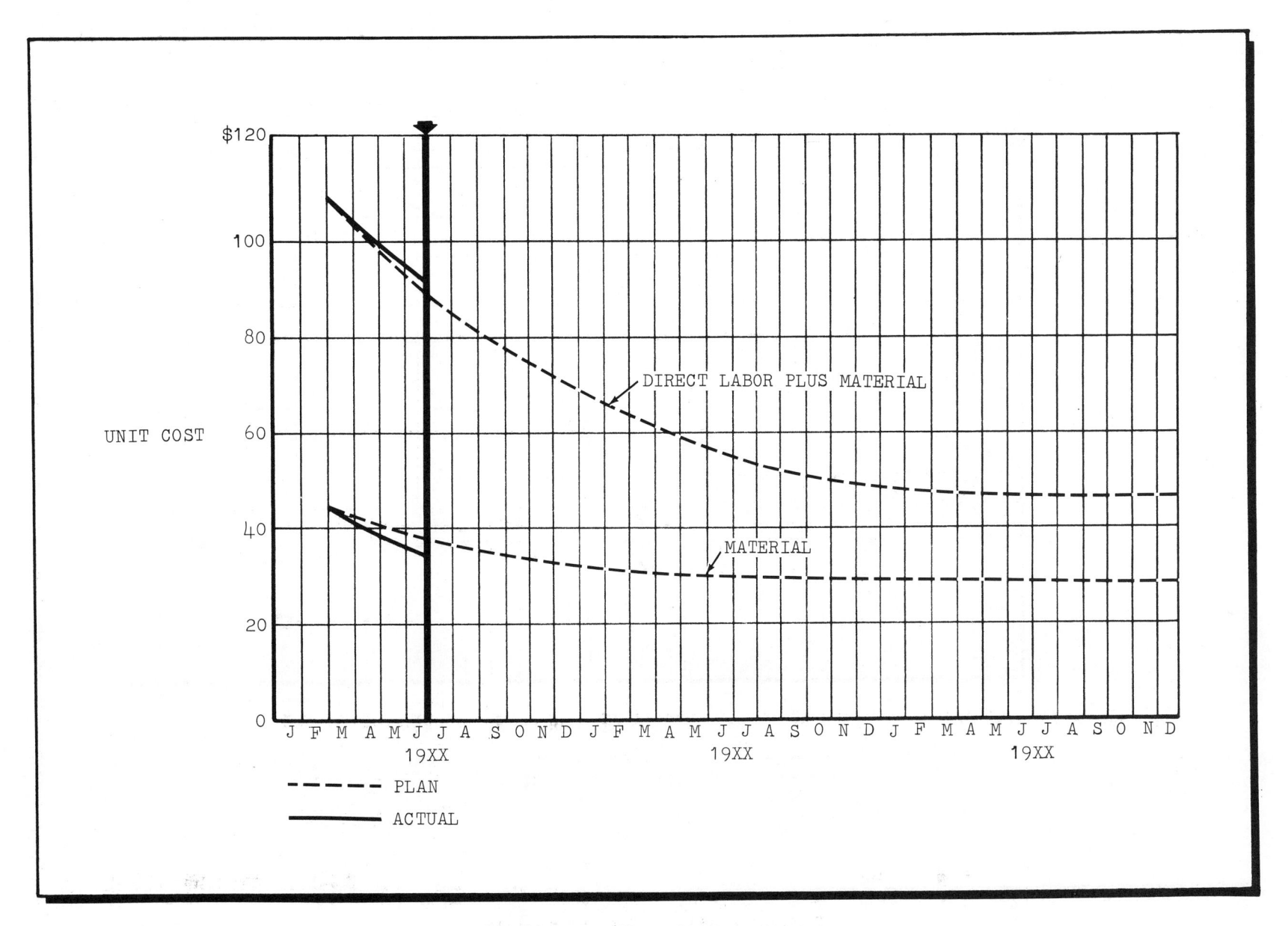

Figure 57.5   Unit Cost/Time—Version 5

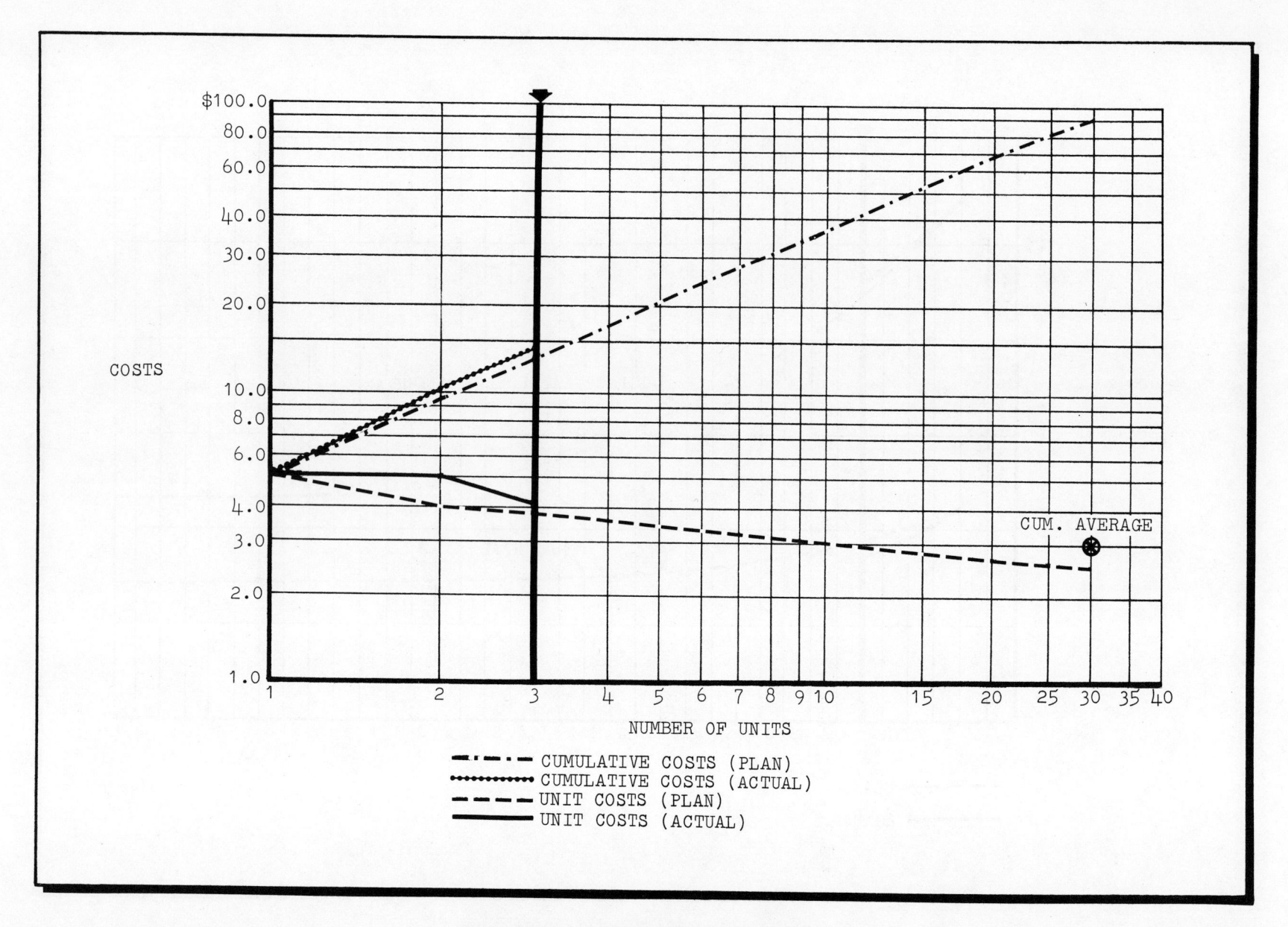

Figure 57.6 Unit Cost/Time—Version 6

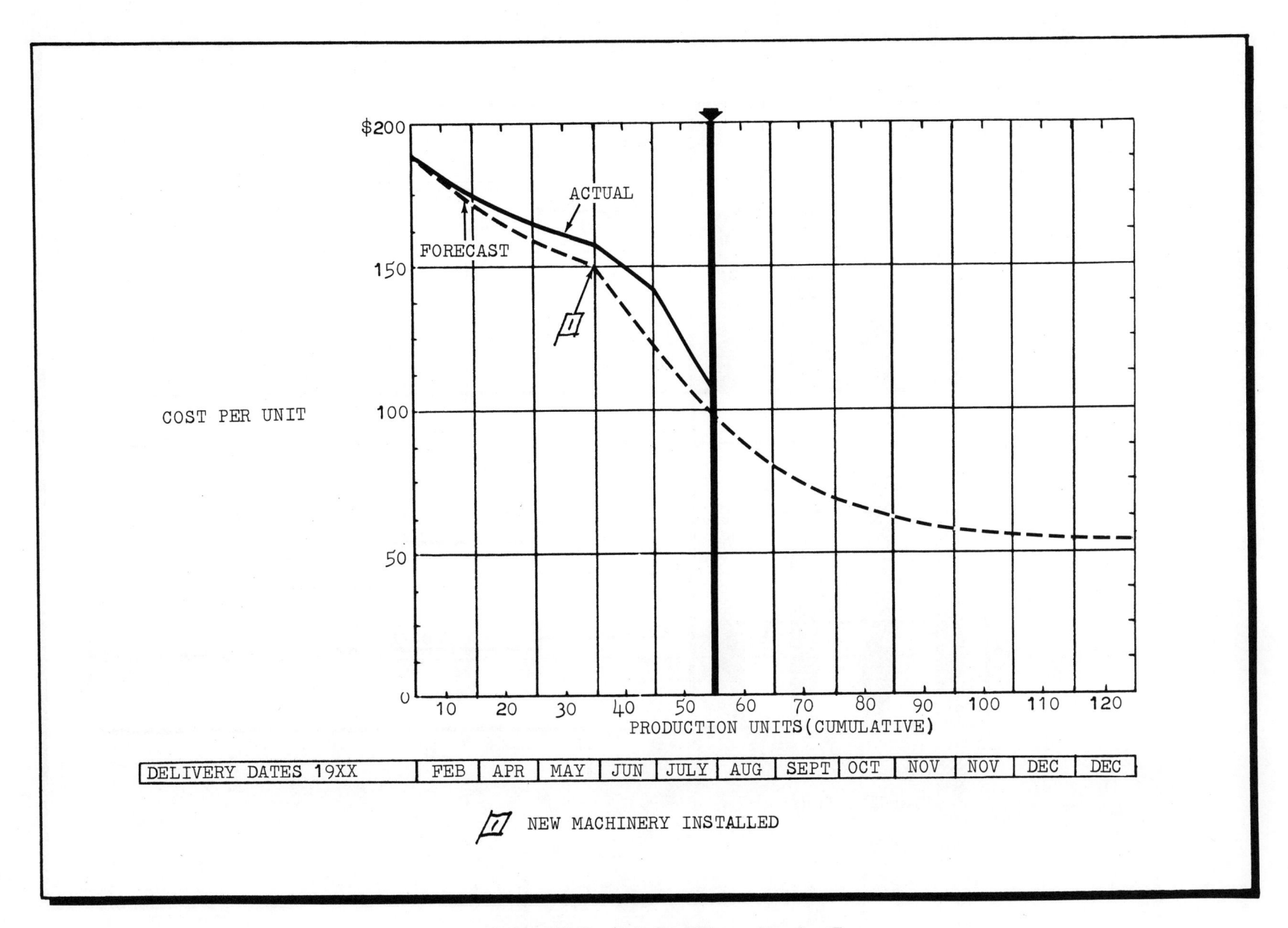

Figure 57.7 Unit Cost/Time—Version 7

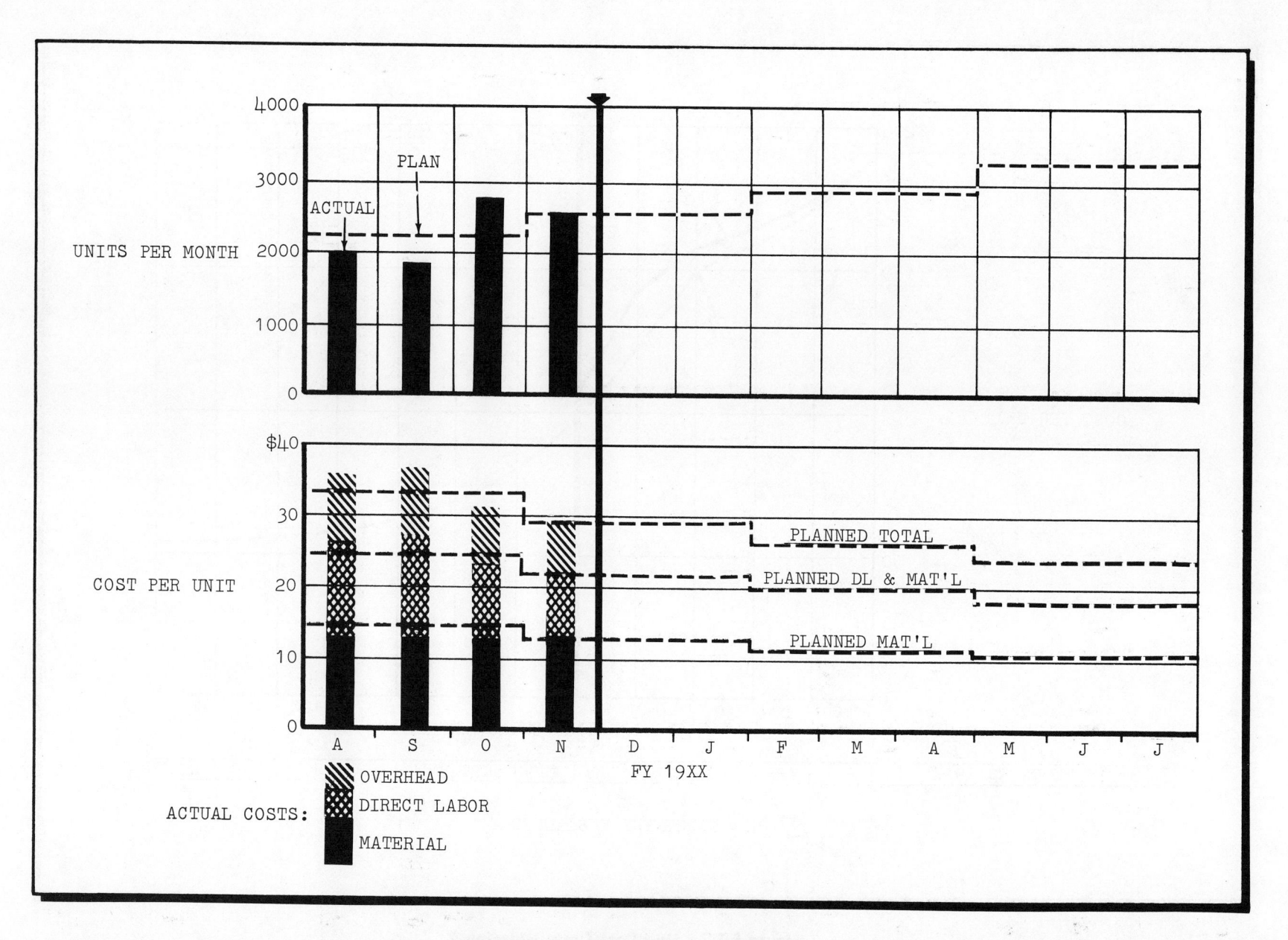

Figure 57.8 Unit Cost/Time—Version 8

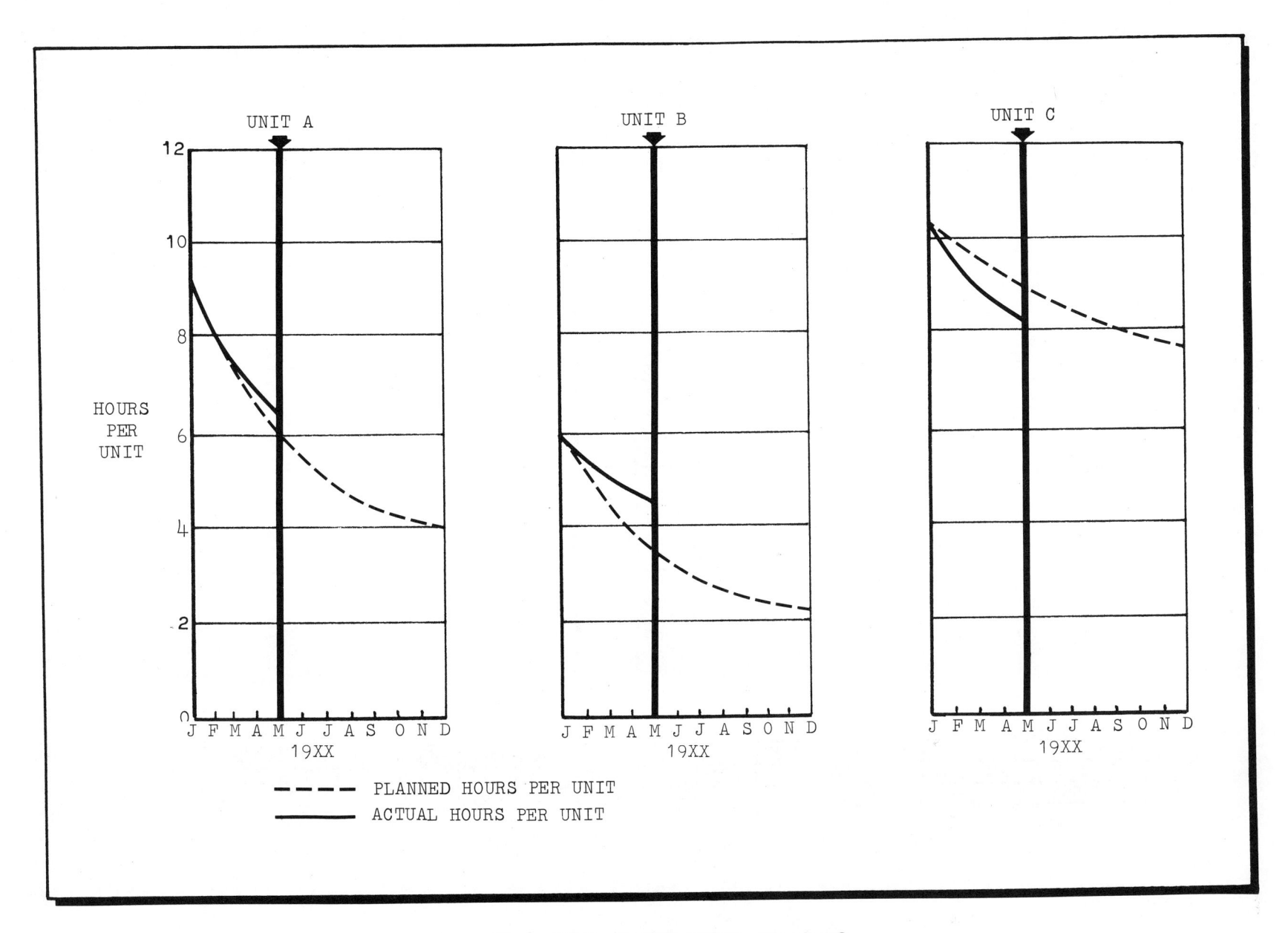

Figure 57.9 Unit Cost/Time—Version 9

COST PER UNIT

		J	F	M	A	M	J	J	A	S	O	N	D
BUDGET	PER MO. – –		213	203	198	194	191	188	186	184	183	182	182	182
ACTUAL	PER MO. ———		216	212	205	195	188							
VARIANCE			+3	+9	+7	+1	-3							

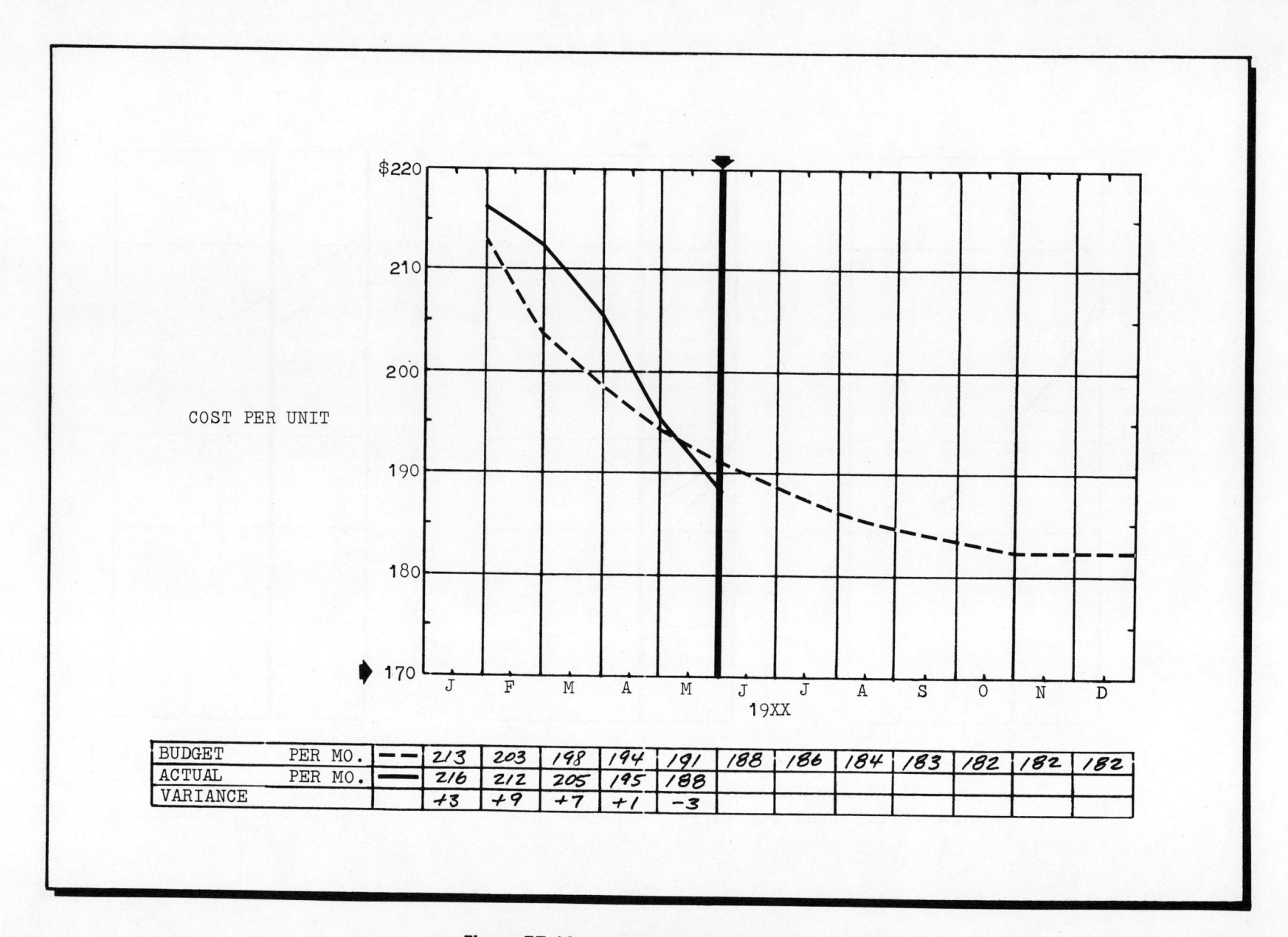

Figure 57.10   Unit Cost/Time—Version 10

DELIVER PRODUCTION LOT NO		1		2		3		4	5	6	7	8
QUANTITY	PER LOT		150		150		150		150	150	150	150	150
	CUM		150		300		450		600	750	900	1050	1200
UNIT COST ($)	FORECAST ---		213		203		198		194	191	188	186	184
	ACTUAL ——		216		212		205		195	188			

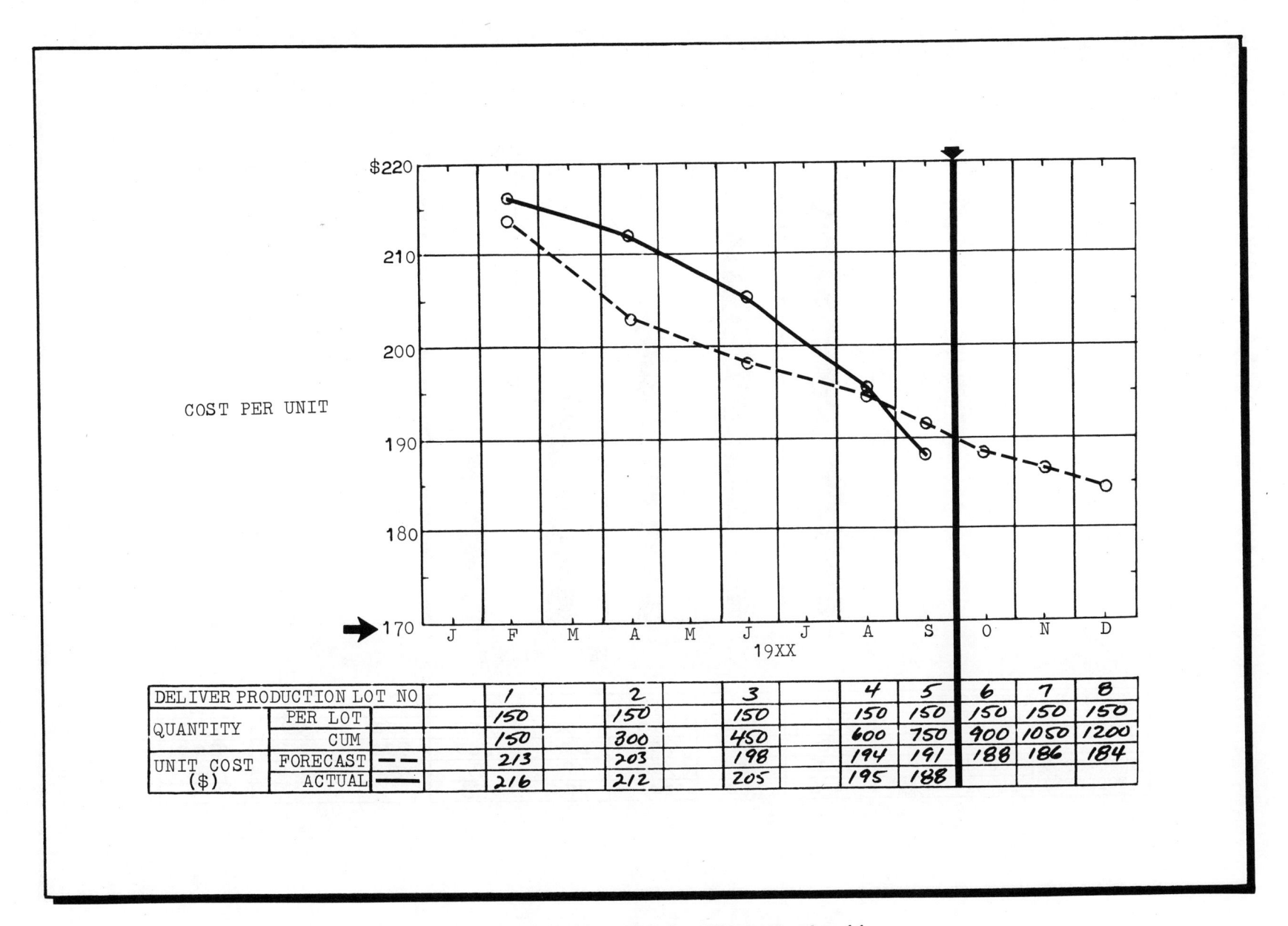

Figure 57.11 Unit Cost/Time—Version 11

DELIVERY DATES 19XX			FEB	APR	JUN	AUG	SEP	OCT	NOV	DEC
QUANTITY	PER LOT		150	150	150	150	150	150	150	150
	CUM		150	300	450	600	750	900	1050	1200
UNIT COST (DOLLARS)	FORECAST	-- --	213	203	198	194	191	188	186	184
	ACTUAL	■	216	212	205	195	188			

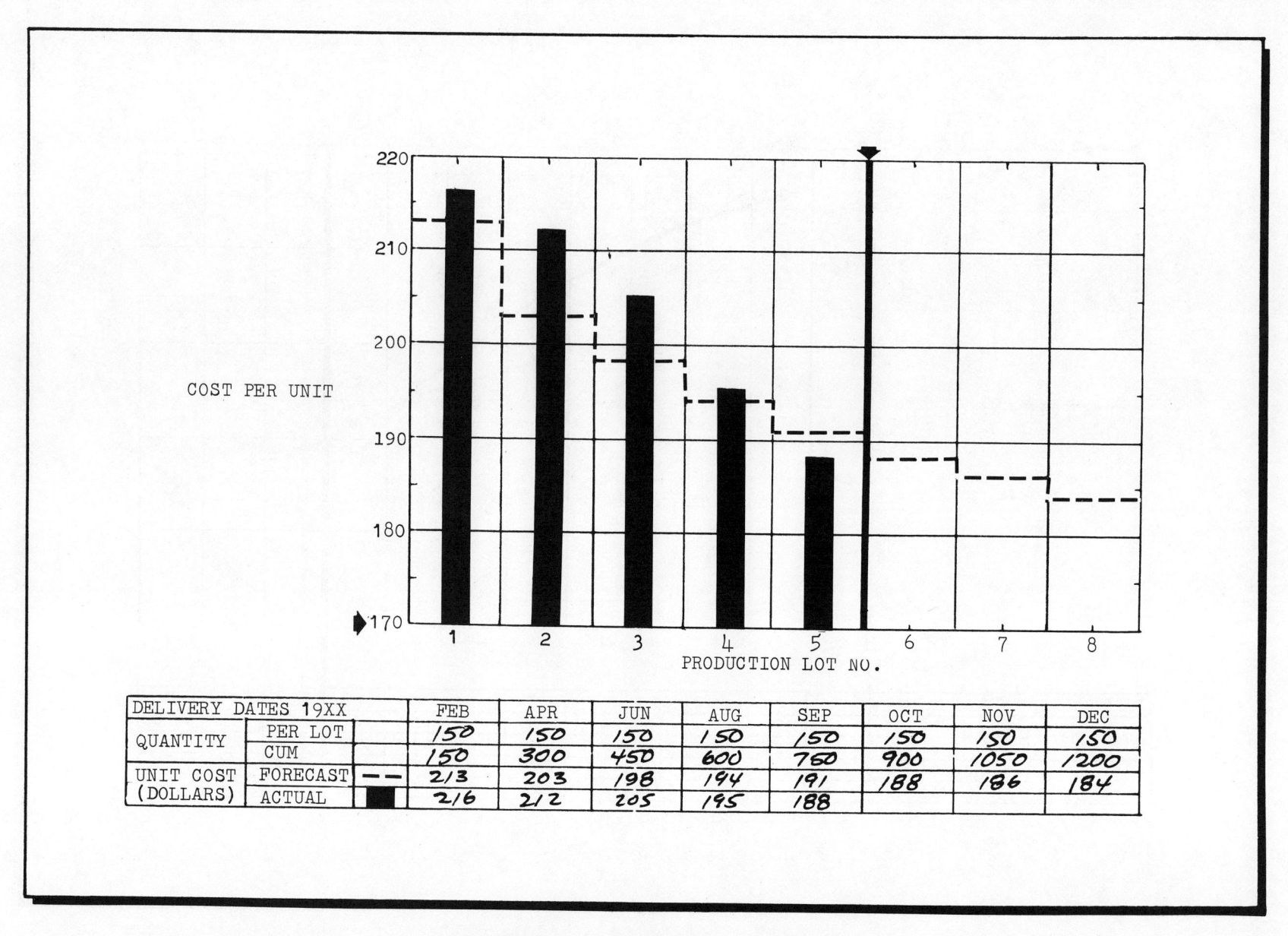

Figure 57.12 Unit Cost/Time—Version 12

ITEM		19XX											
		J	F	M	A	M	J	J	A	S	O	N	D
DELIVER PRODUCTION LOT NO.			1		2		3		4	5	6	7	8
QUANTITY	PER LOT		150		150		150		150	150	150	150	150
	CUMULATIVE		150		300		450		600	750	900	1050	1200
UNIT COST ($)	FORECAST		213		203		198		194	191	188	186	184
	ACTUAL		216		212		205		195	188			
	VARIANCE		+3		+9		+7		+1	−3			

Figure 57.13 Unit Cost/Time—Version 13

UNIT COST STATUS AS OF ___June___

FACTOR	FORECAST	ACTUAL
MATERIALS	$65.60	$75.00 ✓
LABOR	12.50	12.60
TOOLING-PRORATED	5.00	5.00
FACTORY SERVICE	7.40	7.25
TOTAL FACTORY COSTS	$90.50	$99.85
DISTRIBUTION COSTS	36.00	35.00
TOTAL COSTS PER UNIT	$126.50	$134.85

Figure 57.14 Unit Cost/Time—Version 14

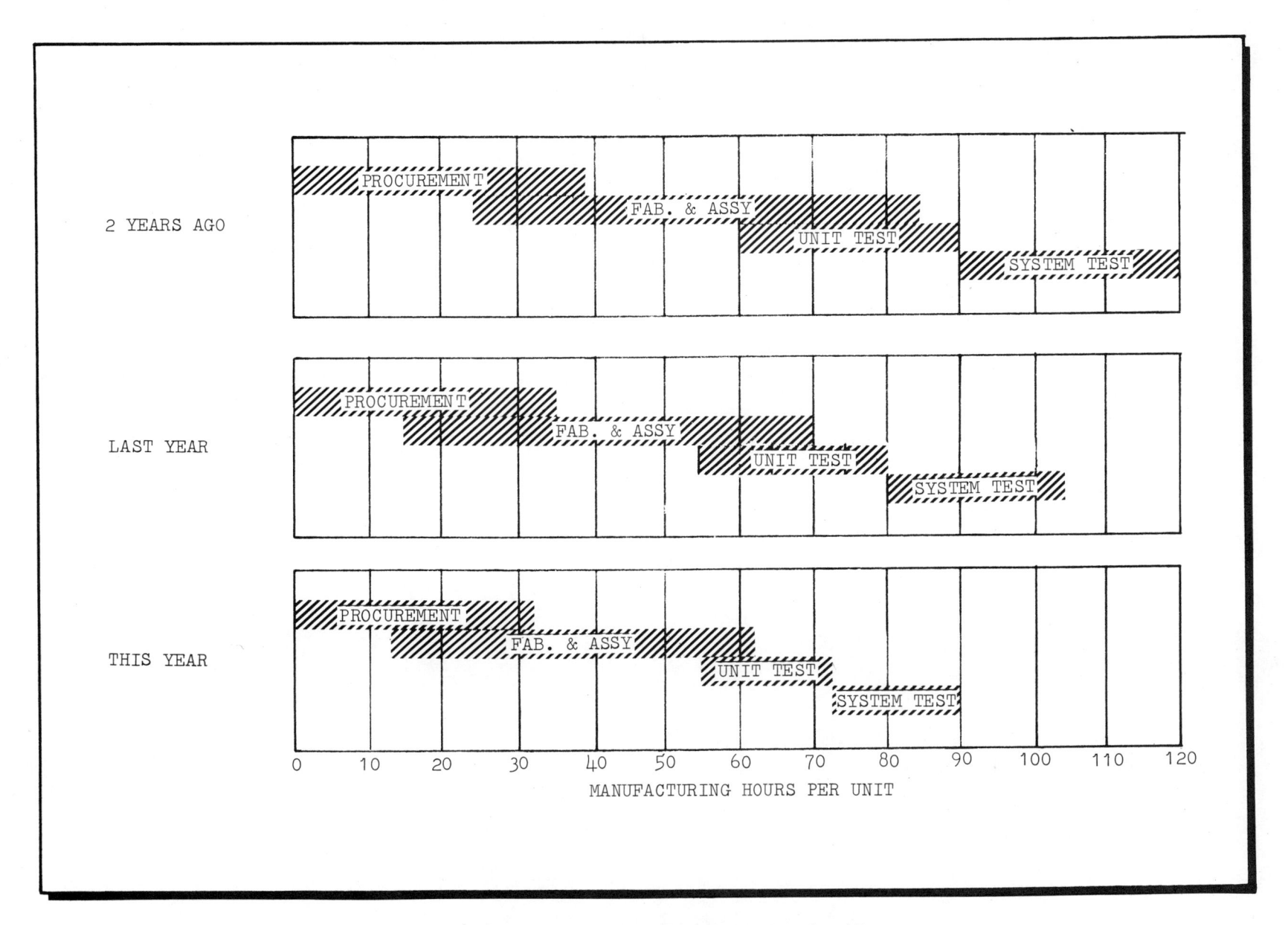

Figure 57.15 Unit Cost/Time—Version 15

775

58.0 WORKING CAPITAL TURNOVER

Charts that display the turnover of working capital, the multiple of net sales to working capital, are shown in this section. Working capital consists of those business assets that can be readily converted into operating funds, the difference remaining after current liabilities have been deducted from current assets. Operating or financial problems are indicated on the chart by an excessively fast or slow turnover.

58.1 Working Capital Turnover—Version 1: A simple version of a working capital turnover chart is shown in Figure 58.1. A goal is shown in this example as a dashed line. This goal could be based on an industry average, or it could be based on a forecast or on performance during the previous time period. Actual performance to date (through April, in this example) is shown with a solid line. The amount scale is in terms of the multiple of net sales to working capital.

58.2 Working Capital Turnover—Version 2: A surface chart style has been used in Version 2 of a working capital turnover chart, Figure 58.2. The problem with this style of chart is the time required to apply the shading.

58.3 Working Capital Turnover—Version 3: Version 3 of a working capital turnover chart, Figure 58.3, is identical to Version 1 except that a line showing the actual year-to-date average statistics has been added.

58.4 Working Capital Turnover—Version 4: A column chart style has been used for Version 4 of a working capital turnover chart, Figure 58.4. Hatched columns are used to show the forecast, while solid columns show actual performance to date.

58.5 Working Capital Turnover—Version 5: A multi-year version of a working capital turnover chart is shown in Figure 58.5. In this example, planned and actual performance is shown for the current year and for four previous years. The coming year's planned performance is shown by quarters.

58.6 Working Capital Turnover—Version 6: A statistical table and a graphic chart have been combined in Version 6 of a working capital turnover chart, Figure 58.6. The graphic portion of the chart shows the goal in dashed line form and the actual performance to date with solid columns. The statistical portion of the display shows net sales, working capital, and the working capital turnover in terms of actual performance, the goal, and the net variance between these latter two figures.

58.7 Working Capital Turnover—Version 7: Figure 58.7 displays a statistical table version of a working capital turnover tracking chart. In this example, the statistics for total current assets and liabilities are given, together with the difference between these two sets of numbers, the working capital. Sales statistics are given on the basis of rate per month, year to date, and annualized.

The working capital turnover (the multiple of sales to working capital) is given in terms of the actual performance, the goal, and the net variance between these latter two figures.

58.8 Working Capital Turnover—Version 8: A one-time status report version of a working capital turnover chart is shown in Figure 58.8. Statistics for planned and actual performance and the variance therefrom are given relative to sales, total current assets and liabilities, working capital, and working capital turnover.

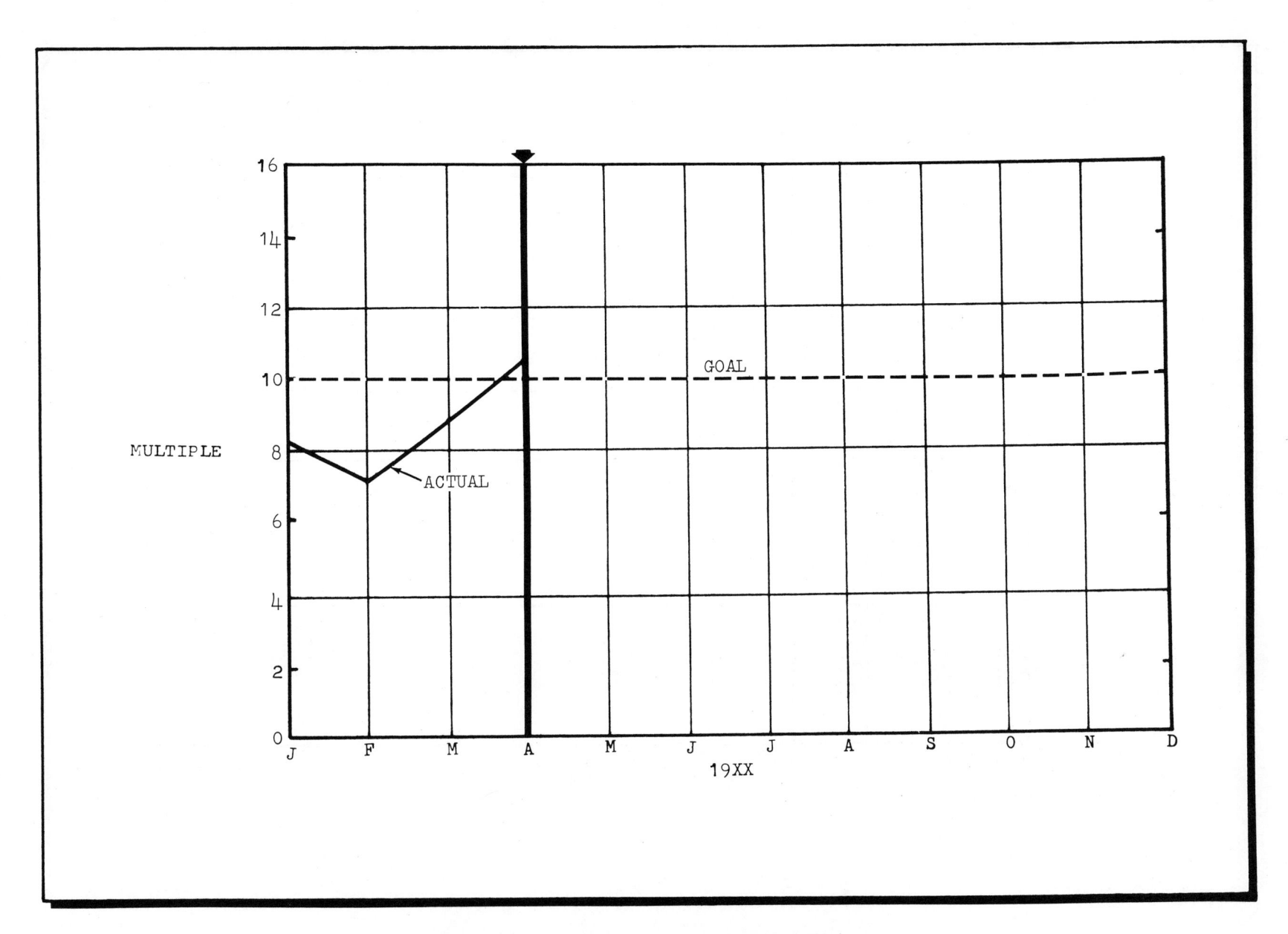

Figure 58.1 Working Capital Turnover—Version 1

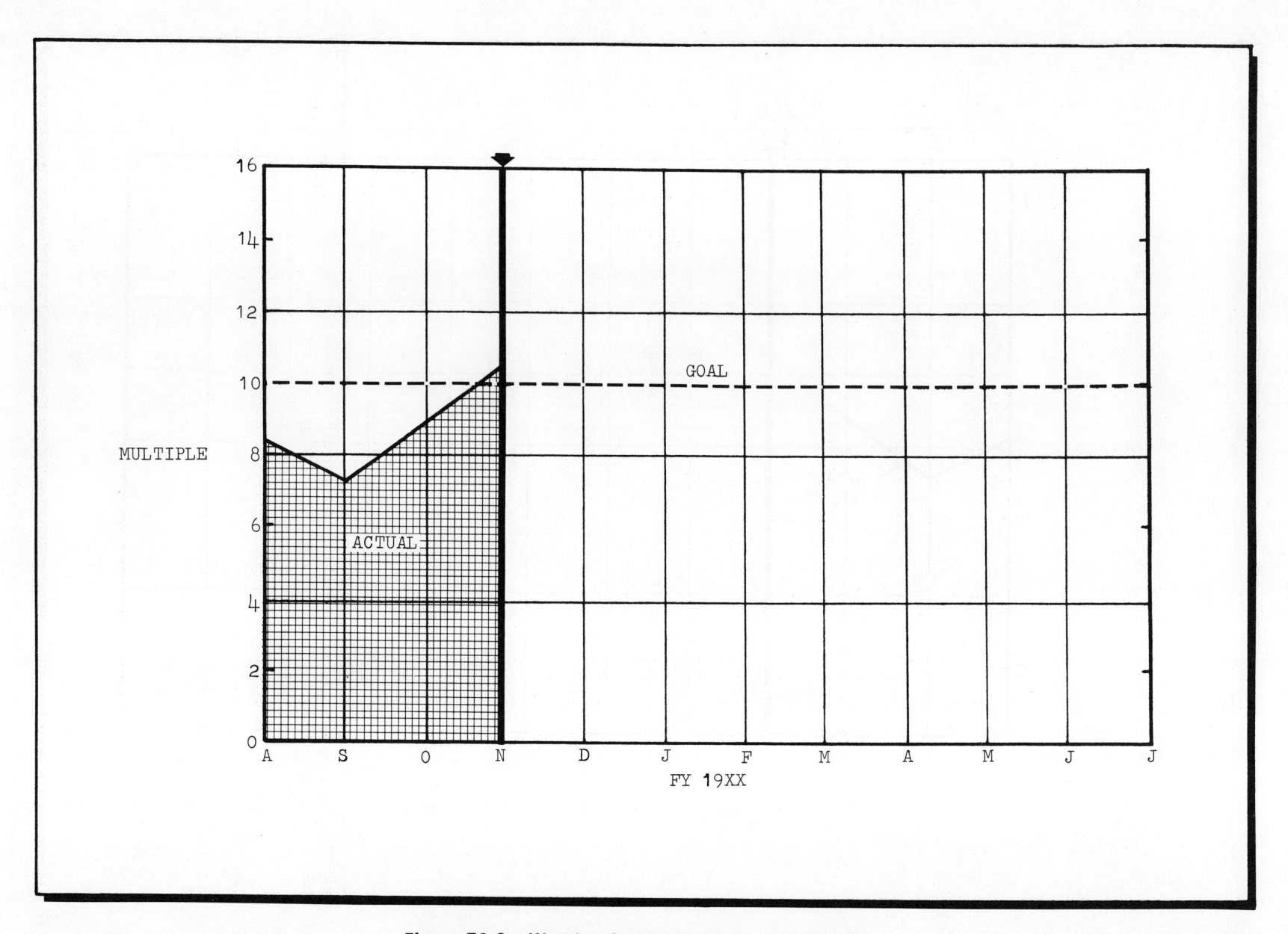

Figure 58.2 Working Capital Turnover—Version 2

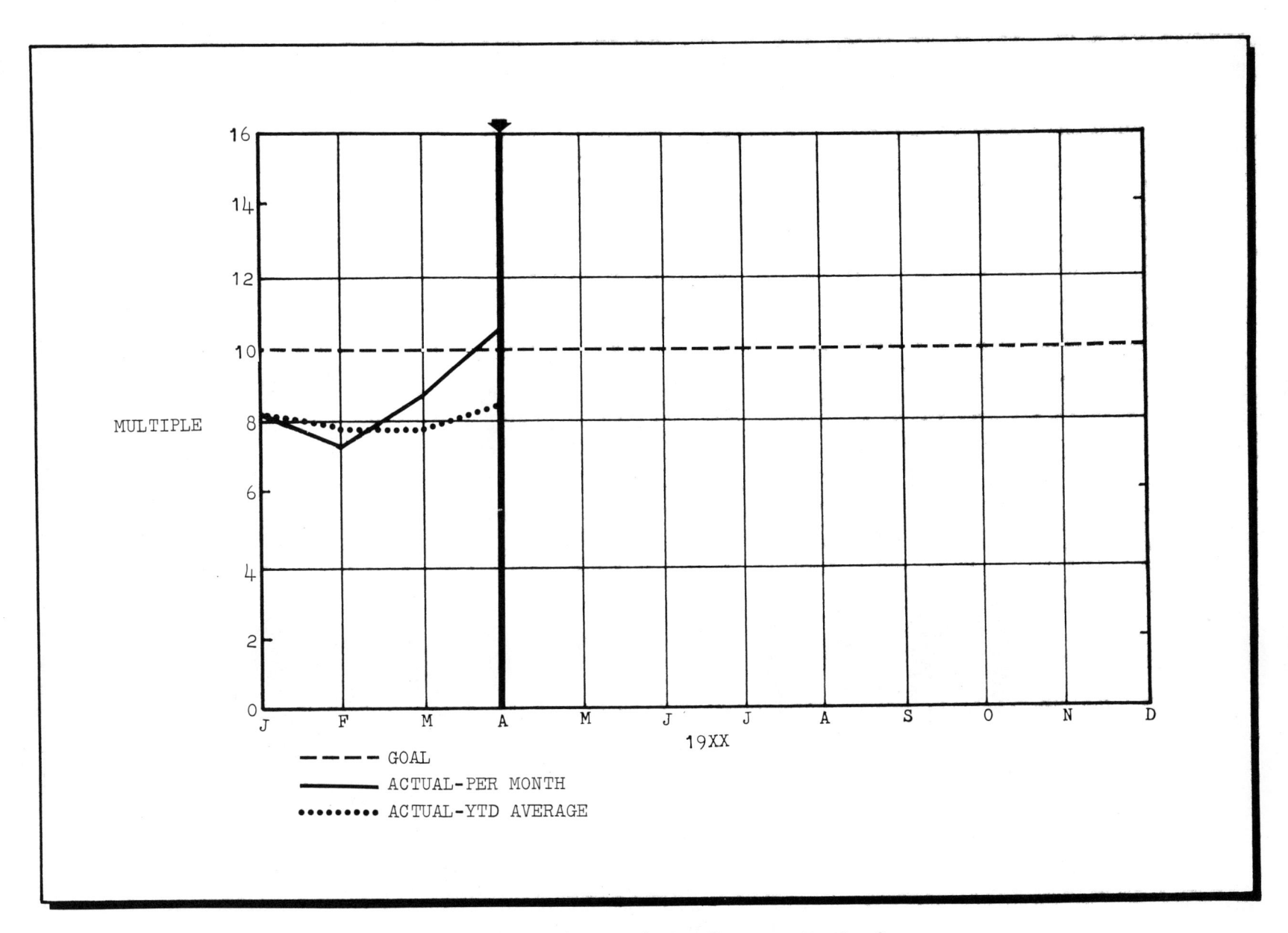

Figure 58.3 Working Capital Turnover—Version 3

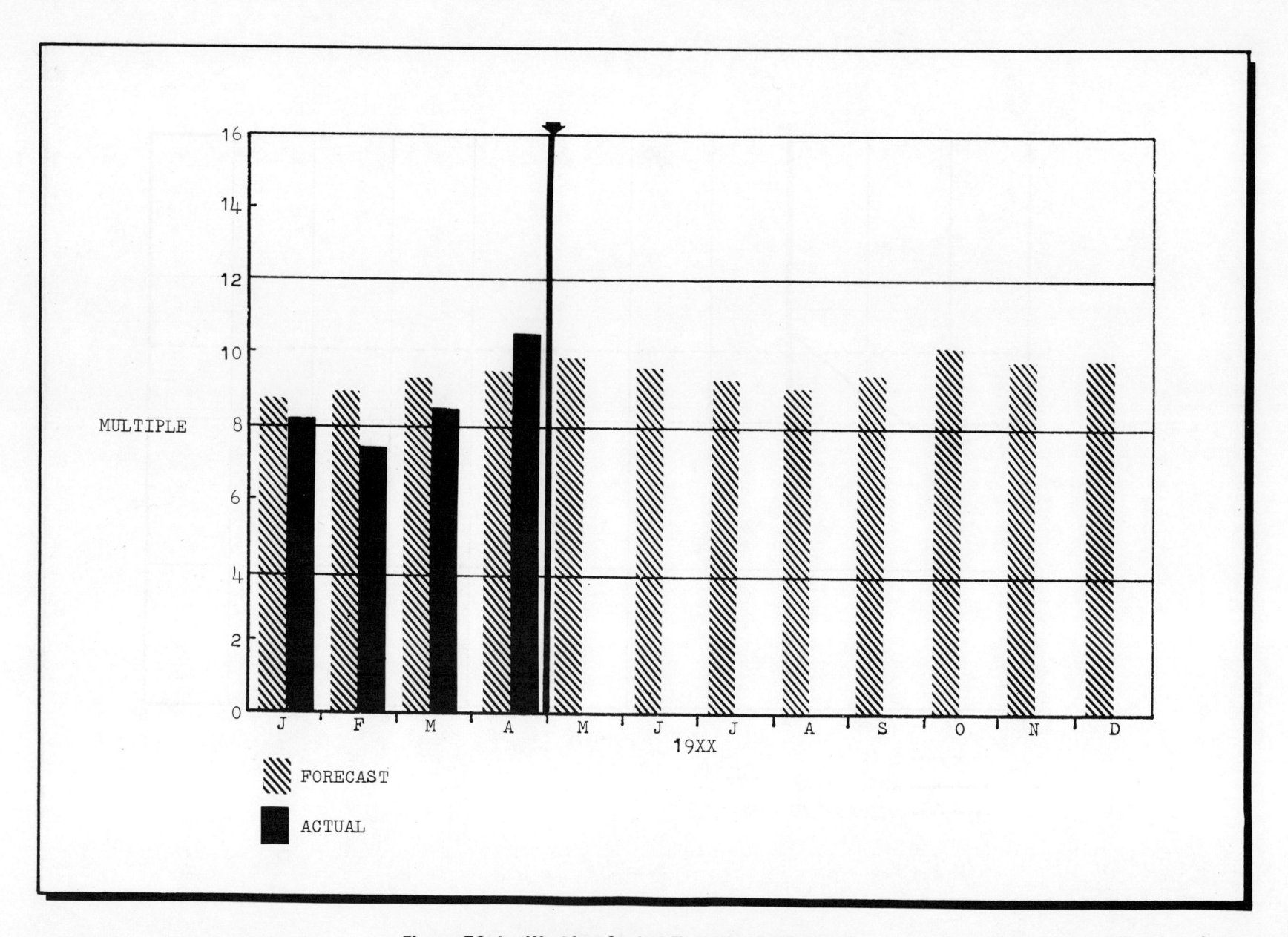

Figure 58.4 Working Capital Turnover—Version 4

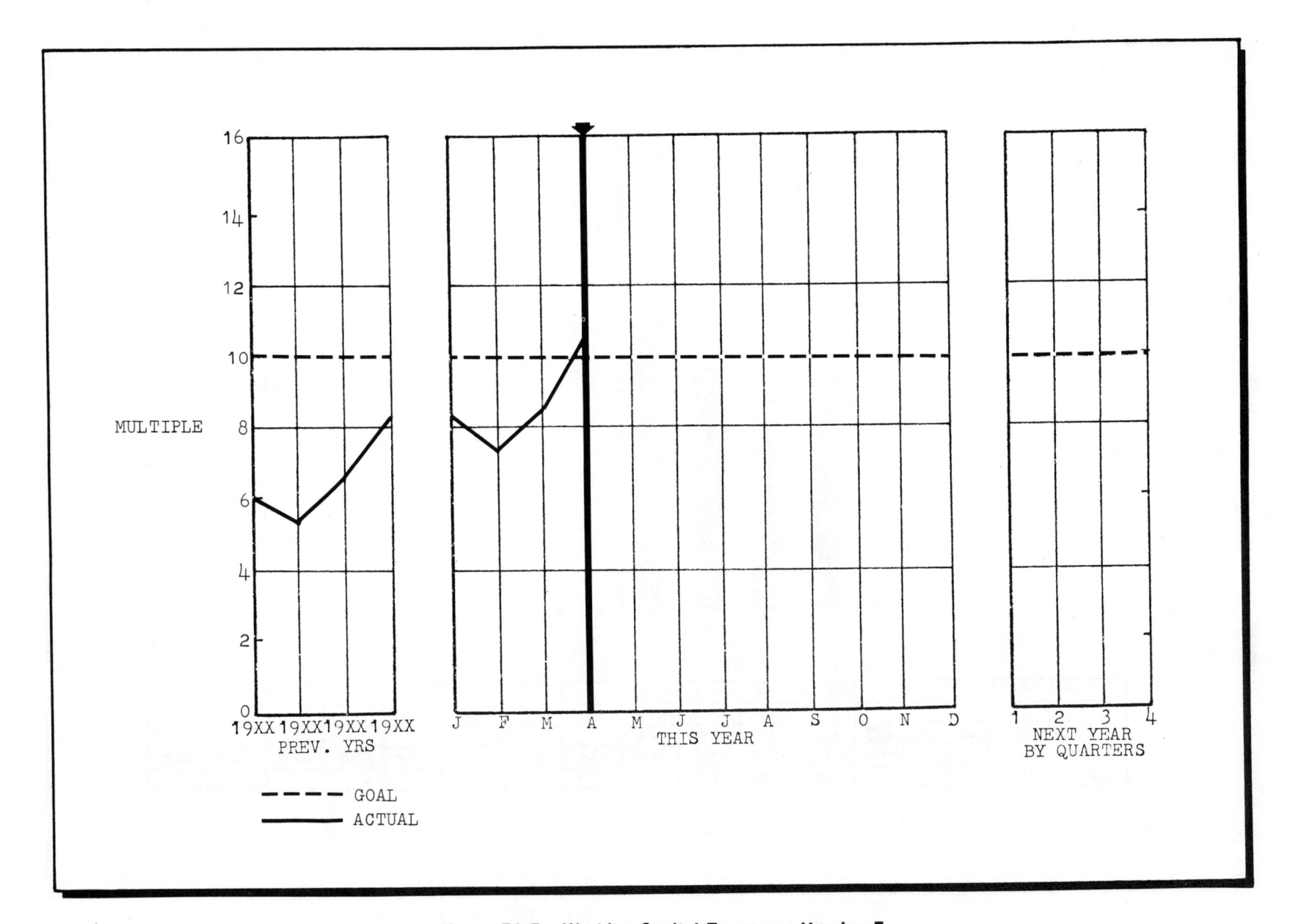

Figure 58.5   Working Capital Turnover—Version 5

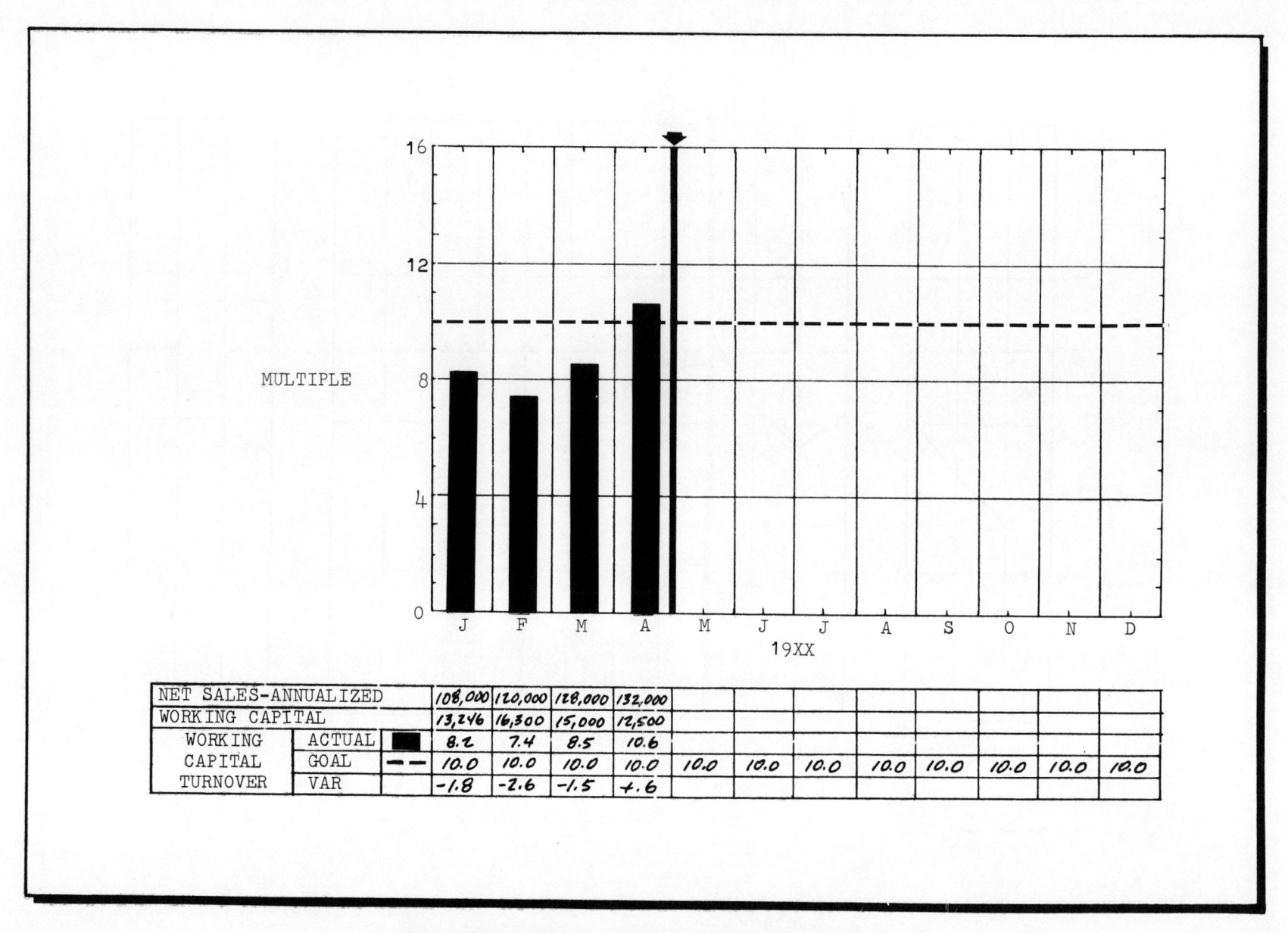

NET SALES-ANNUALIZED		108,000	120,000	128,000	132,000							
WORKING CAPITAL		13,246	16,300	15,000	12,500							
WORKING	ACTUAL ■	8.2	7.4	8.5	10.6							
CAPITAL	GOAL – –	10.0	10.0	10.0	10.0	10.0	10.0	10.0	10.0	10.0	10.0	10.0	10.0
TURNOVER	VAR	-1.8	-2.6	-1.5	+.6							

Figure 58.6 Working Capital Turnover—Version 6

CATEGORY		J	F	M	A	\multicolumn{8}{c}{19XX}							
		J	F	M	A	M	J	J	A	S	O	N	D
TOTAL CURRENT ASSETS ($000)		30.1	33.2	32.0	29.7								
TOTAL CURRENT LIABILITIES ($000)		16.9	16.9	17.0	17.2								
WORKING CAPITAL ($000)		13.2	16.3	15.0	12.5								
NET SALES ($000)	PER MO	9.0	11.0	12.0	12.0								
	YEAR TO DATE	9.0	20.0	32.0	44.0								
	ANNUAL'D	108.0	120.0	128.0	132.0								
WORKING CAPITAL TURNOVER (MULTIPLE)	ACTUAL	8.2	7.4	8.5	10.6								
	GOAL	10.0	10.0	10.0	10.0	10.0	10.0	10.0	10.0	10.0	10.0	10.0	10.0
	NET VAR.	-1.8	-2.6	-1.5	+.6								

Figure 58.7 Working Capital Turnover—Version 7

STATUS AS OF _____

CATEGORY		PLAN	ACTUAL	VARIANCE
NET SALES	THIS MO.	$11,000	$12,000	+$1000
	YTD	$41,000	$44,000	+$3000
	ANNUALIZED	$123,000	$132,000	+$9000
TOTAL CURRENT ASSETS		$30,500	$29,700	-$800
TOTAL CURRENT LIABILITIES		$18,200	$17,200	-$1000
WORKING CAPITAL		$12,300	$12,500	+$200
WORKING CAPITAL TURNOVER		10.0	10.6	+.6

Figure 58.8 Working Capital Turnover—Version 8

II

CHARTSMANSHIP

Introduction

Charts, if well-executed, present complex information in a graphic form where the information can be quickly and easily understood. They are the businessman's "shorthand" and are best when well laid out, well-defined, and stand on their own without the need of lengthy written or oral explanation. In short, charts should be visually fluent.

This part of the encyclopedia has the purpose of setting forth some of the fundamental layout considerations when preparing business charts. These concepts are presented not as "standards," but rather as guidelines in the preparation of effective charts. Many of the suggested practices presented here closely follow the guidelines set forth in the American Society of Mechanical Engineers publication, Time-Series Charts.

The sections under "Chartsmanship" are as follows:

59.0 Basic Types of Business Charts
60.0 Line Chart Variations
61.0 Surface Chart Variations
62.0 Column Chart Variations
63.0 Bar Chart Variations
64.0 Symbol Chart Variations
65.0 Circle Chart Variations
66.0 Format and Nomenclature
67.0 Shape, Position, and Size
68.0 Titles
69.0 Grids
70.0 Line Weight and Shading
71.0 Amount Scales
72.0 Time Scales
73.0 Goals and Limits
74.0 Time-Now Dating
75.0 Notes, Keys, and Authentication
76.0 Emphasizing Key Points
77.0 Data Layout

59.0 BASIC TYPES OF BUSINESS CHARTS

59.1 Basic Chart Types—Two-Scale: There are three basic types of two-scale charts, all shown in Figure 59.1. "Two-scale" means that this category of chart contains both an amount scale (usually vertical) and a time scale (usually horizontal). The line chart is, by far, the most commonly used type of chart. Other names often used for line charts are curve charts, slope curve charts, slope line charts, and line curve charts.

Surface charts are used less often than line charts, often because of the added work involved in shading the surface. They are also called slope surface charts, simple surface charts, and pattern charts.

The column chart is another widely used style. Charts of this type are also sometimes known as simple column charts, area column charts (if the vertical scale is in terms of percentage), ranking charts, and rating charts.

59.2 Basic Chart Types—One-Scale: There are three types of one-scale charts. They are shown in Figure 59.2. The single scale that is used can be in terms of either amount or time. One of the more commonly known one-scale charts is the bar chart. It is also known as a simple bar chart, an area bar chart (when the horizontal scale is in terms of percentage), a ranking chart, and a rating chart.

Another often-used chart in business is the symbol chart. It is also sometimes called a progress chart, and a milestone or Gantt chart, depending upon the symbols and techniques used.

The third type of one-scale chart is the circle chart, also called segmented chart, pie chart, sector chart, divided circle chart, and disc chart.

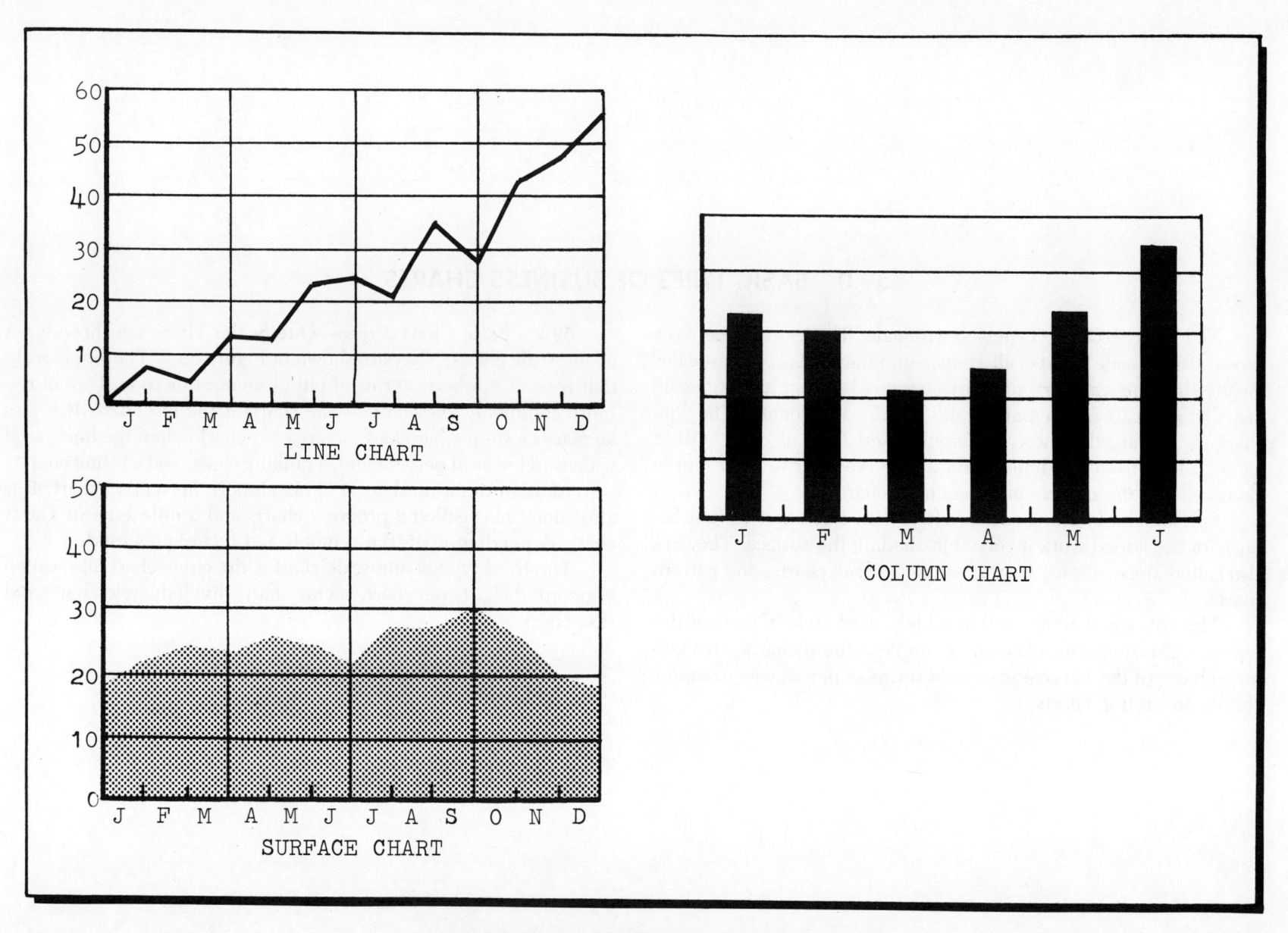

Figure 59.1   Basic Chart Types—Two-Scale

790

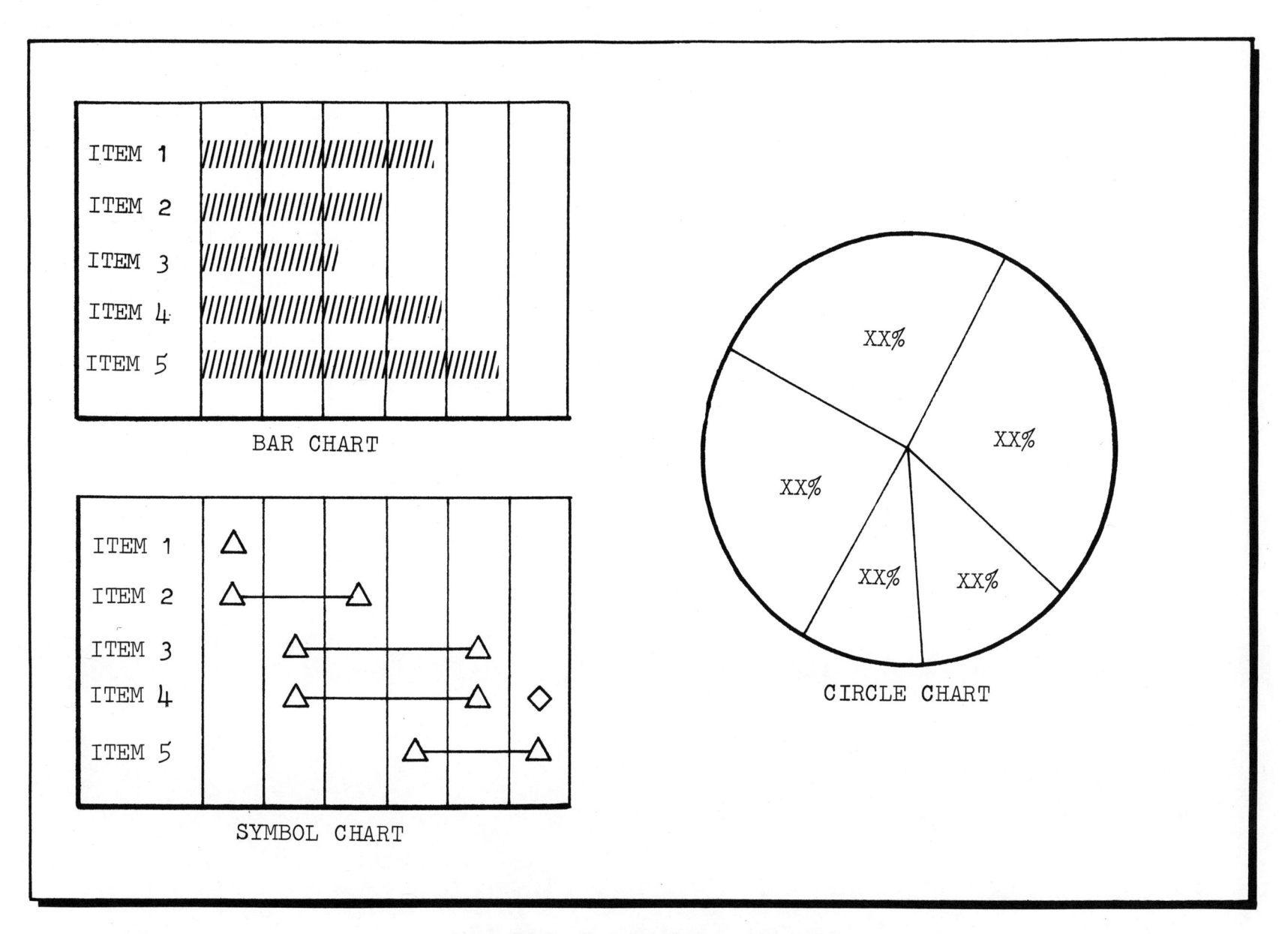

Figure 59.2 Basic Chart Types—One-Scale

60.0 LINE CHART VARIATIONS

60.1 Line Chart Variations—Single Sets of Scales: There is a great number of variations of line charts. The simplest types are shown in Figure 60.1. The most common variation of the basic line chart is the step line chart. This latter type of chart sometimes has the problem, when plotted with other data, of having the vertical lines coincide, thus making the chart difficult to read. The step line chart is also sometimes called a step curve chart or a stair chart.

At the bottom of Figure 60.1 another variation of the line chart is shown. This is the logarithmic amount-scale chart, sometimes called a ratio chart, rate-of-change chart, or semi-log chart.

60.2 Line Chart Variations—Repeated and Multiple Scales: Variations of line charts with repeated or multiple scales are shown in Figure 60.2. Three examples are shown. They are the repeated time-scale line chart, the multiple time-scale line chart, and the multiple amount scale line chart.

60.3 Examples of Uses of Line Charts: Two examples of how line charts can be used are shown in Figure 60.3. At the top of the figure a budget-tracking chart is shown. It displays planned expenditures versus actual expenditures, utilizing a simple, basic line chart format.

An example of the use of a multiple amount-scale step line chart is shown at the bottom of the figure. In this example, sales in terms of dollars (left-hand scale) are compared to the number of sales calls made.

60.4 Examples of Line Charts Used to Display Frequency Distributions: Two variations of line charts used for histograms are shown in Figure 60.4—a curve line form shown at the top, and a step line form. Frequency charts are used in business as analytical tools to examine employment, earnings, and other factors and to measure central tendencies: mode, mean, and median. Mode is the score or amount that occurs most frequently. Mean is the arithmetical average. Median is the score or amount which falls in the middle of the distribution.

60.5 Example of Line Chart Used for Ratio Analysis: The ratio chart (bottom of Figure 60.5) utilizes a logarithmic amount scale where equal distances represent equal ratios; whereas, in the normal arithmetic amount chart (top of Figure 60.5), equal distances represent equal amounts. The ratio chart, also known as a semi-log chart or a rate-of-change chart, is used to picture relative change. The *angle* of change is significant in this graphic method. In the example at the bottom of Figure 60.5 for instance, the straight line upward from left to right indicates a rate-of-change that is increasing at a constant percentage rate. If the line was curved it would indicate an increase at either an increasing or decreasing percentage rate, depending upon the slope of the curve. The reverse would be true, of course, if the lines were sloping downward from left to right.

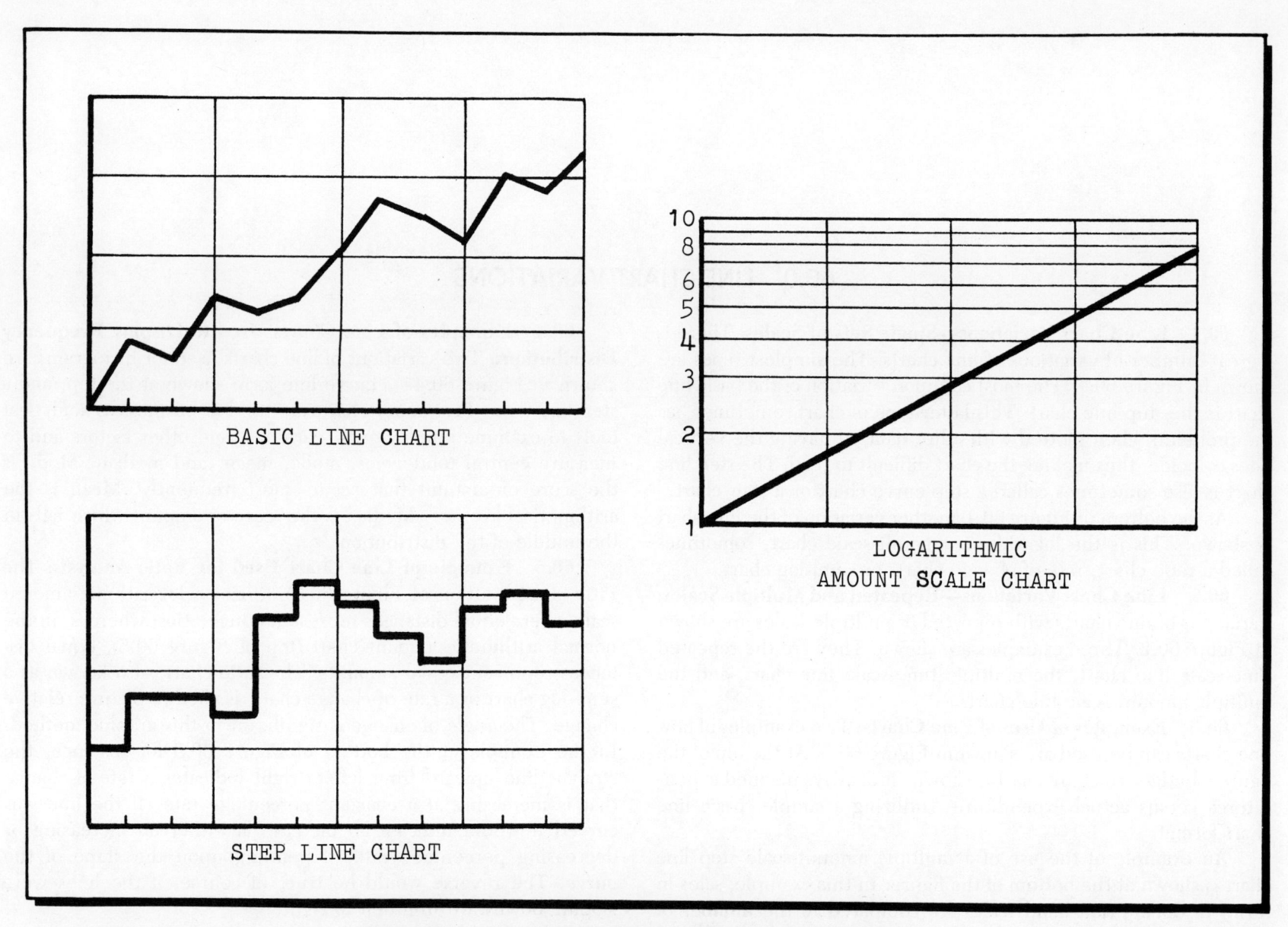

Figure 60.1   Line Chart Variations—Single Sets of Scales

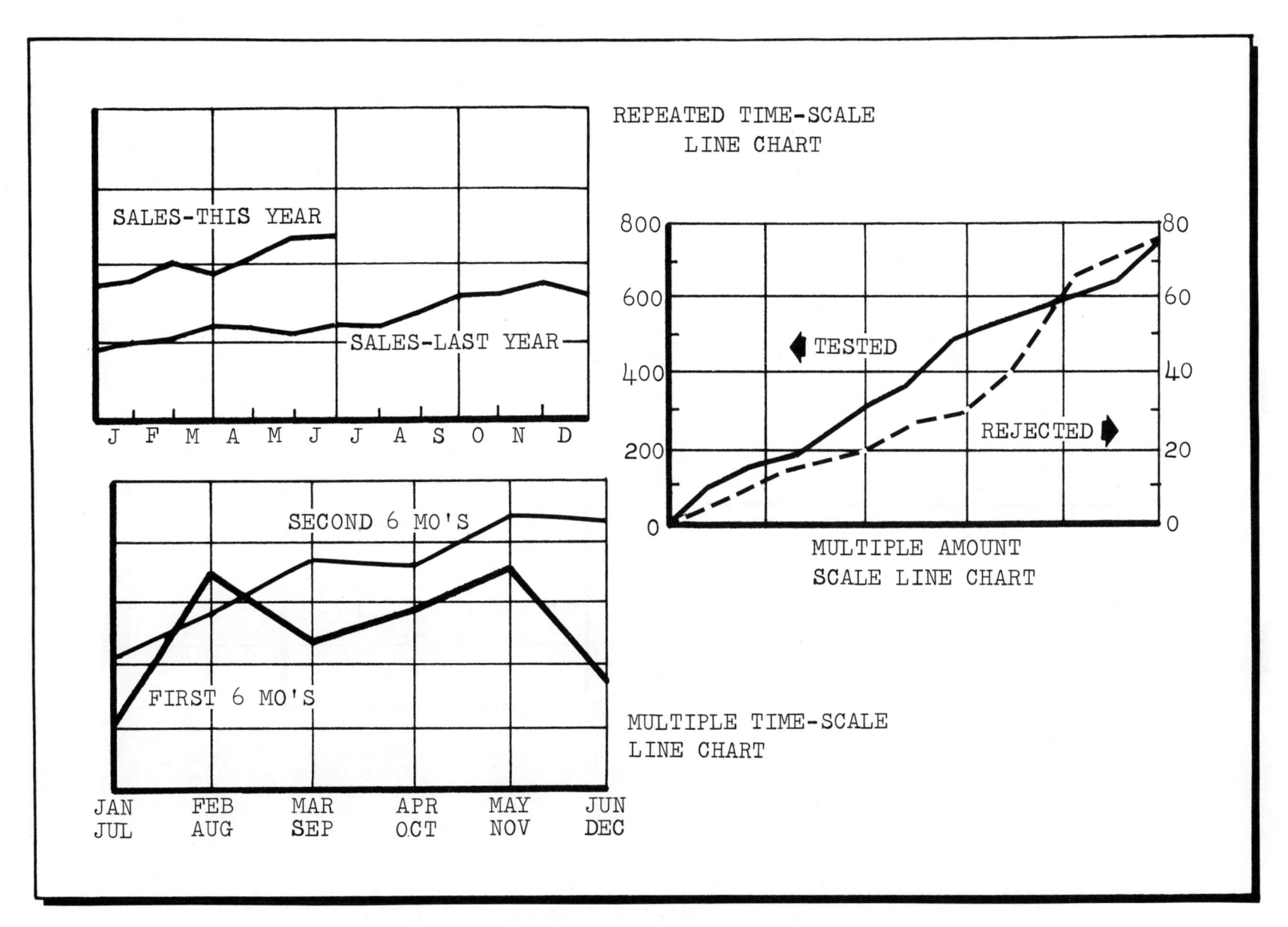

Figure 60.2 Line Chart Variations—Repeated and Multiple Scales

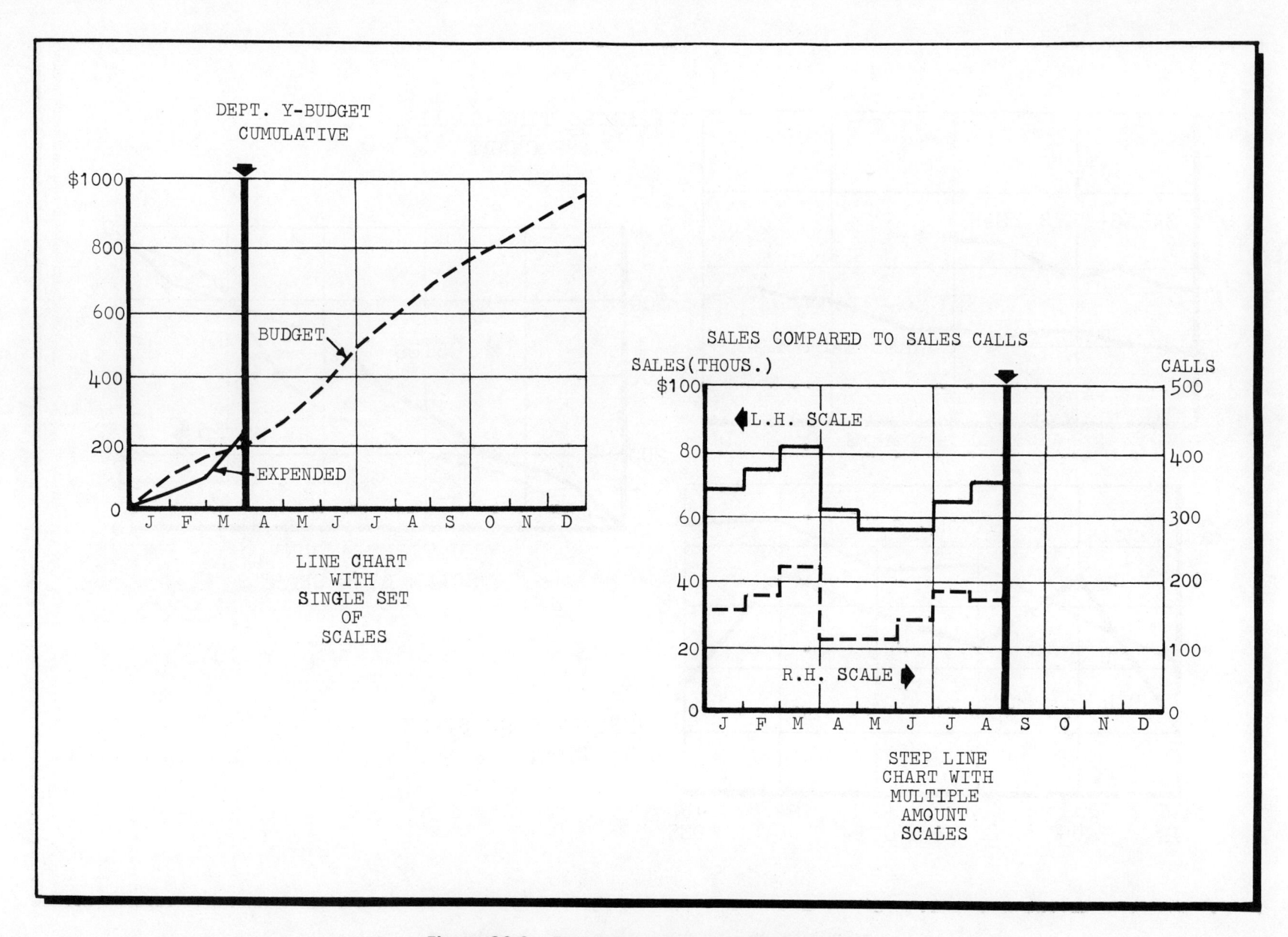

Figure 60.3   Examples of Uses of Line Charts

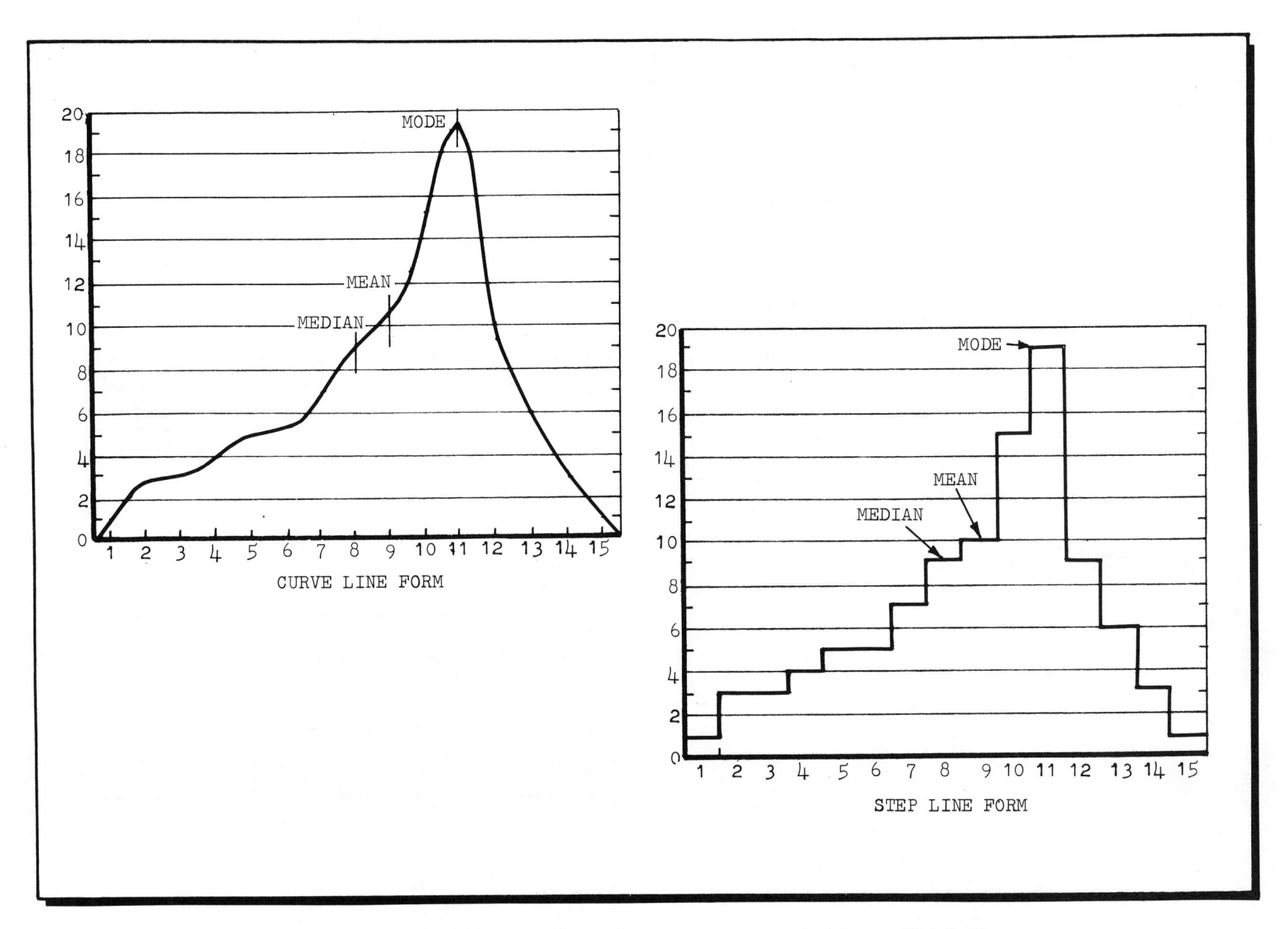

Figure 60.4 Examples of Line Charts Used to Display Frequency Distributions

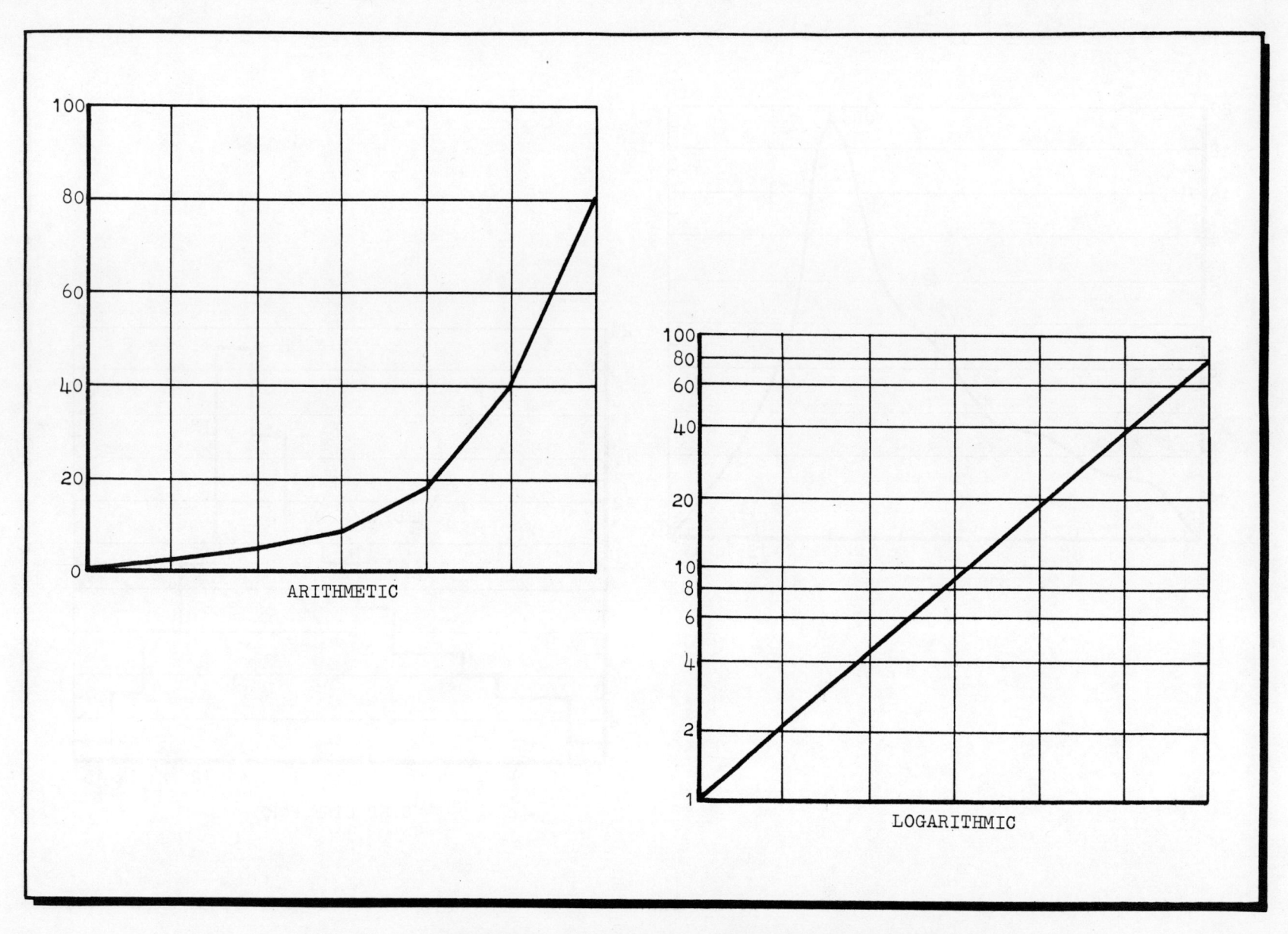

Figure 60.5   Examples of Line Charts Used for Ratio Analysis

61.0 SURFACE CHART VARIATIONS

61.1 Surface Chart Variations—Simple: The more commonly used variations of the surface chart are shown in Figure 61.1. In addition to the basic surface chart (top of figure), there are step surface charts and subdivided line surface charts. The latter type is sometimes called a strata chart or component chart.

61.2 Surface Chart Variations—Band and Variance Styles: Additional variations of surface charts are shown in Figure 61.2. The band surface chart is used to illustrate the margin between two factors. Variations of this are sometimes called correlation charts or line range charts. Similar to the band surface chart is the net-variance surface chart. This is sometimes called a correlation chart or a net-difference chart.

61.3 Examples of Uses of Surface Charts: Two examples of the use of surface charts are shown in Figure 61.3. At the top of the figure, a subdivided surface chart style is used to show sales by category. The categories are "stacked" so that the top line represents total sales.

An example of the use of a band surface chart is shown at the bottom of Figure 61.3. In this example, cumulative deposits and withdrawals have been plotted, the band representing the remaining cash balance.

BASIC SURFACE CHART

STEP SURFACE CHART

SUB-DIVIDED LINE SURFACE CHART

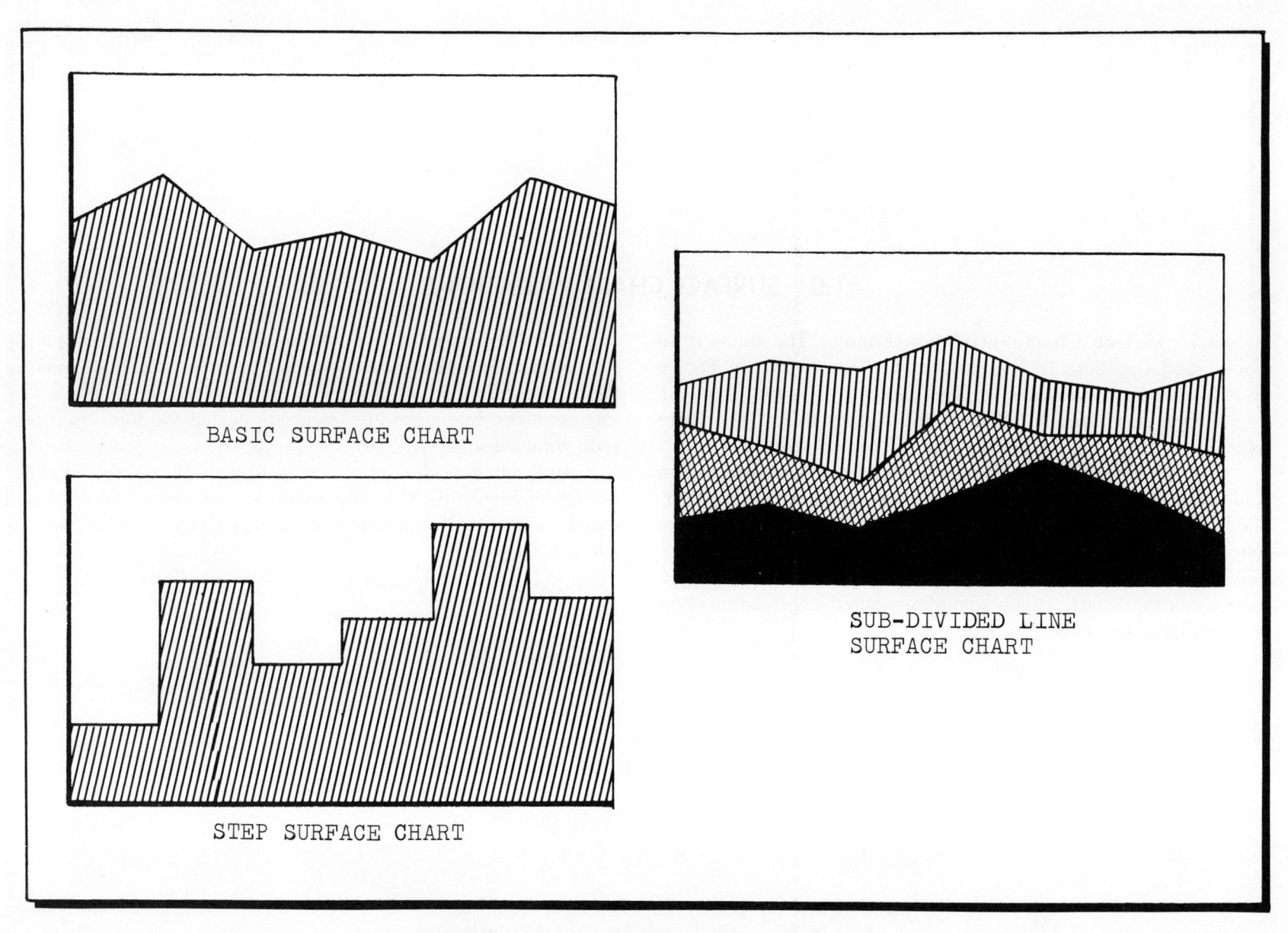

Figure 61.1 Surface Chart Variations—Simple

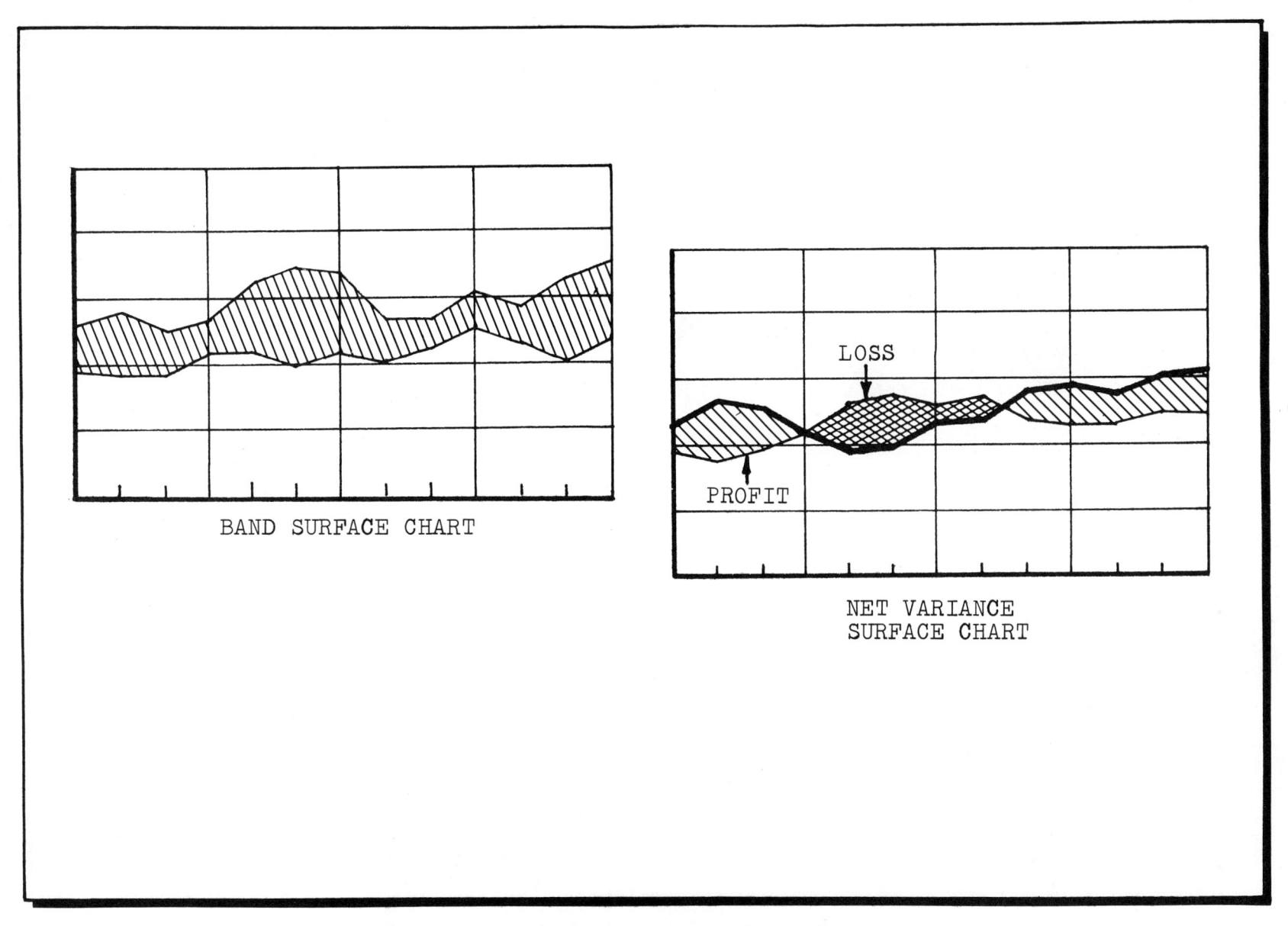

Figure 61.2   Surface Chart Variations—Band and Variance Styles

801

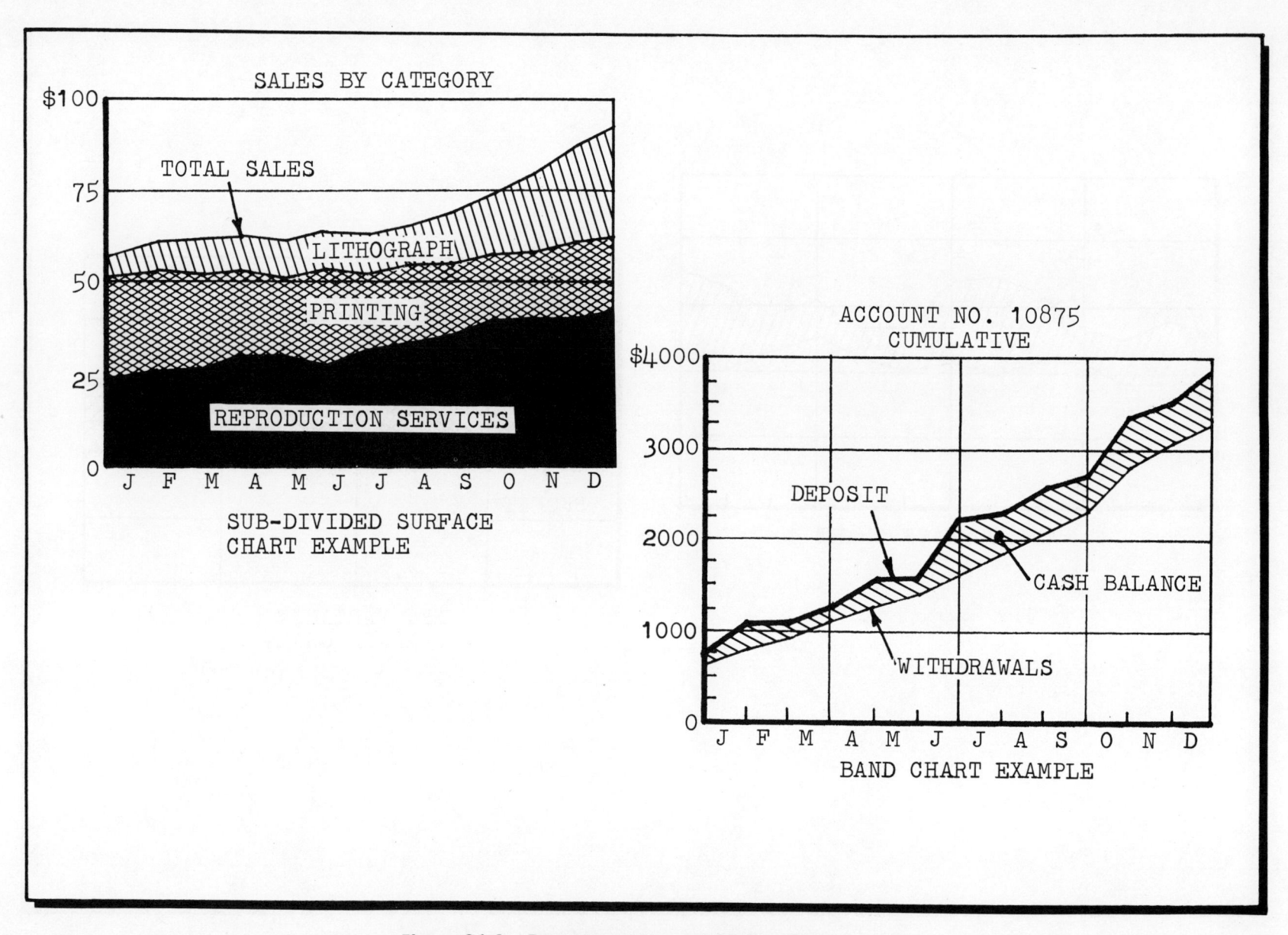

Figure 61.3   Examples of Uses of Surface Charts

62.0 COLUMN CHART VARIATIONS

62.1 Column Chart Variations—Basic: The basic variations of column charts are shown in Figure 62.1 beginning with the simple column chart. When two or more columns are grouped together, they constitute a grouped column chart, sometimes called a compound column chart, relationship chart, double column chart, or multiple column chart. Charts where the columns are segmented are called subdivided column charts. They are also known as component column charts, segmented column charts, and divided column charts. When the amount scale of a column chart is in terms of 100%, it is called an absolute column chart or relative column chart.

Variations not illustrated include pictorial unit column charts where the columns are represented by pictures, such as piles of silver dollars. These are sometimes called pictographs.

62.2 Column Chart Variations—Floating and Area: Additional types of column charts are illustrated in Figure 62.2. Three of them are categorized as floating column charts. The first is a deviation column chart, also called an over-under column chart, used to portray deviations from an average, a norm, or a goal.

Range column charts are familiar in their application to reporting stock market prices. They are sometimes called high-low charts or minimum-maximum charts.

Two-way column charts are used to display the relationship between matching types of data, such as the number of male versus female employees at some location, or at some point in time. This type of chart is also called a bilateral chart, a two-directional column chart, or a paired column chart.

Another variation of the basic column chart is the area column chart, sometimes called a 100% column chart, block chart, or "bucket" chart. The columns are joined and show measurement factors in two planes.

62.3 Examples of Uses of Column Charts: Examples of uses of column charts are shown in Figure 62.3. At the top of the figure, a grouped column chart style is used to display planned versus actual activity as it relates to deliveries. A deviation column chart format is used in the bottom example to display schedule performance.

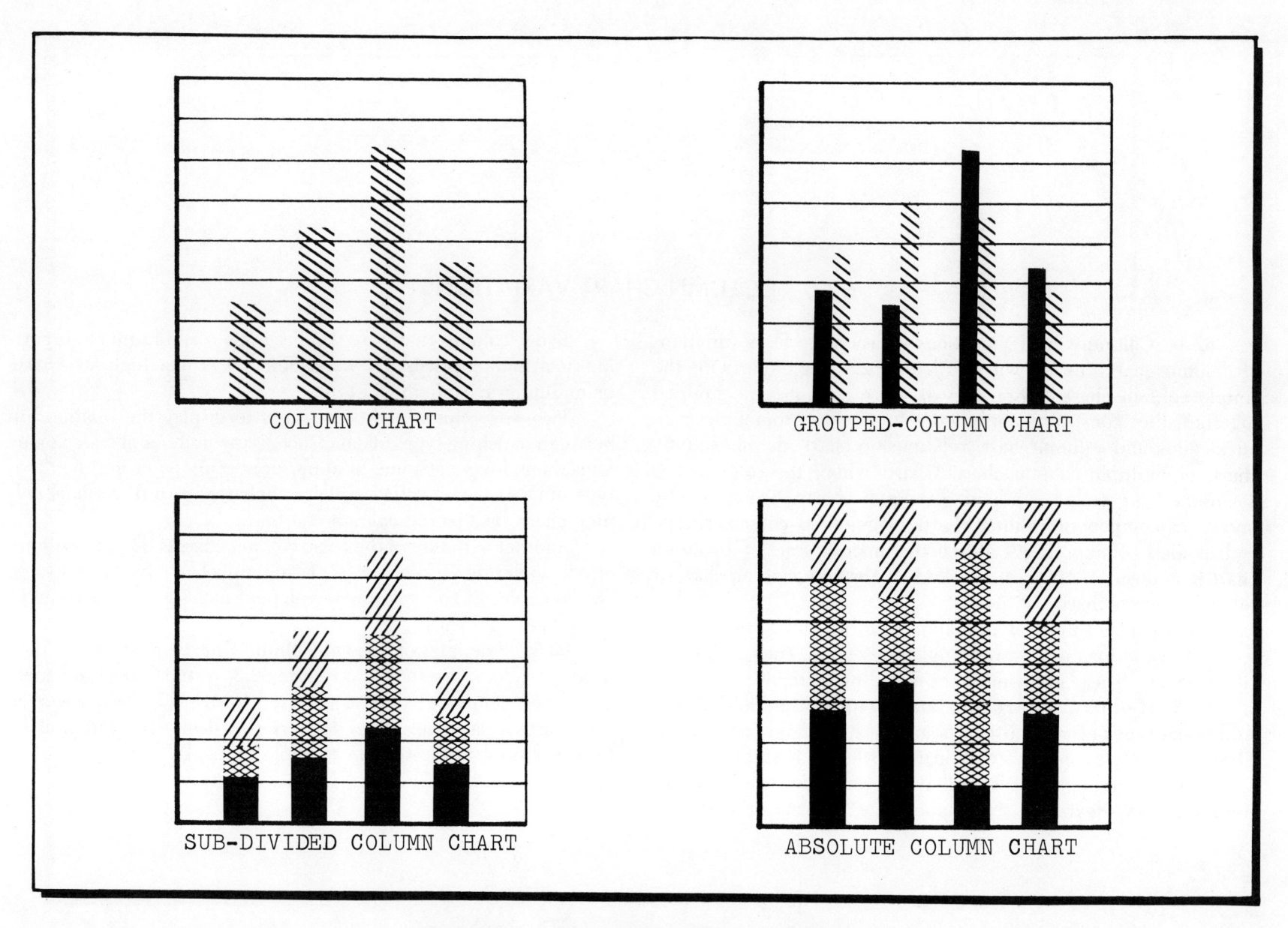

Figure 62.1 Column Chart Variations—Basic

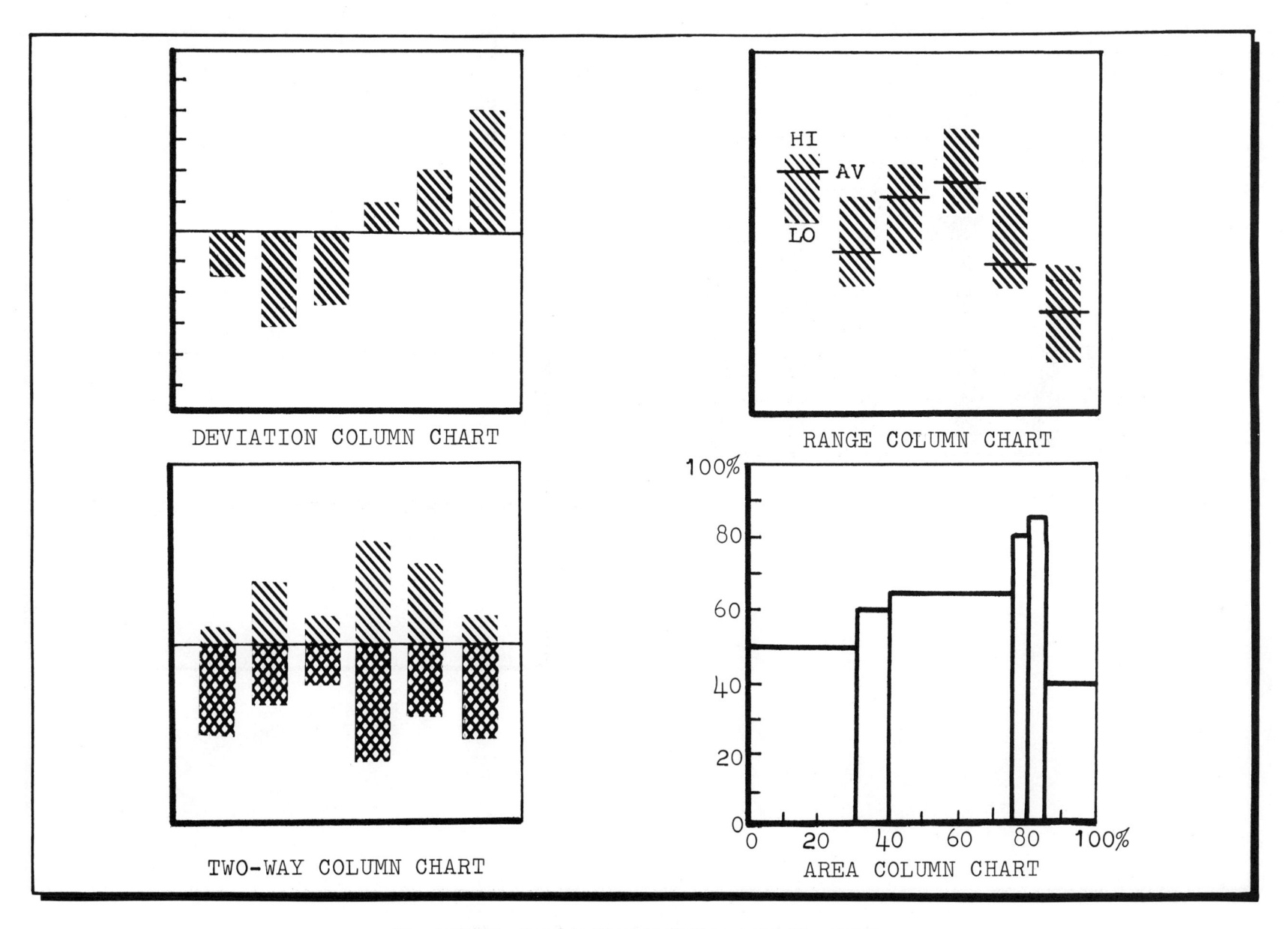

Figure 62.2 Column Chart Variations—Floating and Area

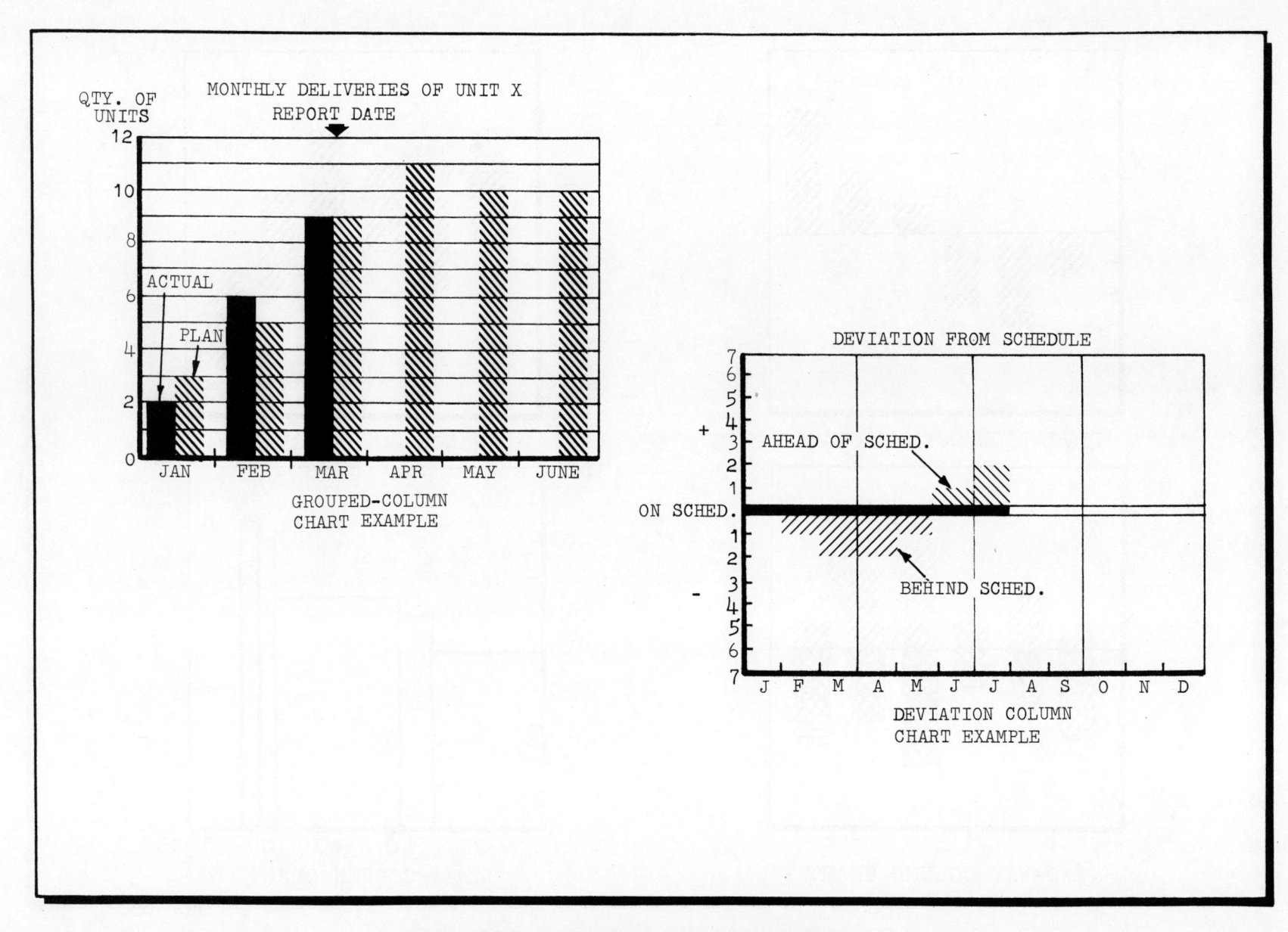

Figure 62.3   Examples of Uses of Column Charts

63.0 BAR CHART VARIATIONS

63.1 Bar Chart Variations—Basic: Figure 63.1 displays the basic bar chart, together with several of the more commonly used variations: subdivided and grouped bar charts. Bar charts are normally used to compare different factors at a given point in time, such as shown, whereas the previously described column charts are normally used for comparisons over a time span.

In Figure 63.1, the subdivided bar chart is also sometimes called a component bar chart or a divided bar chart. The grouped bar chart is also called a compound bar chart, relationship chart, double bar chart, or multiple bar chart.

63.2 Bar Chart Variations—Step Style: Three versions of step-type bar charts are shown in Figure 63.2. All three use time spans as the major scale. The step bar chart at the top of the figure is normally used to compare the same type of item in terms of a single or repeated action over an extended period of time. For instance, the bars could represent the manufacturing time span for each item. If the time spans grew progressively shorter in time, this would signify a learning factor or "learning curve."

The step-grouped bar chart shown in the center of Figure 63.2 adds a second bar to each item, the first representing the plan (P) and the second representing actual performance (A), and designed, in this example, to be shaded to display progress.

A chart style that is often used to display separate processing steps over a period of time is the step-segmented bar chart. This type of chart is also known as a "waterfall" chart, a chronological bar chart, and a component bar chart. As with the previously described step-grouped bar chart, a second set of bars could be added to this type of chart for the purpose of tracking progress.

63.3 Examples of Uses of Bar Charts: Two examples of bar charts are shown in Figure 63.3. At the top of the figure a basic bar chart is shown. It is used, in this example, to compare the performance of a number of separate departments in terms of average number of rejections per month.

The bottom of Figure 63.3 shows a step-grouped bar chart used as a progress-tracking chart. In this example, lot number 159 is shown as behind schedule, whereas lot number 158 is complete and lot number 160 is on schedule.

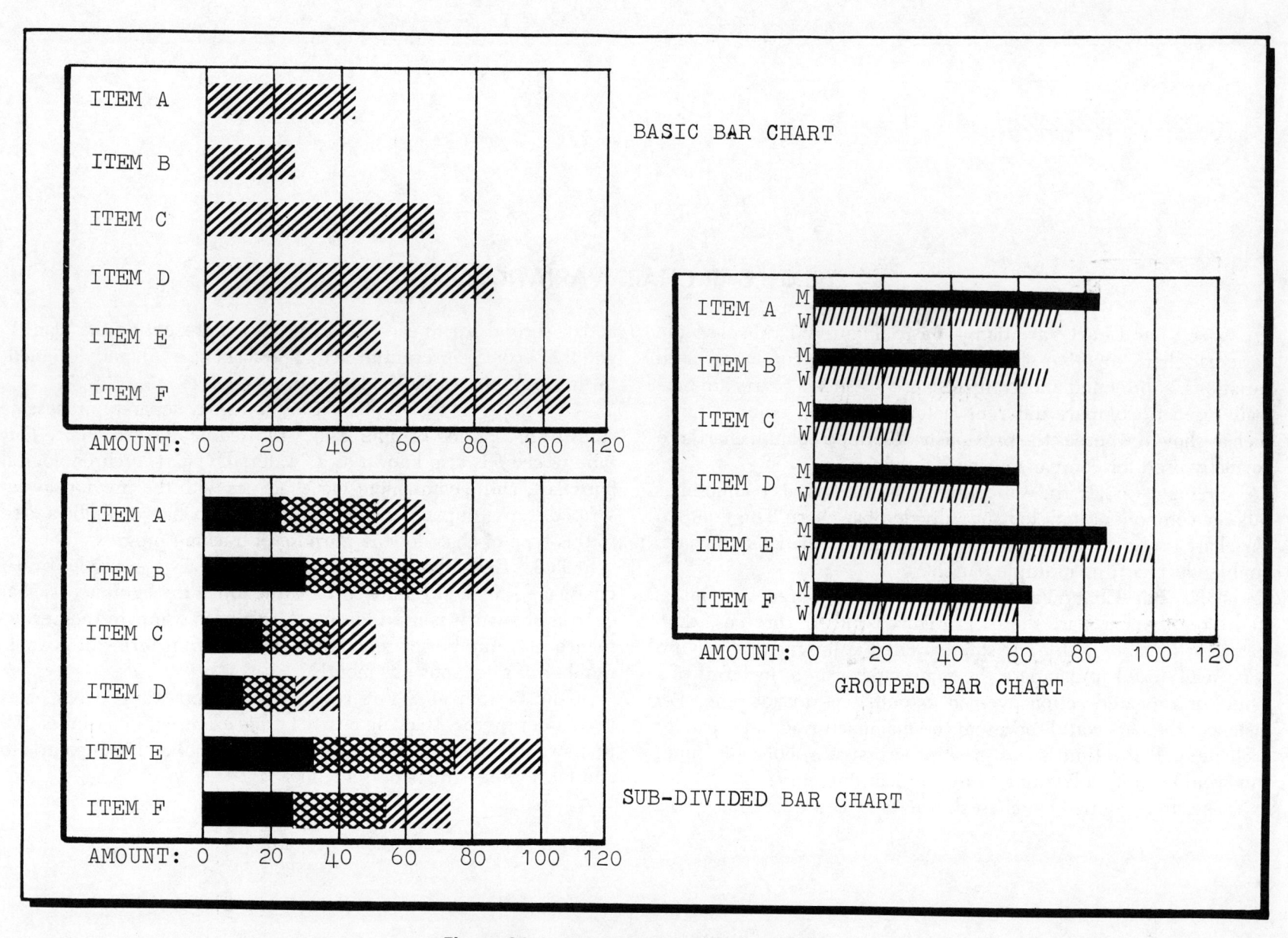

Figure 63.1 Bar Chart Variations—Basic

808

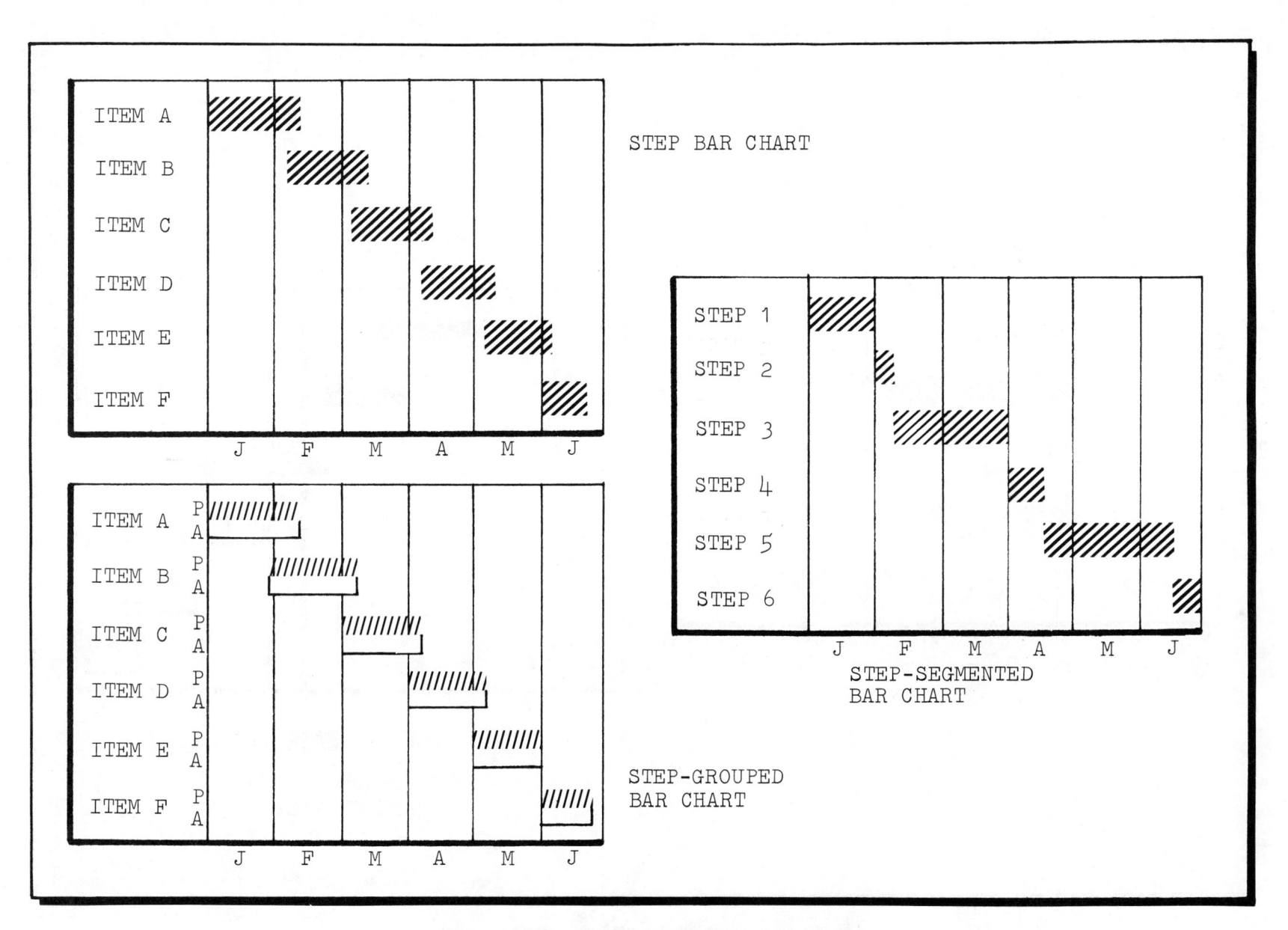

Figure 63.2 Bar Chart Variations—Step Style

809

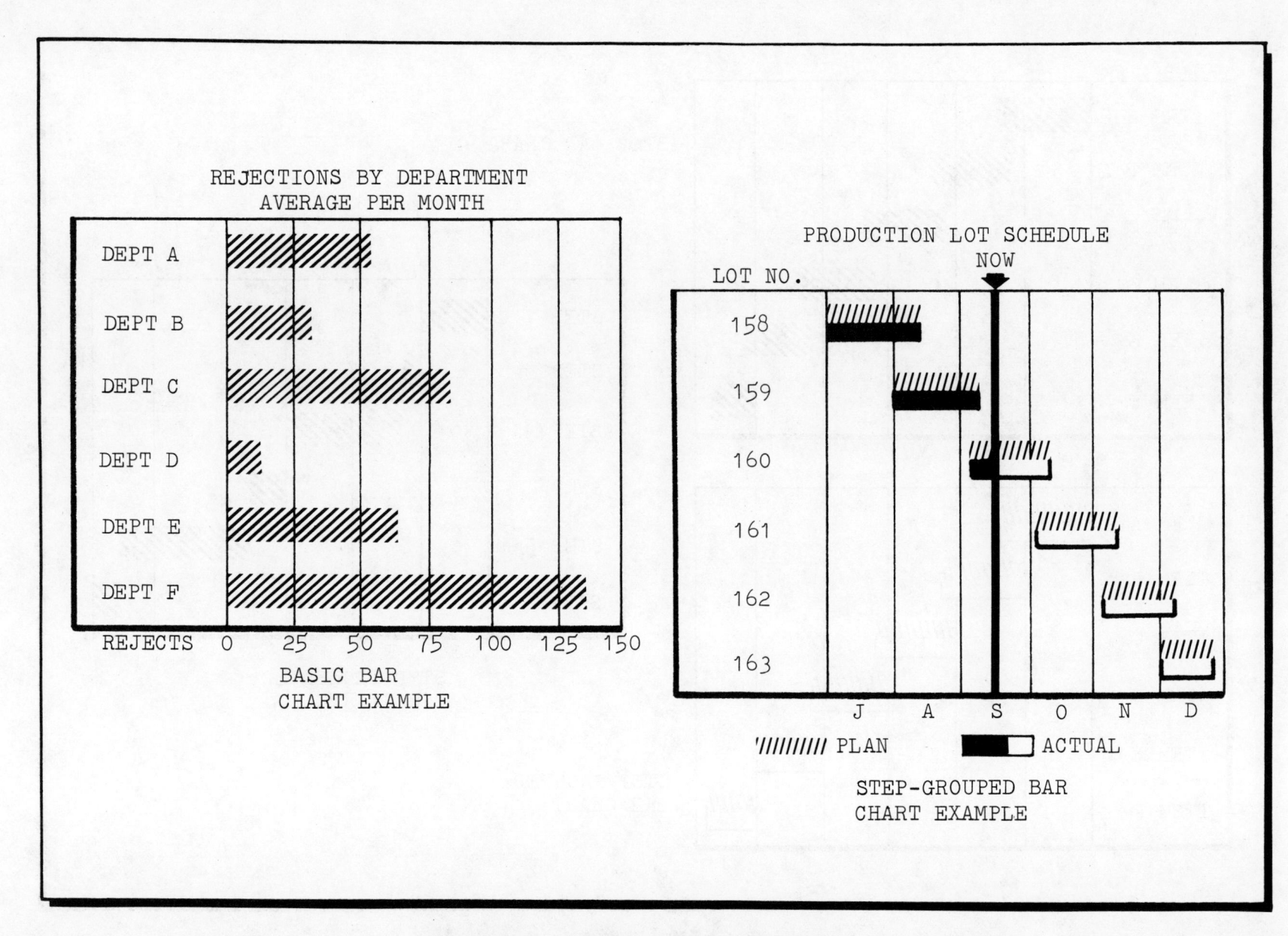

Figure 63.3 Examples of Uses of Bar Charts

64.0 SYMBOL CHART VARIATIONS

64.1 Symbol Chart Variations—Basic: There are many styles of symbol charts. Two of the more common styles are shown in Figure 64.1. Probably the most widely used type is the milestone chart, also called a progress chart. Another variation is the bar and symbol chart, also called a composite chart.

64.2 Milestone Symbol Chart: One of the commonly used charts in business is the "milestone" chart. Generally speaking, there is no standard system of symbology, each user usually developing his own symbols and methods of using them. Some of these systems are relatively simple. Others are complex, with a number of different symbols devised in an attempt to cover all possible contingencies that might be encountered in displaying actual progress versus planned activity. Complex systems usually result in "cluttered" charts that are difficult to interpret. Thus, they defeat the purpose of the chart as a graphic aid.

The symbology shown in Figure 64.2 is one of the more extensively used systems. It enables the display of basic planned and actual accomplishment data. In addition, it provides for displaying major contingency information such as rescheduling and "slipped" schedules. Graphic clarity is achieved by shading all completed items to the left of the "time-now" line, including scheduled events that were completed on a slipped date, as illustrated by lines 3 and 4 on the example. This practice has the tendency to focus attention only on those items to the left of the "time-now" line that remain incomplete, thus, behind schedule. Line 6 is an example of this. It shows this activity as being one week behind schedule. This corresponds to the anticipated slippage symbol which is displayed one week after the originally scheduled completion date. Line 10 illustrates what is to be avoided on milestone charts; i.e., the attempt to indicate quantities of like items. This type of scheduling information fits more appropriately on other types of chart formats.

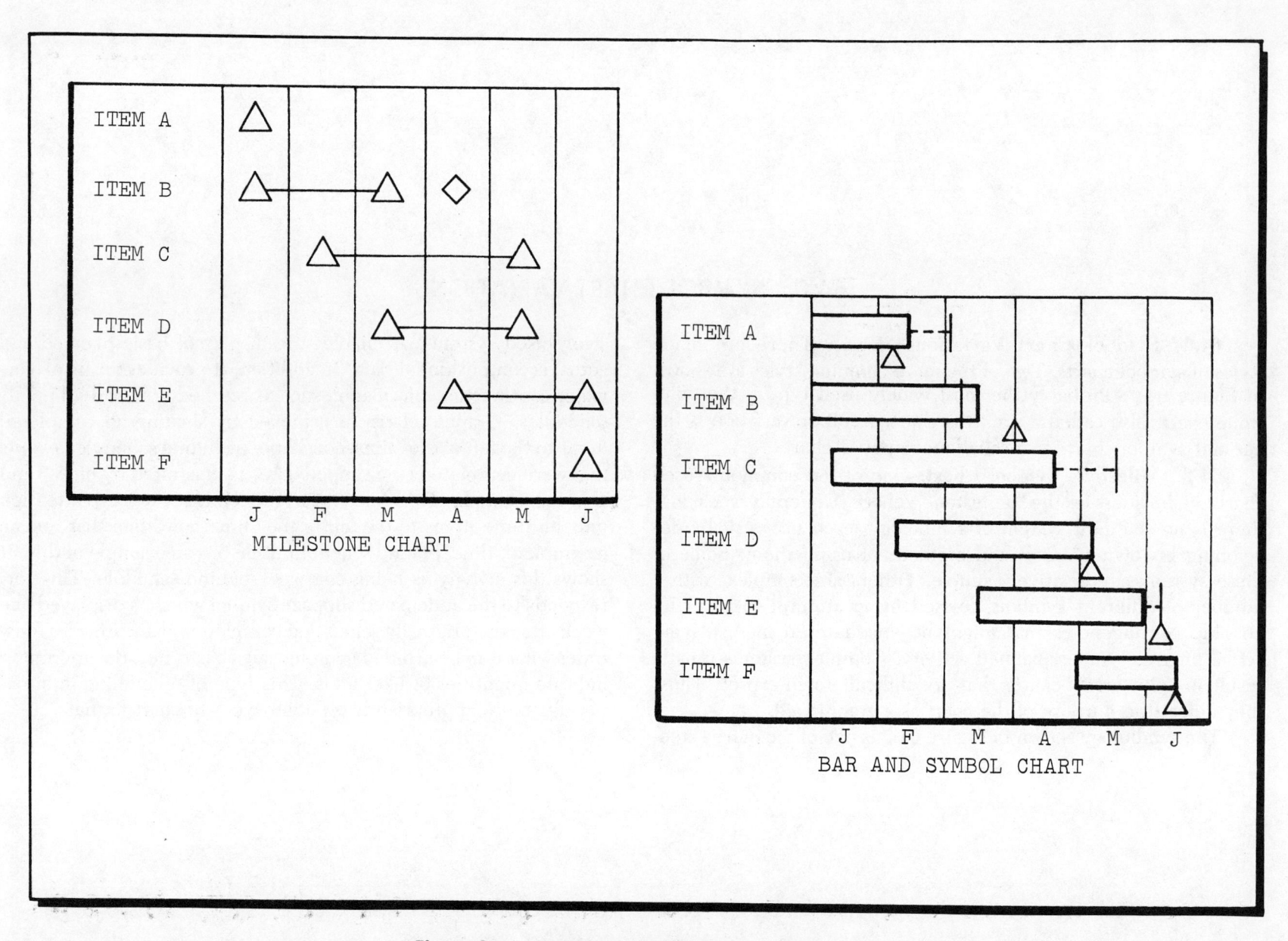

Figure 64.1 Symbol Chart Variations—Basic

812

LEGEND

△ SCHEDULED EVENT, ONE TIME

⚠ RESCHEDULED EVENT. NUMBER INDICATES RESCHEDULED SEQUENCE

▲ COMPLETED EVENT

△—△ SCHEDULED EVENT TIME SPAN

▲—△ PROGRESS ALONG TIME SPAN

△→ CONTINUOUS ACTION

◇ ANTICIPATED SLIPPAGE

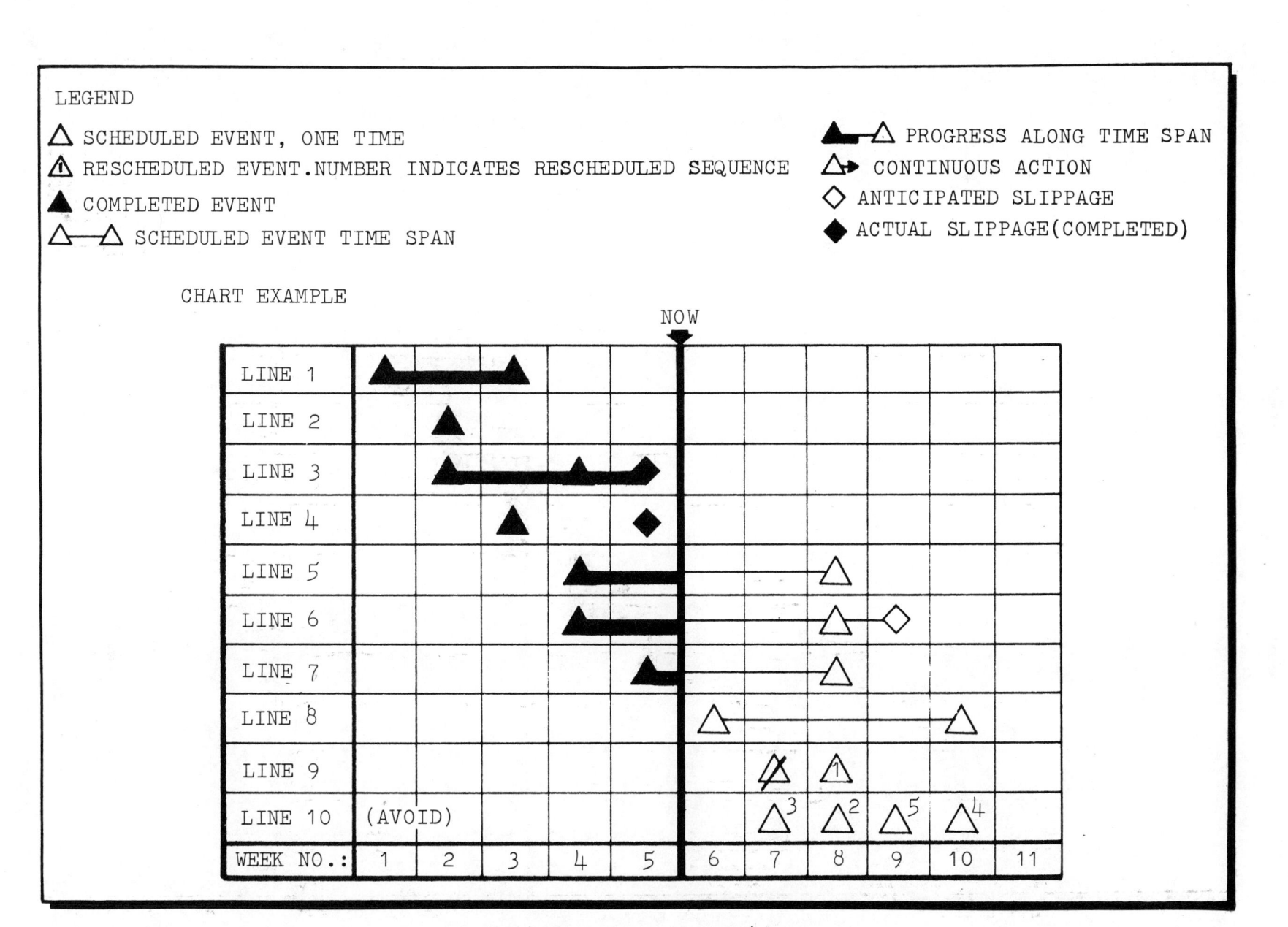

◆ ACTUAL SLIPPAGE (COMPLETED)

CHART EXAMPLE

	1	2	3	4	5	6	7	8	9	10	11
LINE 1	▲━━━━━▲										
LINE 2		▲									
LINE 3		▲━━━▲━━━◆									
LINE 4			▲		◆						
LINE 5				▲━━━━━━△							
LINE 6				▲━━━━━━△—◇							
LINE 7					▲━━△						
LINE 8						△━━━━━━△					
LINE 9							⚠ ⚠₁				
LINE 10	(AVOID)						△³	△²	△⁵	△⁴	
WEEK NO.:	1	2	3	4	5	6	7	8	9	10	11

NOW ▼ (at week 5/6 boundary)

Figure 64.2 Milestone Symbol Chart

813

65.0 CIRCLE CHART VARIATIONS

65.1 Circle Chart Variations—Basic: Three variations of circle charts are shown in Figure 65.1. The first, the most common variation, is the segmented circle chart. Area circle charts, such as the example in the center of Figure 65.1, utilize varying-sized circles to represent sizes or quantities. At the bottom of the illustration is a target circle chart. This type of chart is also known as a polar chart, target chart, scattergram, buckshot chart, shotgun chart, and dot chart.

65.2 Examples of Uses of Circle Charts: Examples of how circle charts might be used are shown in Figure 65.2. The top example shows a segmented circle chart used to display the percent utilization of a particular facility. The bottom example shows a target chart used to display test results.

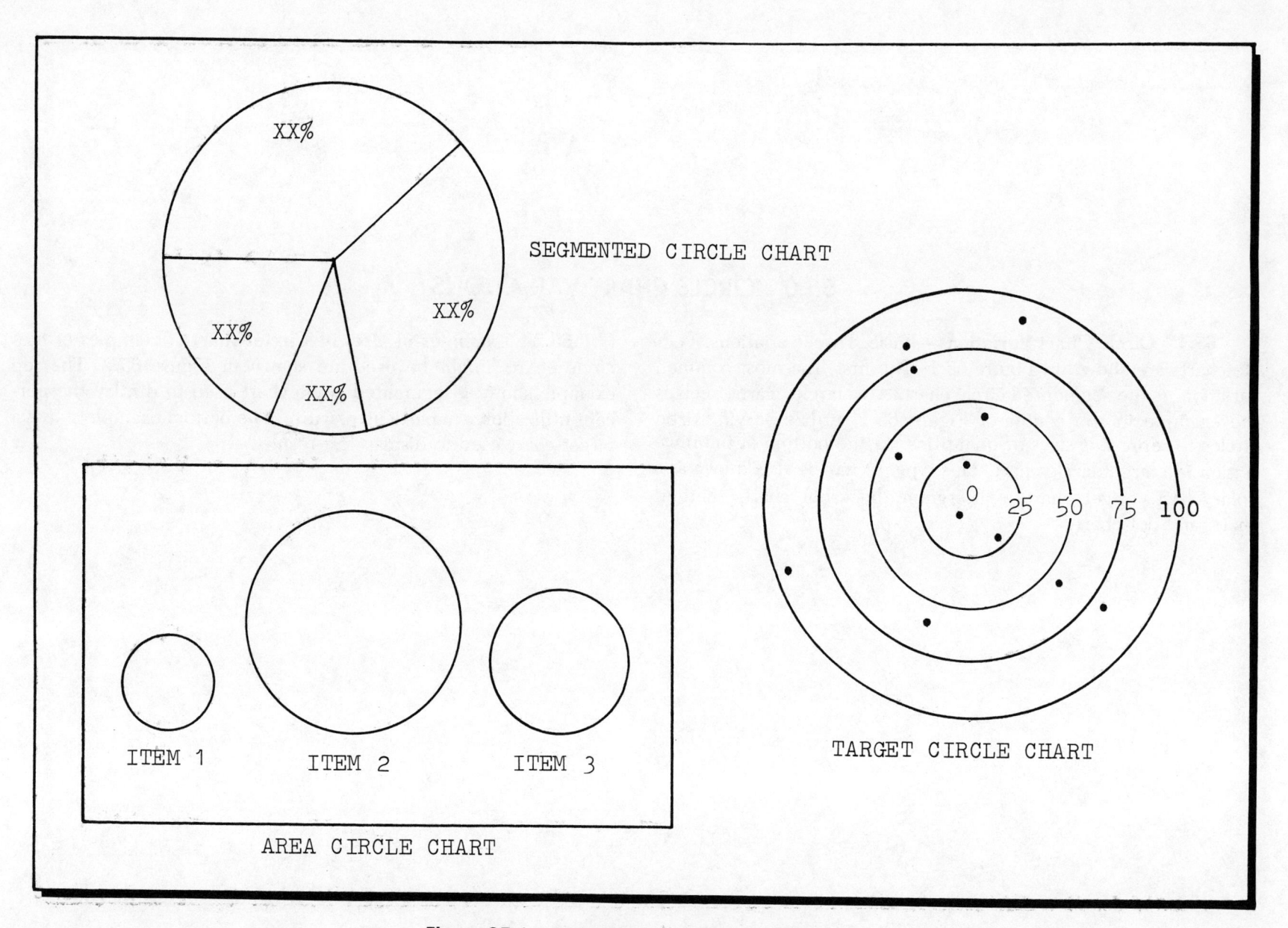

Figure 65.1 Circle Chart Variations—Basic

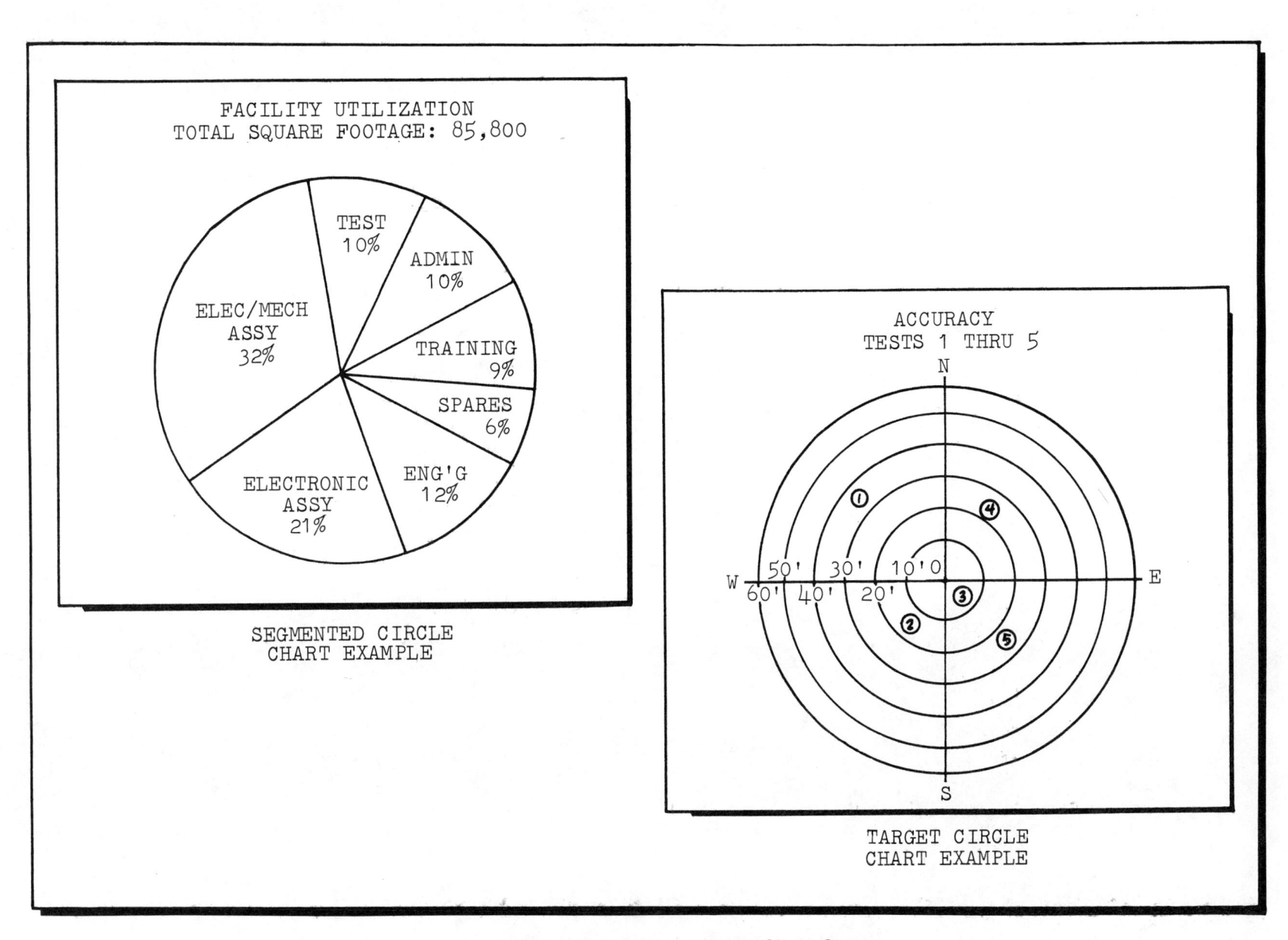

Figure 65.2 Examples of Uses of Circle Charts

66.0 FORMAT AND NOMENCLATURE

66.1 Basic Chart Format: Figure 66.1 displays a basic chart format. In terms of chart identification, space is provided for a chart title and subtitle. Consideration should also be given to identifying the chart with the company or agency designation or logo (or department designation) and, if appropriate, a program or project title or number (or, possibly, the customer name or designation).

Regarding the main body of the chart, it is important to remember to always identify both the horizontal and vertical scales. In the sample format, space is also provided for notes and chart legends or "keys." The notes can be of a general nature, referring to the chart as a whole. They can also be reference notes, calling attention to specific portions of the chart, or notes specifying the source of the data. Space is also provided on the example for a chart (or form) identification or sequence number. There is also a block for approval (authentication) signatures.

66.2 Chart Nomenclature: Chart nomenclature is shown in Figure 66.2. The plotting space of most charts utilizes grid rulings and, sometimes, tick marks. The vertical scale is often also called the quantity scale, amount scale, ordinate, y-axis, or dependent variable. The horizontal scale is sometimes called a time scale, abscissa, x-axis, or independent variable.

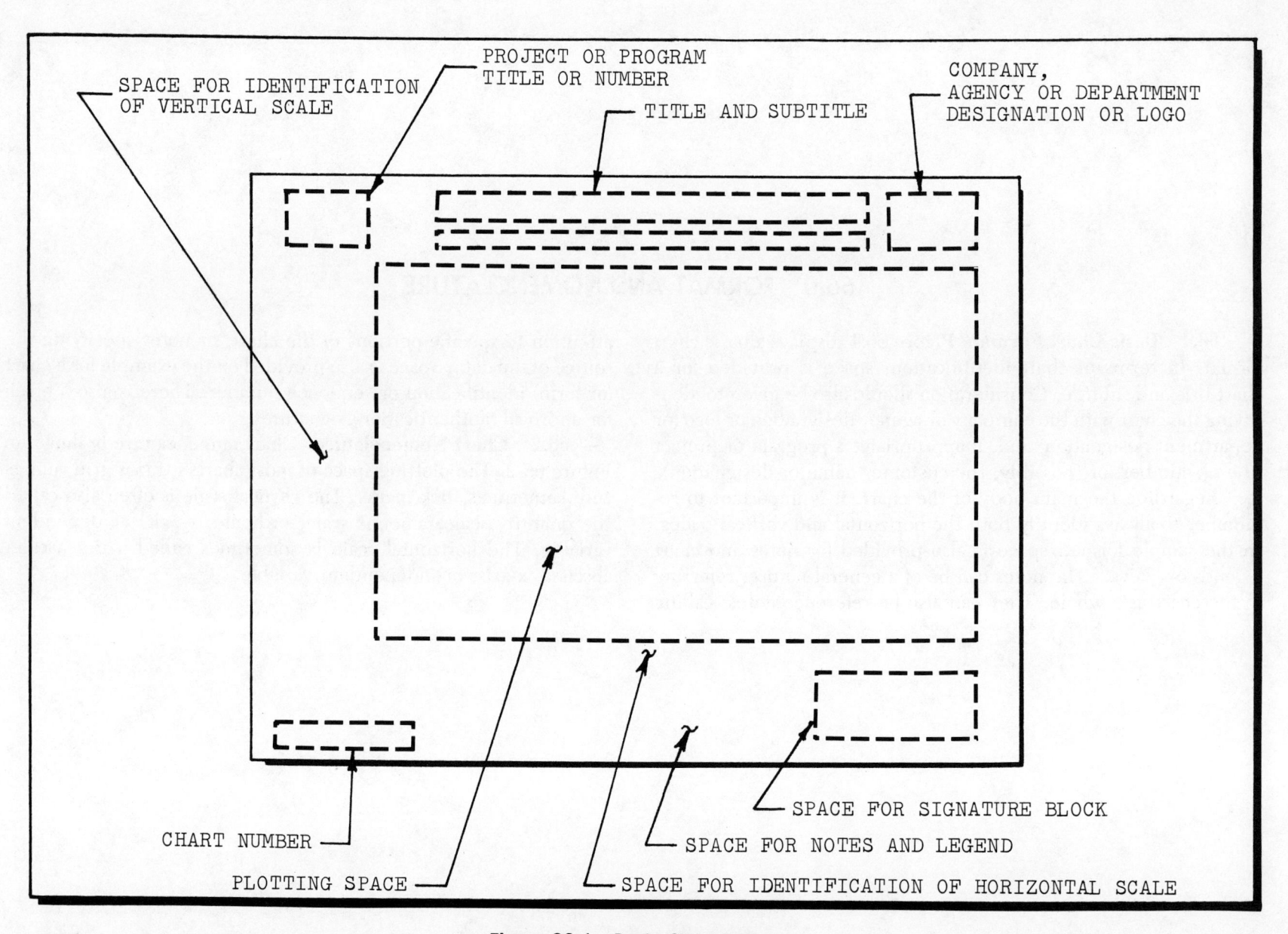

Figure 66.1 Basic Chart Format

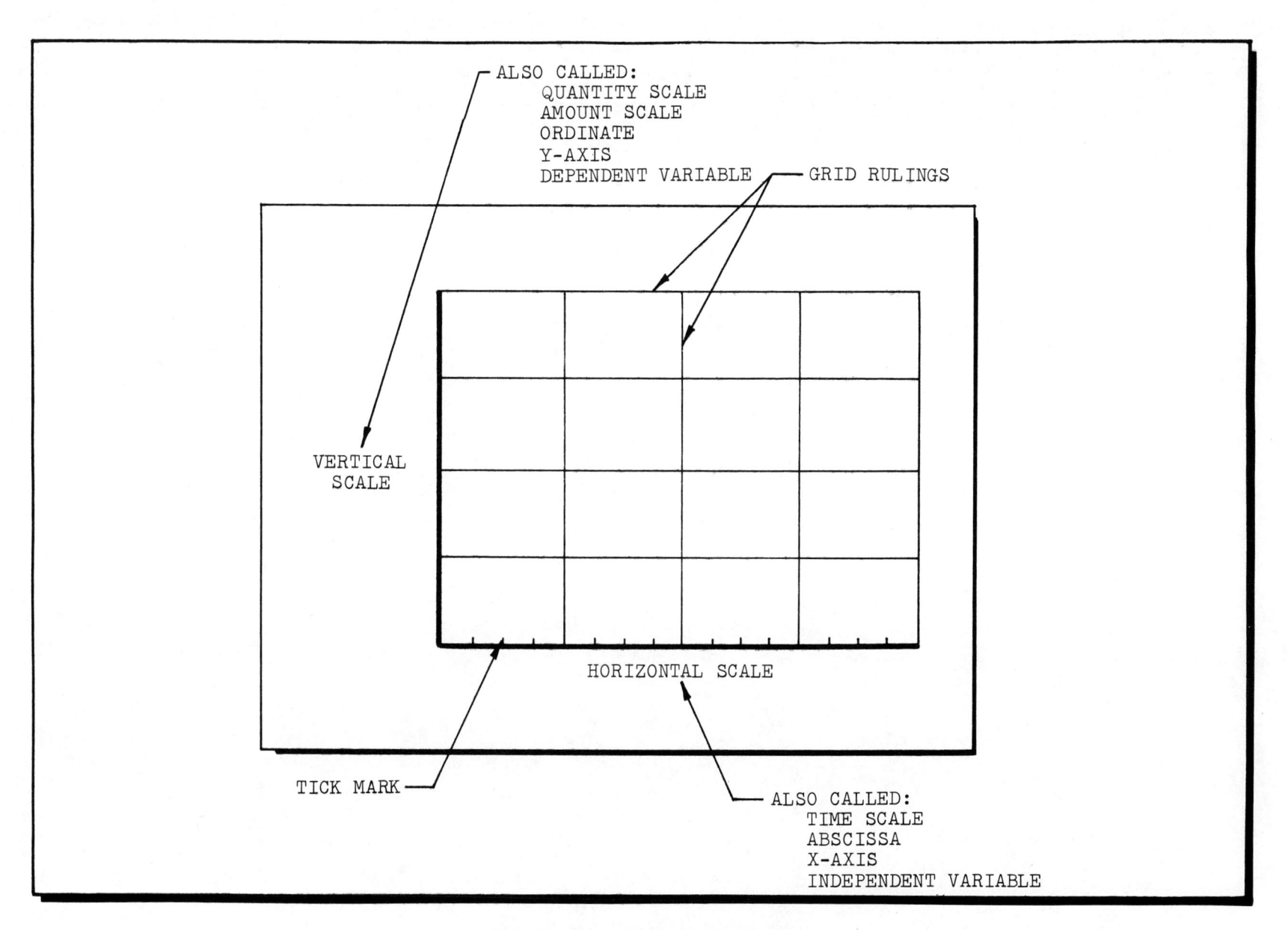

Figure 66.2 Chart Nomenclature

67.0 SHAPE, POSITION, AND SIZE

67.1 Chart Shape: The shape of the chart affects the appearance of the curve. In Figure 67.1, the same data are plotted on three different grids to illustrate this point.

67.2 Chart Position on Page: For charts that are to be presented together with reading material, as in a report, it is preferable to position the chart in the "reading" position rather than sideways which would force the reader to turn the page in order to examine the chart. The bottom portion of Figure 67.2 shows the preferred position for displaying charts that are used in reports.

67.3 Chart Proportions Related to Pages: In positioning charts on report pages, ratios such as shown in Figure 67.3 should be used. Adequate margins on all sides of the chart, or charts, greatly improve the appearance of the chart. If the chart is to be bound with others, all allowance for binding should also be provided.

67.4 Film Projection Proportions: If the chart is to be projected, the shape of the chart should be proportioned to fit within the frame opening of the film or slide. The sizes and ratios of several of the more commonly used projection materials are shown in Figure 67.4.

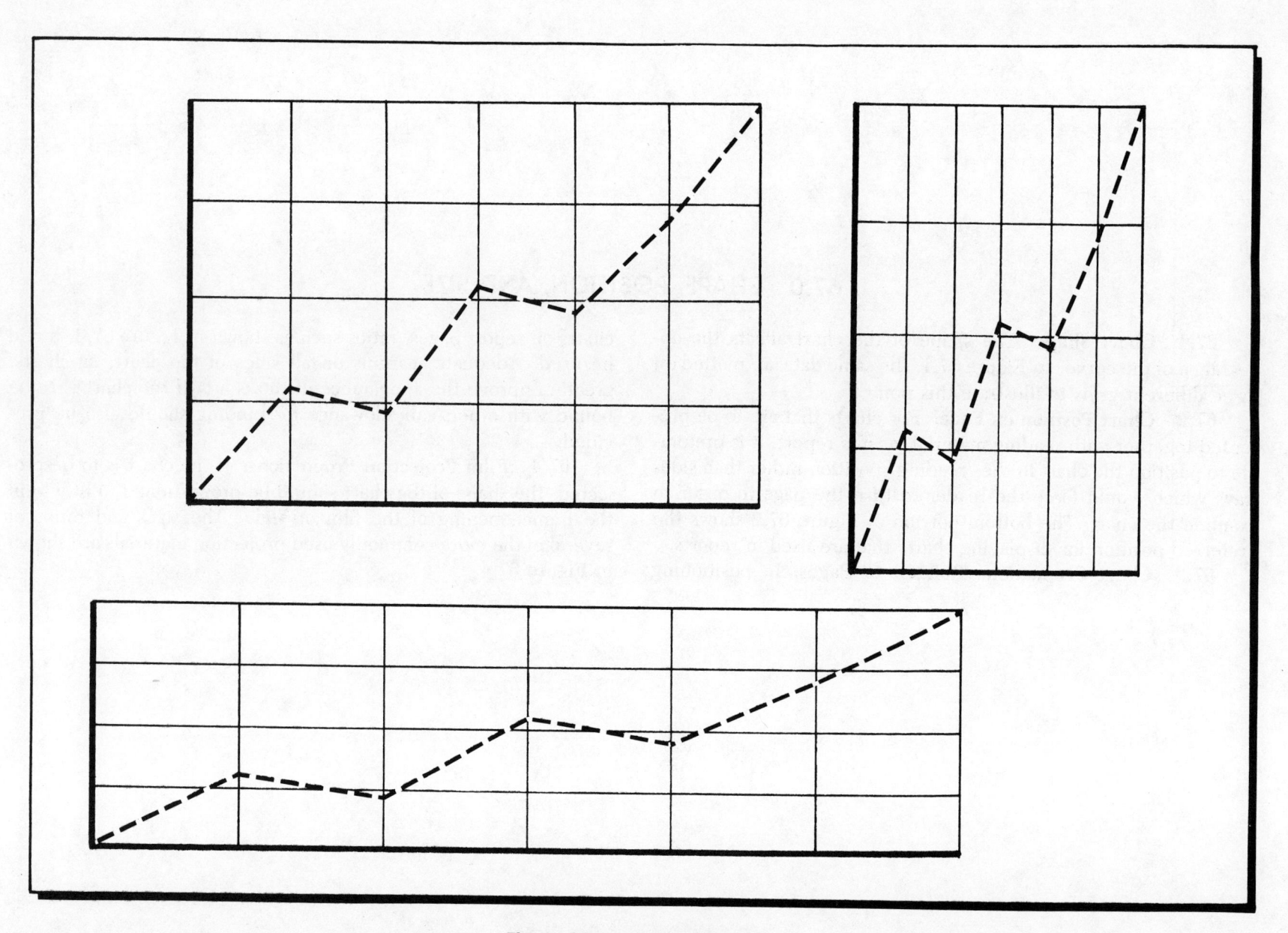

Figure 67.1 Chart Shape

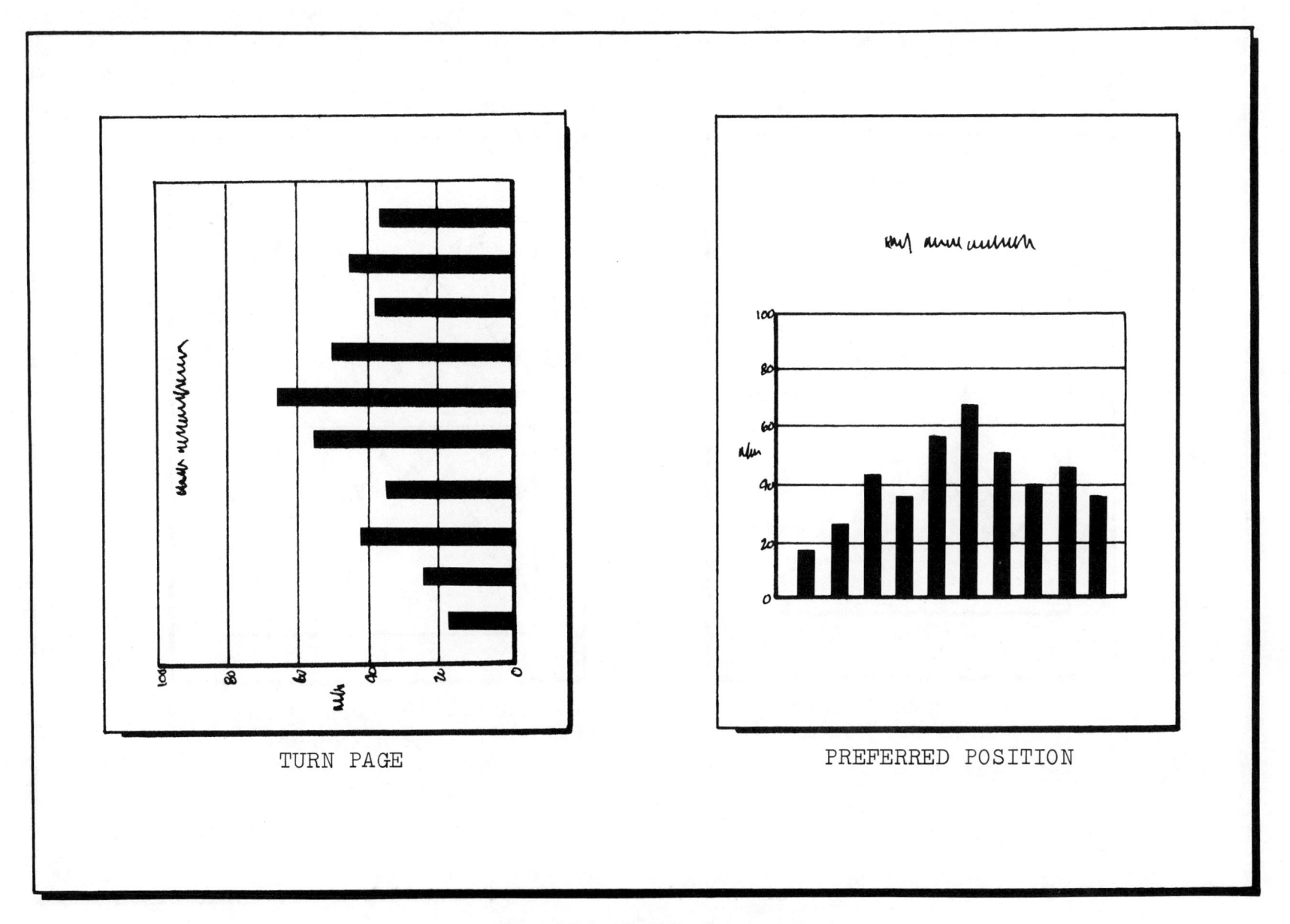

Figure 67.2   Chart Position on Page

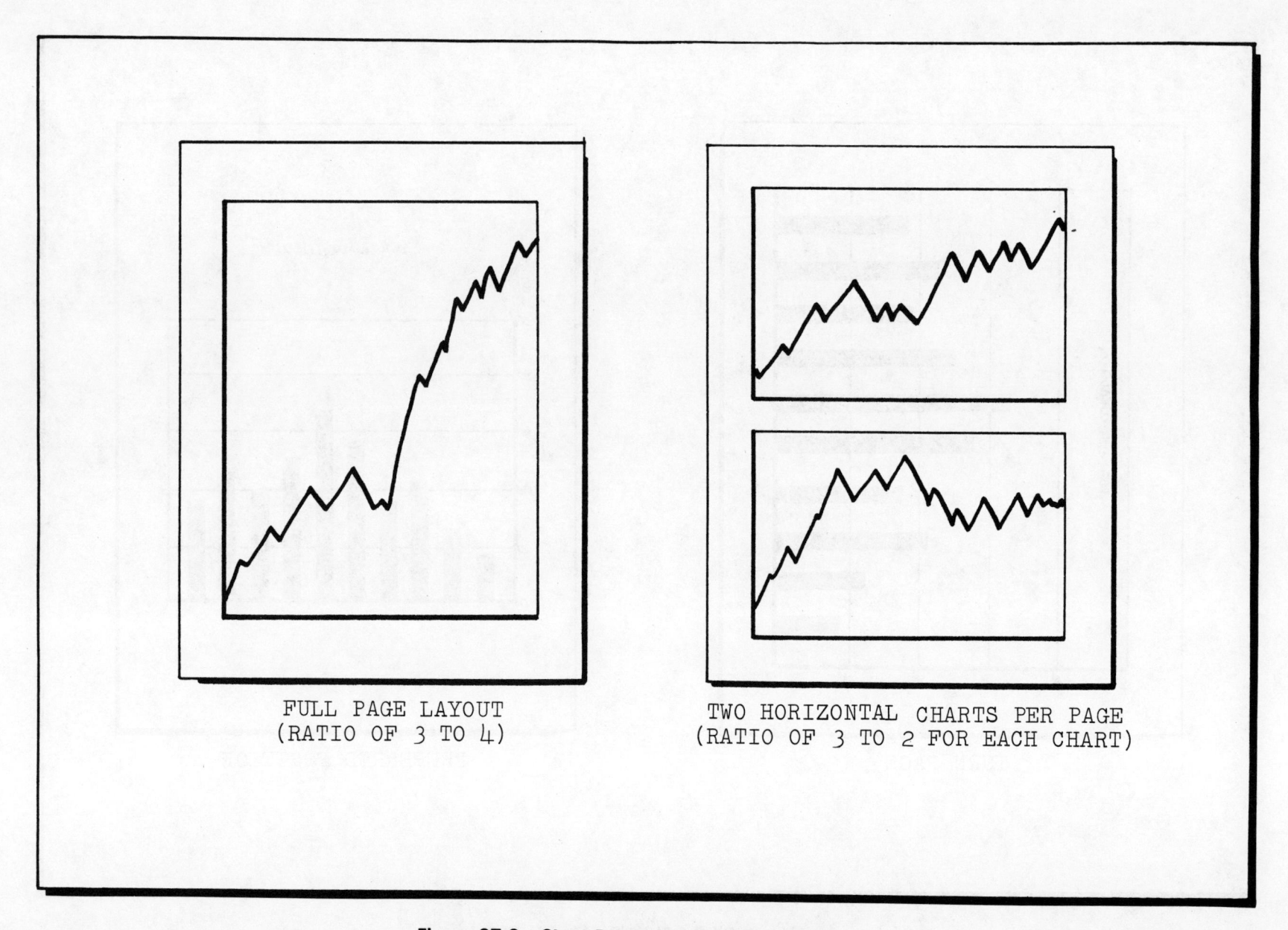

Figure 67.3 Chart Proportions Related to Pages

RATIO:
4 TO 3

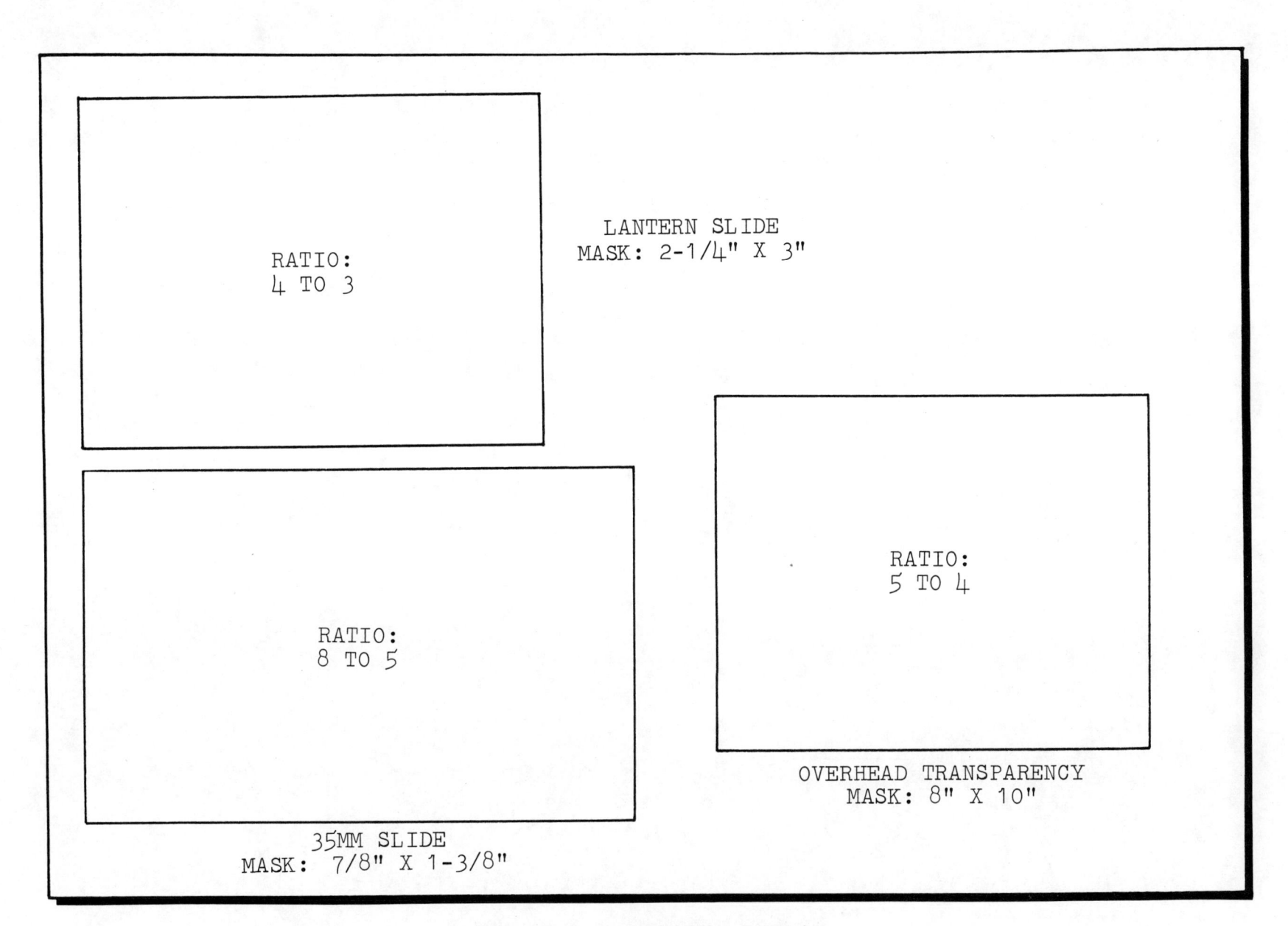

LANTERN SLIDE
MASK: 2-1/4" X 3"

RATIO:
8 TO 5

RATIO:
5 TO 4

OVERHEAD TRANSPARENCY
MASK: 8" X 10"

35MM SLIDE
MASK: 7/8" X 1-3/8"

Figure 67.4   Film Projection Proportions

68.0 TITLES

68.1 Chart Title Location: Two options for locating chart titles and subtitles are shown in Figure 68.1. By locating the title within the grid, as shown at the bottom of the illustration, a larger plotting area can be achieved. However, if at the time that the chart is originally being prepared the plotting data are unknown, it would be safer to use the method shown at the top of the figure so that the title and subtitle won't interfere with the plotted data.

68.2 Chart Title Types: Three types of titles are shown in Figure 68.2. The aim of any title, of course, is to convey to the chart reader a clear understanding of what the chart contains. This can sometimes be done with a simple title such as shown at the top of the illustration. More often than not, an explanatory subtitle is necessary. A variation of the more commonly used title/subtitle approach is the headline title such as illustrated at the bottom of Figure 68.2.

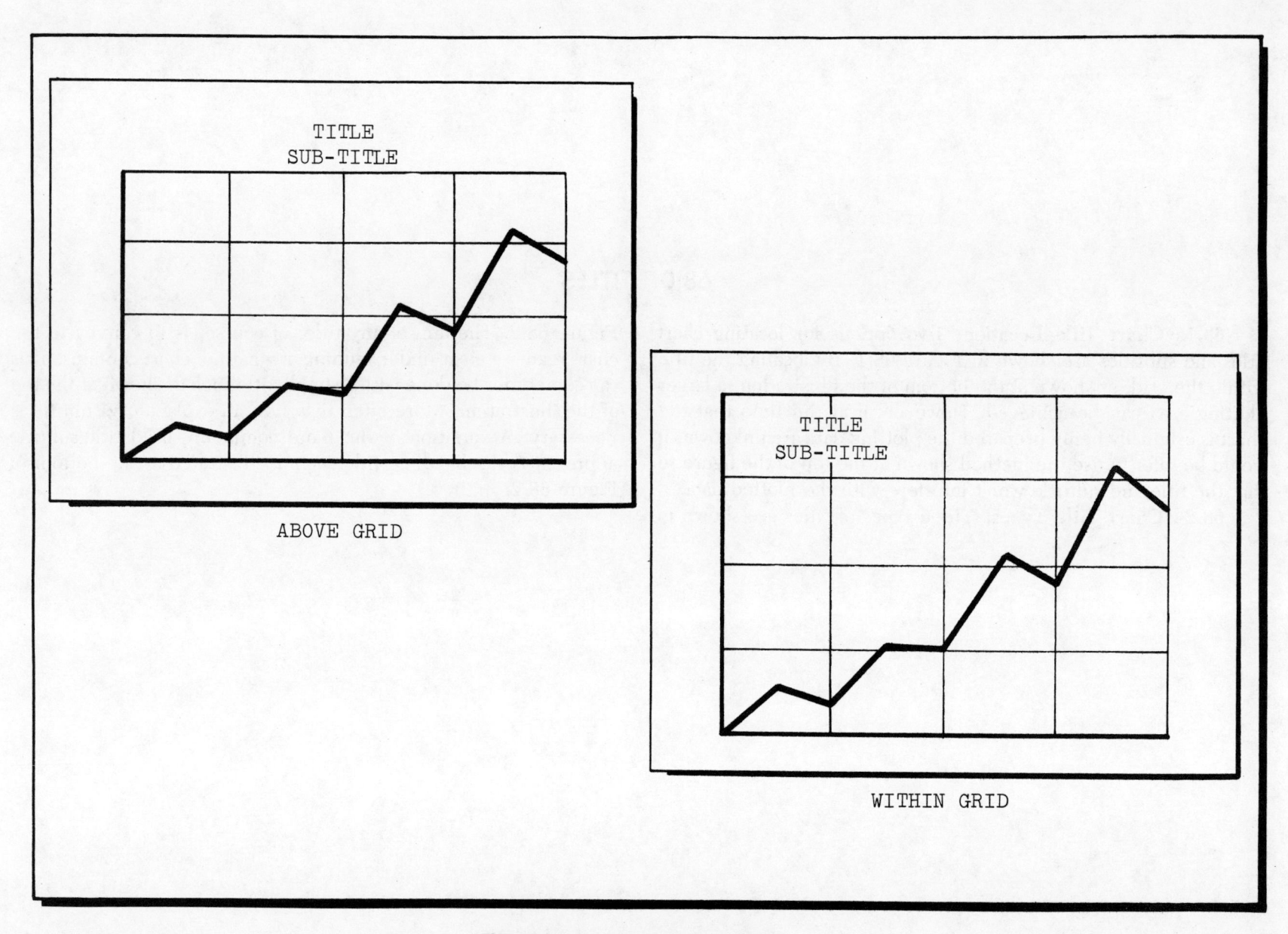

Figure 68.1 Chart Title Location

GYROSCOPE SALES

TITLE

GYROSCOPE SALES
MODEL 10-CUMULATIVE SALES- THIS YEAR

TITLE & SUB-TITLE

THE SALES OF MODEL 10 GYROSCOPES
HAVE BEEN DECLINING SINCE THE
END OF THE SECOND QUARTER

HEADLINE TITLE

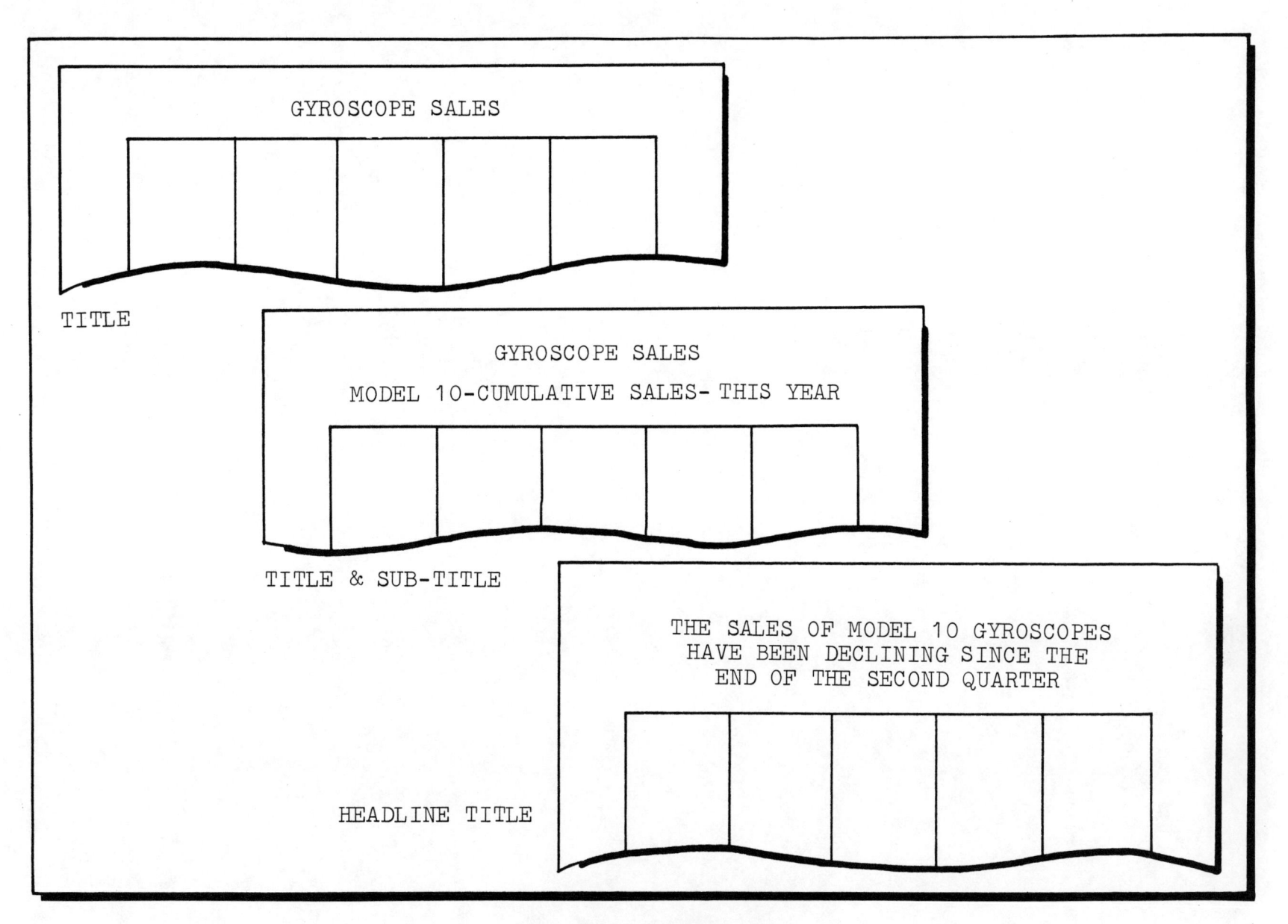

Figure 68.2   Chart Title Types

69.0 GRIDS

69.1 Grid Rulings: The ease or difficulty in interpreting data presented in chart form is directly related to the method of chart ruling. Three basic methods of chart ruling are illustrated in Figure 69.1. At the top of the illustration is an example of a chart that utilizes total ruling. This method normally provides the best background for "reading" a chart.

Using tick marks in lieu of grid lines is illustrated in the center of Figure 69.1. A satisfactory compromise which uses a combination of grid ruling and tick marks is shown at the bottom of the illustration.

Line weight is another important consideration. Grid ruling should be lighter than the plotted data so that the information portion of the chart stands out by contrast.

69.2 Use of Tick Marks: Tick marks should be used on time scales to indicate the points where data are, or are expected to be, plotted. In the example shown at the top of Figure 69.2, Use of Tick Marks, the grid is such as to indicate plottings for January (J), February (tick mark), March (tick mark), April (A), etc. The tick marks and grid at the bottom of Figure 69.2 are structured for plottings for each year from 1910 through 1940.

69.3 Column Chart Grids: Vertical rulings are normally not necessary on column charts, just as horizontal lines are not normally essential to bar charts. The use of horizontal rulings on column charts is illustrated at the top of Figure 69.3. This method, which makes the chart easier to read, is usually preferred over the method of using tick marks, only (bottom of Figure 69.3).

69.4 Grid Patterns for Bar and Symbol Charts: The common practice for bar charts is to use vertical grid rulings, only, as shown at the top of Figure 69.4. Symbol charts, though, are often constructed with both vertical and horizontal rulings as shown at the bottom of the illustration. The horizontal lines are added because in most styles of symbol charts there is a tendency for an ever-widening gap between the symbol and its call-out, and horizontal lines help guide the reader's eyes.

TOTAL RULING

RULING AND TICK
MARKS COMBINED

TICK MARKS IN LIEU
OF RULING

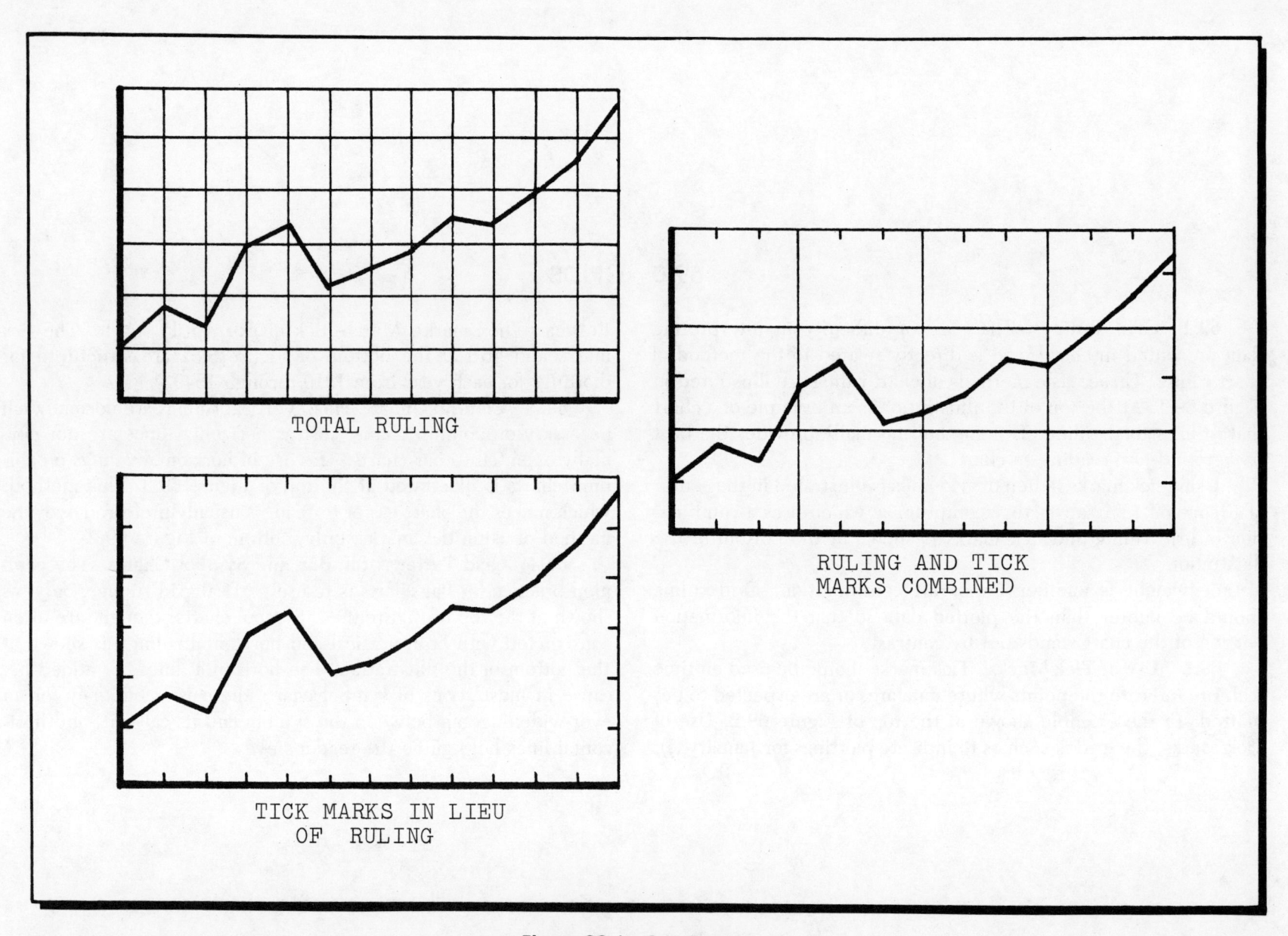

Figure 69.1 Grid Rulings

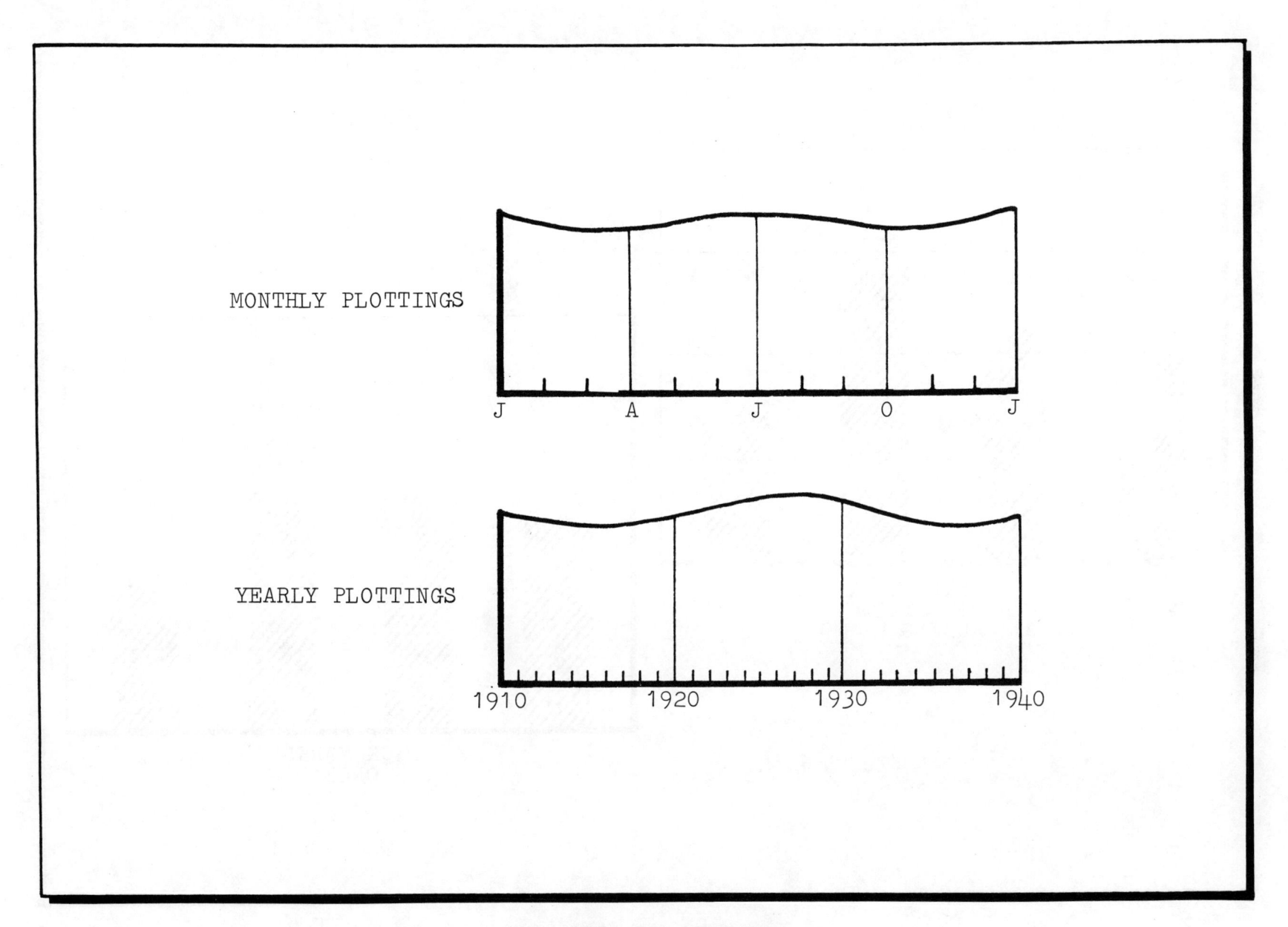

Figure 69.2 Use of Tick Marks

PARTIAL
HORIZONTAL
RULING

TICK MARKS
ONLY

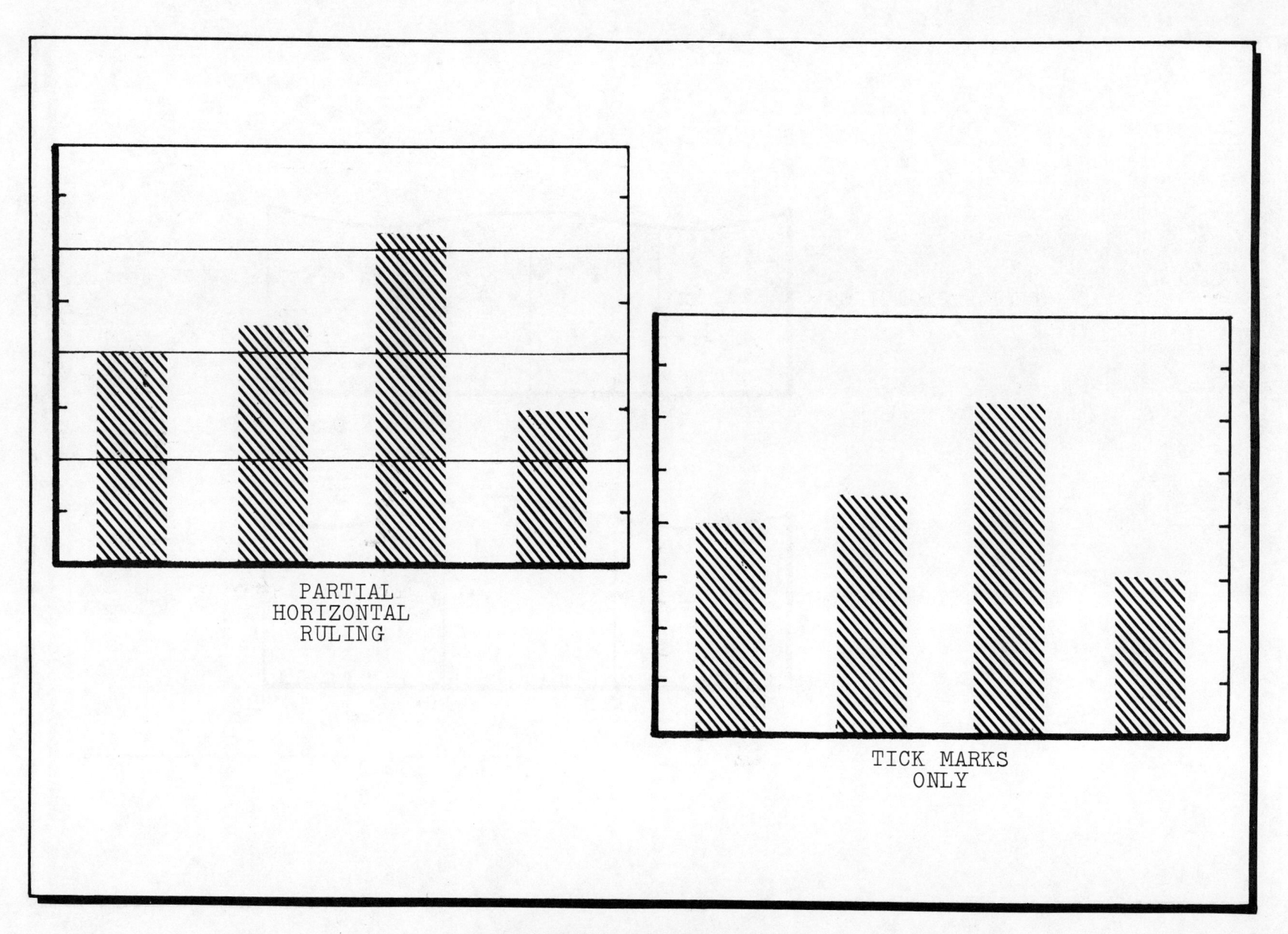

Figure 69.3 Column Chart Grids

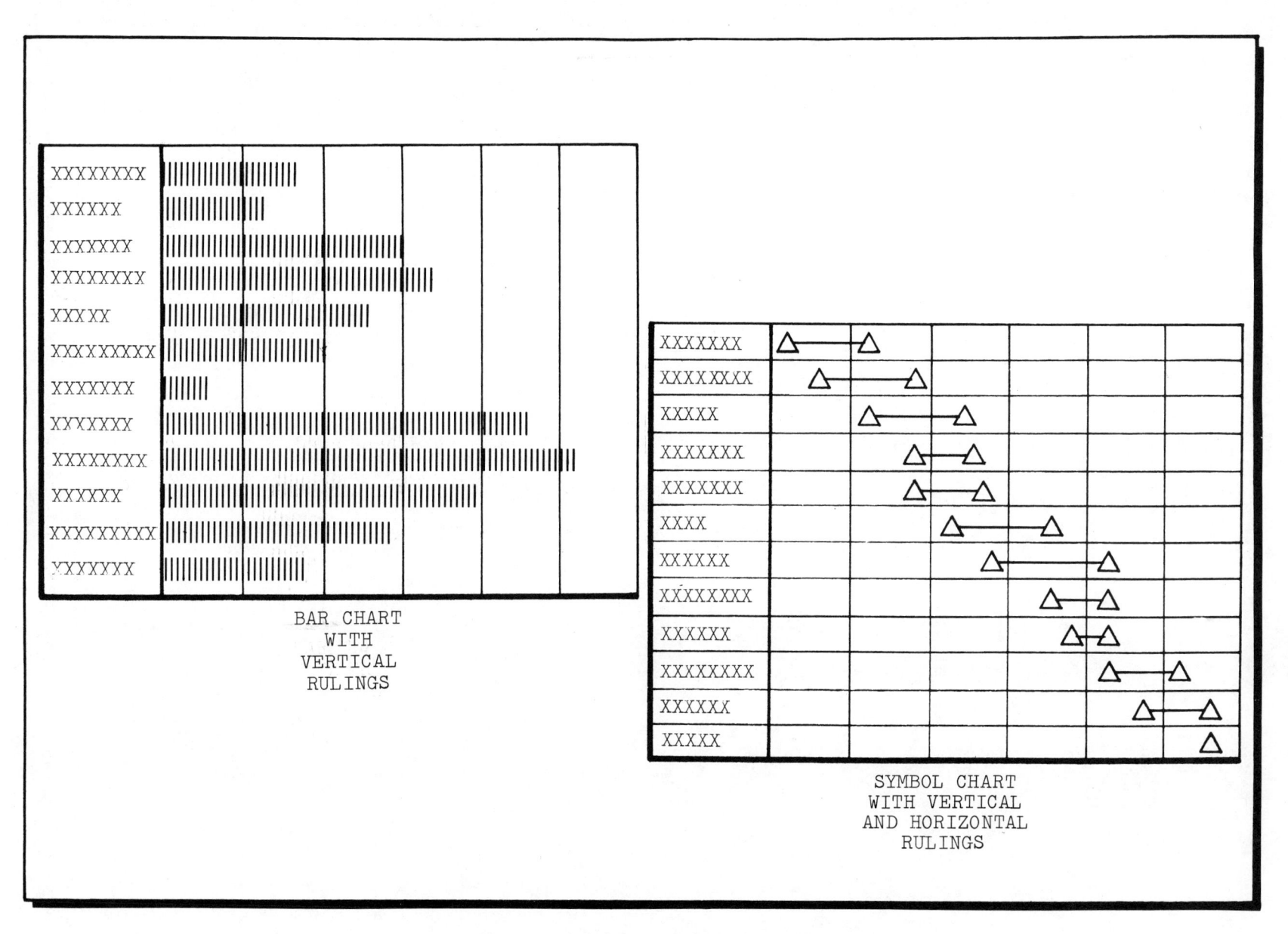

Figure 69.4 Grid Patterns for Bar and Symbol Charts

70.0 LINE WEIGHT AND SHADING

70.1 Line Weight: Chart comprehension can often be enhanced through the use of varying line weights. Figure 70.1 displays several examples of this. In the top example, a major reference line has been made heavier than the grid so as to make it stand out by contrast. The bottom example shows how major time divisions can be made more apparent by using a heavier line.

70.2 Curve Line Weight: Curves should stand out against the grid, as shown in Figure 70.2, through the use of heavier line weights for the curves. Varying line weights can be used, too, with the heaviest used for the primary line and lighter weights used for secondary lines. The use of varying weights for multiple-curve charts is essential to the ease of reading of charts where the lines cross, as illustrated in example 2.

70.3 Preferred Line and Shading Patterns: Figure 70.3 displays preferred line and shading patterns used in chart construction. For lines, the first rule of thumb is to select those that are easiest to draw . . . solid lines and dash lines, for instance. Another important consideration is that, on tracking-type charts, it is common practice to use the dash line or broken patterns to indicate plans or goals, and the solid line or solid pattern to indicate actual performance.

70.4 Effective Shading: In using shading it is good practice to use graduated densities, with the darkest patterns at the bottom of the chart. Examples of this practice are shown for both column and surface charts in Figure 70.4.

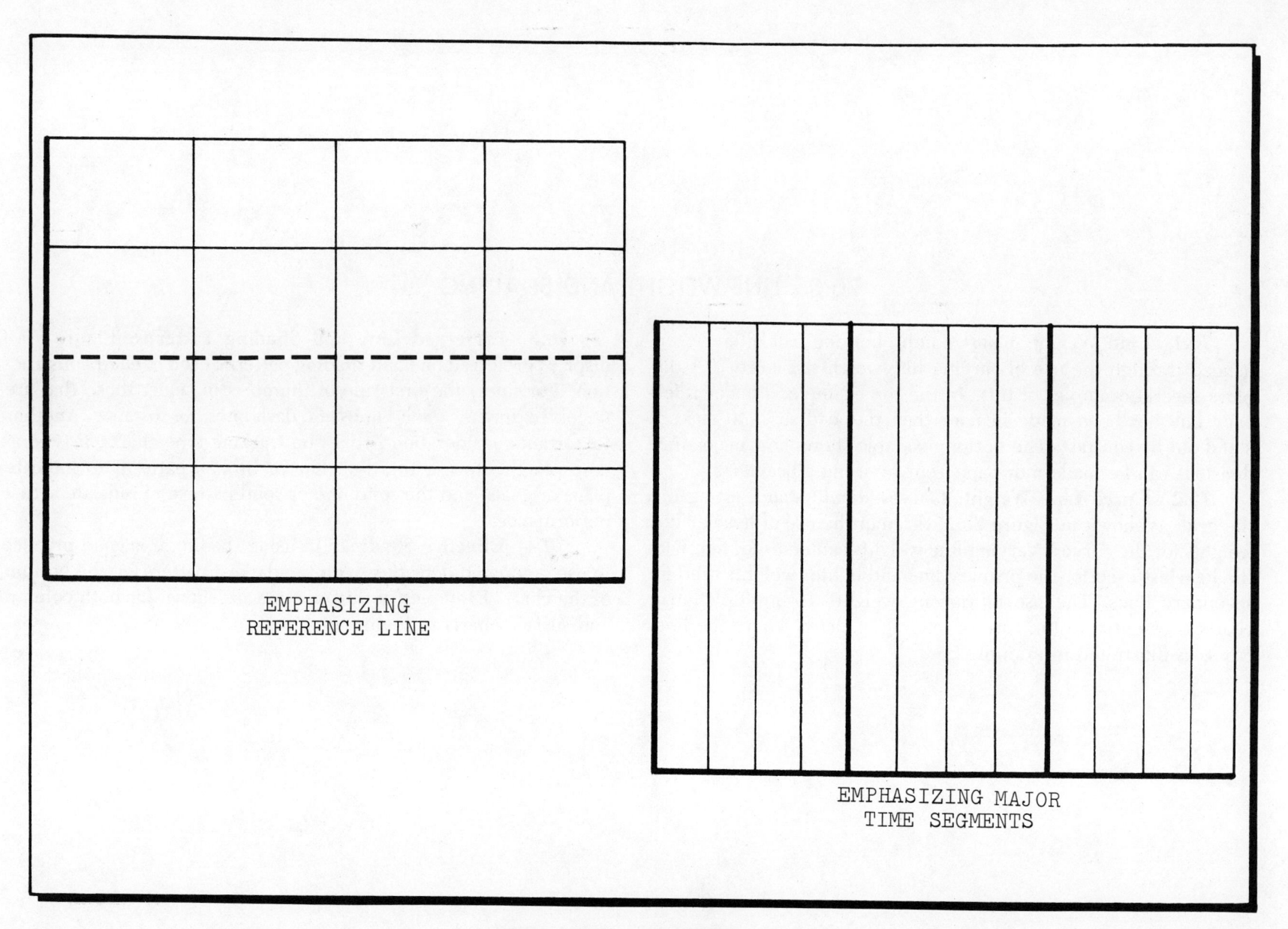

Figure 70.1 Line Weight

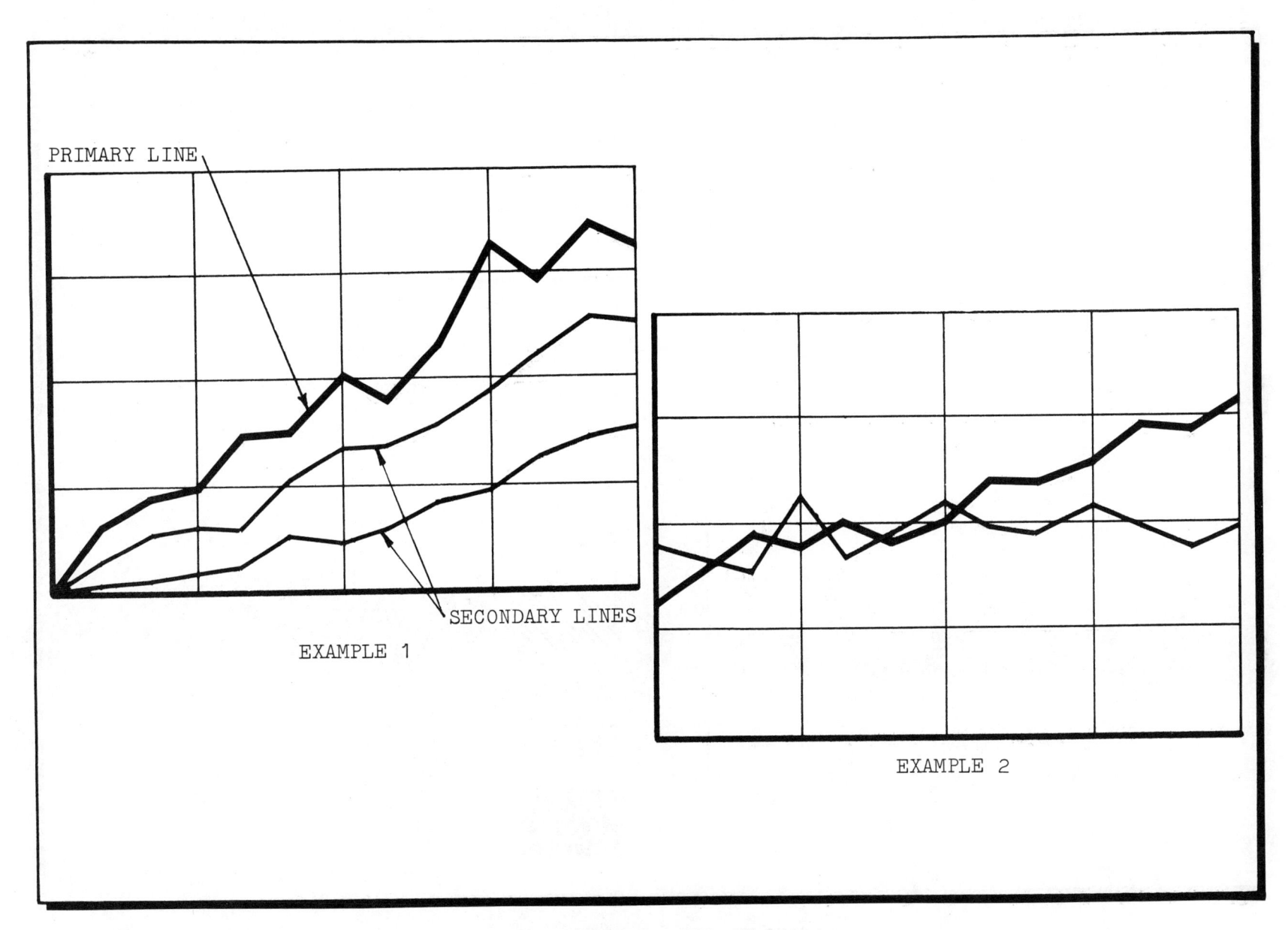

Figure 70.2 Curve Line Weight

PREFERRED LINE PATTERNS
- ———————— SOLID
- — — — — DASH
- ·············· DOT
- •−•−•−•−• BALL & LINE
- —·—·—·— DOT-DASH

PREFERRED SHADING PATTERNS
- DOTTED
- DIAGONAL
- CROSS HATCHED
- SOLID

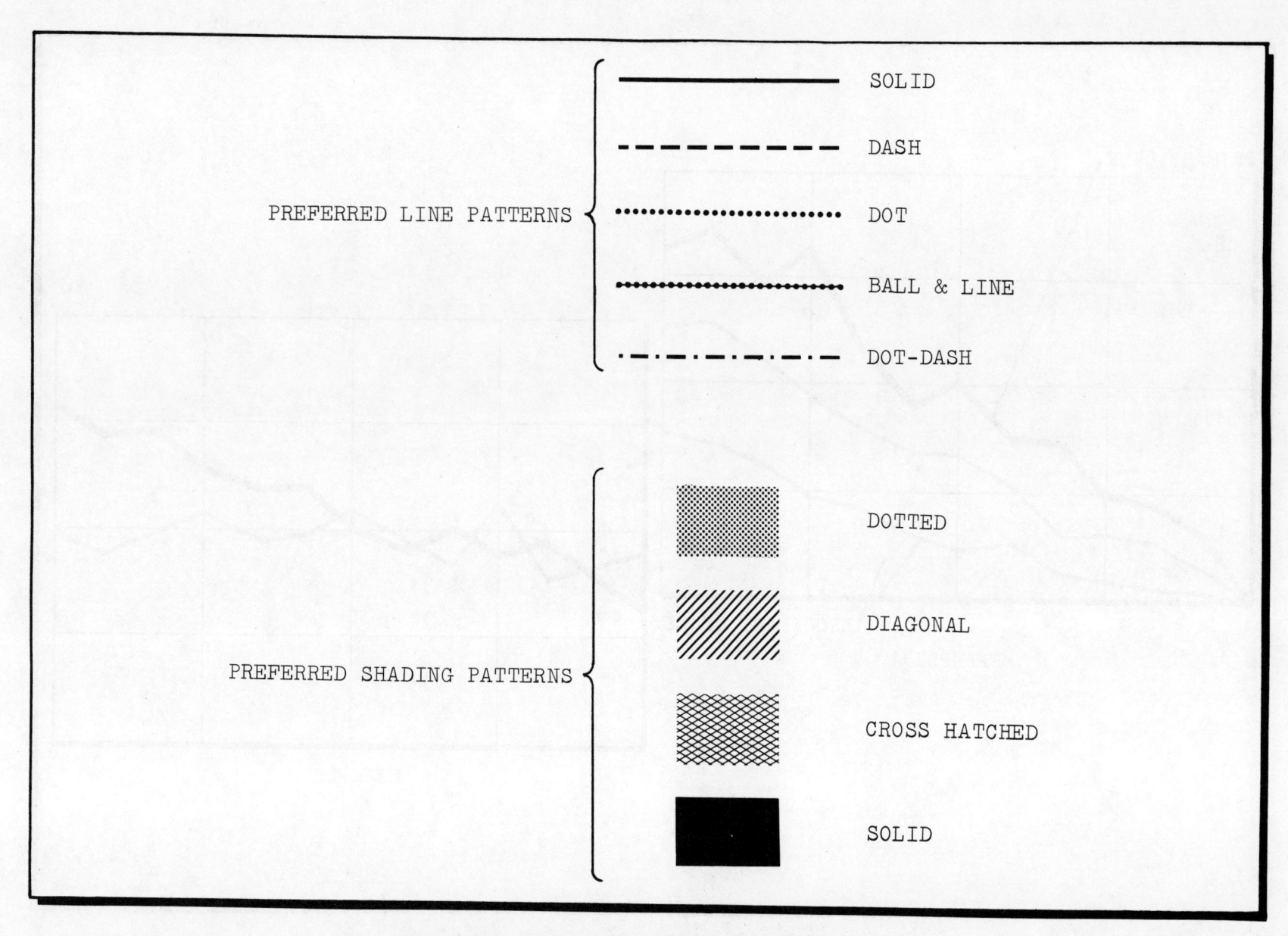

Figure 70.3   Preferred Line and Shading Patterns

EFFECTIVE SHADING -
COLUMN CHART

EFFECTIVE SHADING -
SURFACE CHART

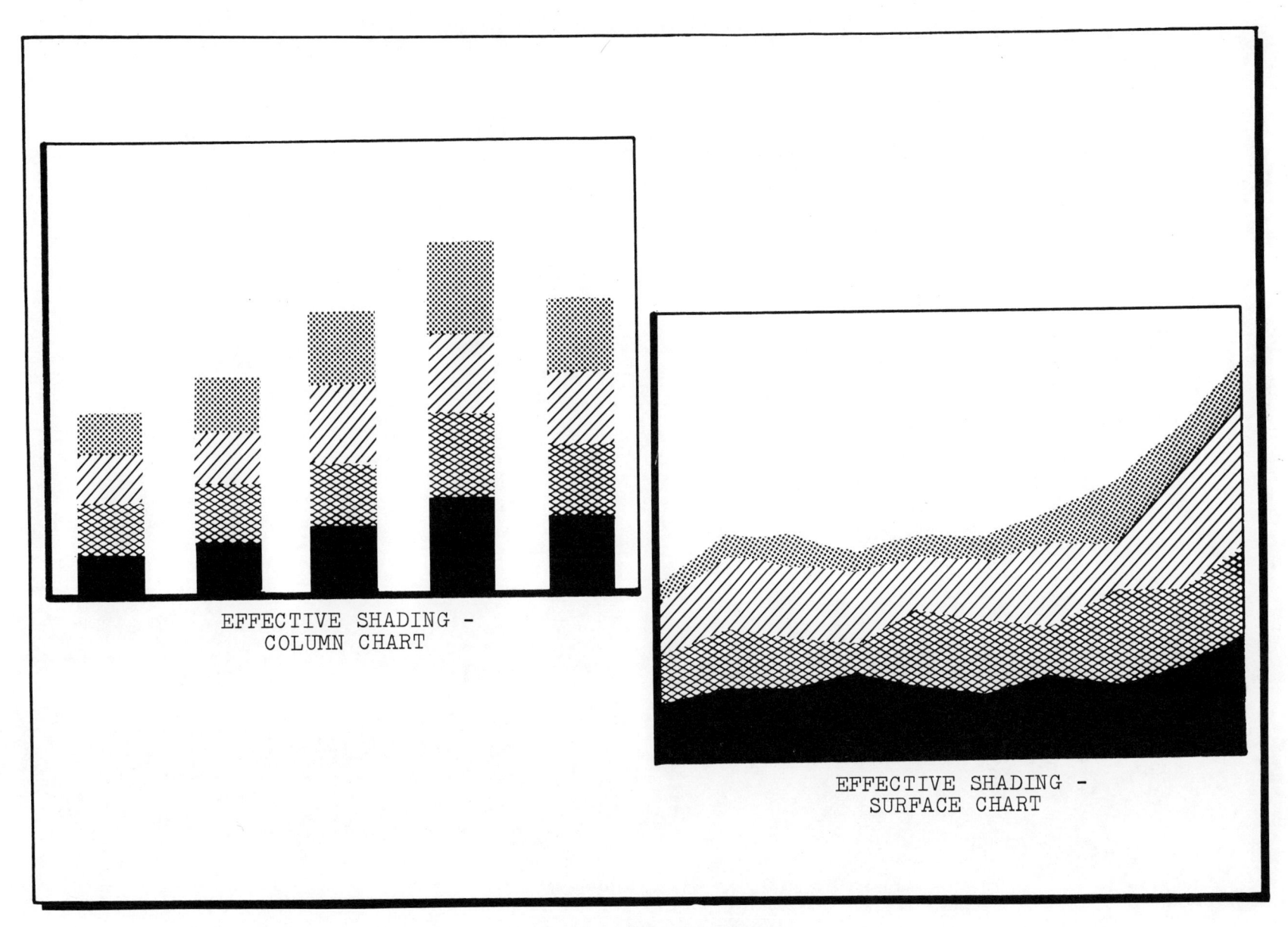

Figure 70.4   Effective Shading

71.0 AMOUNT SCALES

71.1 Amount Scale Selection: At the time that progress tracking charts are prepared, two factors are generally known. One is the period of time that the plan covers, thus enabling the chart maker to properly plan the time scale of the chart. The maximum amount of the plan is also normally known or can be estimated. The amount scale should be selected, such as shown at the bottom of Figure 71.1, to take full advantage of the space available.

71.2 Amount Data Anomalies: Sometimes in plotting data uniformity can be found in all but one or several numbers. If the chart grid was to be selected on the basis of such a single freak number it might distort the balance of the chart information. Examples of how anomalies can be handled in line or column charts are shown in Figure 71.2.

71.3 The Zero Base: Some data do not lend themselves well to an amount scale that has a zero base, such as shown at the top of Figure 71.3. Two alternate methods of handling this situation are shown. In the center of the illustration the example shows a section of the chart removed and the remaining scale expanded so as to display the data over a wider range of the available space. If a zero base is not used, such as shown at the bottom of the figure, some method of highlighting that fact (using an arrow, for instance) should be used.

71.4 Compression of the Amount Scale: Sometimes it is important that two or more elements of data be compared on the same chart. If necessary, these elements can often be better compared if a section of the chart is removed, compressing the amount scale, such as illustrated at the bottom of Figure 71.4.

71.5 Amount Scale Intervals: Care should be exercised in selecting the most appropriate amount scale intervals for the chart. Too many intervals, such as shown at the top of Figure 71.5, can clutter the chart. Too few, as shown in the center of the illustration, can make the chart difficult to interpret.

71.6 Reading Curve or Column Values: Curve or column values can be easy or difficult to read depending on the scale that is selected. It is difficult to interpret mid-point values of odd-numbered graduations, such as shown at the top of Figure 71.6. Even-numbered graduations divisible by two, five, ten, 100, or 1000 are easier to read.

71.7 Location of Amount-Scale Designations: Three different methods of locating amount-scale designations are shown in Figure 71.7. A normal practice in engineering is to use the left-hand side of the chart. The right-hand side is often used in accounting. A method for making the chart easier to read is to use both sides as shown at the bottom of Figure 71.7.

71.8 Line Chart Amount Designations: Several methods for identifying amount scales on line charts are shown in Figure 71.8.

At the top an example of scale designation, only, is shown. In this example, scales are placed on both the right- and left-hand sides of the grids.

The bottom part of Figure 71.8 shows an example of the use of scales plus the numeric identification of specific plotting points on the chart. This clutters the chart but, at the same time, enables a precise reading of the chart data.

71.9 Column Chart Amount Designations: Several of the methods for designating amounts on column charts are illustrated in Figure 71.9. At the top of the figure, the more traditional scale designation is shown. Providing a scale plus captions for each column, as shown at the bottom of the illustration, clutters the chart but, at the same time, enables a precise reading of each column. In this latter approach, the amounts could also be labelled *within* the columns.

71.10 Location of Amount-Scale Caption: The amount-scale identifying caption, if it is brief and concise, such as "dollars" or the symbol for dollars, can be located at the top of the scale as shown at the top of Figure 71.10. This approach permits the maximum amount of horizontal plotting space.

If the amount-scale designation is detailed, it should be located to the left of the scale as shown at the bottom of Figure 71.10. Whatever the location, the caption itself should be clear and abbreviations avoided.

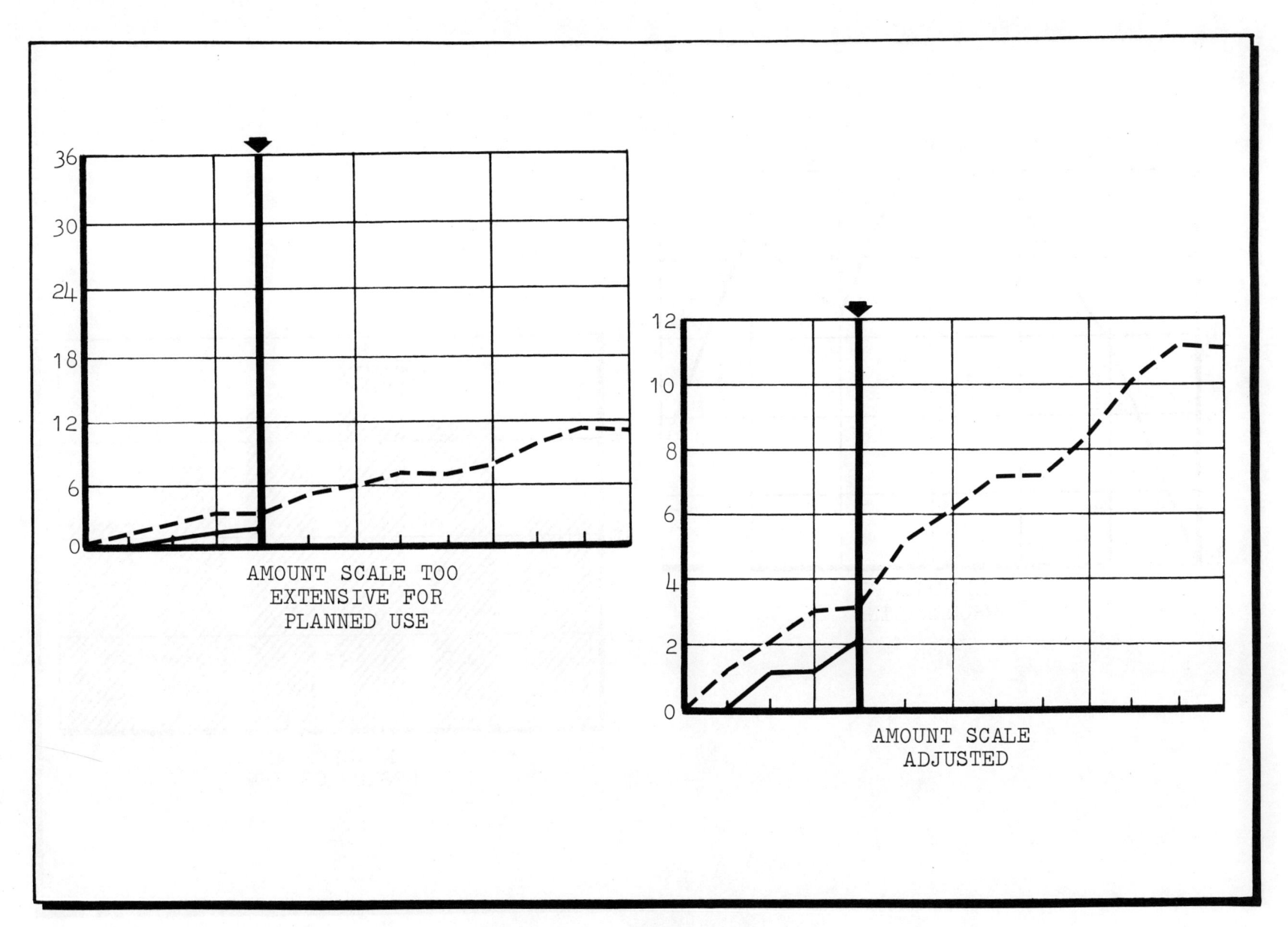

Figure 71.1 Amount Scale Selection

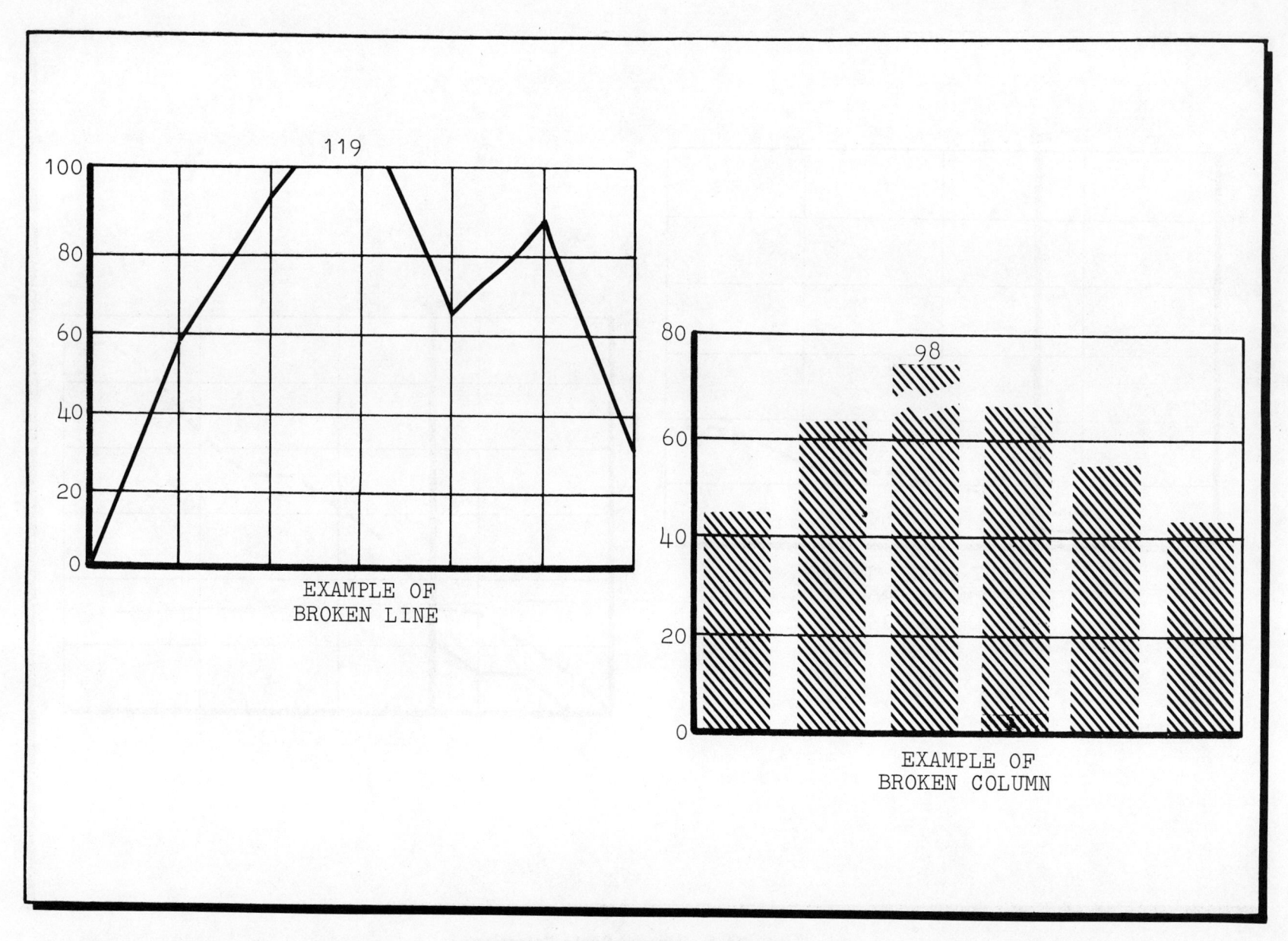

Figure 71.2 Amount Data Anomalies

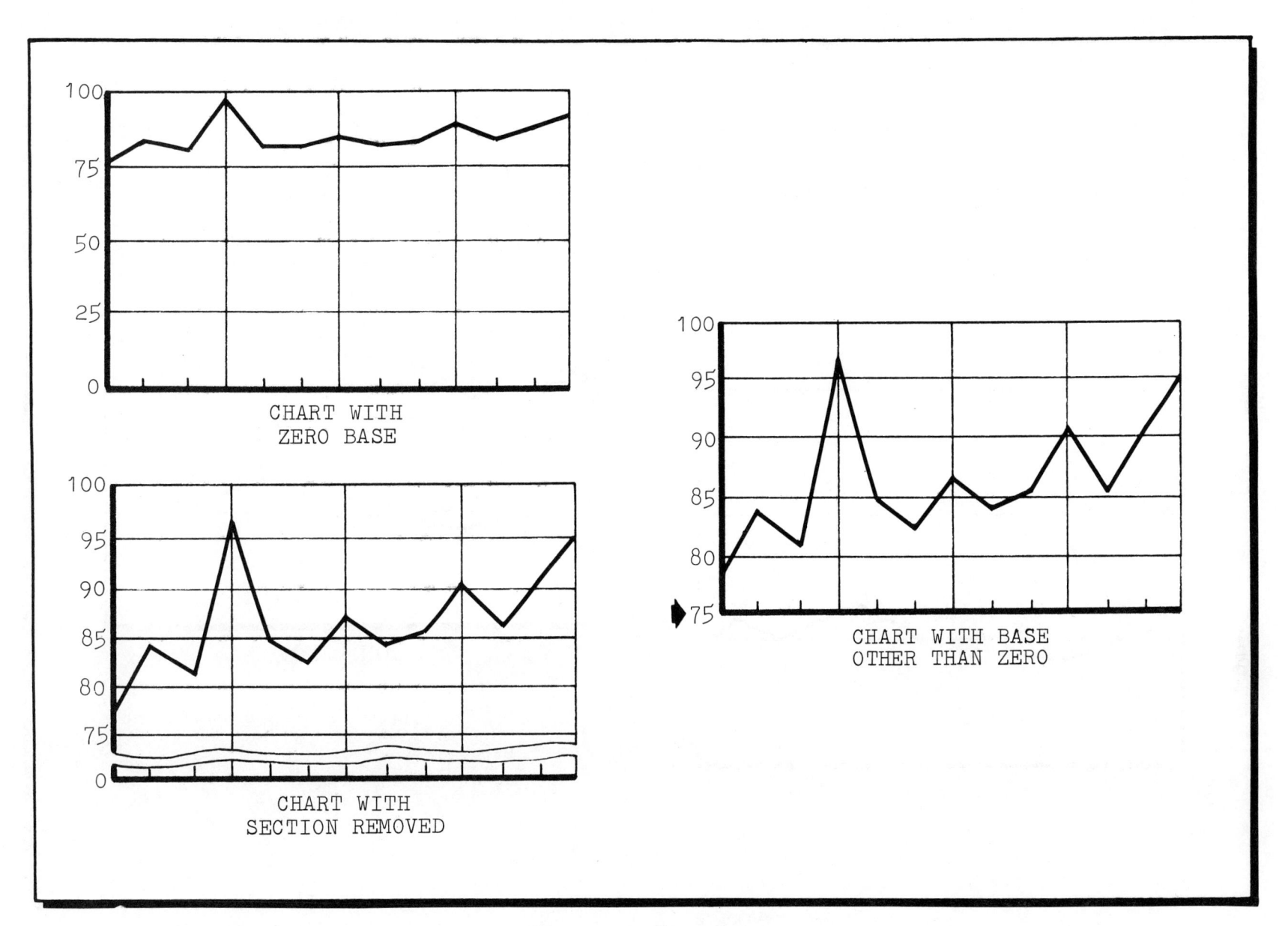

Figure 71.3 The Zero Base

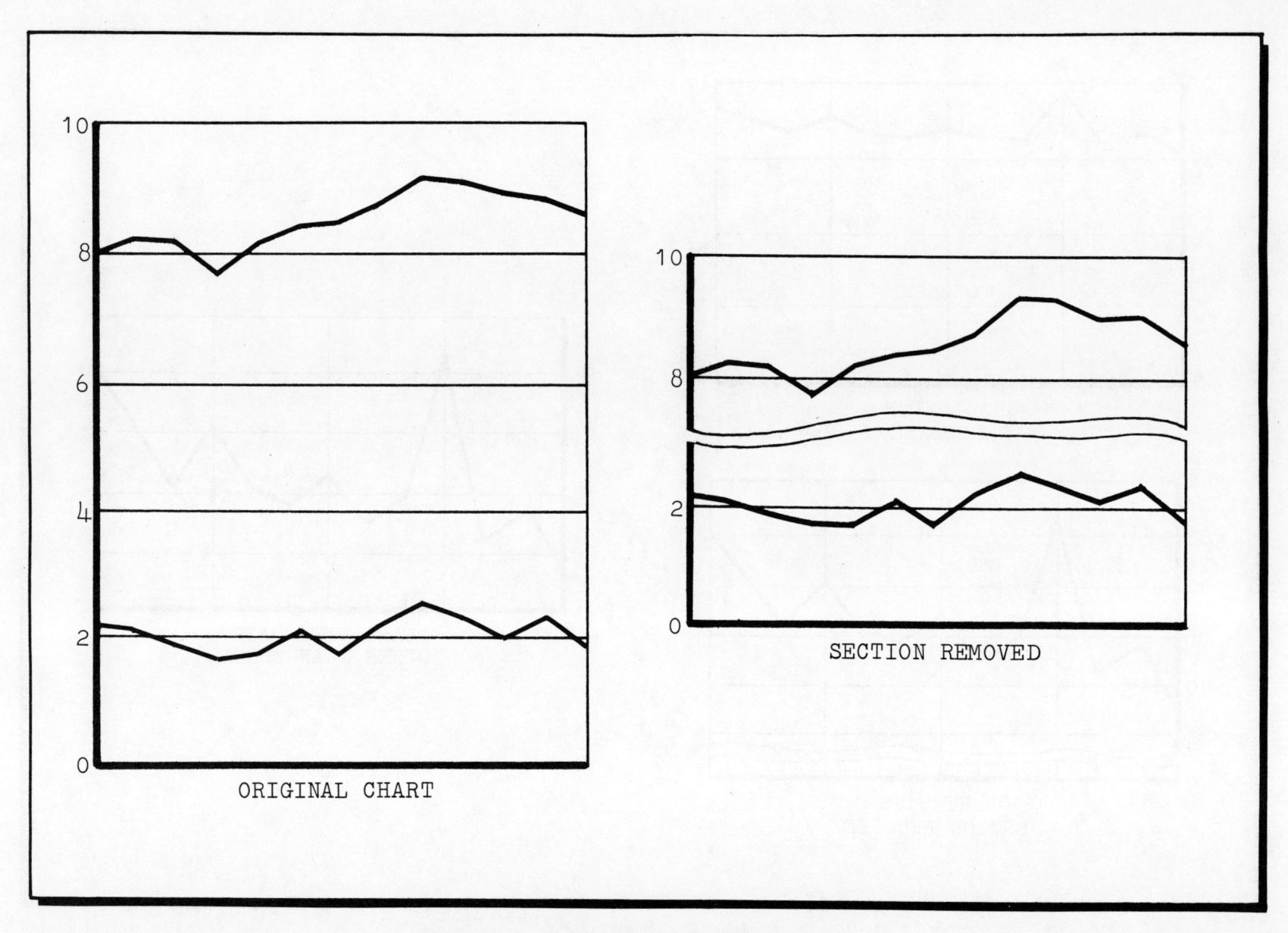

Figure 71.4 Compression of the Amount Scale

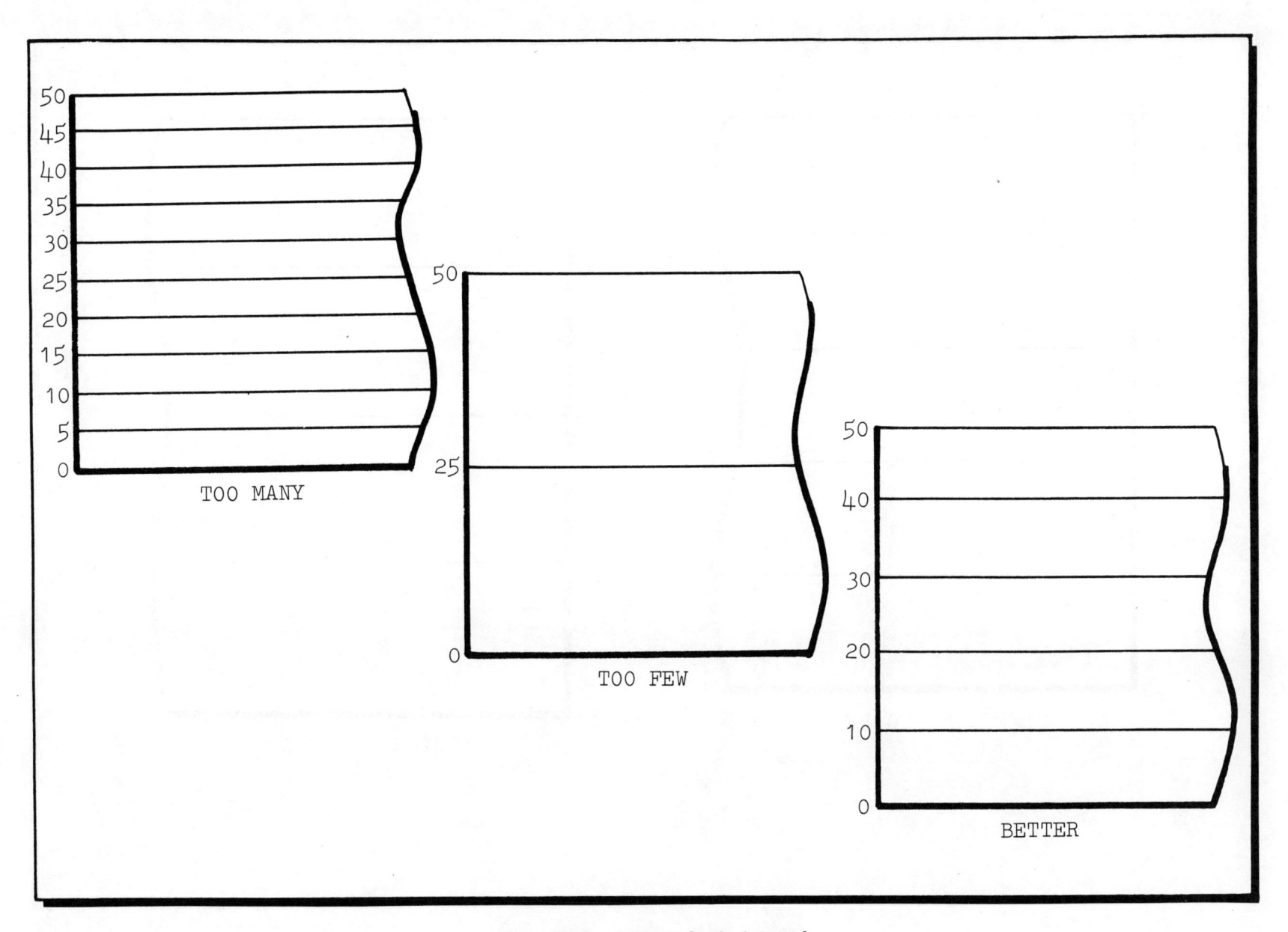

Figure 71.5 Amount Scale Intervals

851

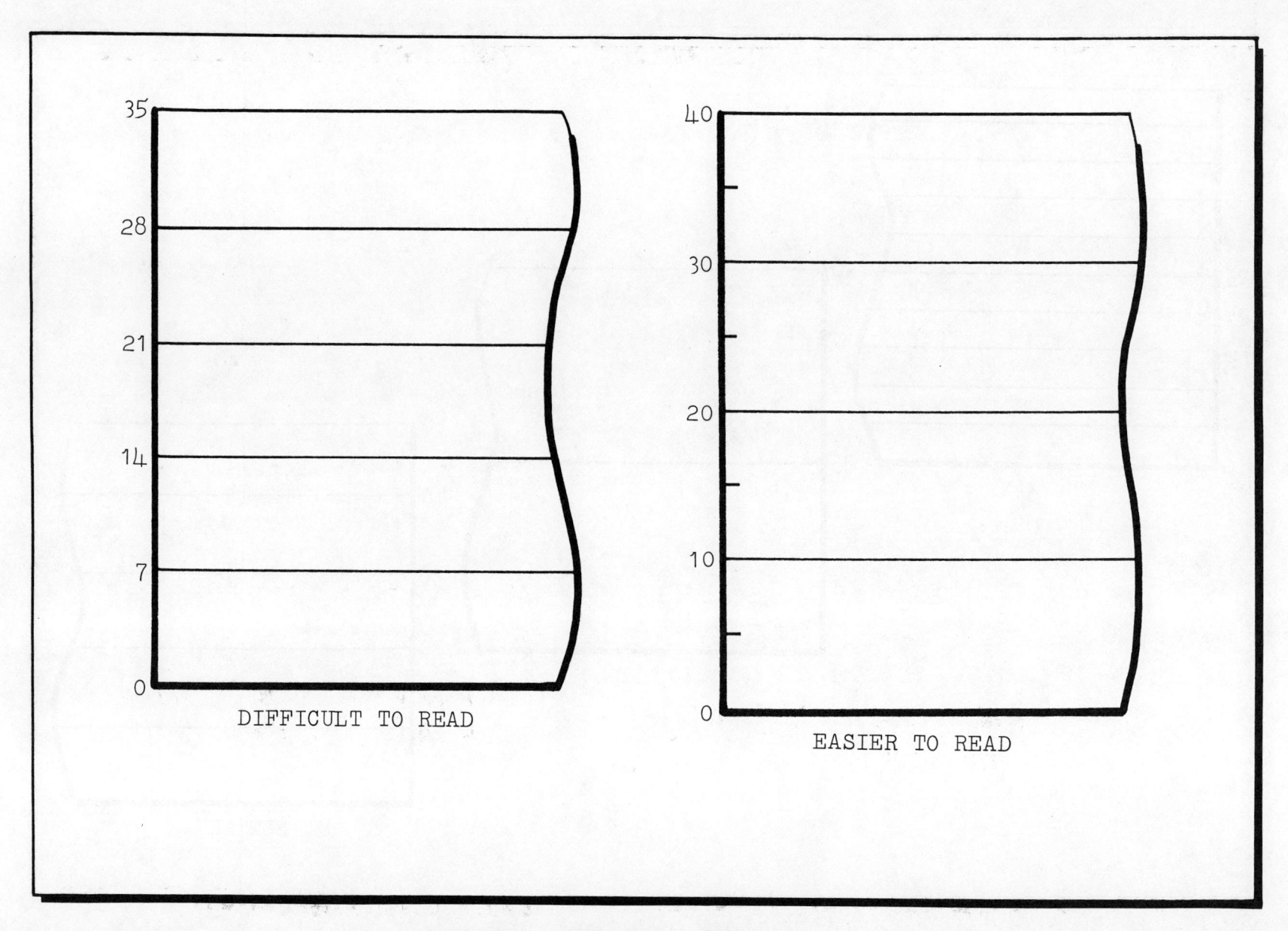

Figure 71.6   Reading Curve or Column Values

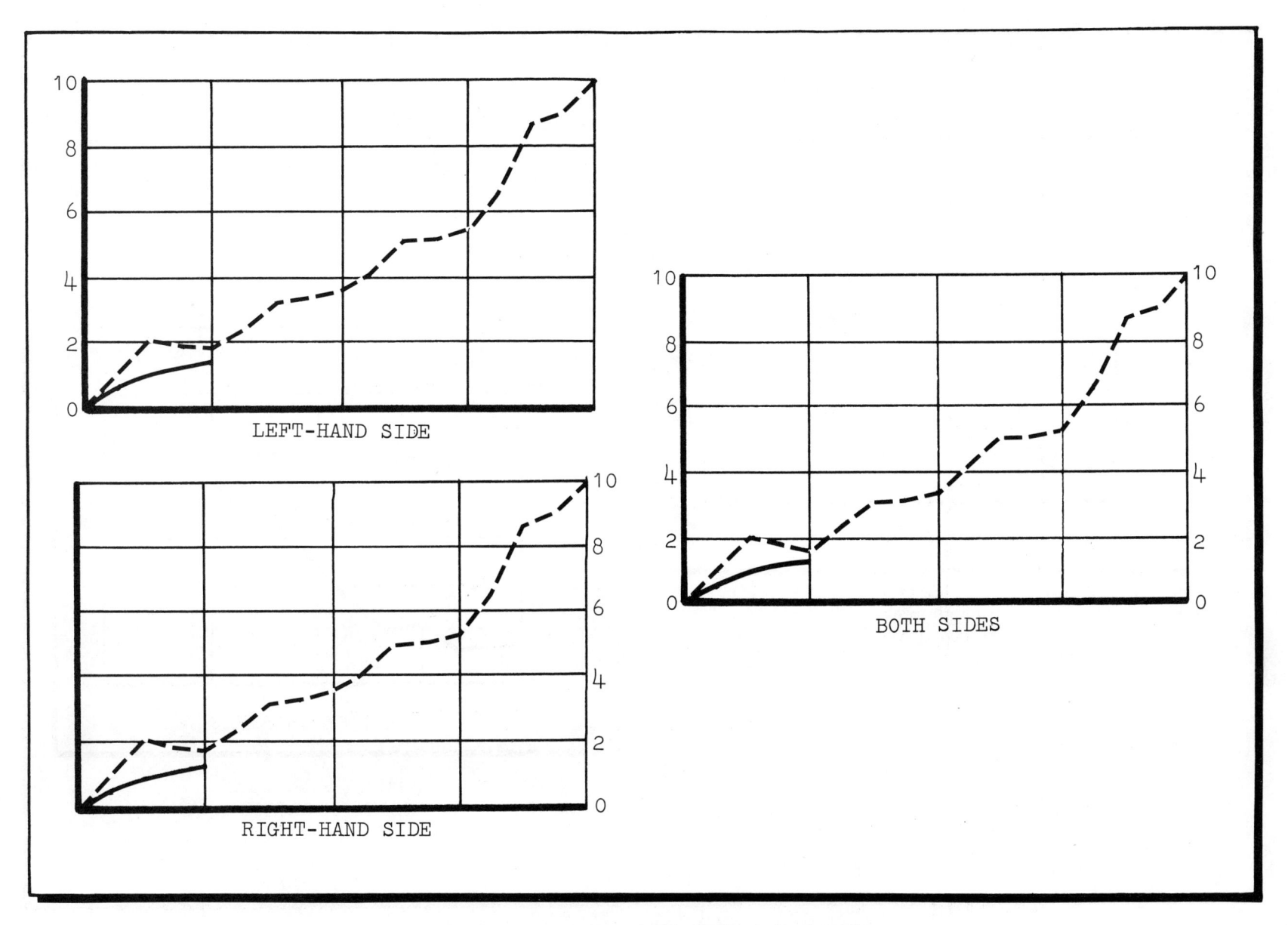

Figure 71.7 Location of Amount Scale Designations

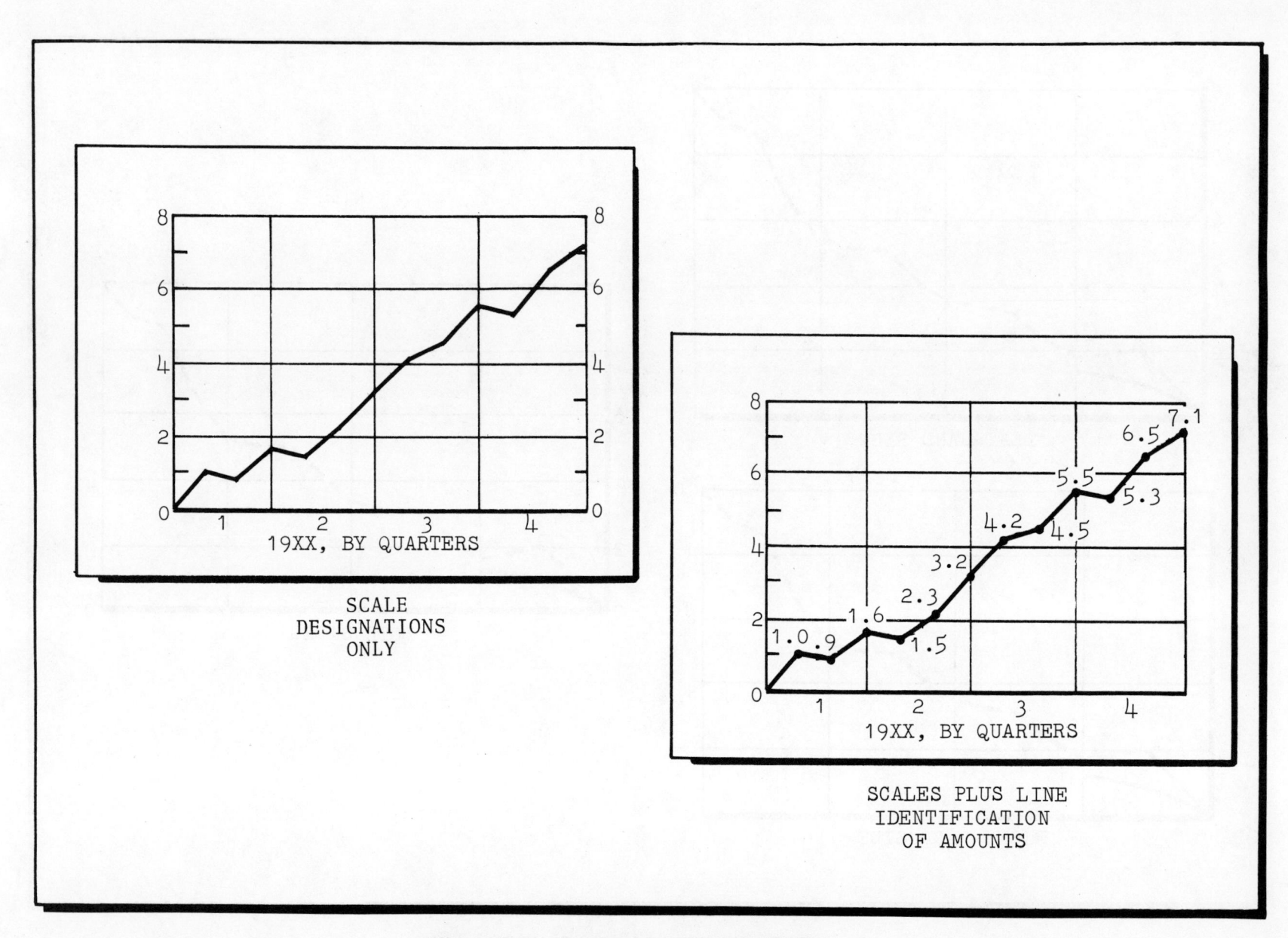

Figure 71.8 Line Chart Amount Designations

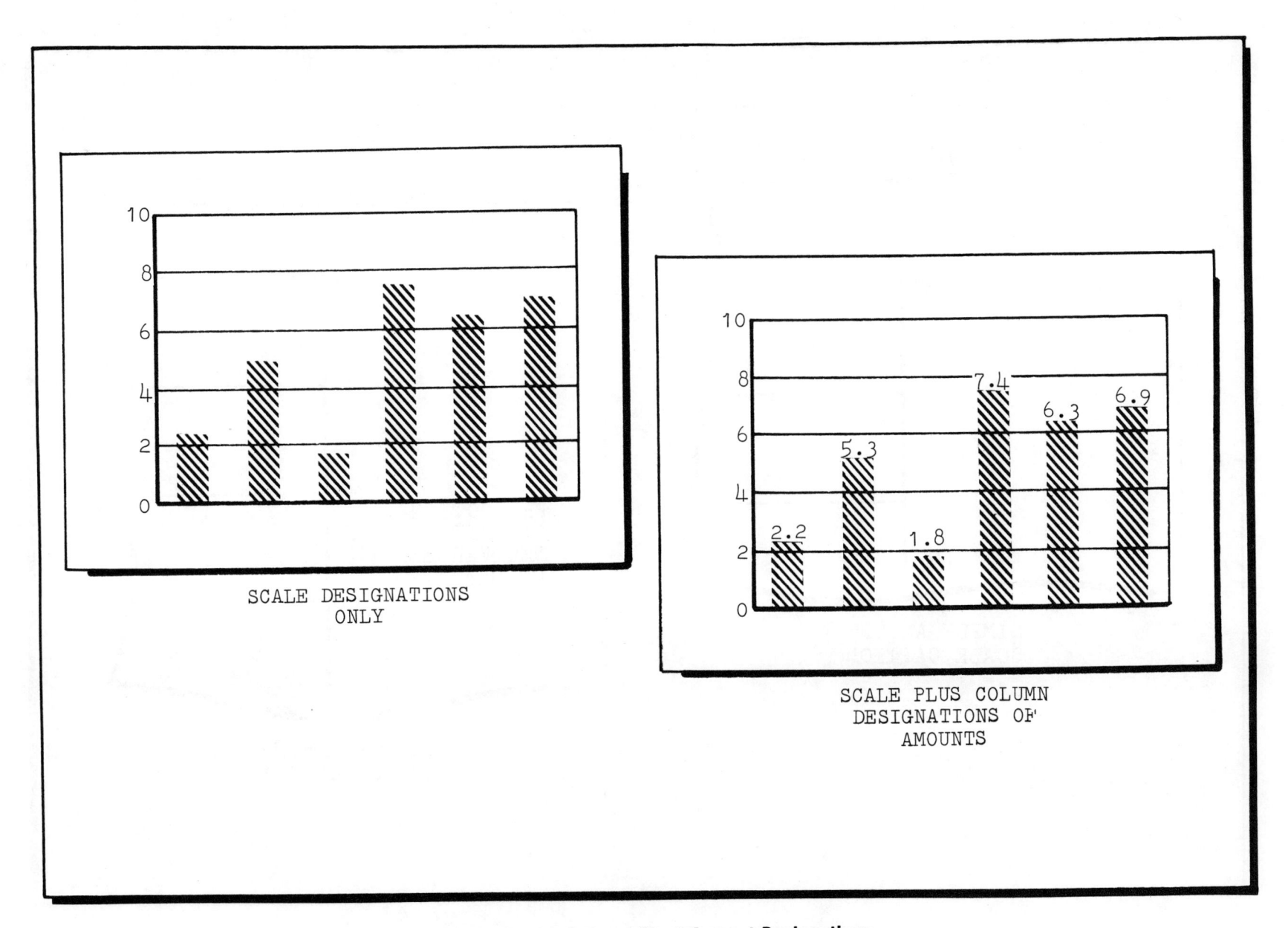

Figure 71.9　Column Chart Amount Designations

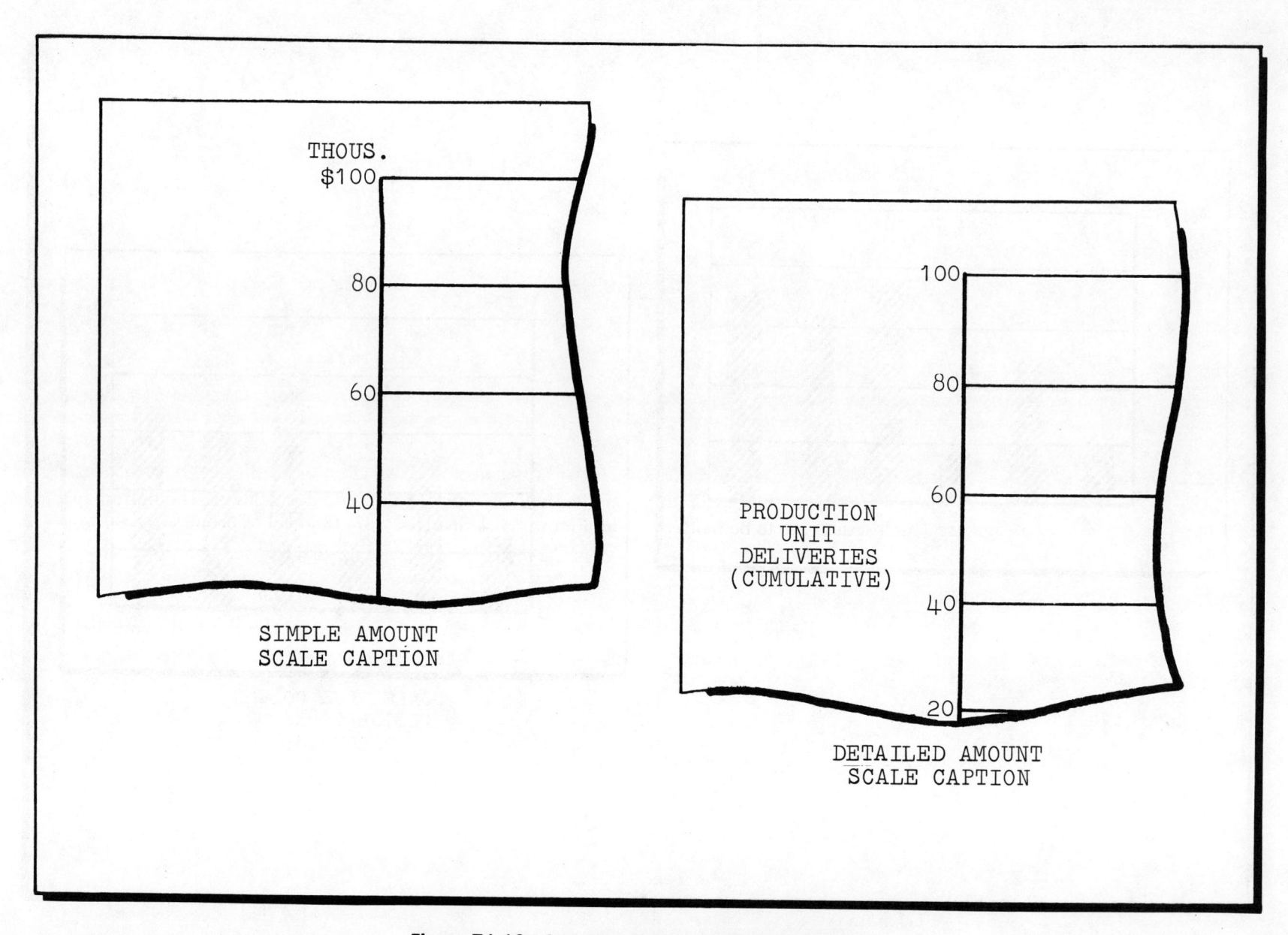

Figure 71.10 Location of Amount Scale Caption

72.0 TIME SCALES

72.1 Time Scale Location: Time scales are normally located below the grid, as shown in both examples in Figure 72.1. When period data are to be plotted, the time scale designations are placed under the grid spaces. For point data the designations are placed directly under the grid lines and/or tick mark lines.

72.2 Time Scale Range: The time scale should be related to the data that are being plotted. In tracking-type charts, for instance, when there is a plan against which actuals are to be plotted, the time scale should be constructed to extend over the full length of the period covered by the plan, as shown at the top of Figure 72.2. To leave a large portion of a chart unused, far beyond current data (as shown at the bottom of the illustration), is not recommended.

72.3 Time Scale Anomalies: When data are missing from some portion of a series, the chart marker should so indicate. Both examples shown in Figure 72.3 are methods for accomplishing this, but the preferred method is the one at the bottom of the figure.

72.4 Time Scale Designations: Various factors involved in identifying time scales are shown in Figure 72.4. The most acceptable way for designating years is shown at the top of the illustration. Two different acceptable ways for abbreviating months are shown in the center of the figure.

It is not necessary to identify each plotting point or plotting period with an alpha or numeric designation. The bottom example in Figure 72.4 displays a method for plotting data by quarters, although only the year designations are given.

72.5 Data Carried Over from Previous Time Period: Two methods of carrying data over from previous time periods are illustrated in Figure 72.5. In example 1, a section line from the last month of the previous reporting period (December) helps to establish continuity between the last data from the previous year's reporting period and the new reporting period. In example 2, another method for carrying over data is shown. In this case, the data from the previous year are shown as an average.

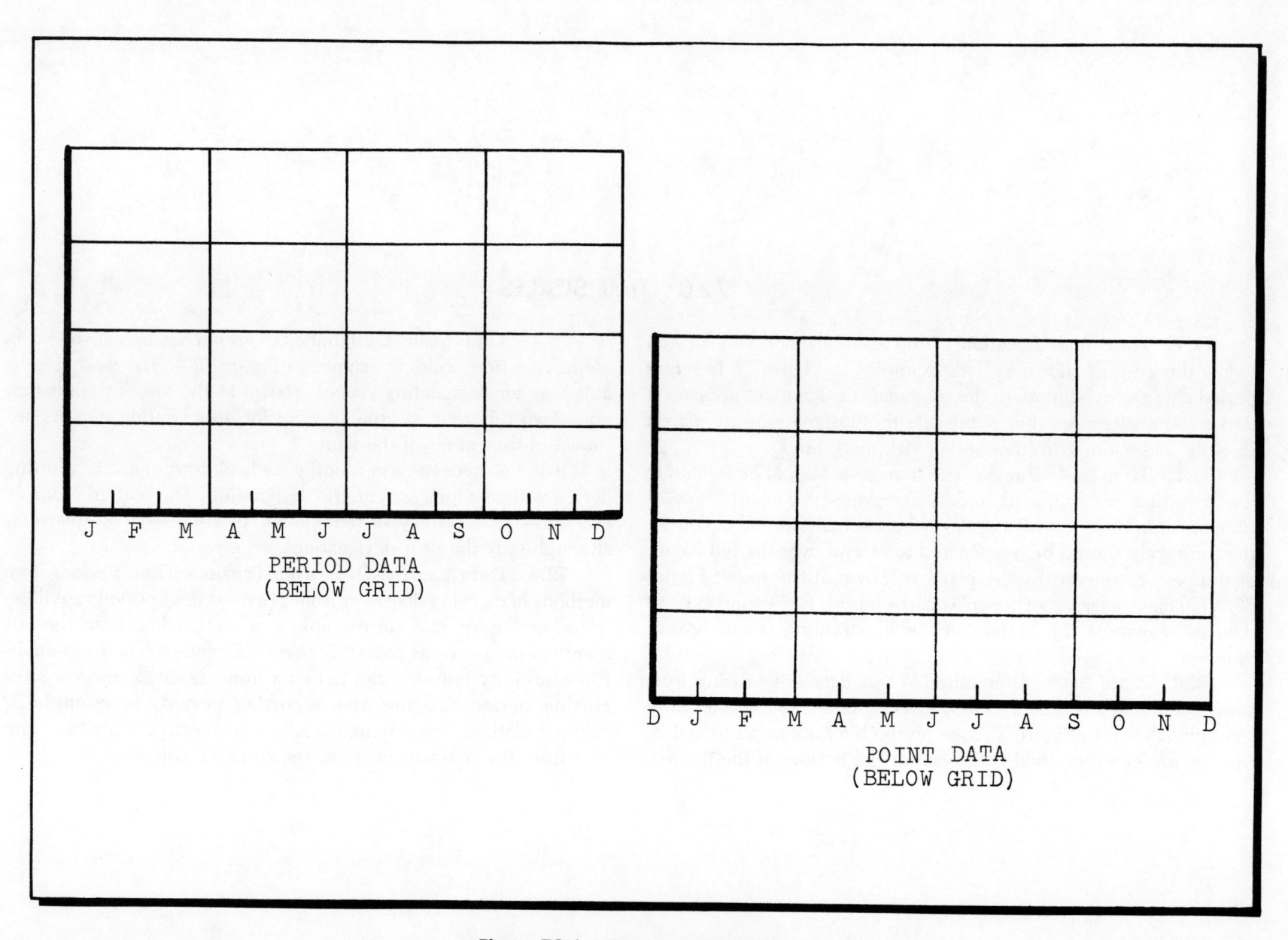

Figure 72.1 Time Scale Location

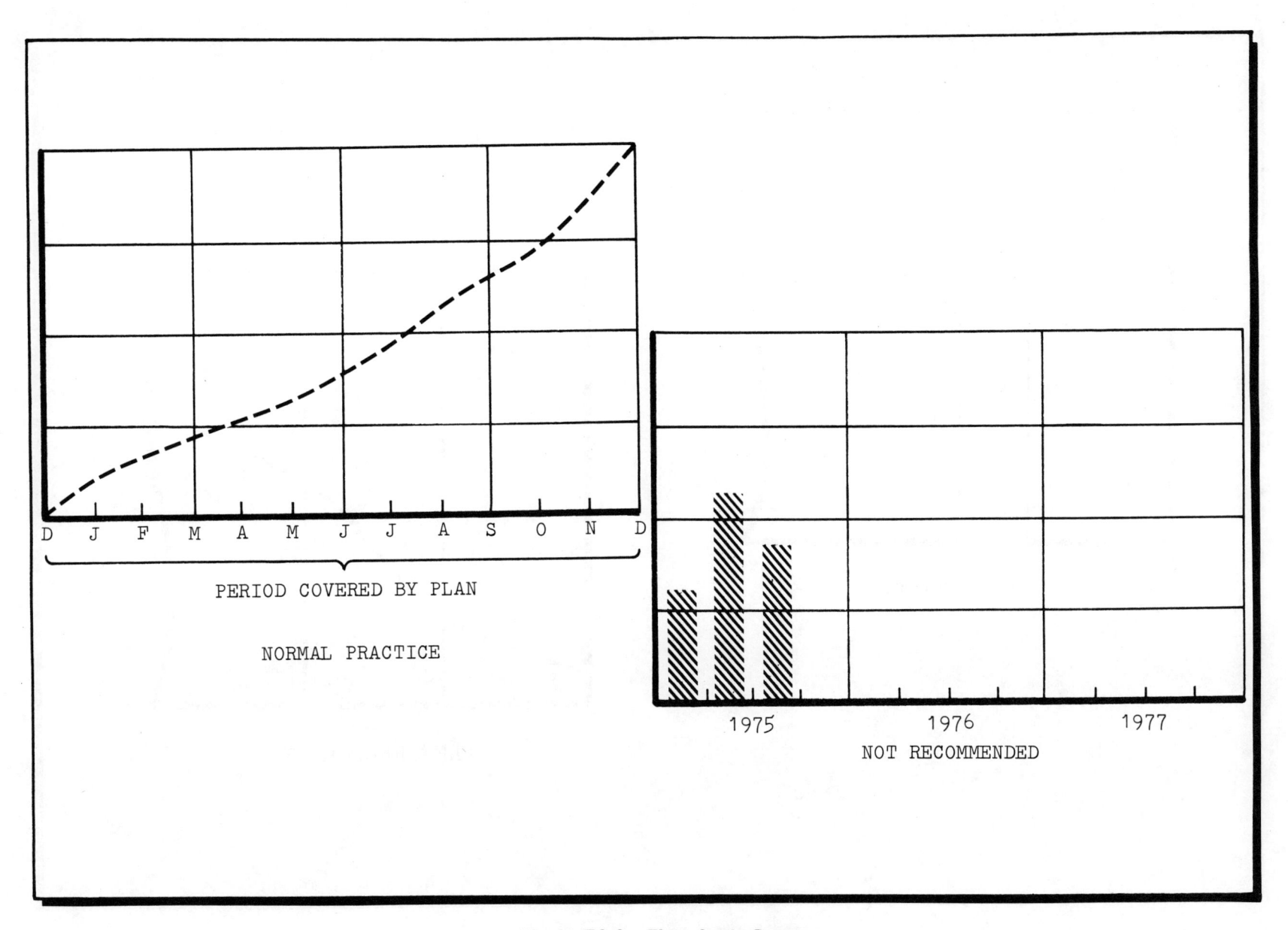

Figure 72.2 Time Scale Range

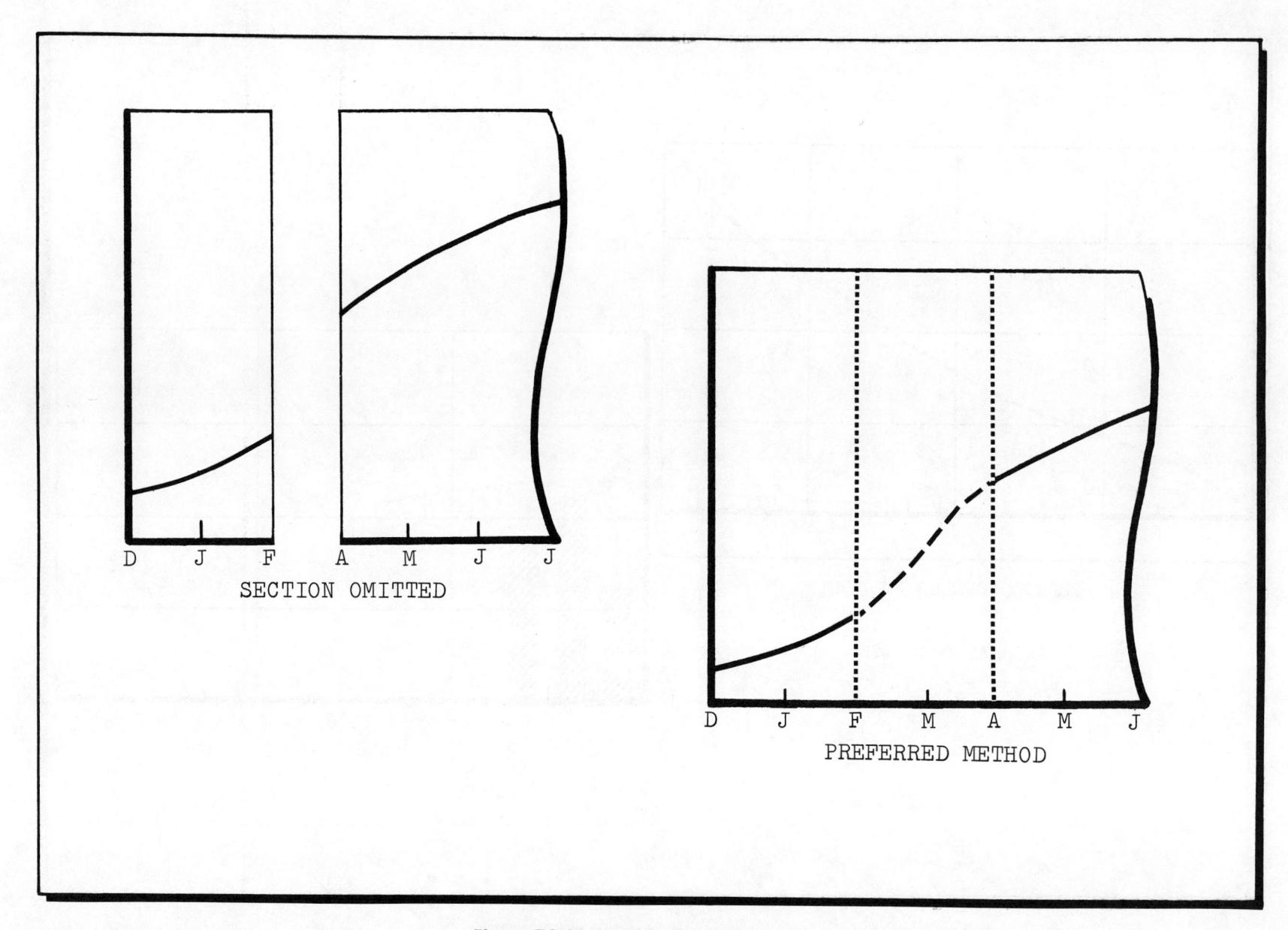

Figure 72.3 Time Scale Anomalies

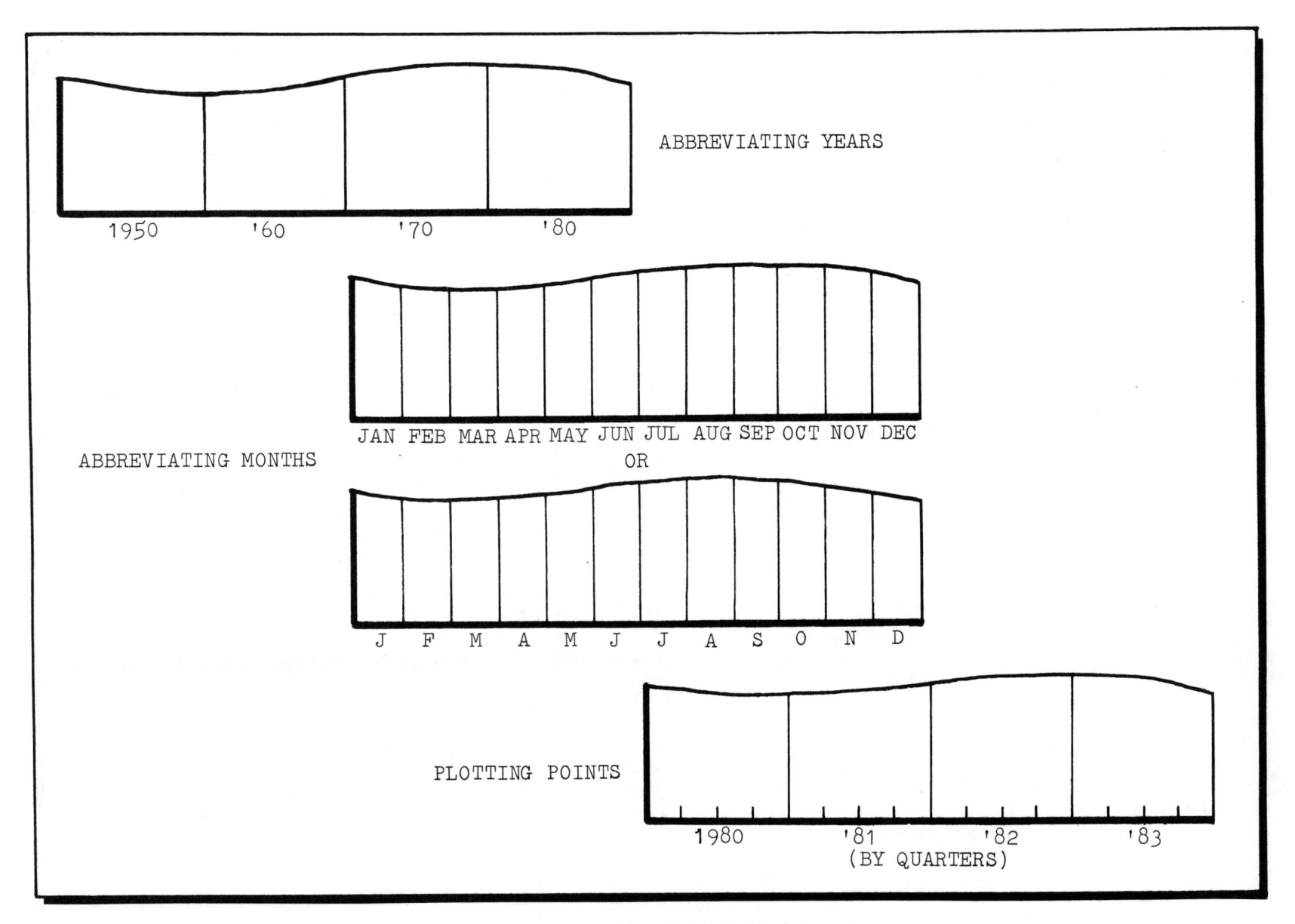

Figure 72.4 Time Scale Designations

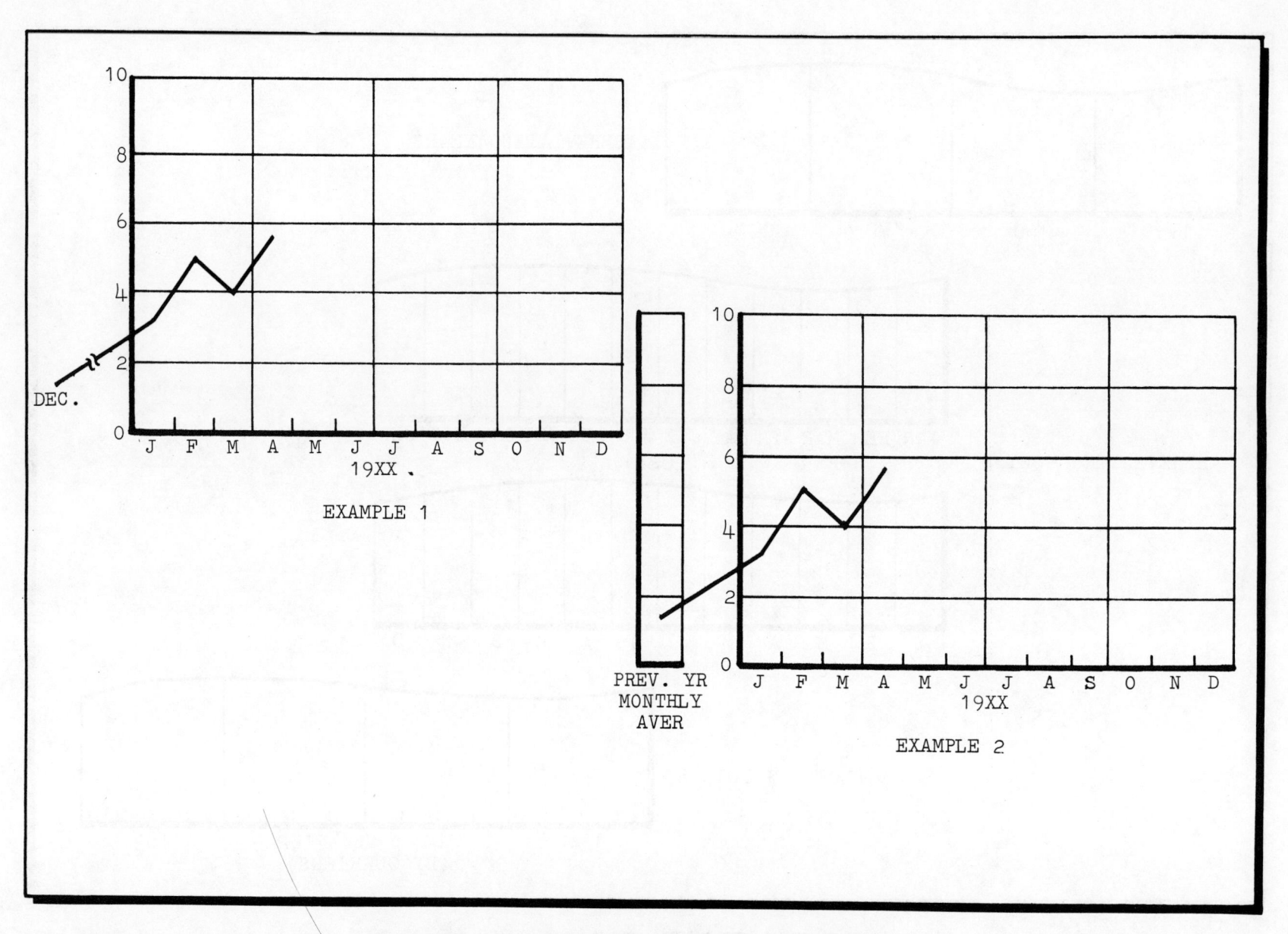

Figure 72.5 Data Carried Over from Previous Time Period

862

73.0 GOALS AND LIMITS

73.1 Goals and Limits—Basic Concepts: Every business tracking chart must contain at least two elements of data: *actual progress* (accomplishment) in relationship to *planned activity*. An example of how these two elements are displayed on a simple line chart is shown at the top of Figure 73.1. Also note that, as previously stated, the common practice of using a dash line for the plan (goal) and a solid line for actual progress, has been used in this example.

Goals can also be stated in terms of limits. An example of this is shown at the bottom of Figure 73.1 where maximum and minimum requirements are graphically displayed in relationship to actual progress.

73.2 Goals as Related to One- and Two-Scale Charts: Goals, or limits (such as "tolerance"), can also be displayed on charts containing a single scale, as shown at the top of Figure 73.2. Although one-scale charts are not *tracking* charts, the use of a goal or limit greatly enhances their usefulness.

An acceptable method for showing a goal on a typical column chart is illustrated at the bottom of Figure 73.2. It should be noted that in this particular style of display, both the *plan* column and the *actual* column for a given month can both be "read" after both elements of data have been plotted.

73.3 Other Examples of Goals and Limits: Additional examples of progress-tracking charts are shown in Figure 73.3. The symbol (or "milestone") chart at the top of the illustration shows how progress is plotted in relationship to the plan by shading that portion of the plan that has been completed.

In the bar chart example, paired bars are used, each pair representing the plan and the actual progress. At the bottom of Figure 73.3, a line chart is shown with minimum-maximum limits narrowing in time.

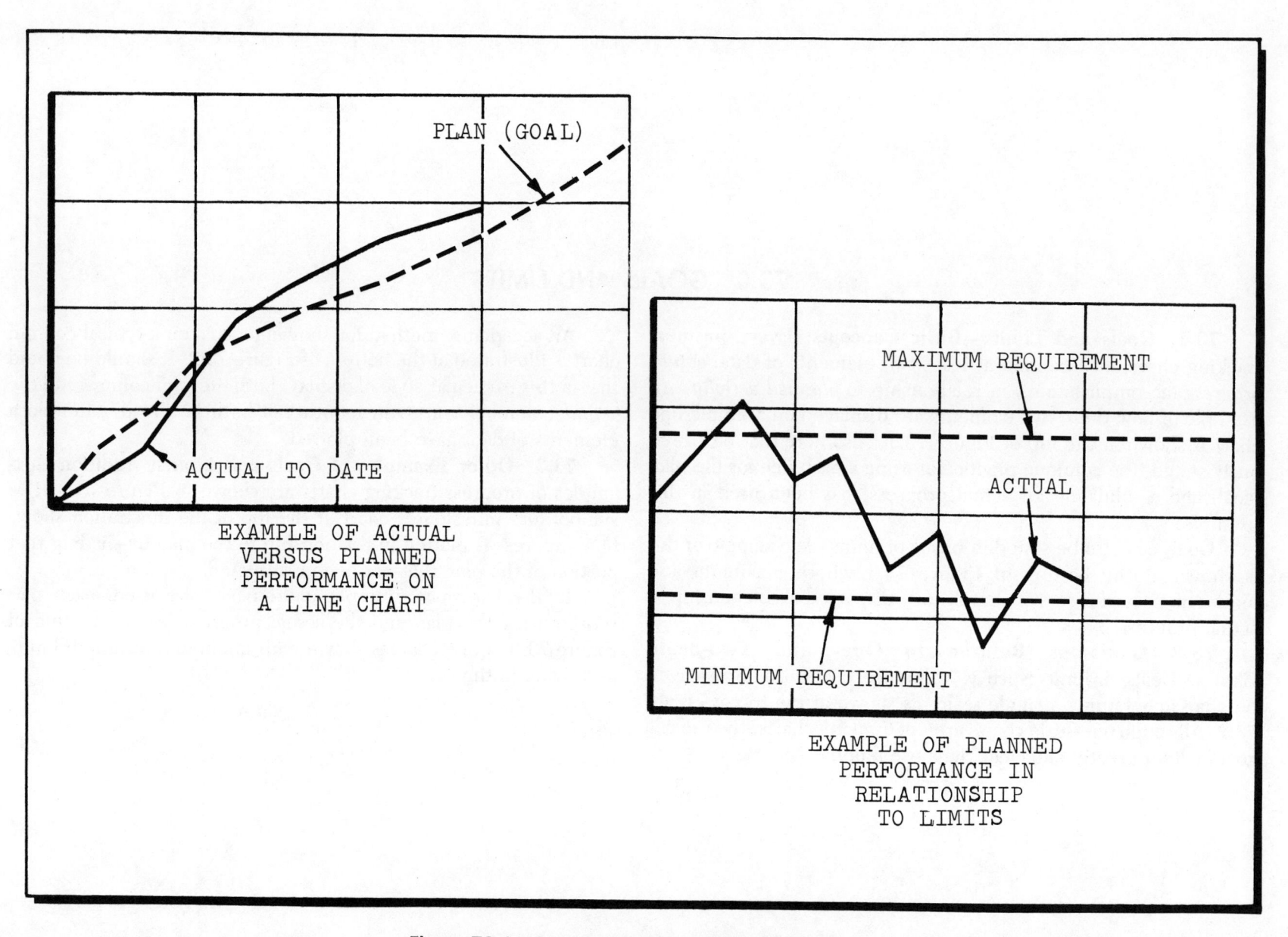

Figure 73.1 Goals and Limits—Basic Concepts

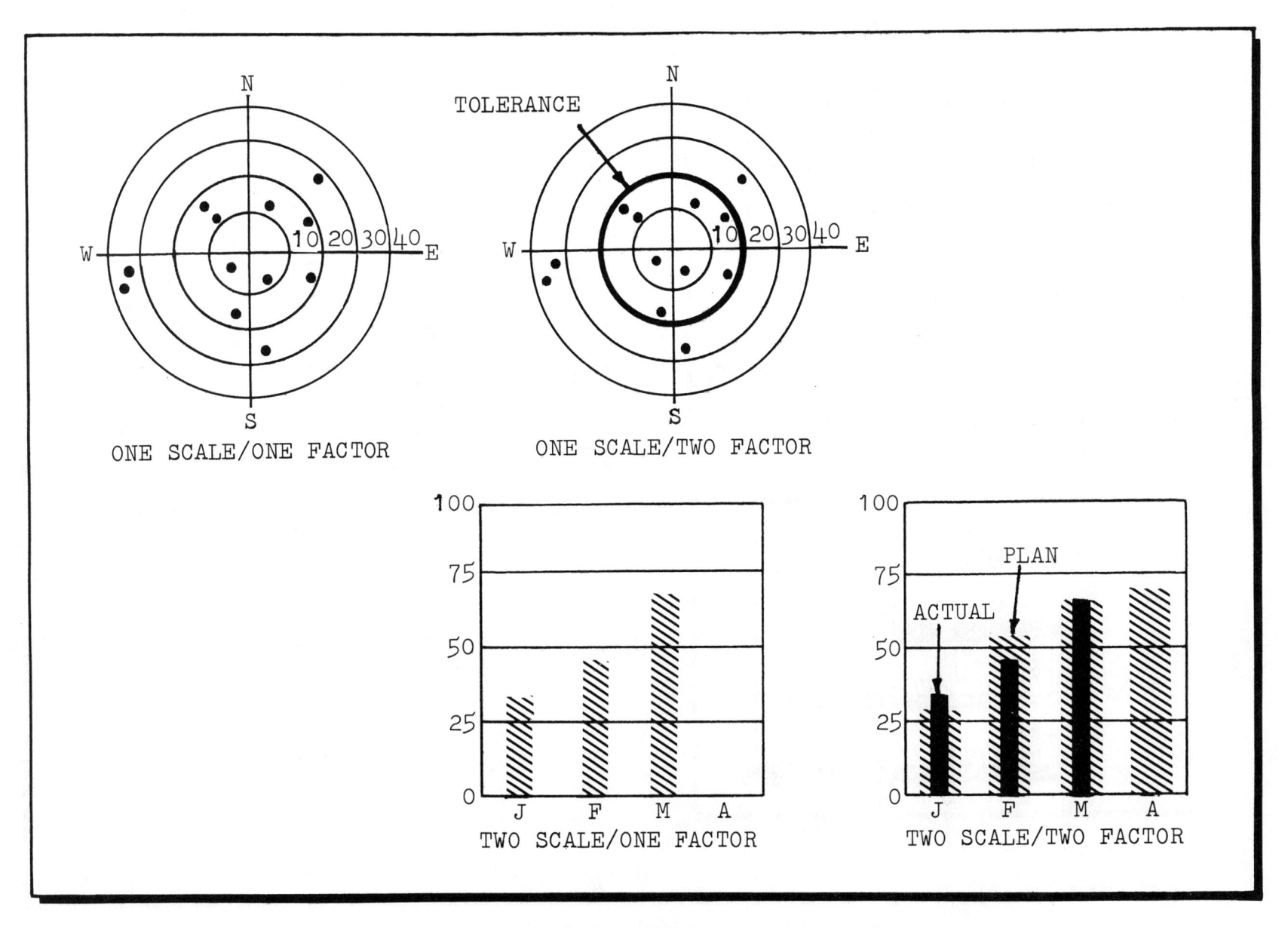

Figure 73.2 Goals as Related to One- and Two-Scale Charts

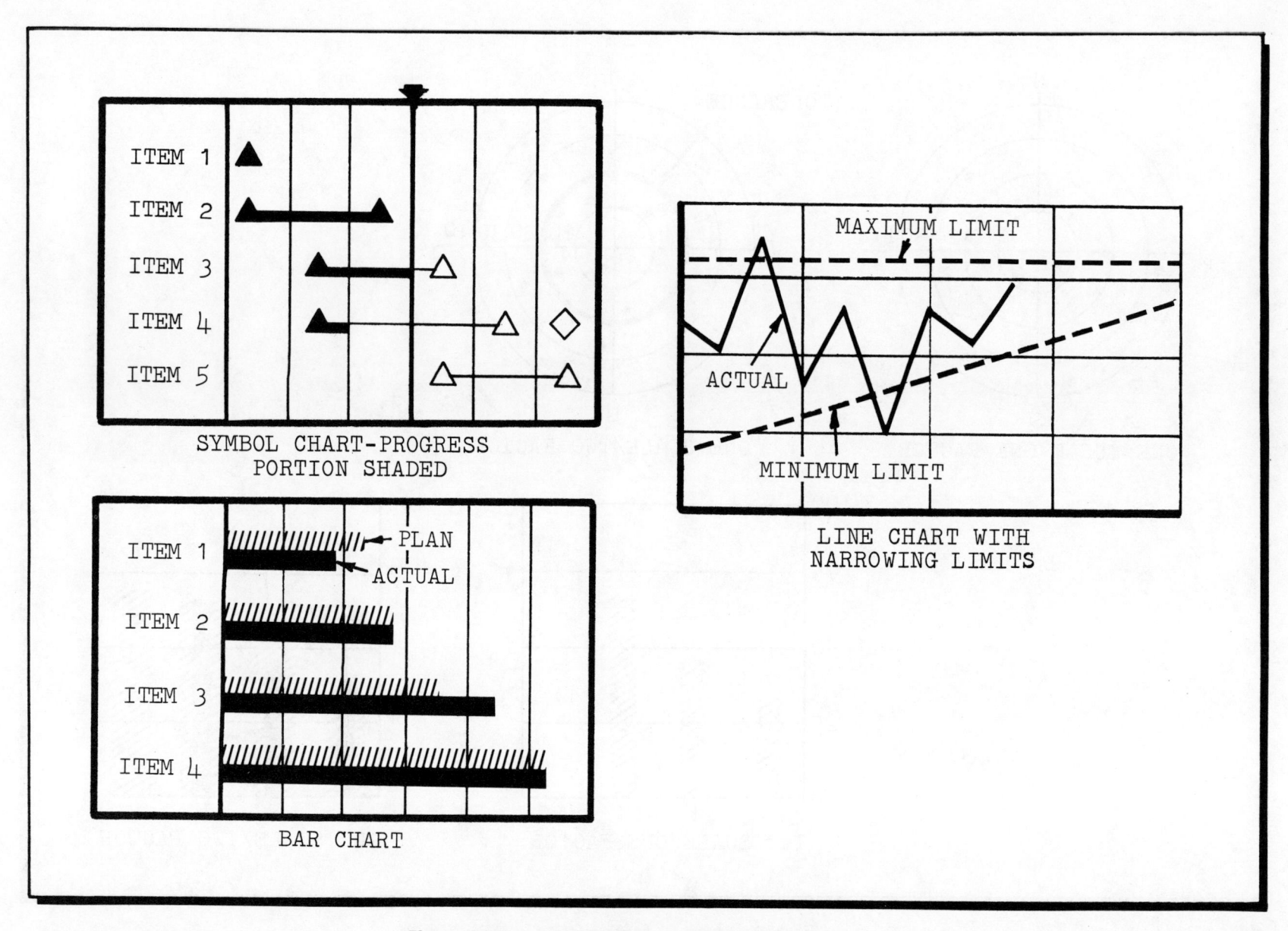

Figure 73.3 Other Examples of Goals and Limits

74.0 TIME-NOW DATING

74.1 Time-Now Dating—Arrows and Lines: Charts with a date scale ordinate should contain an indication of the date to which the information on the chart is valid. Three examples are shown in Figure 74.1.

Time-now lines and arrows should be taped or pressed on to facilitate updating. They should be placed at the date of the latest actual data.

74.2 Time-Now Dating—Shading, Bars, and Call-Outs: Other examples of time-now dating are shown in Figure 74.2. The preferred approach among these three examples is the call-out form illustrated at the top. The least preferred method is the one shown at the bottom because shading is difficult and time-consuming to apply.

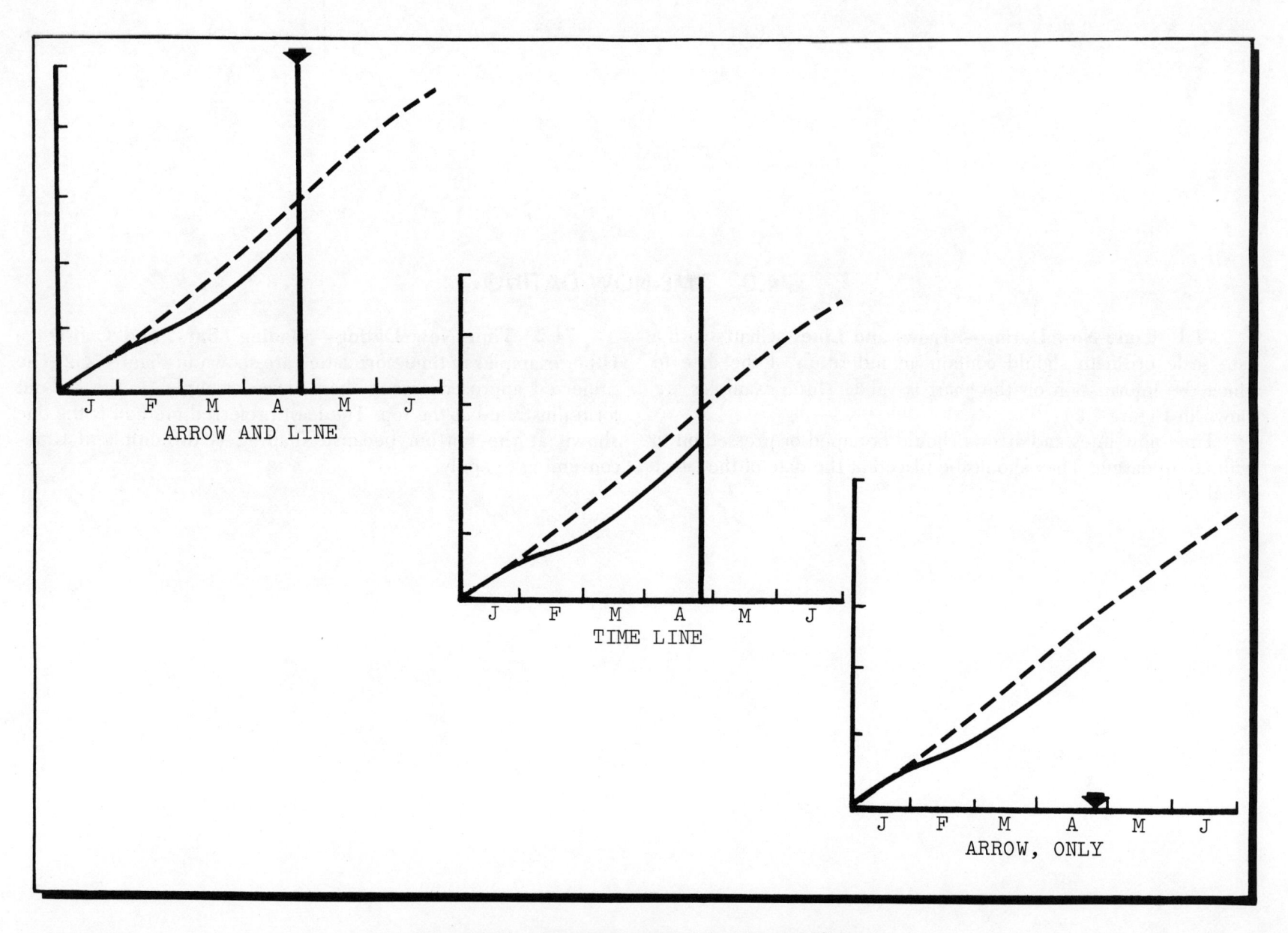

Figure 74.1 Time-Now Dating—Arrows and Lines

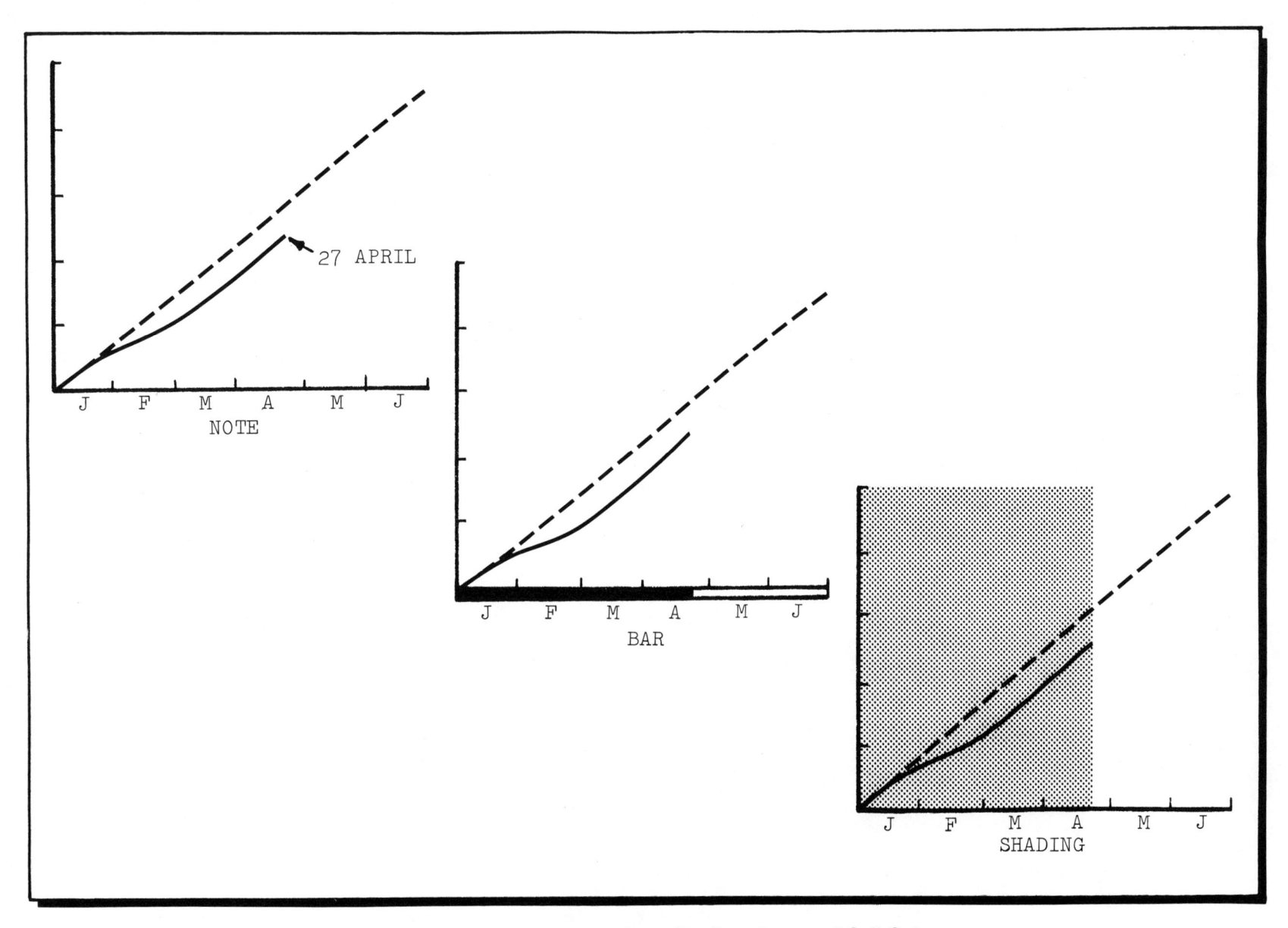

Figure 74.2 Time-Now Dating—Shading, Bars, and Call-Outs

75.0 NOTES, KEYS, AND AUTHENTICATION

75.1 Location for Notes: Charts frequently require source notes, reference notes, and other types of explanatory notations so as to clarify the data that are being displayed. Figure 75.1 shows examples of how such material can be incorporated within the grid (top example), or below the grid (bottom example).

75.2 Labels Versus Keys: Two basic methods for identifying chart information are illustrated in Figure 75.2. At the top of the figure, labels, sometimes referred to as "call-outs," are shown. They could also be placed within the columns, space permitting. A key, also called "legend," is shown at the bottom of the figure. The method selected for any given application should be the one that most clearly presents the information to the chart reader. If abbreviations are used they should be clear and understandable.

75.3 Data Authentication: In some applications it is essential to have the data that are presented on a chart authenticated by some responsible authority. Two methods of doing this are illustrated in Figure 75.3. The use of removable labels should be considered so that a new validation can be made each time the chart is updated.

Other methods for authenticating chart data include utilization of a signed cover sheet for a set of charts or, in extreme cases, the initialing of each single data entry on the chart.

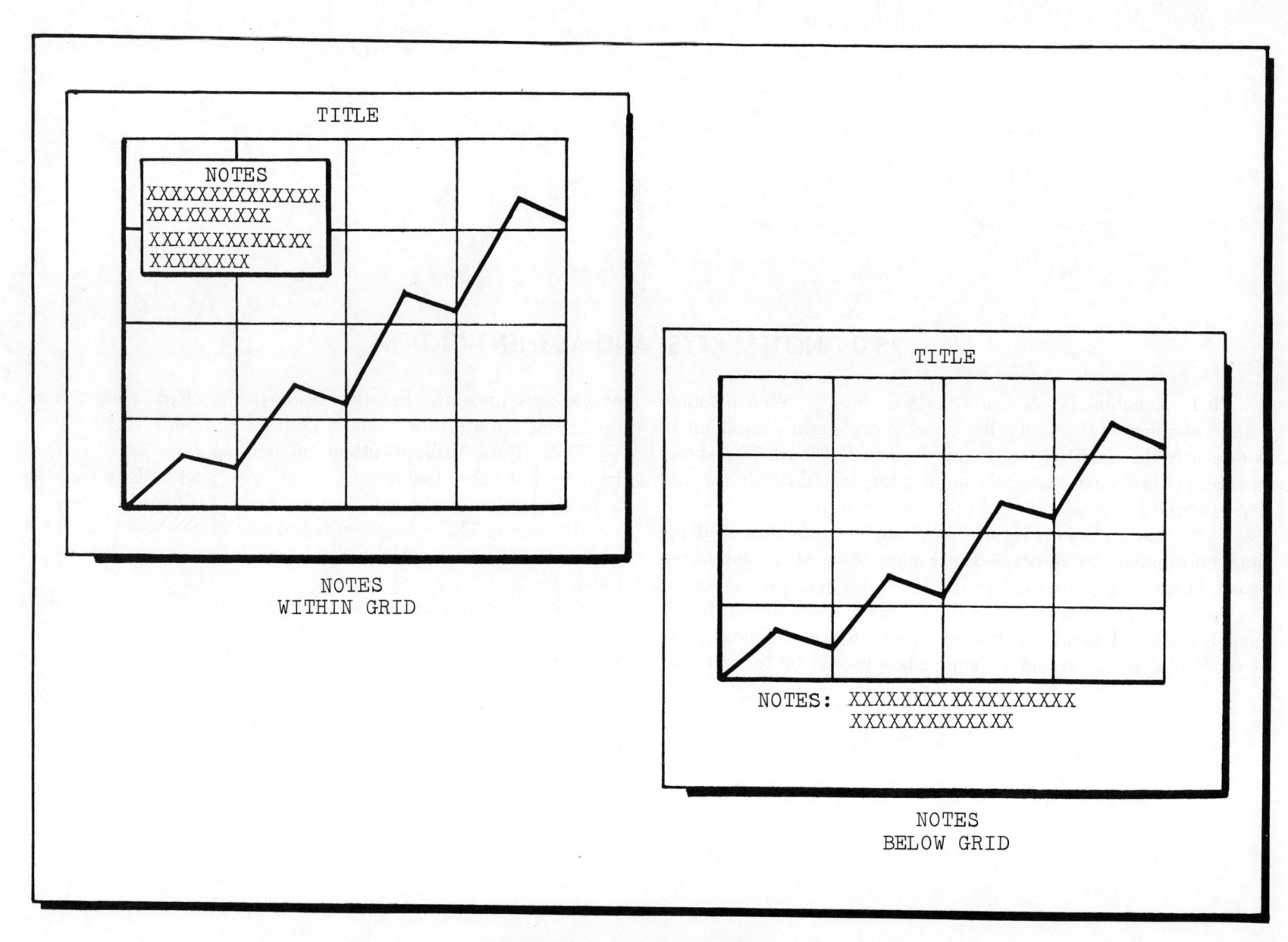

Figure 75.1　Location for Notes

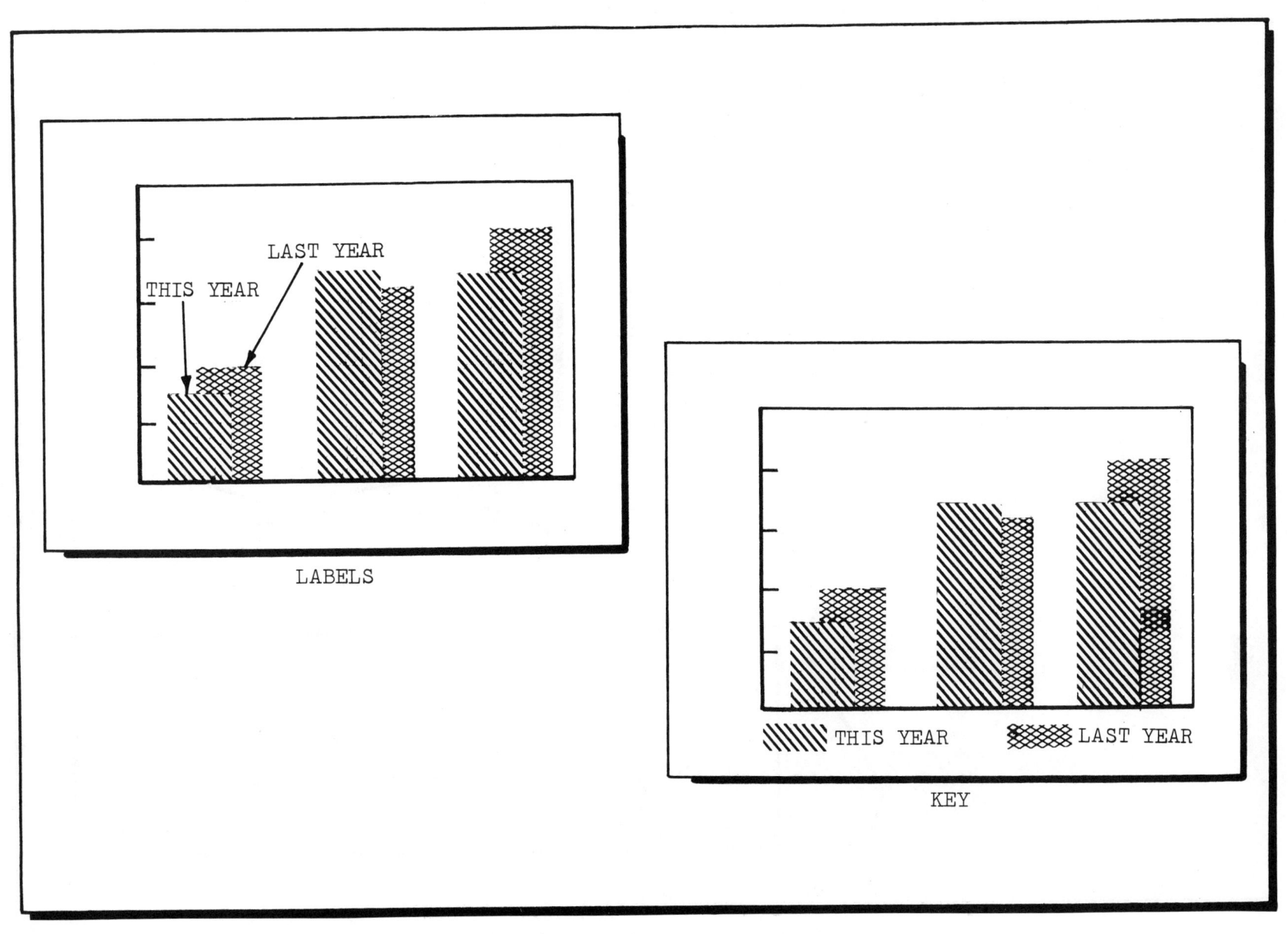

Figure 75.2   Labels Versus Keys

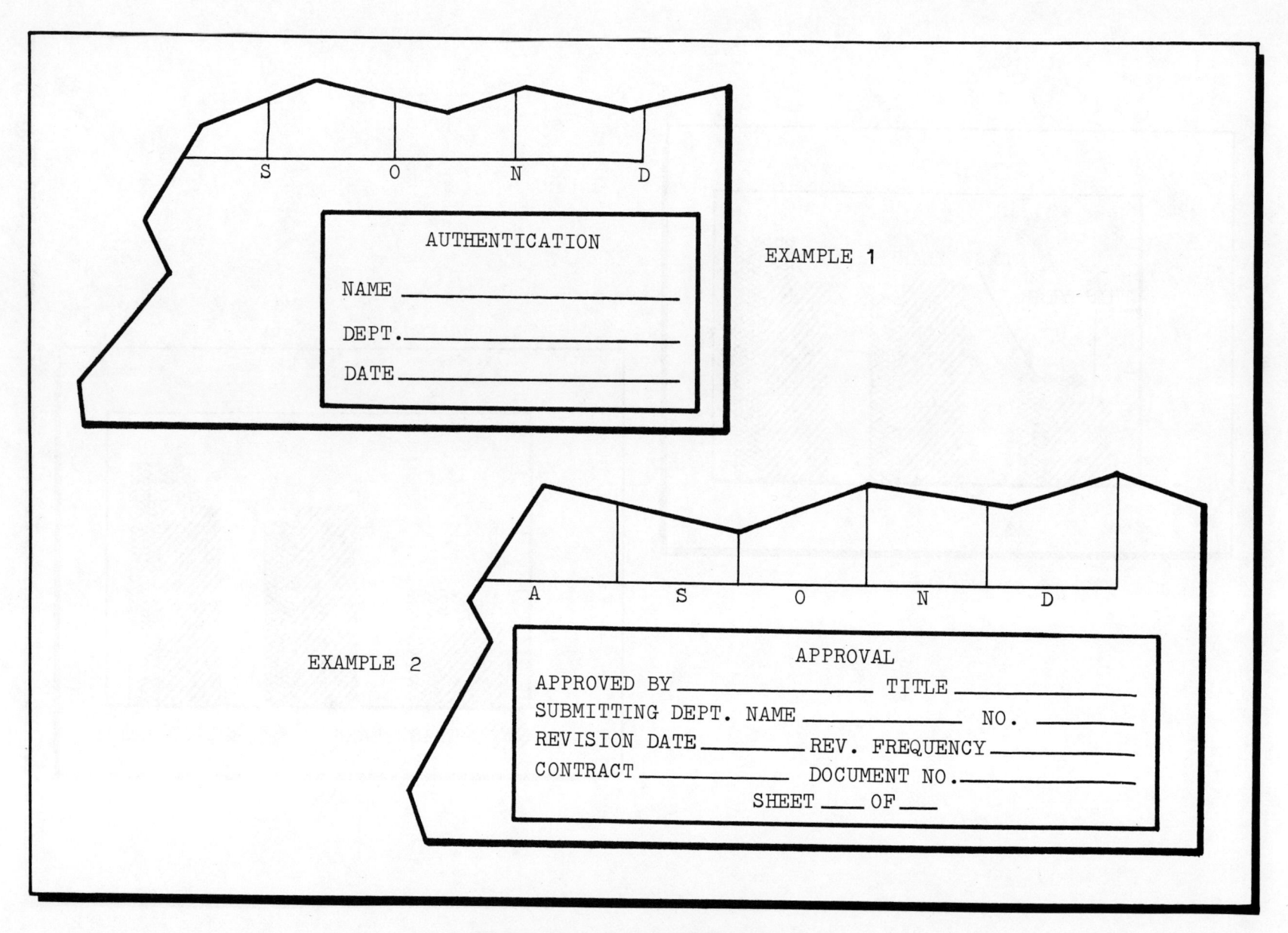

Figure 75.3 Data Authentication

76.0 EMPHASIZING KEY POINTS

76.1 Special Horizontal and Vertical Rulings: Use can be made of special horizontal and vertical rulings to highlight pertinent information. In the example at the top of Figure 76.1, two heavy vertical lines identify a specific time segment as a "strike period," thus shedding light on the significant dip in the plotted data.

Special horizontal rulings can be used to advantage, as well, such as serving as major reference lines.

76.2 Special Uses of Shading: Figure 76.2 illustrates several ways that shading can be productively used in chart layout. Shading is normally a costly, time-consuming technique, but if it serves to greatly clarify the data making the chart easier for the viewer to understand, it can sometimes be considered as cost-effective.

In the top example shading has been used to highlight non-productive periods; in this case, weekends. The bottom example shows shading used to highlight a special condition. Negative/positive charts, such as shown are often confusing. To be under the zero base line in the case of production, for instance, would indicate an unfavorable (behind schedule) condition. On the other hand, to be below the line relative to dollars (under budget), could be a favorable condition. To use shading (possibly color) to indicate an unfavorable condition, whether above or below a reference line, can greatly increase the viewer's understanding of the material presented.

76.3 Highlighting Problems and Exceptions: Various techniques for emphasizing problems or exceptions to the norm are shown in Figure 76.3. At the top of the figure the net variance between the plan and the actual performance is called out with a caption, as one example.

Problems can be "flagged" as shown at the center of the figure. In this manner, the viewer's attention is focused on the main point the chart maker is trying to make with the chart. Color, such as red, can also be used but this is normally an expensive process, especially if reproduction processes are involved.

The bottom example in Figure 76.3 shows how anomalies, or "freaks," in the data can be explained or defined through the use of captions.

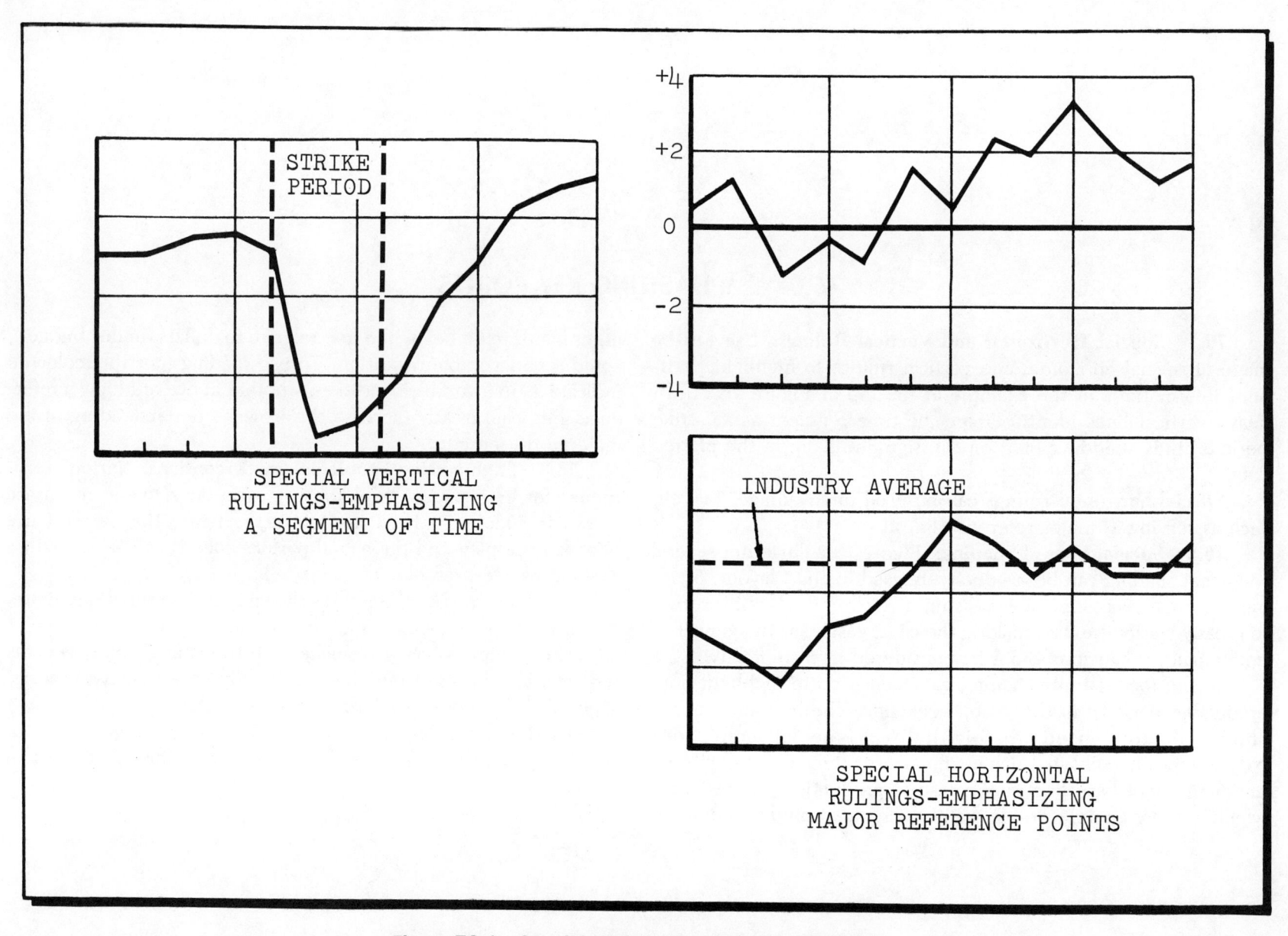

Figure 76.1   Special Horizontal and Vertical Rulings

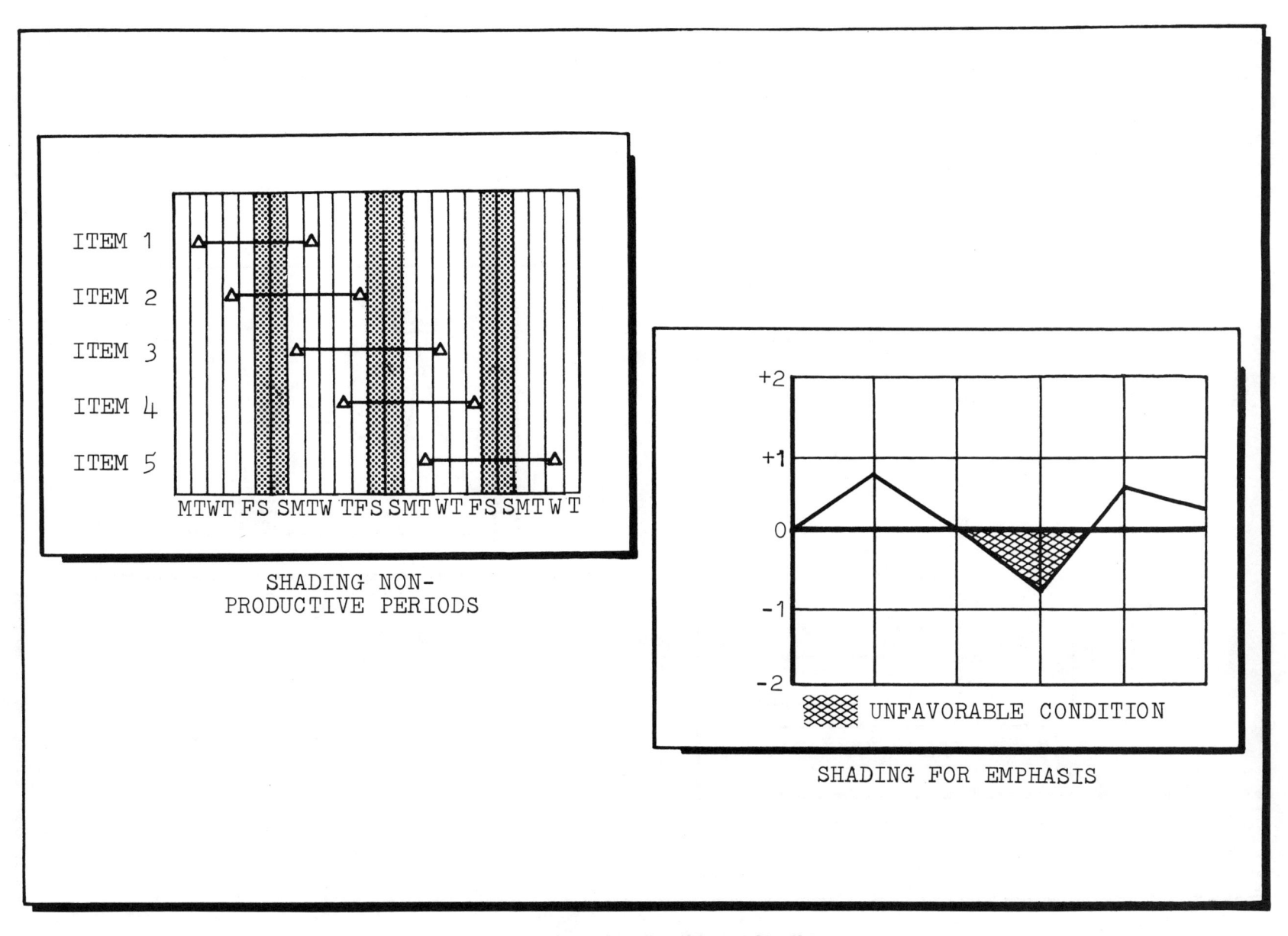

Figure 76.2 Special Uses of Shading

877

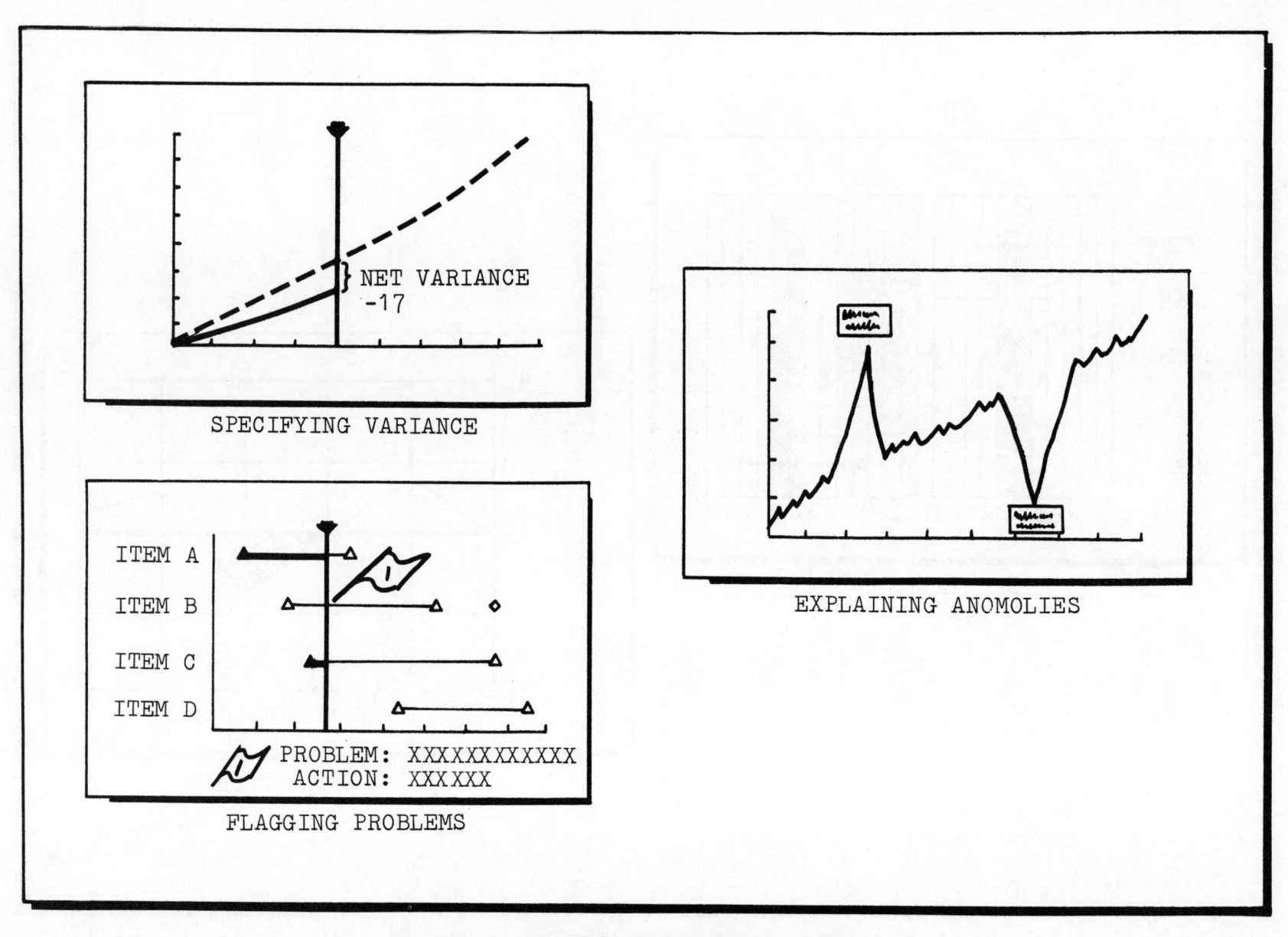

Figure 76.3 Highlighting Problems and Exceptions

878

77.0 DATA LAYOUT

77.1 Trend Versus Detail Charts: Two extremes in chart detail are illustrated in Figure 77.1. It is a matter of application and choice as to the most appropriate form.

Example 1 shows a simple trend-indicating chart. It has been plotted on a background where grid lines have been omitted. The chart's usefulness is enhanced by adding the numerical value (-20) of the variance between scheduled and actual values at the time of the report (end of June in this example).

Example 2 displays a wealth of detailed information in both graphic and statistical form. Scheduled and actual quantities are statistically given in terms of rate per month. The cumulative statistics are also given and plotted on the graph, as well, followed by the net variance between these two figures. Finally, a plan to recover to the original schedule is given both in terms of rate per month and cumulatively.

77.2 Cumulative and Rate Charts: Data can be plotted on charts in terms of rate-per-time segment, as shown at the bottom of Figure 77.2, or in terms of accumulating all preceding values, as shown at the top of the figure. Each method has its usefulness.

People interested in shop-loading factors and capacities, for instance, usually prefer to see data in terms of rates-per-time segment. Those interested in seeing where they stand in terms of a total plan usually prefer the data accumulated so that the net variance from the plan can be more easily determined. Both methods can utilize column, line, or surface chart techniques.

77.3 Plotting Points: Methods of plotting data on the grid are shown in Figure 77.3. Period data, such as the number of units manufactured or the number of sales made during a time period, should be plotted to the space as shown at the top of the illustration. Graphically, this could be done in the form of a step line chart, as shown, or in the form of a slope line curve, or as a column chart.

Point data, such as month-end position, are normally plotted to the line as shown at the center of the illustration. The bottom example of Figure 77.3 shows period data that are combined with tabular data and which are plotted to the line as if indicating the month-end position for each reporting period. This latter technique is to keep both the graphic and tabular information in the same register so that when the time-now line is drawn it includes both elements.

77.4 Surface Versus Column Charts: Care should always be exercised when selecting the graphic method for displaying data. If, for instance, there are radical variations in the data, there is a tendency for vertical distortion if a surface chart approach is taken, such as shown at the top of Figure 77.4. Under such circumstances a column chart can sometimes more clearly present the same data, as illustrated at the bottom of the figure.

77.5 Planning Surface Charts: When two or more elements of data are to be stacked on a surface (strata or band) chart, the chart marker should plan his layout so that the least active data are on the bottom, as shown at the bottom of Figure 77.5. This will minimize the amount of visual distortion, a common fault with this type of chart.

EXAMPLE 1 TREND STYLE

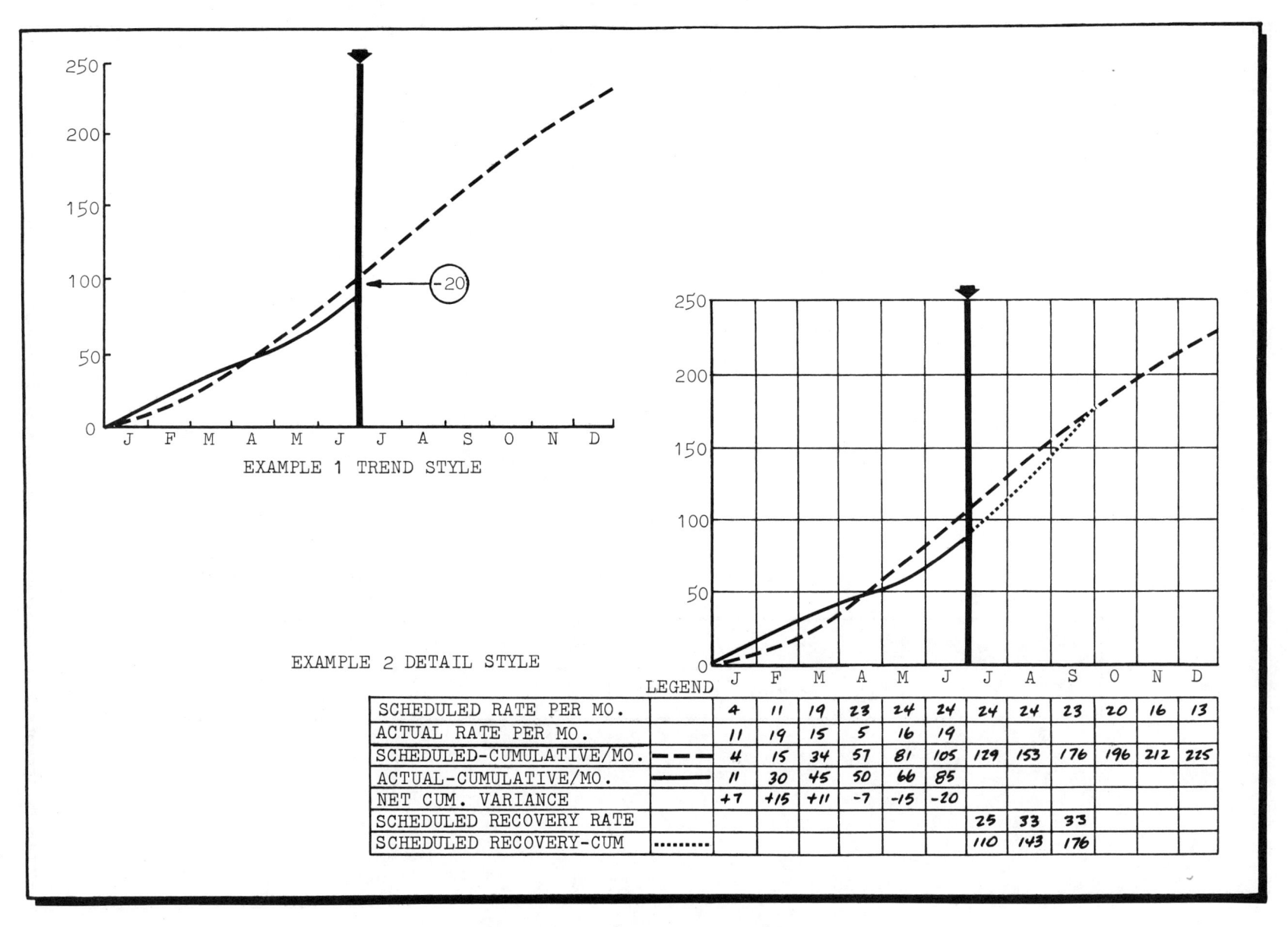

EXAMPLE 2 DETAIL STYLE

LEGEND		J	F	M	A	M	J	J	A	S	O	N	D
SCHEDULED RATE PER MO.		4	11	19	23	24	24	24	24	23	20	16	13
ACTUAL RATE PER MO.		11	19	15	5	16	19						
SCHEDULED-CUMULATIVE/MO.	-----	4	15	34	57	81	105	129	153	176	196	212	225
ACTUAL-CUMULATIVE/MO.	——	11	30	45	50	66	85						
NET CUM. VARIANCE		+7	+15	+11	-7	-15	-20						
SCHEDULED RECOVERY RATE								25	33	33			
SCHEDULED RECOVERY-CUM	········							110	143	176			

Figure 77.1   Trend Versus Detail Charts

LINE CHART
WITH CUMULATIVE
DATA PLOTTED

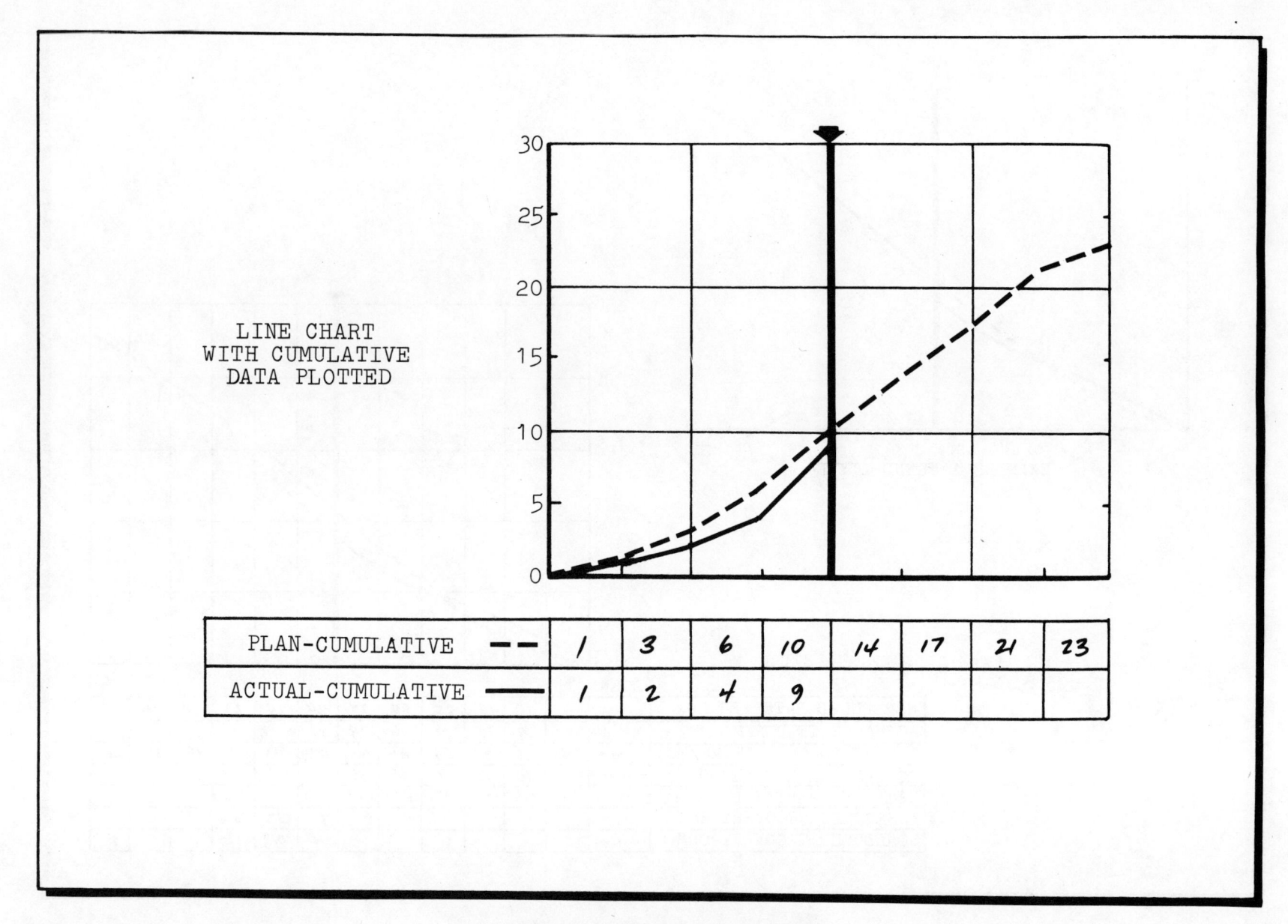

PLAN-CUMULATIVE ----	1	3	6	10	14	17	21	23
ACTUAL-CUMULATIVE ——	1	2	4	9				

Figure 77.2   Cumulative and Rate Charts

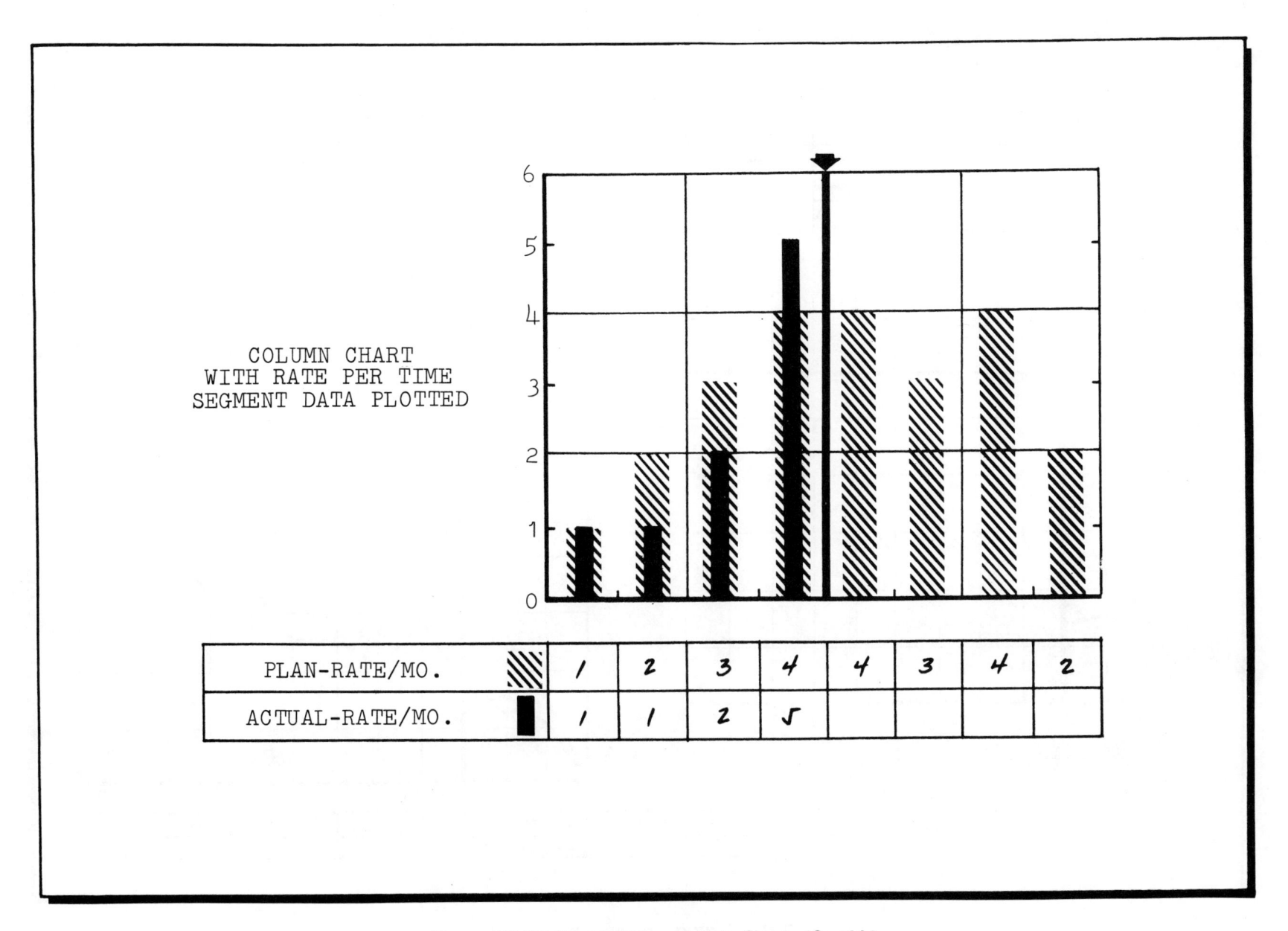

COLUMN CHART
WITH RATE PER TIME
SEGMENT DATA PLOTTED

PLAN-RATE/MO.		1	2	3	4	4	3	4	2
ACTUAL-RATE/MO.		1	1	2	5				

Figure 77.2 Cumulative and Rate Charts (Cont'd.)

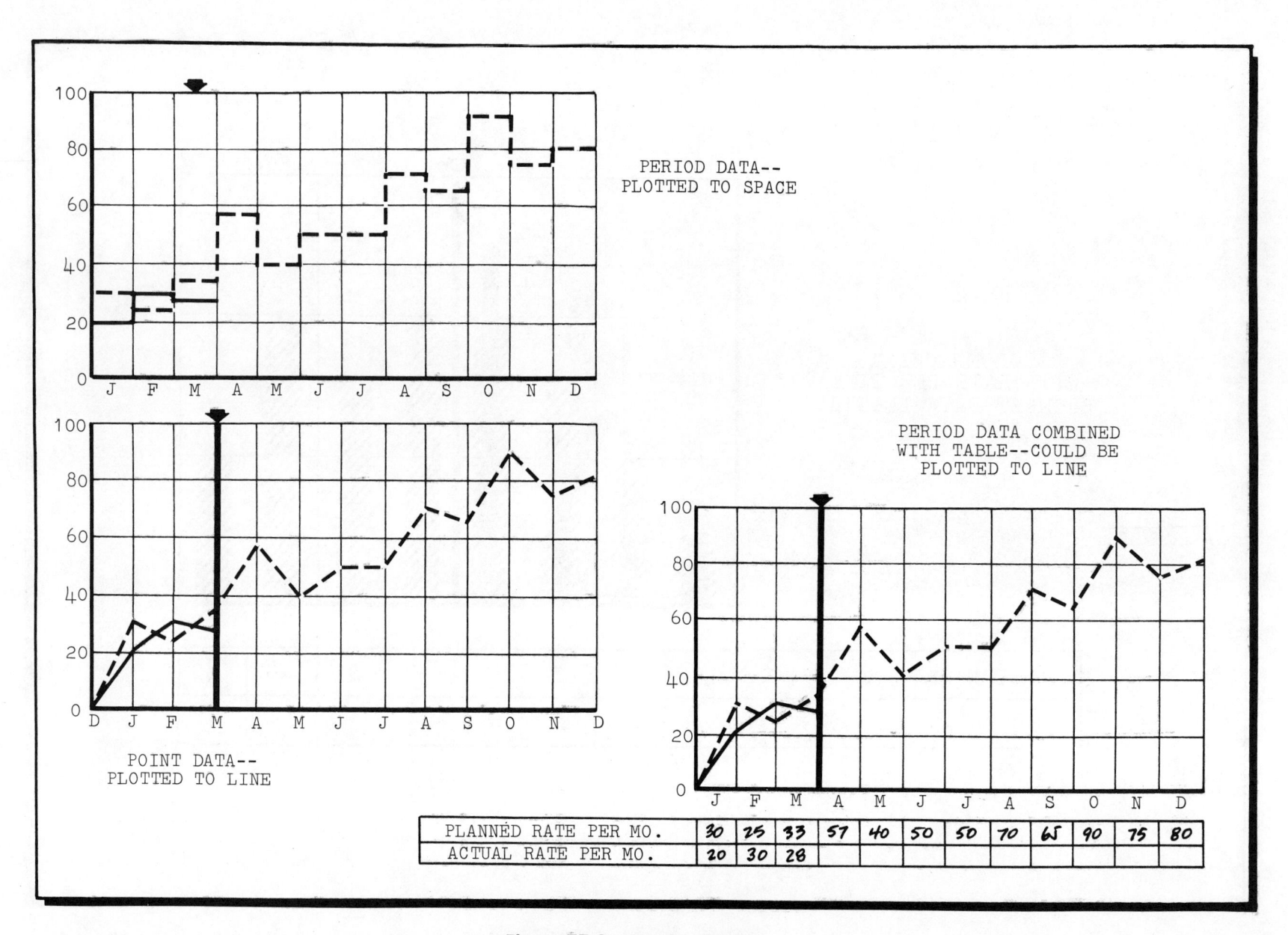

Figure 77.3 Plotting Points

884

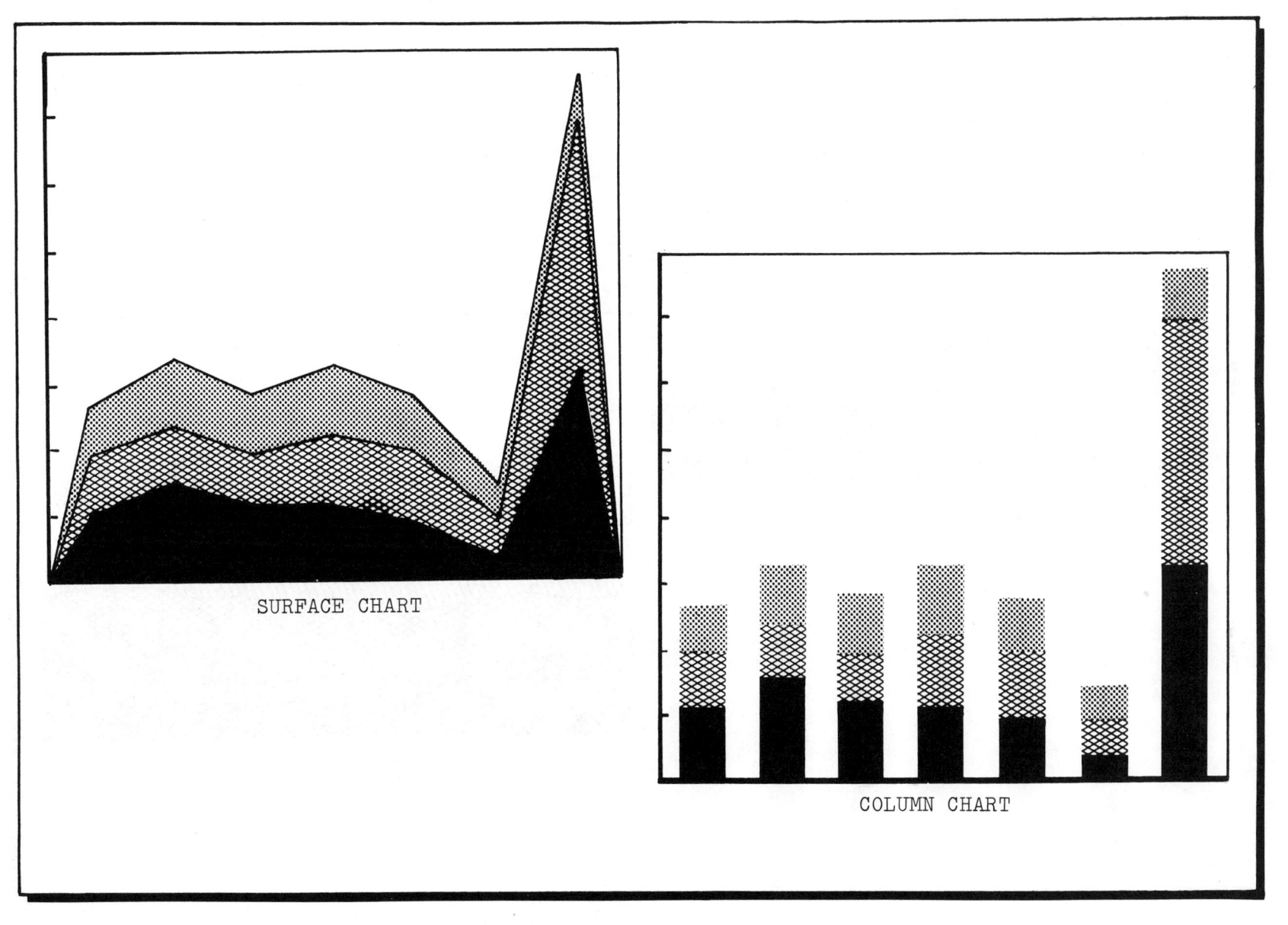

Figure 77.4 Surface Versus Column Charts

WITH THE MOST ACTIVE
DATA ON THE BOTTOM

WITH THE MOST ACTIVE
DATA ON THE TOP

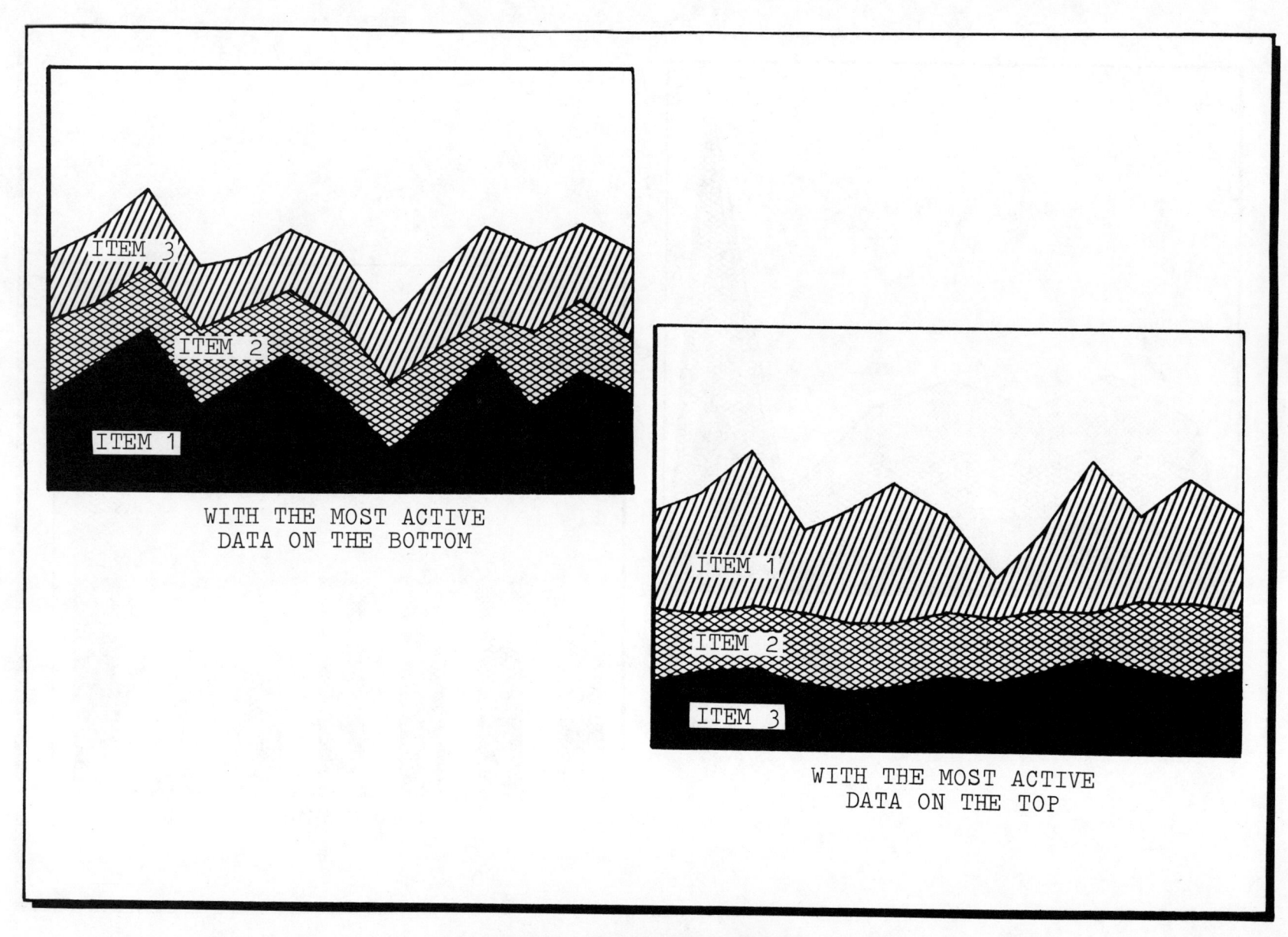

Figure 77.5 Planning Surface Charts